International Business

GLOBAL EDITION

International Business

SEVENTH EDITION
GLOBAL EDITION

Ricky W. Griffin
Texas A&M University

Michael W. Pustay
Texas A&M University

PEARSON

Boston   Columbus   Indianapolis   New York   San Francisco   Upper Saddle River
Amsterdam   Cape Town   Dubai   London   Madrid   Milan   Munich   Paris   Montréal   Toronto
Delhi   Mexico City   São Paulo   Sydney   Hong Kong   Seoul   Singapore   Taipei   Tokyo

Editorial Director: Sally Yagan
Acquisitions Editor: Brian Mickelson
Director of Editorial Services: Ashley Santora
Editorial Project Manager: Sarah Holle
International Senior Acquisitions Editor: Laura Dent
International Editorial Assistant: Toril Cooper
International Marketing Manager: Dean Erasmus
Director of Marketing: Patrice Lumumba Jones
Senior Marketing Manager: Nikki Ayana Jones
Marketing Assistant: Melinda Jensen
Senior Managing Editor: Judy Leale

Production Project Manager: Jacqueline A. Martin
Senior Operations Supervisor: Arnold Vila
Operations Specialist: Cathleen Petersen
Art Director: Steve Frim
Text Designer: Jill Lehan
Photo Researcher: Brandi M. Ford
Manager, Rights and Permissions: Estelle Simpson
Cover Art: Jodi Notowitz
Cover image: © dkimages
Media Editor: Denise Vaughn
Lead Media Project Manager: Lisa Rinaldi

Pearson Education Limited
Edinburgh Gate
Harlow
Essex CM20 2JE
England

and Associated Companies throughout the world

Visit us on the World Wide Web at:
www.pearson.com/uk

© Pearson Education Limited 2013

ISBN-13: 978-0-273-76586-8
ISBN-10: 0-273-76586-8

British Library Cataloguing-in-Publication Data
A catalogue record for this book is available from the British Library

10 9 8 7 6 5 4 3 2
15 14 13 12

Typeset in 10/12 Palatino by Integra Software Services, Inc.
Printed and bound by Courier/Kendallville in United States of America

The publisher's policy is to use paper manufactured from sustainable forests.

To the memory of my father, James P. Griffin, who provided encouragement and guidance in ways he never imagined.

R.W.G.

To the newest members of our family, Sarah Murphy and Scott Currie.
M.W.P.

Brief Contents

Contents

Maps

Preface

We've taught International Business courses for twenty-five years, and enjoyed every moment of the experience. From the instructor's perspective, the joy and excitement of the course lies in its importance and dynamism. Its importance cannot be denied. The jobs, careers, and livelihoods of virtually every human being on the planet are affected by international commerce. For some, that commerce represents an opportunity; for others, a threat. Almost a third of the world's economic activity is attributable to international trade, while foreign direct investment is close to $18 trillion. Nor can its dynamism be denied. Think of the changes that have occurred in the three years between the publication of the sixth edition of International Business: A Managerial Perspective and this seventh edition of the text: a global recession, massive global bank bailouts, record high values for the Swiss franc and the Japanese yen, a major restructuring of the institutions governing the European Union, China's aggressive search for natural resource security, Nokia's shifting from mobile market leader to dead-in-the-water (at least in Wall Street's view), to name but a few examples.

From the student's perspective, however, this dynamism—and the sheer breadth of the subject matter—can be intimidating. We discuss every region of the world and draw on every business discipline—accounting, marketing, management, finance, supply chain management, MIS—and numerous liberal arts disciplines—economics, geography, anthropology, sociology, history, international relations, political science, and the law. It's not surprising that students can feel overwhelmed by the magnitude of the course. We have striven to reduce students' fears of not being able to master this extensive material by providing clear, concise discussions of the principle concepts and challenges of international business and by offering numerous examples of these issues in action.

Our vision in writing this book is to prepare students to be effective participants in the worldwide marketplace. That was the vision we laid out in the preface of the first edition of this book, and it remains so in the seventh. We noted that many of the existing textbooks are written in needlessly technical terms and seem to be concerned only with students who are specializing in international business. However, all students—even those who will never have an overseas assignment—need to be knowledgeable about the global economy.

That is why we feel so strongly about our vision for this book. We want students to attain "cultural literacy" in international business. We want them, for example, to be able to speak comfortably with a visiting foreign exchange student or to ask insightful questions of a visiting executive from a foreign-headquartered multinational corporation. For many students, this textbook and the course that it accompanies is just the first step in a long journey to being an effective businessperson and an informed citizen in a globalizing world. We hope in writing this textbook that that first step will be made a bit easier, a bit more informed, and a bit more exciting.

Like the previous six editions, we have maintained our managerial approach to international business with an emphasis on skills development, emerging markets, and geographical literacy. The seventh edition features new cases, boxes, and analyses reflecting the latest challenges and opportunities confronting international businesses. More specifically, the following content is new or revised to reflect the latest global trends:

- New and updated profiles of the challenges and opportunities provided international firms as they confront and master the complexities of the international marketplace, including new cases featuring LVMH, Lenovo, Cereal Partners Worldwide, and Tata, and updated treatments of Nokia, Disney, Telefónica, Grameen Bank, Astra, Unilever, and Danone, among others.
- New and updated analyses of the impact of globalization on competition within industries, including the global flower industry, the international cinema market, Germany's Mittelstand, the international airline industry, and mobile telephone services.

- New and updated cases exploring how firms address cultural, legal, and technological differences among countries. Students gain deeper and more nuanced understandings of the politics, culture, and social problems of individual countries through in-depth examination of such issues such as Russia and the rule of law, the EU's implementation of the Treaty of Lisbon, Brazil and poverty reduction, Japan and its cultural and demographic challenges, the hidden role of the Communist Party in Chinese businesses, American retailers and Chinese consumers, Islamic finance, and the growth of unionization activity in China.
- New and updated examples and cases assessing the ethical and social responsibilities of international businesses and international businesspeople, including BP and the Gulf oil spill, green energy and free trade, the Chad pipeline, the Siemens bribery scandal, and Grameen Bank.
- New and updated examples of international trade and investment conflicts and the challenges they present international business practitioners, including China's quest for natural resources, Venezuela's Bolivarian Revolution, the global recession of 2008–09, rare earths, tax shelters, sovereign wealth funds, and trade in counterfeit goods.
- The seventh edition also provides up-to-date coverage of the impact of how recent natural disasters and political upheavals have affected international business. Examples include the earthquake and tsunami that shattered Japan and the resultant impact on global supply chains, Toyota's massive recalls and quality problems, and the political unrest that swept through the Middle East in 2011.
- All data and other statistical information in the book have been thoroughly updated, including international trade statistics, exchange rates, and expatriate costs of living in various global business centers.

Pedagogically, we have retained four content boxes that highlight coverage of current issues related to technology, entrepreneurship, and conducting business with a global perspective:

VENTURING ABROAD   Exposes students to the opportunities and challenges of conducting business outside their home country.

E-WORLD   Provides insights into the impact of e-commerce on how business is conducted internationally.

BRINGING THE WORLD INTO FOCUS   Helps students understand the historical, cultural, and political contexts of international business.

EMERGING OPPORTUNITIES   Highlights challenges and opportunities in emerging international markets.

Teaching and Learning Tools for Instructors and Students

MyManagementLab   MyManagementLab gives students the opportunity to test themselves on key concepts and skills, track their own progress through the course, and use personalized study plan activities—all to help them achieve success in the classroom.

Instructor Supplements

Instructors can access downloadable supplemental resources by signing into the Instructor Resource Center at http://www.pearsonglobaleditions.com/griffin.

It gets better.   Once you register, you will not have additional forms to fill out or multiple user names and passwords to remember to access new titles and/or editions. As a registered faculty member, you can log in directly to download resource files and receive immediate access and instructions for installing Course Management content to your campus server.

Need help?   Our dedicated Technical Support team is ready to assist instructors with questions about the media supplements that accompany this text. Visit http://247pearsoned.custhelp.com/ for answers to frequently asked questions and toll-free user support phone numbers. The following supplements are available to adopting instructors.

Instructor's Manual

The helpful Instructor's Manual includes sample syllabi, lecture outlines, and answers to all end-of-chapter and case questions.

Test Item File

The Test Item File boasts over 100 questions per chapter, including multiple choice, true/false, short answer, and essays. The Test Item File includes questions that are tagged Learning Objectives and to AACSB Learning Standards to help measure whether students are grasping the course content that aligns with AACSB guidelines.

TestGen Software

Pearson Education's test-generating software is available via www.pearsonglobaleditions.com/griffin. The software is PC/MAC compatible and preloaded with all of the Test Item File questions. You can manually or randomly view test questions and drag and drop to create a test. You can add or modify test-bank questions as needed.

PowerPoint Slides

Instructor PowerPoints

This presentation includes basic outlines and key points from each chapter. It includes figures from the text but no forms of rich media, which makes the file size manageable and easier to share online or via e-mail. This set was also designed for the professor who prefers to customize PowerPoints and who wants to be spared from having to strip out animation, embedded files, and other media-rich features.

Audio PowerPoints

Pearson's MyManagementLab offers the instructor PowerPoints in an audio format for students taking classes online or as a supplemental teaching aid to the classroom lectures.

Videos

Exciting and high-quality video clips help deliver engaging culture, country, and business programs to the classroom to help students better understand the world around them. Please contact your local representative to receive a copy of these videos.

Acknowledgments

The cover of this book identifies two authors by name. In reality, every edition represents a true team effort involving literally dozens of skilled professionals. While any and all errors of fact, omission, and emphasis are solely our responsibility, we would be remiss if we did not acknowledge those who contributed to this and earlier editions of this book.

We gratefully acknowledge the contributions of John Capela of St. Joseph's College who wrote the Instructor's Manual; Emily Yelverton who wrote the Test Item File; and Myles A. Hassell who prepared the PowerPoint slides to accompany this book.

Thanks go also to our colleagues at other universities who reviewed the manuscript for this edition and previous ones, contributed suggestions, and helped us make this the best international business textbook for students and teachers:

Mohammad Ali	University of Maryland, Eastern Shore
John C. Anderson	University of Tennessee
Madan Annavarjula	Northern Illinois University
Anke Arnaud	University of Central Florida
George Barnes	University of Texas—Dallas
Mack Bean	Franklin Pierce University
Darryl Brown	Indiana University
Dr. Sri Beldona	University of Dallas
Robert Desman	Kennesaw State University
Dante DiGreorio	University of New Mexico
Norb Elbert	Eastern Kentucky University
Allan Ellstrand	California State University—Long Beach
Dan Fogel	Wake Forest University
Tao Gao	Hofstra University
George Gonzales	University of Wisconsin
Basil J. Janavaras	Mankato State University
Sara L. Keck	Pace University
John A. Lehman	University of Alaska—Fairbanks
Lynette Mathur	Southern Illinois University
Roderick J. Matthews	University of Wisconsin—Madison
James McFillen	Bowling Green State University
Claudio Milman	Rollins College
Peter Ping Li	California State University—Stanislaus
Jaime Ortiz	Florida Atlantic University
Christopher J. Robertson	Northeastern University
Carol Sanchez	Grand Valley State University
Michael Shaner	Saint Louis University
Richard M. Steers	University of Oregon
Gregory K. Stephens	Texas Christian University
William Walker	University of Houston

At Texas A&M University, we have had the good fortune to work with one of the finest groups of professional colleagues anyone could imagine. We also appreciate the support of other colleagues, past and present, whose expertise and insights have been incorporated into this manuscript. In addition, we would also like to express our appreciation to the fine team of professionals at Pearson who helped make this revision a reality. Brian Mickelson, Ashley Santora, and Jackie Martin have all played major roles in this revision.

Finally, we would also like to acknowledge the contributions made by our families: Glenda and Dustin Griffin, Ashley and Mathew Hilgemeier, and Zandy, Scott, and Kat Pustay. They didn't write a single word of the book or draw any of the maps or artwork, but their imprint can be found on everything we do. They support us, encourage us, and inspire us. They give our work—and our lives—meaning. It is with all our love and affection that we thank them.

Pearson gratefully acknowledges and thanks the following people for their work on the Global Edition:

Contributors

Nalia Aaijaz, Universiti Kebangsaan Malaysia
Shadi Abouzeid, American University in Dubai
Assad Farah, American University in Dubai
Marie France-Waxin, American University in Sharjah
Kwango Kim, City University of Hong Kong
Goran Milenkovic, Antwerp Management School
Fang Zhao, American University in Sharjah

Reviewers

Abdul Rahim Abu Bakar, Prince Sultan University, Saudi Arabia
Rajah Vellan Komoran, Singapore Management University, Singapore
Richard B. Nyuur, Northumbria University, UK
Davey Yeung, University of South Australia, Australia

About the Authors

Ricky W. Griffin holds the Blocker Chair in Business and is Distinguished Professor of Management in Mays Business School at Texas A&M University. He is serving as Head of the Department of Management; he previously served as both Executive Associate Dean and Interim Dean. After receiving his Ph.D. from the University of Houston in 1978, he joined the faculty at the University of Missouri—Columbia before moving to Texas A&M University in 1981.

Professor Griffin teaches international management, organizational behavior, human resource management, and general management. He has taught both undergraduate and graduate students, participated in numerous executive training programs, and has lectured in London, Paris, Warsaw, Geneva, Berlin, Johannesburg, Tokyo, Hong Kong, and Sydney. A member of the Academy of Management, he has served as division chair of that group's Organizational Behavior division.

Professor Griffin has written several successful textbooks, including *Management*, *Organizational Behavior* (with Greg Moorhead), and *Business Essentials* (with Ron Ebert). He is currently conducting research on workplace violence in Canada, job design differences, and similarities among firms in Japan, Europe, and the United States, and equity employment practices in South Africa.

Michael W. Pustay holds the Anderson Clayton Professorship in Business Administration and is Professor of Management at Texas A&M University. He currently serves as associate director of the Center for International Business Studies and as associate director of the Center for International Business Education and Research at Texas A&M. Professor Pustay, who has taught international business for more than two decades, focuses his teaching and research efforts on international business and business–government relations. His work has appeared in such professional journals as the *Journal of Management*, *Southern Economic Journal*, *Land Economics*, and *Transportation Journal*. He is currently researching the role of regional trading blocs on the world economy and the impact of domestic economic policies on international competition.

Professor Pustay is a member of numerous professional organizations, including the Academy of International Business, the American Economic Association, the Association for Canadian Studies in the United States, and the Transportation Research Forum. He has served as a consultant for a variety of public and private organizations, including the U.S. Department of Transportation, the Small Business Administration, the Civil Aeronautics Board, and Reliant Energy.

CHAPTER 1

An Overview of International Business

AFTER STUDYING THIS CHAPTER, YOU SHOULD BE ABLE TO:

1. Discuss the meaning of international business.
2. Explain the importance of understanding international business.
3. Identify and describe the basic forms of international business activities.
4. Discuss the causes of globalization.
5. Comprehend the growing role of emerging markets in the global economy.

Access a host of interactive learning aids at **www.pearsonglobaleditions.com/ mymanagementlab** to help strengthen your understanding of the chapter concepts.

MyManagementLab

© PCN Photography/Alamy

THE BUSINESS OF THE OLYMPICS

Every two years, the world's attention turns to the Olympic Games. Given that international business and the global economy play such a dominant role in the world today, it is not surprising that the Olympics have come to reflect international business at its most intense. The games are governed by the International Olympic Committee (IOC), which is based in Switzerland. The IOC decides where the games will be held and which sports will be represented, and it oversees the selection of judges and referees. Each country that wants to send athletes to compete in the games establishes a national committee to organize its Olympic effort. These committees are supervised by and report to the IOC.

Potential host cities must give elaborate presentations to the IOC and make substantial commitments in terms of facilities, a volunteer workforce, and related organizational support. For example, as part of their winning bids, Japan promised to build a new high-speed rail line between Tokyo and Nagano, the site of the 1998 winter games, while Greece's proposal featured a new ring road, subway system, and airport in Athens for the 2004 Summer Olympics. China spent over $38 billion on a variety of projects, including 37 new or refurbished sports facilities, transportation improvements, and communications upgrades, for the 2008 Beijing games. The British government plans to spend £9.3 billion to build Olympic facilities and improve the transportation network serving the 2012 games.

The infighting among countries to be selected as the games' host is vicious. French President Jacques Chirac's pique over London's selection over Paris as the host for the 2012 Summer Olympics intensified the squabbles between France and the United Kingdom over European Union policies dealing with agriculture, taxation, and foreign affairs. China threatened a trade war with the United States after the U.S. Senate passed a resolution that hurt Beijing's chances to host the summer games in 2000, a prize eventually seized by Sydney, Australia. (Beijing was later awarded the 2008 games.) After Salt Lake City lost its bid for the 1998 games, the city's local organizing committee launched a massive campaign to procure the 2002 games. Unfortunately, its efforts included widespread gift-giving and the lavish entertaining of IOC delegates, which crossed ethical boundaries. As these facts became public, they triggered a worldwide cry for reform of the IOC.

Why would a city want to host the Olympic Games? Most compete for the privilege because the games would thrust them into the international spotlight and promote economic growth. Further, the tourism benefits are long lived; for example, skiers, skaters, and snowboarders continue to enjoy the facilities at previous Olympic sites such as Turin, Nagano, Lillehammer, Calgary, Albertville, and Lake Placid, pouring money into the local economies long after the Olympic torch has been extinguished. The games also are frequently a catalyst for improving a city's infrastructure. For instance, the high-speed rail line between Tokyo and Nagano halves the travel time between the two cities—a benefit that continues for local residents and for future visitors, as does Athens's new ring road, airport, and subway system. London's Olympic Village will be converted to 3,600 apartments after the completion of the 2012 games, providing much needed housing in one of the world's most expensive real estate markets.

Because of the high cost of running the Olympics, both the IOC and national Olympic committees are always alert for ways to generate revenue. Television coverage provides one significant source of revenue. NBC paid $1.27 billion for the U.S. broadcast rights for the 2000 Sydney summer games and the 2002 Salt Lake City winter games. It then shelled out an additional $2.3 billion to lock up the U.S. broadcast rights for the 2004, 2006, and 2008 games and paid $2.2 billion for the 2010 and 2012 games—even though their sites had not yet been determined. The broadcaster followed a similar strategy in 2011, successfully offering $4.38 billion for rights to broadcast the 2014, 2016, 2018, and 2020 games in the United States. Broadcast rights for Europe, Australia, Asia, and the rest of the Americas sold for smaller but still breathtaking amounts to local broadcasters. NBC and these broadcasters, in turn, sold advertising time to companies eager to market their goods to Olympic fans throughout the world. For instance, despite the high fees it paid, NBC earned $50 to $75 million on its 2006 broadcasts from Turin by spreading its offerings among its NBC, Bravo, MSNBC, and USA outlets so diehard fans would not miss a minute of downhill skiing, hockey, biathlon, or curling. But the network lost an estimated $223 million on the 2010 winter games, as advertising demand and TV ad rates declined due to the slowing U.S. economy.

Not surprisingly, capturing viewers in emerging markets is an important part of the IOC's growth strategy. CCTV, the state-owned TV network, paid $100 million for local broadcasting rights for the 2008 Beijing Olympics. Bidding for TV spots on Chinese television was intense. Yili, a Chinese milk producer, paid CCTV $2.7 million for four 15-second advertisements for the Chinese market; in comparison, NBC charged $800,000 for 30-second commercials in the U.S. market.

Another important source of revenue for the IOC and for national committees is corporate sponsors, who wish to capture the prestige and visibility of being associated with the games. The highest-profile level—and, at $60 to $80 million, the most expensive—is that of "worldwide partner," a designation valuable to firms that market their products to consumers throughout the world, such as Coca-Cola, McDonalds, Acer, Panasonic, and Samsung. The primary benefit of worldwide partnership is that the partners get priority advertising space during Olympic broadcasts, if they choose to buy it. The worldwide partnership program generated $866 million during the 2005–2008 Olympic cycle.[1] ■

The millions of dollars spent on the Olympics by television networks and corporate advertisers reflect the internationalization of business—the result of the desire of firms such as Coca-Cola, Panasonic, and Samsung to market their products to consumers worldwide. The forces that have made the Olympics a growing international business are the same forces that affect firms worldwide as they compete in domestic and foreign markets. Changes in communications, transportation, and information technology not only facilitate domestic firms' foreign expansion but also aid foreign companies in their invasion of the domestic market. These trends have accelerated during the past decade due to the explosive growth of e-commerce, the reduction in trade and investment barriers sponsored by organizations such as the World Trade Organization and the European Union, and the growing importance of emerging markets like China and India. Indeed, these changes are so profound that many futurists now talk about the "boundaryless" global economy—an economy in which national borders are irrelevant.

The global economy profoundly affects your daily life, from the products you buy to the prices you pay to the interest rates you are charged to the kind of job you hold. By writing this book, we hope to help you become more comfortable and effective in this burgeoning international business environment. To operate comfortably in this environment, you need to learn the basic ideas and concepts—the common body of knowledge—of international business. Further, you must understand how these ideas and concepts affect managers as they make decisions, develop strategies, and direct the efforts of others. You also need to be conversant with the fundamental mechanics and ingredients of the global economy and how they affect people, businesses, and industries. You need to understand the evolution of the global economy and the complex commercial and political relationships among Asia, Europe, North America, and the rest of the world.

To help ensure your future effectiveness in the international business world, we plan to equip you with the knowledge, insights, and skills that are critical to your functioning in a global economy. To that end, we have included hundreds of examples to help demonstrate how international businesses succeed—and how they sometimes fail. You also will read tips and extended examples about global companies in special features called "Bringing the World into Focus," "E-World," "Emerging Opportunities," and "Venturing Abroad," and you will have the chance to practice your growing skills in end-of-chapter exercises entitled "Building Global Skills."

What Is International Business?

International business consists of business transactions between parties from more than one country. Examples of international business transactions include buying materials in one country and shipping them to another for processing or assembly, shipping finished products from one country to another for retail sale, building a plant in a foreign country to capitalize on lower labor costs, or borrowing money from a bank in one country to finance operations in another. The parties involved in such transactions may include private individuals, individual companies, groups of companies, and/or governmental agencies.

How does international business differ from domestic business? Simply put, domestic business involves transactions occurring within the boundaries of a single country, while international business transactions cross national boundaries. International business can differ from domestic business for a number of other reasons, including the following:

- The countries involved may use different currencies, forcing at least one party to convert its currency into another.
- The legal systems of the countries may differ, forcing one or more parties to adjust their practices to comply with local law. Occasionally, the mandates of the legal systems may be incompatible, creating major headaches for international managers.

- The cultures of the countries may differ, forcing each party to adjust its behavior to meet the expectations of the other.
- The availability of resources differs by country. One country may be rich in natural resources but poor in skilled labor, while another may enjoy a productive, well-trained workforce but lack natural resources. Thus, the way products are produced and the types of products that are produced vary among countries.

In most cases the basic skills and knowledge needed to be successful are conceptually similar whether one is conducting business domestically or internationally. For example, the need for marketing managers to analyze the wants and desires of target audiences is the same regardless of whether the managers are engaged in international business or domestic business. However, although the concepts may be the same, there is little doubt that the complexity of skills and knowledge needed for success is far greater for international business than for domestic business. International businesspeople must be knowledgeable about cultural, legal, political, and social differences among countries. They must choose the countries in which to sell their goods and from which to buy inputs. International businesses also must coordinate the activities of their foreign subsidiaries, while dealing with the taxing and regulatory authorities of their home country and all the other countries in which they do business.

Why Study International Business?

There are many different reasons why today's students need to learn more about international business. First, almost any large organization you work for will have international operations or be affected by the global economy. You need to understand this increasingly important area to better assess career opportunities and to interact effectively with other managers. For example, in your first job assignment, you could be part of a project team that includes members from Mexico, Uruguay, Canada, and the United States. A basic grasp of international business would help you understand more fully why the team was formed, what the company expects it to accomplish, and how you might most effectively interact with your colleagues. You also need to study international business because you may eventually work for a firm that is owned by a corporation headquartered in another country. For instance, 5.6 million U.S. citizens work for U.S. affiliates of foreign-owned corporations, while foreign subsidiaries of U.S. corporations employ 10.6 million Europeans, Asians, Africans, Australians, Canadians, and Latin Americans.[2]

Small businesses also are becoming more involved in international business. If one day you start your own business, you may find yourself using foreign-made materials or equipment, competing with foreign firms, and perhaps even selling in foreign markets. The growth of e-commerce has also opened up new opportunities for small businesses. Previously, to enter foreign markets, firms often needed to painstakingly build distribution networks and brand recognition country by country, a process that many times favored large firms over small ones. Today, a well-developed website can draw the business of consumers throughout the world without the need to establish a physical presence in each country, making it easier for small businesses to participate in the international marketplace. The Internet may also help small businesses cut their costs, allowing them to better compete against their larger rivals. Consider the Lee Hung Fat Garment Factory, a family-owned Hong Kong manufacturer. It slashed its costs of communicating with its foreign customers by one-third by relying on the Internet rather than faxes and telephone calls. Instead of express mailing product samples to its customers, the company uses a digital camera to transmit photos of garment mock-ups over the Internet. Company managers estimate they save 15 to 20 percent in design costs using this technology.[3]

Another reason for you to study international business is to keep pace with your future competitors. Business students in Europe have traditionally learned multiple languages, traveled widely, and had job experiences in different countries. Many of their programs require them to spend one or more semesters in different countries. Asian students, too, are actively working to learn more about foreign markets and cultures, especially those of North American and European countries. These students, training to become managers, will soon be in direct competition with you, either in jobs with competing companies or in positions within your own company. You need to ensure that your global skills and knowledge will aid your career, rather than allow their absence to hinder it.

All entrepreneurs need to have a basic understanding of standard business, legal, and financial terminology. For an entrepreneur doing business internationally, this terminology takes on additional complexity because different phrases and terms are likely to be used in different countries. Consider, for example, the different terms used to connote business liability in various countries.

Most people in the United States are familiar with the abbreviation *Inc.* and are accustomed to seeing business names such as Southwest Airlines, Inc., and Abercrombie & Fitch, Inc. The term, of course, stands for "incorporated" and means that the financial liability of the company's owners is limited to the extent of their investments if the company fails or encounters financial or legal difficulties. Other countries have different terminology when dealing with this concept of limited liability.

Germany uses three different terms to reflect different forms of limited liability. **Aktiengesellschaft (AG)** is used for a large, publicly held firm that must have a management board and a board of directors. Examples include Deutsche Bank AG and Volkswagen AG. **Kommanditgesellschaft auf Aktien (KGaA)** is used for a firm that is owned by limited partners but has at least one shareholder with unlimited liability. Henkel KGaA, a German adhesives, laundry, and personal care products manufacturer, is an example. Finally, **Gesellschaft mit beschränkter Haftung (GmbH)** applies to smaller, privately held companies.

In Japan **kabushiki kaisha (KK)** is used for all limited-liability companies. In the Netherlands **BV (besloten vennootschap)** refers to a privately held, limited-liability firm, and **NV (naamloze vennootschap)** refers to a publicly held, limited-liability firm, such as Philips NV. The United Kingdom also distinguishes between privately held and publicly held limited-liability companies, using **Ltd.** for the former and **PLC** for the latter. Examples are Swire Pacific Ltd. and GlaxoSmithKline PLC. Italy uses **SpA (la società per azioni)** to denote a limited-liability firm, such as Benetton Group SpA and Fiat SpA. France uses **SA (société anonyme)** for the same purpose, as in Carrefour SA and Hachette SA.

You also need to study international business to stay abreast of the latest business techniques and tools, because no single country has a monopoly on good ideas. For example, Japanese firms pioneered inventory management techniques such as **just-in-time (JIT) systems.** Under JIT, suppliers are expected to deliver necessary inputs just as they are needed. Similarly, European firms such as Volvo and Japanese firms such as Honda were among the first to experiment with such labor practices as empowerment, quality circles, autonomous work groups, and cross-functional teams to raise the productivity and satisfaction of their workforces. Managers who remain ignorant of the innovations of their international competitors are bound to fail in the global marketplace.

Finally, you need to study international business to obtain cultural literacy. As global cultures and political systems become even more intertwined than they are now, understanding and appreciating the similarities and differences of the world's peoples will become increasingly important. You will more often encounter colleagues, customers, suppliers, and competitors from different countries and cultural backgrounds. Knowing something about how and where their countries and companies fit into the global economy can help you earn their respect and confidence as well as give you a competitive edge in dealing with them (see "Bringing the World into Focus"). Conversely, if you know little or nothing about the rest of the world, you may come across as provincial, arrogant, or simply inept. This holds true regardless of whether you are a manager, a consumer, or just an observer of world events.

International Business Activities

Historically, international business activity first took the form of exporting and importing (see "Bringing the World into Focus"). However, in today's complex world of international commerce, numerous other forms of international business activity are also common.

Exporting and Importing

Exporting is the selling of products made in one's own country for use or resale in other countries. **Importing** is the buying of products made in other countries for use or resale in one's own country. Exporting and importing activities often are divided into two groups. One group of activities is trade in goods—tangible products such as clothing, computers, and raw materials. Official U.S. government publications call this type of trade **merchandise exports and imports;** the British call it *visible trade*. The other group of activities is trade in services—intangible

FIGURE 1.1

Exports of Goods and Services as a Percentage of GDP for Some Key Countries (2009 Data)

Source: World Trade Organization (www.wto.org); World Bank, *World Development Report*, 2011.

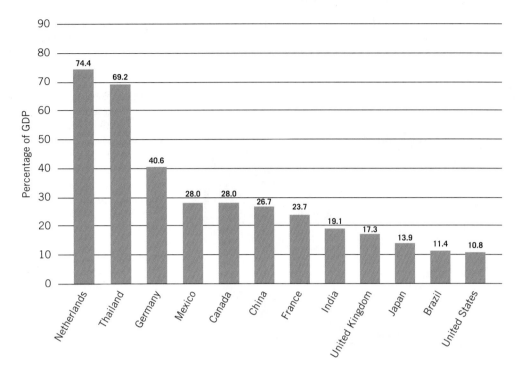

products such as banking, travel, and accounting activities. In the United States this type of trade is called **service exports and imports;** in the United Kingdom it is called *invisible trade.*

Exports are often critical to a firm's financial health. For example, in 2010, 70 percent of Boeing's $33.4 billion in commercial aircraft sales were to foreign customers, creating tens of thousands of jobs at the company and thousands more at the factories of its parts suppliers. International sales often are equally important to smaller firms, such as Task Force Tips, an Indiana manufacturer of fire hose nozzles, which exports one-third of its production.[4] Trade is important to countries as well. As Figure 1.1 shows, exporting accounts for over two-thirds of the gross domestic products (GDP) of the Netherlands and Thailand, and over 25 percent of the GDPs of China, Canada, Germany, and Mexico.

BRINGING THE WORLD INTO FOCUS   **THE EARLY ERA OF INTERNATIONAL BUSINESS**

International business originally consisted of international trade. Trade between nations can be traced back as far as 2000 B.C., when tribes in northern Africa took dates and clothing to Babylonia and Assyria in the Middle East and traded them for spices and olive oil. This trade continued to expand over the years, encompassing more regions and a growing list of resources and products. Even the Olympic Games have their roots in this early era, with the first games being held in Greece in 776 B.C. By 500 B.C. Chinese merchants were actively exporting silk and jade to India and Europe, and common trade routes were being established.

Success in international trade often led to political and military power. First Greece and then the Roman Empire prospered in part because of exploitation of international trade. Ancient wars were fought to maintain trade dominance. For example, the North African city of Carthage became an international business center that rivaled Rome in the third century B.C., as merchants from Europe brought precious metals and glass to trade for the grains, ivory, and textiles offered by African merchants. Over a period of 100 years, Rome fought three bloody wars with Carthage to maintain its trade supremacy, finally defeating the

Carthaginians in 146 B.C. The victorious Romans burned the city and plowed salt into the soil so that crops could not grow, to ensure that Carthage would never again rise as a rival.

During the Middle Ages, Italy became a focal point for international business because of its central location in what was then the world market. The political and military strength of Venice, Genoa, and Florence reflected their roles as major centers of international commerce and banking that linked trade routes between Europe and China. In 1453 these trade routes were severed when the Turks conquered Constantinople (now Istanbul) and gained control of the Middle East. Europe's trade with China had been particularly profitable, so European governments became interested in finding new ocean routes to the Far East. Backed by the Spanish government, Christopher Columbus sailed west from Europe looking for such routes. His landing in the Caribbean islands served instead to identify an important new source of resources and, eventually, led to the colonization of the Americas by European countries.

As this colonization took place, new avenues of trade opened. Settlers throughout the Americas sold raw materials, precious metals, and grains to Europe in exchange for tea, manufactured goods, and other commodities. Most of the American territories eventually became independent countries and important contributors to the world economy.

Another phenomenon of great importance to international business developed during the colonial period and the subsequent Age of Imperialism: the growth of foreign direct investment (FDI) and multina-

tional corporations (MNCs), both of which involve foreigners supplying and controlling investments in a host country. European capitalists from such imperialist powers as the United Kingdom, France, the Netherlands, Spain, Belgium, and Portugal nurtured new businesses in their colonial empires in the Americas, Asia, and Africa, establishing networks of banking, transportation, and trade that persist to this day. The earliest of these firms included the Dutch East India Company (established in 1600), the British East India Company (1602), and the Hudson's Bay Company (1670). These and latter-day trading companies, such as Jardine Matheson Holdings, Ltd., owned copper mines, tea and coffee estates, jute and cotton mills, rubber plantations, and the like as part of their global trading empires.

During the nineteenth century the invention and perfection of the steam engine, coupled with the spread of railroads, dramatically lowered the cost of transporting goods over land and thereby made larger factories more economical. This development in turn broadened the extent of FDI. The forerunners of such large contemporary MNCs as Unilever, Ericsson, and Royal Dutch Shell took their first steps on the path to becoming international giants by investing in facilities throughout Asia, Europe, and the Americas during this period. New inventions promoting technological change further stimulated FDI. For example, in 1852 Samuel Colt built a factory in Great Britain to produce his famous firearms, and later in the century Dunlop built factories in Belgium, France, and Japan to exploit its tire-making expertise.

During the fifth century B.C., international commerce was dominated by Athens and its allies. The Peloponnesian War (431–404 B.C.) brought an end to Athens's power and prosperity. Today's visitors to the Acropolis are reminded of the poignant words of Edgar Allan Poe:

On desperate seas long wont to roam . . . /Thy Naiad airs have brought me home /To the glory that was Greece, /And the grandeur that was Rome.

Sources: S. D. Chapman, "British-based investment groups before 1914," *Economic History Review*, vol. 38 (1985), pp. 230–235; John H. Dunning, *Multinational Enterprises and the Global Economy* (Wokingham, England: Addison-Wesley Publishing Company, 1993), p. 3; Simcha Ronen, *Comparative and Multinational Management* (New York: John Wiley & Sons, 1986).

International Investments

The second major form of international business activity is **international investments**—capital supplied by residents of one country to residents of another. Such investments are divided into two categories: foreign direct investments and foreign portfolio investments. **Foreign direct investments (FDI)** are investments made for the purpose of actively controlling property, assets, or companies located in host countries. (The country in which the parent company's headquarters is located is called the **home country;** any other country in which the company operates is known as a **host country.**) An example of an FDI is the purchase of all the common stock of the U.K.'s Cadbury PLC by Kraft. After the purchase Kraft installed its own executives to oversee Cadbury's operations and integrate them into Kraft's global procurement and marketing programs.

Foreign portfolio investments (FPI) are purchases of foreign financial assets (stocks, bonds, and certificates of deposit) for a purpose other than control. An example of a portfolio investment is the purchase of 1,000 shares of Sony's common stock by a Danish pension fund. With this investment the pension fund is trying to raise the rate of return on its asset portfolio rather than control Sony's decision making. For the same reason many investors in recent years have bought shares of mutual funds that specialize in foreign stocks and bonds.

Other Forms of International Business Activity

International business activity can also take other forms. Licensing, franchising, and management contracts are among the most important. **International licensing** is a contractual arrangement in which a firm in one country licenses the use of its intellectual property (patents, trademarks, brand names, copyrights, or trade secrets) to a firm in a second country in return for a royalty payment. The Walt Disney Company may permit a German clothing manufacturer to market children's pajamas embroidered with Mickey Mouse's smiling face in return for a percentage of the company's sales. **International franchising,** a specialized form of international licensing, occurs when a firm in one country (the franchisor) authorizes a firm in a second country (the franchisee) to utilize its operating systems as well as its brand names, trademarks, and logos in return for a royalty payment. For example, McDonald's Corporation franchises its fast-food restaurants worldwide. Finally, an **international management contract** is an arrangement wherein a firm in one country agrees to operate facilities or provide other management services to a firm in another country for an agreed-upon fee. Management contracts are common, for instance, in the upper end of the international hotel industry. Hoteliers such as Marriott and Hilton often do not own the expensive hotels that bear their brand names throughout the world but rather operate them under management contracts.

A firm that engages in any of these types of transactions can be labeled an international business. More formally, we can define an **international business** as any organization that engages in cross-border commercial transactions with individuals, private firms, and/or public sector organizations. But note that we have also used the term *international business* to mean cross-border commercial transactions. Whenever you see this term, you need to determine, from the context in which it is being used, whether it is referring to a general process involving transactions across borders or to a single organization engaging in specific transactions across borders.

The term **multinational corporation (MNC)** is used to identify firms that have extensive involvement in international business. A more precise definition of a multinational corporation is a firm "that engages in foreign direct investment and owns or controls value-adding activities in more than one country."[5] In addition to owning and controlling foreign assets, MNCs typically buy resources in a variety of countries, create goods and/or services in a variety of countries, and then sell those goods and services in a variety of countries. MNCs generally coordinate their activities from a central headquarters but may also allow their affiliates or subsidiaries in foreign markets considerable latitude in adjusting their operations to local circumstances. Because some large MNCs, such as accounting partnerships and Lloyd's of London, are not true corporations, some writers distinguish between multinational corporations and **multinational enterprises (MNEs).** Further, not-for-profit organizations, such as the IOC and the International Red Cross, are not true enterprises, so the term **multinational organization (MNO)** can be used when one wants to refer to both not-for-profit and profit-seeking organizations. Table 1.1 lists the world's largest corporations in 2010.

TABLE 1.1 The World's Largest Corporations

	Revenues (in millions of U.S. dollars)	
	2010	2002
Wal-Mart	418,952	217,799
Royal Dutch Shell	378,152	179,431
Exxon Mobil	370,125	182,466
BP	308,928	178,721
Sinopec	273,422	44,503
China National Petroleum	240,192	44,864
State Grid	226,294	n.a.
Toyota	221,760	131,754
Japan Post Holdings	203,958	n.a.
ConocoPhillips	198,655	56,748
Chevron	198,198	92,043
Total	186,055	96,944
Volkswagen	168,041	82,203
AXA	162,236	62,050
Fannie Mae	153,825	52,901
General Electric	150,211	79,049
ING Group	147,052	88,102
Glencore International	144,978	n.a.
Berkshire Hathaway	136,185	42,353
General Motors	135,952	186,763

Sources: Fortune, July 25, 2011, p. F1; *Fortune*, July 21, 2003, p. 106; various corporate websites

The Era of Globalization

International business has grown so rapidly in the past decade that many experts believe we are living in the era of globalization. **Globalization** can be defined as "the inexorable integration of markets, nation-states, and technologies … in a way that is enabling individuals, corporations and nation-states to reach around the world farther, faster, deeper, and cheaper than ever before."[6]

There is little doubt that international trade and international direct investment—the two primary vehicles for conducting international business—are becoming increasingly important in the world's economy. Globalization has led to an intensification of the role of international trade in the economies of the world. As Figure 1.2 indicates, the ratio of international trade to economic activity has risen dramatically. In 1950, merchandise trade accounted for about 1 percent of the total GDP of the world's nations; by 2009, it represented 21 percent. International trade in services added another 6 percent to this total. (You may also note the impact of the global recession: In 2009, trade volumes decreased more than the world's GDP did, thus causing the ratio of trade to GDP to fall.)

Some of the rapid growth in international trade in services is due to the development of the Internet and associated technologies, which makes international trade in such diverse industries as banking, consulting, education, retailing, and gambling more feasible. For example, many Canadian and U.S. companies have shifted their customer service and data entry operations to areas with lower labor costs in and outside North America. As long as the transaction can be performed electronically, the physical location of the facility is of little importance. India, for example, has a growing call-center business, providing customer care and troubleshooting services for customers of numerous MNCs throughout the world.

Another manifestation of globalization is the growing importance of foreign direct investment—investments made by citizens of one country to operate and control assets in another. As Figure 1.3 demonstrates, the importance of foreign direct investment (FDI) in the world's economy has risen significantly over time. In 1980, the stock of FDI was only 2.4 percent of the world's GDP; by 2009, the stock of FDI was over 30 percent of that year's GDP.

FIGURE 1.2

World Exports as a Percentage of World GDP

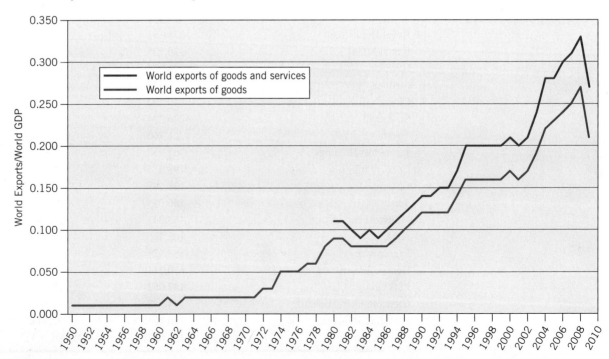

Source: World Trade Organization website, www.wto.org.

FIGURE 1.3

Stock of Foreign Direct Investment (FDI) Relative to World GDP

Source: World Bank, *World Development Report,* various issues; United Nations Conference for Trade and Development, *World Investment Report,* various issues.

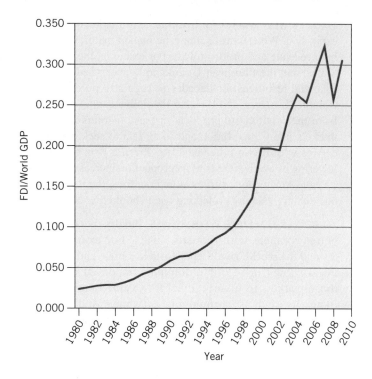

The Contemporary Causes of Globalization

The growth of international business in recent years has been clear and dramatic, as was depicted in Figures 1.2 and 1.3. But why has this growth occurred? And why is international business activity likely to continue to skyrocket during the next decade? There are two broad reasons: strategic imperatives, which motivate globalization, and environmental changes, which facilitate it.

Strategic Imperatives

Several basic motives have compelled firms to become more global in both their orientation and actions. These strategic imperatives include leveraging a firm's core competencies, acquiring resources at low cost, expanding into new markets, and competing with industry rivals.

TO LEVERAGE CORE COMPETENCIES One major motive for globalization is the opportunity to leverage a core competency that a firm has developed in its home market. A **core competency** is a distinctive strength or advantage that is central to a firm's operations. By utilizing its core competency in new markets, the firm is able to increase its revenues and profits. Nokia, for example, developed cutting-edge cellular phone technology that was eagerly adopted by domestic consumers in Finland. Nokia's managers quickly recognized that the firm could increase its revenues and profits by expanding its operations and sales in other countries. Similarly, since its birth in 1972, Singapore Airlines has worked hard to develop award-winning standards of customer satisfaction and reliability that have drawn millions of Asian passengers to its flights. Believing that travelers in other markets would welcome the tender loving care for which the carrier is renowned, Singapore Airlines has deftly expanded its services to more than 60 cities in 30 countries throughout the world.

TO ACQUIRE RESOURCES AND SUPPLIES Another important reason for going international is to acquire resources such as materials, labor, capital, or technology. In some cases organizations must go to foreign sources because certain products or services are either scarce or unavailable locally. For example, North American grocery wholesalers buy coffee and bananas from South America; Japanese firms buy forest products from Canada; and firms worldwide buy oil from the Middle East and Africa. In other cases firms simply find it easier and/or more economical to buy from other countries. For instance, many U.S. advertising agencies shoot commercials overseas. Cape Town, South Africa, has become a popular site, for example, because production crews and equipment can be hired there for less than 40 percent of their cost in Los Angeles.[7] As the chapter's closing case, "Demography Is Destiny," indicates, demographic changes will play a major role in the resource acquisition strategies of MNEs.

TO SEEK NEW MARKETS Seeking new markets is also a common motive for international expansion. When a firm's domestic market matures, it becomes increasingly difficult to generate high revenue and profit growth. For example, the market for toothpaste in Canada, the United States, and the European Union can be classified as mature—most people there have had the financial resources for decades to regularly purchase toothpaste. Thus, firms like Procter & Gamble, Unilever, and Colgate-Palmolive cannot expect to achieve significant growth in sales from their toothpaste products in these markets and have aggressively moved into emerging markets like China, India, and Indonesia to seek expanded sales. Expansion into new markets carries with it two other benefits. First, a firm may be able to achieve economies of scale, lowering its average costs as its production increases. Second, such expansion diversifies a firm's revenue stream. As it serves more countries, the firm becomes less dependent on its sales in any one country, thereby protecting itself should that country's economy turn sour.

TO BETTER COMPETE WITH RIVALS Finally, businesses sometimes enter foreign markets to better compete with industry rivals. For example, as Coca-Cola expands aggressively around the world, rival Pepsi-Cola has little choice but to follow and try to keep up. Should Pepsi allow Coca-Cola to dominate important markets, Coca-Cola could use profits from those markets to finance attacks on Pepsi in still other markets. Such thinking permeates industries such as earthmoving equipment and aircraft manufacturing, where the leading firms continually attack and counterattack each other in every region of the world to prevent their rivals from getting a stranglehold in any country.

The Environmental Causes of Globalization

These strategic imperatives provide firms with the motivation to internationalize their operations. However, firms would not have been able to expand their international activities to the extent we have observed during the post–World War II period without significant changes in two key areas: the political environment and the technological environment.

CHANGES IN THE POLITICAL ENVIRONMENT During the first half of the twentieth century, firms wishing to enter new markets were often frustrated by barriers against foreign trade and investment erected by national governments. After World War I, many countries, including the United States, France, the United Kingdom, and Germany, imposed tariffs and quotas on imported goods and favored local firms on government supply contracts. As a result, international trade and investment declined throughout the 1930s. However, after World War II these policies were reversed. The major trading powers negotiated reductions in tariffs and quotas and eliminated barriers to FDI within their borders. Many of the reductions were negotiated through the General Agreement on Tariffs and Trade (GATT) and its successor, the World Trade Organization (WTO). Regional accords, such as the European Union, the Mercosur Accord, and the North American Free Trade Agreement, also have relaxed trade and investment barriers among their members.

TECHNOLOGICAL CHANGES Changes in governmental policies encouraged international business activity. Improvements in technology—particularly in communication, transportation, and information processing—made international business more feasible and more profitable. Think about the difficulties of conducting business internationally when the primary form of transportation was the sailing ship, the primary form of data processing was pencil and paper, and the primary form of communication was the letter delivered by a postman on horseback. Transportation improvements during the past 150 years—from sailing ship to steamship to seaplane to jet airliner—mean that a manager in London no longer needs to spend weeks traveling in order to confer with colleagues in New Delhi, Toronto, or New York. Advances in transportation also have stimulated growth in international tourism, which is the largest component of international trade in services. The increasing ability of computers to rapidly process vast quantities of information allows firms to manage offices and factories located in every corner of the globe. Exxon Mobil, for example, relies on its computers to continuously adjust the output of its refineries and the sailings of its tankers to meet changes in worldwide demand for its products. Changes in communications technology, such as the advent of electronic mail, smart phones, and tablet computers, enable a manager in Tokyo to receive reports from colleagues in Amsterdam, Abidjan, and Auckland in seconds rather than days. These technological advances make managing distant businesses far easier today than executives would have dreamed possible just a few decades ago, and so have facilitated expansion into international markets.

VENTURING ABROAD | **ABU DHABI AND BRITISH FOOTBALL**

It was the beginning of September 2008 and the usual excitement was mounting as the football transfer window was about to close. Suddenly, out of nowhere it seemed, came the Abu Dhabi United Group for Development and Investment. Headed by Dr. Sulaiman Al Fahim, a billionaire in his own right, the group bought the British Premiership team, Manchester City, from the former Thailand Prime Minister, Thaksin Shinawatra. Negotiations had begun three weeks before and were completed late on Sunday August 31, at the Emirates Palace Hotel in Dubai. The group is believed to have $221 billion at their disposal.

In a stroke, the club's $147 million plus debt was paid off and they began to throw their new financial muscle into the transfer market. They snatched the Real Madrid Brazilian born striker, Robinho, from the cash-rich Chelsea, which is backed by Russian billionaire Roman Abramovitch.

Dr. Sulaiman Al Fahim, who is linked to the Abu Dhabi royal family, made his fortune in a property company known as Hydra. He is an American-educated businessman with projects in Mexico, Abu Dhabi, and Dubai. Hydra Properties already sponsors a football team in Costa Rica and one in Germany. He has financial interests in the creation of a football academy in Abu Dhabi, in partnership with Italian football giants Inter Milan. He is president of the United Arab Emirates Chess Association and is considered the sixteenth most powerful Arab businessman in the world. Dr. Sulaiman Al Fahim won the Visionary Award at the Middle East CEO 2007 awards. He founded Hydra Properties in 2005 and within two years he had secured $2 billion worth of projects.

Apparently, so cash-rich is the doctor and his group that the money required to purchase Manchester City (calculated at around $295 million) was wired from reserves by the brother of the ruler of Abu Dhabi, Sheikh Mansour Bin Zayed Al Nahyan. To put the purchase of Robinho at $47.8 million into perspective, Abu Dhabi generates that amount in surplus revenue in five hours by pumping oil. The doctor intends to make $385 million available to the football club for transfer spending over the next two years. The key aim of acquiring Manchester City is not only to win football glory in the world, but also to raise the profile of Abu Dhabi itself.

Abu Dhabi has been trying to diversify their economy in recent years, specifically by making investments abroad in financial services and in tourism. Abu Dhabi's oil reserves are estimated to be worth around $1 trillion.

Sources: Hydra Properties (www.hydraproperties.com); Arab Business News (www.arabbusiness.com); Manchester City Football Club (www.mcfc.co.uk); Financial Times (www.ft.com); Real Madrid (www.realmadrid.com); United Arab Emirates Government (www.government.ae); Gulf News (www.gulfnews.com).

Globalization and Emerging Markets

We noted that globalization has led to an intensification of international business activity. It is also marked by an expansion of such activity into new markets previously insulated from the international marketplace.

The political changes discussed earlier have played a major role in this process. During the Cold War between the United States and the Soviet Union, many scholars divided the world into three regions: the First World, consisting of the rich, major trading nations from Western Europe, North America, Australia, and parts of Asia, most of which were allied diplomatically with the United States; the Second World, consisting of the Soviet Union and allied Communist states; and the Third World, consisting primarily of the low- to medium-income countries populating Latin America, Africa, and most of Asia. Most international business activity took place between members of the First World. The

The rapid growth enjoyed by emerging markets has created millions of new middle class consumers, like these two shoppers in Beijing. MNCs such as L'Oréal have been quick to profit from these new market opportunities. In 2010, L'Oréal's Asian revenues increased 23 percent compared to only 2.6 percent in its home European market.

© Lou Linwei/Alamy

Second World walled itself off to commerce with the First World, while the Third World was primarily viewed as a supplier of raw materials and commodities to the First World countries.

This is no longer the case: The collapse of European Communism, the ideological and policy changes undertaken by China and India, and the reduction of trade barriers have transformed the global marketplace. Shakespeare once wrote, "All the world's a stage." Today savvy businesspersons recognize that business opportunities are no longer limited to the traditional markets of Western Europe, North America, or Japan. Indeed, today much of the attention of international businesses is focused on the so-called **emerging markets,** countries whose recent growth or prospects for future growth exceed that of traditional markets. Many companies are finding much of their sales and profit growth is attributable to emerging markets. For example, in 2010 L'Oreal's sales in Asia grew 23 percent and 33 percent in Latin America, compared to 13 percent in North America and an anemic 2.6 percent in Western Europe.[8]

There is no universally accepted definition of the countries to be included in the emerging markets category. Some scholars limit the term to the **BRIC countries**—Brazil, Russia, India, and China.

MAP 1.1
China's Regional Challenges

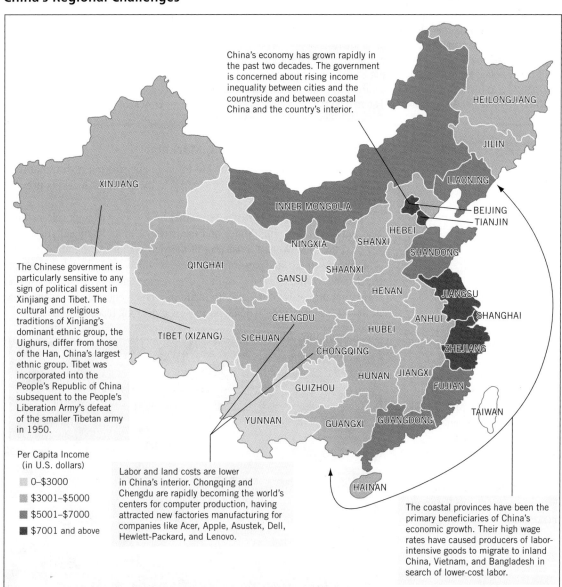

China's economy has grown rapidly in the past two decades. The government is concerned about rising income inequality between cities and the countryside and between coastal China and the country's interior.

The Chinese government is particularly sensitive to any sign of political dissent in Xinjiang and Tibet. The cultural and religious traditions of Xinjiang's dominant ethnic group, the Uighurs, differ from those of the Han, China's largest ethnic group. Tibet was incorporated into the People's Republic of China subsequent to the People's Liberation Army's defeat of the smaller Tibetan army in 1950.

Per Capita Income (in U.S. dollars)
- 0–$3000
- $3001–$5000
- $5001–$7000
- $7001 and above

Labor and land costs are lower in China's interior. Chongqing and Chengdu are rapidly becoming the world's centers for computer production, having attracted new factories manufacturing for companies like Acer, Apple, Asustek, Dell, Hewlett-Packard, and Lenovo.

The coastal provinces have been the primary beneficiaries of China's economic growth. Their high wage rates have caused producers of labor-intensive goods to migrate to inland China, Vietnam, and Bangladesh in search of lower-cost labor.

Sources: "Truckloads of notebooks mark first step of long march inland," *Financial Times*, May 24, 2011, p. 17; "Factory blast roils tech supply chain," *Wall Street Journal*, May 24, 2011, p. B1; "China's rising wage bill poses risk of relocation," *Financial Times*, February 16, 2011, p. 3; Chinese National Statistics Bureau, 2010 Census.

Other researchers have used the term to describe the so-called **Big Ten**—Argentina, Brazil, China, India, Indonesia, Mexico, Poland, South Africa, South Korea, and Turkey.[9] Other experts have a more expansive definition, including most non-high-income countries in Africa, Asia, Eastern Europe, and Latin America. Regardless of the definition, it is clear that international businesses that ignore the emerging markets do so at their own risk. Consider that two of these emerging markets, China (see Map 1.1) and India, together account for more than one-third of the world's population. Their economies are growing significantly faster than that of the world as a whole, as Table 1.2 indicates.

An Overview of the Contents of This Book

In writing this book, we have started with the assumption that most readers will eventually work for or own a firm that is affected by international business activity. Our goal is to help them become more confident and effective managers in the competitive global marketplace. To do so, we provide our readers with the knowledge and skills necessary to succeed in international business.

We have structured the contents of the book to move from relatively macro, or general, issues to increasingly micro, or specific, issues that managers deal with regularly. Our rationale is that managers must fully understand the context of international business to work effectively within it. This broad, general context provides the backdrop within which all international business occurs. At each increasingly specific level within that context, the international manager is faced with specific and operational issues, problems, challenges, and opportunities.

Part 1 comprises Chapters 1 through 5. It provides an overview of the world's marketplaces. Chapter 1 has supplied some background definitions and discussed the contemporary global business environment. Chapter 2 provides a wealth of economic and geographical information about the world's major economies and business centers. Chapters 3 and 4 describe the national environments of international business—the more specific, country-level environmental context that

TABLE 1.2 Characteristics of Selected Emerging Markets, 2009

Country	Total Population (millions)	Total GDP (millions of U.S. dollars)	Gross National Income (per capita) (in U.S. dollars)	Average Annual Growth in GDP, 2000–2009, in percent
BRIC				
Brazil	194	1,571,979	8,040	3.6
Russia	142	1,230,726	9,370	5.9
India	1,155	1,310,171	1,180	7.8
China	1,331	4,984,731	3,590	10.9
Total	**2,822**	**9,097,607**		
Big Ten				
Argentina	40	308,741	7,570	5.4
Brazil	194	1, 571,979	8,040	3.6
China	1,331	4,984,731	3,590	10.9
India	1,155	1,310,171	1,180	7.8
Indonesia	230	540,277	2,230	5.3
Mexico	107	874,902	8,920	2.2
Poland	38	430,076	12,260	4.4
South Africa	49	285,983	5,770	4.1
South Korea	49	832,512	19,830	4.2
Turkey	75	617,099	8,730	4.9
Total	**3,268**	**11,756,471**		
World total	6,775	58,228,178	8,741	2.9

Source: World Bank, *Development Report* 2011.

FIGURE 1.4
Framework for This Book

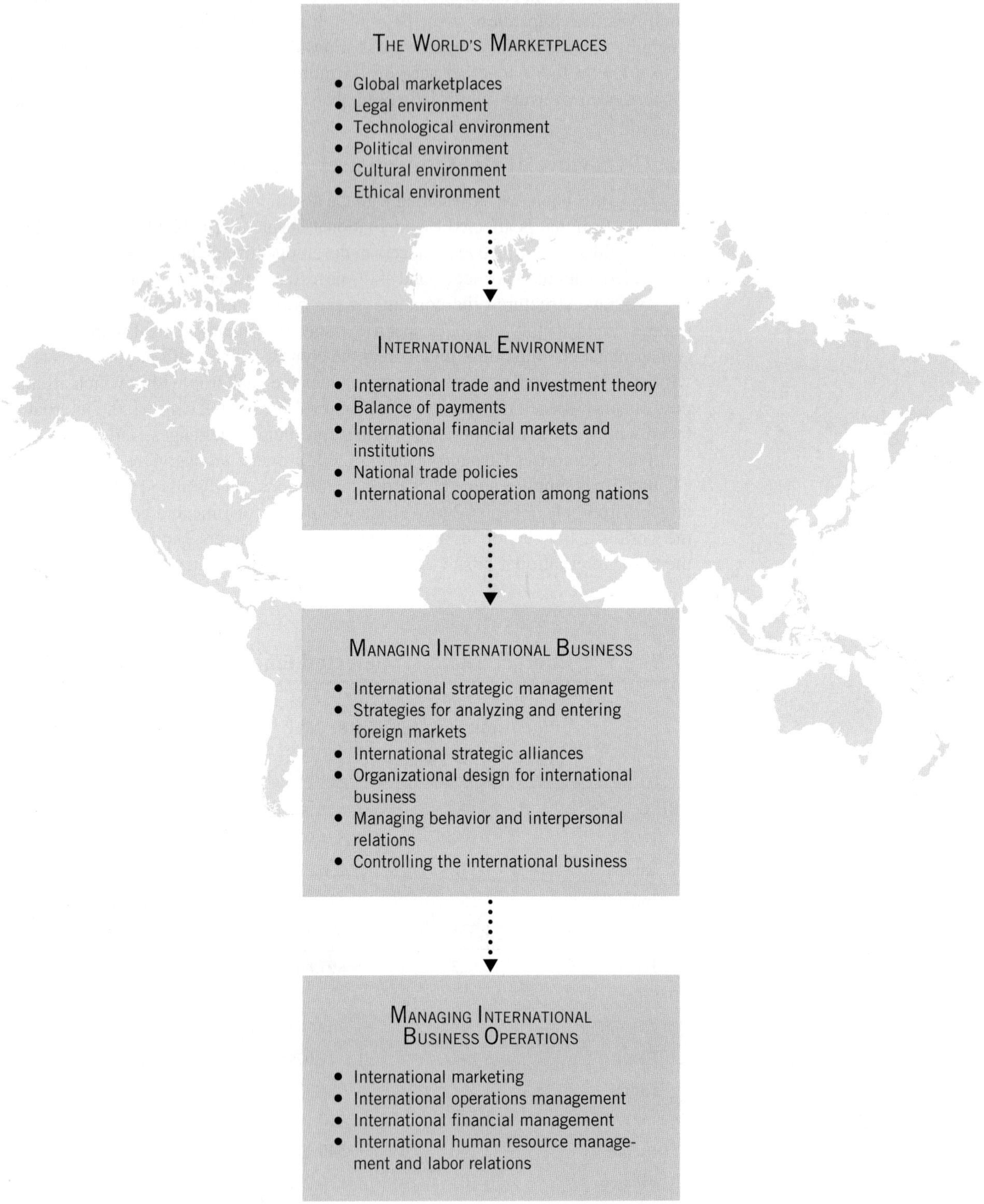

THE WORLD'S MARKETPLACES

- Global marketplaces
- Legal environment
- Technological environment
- Political environment
- Cultural environment
- Ethical environment

INTERNATIONAL ENVIRONMENT

- International trade and investment theory
- Balance of payments
- International financial markets and institutions
- National trade policies
- International cooperation among nations

MANAGING INTERNATIONAL BUSINESS

- International strategic management
- Strategies for analyzing and entering foreign markets
- International strategic alliances
- Organizational design for international business
- Managing behavior and interpersonal relations
- Controlling the international business

MANAGING INTERNATIONAL BUSINESS OPERATIONS

- International marketing
- International operations management
- International financial management
- International human resource management and labor relations

affects and impacts business activity and opportunities. Chapter 5 addresses the social responsibility challenges that international businesses must address in the era of globalization.

Parts 2 through 4 follow a logical progression of topics, moving from the broad, general issues confronting international business to increasingly more specific, focused issues that managers face daily (see Figure 1.4). Part 2 discusses the international environment in more detail, addressing the overall context of international business and introducing many of the global forces and conditions that affect organizations and managers. Part 3 adopts the perspective of a specific organization, focusing on general management issues such as international strategies, modes of entry into foreign markets, joint ventures and strategic alliances, organization design, organizational control, and organizational behavior in international business. Part 4 covers the management of specific international business functions: marketing, operations, finance, and human resource management.

MyManagementLab   Now that you have finished this chapter, go back to **www.pearsonglobaleditions.com/mymanagementlab** to continue practicing and applying the concepts you've learned.

CHAPTER REVIEW

Summary

International business encompasses any business transaction that involves parties from more than one country. These transactions can take various forms and can involve individual companies, groups of companies, and/or government agencies. International business can differ from domestic business because of differences in currencies, legal systems, cultures, and resource availability.

Studying international business is important for several reasons. First, any organization you work for, even if small, is likely to be affected by the global economy. Second, someday you may work for a foreign-owned firm. Further, you need to keep pace with other managers who are learning to function in international settings. Finally, you need to be culturally literate in today's world.

International business activity can take various forms. Exporting involves selling products made in one's own country for use or resale in another country. Importing involves buying products made in other countries for use or resale in one's own country. Foreign direct investments are investments made for the purpose of controlling property, assets, or companies located in foreign countries. Other common forms of international business activity include licensing, franchising, and management contracts.

An international business is one that engages in commercial transactions with individuals, private firms, and/or public sector organizations that cross national boundaries. Firms with extensive international involvement are called multinational corporations, or MNCs.

International business has grown dramatically in recent years because of strategic imperatives and environmental changes. Strategic imperatives include the need to leverage core competencies, acquire resources, seek new markets, and match the actions of rivals. Although strategic imperatives indicate why firms wish to internationalize their operations, significant changes in the political and technological environments have no doubt facilitated the explosive growth in international business activity that has occurred since World War II. The growth of the Internet and other information technologies is likely to redefine global competition and ways of doing international business once again.

Review Questions

1. What is international business? How does it differ from domestic business?
2. Why is it important for you to study international business?
3. What are the basic forms of international business activity?
4. How do merchandise exports and imports differ from service exports and imports?
5. What is portfolio investment?
6. What are the basic reasons for the recent growth of international business activity?

Questions for Discussion

1. Why do some industries become global while others remain local or regional?
2. What is the impact of the Internet on international business? Which companies and which countries will gain as

Internet usage increases throughout the world? Which will lose?
3. Which markets are more important to international businesses—the traditional markets of North America, the

European Union, and Japan, or the emerging markets? Defend your answer.

4. Does your college or university have any international programs? Does this make the institution an international business? Why or why not?

5. What are some of the differences in skills that may exist between managers in a domestic firm and those in an international firm?

6. Would you want to work for a foreign-owned firm? Why or why not?

Building Global Skills

List different products you use on a regular basis, such as your alarm clock, camera, car, coffeemaker, computer, telephone, television, DVD player—perhaps even your favorite CD, shirt, fruit juice, or footwear. Determine which firms made these items. After you have developed your list, go to the library and/or surf the Internet to research the following for each item:

1. In which country is the firm headquartered?
2. What percentage of the firm's annual sales comes from its home market? What percentage comes from other countries?
3. Where was the item most likely manufactured?
4. Why do you think it was manufactured there?

Follow up by meeting with a small group of your classmates and completing these activities:

1. Discuss the relative impact of international business on your daily lives.
2. Compile a combined list of the 10 most common products the average college student might use.
3. Try to identify the brands of each product that are made by domestic firms.
4. Try to identify the brands of each product that are made by foreign firms.
5. Does your list of 10 products include items with components that are both domestically made and foreign made?

CLOSING CASE   **DEMOGRAPHY IS DESTINY**

Recent newspaper headlines trumpeted stories of massive protests in Paris by students and workers denouncing pending labor market reforms; of teachers, policemen, and firefighters in Wisconsin protesting a bill that would truncate their collective bargaining rights; of marches by civil servants in Athens and London denouncing proposed cutbacks in their pensions and working conditions. Meanwhile, the Central Committee of the Communist Party announced new initiatives to promote economic development in China's rural areas. Underlying each of these actions are dramatic demographic changes occurring in these countries.

Demography is the study of the structure of human populations—their size, age composition, gender mix, growth, and so on. Demographers often assert that demography is destiny. By that they mean that a country's demography constrains and shapes the opportunities available to it. If so, then changes in the population, age structure, and gender mix of the world's major economies suggest that significant changes are in store for the world economy.

A traditional way of examining a country's demography is through the use of population pyramids (see Figure 1.5). In olden days, the normal structure of a country's age distribution was a

FIGURE 1.5
Population Pyramids for 2025

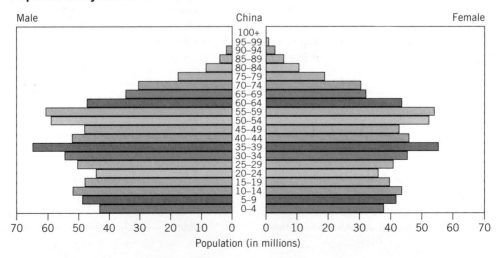

FIGURE 1.5
(Continued)

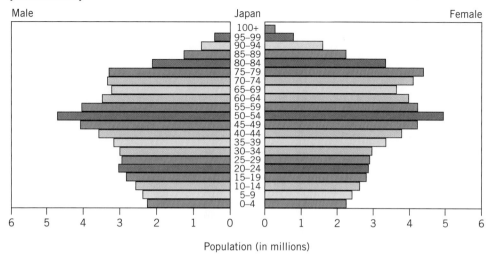

Source: U.S. Census Bureau, International Data Base.

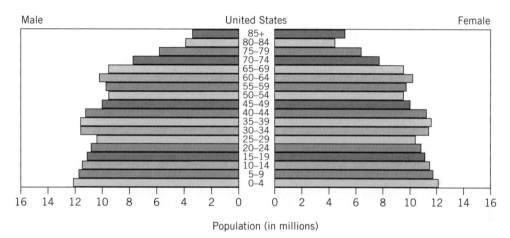

pyramid. Each layer of the pyramid consisted of the number of individuals in an age bracket. The pyramid shape resulted from the fact that the number of people aged 0–4 was slightly larger than the number aged 5–9; 5–9-year-olds slightly outnumbered 10–14-year-olds; and so forth. The declining size was due to the cruel reality of death from disease, famine, and childbirth in a world without modern medicine. Fortunately, better health care, education, and hygiene have freed many societies from this cruel reality, and some population pyramids more closely resemble diamonds or rectangles. But these societies now face the challenge of dealing with graying populations. (The U.S. Census Bureau presents population pyramids for many of the world's countries: see http://www.census.gov/ipc/www/idb.)

These dramatic demographic changes portend major shifts in economic power and competitiveness. The populations of many major economic powers—including France, Italy, Germany, South Korea, and Japan—are predicted to get older and smaller over the next two decades. According to the Organisation for Economic Cooperation and Development (OECD), the old-age dependency ratio will rise dramatically over the next several decades (see Figure 1.6). The old-age dependency ratio is the

ratio of the number of people 65 and older to the number of people between the ages of 20 and 64. A rising old-age dependency ratio indicates that the burden imposed on current workers to support retirees will increase. This burden can take the form of familial transfers or increased taxes. In either case, the monies available to support the consumption of current workers will decline.

The implications of these demographic changes for companies and countries alike are profound. For many companies, when retirees leave work on their last day, a lifetime of experience and knowledge walks out the door as well. Some companies recognize that they will have to change their ways of doing business. For countries, graying of the workforce suggests pressures on the public treasury to support older citizens. Japan is one of the first major economies to face an aging, shrinking population. In 2006, Japan's population began to decline, by a modest 22,000 residents. Japan's population in 2011 was 126.5 million; by 2025, its citizenry will shrink to 117.8 million. In 2011, 22.9 percent of the population is 65 or older; by 2025, that percentage will rise to 29.3 percent, thanks in part to the 83-year life expectancy that its citizens enjoy. It is not surprising, then, that Japanese companies are at the forefront of

FIGURE 1.6
Old Age Dependency Ratios, Selected Countries, 2005, 2025, 2045

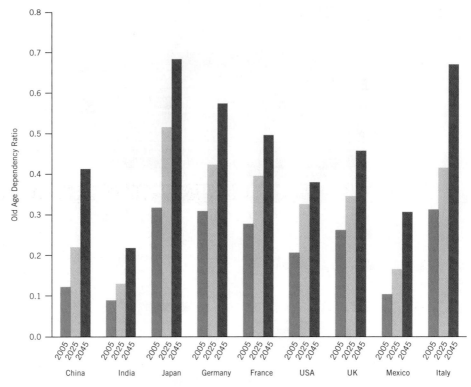

Note: Old age dependency ratio calculated by dividing number of predicted residents 65 and older by predicted residents aged 20–64.
Source: U.S. Census Bureau, International Data Base.

responding to these changes. Toyota has begun to adapt its workstations to make them more comfortable for a workforce that is growing older. Although such changes will help, the reality is that companies operating in countries with shrinking populations are likely to face higher wage and salary costs as the supply of labor contracts. In countries with aging populations, firms are likely to face higher taxes as governments struggle to find revenues to support and care for older citizens. Moreover, an increasing portion of the labor force will be employed caring for retirees, shrinking the availability of labor for other sectors of the economy.

The structure of consumption will also change, because the bundle of goods consumed by retirees differs dramatically from that of younger workers. Retirees demand more medical services, for example, while younger workers buy homes, furniture, household goods, and educational services. Japanese companies appear to be at the forefront of adapting new technologies to meet these demographic challenges. Synclayer, a Nagoya-based supplier of cable television and local area network technology, has developed a system to allow the elderly to self-administer basic medical measurements, which can then be transmitted over the local area network to their doctors. Zojirushi, a leading manufacturer of rice cookers and tea kettles, is equipping its wares with wireless transmitters that send a message to family or friends that the kitchen equipment has been used. Other manufacturers are busily developing service robots to help the elderly lift heavy objects or

monitor their health. A government study predicts that the service robot market could reach $8.4 billion in a decade, thanks to the aging of the Japanese population.

The likely paths of the world's two most populous nations, China and India, diverge. Currently the Chinese labor force is expanding as a result of dramatic declines in infant mortality that occurred in the 1960s and 1970s, providing a ready source of cheap labor for China's manufacturing sector. However, China's working age population will begin shrinking in 2016. Already the number of women between 18 and 35 is declining, as is the population between 20 and 24. These declines suggest that aggregate family formation will decrease within a decade, as will births. India's population, which is much younger than China's, will continue to grow. U.S. government demographers predict that by 2050, India's population will be 1.657 billion (up from 1.189 billion in 2011), while China's population, currently 1.331 billion strong, will peak in 2024 at 1.395 billion and then gradually decline to 1.304 billion by 2050. The median age of Indians in 2050 will be 37.2; Americans, 39.0; Chinese, 48.9. India will face the task of providing employment for these young workers, while China will face the same challenges of a graying population that today confront Japan and most of Western Europe, with two added problems. First, because of its "one-child" policy, which discouraged families from having more than one child, as that one child enters the labor force and his or her parents subsequently retire, the child may need to provide financial support for both parents; and moreover, given the improvements in longevity in China, in some cases the child may also need to support four grandparents. Second, although saving rates in China are quite high, few companies provide pension benefits to their employees. Moreover, because of Chinese cultural values that favor male children, the one-child policy has created a dramatic imbalance in the gender ratio between males and females, with unknown but likely significant impacts on the marriage market, family formation, and elder care. In a decade or two, consumption patterns in young, growing India are likely to dramatically diverge from those in a graying China. Suppliers of video games, big-screen TVs, and child car seats may flock to India, while purveyors of hypertension and anticholesterol medicines, bifocals, and retirement financial services will find China an attractive market.

Case Questions

1. What challenges do graying populations create for companies?
2. What opportunities do graying populations create for firms?
3. How will demographic changes affect the competitiveness of countries in the international marketplace?
4. What can countries do to counteract the impact of these demographic changes on their economic competitiveness?
5. What has been the impact of the one-child policy on China's economic fortunes?

Sources: "China's one-child plan faces new fire," *Financial Times*, April 29, 2011, p. 1; "India passes 1.2 billion mark," *Wall Street Journal*, April 1, 2011, p. A10; http://www.census.gov/ipc/www/idb ; "No babies," *New York Times*, June 29, 2008 (online); "Cautiously, an aging Japan warms to foreign workers," *Wall Street Journal*, May 25, 2007, p. A1; "Bringing up baby," *The Economist*, June 14, 2007, (online); " Population shift is ignored threat," *Wall Street Journal*, June 6, 2006, p. A9; "Labor shortage in China may lead to trade shift," *New York Times*, April 3, 2006 (online); "Chinese president asks senior officials to promote rural development," *People's Daily Online*, February 15, 2006; "Turning boomers into boomerangs," *The Economist*, February 18, 2006, pp. 65–67; "Hey, big-spender," *The Economist*, December 3, 2005, p. 52; "Why China stands to grow old before it gets rich," *Financial Times*, November 10, 2005, p. 13; "China and India: The challenge and the opportunity," *Business Week*, August 22/29, 2005, pp. 51–136; "The factory that has mastered the ageing challenge," *Financial Times*, July 5, 2005, p. 7; "China's golden oldies," *The Economist*, February 26, 2005, p. 65.

Endnotes

1. "NBC Realizes Olympic Dream," *Wall Street Journal*, June 8, 2011, p. B1; "Security is a 'massive challenge'," *USA Today*, March 22, 2011, p. 2C; Olympic Marketing Fact File, www.olympic.org; "In NBC's shadow, Comcast ponders an Olympic plunge," *New York Times*, December 28, 2010; "When the circus leaves town," *The Economist*, July 24, 2010, p. 57; "Gold medal in the race for business," *Financial Times*, September 24, 2009, p. 12; "Olympic marketers seek to soar above politics," *Wall Street Journal*, March 20, 2008, p. B5; "Chinese Olympic ads draw high prices," *Wall Street Journal*, November 20, 2007, p. B3; "GM's pending Olympic exit reshapes marketing arena," *Wall Street Journal*, August 8, 2007, p. B2; "A year out, Beijing games test China's rising power," *Wall Street Journal*, August 7, 2007, p. A1; "Stepping up," *Houston Chronicle*, February 24, 2006, p. C2; "Obscurity takes a holiday," *Wall Street Journal*, February 11–12, 2006, p. A5; "Closing words opened door for London," *Financial Times*, July 7, 2005, p. 2; "A ringing endorsement: Business backing for the Olympics grows as scandals abate," *Financial Times*, July 1, 2005, p. 11; "NBC proud as a peacock of Olympics deal, high-tech focus," *Houston Chronicle*, June 7, 2003, p. 13B; "NBC plans 24-hour coverage of Summer Olympics in 2004," *Wall Street Journal*, February 5, 2003, p. B10; "Sydney already feeling the heat," *USA Today*, February 15, 2000, pp. 1C, 2C; "How the Olympics were bought," *Time*, January 25, 1999; "GM to spend up to $1 billion on Olympics through 2008 in pact with USOC, NBC," *Wall Street Journal*, July 29, 1997, p. B5; "Greek leaders see winning Olympic bid as an endorsement of market reforms," *Wall Street Journal*, September 8, 1997; "NBC wraps up the Olympics through 2008," *Wall Street Journal*, December 13, 1995, p. B1; "Japan's Nagano, site of 1998 games, faces problems of Olympic proportions," *Wall Street Journal*, March 15, 1994, p. A14; "Olympics strategy has its rewards," *USA Today*, February 21, 1994, pp. 1B, 2B; "Going for the gold, merchandisers and retailers promote the Olympics two years in advance," *Wall Street Journal*, December 7, 1993, pp. B1, B16; "Let the bidding begin for the TV rights to '96 Olympics, and watch it heat up," *Wall Street Journal*, August 7, 1992, p. B1; "The Olympics: Brought to you by…," *USA Today*, July 21, 1992, pp. 1B, 2B; "NBC's Olympic gamble," *Newsweek*, January 13, 1992, p. 44.

2. *Survey of Current Business* (Washington, DC: U.S. Department of Commerce), August 2010, p. 205, and November 2010, p. 45.

3. "Family garment business in Hong Kong uses Internet to gain access to global customer pool," *Wall Street Journal*, November 24, 1999, p. B11B.

4. "Surging exports lighten the gloom," *Wall Street Journal*, March 24, 2008, p. A2.

5. John H. Dunning, *Multinational Enterprises and the Global Economy* (Wokingham, England: Addison-Wesley Publishing Company, 1993), pp. 106ff.

6. Thomas L. Friedman, *The Lexus and the Olive Tree* (New York: Anchor Books, 2000), p. 9.

7. "U.S. agencies shift work overseas," *Wall Street Journal*, June 24, 2002, p. B5.

8. "Emerging markets boost L'Oréal profit," *Wall Street Journal*, February 10, 2011 (online).

9. Jeffrey Garten, *The Big Ten: The Big Emerging Markets and How They Will Change Your Life* (New York: HarperCollins, 1998).

CHAPTER 2

Global Marketplaces and Business Centers

AFTER STUDYING THIS CHAPTER, YOU SHOULD BE ABLE TO:

1. Evaluate the impact of the political and economic characteristics of the world's various marketplaces on the opportunities available to international businesses.

2. Appreciate the uses of national income data in making business decisions.

3. Discuss North America as a major marketplace and business center in the world economy.

4. Describe Western Europe as a major marketplace and business center in the world economy.

5. Discuss Asia as a major marketplace and business center in the world economy.

6. Assess the development challenges facing African, Middle Eastern, and South American countries.

Access a host of interactive learning aids at **www.pearsonglobaleditions.com/ mymanagementlab** to help strengthen your understanding of the chapter concepts.

MyManagementLab

© John Warburton-Lee Photography/Alamy

TRADE IS BLOSSOMING

Did you ever wonder where those red roses you gave or received on Valentine's Day came from? If you're a North American, they probably were grown on a mountainside in Colombia or Ecuador. If you're European, they might have come from Ethiopia or Kenya. And if you're Asian, their origin may be Kunming, a city in the rural province of Yunnan, China. Although most recipients of floral bouquets give little thought to where their beautiful blooms are grown, they are beneficiaries of the blossoming international trade in flowers and plants. Once the domain of small mom-and-pop growers focused on serving local markets, the globalization of the floriculture industry is driven by the forces we discussed in Chapter 1: technological change, trade liberalization, the desire to leverage core competencies, and the need to respond to new competitors. The supply chains and technology needed to bring fresh cut roses or mums to a loved one are no less sophisticated than those used by high-tech manufacturers of smart phones, personal computers, and big-screen TVs.

The Netherlands has long been the center of the international commercial flower industry. Dutch farmers began to use greenhouses to grow fruits, flowers, and vegetables during medieval times. Its universities, growers, and floral research centers have been leaders for centuries in developing new breeds of plants. The Dutch remain the most important exporters of flowers and plants, with about 65 percent of the world export market. Much of the country's prominence is attributable to FloraHolland, the most important flower auctioneer in the world. Structured as a cooperative owned by its 5,000 members (primarily growers), FloraHolland was created in 2008 through the merger of six of the country's flower auction markets, the largest of which was Aalsmeer (near Schipol Airport), followed by Naaldwijk and Rijnsburg. In 2009, FloraHolland auctioned over 12 billion plants and flowers worth €3.9 billion. Cut flowers accounted for about 56 percent of these revenues. Not surprisingly, roses were the most important flower, with auction sales valued at €679 million, followed by chrysanthemums and tulips. Most of its cut flowers are destined for EU markets; potted plants and bulbs, being less fragile, have a wider market. For example, the American market absorbs about a quarter of Dutch bulb exports.

Such statistics, however, do not tell the whole story of FloraHolland's significance. Its large trading volumes have allowed it to create a futures market in tulips, roses, and other flowers. By purchasing a flower future, large flower wholesalers can advertise and market flowers for delivery to their clients over the coming months without fear that unexpected changes in flower prices might wipe out their profits when they actually take delivery and pay for the flowers. The availability of flower futures attracts more buyers and sellers to the FloraHolland exchanges, thus increasing their transaction volumes and the liquidity of the market.

To expand its influence beyond the regional market, the flower exchange has integrated e-commerce into its auction system. Now buyers from Germany, France, and other European countries can monitor tulip, rose, and chrysanthemum auctions from their home computers without having to travel to Aalsmeer. The auction's website can also be used to place orders. By melding new technologies with its traditional auction methods, FloraHolland is ensuring that it will continue to play a critical role in the international flower market.

These adaptations are important, because Dutch growers face high labor and land costs, which have created opportunities for growers in other countries. Colombian farmers have benefited from their lower costs, geographic location, and favorable climates to become the primary source of cut flowers to the North American market, accounting for more than half of the flowers imported by U.S. flower wholesalers and retailers. Neighboring Ecuador specializes in roses, which its climate favors. Kenya and Ethiopia are becoming important providers for the European market. China—particulary the city of Kunming in Yunnan province—is growing as a supplier to the Asian market. The Chinese government has encouraged the growth of the industry through low interest loans on greenhouses and refrigerated trucks. Dutch, Korean, and Japanese companies have started to invest in the area, believing it provides a lower cost source of flowers for the Asian market. The domestic Chinese market is also expanding rapidly, in line with the growth of the country's middle class.

The growing international trade in flowers and plants has impacted other industries. The airline industry has been quick to adapt to the changing needs of the floricultural industry. Flowers are perishable, so the reliability of scheduled air service is critical to the buyers' needs. Moreover, most passenger carriers have unused cargo space after accommodating travelers' baggage. Flowers also have a high value-to-weight ratio and are packed in small boxes that easily fit into the cargo hold of a modern jet airliner. And once the flowers arrive at their destination airport, specialized transporters are needed to ensure that flowers are kept refrigerated from the airport to the wholesaler or retailer, creating new opportunities for innovative trucking companies and providers of logistics services to prosper.[1] ◼

FIGURE 2.1

The World Economy: 1970 and 2009

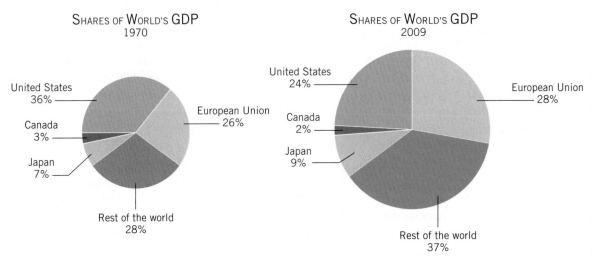

Source: World Bank, *World Development Report* 2011, pp. 312–317.

The blossoming of international trade in flowers is but one example of the myriad opportunities created by globalization. Yet businesses trying to internationalize their operations often blunder because they fail to obtain information vital to their success. Ignorance of basic geography, market characteristics, culture, and politics may lead to lost profits or, in the extreme, doom a venture to failure. Linguistic and cultural ties, past political associations, and military alliances play significant roles in the world pattern of trade and investment and in shaping the opportunities available to businesses today. For example, London's contemporary importance as a world financial center arises from the political and military power of the British Empire in the nineteenth century. Similarly, Austria serves as a bridge between Western and Eastern Europe because of transportation, educational, and cultural linkages that remain from the 600-year reign of the Hapsburg dynasty over the Austro-Hungarian Empire.

Providing an overview of the world economy is a challenge because of its vast size. Much of the world's current economic activity—about 63 percent, as Figure 2.1 indicates—is concentrated in the developed countries of North America, the European Union, and Japan. This is not to suggest that international managers can ignore other markets if they wish to compete successfully. The emerging markets we discussed in Chapter 1—particularly China and India—are responsible for much of the growth in the world economy. In the twenty-first century, the growth rates of China and India, 10.9 percent and 7.8 percent, respectively, have far outpaced Japan's 1.1 percent, Germany's 0.9 percent, or the United States' 2.1 percent. Because astute international managers increasingly need a thorough and sophisticated understanding of the opportunities available in each of the six inhabited continents, we provide a brief overview of all the world's marketplaces in this chapter.

The Marketplaces of North America

North America includes the United States, Canada, Mexico, Greenland, and the countries of Central America and the Caribbean. Home to 531 million people, these countries produce approximately 29 percent of the world's output.

The United States

The United States has only the world's third largest population and fourth largest land mass, yet it possesses the largest economy, accounting for 24 percent of the world's $58.2 trillion GDP in 2009. As Map 2.1 shows, the United States enjoys the highest per capita income of the North

MAP 2.1
North America

Although Greenland is geographically in North America, it is affiliated politically with the Kingdom of Denmark.

- • Cities over 1 million
- ■ Cities of 500,000 to 1 million
- ✪ National capitals
- ⊞ National capitals over 1 million

Country	Population (millions)	2009 GDP (billions)	GDP per capita
CANADA	34	$1,336	$42,170
UNITED STATES	307	$14,119	$47,240
MEXICO	107	$874	$8,920
CENTRAL AMERICA	42	$134	$3,213
CARIBBEAN	41	$259	$6,328

American countries.[2] The United States occupies a unique position in the world economy because of its size and political stability, accounting for about one-tenth of world exports of goods and services and about one-eighth of world imports of goods and services. It is the prime market for lower-income countries trying to raise their standards of living through export-oriented economic development strategies. It is also the prime market for firms from higher-income countries trying to attract business from its large, well-educated middle class. (See "Emerging Opportunities.")

The U.S. dollar serves as the **invoicing currency**—the currency in which the sale of goods and services is denominated—for about half of all international transactions and is an important component of foreign-currency reserves worldwide. Because of its political stability and military strength, the United States also attracts **flight capital**—money sent out of a politically or economically unstable country to one perceived as a safe haven. Citizens unsure of the value of their home country's currency often choose to keep their wealth in dollars. The United States also is an important recipient of long-term foreign investment. Foreigners have invested over $2.3 trillion in U.S. factories, equipment, and property as of 2010.

Although international trade has become increasingly more important during the past decade, it is a relatively small component of the U.S. economy. U.S. exports of goods and services in 2010 totaled $1.8 trillion but were only 12.3 percent of its GDP. However, this figure is somewhat misleading. Because of the country's large size, trade that might be counted as international in smaller countries is considered domestic in the United States. For example, the money spent for a hotel room in neighboring Belgium by a Dutch motorist trapped in a thunderstorm 50 miles from home late at night is counted in the international trade statistics of both Belgium and the Netherlands. A similar expenditure by a Connecticut motorist stuck in New Jersey after watching a football game at the Meadowlands is a purely domestic transaction.

As discussed throughout this book, MNCs heavily influence international trade and investment. In 2010 the world's 500 largest corporations had total sales of $26.0 trillion. Given the importance of the United States in the world economy, it should come as no surprise that 133 of these corporations, or 27 percent, are headquartered in the United States, including 29 of the largest 100 (see Figure 2.2). Walmart is currently the world's largest company, with sales of $419.0 billion in 2010.

FIGURE 2.2

Headquarters of the World's Largest Corporations in 2010 by Country

Source: Fortune, July 25, 2011, p. F1.

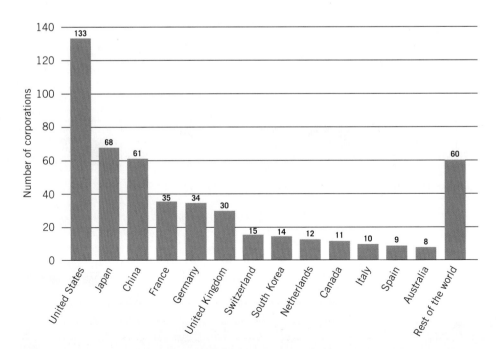

Canada

Canada has the world's second largest land mass, although its population is only 34 million. Eighty percent of the population is concentrated within a 100-mile band along the country's southern border with the United States. Exports are vital to the Canadian economy, accounting for 24 percent of its 2009 GDP of $1,336 billion. Canada's most important exports reflect its rich natural resources: forest products, petroleum, minerals, and grain. The United States is the dominant market for Canadian goods, receiving over three-quarters of Canada's exports in a typical year. Two-way trade between the United States and Canada, which totaled $609 billion in 2010, forms the single largest bilateral trading relationship in the world.

International investors have long been attracted to Canada because of its proximity to the huge U.S. market and the stability of its political and legal systems. Canada's excellent infrastructure and educational systems also contribute to the performance of its economy. However, a lingering threat to Canada's political stability—and to its ability to attract foreign investment—is the long-standing conflict between French-speaking Canadians (many of whom live in the province of Quebec) and English-speaking Canadians. A strong separatist movement has existed in Quebec since the 1960s, and English-speaking Canada has been pressured to adopt policies to diffuse separatism. This conflict has affected domestic and international businesses in many ways. For example, firms exporting products to Canada must be aware of the country's bilingual labeling laws. Also, the riskiness of loans to Quebec firms would increase substantially, at least in the short run, if the province were to become a separate nation, as the 40-year-old separatist movement desires. A more immediate threat to the Canadian economy—the rising value of its currency relative to the U.S. dollar—is explored in Chapter 8's opening case, "The Loonie Takes Flight."

EMERGING OPPORTUNITIES   CLASSIFYING COUNTRIES BY INCOME LEVELS

Often the single most important piece of information needed by international businesspeople about a country is its income level. Income levels provide clues to the purchasing power of residents, the technological sophistication of local production processes, and the status of the public infrastructure.

One important source of income statistics is the World Bank, which divides the world's countries into high-income, middle-income, and low-income categories. High-income countries are those that enjoy annual per capita incomes of at least $12,196. [**Per capita income** is usually measured by dividing a country's **gross domestic product (GDP)** or its **gross national income (GNI)** by its population. GDP is the total market value of all goods and services produced in a country during some time period, such as a year. GNI is GDP plus net income, such as dividends and interest received from residents of other countries minus those paid to residents of other countries.] The high-income group comprises three clusters of countries. The first cluster is drawn from the **Organization for Economic Cooperation and Development (OECD)**, a group of 34 market-oriented democracies formed to promote economic growth. The OECD includes 25 Western European countries (the 15 European Union members prior to its 2004 expansion plus the Czech Republic, Estonia, Hungary, Iceland, Norway, Poland, the Slovak Republic, Slovenia, Switzerland, and Turkey), four Pacific Rim countries (Australia, Japan, New Zealand, and South Korea), and Canada, Mexico, the United States, Israel, and Chile. Thirty-one of the OECD's 34 members fall in the high-income category. (The remaining members—Chile, Mexico, and Turkey—are classified as upper middle income.) The second cluster comprises oil-rich countries such as Bahrain, Brunei, Kuwait, Qatar, Saudi Arabia, and the United Arab Emirates. The third cluster consists of smaller industrialized countries and island states, including Croatia,

Latvia, Hong Kong, Singapore, Taiwan, Bermuda, the Bahamas, and the Cayman Islands.

Middle-income countries have per capita incomes of more than $995 but less than $12,196. The World Bank subdivides this group into lower middle income (per capita income between $996 and $3,945) and upper middle income (per capita income between $3,946 and $12,195). This category includes most of the former Soviet republics, which generally enjoyed high levels of development in the 1930s but fell behind the Western economies economically after World War II. Other countries in this category, such as Chile, Costa Rica, and Mauritius, have been undergoing successful industrialization and economic growth and may be elevated to the high-income category by the end of this decade.

Lower-income countries, often called developing countries, have per capita incomes of $995 or less. This category includes some countries, such as Cambodia and Rwanda, whose economies are growing substantially because of external aid, sound domestic economic policies, foreign direct investment (FDI), and/or exploitation of valuable natural resources. Officially labeled "underdeveloped" by the United Nations General Assembly in 1971, these countries have the potential for above-average economic growth. Other countries, designated "undeveloped" and "least developed" by the United Nations, have low literacy rates, per capita incomes, and economic growth. They are less attractive to international businesses because they offer less consumer demand and lack the public infrastructure necessary for reliable production and distribution of goods and services. A prime example of this latter category is Somalia, an East African country wracked by drought, civil war, and starvation.

Source: World Bank, *World Development Report 2011* (Washington, D.C.: World Bank, 2011).

Mexico

Now the world's most populous Spanish-speaking nation, Mexico declared independence from its Spanish conquerors in 1810. Like the United States, Mexico is a federal system but one whose head of government, a president, is elected by popular vote every six years. For over half a century the Mexican government implemented a program of economic nationalism under which Mexico discouraged foreign investment and erected high tariff walls to protect its domestic industries. During the past three decades, however, Mexico has abandoned these policies and opened its markets to foreign goods and investors. Mexico also reduced the government's role in its economy by selling off many publicly owned firms, such as Aeromexico and Telefonos de Mexico. In 1994, Canada, Mexico, and the United States initiated the North American Free Trade Agreement (NAFTA), which reduced barriers to trade among the three countries over a 15-year period. Thousands of foreign companies have established new factories in Mexico to take advantage of NAFTA, generating hundreds of thousands of new jobs in the process. In 1999, Mexico signed a similar agreement with the European Union, hoping to create additional benefits for its citizens. In 2000, it signed free trade pacts with neighboring El Salvador, Guatemala, and Honduras, and, in 2004, with Japan and Uruguay.[3] The role of trade in Mexico's economy is explored further in Chapter 10's opening case, "Trade and Prosperity: The Case of Mexico."

Central America and the Caribbean

Besides the United States, Canada, and Mexico, the North American continent is occupied by two dozen other countries that are divided geographically into two groups: Central America and the island states of the Caribbean. Collectively their population equals 83 million—more than twice the population of Canada. However, their total GDP of $393 billion is a third of that of Canada. With a few exceptions (notably Costa Rica), the economic development of these countries has suffered from a variety of problems, including political instability, chronic U.S. military intervention, inadequate educational systems, a weak middle class, economic policies that have created large pockets of poverty, and import limitations by the United States and other developed countries on Central American and Caribbean goods, such as sugar and clothing.

The Marketplaces of Western Europe

Western European countries are among the world's most prosperous, attracting the attention of businesses eager to market their products to the region's wealthy consumers. These countries can be divided into two groups: members of the European Union (EU) and other countries in the region (see Map 2.2).

The EU, which we discuss in greater detail in Chapter 10, comprises 27 countries that are seeking to promote European peace and prosperity by reducing mutual barriers to trade and investment. During the past two decades the EU has made tremendous strides in achieving this objective. With a 2009 GDP of $16.4 trillion and a population of 499 million, it is one of the world's richest markets. EU members are free-market-oriented, parliamentary democracies. However, government intervention and ownership generally play a more important role in these countries' economies than in the economy of the United States. Seventeen EU members have eliminated their national currencies, replacing them with a new common currency known as the euro (€).

From an economic perspective, Germany is the EU's most important member. With a 2009 GDP of $3.3 trillion, it possesses the world's fourth largest economy, after the United States, China, and Japan. It is a major player in international business; in 2009 it was the world's second largest exporter of goods (after China), some $1.1 trillion. (Chapter 6's opening case, "The Mittelstand Lead the Way," provides additional insights into Germany's exporting success.) Because of the strength of the German economy and the government's strict anti-inflation policies, Germany has played a major role in formulating the economic policies of the EU.

Politically, France exerts strong leadership within the EU. The French government has been a leading proponent of promoting common European defense and foreign policies and strengthening human rights and workers' rights in the EU. But French leaders have drawn criticism for promoting an agenda of economic nationalism, defending French corporations from takeover efforts by other European firms, contrary to the founding principles of the EU, and protecting the large subsidies paid to French farmers under the EU's Common Agricultural Policy.

MAP 2.2
Western Europe

As the EU's leading voice favoring free trade, the United Kingdom provides a strong counterweight to France's protectionist tendencies.

As the political leader of the EU, France has long been a strong advocate of strengthening human and workers' rights in the EU.

The German central bank had de facto control over the monetary policies of EU members, but its role was taken over by the European Central Bank (ECB) in 1999. The ECB now controls monetary policy for countries using the euro.

Legend:
- EU members using the euro
- EU members using own national currency
- Countries not members of the EU
- Cities over 1 million
- Capitals over 1 million

France's positions have not gone unchallenged, however. The United Kingdom has resisted many of the initiatives to broaden the EU's powers and, as a traditionally strong supporter of free trade, has provided an important counterweight to French protectionist tendencies. The United Kingdom's capital city, London, is a major international finance center, employing over 300,000 in its financial services sector. The United Kingdom is also a major exporter and importer of goods, an important destination for and source of foreign investment, and home to the headquarters or regional divisions of numerous MNCs.

Many of the newest EU members were either part of the Soviet Union (Estonia, Latvia, and Lithuania) or allied with the Soviet Union politically and economically (Bulgaria, Czech Republic, Hungary, Poland, Slovakia, and Romania). (EU member Slovenia declared its independence from communist Yugoslavia in 1991, but Yugoslavia was not part of the Soviet bloc.) After the Soviet bloc began dissolving in 1989 and the Soviet Union disintegrated in 1991, the regional trading system established by the Soviet Union broke down, and the former Soviet satellite states had to adjust to the loss of guaranteed export markets. They also had to restructure their economies from centrally planned communist systems to decentralized market systems and implement necessary political, legal, and institutional reforms, a process facilitated by their joining the European Union. The Czech Republic, Estonia, and Slovenia are the furthest along in this process, already achieving high-income status according to the World Bank's measures.

Rich Western European countries that are not EU members include Iceland, Norway, and Switzerland, plus several small, "postage stamp" countries such as Andorra, Monaco, and Liechtenstein. Classified as high income by the World Bank, these free-market-oriented countries collectively account for 2 percent of the world's GDP. The economies of the Balkan countries of Albania, Bosnia and Herzegovina, Kosovo, Macedonia, Montenegro, and Serbia are classified as middle income by the World Bank, while Croatia is in the high-income category. Their post–Cold War economic progress was slowed by the chaos that surrounded the disintegration of Yugoslavia in 1991. The economies of Serbia, Montenegro, and Bosnia were devastated by the brutal wars over control of Bosnia in the early 1990s and over Kosovo in the late 1990s. These conflicts, needless to say, discouraged most MNCs from investing there during those troubled times.

The Marketplaces of Eastern Europe and Central Asia

No area of the world has undergone as much economic change in the past decade and a half as the countries carved out of the former Soviet Union (see Map 2.3), many of which are still dealing with the aftermath of the painful processes of converting from communism to capitalism and from totalitarianism to democracy. Soviet leader Mikhail Gorbachev's 1986 reform initiatives of *glasnost* (openness) and *perestroika* (economic restructuring) triggered the region's political, economic, and social revolutions.

The area's modern economic history begins with the creation of the Union of Soviet Socialist Republics (Soviet Union or U.S.S.R.), which emerged from the disintegration of the Russian Empire that followed its defeat in World War I. In the chaos that ensued from the 1917 abdication of Czar Nicholas II, the Communist Party seized control of the Russian government and established the Soviet Union in the name of the workers and peasants. The communists outlawed the market system, abolished private property, and collectivized the country's vast rich farmlands. By doing so, they succeeded in reducing the enormous income inequalities that had existed under czarist rule. Despite this success, the population's standard of living increasingly fell behind that of the Western democracies.

Gorbachev's economic and political reforms led to the Soviet Union's collapse in 1991 and subsequent declarations of independence by the 15 Soviet republics, which are now often referred to as the **Newly Independent States,** or **NIS**. In 1992, 12 of the NIS (all but the Baltic countries of Estonia, Latvia, and Lithuania, which are now part of the European Union) formed the **Commonwealth of Independent States (CIS)** as a forum to discuss issues of mutual concern. The most important of these new countries is the Russian Federation (Russia), which was the dominant republic within the former Soviet Union. As an independent state, Russia is the world's largest country in land mass (6.5 million square miles) and the ninth largest in population (142 million people). The country is well endowed with natural resources, including gold, oil, natural gas, minerals, diamonds, and fertile farmland.

MAP 2.3
The Former Soviet Union

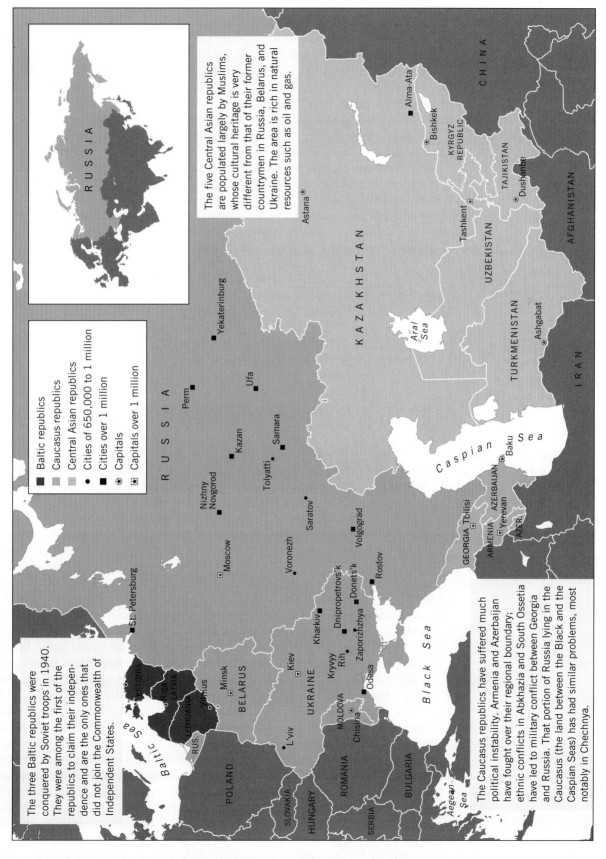

The three Baltic republics were conquered by Soviet troops in 1940. They were among the first of the republics to claim their independence and are the only ones that did not join the Commonwealth of Independent States.

The five Central Asian republics are populated largely by Muslims, whose cultural heritage is very different from that of their former countrymen in Russia, Belarus, and Ukraine. The area is rich in natural resources such as oil and gas.

The Caucasus republics have suffered much political instability. Armenia and Azerbaijan have fought over their regional boundary; ethnic conflicts in Abkhazia and South Ossetia have led to military conflict between Georgia and Russia. That portion of Russia lying in the Caucasus (the land between the Black and the Caspian Seas) has had similar problems, most notably in Chechnya.

Legend:
- Baltic republics
- Caucasus republics
- Central Asian republics
- • Cities of 650,000 to 1 million
- ■ Cities over 1 million
- ⊛ Capitals
- ⊞ Capitals over 1 million

RUSSIA

St. Petersburg
Yekaterinburg
Perm
Ufa
Nizhny Novgorod
Kazan
Tolyatti
Samara
Moscow
Voronezh
Saratov
Volgograd
Rostov

ESTONIA
LATVIA
Riga
LITHUANIA
Vilnius
RUS.
Baltic Sea
Minsk
BELARUS
POLAND
Kiev
UKRAINE
L'viv
Kharkiv
Dnipropetrovs'k
Donets'k
Kryvyy Rih
Zaporizhzhya
Odesa
MOLDOVA
Chisina
ROMANIA
HUNGARY
SLOVAKIA
SERBIA
BULGARIA
Aegean Sea
Black Sea

KAZAKHSTAN
Astana
Aral Sea
Caspian Sea
Alma-Ata
Bishkek
KYRGYZ REPUBLIC
Tashkent
UZBEKISTAN
TAJIKISTAN
Dushanbe
TURKMENISTAN
Ashgabat
Baku
AZERBAIJAN
AZER.
Yerevan
ARMENIA
GEORGIA Tbilisi
CHINA
AFGHANISTAN
IRAN

The transformation of the economies of Russia and many of the other NIS from communism to a free-market system was not easy, to say the least. Boris Yeltsin, Russia's first democratically elected president, tried to privatize many of Russia's state-owned firms. Although some newly privatized firms improved their productivity, many fell into the hands of individuals who were more concerned with looting corporate assets than restoring the companies' economic health and performance. Under Yeltsin's administration, Russia's central government staggered from one financial crisis to another, burdened by an inability to collect taxes and a political need to subsidize the inefficient state-owned enterprises that it was unable to sell to private interests. August 1998 marked the economy's low point: Yeltsin's government was forced to devalue the ruble and imposed a 90-day moratorium on payments to foreign creditors.

Russia's economy has rebounded smartly in the past decade. The country's second president, Vladimir Putin, quickly overhauled the country's taxation system, instituting a flat income tax of 13 percent. This initiative worked, and government revenues increased. Russia, which is the world's second largest oil producer and exporter, has also benefited from the increased prices of oil and other raw materials, which will be discussed in this chapter's closing case. The country's GDP has increased at an annual rate of 5.9 percent per year since 2000. By early 2011, Russia had accumulated $513 billion in currency reserves, the third largest in the world after China and Japan, and its prospects for continued economic growth look strong.

The five Central Asian republics of the former Soviet Union—Kazakhstan, Uzbekistan, Tajikistan, Turkmenistan, and Kyrgyzstan—have much in common. One common feature is the importance of Russia in their recent political history. The five Central Asian republics were part of czarist Russia. Each became a Socialist Republic of the Soviet Union after the communists deposed the czars. When the Soviet Union dissolved in 1991, the five declared their independence. The Muslim faith is the dominant religion in all of them. Their languages share Turkic or Persian roots. All suffer from a scarcity of arable land; mountains and deserts dominate their landscapes. Their peoples are poor, with per capita incomes ranging from $700 in Tajikistan to $6,740 in Kazakhstan. However, extensive fossil fuel reserves can be found throughout Central Asia, particularly in Kazakhstan and Turkmenistan.

The Marketplaces of Asia

Asia is home to over half the world's population, yet it produces only a quarter of the world's GDP (see Map 2.4). Asia's importance to international business cannot be overstated. The region is a source of both high-quality and low-quality products and of both skilled and unskilled labor. Asia is both a major destination for foreign investments by MNCs and a major supplier of capital to non-Asian countries. More important, its aggressive, efficient entrepreneurs have increasingly put competitive pressure on European and North American firms to improve their productivity and the quality of their products.

Japan

Japan, an island country of 126 million people, rose from the ashes of World War II to become one of the world's economic superpowers, with a GDP of $5.1 trillion in 2009. For most of the post-World War II period, Japan's GDP was second only to that of the United States. In 2010, China's GDP surpassed that of Japan, relegating Japan to the number three position. Japan's economic success during the past 60 years is due in part to the partnership between its Ministry of International Trade and Industry (MITI) and its industrial sector. (In 2001, MITI was renamed the Ministry of Economy, Trade, and Industry.) MITI has used its formal and informal powers to guide the production and investment strategies of the country's corporate elite. For example, immediately after World War II, MITI encouraged Japanese firms to concentrate their efforts on such basic industries as steel and shipbuilding. As other countries entered these industries, MITI and Japan's MNCs shifted their focus to producing automobiles, consumer electronics, and machinery.

MITI has been aided by Japan's concentrated industrial structure. Japanese industry is controlled by large families of interrelated companies, called **keiretsu,** that are typically centered on a major Japanese bank. The bank takes primary responsibility for meeting the keiretsu's financing needs. The members often act as suppliers to each other, thus making it more difficult for outsiders to penetrate Japanese markets. Members are also protected from hostile takeovers by an elaborate system of cross-ownership of shares in which keiretsu

MAP 2.4
Asia

The Ural Mountains divide Russia into its European and Asian regions.

Of the top 20 trading nations—based on the sum of imports and exports of goods—7 are countries in East Asia.

China, India, and Indonesia are the first, second, and fourth most populous countries in the world; China alone is home to more than one-fifth of the human race.

Sea of Okhotsk

KURIL ISLANDS

JAPAN
Tokyo
Nagoya
Osaka
Kobe
Kitakyushu

Sea of Japan

N. KOREA
Pyongyang
Seoul
S. KOREA

East China Sea

Taipei
TAIWAN

Pacific Ocean

PAPUA NEW GUINEA

AUSTRALIA

Timor-Leste
Dili

PHILIPPINES
Manila

Celebes Sea

South China Sea

BRUNEI
BORNEO

MALAYSIA
Kuala Lumpur
SINGAPORE

SUMATRA

Jakarta

Ho Chi Minh City

VIETNAM
Phnom Penh
CAMBODIA
Viangchan
LAOS

THAILAND

Rangoon
MYANMAR

HONG KONG
Macao

Guangzhou (Canton)
Changsha
Wuhan
Shanghai
Chongqing (Chungking)
Chengdu

Harbin
Changchun
Shenyang
Beijing (Peking)
Tianjin
Taiyuan

CHINA

RUSSIA

Lake Baikal

Novosibirsk

Ulan Bator
MONGOLIA

Yekaterinburg

Chelyabinsk

Astana

KAZAKHSTAN

Aral Sea

Bishkek
KYRGYZ REPUBLIC
Tashkent
UZBEKISTAN
TAJIKISTAN
Dushanbe
Islamabad

Ashgabat
TURKMENISTAN

Kabul
AFGHANISTAN

Lahore
PAKISTAN

Karachi

Delhi
New Delhi

Ahmadabad
Mumbai

INDIA

Jamshedpur
Kolkata

NEPAL
BHUTAN
BANG.
Dacca
Kolkata

Chennai

SRI LANKA
Colombo

Bay of Bengal

Arabian Sea

Hanoi

Caspian Sea

GEORGIA
Tbilisi
ARMENIA
Yerevan
AZERBAIJAN
Baku

TURKEY
Ankara
Istanbul

Black Sea

LEBANON
Beirut
SYRIA
Damascus
Jerusalem
ISRAEL
Amman
JORDAN

Baghdad
IRAQ

Tehran
IRAN

Kuwait
KUWAIT

BAHRAIN
Manama
QATAR
Doha
U.A.E.
Abu Dhabi
Muscat
OMAN

Riyadh
SAUDI ARABIA

Sanaa
YEMEN

Mediterranean Sea

Legend:

- High-income nations
- Middle-income nations
- Low-income nations
- Major industrial areas
- Capitals ⊛
- Cities over 5 million ■
- Capitals over 5 million ⊞

members own shares in one another's companies. Toyota Motors, for example, owns 10 percent of the common stock of Koito Manufacturing, and other members of Toyota's keiretsu own 25 percent of Koito's stock. Koito in turn is the primary supplier for Toyota's automotive lighting needs. Keiretsu members often rely on a **sogo shosha,** an export trading company, to market their exports worldwide. Typically the sogo shosha is also a keiretsu member.

Japan's economic growth slowed in the 1990s, however. Since 2000, its GDP has grown at an annual rate of 1.1 percent, well below the 2.9 percent average growth in the world economy. Many experts are concerned that the Japanese political and economic systems have not been able to adjust quickly enough to the changes in the world economy created by the growth of e-commerce and the emerging markets. Moreover, Japan has received much international criticism because of the perception that it employs unfair trading practices to market its exports while using numerous nontariff barriers to restrict imports to its domestic market (we will discuss this further in Chapter 9). Perhaps Japan's greatest challenge, however, is dealing with its growing demographic crisis: the aging of its population (see Chapter 1's closing case, "Demography Is Destiny").

Australia and New Zealand

Australia and New Zealand are the other traditional economic powers in Pacific Asia. Although they share a common cultural heritage, significant differences exist between the two countries, which are separated by 1,200 miles of ocean (see Map 2.5). Australia's 22 million people live in

MAP 2.5
Australia and New Zealand

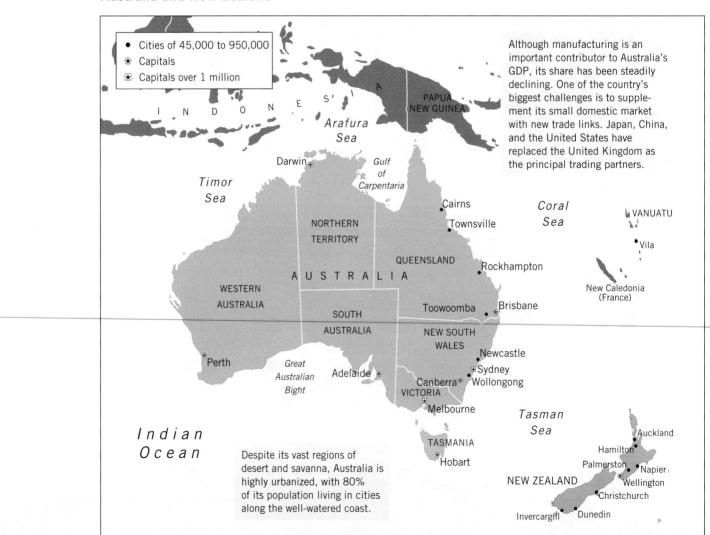

- Cities of 45,000 to 950,000
- ⊛ Capitals
- ⊞ Capitals over 1 million

Although manufacturing is an important contributor to Australia's GDP, its share has been steadily declining. One of the country's biggest challenges is to supplement its small domestic market with new trade links. Japan, China, and the United States have replaced the United Kingdom as the principal trading partners.

Despite its vast regions of desert and savanna, Australia is highly urbanized, with 80% of its population living in cities along the well-watered coast.

New Zealand's temperate but rainy climate provides rich pasture land for the country's 40 million sheep and a prosperous livelihood for its farmers. New Zealand's primary exports are wool, meat, and dairy products.

© Jan Mika/Alamy

an area of 2.97 million square miles. Because much of the continent is arid, most of the population is concentrated in the wetter coastal regions, with approximately 40 percent living in either Sydney or Melbourne. Australia is rich in natural resources but has a relatively small workforce. As a result, its merchandise exports, which in 2009 accounted for 17 percent of its $925 billion GDP, are concentrated in natural resource industries (such as gold, iron ore, and coal) and in land-intensive agricultural goods (such as wool, beef, and wheat).

New Zealand's 4.3 million people live on two main islands—the more populous North Island and the more scenic but less temperate South Island. After systematically deregulating and privatizing its economy in the 1980s, New Zealand gained an international reputation as being in the forefront of the worldwide shift toward greater reliance on market-based policies. Merchandise trade is extremely important to the country; in 2009 exports constituted 20 percent of its $126 billion GDP. Over half of New Zealand's exports are attributable to its extensive pasture lands. These exports include dairy products, meat, and wool. Australia, Japan, and the United States purchase approximately half of New Zealand's exports and imports.

The Four Tigers

Pacific Asia is one of the world's most rapidly industrializing regions. South Korea, Taiwan, Singapore, and Hong Kong in particular have made such rapid strides since 1945 that they are collectively known as the "Four Tigers," a reference to the Chinese heritage that three of the four countries share. They are also referred to as the newly industrialized countries (NICs) or the newly industrialized economies (NIEs). While many publications still classify the Four Tigers as "emerging markets," they have in fact already emerged, as indicated by their having achieved high-income classification by the World Bank for more than a decade.

SOUTH KOREA The Republic of Korea, more commonly known as South Korea, was born of the Cold War, which left the Korean peninsula divided into communist North Korea and capitalist South Korea. Since the end of the Korean War in 1953, South Korea has been one of the world's fastest-growing economies. Merchandise exports accounted for 44 percent of its 2009 GDP of $833 billion. To promote economic development, Korea relied on tight cooperation between the government and 30 or so large, privately owned, and family-centered conglomerates that dominate the Korean economy. The most important of these conglomerates, or **chaebol,** were Samsung, Hyundai, Daewoo Group, and LG (formerly Lucky-Goldstar). In many ways the Korean government tried to follow the economic path established by the Japanese: discouragement of imports, governmental leadership of the economy, and reliance on large economic combines for industrialization.

Unfortunately, Korea's growth came to a screeching halt as a result of the 1997–1998 Asian currency crisis, and many of the chaebol were plunged into financial difficulties. Many observers argued that their problems were due to overexpansion and the poor lending practices of Korean banks. Many of the chaebol seemed to be more interested in size than profitability and borrowed money to enter industries already burdened by overcapacity, such as automobiles, computer chips, and steel manufacturing.

Some of the chaebol learned their lesson and emerged from the crisis as stronger and leaner competitors. Samsung, for example, narrowed its corporate focus. Its senior managers chose to concentrate the company's resources in electronics. Samsung is now a market leader in flash memory, DRAM memory chips, flat-panel displays, color laser printers, and cell phones. The process was painful, however, for Samsung was forced to lay off almost half its workforce and sell off noncore operations. Other chaebol struggle to regain their former glory, such as Ssangyong and Daewoo. Part of their empires were sold off to foreigners or allowed to die in bankruptcy courts.[4]

TAIWAN   Taiwan, as the Republic of China is commonly known, is a small island country off the coast of mainland China that is home to 23 million people. It was born in the aftermath of the civil war between the nationalist forces led by General Chiang Kai-shek and the Chinese communists led by Mao Tse-tung. After their defeat on the mainland in 1949, Chiang's army and government fled to Taiwan. Declaring the island "the Republic of China" and himself the rightful governor of the mainland, Chiang set about developing the Taiwanese economy to support a promised invasion of the mainland. Redistribution of land from large estate holders to peasants increased agricultural productivity. Reliance on family-owned private businesses and export-oriented trade policies has made Taiwan one of the world's fastest-growing economies during the past three decades. Exports were $275 billion in 2009, or 64 percent of the country's GDP of $427 billion.

Taiwan's economic development has been so fast-paced that it can no longer compete as a low-wage manufacturing center. Consequently, Taiwanese businesses more recently have focused on high-value-added industries such as electronics and automotive products. However, the businesses still need low-wage workers. Despite the lack of diplomatic relations between Taiwan and China, Taiwanese businesses increasingly are investing in factories and assembly plants in China to access the low-wage workers they need. For instance, Taiwan's Hon Hai Precision Industries, one of the world's largest contract manufacturers, employs over one million workers in its Chinese factories who produce mobile phones, laptops, and other electronics goods for firms like Apple, Cisco, Nokia, Sony, Vizio, Dell, Intel, and Hewlett-Packard.[5]

SINGAPORE   The Republic of Singapore is a former British colony and a small island country off the southern tip of the Malay Peninsula. To combat the chronic unemployment that plagued the country when it became independent in 1965, Singapore's government initially emphasized development of labor-intensive industries such as textiles. This economic policy proved so successful that Singapore shifted to higher-value-added activities, such as oil refining and chemical processing, and high-tech industries, such as computers and biotechnology. With a population of only 4.7 million, Singapore now suffers from a labor shortage. It can no longer compete with such countries as Honduras and Indonesia in the production of price-sensitive, labor-intensive manufactured goods.

In 2009, Singapore's per capita income was $37,220 and its exports totaled $270 billion, or *148 percent* of its GDP of $182 billion. That figure is not a misprint. Singapore thrives on **reexporting.** Singapore's firms take advantage of the country's excellent port facilities to import foreign goods and then reexport them to other countries (particularly neighboring Malaysia). Besides being an important port and center for oil refining, Singapore provides sophisticated communications and financial services for firms in Pacific Asia and is well on its way to becoming the region's high-technology center.

HONG KONG   Hong Kong was born of the "opium war" (1839–1842) fought between the United Kingdom and China. As a consequence of this war, Hong Kong was ceded to the British. In 1860 the British obtained possession of Kowloon on the Chinese mainland, and in

Hong Kongs deep, sheltered harbor and its dedication to free markets have made it a regional center for international trade and banking. Once a British Crown Colony, it is now a Special Administrative Region of the People's Republic of China.

Chad Ehlers/Stock Connection

1898 they were granted a 99-year lease on an area of the mainland known as the New Territories. The lease expired on July 1, 1997. On that date China again assumed political control of Hong Kong and designated it a special administrative region (SAR). As an SAR, Hong Kong enjoys a fair degree of autonomy. It has its own legislature, economic freedom, free-port status, and a separate taxation system. Hong Kong will enjoy these privileges until 2047. However, China has made it clear that it will impose its own political will on Hong Kong.

Hong Kong's attractiveness to international businesses lies in its deep, sheltered harbor and its role as an entry point to mainland China. Seven million people are packed into Hong Kong's small land area. It offers highly educated, highly productive labor for industries such as textiles and electronics and provides banking and financial services for much of East Asia. As a result of common culture and geography, Hong Kong entrepreneurs often act as intermediaries for companies around the world that want to do business with China. Hong Kong has also traditionally served as a bridge between Taiwan and its political enemy, China. Accordingly, Hong Kong has thrived as an entrepôt for China, receiving goods from it and preparing the goods for shipment to the rest of the world, and vice versa. Export statistics for Hong Kong reflect its role as a reexporter. It exported $330 billion worth of goods in 2009, or 194 percent of its $215 billion GDP.

China

With 1.3 billion people, China is the world's most populous country. It also is one of the world's oldest, ruled by a series of emperors from 2000 B.C. until the early 1900s, when a republic was founded. A chaotic civil war facilitated a Japanese invasion in 1931. After the Japanese were expelled at the end of World War II, the civil war resumed. Finally, in 1949 the communist forces of Mao Tse-tung defeated the nationalist army led by General Chiang Kai-shek.

Communism in China under Mao Tse-tung went through several stages. The Great Leap Forward was a program undertaken from 1958 to 1960 to force industrialization through the growth of small, labor-intensive factories. The program's failure led eventually to the Cultural Revolution in 1966, during which youthful communist cadres indiscriminately purged Communist Party members suspected of deviating from Mao's doctrines. The political chaos that followed set back the country's economic progress, as many of its most productive and educated members were exiled to the countryside to repent their ideological sins.

While many Chinese venerate Chairman Mao, he badly mismanaged the country's economy during his decades of rule. Economic reforms undertaken after his death form the foundation for China's recent spectacular economic growth.

Bettmann

After Mao's death in 1976, the government adopted limited free-market policies. Agriculture was returned to the private sector, and entrepreneurs were allowed to start small businesses such as restaurants and light manufacturing. Foreign companies were permitted to establish joint ventures with Chinese firms. As a result, FDI and economic growth soared, as did hopes for increased political freedom. However, Communist Party leaders were unwilling to relinquish their powers. The massacre of several thousand pro-democracy demonstrators in Beijing's Tiananmen Square in June 1989 chilled economic and political relations between China and the developed countries for several years.

Nonetheless, China is following a unique path. It continues to adopt market-oriented economic policies under the Communist Party's watchful eye, while seemingly abandoning the ideological principles of the party. China's vibrant economy, which grew 10.9 percent a year from 2000 to 2009, has attracted the attention of firms worldwide. FDI in China has exploded since 1992, as Figure 2.3 indicates. Of particular note are the increased investments by overseas Chinese investors living in Taiwan, Hong Kong, and Singapore, who see China as a source of hard-working, low-cost labor, an increasingly scarce commodity in their own communities. While China's cities have boomed economically, this is less the case for the country's estimated 750 million rural residents. A major challenge facing China's leaders is closing the growing income gap between its urban and rural residents.

India

India is the world's second most populous country, having reached the 1 billion mark in 2000. It also is one of the poorest countries, with a per capita GNI of only $1,180. India was part of the British Empire until 1947, when the Indian subcontinent was partitioned along religious lines into India, where Hindus were in the majority, and Pakistan, where Muslims were dominant. The eastern part of Pakistan became the independent nation of Bangladesh in 1971. The new country of India adopted many aspects of British government, including the parliamentary system, a strong independent judiciary, and a professional bureaucracy. For most of

FIGURE 2.3

Annual FDI Flows to China 1982–2009

Source: Data from International Monetary Fund, *International Financial Statistics Yearbook,* various years, and *World Investment Report, 2011.*

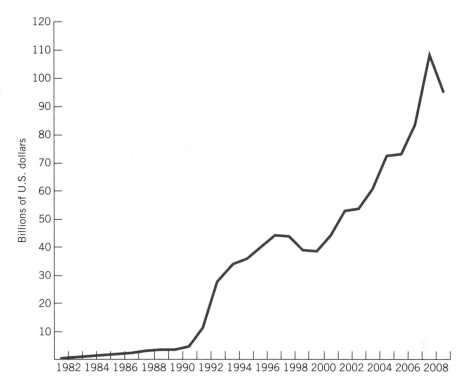

its post–World War II history, the country relied on state ownership of key industries—including power, transportation, and heavy industry—as a critical element of its economic development efforts.

India's bureaucracy can be cumbersome and slow to provide documents necessary to do business in the country. Until 1991, India discouraged foreign investment, limiting foreign owners to minority positions in Indian enterprises and imposing other onerous requirements. For example, as a condition for remaining in the country, the Coca-Cola Company was retroactively required in the 1970s to divulge its secret soft drink formula. Coca-Cola refused and chose to leave the market. Coca-Cola subsequently reentered the Indian market as a result of Prime Minister Rao's 1991 market-opening reforms, which reduced trade barriers, opened the doors to increased FDI, and modernized the country's financial sector.

These reforms have begun to pay off. (See Chapter 11's closing case, "The House of Tata," for a discussion of one company that has thrived as a result of these reforms.) India has attracted much FDI from MNCs based in developed countries, and its GDP growth has averaged 7.8 percent annually since 2000. However, problems remain. Corruption is widespread. The country's infrastructure is overburdened. A lack of clarity in government policy has created enormous confusion for some foreign investors. The World Bank has warned that failure to trim red tape may threaten the flow of foreign capital into sectors that are crucial to India's economic growth.

Southeast Asian Countries

Asia is home to numerous other countries at various stages of economic development. Of particular note are Thailand, Malaysia, and Indonesia, countries with low labor costs that have been recipients of significant FDI in the last three decades. As labor costs have risen in their homeland, many Japanese MNCs have built satellite plants in these three countries to supply low-cost parts to parent factories in Japan. U.S. and European MNCs have used these countries as production platforms as well. The Thai, Malaysian, and Indonesian economies have boomed as a result of exports generated by FDI, although their growth temporarily slowed as a result of the 1997 Asian currency crisis, which is discussed in Chapters 7 and 8. Vietnam, too, is becoming important to MNCs: Intel, for instance, built a billion dollar chip testing and assembly factory in Ho Chi Minh City, which commenced operations in 2010.[6]

The Marketplaces of Africa and the Middle East

Africa covers approximately 22 percent of the world's total land area and is rich in natural resources. Egypt occupies the northeastern tip of the African continent and represents the western boundary of what is commonly known as the Middle East.

Africa

The African continent, shown in Map 2.6, is home to 1.0 billion people and 55 countries. Most of Africa was colonized in the late nineteenth century by the major European powers (Belgium, France, Germany, Italy, Portugal, Spain, and the United Kingdom) for strategic military purposes or to meet domestic political demands. The tide of colonialism began to reverse in the mid-1950s, as one by one the European powers surrendered control of their colonies. Vestiges of colonialism remain in today's Africa, however, affecting opportunities available to international businesses. For example, Chad, Niger, and the Côte d'Ivoire (Ivory Coast) retain close economic and cultural ties to France. They link their currencies to that of France and follow French legal, educational, and governmental procedures. Because of these ties, French manufacturers, financial institutions, and service-sector firms often dominate international commerce with these countries. Similarly, the public institutions of Kenya, Zimbabwe, and the Republic of South Africa are modeled along British lines, giving British firms a competitive advantage in these countries.

The commodity boom, which we discuss in this chapter's closing case, has boosted the economies of many African countries. Algeria, Angola, Gabon, Libya, and Nigeria are major exporters of oil, while Zambia's economy has been bolstered by the rising demand for copper and that of Botswana because of its rich diamond fields. The governments of these countries face the challenge, however, of leveraging the growth in their commodities sector to create broad-based economies capable of benefiting their entire populations. Agriculture also is important to many African countries. It accounts for more than 40 percent of the GDPs of the Central African Republic, Sierra Leone, Tanzania, and Rwanda, for example. Unfortunately, the population in many African countries is largely employed in subsistence farming; these countries include Burkina Faso, Gambia, Mozambique, Sierra Leone, Tanzania, and Zambia.

Many experts believe South Africa will be the dominant economic power and the continent's growth engine during the twenty-first century. South Africa possesses fertile farmland and rich deposits of gold, diamonds, chromium, and platinum. Many MNCs used South Africa as the base for their African operations until the 1970s, when the United Nations imposed trade sanctions against the country because of the government's apartheid policies, which called for the separation of blacks, whites, and Asians. As a result of these external pressures, the government extended voting rights to all its citizens in 1994. Nobel Peace Prize winner Nelson Mandela was elected president in May 1994 in the country's first multiracial elections. In 2009 South Africa's exports—primarily minerals—accounted for 22 percent of its $286 billion GDP.

Middle East

The Middle East includes the region between southwestern Asia and northeastern Africa (see Map 2.7). This area is called the "cradle of civilization" because the world's earliest farms, cities, governments, legal codes, and alphabets originated there. The region was also the birthplace of several of the world's major religions, including Judaism, Christianity, and Islam. The Middle East has had a history of conflict and political unrest; in the last half century it has suffered through several Arab-Israeli wars, the Iran-Iraq war, and two Persian Gulf wars, all of which raised the risk of doing business in the region. In 2011, political unrest swept the area. Protests against the lack of democracy, poor employment opportunities, and high levels of income inequality led to the resignation of the long-time rulers of Egypt and Tunisia and to a civil war in Libya.

In 2009, Saudi Arabia, with a GDP of $369 billion, had the largest economy in the Middle East, but Israel enjoyed the highest per capita income at $25,740 per annum. The region is home to many oil-rich countries. In Saudi Arabia, for example, oil accounts for 45 percent of GDP and 90 percent of total export earnings. Some of the oil-rich nations of the Middle East are attempting to diversify their economies for "life after oil." Dubai, which is one of the seven United Arab

MAP 2.6

Africa and the Middle East

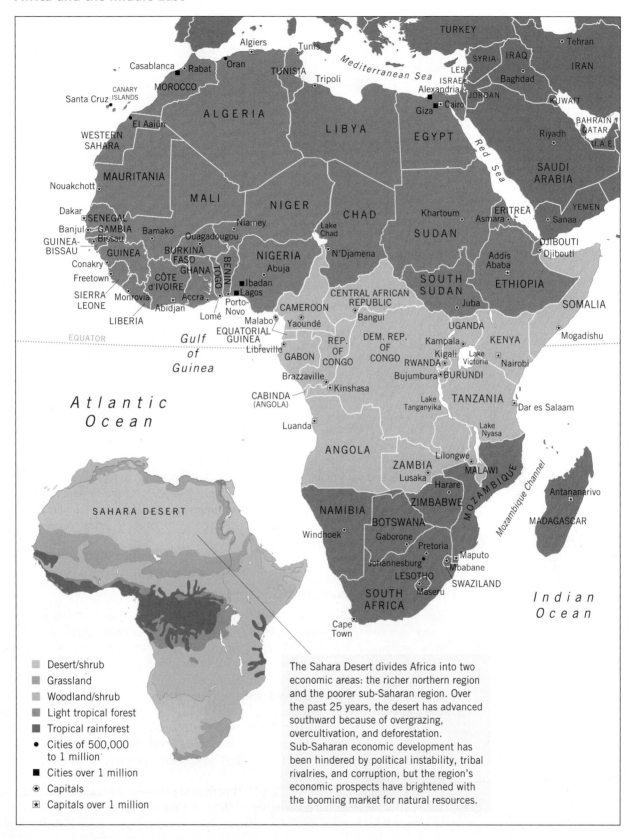

The Sahara Desert divides Africa into two economic areas: the richer northern region and the poorer sub-Saharan region. Over the past 25 years, the desert has advanced southward because of overgrazing, overcultivation, and deforestation. Sub-Saharan economic development has been hindered by political instability, tribal rivalries, and corruption, but the region's economic prospects have brightened with the booming market for natural resources.

Legend:
- Desert/shrub
- Grassland
- Woodland/shrub
- Light tropical forest
- Tropical rainforest
- • Cities of 500,000 to 1 million
- ■ Cities over 1 million
- ✳ Capitals
- ⊞ Capitals over 1 million

MAP 2.7
The Middle East

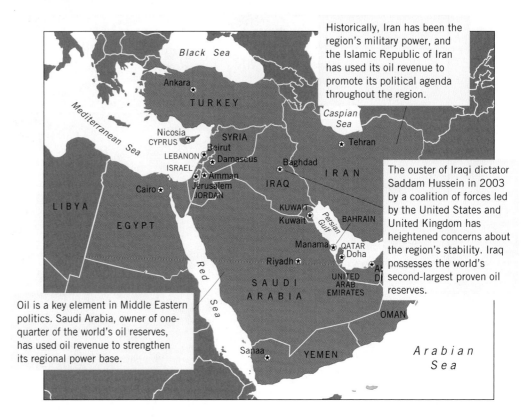

Historically, Iran has been the region's military power, and the Islamic Republic of Iran has used its oil revenue to promote its political agenda throughout the region.

The ouster of Iraqi dictator Saddam Hussein in 2003 by a coalition of forces led by the United States and United Kingdom has heightened concerns about the region's stability. Iraq possesses the world's second-largest proven oil reserves.

Oil is a key element in Middle Eastern politics. Saudi Arabia, owner of one-quarter of the world's oil reserves, has used oil revenue to strengthen its regional power base.

Emirates, offers foreign investors all the benefits of a foreign trade zone (discussed in Chapter 9), an excellent infrastructure, and an entry point for exports to the region.

Many of the so-called petro-states, as well as some of the major Asian trading nations, such as China and Singapore, have constructed impressive portfolios of foreign investments. These **sovereign wealth funds** have grown so large as to create political concerns, as "Venturing Abroad" discusses.

The Marketplaces of South America

South America's 13 countries, shown in Map 2.8, share a common political history as well as many economic and social problems. A 1494 papal decree divided colonization privileges between Portugal, which was allocated Brazil, and Spain, which received the rest of the continent. Spanish and Portuguese explorers subjugated the native populations, exploited their gold and silver mines, and converted their fields to sugar cane, tobacco, and cacao plantations. By the end of the eighteenth century, the hold of the two European powers on their South American colonies had weakened. Led by such patriots as Simon Bolivar, one colony after another won its independence. By 1825 the Spanish flag was flying over Cuba and Puerto Rico only. However, independence did not cure the continent's problems. Many South American countries suffer from huge income disparities and widespread poverty among their peoples, leading to political instability and continual cries for reform.

For much of the post–World War II period, the majority of South American countries followed what international economists call **import substitution policies** as a means of promoting economic development. With this approach, a country attempts to stimulate the development of local industry by discouraging imports via high tariffs and nontariff barriers. (The opposite of import substitution is **export promotion,** whereby a country pursues economic growth by

MAP 2.8

South America

During the late 1980s, many South American governments stimulated economic growth by adopting policies promoting free trade and private enterprise, thereby increasing the continent's appeal to U.S., European, and Asian MNCs. Many South American countries have benefitted recently from the increased prices of raw materials such as copper, iron ore, and tin.

International business in South America is affected by its physical geography. The Andes Mountains make it difficult to transport goods between Pacific Coast countries and their inland neighbors. Other mountain ranges, as well as the dense forests of the Amazon River Basin, similarly limit transport of goods.

- • Cities of 350,000 to 1 million
- ■ Cities over 1 million
- ⊛ Capitals
- ⊠ Capitals over 1 million

Sovereign wealth funds (SWFs) are one of the newest, and perhaps most controversial, sources of capital in the world economy. Sovereign wealth funds, which are government-controlled pools of capital, are estimated to own $4.2 trillion in assets in 2010. Some experts believe that amount may quadruple by 2015, if oil prices remain in the triple digits.

Most of the SWFs are owned by oil-rich governments. The Abu Dhabi Investment Authority is currently the largest, with $627 billion in assets, followed by the Government Pension Fund of Norway with $557 billion. Other SWFs are owned by governments of countries enjoying large balance of payments surpluses, such as the China Investment Corporation ($332 billion), Temasek Holdings of Singapore ($145 billion), and the Government of Singapore Investment Corporation ($247 billion).

China, for example, has accumulated foreign exchange reserves totaling $3.0 trillion as a result of its balance of payments surpluses. The government transferred $200 billion of these reserves to the China Investment Corporation (CIC) to manage in hopes of improving the government's rate of return on its investments. One of the first investments made by the CIC was a $3 billion equity position in the Blackstone Group, a U.S. private equity firm.

The rise of the SWFs reflects the growing role of emerging markets in the global economy. Their ownership of the world's productive assets has grown in conjunction with their increasing share of the world's GDP. The McKinsey Global Institute estimates that in 2006 one-third of the world's $170 trillion in financial assets were held in the United States, while emerging markets owned $24 trillion. However, the growth rate of ownership of assets of emerging markets is double that of developed countries.

Sovereign wealth funds have invested in a variety of industries. For example, Dubai International Capital, owned by the ruler of Dubai, owns stakes in European Aeronautic Defense & Space (the parent of Airbus), Sony, and HSBC Holdings. It has also purchased ownership stakes in the London Stock Exchange, the Nasdaq Stock Market, and OMX AB, which controls seven stock exchanges in Scandinavia and the Baltic region. Similarly, Temasek purchased a controlling interest in Shin Corporation, the largest provider of mobile telephone service in Thailand.

The SWFs were particularly important in shoring up the balance sheets of international banks, hedge funds, and private equity firms hurt by the chaos in the U.S. mortgage market during the global recession of 2008–2009. UBS, which lost $37 billion in the crisis, received $9.7 billion in new equity from the Government of Singapore Investment Corporation, and an additional $1.8 billion from an unidentified strategic investor from the Middle East. The Singapore SWF owns about 9 percent of the Swiss bank as a result of this investment. The China Investment Corporation invested $5 billion in Morgan Stanley, while the Abu Dhabi Investment Authority purchased a 4.9 percent stake in Citigroup for $7.5 billion and a 7.5 percent share of the Carlyle Group for $1.35 billion.

Most of the investments made by SWFs to date have been passive in nature, seeking to earn financial returns rather than actively control assets. Many have purchased equity stakes in investment banks and private equity firms, allowing the SWFs to tap into the sophisticated knowledge of these concerns without having to develop the expertise themselves. They are also attractive to the firms because to date they have not concerned themselves with corporate governance issues or proven to be activist investors. Their investments typically do not entitle the SWF to a board seat, allowing them to avoid political problems and national investment control laws like the Exon-Florio Act. (This act allows the president of the United States to reject certain investments made by foreign nationals for national security reasons.)

Nonetheless, the growth of SWFs has made politicians in many countries uneasy. As a result, the International Monetary Fund is trying to develop a voluntary code of conduct for SWFs. The primary objective of the code is to ensure that investments made by SWFs are solely for commercial purposes, rather than a backdoor means of promoting the political goals of the governmental owner of the SWF.

Sources: "Wealth funds fight for reputation," *Wall Street Journal,* May 10, 2011, p. C3; "Beijing to give wealth fund $200bn," *Financial Times,* April 26, 2011, p. 4; "China's wealth-fund chief warns on global growth," *Wall Street Journal,* April 18, 2011, p. A7; www.swfinstitute.org; "IMF clears way for development of sovereign wealth fund codes," *Wall Street Journal,* March 24, 2008, p. A12; "Code set for state-run funds," *Wall Street Journal,* March 21, 2008, p. A4; "Temasek rising," *TheDeal.com,* February 22, 2008 (online); "Dubai investment fund plans to spend in Asia," *International Herald Tribune,* February 19, 2008 (online); "Ascent of sovereign-wealth funds illustrates new world order," *Wall Street Journal,* January 28, 2008, p. A2; "Asset-backed insecurity," *The Economist,* January 19, 2008, pp. 78ff.; "Gulf states seen raising foreign-asset holdings," *Wall Street Journal,* January 17, 2008, p. A10; "$9.4 billion write-down at Morgan Stanley," *New York Times,* December 20, 2007 (online); "UBS gains two new investors, writes down $10 billion," *Wall Street Journal,* December 10, 2007 (online); "Abu Dhabi to bolster Citigroup with $7.5 billion capital infusion," *Wall Street Journal,* November 27, 2007, p. A3.

expanding its exports. This is the developmental approach successfully adopted by Taiwan, Hong Kong, and Singapore, as discussed earlier in this chapter.) For most South American industries, however, the domestic market is too small to enable domestic producers to gain economies of scale through mass-production techniques or to permit much competition among local producers. Thus, prices of domestically produced goods tend to rise above prices in other markets. These policies benefit domestic firms that face import competition. However, they cripple the ability of a country's exporters to compete in world markets because the companies must pay higher prices for domestically produced inputs than do their foreign competitors. Inevitably, the government must subsidize these firms and often nationalize them to preserve urban jobs. The high costs of doing this are passed on to taxpayers and to consumers through higher prices, but over time the government runs a budget deficit. The result is inflation and destruction of middle-class savings.

Many major South American countries—including Argentina, Brazil, and Chile—adopted these well-intentioned but ultimately destructive import substitution policies. In the late 1980s, however, the countries began to reverse their policies. They lowered tariff barriers, sought free trade agreements with their neighbors, privatized their industries, and positioned their economies to compete internationally. Chile, for example, is now one of the most free-market-oriented economies in the world. The continent's economies boomed during the 1990s as a result of these policies. More recently, the increased demand for raw materials and foodstuffs triggered by China's economic growth has benefited many South American firms, including purveyors of Argentine wheat, Bolivian tin, Brazilian iron ore and soy beans, and Chilean copper. The continent is still plagued, however, by an inability to create policies that bridge the chasm between the rich and the poor. The lack of economic and social mobility has trapped generations of South Americans in poverty and despair and created political instability in many of their countries.

VENTURING ABROAD | **CONNECTING GLOBAL MARKETPLACES: DHL EXPRESS**

International express carriers, frequently referred to as global courier companies, are often cited as being the Business Class of the transportation industry. They offer fast shipping on a door-to-door basis, allowing senders to continually track progress of their packages via the web in near real time. Speed and reliability are achieved by integrating complex but highly standardized logistical systems that link proprietary air and road transport networks. International consignments are typically collected by a courier and driven to a local international airport from where they are flown via one or more hub airports to the destination country and delivered directly to the receiver.

Companies can use this means of transportation to gain a competitive advantage—for example, by sending urgent samples and technical documentation to close a deal or by using express distribution to build just-in-time supply chains. Industry leaders—DHL Express and TNT from Europe and FedEx and UPS from the United States—each connect more than 200 countries and territories with transit times between major economic centers ranging from one to three business days. Over the past two decades, express transportation has grown faster than the world economy and according to the European Express Association, in 2009, the global courier industry directly employed 1.3 million people and indirectly created a further 1.5 million jobs.

DHL Express is recognized by many as having the most extensive global footprint, offering services not only to major cities but also to remote areas and global trouble spots such as Afghanistan, Iraq, or North Korea. It is a business unit of the German-based Deutsche Post DHL Group, a leading global logistics provider with 470,000 employees and revenues of 51 billion euros.

The backbone of DHL's operations, which in 2011 handled 128 million international time-sensitive packages, are its 32,000 service points scattered all over the world, and which are supported by an air network system involving 18 regional airport hubs, 2,000 daily flights, and on-site operations teams at 500 airports.

Naturally, international cargo hubs need to be strategically aligned with global trade lanes. Any significant shift in international business flows requires a reassessment of hub operations. In 2005 DHL carried out an in-depth review of its global air operations. At the time, the European network consisted of one main regional hub, based in Brussels, supported by a number of subhubs. When it was inaugurated in 1985, the Brussels hub was an obvious choice since the majority of the European economic activity was concentrated within an industrial belt, which ranged from the southern United Kingdom, via the Benelux and Western Germany to Northern Italy. DHL's analysis showed, however, that Brussels airport would soon reach saturation point and that the geographical distribution of European economic activity is steadily moving eastwards. Subsequently, Leipzig in Eastern Germany was chosen as the site for the new "super hub." Leipzig is some 600 kilometers east of Brussels, placing the new hub in close proximity of growth markets in Eastern Europe as well as reducing flying times to/from China and Russia, two of Europe's key trading partners. The new facility, which took two years and 300 million euros to build, was opened in 2007.

DHL Express: Airport Hubs (2011)

Marketplace	Main Continental Hub	Regional Sub-hubs
Europe	Leipzig (Germany)	Amsterdam
		Bergamo (Italy)
		Brussels
		Copenhagen
		East Midlands (UK)
		Frankfurt
		London
		Paris
		Vitoria (Spain)
Asia	Hong Kong	Bangkok
		Singapore
United States/ North America	Cincinnati	
Emerging Markets		
Middle East		Bahrain
		Dubai
Africa		Lagos
Latin America		Panama

Source: Adapted from Facts & Figures, www.dhl.com (November 2011).

Sources: Oxford Economics, "The Impact of the Express Delivery Industry on the Global Economy," Report, September 2009 [downloaded from www.eea.org]; www.dhl.com; www.dp-dhl.com; www.fedex.com; www.tnt.com; www.ups.com.

CHAPTER REVIEW

Summary

To compete successfully in the international marketplace, managers need a basic understanding of the world's markets and their interrelationships. Managers also need to assess opportunities available in these markets. A key indicator of a country's desirability to international businesses is its per capita income, which provides information about its consumers and its value as a production site.

The rich developed countries of Japan, the European Union, the United States, and Canada account for about 63 percent of the world's economy. However, emerging markets like China and India cannot be ignored by international businesses, given their rapid growth rates.

The North American market—Canada, Mexico, the United States, Central America, and the island countries of the Caribbean—is one of the world's largest and richest markets. The United States and Canada have the largest bilateral trading relationship in the world. Mexico's economic reforms, initiated in 1982, have made it a more important force in the world economy.

Another large, rich market for international businesses is Western Europe, particularly the 27-member EU. The EU members are free-market-oriented, parliamentary democracies. With the 1989 collapse of European communism, Eastern European and Central European countries are undergoing a transition from communism to capitalism. Most have adopted market-oriented policies to stimulate economic growth. Their growth prospects and unmet consumer demand are attractive to many Asian, North American, and European MNCs.

Asia is home to several of the fastest-growing economies of the post–World War II period. Japan and the Four Tigers—South Korea, Hong Kong, Singapore, and Taiwan—have grown dramatically because of economic policies that focus on export promotion. But the emerging markets of China and India have enjoyed even higher rates of growth during the past decade. Australia and New Zealand are also important economies in this region.

Many African countries regained their independence during the 1950s and 1960s. Their economies primarily rely on natural resources and agriculture. Middle Eastern countries have played an important role in the world economy thanks to their oil wealth, and the growth of their sovereign wealth funds have caught the attention of the world's capital market.

The South American countries have been independent since the early nineteenth century. Although many of them are rich in natural resources and farmlands, the continent's economic development since World War II has been hindered by chronic political unrest and import substitution policies. During the 1980s, however, key South American nations—including Argentina, Brazil, and Chile—shifted toward more market-oriented, export promotion growth strategies. Privatization, reduced governmental regulation, and booming commodity prices have intensified interest in the continent by international businesses.

Review Questions

1. Describe the U.S. role in the world economy.
2. How do differences in income levels and income distribution among countries affect international businesses?
3. What role did MITI serve in the Japanese economy?
4. What is a keiretsu?
5. Who are the Four Tigers? Why are they important to international businesses?
6. What is a chaebol?
7. Discuss the role of natural resources and agriculture in Africa's economy.
8. How did import substitution policies affect the economies of Brazil and Argentina?

Questions for Discussion

1. Regional trading blocs, such as the EU and NAFTA, are growing in importance. What are the implications of these trading blocs for international businesses? Are they helpful or harmful? How may they affect a firm's investment decisions?
2. Many American and European businesspeople argue that the keiretsu system in Japan acts as a barrier to foreign companies entering the Japanese market. Why do you think they believe this?
3. Ethnic ties, old colonial alliances, and shared languages appear to affect international trade. Why

might this be so? If true, how does this affect international businesses' strategies regarding which markets to enter?
4. South Korea is prominently featured in many lists of "emerging markets." (For example, see Table 1.2 on page 43.) Is South Korea an emerging market? Defend your answer. How would you define an "emerging market"?
5. What can African countries do to encourage more foreign investment in their economies?

Building Global Skills

Success in international business often depends on a firm obtaining information about foreign markets so that it can make exporting, importing, and investment decisions. Among the most useful sources are the following:

Survey of Current Business, published monthly by the U.S. Department of Commerce, is a basic source of statistical data on the U.S. economy. It provides detailed analyses of international trade and investment activities affecting the United States.

The World Factbook provides basic geographic, ethnic, religious, political, and economic information on all countries. It is put out by the U.S. Central Intelligence Agency and is particularly useful because it includes data about small, obscure, and politically controversial areas. For example, if you were an executive for Crestone Energy Corporation, which was hired by China's government to hunt for oil and gas around the Spratly Islands, *The World Factbook* is one of the few sources in which you could learn that the islands, many of which are under water at high tide, have no permanent population yet are claimed and garrisoned by five different countries—China, Malaysia, the Philippines, Taiwan, and Vietnam. Armed with this information, you would realize that Crestone's explorations would be extremely sensitive and possibly the target of political conflict.

World Development Report and *World Development Indicators,* published annually by the World Bank, present numerous tables detailing information about World Bank members, including population, income and income distribution, infrastructure, government expenditures, trade, production, living standards, health, education, and urbanization.

Commodity Trade Statistics is an annual United Nations report that provides detailed data on each country's exports and imports, which are classified by commodity and by country of destination or origin. The report is an excellent source of minutiae—for example, the value of pork exports from Denmark

to Portugal in 2010. However, it is rather clumsy to use when time-series information is required—for example, Denmark's total annual exports from 1986 to 2010.

Balance of Payments Statistics, International Financial Statistics, and *Direction of Trade Statistics* are reports published by the International Monetary Fund (IMF). *Balance of Payments Statistics,* issued annually, contains data about balance of payments performances of IMF members. The monthly *International Financial Statistics* offers international and domestic financial data on members' domestic interest rates, money and banking indicators, prices, exports, and exchange rates. *Direction of Trade Statistics* details the exports and imports of each IMF member on a quarterly basis.

World Investment Report is produced annually by the United Nations Conference for Trade and Development. It is a primary source of statistics regarding foreign direct investment flows and stocks into and from countries. It also provides detailed information about the role of transnational corporations (the U.N.'s preferred term for MNCs) in FDI.

Go to your library and/or surf the Internet to examine each of these standard references. Then answer the following questions:

1. What was the total value of U.S. imports from Belgium last year? Of U.S. exports to Belgium?
2. What is the total level of U.S. investments in Belgium? Of Belgian investments in the United States?
3. Profile the economy of Belgium: What is its GDP? What is its per capita income? How fast is its economy growing? What are its major exports and imports? Who are its major trading partners?
4. Profile the people of Belgium: What languages do they speak? What is their average educational level? What is their life expectancy? How fast is the population growing?

CLOSING CASE   CHINA'S QUEST FOR NATURAL RESOURCES

The mining industry is among the world's most cyclical. When times are good, they are very good. When times are bad, they are very bad. The new century has been very, very good to mining companies throughout the world, which are enjoying record or near-record prices and profits. Although prices and profits softened during the global recession of 2008–2009, they have subsequently come roaring back. The revenues of BHP Billiton, the world's largest mining company, rose 35 percent from 2006 to 2010. The profits of Anglo American PLC, the huge London-based mining company that dominates the South

African market, have more than doubled since 2004, reaching $9.3 billion in 2010, thanks to record platinum, coal, and iron prices. And the good times are extending to the industry's suppliers. The profits of Caterpillar, which dominates the market for heavy earthmoving equipment, leapt 678 percent in 2010, on sales growth of 31 percent.

The boom times in mining are attributable in large part to the voracious demands of China and its burgeoning manufacturing sector. China's economy has been growing at double-digit rates for the past decade. The country is undergoing the largest labor migration in the world's history, as rural residents leave their farms to become factory workers. Not only do these factories consume raw materials, but the newly arrived workers must be housed, fed, transported, and entertained, expanding the demand for apartments, automobiles, buses, roadways, electricity, police, restaurants, and every other product imaginable. In Shanghai, for example, the local government is planning nine new communities, each accommodating 800,000 people, to house its growing population.

China is estimated to consume 47 percent of the world's cement output, 37 percent of its cotton, 30 percent of its coal, 26 percent of its steel, and 21 percent of its aluminum. Its insatiable demand for raw materials has impacted commodity prices ranging from aluminum to zinc. Copper prices have reached all time highs, while the price of coal and iron ore has more than doubled since 2006.

These high prices raised two concerns for China's leadership. First, they believed the country was too vulnerable to the pricing power of foreign companies supplying these vital raw materials. Second, they worried that the country's continuing economic growth could be jeopardized if the country's access to these raw materials were threatened.

To reduce their vulnerability to price increases and supply disruptions, Chinese companies have been on a buying binge in the past several years, searching the globe for natural resource producers and mineral reserves to purchase. In 2009 Chinese and Hong Kong companies spent $13 billion on mining acquisitions. Because China is the world's largest steel producer, iron ore is of particular importance to the country's economy. The vice chairman of the China Iron & Steel Association announced a goal to source 40 percent of the country's iron ore imports from Chinese-owned firms. In 2010, Shandong Iron & Steel Group invested $1.5 billion in African Minerals Ltd., which controls an iron ore project in Sierra Leone. Chinalco (China's state-owned aluminum company) and Rio Tinto agreed to a $1.35 billion deal to develop a huge iron ore deposit in Guinea.

China has similar concerns about its energy supplies. Its three big state-owned oil companies—China National Petroleum Corp. (CNPC), China Petroleum & Chemical Corp (Sinopec), and China National Offshore Oil Corp. (CNOC)—have played an important role in its quest for secure energy supplies. CNOC purchased a stake in a major Ugandan oil field from Tullow Oil for $2.5 billion. As part of this deal, CNOC agreed to fund the construction of a 1,200-kilometer pipeline to Mombassa, Kenya's primary port. The company paid $2.16 billion to purchase a one-third interest in a 600,000-acre oil and gas field in South Texas operated by Chesapeake Energy. Similarly, PetroChina, a subsidiary of CNPC, obtained a twenty-year contract to develop Iraq's Halfaya oil field and paid C$1.9 billion to purchase minority interests in two Canadian oilfields owned by Athabasca Oil Sands Corporation.

In the past several years, Chinese firms have signed a series of joint venture agreements to boost the country's refining and petrochemical capacity. Sinopec and Kuwait Petroleum Corp. agreed to build a $9 billion, 300,000 barrels a day refinery in the southern China city of Zhanjiang, along with an accompanying ethylene

plant. CNPC and Russia's OAO Rosneft agreed to construct a 260,000 barrels a day refinery in northern China. In 2011, Sinopec and Saudi Basic Industries Corp. expanded their joint venture in Tianjin, agreeing to invest $1 billion to build a polycarbonate facility to accompany their existing petrochemical plant.

Of course, the booming market for commodities has attracted the attention of firms from other countries as well. For instance, in 2011, China's Minmetal Resources Ltd. offered $6.5 billion to purchase Canada's Equinox Minerals Ltd., an important miner of Zambian copper, but was outbid by Canada's Barrick Gold, which offered $7.6 billion for Equinox. Similarly, Rio Tinto, a British-Australian mining conglomerate, acquired a majority stake in Riversdale Mining, an Australian company with interests in African coal fields, for $3.5 billion.

Some critics have raised concerns about the role of the big state-owned Chinese companies in these purchases. They question whether these companies are commercial, profit-seeking enterprises or whether they are arms of the state, interested primarily in promoting China's national security and foreign policy objectives. This question plays a critical role in many governments' evaluations of whether to allow the companies to buy local firms. For example, China Minmetals Corporation's attempt to purchase Canada's Noranda was blocked by the Canadian government in 2005; similarly, in 2005 the U.S. government did not approve the proposed acquisition of Unocal by CNOC. Australia's prime minister made it known that he would prefer Chinese firms acquire only minority positions in Australian natural resource producers. But these nationalistic approaches affect more than Chinese firms. Canada resisted BHP Billiton's attempt to take over Potash Corp. of Saskatchewan, the world's largest supplier of that critical fertilizer component. BHP Billiton and Rio Tinto withdrew from a proposed joint venture to mine Australian iron ore after the country's government imposed unacceptable restrictions. Zimbabwe is demanding that foreign mining companies transfer majority ownership of their Zimbabwe subsidiaries to local residents.

Case Questions

1. How important is it for nations to control natural resources? Is China's growth threatened if it needs to rely on foreign-owned sources of raw materials?
2. Should countries have special rules for acquisitions of natural resource companies by foreign-based companies?
3. Should there be separate rules for state-owned acquirers like Sinopec?
4. If China's growth slows, what will be the impact on commodity prices?

Sources: "Cnooc sets Canadian deal," *Wall Street Journal*, July 21, 2011, p. B2; "Barrick in $7.6bn bid for miner Equinox," *Financial Times*, April 26, 2011, p. 1; "Rio and Guinea settle mine fight," *Wall Street Journal*, April 25, 2011, p. B4; "Nationalist tide rises for resources," *Wall Street Journal*, April 6, 2011, p. B6; "Minmetals plans $6.5 billion offer for copper miner," *Wall Street Journal*, April 4, 2011; "Zimbabwe shuts out foreign miners," *Wall Street Journal*, March 29, 2011, p. A15; "Commodities to feel kick from China's growth plans," *Financial Times*, March 9, 2011, p. 23; "China hunts for uranium," *Wall Street Journal*, March 9, 2011, p. B3; "Kuwait firm approved to build refinery in China," *Wall Street Journal*, March 9, 2011, p. B6; "China keeping a cool head on uranium," *Wall Street Journal*, March 2, 2011; "Asia bids for Australia's rich resources," *Wall Street Journal*, February 15, 2011, p. B3; "Report: China's big oil no Beijing pet," *Wall Street Journal*, February 21, 2011; "A mining firm snuggles up to its biggest customer," *The Economist*, December 18, 2010, p. 130; "Chinese firms snap up mining assets," *Wall Street Journal*, July 20, 2010; "Let bygones be bygones?," *The Economist*, March 19, 2010; "Asia bids for Australia's rich resources," *Wall Street Journal*, February 15, 2011; "CNOC to buy Uganda oil stake," *Wall Street Journal*, February 6, 2010; "Chinese firms snap up mining assets," *Wall Street Journal*, July 20, 2010; "Mining giants are forces to lessen global ambitions," *Wall Street Journal*, July 17, 2009, p. A12.

Endnotes

1. "With flights grounded, Kenya's produce wilts, *New York Time*, April 19, 2010; "Houston to take on Miami for global flower market," *Houston Chronicle*, October 9, 2009; www.floraholland.com; http://en.kunming.cn; "Yunnan's flower industry blooms," *China International Business*, June 10, 2009; "Flower market has rosy outlook," *Boston Globe*, February 6, 2008.
2. This chapter reports population, GDP, and per capita GDP data for the world's countries. Most of the data are taken from the World Bank's *World Development Report 2011* or from the World Bank's website.
3. "Mexico, 3 neighbors sign free trade pacts," *Houston Chronicle*, May 12, 2000, p. 2C.
4. "Return of the overlord," *The Economist*, April 3, 2010, p. 71; "Back from the brink, Korea Inc. wants a little respect," *Wall Street Journal*, June 13, 2002, p. A1; "The glory of Hyundai sits firmly in past," *Financial Times*, January 29, 2002, p. 22.
5. "Hon Hai reaches out," *Wall Street Journal*, June 9, 2011, p. B4.
6. "Intel to build Vietnam chip plant, raising nation's high-tech profile," *Wall Street Journal*, February 24, 2006, p. A6.

CHAPTER 3

Legal, Technological, Accounting, and Political Environments

AFTER STUDYING THIS CHAPTER, YOU SHOULD BE ABLE TO:

1. Describe the major types of legal systems confronting international businesses.
2. Explain how domestic laws affect the ability of firms to conduct international business.
3. List the ways firms can resolve international business disputes.
4. Describe the impact of the host country's technological environment on international business.
5. Identify the factors that influence national accounting systems.
6. Explain how firms can protect themselves from political risk.

Access a host of interactive learning aids at at **www.pearsonglobaleditions.com/ mymanagementlab** to help strengthen your understanding of the chapter concepts.

MyManagementLab

PETER PARKS/AFP/Getty Images/Newscom

HARRY POTTER GOES TO CHINA

One of the best-known celebrities of the new millennium is Harry Potter, a young wizard and the hero of a series of books written by the British author J. K. Rowling. It's fair to say that Potter has woven a spell over the publishing industry. More than 450 million copies of Harry's seven magical adventures have been sold. Bloomsbury Publishing, Potter's publisher, recognized that the young wizard's appeal was universal and quickly expanded into non-English-speaking markets. Rowling's stories now appear in 67 different languages. China offered a particularly appealing target because children's literature in China often focuses on imparting moral lessons or promoting the latest government policies, rather than entertaining young readers. For example, in "Today I Will Raise the Flag," a teacher tames a mischievous student by promising to let him be in charge of hoisting China's national flag on the school flagpole if he behaves. Another children's story tells of Little Wen, who wants to reforest a local mountain. After accomplishing this task, the story triumphantly concludes, "Little Wen did truly serve the people!"

Given the unappealing nature of such literary fare to most young readers, competition for the Chinese rights to the Potter series was fierce. Notes Wang Ruiqin, an editor at the People's Literature Publishing House in Beijing, "Chinese books exhort children to be courageous, whereas Harry's courage is evident through a story that everyone likes to read." The People's Literature Publishing House beat out 10 domestic rivals by promising to pay a 10 percent licensing fee to the British publisher. The company planned to sell the first three books as a boxed set priced at $10, which is expensive by Chinese standards.

As is the case in any Harry Potter novel, the publisher's path to success was full of obstacles. Translators struggled to maintain the magic of Rowling's writing while converting her words and whimsy into Chinese. Harry Potter, for example, was translated phonetically into "Ha-li Bo-te." More troubles arose when, as Harry was preparing to make his debut in China, the Chinese government initiated a propaganda campaign against "feudal superstition." Ms. Wang became concerned that this government initiative could reduce parents' interest in a book about a young wizard. Despite these obstacles, Harry and his Chinese licensee, the People's Literature Publishing House, quickly tasted success. The company rapidly sold out its initial printing of 600,000 sets of Potter novels. And, not surprisingly, when the first Potter movie, *Harry Potter and the Philosopher's Stone*, was shown in Chinese movie theaters in January 2002, it was an instant hit.

Is there such a thing as being too popular? Within six months of his Chinese debut, the "fifth" Harry Potter novel—*Harry Potter and the Leopard-Walk-Up-To-Dragon*—was being snapped up by eager young readers throughout China. Its success, however, was not happy news for Rowling; she hadn't yet finished writing her fifth installment of Harry's adventures. Apparently, an unknown local author/thief had decided to cash in on Harry's popularity by writing his own Harry Potter novel. Although Chinese police threatened to fine bookstores selling the counterfeit novel, its sales remained brisk. Fortunately, when the real fifth novel—*Harry Potter and the Order of the Phoenix*—was released in June 2003, Chinese children joined their peers around the world in purchasing copies as soon as the novel hit their local bookstores. When July 16, 2005, arrived, Shanghai and Beijing parents and grandparents, like their counterparts in London, Chicago, and New York, dutifully waited in long queues to purchase *Harry Potter and the Half-Blood Prince,* the sixth novel of the series, which was released simultaneously in every country on that date. Within two weeks, however, unauthorized Chinese translations of it were available for sale on the streets of Beijing. The eagerly awaited seventh and final book in the series, *Harry Potter and the Deathly Hallows*, was released worldwide on July 21, 2007. Chinese fans of Harry did not need to wait that long, however, for a book of the same title was already being sold on the streets of Shanghai and Beijing for 10 days—although, of course, J. K. Rowling was not its author. Despite such widespread piracy, to date an estimated 11 million legal copies of Rowling's works have been sold in China.[1] ∎

Virtually all decisions facing international managers—whom to hire, how to market their company's goods in the host market, which technologies to adopt, and so forth—are affected by the national environment of the country in which the transaction occurs. Harry Potter's publisher had to confront cultural, legal, and political issues unique to China in developing its strategy for entering the Chinese market. The goal of this and the next chapter is to understand the impact of the various dimensions of a country's environment on the management of a firm's international business. This chapter discusses the legal, technological, accounting, and political dimensions, while Chapter 4 focuses on the cultural.

The Legal Environment

A domestic firm must follow the laws and customs of its home country. An international business faces a more complex task: It must obey the laws not only of its home country but also the laws of all the host countries in which it operates. Both home and host country laws can critically affect the way international firms conduct their business. These laws determine the markets firms may serve, the prices they can charge for their goods, and the cost of necessary inputs such as labor, raw materials, and technology. The laws may also affect the location of economic activity. For example, some Internet companies have chosen to base their operations outside the People's Republic of China because of the seemingly arbitrary rules imposed by its government. "e-World" discusses some additional effects the rapid growth of the Internet has had on the legal systems of various countries.

Differences in Legal Systems

National legal systems vary dramatically for historical, cultural, political, and religious reasons. The rule of law, the role of lawyers, the burden of proof, the right to judicial review, and, of course, the laws themselves differ from country to country. In the United States, for instance, in times of economic distress firms can lay off workers with minimal notice and severance pay. In Belgium, however, firms wishing to trim their white-collar workforces must provide each worker with three months' notice, three months' severance pay, or some combination of the two for every five years (or fraction of five years) the employee has worked for the firm. Brink's, for example, ran afoul of these laws when its Belgian subsidiary declared bankruptcy as a result of its high labor costs. Affected unions promptly sued the company for failure to negotiate severance pay, as the law required in such cases.[2]

Access to the legal system also may vary from country to country. In the United States, for example, easy availability of lawyers and nondiscriminatory access to its legal system are helpful to international businesses wishing to settle disputes with suppliers and customers. South Korea, in contrast, suffers from a shortage of lawyers because of its tough bar exam—less than 10 percent of the candidates taking it pass. Thus, many international businesses are forced to resolve disputes privately rather than utilize South Korea's courts. Because the Indian court system has an estimated backlog of 30 million cases, many attorneys advise their business clients to settle conflicts out of court rather than wait as long as 10 years to be heard in a court of law (see Map 3.1).[3]

COMMON LAW Common law is the foundation of the legal systems in the United Kingdom and its former colonies, including the United States, Canada, Australia, India, New Zealand, Hong Kong, Barbados, Saint Kitts and Nevis, and Malaysia. **Common law** is based on the cumulative wisdom of judges' decisions on individual cases through history. These cases create legal precedents, which other judges use to decide similar cases.

Brink's ran afoul of Belgium's labor laws after firing or reassigning 60 workers from its money-losing Belgium subsidiary in a cost-cutting move. After workers went on strike in protest, Brink's chose to declare bankruptcy rather than negotiate. Brink's is facing a drawn-out court battle, for workers' rights are more strongly protected in Belgium than they are in Brink's home, the United States.

© imagebroker.net/SuperStock

MAP 3.1

India

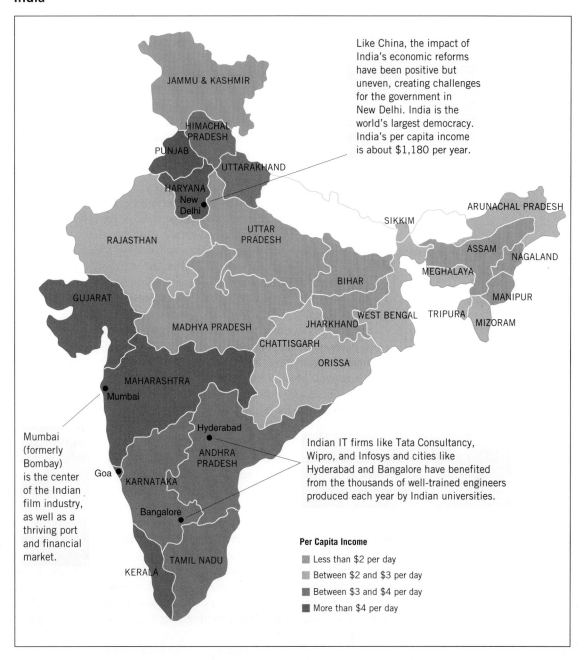

Like China, the impact of India's economic reforms have been positive but uneven, creating challenges for the government in New Delhi. India is the world's largest democracy. India's per capita income is about $1,180 per year.

Indian IT firms like Tata Consultancy, Wipro, and Infosys and cities like Hyderabad and Bangalore have benefited from the thousands of well-trained engineers produced each year by Indian universities.

Mumbai (formerly Bombay) is the center of the Indian film industry, as well as a thriving port and financial market.

Per Capita Income

- Less than $2 per day
- Between $2 and $3 per day
- Between $3 and $4 per day
- More than $4 per day

Common law has evolved differently in each common law country. Thus, laws affecting business practices vary somewhat among these countries, creating potential problems for the uninformed international businessperson. For example, manufacturers of defective products are more vulnerable to lawsuits in the United States than in the United Kingdom as a result of evolutionary differences in the two countries' case law. The U.K.'s libel laws are more plaintiff-friendly than U.S. law. In the United Kingdom, the defendant must prove that a published article is true, whereas in the United States the burden is on the plaintiff to demonstrate that the article is false and malicious in order to win a libel suit.[4]

In addition to evolutionary differences in case law, **statutory laws**—those enacted by legislative action—also vary among the common law countries. For example, many business transactions between firms and the British government are shielded from public scrutiny—and the prying eyes of competitors—by Britain's Official Secrets Act. In contrast, more information about transactions between firms and the U.S. federal government is publicly available because of the U.S. Freedom of Information Act. Even the administration of law may vary. For instance, in the United States the plaintiff and the defendant in a lawsuit generally pay their own legal fees. Often, defendants agree to quick settlements regardless of the strength of their cases to avoid expensive litigation. In the United Kingdom, the losers in trials pay the legal expenses of both parties. Thus, the British have less incentive to file frivolous lawsuits.

CIVIL LAW Another common form of legal system, **civil law**, is based on a codification, or detailed listing, of what is and is not permissible. The civil law system originated in biblical times with the Romans, who spread it throughout the Western world. Its dominance was reinforced by the imposition of the civil-law-based Napoleonic Code on territories conquered by French emperor Napoleon Bonaparte during the early nineteenth century.

One important difference between common law and civil law systems is apparent in the roles of judges and lawyers. In a common law system the judge serves as a neutral referee, ruling on various motions by the opposing parties' lawyers. These lawyers are responsible for developing their clients' cases and choosing which evidence to submit on their clients' behalf. In a civil law system, the judge takes on many of the tasks of the lawyers, determining, for example, the scope of evidence to be collected and presented to the court.

RELIGIOUS LAW **Religious law** is based on the officially established rules governing the faith and practice of a particular religion. A country that applies religious law to civil and criminal conduct is called a **theocracy**. In Iran, for example, a group of mullahs, or holy men, determine legality or illegality through their interpretation of the Koran, the holy book of Islam.

Religious laws can create interesting problems for firms. Consider the teaching of the Koran, which denounces charging interest on loans as an unfair exploitation of the poor. Muslim firms and financial institutions have had to develop alternative financing arrangements to acquire and finance capital. Muslim businesses often rely on leasing arrangements, rather than borrowing money, to obtain long-term assets. In Iran banks often charge up-front fees that act as a substitute for loan interest payments, and owners of bank deposits receive shares of the bank's profits rather than interest payments. Pakistani banks are adopting similar policies—often referred to as Islamic banking—because Pakistan's Supreme Court issued a ruling in 1999 declaring all interest-bearing transactions to be contrary to Islamic law.[5] Family-owned firms are often influential in countries where legal systems are based on the Koran because members of an owner's extended family may be the best available source of capital, given the costs of circumventing the prohibition on interest.

Countries relying on religious law often have other features, such as an absence of due process and appeals procedures, which should make outsiders cautious. In Saudi Arabia, for example, all foreign firms must have a local representative or sponsor, typically a government agency or a person well connected to the royal family. Should a commercial dispute arise between a foreign businessperson and the local representative, the local representative can have the foreigner detained by the local police. Because no independent judiciary exists in the country to protect the foreigner's rights, the foreigner is in a weak bargaining position.

BUREAUCRATIC LAW The legal system in communist countries and in dictatorships is often described as bureaucratic law. **Bureaucratic law** is whatever the country's bureaucrats say it is, regardless of the formal law of the land. Contracts can be made or broken at the whim of those in power. The collapse of Zairean dictator Mobutu Sese Seko's government in 1997, for example, threatened the viability of all existing contracts signed by foreign companies and triggered a mad scramble to revalidate old contracts and negotiate new ones with the government of his successor.[6] Protections that may appear in the country's constitution—such as the right to an attorney and the right to hear witnesses against one—may be ignored if government officials find them inconvenient. For instance, the formalities of Ugandan law afforded Ugandans and foreigners little protection under dictator Idi Amin's regime of terror during the 1970s. Similarly, the elaborate protections detailed in the constitution of the former Soviet Union offered little solace to the victims of Joseph Stalin's political purges during the 1930s.

In countries relying on bureaucratic law, the ability of an international business to manage its operations is often compromised by bureaucrats. International managers are often confronted

E-WORLD   LAW AND THE INTERNET

Most existing laws predate the World Wide Web. Adjusting these laws to the needs of the Internet age is a massive undertaking, to say the least. One basic issue is deciding which country's laws should oversee e-commerce transactions. Activities sponsored by a website may be legal in its home country yet violate the laws of other countries. For example, Yahoo! Inc. was found guilty of allowing neo-Nazi paraphernalia to be sold on its websites in violation of a French law that prohibits the sale of anything that incites racism. Although Yahoo! had carefully excluded such goods from its French portal, it had not done so for its U.S. sites. Because French citizens had access to the U.S. websites over the Internet, Yahoo! was fined $2,800 and given two months to make the site inaccessible to French Internet users.

The responsibility for enforcing intellectual property rights is similarly unresolved. For example, in June 2008, in a lawsuit filed by Hermès a French court ruled that eBay participated in the fraudulent sale of counterfeit goods because it provided a variety of services that facilitated such transactions. Later that month, a different French court ordered eBay to pay LVMH Moët Hennessy Louis Vuitton €40 million in damages, after finding that eBay failed to take sufficient steps to prevent the sale of unauthorized or counterfeit products that damaged the company's brand names. A month later, a U.S. court found in favor of eBay, in a similar lawsuit filed by Tiffany & Co. In August 2008, a Belgian court reached the same conclusion, siding with eBay in a suit filed by L'Oréal SA, as did a third French court and a British court in 2009. In 2011, the European Court of Justice added its opinion, ruling that if an online operator played an "active role" in sale of a fake product it could be held liable for trademark infringements.

National policies toward consumer privacy also need to be adjusted. Many U.S. companies routinely collect information from their customers that the companies then use internally to cross-sell other products or that they sell to third parties. For instance, many websites produce "cookies" that help facilitate repeat online transactions. Cookies allow an online travel vendor to remember customers' frequent flyer numbers, whether the customers prefer an aisle or a window seat, and the billing addresses of their credit cards. However, European laws provide consumers with stronger privacy protection than do U.S. laws. The EU is implementing new rules that require companies to obtain permission from customers before using cookies. U.S.-based web companies must thus alter their marketing and information-gathering practices to accommodate European privacy laws. In a similar vein, Switzerland has demanded that Google obscure every face visible in its Street View mapping application, in order to preserve individual's privacy.

Another issue is what to do with "cybersquatters"—people or firms who try to register domain names of established organizations or famous people and then sell back the names to their owners at inflated prices. For example, when Apple launched the iPhone for the British market in 2007, it discovered that cybersquatters had claimed web addresses such as www.ukiphone.co.uk, which featured nothing more than pay-per-click advertisements for other companies' products. The World Intellectual Property Organization (WIPO) operates an arbitration program to reduce this problem. Although victims are usually successful in reclaiming their property—they win about 85 percent of the cases adjudicated by WIPO—cybersquatting has not gone away. In 2010, for example, 2,696 complaints were filed with WIPO, up 80 percent from their 2006 level.

Sources: "Ebay faces liability on fake goods," *Financial Times*, July 13, 2011, p. 22; "Ebay may be liable for counterfeit goods," *Wall Street Journal*, July 12, 2011 (online); "Cookie laws threaten to unravel web sales," *Financial Times*, May 26, 2011, p. 18; "EU to say location data is private," *Wall Street Journal*, May 13, 2011, p. B6; "Google plans to challenge Swiss ruling on mapping," *Wall Street Journal*, May 12, 2011, p. B5; "EBay wins trademark-infringement case," *Wall Street Journal*, May 22, 2009; "French court says eBay not accountable for sale of L'Oreal fakes," *Wall Street Journal*, May 13, 2009; "L'Oreal loses suit on fakes sold on eBay," *Wall Street Journal*, August 13, 2008, p. B6; "EBay wins fight over Tiffany counterfeits," *Wall Street Journal*, July 15, 2008, p. B1; "E Bay fined over selling counterfeits," *Wall Street Journal*, July 1, 2008, p. B1; "Domain-name complaints rise," *Wall Street Journal*, March 28, 2008, p. B6; "Cybersquatters target iPhone," *Financial Times*, September 27, 2007 (online); "Court setback for French buyers at web auctions," *Financial Times*, May 4, 2000, p. 3; "U.S. in tentative pact protecting Europeans' privacy," *Wall Street Journal*, February 24, 2000, p. B6; "Cybersquatters squeezed as Internet arbitration takes off," *Financial Times*, February 23, 2000, p. 18; "Land of laptops and lederhosen," *Financial Times*, February 17, 2000, p. 14; "Cross-border regulations create hurdle for cyber-shoppers," *Financial Times*, February 16, 2000, p. 7; "Border crossings," *Wall Street Journal*, November 22, 1999, p. R41; "In Europe, surfing a web of red tape," *Wall Street Journal*, October 29, 1999, p. B1; "Judge fines Yahoo! for neo-Nazi auction," *Houston Chronicle*, May 23, 2000, p. A4; www.wipo.int.

---

with arbitrary rules or decisions that have the force of law. This is often the case in China, for example. One study notes:

> Chinese bureaucracies have sometimes been accused of selectively applying regulations. China has many strict rules that are usually ignored in practice until a person or entity falls out of official favor. Governmental authorities can wield their discretionary power to "crack down" on foreign or disfavored investors or make special demands on such investors simply by threatening to wield such power.[7]

Many international managers have learned the hard way that an unfortunate by-product of bureaucratic law is the lack of consistency, predictability, and appeal procedures.

International businesspeople must be aware of these general differences in legal systems to avoid costly misunderstandings. They should also rely on the expertise of local lawyers in each country in which they operate to help them comply with the specific requirements of local laws and to counsel them on substantive differences in due process, legal liabilities, and procedural safeguards.

Domestically Oriented Laws

The laws of the countries in which an international business operates play a major role in shaping the opportunities available to that firm. Some of these laws are primarily designed to regulate the domestic economic environment. Such laws affect all facets of a firm's domestic operations: managing its workforce (recruitment, compensation, and labor relations laws); financing its operations (securities, banking, and credit laws); marketing its products (advertising, distribution, and consumer protection laws); and developing and utilizing technology (patent, copyright, and trademark laws). Although such laws are primarily focused on the domestic marketplace, they may indirectly affect the ability of domestic firms to compete internationally by increasing their costs, thus reducing their price competitiveness relative to foreign firms. For example, labor costs for manufacturers in Germany, France, and Belgium are among the world's highest as a result of government-mandated benefits packages. These manufacturers, therefore, find that their products are less price competitive in export markets; many of them that compete internationally stress their products' quality rather than their price (see Chapter 6's opening case, "The Mittelstand Lead the Way").

Domestically oriented laws may also inadvertently affect the business practices of foreign firms operating outside the country's borders. Often firms whose products are geared to the export market alter their production techniques to meet the regulations of the importing countries, even though the firms' operations are legal within their home country. For example, Grupo Herdez chose to alter its production processes in Mexico in order to sell its goods in the U.S. market. Grupo Herdez is one of Mexico's largest producers of mole (pronounced mo-lay), a spicy but sweet sauce made from chocolate and chili peppers. The firm's traditional way of preparing the chilies for production—laying them out to dry in the sun for several days—failed to meet hygiene standards of the U.S. Food and Drug Administration (FDA). To receive the necessary FDA approval and benefit from the growing U.S. market for Mexican foods, Grupo Herdez had to develop a new technology that uses electronic dryers to prepare the chilies for mole production.[8]

Laws Directly Affecting International Business Transactions

Other national laws are explicitly designed to regulate international business activities. Such laws are often politically motivated and designed to promote the country's foreign policy or military objectives. A country may attempt to induce a second country to change an undesirable policy by imposing **sanctions**—restraints against commerce with that country. Sanctions may take many forms, such as restricting access to high-technology goods, withdrawing preferential tariff treatment, boycotting the country's goods, and denying new loans. For instance, the United Nations imposed financial sanctions against Sierra Leone and Liberia to cut the flow of arms to their war-torn countries, while the United States levied sanctions against Sudan and Myanmar (Burma) for human rights violations and against Iran for nuclear proliferation policy violations.[9]

An **embargo**—a comprehensive sanction against all commerce with a given country—may be imposed by countries acting in unison or alone. For example, the United Nations embargoed all trade with Iraq after Iraq's 1990 invasion of Kuwait. Most countries embargoed goods to or from South Africa during the 1980s to protest its apartheid policies. The United States has unilaterally embargoed trade with Cuba since 1961, when the attempted U.S.-supported overthrow of Fidel Castro died on the beaches of the Bay of Pigs.

A particularly important form of export control involves high-technology goods. Many technologically advanced countries limit the export of so-called **dual-use** products that may be used for both civilian and military purposes. McDonnell Douglas ran afoul of U.S. dual-use controls when it sold sophisticated machine tools to the China National Aero-Technology Import and Export Company, which claimed that the equipment would be used to build civilian aircraft. However, the tools were instead shipped to a military factory that builds ballistic and cruise missiles.[10] Similarly, Boeing agreed to pay a $15 million fine in 2006 because it sold China 94 commercial airliners whose avionics systems contained a tiny gyrochip that could be used to guide air-to-surface missiles, without receiving an export license, in violation of the Arms Control Export Act.[11]

Countries may also attempt to regulate business activities that are conducted outside their borders, a practice known as **extraterritoriality**. For example, firms are vulnerable to U.S. antitrust lawsuits if they engage in activities outside the United States that diminish competition in the U.S. market. In one such case the United States successfully sued Pilkington PLC, the British owner of the most important patents for producing flat glass, for limiting the ability of its U.S. licensees to use the technology in international markets. U.S. authorities claimed that Pilkington's policies hurt U.S. exports and reduced the incentive of U.S. flat glass producers to invest in research and development, thereby lessening competition.[12]

Antiboycott provisions in U.S. trade law also have extraterritorial reach. U.S. antiboycott law prohibits U.S. firms from complying with any boycott ordered by a foreign country that prohibits trade with a country friendly to the United States. This law is primarily directed against a 1954 resolution adopted by the League of Arab States that calls for a boycott of any firm that does business with Israel. Baxter International found itself in deep trouble after a U.S. grand jury investigated it for selling discounted hospital supplies to Syria, allegedly as a bribe for the Arab states terminating their boycott of the company. Baxter pleaded guilty to violating the antiboycott law and paid a fine of $6.6 million.[13]

The Helms-Burton Act is probably the most controversial application of extraterritoriality affecting international business today. This act is directed against international firms that "traffic" in the assets of U.S. companies that were confiscated by the Cuban government when Fidel Castro assumed control in 1959. Over time the Cuban government has leased or sold many of these confiscated assets to foreign companies. The Helms-Burton Act authorizes the U.S. government and the former U.S. owners of the confiscated assets to take action against their new foreign owners. The U.S. government can deny entrance to the United States of officers of companies that benefit from the use of these confiscated assets; such a fate has befallen executives of Canada's Sherritt Corporation, which is producing nickel and cobalt from a mine formerly owned by Freeport McMoRan, a New Orleans–based natural resources company.

In the eyes of the U.S. government the Helms-Burton Act is simply designed to ensure that foreign companies do not profit from Cuban property that was stolen from U.S. owners. In the view of many other countries, such as Canada and the European Union, the Helms-Burton Act is an ill-conceived policy of trying to bludgeon them into joining America's anti-Castro crusade. By some estimates 85 percent of all foreign-owned private property in pre-Castro Cuba was owned by U.S. interests, so it is easy to see why the disposition of confiscated property in Cuba is more important to the United States than to other countries.[14]

Laws Directed Against Foreign Firms

On other occasions countries may pass laws that are explicitly directed against foreign-owned firms. Ownership issues are a particular area of concern. In most countries there is ongoing debate between the political left and right regarding the appropriate balance between governmental control of the economy and reliance on market forces to allocate resources. Often when leftist governments obtain power, they choose to transfer ownership of resources from the private to the public sector, a process known as **nationalization**. Most vulnerable to such actions are industries that lack mobility: natural resource industries such as crude oil production and mining, and capital-intensive industries such as steel, chemicals, and oil refining. For example, in 2008 Hugo Chávez, the president of Venezuela, announced he would nationalize the steel and cement industries on grounds that they constituted "strategic sectors" of the economy. The previous year he nationalized private firms in the oil, power, and telecommunications industries, as this chapter's closing case details.[15] Similarly, Zimbabwe is mandating that foreign-owned mining companies must divest majority ownership of their local subsidiaries to government entities or employee-owned groups.[16]

When the host government compensates the private owners for their losses, the transfer is called **expropriation**. When the host government offers no compensation, the transfer is called **confiscation**. Most governments, including that of the United States, recognize the right of other national governments to mandate the transfer of private property within their borders to the public sector, although nonhost governments do expect that foreign owners will receive suitable compensation for their lost property. For example, many Arab oil-producing countries nationalized the properties of Western oil firms after 1973. These countries, however, offered the Western firms a combination of compensation, continuing operating agreements, and future drilling rights that the firms found acceptable. Conversely, a key element in the U.S. conflict with Cuba is Cuba's lack of compensation for assets seized from U.S. firms.

PRIVATIZATION The conversion of state-owned property to privately owned property is called **privatization**. Although not strictly an issue of host country control, privatization is the opposite of nationalization and creates opportunities for international businesses. Most state-owned enterprises sold to the private sector are unprofitable, undercapitalized, and overstaffed. Nevertheless, they are often attractive to international businesses seeking to expand their operations into new markets located in key sectors of a national economy, such as telecommunications, transportation, and manufacturing.

Privatization, which gained momentum in the 1980s, stems from two primary forces: political ideology and economic pressure. Political ideology prompted Margaret Thatcher, the prime minister of the United Kingdom from 1979 to 1990, to call for diminishing the role of the state in the economy. During the 1980s the British government sold its interests in British Airways, British Telecom, the British Airport Authority, and British Petroleum. Brian Mulroney, head of Canada's Progressive Conservative Party, followed a similar agenda during his tenure as Canada's prime minister from 1984 to 1993, as did the leaders of Argentina, Brazil, Chile, Mexico, and many other countries during the 1990s.

Privatization has also resulted from competitive pressures that firms face in global markets. The telecommunications industry provides a perfect example of this phenomenon. That industry has benefited from rapid technological change, yet many national governments, facing enormous budgetary pressures and deficits, have found it difficult to raise the capital required to upgrade and expand state-owned telecommunications systems. As a result, countries such as Argentina, Mexico, Chile, and the United Kingdom have privatized telecommunications services.

CONSTRAINTS ON FOREIGN OWNERSHIP Many governments limit foreign ownership of domestic firms to avoid having their economies or key industries controlled by foreigners. For example, Mexico restricts foreign ownership in its energy industry, believing that the benefits of its oil reserves, which it views as part of its "national patrimony," should accrue only to its citizens. Canada effectively limits foreign ownership of newspapers to 25 percent as part of its program to protect the country's culture from being inundated by its neighbor to the south. Foreign firms are often excluded from the radio and television broadcasting industries. For example, the United States limits foreigners to 25 percent ownership of U.S. television and radio stations. Similar rules exist in Europe.

Countries can also constrain foreign MNCs by imposing restrictions on their ability to **repatriate** (return to their home countries) the profits earned in the host country. Such restrictions were common in the 1980s, but many countries, such as Botswana and Ethiopia, abolished their repatriation controls during the 1990s as they adopted more free-market-oriented policies.

The Impacts of MNCs on Host Countries

Firms establishing operations beyond the borders of their home country affect and are affected by the political, economic, social, and cultural environments of the host countries in which the firms operate. To compete effectively in these markets and maintain productive relationships with the governments of the host countries, managers of MNCs must recognize how they and their firms should interact with the national and local environments.

ECONOMIC AND POLITICAL IMPACTS MNCs affect every local economy in which they compete and operate. Many of the effects are positive. For instance, as Western supermarket chains like France's Carrefour enter the Chinese market, they offer Chinese consumers greater selection, national brands, and high standards of hygiene. MNCs may make direct investments in new plants and factories, thereby creating local jobs. Such investments provide work for local contractors, builders, and suppliers. MNCs also pay taxes, which benefit the local economy and help to improve educational, transportation, and other municipal services. Technology transfer can also have positive local effects. An important benefit to the Shanghai Automotive Industry Corporation of its joint venture with Volkswagen was access to the latest German automotive technology. Similarly, General Electric raised the productivity of Hungary's largest lightbulb manufacturer by transferring technological knowledge to the Hungarian firm.

MNCs may also have negative effects on the local economy. To the extent that MNCs compete directly with local firms, the MNCs may cause these firms to lose both jobs and profits. For instance, Carrefour's entry into the Chinese market makes it more difficult for mom-and-pop operators in China's open-air food markets to eke out a living.[17] Also, as a local economy becomes more dependent on the economic health of an MNC, the financial fortunes of the firm take on increasing significance. When retrenchment by an MNC is accompanied by layoffs, cutbacks, or a total shutdown of local operations, the effects can be devastating to a local economy.

MNCs also may have a significant political impact, either intentionally or unintentionally. Their sheer size often gives them tremendous power in each country in which they operate. Furthermore, there is always the possibility that this power may be misused. Even when it is not, MNCs are often able to counter efforts by host governments to restrict their activities. The MNCs simply threaten to shift production and jobs to other locations.

CULTURAL IMPACTS MNCs also can exert a major influence on the cultures in which they operate. As they raise local standards of living and introduce new products and services previously unavailable, people in the host cultures develop new norms, standards, and behaviors. Some of these changes are positive, such as the introduction of safer equipment and machinery, better health care and pharmaceuticals, and purer and more sanitary food products. Other changes are not positive. Nestlé, for example, has received much criticism for its promotion of infant formula in the world's developing countries. Mothers in these countries were allegedly enticed into buying the formula but were not trained in its proper use. The mothers diluted the formula to make it go further and often were unable to follow adequate sanitation procedures. As a result, critics argue, infant mortality in these countries increased significantly.

Dispute Resolution in International Business

Disputes in international commerce can be very complicated. Typically, four questions must be answered for an international dispute to be resolved:

1. Which country's law applies?
2. In which country should the issue be resolved?
3. Which technique should be used to resolve the conflict: litigation, arbitration, mediation, or negotiation?
4. How will the settlement be enforced?

Many international business contracts specify answers to these questions to reduce uncertainty and expense in resolving disputes. The courts of most major trading countries will honor and enforce the provisions of these contracts, as long as they are not contrary to other aspects of the country's public policy.

If a contract does not contain answers to the first two questions, each party to the transaction may seek to have the case heard in the court system most favorable to its own interests, a process known as **forum shopping**. Forum shopping allegedly places U.S. manufacturers at a disadvantage in international markets. Monetary awards are higher in U.S. courts, so many plaintiffs' lawyers attempt to use these courts to adjudicate foreign lawsuits for product defects in U.S.-made goods sold internationally. In contrast, a foreign manufacturer of a good sold outside the United States would not face the threat of having to defend its product in a U.S. court because the manufacturer lacked a tie to that forum.

Whether a foreign court order is enforced is determined by the **principle of comity**. The principle of comity provides that a country will honor and enforce within its own territory the judgments and decisions of foreign courts, with certain limitations. For the principle to apply, countries commonly require three conditions to be met:

1. Reciprocity is extended between the countries; that is, country A and country B mutually agree to honor each other's court decisions.
2. The defendant is given proper notice.
3. The foreign court judgment does not violate domestic statutes or treaty obligations.[18]

Because of the costs and uncertainties of litigation, many international businesses seek less expensive means of settling disputes over international transactions. Often business conflicts will be resolved through alternative dispute resolution techniques, such as arbitration. **Arbitration** is the process by which both parties to a conflict agree to submit their cases to a private individual or body whose decision they will honor. Because of the speed, privacy, and informality of such proceedings, disputes can often be resolved more cheaply than through the court system. For example, a five-year-old conflict between IBM and Fujitsu over the latter's unauthorized use of proprietary IBM software that was moving slowly through the U.S. judicial system was settled quickly with the help of two neutral arbitrators from the American Arbitration Association.[19] Similarly, 16 francophone African nations have established a regional commercial arbitration court in Abidjan, Côte d'Ivoire. By providing a site for resolving commercial disputes independent of behind-the-scenes politicking or pressures from a host government, this court should encourage more international trade and investment in the 16 countries.[20]

Another set of issues arises when an international business is in a dispute with a national government. The legal recourse available to international businesses in such disputes is often limited. For example, the U.S. **Foreign Sovereign Immunities Act of 1976** provides that the actions of foreign governments against U.S. firms are generally beyond the jurisdiction of U.S. courts. Thus, if France chose to nationalize IBM's French operations or to impose arbitrary taxes on IBM computers, IBM could not use U.S. courts to seek redress against the sovereign nation of France. However, the Foreign Sovereign Immunities Act does not grant immunity for the commercial activities of a sovereign state. If the French government contracted to purchase 2,000 servers from IBM and then repudiated the contract, IBM could sue France in U.S. courts.

Countries often negotiate bilateral treaties to protect their firms from arbitrary actions by host country governments. These treaties commonly require the host country to agree to arbitrate investment disputes involving the host country and citizens of the other country. The United States and Jamaica have such a treaty. When the Jamaican government announced a tax increase on Alcoa's aluminum refining plant despite a contract between the two parties that prohibited such an increase, Alcoa was able to force the Jamaican government to submit its decision to arbitration.[21]

The Technological Environment

Another important dimension of a country is its technological environment. The foundation of a country's technological environment is its resource base. Some countries, such as Australia, Argentina, and Thailand, are blessed with much fertile agricultural land. Other countries, such as Saudi Arabia, South Africa, and Russia, are endowed with rich natural resources like oil, gold, and diamonds. Countries such as China and Indonesia have abundant labor supplies, while other countries, such as Iceland and New Zealand, do not. The availability or unavailability of resources affects what products are made in a given country. Because of their abundance of fertile land, Australia, Argentina, and Thailand are major exporters of agricultural goods. Similarly, the easy availability of low-cost labor allows firms in China and Indonesia to produce labor-intensive products for the world market. Conversely, firms in Iceland and New Zealand are net importers of such products because these firms lack low-cost labor, which hinders their ability to manufacture labor-intensive goods profitably.

Countries may change or shape their technological environments through investments. Many countries, such as Canada, Germany, and Japan, have invested heavily in their infrastructures—highways, communications systems, waterworks, and so forth—to make producing and distributing products easier. Similarly, many countries have invested heavily in human capital. By improving the knowledge and skills of their citizens, countries improve the productivity and efficiency of their workforces. Investments in infrastructure and human capital have allowed developed countries to continue prospering in world markets despite the high wages paid to workers in those countries.

Another means for altering a country's technological environment is **technology transfer**, the transmittal of technology from one country to another. Some countries have promoted technology transfer by encouraging foreign direct investment (FDI). For instance, Hungary and Poland jump-started their transition from communism to capitalism by using tax and other incentives to entice firms like General Electric and General Motors to build new factories there. Other countries have improved their technological base by requiring companies eager to access a country's resources or consumers to transfer technology as a condition for operating in that country. Saudi Arabia, for example, mandated that oil companies wishing to extract its crude oil hire and train Saudi petroleum engineers, who then learned state-of-the-art exploration and extraction methods on the job. Similarly, the Chinese government approved General Motors' request to build Buicks in Shanghai only after GM agreed to establish five research institutes in China that would train Chinese engineers and advance China's technological know-how in such areas as fuel injection systems and power trains.

An important determinant of a country's technological environment—and the willingness of foreign firms to transfer technology to the country—is the degree of protection that its laws offer to intellectual property rights. Intellectual property—patents, copyrights, trademarks, brand names, and so forth—is an important asset of most MNCs. It often forms the basis of a firm's competitive advantage/core competency in the global marketplace. The value of intellectual property can quickly be damaged unless countries enforce ownership rights of firms. Countries that provide weak protection for intellectual property are less likely to attract technology-intensive foreign investments. Weak intellectual property protection also discourages local firms from developing intellectual property of their own.

Most countries have passed laws protecting intellectual property rights. Protection of such rights has also been promoted by numerous international treaties. Among these are the International Convention for the Protection of Industrial Property Rights (more commonly known as the Paris Convention), the Berne Convention for the Protection of Literary and Artistic Works, the Universal Copyright Convention, and the Trade-Related Intellectual Property Rights agreement (part of the Uruguay Round). On paper these laws and treaties would appear to provide adequate protection to owners of intellectual property. However, not all countries have signed the treaties. Further, their enforcement by many signatories is lax.

Weak protection for intellectual property rights can have high costs for international businesses—as Harry Potter's publisher discovered in this chapter's opening case. According to the Business Software Alliance, piracy of computer software cost its members $51.4 billion in revenues in 2009. Microsoft's revenues in China, for example, are one-twentieth of those it earns in the United States, despite similar PC sales in both countries. Copies of its Windows and Office software are readily available from street sellers for $2 or $3.[22] As Table 3.1 indicates, piracy rates are highest in Georgia, Zimbabwe, and Bangladesh, while they are lowest in the United States, Japan, and Luxembourg. Similarly, music and movie companies estimate that their losses due to illegal duplication of cassettes, CDs, and videos exceed $8 billion annually. Unfortunately for these companies, technology is allowing pirates to move faster than ever. For example, bootleg copies of Hollywood movies routinely appear on the streets of China, Hong Kong, and Indonesia within days of their debuts in theaters.[23] And the monetary costs are but a small part of the problem, as "Bringing the World into Focus" indicates.

Differences in patent practices can also lead to conflicts. For example, Japanese firms tend to file numerous patents, each of which may reflect only a minor modification of an existing patent. Conversely, U.S. patent law requires that patentable inventions be novel, useful, and nonobvious. Accordingly, U.S. firms tend to file far fewer patents than Japanese companies. This has led to trade disputes between the United States and Japan over the use of so-called patent flooding by Japanese firms. With patent flooding, a company files a series of patent applications protecting narrow, minor technical improvements to a competitor's existing patents. Patent flooding makes it difficult for the competitor to improve its own technology without

TABLE 3.1 Software Piracy Rankings

20 Countries with the Highest Piracy Rates				20 Countries with the Lowest Piracy Rates			
Country	2009	2008	2007	Country	2009	2008	2007
Georgia	95%	95%	n.a.	United States	20%	20%	20%
Zimbabwe	92%	92%	91%	Japan	21%	21%	23%
Bangladesh	91%	92%	92%	Luxembourg	21%	21%	21%
Moldova	91%	90%	92%	New Zealand	22%	22%	22%
Armenia	90%	92%	93%	Australia	25%	26%	28%
Yemen	90%	89%	89%	Austria	25%	24%	25%
Sri Lanka	89%	90%	90%	Belgium	25%	25%	25%
Azerbaijan	88%	90%	92%	Finland	25%	26%	25%
Libya	88%	87%	88%	Sweden	25%	25%	25%
Belarus	87%	n.a.	n.a.	Switzerland	25%	25%	25%
Venezuela	87%	86%	87%	Denmark	26%	25%	25%
Indonesia	86%	85%	84%	United Kingdom	27%	27%	26%
Vietnam	85%	85%	85%	Germany	28%	27%	27%
Ukraine	85%	84%	83%	Netherlands	28%	28%	28%
Iraq	85%	85%	85%	Canada	29%	32%	33%
Pakistan	84%	86%	84%	Norway	29%	28%	29%
Algeria	84%	84%	84%	Israel	33%	32%	32%
Cameroon	83%	83%	84%	Ireland	35%	34%	34%
Nigeria	83%	83%	82%	Singapore	35%	36%	37%
Paraguay	82%	83%	82%	South Africa	35%	35%	34%

Source: Seventh, Sixth, and Fifth Annual BSA and IDC Global Software and Piracy Studies (2010, 2009, and 2008, respectively), found on www.bsa.org.

infringing on the intellectual property of the patent flooder. CyberOptics, the small Minneapolis developer of LaserAlign (a software and laser-based technology that helps robots position miniature components on circuit boards), provides an example of a firm that believes it has been harmed by patent flooding by a much larger company. CyberOptics had worked closely with Yamaha for five years to incorporate CyberOptics technology on the pick-and-place robots Yamaha used to produce its motorcycles and other products. Both companies agreed that, without each other's consent, neither would file for patent protection for technology they had developed jointly. However, CyberOptics discovered that Yamaha had filed 26 patent applications in Japan, Europe, and the United States for technology that CyberOptics believed was developed collaboratively based on the LaserAlign system. CyberOptics further discovered that Yamaha was allegedly warning potential CyberOptics customers that they might be in violation of Yamaha's patents if they purchased CyberOptics' services. Consequently, the Minneapolis firm sued Yamaha for breach of contract and infringement of its patents. [24]

Registration of trademarks and brand names can also cause problems for international businesses. Generally, most countries follow a "first to file" approach, which often lends itself to abuses against foreigners. A firm may popularize a brand name or trademark in its home market, only to find, when it attempts to export its product to a second country, that an opportunistic entrepreneur has already applied for the intellectual property rights in that country. Some countries adopt a "use it or lose it" philosophy, which can prove troublesome to foreign firms. For example, J. C. Penney, which had registered its trademark in most markets to establish its "first to file" claim, lost the rights to its name in Singapore to a small entrepreneur who adopted the name "JC Penney Collections" for her two clothing stores. The High Court of Singapore, while acknowledging that J. C. Penney had validly registered its trademark in that

Counterfeiting can cause companies and society problems beyond the mere loss of revenue. In many cases, a company's most valuable asset is its brand name, and counterfeit goods can severely damage that reputation. One well-publicized incident involved a young welder in China who was killed when his Motorola cell phone exploded in his pocket; the presumed cause was that the phone's battery was subjected to extreme heat. After the incident, Chinese regulators ruled that Motorola cell phone batteries failed to meet national safety standards. However, once Motorola examined the evidence, it determined that the battery was not genuine; rather, it was a counterfeit one sold by a Chinese distributor that had no connection to the company.

Colgate-Palmolive Company ran into a similar problem. The U.S. Food and Drug Administration discovered that "Colgate" toothpaste sold in four states contained diethylene glycol, a poisonous substance commonly used in antifreeze. Once again, the product was a counterfeit made in China, but the damage to Colgate's reputation was real. Thanks to the FDA's action, tragedy was avoided.

Such was not the case in Panama, where cough syrup imported from China, laced with diethylene glycol, was responsible for over 40 deaths.

The growth in counterfeiting complicates the ability of overburdened regulators in importing countries to protect their citizens from unsafe products. For example, in 2007 alone the FDA opened up 31 new investigations involving imported counterfeit drugs and was forced to test all imported toothpaste made in China after the fake "Colgate" toothpaste was discovered. Such incidents also raise important questions about the reliability of the complex supply chains that many firms have constructed as a result of globalization.

Sources: "FDA identifies contaminant in heparin batches," *Wall Street Journal*, March 20, 2008, p. A4; "Made in China," *Wall Street Journal*, July 12, 2007, p. A15; "Chinese regulators find mobile phone batteries that can explode," *New York Times*, July 6, 2007 (online); "Colgate warns of fakes," *Wall Street Journal*, June 15, 2007, p. B3; "When fakery turns fatal," *New York Times*, June 5, 2007 (online).

country, determined that the U.S. firm had lost the right to its company name for failure to exercise its use in Singapore.[25] And Starbucks's entry into the Russian market was delayed for several years while it struggled to regain the rights to use its brand name from a trademark squatter. The delay allowed local and foreign rivals to gain a foothold in the Russian market and tie up the best sites for coffeehouses.[26]

Administrative delays may also hurt the rights of intellectual property owners. In Japan approval of a trademark application often takes four times as long for a foreign firm as for a Japanese firm. Approval of foreign patent applications may also take a long time. For example, three decades elapsed before Japanese courts recognized Texas Instruments' (TI) original patents on integrated circuits in 1989, substantially reducing TI's royalty payments from Japanese licensees. Some firms, such as Fujitsu, were able to avoid paying TI any royalties, arguing that Fujitsu's circuit designs rely on newer, more improved technology rather than on TI's original patents. In essence the slowness of Japan's judicial process allowed companies like Fujitsu to benefit from TI's technology during the early days of the semiconductor industry without having to compensate TI for its intellectual property.[27]

The Accounting Environment

Differences in the policies and procedures of national accounting systems can create significant operational and control problems for an international business, which must develop an accounting system that provides both the internal information required by its managers to run the firm and the external information needed by shareholders, lenders, investors, and government officials in all the countries in which the firm operates.

The Roots of National Differences

A country's accounting standards and practices reflect the influence of legal, cultural, political, and economic factors, as Figure 3.1 indicates.[28] Because these factors vary by country, the underlying goals and philosophy of national accounting systems also vary dramatically.

Consider first the difference between common law and code law countries. In common law countries such as the United Kingdom and the United States, accounting procedures normally evolve via decisions of independent standards-setting boards, such as the United Kingdom's Accounting Standards Board or the U.S. Financial Accounting Standards Board (FASB). Each

FIGURE 3.1

Influences on a Country's Accounting System

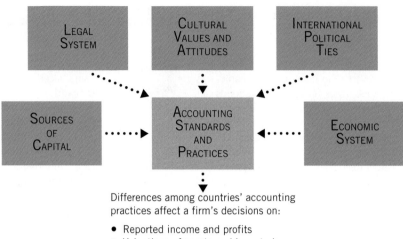

Differences among countries' accounting practices affect a firm's decisions on:

- Reported income and profits
- Valuations of assets and inventories
- Tax reporting
- Desire to operate in a given country
- Use of accounting reserves

board works in consultation with professional accounting groups, such as the U.K.'s various Institutes of Chartered Accountants or the American Institute of Certified Public Accountants. Accountants in common law countries typically follow so-called generally accepted accounting principles (GAAP) that provide a "true and fair" view of a firm's performance based on the standards agreed on by these professional boards. Operating within the boundaries of these principles, accountants have leeway to exercise their professional discretion in reporting a true and fair depiction of a firm's performance.

Conversely, countries relying on code law are likely to codify their national accounting procedures and standards.[29] In these countries accounting practices are determined by the law, not by the collective wisdom of professional accounting groups like the FASB.[30] For example, France's code law system and long tradition of strong central government control over the economy are reflected in its imposition on French firms of a national uniform chart of accounts—the Plan Comptable Général. This accounting system, which dates to 1673, creates accounting records designed to serve as proof in legal procedures. To facilitate this legal role, all corporate accounting records must be officially registered with the government. Similarly, German accounting practices adhere strictly to requirements laid down by law or court decisions.

A country's legal system also influences enforcement of accounting practices. Most developed countries rely on both private and public enforcement of business behavior, although the public/private mixture varies by country. Because French and German accounting procedures are laid down by law, the government plays a major role in monitoring accounting practices in those countries. Indeed, French accountants are legally compelled to report to French prosecutors any criminal acts the accountants uncover when auditing a company's books. In contrast, the U.S. system relies to a greater extent on private litigation to enforce the accuracy and honesty of firms' accounting practices. Any attempt to mislead private investors or creditors in the United States is likely to prompt a lawsuit. Arthur Andersen's fate is a stern reminder of this: Its failure to audit Enron properly led to a blizzard of lawsuits and the quick bankruptcy and collapse of the once venerable accounting firm.

A country's accounting system also may reflect its national culture. The detailed accounting procedures laid down by the French government mirror France's statist tradition. Larger French firms also must publish a "social balance sheet" detailing their treatment and compensation of their workforces. Strong anti-inflation biases are embedded in German accounting procedures, a reaction to the tragic hyperinflation of the early 1920s that wiped out much of the wealth of the German middle class and helped Adolf Hitler rise to the chancellorship in 1932.

International political ties are also important determinants of a country's accounting procedures. Most members of the British Commonwealth have adopted the accounting principles and procedures of the United Kingdom, whereas former colonies of France and the Netherlands have adopted those of their colonial rulers. Similarly, the accounting procedures of the Philippines follow those of the United States, which controlled that country from 1898 to 1946.

A country's economic system also influences its accounting practices. In a centrally planned economy the accounting system is driven by the need to provide output-oriented information to the state planners. Such accounting systems focus on documenting how state funds are used and whether state-mandated production quotas are being met.[31] In market-oriented systems, on the other hand, managers and investors require profit- and cost-oriented information.

Capital markets also may affect national accounting standards. U.S. firms historically have raised capital by relying on public investors. U.S. accounting standards therefore emphasize the provision of accurate and useful information to help outsiders—private shareholders and bondholders—make appropriate investment decisions. As part of this goal, publicly owned firms must satisfy all the disclosure regulations of the Securities and Exchange Commission (SEC). Unfortunately, these disclosure regulations were not perfect, as Enron's bankruptcy demonstrates. To remedy the problems uncovered by the Enron debacle, the Sarbanes-Oxley Act of 2002 (see "Bringing the World into Focus") imposes new corporate governance and financial reporting requirements on companies publicly traded in the United States. The SEC has also issued new regulations addressing these issues, with the goal of making the accounting statements and governance of these companies clearer and more understandable to investors. In contrast, in Germany the dominant role of a few large banks in providing capital results in accounting practices that focus on the needs of creditors, for example, by tending to undervalue assets and overvalue liabilities. This conservative approach is favored by the lending banks. The public capital market has been much less important in Germany than in the United States, and German accounting practices provide less information to public investors than do U.S. methods.[32]

The situation is similar in Japan. Most publicly traded Japanese firms are members of a keiretsu. They have relatively few public shareholders because of the pervasive cross-ownership of shares among keiretsu members and the extensive share ownership by banks and other financial institutions. Most Japanese firms also have large debt-to-equity ratios by Western standards. Thus, Japanese accounting standards are geared toward meeting the needs of a firm's lenders and keiretsu partners, both of which already have privileged access to the firm's financial records, rather than the needs of outside investors. However, the lack of transparent accounting standards often affects the ability of firms in less developed countries to raise capital.

Differences in Accounting Practices

Political, cultural, legal, and economic forces affect each country's philosophy and attitude toward its accounting system. They also affect the way a country's accountants treat different accounting issues. These different treatments in turn impact a firm's reported profits, the value of its assets, its tax bill, and its decision to begin or continue operating in a country. International businesses that rely on foreign accounting records but fail to recognize these differences may make expensive, perhaps fatal, strategic errors and operating mistakes. Let us look at some of the more important national accounting differences that affect international business.

VALUATION AND REVALUATION OF ASSETS Most countries' accounting systems begin with the assumption that a firm's assets should be valued on a historical cost basis. That is, an asset is carried on the firm's books according to the asset's original cost, less depreciation. Because of inflation, however, the market value of an asset is often higher than its historical cost. The resolution of this problem differs among national accounting systems. Dutch firms are permitted to raise the value of such assets on their balance sheets to reflect the assets' true replacement value. British accountants may exercise their professional discretion and value assets on a historical cost basis, a current cost basis, or a mixture of the two. Australia, an inheritor of British accounting philosophy, similarly grants a firm's accountants a great degree of professional discretion. Australian firms may alter the value of long-term assets on their balance sheets to take into account inflation or improved economic conditions. In the United States and Japan, however, such upward revaluations are illegal. These differences in asset revaluation procedures suggest the need for caution when comparing the strength of balance sheets of firms from different countries.

The accounting scandals surrounding Enron, Tyco, and WorldCom threatened more than the accounting profession. The U.S. Congress feared that investors could lose faith in the U.S. capital market if they no longer trusted public accountants or corporate accounting statements. If so, the cost to American firms of acquiring capital could rise, which would lessen their competitiveness in world markets. To restore the public's trust in the capital market, Congress passed the Public Company Accounting Reform and Investor Protection Act of 2002, more commonly known as the Sarbanes-Oxley Act.

The Sarbanes-Oxley Act has several objectives. First, it addresses perceived public accounting problems. The act establishes the Public Company Accounting Oversight Board, which is tasked with developing and enforcing ethical and auditing standards for auditors of public companies. The act forbids accounting firms from providing certain consulting services to firms that they audit. This requirement is a direct response to conflicts of interest that arose between Arthur Andersen and Enron, for Arthur Andersen earned far more from Enron for providing consulting services than auditing services. Many critics believed that Arthur Andersen's willingness to challenge Enron's more dubious accounting practices was compromised by its fear of losing its lucrative consulting business with Enron.

Second, the act strengthens corporate governance of publicly owned corporations by imposing new requirements on corporate executives, auditors, and the company's board of directors. No corporate executive can serve on the audit committee of the board of directors, and any disagreement over accounting procedures between the auditors and company executives must be reported to the audit committee. The chief executive officer and chief financial officer are required to certify that the corporation's financial statements "fairly present, in all material respects, the operations and financial condition" of the corporation. This requirement is designed to eliminate the "I didn't know" defense used by corporate officers in several recent high-profile court cases.

A critical component of the Sarbanes-Oxley Act is Section 404, which mandates that the managers of a publicly traded corporation must create "adequate internal control structure and procedures for financial reporting," which then must be reviewed by the firm's auditor. The CEO, the CFO, and the auditors are required to certify to the company's shareholders and to the SEC their assessment of the quality and adequacy of the company's internal controls.

The act has proven to be highly controversial, particularly because the high costs of complying with Section 404's requirements fall more heavily on small companies than larger ones. The act's passage has also negatively affected the competitiveness of U.S. stock exchanges. Many foreign firms are choosing not to list their shares in the U.S. public capital market, thereby avoiding the costs of complying with Sarbanes-Oxley. In 2000, for example, the New York Stock Exchange was capturing almost 90 percent of the market for new listings of foreign companies when competing against the London and Luxembourg stock exchanges. By 2005, 90 percent of the new listings were acquired by those rivals. The number of stocks listed on U.S. exchanges has fallen by 43 percent since 1997; during that span, listings outside the United States have more than doubled. Ironically, the main beneficiaries of the act—which was passed in part because of their poor performance—are the surviving Big Four accounting firms, whose business is booming because of the additional workload demanded by Sarbanes-Oxley.

Sources: "U.S. falls behind in stock listings," *Wall Street Journal*, May 26, 2011, p. A1; "Please be patient," *Wall Street Journal*, May 25, 2006, p. A14; "Taking their business elsewhere," *BusinessWeek*, May 22, 2006 (online); "New York loses edge in snagging foreign listings," *Wall Street Journal*, January 26, 2006, p. C1; "A price worth paying?" *The Economist*, May 21, 2005, p. 71; "Teething troubles," *The Economist*, May 21, 2005, p. 72.

VALUATION OF INVENTORIES Every introductory accounting course discusses the two principal methods for valuing inventories: LIFO (last in, first out) and FIFO (first in, first out). In times of inflation LIFO tends to raise the firm's reported costs of goods sold, lower the book value of its inventories, and reduce its reported profits (and, presumably, its taxes) more than FIFO does, whereas FIFO produces a clearer estimate of the value of the firm's existing inventories than does LIFO. Thus, in comparing the performance of two firms, one needs to know which technique each uses to value its inventories. There are significant international differences in the use of the two methods. U.S. and Canadian firms may use either approach. In China and India LIFO cannot be used, whereas in Japan LIFO is permitted. Firms in Brazil and the United Kingdom normally use only FIFO.[33]

DEALING WITH THE TAX AUTHORITIES A firm's accounting records form the basis for assessing its income tax burden. In Germany accounting procedures are detailed explicitly in the German Commercial Code and follow the requirements of German tax laws. A German firm's taxable income is measured by the contents of the firm's financial records. Normally no distinction is made between financial statements reported to shareholders and financial statements reported to German tax authorities. The United States follows a very different approach. U.S. firms commonly report two different sets of financial statements—one to the Internal Revenue Service (IRS) and one to shareholders. Such conduct is authorized by U.S. law and allows firms to take advantage of special tax code provisions to reduce their taxable income. For example, U.S. firms often use accelerated depreciation for tax purposes but not for financial-reporting purposes. A German firm normally does not have this option. If it wants to use accelerated depreciation for tax-reporting purposes (to reduce its current-year taxes), the firm also must use accelerated depreciation in reporting to its shareholders (which reduces its reported income).

Forced to choose between higher taxes and lower reported income, most German firms opt for the latter. Managers and investors need to recognize that the reported profits of German firms are thus biased downward. The inflexibility of Germany's accounting system seems to put German firms at a disadvantage in raising capital. However, German firms typically obtain most of their capital from large financial intermediaries like banks and insurance firms. These inside investors have access to more detailed information about the firm's performance than is available in its public financial statements published in its annual report.

Tax laws also play a major role in French accounting practices, which follow well-defined procedures detailed by the French government in the national uniform chart of accounts. As in the German system, no deductions for tax purposes may be taken unless they have been entered into the firm's annual accounting records. Because of the dominance of tax law in accounting judgments, French firms are likely to bias their reported earnings and net assets downward to reduce their tax burdens.

USE OF ACCOUNTING RESERVES Another important difference in national accounting systems is in the use of **accounting reserves**, which are accounts created in a firm's financial reports to record foreseeable future expenses that might affect its operations. An office supplies wholesaler, for example, might establish a reserve account for bad debts and for returned merchandise, knowing that when it ships merchandise, some retailers will ship the goods back and some will fail to pay their bills. The use of accounting reserves by U.S. firms is carefully monitored and limited by the Internal Revenue Service (IRS) and the SEC. The IRS dislikes accounting reserves because charges to them reduce a firm's taxable income. The SEC fears that firms might manipulate their accounting reserves to provide misleading pictures of their financial performance.

In contrast to the restrictive U.S. system, the German Commercial Code liberally permits German firms to establish accounting reserves for various potential future expenses, such as deferred maintenance, future repairs, or exposure to international risks. Because these reserves reduce reported income on which taxes are based, most German firms use them aggressively. In the 1990s, for example, Deutsche Bank admitted that its hidden reserves amounted to over $14 billion.[34]

The use of such reserves hampers outside investors' ability to assess German firms' performance. Often these firms use reserve accounts to smooth out fluctuations in their earning flows by adding large sums to their reserves in good years and dipping into their reserves in poor years. Because of their use of accounting reserves, the reported earnings of German firms often fluctuate less than those of comparable U.S. firms, giving the misleading appearance that the former are less risky than the latter. These accounting differences complicate investors' decision making regarding how to diversify their portfolios internationally to reduce overall investment risk.

OTHER DIFFERENCES Many other differences exist in the way countries treat accounting issues. The following are a few examples:

- *Capitalization of financial leases:* U.S., British, and Canadian firms must capitalize financial leases, whereas Swiss firms may do so but are not required to do so.
- *Capitalization of research and development (R&D) expenses:* Most countries permit firms to capitalize R&D expenses, but this practice is forbidden in the United States except in limited circumstances.
- *Treatment of goodwill:* A firm that acquires a second firm often pays more than the book value of the acquired firm's stock. The excess payment is called **goodwill**. In the Netherlands firms typically amortize goodwill over a five-year period, although they may write it off instantaneously or over a period of up to 20 years. U.K. firms also are allowed to choose between immediately writing off goodwill or capitalizing it on their balance sheets and amortizing it over a period of time. Japanese and French firms may amortize goodwill as well.

Impact on Capital Markets

The various national differences in accounting practices would be little more than a curiosity were it not for international businesspeople's need for information to make decisions. These differences can distort the measured performance of firms incorporated in different countries. As already noted, the earnings of German and French firms often are understated because of the congruency between financial reporting and tax reporting. The price-to-earnings ratios of Japanese firms are frequently higher than those of U.S. firms, primarily because Japanese accounting practices often substantially reduce reported profits. For example, Japanese firms report depreciation expenses on an accelerated basis to their shareholders and are allowed to create generous reserve funds for future pension liabilities. The overall impact of these accounting differences is clear: Comparing the financial reports of firms from different countries is exceedingly complex, making it more difficult for international investors to assess the performance of the world's businesses.

These differences can affect the global capital market in other ways. The New York Stock Exchange (NYSE), for example, is concerned about SEC-mandated accounting rules that must be followed by publicly traded corporations under the SEC's jurisdiction. Those rules emphasize full and comprehensive disclosure of a firm's financial performance information, and the NYSE fears that the rules discourage foreign firms from listing on the exchange, thereby threatening the exchange's global competitiveness.[35] The Sarbanes-Oxley Act of 2002 has worsened this problem, as "Bringing the World into Focus" on page 94 indicated; increasingly, foreign firms are choosing to list their stocks on European or Asian stock exchanges, rather than the NYSE.[36] Consider the plight of Philips NV. As a Dutch company, it must first comply with Dutch accounting standards. To list its stock on the NYSE, Philips must then undergo the expense of reworking its financial statements to meet SEC requirements as well as comply with the requirements of Sarbanes-Oxley.[37]

The information-laden accounting practices used by U.S. firms do offer them certain advantages, however. Many foreign bankers believe that the United States is the easiest foreign locale in which to lend because of U.S. public disclosure policies. Those policies result in reliable numbers for assessing the riskiness of potential loans. In contrast, the German accounting system, which allows firms to lump together various cost categories and establish a variety of reserves, is much less helpful for a potential foreign lender. As one investment manager has noted, "The poor quality of financial information available from many German companies makes it difficult for investors to buy a stock with confidence, since valuations cannot be clearly established."[38] In hopes of improving their standing with institutional investors, many German MNCs adopted either U.S. GAAP or the **International Financial Reporting Standards (IFRS)**, an alternative transparent approach to financial reporting issued by the International Accounting Standards Board (IASB). The Financial Accounting Standards Board (FASB), which establishes American accounting standards, and the IASB have been negotiating to standardize their treatment of accounting issues, but progress has been slow.[39]

The Political Environment

An important part of any business decision is assessing the political environment in which a firm operates. Laws and regulations passed by any level of government can affect the viability of a firm's operations in the host country. Minimum-wage laws affect the price a firm must pay for labor; zoning regulations affect the way it can use its property; and environmental protection laws affect the production technology it can use as well as the costs of disposing of waste materials. Adverse changes in tax laws can slowly destroy a firm's profitability. Civil wars, assassinations, or kidnappings of foreign businesspeople and expropriation of a firm's property are equally dangerous to the viability of a firm's foreign operations.

Political Risk

Most firms are comfortable assessing the political climates in their home countries. However, assessing the political climates in other countries is far more problematic. Experienced international businesses engage in **political risk assessment**, a systematic analysis of the political risks they face in foreign countries. **Political risks** are any changes in the political environment that may adversely affect the value of a firm's business activities. Most political risks can be divided into three categories:

- Ownership risk, in which the property of a firm is threatened through confiscation or expropriation
- Operating risk, in which the ongoing operations of a firm and/or the safety of its employees are threatened through changes in laws, environmental standards, tax codes, terrorism, armed insurrection, and so forth
- Transfer risk, in which the government interferes with a firm's ability to shift funds into and out of the country

As Table 3.2 shows, political risks may result from governmental actions, such as passage of laws that expropriate private property, raise operating costs, devalue the currency, or constrain the repatriation of profits. Political risks may also arise from nongovernmental actions, such as kidnappings, extortion, and acts of terrorism, as "Emerging Opportunities" indicates.

Political risks may affect all firms equally or focus on only a handful. A **macropolitical risk** affects all firms in a country; examples are the civil wars that tore apart Sierra Leone, Zaire, Bosnia, and Rwanda in the 1990s or the recent conflicts in Afghanistan, Iraq, and Libya. A **micropolitical risk** affects only a specific firm or firms within a specific industry. Saudi Arabia's nationalization of its oil industry in the 1970s is an example of a governmentally imposed micropolitical risk, as is the Venezuelan government's recent requirements that foreign oil companies renegotiate their contracts with the government.[40] Nongovernmental micropolitical risks are also important. Disneyland Paris and McDonald's have been the target of numerous symbolic protests by French farmers, who view them as a convenient target for venting their unhappiness with U.S. international agricultural policies. In other instances, protests may turn

TABLE 3.2 Examples of Political Risks

Type	Impact on Firms
Expropriation	Loss of future profits
Confiscation	Loss of assets
	Loss of future profits
Campaigns against foreign goods	Loss of sales
	Increased costs of public relations efforts to improve public image
Mandatory labor benefits legislation	Increased operating costs
Kidnappings, terrorist threats, and other forms of violence	Disrupted production
	Increased security costs
	Increased managerial costs
	Lower productivity
Civil wars	Destruction of property
	Lost sales
	Disruption of production
	Increased security costs
	Lower productivity
Inflation	Higher operating costs
Repatriation	Inability to transfer funds freely
Currency devaluations	Reduced value of repatriated earnings
Increased taxation	Lower after-tax profits

Disneyland Paris is vulnerable to micropolitical risk, given its status as an icon of America. These French farmers have chosen to voice their displeasure with U.S. agricultural trade policies by blocking the entrance to the park with their tractors.

violent, forcing firms to shut down their operations. For instance, Total SA, Royal Dutch Shell, and Chevron have been forced to temporarily suspend their operations in the Niger Delta several times in the past decade because of fighting between the Nigerian government and local ethnic communities who believe that they have not received a fair share of the wealth generated by the oil.[41]

Any firm contemplating entering a new market should acquire basic knowledge of that country, learning, for example, about its political and economic structures in order to control the firm's political risks. The firm needs answers to such questions as:

- Is the country a democracy or a dictatorship? Is power concentrated in the hands of one person or one political party?
- Does the country normally rely on the free market or on government controls to allocate resources? How much of a contribution is the private sector expected to make in helping the government achieve its overall economic objectives? Does the government view foreign firms as a means of promoting or hindering its economic goals?
- Are the firm's customers in the public or private sector? If public, does the government favor domestic suppliers? Are the firm's competitors in the public or private sector? If public, will the government allow foreigners to compete with the public firms on even terms?
- When making changes in its policies, does the government act arbitrarily or does it rely on the rule of law?
- How stable is the existing government? If it leaves office, will there be drastic changes in the economic policies of the new government?

Most MNCs continually monitor the countries in which they do business for changes in political risk. Often the best sources of information are employees. Whether they are citizens of the home country or of the host country, employees possess firsthand knowledge of the local political environment and are a valuable source of political risk information. The views of local staff should be supplemented by the views of outsiders. Embassy officials and international chambers of commerce are often rich sources of information. Governments themselves can supply vital information. Most governments signal their economic and political agendas during the political campaigns that lead to their elections or during the military

Earlier in the chapter we discussed the growth of piracy of intellectual property. Unfortunately, the traditional kind of piracy—attacks at sea—still plagues international business practitioners, endangering sailors and passengers as well as raising the risks and costs of shipping goods by sea. Four hundred eighty-nine acts of piracy or attempted piracy were reported to the International Maritime Organization in 2010, up 20 percent from 2009. The motives for the piracy vary: Some pirates seek cargoes, such as vegetable oils that are easily sold in the black market. Other pirates focus on kidnapping passengers or crew for ransom, while some seek the ships themselves. Piracy costs the world economy an estimated $7 to $12 billion a year. The bulk of the expense is increased insurance premiums ($3.2 billion) and the costs of re-routing shipping out of the most dangerous routes ($2.95 billion).

Two areas are of primary concern to the international maritime industry. The first is the region surrounding the Strait of Malacca, the narrow channel between Malaysia and the Indonesian island of Sumatra (see Map 3.2). The area has been a haven for pirates for two thousand years. The strategic importance of the Strait cannot be overestimated: It is the primary passageway between the Indian and Pacific Oceans, annually traversed by 60,000 ships carrying a quarter of the world's seaborne trade and almost all the oil imported by Korea, Japan, and China. Although the navies of Singapore, Malaysia, and Indonesia routinely patrol the Strait, they have been unable to suppress pirate gangs armed with rocket-propelled grenades and machine guns from preying on shipping.

The second is the Somali coast, which has overtaken the Malacca Strait as the world's most dangerous waters. The International Maritime Organization attributed 265 acts or attempted acts of piracy in 2010 to pirates based in Somali. Somalia descended into anarchy following the 1991 ouster of Mohamed Siad Barre as the country's ruler, creating a perfect environment for piracy to flourish.

In one highly publicized attack, pirates in several speedboats fired upon the *Seabourn Spirit*, a 10,000-ton cruise liner carrying 300 passengers on its way to Mombasa, Kenya, as it traveled 70 miles off the coast of Somalia. The captain successfully evaded the pirates, but other captains in the area have not been so lucky. In 2011, four Americans were murdered by pirates after their yacht was captured off the coast of Oman. Many ship owners refuse to

MAP 3.2

A Map of the Region Surrounding the Malacca Strait

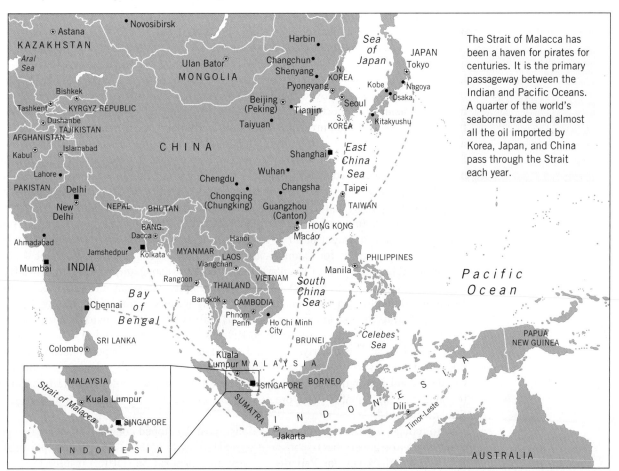

The Strait of Malacca has been a haven for pirates for centuries. It is the primary passageway between the Indian and Pacific Oceans. A quarter of the world's seaborne trade and almost all the oil imported by Korea, Japan, and China pass through the Strait each year.

travel these waters without armed escorts, but despite increased naval patrols from numerous countries the piracy problem continues to grow.

Sources: "Piracy spurs Maersk to raise fee," *Wall Street Journal*, May 9, 2011, p. B3; "Report: Piracy at record high," www.cnn.com, April 14, 2011; "Boarders to control," *Financial Times*, March 2, 2011, p. 7; International Maritime Organization: 2010 Annual Report on Piracy; "Payments to pirates ends tanker hijacking," *Wall Street Journal*, January 9, 2009; "Somali pirates tell their side: They want only money," *New York Times*, September 30, 2008 (online); "U.S. warship fires warning shots over vessel boarded by pirates off Somali Coast," www.foxnews.com, June 5, 2007 (online); "Even hardened sailors fearful of Somali pirates," *Houston Chronicle*, July 3, 2006, p. A17; "For those in peril," *The Economist*, April 22, 2006, p. 73; "Somalia piracy is worst in world," *BBC News*, January 5, 2006 (online); "Pirates shoot at cruise ship off Somalia," *ABC News*, November 6, 2005 (online); "Anti-piracy drive in Malacca Straits," *BBC News*, July 20, 2004 (online).

campaigns that lead to the overthrow of their opponents; once in office, the governments continue to provide useful information about their current and future plans. Moreover, numerous consulting firms specialize in political risk assessment to help firms evaluate the risks of doing business in a particular country. Several international business publications print annual surveys of political risk around the world. Map 3.3 depicts the results of one such survey published in *Euromoney* magazine.

What and how much information a firm needs to assess political risk will depend on the type of business it is and how long it is likely to be in the host country. The greater and longer-lived a firm's investment, the broader its risk assessment should be. A Singapore toy manufacturer that subcontracts with a Chinese firm to assemble toy trucks needs to know about politically influenced factors such as trends in exchange rates, reliability of customs procedures, and the legal recourse available to it should the Chinese subcontractor fail to deliver products that meet contract specifications and deadlines. If the Singapore toy manufacturer wants to build and operate its own toy factory in China, its political risk assessment must be broadened. It needs to scrutinize its vulnerability to changes in laws dealing with labor relations, environmental protection, currency controls, and profit repatriation. It also needs to weigh the likelihood of the Chinese government nationalizing foreigners' property or splitting into warring factions and triggering a civil war.

Some degree of political risk exists in every country, although the nature and importance of these risks vary. The French farmers' protests merely inconvenienced the managers of Disneyland Paris and McDonald's, whereas the ethnic cleansing conducted by Serbian nationalists in Kosovo destroyed the economic viability of firms operating there. In political risk assessment, as in most business decisions, it is a matter of balancing risks and rewards. If a firm is considering an investment in a politically risky environment, it should be sure that it can obtain rates of return that are high enough to offset the risks of entering that market. Firms already operating in a high-risk country may choose to take steps to reduce their vulnerability. A firm can reduce its financial exposure by reducing its net investment in the local subsidiary, perhaps by repatriating the subsidiary's profits to the parent company through dividend payments, by selling shares in the subsidiary to host country citizens, or by utilizing short-term leases to acquire new capital equipment rather than purchasing it outright. Alternatively, a firm might build domestic political support in the host country by being a good corporate citizen; for example, the firm might purchase inputs from local suppliers where possible, employ host country citizens in key management and administrative positions, and support local charities. Alcoa, for example, has spent more than $37 million in Juruti, Brazil, building a hospital and a community water system and improving the technical skills of local residents. Alcoa is investing $1 billion to develop a bauxite mine located near this remote jungle town on the Amazon River, so earning the goodwill of local residents is money well spent.[42] Similarly, Vale and Rio Tinto agreed to support educational, agricultural, and infrastructure projects to ensure that Guinea's newly-elected president, Alpha Condé, would honor the licenses granted by his predecessor allowing the two companies to mine the high-quality iron ore, worth an estimated $2.5 billion, found in Guinea's Simandou field.[43]

To reduce the risk of foreign operations, most developed countries have created government-owned or government-sponsored organizations to insure firms against political risks. For instance, the **Overseas Private Investment Corporation (OPIC)** insures U.S. overseas

MAP 3.3
Countries' Relative Political Riskiness, 2011

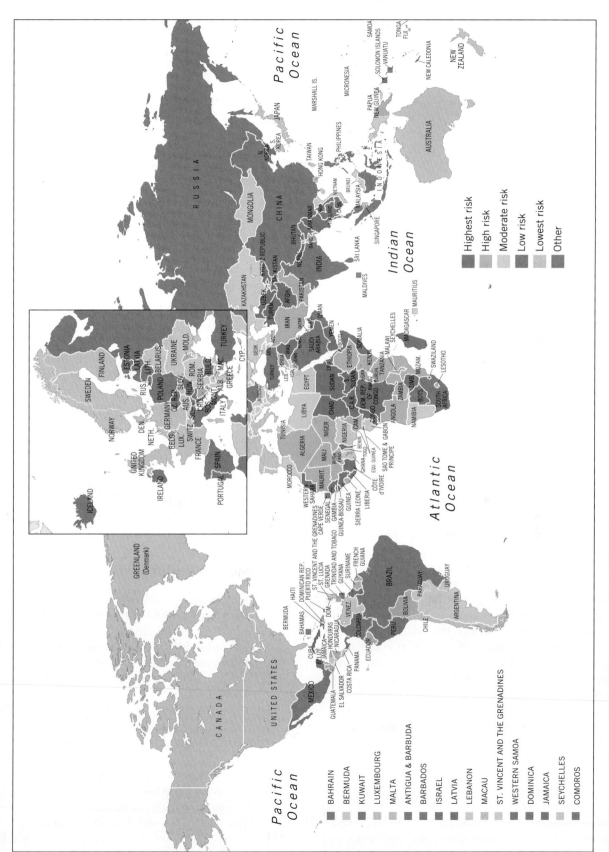

Source: Euromoney's Survey of Country Risk, Euromoney, March 2011 (online).

investments against nationalization, insurrections or revolutions, and foreign-exchange inconvertibility. In a typical transaction, OPIC sold ACD Research, a small Staten Island health care consulting firm, $46.7 million of political risk insurance, allowing it to provide advanced equipment and training to a major oncology center in Russia.[44] However, OPIC insurance is limited to firms operating in countries with which the United States has signed bilateral investment treaties. The **Multilateral Investment Guarantee Agency (MIGA),** a subsidiary of the World Bank, provides similar insurance against political risks. Private insurance firms, such as Lloyd's of London, also underwrite political risk insurance.[45]

MyManagementLab   Now that you have finished this chapter, go back to **www.pearsonglobaleditions.com/mymanagementlab** to continue practicing and applying the concepts you've learned.

CHAPTER REVIEW

Summary

The legal systems used by the world's countries vary dramatically. The former British colonies follow the common law tradition of the United Kingdom, while most other Western countries use the civil law system that originated with the Romans. A few countries, such as Iran and Saudi Arabia, use religious law, while centrally planned economies use bureaucratic law.

Laws adopted by national governments can influence the global marketplace in many ways. A country can impose restrictions on the ability of firms to conduct business internationally and can indirectly affect their competitiveness by raising their costs of doing business. A country's laws may also have extraterritorial reach, affecting transactions conducted beyond the country's borders.

MNCs operating in a host country can influence the country's economic, political, and cultural environments. Often these changes are positive. For example, FDI generates new employment opportunities and raises the productivity of local workers. MNCs can also impact the host country negatively by increasing competition for workers or by introducing products or practices incompatible with the local culture.

Resolution of international disputes is an important dimension of the legal environment. Because of the costliness of international litigation, firms often attempt to resolve disputes through dispute resolution techniques such as arbitration. When U.S. MNCs are dealing with sovereign countries, however, their ability to resolve conflicts is often hindered by the terms of the Foreign Sovereign Immunities Act.

The technological environment is an important facet of the national environment. A country's natural resources, as well as its investments in physical and human capital, affect the country's attractiveness as a location for international business activities. A country's willingness (or unwillingness) to enforce intellectual property rights of foreign firms often plays a major role in their location decisions.

The accounting tasks international businesses confront are more complex than those faced by purely domestic firms. An international firm must meet the accounting requirements of both its home country and all the countries in which it operates. Unfortunately, significant philosophical and operational differences exist in the accounting standards and procedures of the world's countries.

International businesses operating in foreign environments are subject to political risks. To protect themselves from changes in the political environment, firms should continually monitor the political situations in the countries in which they operate by consulting with local staff, embassy officials, and, where appropriate, firms specializing in political risk assessment.

Review Questions

1. Describe the four different types of legal systems with which international businesses must deal.
2. What is extraterritoriality?
3. How can an MNC affect its host country?
4. How do expropriation and confiscation differ?
5. Why do countries impose restrictions on foreign ownership of domestic firms?
6. How do restrictions on repatriation of profits affect MNCs?
7. What factors influence the accounting procedures a country adopts?
8. How do German firms use accounting reserves?
9. What is the impact of differing accounting standards on the international capital market?
10. What is political risk? What forms can it take?
11. What is OPIC's role in promoting international business activity?

Questions for Discussion

1. What options do firms have when caught in conflicts between home country and host country laws?
2. What is the impact of vigorous enforcement of intellectual property rights on the world economy? Who gains and who loses from strict enforcement of these laws?
3. Do you agree with the U.S. government's policies restricting the export of dual-use goods? Why or why not? (You may wish to check out the Bureau of Industry and Security's website, which details how the bureau operates.)
4. What is the impact on the global economy if governments fail to restore investors' faith in firms' accounting statements?
5. What impact would harmonization of national accounting standards have on international businesses?
6. Are U.S. firms at a competitive disadvantage because they cannot use accounting reserves as German firms do?
7. Map 3.3 presents the relative political riskiness of countries in 2011. For which countries has political riskiness changed significantly since then?

Building Global Skills

This exercise will help you better understand the influence of legal and political forces on a firm that is entering a foreign market. Your instructor will divide the class into groups of four or five members each and then assign a different type of firm to each group. Types of firms include food retailers, general merchandisers, auto parts makers, steel producers, paper recyclers, computer manufacturers, beer producers, cigarette makers, filmmakers, and petroleum refineries.

Assume your group is a top management team of a foreign firm. The firm has decided to expand into your country and has selected your local community as its first point of entry. Your task is to find out what legal and political barriers the firm may encounter and to develop a general strategy for dealing with them. Use whatever resources are available. For example, you could interview a member of the city council or a representative from the area's economic development committee. You could also identify potential competitors and discuss what strategies they might adopt to block your entry. As you identify potential barriers, try to determine if they are industry-specific or applicable only to foreign firms.

Finally, carefully assess each potential political or legal barrier and determine how difficult or easy it might be to address it.

1. How easy or difficult was it to identify political or legal forces affecting your firm's proposed entry?
2. What political or legal barriers might exist that you were unable to identify?
3. Are the potential barriers so great as to keep your firm out altogether? Why or why not?
4. Do different levels of government (city, state, and federal) pose different political and legal barriers to your firm? If so, describe these differences.

CLOSING CASE   RISKY BUSINESS IN VENEZUELA

Venezuela has been blessed with huge reserves of oil—nearly 300 billion barrels, about the same size as Saudi Arabia—and a favorable location, close to the huge North American market. However, heavy oil—oil that does not flow easily and is thus expensive to produce—dominates these reserves, particularly those found in the vast Orinoco basin (see Map 3.4). The technology to extract and refine Orinoco oil is well known, but it requires significant investment.

That need for investment has clashed with the political and economic policies of President Hugo Chávez, who was elected president of Venezuela in 1999 and reelected in 2000 and 2006. Chávez has promised to lead a Bolivarian Revolution—named after Simeon Bolivar, one of the South American patriots who liberated the continent from Spanish control in the early nineteenth century. The keystones of the Bolivarian Revolution are Chávez's pledges to promote the country's economic independence and to reduce income inequality. Not surprisingly, he has drawn strong support from voters from the country's poorer districts. As part of this agenda, he has required that state-owned Petróleos de Venezuela SA (PDVSA), the world's fifth largest exporter of oil, divert some of its cash flows to fund his social development goals. To date, PDVSA has contributed over $60 billion for this purpose.

Venezuela has benefited from the recent high price of oil, which was discussed in Chapter 2's closing case, "China's Quest for Natural Resources." An estimated 30 percent of its GDP, 55 percent of government revenues, and 95 percent of its exports are related to oil products. However, PDVSA's

Venezuelan President Hugo Chavez has nationalized many firms in pursuit of his Bolivarian Revolution, which focuses on social justice and reduction of income equality. Much of his electoral support is drawn from the country's working class, which has benefited from his programs. Middle class opponents fear his policies have eroded property rights and democratic principles.

production has been declining, in part because of underinvestment in infrastructure and in development of new fields. Oil industry analysts believe that the PDVSA's output has declined from 3.3 million barrels per day in 1998 to around 2.25 million currently. Its revenues have also been hurt by deals that Chávez has signed to promote his domestic and foreign policy agendas. He ordered PDVSA to sell 115,000 barrels of oil a day to Cuba at preferential prices, in return for the services of 20,000 Cuban medical professionals manning free clinics in poorer areas of Venezuela and the assistance of thousands of Cuban intelligence and security experts. The oil subsidies to Cuba cost PDVSA an estimated $3.5 to $5 billion a year. Similarly, he used petro-diplomacy to build ties with Argentina, Ecuador, and numerous Caribbean nations. To thumb his nose at the Bush administration—he rudely denounced the American president as the devil at a United Nations speech in 2006—Chávez ordered PDVSA to sell 250,000 barrels of heating oil to Massachusetts at prices 40 percent below their market value during the cold winter of 2005–2006. Chávez also signed an agreement to sell China a

million barrels of oil a day, but that is proving difficult to deliver on. It is rumored that China was offered significant discounts to world prices, although that has been officially denied by Rafael Ramirez, the Minister of Energy. Other industry observers argue that it makes little sense to ship Venezuelan oil to China given the distances involved. But the oil is a key part of Chávez's geopolitical vision; moreover, the country needs to pay back a $20 billion line of credit China extended in 2009.

President Chávez has aggressively used political power to punish those firms that stand in the way of his policy goals. He has imposed price controls on a variety of goods. He has frequently nationalized firms who frustrate his political initiatives. Among the industries he has targeted are oil, cement, steel, rice processing and packaging, and supermarkets. Glass container manufacturer Owens-Illinois, which has operated in the country for over 50 years, had its two Venezuelan factories nationalized in 2010 because it was "taking away the money of Venezuelans." The same year Chávez expropriated Sidetur, the country's largest privately owned steel manufacturer. He justified his actions by arguing that the company's prices were illegally high. Sidetur argued this was not the case, but noted price controls have frozen its prices since 2006 despite the country's high inflation rates.

Despite these price controls, Venezuela has been plagued by high inflation, estimated in 2010 to be 28 percent. This high level of inflation has forced Venezuela to devalue its currency, the bolivar, twice in 2010, from 2.15 bolivars per U.S. dollar to 4.3. This devaluation wreaked havoc with the profits of many foreign companies. Mead Johnson Nutrition Co.'s reported earnings were written down by $24 million, while Revlon lost $33 million in sales. The value of Telefonica's investments in Venezuela fell by $1 billion after the devaluation; its profits were estimated to have fallen by 10 percent. Because of the antibusiness tenor of many of the government's policies, capital flight is becoming a problem, as Venezuelan businesspersons seek to invest in greener pastures.

Case Questions

1. Characterize the types of investments that are most vulnerable to political risks. Characterize those that are least vulnerable. What factors influence an investment's vulnerability?
2. Suppose you are employed by a pension fund that has been asked to lend $100 million to PDVSA. PDVSA indicated it is willing to pay an interest rate 5 percent above the rate currently being paid by U.S. Treasury bills, so your boss is definitely interested in examining the proposal. Your boss assigns you the task of conducting a political risk assessment of the project. Begin by listing all the types of political risks that could possibly affect the ability of your pension fund to receive interest payments and the return of its principal in a timely fashion. Having developed this list, assess the likelihood that the risks will arise. Which ones are most critical to you? What can you do to reduce these risks to your pension fund?

MAP 3.4

Venezuela's Orinoco Basin

The Orinoco basin currently yields over 600,000 barrels a day of oil. The area's recoverable oil reserves rival that of Saudi Arabia. Orinoco's extra–heavy crude oil is relatively expensive to extract and refine, however.

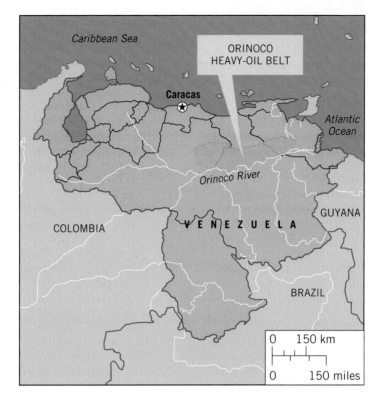

3. What can domestic and foreign investors do to reduce their political risks?
4. What can Venezuela do to restore confidence of potential investors?

Sources: "In Cuba, a Prayer for Chávez," *Wall Street Journal*, July 20, 2011, p. A15; "Chávez's mortality fuels succession speculation," *Financial Times*, July 9/10, 2011, p. 5; "Venezuela's oil pledge to China unlikely to be fulfilled," *Wall Street Journal*, March 22, 2011; "Venezuela roils multinationals," *Wall Street Journal*, March 7, 2011; "Oil leak," *The Economist*, February 26, 2011, p. 43; "Venezuela inflation highest among top emerging markets," *Wall Street Journal*, December 29, 2010; "Venezuela nationalizes private steel plant," *CNN.com*, November 1, 2010; "Venezuelan steel maker to challenge state takeover," *New York Times*, November 1, 2010; "Venezuela says it will take over Owens-Illinois," *Houston Chronicle*, October 27, 2010, p. D8; "Venezuela devaluation hits Telefonica funds," *Wall Street Journal*, January 11, 2010; "Venezuela basks in oil bonanza," news.bbc.co.uk, February 17, 2006; "Venezuela gives US cheap oil deal," news.bbc.co.uk, November 25, 2005.

Endnotes

1. "The fable maker who left books for brand management," *Financial Times*, July 9/10, 2011, p. 9; "The Harry Potter economy," *The Economist*, December 19, 2009, p. 121; "Chinese publishers issue 1.8 million copies of last Harry Potter book," www.startribune.com, November 14, 2007 (online); "Chinese market awash in fake Potter books," *New York Times*, August 1, 2007 (online); "Lots of Harry Potter books in China, not all of them by the author," *International Herald Tribune*, July 31, 2007 (online); "Harry Potter and the secret of success," www.guardian .co.uk, July 22, 2007 (online); "Chinese pirates hawk Harry Potter," www.msnbc.com, July 31, 2005; "Fans queue early for new Harry Potter book," www.chinadaily .com, July 18, 2005; "English *Harry Potter* bewitches Chinese readers," *China Daily*, July 12, 2005; "Wild about Harry: Publisher sets big release of Potter book," *Wall Street Journal*, February 11, 2003; "Rowling says she's polishing fifth 'Potter'," *Wall Street Journal*, September 20, 2002, p. B1; "Harry Potter rides again in bootleg Chinese book," *Bryan-College Station Eagle*, July 6, 2002, p. B1; "Harry Potter film charms Chinese," *Financial Times*, February 9–10, 2002, p. 3; "Harry Potter, meet Ha-li Bo-te," *Wall Street Journal*, September 21, 2000, p. B1.

2. "Brink's retreat in Belgium backfires," *Wall Street Journal*, December 21, 2010, p. B8.

3. "The Hindu rate of self-depreciation," *The Economist*, April 23, 2011, p. 47.

4. "U.K. lawmakers call for end to libel tourism," *Wall Street Journal*, February 24, 2010.

5. "Islamic banking grows, with all sorts of rules," *Wall Street Journal*, May 3, 2005, p. C1; "Court ruling on

Islamic banking poses a challenge for Pakistan inter-ests," *Financial Times*, January 4, 2000, p. 2; "Court orders Islamabad to ban interest," *Financial Times*, December 24–25, 1999, p. 4; "Pakistani court rules that interest is illegal," *Houston Chronicle*, December 24, 1999, p. 2C.

6. "Mining executives woo rebels with billion-dollar min-eral deals," *Houston Chronicle*, April 17, 1997, p. A20; "As Zaire's war wages, foreign businesses scramble for inroads," *Wall Street Journal*, April 14, 1997, p. A1.

7. Office of the U.S. Trade Representative, *National Trade Estimate Report on Foreign Trade Barriers 2002*, p. 70.

8. "U.S. appetite for Mexican food grows, cooking up hotter sales for exporters," *Wall Street Journal*, February 5, 1992, p. A6.

9. "Iranians scheme to elude sanctions," *Wall Street Journal*, February 13, 2008, p. A1.

10. "U.S. plans to indict McDonnell Douglas for alleged violation of export laws," *Wall Street Journal*, October 11, 1999, p. A4.

11. "Boeing, U.S. end charges over sale of sensitive chips," *Wall Street Journal*, April 10, 2006, p. A16.

12. "Pilkington bows to U.S. pressure on process licensing," *Financial Times*, May 27, 1994, p. 1; "Washington's new anti-trust vigor," *Financial Times*, May 27, 1994, p. 6.

13. "Baxter agreed to cut-rate shipments of supplies to Syria, U.S. probe finds," *Wall Street Journal*, December 22, 1992, p. A3; "How Baxter got off the Arab blacklist and how it got nailed," *Wall Street Journal*, March 23, 1993, p. A1.

14. "Keeping the lid on Helms-Burton," *Financial Times*, July 31, 1997, p. 4; "Stet avoids Helms-Burton sanctions," *Financial Times*, July 24, 1997, p. 1; "Property issue harks back to old Cuba," *Houston Chronicle*, October 3, 1996, p. 1C.

15. "Chavez eyes 'strategic sectors' for state control," *Financial Times*, April 11, 2008, p. 5; "Chavez to nation-alize ternium unit," *Wall Street Journal*, April 10, 2008, p. A9.

16. "Zimbabwe shuts out foreign miners," *Wall Street Journal*, March 29, 2011, p. A15.

17. "The bold struggle for China's belly," *New York Times* online, March 6, 2003.

18. Richard Schaffer, Beverley Earle, and Filiberto Agusti, *International Business Law and Its Environment* (St. Paul, MN: West, 1990), p. 196.

19. Ibid., pp. 196–197.

20. "Commercial law plan in francophone Africa," *Financial Times*, May 13, 1999, p. 9.

21. Schaffer, Earle, and Agusti, pp. 429–430.

22. "Ballmer bares China travails," *Wall Street Journal*, May 27, 2011, p. B1.

23. Business Software Alliance, *Fourth Annual BSA and IDC Global Software Piracy Study*; "Movie, music giants try new weapon against pirates: Price," *Wall Street Journal*, March 7, 2005, p. B1; "Video pirates rush out 'Phantom Menace,'" *Wall Street Journal*, May 28, 1999, p. B1.

24. The case was settled with the two firms agreeing to cross-license each other's technology. See Sri Krishna Sankaran, "Patent flooding in the United States and Japan," *IDEA: The Journal of Law and Technology*, 2000, vol. 40, pp. 393ff.; "Patent suit shows small U.S. firms' fears," *Wall Street Journal*, June 5, 1996, p. A10.

25. "Trademark piracy at home and abroad," *Wall Street Journal*, May 7, 1991, p. A20.

26. "From Russia, with lattes: And Russian rivals wait," *Wall Street Journal*, August 31, 2007, p. B1.

27. "Fujitsu backed in patent dispute," *Financial Times*, September 11, 1997, p. 8.

28. Much of the discussion in this section is taken from Frederick D.S. Choi and Gary K. Meek, *International Accounting*, 6th ed. (Upper Saddle River, NJ: Prentice Hall, 2008), Frederick D. S. Choi and Gary K. Meek, *International Accounting*, 5th ed. (Upper Saddle River, NJ: Prentice Hall, 2005), Frederick D. S. Choi, Carol Ann Frost, and Gary K. Meek, *International Accounting*, 4th ed. (Upper Saddle River, NJ: Prentice Hall, 2002), and from reports of the Working Group on Accounting Standards, Organisation for Economic Cooperation and Development, published in 1987: "Accounting Standards Harmonization, No. 2: Consolidation Policies in OECD Nations" and "Accounting Standards Harmonization, No. 3: The Relationship between Taxation and Financial Reporting," Frederick D. S. Choi (ed.), *International Accounting and Finance Handbook* (New York: John Wiley & Sons, 1997).

29. Stephen B. Salter and Timothy D. Doupnik, "The Relationship between Legal Systems and Accounting Practices," in Kenneth S. Most (ed.), *Advances in International Accounting*, vol. 5 (Greenwich, CT: JAI Press, 1992).

30. Hanns-Martin W. Schoenfeld, "International Accounting: Development, Issues, and Future Directions," *Journal of International Business Studies* (Fall 1981), pp. 83–100.

31. "Chinese practitioners ready for their Great Leap Forward," *Financial Times*, August 13, 1993, p. 20.

32. Timothy S. Doupnik, "Recent Innovations in German Accounting Practice," in Kenneth S. Most (ed.), *Advances in International Accounting*, vol. 5 (Greenwich, CT: JAI Press, 1992).

33. Robert Bloom, Jayne Fuglister, and Jeffrey Kantor, "Toward Internationalization of Upper-Level Financial Accounting Courses," in Kenneth S. Most (ed.), *Advances in International Accounting*, vol. 5 (Greenwich, CT: JAI Press, 1992), pp. 239–253; Frederick D. S. Choi and Richard Levich, *The Capital Market Effects of International Accounting Diversity* (Homewood, IL: Dow Jones-Irwin, 1990), pp. 115–117.

34. "Deutsche Bank says Net jumped 24% in 1995, discloses big hidden reserves," *Wall Street Journal*, March 29, 1996, p. A8.

35. "Big board chief renews his pitch on foreign stocks," *Wall Street Journal*, January 7, 1992, p. A2.

36. "New York loses edge in snagging foreign listings," *Wall Street Journal*, January 26, 2006, p. C1.

37. "A price worth paying?" *The Economist*, May 21, 2005, p. 71; S. J. Gray, J. C. Shaw, and L. B. McSweeney, "Accounting Standards and Multinational Corporations," *Journal of International Business Studies* (Spring/Summer 1981), pp. 121–136.

38. "Daimler-Benz gears up for a drive on the freeway," *Financial Times*, April 30, 1993.

39. "A transatlantic divide over the treatment of financial in-struments," *The Economist*, June 12, 2010.

40. "Venezuela warns international oil companies of more tax increases," *Financial Times*, April 11, 2006, p. 8.

41. "In Nigeria's violent delta, hostage negotiators thrive," *Wall Street Journal*, June 7, 2007, p. A1; "As oil supplies are stretched, rebels, terrorists get new clout," *Wall Street Journal*, April 10, 2006, p. A1; "Nigerian militants threaten more attacks," *Houston Chronicle*, March 6, 2006, p. A8; "Violence in Nigeria's oil delta worsens," *Wall Street Journal*, April 1, 2003, p. A13; "Chevron is latest to shut Nigerian operations," *Wall Street Journal*, March 24, 2003, p. A15; "ChevronTexaco evacuates from violence-torn Nigeria," *Houston Chronicle*, March 24, 2003, p. 17A.

42. "Alcoa invests near planned mines," *Wall Street Journal*, March 24, 2008, p. B4.

43. "Vale woos Guinea with social projects," Financial Times, July 7, 2011, p. 14.

44. Overseas Private Investment Corporation, *2005 Annual Report*, p. 19.

45. Schaffer, Earle, and Agusti, pp. 410–421.

The Role of Culture

AFTER STUDYING THIS CHAPTER, YOU SHOULD BE ABLE TO:

1. Discuss the primary characteristics of culture.

2. Describe the various elements of culture and provide examples of how they influence international business.

3. Identify the means by which members of a culture communicate with each other.

4. Discuss how religious and other values affect the domestic environments in which international businesses operate.

5. Describe the major cultural clusters and their usefulness for international managers.

6. Explain Hofstede's primary findings about differences in cultural values.

7. Explain how cultural conflicts may arise in international business.

Access a host of interactive learning aids at **www.pearsonglobaleditions.com/ mymanagementlab** to help strengthen your understanding of the chapter concepts.

MyManagementLab

© AF archive/Alamy

BOLLYWOOD ABROAD

"Bollywood" is a general term that is used to describe the Hindi language film industry, based in Mumbai. Bollywood is undoubtedly the biggest film producer in the world, with at least 900 titles being created, and arguably the most popular entertainment than any other type across the globe. The appeal of Bollywood movies, either dubbed or subtitled, has become a global phenomenon.

Dubai is fast becoming a major international hub for Bollywood films outside India. It features premiers and film production. A number of Bollywood films are premiered in Dubai each year. This has meant that Bollywood stars, such as Salman Khan, Shahrukh Khan, and Amitabh Bachan have become household names in the Arabic-speaking world.

Bollywood film distributors have discovered that there is an enormous appetite for the films from a broad range of different cultural groups and nationalities in Dubai. In 2008, Yash Raj Films, one of India's leading film studios signed a joint venture with Dubai Infinity Holdings, worth several million dollars, to build a theme park and other attractions in Dubai. The development will include hotels, entertainment and leisure complexes, theme park attractions, and a major cinema.

Shahrukh Khan is known by many as the King of Bollywood and his potential audience is 3.5 billion, mainly people of South Asian descent living across the globe. A prime example of the growing strength of Bollywood is the fact that, on average, the Bollywood film industry sells 3.6 billion tickets annually, against which Hollywood can muster just 2.6 billion. Bollywood film stars are obviously massive in South Asian countries, but the appeal is widening, particularly in Germany, Israel and across the Gulf nations, where almost every new Hindi release is dubbed into Arabic. In Germany there are three magazines that are solely devoted to the Bollywood film industry: Bollywood Rapid Eye, Indien and Ishq.

Many believe that the appeal is based on the fact that Bollywood films are fairytales for adults, fantasies or dreams, which release many viewers from the drudgeries of their everyday lives. Many also believe that a Bollywood movie produced in the mid-1990s was the catalyst that has brought Bollywood to the world, Dilwale Dulhania Le Jayenge (a loose translation being "The Brave-hearted One Will Take the Bride"). It was a romance that was set in both India and Britain. It was the debut movie of Aditya Chopra, then just 23 years old, and it also starred Shahrukh Khan. The movie is still breaking box office records and in 2008 enjoyed its six hundredth week in a Mumbai cinema.

Unlike Hollywood, Bollywood did not begin with a view to conquer the global film world. Hollywood spends enormous sums marketing their product to world markets. Bollywood relies on little more than word of mouth and lacks the publicity spending, yet Bollywood is the only film industry in the world to offer Hollywood any kind of competition. In many countries, Hollywood's market share is between 60 and 90 percent, but in India it is barely 5 percent. In many non-European countries it is Bollywood, not Hollywood, that attracts the mass audiences. It extends to television networks, across Africa and Asia, including Indonesia, Egypt, Algeria, Thailand, Malaysia, Singapore and Morocco. Many of the TV networks screen as many as six or more Bollywood films daily.

Just as product placement plays a vital role in the funding of Hollywood films, so too has product placement slowly become an integral part of Bollywood film making. The De Beers Diamond Trading Company has not only used Bollywood legend, Amitabh Bachchan, to promote its solitaire collection, but it has also forged links with Bollywood productions. Other manufacturers of consumer durables and fast-moving consumer goods, including Samsung, Whirlpool, LG Electronics and Aviva life insurance, have all used Bollywood actors and actresses to spearhead their marketing campaigns. The tie-ups between movies and brands in Bollywood are growing by an estimated 70 percent per year. In India it has been shown that cinema advertising is up to six times more effective than television advertising.

Bollywood's appeal has had an influence on Hollywood. Many point to examples of Hollywood and other western film makers borrowing the cultural approach, such as Moulin Rouge, which starred Nicole Kidman and showed dancing in front of an illuminated Taj Mahal. The composer and theatrical producer, Andrew Lloyd Webber, launched Bombay Dreams, a Bollywood-themed musical which opened in London in 2002. It ran for nearly a year on Broadway.

In 2008 the British county of Yorkshire hosted the International Indian Film Academy Awards. The event was screened in 110 countries. Yorkshire and, in particular, Bradford has a long association with the South Asian community. ■

Firms and businesspeople venturing beyond their familiar domestic markets soon recognize that foreign business customs, values, and definitions of ethical behavior differ vastly from their own. Firms that rely on their familiar home culture to compete in a new market can jeopardize their international success. Indeed, virtually all facets of an international firm's business—including contract negotiations, production operations, marketing decisions, and human resource management policies—may be affected by cultural variations. Culture can even confer a competitive advantage—or disadvantage—on firms, as "e-World" suggests. This chapter highlights some of the cultural differences among countries and explains how understanding those differences is invaluable for international businesspeople.

Characteristics of Culture

Business, like all other human activities, is conducted within the context of society. **Culture** is the collection of values, beliefs, behaviors, customs, and attitudes that distinguish one society from another. A society's culture determines the rules that govern how firms operate in the society. Several characteristics of culture are worth noting for their relevance to international business:

- Culture reflects *learned behavior* that is transmitted from one member of a society to another. Some elements of culture are transmitted intergenerationally, as when parents teach their children table manners. Other elements are transmitted intragenerationally, as when seniors educate incoming freshmen about a school's traditions.
- The elements of culture are *interrelated.* For example, Japan's group-oriented, hierarchical society stresses harmony and loyalty, which historically translated into lifetime employment and minimal job switching.
- Because culture is learned behavior, it is *adaptive*; that is, the culture changes in response to external forces that affect the society. For example, after World War II, Germany was divided into free-market-oriented West Germany and communist-controlled East Germany. Despite their having a common heritage developed over centuries, this division created large cultural differences between *Ossis* (East Germans) and *Wessis* (West Germans). The differences resulted from adaptations of the East German culture to the dictates of communist ideology regarding attitudes toward work, risk taking, and fairness of reward systems.
- Culture is *shared* by members of the society and indeed defines the membership of the society. Individuals who share a culture are members of a society; those who do not are outside the boundaries of the society.

E-WORLD **THE INTERNET, NATIONAL COMPETITIVENESS, AND CULTURE**

What does it take to succeed in the Internet age? According to some experts, a country needs "superliquid and vast capital markets, venture-capital networks, world-class universities, risk-taking culture, restructuring ethos, and high-tech talent pools." The Internet, however, threatens to upset numerous culture norms. As you read this chapter, think about the requirements for success in the Internet age and the various elements of culture that are discussed. For example, you might consider the following questions:

- In some business cultures, pay is linked to seniority. Many small high-tech businesses, however, rely heavily on stock options to compensate their employees, and younger workers often have greater technical skills than older workers. How can such cultures reconcile these conflicting norms?

- Can group-oriented cultures that promote a slow, consensus-building style of decision making act quickly enough to compete in the fast-moving e-commerce environment?
- Some cultures dislike uncertainty and risk taking. How can they thrive in the Internet age, which to date has been characterized by high levels of uncertainty and risk?
- Some business cultures stress conducting business with those persons with whom you or your company have developed a long-term, trusting relationship. Is such an approach outmoded in the Internet age?

Source: "Edging Towards the Information Age," *Business Week*, January 31, 2000, p. 90.

Elements of Culture

A society's culture determines how its members communicate and interact with each other. The basic elements of culture (see Figure 4.1) are social structure, language, communication, religion, and values and attitudes. The interaction of these elements affects the local environment in which international businesses operate. They also affect the ability of countries to respond to changing circumstances.

Social Structure

Basic to every society is its social structure, the overall framework that determines the roles of individuals within the society, the stratification of the society, and individuals' mobility within the society.

INDIVIDUALS, FAMILIES, AND GROUPS All human societies involve individuals living in family units and working with each other in groups. Societies differ, however, in the way they define family and in the relative importance they place on the individual's role within groups. The U.S. view of family ties and responsibilities focuses on the nuclear family (father, mother, and offspring). In other cultures, the extended family is far more important. Arabs, for example,

FIGURE 4.1
Elements of Culture

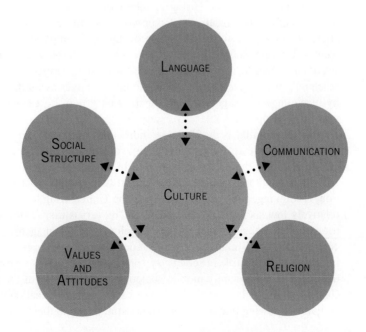

consider uncles, brothers, cousins, and in-laws as parts of their family unit to whom they owe obligations of support and assistance. Other societies utilize an even broader definition of family. For instance, Somalia's society is organized in clans, each of which comprises individuals of the same tribe who share a common ancestor.

These differing social attitudes are reflected in the importance of the family to business. In the United States, firms discourage nepotism, and the competence of a man who married the boss's daughter is routinely questioned by coworkers. In Arab-owned firms, however, family ties are crucial, and hiring relatives is a common, accepted practice. Similarly, in Chinese-owned firms, family members fill critical management positions and supply capital from personal savings to ensure the firms' growth.[1]

Cultures also differ in the importance of the individual relative to the group. U.S. culture, for example, promotes individualism. Schools try to raise the self-esteem of each child and encourage each one to develop individual talents. Because respect for individual authority and responsibility is so strong in the United States, children are trained to believe that their destinies lie in their own hands. Conversely, in group-focused societies such as Japan, children are taught that their role is to serve the group. Virtues such as unity, loyalty, and harmony are highly valued in such societies. These characteristics often are more important in hiring decisions than are personal accomplishments or abilities.[2] Accordingly, when the producers of the hit TV show *The Apprentice* tried to sell a Japanese version of the show to the major local TV networks, they ran into cultural barriers. Not only was there resistance to the public humiliation borne by those that would hear the dreaded words, "You're fired," but no high-profile CEO was willing to assume the Donald Trump role. Noted one expert, "Most Japanese companies are presented as the cumulative effort of many individuals rather than the creation of a single person."[3]

SOCIAL STRATIFICATION Societies differ in their degree of **social stratification.** All societies categorize people to some extent on the basis of their birth, occupation, educational achievements, or other attributes. However, the importance of these categories in defining how individuals interact with each other within and between these groups varies by society. In medieval Europe, for example, the roles and obligations of peasants, craftsmen, tradesmen, and nobles were carefully delineated by custom and law. The British class structure and the Indian caste system provide more recent examples of the same phenomenon, in which one's social position may affect many facets of one's dealings with other people. In other societies, social stratification is less important. For instance, a U.S. bank president may haughtily bark orders at the janitorial staff when on the job yet willingly take orders from those same individuals when cleaning up after a church fund-raiser.

Multinational corporations (MNCs) operating in highly stratified societies often must adjust their hiring and promotion procedures to take into account class or clan differences among supervisors and workers. Hiring members of one group to do jobs traditionally performed by members of another group may lower workplace morale and productivity. In less stratified societies, firms are freer to seek out the most qualified employee, regardless of whether that person went to the right school, goes to the proper church, or belongs to all the best clubs. In highly stratified societies, advertisers must tailor their messages more carefully to ensure that they reach only the targeted audience and do not spill over to another audience that may be offended by receiving a message intended for the first group. In less stratified societies, such concerns may be less important.

Social mobility is the ability of individuals to move from one stratum of society to another. Social mobility tends to be higher in less stratified societies. It is higher in the United States, for example, than in the United Kingdom or India. Social mobility (or the lack thereof) often affects individuals' attitudes and behaviors toward such factors as labor relations, human capital formation, risk taking, and entrepreneurship. The United Kingdom's formerly rigid class system and relatively low social mobility created an "us versus them" attitude among many British industrial workers, causing them to eye suspiciously any management efforts to promote workplace cooperation. Until relatively recently, some British working-class youth dropped out of school, believing that their role in society was preordained and thus investment in education was a waste of time. In more socially mobile societies, such as those of the United States, Singapore, and Canada, individuals are more willing to seek higher education or to engage in entrepreneurial activities, knowing that if they are successful, they and their families are free to rise in society.

BRINGING THE WORLD INTO FOCUS · THE IMPACT OF JAPANESE CULTURE ON BUSINESS

The first cultural element that plays a major role in Japanese business practices is the hierarchical structure of Japanese society. The social hierarchy strictly defines how people deal with each other.

A second cultural element is groupism. The person is identified as a member of a group rather than as an individual. This group identity is engrained in Japanese children. Strong group identity is reinforced by Japan's ethnic homogeneity and its relative isolation from the rest of the world until the 1850s.

The third element of the Japanese culture is wa, or social harmony. The goal of each group member is to promote harmony, or consensus, within the group. Decisions are not made within Japanese organizations by upper-management because that would upset the wa. The need to preserve wa is one reason many Japanese firms encourage after-work socializing and partying by Japanese salarymen.

A fourth cultural element is obligation, or duty. The individual, once hired, becomes indebted to the firm. The debt owed to the firm for agreeing to employ the person is so great that the person can never repay it. The person owes everything to the firm, and the firm's needs come first, even before personal and familial needs. The strong cultural disapproval of an employee moving to another firm stems from this facet of Japanese culture.

Sources: "Fujitsu to Institute Merit-Based Pay for All Employees." *Wall Street Journal,* March 26, 1998. P. B5; Richard G. Newman and K. Anthony Rhee, "Self-Styled Barriers Inhibit Transferring Management Methods," *Business Horizons,* May-June 1989, pp. 17–21.

The Image Works.

Japanese culture stresses the importance of working together within groups and maintaining social harmony, or *wa*. An important task of this Japanese preschool is to teach its students the norms of the country's group-oriented, harmonious culture, so that they can grow up to be productive members of Japanese society

Language

Language is a primary delineator of cultural groups because it is an important means by which a society's members communicate with each other. Experts have identified some 3,000 different languages and as many as 10,000 distinct dialects worldwide (see Map 4.1).[4]

Language organizes the way members of a society think about the world. It filters observations and perceptions and thus affects unpredictably the messages that are sent when two individuals try to communicate. In one famous experiment in Hong Kong, 153 undergraduate students, bilingual in English and Chinese, were divided into two groups. One group was given a class assignment written in English; the other was given the same assignment written in Chinese. The professor in charge of the experiment took every precaution to ensure that the translations were perfect, yet the answers given by the two groups differed significantly, indicating that the language itself altered the nature of the information being conveyed.[5]

In addition to shaping one's perceptions of the world, language provides important clues about the cultural values of the society and aids acculturation. For example, many languages, including French, German, and Spanish, have informal and formal versions of the word *you*, the use of which depends on the relationship between the speaker and the person addressed.[6] Existence of these language forms provides a strong hint that one should take care in maintaining an appropriate level of formality when dealing with business people from countries in which those languages predominate.

The presence of more than one language group is an important signal about the diversity of a country's population and suggests that there may also be differences in income, cultural values, and educational achievement. For instance, India recognizes 16 official languages, and approximately 3,000 dialects are spoken within its boundaries, a reflection of the heterogeneity of its society. In several mountainous countries of South America, including Bolivia, Paraguay, and Peru, many poor rural residents speak local Indian dialects and have trouble communicating with the Spanish-speaking urban elites. Generally, countries dominated by one language group tend to have a homogeneous society, in which nationhood defines the society. Countries with multiple language groups tend to be heterogeneous, with language providing an important means of identifying cultural differences within the country.

Savvy businesspeople operating in heterogeneous societies adapt their marketing and business practices along linguistic lines to account for cultural differences among their prospective customers. For example, market researchers discovered that English Canadians favor soaps that promise cleanliness, while French Canadians prefer pleasant- or sweet-smelling soaps. Thus, Procter & Gamble's English-language Canadian ads for Irish Spring soap stress the soap's deodorant value, while its French-language ads focus on the soap's pleasant aroma.[7] Generally, advertisers should seek out the media—newspapers, radio, cable television, and magazines—that allow them to customize their marketing messages to individual linguistic groups. For instance, in the United States the development of Spanish-language television networks such as Univision and Telemundo has allowed advertisers to more easily customize their advertisements to reach the Hispanic market, without confusing their marketing messages to the larger, English-speaking audience.

LANGUAGE AS A COMPETITIVE WEAPON Linguistic ties often create important competitive advantages because the ability to communicate is so important in conducting business transactions. Commerce among Australia, Canada, New Zealand, the United Kingdom, and the United States is facilitated by their common use of English. For example, when Giro Sport Design, a Soquel, California, manufacturer of bicycle helmets, decided to manufacture its products in Europe rather than export from the United States, the firm told its location consultants to find a plant site in an English-speaking country. Its president noted, "With all the problems you have in running a business abroad, we didn't want to be bothered by language."[8] The firm located its European production facilities in Ireland, where it enjoyed a plentiful supply of well-trained English-speaking labor, economic development incentives, and tax benefits.

Similarly, Spain's Telefónica SA moved aggressively into Latin America as part of its internationalization strategy. Benefiting from the region's privatization programs, it has bought controlling interests in the formerly state-owned telephone monopolies of Colombia and Peru. Spanish banks such as Banco Santander, Banco Bilbao Vizcaya, and Banco Central Hispano adopted a comparable approach, investing heavily in Argentina, Chile, Mexico,

MAP 4.1
World Languages

MAJOR LANGUAGES

Arabic
Chinese dialects
English
French
German
Hindi
Portuguese
Russian and other Slavic
Scandinavian
Spanish
Turkic
Other

ANDORRA
LIECHTENSTEIN
LUXEMBOURG
MONACO

BAHAMAS
BARBADOS
BRUNEI
JAMAICA
MARTINIQUE
MAURITIUS
TRINIDAD & TOBAGO
VIRGIN ISLANDS

CANADA
UNITED STATES
GREENLAND (Denmark)
MEXICO
GUATEMALA
EL SALVADOR
COSTA RICA
BELIZE
HONDURAS
NICARAGUA
PANAMA
CUBA
BAHAMAS
HAITI
ECUADOR
COLOMBIA
VENEZ.
GUYANA
SURINAME
FRENCH GUIANA
PERU
BRAZIL
BOLIVIA
PARAGUAY
CHILE
ARGENTINA
URUGUAY

IRELAND
UNITED KINGDOM
NETH.
BELG.
LUX.
FRANCE
SPAIN
PORTUGAL
NORWAY
SWEDEN
FINLAND
DEN.
GERMANY
SWITZ.
ITALY
POLAND
CZ. REP.
AUS.
SLOV.
HUN.
CRO.
BOS.
SERB.
MONT.
ALB.
SI.
ESTONIA
LATVIA
LITH.
RUS.
BELARUS
UKRAINE
MOLDOVA
ROM.
BULG.
GREECE
TURKEY
MALTA
CYP.

RUSSIA
MONGOLIA
CHINA
N. KOREA
S. KOREA
JAPAN
TAIWAN
MYANMAR
BHUTAN
NEPAL
INDIA
BANG.
LAOS
THAILAND
VIETNAM
CAMB.
MALAYSIA
BRUNEI
SINGAPORE
PHILIPPINES
INDONESIA
PAPUA NEW GUINEA
AUSTRALIA
NEW ZEALAND
SRI LANKA

KAZAKHSTAN
UZBEK.
TURKM.
TAJIKISTAN
KYRGYZSTAN
AFGH.
PAKISTAN
IRAN
GEOR.
ARM.
AZERB.
TURKEY
SYRIA
IRAQ
ISR.
LEB.
JORDAN
KUWAIT
QATAR
U.A.E.
SAUDI ARABIA
OMAN
YEMEN

MOROCCO
WESTERN SAHARA
ALGERIA
TUNISIA
LIBYA
EGYPT
MAURIT.
MALI
NIGER
CHAD
SUDAN
ERIT.
DJIBOUTI
ETHIOPIA
SOMALIA
SENEGAL
GAMBIA
GUINEA-BISSAU
GUINEA
SIERRA LEONE
LIBERIA
CÔTE d'IVOIRE
BURKINA FASO
GHANA
TOGO
BENIN
NIGERIA
CAM.
EQU. GUINEA
GABON
CONGO
D.R. OF THE CONGO
C.A.R.
UGANDA
RWANDA
BUR.
KENYA
TANZANIA
ANGOLA
ZAMBIA
MALAWI
MOZAM.
ZIMB.
NAMIBIA
BOTS.
SOUTH AFRICA
SWAZILAND
LESOTHO
MADAGASCAR
MAURITIUS

MAP 4.2
Africa's Colonial Heritage

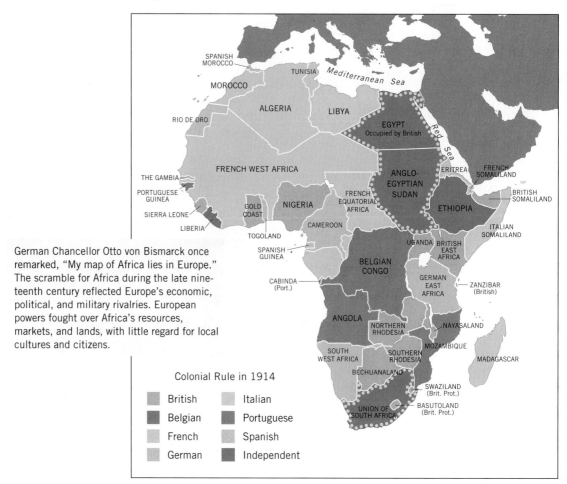

German Chancellor Otto von Bismarck once remarked, "My map of Africa lies in Europe." The scramble for Africa during the late nineteenth century reflected Europe's economic, political, and military rivalries. European powers fought over Africa's resources, markets, and lands, with little regard for local cultures and citizens.

Colonial Rule in 1914

British
Belgian
French
German
Italian
Portuguese
Spanish
Independent

Peru, Puerto Rico, and Uruguay.[9] Turkey is fast becoming the jumping-off point for doing business in the Turkic areas of the former Soviet Union, such as Azerbaijan, Kazakhstan, and Turkmenistan. The linguistic legacy of colonialism also affects international business, as Map 4.2 indicates.

LINGUA FRANCA To conduct business, international businesspeople must be able to communicate. As a result of British economic and military dominance in the nineteenth century and U.S. dominance since World War II, English has emerged as the predominant common language, or **lingua franca,** of international business. Most European and Japanese public school students study English for many years. Some countries that have multiple linguistic groups, such as India and Singapore, have adopted English as an official language to facilitate communication among the diverse groups. Similarly, firms with managers from many different countries may use English as the official corporate language. For example, Philips, the Dutch-based electronics MNC, has used English for intracorporate communications since 1983. Switzerland's Brown Boveri and Sweden's Asea adopted English as their corporate language after their merger in 1987, as did Luxembourg's ArcelorMittal, even though less than 10 percent of its employers are native English-speakers.[10] Even some French companies, like Total, Air Liquide, and France Telecom, use English when their boards of directors meet.[11]

The use of English as a lingua franca does not eliminate all cross-cultural misunderstandings, however. In some cultures—British, Danish, and American, for example—self-deprecating humor is often used to show the speaker is neither pompous nor arrogant, while in others, such as France or Germany, it may convey a lack of seriousness. And cultural differences can affect the interpretation of the meaning of common words. An American executive might say that she'd "like" something done by next Thursday. An American colleague would interpret this to mean that Thursday is the deadline, whereas a colleague in Thailand might view it as a preference rather than a demand.[12]

The dominance of English seemingly gives an advantage in international commerce to people whose native language is English, particularly when transactions are done in Canada, the United Kingdom, or the United States. However, failure by native English speakers to learn a second language puts them and their firms at a decided disadvantage when negotiating or operating on foreign turf. For example, a few years ago Lionel Train Company moved its manufacturing facilities to Mexico to take advantage of lower labor costs, but it could not find enough bilingual managers to run the plant. As a result, the firm eventually shut down the plant and moved its operations back to the United States.[13]

Because language serves as a window on the culture of a society, many international business experts argue that students should be exposed to foreign languages, even if they are unable to master them. Although mastery is best, even modest levels of language training provide students with clues about cultural norms and attitudes that prove helpful in international business.

TRANSLATION Of course, some linguistic differences may be overcome through translation. The process, however, requires more than merely substituting words of one language for those of another. Translators must be sensitive to subtleties in the connotations of words and focus on translating ideas, not the words themselves. Far too often, translation problems create marketing disasters. A classic case is KFC's initial translation of "Finger Lickin' Good" into Chinese, which came out as the far less appetizing "Eat Your Fingers Off." Similarly, the original translation of Pillsbury's Jolly Green Giant for the Saudi Arabian market was "intimidating green ogre"—a very different image from what the firm intended (although it still might encourage children to eat their peas).

Firms can reduce the chances that they are sending the wrong message to their customers by using a technique known as backtranslation. With **backtranslation,** one person translates a document, then a second person translates the translated version back into the original language. This technique provides a check that the intended message is actually being sent, thus avoiding communication mistakes.

When communications to nonnative speakers must be made in the home country's language, speakers and writers should use common words, use the most common meanings of those words, and try to avoid idiomatic phrases. Caterpillar is faced with the problem of communicating with the diverse international users of its products. It developed its own language instruction program called Caterpillar Fundamental English (CFE), which it uses in its overseas repair and service manuals. CFE is a simplified, condensed version of English that can be taught to non-English-speaking people in 30 lessons. It consists of 800 words that are necessary to repair Cat's equipment: 450 nouns, 70 verbs, 100 prepositions, and 180 other words.[14] A similar approach developed by the European Association of Aerospace Industries, "Simplified English," is required to be used in aircraft maintenance manuals written for its members. It has subsequently been adopted as an international standard in the industry.[15]

SAYING NO Another cultural difficulty international businesspeople face is that words may have different meanings to persons with diverse cultural backgrounds. North Americans typically translate the Spanish word *mañana* literally to mean "tomorrow," but in parts of Latin America, the word is used to mean "some other day—not today."

Even the use of yes and no differs across cultures. In contract negotiations, Japanese businesspeople often use yes to mean "Yes, I understand what is being said." Foreign negotiators often assume that their Japanese counterparts are using yes to mean "Yes, I agree with you" and are disappointed when the Japanese later fail to accept contract terms that the foreigners had assumed were agreed to. Misunderstandings can be compounded because directly uttering "no" is considered very impolite or inhospitable in Japan, as well as in China, India, and the Middle East. In such cultures, negotiators who find a proposal unacceptable will, in order to be polite, suggest that it "presents many difficulties" or requires "further study."[16] Foreigners waiting for a definitive "no" may have to wait a long time. Such behavior may be considered evasive in U.S. business culture, but it is the essence of politeness in these business cultures.

Communication

Communicating across cultural boundaries, whether verbally or nonverbally, is a particularly important skill for international managers. Although communication can often go awry between people who share a culture, the chances of miscommunication increase substantially when the people are from different cultures. In such cases, the senders encode messages using their cultural filters and the receivers decode the same messages using their filters. The result of using different cultural filters is often a misunderstanding that is expensive to resolve. For example, a contract between Boeing and a Japanese supplier called for the fuselage panels for Boeing's 767 aircraft to have a "mirror finish." Labor costs for the part were higher than expected because the Japanese supplier polished and polished the panels to achieve what it believed to be the desired finish, when all Boeing wanted was a shiny surface.[17]

NONVERBAL COMMUNICATION Members of a society communicate with each other using more than words. In fact, some researchers believe 80 to 90 percent of all information is transmitted among members of a culture by means other than language.[18] This nonverbal communication includes facial expressions, hand gestures, intonation, eye contact, body positioning, and body posture. In America, for example, businesspersons often greet colleagues, customers, or suppliers with a handshake. In Brazil, hugs, backclasps, and cheek-kisses, as well as handshakes, would be expected, depending on the gender, length of relationship, and level of trust between the two individuals.[19] Although most members of a society quickly understand nonverbal forms of communication common to their society, outsiders may find the nonverbal communication difficult to comprehend. Table 4.1 lists some of the many common forms of nonverbal communication.

Because of cultural differences, nonverbal forms of communication often can lead to misunderstandings. For example, in the United States, people discussing business at a party typically stand 20 inches from each other. In Saudi Arabia, the normal conversational distance is 9 to 10 inches. A U.S. businessperson conversing with a Saudi counterpart at a party will respond to the Saudi's polite attempts to move in closer by politely moving back. Each is acting politely within the context of his or her own culture—and insulting the other in the context of that person's culture.[20]

Differences in the meanings of hand gestures and facial expressions also exist among cultures. Nodding one's head means "yes" in the United States but "no" in Bulgaria. Joining the thumb and forefinger in a circle while extending the remaining three fingers is the signal for "okay" in the United States; however, it symbolizes money to the Japanese, worthlessness to the French, male homosexuals to the Maltese, and a vulgarity in many parts of Eastern Europe.[21] Needless to say, international businesspeople should avoid gesturing in a foreign culture unless they are sure of a gesture's meaning in that culture.

Even silence has meaning. People in the United States tend to abhor silence at meetings or in private conversation, believing that silence reflects an inability to communicate or to empathize. In Japan silence may indicate nothing more than that the individual is thinking or that

TABLE 4.1 Forms of Nonverbal Communication

Dress: fashionable, flashy, or conservative

Hand gestures

Facial expressions: smiles, frowns, nods, eye contact (or lack of it)

Hair styles

Greetings: bows, hugs, kisses, and hand shakes

Perfumes and colognes

Physical contact: hand holding, pats on the back

Posture: formal or relaxed?

Time: arrive promptly, early, or late?

Waiting your turn: queue up? or not?

Walking: fast, slow; in group or single file; position of leader within group

Source: Based on Gary Ferraro, *The Cultural Dimension of International Business*, 6th ed., Prentice Hall, 2010, pp. 82–105; Lillian Chaney and Jeanette Martin, *Intercultural Business Communication*, 2nd ed., Prentice Hall, 2000, pp. 105–128.

additional conversation would be disharmonious. U.S. negotiators have often misinterpreted the silence of their Japanese counterparts and offered contract concessions when none were needed, simply to end a lull in the discussion. Attitudes toward silence also affect management styles. In the United States good managers solve problems. Thus, U.S. managers often attempt to dominate group discussions to signal their competence and leadership abilities. In Japan good managers encourage their subordinates to seek solutions that are acceptable to all involved parties. A Japanese manager therefore will demonstrate leadership by silence, thereby encouraging full participation by subordinates attending a meeting and promoting group consensus.[22]

GIFT-GIVING AND HOSPITALITY Gift-giving and hospitality are important means of communication in many business cultures. Japanese business etiquette requires solicitous hospitality. Elaborate meals and after-hours entertainment serve to build personal bonds and group harmony among the participants. These personal bonds are strengthened by the exchange of gifts, which vary according to the occasion and the status of the giver and the recipient. However, business gifts are opened in private so as not to cause the giver to lose face should the gift be too expensive or too cheap relative to the gift offered in return. Because the rules for gift-giving can be quite complicated, even to native Japanese, etiquette books that detail the appropriate gift for each circumstance are available.

Arab businesspeople, like the Japanese, are very concerned about their ability to work with their proposed business partners; the quality of the people one deals with is just as important as the quality of the project. Thus, the business culture of Arab countries also includes gift-giving and elaborate and gracious hospitality as a means of assessing these qualities. Unlike in Japan, however, business gifts are opened in public so that all may be aware of the giver's generosity.

Hospitality customs also differ. When wooing clients, power-lunching American executives often seek the most conspicuous table in a fancy restaurant as a means of communicating their status and clout. Conversely, in China business banquets are an important mechanism for developing the personal relationships so important in that business culture. However, such events, which typically feature rounds of toasting interspersed with numerous courses of expensive delicacies, are normally located in a private dining room of an expensive restaurant. The American executive's "see and be seen" desire is the antithesis of the Chinese executive's desire for privacy.[23]

Norms of hospitality even affect the way bad news is delivered in various cultures. In the United States bad news is typically delivered as soon as it is known. In Korea it is delivered at day's end so it will not ruin the recipient's whole day. Further, in order not to disrupt personal relationships, the bad news is often only hinted at. In Japan maintaining harmony among participants in a project is emphasized, so bad news often is communicated informally from a junior member of one negotiating team to a junior member of the other team. Even better, a third party may be used to deliver the message to preserve harmony within the group.

Religion

Religion is an important aspect of most societies. It affects the ways in which members of a society relate to each other and to outsiders. Approximately 85 percent of the world's 6.8 billion people claim some religious affiliation. As reflected in Map 4.3, 74 percent of the world's population adheres to one of four religions: Christianity, comprising Roman Catholic (17 percent), Protestant (12 percent), and Eastern Orthodox (4 percent); Islam (22 percent); Hinduism (13 percent); and Buddhism (6 percent).

Religion shapes the attitudes its adherents have toward work, consumption, individual responsibility, and planning for the future. Sociologist Max Weber, for example, has associated the rise of capitalism in Western Europe with the **Protestant ethic**, which stresses individual hard work, frugality, and achievement as means of glorifying God. The Protestant ethic makes a virtue of high savings rates, constant striving for efficiency, and reinvestment of profits to improve future productivity, all of which are necessary for the smooth functioning of a capitalist economy.

In contrast, Hinduism emphasizes spiritual accomplishment rather than economic success. The goal of a Hindu is to achieve union with Brahma, the universal spirit, by leading progressively more ascetic and pure lives as one's reincarnated soul goes through cycles of death and rebirth. The quest for material possessions may delay one's spiritual journey. Thus, Hinduism provides little support for capitalistic activities such as investment, wealth accumulation, and the constant quest for higher productivity and efficiency.

MAP 4.3
Major World Religions

MAJOR RELIGIONS

- Buddhist
- Buddhist/Confucian
- Eastern Orthodox
- Hindu
- Muslim
- Mixed Christian (Catholic, Protestant, and other Christian groups)
- Protestant
- Roman Catholic
- Other

Map labels:

NEW ZEALAND
PAPUA NEW GUINEA
AUSTRALIA
RUSSIA
JAPAN
N. KOREA
S. KOREA
TAIWAN
HONG KONG
PHILIPPINES
MONGOLIA
CHINA
VIETNAM
BRUNEI
INDONESIA
MALAYSIA
SINGAPORE
MYANMAR
THAILAND
CAMB.
BHUTAN
BANG.
NEPAL
INDIA
SRI LANKA
KAZAKHSTAN
KYRGYZSTAN
TAJIKISTAN
UZBEK.
TURKM.
AFGH.
PAKISTAN
FINLAND
ESTONIA
LATVIA
LITH.
BELARUS
UKRAINE
MOLDOVA
ROM.
TURKEY
CYP.
SWEDEN
NORWAY
DEN.
NETH.
UNITED KINGDOM
IRELAND
GERMANY
BELG.
LUX.
POLAND
CZECH REP.
AUS.
SWZ.
SLK.
HUN.
SLO.
CRO.
BOS.
SERBIA
MAC.
ALB.
BULG.
GREECE
MALTA
ITALY
FRANCE
SPAIN
PORTUGAL
GEOR.
ARM.
AZER.
IRAN
IRAQ
SYRIA
LEB.
ISR.
JORDAN
KUWAIT
QATAR
U.A.E.
SAUDI ARABIA
OMAN
YEMEN
EGYPT
LIBYA
TUNISIA
ALGERIA
MOROCCO
WESTERN SAHARA
MAURIT.
MALI
NIGER
CHAD
SUDAN
ERIT.
DJIBOUTI
ETHIOPIA
SOMALIA
KENYA
UGANDA
DR. OF THE CONGO
CONGO
GABON
EQUI. GUINEA
CAM.
C.A.R.
NIGERIA
BENIN
TOGO
GHANA
CÔTE d'IVOIRE
LIBERIA
SIERRA LEONE
GUINEA
GUINEA-BISSAU
GAMBIA
SENEGAL
BRK. FASO
RWA.
BURU.
TANZANIA
MALAWI
MOZAM.
ZAMBIA
ANGOLA
NAMIBIA
BOTS.
ZIMB.
SWAZILAND
LESOTHO
SOUTH AFRICA
MADAGASCAR
MAURITIUS
GREENLAND (Denmark)
CANADA
UNITED STATES
MEXICO
GUATEMALA
EL SALVADOR
COSTA RICA
PANAMA
BELIZE
HONDURAS
NICARAGUA
CUBA
BAHAMAS
COLOMBIA
ECUADOR
VENEZ.
GUYANA
SURINAME
FRENCH GUIANA
PERU
BRAZIL
BOLIVIA
PARAGUAY
CHILE
ARGENTINA
URUGUAY

Islam, while supportive of capitalism, places more emphasis on the individual's obligation to society. According to Islam, profits earned in fair business dealings are justified, but a firm's profits may not result from exploitation or deceit, for example, and all Muslims are expected to act charitably, justly, and humbly in their dealings with others. The Islamic prohibition against payment or receipt of interest, noted in Chapter 3, results from a belief that the practice represents exploitation of the less fortunate. Firms wishing to do business with Muslim customers must often adapt their policies and procedures even in non-Muslim countries, as "Bringing the World into Focus" demonstrates.

Religion affects the business environment in other important ways. Often religions impose constraints on the roles of individuals in society. For example, the caste system of Hinduism traditionally has restricted the jobs individuals may perform, thereby affecting the labor market and foreclosing business opportunities.[24] Countries dominated by strict adherents to Islam, such as Saudi Arabia, limit job opportunities for women, in the belief that their contact with adult males should be restricted to relatives. Religion may also affect the way products are sold. In Nigeria, advertisements in the predominantly Christian south might feature attractive women mouthing double entendres, following the old Madison Avenue precept that "sex sells"; in the predominantly Muslim north that approach would not be beneficial.[25]

Religion also affects the types of products consumers may purchase as well as seasonal patterns of consumption. In most Christian countries, for example, the Christmas season represents an important time for gift-giving, yet very little business is done on Christmas Day itself. While consumption booms during the Christmas holidays, production plummets as employees take time off to visit friends and family.

BRINGING THE WORLD INTO FOCUS | **ISLAMIC FINANCE**

Islam, one of the great religions of the world, was nurtured within the trading traditions of the Arabian peninsula. The Prophet Mohammed was a trader, as was his immediate successor, Abu Bakr. Islamic traders dominated the critical trade routes between the Mediterranean and Asia from the mid-seventh century until the end of the fifteenth century, when Vasco da Gama's voyages pioneered new sea routes that were soon controlled by European merchants and naval vessels.

The Prophet Mohammed emphasized that commerce must be conducted fairly and honestly. One important tenet of Islamic, or Sharia law, forbids receipt or payment of interest, viewing such transactions as exploitation of the poor by the rich. Yet credit is an important component of modern commerce, and adherents of Islam are important contributors to the growth of world commerce. Islamic banking, sukuk (Islamic) bonds, and even hedge funds operating within Islamic tenets are growing leaps and bounds.

Sharia law may forbid interest payments, but it recognizes that it is appropriate that those who take risks be rewarded. Accordingly, sharia-compliant loans typically are structured as risk-sharing arrangements. Often the banker buys the property or item in question from the seller, takes title to the property, and then resells it to the borrower at a higher price. The mark-up charged by the banker is equivalent to the interest payments the banker would have received had the loan been drawn up by a Western bank. As in a traditional auto loan or home mortgage loan, the borrower makes periodic payments to the bank. The payments compensate for the use of the property (a rental payment) and purchase a portion of the lender's ownership interest in the property. The banker retains the title to the property in question until the borrower purchases all of its ownership interest in the property. Once this occurs, the banker transfers the property title to the borrower. The payments are equivalent to what the bank

would have received under a more traditional loan. Such a loan is acceptable, because the bank is earning its profit through trading, not interest.

Another common approach is to structure the purchase and loan as a lease-buyback transaction. The borrower makes a series of fixed payments to the lender for the use of the property over the agreed upon period of time. At the end of the contract, the borrower buys the good in question for a previously agreed upon price. The rental payments and the final price allow the lender to recoup the initial cost of the good plus a profit.

Some sharia lenders have pioneered a different model for financing home purchases. Conceptually, the lender and the borrower form a partnership to purchase the home. They then establish a fair rental value for the home. The rental payments that the borrower makes are split between the borrower and lender, in proportion to their equity share. The borrower also agrees to make periodic payments to buy out the lender's equity ownership over time. This joint rental and equity payment, which sounds similar to the "principal and interest" payments made by millions of non-Muslim homeowners in Asia, Europe, and the Americas, is nonetheless compatible with the requirements of sharia law. (For more information on this technique, you might wish to visit the website of the largest sharia-compliant mortgage lender in the United States, American Finance House Lariba at www.lariba.com.)

Sources: www.lariba.com; "Savings and souls," *The Economist*, September 6, 2008; "Faith-based finance," *The Economist*, September 6, 2008; "Turning towards Mecca," *The Economist*, May 10, 2008; William J. Bernstein, *A Splendid Exchange: How Trade Shaped the World* (New York: Atlantic Monthly Press, 2008); "When interest is forbidden by religion," *Wall Street Journal*, March 9, 2003, p. E5.

The impact of religion on international businesses varies from country to country, depending on the country's legal system, its homogeneity of religious beliefs, and its toleration of other religious viewpoints. Consider Saudi Arabia, home of the holy city of Mecca, to which all Muslims are supposed to make a pilgrimage sometime in their lives. The teachings of the Koran form the basis of the country's theocratic legal system, and 99 percent of the Saudi population is Muslim. Strong political pressure exists within the country to preserve its religious traditions. It is impossible to overstate the importance to foreign businesspeople of understanding the tenets of Islam as they apply to exporting, producing, marketing, or financing goods in the Saudi market. For example, work stops five times a day when the faithful are called to pray to Allah. A non-Muslim manager would be foolish to object to the practice even though it seemingly leads to lost production. Foreigners must also be considerate of their Saudi hosts during the holy month of Ramadan, when the Muslim faithful fast from sunrise to sunset. Female executives of Western firms face additional obstacles because of Saudi attitudes toward the appropriate roles for women, attitudes that stem from their religion. Even actions taken outside Saudi borders may affect commercial relations with the country. For example, McDonald's made a major faux pas when it printed the flags of the 24 soccer teams participating in the World Cup finals, including that of Saudi Arabia, on its paper takeout bags. The Saudi flag includes a sacred inscription that reads, "There is no God but Allah, and Mohammed is His Prophet." Muslims in Saudi Arabia and other countries were outraged, believing that Islam had been insulted by including the name of Allah on a container that would be thrown into garbage cans. McDonald's quickly apologized and pledged to stop using the bags, thereby diffusing a controversy that would have affected its business in Saudi Arabia and other Muslim countries. Nike made a similar gaffe when Muslim groups protested that the logo designed for a line of athletic shoes it was introducing resembled the Arabic word for God, Allah. Nike quickly pulled the footwear from production and redesigned the offending logo.[26]

In many other countries, however, religion, while important, does not permeate every facet of life. For example, in many South American countries most of the population is Roman Catholic. But other religions are also practiced, and tolerance of those religions is high. The Catholic Church is an important pillar of these societies, but only one of many institutions that affect and shape the daily lives of the citizens. Yet public holidays reflect Christian theology (Easter, Christmas), as does the workweek (Sunday is the day of rest). A firm operating in these countries thus needs to adjust its production and employee scheduling to meet the expectations of its workers and customers. Firms operating in Sweden, which is 97 percent Lutheran, must make similar adjustments.

Ironically, countries characterized by religious diversity may offer even greater challenges. Firms that operate in the cosmopolitan cities of London and New York, such as Barclays Bank, Hoffmann-LaRoche, and IBM, must accommodate the religious needs of their Jewish, Christian, Muslim, and Hindu employees and customers by taking into account differences in religious holidays, dietary restrictions or customs, and Sabbath days. Firms that fail to adjust to these needs may suffer from absenteeism, low morale, and lost sales.

Values and Attitudes

Culture also affects and reflects the secular values and attitudes of the members of a society. Values are the principles and standards accepted by the members; attitudes encompass the actions, feelings, and thoughts that result from those values. Cultural values often stem from deep-seated beliefs about the individual's position in relation to his or her deity, the family, and the social hierarchy that we discussed earlier. Cultural attitudes toward such factors as time, age, education, and status reflect these values and in turn shape the behavior of and opportunities available to international businesses operating in a given culture.

TIME Attitudes about time differ dramatically across cultures. In Anglo-Saxon cultures, the prevailing attitude is "time is money." Time represents the opportunity to produce more and to raise one's income, so it is not to be wasted. Underlying this attitude is the Protestant ethic, which encourages people to better their positions in life through hard work, and the puritanical belief that "idle hands are the Devil's workshop." As a result, U.S. and Canadian businesspeople expect meetings to start on time, and keeping a person waiting is considered extremely rude.

In Latin American cultures, however, few participants would think it unusual if a meeting began 45 minutes after the appointed time.[27] In Arab cultures, meetings not only often start later than the stated time, but they also may be interrupted by family and friends who wander in to exchange pleasantries. Westerners may interpret their host's willingness to talk to these unscheduled visitors as a sign of rudeness and as a subtle device to undermine the Westerners' dignity. Nothing could be further from the truth. This open-door policy reflects the hospitality of the host and the respect the host offers to all guests—just the sort of person with whom the Arab presumes the Westerners want to do business.[28]

Even the content of business meetings can vary by country. If a meeting is scheduled for 2 P.M., U.S., Canadian, and British businesspeople arrive at 1:55 P.M. and expect the meeting to start promptly at 2 P.M. After exchanging a few pleasantries, they then get down to business, following a well-planned agenda that has been distributed in advance to the participants. At the meeting the positions of the parties are set forth and disagreement is common. In contrast, in Japan or Saudi Arabia the initial meeting often focuses on determining whether the parties can trust each other and work together comfortably, rather than on the details of the proposed business. This time, however, is not being wasted. Because these cultures value personal relationships so highly, time is being utilized for an important purpose—assessing the qualities of potential business partners.

AGE Important cultural differences exist in attitudes toward age. Youthfulness is considered a virtue in the United States. Many U.S. firms devote much time and energy to identifying young "fast-trackers" and providing them with important, tough assignments, such as negotiating joint ventures with international partners. In Asian and Arab cultures, however, age is respected and a manager's stature is correlated with age. These cultural differences can lead to problems. For example, many foreign firms mistakenly send young, fast-track executives to negotiate with government officials of China. The Chinese, however, prefer to deal with older and more senior members of a firm, and thus may be offended by this approach.

In Japan's corporate culture, age and rank are highly correlated, but senior (and, by definition, older) managers will not grant approval to a project until they have achieved a consensus among junior managers. Many foreign firms mistakenly focus their attention in negotiations on the senior Japanese managers, failing to realize that the goal should be to persuade the junior managers. Once the junior managers consent to a project, the senior managers will grant their approval as well.

EDUCATION A country's formal system of public and private education is an important transmitter and reflection of the cultural values of its society. For instance, U.S. primary and secondary schools emphasize the role of the individual and stress the development of self-reliance, creativity, and self-esteem. The United States prides itself on providing widespread access to higher education. Research universities, liberal arts colleges, and community colleges coexist to meet the educational needs of students with disparate incomes and intellectual talents. In contrast, the United Kingdom, reflecting its past class system, has historically provided an elite education to a relatively small number of students. Germany has well-developed apprenticeship programs that train new generations of skilled craftspeople and machinists for its manufacturing sector (see Chapter 6's opening case, "The Mittelstand Lead the Way"). The Japanese and French educational systems share a different focus. Their primary and secondary schools concentrate on preparing students to take a nationwide college entrance exam. The top-scoring students gain entry to a handful of prestigious universities—such as Tokyo University or Kyoto University in Japan and the five grandes écoles in France—which virtually guarantee their graduates placement in the most important corporate and governmental jobs in their societies.[29]

STATUS The means by which status is achieved also vary across cultures. In some societies status is inherited as a result of the wealth or rank of one's ancestors. In others it is earned by the individual through personal accomplishments or professional achievements. In some European countries, for example, membership in the nobility ensures higher status than does mere personal achievement, and persons who inherited their wealth look down their noses at the nouveau riche. In the United States, however, hard-working entrepreneurs are honored, and their children are often disdained if they fail to match their parents' accomplishments.

In Japan a person's status depends on the status of the group to which he or she belongs. Thus, Japanese businesspeople often introduce themselves by announcing not only their names but also their corporate affiliation. Attendance at elite universities such as Tokyo University or employment in elite organizations such as Toyota Motor Corporation or the Ministry of Finance grants one high status in Japanese society.

In India status is affected by one's caste. The caste system divides society into various groups including *Brahmins* (priests and intellectuals), *Kshatriyas* (soldiers and political leaders), *Vaishyas* (businesspeople), *Sudras* (farmers and workers), and untouchables, who perform the dirtiest and most unpleasant jobs. According to Hinduism, one's caste reflects the virtue (or lack of virtue) that one exhibited in a previous life. Particularly in rural areas, caste used to affect every facet of life, from the way a man shaped his mustache to the food the family ate to the job a person could hold.[30] However, the power of the caste system in rural areas is slowly eroding due to government affirmative action policies and the growing scarcity of high-skilled employees needed by India's high-tech industries. Infosys, for example, has been forced to broaden its recruiting efforts to 700 colleges, many of which are located in semirural areas where lower-caste individuals often live, in order to acquire the talented workers it requires. A decade ago, the high-tech firm could meet its hiring needs by recruiting at 50 Indian universities, most of which were located in urban areas.[31]

Seeing the Forest, Not the Trees

The various elements of national culture affect the behavior and expectations of managers and employees in the workplace. International businesspeople, who face the challenge of managing and motivating employees with different cultural backgrounds, need to understand these cultural elements if they are to be effective managers. To a beginning student in international business, however, this discussion of the elements of culture can be very confusing. Moreover, many students and businesspeople panic at the thought of memorizing a bunch of rules—"the French do this," "the Saudis do that," and so on. Fortunately, numerous scholars have tried to make sense of the various elements of culture. Their efforts make it easier for international managers to understand the big picture regarding a country's culture and how it affects their ability to manage their firms. In this section, we present the work of several of these scholars.

Hall's Low-Context–High-Context Approach

One useful way of characterizing differences in cultures is the low-context–high-context approach developed by Edward and Mildred Hall.[32] In a **low-context culture,** the words used by the speaker explicitly convey the speaker's message to the listener. Anglo-Saxon countries, such as Canada, the United Kingdom, and the United States, and Germanic countries are good examples of low-context cultures (see Table 4.2). In a **high-context culture,** the context in which a conversation occurs is just as important as the words that are actually spoken, and cultural clues are important in understanding what is being communicated. Examples are Arab countries and Japan.

Business behaviors in high-context cultures often differ from those in low-context cultures. For example, German advertising is typically fact oriented, while Japanese advertising is more emotion oriented.[33] High-context cultures place higher value on interpersonal relations in deciding whether to enter into a business arrangement. In such cultures preliminary meetings are often held to determine whether the parties can trust each other and work together comfortably. Low-context cultures place more importance on the specific terms of a transaction.[34] In low-context cultures such as Canada, the United Kingdom, and the United States, lawyers are often present at negotiations to ensure that their clients' interests are protected. Conversely, in high-context cultures such as Saudi Arabia, Japan, and Egypt, the presence of a lawyer, particularly at the initial meeting of the participants, would be viewed as a sign of distrust. Because these

TABLE 4.2

Low-Context Cultures	High-Context Cultures
German	Chinese
Swiss	Korean
Austrian	Japanese
Scandinavian	Vietnamese
U.S./Canadian	Arab
British	Greek
Australian	Spanish

TABLE 4.3 Differences in Negotiating Styles Across Cultures

Japanese	North American	Latin American
Emotional sensitivity highly valued.	Emotional sensitivity not highly valued.	Emotional sensitivity valued.
Hiding of emotions.	Dealing straightforwardly or impersonally.	Emotionally passionate.
Subtle power plays; conciliation.	Litigation not as much as conciliation.	Great power plays; use of weakness.
Loyalty to employer. Employer takes care of its employees.	Lack of commitment to employer. Breaking of ties by either if necessary.	Loyalty to employer (who is often family).
Group decision-making consensus.	Teamwork provides input to a decision maker.	Decisions come down from one individual.
Face-saving crucial. Decisions often made on basis of saving someone from embarrassment.	Decisions made on a cost-benefit basis. Face-saving does not always matter.	Face-saving crucial in decision making to preserve honor; dignity.
Decision makers openly influenced by special interests.	Decision makers influenced by special interests but often this is not considered ethical.	Execution of special interests of decision maker expected, condoned.
Not argumentative. Quiet when right.	Argumentative when right or wrong, but impersonal.	Argumentative when right or wrong; passionate.
What is down in writing must be accurate, valid.	Great importance given to documentation as evidential proof.	Impatient with documentation as obstacle to understanding general principles.
Step-by-step approach to decision making.	Methodically organized decision making.	Impulsive, spontaneous decision making.
Good of group is the ultimate aim.	Profit motive or good of individual ultimate aim.	What is good for the group is good for the individual.
Cultivate a good emotional social setting for decision making. Get to know decision makers.	Decision making impersonal. Avoid involvements, conflicts of interest.	Personalism necessary for good decision making.

Source: Pierre Casse, *Training for the Multicultural Manager: A Practical and Cross-Cultural Approach to the Management of People.* Sietar International © 1982.

cultures value long-term relationships, an assumption by a potential partner that one cannot be trusted may be sufficient grounds to end the negotiations. Table 4.3 provides additional information about differences in negotiating styles across cultures.

The Cultural Cluster Approach

The cultural cluster approach is another technique for classifying and making sense of national cultures. Similarities exist among many cultures, thereby reducing some of the need to customize business practices to meet the demands of local cultures. Anthropologists, sociologists, and international business scholars have analyzed such factors as job satisfaction, work roles, and interpersonal work relations in an attempt to identify clusters of countries that share similar cultural values that can affect business practices. Map 4.4 shows the eight country clusters developed by one such team of researchers, Ronen and Shenkar. (In their study, four countries—Brazil, India, Israel, and Japan—were not placed in any cluster.) A **cultural cluster** comprises countries that share many cultural similarities, although differences do remain. Many clusters are based on language similarities, as is apparent in the Anglo, Germanic, Latin American, and Arab clusters and, to a lesser extent, in the Nordic and Latin European clusters. Of course, one can disagree with some ments of countries within clusters. Spain and the countries of Latin America share many values, as do Israel and the United States.

MAP 4.4
A Synthesis of Country Clusters

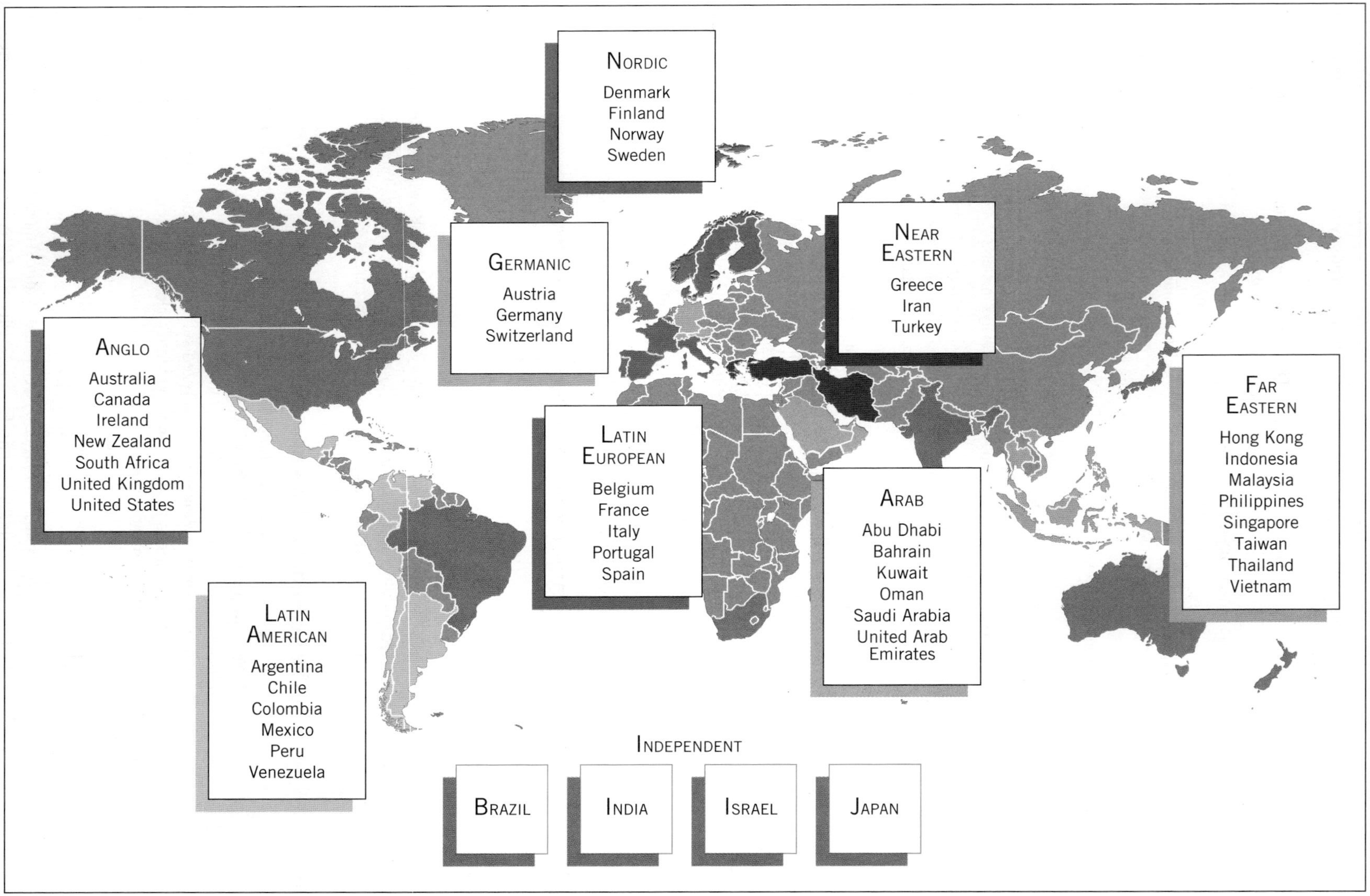

FAR EASTERN
Hong Kong
Indonesia
Malaysia
Philippines
Singapore
Taiwan
Thailand
Vietnam

NEAR EASTERN
Greece
Iran
Turkey

ARAB
Abu Dhabi
Bahrain
Kuwait
Oman
Saudi Arabia
United Arab Emirates

JAPAN

ISRAEL

INDEPENDENT

INDIA

BRAZIL

NORDIC
Denmark
Finland
Norway
Sweden

LATIN EUROPEAN
Belgium
France
Italy
Portugal
Spain

GERMANIC
Austria
Germany
Switzerland

LATIN AMERICAN
Argentina
Chile
Colombia
Mexico
Peru
Venezuela

ANGLO
Australia
Canada
Ireland
New Zealand
South Africa
United Kingdom
United States

Source: Based on Simcha Ronen and Oded Shenkar, "Clustering countries on attitudinal dimensions: A review and synthesis," *Academy of Management Review,* vol. 10, no. 3 (1985).

Many international businesses instinctively utilize the cultural cluster approach in formulating their internationalization strategies. U.S. firms' first exporting efforts often focus on Canada and the United Kingdom. Hong Kong and Taiwanese firms have been very successful in exploiting China's markets. Similarly, many Spanish firms have chosen to focus their international expansion efforts on Spanish-speaking areas in the Americas.

Closeness of culture may affect the form that firms use to enter foreign markets. Researchers have found, for example, that Canadian firms are more likely to enter the British market by establishing joint ventures with British firms, while Japanese firms are more likely to enter the British market via a **greenfield investment,** that is, a brand-new investment. The likely reason for the difference? Because of the relative closeness of their national cultures, Canadian firms are more comfortable working with British partners than are Japanese firms.[35]

Hofstede's Five Dimensions

The most influential studies analyzing cultural differences and synthesizing cultural similarities are those performed by Geert Hofstede, a Dutch researcher who studied 116,000 people working for IBM in dozens of different countries.[36] Although Hofstede's work has been criticized for methodological weaknesses and his own cultural biases, it remains the largest and most comprehensive work of its kind. Hofstede's work identified five important dimensions along which people seem to differ across cultures. These dimensions are shown in Figure 4.2. Note that these dimensions reflect tendencies within cultures, not absolutes. Within any given culture, there are likely to be people at every point on each dimension.

FIGURE 4.2
Hofstede's Five Dimensions of National Culture

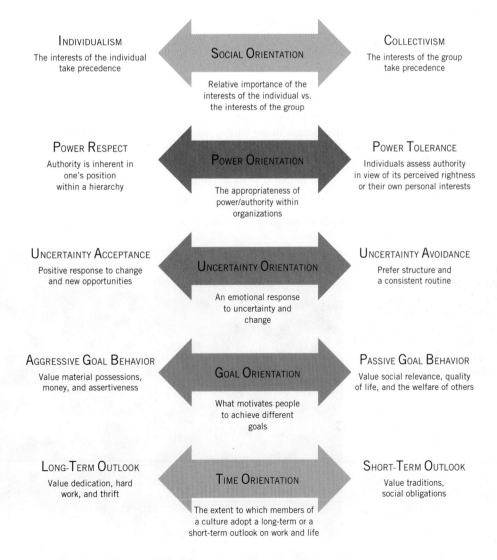

TABLE 4.4 Extremes of Social Orientation

Collectivism	Individualism
Children learn to think in terms of "we"; use of the word "I" is avoided	Children learn to think in terms of "I"; use of the word "I" is encouraged
Interdependent self	Independent self
Education focuses on learning how to do	Education focuses on learning how to learn
Employer–employee relationship essentially moral, like a family relationship	Employer–employee relationship is a contract in the labor market
Value standards differ for in-groups and out-groups: exclusionism	Same values apply to everyone: universalism
Harmony should be maintained; avoid confrontation	An honest person speaks one's mind
Relationship prevails over task	Task prevails over relationship
High-context communication prevails	Low-context communication prevails
Social network is primary source of information	Media is primary source of information

Source: Geert Hofstede, Gert Jan Hofstede, and Michael Minkov. *Cultures and Organizations: Software of the Mind*, Third Edition. New York: McGraw-Hill, 2010.

Social Orientation

The first dimension identified by Hofstede is social orientation.[37] **Social orientation** is a person's beliefs about the relative importance of the individual and the groups to which that person belongs. The two extremes of social orientation, summarized in Table 4.4, are individualism and collectivism. **Individualism** is the cultural belief that the person comes first. Key values of individualistic people include a high degree of self-respect and independence. These people often put their own career interests before the good of their organizations, and they tend to assess decisions in terms of how those decisions affect them as individuals. Hofstede's research suggested that people in the United States, the United Kingdom, Australia, Canada, New Zealand, and the Netherlands tend to be relatively individualistic.

Collectivism, the opposite of individualism, is the belief that the group comes first. Societies that tend to be collectivistic are usually characterized by well-defined social networks, including extended families, tribes, and coworkers. People are expected to put the good of the

These Bangladeshi women are attending a weekly meeting at which they collect monies to repay the GrameenBank. This bank, a pioneer in the microfinance movement, relies on peer pressure and the country's collectivist norms to ensure that the loans it extends to poor villagers (mostly women) are paid promptly and in full.

Shehzad Noorani/Photolibrary/Peter Arnold, Inc.

group ahead of their own personal welfare, interests, or success. Individual behavior in such cultures is strongly influenced by the emotion of shame; when a group fails, its members take the failure very personally and experience shame. In addition, group members try to fit into their group harmoniously, with a minimum of conflict or tension. Hofstede found that people from Mexico, Greece, Hong Kong, Taiwan, Peru, Singapore, Colombia, and Pakistan tend to be relatively collectivistic in their values.

International firms must be aware of differences in the social orientations of countries. Nepotism is often frowned on in individualistic cultures but may be a normal hiring practice in collectivistic cultures. In countries such as the United States, where individualism is a cultural norm, many workers believe they should be compensated according to their individual achievements. They judge the fairness of any compensation system by whether it achieves this objective. U.S. firms thus spend much time and resources assessing individual performance in order to link pay and performance. A firm that fails to do this will likely lose its more productive employees to firms that do.

Because of its group-oriented culture, prevailing compensation practices in Japan are very different. In many Japanese corporations a person's compensation reflects the group to which he or she belongs, not personal achievements. For example, all individuals who join the company's engineering staff in 2010 will receive the same compensation, regardless of their individual talents, insights, and efforts. The salaries received by each cohort within the corporation reflect seniority: Engineers who join the company in 2010 will receive higher salaries than engineers who join the firm in 2011, but lower salaries than engineers who start in 2009. This compensation structure, which lasts for the first six to eight years the employee works for the firm, encourages employees to focus on group goals. Although some Japanese corporations have begun to abandon these group-oriented approaches in favor of more merit-oriented ones, individual-oriented approaches remain the exception, not the rule.

These cultural differences help to explain the widely publicized differences in CEO pay between the United States and Japan. In group-oriented Japan the CEO's pay symbolically reflects the performance of the group. In the United States the CEO's pay is presumed to measure the CEO's contribution to the firm. Even the way the issue is framed reflects the cultural values of the United States: The question "How can President Smith of the XYZ Corporation be worth $10 million?" implicitly assumes that the CEO's pay should measure his or her individual contribution to the organization.

A similar pattern characterizes the career progression and job mobility of employees. In individualistic societies a person's career path often involves switching employers in search of higher-paying and more challenging jobs so that the person can prove his or her capabilities in new and changing circumstances. Indeed, in the United States a person's failure to accept a better-paying job at another firm raises suspicions about the person's ambition, motivation, and dedication to his or her career. However, in collectivistic cultures, such as Japan, changing jobs is often interpreted as reflecting disloyalty to the collective good (the firm) and may brand the person as unworthy of trust.[38] Because of this stigma, job switchers traditionally have had difficulties finding appropriate jobs in other Japanese companies. Although this norm is changing because of the economic stresses Japan underwent in the 1990s, job mobility is much lower in Japan than in the United States.

Power Orientation

The second dimension Hofstede proposed is power orientation. **Power orientation** refers to the beliefs that people in a culture hold about the appropriateness of power and authority differences in hierarchies such as business organizations. The extremes of the dimension of power orientation are summarized in Table 4.5.

Some cultures are characterized by **power respect**. This means that people in a culture tend to accept the power and authority of their superiors simply on the basis of the superiors' positions in the hierarchy. These same people also tend to respect the superiors' right to that power. People at all levels in a firm accept the decisions and mandates of those above them because of the implicit belief that higher-level positions carry the right to make decisions and issue mandates. Hofstede found people in France, Spain, Mexico, Japan, Brazil, Indonesia, and Singapore to be relatively power respecting.

In contrast, people in cultures characterized by **power tolerance** attach much less significance to a person's position in the hierarchy. These people are more willing to question a decision or mandate from someone at a higher level or perhaps even refuse to accept it. They are

TABLE 4.5 Extremes of Power Orientation

Power Tolerance	Power Respect
Parents treat children as equals	Parents treated as superiors
Teachers are experts who transfer impartial truths	Teachers are gurus who transfer personal wisdom
Managers rely on experience and subordinates	Managers rely on superiors and formal rules
Hierarchy means inequality of roles, established for convenience	Hierarchy reflects existential inequality between higher- and lower-level employees
Subordinates expect to be consulted	Subordinates expect to be told what to do
Decentralization is popular	Centralization is popular
All people should have equal rights	The powerful should have privileges
Inequalities among people should be minimized	Inequalities among people are expected and desired

Source: Geert Hofstede, Gert Jan Hofstede, and Michael Minkov, *Cultures and Organizations: Software of the Mind*, Third Edition. New York: McGraw-Hill, 2010.

willing to follow a leader when that leader is perceived to be right or when it seems to be in their own self-interest to do so but not because of the leader's intangible right to issue orders. Hofstede's work suggested that people in the United States, Israel, Austria, Denmark, Ireland, Norway, Germany, and New Zealand tend to be more power tolerant.

Persons from power-tolerant cultures believe that hierarchies exist to solve problems and organize tasks within organizations. Power-respecting business cultures, such as those in Indonesia and Malaysia, assume that hierarchies are developed so that everyone knows who has authority over whom. In approaching a new project, power-tolerating Americans would first define the tasks at hand and then assemble the project team. Conversely, power-respecting Indonesians would first determine who would be in charge and then assess whether the project would be feasible under that manager's leadership. Such attitudes obviously have important consequences for international businesses. As "e-World" noted earlier in this chapter, a power-tolerant culture may be more suited to the needs of Internet start-ups than a power-respecting one.

These cultural differences regarding the role of hierarchies were highlighted in a survey that asked international managers to respond to the following statement: "In order to have efficient work relationships, it is often necessary to bypass the hierarchical line." Swedish, British, and U.S. managers agreed with the statement. They believe that superiors do not necessarily have all the information subordinates need to make decisions and that it is efficient for a subordinate to seek out the person who has the relevant information regardless of the firm's formal hierarchy. Italian managers, on the other hand, disagreed: Bypassing a superior is a sign of insubordination, not efficiency, in the Italian business culture.[39]

Differing cultural attitudes toward power orientation can lead to misunderstandings in business. For example, when firms are negotiating with each other, a firm from a power-tolerant country will often send a team composed of experts on the subject, without concern for rank or seniority. However, a team composed of junior employees, no matter how knowledgeable they are about the problem at hand, may be taken as an insult by managers from a power-respecting culture, who expect to deal with persons of rank equal to their own. Also, the use of informalities by U.S. managers—for example, calling a counterpart by that person's first name—may be misinterpreted by managers from power-respecting cultures as an insulting attempt to diminish another's authority. Similarly, the willingness of U.S. managers to roll up their sleeves and pitch in on the factory floor during an emergency is likely to win praise from U.S. production workers. Conversely, Indian managers would find performing such menial tasks beneath their dignity. Worse, managers so lacking in self-respect would be deemed unworthy of respect or obedience from their peers and subordinates.[40]

At other times such cultural norms may lead to tragedy. During the late 1990s, for example, Korean Airlines (KAL) suffered an abnormally high number of fatal accidents. Some aviation safety experts attributed the problem to the power-respecting norms of Korean culture. Behavioral scientists found that KAL first officers (the second-in-command pilots) were often unwilling to suggest to their captains that the captain might be making a mistake even if the mistake was putting the aircraft in danger. KAL's reliance on ex-military pilots exacerbated the problem because

FIGURE 4.3

Power Distance Versus Individualism

Source: Reprinted with permission from Geert Hofstede, Gert Jan Hofstede, and Michael Minkov, *Cultures and Organizations: Software of the Mind*, Third Edition. New York: McGraw-Hill, 2010.

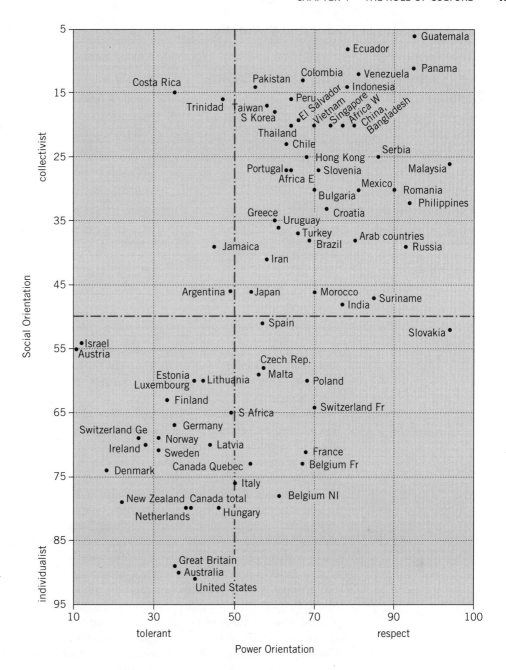

military pilots have been trained to obey the orders issued by the chain of command. To remedy this problem, KAL changed its cockpit recruitment strategies, focusing on hiring foreign pilots and nonmilitary pilots who would be more likely to question the captain in case of emergency. It also altered its training strategies for pilots and first officers, forcing them to work as a team.[41]

We can gain additional perspectives on Hofstede's dimensions by viewing them in combinations. For example, when social orientation and power orientation are superimposed, individualistic and power-tolerant countries seem to cluster, as do collectivistic and power-respecting countries (see Figure 4.3).

Uncertainty Orientation

The third basic dimension of cultural differences Hofstede studied is uncertainty orientation. **Uncertainty orientation** is the feeling people have regarding uncertain and ambiguous situations. The extremes of this dimension are summarized in Table 4.6.

People in cultures characterized by **uncertainty acceptance** are stimulated by change and thrive on new opportunities. Ambiguity is seen as a context within which an individual can grow,

TABLE 4.6 Extremes of Uncertainty Orientation

Uncertainty Acceptance	Uncertainty Avoidance
Comfortable with ambiguous situations and with unfamiliar risks	Fear of ambiguous situations and unfamiliar risks
Tolerance for ambiguity and chaos	Need for precision and formalization
Students prefer open-ended learning situations and are concerned with good discussions	Students prefer structured learning situations and are concerned with the right answers
Teachers may say, "I don't know"	Teachers are supposed to have all the answers
Teachers involve parents	Teachers inform parents
What is different is curious	What is different is dangerous
There should be no more rules than strictly necessary	There is an emotional need for rules
Top managers are concerned with strategy	Top managers are concerned with daily operations

Source: Geert Hofstede, Gert Jan Hofstede, and Michael Minkov, *Cultures and Organizations: Software of the Mind*, Third Edition. New York: McGraw-Hill, 2010.

develop, and carve out new opportunities. In these cultures certainty carries with it a sense of monotony, routineness, and overbearing structure. Hofstede suggested that many people from the United States, Denmark, Sweden, Canada, Singapore, Hong Kong, and Australia are uncertainty accepting.

In contrast, people in cultures characterized by **uncertainty avoidance** dislike ambiguity and will avoid it whenever possible. Ambiguity and change are seen as undesirable. These people tend to prefer a structured and routine, even bureaucratic, way of doing things. Hofstede found that many people in Austria, Japan, Italy, Colombia, France, Peru, and Belgium tend to avoid uncertainty whenever possible.

Uncertainty orientation affects many aspects of managing international firms. Those operating in uncertainty-avoiding countries, for example, tend to adopt more rigid hierarchies and more elaborate rules and procedures for doing business. Conversely, uncertainty-accepting cultures are more tolerant of flexible hierarchies, rules, and procedures. Risk taking ("nothing ventured, nothing gained") is highly valued in uncertainty-accepting cultures such as that of the United States and Hong Kong, whereas preserving the status and prestige of the firm through conservative, low-risk strategies is more important in uncertainty-avoiding countries such as Spain, Belgium, and Argentina. Not surprisingly, uncertainty-accepting cultures may be more attuned with the needs of the new e-commerce economy than uncertainty-avoiding ones. And recent research suggests that firms operating in uncertainty-avoiding cultures, such as France or Germany, tend to rely on banks to raise capital, whereas firms in uncertainty-accepting cultures are more likely to rely on the stock market.[42]

The second-guessing that followed the 1998 crash of Swissair 111 off the coast of Nova Scotia provides a dramatic example of how uncertainty orientation influences business practices. Smoke suddenly filled the cabin of the plane as it was en route from New York to Geneva. The Swissair pilot swung the troubled aircraft out to sea in order to dump excess fuel before landing. Unfortunately, the plane plunged into the sea before it could reach safety. A controversy broke out over whether the pilot's decision to circle and dump fuel before landing was correct. Some U.S. airline pilots interviewed by the media suggested that the pilot should have landed the plane as soon as possible once smoke was detected. Swissair officials defended their pilot, noting that the captain followed Swissair's emergency procedures published in the carrier's operating manual. The U.S. pilots retorted that in such emergencies pilots should exercise their independent judgment, regardless of what is contained in the company manual. Swissair officials countered that the procedures detailed in the manual reflected the state-of-the-art understanding of what to do in an emergency, and thus its pilots did the right thing in adhering to the manual. The "rules are there to be obeyed" viewpoint of Swissair's officials reflects their country's uncertainty-avoiding culture, while the "rules are made to be broken" attitude of U.S. pilots reflects the uncertainty-accepting norms of the United States.

It is interesting to consider uncertainty orientation along with the social orientation dimension. Job mobility is likely to be higher in uncertainty-accepting countries than in those characterized by uncertainty avoidance. Some Japanese firms have traditionally used lifetime employment practices partly in response to the uncertainty-avoiding and collectivistic tendencies of the Japanese culture. Because of the lifetime employment relationship, Japanese firms take considerable care in selecting employees and force job applicants to undergo rigorous testing and interviewing prior to being hired. Once hired, employees recognize that their jobs depend on the long-term survival of their employer and that their jobs are secure as long as the firm is secure.

However, lifetime employment—as well as the seniority-based pay and promotion policies traditionally used by Japanese firms—may not be an effective policy when transplanted to individualistic and uncertainty-accepting countries. For example, Japanese firms operating in uncertainty-accepting Canada and the United States have been forced to modify their pay and promotion policies because North American workers are more oriented toward an individualistic "pay me what I'm worth" attitude and are less worried about job security than are their counterparts in Japan.

Goal Orientation

Hofstede's fourth dimension, **goal orientation,** is the manner in which people are motivated to work toward different kinds of goals. One extreme on the goal orientation continuum is **aggressive goal behavior** (see Table 4.7). People who exhibit aggressive goal behavior tend to place a high premium on material possessions, money, and assertiveness. At the other extreme, people who adopt **passive goal behavior** place a higher value on social relationships, quality of life, and concern for others.

According to Hofstede, cultures that value aggressive goal behavior also tend to define gender-based roles somewhat rigidly, whereas cultures that emphasize passive goal behavior do not. In cultures characterized by extremely aggressive goal behavior, men are expected to work and to focus their careers in traditionally male occupations; women are generally expected not to work outside the home and to focus on their families. If they do work outside the home, they are usually expected to pursue work in areas traditionally dominated by women. According to Hofstede's research, many people in Japan tend to exhibit relatively aggressive goal behavior, whereas many people in Germany, Mexico, Italy, and the United States exhibit moderately aggressive goal behavior. Men and women in passive goal behavior cultures are more likely both to pursue diverse careers and to be well represented within any given occupation. People from the Netherlands, Norway, Sweden, Denmark, and Finland tend to exhibit relatively passive goal behavior. Norway, for example, was the first country to mandate that at least 40 percent of corporate board directors be female.[43] A minimum of two months of the 13 months of paid parental leave provided by Swedish law is reserved for the father; an estimated 85 percent of Swedish fathers take advantage of the paid leave. The program is credited with boosting women's wages and reducing the country's divorce rate.[44]

TABLE 4.7 Extremes of Goal Orientation

Passive Goal Behavior	Aggressive Goal Behavior
Relationships and quality of life are important	Challenge, earnings, recognition, and advancement are important
Average student is the norm; praise for weak students	Best student is the norm; praise for excellent students
Failing in school is a minor incident	Failing in school is a disaster
Job choice is based on intrinsic interest	Job choice is based on career opportunities
Resolution of conflict through compromise and negotiation	Resolution of conflict by letting the strongest win
Rewards based on equality	Rewards based on equity
People work in order to live	People live in order to work
Leisure time is preferred over money	Money is preferred over leisure time

Source: Geert Hofstede, Gert Jan Hofstede, and Michael Minkov, *Cultures and Organizations: Software of the Mind*, Third Edition. New York: McGraw-Hill, 2010.

Passive goal behavior cultures place more emphasis on social relationships, quality of life, and concern for others than on the accumulation of material possessions. Sweden, a passive goal behavior culture, has made early childhood education and care a national priority.

These cultural attitudes affect international business practices in many ways. One study showed that decisions made by Danish managers (a passive goal behavior culture) incorporate societal concerns to a greater extent than decisions made by more profit-oriented U.S., British, and German executives (from more aggressive goal behavior cultures).[45] Similarly, studies of the Swedish workforce indicate that the country's egalitarian traditions, as well as workers' desires to maintain comfortable work schedules, often make promotions less desirable than in other countries. Many Swedish workers prefer more fringe benefits rather than higher salaries.[46] Or consider the impact of the role of women in business. In Sweden the high proportion of dual-career families makes it difficult for many workers to accept a promotion if it entails moving. Not surprisingly, Swedish firms are among the world's leaders in providing fringe benefits such as maternity and paternity leave and company-sponsored child care.

Time Orientation

Hofstede's fifth dimension, **time orientation**, is the extent to which members of a culture adopt a long-term versus a short-term outlook on work, life, and other aspects of society. Some cultures, such as those of Japan, Hong Kong, Taiwan, and South Korea, have a long-term, future orientation that values dedication, hard work, perseverance, and thrift. Other cultures, including those of Pakistan, Nigeria, and the Philippines, tend to focus on the past and present, emphasizing respect for traditions and fulfillment of social obligations. Hofstede's work suggests that the United States and Germany tend to have an intermediate time orientation.

International Management and Cultural Differences

Some experts believe the world's cultures are growing more similar as a result of improvements in communication and transportation. Thanks to MTV and CNN, teenagers worldwide have been able to enjoy the wit and wisdom of JWoww, Snooki, and Pauly D, while their parents can learn about politics, scandals, disasters, and culture in other countries. Lower airfares generated by increased airline competition mean that more tourists can learn about other cultures firsthand. MNCs facilitate this process of **cultural convergence,** for better or worse, through their advertisements that define appropriate lifestyles, attitudes, and goals and by bringing new management techniques, technologies, and cultural values to the countries in which they operate.

Understanding New Cultures

Nonetheless, cultural differences do exist. When dealing with a new culture, many international businesspeople make the mistake of relying on the **self-reference criterion,** the unconscious use of one's own culture to help assess new surroundings. A U.S. salesperson who calls on a German customer in Frankfurt and asks about the customer's family is acting politely according to U.S. culture—the salesperson's reference point—but rudely according to German culture, thereby generating ill will and the potential loss of a customer.[47] In behaving as is usual in the United States, the salesperson forgot the answer to a critical question: "Who is the foreigner?"

To be successful, international businesspeople traveling abroad must remember that they are the foreigners and must attempt to behave according to the rules of the culture at hand. There are numerous ways to obtain knowledge about other cultures to achieve **cross-cultural literacy.** The best and most common way, not surprisingly, is through personal experience that results from conducting business abroad—as part of either a business trip or a long-term assignment—or from nonbusiness travel.[48] Many firms, such as Motorola, offer cross-cultural training programs to their employees headed for foreign assignments.[49] Information about specific cultures can also be obtained from various published sources. For example, ProQuest provides a series of highly regarded *Culturegrams* on more than 200 countries, and the U.S. government publishes detailed descriptions and analyses of the economies, political systems, natural resources, and cultures of the world's countries in a series of volumes called *Country Studies.*

Cross-cultural literacy is the first step in **acculturation,** the process by which people not only understand a foreign culture but also modify and adapt their behavior to make it compatible with that culture. Acculturation is of particular importance to home country managers who frequently interact with host country nationals—for example, a plant manager from the home country or a marketing director working overseas at a foreign subsidiary.

To complicate matters further, many countries have more than one culture, although the level of such cultural diversity varies by country. Japan, with a population consisting of 99.4 percent ethnic Japanese, is extremely homogeneous. Conversely, the United States is culturally heterogeneous, with significant Caribbean, Latin American, Middle Eastern, Hispanic, African, and Asian communities complementing the dominant Anglo-Saxon culture. Successful international businesspeople must recognize the attributes of the primary national culture as well as any important subcultures in culturally heterogeneous societies.

MyManagementLab

Now that you have finished this chapter, go back to **www.pearsonglobaleditions.com/mymanagementlab** to continue practicing and applying the concepts you've learned.

CHAPTER REVIEW

Summary

Understanding cultural differences is critical to the success of firms engaging in international business. A society's culture affects the political, economic, social, and ethical rules a firm must follow in its business dealings within that society.

A society's culture reflects its values, beliefs, behaviors, customs, and attitudes. Culture is learned behavior that is transmitted from one member of a society to another. The elements of culture are interrelated and reinforce each other. These elements are adaptive, changing as outside forces influence the society. Culture not only is shared by the society's members but also defines the society's membership.

A society's culture comprises numerous elements. The social structure reflects the culture's beliefs about the individual's role in society and the importance of mobility within that society. Language is another important cultural element because it allows members of the society to communicate with each other. Approximately 85 percent of the world's population claims some

religious affiliation. Religion influences attitudes toward work, investment, consumption, and responsibility for one's behavior. Religion may also influence the formulation of a country's laws.

A society's culture reflects and shapes its values and attitudes, including those toward time, age, status, and education. These affect business operations in numerous ways, such as in hiring practices, job turnover, and the design of compensation programs.

Researchers have grouped countries according to common cultural characteristics. Hall and Hall developed the low-context–high-context classification scheme, which focuses on the importance of context within a culture. To some extent, the existence of cultural clusters eases the difficulties of doing business internationally. Researchers have discovered that many countries share similar attitudes toward work roles, job satisfaction, and other work-related aspects of life. Often countries within a cultural cluster share a common language.

The pioneering research of Geert Hofstede has identified five basic cultural dimensions along which people may differ: social orientation, power orientation, uncertainty orientation, goal orientation, and time orientation. These differences affect business behavior in numerous ways and often lead to cross-cultural misunderstandings.

Review Questions

1. What is culture?
2. What are the primary characteristics of culture?
3. Describe the difference between high-context and low-context cultures.
4. What are cultural clusters?
5. What are individualism and collectivism? How do they differ?
6. Discuss the differences in pay systems between U.S. and Japanese firms. To what extent are these differences culturally determined?
7. What is power orientation?
8. What is uncertainty orientation?
9. What are aggressive and passive goal behaviors? How do they differ?
10. What is the self-reference criterion?

Questions for Discussion

1. How can international businesspeople avoid relying on the self-reference criterion when dealing with people from other cultures?
2. U.S. law protects women from job discrimination, but many countries do not offer women such protection. Suppose several important job opportunities arise at overseas factories owned by your firm. These factories, however, are located in countries that severely restrict the working rights of women, and you fear that female managers will be ineffective there. Should you adopt gender-blind selection policies for these positions? Does it make a difference if you have good reason to fear for the physical safety of your female managers? Does it make a difference if the restrictions are cultural rather than legal in nature?
3. Under what circumstances should international businesspeople impose the values of their culture on foreigners with whom they do business? Does it make a difference if the activity is conducted in the home or the host country?
4. How would you evaluate yourself on each of Hofstede's dimensions?
5. Assume you have just been transferred by your firm to a new facility in a foreign location. How would you go about assessing the country's culture along Hofstede's dimensions? How would you incorporate your findings into conducting business there?

Building Global Skills

This exercise will help give you insights into how cultural and social factors affect international business decisions. Your instructor will divide the class into groups of four or five people. Each group then picks any three products from the first column of the following list and any three countries from the second column. (Your instructor may instead assign each group three products and three countries.)

Products	Countries
swimsuits	France
CD players	Singapore
desks and bookcases	Poland
men's neckties	Saudi Arabia
women's purses	Taiwan
throat lozenges	Italy
digital cameras	South Africa
shoes	Russia

Assume that your firm already markets its three products in your home country. It has a well-known trademark and slogan for each product, and each product is among the market leaders. Assume further that your firm has decided to begin exporting each product to each of the three countries. Research the cultures of those three countries to determine how, if at all, you may need to adjust packaging, promotion, advertising, and so forth in order to maximize your firm's potential for success. Do not worry too much about whether a market truly exists (assume that market research has already determined that one does). Focus instead on how your product will be received in each country given that country's culture.

1. What were your primary sources of information about the three countries? How easy or difficult was it to find information?
2. Can you think of specific products that are in high demand in your home country that would simply not work in other specific countries because of cultural factors?
3. How do you think foreign firms assess your home culture as they contemplate introducing their products into your market?

Ten years ago, most Americans had never heard of AFLAC, a $21-billion insurance company based in Columbus, Georgia. Thanks to AFLAC's new mascot, this is no longer the case. The company's attention-grabbing advertising campaign, which began in 2000, features a helpful but frustrated duck that fails to get people to acknowledge his presence or the company's name. Nonetheless, the duck's efforts appear to be paying off. According to advertising surveys, 90 percent of Americans are now aware of the AFLAC brand; more importantly, policies in force have risen more than 50 percent and annual premiums have more than doubled since the duck commercials began in the United States. And the AFLAC duck has done more than simply increase the company's American sales. AFLAC now sells the duck on its website and donates the proceeds to a children's cancer center in Atlanta. During the Christmas season, AFLAC teams up with a major department store chain to sell special-edition AFLAC holiday ducks. To date, $3 million has been donated to 40 children's hospitals around the country from their sale.

Despite the duck's efforts, AFLAC is still a small player in the U.S. market. Its $5.1 billion of revenue in the United States is dwarfed by such insurers as AIG, Prudential, or MetLife. Such is not the case in Japan, where an estimated 25 percent of the populace has purchased AFLAC insurance. AFLAC does more than 70 percent of its business in Japan. Its assets in Japan are huge—$87.1 billion—compared to only $13.1 billion in the United States. Thus, AFLAC is a rarity among American multinational corporations—its dominant market is Japan, not the United States.

AFLAC specializes in supplemental insurance—insurance that covers specific types of problems, such as cancer, disability, or accidents. The company was founded on a shoestring in 1955 as the American Family Life Assurance Company. The three founding brothers—Paul, Bill, and John Amos—scraped together $40,000 to launch the enterprise. In its early years the company struggled through many crises; once the Amos brothers were so short of cash they had to sell off the office furniture.

AFLAC's big break came when John Amos visited the Osaka World's Fair in 1970. He noticed that many Japanese walked around in surgical masks to reduce the spread of respiratory infections. Amos believed that such health-conscious consumers would be prime candidates for supplemental insurance. Entering the Japanese market was no picnic, however. It took AFLAC four years to receive regulatory clearance to begin marketing its products there.

AFLAC initially focused on selling cancer life insurance in Japan. As its knowledge of the market grew, it added accident, nursing care, medical, and other specialty policies to its product line. It has enjoyed continual growth in the years it has operated in Japan. AFLAC's competitive strength lies in its distribution network. Its products are sold by an army of licensed sales associates, some 115,000 strong, working through 19,600 independent insurance agencies. Ninety-one percent of the companies listed on the Tokyo Stock Exchange offer AFLAC products to their employees through payroll deduction programs.

AFLAC strives to deliver high-quality service to its customers. In 2010, the average claim was settled by AFLAC in four business days. The company has also adapted its operating procedures to the needs of the local market. Consider its human resource practices. When the company first ventured into Japan, it copied the lifetime employment and seniority-based pay and promotion policies then current in Japan. In the past several years, some Japanese companies have switched to job-based reward systems, in which salaries are based upon the skill requirements and difficulties of the job. So too has AFLAC.

AFLAC has added some "made in USA" features to its Japanese operations. Nearly half of its Japanese employees have been granted stock options, reinforcing their commitment to the company's future. It has funded AFLAC Parents' House in Tokyo, providing a place to stay for families whose children have been sent to Tokyo to receive medical treatment for pediatric cancer and other life-threatening diseases. AFLAC also funds college scholarships for Japanese high school students who have lost a parent to cancer.

AFLAC is the largest provider of supplemental insurance in Japan. Its Japanese revenues reached $16 billion in 2010. Given the graying of the Japanese market—older folks tend to buy more insurance—the high profit margins of its product line, and an overburdened Japanese health care system that is shifting costs to consumers, AFLAC believes that the profitability of its Japanese operations will continue to grow.

AFLAC does face numerous challenges, of course. For many years it benefited from the Japanese government's restrictive regulation of the country's financial services sector, which discouraged competition and price-cutting. To combat Japan's decade-long economic slump, the government relaxed its regulation of financial services, a process known as the Regulatory Big Bang. In 2001, the Ministry of Finance allowed additional firms to begin selling supplemental insurance, including domestic giants like Tokio Marine & Fire and Nippon Life. To date, the increased competition hasn't dethroned AFLAC from its market-leading perch. Its operating costs are less than those of its rivals. To maintain this edge, AFLAC has streamlined its operations, allowing sales agents to submit policy applications online and introducing new online billing techniques. To bolster its sales position, AFLAC stepped up its recruitment and training of sales agents and developed new products for them to sell. It entered into a strategic alliance with Dai-ichi Mutual Life, the second-largest life insurance company in Japan. Dai-ichi Mutual's 50,000-person sales force helps market AFLAC's supplemental policies to retail customers; in 2010, Dai-ichi agents sold 97,000 AFLAC cancer policies.

In 2001, AFLAC took another bold step—it brought the duck to Japan! The Japanese translation for "quack" is *ga-ga,* and Japanese consumers proved to be as "gaga" for the duck as

Americans were. Surveys of Japanese consumers report that TV commercials featuring the AFLAC duck consistently rank first or second in popularity in the insurance category. In 2009, AFLAC tinkered with the duck's design, blending it with the traditional *maneki neko* cat (the ceramic figurine of a cat with a raised paw) to create the *maneki neko* duck, which AFLAC now features in many of its advertisements for family-oriented insurance products. (You might wish to watch http://www.youtube.com/watch?v=cZLK04-4ZfU&feature=related or http://www.youtube.com/watch?v=LOnTM88qSO4&feature=related.)

Case Questions

1. AFLAC introduced the AFLAC duck in the U.S. market to build brand awareness there. However, AFLAC's brand awareness is very high in Japan. Should AFLAC use the same advertising campaign in Japan as it does in the United States? Is there any value to having identical advertising in both markets? Having introduced the *maneki neko* duck in Japan, should it now introduce it in the U.S. market as well?

2. How important is it for AFLAC to adapt its business practices to the Japanese way of doing things? Should AFLAC act more Japanese or more American in doing business in Japan?

3. AFLAC built its dominant position in the Japanese supplemental insurance market because Japanese regulators actively discouraged new entrants into this market. The Financial Big Bang policy now encourages new entrants into the supplemental insurance market. What has AFLAC done to protect its market position? What else can AFLAC do?

4. AFLAC is a rarity among U.S. companies inasmuch as the Japanese market accounts for more than 70 percent of its business. Does this reliance on the Japanese market create any special challenges for AFLAC? Does it present any unique opportunities for the company?

Sources: AFLAC Incorporated Annual Report for 2010; "AFLAC: Its Ducks Are Not in a Row," *Business Week*, February 2, 2004, p. 52; "AFLAC Duck Loses Some Quacking on Way to Japan," *USA Today*, May 7, 2003 (online); *AFLAC Incorporated Annual Report for 2002*; Charles D. Lake II, "Developing new opportunities in a weak Japanese economy: AFLAC adapts to change," *Japan Economic Currents*, May 2002, No. 20, pp. 4ff.; "Bullish on AFLAC's duck," *Business Week Online*, April 30, 2002; "AFLAC reaches new milestone," *Columbus Ledger-Enquirer*, March 19, 2002 (online); "Duck and coverage," *Fortune*, August 13, 2001 (online); "Duck ads have 'em flocking to AFLAC," *USA Today*, September 18, 2000 (online).

Endnotes

1. "The overseas Chinese: A driving force," *The Economist*, July 18, 1992, pp. 21–24.
2. Nancy Adler, *International Dimensions of Organizational Behavior*, 3rd ed. (Cincinnati: South-Western College Publishing, 1997), pp. 15–16.
3. "Show of raw capitalism fails to fire Japan's bosses," *Financial Times*, April 19, 2006, p. 6.
4. Vern Terpstra and Kenneth David, *The Cultural Environment of International Business* (Cincinnati: South-Western College Publishing, 1985), p. 20.
5. John R. Schermerhorn, Jr., "Language effects in cross-cultural management research: An empirical study and a word of caution," *Proceedings of the Academy of Management*, 1987, p. 103.
6. John C. Condon and Fathi Yousef, *An Introduction to Intercultural Communication* (New York: Bobbs-Merrill, 1975), p. 174; Jon P. Alston, *The American Samurai: Blending American and Japanese Business Practices* (New York: Walter de Gruyter, 1986), p. 325.
7. Adler, p. 16.
8. "Going global," *Wall Street Journal*, October 16, 1992, p. R20.
9. "Spanish firms discover Latin American business as new world of profit," *Wall Street Journal*, May 23, 1996, p. A1.
10. "Plain English gets harder in global era," *Wall Street Journal*, November 5, 2007, p. B1.
11. "French not the lingua franca in the boardroom," *Financial Times*, March 25–26, 2006, p. 1.
12. "Plain English gets harder in global era," *Wall Street Journal*, November 5, 2007, p. B1.
13. "Some firms resume manufacturing in U.S. after foreign fiascoes," *Wall Street Journal*, October 14, 1986, p. 1, 27.
14. Terpstra and David, p. 37.
15. "A word in your ear: keep it slow and simple," *Financial Times*, August 25, 2008 (online).
16. "How to tell when yes really means no," *Wall Street Journal*, October 31, 2007 (online).
17. Henry W. Lane and Joseph J. Distefano, *International Management Behavior* (Boston: PWS-Kent Publishing, 1992), p. 214.
18. Ibid., p. 3.
19. "Touchy subject: Doing business where hugs replace handshakes," *Wall Street Journal*, December 19, 2007 (online).
20. Gary P. Ferraro, *The Cultural Dimension of International Business* (Upper Saddle River, NJ: Prentice Hall, 1990), p. 82.
21. Ibid., p. 76.
22. Jon P. Alston, "Wa, Guanxi, and Inhwa: Managerial principles in Japan, China, and Korea," *Business Horizons*, March–April 1989, pp. 26–31.
23. "Inside a 'power lunch'," *Wall Street Journal*, January 7, 2008 (online).

24. "A village in a million," *The Economist*, December 18, 2010, pp. 59ff.

25. "Nigeria's mad men," *The Economist*, April 28, 2011 (online).

26. "Nike tries to quell two of its disputes," *Houston Chronicle*, June 25, 1997, p. 5C.

27. Ferraro, p. 99.

28. Gavin Kennedy, *Doing Business Abroad* (New York: Simon & Schuster, 1985), pp. 97–98.

29. "Miyazawa, making waves, seeks to cut the clout of Tokyo University's alumni," *Wall Street Journal*, March 5, 1992, p. A12.

30. "India's languishing countryside," *The Economist*, December 18, 2010, pp. 59ff.

31. "The caste buster," *New York Times*, December 30, 2010 (online); "Caste away," *Wall Street Journal*, June 23, 2007, p. A1.

32. Edward T. Hall, *Beyond Culture* (Garden City, NY: Anchor Press, 1976).

33. Edward T. Hall and Mildred Reed Hall, *Understanding Cultural Differences* (Yarmouth, ME: Intercultural Press, 1990), pp. 72–73.

34. Edward T. Hall and Mildred Reed Hall, *Hidden Differences* (Garden City, NY: Doubleday, 1987), pp. 9–10.

35. Bruce Kogut and Harbir Singh, "The effect of national culture on the choice of entry mode," *Journal of International Business Studies*, Fall 1988, pp. 411–432.

36. Geert Hofstede, *Culture's Consequences: International Differences in Work Related Values* (Beverly Hills, CA: Sage, 1980).

37. We have taken the liberty of changing some of the labels Hofstede applied to each of the dimensions. The terms we have chosen are more descriptive, simpler, and more self-evident in their meaning.

38. Ferraro, p. 157.

39. Adler, pp. 45–46; Andre Laurent, "The cultural diversity of Western conceptions of management," *International Studies of Management and Organization*, vol. XIII, no. 1–2 (Spring–Summer 1983), pp. 75–96.

40. Ferraro, p. 162.

41. "Korean Air bucks tradition to fix problems," *Wall Street Journal*, January 9, 2006, p. B1; "Crash near London points to Korean Air poor safety record," *Financial Times*, December 24, 1999, p. 2; "Pilot error is cited in Korea Air crash; FAA is criticized on foreign oversight," *Wall Street Journal*, November 3, 1999, p. A6; "Korean Air confronts dismal safety record rooted in its culture," *Wall Street Journal*, July 7, 1999, p. A1; "Korean Air to hire more foreign pilots," *Wall Street Journal*, April 15, 1999, p. A14.

42. Chuck C.Y. Kwok and Solomon Tadesse, "National culture and financial systems," *Journal of International Business Studies*, vol. 37 (2006), pp. 227–247.

43. "Behind the rush to add women to Norway's boards," *Wall Street Journal*, December 10, 2007, p. B1.

44. "In Sweden, men can have it all," *New York Times*, June 9, 2010 (online).

45. B. Bass and L. Eldridge, "Accelerated managers' objectives in twelve countries," *Industrial Relations*, vol. 12 (1973), pp. 158–171.

46. Susan C. Schneider, "National versus corporate culture: Implications for human resource management," *Human Resource Management*, vol. 27, no. 2 (Summer 1988), pp. 231–246.

47. Kathleen K. Reardon, "It's the thought that counts," *Harvard Business Review* (September–October 1984), pp. 136–141.

48. Stephen Kobrin, *International Expertise in American Business* (New York: Institute of International Education, 1984), p. 38.

49. "Firms grapple with language," *Wall Street Journal*, November 7, 1989, pp. B1, B10.

CHAPTER 5

Ethics and Social Responsibility in International Business

AFTER STUDYING THIS CHAPTER, YOU SHOULD BE ABLE TO:

1. Describe the nature of ethics.

2. Discuss ethics in cross-cultural and international contexts.

3. Identify the key elements in managing ethical behavior across borders.

4. Discuss social responsibility in cross-cultural and international contexts.

5. Identify and summarize the basic areas of social responsibility.

6. Discuss how organizations manage social responsibility across borders.

7. Identify and summarize the key regulations governing international ethics and social responsibility.

Access a host of interactive learning aids at **www.pearsonglobaleditions.com/ mymanagementlab** to help strengthen your understanding of the chapter concepts.

MyManagementLab

© US Coast Guard Photo/Alamy

BP: SAFETY FIRST OR PROFITS FIRST?

On April 20, 2010, the *Deepwater Horizon*, a drilling rig operating in the Gulf of Mexico, exploded, killing 11 workers and injuring another 17. Investigators determined that the likely cause was a column of methane gas that rose through the borehole under extremely high pressure, expanded upon reaching the surface, and then ignited, with catastrophic consequences. After burning for 36 hours, the rig collapsed and sank into the Gulf. It triggered one of the worst environmental disasters in recent American history, devastated the tourism and fishing industries throughout the Gulf Coast, and raised serious questions about the efficacy of government regulation and the safety of deepwater drilling.

The Deepwater Horizon was owned and operated by Swiss-headquartered Transocean. Under contract to BP, it was in the final stages of completing an exploratory well in mile-deep water in the Macondo Prospect. Halliburton, an experienced oil well service company, had just finished cementing in the well. Later testimony indicated that the rig technicians had failed to react to a buildup of gas pressures in the well; they also ignored a critical test of the cement job itself. A few days after the explosion, Coast Guard officials noticed that oil was leaking from the drill site. Initial estimates provided by BP officials were 1,000 barrels a day; over time the estimate progressively rose to between 35,000 and 60,000 barrels per day. In total, about 5 million barrels of oil leaked into the Gulf before BP finally capped the well after 87 days on July 15.

While officials of BP, Transocean, and Halliburton found fault with each other's performance—and independent investigations indicated that all three made mistakes—ultimate responsibility lay with BP, as owner of the Macondo well. Investigators uncovered a series of decisions by BP officials that—at least in hindsight—suggested that the company was more worried about controlling costs than promoting safety. The Macondo project was $58 million over budget and six weeks behind schedule, and internal memos indicated that BP managers on the rig were under increasing pressure to complete the project quickly. The National Commission on the BP Deepwater Oil Spill and Offshore Drilling, a group of independent experts selected by President Obama, concluded that "systematic failures in risk management ... place in doubt the safety culture of the entire industry" (report at p. vii).

Unfortunately, the Deepwater Horizon tragedy was not the first time that BP's commitment to safety was called into question. BP's Texas City refinery suffered a fire in 2004; in 2005 a deadly explosion at the same plant killed 15 individuals and injured 170 workers. A U.S. Department of Energy study cited deficiencies in the safety culture at BP as the root cause of the incident. OSHA fined BP $87 million after conducting a safety audit of the refinery in 2009, despite BP's claim that they had spent $1 billion improving the refinery. OSHA inspectors discovered problems with pressure-relief values during a 2006 inspection at BP's refinery in Toledo, Ohio, that the company jointly owned with Husky Oil. When OSHA returned to the Toledo facility in 2009, its inspectors determined that BP had replaced the problem valves that OSHA had cited in the 2006 inspection, but not other valves that suffered from the same problem. BP's safety performance at Prudhoe Bay in the Alaskan North Slope field has also raised concerns. In 2006, over 5,000 barrels of oil leaked from corroded pipelines there in two separate incidents; the leakage was attributed to poor maintenance and inadequate inspections. In 2011, BP agreed to settle a civil lawsuit over these spills for $25 million, after having previously paid a $20 million fine for violating the Clean Water Act.

To address these concerns, the BP Board of Directors replaced CEO John Browne with Tony Hayward in May 2007. Hayward was often quoted as saying he had two primary challenges, to cut costs and to improve the company's safety record, both of which were below industry standards. However, BP continued to have problems. The Macondo spill was preceded by a small spill at its Atlantis platform in the Gulf of Mexico in 2008. The spill—only 193 barrels—was caused by a rupture in a piece of steel tubing, which was connected to a defective pump, which the company had chosen not to repair in order to control costs. Company executives praised employees for the lean operations at the Atlantis operation—4 percent below budget—instead of criticizing them for the spill. Its North Slope operations also continued to experience problems. In September 2008, two segments of pipe flew 900 feet after a high-pressure natural gas pipeline ruptured. That pipeline had not been inspected for over a decade. A two-foot gash in an oil pipeline in November 2009 resulted in a 1,000 barrel-spill of oil, gas, and water, damaging the tundra. Poor or deferred maintenance again appears to be the culprit.

BP's commitment to safety was further called into question when it suspended Phil Dziubinski, BP's ethics and compliance officer in Alaska—a position the company created as part of its renewed commitment to safety—the day after the Macondo well exploded. The company claimed the action was part of a corporate reorganization in which 200 of its professional staff were let go. Dziubinski believes he was drummed out of the company for pushing safety issues too aggressively. He was particularly concerned that the company's heavy use of overtime was endangering safety due to worker fatigue. Dziubinski filed suit against BP for wrongful dismissal. The case was later settled out of court.

Despite its safety performance, BP executives continue to assert that "BP's absolute No. 1 priority is safe and reliable operations."[1] ■

Globalization offers businesses, employees, and entrepreneurs myriad new opportunities to seek new markets, broaden their product lines, and lower their cost of production. And the introduction of new products and new ways of doing business can bring major improvements in the lives of the world's poorest people. But globalization also presents international businesses with new challenges, such as the need to define appropriate ethical standards and to operate in a socially responsible manner in all the markets and countries in which the firm does business.

One important issue is the firm's responsibility to provide a safe working environment for its employees and diligent protection of the natural environment, as the chapter's opening case highlighted. Another issue is the appropriate response to the cost pressures that firms face as a result of globalization. It has long been common for firms to move production and low-skill jobs from their home country to other countries, often to capitalize on lower labor costs. But these practices sometimes result in unfavorable publicity and may even expose fundamental issues associated with potential human rights violations. For instance, for years large fruit juice distributors like Minute Maid, Tropicana, and Nestlé bought fruit juices from suppliers in South America. Many of these suppliers relied heavily on child labor to harvest oranges, lemons, and other fruits. Children as young as nine years old were commonly taken out of school by their impoverished parents and put to work in the citrus groves. These parents often saw no problem with this behavior because they themselves had also picked fruit as children. A similar set of issues were raised regarding Nestlé's, Cargill's, and Archer Daniels Midland's purchasing of cocoa from West African plantations that employed 280,000 children, some of whom were allegedly treated no better than slaves.[2]

However, the issues may not be as clear as they might at first seem. For example, many people from developed countries would agree that it is unethical for a business to outsource production to an offshore factory that relies on child labor and/or that maintains unsafe working conditions. But

Danone SA, France's largest food conglomerate, has teamed with Bangladesh's Grameen Bank to create Shoktidoi yogurt as a means of addressing the twin problems of malnutrition and rural poverty. The fortified yogurt provides children with 30 percent of their daily nutritional needs. The company is recruiting local villagers as distribution agents, thus providing a new source of employment for the rural population.

HALEY/SIPA/Newscom

people in that country might argue that as unattractive as they might seem to outsiders, those jobs are superior to the ones that would otherwise be available.

This chapter explores these and other issues from an international business perspective. We first examine the nature of ethics and social responsibility in international business. We then discuss ethics in cross-cultural and international contexts. Next, we describe how firms attempt to manage ethical behavior across borders. Social responsibility in cross-cultural and international contexts is then introduced and discussed. After describing the major areas of social responsibility, we discuss how firms manage social responsibility across borders. Finally, we conclude with a summary of some of the major laws that attempt to regulate international ethics and social responsibility.

The Nature of Ethics and Social Responsibility in International Business

The fundamental reason for the existence of a business is to create value (usually in the form of profits) for its owners. Furthermore, most individuals work in order to earn income to support themselves and/or their families. As a result, the goal of most of the decisions made on behalf of a business or an individual within a business is to increase income (for the business and/or the individual) and/or reduce expenses (again, for the business and/or the individual). In most cases businesspeople make decisions and engage in behaviors, for both their personal conduct and the conduct of their organizations, that are acceptable to society. But sometimes they deviate too much from what others see as acceptable.

In recent years, it seems that the incidence of unacceptable behaviors on behalf of businesses and/or people within businesses has increased. Regardless of whether this increase is real or only illusory, such high-profile and well-documented cases as Enron, WorldCom, Tyco, and Arthur Andersen have certainly captured the attention of managers, investors, and regulators everywhere. Nor has this been a distinctly American problem. Businesses such as Satyam Computer Services (an Indian computer services firm engaged in wholesale accounting fraud), Royal Ahold NV (a Dutch grocery chain admitting to accounting irregularities), and Nestlé (a Swiss firm accused of violating World Health Organization codes controlling the marketing of infant formula in less-developed countries) have also caught their share of attention for improprieties, real or imagined.[3] Hence, just as the business world is becoming increasingly internationalized, so too is the concern for ethical and socially responsible conduct by managers and the businesses they run.

We define **ethics** as an individual's personal beliefs about whether a decision, behavior, or action is right or wrong.[4] Hence, what constitutes ethical behavior varies from one person to another. For instance, one person who finds a 20-euro banknote on the floor of an empty room may believe that it is okay to simply keep it, whereas another may feel compelled to turn it in to the lost-and-found department and a third to give it to charity. Further, although ethics is defined in the context of an individual's belief, the concept of **ethical behavior** usually refers to behavior that conforms to generally accepted social norms. **Unethical behavior**, then, is behavior that does not conform to generally accepted social norms.

An individual's ethics are determined by a combination of factors. People start to form ethical frameworks as children in response to their perceptions of the behavior of their parents and other adults they deal with. As children grow and enter school, they are influenced by peers with whom they interact in the classroom and playground. Everyday occurrences that force the participants to make moral choices—a friend asking to copy homework, a father accidently denting a parked car when the only witness is his child, or a child who sees his mother receive too much change from the supermarket cashier—shape people's ethical beliefs and behavior as they grow into adulthood. Similarly, a person's religious training contributes to his or her ethics. Some religious beliefs, for instance, promote rigid codes of behaviors and standards of conduct, while others provide for more flexibility. A person's values also influence ethical standards. People who place financial gain and personal advancement at the top of their list of priorities, for example, will adopt personal codes of ethics that promote the pursuit of wealth. Thus, they may be ruthless in efforts to gain these rewards, regardless of the costs to others. In contrast, people who clearly establish their family and/or friends as their top priority will adopt different ethical standards.

A society generally adopts formal laws that reflect the prevailing ethical standards—the social norms—of its members. For example, because most people consider theft to be unethical, laws have been passed in most countries to make such behaviors illegal and to proscribe ways of punishing those who do steal. But although laws attempt to be clear and unambiguous, their application and interpretation still lead to ethical ambiguities. For example, most people would agree that forcing employees to work excessive hours, especially for no extra compensation, is unethical. Accordingly, laws have been passed in some countries to define work and pay standards. But applying that law to organizational settings can still result in ambiguous situations that can be interpreted in different ways. In Japan, for example, by custom a junior employee cannot leave the office until the more senior person departs, whereas in the United States the boss is often supposed to be the last to leave. These expectations are often more powerful in shaping behavior than the mere existence of a law.

These definitions suggest the following generalizations:

- Individuals have their own personal belief system about what constitutes ethical and unethical behavior. For example, most people will be able to readily describe simple behaviors (such as stealing or returning found property) as ethical or unethical.
- People from the same cultural contexts are likely to hold similar—but not necessarily identical—beliefs as to what constitutes ethical and unethical behavior. For example, a group of middle-class residents of Brazil will generally agree with one another as to whether a behavior such as stealing from an employer is ethical or unethical.
- Individuals may be able to rationalize behaviors based on circumstances. For instance, the person who finds a 20-euro banknote and knows who lost it may quickly return it to the owner. But if the money is found in an empty room, the finder might justify keeping it on the grounds that the owner is not likely to claim it anyway.
- Individuals may deviate from their own belief systems based on circumstances. For instance, in most situations people would agree that it is unethical to steal and therefore they do not steal. But if a person has no money and no food, that individual may steal food as a means of survival.
- Ethical values are strongly affected by national cultures and customs. **Values** are the things a person feels to be important. As we discussed in Chapter 4, values often center on such things as time, age, education, and status. Culture has a direct impact on the value systems of the members of that culture. Values in turn affect how those individuals define ethical versus unethical behavior. For instance, in Japan status is often reflected by group membership. As a result, behavior that helps the group is more likely to be seen as ethical, whereas behavior that harms the group is likely to be viewed as unethical. For example, many Americans condoned the looting that occurred in New Orleans in the chaos that followed Hurricane Katrina in 2005, in the belief that an individual's rights to survival superseded property rights. Yet under similar dire circumstances, looting was far less prevalent in Japan after its devastating 2011 earthquake and tsunami.

Members of one culture may view a behavior as unethical, whereas members of another may view that same behavior as perfectly reasonable. An American businessman might report to the police an American customs officer who requested $100 in a envelope to clear a shipment of imported goods, whereas his Kenyan or Indonesian counterparts would likely make the payment without even being asked. These differences can create worrisome ethical dilemmas for international business practitioners when the ethical standards of their home country differ from that of the host country. Nonetheless, we want to emphasize that ethics is a distinctly individual concept, rather than an organizational one. In general, the relationship between an organization and its environment revolves around the concept of social responsibility, a topic we address later in this chapter. But as we discuss ethics per se in the first part of the chapter, keep in mind that we are focusing on individuals in organizations, as opposed to the organization itself.

Ethics in Cross-Cultural and International Contexts

A useful way to characterize ethical behaviors in cross-cultural and international contexts is in terms of how an organization treats its employees, how employees treat the organization, and how both the organization and its employees treat other economic agents. These relationships are illustrated in Figure 5.1.

FIGURE 5.1

Ethics in a Cross-Cultural Context

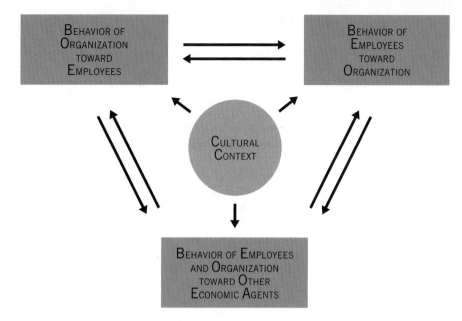

How an Organization Treats Its Employees

One important area of cross-cultural and international ethics is the treatment of employees by the organization. At one extreme, an organization can strive to hire the best people, to provide ample opportunity for skills and career development, to provide appropriate compensation and benefits, and to generally respect the personal rights and dignity of each employee. At the other extreme, a firm can hire using prejudicial or preferential criteria, can intentionally limit development opportunities, can provide the minimum compensation allowable, and can treat employees callously and with little regard to personal dignity.

In practice, the areas most susceptible to ethical variation include hiring and firing practices, wages and working conditions, and employee privacy and respect. In some countries both ethical and legal guidelines suggest that hiring and firing decisions should be based solely on an individual's ability to perform the job. But in other countries it is perfectly legitimate to give preferential treatment to individuals based on gender, ethnicity, age, or other non-work-related factors. Consider the case of Daslu, a São Paulo high-fashion women's clothing store catering to the wealthiest of Brazil's wealthy. Its sales staff is drawn exclusively from the same social circles as its clientele. Daslu also hires a small army of assistants—colloquially known as *aventalzinhos*, or "little aprons"—to aid the sales staff. The typical *aventalzinho* works longer hours, gets paid less, has worked for the store more years, and is more knowledgeable about the merchandise than the sales staff. Yet *aventalzinhos* are unlikely to be promoted to sales positions, because these individuals come from the wrong social class.[5]

Wages and working conditions, while regulated in some countries, are also areas for potential controversy. A manager paying an employee less than he or she deserves, simply because the manager knows the employee cannot afford to quit and so will not risk losing his or her job by complaining, might be considered unethical. Similarly, in some countries people would agree that an organization is obligated to protect the privacy of its employees. A manager spreading a rumor that an employee has AIDS or is having an affair with a coworker is generally seen as an unethical breach of privacy. Likewise, the manner in which an organization responds to and addresses issues associated with sexual harassment also involves employee privacy and related rights.

Managers in international organizations face a number of clear challenges with regard to these matters. The firm must deal with country-specific ethical issues regarding its treatment of employees, but must also be prepared to contend with international comparisons as well. Consider the myriad ethical dilemmas posed by the practice of outsourcing production to overseas locations. From one perspective it can be argued that firms are ethically bound to move jobs wherever they can be performed for the least cost. But some critics would argue that this practice is unethical, for it devalues the workers' numerous contributions to the firm and ignores the hardships imposed on displaced workers. In some countries, such as Japan, aggressive outsourcing that results in domestic layoffs violates the firm's implicit agreement to provide lifetime employment. The ethical issues facing the firm's managers do not end once the production is moved overseas. Contemplate the following passage from *Fortune*, a U.S. business magazine that does not have the reputation of being unsympathetic to the virtues of free markets:

> For the privilege of working 12-hour shifts seven days a week in a factory where she makes plastic casings for Motorola cellphones, Mary, 30, will be in debt for years to come. To secure work at the Motorola subcontractor, which is in Taiwan, Mary had to pay $2,400 to a labor broker in her native Philippines. She didn't have that kind of money, so she borrowed from a local money lender at an interest rate of 10% per month. That payment, however, got her only as far as Taiwan. A second labor broker met Mary at the Taipei airport and informed her of his separate $3,900 fee before delivering her to the new job.
>
> Before she left the Philippines, Mary rejoiced at the $460 she would be earning in Taiwan; it was more than five times what she could make doing similar work, if she could find it, in her own country. But once in Taiwan she began to realize that after the brokers' fees and other deductions, she would be left with almost nothing. Out of her monthly check came $215 to pay the Taiwanese broker, $91 for Taiwanese income tax, $72 for her room and board at the factory dorm, and $86 for a compulsory contribution to a savings bond she will get only if she completes her three-year contract. After 18 months she will have repaid the Taiwanese labor broker. But she still must contend with her Philippine debt and its rapidly compounding interest.[6]

Hundreds of thousands of workers have obtained their jobs in Asian factories through brokers similar to the ones used by this Philippine woman. She entered into these arrangements willingly, although out of economic desperation. However, the Philippine law that limits a broker to charging only one month's pay for his service was ignored. Managers of multinational corporations that outsource their production to these facilities need to consider carefully their ethical responsibilities to workers, such as Mary, who are snared in debt bondage.

How Employees Treat the Organization

Numerous ethical issues also relate to how employees treat the organization. The central ethical issues in this relationship include conflicts of interest, secrecy and confidentiality, and honesty. A conflict of interest occurs when a decision potentially benefits the individual to the possible detriment of the organization. Ethical perceptions of the importance of conflicts of interest vary from culture to culture. Consider the simple example of a supplier offering a gift to a company employee. Some companies believe that such a gift can create conflicts of interest. They fear that the employee will begin to favor the supplier that offers the best gifts, rather than the supplier whose product is best for the firm. To guard against such dangers, many companies have policies that forbid their buyers from accepting gifts from suppliers. Some U.S. newspapers and broadcast media, such as the *New York Times*, even refuse to allow their employees to accept free meals for fear that their journalistic judgments and integrity might be compromised. But in other countries exchanges of gifts between a company's employees and its customers or suppliers is perfectly acceptable. In Japan, for instance, such exchanges are common (and expected) during the *ochugen* and *oseibo* gift-giving periods. *Ochugen*, which occurs in July, originally developed to pay homage to the spirit of one's ancestors, although it has evolved to reflect one's best wishes for summer. *Oseibo* gifts, which are offered in December, represent a token of gratitude for favors and loyalty shown throughout the year. Japanese department stores helpfully stock their shelves with appropriate goods at every price level during *ochugen* and *oseibo*, as well-defined cultural norms govern the level and appropriateness of the gifts to be exchanged by businesspersons, which depends upon the nature of the business relationship, its length, and the amount of business transacted. Note, however, that determining an appropriate gift by the amount of business transacted is exactly the kind of behavior that arouses suspicion of conflict of interest in many North American and European companies.

China offers a similar set of challenges to firms wishing to control conflicts of interest. Much business in China is conducted through *guanxi*, which is based on reciprocal exchanges of favors. Because of the importance of *guanxi*, North American and European firms operating in China often face a difficult task in adapting to the norms of Chinese business culture while continuing to honor company policy regarding conflicts of interest. Typically one finds that in high-context, collectivist, and power-respecting cultures, gift exchanges are a more important part of the way business is done than in low-context, individualistic, and power-tolerant cultures.

Divulging company secrets is viewed as unethical in some countries, but not in others. Employees who work for businesses in highly competitive industries—electronics, software, and fashion apparel, for example—might be tempted to sell information about company plans to competitors. Consider the plight of Durawool, an American steel-wool manufacturer. It was shocked to learn that Chinese law offered it little protection when one of its local employees left the company's Chinese subsidiary and promptly started a rival firm using Durawool's technology.[7] Motorola and SI Group, a U.S. chemical manufacturer, are currently engaged in legal struggles with former Chinese managers they accuse of similar behavior.[8]

A third area of concern is honesty in general. Relatively common problems in this area include such things as using a business telephone to make personal long distance calls, stealing supplies, and padding expense accounts. In some business cultures, such actions are viewed as unethical; in others, employees may develop a sense of entitlement and believe that "if I'm working here, then it's the company's responsibility to take care of my needs." The potential for conflict is clear when individuals from such divergent ethical perspectives work together.

How Employees and the Organization Treat Other Economic Agents

The third major perspective for viewing ethics involves the relationship between the firm and its employees with other economic agents. The primary agents of interest include customers, competitors, stockholders, suppliers, dealers, and labor unions. The behaviors between the organization and these agents that may be subject to ethical ambiguity include advertising and promotions, financial disclosures, ordering and purchasing, shipping and solicitations, bargaining and negotiation, and other business relationships.

For example, businesses in the global pharmaceuticals industry have been under growing criticism because of the rapid escalation of the prices they charge for their newest and most powerful drugs.[9] These firms argue that they need to invest heavily in research and development programs to develop new drugs, and higher prices are needed to cover these costs. Yet given the extent of the public health crises that plague some areas of the world—such as HIV/AIDS in sub-Saharan Africa—some activists argue that the pharmaceutical manufacturers should lower their prices and/or relax their patent protection so that patients in poorer countries can afford to purchase the drugs needed to treat such diseases. Another growing concern in recent years involves financial reporting by businesses. Because of the complexities inherent in the finances of large multinational corporations, some of them have been very aggressive in presenting their financial positions in a very positive light. And in at least a few cases, some managers have substantially overstated their earnings projections and/or hidden financial problems so as to entice more investors.[10]

Differences in business practices across countries create additional ethical complexities for firms and their employees. In some countries small bribes and side payments are a normal and customary part of doing business; foreign companies often follow the local custom regardless of what is considered an ethical practice at home. In China, for instance, local journalists expect their cab fare to be paid if they are to cover a business-sponsored news conference. In Indonesia the normal time for a foreigner to get a driver's license is over a year, but it can be "expedited" for an extra $100. And in Romania, building inspectors routinely expect a "tip" for a favorable review.[11]

At times, however, the sums involved are not small. A U.S. power-generating company lost a $320 million contract in the Middle East because government officials demanded a $3 million bribe. A Japanese firm paid the bribe and won the contract. Enron allegedly had a big project in India canceled because newly elected officials demanded bribes. Although such payments are illegal under U.S. law (as well as the laws of several other countries), managers nonetheless dislike losing important contracts to less ethical rivals.

Managing Ethical Behavior Across Borders

Ethics reside in individuals, but many businesses nevertheless endeavor to manage the ethical behavior of their managers and employees by clearly establishing the fact that they expect them to engage in ethical behaviors. They also want to take appropriate steps to eliminate as much ambiguity as possible about what the companies view as ethical versus unethical behavior. The most common ways of doing this are through the use of guidelines or codes of ethics, ethics training, and organizational practices and the corporate culture.

Guidelines and Codes of Ethics

Many large multinationals, including Toyota, Siemens, General Mills, and Johnson & Johnson, have written guidelines that detail how employees are to treat suppliers, customers, competitors, and other stakeholders. Others, such as Philips, Nissan, Daewoo, Whirlpool, and Hewlett-Packard, have developed formal **codes of ethics**—written statements of the values and ethical standards that guide the firms' actions. However, the mere existence of a code of ethics does not ensure ethical behavior. It must be backed up by organizational practices and the company's corporate culture. (See "Venturing Abroad," *Siemens Pays—and Pays and Pays.*)

A multinational firm must make a decision as to whether to establish one overarching code for all of its global units or to tailor each one to its local context. Similarly, if a firm acquires a new foreign subsidiary, it must also decide whether to impose its corporate code on that subsidiary or allow it to retain the one it may have already been following. In order for a code to have value, of course, it must be clear and straightforward, it must address the major elements of ethical conduct relevant to its environment and business operations, and it must be adhered to when problems arise. In one classic folly, Enron's board of directors was once presented with a potentially lucrative venture that contradicted the firm's code of ethics. So what did the board do? It voted to set aside the code of ethics, approved the business venture, and then reinstated the code of ethics!

Ethics Training

Some multinational corporations address ethical issues proactively, by offering employees training in how to cope with ethical dilemmas. At Boeing, for example, line managers lead training sessions for other employees, and the company also has an ethics committee that reports directly to the board of directors. The training sessions involve discussions of different ethical dilemmas that employees might face and how they might best handle those dilemmas.

Again, one decision for international firms is whether to make ethics training globally consistent or tailored to local contexts. Regardless of which approach they use, though, most multinationals provide expatriates with localized ethics training to better prepare them for their foreign assignments. BP, for instance, prepares managers at its headquarters in London for future assignments to Russia by having them undergo training in the Russian language as well as in local business customs and practices and ethics.

Organizational Practices and the Corporate Culture

Organizational practices and the corporate culture also contribute to the management of ethical behavior. If the top leaders in a firm behave in an ethical manner and violations of ethical standards are promptly and appropriately addressed, then everyone in the organization will understand that the firm expects them to behave in an ethical manner—to make ethical decisions and to do the right things. But if top leaders appear to exempt themselves from ethical standards or choose to ignore or trivialize unethical behaviors, then the opposite message is being sent—that it's acceptable to do something that's unethical if you can get away with it.

One recent survey sheds some interesting light on how these practices are implemented in various countries. The survey focused specifically on the acceptability of bribing officials when doing business in foreign countries. This survey found that Russian, Chinese, Taiwanese, and South Korean firms found bribery to be relatively acceptable. Among the countries that found bribery to be unacceptable were Australia, Sweden, Switzerland, Austria, and Canada. Italy, Japan, and the United States fell in between the extremes.[12]

Kenya is one of the countries where bribery is almost a way of life. One study estimates that as many as two-thirds of individual and business involvements with Kenyan public officials involve paying a bribe.[13] Bribery and corruption is so extensive in China that some studies estimate that the costs of corruption have wiped out the equivalent of 13 to 16 percent of the country's GDP.[14] Many of the former Soviet republics face similar problems.

Yet firms should think twice—or more than twice—before engaging in such behavior, as "Venturing Abroad" indicates. Firms that gain reputations as bribe payers are asked to pay bribes; firms with the opposite reputation often are not. As one expert in the area notes:

> Viable companies can say "no." … [T]he U.S. electronics group Motorola not only refused a bribe request from a Latin American official but also said it would not conduct business in that country until the regime changed. Refusal of bribe requests requires a corporate culture

that supports the refusal of such requests. One of the most effective means of doing this is with a simple corporate code for managers and employees, affiliates and potential business partners. At a minimum, the code should refer to the laws that bind the company and prohibit bribery of foreign officials. The code should also describe the decision-making line for bribe requests and assure managers the company will back them when they refuse to pay a bribe.

Building this into the corporate culture ... can bring competitive advantage. The leading oil company Texaco (now part of Chevron), for example, earned such a fearsome reputation for not acceding to bribe requests that even at remote African border crossings Texaco's jeeps are sometimes waved through without any requests for a bribe.[15]

Social Responsibility in Cross-Cultural and International Contexts

As we have seen, ethics in business relate to individual managers and other employees and their decisions and behaviors. Organizations themselves do not have ethics but do relate to their environment in ways that often involve ethical dilemmas and decisions by individuals within the organization. These situations are generally referred to within the context of the organization's social responsibility. Specifically, **social responsibility** (sometimes called corporate social responsibility, or CSR) is the set of obligations an organization undertakes to protect and

---

VENTURING ABROAD | **SIEMENS PAYS—AND PAYS AND PAYS**

The saga of Siemens AG, the €76 billion Munich-based manufacturer of steam turbines, telecommunications equipment, medical scanners, and other sophisticated technology, provides a morality tale for firms pondering whether they should offer under-the-table payments to win lucrative international contracts. In October 2007, a German court fined Siemens €201 million ($284 million) for paying bribes. According to German court records, at least 77 separate bribes, totaling €12 million, were made by managers of Siemens's telecommunications equipment subsidiary to cabinet ministers and bureaucrats in Libya, Russia, and Nigeria. The court estimated the bribes generated €200 million in "unlawful economic advantages" for Siemens, which formed the basis for the magnitude of the fine. And earlier that year, another German court fined Siemens €38 million for bribes paid to Italian officials in the company's power generation subsidiary. Nor were the German prosecutors finished: In April 2008, they announced they were broadening their inquiries and contemplating criminal proceedings.

But the worst was not over for Siemens. The company was then investigated by the U.S. Justice Department and the Securities and Exchange Commission for violation of the Foreign Corrupt Practices Act and securities regulations. The SEC alleged that "Siemens created elaborate payment schemes to conceal the nature of its corrupt payments, and the Company's inadequate controls allowed the illicit conduct to flourish. The misconduct involved employees at all levels of the Company, including former senior management, and reveals a corporate culture that had long been at odds with the FCPA." The SEC uncovered 4,238 payments totaling $1.4 billion to bribe government officials in such countries as Venezuela, China, Israel, Bangladesh, Nigeria, Argentina, Vietnam, Russia, Mexico, and Iraq. In December 2008, Siemens agreed to pay the U.S. government $800 million to settle the charges against it: $350 million to the SEC for the securities charges and $450 million to the Department of Justice for the criminal charges. Siemens also paid an additional $569 million fine to the

German government. In addition, the company also agreed to pay the World Bank $100 million and to forgo bidding on World Bank contracts for two years.

Acknowledging the extent of the problem, Siemens's supervisory board replaced several of the firm's top executives with outsiders. The company's new general counsel, Peter Solmssen—like the new CEO Peter Löscher, he is a former General Electric executive—recognizes the challenges he and the company face. Notes Solmssen, "Corruption at Siemens was 'systemic' in recent years. There was a cultural acceptance that this was the way to do business around the world, and we have to change that." Among Löscher and Solmssen's first acts was an overhaul of the company's code of conduct and its compliance programs. In addition to transforming the firm's corporate culture, they face the task of restoring the firm's external reputation and credibility. And, of course, they need to maintain Siemens's competitiveness in the marketplace: No small trick, given the distraction of the company's legal problems and the ensuing drain on managerial attention and company resources. There is little doubt that Siemens will continue to pay for its misdeeds for a very long time.

Sources: "Siemens settles with World Bank on bribes," *Wall Street Journal*, July 3, 2009; "SEC charges Siemens AG for engaging in worldwide bribery," U.S. Securities and Exchange Commission, Press Release 2008-294 (December 15, 2008); U.S. District Court for the District of Columbia, *U.S. Securities and Exchange Commission v. Siemens Aktiengesellschaft*, Case: 1:08-cv-02167; "Siemens power unit investigated," *Wall Street Journal*, April 15, 2008 (online); "Siemens amnesty plan assists bribery probe," *Wall Street Journal*, March 5, 2008, p. A12 (includes Solmssen's quote); "Siemens internal review hits hurdles," *Wall Street Journal*, January 23, 2008, p. A18; "Inside bribery probe of Siemens," *Wall Street Journal*, December 28, 2007, p. A4; "Siemens ruling details bribery across the globe," *Wall Street Journal*, November 16, 2007, p. A1; "Siemens fine ends a bribery probe," *Wall Street Journal*, October 5, 2007, p. A2; "Siemens probe spotlights murky role of consultants," *Wall Street Journal*, April 20, 2007, p. A1.

enhance the society in which it functions. The complexities for managers in an international business are clear—balancing the ideal of a global stance on social responsibility against the local conditions that may compel differential approaches in the various countries where the firm does business.

A classic example of this relates to the tobacco industry. In several countries, such as the United States, South Africa, and the United Kingdom, tobacco companies are limited in their ability to advertise cigarettes and are required to post health warnings on cigarette packages. But many countries either have less restrictive limitations or no limitations whatsoever. The issue, then, is the extent to which a tobacco company should apply the most restrictive approach to all markets or else take advantage of the flexibility offered in some markets to actively promote the sale and use of tobacco products.

Areas of Social Responsibility

Organizations may exercise social responsibility toward their stakeholders, toward the natural environment, and toward general social welfare. Some organizations acknowledge their responsibilities in all three areas and strive diligently to meet each of them, but others emphasize only one or two areas of social responsibility. And a few acknowledge no social responsibility at all.

Organizational Stakeholders

Organizational stakeholders are those people and organizations that are directly affected by the practices of an organization and that have a stake in its performance.[16] Most companies that strive to be responsible to their stakeholders concentrate first and foremost on three main groups: customers, employees, and investors. They then select other stakeholders that are particularly relevant or important to the organization and then attempt to address their needs and expectations as well.

Organizations that are responsible to their customers strive to treat them fairly and honestly. They pledge to charge fair prices, to honor product warranties, to meet delivery commitments, and to stand behind the quality of the products they sell. Companies that have established excellent reputations in this area include L. L. Bean, Toyota, Land's End, Dell Computer, Daimler, and Volkswagen.

Organizations that are socially responsible in their dealings with employees treat their workers fairly, make them a part of the team, and respect their dignity and basic human needs. Organizations such as 3M Company, Hoechst AG, and Honda have all established strong reputations in this area. In addition, they also go to great lengths to find, hire, train, and promote qualified minorities.

To maintain a socially responsible stance toward investors, managers should follow proper accounting procedures, provide appropriate information to shareholders about the financial performance of the firm, and manage the organization to protect shareholder rights and investments. Moreover, they should be accurate and candid in their assessment of future growth and profitability and avoid even the appearance of improprieties involving such sensitive areas as insider trading, stock price manipulation, and the withholding of financial data.

The Natural Environment

A second critical area of social responsibility relates to the natural environment.[17] Not long ago, many organizations indiscriminately dumped sewage, waste products from production, and trash into streams and rivers, into the air, and on vacant land. When Royal Dutch Shell first explored the Amazon River Basin for potential drilling sites in the late 1980s, its crews ripped down trees and left a trail of garbage in their wake. Now, however, many laws regulate the disposal of waste materials. In many instances, companies themselves have become more socially responsible in their release of pollutants and general treatment of the environment. For example, when Shell launched its most recent exploration expedition into another area of the Amazon Basin, the group included a biologist to oversee environmental protection and an anthropologist to help the team more effectively interact with native tribes.[18] Similarly, lumber retailers like Home Depot and Wickes have agreed to sell only wood products certified as having been harvested using environment-friendly techniques.[19] Yet companies need to do more than "talk the talk." BP, for example, spent millions of pounds touting its concerns for the environment in a series of ads that played off its former name of British Petroleum, claiming BP meant "beyond petroleum" and promising innovative efforts to develop green energy sources. Gulf Coast shrimpers, crabbers, and motel owners and the Inupiat people of northern Alaska might rightly be skeptical of BP's environmental pledges.

Rainforests, such as this one on the Indonesian island of Bali, play a critical role in reducing greenhouse gases by absorbing atmospheric carbon through photosynthesis. Many lumber retailers, such as Home Depot and Wickes, have pledged to sell only wood products harvested using environmental-friendly methods.

© Leo Bruce Hempell/Dreamstime.com

Much remains to be done. Companies need to develop economically feasible ways to reduce acid rain and global warming; to avoid depleting the ozone layer; and to create alternative methods of handling sewage, hazardous wastes, and ordinary garbage.[20] Procter & Gamble, for example, is an industry leader in using recycled materials for containers, while many German firms aggressively use recycled materials whenever possible. Hyatt Corporation established a new company to help recycle waste products from its hotels. Conservation Corporation of Africa, a game lodge firm based in Johannesburg, strives to make its lodges as environmentally friendly as possible. And Starbucks pays its coffee suppliers a premium of 10 cents additional per pound if they demonstrate a commitment to protect the environment. The Internet is also seen as potentially playing an important role in resource conservation. This is due to the fact that many e-commerce businesses and transactions reduce both energy costs and pollution.[21]

General Social Welfare

Some people believe that in addition to treating their stakeholders and the environment responsibly, business organizations also should promote the general welfare of society. Examples include making contributions to charities, philanthropic organizations, and not-for-profit foundations and associations; supporting museums, symphonies, and public radio and television; and taking a role in improving public health and education. Some people also believe that organizations should act even more broadly to correct the political and/or social inequities that exist in the world. For example, these observers would argue that businesses should not conduct operations in countries with a record of human rights violations, such as Myanmar (Burma) or Sudan. Recent interest by U.S. firms in oil reserves in western and central Africa have sparked concerns about human rights issues in those areas as well, an issue discussed in more depth in the chapter's closing cases, "A Pipeline of Good Intentions."[22] A related but distinct problem that also is receiving renewed attention is global poverty and the potential role of business in helping to address it. In Cambodia, for instance, 28 percent of the population lives below the poverty level. Thirty-nine percent lack clean drinking water, and 29 percent are malnourished. But there are also emerging signs that some countries are beginning to address poverty-related issues. Uganda, for example, is still a very poor country; foreign aid constitutes a significant portion of its national budget. But since 1990 the percentage of its population living with HIV has dropped from 10.2 percent to 6.5 percent. Primary school enrollment has jumped from 58 percent in 1986 to over 92 percent of school-age children today. And the proportion of its population living on less than $1.25 per day has fallen from 69 percent in 1988 to 29 percent.[23] Yet, as illustrated in Map 5.1, numerous problem areas still exist.

MAP 5.1

Social Responsibility Hot Spots: Some Successes, But Many Challenges Remain

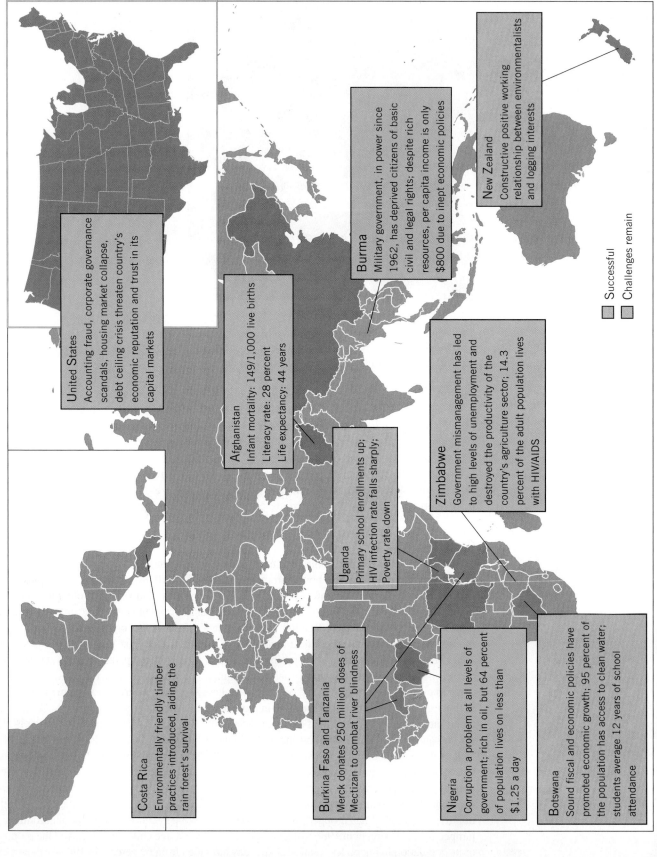

United States
Accounting fraud, corporate governance scandals, housing market collapse, debt ceiling crisis threaten country's economic reputation and trust in its capital markets

Afghanistan
Infant mortality: 149/1,000 live births
Literacy rate: 28 percent
Life expectancy: 44 years

Burma
Military government, in power since 1962, has deprived citizens of basic civil and legal rights; despite rich resources, per capita income is only $800 due to inept economic policies

New Zealand
Constructive positive working relationship between environmentalists and logging interests

Zimbabwe
Government mismanagement has led to high levels of unemployment and destroyed the productivity of the country's agriculture sector; 14.3 percent of the adult population lives with HIV/AIDS

Uganda
Primary school enrollments up; HIV infection rate falls sharply; Poverty rate down

Costa Rica
Environmentally friendly timber practices introduced, aiding the rain forest's survival

Burkina Faso and Tanzania
Merck donates 250 million doses of Mectizan to combat river blindness

Nigeria
Corruption a problem at all levels of government; rich in oil, but 64 percent of population lives on less than $1.25 a day

Botswana
Sound fiscal and economic policies have promoted economic growth; 95 percent of the population has access to clean water; students average 12 years of school attendance

☐ Successful
☐ Challenges remain

Managing Social Responsibility Across Borders

As with attempts to manage ethical conduct, businesses usually make some effort to actively address social responsibility. As we will discuss, firms generally adopt one of four different basic approaches to social responsibility. The basic approach they adopt shapes how they manage issues of compliance, the informal dimensions of social responsibility, and the evaluation of their social responsibility efforts.

Approaches to Social Responsibility

As "Bringing the World into Focus" indicates, some people advocate for a larger social role for organizations, while others argue that the role is already too large. Not surprisingly, organizations themselves adopt a wide range of positions on social responsibility. The four stances that an organization can take concerning its obligations to society, as shown in Figure 5.2, fall along a continuum ranging from the lowest to the highest degree of socially responsible practices.

OBSTRUCTIONIST STANCE Organizations that take what might be called an **obstructionist stance** to social responsibility usually do as little as possible to address social or environmental problems. When they cross the ethical or legal line that separates acceptable from unacceptable practices, their typical response is to deny or avoid accepting responsibility for their actions. For example, a few years ago top managers in several foreign affiliates of Astra, a Swedish firm, were accused of a host of improprieties ranging from sexual harassment to the diversion of company resources for personal use. When these problems first began to surface, top officials in Sweden denied any wrongdoing before they even bothered to conduct an investigation. Similarly, both Nestlé and Danone have been accused of violating international agreements signed in 1981 to control the marketing of infant formulas that serve as substitutes for breast milk. Those agreements stress the importance of breast-feeding. Nestlé and Danone allegedly provided mothers in West Africa with free samples of milk powder and violated labeling standards on infant formula in the countries of Togo and Burkina Faso. The firms, however, deny any such violations and argue that their actions were all technically within the parameters of the agreements.[24] Moreover, both companies now believe that the treaties are outmoded as a result of the HIV/AIDS crisis, arguing that utilization of infant formulas may reduce the transmission of the virus from infected breast-feeding mothers to their infants.

DEFENSIVE STANCE One step removed from the obstructionist stance is the defensive stance, whereby the organization will do everything that is required of it legally but nothing more. This approach is often adopted by companies that are unsympathetic to the concept of social responsibility. Managers in organizations that take a defensive stance insist that their job is to generate profits. For example, such a firm would install pollution control equipment dictated by law but would not install higher-quality equipment even though it might limit pollution

---

BRINGING THE WORLD INTO FOCUS **SHOULD FIRMS PRACTICE CORPORATE SOCIAL RESPONSIBILITY?**

In the eyes of advocates of corporate social responsibility, the case for CSR is overwhelming. The corporate sector must be mindful of the "triple bottom line" and must continually evaluate its environmental and social performance as well as its economic achievements. The corporate sector must promote global sustainability, meeting the needs of the present without compromising the needs of the future. In short, the goal of CSR is to promote a humane and just society, and corporations must play an appropriate role in achieving this objective. After all, corporations are granted a license to operate by society; therefore, they owe something to society in return. The unconstrained pursuit of profit breeds abuses, excesses, greed, and failure to consider the needs of future generations. Moreover, corporations have unique talents and resources to solve society's ills and should be expected to contribute them when necessary to address these problems.

Some experts, however, believe that the CSR movement is unethical, misguided, and inappropriate. Their case rests on a belief that in an economic system relying on shareholder capitalism, the corporate goal is (and should be) to maximize profits for shareholders. Requiring managers to promote social goals in addition to economic goals may cause managers to lose focus, thereby abandoning their fiduciary duty to shareholders. Moreover, these critics argue that the CSR movement rests on a fundamental misunderstanding of the functioning of free markets. True, firms are motivated to earn profits. But they can earn profits only by providing consumers with products that consumers are willing to buy at a price they are willing to pay; moreover, they are pressured to produce these products while using as few of society's scarce resources as possible. In a world of global competition, this is no easy task.

FIGURE 5.2

Approaches to Social Responsibility

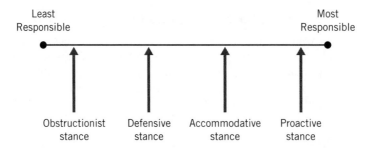

further. Tobacco companies take this position in their marketing efforts. In the United States, they are legally required to include warnings to smokers on their products and to limit their advertising to prescribed media. Domestically they follow these rules to the letter of the law but use stronger marketing methods in countries that have no such rules. In many African countries, for example, cigarettes are heavily promoted, contain higher levels of tar and nicotine than those sold in the United States, and carry few or no health warning labels.[25] Firms that take this position are less likely to cover up wrongdoing than obstructionist firms and will generally admit to mistakes when they are identified and then take appropriate corrective actions.

ACCOMMODATIVE STANCE A firm that adopts an **accommodative stance** meets its legal and ethical requirements but will also go beyond these requirements in selected cases. Such firms voluntarily agree to participate in social programs, but solicitors have to convince the organization that the programs are worthy of their support. Some firms will match contributions made by their employees to selected charitable causes. And many organizations will respond to requests for donations to Little League baseball, youth football programs, and so forth. Vodafone's local affiliate, for example, sponsors a youth cricket league in Pretoria, South Africa. The point, though, is that someone generally has to knock on the door and ask—the organizations do not proactively seek such avenues for contributing.

PROACTIVE STANCE The highest degree of social responsibility that a firm can exhibit is the proactive stance. Firms that adopt this approach take to heart the arguments in favor of social responsibility. They view themselves as citizens in a society and proactively seek opportunities to contribute. An excellent example of a proactive stance is the Ronald McDonald House program undertaken by McDonald's Corp. These houses, located close to major medical centers, can be used by families for minimal cost while their sick children are receiving medical treatment nearby. Likewise, Aquafinca, a Honduran subsidiary of Florida's Regal Springs Tilapia, teamed up with the World Wildlife Foundation and two important American distributors, Sysco and Costco, to become the first supplier of tilapia to meet the International Standards for Responsible Tilapia Aquaculture.[26] These and related activities and programs exceed the accommodative stance—they indicate a sincere and potent commitment to improving general social welfare in a country and thus represent a proactive stance to social responsibility. The Body Shop, Ben & Jerry's, Patagonia, and Timberland are four other companies widely admired for their proactive stances regarding social responsibility.[27]

Remember that these categories are not discrete but merely define stages along a continuum of approach. Organizations do not always fit neatly into one category. The Ronald McDonald House program has been widely applauded, for example, but McDonald's has also come under fire for allegedly misleading consumers about the nutritional value of its food products. And even though Astra took an obstructionist stance in the example cited above, many individual employees and managers at the firm have no doubt made substantial contributions to society in a number of different ways.

Managing Compliance

The demands for social responsibility placed on contemporary organizations by an increasingly sophisticated and educated public grow stronger every day. As we have seen, there are pitfalls for managers who fail to adhere to high ethical standards and for companies that try to circumvent their legal obligations. Organizations therefore need to fashion an approach to social responsibility the same way that they develop any other business strategy. That is, they should view social responsibility as a major challenge that requires careful planning, decision making, consideration, and evaluation. They may manage social responsibility through both formal and informal dimensions. Formal organizational dimensions used to implement a firm's social responsibility include legal compliance, ethical compliance, and philanthropic giving.

LEGAL COMPLIANCE **Legal compliance** is the extent to which the organization conforms to regional, national, and international laws. The task of managing legal compliance is generally assigned to the appropriate functional managers. For example, the organization's top human resource executive is responsible for ensuring compliance with regulations concerning hiring, pay, and workplace safety and health. Likewise, the top finance executive generally oversees compliance with securities and banking regulations. The organization's legal department is also likely to contribute to this effort by providing general oversight and answering queries from managers about the appropriate interpretation of laws and regulations.

ETHICAL COMPLIANCE **Ethical compliance** is the extent to which the members of the organization follow basic ethical (and legal) standards of behavior. We noted earlier that organizations have increased their efforts in this area—providing training in ethics and developing guidelines and codes of conduct, for example. These activities serve as vehicles for enhancing ethical compliance. Many organizations also establish formal ethics committees, which may be asked to review proposals for new projects, help evaluate new hiring strategies, or assess new environmental protection plans. They might also serve as a peer review panel to evaluate alleged ethical misconduct by an employee.[28]

PHILANTHROPIC GIVING Finally, **philanthropic giving** is the awarding of funds or gifts to charities or other social programs. Giving across national boundaries is becoming more common. For example, Alcoa gave $112,000 to a small town in Brazil to build a sewage treatment plant. And Japanese firms like Sony and Mitsubishi make contributions to a number of social programs in the United States. BP has chosen to support numerous social programs in Russia and other former republics of the former Union of Soviet Socialist Republics.

Perhaps the most significant international philanthropic program to date is that of Merck, the big U.S. pharmaceutical company, which had developed a heartworm medicine for dogs. In the affluent U.S. market Merck charged $20 to $30 for a dose of the drug. But Merck scientists discovered that their heartworm medicine could also cure onchocerciasis, a disease more commonly known as river blindness. This parasitic disease, spread by biting black flies, causes maddening itching, muscle pains, and weakness. Half of its victims suffer impaired vision, and a sixth lose their eyesight entirely. Yet the people who inhabit the lands that are plagued by river blindness are among the world's poorest. Merck decided to provide the drug, called Mectizan, for free. Since 1987, Merck has donated over 2.5 billion doses of Mectizan to people in 33 countries, sparing an estimated 80 million people annually from this terrifying disease.[29]

Unfortunately, in this age of cutbacks, many corporations have also had to limit their charitable gifts over the past several years as they continue to trim their own budgets. And many firms that continue to make contributions are increasingly targeting them to programs or areas where the firm will get something in return. For example, firms today are more likely to give money to job training programs than to the arts than was the case just a few years ago. The logic is that they get more direct payoff from the former type of contribution—in this instance, a better trained workforce from which to hire new employees—than the latter.[30]

Informal Dimensions of Social Responsibility

In addition to these formal dimensions for managing social responsibility, there are also informal ones. Leadership, organization culture, and how the organization responds to whistle-blowers each helps shape and define people's perceptions of the organization's stance on social responsibility.

ORGANIZATION LEADERSHIP AND CULTURE Leadership practices and organization culture can go a long way toward defining the social responsibility stance an organization and its members will adopt.[31] Consider Patagonia, a supplier of high-quality outdoor gear that started as a small specialist provider of mountain-climbing equipment. Its founder, Californian Yvon Chouinard, was a pioneer in the clean climbing movement, which sought to minimize the sport's impact on the wilderness. Under Chouinard's leadership, the firm has made an explicit and comprehensive commitment to environment protection. Its mission statement is straightforward: "Build the best products, cause no unnecessary harm, use business to inspire and implement solutions to the environmental crisis." It has matched these words with deeds that send a clear message to its employees, customers, and suppliers. In 1989, it cofounded the Conservation Alliance with other firms in the outdoor industry to promote protection of the environment. Patagonia organizes workshops to train grassroots environmental groups, gives monies to environmental causes, and funds its employees who wish to serve internships in environmental groups. In 2010, for example 50 Patagonia employees interned for groups as diverse as Kenya's Watamu Turtle Programme, Maine's Friends of Casco Bay, and Guatemala's Smithsonian Migratory Bird Center.[32] By contrast, the message sent to BP employees regarding the trade-offs among costs, safety, and environmental protection communicated a very different set of priorities.

WHISTLE-BLOWING **Whistle-blowing** is the disclosure by an employee of illegal or unethical conduct on the part of others within the organization.[33] How an organization responds to this practice often indicates its stance toward social responsibility. In a typical North American company, whistle-blowers may have to proceed through a number of channels to be heard. Some have even been fired for their efforts, a fate that befell James Bingham, a former executive with Xerox. He attempted to blow the whistle on alleged financial mismanagement in several of the firm's foreign subsidiaries. He claimed that the firm illegally set aside $100 million when it acquired a British firm in order to use those funds to boost future earnings. He also cited a corporate culture at Xerox that, in his words, "cut bookkeeping corners to make up for deteriorating business fundamentals and to maximize short-term results." Shortly after he made his allegations, Bingham was fired.[34]

Many organizations, however, welcome the contributions of whistle-blowers. A person who observes questionable behavior typically first reports the incident to his or her boss. If nothing is done, the whistle-blower may then inform higher-level managers or an ethics committee if one exists. Eventually, the person may have to go to a regulatory agency or even the media to be heard.

Not surprisingly, attitudes toward whistle-blowing are affected by culture. Because of the traditional strong attachment of the individual to the organization in Japan, for instance, whistle-blowing is often viewed as an act of betrayal, rather than one of integrity. Back in the 1970s, one Japanese salesman discovered that his boss was engaging in price-fixing. He reported the incident to higher-ups in the organization, who told him to ignore the problem. The salesman persisted in his whistle-blowing efforts. The company's response was to exile him to a remote subsidiary, where he continued to work in a tiny office—only nine square feet—without a telephone or a pay raise for 27 years. Although whistle-blowing has become more common in Japan in the past decade, it is still frowned upon, for it disturbs the harmony of the group, or *wa*, a value much prized in Japanese culture.[35] One Japanese religious scholar notes, "Traditionally, betrayal is the biggest crime in Japan, almost worse than murder. The price was *mura hachibu*, or exile from the village."[36] One survey of 101 Japanese corporations indicated that only 29 have an in-house

Over 80 million residents of Africa, Latin America, and the Middle East are threatened by river blindness, a debilitating disease spread by black flies. Merck has donated over 2.5 billion doses of Mectizan to help clinics like this one in Togo halt the disease's progress.

hotline for whistle-blowers. Although 20 companies replied that they were planning on installing a hotline, 49 adamantly reported they had no intention of doing so.[37]

Evaluating Social Responsibility

Any organization that is serious about social responsibility must ensure that its efforts are producing the desired benefits. Essentially this requires applying the concept of control to social responsibility. Many organizations now require current and new employees to read their guidelines or code of ethics and then sign a statement agreeing to abide by it. An organization should also evaluate how it responds to instances of questionable legal or ethical conduct. Does it follow up immediately? Does it punish those involved? Or does it use delay and cover-up tactics? Answers to these questions can help an organization diagnose any problems it might be having in meeting its social responsibilities.

Many organizations choose to conduct formal evaluations of the effectiveness of their social responsibility efforts. Some organizations, for instance, routinely conduct corporate social audits. A **corporate social audit** is a formal and thorough analysis of the effectiveness of the firm's social performance. The audit is usually undertaken by a task force of high-level managers from within the firm. It requires that the organization clearly define all its social goals, analyze the resources it devotes to each goal, determine how well it is achieving the various goals, and make recommendations about which areas need additional attention.

Difficulties of Managing CSR Across Borders

Another challenge facing corporations in establishing their policy toward corporate social responsibility is that the role of the corporation in society varies across countries. Multinational corporations, which by definition operate in multiple political and legal jurisdictions, are continually attempting to find the proper balance between the roles and behaviors expected by their home government and those expected by all of the host governments in the countries in which they operate. This is particularly complex in the case of corporate social responsibility, because corporations play very different roles in the political process of individual countries. How does an MNC please all of them? Indeed, companies are often criticized both for too much involvement in local politics and for not enough involvement. Many critics argue, for example, that oil companies play too large a role in the formulation of energy and environmental policies in the United States. Yet other critics have complained that these companies do too little to influence public policy in such countries as Nigeria or Myanmar. Shell's official policy is to support CSR "within the legitimate role of business," although that policy probably creates more questions than answers in interpreting what it means in practice.

A model developed by two Dutch CSR experts, Rob van Tulder and Alex van der Zwart, showcases this problem.[38] Their approach suggests there are three main actors in the policy formulation process:

1. The *state*, which passes and enforces laws;
2. The *market*, which through the process of competition and the pricing mechanism utilizes inputs and allocates outputs to members of the society; and
3. *Civil society*, which includes churches, charitable organizations, the Boy Scouts, labor unions, NGOs (nongovernmental organizations), and so on. Civil society in many ways manifests the cultural values of the citizens of the country.

The interplay among these three actors establishes public policy and the norms of social interaction, including, of course, accepted business behaviors. As is the case with culture, however, these social norms vary from country to country. Van Tulder and van der Zwart's model develops stereotypical behaviors in three regions of the world.

The Anglo-Saxon Approach

In van Tulder and van der Zwart's analysis, Anglo-Saxon countries view the state, the market, and civil society as separate, competitive, and antagonistic. Thus, when the government must contract with the private sector to purchase goods or services, such contracting should be done through an open and competitive bidding process. When business and government fail to maintain sufficient separation, Anglo-Saxons deem that failure as corruption. Similarly, when Americans look at the relationship between civil society and government, members of the former are labeled "special interest groups." As articulated by James Madison in the *Federalist Papers*, democracy entails political competition among these special interest groups. So the U.S.–Anglo-Saxon approach focuses on competition, not cooperation, among the three groups as the means to promote social goals.

The Asian Approach

The relationship between these three actors is very different in Asia. Many Asian countries—Japan, Korea, China, and Indonesia come to mind—rely on close cooperation between the private sector and the government. Indeed, the economic clout of Japan's *keiretsu* and Korea's *chaebol* rests on their willingness to do the government's bidding and vice versa. Many Asian leaders view this cooperation as the linchpin of their successful development strategies—the so-called "Asian Way." Note two things: First, from the perspective of the Anglo-Saxon approach, this symbiotic relationship between business and government is viewed as "crony capitalism," a polite term for corruption. Second, civil society plays a minor role in this process.[39]

The Continental European Approach

In the European Union—particularly in continental European countries such as Austria, Germany, France, and the Netherlands—the three actors have much more cooperative ways of working with one another. In Germany, for example, large employer associations bargain with umbrella labor organizations under the watchful supervision of the government. Similarly, Germany's codetermination policy gives workers a well-defined role in the governance of large German businesses (see page 560). And, in general, the public policy process is based upon creating consensus among the three actors. Cooperation, not competition, is the hallmark of this approach.

Clearly each of the three approaches—Continental European, Asian, and Anglo-Saxon—conceptualizes the responsibilities of government, business, and civil society quite differently. This leaves MNCs that operate in all three areas with the difficult and complex task of triangulating between their own interests, the proper way of doing things according to the perspective of their home society, and the proper way of doing things according to the perspective of the society of the host countries in which they operate.

Regulating International Ethics and Social Responsibility

Not surprisingly, there have been many attempts to mandate and regulate ethical and socially responsible behavior by businesspeople and businesses. A detailed discussion of the myriad laws and regulations is beyond the scope of this discussion. However, we will describe a few of the more important and representative regulations.

The **Foreign Corrupt Practices Act (FCPA)** was passed by the United States Congress in 1977. The FCPA prohibits U.S. firms, their employees, and agents acting on their behalf from paying or offering to pay bribes to any foreign government official in order to influence the official actions or policies of that individual to gain or retain business. This prohibition applies even if the transaction occurs entirely outside U.S. borders. We already noted the fines paid by Siemens for violating the FCPA. Other examples abound. For instance, two former executives of Mobil Oil were indicted in 2003 for violating the FCPA. Allegedly they participated in an agreement to pay $78 million to several government leaders in Kazakhstan in return for control of the country's giant Tengiz oil fields; one of the executives allegedly received a $2 million kickback in the deal.[40] Similarly, Baker Hughes, a Texas-based oil field services provider, paid a $44 million fine to settle charges it violated the FCPA in Angola, Indonesia, Nigeria, Russia, and Uzbekistan, as well as Kazakhstan.[41] However, the FCPA does not outlaw routine payments, regardless of their size, made to government officials to expedite normal commercial transactions, such as issuance of customs documents or permits, inspection of goods, or provision of police services.

In 2010, the British government passed the **Bribery Act**, which applies to corrupt actions done anywhere in the world by firms with a business presence in the United Kingdom. In many ways, this British law is more extensive and comprehensive than the FCPA. Like the

FCPA, it applies to transactions involving government officials. Unlike the FCPA, the Bribery Act also applies to transactions between two businesses and it outlaws facilitation payments.[42]

The **Alien Tort Claims Act** was passed in the United States in 1789 but has recently emerged as a potentially significant law affecting U.S. multinational corporations. Under some recent interpretations of this law, U.S. multinationals may be responsible for human rights abuses by foreign governments if the companies benefited from those abuses. For instance, the U.S. Court of Appeals for the Ninth Circuit allowed citizens of Burma to proceed with a case accusing Unocal of knowingly using forced labor supplied by the Burmese military. (The case was settled out of court.) Other suits have been filed in New York and New Jersey accusing IBM, Citigroup, and other corporations of benefiting from apartheid in South Africa.[43]

The **Anti-Bribery Convention of the Organization for Economic Cooperation and Development** was developed in and first ratified by Canada in 2000; it has since been ratified by 37 other countries. The Convention is an attempt to eliminate bribery in international business transactions. Its centerpiece mandates jail time for those convicted of paying bribes.[44]

Finally, the **International Labor Organization (ILO)** has become a major watchdog for monitoring working conditions in factories in developing countries. Spurred by both Western corporations and the factories themselves, the ILO has begun to systematically inspect working conditions in countries such as Bangladesh, Cambodia, and the Philippines. Corporations find that such an independent inspection mechanism helps allay concerns from human rights and workers rights activist groups; factory owners are also finding that subjecting themselves to regular ILO inspections helps them establish new business relationships with multinational corporations.[45]

There are numerous other laws and international agreements to promote socially responsible international business practices. "Emerging Opportunities" describes one such agreement, which is attempting to control trade in conflict diamonds, in order to bring peace to Sierra Leone, Congo, and other African nations.

EMERGING OPPORTUNITIES | CONFLICT DIAMONDS

According to Western custom, diamonds are a perfect way for a young man to demonstrate his undying love to his fiancée. But diamonds are also perfect for smuggling. They are small, easily concealed, and very valuable relative to their bulk and weight. A nasty little secret of the diamond trade is that diamond smugglers have financed some of the world's most vicious civil wars, including those that devastated Sierra Leone, Côte d'Ivoire, Congo, and Angola. Officials of nongovernmental organizations (NGOs) that are trying to aid the victims of these wars, such as CARE, Médecins Sans Frontières, Global Witness, and the International Red Cross, realized that peace would be impossible unless trade in these so-called "conflict diamonds" ceased. They began publicizing the linkage between diamonds and these civil wars. Experts estimate that conflict diamonds constitute between 2 and 20 percent of the world's trade in the precious stones.

The diamond industry quickly realized that they faced a public relations disaster, fearing that consumers might shun diamond earrings or bracelets if they knew that their glittery purchases were helping warlords to buy bullets and machine guns. In 2000, the major countries involved in the diamond trade as producers, traders, or consumers commenced the Kimberley Process (named for the famed South African mining town) to halt trade in conflict diamonds. Seventy-five countries have agreed that, beginning in 2003, trade in diamonds would be limited to those stones that carry a certificate of origin from their country of production, guaranteeing that they were produced legally and outside the zones of conflict. However, the real problem is in enforcing the good intentions of the Kimberley Process. Some NGOs fear that smugglers will bribe corrupt officials to issue the certificates, or that they will devise other ways to circumvent the agreement. (The plot of a 2002 James Bond movie, *Die Another Day*, involved just such a scheme.)

Other countries believe that conflict over conflict diamonds gives them an opportunity to promote their own industry. Canada, for instance, now produces 6 percent of the world's gem-quality diamonds, thanks to a discovery in the Northwest Territory in 1991. To demonstrate that their gems are produced in a conflict-free zone, one Canadian producer engraves a tiny polar bear in its diamonds, and another inscribes a maple leaf.

Sources: "Zimbabwe auctions diamonds amid controversy," *Wall Street Journal*, August 11, 2010; "The 'Blood Diamond' resurfaces," *Wall Street Journal*, June 19, 2010; "The dark core of a diamond," *Time* (Global Business bonus section), May 2006, p. A3; "Accord on conflict diamond smuggling," *Financial Times*, November 11, 2005, p. 4; "Warning to 'conflict diamond' traders," *Financial Times*, April 29, 2003, p. 6; "Political correctness by the carat," *Wall Street Journal*, April 17, 2003, p. B1; "Talks end in agreement to track diamond shipments," *Houston Chronicle*, November 30, 2001, p. 36A; "Diamond town in the rough," *Wall Street Journal*, July 5, 2001, p. B1; Jon Lee Anderson, "Oil and blood," *The New Yorker*, August 14, 2000, pp. 45ff.

MyManagementLab   Now that you have finished this chapter, go back to **www.pearsonglobaleditions.com/mymanagementlab** to continue practicing and applying the concepts you've learned.

CHAPTER REVIEW

Summary

Ethics are an individual's personal beliefs about whether a decision, behavior, or action is right or wrong. What constitutes ethical behavior varies from one person to another. But even though ethical behavior is in the eye of the beholder, it usually refers to behavior that conforms to generally accepted social norms. Unethical behavior is behavior that does not conform to generally accepted social norms. A society generally adopts formal laws that reflect the prevailing ethical standards—the social norms—of its members. Cultural differences often create ethical complications. Acceptable behavior in one culture may be viewed as immoral in another.

One important area of cross-cultural and international ethics is the treatment of employees by the organization. In practice, the areas most susceptible to ethical variation include hiring and firing practices, wages and working conditions, and employee privacy and respect. Numerous ethical issues also relate to how employees treat the organization. The central ethical issues in this relationship include conflicts of interest, secrecy and confidentiality, and honesty. A third major perspective for viewing ethics involves the relationship between the firm and its employees with other economic agents. The primary agents of interest include customers, competitors, stockholders, suppliers, dealers, and unions.

While ethics reside in individuals, many businesses nevertheless endeavor to manage the ethical behavior of their managers and employees. They want to clearly establish the fact that they expect their managers and other employees to engage in ethical behaviors. They also want to take appropriate steps to eliminate as much ambiguity as possible in what the company views as ethical versus unethical behavior. The most common ways of doing this are through the use of guidelines or a code of ethics, ethics training, and organizational practices and the corporate culture.

Organizations need to define their policies toward corporate social responsibility—the set of obligations an organization has to protect and enhance the society in which it functions. Organizations may exercise social responsibility toward their stakeholders, toward the natural environment, and toward general social welfare. Some organizations acknowledge their responsibilities in all three areas and strive diligently to meet each of them, while others emphasize only one or two areas of social responsibility. And a few acknowledge no social responsibility at all.

As with attempts to manage ethical conduct, businesses usually make some effort to actively address social responsibility. This generally starts from their basic approach to social responsibility. It then extends to how they manage issues of compliance, the informal dimensions of social responsibility, and how they evaluate their efforts regarding social responsibility.

There have been many attempts to regulate ethical and socially responsible international business conduct. Five illustrative examples are the Foreign Corrupt Practices Act, the Bribery Act, the Alien Tort Claims Act, the Anti-Bribery Convention of the Organization for Economic Cooperation and Development, and the International Labor Organization (ILO).

Review Questions

1. What are ethics?
2. Distinguish between ethical and unethical behavior.
3. What role does culture play in the formation of ethics?
4. How do organizations attempt to manage ethical behavior across borders?
5. What is social responsibility?
6. What is the difference between ethics and social responsibility?
7. Identify the major areas of social responsibility for international business.
8. What are the four general approaches a firm can take with regard to social responsibility?
9. What is a whistle-blower?
10. Identify and briefly summarize representative laws and regulations that attempt to address international ethics and social responsibility.

Questions for Discussion

1. While people from the same culture are likely to have similar views of what constitutes ethical versus unethical behavior, what factor or factors would account for differences within a culture?
2. Is it valid to describe someone as having "no ethics"? Why or why not?
3. People from which countries would likely have similar ethical beliefs as people from the United Kingdom? Why?
4. Under what circumstances is a code of ethics most and least likely to be effective? Why?
5. What do you think is most likely to happen if the ethical behaviors and decisions of a new team of top managers of

a firm are inconsistent with the firm's long-entrenched corporate culture?

6. Do you think social responsibility for a multinational corporation is something best managed locally or best managed globally?

7. Do multinational businesses ever do socially responsible things that are clearly of no benefit whatsoever to themselves?

8. What are the dangers or pitfalls that might be encountered if a multinational business attempts to be socially responsible, but only in ways that provide direct benefits to its profitability?

9. Under what circumstances, if any, might you see yourself as a whistle-blower? Under what circumstances, if any, might you keep quiet about illegal acts by your employer?

10. Do you think there should be more or fewer attempts to regulate international ethics and social responsibility? Why?

11. Consider the plight of Mary, the Philippine woman discussed on page 146. In response to the inquiries of *Fortune*'s reporter, Motorola issued a statement saying it "has a strict policy of adherence to the laws and labor practices in the countries where it operates, in addition to a rigorous code of conduct." Is this an adequate response? In your opinion, what responsibility does Motorola have to workers like Mary? Defend your answer.

12. Are the ethics of gift-giving different between high-context and low-context cultures?

13. Consider the following scenarios:

- To assist the sale of your products in a particular foreign market, it is suggested that you pay a 10 percent commission to a "go-between" who has access to high-ranking government officials in that market. You suspect, but do not know, that the go-between will split the commission with the government officials who decide which goods to buy. Should you do it? Does it make a difference if your competitors routinely pay such commissions?

- You have a long-standing client in a country that imposes foreign exchange controls. The client asks you to pad your invoices by 25 percent. For example, you would ship the client $100,000 worth of goods but would invoice the client for $125,000. On the basis of your invoice, the client would obtain the $125,000 from the country's central bank. The client then would pay you $100,000 and have you put the remaining $25,000 in a Swiss bank account in the client's name. Should you do it? Would it make a difference if your client is a member of a politically unpopular minority and might have to flee the country at a moment's notice?

Building Global Skills

Identify an industry that interests you personally and that has a number of major multinational companies. Potential examples include energy, automobiles, and consumer electronics. Visit the websites of three firms in that industry and learn as much as possible about their stances regarding ethical conduct and social responsibility. Identify commonalities and differences across the three firms. Next, develop observations about the likely effectiveness of the firms' efforts to promote ethical conduct and social responsibility based on their websites. Finally, respond to the following questions:

1. Symbolically, what potential role does the Internet serve in helping to promote ethical conduct and social responsibility as evidenced by the websites you visited?

2. Which firm has the most effective website vis-à-vis ethics and social responsibility? In your opinion, what makes it the best?

3. Which firm has the least effective website vis-à-vis ethics and social responsibility? In your opinion, what makes it the worst?

4. How do the websites affect your view of each company from the standpoint of a potential investor? A potential employee? A potential supplier?

5. If asked, what advice might you offer to each company to improve its attention to ethical conduct and social responsibility as reflected by its website?

CLOSING CASE   A PIPELINE OF GOOD INTENTIONS

Development economists and poverty specialists often talk about the "oil curse," a phrase reflecting the numerous instances when the discovery of oil in poor countries has paradoxically led to increases in poverty and social problems. When oil was discovered in the Doba basin in southern Chad in the 1990s, many predicted the oil curse would strike Chad as well. Chad, which is primarily desert with few natural resources, is one of the poorest countries on earth. With only a few hundred doctors to serve a population of 11 million, one-third of its children suffer from malnutrition. Since gaining independence from France in 1960, the country has been plagued by dictatorships and civil wars, as well as invasions by Libya and incursions by Sudanese rebel groups. Four times French troops have had to be sent to the former colony to restore a semblance of order.

While the Doba basin was estimated to hold 2 billion barrels of oil, Chad is landlocked. To get the oil to market, an expensive, 650-mile (1,070-kilometer) pipeline would have to be built from Chad to a port in Cameroon, where the oil could then be shipped from the Gulf of Guinea to world markets (see Map 5.2). Despite a relatively low royalty rate to be paid to Chad's government—one-eighth of the value of production—the consortium of foreign companies who had discovered the oil field—Exxon Mobil, PETRONAS of Malaysia, and Chevron—were hesitant to develop the Doba basin because of the political risks of operating in Chad, the costliness of the pipeline, and the low quality of the oil produced there.

The consortium members and the governments of Chad and Cameroon approached the World Bank to provide financing for the $4.1 billion project. In 1999, the World Bank agreed to provide $400 million of financing; the oil companies anted up $3.5 billion. Exxon Mobil, which operates the wells, supplied 40 percent; Chevron put up 25 percent; and PETRONAS of Malaysia, 35 percent. The remaining funds were supplied by the European Investment Bank. The pipeline itself was to be owned and operated by two joint-venture companies, one in Chad and one in Cameroon. The two governments owned minority interests in their respective companies, with a majority stake in both taken by the consortium of oil companies.

While the Bank's share of the $4.1 billion cost was small, its participation in the deal was critical. Because the World Bank had other loans outstanding to Chad, Exxon Mobil and the other oil companies believed that the World Bank's participation would lower their political risks, for Chad would be unlikely to jeopardize its relationship with the World Bank. However, two recent World Bank presidents, James Wolfensohn and Paul Wolfowitz, were growing increasingly concerned about corruption's corrosive impact on economic development. This issue was certainly germane to Chad. Transparency International, an NGO (nongovernmental organization) that annually conducts surveys of corruption, ranks Chad's government as one of the most corrupt in Africa. Facilitating corruption was the lack of accountability and transparency in the use of oil revenues by many governments. And the revenues generated by the pipeline would provide sufficient temptation: Over its estimated 25-year life, the project was expected to yield $2 billion for Chad and $500 million for Cameroon.

Given these circumstances, the World Bank agreed to lend money for the project only if it received assurances that the revenues from the oil field would be devoted to alleviating the country's poverty. To gain the World Bank's approval for the loan, Chad agreed to enact the Petroleum Revenue Management Law. Under this law, Chad's royalties were to be deposited in an escrow account at Citibank's London branch. Ten percent of the royalties were to be put in a separate fund to benefit future generations of Chadians. The remaining royalty revenues were to be spent according to a formula—15 percent for general governmental needs, 80 percent for health and education services, and 5 percent in the oil-producing region, Doba.

For the first several years of the program, everything went according to plan. The oil companies drilled over 200 wells in Doba, and soon oil was flowing through the pipeline. The pipeline boosted the local economy and the government's coffers. The pipeline employs 7,300 people in Chad, 83 percent of whom are Chad nationals; the comparable figures for Cameroon are 1,100 and 90 percent. The pipeline consortium also sponsored a variety of health initiatives, including anticholera, antimalaria, and HIV/AIDS awareness programs. Exxon has purchased more than $2 billion from local suppliers and refurbished 300 miles of local roads and bridges. The company also funded the construction of several local clinics, which treat more than 12,000 patients

MAP 5.2
Chad Pipeline

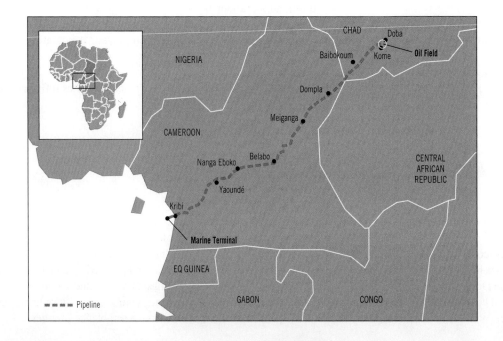

a year. In its first year of production, the pipeline generated $131 million for Chad's government, about 42 percent of its budget. By mid-2006, Chad had earned $537 million from the pipeline. Of these monies, $295 million had been directed to the priority sectors of health, education, and road rehabilitation, and $19 million had been devoted to community-development projects in the Doba region, where the oil fields were located.

Unfortunately, Chad's government began to suffer budget difficulties. President Idriss Déby argued that his government could no longer honor its deal with the World Bank, in part because of the rising costs of administering to the flood of refugees fleeing the conflict in the Darfur region of neighboring Sudan. In December 2005 Chad's National Assembly voted to amend the Petroleum Revenue Management Law. The new amendments abolished the special fund that would preserve oil revenues for the benefit of future generations. In addition, the legislation doubled the percentage of oil revenues that the country could spend without outside oversight to 30 percent. It also added national security to the priority areas of education, health, and road rehabilitation.

The World Bank acted swiftly in response to this legislation, which it viewed as abandoning Chad's obligations under the agreement. In January 2006, it suspended all new grants and loans to Chad and cut off additional disbursements under existing projects with Chad. The World Bank's actions affected some $124 million in undisbursed funds in eight Bank-funded projects with Chad. To make matters worse, in April 2006, a rebel army, allegedly backed by the government of Sudan, attacked N'Djamena, Chad's capital. Although this incursion was defeated, it heightened the resolve of President Déby to relax the constraints on the oil revenues.

The Exxon-led consortium was now caught in the middle. It decided to withhold all revenues until the dispute between the World Bank and Chad's government was resolved. However, President Déby announced that if the consortium failed to deliver the funds to Chad's government, he would demand that oil production cease in Doba. Ultimately, the consortium could lose its rights to operate in the country. However, if the consortium delivered the funds to the Déby government, it faced the wrath of the World Bank and various activist groups like Transparency International.

Case Questions

1. What is the "oil curse"? Why do you think it develops?
2. Why was the World Bank's participation in the Chad-Cameroon pipeline critical?
3. Does the World Bank have a right to demand that sovereign countries like Chad spend their oil revenues in ways the World Bank deems appropriate?
4. If the World Bank and Chad's government fail to settle their dispute over amendments to the Petroleum Revenue Management Law, what should the consortium do? Should they make funds available to Chad's government in defiance of the World Bank's wishes?
5. Subsequent to the signing of the pipeline agreement, world oil prices have increased substantially. Given the abject poverty of Chad, should the oil companies offer to increase the royalties paid to Chad's government once its dispute with the World Bank is settled?
6. In September 2008, Chad repaid all of the World Bank's loans, effectively nullifying all of the pledges it made to the bank regarding the use of its oil revenues. Had the various actors known that would happen when the project was first conceived, should they have proceeded in the first place?

Sources: www.worldbank.org; Chad/Cameroon Development Project Update 29, Annual Report 2010; International Advisory Group, Chad-Cameroon Petroleum Development and Pipeline Project: Final Report (September 3, 2009), Esso Exploration and Production Chad, Inc.; "A vaunted model development project goes awry," *The Economist*, September 27, 2008 (online); "A regime saved, for the moment," *The Economist*, February 9, 2008, p. 53; "Chad Export Project: Project Update No. 22," Esso Exploration and Production Chad, Inc. (2007); "An ill-advised leap into the unknown?" *Financial Times*, March 1, 2006, p. 7; "Exxon faces a dilemma on Chad project," *Wall Street Journal*, February 28, 2006, p. A4; "The 'resource curse' anew: Why a grand World Bank oil project has fast run into the sand," *Financial Times*, January 23, 2006, p. 13; "World Bank pulls Chad pipeline loan," *Houston Chronicle*, January, 2006, p. D3; "As Exxon pursues African oil, charity becomes political issue," *Wall Street Journal*, January 10, 2006, p. A1; "Chad Export Project: Project Update No. 19, Annual Report 2005," Esso Exploration and Production Chad, Inc. (2006); "A regime change," *The Economist*, June 4, 2005, p. 65; "African pipeline has yet to deliver lasting benefits," *Houston Chronicle*, June 29, 2003, p. 5D; "In war on poverty, Chad's pipeline plays unusual role," *Wall Street Journal*, June 24, 2003, p. A8.

PART 1 CLOSING CASES   *KFC IN CHINA*

KFC opened its first western-style restaurant in Beijing in 1987. It has rapidly expanded using a blend of franchising and localization strategies. It has grown from small beginnings to become China's largest foreign fast food chain. It has over 2,200 branches in 450 Chinese cities. It is a far bigger enterprise than any of the other multinational fast food chains that have tried to trade in the potentially high-risk Chinese market.

The first KFC store in China was opened close to Tiananmen Square. It is still the largest KFC outlet worldwide.

Such has been the transition in fortunes for KFC and other multinational fast food outlets that initially, when they were opened, the most frequent customers were foreigners living in China. Local consumers could not afford to eat there.

The Yum Brands owns the KFC and Pizza Hut brands. It quickly discovered that it is not enough to rely on a well-known foreign brand name to ensure growth. Instead, it is important to adapt to local tastes and lifestyles. KFC has, therefore, adapted its menu by adding a variety of dishes that are familiar to the Chinese.

Year on year, Yum's sales in China have increased; it was the first foreign fast food company to move into China and including the Pizza Hut stores it has 2,500 branches with annual sales of $2 billion. The nearest multinational competitor is McDonald's with just 900 branches. There is still considerable room for expansion, as China's fast food market is estimated to be worth $28 billion per year.

During 2008, with the Beijing Olympics and the higher profile that China enjoyed, Yum intended to add 425 new branches, while McDonald's aimed to top the 1,000 mark with 125 new stores. In 2007 Yum's China Division's operating profit rose by 30 percent to $375 million. This was a quarter of the entire multinationals operating profit. The Chief Executive of Yum, David Novak, predicted that by 2017 the Chinese operation would contribute 40 percent of the overall profits.

Perceptions of Pizza Hut, in particular, are very different in China than in many other markets. In Europe and the United States, for example, Pizza Huts are regarded as being relatively inexpensive, but in China they are considered to be up-market and, therefore, Yum has targeted the estimated 250 million middle class Chinese consumers.

In a unique reverse strategy the success of Yum's Chinese business, particularly by introducing healthier products and breaking away from the notion that KFC produces junk food, Novak explained to shareholders in December 2007: Let's learn from our most successful business. Let's learn from our China business.

The idea will be to adapt the China model across the rest of the world and increase the emphasis on breakfast and evening sales and provide broader menus.

Yum China is not content with simply taking China's fast food chicken market by storm. They are now planning the expansion of a traditional Chinese fast food chain called East Dawning. This will take on Kung Fu Catering Management and the hotpot chain, Inner Mongolia Little Sheep. Ten East Dawning branches have been operating in Shanghai since 2005. Yum tested the Beijing market prior to the Olympics. The branches offer traditional Chinese dishes.

Initially, the novelty of KFC restaurants won over many Chinese customers. Fast food was considered to be exotic and Chinese consumers were curious. At first, KFC took advantage of the situation, charging relatively high prices. By the mid-1990s there were about 100 fast food restaurants around Beijing. It quickly became obvious that the market was not growing fast enough, as many Chinese considered that the fast food was not as good as their own Chinese cuisine. During Chinese festivals traditional Chinese restaurants were full to bursting, while KFC restaurants and McDonald's were almost empty. There were a number of reasons for this; some economic, some social and others ideological, but culture played the most important role.

The Chinese have a traditional culture of food and drink and fast food could not compare with it. Once the curiosity of the newfast food restaurants had waned, Chinese people returned to their own cuisine. In order to first survive and then to prosper, KFC had to combine the elements of the two different cuisine cultures. In other words, it had to absorb elements of Chinese cuisine.

In 2001 KFC introduced Chinese food to their menus. They started with preserved Sichuan pickle and shredded pork soup. This was a success and mushroom rice, tomato and egg soup and Peking chicken rolls were also added to the menu. McDonald's tried to follow suit and began to modify the design of the restaurants and add distinctly Chinese style soups to their menu. In effect, both KFC and McDonald's had developed intercultural management. They had retained American business culture but supplemented it with Chinese traditional culture. The businesses had used localization strategies to reinterpret American business culture.

Why then is KFC far more popular in China than McDonald's? Certainly, KFC has stressed that their own version of fast food is far healthier than other fast food options. China also is an enormous consumer of fried chicken and customers prefer it to hamburgers. KFC also has a far more Chinese-specific menu than McDonald's and, finally, KFC has made great use of deals and coupons and around 50 percent of their customers use coupons to purchase food from their branches.

On January 16, 2004, KFC had opened its one thousandth restaurant in China. The success of KFC was certainly linked to both its franchise policy and the scientific nature of its managerial operations. This was known as CHAMPS. It measures operational basics of Cleanliness, Hospitality, Accuracy, Maintenance, Product quality and Speed.

From the outset KFC took advantage of the political changes in China and the different approach of the Chinese government that began to welcome western investors. KFC certainly had a synergy with China from the very beginning.The poultry industry in China was one of the major priorities of the agricultural modernization plans and KFC, as a predominantly poultry food chain, gained enormous support from the Chinese government.

Financially, KFC's entry into the Chinese market came at an ideal time. PepsiCo had only recently purchased the company and the business now had enormous financial muscle. The market potential in China was enormous and chicken was not only more popular, but cheaper and more widely available than beef. KFC also had the ideal image as far as the Chinese consumer was concerned; the clean branches were considered to be hygienic and KFC stressed the high levels of quality and service throughout all of their outlets.

There were, however, some weaknesses and potential threats. The Chinese government provides far more support to businesses that are bringing technology into their country and KFC was a service provider. The setting up of each new restaurant was a high-cost venture and initially KFC had problems in ensuring high quality supplies from local producers. Human resource management was difficult in a culture where family contacts are often used to obtain sought-after jobs. There was also a lack of Chinese-speaking store outlet managers and initially there were problems with the management and local employees. KFC's imposed quality standards were at variance with Chinese partners, who believed that they knew what Chinese customers wanted more than KFC.

In order to adapt and to cater for the Chinese market, KFC's strategy was to offer a blend of western style products, which would appeal to younger consumers that were eager to try foreign food, while at the same time developing traditional Chinese-style fast food. The net outcome was a blend of both east and west, with Chinese seafood and Hong Kong milk tea sitting alongside orange juice, fries and western chicken burgers. The U.S. brand image was retained, which was consistent with KFC's globalization strategy, but the incorporation of Chinese side dishes was a key localization strategy.

One of the major cultural differences between the United States and China is the perceived gulf between American individualism and Chinese collectivism. Taking this into account, it was obviously a key influence on the advertising and on the strategies used by KFC in China. Individualism emphasizes achievement, freedom, competition, pleasure and independence. On the other hand, collectivism suggests security, hierarchy, cooperation, low competition and interdependence. Harmony and conformity are also a key aspect of collectivism. KFC therefore had to adapt its advertising, in order to communicate how their products would satisfy these customer needs. The first key aspect was to become family and group orientated. Commercials promoted the KFC bucket, which could be enjoyed by the whole family; this fitted well with the value systems in China. Big families with three generations and relatives were targeted by the advertising. As far as groups were concerned, KFC commercials targeted friends having fun and work colleagues. KFC also used emotional appeals, which would find resonance in the Chinese market. They focused on patriotism, respect for the elderly, cherishing the young, friendship and romantic love.

In December 2003 KFC made a major mistake when it promoted a new chicken wrap. It featured an empty Cantonese restaurant and a packed KFC outlet and caused enormous reaction; KFC was accused of being arrogant and there was considerable backlash. KFC has since been extremely careful to avoid offending Chinese culture.

As with any foreign product or service, there is always the question of cultural imperialism and the fact that western-style fast food can be seen as an invisible cultural invasion that is trying to overwhelm traditional Chinese culture. The Chinese were particularly concerned about the influence of fast food on the young and whether it would, in effect, separate the young from their own cultural heritage. Much of this attitude has changed, as China is no longer isolationist and there is no longer a fascination for fast food just because it is foreign. KFC is a prime example of how its convenience fits in with Chinese lifestyle and the fact that it has adapted to the fast pace of modern Chinese life. Understandably, there have also been health concerns and in China there was a belief that too much fast food would cause obesity and other health problems. So far, KFC has tried to mitigate any particular problems in relation to health issues by focusing on the nutritional value.

KFC's success in China has undoubtedly been a result of understanding the country and its culture. The company has recognized that the host culture is an important consideration and cannot be overwhelmed by standardized global marketing and advertising. Undoubtedly, KFC is the most popular international brand in China. The localization strategy has certainly worked.

Yum Brands are also trying to replicate their success with KFC across their other brands. Su believes that Pizza Hut will be the next major success story. China has rising incomes and economic growth; both key drivers in helping Pizza Hut to become a major brand.

Taco Bell is also being tested in the Chinese market, with a test restaurant in Shanghai. They hope the model will work across China and if it does it will be another big success story.

Questions

1. Real Kung Fu is a Chinese fast food chain with around 200 stores across China. What are their short-term growth plans and possible problems?
2. Where is Yum Brands based and which countries does the Yum China Division cover?
3. When did KFC open its first ever drive through restaurant and how many Pizza Hut home delivery services are operating in mainland China?
4. When did KFC open its first ever drive through restaurant and how many Pizza Hut home delivery services are operating in mainland China?

Sources: China Economic Net (www.en.ce.cn); China Daily (www.chinadaily.com); The China Ex Pat (www.thechinaexpat.com); China Herald (www.chinaherald.net); People's Daily (www.english.peopledaily.com.cn); All Business (www.allbusiness.com); Eats Online (www.eats.com).

The Oil Curse

In Chapter 5's closing case, we noted that development economists and poverty specialists often view the discovery of oil as a curse rather than a blessing. Consider the case of Nigeria. Its 155 million citizens make it Africa's most populous country. Declared a British protectorate in 1914, it is home to more than 250 ethnic groups, although four groups—the Hausa and Fulani in northern Nigeria (29 percent), the Yoruba in the southwest (21 percent), and the Igbo (Ibo) and Ijaw in the southeast (18 percent and 10 percent, respectively)—account for the majority of the population.

Oil was first discovered in the Niger Delta in 1958, shortly before Nigeria became an independent nation in 1960. In 1967 the Ibo and other ethnic groups in the southeastern coastal region attempted to secede from Nigeria, declaring their lands the Republic of Biafra. Biafra's secession met with fierce opposition from the Hausa/Fulani and Yoruba leadership, who quickly realized that an independent Biafra would control the Niger Delta oil fields and the area's primary source of revenue. Federal troops suppressed the secession attempt in a bloody, two-year war. A cease-fire was instituted in early 1970, and Biafra was reabsorbed into Nigeria.

The Nigerian oil industry, then as now, is centered on Port Harcourt in the Niger Delta. Capable of producing 2.4 million barrels of oil a day, Nigeria is Africa's largest oil producer. Oil revenues account for 95 percent of the country's exports, 20 percent of its GDP, and 80 percent of the government's revenues. However, the country remains poor, with an estimated per capita income of $1,140 and a life expectancy at birth of only 47.

Unfortunately, during its brief history Nigeria has been plagued by high levels of corruption, fueled in part by the misuse of its oil revenues. Nor has Nigeria been blessed with good governments. Among the worst was the military regime of Sani Abacha, a dictator who ruled the country from 1993 to 1998. One of the low points of Abacha's reign was the sham trial and execution of Ken Saro-Wiwa, a political activist who fought to protect the environment and the human rights of the people in the Niger Delta. After 16 years of military government, in 1999 Olusegun Obasanjo was elected president of the country in what has been described as a relatively fair election by local standards. He was reelected in 2003. In 2007, he was succeeded by Umaru Musa Yar'Adua in an election that international observers characterized as tainted. Yar'Adua died in office in 2010; his vice-president, Jonathan Goodluck, became president and was subsequently elected as president in 2011 in a relatively clean election.

Local citizens in the Niger Delta have benefited little from the oil boom. Despite the wealth generated by the Niger Delta's oil fields, much of the local population lives in desperate poverty, lacking adequate hospitals, schools, and electricity. Pollution from drilling operations and inevitable spills have despoiled the local mangrove swamps and harmed the fisheries and the fishing industry that depends on them.

Although Presidents Obasanjo, Yar'Adua, and Goodluck have tried to address the issues raised by community leaders in the Niger Delta, violence is increasingly supplanting political dialogue. In 2002, hundreds of Nigerian women invaded Chevron's oil processing facilities on Escravos Island, demanding that the company provide schools, clinics, and jobs for the local citizens; three months earlier a Chevron offshore drilling platform was the target of a similarly motivated raid.

In 2004, a rebel group called the Niger Delta People's Volunteer Force demanded that foreign oil companies terminate their operations in the area or face the threat of all-out war. Armed militias clashed with government forces in Port Harcourt and the surrounding Rivers State, leading to the deaths of several hundred Nigerians and making it more difficult for Shell, Chevron, and other oil companies to maintain and repair their facilities and produce and transport their products. The group's stated aim is to liberate the local Ijaw people from control of the central government and allow the Ijaws to benefit from the oil wealth that their region generates. The Nigerian government dismissed such claims, scoffing that the group was nothing more than a front for oil thieves.

There is little doubt that much oil thievery takes place in the Niger Delta. Armed gangs divert as much as 5 percent of the oil through a practice called bunkering, maneuvering small boats at night to siphon off oil from lightly guarded pipelines in remote areas. The stolen oil eventually reaches the international market, first passing through layers of middlemen. Human rights activists, however, claim the problem is not limited to local thugs, alleging that the army, the police, local politicians, and even the oil companies participate in bunkering schemes. Such lawlessness costs more than money. In

2006, nearly 200 villagers were killed when a gasoline pipeline exploded in Inagbe, a fishing community 30 miles east of Lagos. Officials believe the explosion occurred because of the common practice of puncturing the pipeline to siphon off gasoline.

The security situation continued to deteriorate. In early 2006, the commander of another group, the Movement for the Emancipation of the Niger Delta (MEND), declared total war on foreign oil operations. MEND demanded the return of control of Nigeria's oil wealth to the region where it is produced and the release of two ethnic Ijaw leaders being held by the central government on money laundering and treason charges. To further its goals, it sabotaged oil-pumping stations, attacked transport barges, and kidnapped foreign oil workers, snatching them from offshore drilling rigs. MEND's actions have cut production in the Niger Delta by 455,000 barrels a day, costing the government, the industry, and the country billions of dollars of lost revenues. Shell, for example, abandoned one field in the southern Niger Delta producing 115,000 barrels per day, citing safety concerns for its employees.

Nor is the violence limited to MEND. In May 2006, three expatriate employees of ENI, the Italian oil company, were kidnapped in Port Harcourt, and an American employee of Baker Hughes was murdered in that city. In June 2006 eight foreign oil workers were kidnapped from an oil rig located 40 miles offshore operated by a subsidiary of Norway's Fred Olsen Energy Company. The eight were released a day later. MEND claimed it was not responsible for the murder or the kidnappings, alleging that another group had done so, motivated by the lure of ransom money. However, later in the week, MEND, the Niger Delta People's Volunteer Force, and another group, the Martyrs Brigade, launched a coordinated, 10-boat-strong attack on an oil facility in Port Harcourt, destroying a drilling rig, sinking two naval vessels, killing several soldiers, and abducting five South Korean workers. Six Chevron employees were kidnap victims in May 2007; fortunately they were released a month later unharmed. In 2008, MEND launched an assault on Shell's Bonga oil platform, located 120 kilometers offshore, thereby serving notice that no oil facility was safe from its attacks. In 2009, MEND and the government agreed to an amnesty. While violence has diminished, other rebel groups, some led by former MEND officials, rejected the peacemaking initiative. For example, in November 2010, seven workers were kidnapped off an Exxon offshore oil platform, while an onshore oil rig owned by Italy's AGIP was bombed in March 2011.

As if this operating environment were not difficult enough, the reputation of the oil companies operating in the region has also come under attack. Royal Dutch Shell has drawn the bulk of the blame by Western activists and local citizens, although other Western companies, such as Chevron, have been targeted as well. Environmental groups and NGOs like Global Exchange and Essential Action have argued that the oil companies are taking advantage of lax enforcement of environmental laws to pollute the area and ignore the damage caused by oil and gasoline spills. Other activists have argued that Shell has alleged sabotage of the pipelines to cover up spills resulting from the company's lack of maintenance. Human rights activists claim that the foreign oil companies are complicit in human rights violations by the Nigerian government as it attempts to suppress political dissent and insurgent activity in the region.

Questions

1. Assess the political risks facing foreign oil companies operating in the Niger Delta. Should they shut down operations in the area until security improves?
2. What is the responsibility of Western oil companies like Royal Dutch Shell and Chevron to the local community?
3. What responsibility does a drilling company like Fred Olsen Energy have to its employees? In the case of kidnappings motivated by profit, should a company pay ransom?
4. Is the discovery of oil a blessing or a curse?

Sources: "The real thing," *The Economist*, April 23, 2011, p. 50; "Shell stands firm on Nigerian spill," *Houston Chronicle*, January 27, 2011, p. D6; "The president is threatened by a fraying amnesty," *The Economist*, January 1, 2011; "Hints of a new chapter," *The Economist*, November 14, 2010; "Nigeria's oil-export reliability at risk," *Wall Street Journal*, February 11, 2008, p. A14; "Nigeria's gang violence escalates," *New York Times*, November 9, 2007 (online); "In Nigeria's violent delta, hostage negotiators thrive," *Wall Street Journal*, June 7, 2007, p. A1; "Militants attack Nigeria oil field," *CNN.com*, June 7, 2006; "Nigerian kidnappers release foreign oil workers," *Wall Street Journal*, June 4, 2006 (online); "Nigerian gunmen abduct 8 workers from oil platform," *Wall Street Journal*, June 3, 2006, p. A5; "Gasoline pipeline explodes in Nigeria, killing about 200," *New York Times*, May 13, 2006, p. A3; "Africa: Nigeria: Gunmen kidnap 3 foreign oil workers," *New York Times*, May 12, 2006 (online); "As oil supplies are stretched, rebels, terrorists get new clout," *Wall Street Journal*, April 10, 2006, p. A1; "Oil giants to steer clear until Nigeria has a truce," *Houston Chronicle*, April 6, 2006, p. D8; "Insecurity in Nigerian oil delta here to stay," *Houston Chronicle*, March 24, 2006, p. A19; "Nigeria militants threaten more attacks," *Houston Chronicle*, March 6, 2006, p. A8; "Poverty in the midst of wealth," *Houston Chronicle*, March 1, 2006, p. D8; "Militants say the plan is to take more hostages," *Houston Chronicle*, February 23, 2006, p. D3; "Nigeria oil 'total war' warning," *BBC News*, February 17, 2006 (online); "SEC widens Nigeria bribery probe with Shell subpoena," *Financial Times*, October 13, 2005, p. 4; "Nigerian army warns oil rebels," *BBC News*, September 28, 2004 (online); "Nigeria's oil capital under siege," *BBC News*, September 8, 2004 (online); "Women storm Nigeria oil plant," *BBC News*, July 9, 2002 (online); "Nigeria oil rig workers seized," *BBC News*, April 23, 2002 (online); *The World Factbook*, www.cia.gov (online).

The Power of Microfinance: The Grameen Bank

The lack of a well-functioning credit market is often a hindrance to rural villagers and farmers in developing countries. Living from harvest to harvest, the rural poor are vulnerable to the vagaries of the weather. When the previous harvest fails, far too often rural farmers are forced to borrow sums to plant the next crop at extortionate interest rates that keep them indebted to the money lenders.

To break this cycle of poverty, a new form of lending to the poor has emerged: microfinance. Microfinance institutions typically focus on making very small loans—typically from $25 to $200—to rural entrepreneurs to begin or expand a small business. Microfinance lenders oftentimes provide other services to the rural villagers they serve, including offering savings accounts, life insurance, and basic health care.

The founder of the microfinance movement is Muhammad Yunus, an economics professor at Bangladesh's Chittagong University. In 1976, he made a small loan out of his own pocket to local craft makers in a nearby village. That $27 loan was the inspiration for the Grameen Bank, the world's most successful microfinance institution. Since its founding in 1983, the Grameen Bank has lent more than $5 billion to 5.3 million people and inspired over 3,000 imitators who have reached an additional 93 million clients. Yunus and the Grameen Bank were awarded the 2006 Nobel Peace Prize in recognition of their accomplishments.

Traditional banks focus on making large loans to creditworthy, ongoing businesses. Yunus turned Grameen's attention to the needs of the rural poor in Bangladesh. Most bank loans are to men. Yunus believed that Grameen should focus on lending to women, as they were more likely to recognize the needs of their families and their communities: 96 percent of Grameen's loans are to women. Often they were illiterate, so Grameen dispensed with paperwork. Often they lacked collateral, so Grameen developed a new lending model based on trust and peer pressure. Loans are made to individuals in lending groups, consisting of five to ten members. Social pressure from members of the group encourages each borrower to make her loan payments on time. Default rates on Grameen loans are remarkably small: 1 to 2 percent, on average, although they soared after the catastrophic 1998 flood that devastated Bangladesh.

Buoyed by the success of its microfinance operations, the Grameen group has developed new ways to alleviate rural poverty. Grameen Telecom has teamed with Norway's Telenor to provide cell phone service in rural villages. The Grameen Bank provides small loans to "village telephone ladies" to buy a cell phone. The telephone lady then charges villagers a small fee to use the cell phone, which has allowed local entrepreneurs to identify new markets and lower their costs of doing business (see Chapter 16's closing case, "A Call for Progress"). The Grameen Group also created a joint venture with Danone SA, the giant French food conglomerate, to improve nutrition in Bangladesh through the provision of healthier foods and to reduce poverty by developing new markets for poor local farmers. Grameen Danone's first product is low-priced Shoktidoi yogurt (Bengali for "yogurt that makes you strong"), which sells for about 6 eurocents a cup. Shoktidoi yogurt is formulated to address nutritional deficiencies of the local children—an estimated 56 percent of Bangladeshi children suffer from malnutrition—using locally sourced milk and molasses made from dates.

Case Questions

1. How transferable is the Grameen Bank's business model? Would it work in your country? How important are the cultural values of Bangladeshi society to its success?
2. Numerous banks and venture capitalists have established for-profit microfinance companies to provide small loans

to villagers in India and in numerous African nations. Yet some critics have argued it is immoral to profit from the poverty of these impoverished peoples. Do you agree? Should microfinance be limited to not for profit organizations like Grameen Bank?

3. Grameen Bank has teamed with Telenor and Danone to provide telephone service and a low-priced, but nutritious yogurt. Can you think of any other goods or services that could benefit the rural poor through joint ventures between nonprofit organizations and for-profit international businesses?

Sources: "Microfinance falls short of initial promise," *Houston Chronicle*, March 13, 2011, D6; Danone Social and Economic Report 2006; "Nobel winner Yunus: Microcredit missionary," *Business Week*, December 26, 2005 (online); Mainsah, Evaristus, Heuer, Schuyler, Kalra, Aprajita, and Zhang, Qiulin, "Grameen Bank: Taking capitalism to the poor," *Chazen Web Journal of International Business*, Spring 2004, Columbia Business School (online); http://www.grameenfoundation.org

Endnotes

1. "BP agrees to penalty in North Slope spill lawsuit settlement," *Anchorage Daily News*, May 4, 2011 (online); "BP will pay fine in spills," *Wall Street Journal*, May 4, 2011, p. B3; "The shores of recovery," *The Economist*, April 23, 2011, p. 31; "BP's safety drive faces rough road," *Wall Street Journal*, February 1, 2011, p. A1; National Commission on the BP Deepwater Oil Spill and Offshore Drilling, *Deep Water: The Gulf Oil Disaster and the Future of Offshore Drilling: Report to the President*, January 2011; "In BP's record, a history of boldness and costly blunders," *New York Times*, July 12, 2010; "As CEO Hayward remade BP, safety, cost drives clash," *Wall Street Journal*, June 29, 2010; U.S. Department of Labor press release 10-234-CHI, March 8, 2010; U.S. Department of Energy, April 2007 at www.hss.doe.gov/csa/csp/advisory/SAd_2007-02.pdf.

2. "Slave chocolate?," *Forbes*, April 24, 2006, p. 96; "Can we talk?" *Fortune*, September 2, 2002, pp. 102-110; "'Tradition' perpetuating poverty," *Houston Chronicle*, June 23, 2002, p. 28A; "U.S. Child-Labor Law sparks a trade dispute over Brazilian oranges," *Wall Street Journal*, September 9, 1998, p. A1.

3. "Supermarket giant Ahold ousts CEO in big accounting scandal," *Wall Street Journal*, February 25, 2003, pp. A1, A10; "Milk powder makers accused over Africa," *Financial Times*, January 18–19, 2003, p. 4; "As UNICEF battles baby-formula makers, African infants sicken," *Wall Street Journal*, December 5, 2000, p. A1.

4. See Norman Barry, *Business Ethics* (West Lafayette, IN: Purdue University Press, 1999).

5. Rebecca Mead, "Dressing for Lula," *The New Yorker*, March 17, 2003, pp. 82ff.

6. "No way out," *Fortune*, January 20, 2003, pp. 102ff.

7. "For steel-wool maker, Chinese lessons," *New York Times*, May 28, 1996, p. C5.

8. "Tire suit treads loudly in China," *Wall Street Journal*, May 4, 2011, p. B1; "Data out of the door," *Financial Times*, February 2, 2011, p. 8.

9. "AIDS gaffes in Africa come back to haunt drug industry at home," *Wall Street Journal*, April 23, 2001, p. A1; "Drug companies face assault on prices," *Wall Street Journal*, May 11, 2000, pp. B1, B4.

10. Jeremy Kahn, "Presto chango! Sales are huge," *Fortune*, March 20, 2000, pp. 90–96; "More firms falsify revenue to boost stocks," *USA Today*, March 29, 2000, p. 1B.

11. "How U.S. concerns compete in countries where bribes flourish," *Wall Street Journal*, September 29, 1995, pp. A1, A14; Patricia Digh, "Shades of gray in the global marketplace," *HRMagazine*, April 1997, pp. 90–98.

12. "Corporate Canada wary of using bribery," *Financial Post*, May 15, 2002, p. FP5.

13. "Bribery drives up the cost of living in Kenya," *Financial Times*, January 19–20, 2002, p. 4.

14. "Cancer of corruption spreads throughout the country," *Financial Times*, November 1, 2002, p. 6; "Chinese corruption has sliced up to 16% off GDP over decade, study estimates," *Wall Street Journal*, March 8, 2001, p. A10.

15. "Dealing with an eruption of corruption," *Financial Times*, May 30, 2000, Managing Risk Supplement, p. 15.

16. Thomas Donaldson and Lee E. Preston, "The stakeholder theory of the corporation: Concepts, evidence, and implications," *Academy of Management Review*, vol. 20, no. 1 (1995), pp. 65–91. See also Jeffrey S. Harrison and R. Edward Freeman, "Stakeholders, social responsibility, and performance: Empirical evidence and theoretical perspectives," *Academy of Management Journal*, vol. 42, no. 5 (1999), pp. 479–495.

17. Aseem Prakash, *Greening the Firm* (Cambridge: Cambridge University Press, 2000); Forest L. Reinhardt, *Down to Earth* (Boston: Harvard Business School Press, 2000).

18. "Oil companies strive to turn a new leaf to save rain forest," *Wall Street Journal*, July 17, 1997, pp. A1, A8.

19. "How Home Depot and activists joined to cut logging abuse," *Wall Street Journal*, September 26, 2000, p. A1.

20. Petra Christmann and Glen Taylor, "Globalization and the environment: Strategies for international voluntary environmental initiatives," *Academy of Management Executive*, vol. 16, no. 3 (2002), pp. 121–130.

21. Christine Y. Chen and Greg Lindsay, "Will Amazon(.com) save the Amazon?" *Fortune*, March 20, 2000, pp. 224–226.

22. "Human rights in focus as US interest in African oil surges," *Financial Times*, October 29, 2002, p. 8.

23. World Bank, World Development Indicators database, May 26, 2011.

24. "Milk powder makers accused over Africa," *Financial Times*, January 18–19, 2003, p. 4.

25. "Inside America's most reviled company," *BusinessWeek*, November 29, 1999, pp. 176–192.

26. "Another side of tilapia, the perfect factory fish," *Wall Street Journal*, May 2, 2011; Regal Springs Tilapia press release, "Regal Springs farm first to be Aquaculture Dialogue compliant," October 22, 2010; Regal Springs Tilapia press release, "Sysco, WWF deal a big boost for 'green' seafood," April 17, 2009.

27. "Doing good and doing well at Timberland," *Wall Street Journal*, September 9, 2003, p. B1.

28. Lynn Sharp Paine, "Managing for organizational integrity," *Harvard Business Review* (March–April 1994), pp. 106–115.

29. http://www.merck.com/responsibility/access/access-feature-mectizan.html (accessed April 26, 2011); *Merck 2007 Annual Review*, p. 12; "Africa recovery," allAfrica.com, April 22, 2003 (online); www.merck.com, press release 090502 (online).

30. "A new way of giving," *Time*, July 24, 2000, pp. 48–51.

31. David M. Messick and Max H. Bazerman, "Ethical leadership and the psychology of decision making," *Sloan Management Review* (Winter 1996), pp. 9–22.

32. www.patagonia.com, accessed on May 26, 2011.

33. See Janet P. Near and Marcia P. Miceli, "Whistle-blowing: Myth and reality," *Journal of Management*, vol. 22, no. 3 (1996), pp. 507–526, for a review of the literature on whistle-blowing.

34. "Executive challenges Xerox's books, is fired," *Wall Street Journal*, February 6, 2001, p. C1.

35. "A louder blast from Japan's whistle-blowers," *BusinessWeek*, September 2, 2002 (online).

36. Mark Magnier, "Speaking out has high cost," *Los Angeles Times*, at www.soeken.lawsonline.net (online).

37. "Scandals put whistle-blowers in heroic light," *Nikkei Weekly*, September 9, 2002 (online).

38. Rob van Tulder and Alex van der Zwart, *International Business-Society Management* (London: Taylor & Francis, 2006).

39. "Charity at home," *The Economist*, July 9, 2011, p. 38.

40. "Swiss launch bribery probe in Kazakh case," *Wall Street Journal*, May 6, 2003, p. A22; "U.S. bribery probe looks at Mobil," *Wall Street Journal*, April 23, 2003, p. A2; "Former Mobil executive pleads not guilty to Kazak oil kickback," *Wall Street Journal*, April 8, 2003, p. A12.

41. "Lines less blurred," *Financial Times*, July 18, 2011, p. 7; "Cost of turning a blind eye to graft: Corruption probes teach US oil services company a $44m lesson," *Financial Times*, April 10, 2008, p. 12.

42. "U.K. outlines bribery laws," *Wall Street Journal*, March 31, 2011; "Exports warning as bribery law is delayed," *Financial Times*, January 31, 2011; "U.K. law on bribes has firms in a sweat," *Wall Street Journal*, December 28, 2010.

43. "Slave chocolate?" *Forbes*, April 24, 2006, p. 96; "Making a federal case out of overseas abuses," *BusinessWeek*, November 25, 2002, p. 78.

44. "Corporate Canada wary of using bribery," *Financial Post*, May 15, 2002, p. FP5.

45. "Do-it-yourself labor standards," *BusinessWeek*, November 19, 2001, pp. 74–76, 108.

CHAPTER 6

International Trade and Investment

AFTER STUDYING THIS CHAPTER, YOU SHOULD BE ABLE TO:

1. Understand the motivation for international trade.

2. Summarize and discuss the differences among the classical country-based theories of international trade.

3. Use the modern firm-based theories of international trade to describe global strategies adopted by businesses.

4. Describe and categorize the different forms of international investment.

5. Explain the reasons for foreign direct investment.

6. Summarize how supply, demand, and political factors influence foreign direct investment.

Access a host of interactive learning aids at **www.pearsonglobaleditions.com/ mymanagementlab** to help strengthen your understanding of the chapter concepts.

MyManagementLab

© vario images GmbH & Co.KG/Alamy

THE MITTELSTAND LEAD THE WAY

During the 2008–2009 global recession, Germany's economy suffered a deeper downturn but recovered more quickly and strongly than most developed countries. In 2010, its 3.6 percent real GDP growth exceeded that of Japan (3.0 percent), the United States (2.9 percent), and the United Kingdom (1.6 percent). The German economy's solid performance is attributable in part to the exporting prowess of the so-called Mittelstand, which are the backbone of Germany's manufacturing sector. A typical Mittelstand firm is a small- to medium-sized, family-owned enterprise, often located in a small town or city. Many of the Mittelstand compete on quality, innovation, reliability, and craftsmanship, not price. German labor costs are high, but the labor force is well educated and quality oriented. The Mittelstand account for about 60 percent of Germany's private sector workforce and 38 percent of corporate sales.

Many Mittelstand firms specialize in product niches, but then aim to be the world's best in that niche. Some of them make the machines that make things. For example, Kugler-Womako is a world leader in crafting the machines that make passports; Wirtgen specializes in manufacturing machines that make new tar roads out of old ones; Koenig & Bauer fabricates printing presses. Other Mittelstand firms focus on more mundane products. Tente produces casters for hospital beds, while Aeroxon is a leader in manufacturing flycatchers. The emphasis is on making durable, well-engineered products. Devotion to customer service is another hallmark of the Mittelstand, as is their export orientation. Over 90 percent of Koenig & Bauer's revenue is generated from exporting, for example.

Mittelstand firms are known for their resourcefulness. Heidelberger Druckmaschinen, one of the world's leading makers of offset printing presses, has created a profitable contract manufacturing business. Unternehmensgruppe Fischer has leveraged its manufacturing acumen to develop a lucrative consulting business teaching other manufacturers how to improve their operating efficiency.

The Mittelstand do face many challenges, of course. Labor costs in Germany are much higher than in emerging manufacturing powerhouses like China or Brazil, so they must continually innovate and improve their product lines. They also must confront Germany's demographic challenges. They rely on the skilled craftspeople produced by Germany's educational system, but Germany's low birth rate has raised concerns about the size and composition of its future labor force. To make matters worse, for the past several years, Germany has experienced net outmigration, particularly among its scientists, engineers, and other highly skilled workers who have been targeted by recruiters from other countries. The small size of some members of the Mittelstand means they lack the resources to establish their own personnel recruiting offices in other countries. Moreover, Germany's restrictive immigration laws make it difficult to recruit new employees from non-EU countries.[1] ■

The Mittelstand are prime examples of the firms throughout the world who have utilized technology, knowledge, and the resources at their disposal to compete successfully in the global marketplace. In this chapter we analyze the underlying economic forces that shape and structure the international business transactions conducted by the Mittelstand and thousands of other firms. We discuss the major theories that explain and predict international trade and investment activity. These theories help firms sharpen their global business strategies, identify promising export and investment opportunities, and react to threats posed by foreign competitors. As they introduce you to the economic environment in which firms compete, the theories help you understand why Mittelstand firms, despite their high labor costs, have proved to be so successful in international markets.

International Trade and the World Economy

Trade is the voluntary exchange of goods, services, assets, or money between one person or organization and another. Because it is voluntary, both parties to the transaction must believe they will gain from the exchange or else they would not complete it. **International trade** is trade between residents of two countries. The residents may be individuals, firms, not-for-profit organizations, or other forms of associations.

Why does international trade occur? The answer follows directly from our definition of trade: Both parties to the transaction, who happen to reside in two different countries, believe they benefit from the voluntary exchange. Behind this simple truth lies much economic theory, business practice, government policy, and international conflict—topics we cover in this and the next four chapters.

FIGURE 6.1

The Growth of World Exports since 1950

Source: International Monetary Fund Supplement on Trade Statistics (International Monetary Fund, Washington, DC: 1990); World Trade Organization website (www.wto.org), June 2011.

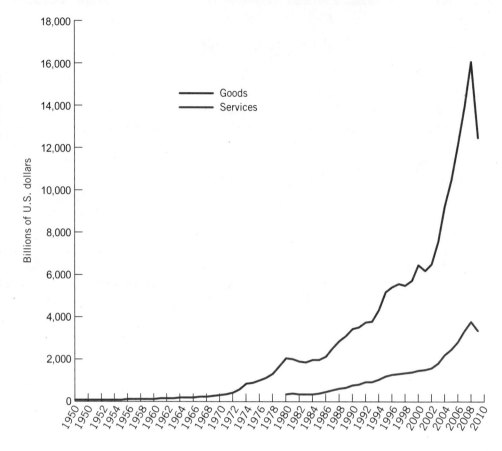

As Figure 6.1 indicates, world trade has grown dramatically in the half century since the end of World War II. Total international merchandise trade in 2009 was $12.5 trillion, or approximately 21 percent of the world's $58.2 trillion gross domestic product (GDP); trade in services that year amounted to $3.4 trillion. The European Union, the United States, Canada, and Japan accounted for 52.4 percent of the world's merchandise exports (see Figure 6.2); China, 9.6 percent; and other countries, 38 percent. Such international trade has important direct and indirect effects on national economies. On the one hand, exports spark additional economic activity in the domestic economy. Consider a leading exporter like Caterpillar. Its $13.4 billion in exports generates orders for its U.S. suppliers, wages for its U.S. workers, and dividend payments for its U.S. shareholders, all of which then create income for local automobile dealers, grocery stores, and others, which in turn add to their own payrolls. On the other hand, imports can pressure domestic suppliers to cut their prices and improve their competitiveness. Failure to respond to foreign competition may lead to closed factories and unemployed workers.

FIGURE 6.2

Source of the World's Merchandise Exports, 2009

Source: World Trade Organization (www.wto.org), April 2009.

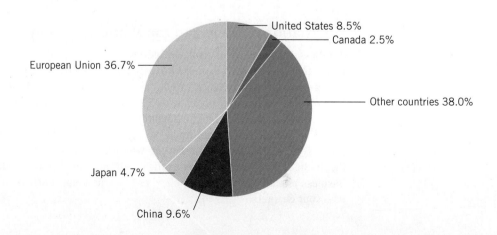

Because of the obvious significance of international trade to businesses, consumers, and workers, scholars have attempted to develop theories to explain and predict the forces that motivate such trade. Governments use these theories when they design policies they hope will benefit their countries' industries and citizens. Managers use them to identify promising markets and profitable internationalization strategies.

Classical Country-Based Trade Theories

The first theories of international trade developed with the rise of the great European nation-states during the sixteenth century. Not surprisingly, these early theories focused on the individual country in examining patterns of exports and imports. As we discuss in more detail later in this chapter, these country-based theories are particularly useful for describing trade in commodities—standardized, undifferentiated goods such as oil, sugar, or lumber that are typically bought on the basis of price rather than brand name. However, as multinational corporations (MNCs) rose to power in the middle of the twentieth century, scholars shifted their attention to the firm's role in promoting international trade. The firm-based theories developed after World War II are useful in describing patterns of trade in differentiated goods—those such as automobiles, consumer electronics, and personal care products, for which brand name is an important component of the customer's purchase decision. In this section, we examine the classical country-based theories of international trade; in the next section, we explore the more modern firm-based theories.

Mercantilism

Mercantilism is a sixteenth-century economic philosophy that maintains that a country's wealth is measured by its holdings of gold and silver. According to mercantilists, a country's goal should be to enlarge these holdings by promoting exports and discouraging imports. The logic was transparent to sixteenth-century policymakers: If foreigners buy more goods from you than you buy from them, then the foreigners have to pay you the difference in gold and silver, enabling you to amass more treasure. Mercantilist terminology is still used today, for example, when television commentators and newspaper headlines report that a country suffered an "unfavorable" balance of trade—that is, its exports were less than its imports.

At the time mercantilism seemed to be sound economic policy. Large gold and silver holdings meant the reigning monarchs could afford to hire armies to fight other countries and thereby expand their realms. Politically, mercantilism was popular with many manufacturers and their workers. Export-oriented manufacturers favored mercantilist trade policies, such as those establishing subsidies or tax rebates, which stimulated sales to foreigners. Domestic manufacturers threatened by foreign imports endorsed mercantilist trade policies, such as those imposing tariffs or quotas, which protected the manufacturers from foreign competition. These businesses, their workers, their suppliers, and the local politicians representing the communities in which the manufacturers had production facilities all praised the wisdom of the monarchs' mercantilist policies.

Most members of society, however, are hurt by such policies. Governmental subsidies of the exports of certain industries are paid by taxpayers in the form of higher taxes. Governmental import restrictions are paid for by consumers in the form of higher prices because domestic firms face less competition from foreign producers. During the age of imperialism, governments often shifted the burden of mercantilist policies onto their colonies. For example, under the Navigation Act of 1660 all European goods imported by the American colonies had to be shipped from Great Britain. The British prohibited colonial firms from exporting certain goods that might compete with those from British factories, such as hats, finished iron goods, and woolens. To ensure adequate supplies of low-cost inputs for British merchants, the British required some colonial industries to sell their output only to British firms. This output included rice, tobacco, and naval stores (forest products used in shipbuilding).[2] This particular mercantilist strategy ultimately backfired—it contributed to the grievances that led to the overthrow of the British Crown in the American colonies.

Because mercantilism does benefit certain members of society, mercantilist policies are still politically attractive to some firms and their workers. Modern supporters of such policies, called

neomercantilists or **protectionists**, include such diverse U.S. groups as the American Federation of Labor–Congress of Industrial Organizations, textile manufacturers, steel companies, sugar growers, and peanut farmers.

Protectionist attitudes are not limited to the United States. North Americans and Europeans have long complained that Japan limits the access of foreign goods to its market. For instance, it took 40 years of negotiations before Japan grudgingly agreed in the 1990s to allow the importation of foreign rice, and even then it limited rice imports to less than 10 percent of its market. Asian and North American firms criticize the Europeans for imposing barriers against imported goods such as beef, bananas, and other agricultural products. Such finger-pointing is amply justified: Nearly every country has adopted some neomercantilist policies to protect key industries in its economy.

Absolute Advantage

Neomercantilism has superficial appeal, particularly to patriots who want to strengthen their country's economy. Why shouldn't a country try to maximize its holdings of gold and silver? According to Adam Smith, the Scottish economist who is viewed as the father of free-market economics, mercantilism's basic problem is that it confuses the acquisition of treasure with the acquisition of wealth. In *An Inquiry into the Nature and Causes of the Wealth of Nations* (1776), Smith attacked the intellectual basis of mercantilism and demonstrated that it actually weakens a country, because it robs individuals of the ability to trade freely and to benefit from voluntary exchanges. Moreover, in the process of avoiding imports at all costs, a country must squander its resources producing goods it is not suited to produce. The inefficiencies caused by mercantilism reduce the wealth of the country as a whole, even though certain special interest groups may benefit.

Smith advocated free trade among countries as a means of enlarging a country's wealth. Free trade enables a country to expand the amount of goods and services available to it by specializing in the production of some goods and services and trading for others. But which goods and services should a country export and which should it import? To answer this question, Smith developed the **theory of absolute advantage**, which suggests that a country should export those goods and services for which it is more productive than other countries are and import those goods and services for which other countries are more productive than it is.

This statue of Adam Smith enjoys a prominent location on Edinburgh's Royal Mile. His influential 1776 work, *The Wealth of Nations,* promoted the virtues of free trade and undermined public and intellectual support for mercantilism.

Liz Leyden/iStockphoto

TABLE 6.1 The Theory of Absolute Advantage: An Example

	Output Per Hour of Labor	
	France	Japan
Wine	2	1
Clock radios	3	5

Absolute advantage can be demonstrated through a numerical example. Assume, for the sake of simplicity, that there are only two countries in the world, France and Japan; only two goods, wine and clock radios; and only one factor of production, labor. Table 6.1 shows the output of the two goods per hour of labor for the two countries. In France 1 hour of labor can produce either 2 bottles of wine or 3 clock radios. In Japan 1 hour of labor can produce either 1 bottle of wine or 5 clock radios. France has an absolute advantage in the production of wine: One hour of labor produces 2 bottles in France but only 1 in Japan. Japan has an absolute advantage in the production of clock radios: One hour of labor produces 5 clock radios in Japan but only 3 in France.

If France and Japan are able to trade with each other, both will be better off. Suppose France agrees to exchange 2 bottles of wine for 4 clock radios. Only 1 hour of French labor is needed to produce the 2 bottles of wine bound for Japan. In return, France will get 4 clock radios from Japan. These 4 clock radios would have required 1.33 hours of French labor had France produced them rather than buy them from Japan. By trading with Japan rather than producing the clock radios itself, France saves 0.33 hour of labor. France can use this freed-up labor to produce more wine, which in turn can be consumed by French citizens or traded to Japan for more clock radios. By allocating its scarce labor to produce goods for which it is more productive than Japan and then trading them to Japan, France can consume more goods than it could have done in the absence of trade.

Japan is similarly better off. Japan uses 0.8 hour of labor to produce the 4 clock radios to exchange for the 2 bottles of French wine. Producing the 2 bottles of wine itself would have required 2 hours of labor. By producing clock radios and then trading them to France, Japan saves 1.2 hours of labor, which can be used to produce more clock radios that the Japanese can consume themselves or trade to France for more wine.

Comparative Advantage

The theory of absolute advantage makes intuitive sense. Unfortunately, the theory is flawed. What happens to trade if one country has an absolute advantage in both products? The theory of absolute advantage incorrectly suggests that no trade would occur. David Ricardo, an early-nineteenth-century British economist, solved this problem by developing the **theory of comparative advantage**, which states that a country should produce and export those goods and services for which it is *relatively* more productive than other countries are and import those goods and services for which other countries are *relatively* more productive than it is.[3]

The difference between the two theories is subtle: Absolute advantage looks at absolute productivity differences; comparative advantage looks at relative productivity differences. The distinction occurs because comparative advantage incorporates the concept of opportunity cost in determining which good a country should produce. The **opportunity cost** of a good is the value of what is given up to get the good. Most of us apply the principles of comparative advantage and opportunity cost without realizing it. Consider a brain surgeon who is better at both brain surgery and lawn mowing than her neighbor's teenaged son is. If the surgeon is comparatively better at surgery than at lawn mowing, she will spend most of her time at the operating table and pay the teenager to mow her lawn. The brain surgeon behaves this way because the opportunity cost of mowing the lawn is too high: Time spent mowing is time unavailable for surgery.

Let us return to the example in Table 6.1 to contrast absolute and comparative advantage. Recall that France has an absolute advantage in wine and Japan has an absolute advantage in

TABLE 6.2 The Theory of Comparative Advantage: An Example

	Output Per Hour of Labor	
	France	Japan
Wine	4	1
Clock radios	6	5

clock radios. The theory of absolute advantage says that France should export wine to Japan and Japan should export clock radios to France. As Table 6.1 shows, France also has a comparative advantage in wine: With 1 hour of labor it produces 2 times as much wine as Japan does but only 0.6 times as many clock radios. Thus, France is relatively more productive in wine. Japan has a comparative advantage in clock radios: With 1 hour of labor it produces 1.67 times as many clock radios as France does but only 0.5 times as much wine. So Japan is relatively more productive in clock radios. The theory of comparative advantage says that France should export wine to Japan and Japan should export clock radios to France. For the example in Table 6.1, the theory of absolute advantage and the theory of comparative advantage both yield the same outcome.

Now let us change the facts. Suppose productivity stays the same in Japan but doubles in France as the result of new job training programs. Table 6.2 shows this new situation. France now can produce 4 bottles of wine or 6 clock radios per hour of labor. France now has an absolute advantage in both wine and clock radios: For each hour of labor, France can produce 3 more bottles of wine (4 minus 1) or 1 more clock radio (6 minus 5) than Japan can. According to the theory of absolute advantage, no trade should occur, because France is more productive than Japan in producing both goods.

The theory of comparative advantage, on the other hand, indicates that trade should still occur. France is 4 times better than Japan is in wine production but only 1.2 times better in clock radio production. (Alternatively, Japan is only 0.25 times as good as France in wine production but 0.83 times as good in clock radio production.) France is comparatively better than Japan in wine production, while Japan is comparatively better than France in clock radio production.

By the theory of comparative advantage, France should export wine to Japan and Japan should export clock radios to France. If they do so, both will be better off. In the absence of trade, 1 bottle of wine will sell for 1.5 clock radios in France and for 5 clock radios in Japan. If Japan offers to trade 2 clock radios for 1 bottle of wine, France will be better off—even though France has an absolute advantage in clock radio production. Without trade, sacrificing 1 bottle of wine domestically would yield France only 1.5 clock radios in increased production. With trade, France could get 2 clock radios by giving up 1 bottle of wine to Japan. France gets more clock radios per bottle of wine given up by trading with Japan than by producing the clock radios domestically.

Japan also gains. Without trade, Japan has to give up 5 clock radios to get 1 more bottle of wine. With trade, Japan has to give up only 2 clock radios to obtain 1 more bottle. Japan gets more wine per clock radio given up by trading with France than by producing the wine domestically. Even though France has an absolute advantage in both wine and clock radio production, both countries gain from this trade. It is comparative advantage that motivates trade, not absolute advantage. For another insight into comparative advantage and the problems inherent in neomercantilism, see "Bringing the World into Focus."

Comparative Advantage with Money

The lesson of the theory of comparative advantage is simple but powerful: *You are better off specializing in what you do relatively best. Produce (and export) those goods and services you are relatively best able to produce, and buy other goods and services from people who are relatively better at producing them than you are.*

Of course, Tables 6.1 and 6.2 are both simplistic and artificial. The world economy produces more than two goods and services and is made up of more than two countries. Barriers to trade may exist, someone must pay to transport goods between markets, and inputs other than labor are necessary to produce goods. Even more important, the world economy uses

Foreign trade policy has been debated by politicians, pundits, and professors for centuries. Proponents of free trade see little distinction between domestic trade and foreign trade: If the voluntary exchange of good, services, and assets between two residents of the same country is to be encouraged because it benefits both parties to the transaction, the same logic should hold true for voluntary exchanges between a domestic resident and a foreigner. But other groups argue that government policy should favor domestic producers over foreign producers. In their view, foreign trade builds up the economies of foreign countries while weakening the domestic economy. Abraham Lincoln, for example, endorsed this position with his characteristic clarity: "I know this much. When we buy goods manufactured abroad, we get the goods and the foreigner gets the money. When we buy goods manufactured at home, we get both the goods and the money."

While Lincoln's statements may seem like common sense to patriots concerned about strengthening their nation's economy and promoting job opportunities for their fellow citizens, trade experts find his argument misleading and incomplete. Lincoln is correct in asserting that buying goods from foreign producers sends our money abroad, while buying goods from domestic producers keeps our money in our country. What his argument fails to consider is the resources—the factors of production—needed to create the goods. When we buy goods produced domestically, domestic factors of production, such as labor, land, and natural resources, must be consumed and thus are unavailable for other uses. When we buy goods produced by foreigners, foreign resources are used, leaving the domestic factors of production available to be used for other purposes. That, of course, is the benefit of free trade in the eyes of proponents like Adam Smith and David Ricardo: it allows a country to allocate its domestic resources to produce goods for which the country has a comparative advantage.

Thus, a more complete and appropriate analysis would be: "When we buy goods from domestic producers, we (or our countrymen) get the goods and the money, but to do so we have to consume some of our country's resources that could have been used to make other goods. When we buy goods from foreign producers, we get the goods and we get to keep the resources that would otherwise be needed to produce those goods domestically; the foreigners get our money, but they have to consume their resources to make the goods they sold to us." If we utilize those freed resources to specialize in the production of goods for which we have a comparative advantage—and so do our foreign trading partners—both we and our foreign trading partners will have more goods to consume after we engage in international trade.

The gains from specialization and trade are reflected in how most of us spend our daily lives. As producers, we spend our workweek specializing in providing a single service, whether it's unclogging a drain as a plumber or writing code as a computer programmer. As consumers, we buy almost everything we consume from other specialists. To obtain food, we trade money for groceries from the supermarket; to obtain clothing, we trade money for jeans or shirts from the clothing retailer. It is certainly true that when we purchase our food from the grocer, we get the food and the grocer gets our money, but both of us benefit from this transaction. If we had to grow our own food, we would have to devote more of our time and energies to that task and less time to our own productive specialty, be it computer programming or plumbing. Most of us quickly determine that our standard of living will be higher if we focus our energies on our productive specialty and then trade for goods and services produced by others. This concept applies to countries as well as individuals. By specializing in products for which they have a comparative advantage and trading freely, countries' productivity increases and, therefore, their citizens have more to consume and a higher standard of living than they would if trade were restricted by tariffs, quotas, and other barriers

money as a medium of exchange. Table 6.3 introduces money into our discussion of trade and incorporates the following assumptions:

1. The output per hour of labor in France and Japan for clock radios and wine is as shown in Table 6.2.
2. The hourly wage rate in France is 12 euros (€).
3. The hourly wage rate in Japan is 1,000 yen (¥).
4. One euro is worth 125 yen.

TABLE 6.3 The Theory of Comparative Advantage with Money: An Example

	Cost of Goods in France		Cost of Goods in Japan	
	French Made	Japanese Made	French Made	Japanese Made
Wine	€3	€8	¥375	¥1,000
Clock radios	€2	€1.6	¥250	¥200

Note: For example, 1 hour's worth of French labor can produce 4 bottles of wine at a total cost of €12 or an average cost of €3 per bottle. At an exchange rate of 125 yen per euro, a bottle of French-made wine will cost ¥375 (375 = 3 × 125).

Given these assumptions, in the absence of trade, a bottle of wine in France costs €3, the equivalent of ¥375, and clock radios cost €2, the equivalent of ¥250. In Japan a bottle of wine costs ¥1,000 (€8), and clock radios cost ¥200 (€1.60).

In this case, trade will occur because of the self-interest of individual entrepreneurs (or the opportunity to make a profit) in France and Japan. Suppose buyers for Galeries Lafayette, a major Paris department store, observe that clock radios cost €2 in France and the equivalent of only €1.60 in Japan. To keep their cost of goods low, these buyers will acquire clock radios in Japan, where they are cheap, and sell them in France, where they are expensive. Accordingly, clock radios will be exported by Japan and imported by France, just as the law of comparative advantage predicts. Similarly, wine distributors in Japan observe that a bottle of wine costs ¥1,000 in Japan but the equivalent of only ¥375 in France. To keep their cost of goods as low as possible, buyers for Japanese wine distributors will buy wine in France, where it is cheap, and sell it in Japan, where it is expensive. Wine will be exported by France and imported by Japan, as predicted by the law of comparative advantage.

Note that none of these businesspeople needed to know anything about the theory of comparative advantage. They merely looked at the price differences in the two markets and made their business decisions based on the desire to obtain supplies at the lowest possible cost. Yet they benefit from comparative advantage because prices set in a free market reflect a country's comparative advantage.

The elegant Galeries Lafayette department store on Boulevard Haussmann, a Parisian fixture for over a century, is a magnet for international shoppers desiring the latest in fashion and design from around the world.

Relative Factor Endowments

The theory of comparative advantage begs a broader question: What determines the products for which a country will have a comparative advantage? To answer this question, two Swedish economists, Eli Heckscher and Bertil Ohlin, developed the **theory of relative factor endowments**, now often referred to as the **Heckscher-Ohlin theory**. These economists made two basic observations:

1. *Factor endowments (or types of resources) vary among countries.* For example, Argentina has much fertile land, Saudi Arabia has large crude oil reserves, and Bangladesh has a large pool of unskilled labor.
2. *Goods differ according to the types of factors that are used to produce them.* For example, wheat requires fertile land, oil production requires crude oil reserves, and apparel manufacturing requires unskilled labor.

From these observations, Heckscher and Ohlin developed their theory: *A country will have a comparative advantage in producing products that intensively use resources (factors of production) it has in abundance.* Thus, Argentina has a comparative advantage in wheat growing because of its abundance of fertile land; Saudi Arabia has a comparative advantage in oil production because of its abundance of crude oil reserves; and Bangladesh has a comparative advantage in apparel manufacture because of its abundance of unskilled labor.

The Heckscher-Ohlin theory suggests a country should export those goods that intensively use those factors of production that are relatively abundant in the country. The theory was tested empirically after World War II by economist Wassily Leontief using input-output analysis, a mathematical technique for measuring the interrelationships among the sectors of an economy. Leontief believed the United States was a capital-abundant and labor-scarce economy. Therefore, according to the Heckscher-Ohlin theory, he reasoned that the United States should export capital-intensive goods, such as bulk chemicals and steel, and import labor-intensive goods, such as clothing and footwear.

Leontief used his input-output model of the U.S. economy to estimate the quantities of labor and capital needed to produce "bundles" of U.S. exports and imports worth $1 million in 1947 (see Figure 6.3). (Each bundle was a weighted average of all U.S. exports or imports in 1947.) He determined that in 1947 U.S. factories utilized $2.551 million of capital and 182.3 person-years of labor, or $13,993 of capital per person-year of labor, to produce a bundle of exports worth $1 million. He also calculated that $3.093 million of capital and 170.0 person-years of labor, or $18,194 of capital per person-year of labor, were used to produce a bundle of U.S. imports worth $1 million in that year. Thus, U.S. imports were more capital-intensive than U.S. exports. Imports required $4,201 ($18,194 – $13,993) more in capital per person-year of labor to produce than exports did.

These results were not consistent with the predictions of the Heckscher-Ohlin theory: U.S. imports were nearly 30 percent more capital-intensive than were U.S. exports. The economics profession was distraught. The Heckscher-Ohlin theory made such intuitive sense, yet Leontief's findings were the reverse of what was expected. Thus was born the **Leontief paradox**.

FIGURE 6.3

U.S. Imports and Exports, 1947: The Leontief Paradox

$3.093 million of capital + 170.0 person-years of labor produces . . . ▶ A bundle of U.S. imports worth **$1 million**

$2.551 million of capital + 182.3 person-years of labor produces . . . ▶ A bundle of U.S. exports worth **$1 million**

During the past 50 years numerous economists have repeated Leontief's initial study in an attempt to resolve the paradox. The first such study was performed by Leontief himself. He thought trade flows might have been distorted in 1947 because much of the world economy was still recovering from World War II. Using 1951 data he found that U.S. imports were 6 percent more capital-intensive than U.S. exports were. Although this figure was less than that in his original study, it still disagreed with the predictions of the Heckscher-Ohlin theory.

Some scholars argue that measurement problems flaw Leontief's work. Leontief assumed there are two homogeneous factors of production: labor and capital. Yet other factors of production exist, most notably land, human capital, and technology—none of which were included in Leontief's analysis. Failure to include these factors might have caused him to mismeasure the labor intensity of U.S. exports and imports. Many U.S. exports are intensive in either land (such as agricultural goods) or human knowledge (such as computers, aircraft, and services). Consider the products sold by one of the leading U.S. exporters, Boeing. Leontief's approach measures the physical capital (the plants, property, and equipment) and the physical labor used to construct Boeing aircraft but fails to gauge adequately the role of human capital and technology in the firm's operations. Yet human capital (the well-educated engineers who design the aircraft and the highly skilled machinists who assemble it) and technology (the sophisticated management techniques that control the world's largest assembly lines) are more important to Boeing's success than mere physical capital and physical labor. Leontief's failure to measure the role that these other factors of production play in determining international trade patterns may account for his paradoxical results.

Modern Firm-Based Trade Theories

Since World War II, international business research has focused on the role of the firm rather than the country in promoting international trade. Firm-based theories have developed for several reasons: (1) the growing importance of MNCs in the postwar international economy; (2) the inability of the country-based theories to explain and predict the existence and growth of intraindustry trade (defined in the next section); and (3) the failure of Leontief and other researchers to empirically validate the country-based Heckscher-Ohlin theory. Unlike country-based theories, firm-based theories incorporate factors such as quality, technology, brand names, and customer loyalty into explanations of trade flows. Because firms, not countries, are the agents for international trade, the newer theories explore the firm's role in promoting exports and imports.

Product Life Cycle Theory

Product life cycle theory, which originated in the marketing field to describe the evolution of marketing strategies as a product matures, was modified by Raymond Vernon of the Harvard Business School to create a firm-based theory of international trade (and, as we will see, of international investment). International product life cycle theory traces the roles of innovation, market expansion, comparative advantage, and strategic responses of global rivals in international production, trade, and investment decisions. According to Vernon's theory, and as illustrated in Figure 6.4, the international product life cycle consists of three stages: new product, maturing product, and standardized product.

In stage 1, the *new product stage*, a firm develops and introduces an innovative product, such as a photocopier or a personal computer, in response to a perceived need in the domestic market. Because the product is new, the innovating firm is uncertain whether a profitable market for the product exists. The firm's marketing executives must closely monitor customer reactions to ensure that the new product satisfies consumer needs. Quick market feedback is important, so the product is likely to be initially produced in the country where its research and development occurred, typically a developed country such as Japan, Germany, or the United States. Further, because the market size also is uncertain, the firm usually will minimize its investment in manufacturing capacity for the product. Most output initially is sold in the domestic market, and export sales are limited.

FIGURE 6.4

The International Product Life Cycle

Source: Raymond Vermon and Louis T. Wells, Jr., *The Economic Environment of International Business*, 5th ed. (©1991, p. 85. Adapted by permission of Prentice Hall, Upper Saddle River, NJ).

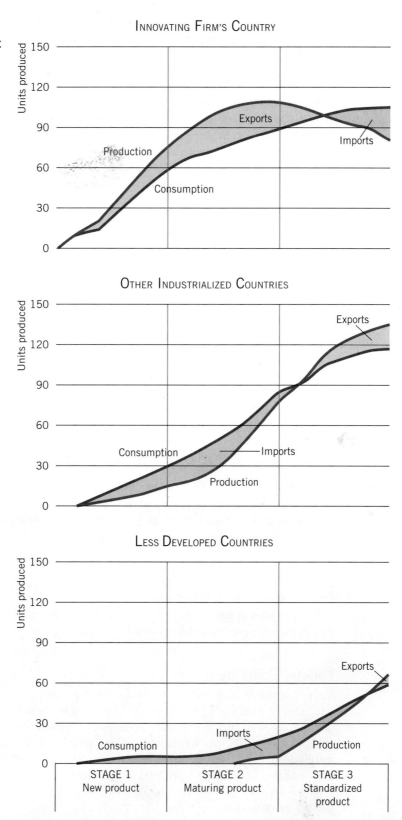

For example, during the early days of the personal computer industry the small producers that populated the industry had their hands full trying to meet the burgeoning demand for their product. Apple Computer typified this problem. Founded on April Fool's Day in 1976, its initial assembly plant was located in the garage of cofounder Steve Jobs. The first large order for its homemade computers—50 units from a local computer hobbyist store—almost bankrupted the firm because it lacked the financing to buy the necessary parts.[4] Apple survived because of the nurturing environment in which it was born, California's Silicon Valley. Home to major electronics firms such as Hewlett-Packard, Intel, and National Semiconductor, Silicon Valley was full of electrical engineers who could design and build Apple's products and venture capitalists who were seeking the "next Xerox." It was the perfect locale for Apple's sales to grow from zero in 1976 to $7.8 million in 1978 and $65 billion in 2010.

In stage 2, the *maturing product stage*, demand for the product expands dramatically as consumers recognize its value. The innovating firm builds new factories to expand its capacity and satisfy domestic and foreign demand for the product. Domestic and foreign competitors begin to emerge, lured by the prospect of lucrative earnings. In the case of Apple, the firm introduced a hand-assembled version of its second model, the Apple II, at a San Francisco computer fair in the spring of 1977. Within three years Apple had sold 130,000 units and expanded its production facilities beyond Jobs's garage. To serve domestic and foreign customers, Apple IIs were manufactured in California and Texas and distributed from warehouses in the United States and the Netherlands.

In stage 3, the *standardized product stage*, the market for the product stabilizes. The product becomes more of a commodity, and firms are pressured to lower their manufacturing costs as much as possible by shifting production to facilities in countries with low labor costs. As a result, the product begins to be imported into the innovating firm's home market (by either the firm or its competitors). In some cases, imports may result in the complete elimination of domestic production.

The personal computer industry has entered the standardized product stage. Chinese computer companies like Lenovo and Taiwanese manufacturers such as Asustek, Hon Hai, Tatung, Mitac International, and First International—none of them household names in the United States—annually export to the United States and to other countries millions of personal computers, many of which are produced under contract for leading PC vendors like Apple, Dell, and HP. Such an arrangement is typical in this stage of the product life cycle: the production of the good shifts to lower-cost manufacturing sites, but the branding and marketing functions remain in the innovating country.[5]

According to the international product life cycle theory, domestic production begins in stage 1, peaks in stage 2, and slumps in stage 3. Exports by the innovating firm's country also begin in stage 1 and peak in stage 2. By stage 3, however, the innovating firm's country becomes a net importer of the product. Foreign competition begins to emerge toward the end of stage 1, as firms in other industrialized countries recognize the product's market potential. In stage 2, foreign competitors expand their productive capacity, thus servicing an increasing portion of their home markets and perhaps becoming net exporters. As competition intensifies in stage 2, however, the innovating firm and its domestic and foreign rivals seek to lower their production costs by shifting production to low-cost sites in less-developed countries. Eventually, in stage 3, the less-developed countries may become net exporters of the product.

Country Similarity Theory

Country-based theories, such as the theory of comparative advantage, do a good job of explaining interindustry trade among countries. **Interindustry trade** is the exchange of goods produced by one industry in country A for goods produced by a different industry in country B, such as the exchange of French wines for Japanese clock radios. Yet much international trade consists of **intraindustry trade**, that is, trade between two countries of goods produced by the same industry. For example, Japan exports Toyotas to Germany, while Germany exports BMWs to Japan. Intraindustry trade accounts for approximately 40 percent of world trade, and it is not predicted by country-based theories.

In 1961, Swedish economist Steffan Linder sought to explain the phenomenon of intraindustry trade. Linder hypothesized that international trade in manufactured goods results from similarities of preferences among consumers in countries that are at the same stage of economic development. In his view, firms initially manufacture goods to serve the firms' domestic market. As they explore exporting opportunities, they discover that the most promising foreign markets are in countries where consumer preferences resemble those of their own domestic market. The Japanese market, for example, provides BMW with well-off, prestige- and performance-seeking automobile buyers similar to the ones who purchase its cars in Germany. The German market provides Toyota with quality-conscious and value-oriented customers similar to those found in its home market. As each company targets the other's home market, intraindustry trade arises. Linder's **country similarity theory** suggests that most trade in manufactured goods should be between countries with similar per capita incomes and that intraindustry trade in manufactured goods should be common. This theory is particularly useful in explaining trade in **differentiated goods** such as automobiles, expensive electronics equipment, and personal care products, for which brand names and product reputations play an important role in consumer decision making. (**Undifferentiated goods**, such as coal, petroleum products, and sugar, are those for which brand names and product reputations play a minor role at best in consumer purchase decisions.)

New Trade Theory

The so-called **new trade theory** developed by Elhanen Helpman, Paul Krugman,[6] and Kelvin Lancaster,[7] in the 1970s and 1980s extends Linder's analysis by incorporating the impact of economies of scale on trade in differentiated goods. **Economies of scale** occur if a firm's average costs of producing a good decrease as its output of that good increases. Suppose automobile manufacturing and marketing benefits from economies of scale. If both BMW and Toyota are able to expand their sales beyond their home market, each will benefit from lower average costs and each will improve its competitiveness vis-à-vis smaller firms. In industries where economies of scale are important, we would expect firms to be particularly aggressive in expanding beyond their domestic markets.

Like Linder's approach, the new trade theory predicts that intraindustry trade will be commonplace. It also suggests multinational corporations within the same industry, such as Caterpillar and Komatsu, Unilever and Procter & Gamble, and Airbus and Boeing, will continually play cat-and-mouse games with one another on a global basis as they attempt to expand their sales to capture scale economies. Often they seek to harness some sustainable competitive advantage they enjoy as a means of leveraging their own strengths and neutralizing those of their rivals.

Firms competing in the global marketplace have numerous ways of obtaining a sustainable competitive advantage. The more popular ones are owning intellectual property rights, investing in research and development (R&D), achieving economies of scope, and exploiting the experience curve. We discuss each of these options next.

OWNING INTELLECTUAL PROPERTY RIGHTS A firm that owns an intellectual property right—a trademark, brand name, patent, or copyright—often gains advantages over its competitors. For instance, owning prestigious brand names enables Ireland's Waterford Wedgwood Company and France's LVMH Moët Hennessy Louis Vuitton to charge premium prices for their upscale products. And Coca-Cola and PepsiCo compete for customers worldwide on the basis of their trademarks and brand names.

INVESTING IN RESEARCH AND DEVELOPMENT R&D is a major component of the total cost of high-technology products. For example, Airbus has spent over $12 billion developing its new superjumbo jet, the A380. Firms in the computer, pharmaceutical, and semiconductor industries also spend large amounts on R&D to maintain their competitiveness. Because of such large "entry" costs, other firms often hesitate to compete against established firms. Thus, the firm that acts first often gains a first-mover advantage.

However, knowledge does not have a nationality. Firms that invest up front and secure the first-mover advantage have the opportunity to dominate the world market for goods that are intensive in R&D. Thus, national competitiveness and trade flows may be determined by which firms make the necessary R&D expenditures. Why is the European Union a large exporter of commercial aircraft? Because Airbus is one of the few firms willing to spend the large sums of money required to develop new aircraft and because it is headquartered in Europe.

Firms with large domestic markets may have an advantage over their foreign rivals in high-technology markets because these firms often are able to obtain quicker and richer feedback from customers. With this feedback the firms can fine-tune their R&D efforts, enabling the firms to better meet the needs of their domestic customers. This knowledge can then be utilized to serve foreign customers. For example, U.S. agricultural chemical producers such as Monsanto and Eli Lilly have an advantage over Japanese rivals in developing soybean pesticides because the U.S. market for such pesticides is large but the Japanese market is small. Knowledge gained in the U.S. pesticide market can be readily transferred to meet the needs of Japanese farmers.

ACHIEVING ECONOMIES OF SCOPE Economies of scope offer firms another opportunity to obtain a sustainable competitive advantage in international markets. Economies of scope occur when a firm's average costs decrease as the number of different products it sells increases. Firms that are able to achieve economies of scope enjoy low average costs, which give the firms a competitive advantage over their global rivals. Consider the e-retailer Amazon.com, which has benefited from both economies of scale and scope. It has spent enormous sums developing and maintaining its website and building its customer base. Because many of these costs are fixed, the company's average costs per sale decline as the company expands its sales. In its quest to capture the volume-driven economies of scale, Amazon.com has been expanding its operations into the international marketplace. Moreover, the marginal cost of adding an additional product line to its website is relatively small. Accordingly, the company has expanded from books to compact discs to DVDs to myriad other goods in order to capture such economies of scope.

EXPLOITING THE EXPERIENCE CURVE Another source of firm-specific advantages in international trade is exploitation of the experience curve. For certain types of products production costs decline as the firm gains more experience in manufacturing the product. Experience curves may be so significant that they govern global competition within an industry. For instance, in semiconductor chip production, unit cost reductions of 25 to 30 percent with each doubling of a firm's cumulative chip production are not uncommon.[8] Any firm attempting to be a low-cost producer of so-called commodity chips—such as DRAM memory chips—can achieve that goal only if it moves further along the experience curve than its rivals do. Both U.S. and Asian chip manufacturers have often priced their new products below current production costs to capture the sales necessary to generate the production experience that will in turn enable the manufacturers to lower future production costs. Because of their technological leadership in manufacturing and their aggressive, price-cutting strategies, Asian semiconductor manufacturers such as Hynix and Samsung dominate the production of low-cost, standardized semiconductor chips.[9] Similarly, innovative U.S. semiconductor firms such as Intel and Advanced Micro Devices utilize the experience curve to maintain leadership in the production of high-priced, proprietary chips that form the brains of newer microcomputers.

Porter's Theory of National Competitive Advantage

Harvard Business School professor Michael Porter's **theory of national competitive advantage** is the newest addition to international trade theory. Porter believes that success in international trade comes from the interaction of four country- and firm-specific elements: factor conditions; demand conditions; related and supporting industries; and firm strategy, structure, and rivalry.

FACTOR CONDITIONS A country's endowment of factors of production affects its ability to compete internationally. Although factor endowments were the centerpiece of the Hecksher-Ohlin theory, Porter goes beyond the basic factors—land, labor, capital—considered by the classical trade theorists to include more advanced factors such as the educational level of the workforce and the quality of the country's infrastructure. His work stresses the role of factor creation through training, research, and innovation.

DEMAND CONDITIONS The existence of a large, sophisticated domestic consumer base often stimulates the development and distribution of innovative products as firms struggle for dominance in their domestic markets. In meeting their domestic customers' needs, however, firms continually develop and fine-tune products that also can be marketed internationally. Thus, pioneering firms can stay ahead of their international competitors as well. For example, Japanese consumer electronics producers maintain a competitive edge internationally because of the willingness of Japan's large, well-off middle class to buy the latest electronic creations of Sony, Toshiba, and Matsushita. After being fine-tuned in the domestic market, new models of

Japanese digital cameras, big-screen TVs, and Blu-ray players are sold to eager European and North American consumers. A similar phenomenon is occurring in the telecommunications market, where the rapid adoption of the Internet and smart phones by North American consumers and companies has created a fertile climate for companies such as Twitter, Facebook, eBay, and Amazon to develop and tailor new products to meet the needs of this market domestically and internationally.

RELATED AND SUPPORTING INDUSTRIES The emergence of an industry often stimulates the development of local suppliers eager to meet that industry's production, marketing, and distribution needs. An industry located close to its suppliers will enjoy better communication and the exchange of cost-saving ideas and inventions with those suppliers. Competition among these input suppliers leads to lower prices, higher-quality products, and technological innovations in the input market, in turn reinforcing the industry's competitive advantage in world markets. For example, Hollywood's dominance of the world film industry is based in part on the local availability of specialist input suppliers, such as casting directors, stunt coordinators, costume and set designers, demolition experts, animators, special-effects firms, and animal wranglers.

FIRM STRATEGY, STRUCTURE, AND RIVALRY The domestic environment in which firms compete shapes their ability to compete in international markets. To survive, firms facing vigorous competition domestically must continuously strive to reduce costs, boost product quality, raise productivity, and develop innovative products. Firms that have been tested in this way often develop the skills needed to succeed internationally. Further, many of the investments they have made to succeed in the domestic market (for example, in R&D, quality control, brand image, and employee training) are transferable to international markets at low cost. Such firms have an edge as they expand abroad. Thus, according to Porter's theory, the international success of Japanese automakers and consumer electronics manufacturers and of Hollywood film studios is aided by intense domestic competition in these firms' home countries.

Porter holds that national policies may also affect firms' international strategies and opportunities in more subtle ways. Consider the German automobile market. German labor costs are very high, so German automakers find it difficult to compete internationally on the

The Netherlands' rich farmland and favorable climate makes it the world's largest producer of tulip and daffodil bulbs—an estimated 9 billion per year. Dutch producers in turn benefit from sophisticated supporting industries and trade associations, such as the Dutch Flower Council, the Association of Dutch Flower Growers Research Groups, and the FloraHolland flower auctions, which facilitate the competitiveness of Dutch flower growers.

Scott Pustay

basis of price. As most auto enthusiasts know, however, there are no speed limits on many stretches of Germany's famed autobahns. So German automakers such as Daimler-Benz, Porsche, and BMW have chosen to compete on the basis of quality and high performance by engineering chassis, engines, brakes, and suspensions that can withstand the stresses of high-speed driving. Consequently, these firms dominate the world market for high-performance automobiles.

Porter's theory is a hybrid: It blends the traditional country-based theories that emphasize factor endowments with the firm-based theories that focus on the actions of individual firms. Countries (or their governments) play a critical role in creating an environment that can aid or harm the ability of firms to compete internationally, but firms are the actors that actually participate in international trade. Some firms succeed internationally; others do not. Porsche, Daimler-Benz, and BMW successfully grasped the opportunity presented by Germany's decision to allow unlimited speeds on its highways and captured the high-performance niche of the worldwide automobile industry. Conversely, Volkswagen and Opel chose to focus on the broader middle segment of the German automobile market, ultimately limiting their international options.

In summary, no single theory of international trade explains all trade flows among countries. The classical country-based theories are useful in explaining interindustry trade of homogeneous, undifferentiated products, such as agricultural goods, raw materials, and processed goods like steel and aluminum. The firm-based theories are more helpful in understanding intraindustry

---

EMERGING OPPORTUNITIES | **MULTIMEDIA AND OIL CLUSTERS IN MALAYSIA**

Michael Porter describes three basic mechanisms through which economic clusters—the regional grouping of firms within an industry—improve the competitiveness of its firms. First, it increases the productivity of firms based within a cluster by providing them access to shared best practices, labor and management pools, and training resources. Second, it drives the direction and pace of innovation within the cluster, which in turn leads to productivity enhancement in firms. Third, it speeds up the entrepreneurial process and new firm formation within clusters.

Many countries in the developing world have also embarked on cluster initiatives of their own such as Panama's Knowledge City, Doha's Education City, Oman's Knowledge Oasis, and Malaysia's Cyberjaya. Malaysia is one of the most dramatic and comprehensive economic success stories in the Islamic world. Malaysia's Multimedia Super Corridor represents the crown jewel of Malaysia's economic miracle. Conceptualized in 1996, the Multimedia Super Corridor (MSC) has grown into a thriving hub of over 900 IT companies—including several multinationals—from all across Malaysia and around the world.

The MSC is a 50-km-long high-tech zone stretching from the Petronas Twin Towers in the north, to the Kuala Lumpur International Airport in the south, offering distinct benefits to foreign-owned and home-grown Malaysian companies focused on multimedia and communications products, solutions, services, and research and development. The corridor today consists of five cybercities, which are Cyberjaya, Technology Park Malaysia, University Putra Malaysia–Malaysian Technology Development Corporation (UPM–MTDC), Kuala Lumpur City Centre (KLCC), and KL Tower. Cyberjaya serves as the center of the MSC.

Malaysia's East Coast Economic Region (ECER) also features an oil, gas, and petrochemical cluster. These industries are capital intensive and technology driven, have a long gestation period, and are cyclical in nature; hence, the industry has been dominated by big players. A key initiative in the downstream petrochemical industry includes the proposed Kertih Plastics Park (KPP), which is the first of its kind in the country. Located within the Petronas Petroleum Industry Complex (PPIC), the Plastics Park will expand employment and entrepreneurship opportunities as well as create demand for other ancillary services. It will also attract domestic and foreign investments in plastics and plastics-related industries.

The Plastics Park's development will be supported by world class research and development input from the PETRONAS Polymer Technology Centre (PPTC), a market-driven technology center that will enhance customer technical services and product improvement for plastics applications.

Despite their widespread popularity and prevalence, developing successful cluster strategies is challenging. Many of the clusters are at the preliminary stages of their development and will require considerable hard work before they can deliver on their promised potential. They are, nonetheless, a step in the right direction to diversify the natural resource-dependent economies in the Middle East and elsewhere. Malaysia's plans will focus on rationalizing existing government organizations and structures; building capacity in organizations focused on national priorities; establishing high performance monitoring units, and attracting, developing, and retaining top talent in the public services. Realizing the promise of these clusters would effectively link these countries with the rest of the world through trading relationships, thus ensuring a prosperous and viable economic future for the developing world in the twenty-first century and beyond.

Sources: http://dinarstandard.com/innovation/creating-economic-clusters-in-the-muslim-world/ author Santa Monica-based (California) Athar Osama. (Accessed on November 24, 2011); http://www.discoverpetronas.com/experienced_professionals/overview.aspx (Accessed on November 24, 2011); http://www.ecerdc.com/ecerdc/oil4.htm (Accessed on November 24, 2011).

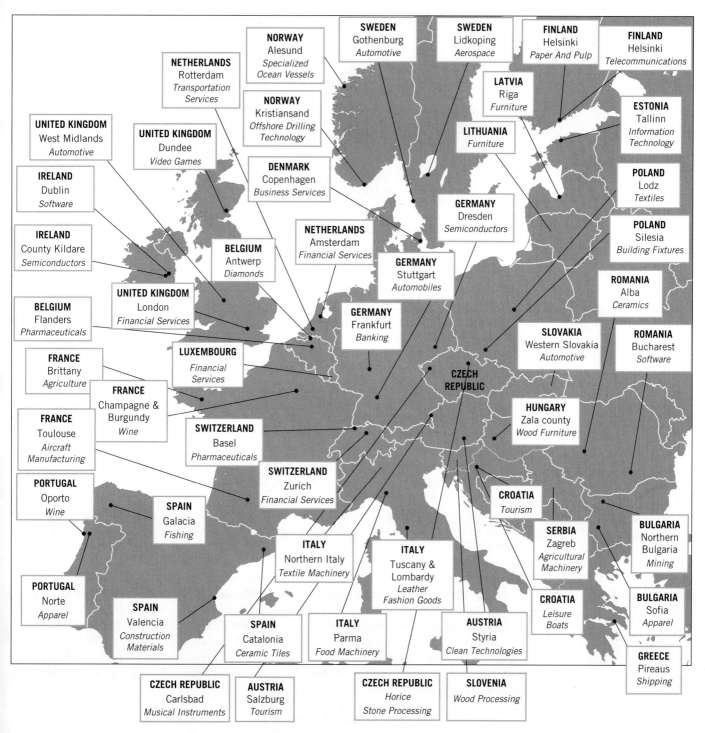

MAP 6.1

Key Industrial Clusters in Western Europe

trade of heterogeneous, differentiated goods, such as Sony televisions and Caterpillar bulldozers, many of which are sold on the basis of their brand names and reputations. Further, in many ways, Porter's theory synthesizes the features of the existing country-based and firm-based theories. Figure 6.5 summarizes the major theories of international trade.

FIGURE 6.5

**Theories of
International Trade**

Country-Based Theories	**Firm-Based Theories**

Country is unit of analysis
Emerged prior to World War II
Developed by economists
Explain interindustry trade
Include:
    Mercantilism
    Absolute advantage
    Comparative advantage
    Relative factor endowments
    (Heckscher-Ohlin)
	Firm is unit of analysis
	Emerged after World War II
	Developed by business school professors
	Explain intraindustry trade
	Include:
	    Country similarity theory
	    Product life cycle
	    New trade theory
	    National competitive advantage

An Overview of International Investment

Trade is the most obvious but not the only form of international business. Another major form is international investment, whereby residents of one country supply capital to a second country.

Types of International Investments

International investment, as discussed in Chapter 1, is divided into two categories: foreign portfolio investment (FPI) and foreign direct investment (FDI). The distinction between the two rests on the question of control: Does the investor seek an active management role in the firm or merely a return from a passive investment?

Foreign portfolio investments represent passive holdings of securities such as foreign stocks, bonds, or other financial assets, none of which entails active management or control of the securities' issuer by the investor. Modern finance theory suggests that foreign portfolio investments will be motivated by attempts to seek an attractive rate of return as well as the risk reduction that can come from geographically diversifying one's investment portfolio. Sophisticated money managers in New York, London, Frankfurt, Tokyo, and other financial centers are well aware of the advantages of international diversification. In 2010, for example, private U.S. citizens purchased $112.8 billion worth of foreign securities, bringing their total holdings of such securities to $6.2 trillion. Foreign official and private investors purchased $834 billion worth of U.S. corporate, federal, state, and local securities, raising their total holdings of such securities to $10.2 trillion.[10]

Foreign direct investment (FDI) is acquisition of foreign assets for the purpose of controlling them. U.S. government statisticians define FDI as "ownership or control of 10 percent or more of an enterprise's voting securities or the equivalent interest in an unincorporated business."[11] FDI may take many forms, including purchase of existing assets in a foreign country, new investment in property, plant, and equipment, and participation in a joint venture with a local partner. Perhaps the most historically significant FDI in the United States was the $24 that Dutch explorer Peter Minuet paid local Native Americans for Manhattan Island.[12] The result: New York City, one of the world's leading financial and commercial centers.

The Growth of Foreign Direct Investment

The growth of foreign direct investment during the past 30 years has been phenomenal. As Figure 6.6 indicates, in 1967 the total stock (or cumulative value) of FDI received by countries worldwide was slightly over $100 billion. Worldwide FDI as of 2009 topped $17.7 trillion. This stunning growth in FDI—and its acceleration beginning in the 1990s—reflects the globalization of the world's economy. As you might expect, most FDI comes from developed countries. Surprisingly, most FDI also goes to developed countries. We discuss later in this chapter reasons for this explosive growth in FDI.

Foreign Direct Investment and the United States

We can gain additional insights into FDI by looking at individual countries. Consider the stock of FDI in the United States, which totaled $2.3 trillion (measured at historical cost) at the end of 2010 (see Table 6.4[a]). The United Kingdom was the most important source of this FDI,

FIGURE 6.6

Stock of Foreign Direct Investment, by Recipient (in billions of dollars)

Sources: John H. Dunning, *Multinational Enterprises and the Global Economy.* Wokingham, England: Addison-Wesley Publishers Ltd., 1993; United Nations Conference on Trade and Development, *World Investment Report* (online at www.unctad.org/wir).

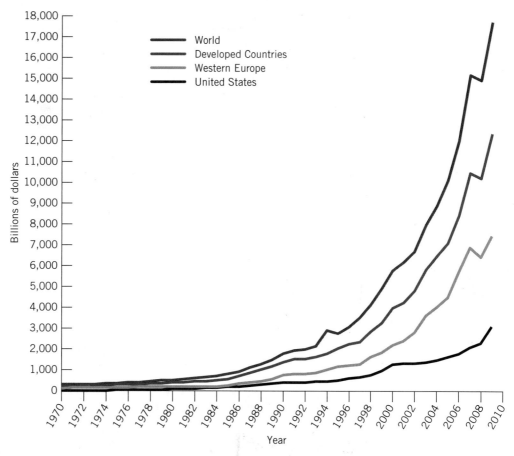

accounting for $432.5 billion, or 18 percent, of the total. The countries listed by name in Table 6.4(a) account for 86 percent of total FDI in the United States.

The stock of FDI by U.S. residents in foreign countries totaled $3.9 trillion at the end of 2010 (see Table 6.4[b]). Most of this FDI was in other developed countries, particularly the Netherlands ($521.4 billion) and the United Kingdom ($508.4 billion). The countries listed by name in Table 6.4(b) account for 72 percent of total FDI from the United States.

Looking at Table 6.4, you may wonder why Bermuda, the Bahamas, and other small Caribbean islands are so important. They serve as offshore financial centers, which we will discuss in Chapter 8. Many U.S. companies set up finance subsidiaries in such centers to take advantage of low taxes and business-friendly regulations. Similarly, many financial services companies from other countries establish such subsidiaries as the legal owners of their U.S. operations.

During the past decade outward FDI has remained larger than inward FDI for the United States (see Figure 6.7), but both categories have tripled in size. Although inward and outward flows of FDI are not perfectly matched, the pattern is clear: Most FDI is made by and destined for the most prosperous countries. In the next section we discuss how this pattern suggests the crucial role MNCs play in FDI.

International Investment Theories

Why does FDI occur? A sophomore taking his or her first finance course might answer with the obvious: Average rates of return are higher in foreign markets. Yet given the pattern of FDI between countries that we just discussed, this answer is not satisfactory. Canada and the United Kingdom are both major sources of FDI in the United States and important destinations for FDI from the United States. Average rates of return in Canada and the United Kingdom cannot be simultaneously below that of the United States (which would justify inward U.S. FDI) and above that of the United States (which would justify outward U.S. FDI). The same pattern of two-way investment occurs on an industry basis. By the end of 2010, for example, U.S. firms had invested $7.8 billion in the chemical

TABLE 6.4 Stock of FDI for the United States, end of 2010 (billions of dollars)

a. Sources of FDI in the United States

United Kingdom	432.5
Japan	257.3
Netherlands	217.1
Germany	212.9
Canada	206.1
Switzerland	192.2
France	184.8
Luxembourg	181.2
Australia	49.5
Belgium	43.2
Bermuda, The Bahamas, and other Caribbean Islands	40.1
Other European countries	233.3
All other countries	92.6
Total	2342.8

b. Destination of FDI from the United States

Netherlands	521.4
United Kingdom	508.4
Bermuda, The Bahamas, and other Caribbean Islands	420.4
Canada	296.7
Luxembourg	274.9
Ireland	190.5
Switzerland	143.6
Australia	134.0
Japan	113.3
Singapore	106.0
Germany	105.8
Other European countries	441.3
All other countries	651.9
Total	3908.2

Source: Survey of Current Business, July 2011, pp. 139 and 141.

industry in the Netherlands, while Dutch firms had invested $2.6 billion in the U.S. chemical industry. This pattern cannot be explained by national or industry differences in rates of return. We must search for another explanation for FDI.

Ownership Advantages

More powerful explanations for FDI focus on the role of the firm. Initially researchers explored how firm ownership of competitive advantages affected FDI. The **ownership advantage theory** suggests that a firm owning a valuable asset that creates a competitive advantage domestically can use that advantage to penetrate foreign markets through FDI. The asset could be, for example, a superior technology, a well-known brand name, or economies of scale. This theory is consistent with the observed patterns of international and intraindustry FDI discussed earlier in this chapter. Caterpillar, for example, built factories in Asia, Europe, Australia, South America, and North America to exploit proprietary technologies and its brand name. Its chief rival, Komatsu, constructed plants in Asia, Europe, and the United States for the same reason.

FIGURE 6.7

Outward and Inward U.S. FDI, 1982–2010

Source: Survey of Current Business, July 2011, p. 125.

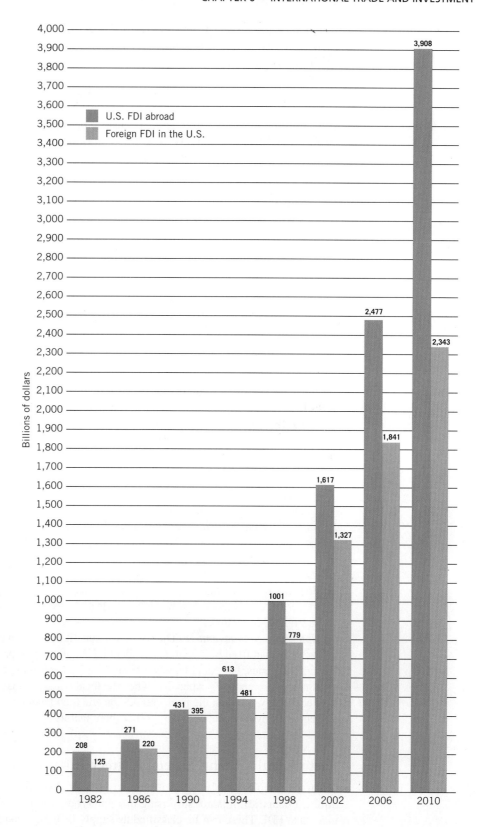

Internalization Theory

The ownership advantage theory only partly explains why FDI occurs. It does not explain why a firm would choose to enter a foreign market via FDI rather than exploit its ownership advantages internationally through other means, such as exporting its products, franchising a brand name, or licensing technology to foreign firms. For example, McDonald's has successfully internationalized by franchising its fast-food operations outside the United States, while Boeing has relied on exporting to serve its foreign customers.

Internalization theory addresses this question. In doing so, it relies heavily on the concept of transaction costs. **Transaction costs** are the costs of entering into a transaction, that is, those connected to negotiating, monitoring, and enforcing a contract. A firm must decide whether it is better to own and operate its own factory overseas or to contract with a foreign firm to do this through a franchise, licensing, or supply agreement. **Internalization theory** suggests that FDI is more likely to occur—that is, international production will be internalized within the firm—when the costs of negotiating, monitoring, and enforcing a contract with a second firm are high. For example, Toyota's primary competitive advantages are its reputation for high quality and its sophisticated manufacturing techniques, neither of which is easily conveyed by contract. As a result, Toyota has chosen to maintain ownership of its overseas automobile assembly plants.

Conversely, internalization theory holds that when transaction costs are low, firms are more likely to contract with outsiders and internationalize by licensing their brand names or franchising their business operations. For example, McDonald's is the premier expert in the United States in devising easily enforceable franchising agreements. Because McDonald's is so successful in reducing transaction costs between itself and its franchisees, it has continued to rely on franchising for its international operations.

Dunning's Eclectic Theory

Although internalization theory addresses why firms choose FDI as the mode for entering international markets, the theory ignores the question of why production, by either the company or a contractor, should be located abroad. In other words, is there a location advantage to producing abroad? This issue was incorporated by John Dunning in his **eclectic theory**, which combines ownership advantage, location advantage, and internalization advantage to form a unified theory of FDI. This theory recognizes that FDI reflects both international business activity and business activity internal to the firm. According to Dunning, FDI will occur when three conditions are satisfied:

1. *Ownership advantage.* The firm must own some unique competitive advantage that overcomes the disadvantages of competing with foreign firms on their home turfs. This advantage may be a brand name, ownership of proprietary technology, the benefits of economies of scale, and so on. Caterpillar, for example, enjoys all three of these advantages in competing in Brazil against local firms.
2. *Location advantage.* Undertaking the business activity must be more profitable in a foreign location than undertaking it in a domestic location. For example, Caterpillar produces bulldozers in Brazil to enjoy lower labor costs and avoid high tariff walls on goods exported from its U.S. factories.
3. *Internalization advantage.* The firm must benefit more from controlling the foreign business activity than from hiring an independent local company to provide the service. Control is advantageous, for example, when monitoring and enforcing the contractual performance of the local company is expensive, when the local company may misappropriate proprietary technology, or when the firm's reputation and brand name could be jeopardized by poor behavior by the local company. All of these factors are important to Caterpillar.

Factors Influencing Foreign Direct Investment

Given the complexity of the global economy and the diversity of opportunities that firms face in different countries, it is not surprising that numerous factors may influence a firm's decision to undertake FDI. These can be classified as supply factors, demand factors, and political factors (see Table 6.5).

Supply Factors

A firm's decision to undertake FDI may be influenced by supply factors, including production costs, logistics, availability of natural resources, and access to key technology.

TABLE 6.5 Factors Affecting the FDI Decision

Supply Factors	Demand Factors	Political Factors
Production costs	Customer access	Avoidance of trade barriers
Logistics	Marketing advantages	Economic development incentives
Resource availability	Exploitation of competitive advantages	
Access to technology	Customer mobility	

PRODUCTION COSTS Firms often undertake FDI to lower production costs. Foreign locations may be more attractive than domestic sites because of lower land prices, tax rates, commercial real estate rents, or because of better availability and lower cost of skilled or unskilled labor. For example, Intel built a new chip fabrication facility in Chengdu in China's remote Sichuan province because labor and land costs were much lower than in Shanghai, where the company already operates three facilities.[13] Similarly, Nokia announced in 2011 it will build a $275 million mobile phone assembly plant in northern Vietnam to take advantage of the area's low labor costs.[14]

LOGISTICS If transportation costs are significant, a firm may choose to produce in the foreign market rather than export from domestic factories. For example, Heineken has utilized FDI extensively as part of its internationalization strategy because its products are primarily water. Brewing its beverages close to where its foreign consumers live is cheaper for Heineken than transporting the beverages long distances from the company's Dutch breweries. International businesses also often make host-country investments to reduce distribution costs. For example, Citrovita, a Brazilian producer of orange juice concentrate, operates a storage and distribution terminal at the Port of Antwerp rather than ship to European grocery chains directly from Brazil. Citrovita can take advantage of low ocean-shipping rates to transport its goods in bulk from Brazil to the Belgian port. The company then uses the Antwerp facility to repackage and distribute concentrate to its customers in France, Germany, and the Benelux countries.

AVAILABILITY OF NATURAL RESOURCES Firms may utilize FDI to access natural resources that are critical to their operations. For instance, because of the decrease in oil production in the United States, many U.S.-based oil companies have been forced to make significant investments worldwide to obtain new oil reserves. Often international businesses negotiate with host governments to obtain access to raw materials in return for FDI. For example, in 2007 the China National Petroleum Company created a joint venture with state-owned Petróleos de Venezuela that will invest $10 billion to extract, refine, and transport 1 million barrels of oil a day from Venezuela's Orinoco basin.[15]

ACCESS TO KEY TECHNOLOGY Another motive for FDI is to gain access to technology. Firms may find it more advantageous to acquire ownership interests in an existing firm than to assemble an in-house group of research scientists to develop or reproduce an emerging technology. For instance, many Swiss pharmaceutical manufacturers have invested in small U.S. biogenetics companies as an inexpensive means of obtaining cutting-edge biotechnology. Similarly, in 2007 Korea's Doosan Infracore paid $4.9 billion for the Bobcat division of Ingersoll-Rand, in order to benefit from Bobcat's superior technology, outstanding distribution network, and skilled management team.[16]

Demand Factors

Firms also may engage in FDI to expand the market for their products. The demand factors that encourage FDI include customer access, marketing advantages, exploitation of competitive advantages, and customer mobility.

CUSTOMER ACCESS Many types of international business require firms to have a physical presence in the market. For example, fast-food restaurants and retailers must provide convenient access to their outlets for competitive reasons. KFC cannot provide its freshly prepared fried chicken to Japanese customers from its restaurants in the United States; it must locate outlets in Japan to do so. Similarly, IKEA's success in broadening its customer base beyond its home market in Sweden is due to its opening a number of new stores worldwide.

MARKETING ADVANTAGES FDI may generate several types of marketing advantages. The physical presence of a factory may enhance the visibility of a foreign firm's products in the host market. The foreign firm also gains from "buy local" attitudes of host country consumers. For example, through ads in such magazines as *Time* and *Sports Illustrated*, Toyota has publicized the beneficial impact of its U.S. factories and input purchases on the U.S. economy. Firms may also engage in FDI to improve their customer service. Taiwan's Delta Products, which makes battery packs for laptop computers, was concerned that it could not respond quickly and flexibly enough from its factories in China and Thailand to meet the changing needs of its U.S. customers. As one of its executives noted, if you "build in the Far East, you're too far away. You can't do a last-moment modification while the product is on the ocean." Accordingly, Delta shifted some of its production to a Mexican factory just across the border from Nogales, Arizona, to better serve its U.S. customers.[17]

EXPLOITATION OF COMPETITIVE ADVANTAGES FDI may be a firm's best means to exploit a competitive advantage that it already enjoys. An owner of a valuable trademark, brand name, or technology may choose to operate in foreign countries rather than export to them. Often this decision depends on the product's nature. For instance, companies like Procter and Gamble, Nestlé, and Unilever often choose to site factories in the countries in which they sell their products. By so doing, they enhance their ability to customize their products to meet local tastes while still benefitting from the power of their brand names and manufacturing prowess.

CUSTOMER MOBILITY A firm's FDI also may be motivated by the FDI of its customers or clients. If one of a firm's existing customers builds a foreign factory, the firm may decide to locate a new facility of its own nearby, thus enabling it to continue to supply its customers promptly and attentively. Equally important, establishing a new facility reduces the possibility that a competitor in the host country will step in and steal the customer. For example, Japanese parts suppliers to the major Japanese automakers have responded to the construction of Japanese-owned automobile assembly plants in the United States by building their own U.S. factories, warehouses, and research facilities. Their need to locate facilities in the United States is magnified by the automakers' use of just-in-time (JIT) inventory management techniques; JIT minimizes the amount of parts inventory held at an assembly plant, putting a parts-supply facility located in Japan at a severe disadvantage. Likewise, after Samsung decided to construct and operate an electronics factory in northeast England, six of its Korean parts suppliers also established factories in the vicinity.[18]

Political Factors

Political factors may also enter into a firm's decision to undertake FDI. Firms may invest in a foreign country to avoid trade barriers by the host country or to take advantage of economic development incentives offered by the host government. But, as "Venturing Abroad" indicates, political factors may also discourage FDI.

AVOIDANCE OF TRADE BARRIERS Firms often build foreign facilities to avoid trade barriers. For example, in 2011 Hon Hai Precision Industries, a leading Taiwanese contract manufacturing firm, announced it would build a new electronics manufacturing plant in Brazil to avoid that country's high tariffs on imported consumer electronics goods. Other types of government policies may also impact FDI. Microsoft, for example, located a software development center in Richmond, British Colombia, in part to avoid limitations placed by the U.S. government on the number of highly skilled immigrant workers who can obtain H-1B work visas in any given year.[19]

ECONOMIC DEVELOPMENT INCENTIVES Most democratically elected governments—local, state, and national—are vitally concerned with promoting the economic welfare of their citizens,

HOW IMPORTANT IS THE RULE OF LAW?

As the eminent scholar and jurist Richard Posner has defined it, the rule of law means "that judges decide cases 'without respect to persons', that is, without considering the social status, attractiveness, etc. of the parties or of their lawyers." A well-functioning legal system with clearly defined rules and procedures often encourages foreign firms to invest in a country. But the opposite may also be true.

One country where a lack of the rule of law appears to be affecting FDI is Russia. Russian authorities are notorious for manipulating the Russian legal system to promote their personal agendas. For example, despite a constitutional guarantee for freedom of assembly, Russian officials arrested Brian Nemtsov, a former deputy prime minister, for attending a rally promoting freedom of assembly on New Year's Eve 2010. According to some human rights activists, the motive for his arrest was simply to demonstrate to political dissidents that the authorities could do what they wish.

Perhaps the most brazen example of the deficiency of the Russian rule of law is the second trial and conviction of former oil magnate Mikhail Khodorkovsky. He was the founder of OAO Yukos, once Russia's largest oil company. Yukos was a creation of the privatization process that followed the collapse of the Soviet Union. The selling off of state-owned assets created much controversy, as critics charged that favored insiders benefited from a lack of transparency that characterized this privatization process. Khodorkovsky, once the richest man in the new Russia and the most powerful of the new oligarchs (the term used to describe the business leaders made rich by the privatization process), committed the fatal mistake of making a political enemy of Vladimir Putin, the Russian Federation's second president and its most powerful political force. Khodorkovsky provided financing for political parties not friendly to Putin and argued for a strong, independent media. Khodorkovsky was arrested in 2003, convicted in 2005 of tax evasion, and sentenced to eight years in a Siberian prison. After the conviction, Yukos was forced into bankruptcy. Most of its assets were sold off at bargain basement prices to state-owned companies controlled by political allies of Putin to pay for the alleged unpaid taxes.

As his release date from prison drew nearer, Khodorkovsky and his partner Platon Lebedev were charged with stealing all the oil that Yukos produced. Khodorkovsky was convicted in December 2010 and sentenced to another six years in prison. Many observers viewed this second trial as a clear case of double jeopardy. They also viewed it as logically inconsistent with the charges filed in his first trial. If Khodorkovsky stole the oil, then Yukos wouldn't have had any profits in the first place and thus couldn't have underpaid its taxes. If Yukos was guilty of tax evasion, then it must have owned the oil and then Khodorkovsky couldn't have stolen the oil. The suspicion that his original and subsequent arrest were politically motivated was heightened when in February 2011 an assistant to the presiding judge in the second trial claimed that the judge was pressured by his superior to deliver a guilty verdict and a harsh sentence. The Obama administration denounced the verdict as an "abusive use of the legal system for improper ends."

Many Russian citizens viewed Khodorkovsky's first conviction favorably. The oligarchs who rose to prominence in the 1990s after the breakup of the Soviet Union were perceived as benefiting from insider deals as state-owned assets were transferred to the private sector. But in the 2000s economic power appears to have been transferred from the oligarchs to bureaucrat-entrepreneurs, that is, government officials who used their government positions to enrich themselves and their friends. Administrative power, rather than property rights, became the basis of wealth. The concern is that firms, foreign and domestic, in such an environment will fail to make the long-term investments that are the basis of economic growth in developed economies. Other investors fear that if their investments become too profitable they will attract the attention of state authorities, who will then use their positions to loot those assets: Such a fate befell Hermitage Capital, a foreign-financed firm that at one time was the largest investor in the Russian stock market.

Sources: "Khodorkovsky derides reforms," *Financial Times*, May 25, 2011, p. 2; "Russian tycoon's sentence is upheld," *Wall Street Journal*, May 25, 2011, p. A11; "Sergei Magnitsky and the rule of law in Russia," *Wall Street Journal*, February 24, 2011; Dafna Linzer, "The problem with question 36," *Slate*, February 23, 2011 (online); "Mikhail B. Khodorkovsky," *New York Times*, February 15, 2011 (online); "Opposition battles repression in Russia," *Washington Post*, January 28, 2011; "Doing things the Putin way," *The Economist*, January 1, 2011; "White House criticizes Moscow court," *Wall Street Journal*, December 27, 2010; "Frost at the core," *The Economist*, December 11, 2010; "The trial, part two," *The Economist*, April 24, 2010.

many of whom are, of course, voters. Many governments offer incentives to firms to induce them to locate new facilities in the governments' jurisdictions. Governmental incentives that can be an important catalyst for FDI include reduced utility rates, employee training programs, infrastructure additions (such as new roads and railroad spurs), and tax reductions or tax holidays. Often MNCs benefit from bidding wars among communities eager to attract the companies and the jobs they bring. For instance, Georgia agreed to provide Kia Motors $400 million in incentives to capture that firm's first U.S. plant, which now employs 3,000 workers.[20] Likewise, Samsung Electronics announced it would locate its latest chip factory in Austin, Texas, after the city and the state granted it a $233 million incentive package.[21]

MyManagementLab   Now that you have finished this chapter, go back to **www.pearsonglobaleditions.com/mymanagementlab** to continue practicing and applying the concepts you've learned.

CHAPTER REVIEW

Summary

International trade is an important form of international business—over $15.9 trillion of goods and services were traded among residents of different countries in 2009. International trade affects domestic economies both directly and indirectly. Exports stimulate additional demand for products, thus generating income and employment gains. Imports lower consumer prices and pressure domestic firms to become more efficient and productive.

Because of the importance of trade to businesses and governments worldwide, scholars have offered numerous explanations for its existence. The earliest theories, such as absolute advantage, comparative advantage, and relative factor endowments, relied on characteristics of countries to explain patterns of exports and imports. These country-based theories help explain trade in undifferentiated goods such as wheat, sugar, and steel.

Coincident with the rise of MNCs, post–World War II research focused on firm-based explanations for international trade. Product life cycle, country similarity, and new trade theories focus on the firm as the agent for generating trade and investment decisions. These firm-based theories help explain intraindustry trade and trade in differentiated goods such as automobiles, personal care products, and consumer electronics goods.

International investment is the second major way in which firms participate in international business. International investments fall into two categories: foreign portfolio investments and FDI. FDI has risen in importance as MNCs have increased in size and number.

Dunning's eclectic theory suggests that FDI will occur when three conditions are met: (1) The firm possesses a competitive advantage that allows it to overcome the disadvantage of competing on the foreign firm's home turf; (2) the foreign location is superior to a domestic location; and (3) the firm finds it cheaper

(because of high transaction costs) to produce the product itself rather than hire a foreign firm to do so.

Numerous factors can influence a firm's decision to undertake FDI. Some FDI may be undertaken to reduce the firm's costs. Such supply factors include production costs, logistics, availability of natural resources, and access to key technology. The decision to engage in FDI may be affected by such demand factors as developing access to new customers, obtaining marketing advantages through local production, exploiting competitive advantages, and maintaining nearness to customers as they internationalize their operations. Political considerations may also play a role in FDI. Often firms use FDI to avoid host country trade barriers or to capture economic development incentives offered by host country governments.

Review Questions

1. What is international trade? Why does it occur?
2. How do the theories of absolute advantage and comparative advantage differ?
3. Why are Leontief's findings called a paradox?
4. How useful are country-based theories in explaining international trade?
5. How do interindustry and intraindustry trade differ?
6. Explain the impact of the product life cycle on international trade and international investment.
7. What are the primary sources of the competitive advantages firms use to compete in international markets?
8. What are the four elements of Porter's theory of national competitive advantage?
9. How do foreign portfolio investments and FDI differ?
10. What are the three parts of Dunning's eclectic theory?
11. How do political factors influence international trade and investment?

Questions for Discussion

1. In our example of France trading wine to Japan for clock radios, we arbitrarily assumed that the countries would trade at a price ratio of 1 bottle of wine for 2 clock radios. Over what range of prices can trade occur between the two countries? (Hint: In the absence of trade, what is the price of clock radios in terms of wine in France? In Japan?) Does your answer differ if you use Table 6.2 instead of Table 6.1?

2. In the public debate over ratification of the North American Free Trade Agreement, Ross Perot said he heard a "giant sucking sound" from U.S. jobs headed south because of low wage rates in Mexico. Using the

theory of comparative advantage, discuss whether Perot's fears are valid.

3. Why is intraindustry trade not predicted by country-based theories of trade?

4. Hyundai decided to build a new automobile assembly plant in Alabama.
   a. What factors do you think Hyundai considered in selecting Alabama as the site for the factory?
   b. Who benefits and who loses from the new plant in Alabama?
   c. Is the firm's decision to build the new plant consistent with Dunning's eclectic theory?

Building Global Skills

The U.S. market for computers is dominated by domestic firms such as Dell, Hewlett-Packard, and Apple. The U.S. market for consumer electronics is dominated by Japanese firms and brands such as Sony, JVC, Panasonic, Mitsubishi, and Toshiba. However, the U.S. automobile market includes both domestic firms like Ford and General Motors and formidable Japanese competitors like Toyota and Honda.

Your instructor will divide the class into groups of four or five and assign each group one of the three industries just noted. To begin, discuss within your group your individual views on why different patterns exist for these industries.

Next, analyze the industry assigned to your group from the standpoint of each country-based and firm-based theory of international trade discussed in this chapter. Try to agree on which theory is the best predictor and which is the worst predictor of reality for your specific industry.

Now reconvene as a class. Each group should select a spokesperson. Each spokesperson should indicate the industry that the person's group discussed and identify the best and worst theories selected. Note the points on which the groups who analyzed the same industries agree.

Finally, separate again into your small groups and discuss the areas of common disagreements. Also discuss the following questions:

1. Do some theories work better than others for different industries? Why?
2. What other industries can you think of that fit one of the three patterns noted in the opening paragraph?
3. Do the same theories work as well in making predictions for those industries?
4. Based on what you know about the Japanese market, decide whether the same pattern of competitiveness that exists in the United States for the computer, consumer electronics, and automobile industries also holds true for the Japanese market. Why or why not?

CLOSING CASE   **TWENTY-FIRST CENTURY PIRATES**

Most economists would agree that intellectual property rights (IPR) are critical components of a well-functioning market system. They encourage inventors to develop new technologies to benefit consumers or lower production costs and motivate firms to develop products and brand names that consumers can trust. For many firms, ownership of IPR forms the basis on which they compete in world markets. Yet one of the unexpected consequences of globalization is increased levels of product piracy, which threaten the profitability and sometimes the existence of firms that have invested heavily in intellectual property. A pharmaceutical company that spends 20 percent of its revenues on R&D, for example, is at a cost disadvantage to a rival who steals its innovations but invests nothing itself in R&D.

The Business Software Alliance believes that $51 billion of software is illegally sold by pirates each year. Piracy of recorded music is estimated to cost studios $3.5 billion a year, while U.S. movie studios lose $4.6 billion a year due to illegally duplicated DVDs. Counterfeit drugs yearly cost legitimate pharmaceutical manufacturers $37 billion in sales. The fake Rolex watches, Louis Vuitton luggage, Prada handbags, and other faux luxury goods peddled on the streets of Asia, Europe, and the Americas amount to additional untold billions of losses for the companies whose IP has been stolen.

China appears to be the home of many of the worst offenders. According to the Business Software Alliance, 79 percent of the software sold in China has been pirated, as is an estimated 85–90 percent of recorded music. Movie studios lose an estimated $280 million annually to Chinese counterfeiters. Entertainment firms have adopted a variety of approaches to try to cut their losses. Warner Brothers slashed the prices it charges in China for DVDs featuring its newest movies to $2 to $4, in hopes of reducing the street trade for illegal copies, which normally sell for $1. The company also altered the release schedules of its movies, opening them simultaneously in China and in the United States, to reduce the ability of the pirates to illegally tape movies in U.S. theaters for duplication and distribution in China. Electronic Arts, the California-based developer and marketer of video games, decided to shift its distribution strategy in China to combat pirates. Instead of distributing its games on easily copied CDs or DVDs, the California company decided to focus on online, live multiplayer games, which is already a $540 million business in China.

The problem isn't limited to entertainment products. Some Chinese firms have begun to manufacture counterfeit drugs, which threaten public safety and the reputation of companies should the counterfeited drugs contain contaminants or improper dosages of their active ingredients. Chinese authorities seized over 2 million tablets of fake Viagra, Lipitor, and Norvasc; however, in most cases the investigations that led to the seizures were initiated by Pfizer, the patent owner of these drugs, rather than the Chinese police.

One Indiana company, Abro Industries, which sells adhesive products such as epoxies, glues, and sticky tape, didn't have just its products pirated; the company seemingly was pirated as well. A Chinese company with no connection to Abro, Hunan Magic Power Industrial Company, marketed and distributed over 40 different products bearing the Abro brand; the CEO of Hunan even used business cards with Abro's logo. Abro has spent over $600,000 suing Hunan Magic Power and other pirates, but has been frustrated by the Chinese legal system. To date, the total penalty imposed by Chinese authorities on Hunan for its actions is a fine of $600.

This is not to say that Chinese authorities never enforce IP rights. For example, the Intermediate Court of Nantong (a city near Shanghai) sentenced two men to jail terms of three and four years and fined them a total of $105,000 for shipping counterfeit versions of luxury perfumes made by LVMH Moët Hennessy Louis Vuitton. However, such sentences are rare. A report issued in 2006 by the Office of the U.S. Trade Representative noted, "In the IPR area, while China has made noticeable improvements to its framework of laws and regulations, the lack of effective IPR enforcement remains a major challenge" (p. 93). The same report went on to say, "Counterfeiting and piracy in China remain at epidemic levels and cause serious economic harm to U.S. businesses in virtually every sector of the economy" (p. 121). Most local firms who are prosecuted face minor fines in administrative courts, which they write off as a cost of doing business. The risk of serious punishment for IPR violations is small: In 2004, less than 200 trademark or copyright infringement cases investigated by Chinese officials—out of a total of over 60,000—were forwarded to criminal courts. Many of the major violators, particularly counterfeiters of CDs and DVDs, are allegedly owned by companies linked to the state, government officials, or the military. Not surprisingly, local officials are oftentimes unwilling to aggressively prosecute firms that are so well connected politically.

The problem of counterfeit goods is not limited to China, of course. North Korea, for instance, is a primary source of counterfeit cigarettes—an estimated 2 billion packs a year. Major tobacco companies believe that the North Korean government is earning $80 to $160 million annually in payoffs from the crime gangs that control this trade. But China has attracted the most attention for IPR violations because of its growing presence in the world economy. Some experts fear that China won't truly protect intellectual property until the issue becomes important for local firms. To this end, Microsoft, one of the largest victims of Chinese IP theft, decided to help build a Chinese software industry, in hopes that local entrepreneurs would encourage the government to more aggressively attack IP thieves. For example, it created a Shanghai-based joint venture, Wicresoft, which provides customer support for other Chinese software firms.

In 2006, Chinese officials once again agreed to reinvigorate their pursuit of intellectual property thieves. They pledged to increase fines for IPR violations, lower the hurdles for prosecuting IPR violations in criminal rather than civil courts, and establish new offices in 50 cities to handle IPR complaints. Another important step involves computer operating systems. Bowing to government pressure, China's three largest manufacturers of PCs—Lenovo, Founder, and Tsinghua Tongfang—have agreed to ship their products with pre-installed operating systems. Previously, most PCs sold in China came without an operating system; consumers simply loaded a pirated copy of Windows 7 or similar product onto their computers, which they could buy from a street vendor for a dollar or two. This policy ensures that software companies like Microsoft will be compensated for the use of their intellectual property.

Case Questions

1. How important is intellectual property to the world economy?
2. Should the average consumer concern himself or herself with theft of intellectual property? What about the average citizen? The average worker?
3. Does intellectual property theft undermine the workings of the free-market system?
4. What is the impact of China's lack of aggressive enforcement of intellectual property rights on its economic development in the short run? In the long run?

Sources: "A cloud up in the air," *Financial Times*, August 1, 2011, p. 5; Seventh Annual BSA Global Software Piracy Study, 2010; "Disney tries new antipiracy tack," *Wall Street Journal*, May 31, 2006, p. B3; "Handbags at dawn," *The Economist*, April 21, 2006 (online); "U.S., China begin talks to ease tensions on market access, piracy," *Wall Street Journal*, April 12, 2006, p. A4; "China to crack down on computer piracy," *Houston Chronicle*, April 12, 2006, p. D8; "Chinese PC maker agrees to address Microsoft piracy," *Wall Street Journal*, April 6, 2006, p. B5; Office of the U.S. Trade Representative, *2006 National Trade Estimate Report on Foreign Trade Barriers*; "China jails two for luxury goods piracy," *Financial Times*, March 4/5, 2006, p. 3; "As luxury industry goes global, knock-off merchants follow," *Wall Street Journal*, January 31, 2006, p. A1; "Tobacco firms trace fakes to North Korea," *Wall Street Journal*, January 27, 2006, p. B1; "As Pfizer battles fakes in China, nation's police are uneasy allies," *Wall Street Journal*, January 24, 2006, p. A1; "Media counter piracy in China in new ways," *Wall Street Journal*, September 26, 2005, p. B1; "China won't protect IP until it gets its own IT," *Fortune*, June 27, 2005, p. 54; "Movie, music giants try new weapon against pirates: Price," *Wall Street Journal*, March 7, 2005, p. B1; James McGregor, *One Billion Customers* (New York: Free Press, 2005); "Stuck on you: A tiny glue seller claims identity theft," *Wall Street Journal*, November 22, 2004, p. A1.

Endnotes

1. "The engines of growth," *Wall Street Journal*, June 27, 2011, p. R4; "Anybody home?," *Wall Street Journal*, June 27, 2011, p. R6; "The German drive to globalise," *Financial Times*, June 1, 2011, p. 6; "China blunts Germany's edge," *Wall Street Journal*, May 12, 2011, p. B11; "Profits of inside knowledge," *Financial Times*, April 5, 2011, p. 14; "Exodus of skilled labor saps Germany," *Wall Street Journal*, March 11, 2011, p. A12; "A machine running smoothly," *The Economist*, February 5, 2011; "Reflected glory," *Financial Times*," January 19, 2011, p. 9; "Mittel-management," *The Economist*, November 27, 2010; "How Germany got it right on the economy," *Washington Post*, November 24, 2010; "Mittelstand style still limited in UK," *Financial Times*, September 26, 2010.

2. Arthur M. Schlesinger, *The Colonial Merchants and the American Revolution 1763–1776* (New York: Facsimile Library, 1939), pp. 16–20.

3. David Ricardo, *The Principles of Political Economy and Taxation* (Homewood: Irwin, 1963). (Ricardo's book was first published in 1817.)

4. Michael Moritz, *The Little Kingdom: The Private Story of Apple Computer* (New York: William Morrow, 1984).

5. "Taiwan eases rules for Chinese investors," *Financial Times*, February 28, 2011, p. 20.

6. P. Krugman, "Intraindustry specialization and the gains from trade," *Journal of Political Economy*, vol. 89 (October 1981), pp. 959–973.

7. K. Lancaster, "Intra-industry trade under perfect monopolistic competition," *Journal of International Economics,* vol. 10 (May 1980), pp. 151–175.

8. Andrew R. Dick, "Learning by doing and dumping in the semiconductor industry," *Journal of Law and Economics,* vol. 34, no. 1 (April 1991), p. 134.

9. Fred Warshofsky, *The Chip War* (New York: Scribner's, 1989), pp. 131–132.

10. The investment statistics for this section are taken from the *Survey of Current Business*, July 2011, pp. 113ff.

11. A. Quijana, "A guide to BEA statistics on foreign direct investment in the United States," *Survey of Current Business*, February 1990, pp. 29–37.

12. Grant T. Hammond, *Countertrade, Offsets and Barter in International Political Economy* (St. Martin's Press: New York, 1990), p. 3.

13. "Intel pushes chip production deep into China's hinterland," *Wall Street Journal*, May 23, 2006, p. B1.

14. "Nokia to establish new manufacturing site in Vietnam," Nokia press release dated March 1, 2011.

15. "China joins Venezuela in heavy-oil venture," *Houston Chronicle*, September 11, 2007 (online).

16. "Korea finds a new way to exploit expertise," *Financial Times*, August 16, 2007 (www.ft.com).

17. "Asian investment floods into Mexican border region," *Wall Street Journal*, September 6, 1996, p. A10.

18. "Samsung attracts six Korean suppliers," *Financial Times*, April 24, 1996, p. 9.

19. "Limit reached on Visas for skilled workers after one week," *Wall Street Journal*, April 9, 2008, p. A12; "Firms get creative to work around Visa bottlenecks," *Wall Street Journal*, August 27, 2007, p. B1; "Microsoft plans Canada software enter," *Wall Street Journal*, July 6, 2007 (online).

20. "US states become addicted to use of economic sweeteners," *Financial Times*, March 23, 2006, p. 19.

21. "Samsung electronics to begin construction of new Austin plant," *Wall Street Journal*, April 19, 2006, p. B5C.

CHAPTER 7

The International Monetary System and the Balance of Payments

AFTER STUDYING THIS CHAPTER, YOU SHOULD BE ABLE TO:

1. Discuss the role of the international monetary system in promoting international trade and investment.

2. Explain the evolution and functioning of the gold standard.

3. Summarize the role of the World Bank Group and the International Monetary Fund in the post–World War II international monetary system established at Bretton Woods.

4. Explain the evolution of the flexible exchange rate system.

5. Describe the function and structure of the balance of payments accounting system.

6. Differentiate among the various definitions of a balance of payments surplus and deficit.

Access a host of interactive learning aids at **www.pearsonglobaleditions.com/mymanagementlab** to help strengthen your understanding of the chapter concepts.

MyManagementLab

Nik Wheeler/CORBIS

WILL THE STARS SHINE ON ASTRA AGAIN?

PT Astra International is one of the oldest and largest conglomerates in Southeast Asia, employing at its peak 125,000 people. For many years the company thrived as Indonesia's dominant automobile assembler, producing about 400,000 vehicles a year. Other Astra subsidiaries build and sell motorcycles and tractors, operate coal mines, run plantations (tea, cocoa, and rubber), and offer financial services (banking, leasing, and insurance). Astra benefited from the phenomenal growth of Indonesia's economy during the 1980s and much of the 1990s, when the country's annual growth in per capita gross domestic product (GDP) averaged 4 percent, more than triple the world's average during that time span. High tariff walls and government procurement policies that favored domestically produced goods shielded many of Astra's factories from foreign competitors.

This producers' paradise came to an abrupt end in the late 1990s. One set of problems arose from the "crony capitalism" that characterized Indonesia during the 32-year rule of President Suharto (1966 to 1998). Crony capitalism refers to the common practice in some countries of government agencies favoring businesses with close ties to high-ranking government officials. In 1996 the Suharto government launched its "national car" program, granting favorable tax treatment to cars built in Indonesia using Indonesian-made parts. Only one company initially qualified for these tax preferences—a company controlled by Suharto's son Tommy. To avoid losing the Indonesian market to this upstart, Astra's managers borrowed $800 million from foreign bankers to expand its production of auto parts, allowing it to qualify for the preferential tax treatment as well. This task was essentially completed by the end of 1997. But Astra's timing was lousy. The Asian currency crisis erupted that year, ultimately leading to a 74 percent devaluation of Indonesia's currency, the rupiah. Astra's bank borrowings threatened to crush the company because most of these new loans were denominated in foreign currencies like the U.S. dollar and the Japanese yen. Because of the rupiah's loss of value, Astra would need to generate many more rupiah in profits than it had planned on to obtain the dollars and yen needed to repay its loans. Unfortunately, the Asian currency crisis traumatized Indonesia's banks, real estate industry, and stock market. As a result of the government-ordered restructuring of Indonesia's banking industry, 39 percent of Astra's stock fell into the hands of the Indonesian Bank Restructuring Agency (IBRA). Furthermore, as Indonesia's economy imploded, many companies laid off employees, and the demand for automobiles—Astra's main product—collapsed. Its automobile sales shrank

by almost 90 percent within the year. To make matters worse, as a condition for extending $18 billion in emergency loans, the International Monetary Fund (IMF) demanded that Indonesia dismantle the trade barriers that the country had constructed to encourage domestic industry. The impact was painful: Thai-made automobiles became available in the Indonesian market at prices 30 percent less than Astra's costs.

Into this mess stepped Rini Soewandi. Although relatively young—only 40 at the time of her appointment as Astra's president in June 1998—she understood the company and its problems. Soewandi recognized that Astra would have to restructure itself if it was to survive the cataclysmic changes in its operating environment. Her first action was to slash the company's workforce by 20 percent. She then went to work cleaning up Astra's balance sheet, spending many long and tense hours renegotiating the company's debt with its 70 bankers. To free up cash, she sold off nonstrategic assets like Astra Microtronics Technology, reaping $90 million on that sale alone.

Soewandi faced even more thorny challenges in reforming the company's culture. When Astra's autos were protected from foreign competition by Indonesia's high tariffs, it could easily sell every car it produced. The concept of customer service was a bitter joke. "Go wait in line" was the common retort to most customers' questions. Soewandi beefed up salesforce training and encouraged the Astra sales staff to go door-to-door to uncover potential buyers. Even more important changes were made in the executive suite. Soewandi introduced new compensation programs that linked pay with performance. Under her direction Astra became the first company in Indonesia to introduce stock options to compensate and motivate managers. Soewandi also targeted conflicts of interest—many senior executives had owned stock in companies that supplied parts to Astra—by strengthening the powers of internal auditors and by imposing a new corporate code of ethics that frowned on such financial ties.

Soewandi's initiatives paid off, and Astra's damaged operations and balance sheet slowly began to mend. Unfortunately for Soewandi, Astra became entwined in a complex loan negotiation between Indonesia's government and the IMF. As a condition for offering additional aid, the IMF demanded that the Indonesian government sell off assets held by various state holding companies. Ironically, as a result of Soewandi's efforts, Astra was one of the more desirable companies in the IBRA's $81 billion portfolio. The IBRA announced it would sell its stake in Astra to foreign investors. Soewandi fought this decision, arguing that Astra was well on the road to recovery and deserved a chance to remain independent. Fearing the wrath of the IMF more than that of Soewandi, the IBRA squeezed her out of office and proceeded with the stock sale. Yet, as Soewandi predicted, a slimmed-down Astra would thrive. In 2010, for example, it earned $1.6 billion on sales of $14.5 billion.[1] ■

As its managers learned the hard way, even a domestically oriented company like PT Astra International must be attuned to changes in the global economy. Astra's crisis was not home-grown. Events outside the country's borders triggered a crisis in the international monetary system, which led to the collapse of the Indonesian economy and decimated the value of its currency. These circumstances caused the domestic market for Astra's products to dry up and its debt burden to balloon to unsustainable levels. Officials of multilateral organizations like the IMF were then able to dictate economic reforms to the government, reforms that caused a controlling interest in the company to be sold to foreign investors. The lesson of Astra's travails is clear. Managers—even those focused on the domestic marketplace—who ignore the workings of the international monetary system and the international institutions that monitor it do so at their own peril.

The international monetary system exists because most countries have their own currencies. A means of exchanging these currencies is needed if business is to be conducted across national boundaries. The **international monetary system** establishes the rules by which countries value and exchange their currencies. It also provides a mechanism for correcting imbalances between a country's international payments and its receipts. Further, the cost of converting foreign money into a firm's home currency—a variable critical to the profitability of international operations—depends on the smooth functioning of the international monetary system.

International businesspeople also monitor the international monetary system's accounting system, the balance of payments. The **balance of payments (BOP) accounting system** records international transactions and supplies vital information about the health of a national economy and likely changes in its fiscal and monetary policies. BOP statistics can be used to detect signs of trouble that could eventually lead to governmental trade restrictions, higher interest rates, accelerated inflation, reduced aggregate demand, and general changes in the cost of doing business in any given country.

History of the International Monetary System

Today's international monetary system can trace its roots to the ancient allure of gold and silver, both of which served as media of exchange in early trade between tribes and in later trade between city-states. Silver, for example, was used in trade among India, Babylon, and Phoenicia as early as the seventh century B.C.[2] As the modern nation-states of Europe took form in the sixteenth and seventeenth centuries, their coins were traded on the basis of their relative gold and silver content.

The Gold Standard

Ancient reliance on gold coins as an international medium of exchange led to the adoption of an international monetary system known as the gold standard. Under the **gold standard**, countries agree to buy or sell their paper currencies in exchange for gold on the request of any individual or firm and, in contrast to mercantilism's hoarding of gold, to allow the free export of gold bullion and coins. In 1821 the United Kingdom became the first country to adopt the gold standard. During the nineteenth century, most other important trading countries—including Russia, Austria-Hungary, France, Germany, and the United States—did the same.

The gold standard effectively created a fixed exchange rate system. An **exchange rate** is the price of one currency in terms of a second currency. Under a **fixed exchange rate system**, the price of a given currency does not change relative to each other currency. The gold standard created a fixed exchange rate system because each country tied, or **pegged**, the value of its currency to gold. The United Kingdom, for example, pledged to buy or sell an ounce of gold for 4.247 pounds sterling, thereby establishing the pound's **par value**, or official price in terms of gold. The United States agreed to buy or sell an ounce of gold for a par value of $20.67. The two currencies could be freely exchanged for the stated amount of gold, making £4.247 = 1 ounce of gold = $20.67. This implied a fixed exchange rate between the pound and the dollar of £1 = $4.867, or $20.67/£4.247.

As long as firms had faith in a country's pledge to exchange its currency for gold at the promised rate when requested to do so, many actually preferred to be paid in currency. Transacting in gold was expensive. Suppose Jardine Matheson, a Hong Kong trading company, sold £100,000 worth of tea to Twining & Company, a London distributor of fine teas. If it wanted to be paid in gold by Twining & Company upon delivery of the tea, Jardine Matheson had to bear the costs of loading the gold into the cargo hold of a ship, guarding it against theft, transporting it, and insuring it against possible disasters. Moreover, because of the slowness of sailing ships, Jardine Matheson would be unable to earn interest on the £100,000 payment while the gold was in transit from London to Hong Kong. However, if Jardine Matheson was willing to be paid in British pounds, Twining could draft a check to Jardine Matheson and give it to the firm's London agent. The London agent could then either immediately deposit the check in Jardine Matheson's interest-bearing London bank account or transfer the funds via telegraph to the firm's account at its Hong Kong bank.

From 1821 until the end of World War I in 1918, the most important currency in international commerce was the British pound sterling, a reflection of the United Kingdom's emergence from the Napoleonic Wars as Europe's dominant economic and military power. Most firms worldwide were willing to accept either gold or British pounds in settlement of transactions. As a result, the international monetary system during this period is often called a **sterling-based gold standard**. The pound's role in world commerce was reinforced by the expansion of the British Empire. The Union Jack flew over so many lands (see Map 7.1)—for example, present-day Canada, Australia, New Zealand, Hong Kong, Singapore, India, Pakistan, Bangladesh, Kenya, Zimbabwe, South Africa, Gibraltar, Bermuda, and Belize—that the claim was made that "the sun never sets on the British Empire." In each colony British banks established branches and used the pound sterling to settle international transactions among themselves. Because of the international trust in British currency, London became a dominant international financial center in the nineteenth century, a position it still holds. The international reputations and competitive strengths of such British firms as Barclays Bank, Thomas Cook, and Lloyd's of London stem from the role of the pound sterling in the nineteenth-century gold standard.

The Collapse of the Gold Standard

During World War I, the sterling-based gold standard unraveled. With the outbreak of war, normal commercial transactions between the Allies (France, Russia, and the United Kingdom) and the Central Powers (Austria-Hungary, Germany, and the Ottoman Empire) ceased. The economic pressures of war caused country after country to suspend their pledges to buy or sell gold at their currencies' par values. After the war, conferences at Brussels (1920) and Genoa (1922) yielded general agreements among the major economic powers to return to the prewar gold standard. Most countries, including the United States, the United Kingdom, and France, readopted the gold standard in the 1920s despite the high levels of inflation, unemployment, and political instability that were wracking Europe.

The resuscitation of the gold standard proved to be short-lived, however, due to the economic stresses triggered by the worldwide Great Depression. The Bank of England, the United Kingdom's central bank, was unable to honor its pledge to maintain the value of the pound. On September 21, 1931, it allowed the pound to **float**, meaning that the pound's value would be determined by the forces of supply and demand and the Bank of England would no longer redeem British paper currency for gold at par value.

After the United Kingdom abandoned the gold standard, a "sterling area" emerged as some countries, primarily members of the British Commonwealth, pegged their currencies to the pound and relied on sterling balances held in London as their international reserves.

MAP 7.1
The British Empire in 1913

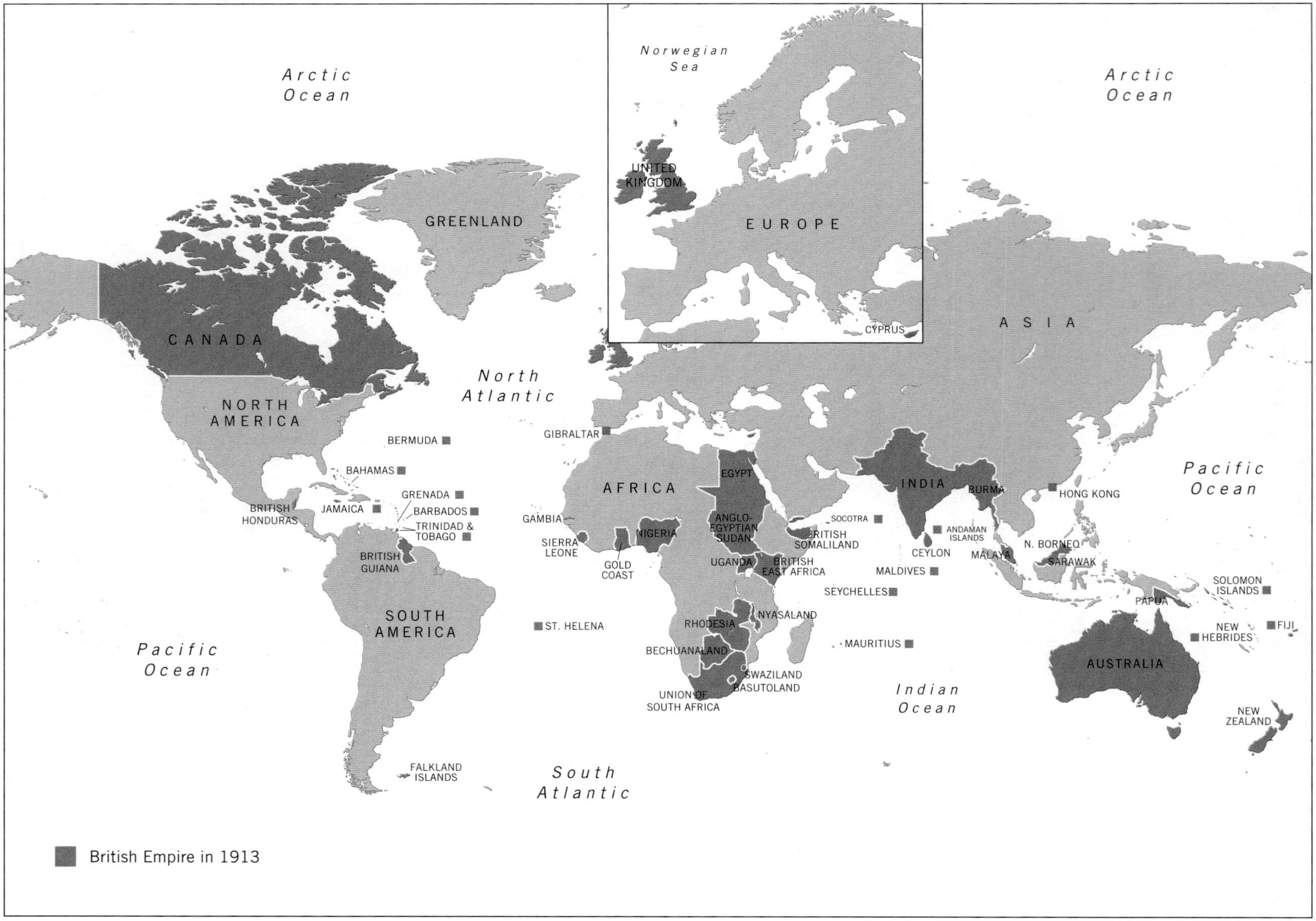

Arctic Ocean

Pacific Ocean

SOLOMON ISLANDS
NEW HEBRIDES
FIJI
NEW ZEALAND

A S I A

PAPUA
AUSTRALIA

HONG KONG
N. BORNEO
SARAWAK
MALAYA

BURMA
ANDAMAN ISLANDS
CEYLON
MALDIVES
SEYCHELLES
MAURITIUS

INDIA

Indian Ocean

CYPRUS

E U R O P E

Norwegian Sea

UNITED KINGDOM

SOCOTRA
BRITISH SOMALILAND
BRITISH EAST AFRICA
UGANDA
EGYPT
ANGLO-EGYPTIAN SUDAN
NYASALAND
SWAZILAND
BASUTOLAND
RHODESIA
BECHUANALAND
UNION OF SOUTH AFRICA

A F R I C A

NIGERIA
GOLD COAST
GAMBIA
SIERRA LEONE
ST. HELENA

GIBRALTAR

North Atlantic

South Atlantic

GREENLAND

Arctic Ocean

BERMUDA
BAHAMAS
JAMAICA
GRENADA
BARBADOS
TRINIDAD & TOBAGO
BRITISH GUIANA
BRITISH HONDURAS

FALKLAND ISLANDS

SOUTH AMERICA

CANADA
NORTH AMERICA

Pacific Ocean

■ British Empire in 1913

Other countries tied the value of their currencies to the U.S. dollar or the French franc. The harmony of the international monetary system degenerated further as some countries—including the United States, France, the United Kingdom, Belgium, Latvia, the Netherlands, Switzerland, and Italy—engaged in a series of competitive devaluations of their currencies. By deliberately and artificially lowering (devaluing) the official value of its currency, each nation hoped to make its own goods cheaper in world markets, thereby stimulating its exports and reducing its imports. Any such gains were offset, however, when other countries also devalued their currencies. (If two countries each devalue their currency by 20 percent, neither gains an advantage because each currency's value relative to the other remains the same.) Most countries also raised the tariffs they imposed on imported goods in the hope of protecting domestic jobs in import-competing industries. Yet as more and more countries adopted these **beggar-thy-neighbor policies**, international trade contracted (see Figure 7.1), hurting employment in each country's export industries. More ominously, this international economic conflict was soon replaced by international military conflict—the outbreak of World War II in 1939.

The Bretton Woods Era

Many politicians and historians believe the breakdown of the international monetary system and international trade after World War I created economic conditions that helped bring about World War II. Inflation, unemployment, and the costs of rebuilding war-torn economies created political instability that enabled fascist and communist dictators to seize control of their respective governments. Determined not to repeat the mistakes that had caused World War II, Western diplomats desired to create a postwar economic environment that would promote worldwide peace and prosperity. In 1944 the representatives of 44 countries met at a resort in Bretton Woods, New Hampshire, with that objective in mind. The Bretton Woods conferees agreed to renew the gold standard on a greatly modified basis. They also agreed to the creation of two new international organizations that would assist in rebuilding the world economy and the international monetary system: the International Bank for Reconstruction and Development and the International Monetary Fund.

FIGURE 7.1

Down the Tube: The Contraction of World Trade, 1929–1933

Source: Charles Kindleberger, *The World in Depression* (Berkeley: University of California Press, 1986), p. 170.

Note: Total imports of 75 countries (monthly values, millions of dollars)

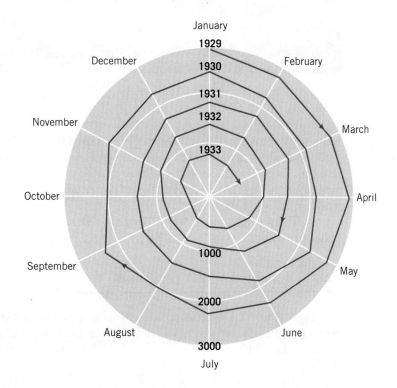

The defeat of Napoleon's Grande Armée at the Battle of Waterloo in 1815 by British and Prussian armies under the leadership of the Duke of Wellington led to the century-long dominance of world commerce by the United Kingdom. While the onset of World War I eroded the U.K.'s military and economic power, London remains at the center of the international capital market.

SuperStock/SuperStock

THE INTERNATIONAL BANK FOR RECONSTRUCTION AND DEVELOPMENT The **International Bank for Reconstruction and Development (IBRD)** is the official name of the **World Bank**. Established in 1945, the World Bank's initial goal was to help finance reconstruction of the war-torn European economies. With the assistance of the Marshall Plan, the World Bank accomplished this task by the mid-1950s. It then adopted a new mission—to build the economies of the world's developing countries.

As its mission has expanded over time, the World Bank has created three affiliated organizations:

1. The International Development Association
2. The International Finance Corporation
3. The Multilateral Investment Guarantee Agency

Together with the World Bank, these constitute the **World Bank Group** (see Figure 7.2). The World Bank, which currently has $120.1 billion in loans outstanding, is owned by its 187 member countries. In reaching its decisions, the World Bank uses a weighted voting system that reflects the economic power and contributions of its members. The United States currently controls the largest bloc of votes (16.0 percent), followed by Japan (9.6 percent), Germany (4.4 percent),

FIGURE 7.2

Organization of the World Bank Group

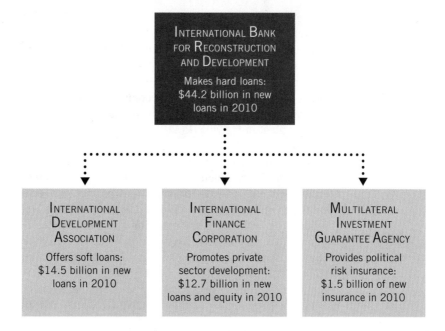

the United Kingdom (4.2 percent), France (4.2 percent), and six countries with 2.7 percent each: Canada, China, India, Italy, Russia, and Saudi Arabia. From time to time the voting weights are reassessed as economic power shifts or as new members join the World Bank. To finance its lending operations, the World Bank borrows money in its own name from international capital markets. Interest earned on existing loans it has made provides it with additional lending power. The World Bank made $44.2 billion in new loan commitments in 2010.

According to its charter, the World Bank may lend only for "productive purposes" that will stimulate economic growth within the recipient country. An example of such a loan is the $200 million provided to Indonesia to modernize its national highways and improve traffic safety. The World Bank cannot finance a trade deficit, but it can finance an infrastructure project, such as a new railroad or harbor facility, that will bolster a country's economy. It may lend only to national governments or for projects that are guaranteed by a national government, and its loans may not be tied to the purchase of goods or services from any country. Most important, the World Bank must follow a **hard loan policy**; that is, it may make a loan only if there is a reasonable expectation that the loan will be repaid.

The hard loan policy was severely criticized in the 1950s by poorer countries, which complained it hindered their ability to obtain World Bank loans. In response, the World Bank established the **International Development Association (IDA)** in 1960. The IDA offers **soft loans**, loans that bear some significant risk of not being repaid. IDA loans carry no interest rate, although the IDA collects a small service charge (currently 0.75 percent) from borrowers. The loans also have long maturities (normally 35 to 40 years), and borrowers are often granted a 10-year grace period before they need to begin repaying their loans. The IDA's lending efforts focus on the least-developed countries. A typical loan is the $25 million provided to Guinea to reduce water pollution and lessen waterborne diseases. The IDA obtains resources from the initial subscriptions its members make when joining it, from transferred World Bank profits, and from periodic replenishments contributed by richer countries. In 2010, the IDA made new loan commitments amounting to $14.5 billion.

The two other affiliates of the World Bank Group have narrower missions. The **International Finance Corporation (IFC)**, created in 1956, is charged with promoting the development of the private sector in developing countries. Acting like an investment banker, the IFC, in collaboration with private investors, provides debt and equity capital for promising commercial activities. For example, the IFC provided Bangladesh's Lafarge Surma Cement Ltd. with $10 million in equity and $35 million in loans to help it build a $60-million plant capable of producing 1.2 million tons of cement annually. The IFC is also interested in helping small entrepreneurs. In total the IFC provided $12.7 billion of financing in 2010.

The other World Bank affiliate, the **Multilateral Investment Guarantee Agency (MIGA)**, was set up in 1988 to overcome private sector reluctance to invest in developing countries because of perceived political riskiness—a topic covered in Chapter 3. MIGA encourages direct investment in developing countries by offering private investors insurance against noncommercial risks. For example, MIGA issued $18 million of political risk insurance to Société Nationale de Télécommunications du Sénégal to protect its investment in Ikatel SA, a Mali telephone company, and $115 million in support of the Bujagali hydropower plant in Uganda. In 2010, MIGA underwrote a total of $1.5 billion in political risk insurance.

Paralleling the efforts of the World Bank are the **regional development banks**, such as the African Development Bank, the Asian Development Bank, and the Inter-American Development Bank. These organizations promote the economic development of the poorer countries in their respective regions. The most recently created regional development bank is the European Bank for Reconstruction and Development. It was established by the Western countries to assist in the reconstruction of Central Europe and Eastern Europe after the regions' communist regimes collapsed. The regional development banks and the World Bank often work together on development projects. For example, the Asian Development Bank, in conjunction with the World Bank and several other agencies, helped fund and insure a hydro-electric power plant near Kathmandu, Nepal, which will supply 25 percent of Nepal's electrical power.

THE INTERNATIONAL MONETARY FUND The Bretton Woods attendees believed that the deterioration of international trade during the years after World War I was attributable in part to the competitive exchange rate devaluations that plagued international commerce. To ensure that the post–World War II monetary system would promote international commerce, the Bretton Woods Agreement called for the creation of the **International Monetary Fund (IMF)** to oversee the functioning of the international monetary system. Article I of the IMF's Articles of Agreement lays out the organization's objectives:

1. To promote international monetary cooperation
2. To facilitate the expansion and balanced growth of international trade
3. To promote exchange stability, to maintain orderly exchange arrangements among members, and to avoid competitive exchange depreciation
4. To assist in the establishment of a multilateral system of payments
5. To give confidence to members by making the general resources of the IMF temporarily available to them and to correct maladjustments in their balance of payments
6. To shorten the duration and lessen the degree of disequilibrium in the international balance of payments of members

Membership in the IMF is available to any country willing to agree to its rules and regulations. As of 2011, 187 countries were members. To join, a country must pay a deposit, called a **quota**, partly in gold and partly in the country's own currency. The quota's size primarily reflects the global importance of the country's economy, although political considerations may also have some effect. The size of a quota is important for several reasons:

1. A country's quota determines its voting power within the IMF. Currently the United States controls 16.8 percent of the votes in the IMF, Japan 6.2 percent, and Germany 5.8 percent, followed by France and the United Kingdom (4.3 percent), China (3.8 percent), Italy (3.2 percent), Saudi Arabia (2.8 percent), Canada (2.6 percent), and Russia (2.4 percent). However, these voting powers are likely to change: In 2010 the IMF's Executive Board proposed to shift 6 percent of the organization's voting power from developed countries to the emerging and developing countries in recognition of their growing importance in the world economy.[3]
2. A country's quota serves as part of its official reserves (we discuss official reserves later in this chapter).
3. The quota determines the country's borrowing power from the IMF. Each IMF member has an unconditional right to borrow up to 25 percent of its quota from the IMF. IMF policy allows additional borrowings contingent on the member country's agreeing to

IMF-imposed restrictions—called **IMF conditionality**—on its economic policies. For example, in return for an IMF loan of $21 billion during the Asian currency crisis, South Korea agreed to undertake major economic reforms, including permitting foreign banks to take over their Korean counterparts, closing insolvent merchant banks, reducing government favoritism toward the larger *chaebols*, and lowering tariffs on many goods. The IMF consented to lend Indonesia $10 billion after that country pledged to scrap state monopolies controlling certain foodstuffs, reform its banking industry, and cut trade barriers directed against imported goods.[4] As noted in the opening case, the IMF also pressured Indonesia's government to liquidate its holdings in various companies, which led to the sale of PT Astra International to a Singapore consortium. Local politicians and interest groups often bitterly protest the IMF's conditionality requirements, arguing that foreigners, working through the IMF, are taking advantage of the country's short-term problems to extract changes favorable to the foreigners. At times, the situation can turn uglier. For example, Indonesia was wracked by rioting after prices and unemployment soared as a result of the austerity measures demanded by the IMF, and longtime President Suharto was forced to resign his office.

A DOLLAR-BASED GOLD STANDARD The IMF and the World Bank provided the institutional framework for the post–World War II international monetary system. The Bretton Woods participants also addressed the problem of how the system would function in practice. All countries agreed to peg the value of their currencies to gold. For example, the par value of the U.S. dollar was established at $35 per ounce of gold. However, only the United States pledged to redeem its currency for gold at the request of a foreign central bank. Thus, the U.S. dollar became the keystone of the Bretton Woods system. Why this central role for the U.S. dollar? During the early postwar years, only the U.S. and Canadian dollars were **convertible currencies**, that is, ones that could be freely exchanged for other currencies without legal restrictions. Countries had faith in the U.S. economy and so were willing to accept U.S. dollars to settle their transactions. As the British pound sterling had been in the nineteenth century, the U.S. dollar became the preferred vehicle for settling most international transactions. The effect of the Bretton Woods conference was thus to establish a U.S. dollar–based gold standard.

Because each country established a par value for its currency, the Bretton Woods Agreement resulted in a fixed exchange rate system. Under the agreement each country pledged to maintain the value of its currency within ± 1 percent of its par value. If the market value of its currency fell outside that range, a country was obligated to intervene in the foreign-exchange market to bring the value back within ± 1 percent of par value. This stability in exchange rates benefited international businesses because the Bretton Woods system *generally* provided an assurance that the value of each currency would remain stable.

Note the use of the qualifier *generally*. Under extraordinary circumstances the Bretton Woods Agreement allowed a country to adjust its currency's par value. Accordingly, the Bretton Woods system is often described as using an **adjustable peg** because currencies were pegged to gold but the pegs themselves could be altered under certain conditions. Under the system, for example, the British pound's par value was first set at $2.80. (Technically, the par value was pegged to an ounce of gold, which then could be translated into dollars at a rate of $35.00 per ounce. Most businesspeople ignored this technicality, however, and focused on the implicit par value of a currency in terms of the U.S. dollar.) Thus, the Bank of England was obligated to keep the pound's value between $2.772 and $2.828 (±1 percent of $2.80). In the event that pessimism about the British economy caused the pound's market price to fall to $2.76, the Bank of England would be required to defend the value of the pound by selling some of its gold or U.S. dollar holdings to buy pounds. This move would increase the demand for pounds, and the market price would return to within the legal range—from $2.772 to $2.828.

The End of the Bretton Woods System

This arrangement worked well as long as pessimism about a country's economy was temporary, but if a country suffered from structural macroeconomic problems, major difficulties could arise. For example, in the 1960s, Labour governments striving for social justice dominated British politics, and British unions secured higher wages, better working conditions, and protective work rules. At the same time, however, British productivity decreased relative to that of its major international competitors, and the pound's value weakened. The Bank of England had to intervene continually in the foreign currency market, selling gold and foreign currencies to support the pound. In so doing, however, the Bank's holdings of official reserves, which were needed to back up the country's Bretton Woods pledge, began to dwindle. International currency traders began to fear the Bank would run out of reserves. As that fear mounted, international banks, currency traders, and other market participants became unwilling to hold British pounds in their inventory of foreign currencies. They began dumping pounds on the market as soon as they received them. A vicious cycle developed: As the Bank of England continued to drain its official reserves to support the pound, the fears of the currency-market participants that the Bank would run out of reserves were worsened.

The situation resembles a run on a bank. Banks never have enough cash on hand to honor all their liabilities. However, as long as people trust that their bank will give them their money if they need it, no one worries. If people lose that trust and withdraw more of their money than the bank has on hand, the bank could be in trouble. The Bretton Woods system was particularly susceptible to speculative "runs on the bank" because there was little risk in betting against a currency in times of doubt. For example, speculators distrustful of the Bank of England's ability to honor the U.K.'s Bretton Woods pledge could convert their pounds into dollars. If they guessed right and the pound was devalued, they could make a quick financial killing. If they guessed wrong and the Bank of England maintained the pound's par value, the speculators could always reconvert their dollar holdings back into pounds with little penalty.

The United Kingdom faced this type of bank run in November 1967. The Bank of England could not counter the flood of pounds dumped on the market by speculators and was forced to devalue the pound by 14.3 percent (from $2.80 to $2.40 per pound). France faced a similar run in 1969 and had to devalue the franc. These devaluations tested the international business community's faith in the Bretton Woods system. But the system faced its true Waterloo when the dollar came under attack in the early 1970s.

These runs on the British and French central banks were a precursor to a run on the most important bank in the Bretton Woods system—the U.S. Federal Reserve Bank. Ironically, the reliance of the Bretton Woods system on the dollar ultimately led to the system's undoing. Because the supply of gold did not expand in the short run, the only source of the liquidity needed to expand international trade was the U.S. dollar. Under the Bretton Woods system, the expansion of international liquidity depended on foreigners' willingness to continually increase their holdings of dollars. Foreigners were perfectly happy to hold dollars as long as they trusted the integrity of the U.S. currency, and during the 1950s and 1960s the number of dollars held by foreigners rose steadily.

As foreign dollar holdings increased, however, people began to question the ability of the United States to live up to its Bretton Woods obligation. This led to the **Triffin paradox**, named after the Belgian-born Yale University economist Robert Triffin, who first identified the problem. The paradox arose because foreigners needed to increase their holdings of dollars to finance expansion of international trade, but the more dollars they owned, the less faith they had in the ability of the United States to redeem those dollars for gold. The less faith foreigners had in the United States, the more they wanted to rid themselves of dollars and get gold in return. If they did this, however, international trade and the international monetary system might collapse because the United States did not have enough gold to redeem all the dollars held by foreigners.

As a means of injecting more liquidity into the international monetary system while reducing the demands placed on the dollar as a reserve currency, IMF members agreed in 1967 to create **special drawing rights (SDRs)**. IMF members can use SDRs to settle official transactions at the IMF. Thus, SDRs are sometimes called "paper gold." IMF members currently hold approximately 204 billion SDRs. (About 90 percent of these SDRs were created in 2008 and 2009 by the IMF to address the recent global recession.)[5] An SDR's value is currently calculated daily as a weighted average of the market value of four major currencies—U.S. dollar, euro, Japanese yen, and British pound sterling—with the weights revised every five years. As of August 2011, the SDR was worth $1.60 in U.S. dollars.

TABLE 7.1 The Groups of Five, Seven, and Ten

	Group of Five	Group of Seven	Group of Ten*	Percentage of World GDP
	United States	United States	United States	24.5
	Japan	Japan	Japan	8.7
	Germany	Germany	Germany	5.8
	France	France	France	4.6
	United Kingdom	United Kingdom	United Kingdom	3.7
		Italy	Italy	3.6
		Canada	Canada	2.3
			Netherlands	1.4
			Switzerland	.9
			Belgium	.8
			Sweden	.7
Cumulative Percentage of World GDP	47.3	53.2	57.0	

*The Group of Ten has 11 members.

Although SDRs did provide new liquidity for the international monetary system, they did not reduce the fundamental problem of the glut of dollars held by foreigners. By mid-1971, the Bretton Woods system was tottering, the victim of fears about the dollar's instability. During the first seven months of 1971, the United States was forced to sell one-third of its gold reserves to maintain the dollar's value. It became clear to the marketplace that the United States did not have sufficient gold on hand to meet the demands of those who still wanted to exchange their dollars for gold. In a dramatic address on August 15, 1971, President Richard M. Nixon announced that the United States would no longer redeem gold at $35 per ounce. The Bretton Woods system was ended. In effect, the bank was closing its doors.

After Nixon's speech most currencies began to float, their values being determined by supply and demand in the foreign-exchange market. The value of the U.S. dollar fell relative to most of the world's major currencies. The nations of the world, however, were not yet ready to abandon the fixed exchange rate system. At the **Smithsonian Conference**, held in Washington, D.C., in December 1971, central bank representatives from the Group of Ten (see Table 7.1) agreed to restore the fixed exchange rate system but with restructured rates of exchange between the major trading currencies. The U.S. dollar was devalued to $38 per ounce but remained inconvertible into gold, and the par values of strong currencies such as the yen were revalued upward. Currencies were allowed to fluctuate around their new par values by ±2.25 percent, which replaced the narrower ±1.00 percent range authorized by the Bretton Woods Agreement.

Performance of the International Monetary System Since 1971

Free-market forces disputed the new set of par values established by the Smithsonian conferees. Speculators sold both the dollar and the pound, believing they were overvalued, and hoarded currencies they believed were undervalued, such as the Swiss franc and the German mark. The Bank of England was unable to maintain the pound's value within the ±2.25 percent band and in June 1972 had to allow the pound to float downward. Switzerland let the Swiss franc float upward in early 1973. The United States devalued the dollar by 10 percent in February 1973. By March 1973 the central banks (see Table 7.2 for a list of the most important of today's central banks) conceded they could not successfully resist free-market forces and so established a flexible exchange rate system. Under a **flexible (or floating) exchange rate system**, supply and demand for a currency determine its price in the world market. Since 1973, exchange rates

TABLE 7.2 Key Central Banks

Country	Bank
Canada	Bank of Canada
European Union (members using the euro)	European Central Bank
Japan	Bank of Japan
United Kingdom	Bank of England
United States	Federal Reserve Bank

among many currencies have been established primarily by the interaction of supply and demand. We use the qualifier *primarily* because central banks sometimes try to affect exchange rates by buying or selling currencies on the foreign-exchange market. Thus, the current arrangements are often called a **managed float** (or, more poetically, a **dirty float**) because exchange rates are not determined purely by private sector market forces. "Bringing the World into Focus" discusses other differences between fixed and flexible exchange rates.

The new flexible exchange rate system was legitimized by an international conference held in Jamaica in January 1976. According to the resulting **Jamaica Agreement**, each country was free to adopt whatever exchange rate system best met its own requirements. The United States adopted a floating exchange rate. Other countries adopted a fixed exchange rate by pegging their currencies to the dollar, the French franc, or some other currency. Still others utilized **crawling pegs**, allowing the peg to change gradually over time.

Of particular note is the strategy adopted by European Union (EU) members in the belief that flexible exchange rates would hinder their ability to create an integrated European economy. In 1979 EU members created the **European Monetary System (EMS)** to manage currency relationships among themselves. Most EMS members chose to participate in the EU's **exchange rate mechanism (ERM)**. ERM participants pledged to maintain fixed exchange rates among their currencies within a narrow range of ± 2.25 percent of par value and a floating rate against the U.S. dollar and other currencies. The exchange rate mechanism facilitated the creation of the EU's single currency, the euro, in 1999, a topic we will cover more thoroughly in Chapter 10.

Map 7.2 shows the current status of the world's exchange rate arrangements. The current international monetary system is an amalgam of fixed and flexible exchange rates. For example,

---

BRINGING THE WORLD INTO FOCUS   **FIXED VERSUS FLEXIBLE EXCHANGE RATES**

One important difference between fixed and flexible exchange rate systems is the way they reach equilibrium. Under the fixed exchange rate system, such as the gold standard (1821 to 1914) and the Bretton Woods system (1945 to 1971), each country pledges to maintain the value of its currency against some standard, such as gold or another currency. If the value of the country's currency falls below par value, the country's central bank boosts the currency's price by buying it in the foreign-exchange market, selling off its gold reserves or stock of convertible currencies in the process. If the currency's value rises above par value, the central bank sells the currency in the foreign-exchange market, acquiring additional gold or foreign currency in the process. Long-run equilibrium is supposed to occur through the deflationary or inflationary impact of changes in the country's money supply attributable to the central bank's actions in the foreign-exchange market.

Although this automatic adjustment process worked reasonably well under the nineteenth-century gold standard, it did not work well under the Bretton Woods system. In practice, the adjustment process under the Bretton Woods system was asymmetric. A country

with a BOP surplus did not need to do anything, provided it was willing to accumulate foreign exchange or gold. A country suffering a BOP deficit saw a continuing decrease in its official reserves. It had to cure its BOP problems well before it ran out of reserves. If the country did nothing, other countries (and investors), seeing its reserves dwindling, would begin to distrust the country's ability to honor its pledge to maintain its currency's par value. These foreigners would rush to sell their holdings of the currency, thereby worsening the drain on the country's reserves. Ultimately, the government would have to renege on its promise to convert at the fixed rate and would resort to devaluing its currency. This is what happened to the United Kingdom in 1967, France in 1969, and the United States in 1971.

Conversely, under a flexible exchange rate system, the exchange rate is determined by the forces of supply and demand for each currency. Assuming a country's central bank is willing to live with the outcome of these market forces, its official reserves need not be depleted because consumers and investors are determining the currency's value through their self-interested transactions.

MAP 7.2

Exchange Rate Arrangements as of 2010

Source: www.imf.org, www.state.gov, accessed August 5, 2011.

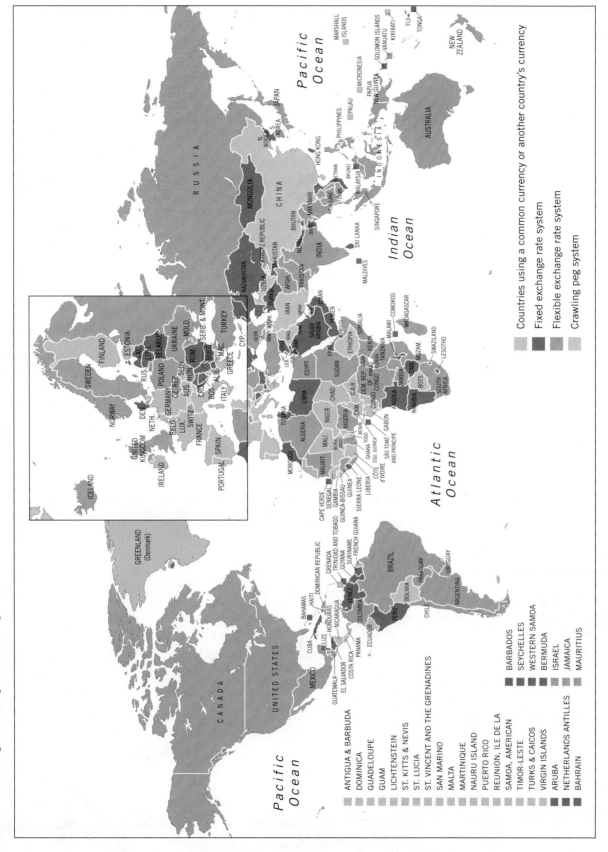

as just discussed, most members of the EU have adopted a common currency, while other countries have voluntarily adopted a fixed exchange rate against the U.S. dollar, the euro, or some other currency. Still other countries, such as Canada, Japan, the United Kingdom, and the United States, have chosen to let their currencies float. Accordingly, under the current international monetary system, the currencies of one country grouping float against the currencies of other country groupings. For example, the U.S. dollar and currencies fixed to the U.S. dollar float against the euro and currencies fixed to it. The U.S. dollar and the euro in turn float against numerous independently floating currencies, such as the Canadian dollar, the Australian dollar, the British pound, and the Swiss franc.

OTHER POST–WORLD WAR II CONFERENCES The international monetary system that has grown out of the Jamaica Agreement has not pleased all of the world's central banks all the time. Since 1976, the central banks have met numerous times to iron out policy conflicts among themselves. For example, U.S. complaints that an overvalued dollar was hurting the competitiveness of U.S. exports and allowing cheap imports to damage U.S. industries prompted finance ministers of the Group of Five (see Table 7.1) to meet in September 1985 at the Plaza Hotel in New York City. The meeting led to the **Plaza Accord**, in which the central banks agreed to let the dollar's value fall on currency markets—and fall it did. From its peak in February 1985 the dollar plummeted almost 46 percent against the German mark and 41 percent against the yen by the beginning of 1987. Fearing that continued devaluation of the dollar would disrupt world trade, finance ministers from the Group of Five met again, this time at the Louvre in Paris in February 1987. The **Louvre Accord** signaled the commitment of these five countries to stabilizing the dollar's value. However, the foreign-exchange market was once again thrown into turmoil in 1990, this time by the onset of the Persian Gulf hostilities. The values of key currencies continued to fluctuate through the end of the century. Figure 7.3 shows changes in the dollar's value against the Japanese and German currencies since the collapse of the Bretton Woods system.

These fluctuations in currency values are of great importance to international businesses. When the value of their domestic currency increases in the foreign-exchange market, firms find it harder to export their goods, more difficult to protect their domestic markets from the threat of foreign imports, and more advantageous to shift their production from domestic factories to foreign factories. A decrease in the domestic currency's value has the opposite effect. Savvy international businesspeople are mindful of the impact of these currency fluctuations on their

FIGURE 7.3

Exchange Rates of the Dollar Versus the Yen, the Euro, and the Deutsche Mark, 1960–2010

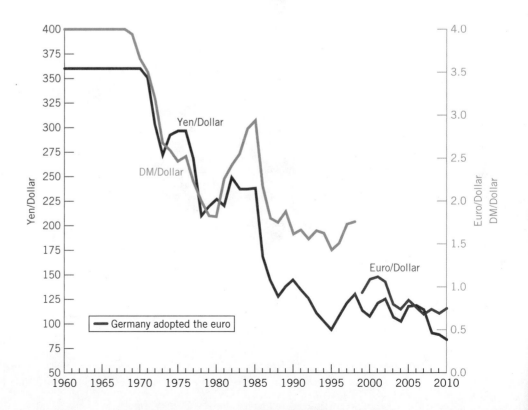

business opportunities. For example, Mittelstand firms find it easier to export their goods and services when the value of the euro falls in the foreign exchange market. Conversely, increases in the value of the euro make it harder for German and other euro-based firms to compete with rivals from North America or Asia. The problems caused by these exchange rate fluctuations have motivated some experts to call for a restoration of the Bretton Woods system (see "Bringing the World into Focus").

THE INTERNATIONAL DEBT CRISIS The flexible exchange rate system instituted in 1973 was immediately put to a severe test. In response to the Israeli victory in the Arab-Israeli War of 1973, Arab nations imposed an embargo on oil shipments to countries such as the United States and the Netherlands, which had supported the Israeli cause. As a result, the Organization of Petroleum Exporting Countries (OPEC) succeeded in quadrupling world oil prices from $3 a barrel in October 1973 to $12 a barrel by March 1974. This rapid increase in oil prices caused inflationary pressures in oil-importing countries. For example, in the United States inflation rose from 6.1 percent in 1973 to 11.1 percent in 1974. In 1974 alone $60 billion in wealth was transferred from oil-importing countries to oil-exporting countries. The new international monetary arrangements absorbed some of the shock caused by this upheaval in the oil market, as exchange rates adjusted to account for changes in the value of each country's oil exports or imports. In general, the currencies of the oil exporters strengthened, while those of the oil importers weakened.

This enormous transfer of wealth raised certain economic concerns. The higher oil prices acted as a tax on the economies of the oil-importing countries. Some economists feared that worldwide depression would develop as consumer demand fell in the richer countries. Other economists worried that because trade in oil was denominated in dollars, international liquidity would dry up as dollars piled up in OPEC bank accounts. Neither of these fears was realized. Many of the oil-exporting countries went on spending sprees, using their new wealth to improve their infrastructures or to invest in new facilities (such as petroleum refineries) to produce wealth for future generations. The unspent petrodollars were deposited in banks in international money centers such as London and New York City. The international banking community then recycled these petrodollars through its international lending activities to help revive the economies damaged by rising oil prices.

Unfortunately, the international banks were too aggressive in recycling these dollars. Many countries borrowed more than they could repay. Mexico, for example, borrowed $90 billion, while Brazil took on $67 billion in new loans. The financial positions of these borrowers became precarious after the oil shock of 1978–1979, which was triggered by the toppling of the Shah of Iran from power. The price of oil skyrocketed from $13 a barrel in 1978 to over $30 a barrel in 1980, triggering another round of worldwide inflation. Interest rates on these loans rose, as most carried a floating interest rate, further burdening the heavily indebted nations. The international debt crisis formally began when Mexico declared in August 1982 that it could not service its external debts. Mexico requested a rescheduling of its debts, a moratorium on repayment of principal, and a loan from the IMF to help it through its debt crisis. Mexico was soon joined by Brazil and Argentina. In total more than 40 countries in Asia, Africa, and Latin America sought relief from their external debts. Negotiations among the debtor countries, creditor countries, private banks, and international organizations continued through the rest of the 1980s.

Various approaches were used to resolve the crisis. The 1985 **Baker Plan** (named after then U.S. Treasury Secretary James Baker) stressed the importance of debt rescheduling, tight IMF-imposed controls over domestic monetary and fiscal policies, and continued lending to debtor countries in hopes that economic growth would allow them to repay their creditors. In Mexico's case the IMF agreed to provide a loan package only if private foreign banks holding Mexican debt agreed to reschedule their loans and provide Mexico with additional financing. However, the debtor nations made little progress in repaying their loans. Debtors and creditors alike agreed that a new approach was needed. The 1989 **Brady Plan** (named after the first Bush administration's treasury secretary, Nicholas Brady) focused on the need to reduce the debts of the troubled countries by writing off parts of the debts or by providing the countries with funds to buy back their loan notes at below face value.

The international debt crisis receded during the 1990s as the debt-servicing requirements of debtor countries were made more manageable via a combination of IMF loans, debt rescheduling,

International policymakers have debated the value of resurrecting the Bretton Woods system. Proponents of the system believe fixed exchange rates offer international businesses several advantages. Exchange rates are not subject to wide daily, weekly, and monthly fluctuations. The riskiness of international trade transactions is thus reduced, and firms have greater assurance of stability in the values of foreign currencies. Also, fixed exchange rates are an important anti-inflationary tool because the loss of official reserves forces a country to counteract inflationary tendencies in its economy. Bretton Woods proponents also are distressed because the wild swings in the values of key currencies that occur in flexible exchange rate systems can disrupt sound international investment decision making.

Advocates of flexible exchange rates look at the other side of the coin. If balance of payments (BOP) equilibrium can be reached through changes in exchange rates, then domestic policymakers are free to focus on domestic economic concerns without worrying about the BOP consequences of their actions. Flexible exchange rates also reduce the need for international coordination of domestic economic policies and allow each country to follow its own economic destiny. For example, if Mexico's monetary authorities choose more inflationary, growth-oriented economic policies than those adopted by its major trading partners, changes in exchange rates will bring about BOP equilibrium. Flexible exchange rates can absorb the impact of damaging external economic events, such as occurred during the two oil embargoes in the 1970s. Proponents of flexible exchange rates also suggest that fixed exchange rate systems are not invulnerable to disorderly changes in currency values and cite the depreciation of the pound in 1967, the French franc in 1969, and the U.S. dollar in 1971. Similarly, they point out the chaos and hardships created by the 1997–1998 collapse of the fixed exchange rate systems used by Thailand, Indonesia, and other Southeast Asian countries.

and changes in governmental economic policies (see the discussion of economic reforms in Mexico, Argentina, and Brazil in Chapter 2). The impact of the crisis cannot be overstated. Many experts consider the 1980s the "lost decade" for economic development in Latin America.

The Asian currency crisis erupted in July 1997, when Thailand, which had pegged its currency to a dollar-dominated basket of currencies, was forced to unpeg its currency, the baht, after investors began to distrust the abilities of Thai borrowers to repay their foreign loans and of the Thai government to maintain the baht's value. Not wanting to hold a currency likely to be devalued, foreign and domestic investors converted their baht to dollars and other currencies. The Thai central bank spent much of its official reserves desperately trying to maintain the pegged value of the baht. After Thailand was forced to abandon the peg on July 2, the baht promptly fell 20 percent in value. As investors realized that other countries in the region shared Thailand's overdependence on foreign short-term capital, their currencies also came under attack and their stock markets were devastated. Indonesia was hit the worst by the so-called Asian contagion, as our earlier discussion of PT Astra International indicated. The value of the Indonesian rupiah fell by 73 percent and its stock market plunged by more than 80 percent. Aftershocks of the crisis spread to Latin America and Russia, and the Russian government effectively defaulted on its foreign debts. All told, the IMF and the developed countries pledged over $100 billion in loans to help restore these countries to economic health.

The latest financial crisis to plague the international capital market began with the so-called subprime meltdown, which resulted from the bursting of the U.S. housing bubble. The financial problems created by this collapse affected financial markets throughout the world. This is the subject of the closing case of Chapter 8.

These crises did not come as a surprise to the analysts who had been monitoring the affected countries' balance of payments accounts for danger signs. The BOP accounting system provided clear warning of the deteriorating performance of the countries in crisis and the increasing riskiness of their overextended external debt positions. A careful reading of BOP statistics could have protected international bankers from bad investments and risky loans. Because the BOP accounting system provides such valuable economic intelligence information, the next section discusses it in detail.

The Balance of Payments Accounting System

Each year countries purchase trillions of dollars of goods, services, and assets from each other. The BOP accounting system is a double-entry bookkeeping system designed to measure and record all economic transactions between residents of one country and residents of all other countries during a particular time period. It helps policymakers understand the performance of each country's economy in international markets. It also signals fundamental changes in the competitiveness of countries and assists policymakers in designing appropriate public policies to respond to these changes.

International businesspeople need to pay close attention to countries' BOP statistics for several reasons, including the following:

1. BOP statistics help identify emerging markets for goods and services.
2. BOP statistics can warn of possible new policies that may alter a country's business climate, thereby affecting the profitability of a firm's operations in that country. For example, sharp rises in a country's imports may signal an overheated economy and portend a tightening of the domestic money supply. In this case attentive businesspeople will shrink their inventories in anticipation of a reduction in customer demand.
3. BOP statistics can indicate reductions in a country's foreign-exchange reserves, which may mean that the country's currency will depreciate in the future, as occurred in Thailand in 1997. Exporters to such a country may find that domestic producers will become more price competitive.
4. As was true in the international debt crisis, BOP statistics can signal increased riskiness of lending to particular countries.

Four important aspects of the BOP accounting system need to be highlighted:

1. The BOP accounting system records international transactions made during some time period, for example, a year.
2. It records only economic transactions, those that involve something of monetary value.
3. It records transactions between residents of one country and residents of all other countries. Residents can be individuals, businesses, government agencies, or nonprofit organizations, but defining residency is sometimes tricky. Persons temporarily located in a country—tourists, students, and military or diplomatic personnel—are still considered residents of their home country for BOP purposes. Businesses are considered residents of the country in which they are incorporated. Firms often conduct international business by locating either a branch or a subsidiary in a foreign country. A branch, which by definition is an unincorporated operation and thus not legally distinct from its parent corporation, is a resident of the parent's home country. A subsidiary, which by definition is a separately incorporated operation, is a resident of the country in which it is incorporated. In most cases the subsidiary is incorporated in the host country to take advantage of legally being a resident of the country in which it is operating.
4. The BOP accounting system is a double-entry system. Each transaction produces a credit entry and a debit entry of equal size. In most international business dealings the first entry in a BOP transaction involves the purchase or sale of something—a good, a service, or an asset. The second entry records the payment or receipt of payment for the thing bought or sold. Figuring out which is the BOP debit entry and which is the BOP credit entry is not a skill that most people are born with. Many experts compare a BOP accounting statement to a statement of sources and uses of funds. Debit entries reflect uses of funds; credit entries indicate sources of funds. Under this framework, buying things creates debits, and selling things produces credits.

The Major Components of the Balance of Payments Accounting System

The BOP accounting system can be divided conceptually into four major accounts. The first two accounts—the current account and the capital account—record purchases of goods, services, and assets by the private and public sectors. The official reserves account reflects the impact of central bank intervention in the foreign-exchange market. The last account—errors and omissions—captures mistakes made in recording BOP transactions.

CURRENT ACCOUNT   The current account records four types of transactions among residents of different countries:

1. Exports and imports of goods (or merchandise)
2. Exports and imports of services

TABLE 7.3 BOP Entries, Current Account

	Debit	Credit
Goods	Buy	Sell
Services	Buy	Sell
Dividends and interest (investment income)	Pay	Receive
Gifts	Give	Receive

3. Investment income
4. Gifts (or unilateral transfers)

Table 7.3 summarizes debit and credit entries for transactions involving the current account.

For example, to Germany the sale of a Mercedes-Benz automobile to a doctor in Marseilles is a **merchandise export**, and the purchase by a German resident of Dom Perignon champagne from France is a **merchandise import**. (The British use the term **trade in visibles** to refer to merchandise trade.) The difference between a country's exports and imports of goods is called the **balance on merchandise trade**. The United States, which has been importing more goods than it has been exporting, has a *merchandise trade deficit*; Japan, which has been exporting more goods than it has been importing, has a *merchandise trade surplus*.

The services account records sales and purchases of such services as transportation, tourism, medical care, telecommunications, advertising, financial services, and education. The sale of a service to a resident of another country is a **service export**, and the purchase by a resident of a service from another country is a **service import**. (The British use the term **trade in invisibles** to denote trade in services.) For example, for Germany a German student spending a year studying at the Sorbonne in Paris is an import of services, and the telephone call home that an Italian tourist makes during the Oktoberfest in Munich represents a service export. The difference between a country's exports of services and its imports of services is called the **balance on services trade**.

The third type of transaction recorded in the current account is investment income. Income German residents earn from their foreign investments is viewed as an **export of the services of capital** by Germany. This income takes the form of either interest and dividends

International trade in services totaled $3.4 trillion in 2009. The monies that foreign tourists who visit the medieval Belgian town of Bruges annually spend on food, lodging, and transportation are recorded as a service export in the Belgian balance of payments.

Medioimages/Photodisc

earned by German residents on their investments in foreign stocks, bonds, and deposit accounts, or profits that are repatriated back to Germany from incorporated subsidiaries in other countries that are owned by German firms. Of course, foreigners also make investments in Germany. Income earned by foreigners from their investments in Germany is viewed as an **import of the services of capital** by Germany. This income includes interest and dividends paid by firms in Germany on stocks, bonds, and deposit accounts owned by foreign residents, as well as profits that are repatriated by foreign-owned incorporated subsidiaries in Germany back to their corporate parents.

The fourth type of transaction in the current account is **unilateral transfers**, or gifts between residents of one country and another. Unilateral transfers include private and public gifts. For example, Pakistani-born residents of Kuwait who send part of their earnings back home to their relatives are engaging in private unilateral transfers. In contrast, governmental aid from the United Kingdom used for a flood control project in Bangladesh is a public unilateral transfer. In both cases, the recipients need not provide any compensation to the donors.

The **current account balance** measures the net balance resulting from merchandise trade, service trade, investment income, and unilateral transfers. It is closely scrutinized by government officials and policymakers because it broadly reflects the country's current competitiveness in international markets.

CAPITAL ACCOUNT. The second major account in the BOP accounting system is the **capital account**, which records capital transactions—purchases and sales of assets—between residents of one country and those of other countries. (The U.S. BOP accounting system makes a distinction between the capital account and the financial account. To simplify our discussion, we will combine the two.)[6] Capital account transactions (summarized in Table 7.4) can be divided into two categories: foreign direct investment (FDI) and foreign portfolio investment.

FDI is any investment made for the purpose of controlling the organization in which the investment is made, typically through ownership of significant blocks of common stock with voting privileges. Under U.S. BOP accounting standards, control is defined as ownership of at least 10 percent of a company's voting stock. A foreign portfolio investment is any investment made for purposes other than control. Foreign portfolio investments are divided into two subcategories: short-term investments and long-term investments. **Short-term foreign portfolio investments** are financial instruments with maturities of one year or less. Included in this category are commercial paper; checking accounts, time deposits, and certificates of deposit held by residents of a country in foreign banks or by foreigners in domestic banks; trade receivables and deposits from international commercial customers; and banks' short-term international lending activities, such as commercial loans. **Long-term foreign portfolio investments** are stocks, bonds, and other financial instruments issued by private and public organizations that have maturities greater than one year and that are held for purposes other than control. For example, when IBM invests excess cash balances overnight in a Paris bank to earn a higher interest rate than it could earn in New York, it is making a short-term portfolio investment. When the California Public Employees' Retirement System Pension Fund buys stock in British Airways, it

TABLE 7.4 Capital Account Transactions

	Maturity	Motivation	Typical Investments
Portfolio (short-term)	One year or less	Investment income or facilitation of international commerce	Checking account balances Time deposits Commercial paper Bank loans
Portfolio (long-term)	More than one year	Investment income	Government notes and bonds Corporate stocks and bonds
Foreign direct investment	Indeterminate	Active control of organization (own at least 10 percent of voting stock)	Foreign subsidiaries Foreign factories International joint ventures

is making a long-term portfolio investment. When Kraft purchases all of the common stock of Cadbury PLC, it is making an FDI.

Current account transactions often affect the short-term component of the capital account. Why? As noted earlier in this chapter, the first entry in the double-entry BOP accounting system records the purchase or sale of something—a good, a service, or an asset. The second entry typically records the payment or receipt of payment for the thing bought or sold. In most cases this second entry reflects a change in someone's checking account balance, which in the BOP accounting system is a short-term capital account transaction. ("Building Global Skills" at the end of this chapter walks you through this linkage between the current account and the capital account in more detail.)

Capital inflows are credits in the BOP accounting system. They can occur in two ways:

1. *Foreign ownership of assets in a country increases.* An example of a capital inflow into the United States is the purchase of Cephalon, a Pennsylvania-based biopharmaceutical company, by Teva Pharmaceuticals, an Israeli generic drug manufacturer, for $6.8 billion in 2011.[7] A capital inflow also occurs if a foreign firm deposits a check in a U.S. bank. In this case, the asset being purchased is a claim on a U.S. bank, which of course is all that a checking account balance represents.

2. *Ownership of foreign assets by a country's residents declines.* When the Ford Motor Company sold its Jaguar and Land Rover brands to India's Tata Motors for $2.5 billion in 2008, the United States experienced a capital inflow. Similarly, when IBM pays a Japanese flash drive supplier with a check drawn on IBM's account at a Tokyo bank, IBM's Japanese checking account balance declines and the United States experiences a capital inflow because IBM is partially liquidating its ownership of foreign assets.

Capital outflows are debits in the BOP accounting system. They also can occur in two ways:

1. *Ownership of foreign assets by a country's residents increases.* Pepsi's $1.4 billion purchase of 74 percent of the shares of Russian beverage company OAO Lebedyansky represented a capital outflow from the United States. A U.S. capital outflow also occurs when Delta Air Lines deposits a check from a London businessperson into an account it holds in an English bank.

2. *Foreign ownership of assets in a country declines.* A German mutual fund that sells 100,000 shares of GM common stock from its portfolio to a U.S. resident causes a capital outflow from the United States. A U.S. capital outflow also occurs if Japan Air Lines writes a check drawn on its account at a Hawaiian bank to pay its fuel supplier at Honolulu Airport. In both cases foreigners are liquidating a portion of their U.S. assets.

Table 7.5 summarizes the impact of various capital account transactions on the BOP accounting system.

TABLE 7.5 BOP Entries, Capital Account

	Debit (Outflow)	Credit (Inflow)
Portfolio (short-term)	Receiving a payment from a foreigner	Making a payment to a foreigner
	Buying a short-term foreign asset	Selling a domestic short-term asset to a foreigner
	Buying back a short-term domestic asset from its foreign owner	Selling a short-term foreign asset acquired previously
Portfolio (long-term)	Buying a long-term foreign asset (not for purposes of control)	Selling a domestic long-term asset to a foreigner (not for purposes of control)
	Buying back a long-term domestic asset from its foreign owner (not for purposes of control)	Selling a long-term foreign asset acquired previously (not for purposes of control)
Foreign direct investment	Buying a foreign asset for purposes of control	Selling a domestic asset to a foreigner for purposes of control
	Buying back from its foreign owner a domestic asset previously acquired for purposes of control	Selling a foreign asset previously acquired for purposes of control

OFFICIAL RESERVES ACCOUNT The third major account in the BOP accounting system, the **official reserves account**, records the level of official reserves held by a national government. These reserves are used to intervene in the foreign-exchange market and in transactions with other central banks. Official reserves comprise four types of assets:

1. Gold
2. Convertible currencies
3. SDRs
4. Reserve positions at the IMF

Official gold holdings are measured using a par value established by a country's treasury or finance ministry. Convertible currencies are currencies that are freely exchangeable in world currency markets. The convertible currencies most commonly used as official reserves are the U.S. dollar, the euro, and the yen. The last two types of reserves—SDRs and reserve positions (quotas minus IMF borrowings) at the IMF—were discussed earlier in this chapter.

ERRORS AND OMISSIONS The last account in the BOP accounting system is the errors and omissions account. One truism of the BOP accounting system is that the BOP must balance. In theory the following equality should be observed:

$$\text{Current Account} + \text{Capital Account} + \text{Official Reserves Account} = 0$$

However, this equality is never achieved in practice because of measurement errors. The **errors and omissions account** is used to make the BOP balance in accordance with the following equation:

$$\text{Current Account} + \text{Capital Account} + \text{Official Reserves Account}$$
$$+ \text{ Errors and Omissions} = 0$$

The errors and omissions account can be quite large. In 2010, for example, the U.S. errors and omissions account totaled $216.8 billion. Experts suspect that a large portion of the errors and omissions account balance is due to underreporting of capital account transactions. Such innovations as instantaneous, round-the-clock foreign-exchange trading, sophisticated monetary swaps and hedges, and international money market funds have made it difficult for government statisticians to keep up with the growing volume of legal short-term money flowing between countries in search of the highest interest rate.

Sometimes, errors and omissions are due to deliberate actions by individuals who are engaged in illegal activities such as drug smuggling, money laundering, or evasion of currency and investment controls imposed by their home governments. Politically stable countries, such as the United States, are often the destination of **flight capital**, money sent abroad by foreign residents seeking a safe haven for their assets, hidden from the sticky fingers of their home governments. Given the often illegal nature of flight capital, persons sending it to the United States often try to avoid any official recognition of their transactions, making it difficult for government BOP statisticians to record such transactions. Residents of other countries who distrust the stability of their own currency may also choose to use a stronger currency, such as the dollar or the euro, to transact their business or keep their savings, as "Bringing the World into Focus" suggests.[8]

Some errors may crop up in the current account as well. Statistics for merchandise imports are generally thought to be reasonably accurate because most countries' customs services scrutinize imports to ensure that all appropriate taxes are collected. This scrutiny generates paper trails that facilitate the collection of accurate statistics. However, few countries tax exports, so customs services have less incentive to assess the accuracy of statistics concerning merchandise exports. Statistics for trade in services also may contain inaccuracies. Many service trade statistics are generated by surveys. For example, U.S. tourism exports are measured in part by surveying foreign tourists on how many days they spent in the United States and how many dollars they spent per day. If tourists underestimate their daily spending, then U.S. service exports are underestimated. To help you gain a better understanding of the BOP accounts, we next review the international transactions of the United States in 2010.

BEN FRANKLIN, WORLD TRAVELER

Who is the most well-known American outside the borders of the United States? Barack Obama? Madonna? Gwyneth Paltrow? A good argument can be made for Ben Franklin, whose face adorns the U.S. $100 bill. Economists and accountants at the U.S. Federal Reserve Bank (FRB) estimate that $342 billion of U.S. currency is held by foreigners. Most of this foreign-held currency is in $100 bills; U.S. consumers prefer to utilize smaller denomination bills.

Tracking down the total number of dollars held overseas is rather complex and is based on a mixture of sophisticated economic modeling, consumer surveys, and educated guesswork. A 1995 FRB survey of U.S. households could account for only 3 percent of the $100 bills printed by the U.S. government, yet the number of such bills in circulation has increased by $143 billion since 1990. FRB staffers also know that the Los Angeles and New York City branches of the FRB distribute enormous numbers of $100 bills relative to the other branches. From 1990 to 1996 these two branches accounted for 84 percent of the new $100 bills placed in circulation. Experts believe that most of this currency flows to citizens of countries where economic and/or political unrest is high. For instance, because of their country's struggle with controlling inflation, Vietnam residents hold an estimated $5 billion in U.S. currency secreted under floorboards or hidden in closets. Russia, other former Soviet Republics, the Middle East, and Latin America are also important destinations for U.S. dollar bills.

Another contributing factor is the increasing "dollarization" of Latin America. On New Year's Day 2001, El Salvador made the U.S.

dollar legal tender there. El Salvador's Central Reserve Bank purchased $450 million worth of U.S. currency to implement this change. Ecuador adopted a similar policy in mid-2000, and Guatemala has taken steps to dollarize its economy as well.

These foreign holdings of U.S. paper currency provide an important benefit to the U.S. Treasury and ultimately to the U.S. taxpayer because they effectively serve as an interest-free loan. Normally, to fund the U.S. debt, the U.S. Treasury must float loans in the form of bonds, notes, and bills. Currency holdings substitute for such loans and reduce the amount the treasury must borrow. If 30-year treasury bonds bear an interest rate of 5 percent, then the U.S taxpayer saves $17.1 billion (5 percent times $342 billion) in interest payments annually as a result of foreign holdings of U.S. currency. This is one of the benefits American citizens receive as a result of the country's economic and political stability. Other countries—particularly those members of the European Union using the euro—also benefit from large holdings of their paper currencies by residents of other countries.

Sources: Survey of Current Business, July 2011, p. 119; "Vietnam battles dark side of boom," *Wall Street Journal*, December 16, 2010, p. C1; "El Salvador switching to U.S. dollar," *Houston Chronicle*, December 30, 2000, p. 1C; "Dollar's share of world reserves grows," *Wall Street Journal*, September 10, 1997, p. A2; "Russia counts cost of change as U.S. set to issue new $100 bill," *Financial Times*, January 16, 1996, p. 20; "Where's the buck? Dollars make the world go around, Fed says," *Houston Chronicle*, October 13, 1995, p. 2C.

The U.S. Balance of Payments in 2010

The first component of the current account is merchandise (goods) exports and imports. As shown in Table 7.6, U.S. merchandise exports totaled $1,288.7 billion in 2010. Figure 7.4(a) presents a more detailed picture of the leading U.S. exports. Automobiles and auto parts were the largest component of U.S. merchandise exports, generating $112.0 billion in sales. Of U.S. automobile exports, 44 percent were to Canada, a reflection of the integrated nature of North American automobile production that resulted from the 1965 Auto Pact between the United States and Canada. (Canada—meaning primarily GM, Ford, and Chrysler plants that are located in Canada—exported $52.4 billion in automobiles and auto parts to the United States.) The six industries shown in Figure 7.4(a) accounted for 41 percent of U.S. merchandise exports in 2010.

From Table 7.6, you can see that U.S. merchandise imports totaled $1,934.6 billion in 2010. From Figure 7.4(b) you can see that the leading import was petroleum products, at $353.7 billion, or 18 percent of imports. Six industries accounted for $977.3 billion, or 51 percent of total U.S. merchandise imports.

The second component of the current account is trade in services. U.S. exports of services totaled $548.9 billion in 2010, with travel and tourism being the largest portion ($134.4 billion). U.S. service imports equaled $403.0 billion, with travel and tourism again being the largest portion ($102.8 billion). The United States had a positive balance on services trade of $145.9 billion (see Table 7.6).

Figure 7.5 shows exports and imports for the major trading partners of the United States and includes trade in both goods and services. From this figure, you can see that the United States tends to import more goods from its major trading partners than it exports to them; you can also see that the United States tends to export more services to its trading partners than it imports from them.

TABLE 7.6 U.S. BOP, 2010 (in billions of dollars)

Current Account		
Goods		
Exports	1288.7	
Imports	−1934.6	
Balance on Merchandise Trade	−645.9	
Services		
Exports	548.9	
Imports	−403.0	
Balance on Services Trade	145.9	
Investment Income		
Received	663.2	
Paid	−498.0	
Balance on Investment Income	165.2	
Unilateral Transfers (net)	−136.1	
(−means outward gifts greater than inward)		
Balance on Current Account		−470.9
Capital Account		
Portfolio, Short-Term (Net Outflow)	−295.2	
Portfolio, Long-Term		
New Foreign Investment in United States	813.5	
New U.S. Investment Abroad	−147.2	
Foreign Direct Investment		
New FDI in United States	236.2	
New U.S. FDI Abroad	−351.4	
Balance on Capital Account		255.9
Official Reserves Account		−1.8
Errors and Omissions		216.8
Net Balance		0

FIGURE 7.4

Leading U.S. Merchandise Exports and Imports, 2010

Source: Survey of Current Business, July 2011, pp. 82 and 84.

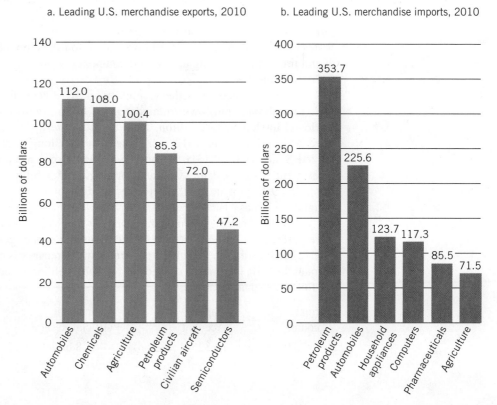

a. Leading U.S. merchandise exports, 2010

b. Leading U.S. merchandise imports, 2010

FIGURE 7.5

Trade Between the United States and Its Major Trading Partners, 2010

Source: Survey of Current Business,
July 2011, pp. 100ff.

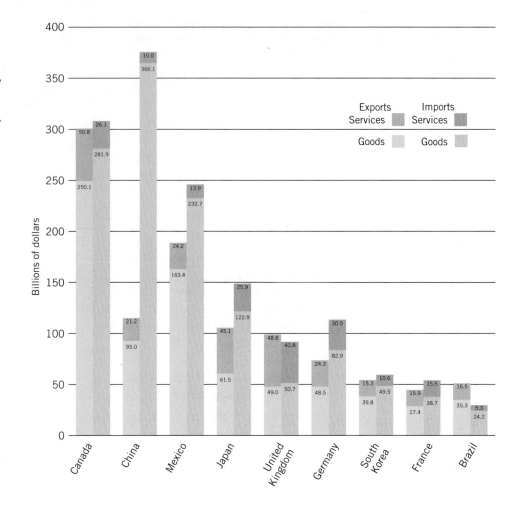

The third component of the current account is investment income (see Table 7.6). In 2010 U.S. residents received $663.2 billion from foreign investments and paid out $498.0 billion to foreigners for a net balance on investment income of $165.2 billion. The United States had a net deficit of $136.1 billion in the fourth component of the current account, unilateral transfers. Summing up the four components yielded a 2010 current account deficit of $470.9 billion.

The capital account is the second major BOP account (see Table 7.6). In 2010 new U.S. FDI abroad (outflows) totaled $351.4 billion, while new FDI in the United States (inflows) totaled $236.2 billion. New U.S. long-term international portfolio investments were $147.2 billion in 2010, while new foreign long-term portfolio investments in the United States were $813.5 billion. There was also a net outflow of short-term portfolio investment from the United States, totaling $295.2 billion. The capital account balance was $255.9 billion in 2010, as foreigners bought more U.S. assets than U.S. residents bought foreign assets.

U.S. official reserves account transactions were −$1.8 billion. If the BOP statistical data net were perfect, the current account balance plus the capital account balance plus the official reserves account balance should equal zero. Any discrepancy is put into the errors and omissions account. In 2010, there was a discrepancy of $216.8 billion. Therefore, for the U.S. BOP in 2010 the following equation applies:

Current Account	Capital +Account	Changes in +Official Reserves	Errors and +Omissions = 0
(−$470.9 billion)	(+$255.9 billion)	(−$1.8 billion)	(+$216.8 billion)

Defining Balance of Payments Surpluses and Deficits

Every month the federal government reports the performance of U.S. firms in international markets when it releases the monthly BOP statistics. In most months during the past decade, newscasters have solemnly reported on the evening news that the U.S. BOP is in deficit.

What do the newscasters mean? We just said that the BOP always balances (equals zero), so how can there be a BOP deficit? In reality when knowledgeable people (or even newscasters) talk about a BOP surplus or deficit, they are referring only to a subset of the BOP accounts. Most newscasters are in fact reporting on the balance on trade in goods and services. When a country exports more goods and services than it imports, it has a trade surplus. When it imports more goods and services than it exports, it has a trade deficit.

Because the balance on trade in goods and services is readily understandable and quickly available to the news media, it receives the most public attention. However, other balances also exist, such as the balance on services, the balance on merchandise trade, and the current account balance. Another closely watched BOP balance is the official settlements balance. The **official settlements balance** reflects changes in a country's official reserves; essentially, it records the net impact of the central bank's interventions in the foreign-exchange market in support of the local currency.

Which of these BOP balances is *the* balance of payments? That is really a trick question. There is no single measure of a country's global economic performance. Rather, as in the parable of the blind men touching the elephant, each balance presents a different perspective on the nation's position in the international economy. Knowing which BOP concept to use depends on the issue confronting the international businessperson or government policymaker. The balance on merchandise trade reflects the competitiveness of a country's manufacturing sector. The balance on services reflects the service sector's global competitiveness. Although the balance on merchandise trade often receives more publicity, the balance on services is growing in importance because of the expansion of the service sector in many national economies. The balance on goods and services reflects the combined international competitiveness of a country's manufacturing and service sectors. The current account balance shows the combined performance of the manufacturing and service sectors and also reflects the generosity of the country's residents (unilateral transfers) as well as income generated by past investments. The official settlements balance reflects the net quantity demanded and supplied of the country's currency by all market participants, other than the country's central bank.[9]

Figure 7.6 shows the U.S. balance of payments since 1969 according to these various measures.

In 2010 China exported $366 billion of merchandise to the United States while importing $93 billion. This large imbalance in trade between the two countries has attracted the attention of many American politicians, who worry about the loss of domestic jobs. American consumers, however, benefit from the lower prices and increased choices that international trade creates.

Emmanuel Lacoste/Alamy Images

FIGURE 7.6

The U.S. BOP According to Various Reporting Measures

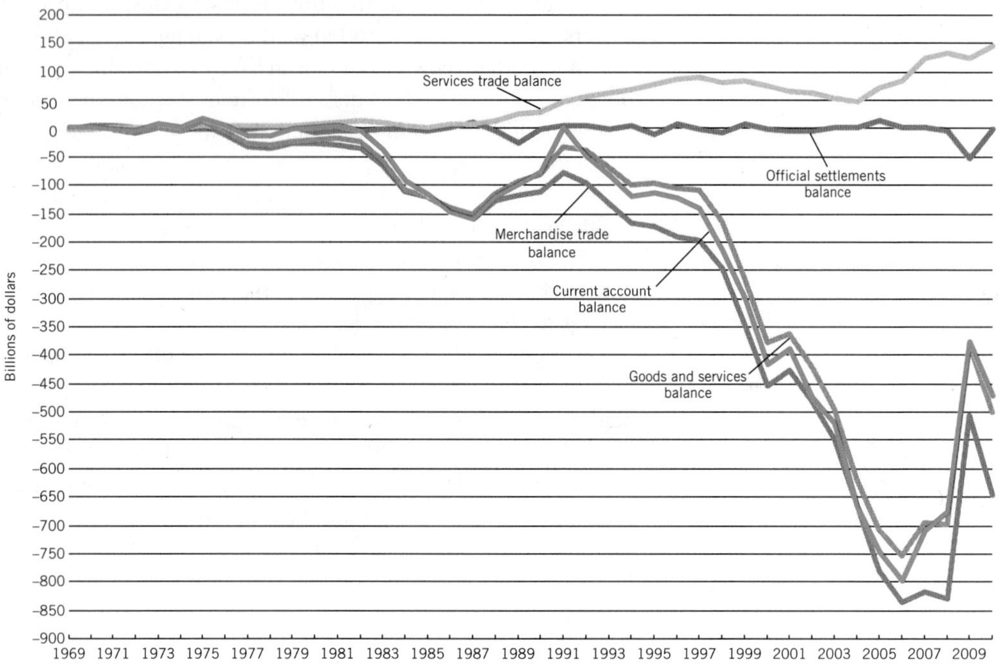

Now that you have finished this chapter, go back to **www.pearsonglobaleditions.com/mymanagementlab** to continue practicing and applying the concepts you've learned.

CHAPTER REVIEW

Summary

In their normal commercial activities international businesses often deal with currencies other than those of their home countries. For international commerce to thrive, some system for exchanging and valuing different currencies, preferably at low cost, must exist. The international monetary system accomplishes this by establishing the rules for valuing and exchanging different currencies.

The economic growth of the nineteenth century is attributable in part to the success of the gold standard in providing a stable, reliable international monetary system based on fixed exchange rates. However, the gold standard broke down during World War I and could not be satisfactorily revived in the years between the two world wars.

The Bretton Woods Agreement of 1944 structured the post–World War II international monetary system. In addition to creating the International Bank for Reconstruction and Development (the World Bank) and the IMF, the agreement reinstituted a fixed exchange rate system, with the U.S. dollar playing a key role in international transactions. As the number of dollars held by foreigners increased, however, the marketplace began to distrust the ability of the United States to redeem its currency at $35 per ounce of gold as required by the agreement. After

fending off waves of speculation against the dollar, the United States abandoned the Bretton Woods Agreement in August 1971.

Since then, the international monetary system has relied on a combination of fixed and flexible exchange rate systems. Some countries have allowed their currencies to float; others, such as the EU members, have attempted to maintain fixed exchange rates among their currencies. The system has proven responsive to major shocks to the world economy, such as the shift of wealth from oil-consuming to oil-producing countries after the 1973–1974 oil embargo, the 1980s international debt crisis, the 1997–1998 Asian currency crisis, and the 2008–2009 global recession.

The BOP accounting system, which is used to record international transactions, is important to international businesspeople. The BOP system provides economic intelligence data about the international competitiveness of a country's industries, likely changes in its fiscal and monetary policies, and its ability to repay its international debts.

The BOP accounting system comprises four accounts. The current account reflects exports and imports of goods, exports and imports of services, investment income, and gifts. The capital account records financial and capital transactions among countries and includes FDI and portfolio investments. Portfolio investments in turn can be divided into long-term and short-term investments. The official reserves account is a record of changes in a country's official reserves, which include central bank holdings of gold, convertible currencies, SDRs, and reserves at the IMF. The errors and omissions account captures statistical discrepancies that often result from transactions that participants want to hide from government officials.

There are numerous ways to measure a balance of payments surplus or deficit. Each presents a different perspective on a country's global economic performance. The balance on merchandise trade measures the difference between a country's exports and imports of goods. The balance on services is growing in importance because of the rapid expansion of the service sector in many economies. The balance on goods and services measures a country's trade in goods and services. The current account balance reflects both trade in goods and trade in services, as well as net investment income and gifts. The official settlements balance shows changes in a country's official reserves.

Review Questions

1. What is the function of the international monetary system?
2. Why is the gold standard a type of fixed exchange rate system?
3. What were the key accomplishments of the Bretton Woods conference?
4. Why was the IFC established by the World Bank?
5. Why are quotas important to IMF members?
6. Why did the Bretton Woods system collapse in 1971?
7. Describe the differences between a fixed exchange rate system and a flexible exchange rate system.
8. List the four major accounts of the BOP accounting system and their components.
9. What factors cause measurement errors in the BOP accounts?
10. Identify the different types of balance of payments surpluses and deficits.

Questions for Discussion

1. What parallels exist between the role of the British pound in the nineteenth-century international monetary system and that of the U.S. dollar since 1945?
2. Did the key role that the dollar played in the Bretton Woods system benefit or hurt the United States?
3. Under what conditions might a country devalue its currency today?
4. Are there any circumstances under which a country might want to increase its currency's value?
5. Can international businesses operate more easily in a fixed exchange rate system or in a flexible exchange rate system?
6. What connections exist between the current account and the capital account?

Building Global Skills

This exercise explains how U.S. governmental statisticians account for international transactions. You may want to refer to Tables 7.3 and 7.5 and to the definitions of capital inflows and capital outflows on page 220.

Example 1

Suppose Walmart imports $1 million worth of Blu-ray players from the Sony Corporation of Japan. The debit entry is a merchandise import of $1 million.

Here is the tough part. What is the offsetting credit entry? The answer is a capital inflow affecting the short-term portfolio account. Recall that a capital inflow occurs because of either an increase in foreign-owned U.S. assets or a decrease in U.S.-owned foreign assets. If Walmart pays Sony with a $1-million check that Sony deposits in its U.S. bank, foreign ownership of assets in the United States increases, which is a short-term capital inflow. If Walmart pays Sony in yen by drawing down a Walmart checking account balance at a Tokyo bank, a decrease of U.S.-owned assets in foreign countries occurs, which is also a short-term capital inflow. Either way, a short-term capital inflow occurs because the Blu-ray players are being exchanged for a change in a checking account balance.

What if Walmart pays Sony with a $1-million check, but Sony wants yen? Sony will take the check to its U.S. bank and ask the bank to convert the $1-million check to yen. The U.S. bank can accommodate Sony in one of two ways:

1. Give Sony yen that the U.S. bank already owns—this represents a decrease in U.S.-owned foreign assets.
2. Pass along the check to a Japanese bank that keeps the $1 million but gives Sony the equivalent in yen—this represents an increase in U.S. assets owned by foreigners (the Japanese bank).

In either case, a capital inflow occurs. Thus, Walmart's purchase of the Blu-ray players from Sony enters the U.S. BOP accounts as follows:

	Debit	**Credit**
Merchandise imports account	$1 million	
Short-term portfolio account		$1 million

The merchandise import account is debited to reflect a use of funds. The payment itself is credited because effectively a foreigner has purchased a U.S. asset (either an increase in foreign claims on the United States or a decrease in U.S. claims on foreigners). Note the linkage between the current account and the capital account.

Example 2

A North Korean restaurant owner in Los Angeles who escaped her homeland smuggles $1,000 in cash back to her relatives in Pyongyang. The U.S. BOP accounts should record this transaction as follows:

	Debit	Credit
Unilateral transfer account	$1,000	
Short-term portfolio account		$1,000

The transaction involves a unilateral transfer because the $1,000 is a gift. Because the gift is being given by a U.S. resident, it is a debit. The capital account is credited because foreigners have increased their claims on the United States. (A country's currency reflects a claim on its goods, services, and assets.) Had the restaurant owners sent a $1,000 stereo system instead of cash, the credit entry would have been a merchandise export.

Note the use of the qualifier *should* in the first paragraph. If U.S. governmental statisticians were omniscient, the transaction would be recorded as just explained. However, if the restaurant owner wished to hide her transaction from the government, it is unlikely U.S. statisticians would ever learn of it. When you consider the widespread usage of the dollar in countries suffering political turmoil, it is not surprising that the errors and omissions account is as large as it is.

Example 3

Mitsubishi buys 51 percent of Rockefeller Center for $846 million from a Rockefeller family trust. This transaction will be recorded in the U.S. BOP accounts as follows:

	Debit	Credit
Foreign direct investment account		$846 million
Short-term portfolio account	$846 million	

In this transaction two assets are being exchanged. Japan is buying a long-term asset—Rockefeller Center—for purposes of control, and the United States is buying a short-term asset called an "increase of claims on foreigners or a decrease of foreign claims on the United States." The U.S. BOP is credited with a long-term FDI capital inflow of $846 million because foreign ownership of U.S. assets (for purposes of control) has increased. However, the actual payment of the $846 million is debited as a short-term capital outflow: Either Japanese-owned checking account balances in the United States declined by $846 million or U.S.-owned checking account balances in Japan rose by $846 million.

Unlike Examples 1 and 2, this transaction does not involve a current account entry and a capital account entry. Both the debit entry and the credit entry affect the capital account. However, a balance in someone's checking account is affected by this transaction, as was the case in Example 1.

Do the following exercises on your own. How will the following transactions be recorded in the U.S. BOP accounts?

1. An American entrepreneur seeking to sell souvenirs at the 2012 summer Olympics in London pays British Airways, a U.K. carrier, $1,500 for a Los Angeles–London round-trip ticket.
2. The American entrepreneur instead pays United Airlines (an American airline) $1,500 for a Los Angeles–London round-trip ticket.
3. Ford Motor Company (U.S.) pays $2.5 billion to purchase all the common stock of the Jaguar Motor Co. (U.K.).
4. The U.S. government gives Rwanda $500 million worth of food to feed starving refugees.

CLOSING CASE   RECENT U.S. BOP PERFORMANCE: IS THE SKY FALLING?

During the past decade the U.S. BOP performance could be characterized as follows:

- The U.S. current account recorded large annual deficits.
- The U.S. capital account recorded large annual surpluses of roughly the same magnitude as the current account deficits.
- Changes in the official reserves account were small relative to the magnitude of the current account deficits.

Two scenarios can be developed from the facts just cited:

1. The sky is falling. U.S. industries are uncompetitive in international markets (as indicated by the first fact), and foreigners are taking over the country by buying up valuable U.S. assets and transforming the country into the largest debtor in international history (as indicated by the second fact).
2. Everything is wonderful. Foreigners are so enthralled with the future prospects of the U.S. market, which is a showcase of economic democracy, that they are eagerly investing in the U.S. economy (the second fact). The only way they can do so, however, is by running a current account surplus with the United States (the first fact).

Needless to say, these two scenarios conflict, even though both are consistent with the data. They reflect a policy war that is occurring between protectionists and free traders, between unions and MNCs, between liberals and conservatives, and between firms threatened by foreign imports and export-oriented firms.

People who believe the sky is falling argue that the United States must reduce its balance of trade deficit. They argue that U.S. firms are increasingly uncompetitive in global markets and must be strengthened via aggressive government policies, such as those calling for worker-training programs, increased investment in infrastructure, and tax credits for R&D and investment expenditures. These people assert that U.S. firms are victimized by the unfair trade practices of foreign firms and governments. They propose stiffer tariffs and quotas on imported goods and believe that the federal government should do more to promote U.S. exports and restrict foreign ownership of U.S. assets.

People who believe everything is wonderful say the best policy is to continue to make the United States an attractive economy in which to invest. By keeping tax rates low and governmental regulation modest, the United States will attract foreign capital. U.S. industries, consumers, and workers will then benefit from increased capital investment and the enhancements in productivity that will ensue from this investment. U.S. consumers will benefit from the availability of low-priced, high-quality imported goods and services. Moreover, U.S. firms will become "leaner and meaner" as they respond to foreign competitors.

A variant of this "everything is wonderful" argument has been offered by the late Nobel laureate Milton Friedman, the provocative free-market advocate from the University of Chicago. Friedman argued that foreign companies have been busily producing Blu-ray players, luxury automobiles, and smartphones in return for dollar bills from U.S. consumers. If these companies are happy voluntarily exchanging their goods for pieces of paper (that is, dollar bills), and U.S. citizens are happy voluntarily exchanging pieces of paper for goods, why should anyone worry?

As you ponder these divergent perspectives, recognize that they have developed because of two very different views of what represents a BOP deficit. The "sky is falling" crowd is focusing on the balance on merchandise trade and assessing whether U.S. firms are able to sell as many goods to foreigners as foreigners sell to Americans. The "everything is wonderful" folks are focusing on voluntary transactions in the marketplace. In their view, if U.S. citizens find that being net buyers of foreign goods is in their self-interest and foreigners find that being net buyers of U.S. assets is in their self-interest, then what is the problem?

Because BOP statistics affect the ongoing domestic political battle over international trade policy, they are important to virtually every U.S. firm. Export-oriented firms and workers benefit from the free trade policies promoted by the "everything is wonderful" crowd, as do communities that benefit from jobs created by inward FDI. Firms and workers threatened by imported goods or by the output of new domestic factories built by foreign competitors are more likely to support the "sky is falling" view.

Case Questions

1. What is more important to an economy—exports or foreign capital inflows?
2. What is the connection between the U.S. current account deficit and capital account surplus?
3. Which of the following groups are likely to endorse the "sky is falling" view of the U.S. BOP?

- Import-threatened firms such as textile producers
- Textile workers
- A cash-starved California biotechnology company
- Merrill Lynch
- Boeing Aircraft, one of the country's largest exporters
- Consumers

Endnotes

1. Astra International investor update, December 31, 2010; Astra International press release, March 23, 2006 (http://www.astra.co.id); "Foreign exchange gains lift Astra," *Financial Times*, March 31, 2003, p. 19; "Toyota set for investment in Indonesia," *Financial Times*, February 21, 2003, p. 20; "Astra gets ready to move to higher gear," *Financial Times*, November 25, 2002, p. 17; "Indonesia sells stake in Astra car maker," *Wall Street Journal*, March 27, 2000, p. A24; "Indonesia removes top Astra officials," *Wall Street Journal*, February 9, 2000, p. A22; "Astra abandons opposition to sell-off," *Financial Times*, February 8, 2000, p. 23; "The woman steering Indonesia's Astra sets a modernizing course," *Wall Street Journal*, October 28, 1999, p. A1.
2. Del Mar, *A History of Money in Ancient Countries* (New York: Burt Franklin, 1968; originally published in 1885), p. 71.
3. "IMF executive board approves major overhaul of quotas and governance," IMF Press Release No. 10/418, November 5, 2010.
4. "South Korea reaches accord with IMF over terms of bailout," *Wall Street Journal*, December 1, 1997, p. A15; "Group offers Indonesia loans of up to $40 billion," *Houston Chronicle*, November 1, 1997, p. 1C.
5. International Monetary Fund, Factsheet: Special Drawing Rights, March 31, 2011.
6. In the U.S. accounting system, the Capital Account measures transfers of capital assets between foreign residents and U.S. residents. The Financial Account measures changes in the level of financial claims between foreign residents and U.S. residents.
7. "Teva agrees $6.8bn Cephalon deal," *Financial Times*, May 3, 2011, p. 19; "Teva buying Cephalon for $6.8 billion," *Wall Street Journal*, May 2, 2011 (online).
8. *Survey of Current Business*, July 2008, p. 44.
9. "Basic truths," *The Economist*, August 24, 1991, p. 68.

CHAPTER 8

Foreign Exchange and International Financial Markets

AFTER STUDYING THIS CHAPTER, YOU SHOULD BE ABLE TO:

1. Describe how demand and supply determine the price of foreign exchange.

2. Discuss the role of international banks in the foreign-exchange market.

3. Assess the different ways firms can use the spot and forward markets to settle international transactions.

4. Summarize the role of arbitrage in the foreign-exchange market.

5. Discuss the important aspects of the international capital market.

Access a host of interactive learning aids at **www.pearsonglobaleditions.com/ mymanagementlab** to help strengthen your understanding of the chapter concepts.

MyManagementLab

Phillip MacCallum/Stringer/Newscom

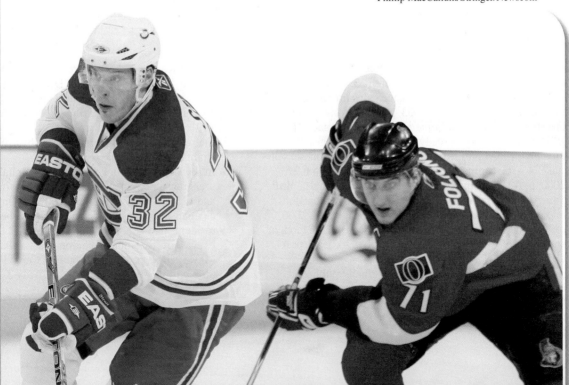

THE LOONIE TAKES FLIGHT

There's an old adage: Be careful of what you ask for. For many years, Canadian citizens bemoaned the fact that the Canadian dollar sold at a discount from the U.S. dollar. But in September 2007, the Canadian dollar reached parity with its southern neighbor's: one Canadian dollar equaled one U.S. dollar. By November, it took US $1.10 to buy a loonie—the affectionate nickname for the Canadian one-dollar coin, which features a loon on one side. All told, in 2007, the loonie soared 24 percent against the U.S. dollar.

This was not always the case. In 2002, it took 1.6143 Canadian dollars to buy an American dollar. But in the following five years the loonie rose 38 percent relative to the U.S. dollar. Much of the loonie's ascent is due to the boom in commodity prices (see Chapter 2's closing case), which has benefited producers of raw materials like Canada. And high oil prices have attracted enormous investments in Alberta's Athabascan tar sands, which contain an estimated 1.6 trillion barrels of oil, of which 350 billion barrels are judged to be recoverable. When commodity prices softened in the global recession of 2008–2009, the loonie fell in value against the U.S. dollar. Renewed global economic growth restored the loonie's luster. In August 2011, for example, the loonie was worth $1.04 in U.S. dollars. The value of the currencies of other commodity-rich countries, like the Australian dollar, the Brazilian real, and the Chilean peso, have exhibited similar correlation with commodity prices.

The rising value of the loonie affects numerous individuals, firms, and markets on both sides of the border. Canadian consumers pay lower prices for goods made in the United States, while Canadian vacationers enjoy lower costs on their winter trips to Florida and Arizona. The increased value of the loonie may even affect who wins the World Series and the Stanley Cup. When the U.S. dollar was riding high, Canadian baseball and hockey teams were at a disadvantage because their ticket revenues were denominated in Canadian currency while their player costs were tied to the U.S. dollar. With the value of the loonie rising,

this drawback is disappearing. The Toronto Blue Jay's costs, for example, are reduced US $600,000 for every one cent rise in the value of the Canadian dollar, allowing them to bid more aggressively for free agents and offer higher salaries to retain key starters. Similarly, the six Canadian teams in the National Hockey League had been at a decided disadvantage because of the low value of the Canadian dollar. Its recent rise, however, has allowed these teams to improve their locker rooms, offices, and training facilities to better match those of U.S.-based hockey teams, as well as compete for talented players.

But the high value of the loonie has a downside. As Chapter 2 noted, Canada's economy is export-oriented, and the vast majority of its exports are destined for the United States. Some economists estimate that Canada could lose 150,000 jobs due to declining exports to the United States. Fewer Americans are frequenting Windsor's casinos, and Canadian retailers in border towns are losing customers to American shops. The Retail Council of Canada believes that the rise in the number of Canadians heading south to take advantage of now-cheaper American goods has trimmed retail sales in Canada by 5 percent. Many Canadian retailers have slashed their prices to stop this hemorrhaging of customers, but these price cuts harm their profit margins. Canadian auto dealers have been particularly vulnerable to this bargain-seeking behavior. And companies like Dofasco, a steel manufacturer in Hamilton, Ontario, are hurt because their sales are denominated in U.S. dollars but their costs are in Canadian currency. The loonie's soaring value has cut deeply into such export-oriented firms' profit margins. And pity Canada's Christmas tree growers. They normally greet the yuletide season with a hearty, "Merry Christmas," exporting in a typical year some 2.5 million trees to the United States. But the loonie's rise has changed that to "Bah, humbug," as Canadian Christmas tree exports to the United States have fallen by 20 percent, forcing some firms, such as Kirk Forest Products of Nova Scotia, out of business and slashing the profits of most other Canadian growers.[1] ∎

One factor that obviously distinguishes international business from domestic business is the use of more than one currency in commercial transactions. If Marks and Spencer, one of the United Kingdom's leading department stores, purchases kitchen appliances from a British supplier, that is a domestic transaction that will be completed entirely in pounds. However, if Marks and Spencer chooses to purchase the appliances from Michigan-based Whirlpool Corporation, this international transaction will require some mechanism for exchanging pounds (Mark and Spencer's home currency) and U.S. dollars (Whirlpool's home currency). The foreign-exchange market exists to facilitate this conversion of currencies, thereby allowing firms to conduct trade more efficiently across

The millions of foreign tourists who visit Rio de Janeiro and its iconic Christ the Redeemer monument benefit from the efficiency of the foreign exchange market, which allows them to convert their home currencies into Brazilian reals at low cost.

national boundaries. The foreign-exchange market also facilitates international investment and capital flows. Firms can shop for low-cost financing in capital markets around the world and then use the foreign-exchange market to convert the foreign funds they obtain into whatever currency they require. But changes in exchange rates also affect the prices that consumers pay, the markets in which they shop, and the profits of firms, as the opening case indicates.

The Economics of Foreign Exchange

Foreign exchange is a commodity that consists of currencies issued by countries other than one's own. Like the prices of other commodities, the price of foreign exchange—given a flexible exchange rate system—is set by demand and supply in the marketplace.

Let us look more closely at what this means by using the market between U.S. dollars and Japanese yen as an example. Figure 8.1 presents the demand curve for Japanese yen. Economists call this demand curve a *derived demand* curve because the demand for yen is derived from foreigners' desire to acquire Japanese goods, services, and assets. To buy Japanese goods, foreigners first need to buy Japanese yen. Like other demand curves, it is downward sloping, so as the

FIGURE 8.1

The Demand for Japanese Yen Is Derived from Foreigners' Demand for Japanese Products

FOREIGNERS' DEMAND FOR YEN

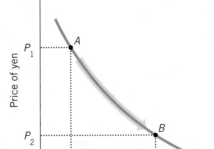

FIGURE 8.2

The Supply of Yen Is Derived from Japanese Demand for Foreign Products

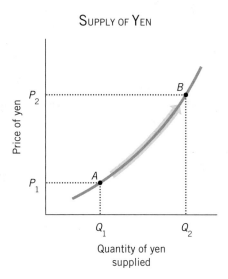

SUPPLY OF YEN

price of the yen falls, the quantity of yen demanded increases. This is shown as a movement from point A to point B on the demand curve.

Figure 8.2 presents the supply curve for yen. Underlying the supply curve for yen is the desire by the Japanese to acquire foreign goods, services, and assets. To buy foreign products, Japanese need to obtain foreign currencies, which they do by selling yen and using the proceeds to buy the foreign currencies. Selling yen has the effect of supplying yen to the foreign-exchange market. As with other goods, as the price of the yen rises, the quantity supplied also rises; you can see this when you move from point A to point B along the supply curve in Figure 8.2. The supply curve for the yen thus behaves like most other supply curves: People offer more yen for sale as the price of the yen rises.[2] Figure 8.3 depicts the determination of the equilibrium price of yen. Points along the vertical axis show the price of the yen in dollars—how many dollars one must pay for each yen purchased. Points along the horizontal axis show the quantity of yen. As in other markets, the intersection of the supply curve (S) and the demand curve (D) yields the market-clearing, equilibrium price ($.009/yen in this case) and the equilibrium quantity demanded and supplied (200 million yen). Recall from Chapter 7 that this equilibrium price is called the *exchange rate*, the price of one country's currency in terms of another country's currency.

Although Figure 8.3 illustrates the dollar-yen foreign-exchange market, a similar figure could be drawn for every possible pair of currencies in the world, each of which would constitute a separate market, with the equilibrium prices of the currencies determined by the supply of and demand for them. Foreign-exchange rates are published daily in most major newspapers

FIGURE 8.3

The Market for Yen

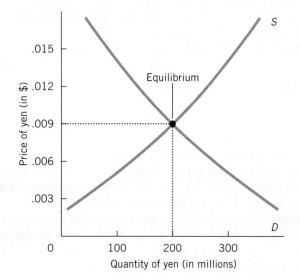

FIGURE 8.4

Direct and Indirect Exchange Rates

Source: Various newspapers.

Exchange Rates

August 3, 2011

The foreign exchange rates below reflect wholesale transactions, typically in amounts of at least $1 million, between major international banks.

Country/currency	U.S. DOLLAR EQUIVALENT		CURRENCY PER U.S. DOLLAR	
	Wed	Tues	Wed	Tues
Argentina (peso)	0.2409	0.2421	4.1514	4.1300
Australia (dollar)	1.0756	1.0780	0.9297	0.9276
1-mos forward	1.0713	1.0736	0.9334	0.9315
3-mos forward	1.0634	1.0658	0.9404	0.9383
6-mos forward	1.0525	1.0544	0.9501	0.9484
Bahrain (dinar)	2.6520	2.6523	0.3771	0.3770
Bolivia (boliviano)	0.14451	0.14451	6.92	6.92
Brazil (real)	0.6385	0.6402	1.5662	1.5621
Canada (dollar)	1.0392	1.0403	0.9622	0.9612
Chile (peso)	0.002195	0.002185	455.64	457.76
China (yuan)	0.1553	0.1554	6.4392	6.4356
Colombia (peso)	0.0005674	0.0005624	1762.4	1778.05
Costa Rica (colon)	0.00198	0.00198	505.25	505.25
Czech Rep. (koruna)	0.05904	0.05845	16.936	17.108
Denmark (krone)	0.1923	0.1906	5.2004	5.2458
Ecuador US (dollar)	1	1	1	1
Egypt (pound)	0.16799	0.16800	5.9528	5.9525
Euro area (euro)	1.4323	1.4202	0.6982	0.7041
Hong Kong (dollar)	0.1282	0.1283	7.7994	7.7955
Hungary (forint)	0.005270	0.005236	189.75	191.00
India (rupee)	0.02259	0.02269	44.2705	44.0705
Indonesia (rupiah)	0.0001186	0.0001182	8435	8460
Iran (rial)	0.00009	0.00009	10555.5	10544.0
Israel (shekel)	0.2887	0.2889	3.4641	3.4618
Japan (yen)	0.012978	0.012960	77.06	77.16
1-mos forward	0.012982	0.012965	77.03	77.13
3-mos forward	0.012990	0.012972	76.98	77.09
6-mos forward	0.013006	0.012990	76.89	76.98
Jordan (dinar)	1.4107	1.4107	0.7089	0.7089
Kenya (shilling)	0.01098	0.01097	91.11	91.15
Kuwait (dinar)	3.6593	3.6571	0.2733	0.2734
Lebanon (pound)	0.0006627	0.0006609	1509.05	1513.05
Malaysia (ringgit)	0.3370	0.3372	2.9670	2.9654

Country/currency	U.S. DOLLAR EQUIVALENT		CURRENCY PER U.S. DOLLAR	
	Wed	Tues	Wed	Tues
Mexico (peso)	0.08460	0.08440	11.8205	11.8439
New Zealand (dollar)	0.8635	0.8666	1.1580	1.1539
Nigeria (naira)	0.00656	0.00656	152.55	152.55
Norway (krone)	0.1864	0.1844	5.3646	5.4223
Pakistan (rupee)	0.01155	0.01153	86.570	86.725
Peru new (sol)	0.3655	0.3652	2.7358	2.7381
Philippines (peso)	0.0237	0.0238	42.128	41.940
Poland (zloty)	0.3557	0.3526	2.8111	2.8361
Romania (leu)	0.3357	0.3353	2.9787	2.9821
Russia (ruble)	0.03591	0.03594	27.848	27.822
Saudi Arabia (riyal)	0.2666	0.2666	3.7503	3.7503
Singapore (dollar)	0.8296	0.8291	1.2054	1.2061
South Africa (rand)	0.1488	0.1474	6.7217	6.7840
South Korea (won)	0.0009439	0.0009474	1059.45	1055.55
Sweden (krona)	0.1577	0.1559	6.3420	6.4142
Switzerland (franc)	1.2983	1.3115	0.7703	0.7625
1-mos forward	1.2992	1.3120	0.7697	0.7621
3-mos forward	1.3008	1.3131	0.7687	0.7616
6-mos forward	1.3017	1.3150	0.7682	0.7605
Taiwan (dollar)	0.03475	0.03475	28.775	28.775
Thailand (baht)	0.03362	0.03357	29.747	29.787
Tunisia (dinar)	0.7257	0.7235	1.3779	1.3821
Turkey (lira)	0.5848	0.5907	1.7101	1.6929
UAE (dirham)	0.2723	0.2723	3.6731	3.6731
UK (pound)	1.6426	1.6299	0.6088	0.6135
1-mos forward	1.6422	1.6294	0.6090	0.6137
3-mos forward	1.6411	1.6284	0.6093	0.6141
6-mos forward	1.6396	1.6269	0.6099	0.6146
Ukraine (hryvnja)	0.12509	0.12502	7.9945	7.9990
Uruguay (peso)	0.05464	0.05435	18.3016	18.3993
Venezuela b. (fuerte)	0.22989	0.22989	4.35	4.35
Vietnam (dong)	0.00005	0.00005	20541	20606

worldwide. Figure 8.4 presents rates for August 3, 2011. These rates are quoted in two ways. A **direct exchange rate** (or **direct quote**) is the price of the foreign currency in terms of the home currency. For instance, from the perspective of a U.S. resident, the direct exchange rate between the U.S. dollar and the yen (¥) on Wednesday, August 3, was $.012978/¥1. An **indirect exchange rate** (or **indirect quote**) is the price of the home currency in terms of the foreign currency. From the U.S. resident's perspective, the indirect exchange rate on Wednesday, August 3, was ¥77.06/$1. Mathematically, the direct exchange rate and the indirect exchange rate are reciprocals of each other. By tradition—and sometimes for convenience—certain exchange rates are typically quoted on a direct basis and others on an indirect basis. Common U.S. practice is to quote British pounds on a direct basis but Japanese yen on an indirect basis.

If you get confused about which is the direct rate and which is the indirect rate, just remember that you normally buy things using the direct rate. If you go to the store to buy bread, it is typically priced using the direct rate: A loaf of bread costs $2.89. The indirect rate would be .346 loaves of bread per dollar. "Bringing the World into Focus" provides additional hints for understanding the foreign-exchange market.

The Structure of the Foreign-Exchange Market

The foreign-exchange market comprises buyers and sellers of currencies issued by the world's countries. Anyone who owns money denominated in one currency and wants to convert that money to a second currency participates in the foreign-exchange market. Pakistani tourists exchanging rupees for British pounds at London's Heathrow Airport utilize the foreign-exchange market, as does Toyota when it exports automobiles to Canada from its factories in Japan, and the British government when it arranges a multimillion-pound loan to rebuild the monsoon-ravaged economy of Bangladesh. The world wide volume of foreign-exchange trading is estimated at $4.0 trillion per day. Foreign exchange is being traded somewhere in the world every minute of the day (see Map 8.1). The largest foreign-exchange market is in London, followed by New York, Tokyo,

MAP 8.1
A Day of Foreign-Exchange Trading

Traditionally, the trading day begins in Auckland, New Zealand, which lies just west of the international date line. As the earth rotates, foreign-exchange markets open in other cities, including Sydney, Tokyo, Hong Kong, Singapore, Bahrain, Frankfurt, Zurich, Paris, London, New York, Chicago, and San Francisco.

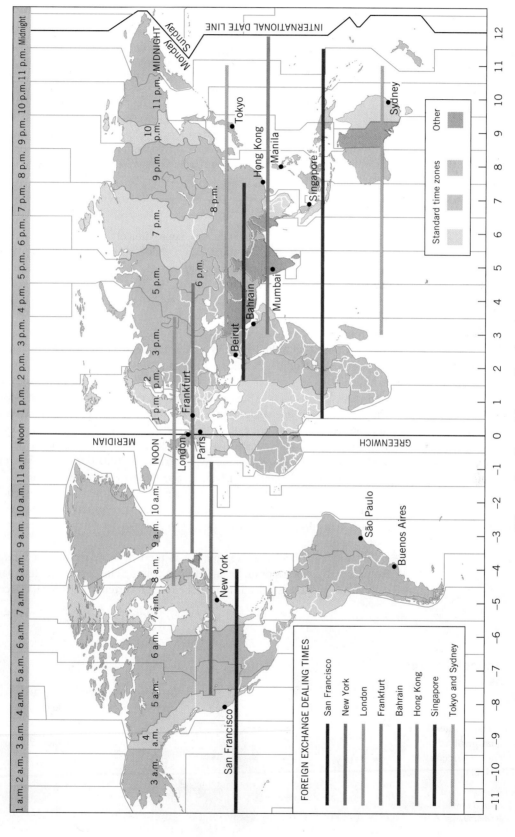

Not everyone reading this book is a finance major. Some readers may have difficulty with the concept of using money to buy money and what is meant by a currency's value rising or falling. If you are having trouble with this, here is a simple trick. In Figure 8.3 replace the currency that is being bought and sold with the phrase "loaf of bread" (or the name of any other tangible good). If you do this, then the vertical axis is the price in dollars of one unit of bread and the horizontal axis is the quantity of bread sold—a standard supply and demand graph that you encountered in your basic economics course. Nothing has changed in the supply and demand graph except the label. Think about this until you feel comfortable with the notion that yen are merely a good, like bread or widgets.

As you read the rest of this book, if you get confused about what is up and what is down when we say a currency is rising or falling in value, you can use the same trick. For example, suppose on Monday the British pound is worth $2.01 and on Tuesday it is worth $2.02. From Monday to Tuesday the pound rose in value, while the dollar fell in value. If that is obvious to you, fine. If it is not, substitute "a loaf of bread" for "pound." A statement about this example would then read, "On Monday a loaf of bread is worth $2.01, and on Tuesday a loaf of bread is worth $2.02." The conclusion is that a loaf of bread has gone up in value because more dollars are needed to buy it on Tuesday. Conversely, you can say the dollar has gone down in value because each dollar on Tuesday buys less bread.

and Singapore. As Figure 8.5 indicates, approximately 85 percent of the transactions involve the U.S. dollar, a dominance stemming from the dollar's role in the Bretton Woods system. Because the dollar is used to facilitate most currency exchange, it is known as the primary **transaction currency** for the foreign-exchange market.

The Role of Banks

The foreign-exchange departments of large international banks such as JPMorgan Chase, Barclays, and Deutsche Bank in major financial centers like New York, London, Tokyo, Singapore, and Hong Kong play a dominant role in the foreign-exchange market. These banks stand ready to buy or sell the major traded currencies. They profit from the foreign-exchange market in several ways. Much of their profits come from the spread between the bid and ask prices for foreign exchange. Suppose JPMorgan Chase buys 10 million Swiss francs (SwFr) from one customer at a price of SwFr 1.649/$1 and sells those Swiss francs to a second customer at SwFr 1.648/$1; JPMorgan Chase makes $3,679.78. (Get out your calculator and do the arithmetic! JPMorgan Chase buys the Swiss francs for 10,000,000 ÷ 1.649, or $6,064,281.38, and sells them for 10,000,000 ÷ 1.648, or $6,067,961.16, thereby earning a profit of $3,679.78.) Sometimes international banks act as speculators, betting that they can guess in which direction exchange rates are headed. Such speculation can be enormously profitable, although it is always risky. And, as discussed later in this chapter, banks also may act as arbitrageurs in the foreign-exchange market.

International banks are key players in the wholesale market for foreign exchange, dealing for their own accounts or on behalf of large commercial customers. Interbank transactions, typically involving at least $1 million (or the foreign currency equivalent), account for a majority of

FIGURE 8.5

Currencies Involved in Foreign-Exchange Market Transactions

Percentage share of foreign-exchange transactions involving selected currencies. Because there are two currencies involved in each transaction, the percentages add up to 200 percent.

Source: Bank for International Settlements, *Central Bank Survey of Foreign Exchange and Derivatives Market* Activity (Basle, December 2010), p. 12.

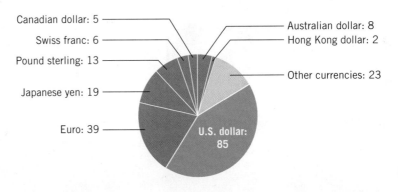

Canadian dollar: 5
Swiss franc: 6
Pound sterling: 13
Japanese yen: 19
Euro: 39
Australian dollar: 8
Hong Kong dollar: 2
Other currencies: 23
U.S. dollar: 85

foreign-exchange transactions. Corporate treasurers, pension funds, hedge funds, and insurance companies are also major players in the foreign exchange market. Using the Internet, computers, telephones, e-mail, and fax machines, banks and institutional investors in one market are in constant contact with their counterparts in other markets to seek the best currency prices. Online currency trading is a growing component of this market, as "e-World" indicates, as is the role of institutional investors like hedge funds and mutual funds.[3] International banks also play a key role in the retail market for foreign exchange, dealing with individual customers who want to buy or sell foreign currencies in large or small amounts. Typically, the price paid by retail customers for foreign exchange is the prevailing wholesale exchange rate plus a premium. The size of the premium is in turn a function of the size of the transaction and the importance of the customer to the bank. A Danish music store chain that needs $50,000 to pay for 10,000 compact discs of Lady Gaga's or M.I.A.'s latest release will pay a higher premium for its foreign currency than will General Motors when it needs £20 million to repay British investors. And, of course, foreign tourists cashing in a traveler's check for local currency at a bank or exchange office pay an even higher premium.

The clients of the foreign-exchange departments of banks fall into several categories:

- *Commercial customers* engage in foreign-exchange transactions as part of their normal commercial activities, such as exporting or importing goods and services, paying or receiving dividends and interest from foreign sources, and purchasing or selling foreign assets and investments. Some commercial customers may also use the market to hedge, or reduce, their risks due to potential unfavorable changes in foreign-exchange rates for moneys to be paid or received in the future.
- *Speculators* deliberately assume exchange rate risks by acquiring positions in a currency, hoping that they can correctly predict changes in the currency's market value. Foreign-exchange speculation can be very lucrative if one guesses correctly, but it is also extremely risky.
- *Arbitrageurs* attempt to exploit small differences in the price of a currency between markets. They seek to obtain riskless profits by simultaneously buying the currency in the lower-priced market and selling it in the higher-priced market.

Countries' central banks and treasury departments are also major players in the foreign-exchange market. As discussed in Chapter 7, under the gold standard and the Bretton Woods system, a country's central bank was required to intervene in the foreign-exchange market to ensure

---

E-WORLD   THE BIGGEST ONLINE MARKET

The foreign-exchange market is the world's biggest single market—some $4.0 trillion a day in volume. It is no surprise that this market is moving online, because electronic trading lowers the cost of completing foreign-exchange (FX) transactions. Already online sales of foreign exchange dwarf the sales of any other product sold on the Internet.

Many major international banks, such as JPMorgan Chase, Deutsche Bank, Citigroup, and UBS, initially responded to the opportunities provided by the advent of the Internet by developing their own proprietary FX trading platforms to serve their retail customers. However, most soon recognized that these go-it-alone approaches would be likely to lose out to multibank services like FXall.com, a joint venture founded by several of the largest players in the foreign-exchange market—Bank of America, Goldman Sachs, Credit Suisse, Morgan Stanley Dean Witter, UBS Warburg, and HSBC—who believed that most currency traders would prefer to go to one website rather than surf numerous single-vendor sites. To date, that belief seems to be correct. More than 75 large international banks have joined the FXall network, as have 1,000 institutions. In 2003, $2.4 trillion of foreign exchange was traded over FXall's platform; in 2004, $4.9 trillion; in 2005, $6.7 trillion; in 2006, $9.8 trillion; and in 2007, $13.4 trillion. In 2010, the company's trading volume reached $100 billion a day. This increased volume bodes well for FXall's future, because the more transactions the platform executes, the more liquidity it provides to FX traders, which encourages them to execute more transactions on it, which creates more liquidity, and so on. Indeed, numerous surveys conducted by trade magazines such as *Euromoney* or *Global Investor* have named FXall the leading multibank foreign exchange portal.

Sources: "FXall surpasses $100 billion daily trading milestone," FXall press release, May 26, 2010, www.fxall.com, June 7, 2011; "Foreign exchange banks charge into online battle," *Financial Times*, August 15, 2000, p. 19; "Banks move towards online currency trading," *Financial Times*, June 7, 2000, p. 20; "Deutsche Bank, Chase Manhattan join move toward online currency dealing," *Wall Street Journal*, April 3, 2000, p. A43D.

This Tel Aviv foreign-exchange trader is an important link in the $4 trillion-per-day global foreign exchange market. The largest center for foreign exchange trading is London, followed by New York and Tokyo.

David Silverman/Getty Images

that the market value of the country's currency approximated the currency's par value. Countries that have chosen to peg their currencies to that of another country must do the same. And, of course, central banks of countries that allow their currencies to float are free to intervene in the foreign-exchange market to influence the market values of their currencies if they so desire.

Active markets exist for relatively few pairs of currency other than those involving the U.S. dollar, the euro, the British pound, and the Japanese yen. Suppose a Swedish knitting mill needs New Zealand dollars to pay for 100,000 pounds of merino wool. The foreign-exchange market between the Swedish krona and the New Zealand dollar is very small—in fact, no active market exists for the direct exchange of these two currencies. Usually, the U.S. dollar would be used as an intermediary currency to facilitate this transaction. The knitting mill's Swedish banker would obtain the necessary New Zealand dollars by first selling Swedish krona to obtain U.S. dollars and then selling the U.S. dollars to obtain New Zealand dollars. Such transactions are routine for international banks.

Domestic laws may constrain the ability to trade a currency in the foreign-exchange market. Currencies that are freely tradable are called **convertible currencies**. Also called **hard currencies,** these include the euro, the British pound, the Swedish krona, the Canadian dollar, the Swiss franc, the Japanese yen, and the U.S. dollar. Currencies that are not freely tradable because of domestic laws or the unwillingness of foreigners to hold them are called **inconvertible currencies** or **soft currencies**. The currencies of many developing countries fall in the soft category.

Spot and Forward Markets

Many international business transactions involve payments to be made in the future. Such transactions include lending activities and purchases on credit. Because changes in currency values are common, such international transactions would appear to be risky in the post–Bretton Woods era. How can a firm know for sure the future value of a foreign currency? Fortunately, in addition to its geographic dimension, the foreign-exchange market also has a time dimension. Currencies can be bought and sold for immediate delivery or for delivery at some point in the future. The **spot market** consists of foreign-exchange transactions that are to be consummated immediately. (*Immediately* is normally defined as two days after the trade date because of the time historically needed for payment to clear the international banking system.) Spot transactions account for 33 percent of all foreign-exchange transactions.

The **forward market** consists of foreign-exchange transactions that are to occur sometime in the future. Prices are often published for foreign exchange that will be delivered one month, three months, and six months in the future. For example, on Wednesday, August 3, 2011, the spot price of the British pound was $1.6426, whereas the forward price for pounds for delivery in one month was $1.6422 and for delivery in six months was $1.6396.

Currency	U.S. $ equiv.		per U.S. $	
	Wed.	Tues.	Wed.	Tues.
Britain (Pound)	1.6426	1.6299	.6088	.6135
1-month Forward	1.6422	1.6294	.6090	.6137
3-month Forward	1.6411	1.6284	.6093	.6141
6-month Forward	1.6396	1.6269	.6099	.6146

Many users of the forward market engage in swap transactions. A **swap transaction** is a transaction in which the same currency is bought and sold simultaneously, but delivery is made at two different points in time. For example, in a typical "spot against forward" swap, a U.S. manufacturer borrowing £10 million from a British bank for one month but needing dollars will sell the £10 million in the spot market to obtain U.S. dollars and simultaneously buy £10 million (plus the number of pounds it owes in interest payments) in the one-month forward market to repay its pound-denominated loan.

Normally, an international business that wants to buy or sell foreign exchange on a spot or forward basis will contract with an international bank to do so. The bank will charge the firm the prevailing wholesale rate for the currency, plus a small premium for its services. Because of the bank's extensive involvement in the foreign-exchange market, it is typically willing and able to customize the spot, forward, or swap contract to meet the customer's specific needs. For example, if Siemens expects to receive 10.7 million francs from Swiss customers in 42 days, its bank will usually agree to enter into a forward contract to buy those Swiss francs from Siemens with delivery in 42 days.

The foreign-exchange market has developed two other mechanisms to allow firms to obtain foreign exchange in the future. Neither, however, provides the flexibility in amount and in timing that international banks offer. The first mechanism is the **currency future**. Publicly traded on many exchanges worldwide, a currency future is a contract that resembles a forward contract. However, unlike the forward contract, the currency future is for a standard amount (for example, ¥12.5 million or SwFr 125,000) on a standard delivery date (for example, the third Wednesday of the contract's maturity month). As with a forward contract, a firm signing a currency-future contract must complete the transaction by buying or selling the specified amount of foreign currency at the specified price and time. This obligation is usually not troublesome, however; a firm wanting to be released from a currency-future obligation can simply make an offsetting transaction. In practice, 98 percent of currency futures are settled in this manner. Currency futures represent only 1 percent of the foreign-exchange market.

The second mechanism, the **currency option** allows, but does not require, a firm to buy or sell a specified amount of a foreign currency at a specified price at any time up to a specified date. A **call option** grants the right to buy the foreign currency in question; a **put option** grants the right to sell the foreign currency. Currency options are publicly traded on organized exchanges worldwide. For example, put and call options are available for Canadian dollars on the Chicago Mercantile Exchange (in contract sizes of Can $100,000) and on the Philadelphia Exchange (in contract sizes of Can $50,000). Because of the inflexibility of publicly traded options, international bankers often are willing to write currency options customized as to amount and time for their commercial clients. Currency options account for 5 percent of foreign-exchange market activity.

The forward market, currency options, and currency futures facilitate international trade and investment by allowing firms to hedge, or reduce, the foreign-exchange risks inherent in international transactions. Suppose Best Buy purchases Sony PlayStation 3 game consoles for ¥800 million for delivery three months in the future, with payment due at delivery. Rather than having to buy yen today and hold them for three months, Best Buy can simply go to its bank and contract to buy the ¥800 million for delivery in three months. The firm's bank will in turn charge Best Buy for those yen based on the yen's current price in the three-month forward wholesale market. Best Buy could also protect itself from increases in the yen's price by purchasing a currency future or a currency option. (We discuss the advantages and disadvantages of these different hedging techniques more thoroughly in Chapter 18.)

The forward price of a foreign currency often differs from its spot price. If the forward price (using a direct quote) is less than the spot price, the currency is selling at a **forward discount**. If the forward price is higher than the spot price, the currency is selling at a **forward premium**. For example, as Figure 8.4 indicates, the spot price of the British pound on August 3, 2011, was $1.6426. On the same day the three-month forward price was $1.6411, indicating that the pound was selling at a forward discount. The annualized forward premium or discount on the pound can be calculated by using the following formula:

$$\text{Annualized forward premium or discount} = \frac{P_f - P_s}{P_s} \times n$$

where, using our example,

P_f = three-month forward price = $1.6411
P_s = spot price = $1.6426
n = the number of periods in a year = 4

(Because the example calls for a three-month forward rate, n equals 4; there are four three-month periods in a year.) Thus,

$$\text{Annualized forward premium or discount} = \frac{\$1.6411 - \$1.6426}{\$1.6426} \times 4$$
$$= -.0037 = -.37\%$$

Because the equation results in a negative number, the pound is selling at a forward discount. Had the forward price of the pound been higher than the spot price (using the direct quote), the sign of the equation would have been positive and the formula would have yielded the annualized forward premium for the pound.

The forward price represents the marketplace's aggregate prediction of the spot price of the exchange rate in the future. Thus, the forward price helps international businesspeople forecast future changes in exchange rates. These changes can affect the price of imported components as well as the competitiveness and profitability of the firm's exports. If a currency is selling at a forward discount, the foreign-exchange market believes that the currency will depreciate over time. Firms may want to reduce their holdings of assets or increase their liabilities denominated in such a currency. The currencies of countries suffering balance of payment (BOP) trade deficits or high inflation rates often sell at a forward discount. Conversely, if a currency is selling at a forward premium, the foreign-exchange market believes the currency will appreciate over time. Firms may want to increase their holdings of assets and reduce their liabilities denominated in such a currency. The currencies of countries enjoying BOP trade surpluses or low inflation rates often sell at a forward premium. Thus, the difference between the spot and forward prices of a country's currency often signals the market's expectations regarding that country's economic policies and prospects.

Arbitrage and the Currency Market

Another important component of the foreign-exchange market is arbitrage activities. **Arbitrage** is the riskless purchase of a product in one market for immediate resale in a second market in order to profit from a price discrepancy. We explore two types of arbitrage activities that affect the foreign-exchange market: arbitrage of goods and arbitrage of money.

ARBITRAGE OF GOODS—PURCHASING POWER PARITY Underlying the arbitrage of goods is a very simple notion: If the price of a good differs between two markets, people will tend to buy the good in the market offering the lower price, the "cheap" market, and resell it in the market offering the higher price, the "expensive" market. Under the *law of one price,* such arbitrage activities will continue until the price of the good is identical in both markets (excluding transactions costs, transportation costs, taxes, and so on). This notion induced purchasing agents for Galeries Lafayette to buy clock radios in Japan and export them to France in the example in Chapter 6.

The arbitrage of goods across national boundaries is represented by the **theory of purchasing power parity (PPP)**. This theory states that the prices of tradable goods, when expressed in a common currency, will tend to equalize across countries as a result of exchange rate changes. PPP occurs because the process of buying goods in the cheap market and reselling them in the expensive market affects the demand for, and thus the price of, the foreign currency, as well as the market price of the good itself in the two product markets in question. For example, assume the exchange rate between U.S. and Canadian dollars is US $0.80 = Can $1. Suppose Levi's jeans sell for US $48 in the United States and Can $60 in Canada. PPP would exist in this case. At the existing exchange rate

$$\frac{\text{US } \$0.80}{\text{Can } \$1} \times \text{Can } \$60 = \text{US } \$48.$$

Thus, the Levi's jeans are the same price in both markets (expressed in either U.S. or Canadian dollars), and neither U.S. nor Canadian residents would have any reason to cross their shared border to purchase the jeans in the other country.

Now suppose Canadian firms decide to increase their investments in Mexico as a result of opportunities created by the North American Free Trade Agreement (NAFTA). As Canadians sell their currency to buy Mexican pesos, they increase the supply of Canadian dollars in the foreign-exchange market, causing the value of the Canadian dollar to fall. Suppose the new exchange rate between U.S. and Canadian dollars is US $0.60 = Can $1. PPP would no longer exist. At this new exchange rate U.S. residents could cross the border, exchange US $36 for Can $60, and buy their Levi's in Canada, thereby saving themselves US $12.

This arbitrage process affects three markets: the foreign-exchange market between U.S. and Canadian dollars; the market for Levi's in the United States; and the market for Levi's in Canada. First, by buying their jeans in Canada, U.S. residents increase the supply of U.S. dollars in the foreign-exchange market, thereby raising the value of the Canadian dollar relative to the U.S. dollar. Second, the behavior of the U.S. residents reduces the demand for Levi's in the United States, lowering their price there. Third, the actions of the U.S. residents increase the demand for Levi's in Canada, thereby raising their price there. This arbitrage behavior will continue until the law of one price is met—the price of Levi's jeans, stated in either Canadian dollars or U.S. dollars, is the same in both countries. This will occur through some combination of changes in the exchange rate and changes in the two product markets.

Does this really happen? Obviously, teenagers from Miami, Florida, do not fly to Calgary, Alberta, just to save US $12 on a pair of jeans. However, for residents of Sault Ste. Marie, Ontario, and Sault Ste. Marie, Michigan; Calais, Maine, and St. Stephen, New Brunswick; and Seattle, Washington, and Vancouver, British Columbia, the border is but a short trip away, making arbitrage-driven cross-border shopping feasible. Spring-break skiers and snowboarders may choose Whistler Mountain over Crested Butte or Tremblant over Killington, depending on the exchange rate between Canadian and U.S. dollars.

Of course, the Canadian-U.S. exchange rate is determined by much more than the relative price of jeans in the two countries, border trade between cities like the two Sault Ste. Maries, or spring-break skiers. Nonetheless, if PPP does not exist in the two countries for jeans (or any other tradable good), people will buy the good in the cheap market and transport it to the expensive market, thereby affecting prices in the two product markets, as well as supply and demand in the foreign-exchange market. That is why the PPP theory states that prices of tradable goods will *tend* to equalize.

International economists use PPP to help them compare standards of living across countries. Consider, for example, France and Canada. Converting France's 2009 per capita income measured in euros into U.S. dollars using the average 2009 exchange rate between the euro and the dollar would yield $42,680. Canadian per capita income in 2009, when converted to U.S. dollars, was $42,170. These figures suggest that the average French citizen enjoys a higher income than the average Canadian citizen. However, this comparison fails to take into account differences in price levels between the two countries. After adjusting for purchasing power, France's per capita income falls to $33,980, while Canada's falls to $37,590, indicating that the average Canadian is better off than the average French citizen. Because of such distortions due to price levels, international businesspeople who use international income data to make decisions, such as which market to enter or how to position a product, must pay close attention to whether the data are reported with or without PPP adjustments.

Foreign-exchange analysts also use the PPP theory to forecast long-term changes in exchange rates. The analysts believe that broad purchasing power imbalances between countries

The Big Mac Index

	Price of a Big Mac		Implied exchange rate for PPP to exist	Actual exchange rate July 15, 2011	Under (-) or over (+) valuation versus the U.S. dollar
	in local currency	in US dollars			
United States	US $4.07	$4.07	–	–	–
Argentina	Peso 20.0	$4.85	4.92	4.12	19%
Australia	A$4.56	$4.86	1.12	0.94	19%
Brazil	Real 9.50	$6.02	2.34	1.58	48%
Canada	C$4.73	$4.96	1.16	0.95	22%
Chile	Peso 1,850	$4.00	455	462	−2%
China	Yuan 14.7	$2.28	3.60	6.44	−44%
Colombia	Peso 8,400	$4.81	2,066	1,747	18%
Czech Republic	Koruna 69.3	$4.01	17.1	17.3	−1%
Denmark	DK 28.5	$5.41	7.01	5.27	33%
Egypt	Pound 14.1	$2.37	3.47	5.95	−42%
Euro zone	€ 3.44	$4.87	0.85	0.71	20%
Hong Kong	HK$15.1	$1.94	3.71	7.79	−52%
Hungary	Forint 760	$3.99	187	191	−2%
India	Rupee 84.0	$1.89	20.7	44.4	−53%
Indonesia	Rupiah 22,534	$2.64	5543	8537	−35%
Israel	Shekel 15.9	$4.64	3.91	3.43	14%
Japan	¥320	$4.04	78.7	79.1	−1%
Malaysia	Ringgit 7.2	$2.39	1.77	3.01	−41%
Mexico	Peso 32.0	$2.73	7.87	11.74	−33%
New Zealand	NZ$5.10	$4.31	1.25	1.18	6%
Norway	Kroner 45.0	$8.10	11.1	5.56	100%
Pakistan	Rupee 205	$2.38	50.5	86.1	−41%
Peru	Sol 10.0	$3.65	2.46	2.74	−10%
Philippines	Peso 118	$2.75	29.0	42.9	−32%
Poland	Zloty 8.63	$3.04	2.12	2.83	−25%
Russia	Rouble 75.0	$2.67	18.5	28.1	−34%
Saudi Arabia	Riyal 10.0	$2.67	2.46	3.75	−34%
Singapore	S$4.41	$3.62	1.08	1.22	−11%
South Africa	Rand 19.45	$2.82	4.78	6.89	−31%
South Korea	Won 3,700	$3.50	910	1058	−14%
Sweden	SKr 48.4	$7.46	11.9	6.49	83%
Switzerland	SFr 6.50	$7.98	1.60	0.81	96%
Taiwan	NT$76.0	$2.64	18.5	28.8	−36%
Thailand	Baht 70.0	$2.33	17.2	30.1	−43%
Turkey	Lira 6.50	$3.95	1.60	1.65	−3%
United Kingdom	£2.39	$3.86	0.59	0.62	−5%

Sources: The Economist (online, accessed August 5, 2011); Wall Street Journal (online, accessed August 5, 2011)

Taking advantage of the presence of McDonald's restaurants in 117 countries, *The Economist* magazine periodically publishes its Big Mac Index, which provides a quick-and-dirty estimate of the undervaluation or overvaluation of a country's currency. In 2010, it judged that the currencies of commodity-rich countries like Australia, Brazil, and Canada were overvalued, a result of the booming demand for their iron ore, coal, potash, and other raw materials.

@Xiye/Dreamstime.com

signal possible changes in exchange rates. As a quick and dirty way of assessing misalignments in exchange rates, the British business weekly *The Economist* periodically reports the prices of McDonald's Big Macs around the world (see "Bringing the World into Focus"). Although not a perfect indicator—the price of a Big Mac is affected by taxes and nontraded inputs like local rents—the Big Mac index has proven to provide helpful signals whether a currency is overvalued or undervalued in the foreign-exchange market.

ARBITRAGE OF MONEY Although we do not want to diminish the long-run importance of the arbitrage of goods, its impact on the foreign-exchange market is dwarfed by that of the short-term arbitrage of money. Much of the $4.0 trillion in daily trading of foreign exchange stems from financial arbitrage. Professional traders employed by money market banks and other financial organizations seek to profit from small differences in the price of foreign exchange in different markets. Although not all the volume in currency markets reflects arbitrage activities, the importance of financial activities relative to real activities (purchases of goods and services) in foreign-exchange markets is indicated by the ratio of daily foreign currency trading ($4.0 trillion) to daily international trade ($44 billion).

Whenever the foreign-exchange market is not in equilibrium, professional traders can profit through arbitraging money. Numerous forms of foreign-exchange arbitrage are possible, but we discuss three common examples: two-point, three-point, and covered interest.

Two-point arbitrage, also called **geographic arbitrage,** involves profiting from price differences in two geographically distinct markets. Suppose £1 is trading for $2.00 in New York City and $1.80 in London. A profitable arbitrage opportunity is available. A foreign-exchange trader at JPMorgan Chase could take $1.80 and use it to buy £1 in London's foreign-exchange market. The trader could then take the pound she just bought and resell it for $2.00 in New York's foreign-exchange market. Through this two-point, or geographic, arbitrage, the trader at JPMorgan Chase transforms $1.80 into $2.00 at no risk whatsoever.

Of course, currency traders at other banks will also note the opportunity for quick profits. As arbitrageurs sell dollars and buy pounds in London, the dollar falls in value relative to the pound in the London market. As arbitrageurs sell pounds and buy dollars in New York, the pound falls in value relative to the dollar in that market. This process will continue until the pound-dollar exchange rate is identical in both markets. Only when there is no possibility of profitable arbitrage will the foreign-exchange market be in equilibrium.

We add one caveat: If the costs of making an arbitrage transaction were large, there could be differences in the exchange rates in the two markets that reflected the size of the transaction costs. However, for major currencies foreign exchange is sold in large amounts by very large, well-known, and trustworthy international banks. Accordingly, transaction costs are extremely small, and two-point arbitrage generally will cause exchange rates between any two major currencies to be identical in all markets.

Consider another example. Suppose that £1 can buy $2 in New York, Tokyo, and London, $1 can buy ¥120 in those three markets, and £1 can buy ¥200 in all three. Because the exchange rate between each pair of currencies is the same in each country, no possibility of profitable two-point arbitrage exists. However, profitable **three-point arbitrage** opportunities exist. Three-point arbitrage is the buying and selling of three different currencies to make a riskless profit. Figure 8.6 shows how this can work:

Step 1: Convert £1 into $2.

Step 2: Convert the $2 into ¥240.

Step 3: Convert the ¥240 into £1.2.

Through these three steps, £1 has been converted into £1.2, for a riskless profit of £0.2.

Professional currency traders can make profits through three-point arbitrage whenever the cost of buying a currency directly (such as using pounds to buy yen) differs from the cross rate of exchange. The **cross rate** is an exchange rate between two currencies calculated through the use of a third currency (such as using pounds to buy dollars and then using the dollars to buy yen). Because of the depth and liquidity of dollar-denominated currency markets, the U.S. dollar is the primary third currency used in calculating cross rates. In the earlier example, the direct quote between pounds and yen is £1/¥200, while the cross rate is

$$\frac{£1}{\$2} \times \frac{\$1}{¥120} = \frac{£1}{¥240}$$

The difference between these two rates offers arbitrage profits to foreign-exchange market professionals. The market for the three currencies will be in equilibrium only when arbitrage profits do not exist, which occurs when the direct quote and the cross rate for each possible pair of the three currencies are equal.

The real significance of three-point arbitrage is that it links together individual foreign-exchange markets. Changes in the pound/dollar market will affect both the yen/pound market and the dollar/yen market because of the direct quote–cross rate equilibrium relationship. These changes will in turn affect other markets, such as the dollar/euro market, the yen/euro market, and the pound/euro market. Because of three-point arbitrage, changes in any one foreign-exchange market can affect prices in all other foreign-exchange markets.

The third form of arbitrage we discuss is covered-interest arbitrage. **Covered-interest arbitrage** is arbitrage that occurs when the difference between two countries' interest rates is not equal

FIGURE 8.6
Three-Point Arbitrage

to the forward discount/premium on their currencies. In practice, it is the most important form of arbitrage in the foreign-exchange market. It occurs because international bankers, insurance companies, and corporate treasurers are continually scanning money markets worldwide to obtain the best returns on their short-term excess cash balances and the lowest rates on short-term loans. In doing so, however, they often want to protect, or cover (hence, the term *covered-interest arbitrage*), themselves from exchange rate risks.

A simple example demonstrates how covered-interest arbitrage works. Suppose the annual interest rate for three-month deposits is 12 percent in London and 8 percent in New York. New York investors will be eager to earn the higher returns available in London. To do so, they must convert their dollars to pounds today in order to invest in London. However, the New York investors ultimately want dollars, not pounds, so they must reconvert the pounds back to dollars at the end of three months. But what if the pound's value were to fall during that period? The extra interest the New Yorkers will earn in London might then be wiped out by losses suffered when they exchange pounds for dollars in three months.

The New York investors can capture the higher London interest rates but avoid exchange rate dangers by covering in the forward market their exposure to potential drops in the pound's value. Suppose they have $1 million to invest, the spot pound is selling for $2.00, and the three-month forward pound is selling for $1.99. They have two choices:

1. They can invest their money in New York at 8 percent interest.
2. They can convert their dollars into pounds today, invest in London at 12 percent interest, and in three months liquidate their London investment and convert it back to dollars.

If the New York investors choose the first option and invest their funds in the New York money market for three months at 8 percent annual interest (or 2 percent for three months), at the end of the three months their investment will be

$$\$1,000,000 \times 1.02 = \$1,020,000$$

Or they can invest their money in London for three months. To do so, they first convert their $1,000,000 into £500,000 at the spot rate of $2.00/£1. At the 12 percent annual interest rate available in London (or 3 percent for three months), their investment will grow in three months to

$$£500,000 \times 1.03 = £515,000$$

If they want to avoid exposure to exchange rate fluctuations, they can sell the £515,000 today in the three-month forward market at the current three-month forward rate of $1.99/£1, which, at the end of three months, yields

$$£515,000 \times \$1.99/£1 = \$1,024,850$$

The New Yorkers thus earn more money by investing in London than they would at home ($24,850 versus $20,000). Covered-interest arbitrage allows them to capture the higher interest rate in London while covering themselves from exchange rate fluctuations by using the forward market. So short-term investment money, seeking the higher covered return, will flow from New York to London.

What happens in the two lending markets and the foreign-exchange market when such arbitrage occurs? When funds are transferred from New York to London, interest rates will rise in New York because the supply of lendable money in New York decreases. Interest rates will fall in London because the supply of lendable money increases there. In the spot market the demand for pounds increases, thereby raising the spot price of pounds. In the three-month forward market the supply of pounds increases, thereby lowering the forward price of pounds. Lendable funds will continue to flow from New York to London until the return on the covered investment is the same in London as it is in New York. Only then will all possibilities for profitable covered-interest arbitrage be exhausted. ("Venturing Abroad" discusses the growing role of uncovered interest arbitrage, known as the carry trade.)

Returns to international investors will be equal—and arbitrage-driven, short-term international capital flows will end—when the interest rate difference between the two markets equals the three-month forward discount on the pound. Said another way, covered-interest arbitrage will end if the gains investors capture from the higher interest rates in the London market are just offset by the exchange rate losses they suffer from the conversion of their dollars to pounds today and reconversion of their pounds back to dollars in three months. (Note that the pound's forward discount measures in percentage terms the exchange rate loss on this "spot against forward" swap transaction.)

The short-term capital flows that result from covered-interest arbitrage are so important to the foreign-exchange market that, in practice, the short-term interest rate differential between two countries determines the forward discount or forward premium on their currencies.

This last statement raises another question: Why should interest rates vary among countries in the first place? Addressing this question in 1930, Yale economist Irving Fisher demonstrated that a country's nominal interest rate reflects the real interest rate (which he assumed to be constant across countries) plus expected inflation in that country. National differences in expected inflation rates thus yield differences in nominal interest rates among countries, a phenomenon known as the **international Fisher effect**. Because of the international Fisher effect and covered-interest arbitrage, an increase in a country's expected inflation rate implies higher interest rates in that country. This in turn will lead to either a shrinking of the forward premium or a widening of the forward discount on the country's currency in the foreign-exchange market. Because of this linkage between inflation and expected changes in exchange rates, international businesspeople and foreign currency traders carefully monitor countries' inflation trends. The connection between inflation and exchange rates also affects the international monetary system. For example, a fixed exchange rate system functions poorly if inflation rates vary widely among countries participating in the system.

In summary, arbitrage activities are important for several reasons. Arbitrage constitutes a major portion of the $4.0 trillion in currencies traded globally each working day. It affects the supply and demand for each of the major trading currencies. It also ties together the foreign-exchange markets, thereby overcoming differences in geography (two-point arbitrage), currency type (three-point arbitrage), and time (covered-interest arbitrage). Arbitrage truly makes the foreign-exchange market global.

The International Capital Market

Not only are international banks important in the functioning of the foreign-exchange market and arbitrage transactions, but they also play a critical role in financing the operations of international businesses, acting as both commercial bankers and investment bankers. As commercial bankers,

---

VENTURING ABROAD | **THE CARRY TRADE**

While covered-interest arbitrage is an important component of the foreign-exchange market, uncovered-interest arbitrage—the so-called **carry trade**—is a growing phenomenon. The carry trade tries to exploit differences in the interest rates between countries. Because Japan's interest rates have been among the lowest of the major trading nations, the yen is a favorite currency of the carry trade. The strategy is simple: Borrow yen at a low interest rate, and use the borrowed yen to buy bonds, notes, or certificates of deposit denominated in currencies that are paying higher interest rates, such as the Australian dollar or the New Zealand dollar. The strategy is risky: If the yen rises in value relative to the second currency, the carry trader can lose lots of money very quickly. Some experts have compared it to picking up nickels in front of a moving steamroller—easy money, as long as nothing goes wrong. In their view, the carry trade is high risk, low reward.

Nonetheless, investors and speculators are often seduced by the lure of the carry trade, particularly in times of low volatility in the foreign-exchange market. FX Concepts, a $13 billion New York–based hedge fund, often invests in the carry trade. In 2007, for example, it borrowed yen, paying an interest rate of less than 1 percent, and invested them in Australian- and New Zealand-dollar based securities yielding 6 to 8 percent. But the carry trade has also enticed less professional investors as well. Trying to escape the low interest rates offered by Japanese banks, tens of thousands of Japanese married women, who by custom manage their households' finances, routinely trade currencies and engage in carry trade transactions using online trading platforms. A cottage industry of investing clubs, books, and online blogs has mushroomed to aid these legions of housewife currency traders. All told, private Japanese investors were estimated to account for 30 percent of the spot trading in the yen, 5 percent of trading in the Australian dollar, and 4 percent in the British pound in 2009.

Volatile currency markets are poisonous to the carry trade. For instance, as the problems with subprime mortgages became more widely known during the summer of 2007 (see this chapter's closing case), the currency and capital markets became increasingly skittish. During one week in August 2007, the yen rose 4 percent versus the U.S. dollar, 9 percent against the Australian dollar, and 11 percent relative to the New Zealand dollar. When the yen began to rise, many carry traders tried to cut their losses by buying yen to close out their open positions. The sudden deluge of buy orders elevated the yen's value, worsening the squeeze on the carry traders. Private online Japanese currency traders lost an estimated $2.5 billion that month.

Sources: "Forex tips from the Far East," *Wall Street Journal*, February 25, 2011; "Japan limits Forex trades of 'Mrs Watanabes'," *Financial Times*, August 2, 2010, p. 13; "In Japan, currency traders stay in game," *Wall Street Journal*, November 28, 2008; "Japanese housewives sweat in secret as markets reel," *New York Times*, September 16, 2007 (online); "Currency 'carry trade' becomes harder play amid aversion to risk," *Wall Street Journal*, August 18, 2007, p. B1; "Japan faces scrutiny over carry trade," *Financial Times*, August 2, 2007 (online); "Two-thirds of a problem," *Financial Times*, July 1, 2007 (online).

they finance exports and imports, accept deposits, provide working capital loans, and offer sophisticated cash management services for their clients. As investment bankers, they may underwrite or syndicate local, foreign, or multinational loans and broker, facilitate, or even finance mergers and joint ventures between foreign and domestic firms. The big international banks are continually developing new products to meet the needs of borrowers worldwide. Unfortunately, market participants may not fully appreciate the risks inherent is some of these new financial instruments, as the chapter's closing case, "Subprime Meltdown, Global Recession" reports.

Major International Banks

The international banking system is centered in large money market banks headquartered in the world's financial centers—Japan, the United States, and the European Union. These banks are involved in international commerce on a global scale (see Table 8.1).

International banking takes many forms. Originally, most international banking was done through reciprocal correspondent relationships among banks located in different countries. A **correspondent relationship** is an agent relationship whereby one bank acts as a correspondent, or agent, for another bank in the first bank's home country, and vice versa. For example, a U.S. bank could be the correspondent for a Danish bank in the United States, while the Danish bank could be the U.S. bank's correspondent in Denmark. Services performed by correspondent banks include paying or collecting foreign funds, providing credit information, and honoring letters of credit. To facilitate these transactions, each bank maintains accounts at the other bank denominated in the local currency.

As the larger banks have internationalized their operations, they have increasingly provided their own overseas operations, rather than utilizing correspondent banks, to improve their ability to compete internationally. A bank that has its own foreign operations is better able to access new sources of deposits and profitable lending opportunities. Equally important, as its domestic clients internationalize, the bank can better meet those clients' international banking needs. Thus, it retains the international business of its domestic clients and reduces the risk that some other international bank will steal them away.

TABLE 8.1 The World's 20 Largest Banks

Rank	Company	Country	Revenues ($ Mil)
1	ING Group	Netherlands	147,052
2	Bank of America	United States	134,194
3	BNP Paribas	France	128,726
4	J.P. Morgan Chase & Co	United States	115,475
5	Citigroup	United States	111,055
6	Crédit Agricole	France	105,003
7	HSBC Holdings	United Kingdom	102,680
8	Banco Santander	Spain	100,350
9	Lloyds Banking Group	United Kingdom	95,682
10	Société Générale	France	84,350
11	Industrial & Commercial Bank of China	China	80,501
12	Dexia Group	Belgium	69,491
13	Groupe BPCE	France	69,297
14	Royal Bank of Scotland	United Kingdom	68,088
15	China Construction Bank	China	67,081
16	Barclays	United Kingdom	63,661
17	Banco do Brasil	Brazil	62,891
18	Agricultural Bank of China	China	60,536
19	Bank of China	China	59,212
20	Deutsche Bank	Germany	55,314

Source: Fortune, July 25, 2011, p. F1ff; annual reports, various companies.

An overseas banking operation can be established in several ways. If it is separately incorporated from the parent, it is called a **subsidiary bank**; if it is not separately incorporated, it is called a **branch bank**. Sometimes an international bank may choose to create an **affiliated bank,** an overseas operation in which it takes part ownership in conjunction with a local or foreign partner.

COMMERCIAL BANKING SERVICES International banks and their overseas operations are important providers of international commercial banking services. Exporters and tourists utilize such banking services when they exchange their home currency or traveler's checks for local currency. Although the physical exchange of one country's paper currency for another's is part of international banking operations, a far more important part entails financing and facilitating everyday commercial transactions. For example, when Hallmark orders ¥100 million worth of Hello Kitty merchandise from its Japanese manufacturer Sanrio, with payment due in 90 days, Hallmark may require any of the following banking services:

- Short-term financing of the purchase
- International electronic funds transfer
- Forward purchases of Japanese yen
- Advice about proper documentation for importing and paying for the goods

The international department of the firm's bank will provide any or all of these services as part of its normal commercial banking operations.

INVESTMENT BANKING SERVICES In addition to commercial banking services, most international banks provide investment banking services. Investment banking services are also furnished by large securities firms like Nomura, Morgan Stanley, Goldman Sachs, and Merrill Lynch. Corporate clients hire investment bankers to package and locate long-term debt and equity funding and to arrange mergers and acquisitions of domestic and foreign firms. Competition has forced investment bankers to globalize their operations to secure capital for their clients at the lowest possible cost.

The Eurocurrency Market

Another important facet of the international financial system is the Eurocurrency market. Originally called the Eurodollar market, the Eurocurrency market originated in the early 1950s when the communist-controlled governments of Central Europe and Eastern Europe needed dollars to finance their international trade but feared that the U.S. government would confiscate or block their holdings of dollars in U.S. banks for political reasons. The communist governments solved this problem by using European banks that were willing to maintain dollar accounts for them. Thus, **Eurodollars**—U.S. dollars deposited in European bank accounts—were born. As other banks worldwide, particularly in Canada and Japan, began offering dollar-denominated deposit accounts, the term *Eurodollar* evolved to mean U.S. dollars deposited in any bank account outside the United States. As other currencies became stronger in the post–World War II era— particularly the yen, the pound, and the German mark—the Eurocurrency market broadened to include Euroyen, Europounds, and other currencies. Today a **Eurocurrency** is defined as a currency on deposit outside its country of issue.

The Euroloan market has grown up with the Eurocurrency market. The Euroloan market is extremely competitive, and lenders operate on razor-thin margins. Euroloans are often quoted on the basis of the **London Interbank Offer Rate (LIBOR),** the interest rate that London banks charge each other for short-term Eurocurrency loans. The Euroloan market is often the low-cost source of loans for large, creditworthy borrowers, such as governments and large multinational enterprises (MNEs), for three reasons. First, Euroloans are free of costly government banking regulations, such as reserve requirements, that are designed to control the domestic money supply but that drive up lending costs. Second, Euroloans involve large transactions, so the average cost of making the loans is lower. Third, because only the most creditworthy borrowers use the Euroloan market, the risk premium that lenders charge also is lower.

During the 1970s, U.S. banks complained that reserve requirements and other expensive regulations imposed by the Federal Reserve Board prevented them from competing with European and Asian banks in issuing dollar-denominated international loans, which at the time accounted for more than half of the Euroloan market. Foreign banks lending in Eurodollars were not subject to the regulations. To counter this problem, in 1981 the Federal Reserve Board authorized the creation of international banking facilities. An **international banking facility (IBF)** is an entity of a U.S. bank that is legally distinct from the bank's domestic operations and that may offer only international banking services. IBFs do not need to observe the numerous U.S. domestic banking regulations. Of course, the Federal Reserve Board has issued various regulations to ensure that IBFs do not engage in domestic banking services. For example, IBFs may accept deposits from or make loans to only non–U.S. residents. Nonetheless, IBFs enable U.S. banks to compete with other international bankers on a more equal footing in the critical Euroloan market.

The International Bond Market

The international bond market represents a major source of debt financing for the world's governments, international organizations, and larger firms. This market has traditionally consisted of two types of bonds: foreign bonds and Eurobonds. **Foreign bonds** are bonds issued by a resident of country A but sold to residents of country B and denominated in the currency of country B. For example, the Nestlé Corporation, a Swiss resident, might issue a foreign bond denominated in yen and sold primarily to residents of Japan. A **Eurobond** is a bond issued in the currency of country A but sold to residents of other countries. For example, American Airlines could borrow $500 million to finance new aircraft purchases by selling Eurobonds denominated in dollars to residents of Denmark and Germany. The euro and the U.S. dollar are the dominant currencies in the international bond market (see Figure 8.7).

As the global capital market has evolved, the international bond market has grown increasingly sophisticated. Syndicates of investment banks, securities firms, and commercial banks put together complex packages of international bonds to serve the borrowing needs of large, creditworthy borrowers, such as major MNEs, national governments, and international organizations. The global bond is one such innovative financial instrument. A **global bond** is a large, liquid financial asset that can be traded anywhere at any time. Its use was pioneered by the World Bank, which simultaneously sold $1.5 billion of U.S. dollar–denominated global bonds in North America, Europe, and Japan and succeeded in lowering its interest costs on the bond issue by about 0.225 percentage point. Although 0.225 percentage point may not seem like much, multiplying that amount by $1.5 billion reveals that the bank reduced its annual financing costs by $3,375,000. Attracted by the World Bank's success, many other large organizations, such as Matsushita Electric, the Province of Ontario, Citicorp, and Household Finance, have also issued global bonds.

Other innovative opportunities exist in the bond market. For example, at the borrower's option, bond interest may be paid in one currency and the principal paid in another currency. Or the borrower may secure a lower interest rate by offering inflation protection that pegs the principal repayment to the value of gold or special drawing rights.

Like the Euroloan market, the international bond market is highly competitive, and borrowers are often able to obtain funds on very favorable terms. Large transaction sizes, creditworthy borrowers, and freedom from costly regulations imposed on domestic capital markets all help to lower the interest rates charged on such loans.

Global Equity Markets

The growing importance of multinational operations and improvements in telecommunications technology have also made equity markets more global. Start-up companies are no longer restricted to raising new equity solely from domestic sources. For example, Swiss pharmaceutical firms are a

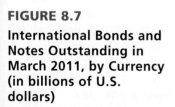

FIGURE 8.7

International Bonds and Notes Outstanding in March 2011, by Currency (in billions of U.S. dollars)

Source: Bank of International Settlements, "International bonds and notes, Table 13B," *BIS Quarterly Review*, June 2011, p. A119.

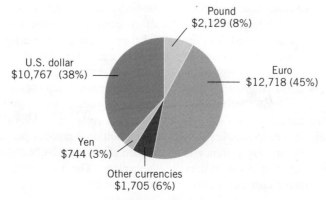

major source of equity capital for new U.S. biotechnology firms. Established firms also tap into the global equity market. When expanding into a foreign market, a firm may choose to raise capital for its foreign subsidiary in the foreign market. The Walt Disney Company, for example, initially sold 51 percent of its Disneyland Paris project to French investors. Numerous MNEs also cross-list their common stocks on multiple stock exchanges. Toyota, for instance, is listed on the Tokyo, London, and New York stock exchanges, thereby enabling Asian, European, and American investors to purchase its shares conveniently. Another innovation is the development of country funds. A **country fund** is a mutual fund that specializes in investing in a given country's firms.

The globalization of equity markets has been facilitated by the globalization of the financial services industry. Most major financial services firms, such as Merrill Lynch, Daiwa Securities, and Deutsche Bank, have expanded operations from their domestic bases into the major international financial centers. These financial services firms are eager to raise capital, provide investment advice, offer stock market analyses, and put together financing deals for clients anywhere around the world.

Offshore Financial Centers

Offshore financial centers focus on offering banking and other financial services to nonresident customers. Many of these centers are located on island states, such as the Bahamas, Bahrain, the Cayman Islands, Bermuda, the Netherlands Antilles, and Singapore. Luxembourg and Switzerland, although not islands, are also important "offshore" financial centers.

MNEs often use offshore financial centers to obtain low-cost Eurocurrency loans. Many MNEs locate financing subsidiaries in these centers to take advantage of the benefits they offer: political stability, a regulatory climate that facilitates international capital transactions, excellent communications links to other major financial centers, and availability of legal, accounting, financial, and other expertise needed to package large loans. The efficiency of offshore financial centers in attracting deposits and then lending these funds to customers worldwide is an important factor in the growing globalization of the capital market.

MyManagementLab
Now that you have finished this chapter, go back to **www.pearsonglobaleditions.com/mymanagementlab** to continue practicing and applying the concepts you've learned.

CHAPTER REVIEW

Summary

A currency's price in the foreign-exchange market is determined by the interaction of the demand for and supply of the currency. Underlying the demand for a particular currency is the desire of foreigners to buy goods, services, and assets of the issuing country. Underlying the supply is the desire of residents to purchase goods, services, and assets owned by foreigners.

Major international banks in financial centers such as London, Hong Kong, Singapore, Tokyo, and New York City play a critical role in the functioning of the foreign-exchange market. Key players in the wholesale market, these banks account for the vast majority of foreign-exchange transactions. In serving their clients' needs, the banks are also an important component of the retail market. They assist commercial customers, speculators, and arbitrageurs in acquiring foreign currency on both the spot and forward markets.

An important feature of the foreign-exchange market is its time dimension. International businesses may buy currency in the spot market for immediate delivery or in the forward market for future delivery. The forward market, currency futures,

and currency options enable firms to protect themselves from unfavorable future exchange rate movements.

Arbitrage activities affect the demand for and supply of foreign exchange. The theory of purchasing power parity (PPP) states that the prices of tradable goods will tend to equalize among countries. Arbitrage of foreign exchange itself is even more important. Two-point arbitrage implies that the exchange rate between two currencies will be the same in all geographic markets. Three-point arbitrage links individual foreign-exchange markets together. Covered-interest arbitrage causes geographic differences in interest rates to equal differences between spot and forward exchange rates.

The international capital market is growing in sophistication as a result of technological advances in telecommunications and computers. Major international banks still utilize their traditional correspondent relationships with other banks but are also increasingly engaged in overseas bank operations themselves. The Eurocurrency market allows banks of any country to conduct lending operations in whatever currencies their clients require. MNEs now commonly raise capital, both debt and equity, on a global basis, wherever its cost is lowest.

Review Questions

1. What determines the demand for any given currency in the foreign-exchange market?
2. What determines the supply of any given currency in the foreign-exchange market?
3. How are prices established in the foreign-exchange market?
4. What is the role of international banks in the foreign-exchange market?
5. Explain the different techniques that firms can use to protect themselves from future changes in exchange rates.
6. Discuss the major types of arbitrage activities that affect the foreign-exchange market.
7. Describe the various forms a bank's overseas operations may take.
8. What are Eurocurrencies?
9. What are the major characteristics of offshore financial centers?

Questions for Discussion

1. Suppose the Federal Reserve Board unexpectedly raises interest rates in the United States. How will this action affect the foreign-exchange market?
2. How important are communications and computing technologies to the smooth functioning of the foreign-exchange market? If the technological advances of the past four decades were eliminated—for example, no PCs or satellite telecommunications—how would the foreign-exchange market be affected?
3. Do you expect the U.S. dollar to maintain its position as the dominant currency in the foreign-exchange market or will the euro or the Chinese yuan supplant it? Explain your answer.
4. Suppose the spot pound and the three-month forward pound are both selling for $2.00, while U.S. interest rates are 10 percent and British interest rates are 6 percent. Using covered-interest arbitrage theory, describe what will happen to the spot price of the pound, the three-month forward price of the pound, interest rates in the United States, and interest rates in the United Kingdom when arbitrageurs enter this market.
5. How important is the creation of international banking facilities to the international competitiveness of the U.S. banking industry?
6. What would be the impact on world trade and investment if there were only one currency?

Building Global Skills

Please refer to Figure 8.4 to answer the following questions:
1. What is the spot rate for the British pound on Wednesday in terms of the U.S. dollar? (Or, stated differently, how many dollars does a pound cost? Or, from the U.S. perspective, what is the direct quote on pounds?)
2. What is the spot price for the dollar on Wednesday in terms of the Swiss franc? (Or, from the U.S. perspective, what is the indirect rate on Swiss francs?)
3. Calculate the cross rate of exchange between the British pound and the Swiss franc.
4. Calculate the annualized forward premium or discount on six-month forward yen.
5. If you are planning to go to Japan this summer, should you buy your yen today? Why or why not?
6. According to the covered-interest arbitrage theory, is the United States or Japan expected to have higher interest rates?
7. According to the covered-interest arbitrage theory, what is the expected difference between interest rates in the United States and Japan?
8. According to the international Fisher effect, is expected inflation higher in Japan or the United States?
9. Did the value of the Canadian dollar rise or fall between Tuesday and Wednesday?

CLOSING CASE · SUBPRIME MELTDOWN, GLOBAL RECESSION

The recession of 2008–2009 was truly global: World GDP fell from $60.6 trillion in 2008 to $58.2 trillion in 2009, while world merchandise trade plummeted from $16.2 trillion to $12.5 trillion. Unemployment in the United States reached 10.4 percent; the United Kingdom, 8.0 percent; Ireland, 14.8 percent; France, 10.0 percent; and Spain, 20.7 percent. Few countries escaped this economic tsunami: Every EU member save Poland suffered a contraction in its GDP, as did Brazil, Canada, Japan, the United States, and numerous other countries. Among the few countries to be spared were China, India,

and South Korea, which nonetheless suffered decreases in their GDP growth rates.

One key cause of the global recession was the globalization of financial markets that allowed bursting real estate bubbles in numerous countries—including Australia, Ireland, Italy, Spain, the United Kingdom, and the United States—to spew their damage well beyond their national borders. Much of the blame can be laid at the feet of the United States, where housing prices boomed as a result of the cheap credit policies of the Federal Reserve Bank, declining lending standards, and regulatory inattention. When the

American housing bubble finally burst, the ensuing "subprime meltdown" traumatized the global financial services industry, damaging banks, brokerage houses, hedge funds, mortgage brokers, and municipal bond issuers throughout the world.

Over the past 10 years, some $2 trillion worth of securities backed by American home mortgages were sold globally by highly paid investment bankers to customers worldwide. Pension funds and hedge funds around the world were eager to get their piece of the action, secure in the belief that American housing prices would continue to rise and that homeowners would continue to make their house payments. Unfortunately, those beliefs proved to be inaccurate, and the global nature of the capital market ensured that the pain created by the meltdown in the American housing market would cascade throughout the world.

The problem began with the low interest rate policy that the Federal Reserve System adopted in 2001 to combat a developing recession. These low interest rates made it cheaper to purchase homes, and many Americans took advantage of this opportunity. Other homeowners, lured by a barrage of TV advertising, chose to refinance their homes, many taking advantage of rising home prices to extract equity from their homes. In hot markets like Southern California and southern Florida, newspaper articles abounded about real estate speculators who would put a small deposit on a condo unit during the preconstruction phase of a new development and make a quick profit by selling their unit to a new buyer when the condo project was completed. TV shows like *Flip This House* provided step-by-step instructions for their viewers to get their share of the action.

In this frenzied market—where housing prices were rising and were a "sure thing" to continue to rise—many mortgage lenders relaxed their traditional 20 percent down payment requirement and began to offer no down payment, interest-only, adjustable rate mortgages. These so-called subprime mortgages began to become increasingly common. Of course, the easy lending standards of the subprime market boosted demand for homes, further raising prices. This boom-time mentality encouraged developers to build more inventory; by the third quarter of 2007 there were a record 2.1 million housing units available for sale.

The flow of money into home mortgages was facilitated by innovative investment bankers in money markets like New York and London. Banks pooled the mortgages of thousands of homeowners and packaged them into new financial instruments called collateralized debt obligations (CDOs). A bank might pool a thousand mortgages, for example, worth a total of $300 million, into a CDO. The cash flow rights from these CDOs would be subdivided into different pieces, or tranches. Each tranche would carry a different risk-reward profile. The most senior tranche would enjoy the right to the first cash flows generated by the underlying mortgages. This tranche would be relatively risk free, so it would offer a relatively low rate of return. Conversely, the most junior tranche of the CDO would enjoy the highest rates of return, but would also be highly risky, for it would be the first to be affected if any of the mortgagees defaulted. Nonetheless, the creation of the tranches allowed investors to choose the risk-reward trade-off that best met their needs and preferences.

The growth of the subprime CDO market, which ultimately reached $400 billion, was stimulated by another financial innovation, specialized investment vehicles (SIVs), which were created by investment bankers and hedge funds to invest in CDOs. The banks and hedge funds collected lucrative fees to create, market, and operate the SIVs on the behalf of the investors to whom they were sold. And SIVs had a particular advantage to banks: Because the banks were not owners of the SIVs, the SIVs were not on the banks' balance sheets. Citigroup, for example, created seven separate SIVs, with combined assets of $80 billion, specializing in subprime CDOs. Of course, foreign banks were eager to crash the lucrative subprime SIV market. Switzerland's UBS invested more than $40 billion in SIVs, CDOs, and other subprime holdings. SIVs were also created by the Bank of Montreal, Germany's Dresdner Kleinwort, the Netherlands' Rabobank, and HSBC and Standard Chartered of the United Kingdom. One German state-owned bank, Sachsen LB, established an office in Dublin, Ireland, to trade and market CDOs, while the Bank of China purchased $9.7 billion of CDOs backed by U.S. subprime mortgages. Even smaller banks got involved, such as IKB Deutsche Industriebank, whose primary business was lending money to small German companies. In 2002, it established a subsidiary, Rhineland Funding Capital Corporation, to invest in high yielding bonds. Most of Rhineland's investments were in CDOs backed by American subprime mortgages.

Unfortunately, Rhineland and other purveyors of SIVs fell into the classic trap of borrowing short and lending long. Most SIVs were financed by issuing commercial paper, a form of short-term financing that typically carries low interest rates. They then invested in high-yielding CDOs backed by subprime mortgages. In normal times, the SIVs benefited from the spread between the two interest rates. But a perfect storm soon hit the U.S. mortgage market. The Federal Reserve Bank began to worry more about inflation than recession. In June 2004, it raised the federal funds rate, then 1.00 percent, a quarter of a point. This modest increase was a harbinger of future rate hikes. In the ensuing two years, the Federal Reserve Bank increased the federal funds rate 16 times, reaching a peak of 5.25 percent in June 2006. As the federal funds rate rose, so too did other short-term interest rates, raising the borrowing costs of many SIVs. These higher short-term interest rates also elevated the borrowing costs of homeowners who had utilized an adjustable rate mortgage to finance their home purchases. Higher borrowing costs caused housing prices to begin to fall in many markets—particularly ones that had enjoyed the greatest increases in prices, such as in Florida or Southern California—leaving some borrowers who put little or no money down for the homes in the unhappy position of owing more on their mortgage loan than their home was worth. Homeowners increasingly choose to—or were forced to—default on their mortgages. A vicious cycle developed: As defaults increased, the inventory of unsold housing rose, which intensified the downward pressure on housing prices, which then caused more homeowners to default.

Rising default rates triggered a decline in the value of CDOs backed by subprime loans. Soon SIVs found it more difficult and more expensive—sometimes even impossible—to issue new commercial paper to replace their short-term loans as they matured. Unable to secure short-term financing, the SIVs were forced to dump their CDOs on the market at distressed prices.

The result was a flood of red ink, massive loan write-offs, and concerns that the world economy might plunge into recession. UBS alone lost $37 billion on loans associated with CDOs and SIVs backed by subprime mortgages. To restore its shattered balance sheet, it sold a 12.4 percent share of the company to the Singapore Investment Corporation, a sovereign wealth fund, and an unidentified investor from the Middle East for $11.5 billion. Morgan Stanley wrote off $13.1 billion of bad subprime loans. It too was forced to restore its balance sheet by selling a 10 percent ownership share of the firm to the China Investment Corporation for $5 billion. Citigroup's potential exposure was over $21 billion, forcing it to seek new capital as well—$7.5 billion from the Abu Dhabi Investment Authority, in return for a 4.9 percent ownership share. And the list of losses goes on: Merrill Lynch, $25.1 billion; HSBC, $7.5 billion; IKB Deutsche Industriebank, €3.5 billion; Deutsche Bank, $7.4 billion; Société Général, $4.8 billion; Royal Bank of Scotland, $6.0 billion; Barclays, $4.5 billion; Swiss Reinsurance, $875 million—a Who's Who of the international financial world. And a host of smaller investors, such as the city governments of Manley, Australia, and Narvik, Norway, got clobbered as well. Manley's losses were relatively mild, for its council had invested only A$3 million in CDOs. But Narvik invested $44 million in CDOs and related products—an amount equal to a quarter of the town's annual budget. Its employees went without paychecks in the weeks before Christmas as a result.

The worst was yet to come. In September 2008, new crises erupted. The U.S. government effectively took over control of the Federal National Mortgage Association (often referred to as Fannie Mae) and the Federal Home Loan Mortgage Corporation (known as Freddie Mac), two huge players in the U.S. mortgage market, and granted a $85 billion bridge loan to American International Group, an insurance conglomerate. The venerable investment house Lehman Brothers slipped into bankruptcy; to avoid a similar fate, Merrill Lynch arranged to sell itself to Bank of America.

Unfortunately, the United States was not the only country to suffer from a real estate bubble. The construction and housing markets in Ireland and Spain, for example, boomed as a result of the low-interest rate policies of the European Central Bank, which were designed to stimulate the then stagnating economies of the majority of the eurozone members. Other EU members, including France, Italy, and the United Kingdom, also experienced housing bubbles, as did dozens of other countries in Asia, Europe, and Latin America. As their bubbles burst, governments were forced to bail out their crippled financial services industries. The United Kingdom's bank bailout bore a price tag of more than £500 billion. Ireland was forced to nationalize or recapitalize the country's three largest banks, as did Iceland.

Case Questions

1. The case refers to the "classic trap of borrowing short and lending long." Explain what this means. What are the advantages of borrowing short and lending long? What are the disadvantages?
2. Why did the sovereign wealth funds of Singapore, Abu Dhabi, and China choose to invest in UBS, Citigroup, and Morgan Stanley at a time when they were performing so poorly? Do these investments create any public policy issues? If so, what are they?
3. What happens to an economy when a housing bubble bursts?
4. The change in mortgage lending standards in the United States created a global financial crisis. Do you think an international financial regulatory agency should be created to reduce the likelihood that such crises will arise in the future? Why or why not?

Sources: "Bank bail-out adds £1.5 trillion to debt," *The Telegraph,* January 16, 2011 (online); "Mounting fears pummel world markets as banking giants rush to find buyers," *Wall Street Journal,* September 18, 2008, p. A1; "Stocks surge as 2 major banks advance turnaround plans," *Wall Street Journal,* April 2, 2008, p. A1; "S&P lowers rating on Alabama County," *Wall Street Journal,* April 1, 2008 (online); "Crunch, from Alabama to stocks," *Wall Street Journal,* March 7, 2008, p. C1; "France presses bank to dump besieged chief over trading," *Wall Street Journal,* January 30, 2008, p. A1; "UBS takes a $14 billion write-off," *New York Times,* January 30, 2008 (online); "Credit scare spreads in U.S., abroad," *Wall Street Journal,* January 22, 2008, p. A1; "Loss pressures Morgan Stanley CEO," *Wall Street Journal,* December 20, 2007, p. A1; "$9.4 billion write-down at Morgan Stanley," *New York Times,* December 20, 2007 (online); "U.S. mortgage crisis rivals S&L meltdown," *Wall Street Journal,* December 10, 2007, p. A1; "Societe General to bail out SIV," *New York Times,* December 10, 2007 (online); "U.S. credit crisis adds to gloom in Arctic Norway," *New York Times,* December 2, 2007 (online); "Abu Dhabi to bolster Citigroup with $7.5 billion capital infusion," *Wall Street Journal,* November 27, 2007, p. A3; "$75 billion fund is seen as stopgap," *New York Times,* November 1, 2007 (online); "How London created a snarl in global markets," *Wall Street Journal,* October 18, 2007, p. A1; "How subprime mess ensnared German bank; IKB gets a bailout," *Wall Street Journal,* August 10, 2007, p. A1.

Endnotes

1. "Rise and rise of the Canadian dollar," *Wall Street Journal,* January 12, 2011; "Currency rise helps Canadian N.H.L. teams," *New York Times,* December 1, 2009; "Wallet check: It's pain or gain," *Wall Street Journal,* October 19, 2009, p. C1; "Development interest lacking in Kirk Forest Products land," *Bridgewater Bulletin,* February 19, 2008, p. A10; "Land of the spree," *Wall Street Journal,* December 15, 2007, p. W1: "They can only dream of a green Christmas," *Houston Chronicle,* December 9, 2007, p. D6; "Loonie's rise yields splitting pain for Canada,"

Wall Street Journal, November 12, 2007, p. C1; "Canada is giddy about the loonie and twitting U.S.," *Wall Street Journal,* September 22, 2007, p. A1.

2. To simplify the exposition, we assumed the foreign-exchange supply curve is upward sloping like most supply curves. Unfortunately, foreign-exchange supply curves may bend backward, a complication that can be left for graduate students in economics and finance to deal with.

3. "Currency trading soars," *Wall Street Journal,* September 1, 2010, p. A1.

Formulation of National Trade Policies

AFTER STUDYING THIS CHAPTER, YOU SHOULD BE ABLE TO:

1. Present the major arguments in favor of and against governmental intervention in international trade.

2. Identify the advantages and disadvantages of adopting an industrial policy.

3. Analyze the role of domestic politics in formulating a country's international trade policies.

4. Describe the major tools countries use to restrict trade.

5. Specify the techniques countries use to promote international trade.

6. Explain how countries protect themselves against unfair trade practices.

Access a host of interactive learning aids at **www.pearsonglobaleditions.com/ mymanagementlab** to help strengthen your understanding of the chapter concepts.

MyManagementLab

Michael Webberley/UPPA/Photoshot/Newscom

JUMBO BATTLE OVER JUMBO JETS

Since its initial commercial flight in 1969, the Boeing 747 benefited from its status as the world's largest commercial aircraft. Its costs per seat mile were lower than that of any other aircraft available, largely because the 747 can seat as many as 495 people. Although its low costs were attractive on transatlantic and transcontinental routes, they were of particular importance in charter, transpacific, and freighter operations. Boeing's monopoly in the jumbo jet market gave it an advantage over Airbus in selling smaller aircraft as well. Spare parts can often be used for different models of aircraft produced by the same manufacturer, which sometimes is enough of an advantage to sway an airline to purchase a Boeing product over the comparable one manufactured by Airbus.

Airbus targeted the 747 for years. In 2000, its engineers finalized the plans for a 650-seat aircraft, the A380, which dwarfs the 747. The A380 then underwent extensive design, testing, and certification procedures. In October 2007, Singapore Airlines offered the first commercial flight of an A380, from Singapore to Sydney.

Airbus executives believe this aircraft will destroy the lucrative monopoly that the Boeing 747 held in the jumbo jet market. Airbus calculates the A380's costs per seat mile are 17 percent less than those of the 747. However, R&D costs for the A380 are estimated to have run between $12 billion and $16 billion. To help finance these up-front costs, Airbus obtained $3.5 billion in low-cost loans—called "launch aid"—from the German, French, and British governments. (Airbus's original investors were from France, Germany, Spain, and the United Kingdom.) Boeing officials asserted these loans to Airbus were nothing more than government subsidies and should be barred under international trade law. Moreover, Boeing believed that Airbus officials vastly overestimated the size of the market. Airbus judged the market for superjumbo jets will reach 1,500 in the next 20 years, and thus the A380 has a bright future. Boeing argued that the true market is only one-quarter to one-third of that estimate, and thus the A380 will be a financial disaster. Should Boeing be correct, it fears that the government loans to its rival will be forgiven. Worse, the A380 would then continue in production, dragging down the profitability of Boeing's 747 operations.

The European Union (EU) and the United States have fought over this issue before. The U.S. government has argued that previous European loans to Airbus have been written off as worthless, thereby providing the airframe manufacturer with illegal subsidies. For example, in early 1999 the German Finance Ministry relieved DaimlerChrysler Aerospace AG of an obligation to repay $750 million in loans to design Airbus's A330 and A340 jets. EU officials respond that Boeing's commercial aircraft division has benefited from hidden subsidies from the U.S. government. EU officials believe that Boeing has been able to develop new aircraft technologies by winning U.S. Defense Department contracts that are limited to U.S. firms. Having acquired that technology from its defense contracts, Boeing then can transfer the technology to its commercial aircraft operations.

A 1992 agreement between the EU and the United States led to a truce in this verbal war. That accord limited the amount of indirect subsidies the United States could grant Boeing through military contracts, while European governments were allowed to provide limited loans to Airbus for development of new aircraft. However, this agreement predates the World Trade Organization (WTO) and the new obligations imposed on members of that organization (see the next chapter for a full discussion of the WTO). In 2004, U.S. officials withdrew from the 1992 accord and filed a complaint with the WTO, arguing that the A380 has indeed benefited from illegal subsidies. The EU quickly filed a countercomplaint against Boeing. In 2010 the WTO ruled that the EU's launch aid for the A380, as well as for the A300, A310, A320, A330, and A340 series of Airbus aircraft violated its rules. In total, the WTO deemed a total of some $20 billion in government loans an improper export subsidy, as they offered terms to Airbus unavailable in normal commercial lending markets. In 2011, the WTO ruled that Boeing received $5.3 billion in subsidies through contracts awarded by the U.S. Department of Defense and the National Aeronautics and Space Administration. Both parties have appealed the WTO's decisions, but most expert observers believe the United States and the European Union will ultimately have to negotiate a settlement, as the monies involved are so large.[1] ■

In today's global economy, many firms benefit from international trade, finding foreign markets a rich source of additional customers. Exports generate domestic jobs, so many national governments promote the success of their countries' domestic firms in international markets. But at times firms believe that their foreign competitors have gained an unfair advantage as a result of policies adopted by their governments. As a result, as is the case in the commercial aircraft market, a firm may ask its national government for protection against the foreigners. In this chapter, we discuss the development of national trade policies that protect domestic firms from foreign competition and help promote the country's exports. We also explore the rationale for these policies and the means by which governments implement them.

Rationales for Trade Intervention

Politicians, economists, and businesspeople have been arguing for centuries over government policy toward international trade. Two principal issues have shaped the debate on appropriate trade policies:

1. Whether a national government should intervene to protect the country's domestic firms by taxing foreign goods entering the domestic market or constructing other barriers against imports
2. Whether a national government should directly help the country's domestic firms increase their foreign sales through export subsidies, government-to-government negotiations, and guaranteed loan programs

In North America, the trade policy debate has recently focused on the issue of whether the government should promote "free" trade or "fair" trade. **Free trade** implies that the national government exerts minimal influence on the exporting and importing decisions of private firms and individuals. **Fair trade**, sometimes called **managed trade**, suggests that the national government should actively intervene to ensure that domestic firms' exports receive an equitable share of foreign markets and that imports are controlled to minimize losses of domestic jobs and market share in specific industries. Some fair traders also argue that the government should ensure a "level playing field" on which foreign and domestic firms can compete on equal terms. Although sounding reasonable, the "level playing field" argument is often used to justify policies that restrict foreign competition.

The outcome of the debate is critical to international managers. The policies individual countries adopt affect the size and profitability of foreign markets and investments, as well as the degree to which firms are threatened by foreign imports in their domestic markets. Governments worldwide are continually pressured by successful and efficient firms that produce goods for export, as well as by the firms' labor forces and the communities in which their factories are located, to adopt policies supporting freer trade. Companies such as Sony, Volkswagen, and Caterpillar gain increased sales and investment opportunities in foreign markets when international trade barriers are lowered. At the same time, governments are petitioned by firms beleaguered by foreign competitors, as well as by these firms' labor forces and the communities in which their factories are located, to raise barriers to imported goods by adopting fair-trade policies, for they gain increased sales opportunities in their domestic markets when international trade barriers exist.

The debate also affects consumers in every country, influencing the prices they pay for automobiles, clothing, televisions, and thousands of other goods. Barriers erected by the U.S. government against free trade in textiles and sugar, for example, raise the prices that parents must pay to clothe and feed their children.

Industry-Level Arguments

The argument for free trade follows Adam Smith's analysis outlined in Chapter 6: Voluntary exchange makes both parties to the transaction better off and allocates resources to their highest valued use. In Smith's view the welfare of a country and its citizens is best promoted by allowing self-interested individuals, regardless of where they reside, to exchange goods, services, and assets as they see fit. However, many businesspeople, politicians, and policymakers believe that, under certain circumstances, deviations from free trade are appropriate. In this section, we review the primary arguments against free trade and for government intervention, and we discuss trade policies that focus on the needs of individual industries. In the next section, we explore broader, national-level policies.

THE NATIONAL DEFENSE ARGUMENT National defense has often been used as a reason to support governmental protection of specific industries. Because world events can suddenly turn hostile to a country's interests, the **national defense argument** holds that a country must be self-sufficient in critical raw materials, machinery, and technology or else be vulnerable to foreign threats. For instance, the vulnerability of Japan's supply lines was demonstrated by the extensive damage done to its merchant marine fleet by Allied submarines during World War II. After the war, Japan banned the importation of rice as a means of promoting domestic self-sufficiency in the country's dietary staple. Similarly, the United States, to retain shipbuilding skills and expertise within the country in case of war, has developed numerous programs to support its domestic shipbuilding industry. For example, all U.S. naval vessels must be built in U.S. shipyards, and ocean transportation between U.S. ports must be conducted by U.S.-built ships. Many of the jobs in the U.S. shipbuilding industry would be lost without these federal protections because U.S. shipyards are not competitive with those of Korea, Norway, China, or Vietnam. One federal study found that the average bid by U.S. shipyards on commercial contracts was 97 percent higher than the lowest foreign bid.[2]

The national defense argument appeals to the general public, which is concerned that its country will be pushed around by other countries that control critical resources. Many special-interest groups have used this politically appealing argument to protect their industries from foreign competition. The U.S. mohair industry, for example, produces wool that was once used in military uniforms. It benefited from federal subsidies after passage of the 1954 National Wool Act, which protected the industry purportedly in the country's strategic interest. Even though the military had long since replaced mohair with synthetic fabrics, the subsidy remained in effect for more than 40 years. Other U.S. industries receiving favorable treatment for national defense reasons include steel, electronics, machine tools, and the merchant marine.[3]

THE INFANT INDUSTRY ARGUMENT Alexander Hamilton, the first U.S. secretary of the treasury, articulated the **infant industry argument** in 1791. Hamilton believed that the newly independent country's infant manufacturing sector possessed a comparative advantage that would ultimately allow it to thrive in international markets. He feared, however, that the young nation's manufacturers would not survive their infancy and adolescence because of fierce competition from more mature European firms. Hamilton thus fought for the imposition of tariffs on numerous imported manufactured goods to give U.S. firms temporary protection from foreign competition until they could fully establish themselves. His philosophy has been adopted by countries worldwide. Japan has been particularly effective in nurturing its domestic industries. Since the end of World War II, Japan has developed thriving metal fabrication industries (iron and steel, aluminum, copper, and zinc) despite its lack of significant natural resources. Japan has done this

To ensure that critical technology and skills remain in the country, the United States government requires that all American naval vessels be built in American shipyards, such as this guided missile destroyer constructed at the Bath Iron Works in Maine.

Reuters/CORBIS

by eliminating tariffs on imports of raw ores and ore concentrates while imposing high tariffs on processed and fabricated metals. For instance, in 1970 no tariff was imposed on copper ore imported in Japan, but fabricated copper products bore tariffs as high as 22 percent. As its metal fabrication industry matured, Japan reduced the level of import protection. Today its tariffs on copper products are negligible.[4]

Governmental nurturing of domestic industries that will ultimately have a comparative advantage can be a powerful economic development strategy, as Japan's postwar economic success indicates. However, determination of which industries deserve infant industry protection is often done on a political rather than an economic basis. Firms, workers, and shareholders are not shy about using the infant industry argument to bolster support for import protection or export subsidies for their industries. Moreover, once an industry is granted protection, it may be reluctant to give it up. Many infant industries end up being protected well into their old age.

MAINTENANCE OF EXISTING JOBS Well-established firms and their workers, particularly in high-wage countries, are often threatened by imports from low-wage countries. To maintain existing employment levels, firms and workers often petition their governments for relief from foreign competition. Government officials, eager to avoid the human and economic misery inflicted on workers and communities when factories are shut down, tend to lend a sympathetic ear to such pleas. Assistance may come in the form of tariffs, quotas, or other barriers, which we discuss in more detail in the next section. The assistance may be temporary, as was the case when Harley-Davidson received tariff protection from Japanese imports for five years in the mid-1980s to allow the firm to revamp its operations and restore its image in the marketplace. Conversely, the assistance may be long lived, as in the case of governmental protection of the U.S. commercial shipbuilding industry, which has extended that industry's life by over 40 years.

STRATEGIC TRADE THEORY When firms and labor union officials plead for government intervention to help them compete internationally, their efforts are usually criticized by economists, who claim that such intervention ultimately harms the economy. The economists base this claim on the theoretical predictions of the classical trade theories—absolute advantage and comparative advantage—discussed in Chapter 6. These trade theories, however, assume that firms operate in perfectly competitive markets of the sort that exist only in economics textbooks. The theories also assume that each country's consumers are able to buy goods and services at the lowest possible prices from the world's most efficient producers. According to the classical theories, any governmental intervention that denies consumers these buying opportunities will make the country as a whole worse off, although it could make certain groups within the society better off.

In the early 1980s, however, new models of international trade—known collectively as **strategic trade theory**—were developed. These models provide a new theoretical justification for government trade intervention, thereby supporting firms' requests for protection. Strategic trade theory makes very different assumptions about the industry environment in which firms operate than do the classical theories. Strategic trade theory applies to those industries capable of supporting only a few firms worldwide, perhaps because of high product development costs or strong experience curve effects. A firm can earn monopoly profits if it can succeed in becoming one of the few firms in such a highly concentrated industry. Strategic trade theory suggests that a national government can make its country better off if it adopts trade policies that improve the competitiveness of its domestic firms in such oligopolistic industries.

Consider the potential market for a new nuclear power plant design, one that could safely and cheaply supply electrical energy. Assume that because of economies of scale, the market will be extremely profitable if one—and only one—firm decides to enter it. Further assume that only two firms, France's Areva and Japan's Toshiba, have the engineering talent and financial resources to develop the new plant design and that both are equally capable of successfully completing the project. Figure 9.1 shows the payoff matrix for the two firms. If Toshiba decides to develop the plant design and Areva decides not to (see the lower left-hand corner), Toshiba profits by $10 billion, while Areva makes nothing. If Areva decides to develop the plant design and Toshiba does not, Areva profits by $10 billion, while Toshiba makes nothing (see the upper right-hand corner). If neither firm chooses to develop the design,

FIGURE 9.1

Payoff Matrix: Profits from Developing a Nuclear Power Plant Design (in billions of dollars)

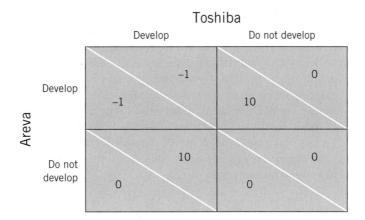

they both make nothing (see the lower right-hand corner). If both decide to develop the design, both will lose $1 billion because the market is too small to be profitable for both of them. Neither firm has a strategy that it should follow regardless of what its rival does.

Now suppose the French government learns of the large profits that one of its country's firms could earn if that firm were the sole developer of the new plant design. If France were to offer Areva a subsidy of $2 billion to develop the new nuclear technology, the payoff matrix would change to that shown in Figure 9.2. Because of the subsidy, Areva's payoff is increased by $2 billion if and only if it develops the technology (see the first row). With the subsidy, Areva will develop the technology regardless of what Toshiba does because Areva makes more money by developing than by not developing. If Toshiba chooses to develop, Areva makes nothing if it does not develop and $1 billion if it does develop. If Toshiba does not develop, Areva makes nothing if it does not develop and $12 billion if it does develop. Thus, Areva will always choose to develop. But if Toshiba knows that Areva will always choose to develop, then the best strategy for Toshiba is not to develop.

What has the French government accomplished with its $2 billion subsidy?

1. It has induced Areva to develop the new nuclear power plant technology.
2. It has induced the Japanese firm to stay out of the market.
3. It has succeeded in allowing a French firm to make a $12 billion profit at a cost to French taxpayers of only $2 billion.

By adopting a strategic trade policy in a market where monopoly profits are available, the French government has made French residents as a group better off by $10 billion ($12 billion in profits minus $2 billion in subsidies).

However, strategic trade theory applies only to markets that are incapable of supporting more than a handful of firms on a worldwide basis. (One industry that may meet the requirements of strategic trade theory is the commercial aircraft industry; see the chapter's opening case, "Jumbo Battle over Jumbo Jets.") Most global industries are more competitive than this. A

FIGURE 9.2

Payoff Matrix: Profits Resulting from a $2 Billion Subsidy to Areva (in billions of dollars)

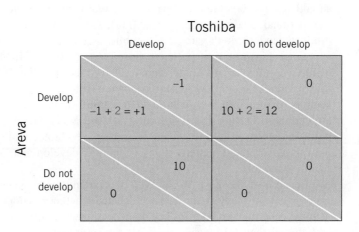

country's wholesale adoption of strategic trade policies to cover a broad group of industries may actually reduce the country's overall international competitiveness because favoring certain industries inevitably hurts others. For example, if the French government chooses to subsidize the nuclear power industry, the demand for and the salaries paid to the mechanical engineers, computer programmers, and systems analysts needed by the nuclear power industry will rise, thereby reducing the international competitiveness of other French industries requiring such skilled personnel. Further, the benefit of the subsidy could be neutralized if another country adopts a similar strategy. If Japan responded to France's $2 billion subsidy by giving a $3 billion subsidy to Toshiba, the payoff matrix would change: Toshiba would be encouraged to develop the power plant as well. Any anticipated monopoly profits might be dissipated if the two countries engaged in an all-out subsidy war.

National Trade Policies

The policies just discussed address the needs of individual industries. A national government may also develop trade policies that begin by taking an economy-wide perspective. After assessing the needs of the national economy, the government then adopts industry-by-industry policies to promote the country's overall economic agenda.

ECONOMIC DEVELOPMENT PROGRAMS An important policy goal of many governments, particularly those of developing countries, is economic development. International commerce can play a major role in economic development programs. Countries that depend on a single export often choose to diversify their economies to reduce the impact of, say, a bad harvest or falling prices for the dominant export. For example, the West African country of Ghana, which once depended heavily on cocoa, began an industrialization program to protect itself from fluctuations in cocoa prices. Dubai chose to diversify away from its heavy dependency on oil sales, electing to do so by making the emirate a business center and aviation hub. Dubai's international airport, already the world's third largest, is on track to handle 160 million passengers a year once its $8 billion expansion program is completed.[5]

As discussed in Chapter 2, some countries, such as Singapore, South Korea, and Taiwan, based their post–World War II economic development on heavy reliance on exports. According to this **export promotion strategy**, a country encourages firms to compete in foreign markets by harnessing some advantage the country possesses, such as low labor costs. Other countries, such as Australia, Argentina, India, and Brazil, adopted an **import substitution strategy** after World War II; such a strategy encourages the growth of domestic manufacturing industries by erecting high barriers to imported goods. Many multinational corporations (MNCs) responded by locating production facilities within these countries to avoid the costs resulting from the high barriers. In general, the export promotion strategy has been more successful than the import substitution strategy, as Chapter 2 indicated.

INDUSTRIAL POLICY In many countries the government plays an active role in managing the national economy. Often an important element of this task is determining which industries should receive favorable governmental treatment. Bureaucrats within Japan's Ministry of International Trade and Industry (MITI), for example, identify emerging technologies and products and through subsidies, public statements, and behind-the-scenes maneuvering encourage Japanese firms to enter those markets. (In 2001, MITI's name was changed to the Ministry of Economy, Trade, and Industry.) During the 1950s and 1960s, MITI actively diverted scarce credit and foreign exchange from low-value-added, labor-intensive industries such as textiles into high-value-added, capital-intensive heavy industries such as steel and automobiles. During the 1970s and 1980s, MITI targeted industries with high growth potential, such as semiconductors, aerospace, biotechnology, and ceramics. The South Korean government patterned its economic development strategies after the successful Japanese model.

Because of the post–World War II economic successes of Japan and South Korea, the governments of many countries have debated whether to adopt **industrial policy**, by which the national government identifies key domestic industries critical to the country's future economic growth and then formulates programs that promote their competitiveness. Ideally, industrial policy assists a country's firms in capturing large shares of important, growing global markets, as MITI has done for Japanese multinational corporations (MNCs).

Many experts, however, do not view industrial policy as a panacea for improving the global competitiveness of a country's firms. They argue that government bureaucrats cannot perfectly identify the right industries to favor under such a policy. As an example, they cite France, where postwar industrial policies targeting automobiles, computers, military and commercial aircraft, and telecommunications created some spectacularly unprofitable enterprises that required large government subsidies. These industries became a drag on the French economy rather than a generator of new wealth. Even Japan has not been infallible. During the early 1980s, MITI bureaucrats encouraged domestic consumer electronics firms to develop high-definition television (HDTV), which relied on Japan's lead in analog-based TV technology. Unfortunately, the technical transmission standards for HDTV adopted by U.S. and European regulators relied on more sophisticated digital technology being developed by Western firms rather than the dated analog technology imposed on Japanese firms by MITI. Consequently, the multibillion-dollar investment of the leading Japanese consumer electronics firms in analog-based HDTV turned out to be a total loss.

Opponents of industrial policy also fear that the choice of industries to receive governmental largesse will depend on the domestic political clout of those industries, rather than on their potential international competitiveness. Instead of selecting future winners in the international marketplace, opponents say, industrial policy will become a more sophisticated-sounding version of pork barrel politics.

At the heart of the industrial policy debate is the question of what is the proper role of government in a market economy. Not surprisingly, in the United States recent Republican administrations have rejected formally adopting an industrial policy, on the grounds that the government should limit its role in the economy.[6] Conversely, the Clinton administration believed that improving the global competitiveness of the country's firms was too important to be left to the private sector. To further this belief, during its first term the Clinton administration designated five emerging technologies that would receive increased federal R&D support: genetics, health care information systems, electronics, automobiles and highway systems, and computer software.[7]

PUBLIC CHOICE ANALYSIS Although many arguments favoring governmental trade intervention are couched in terms of national interest, such intervention typically helps some special-interest groups but invariably hurts other domestic interests and the general public. For example, President Bush's decision to impose tariffs on imported steel during his first term in office helped U.S. steel producers but jeopardized the more numerous steel-using domestic firms. It also reduced the work available to dockworkers who unload foreign steel in Baltimore, New York, Houston, Long Beach, and other port cities and raised the prices that American consumers pay for automobiles, refrigerators, and other goods made of steel.

Why do national governments adopt public policies that hinder international business and hurt their own citizenry overall, even though the policies may benefit small groups within their societies? According to **public choice analysis**, a branch of economics that analyzes public decision making, the special interest will often dominate the general interest on any given issue for a simple reason: Special-interest groups are willing to work harder for the passage of laws favorable to their interests than the general public is willing to work for the defeat of laws unfavorable to its interests. For example, under the 1920 Jones Act, the United States restricts foreign ships from providing transportation services between U.S. ports. This restriction is supported by owners of U.S. oceangoing vessels, who gain increased profits estimated at $630 million per year. However, the Jones Act is also estimated to increase the transportation costs that consumers pay by $10.5 billion annually, or $35 per person. Further, like other restrictions on free trade, the Jones Act has had unintended consequences, as Map 9.1 suggests.

Public choice analysis suggests that few consumers will be motivated to learn how the Jones Act impacts them or to write or call their elected officials to save a trivial sum like $35. The special interests, however, such as shipowners and members of U.S. maritime unions, are motivated to know all the ins and outs of the Jones Act and to protect it from repeal because what they gain makes it worth their while to do so. As a result, members of Congress constantly hear from special-interest groups about the importance of preserving

MAP 9.1

An Effect of the Jones Act

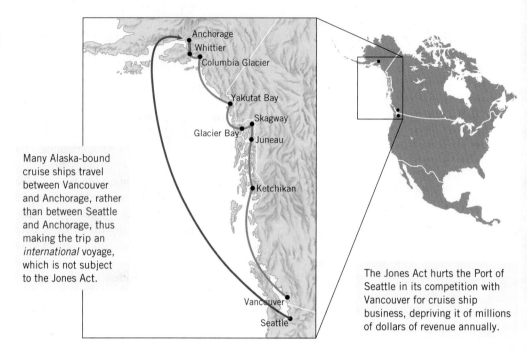

Many Alaska-bound cruise ships travel between Vancouver and Anchorage, rather than between Seattle and Anchorage, thus making the trip an *international* voyage, which is not subject to the Jones Act.

The Jones Act hurts the Port of Seattle in its competition with Vancouver for cruise ship business, depriving it of millions of dollars of revenue annually.

the Jones Act, while the average consumer is silent on the issue.[8] Knowing that they will be harmed by the special-interest groups and will not be rewarded by the general public if they repeal the Jones Act, members of Congress will rationally vote with the special interests on this issue.

According to public choice analysis, domestic trade policies that affect international business stem not from some grandiose vision of a country's international responsibilities but rather from the mundane interaction of politicians trying to get elected. And who elects the politicians? The people in their legislative districts. Hence, former Speaker of the House of Representatives Tip O'Neill's brilliant insight: "All politics is local." A good example is Japan's unwillingness to open its markets to imported rice because of the need of Japan's ruling party in the Diet (Japan's parliament) to retain the votes of local farmers. The impact of this policy on Texas rice farmers, the port of Houston, or the world economy is of little concern to the domestic politicians.

Savvy international businesspeople recognize these political realities. Often a foreign firm needs to find domestic political allies to run interference for it. For example, Nissan and Toyota received much criticism for the size of their exports to the U.S. market, so in the 1980s they began building new factories in the United States. The congressional delegations of the states where factories are located can now be expected to support the firms legislatively to protect the jobs of their constituents working for the Japanese firms.

Barriers to International Trade

We have seen that domestic politics often causes countries to try to protect their domestic firms from foreign competitors by erecting barriers to trade. Such forms of government intervention can be divided into two categories: tariffs and nontariff barriers. Countries have been erecting trade barriers since the creation of the modern nation-state in the sixteenth century in hopes of increasing national income, promoting economic growth, and/or raising their citizens' standard of living. Sometimes, as you just read, national trade policies that benefit special-interest groups are adopted at the expense of the general public or society at large.

Tariffs

A **tariff** is a tax placed on a good that is traded internationally. Some tariffs are levied on goods as they leave the country (an **export tariff**) or as they pass through one country bound for another (a **transit tariff**). Most, however, are collected on imported goods (an **import tariff**). Three forms of import tariffs exist:

| VENTURING ABROAD | EMIRATES AIRLINE EXPANSION: THE CASE OF THE CANADIAN MARKET |

Dubai's flagship carrier "Emirates Airline" represents one of the fastest-growing corporations in the United Arab Emirates (UAE) and has received more than 400 global awards for service excellence in linking Asia to Europe and the Americas. In its effort to further expand internationally and cater to the increasing demand of its Asian customers, Emirates requested that the Canadian government enables it to increase its current quota of three flights per week to Pearson International Airport in Toronto to daily service from Dubai to Toronto, Calgary, and Vancouver airports.

Negotiations between the two lasted for few years. In the fourth quarter of 2010, the Canadian government decided to retain the non-tariff barrier (NTB) on Emirates' flights to Canada, claiming that more landing rights will result in an unfair "capacity dumping" into its airline market.

Unlike Emirates Airline, Canada's leading airline (Air Canada) does not offer services to most key cities in Southeast Asia, Africa, and the Middle East and relies on its European partners to transport passengers onto these routes. Therefore, by protecting a prime national firm against a foreign competitor the Canadian government has deprived travelers (mostly Canadian) from shorter journey times and more choice in prices and services. Furthermore, in retaliation to Canada's action, the UAE government placed restrictions on several Canadian firms dealing with the UAE (that is ranked seventeenth largest export market for Canada) and removed it from the Visa waiver program, thus forcing all its citizens to obtain an entry Visa to the UAE prior to travelling.

Emirates argued that increasing the current frequency and adding more cities to its network would create 2,800 jobs in Canada, while keeping its share to just under 2 percent of the country's international airline services. On the other hand, Air Canada is facing increasing criticism from customers relating to bad service, despite it being supported by millions of dollars provided by the Canadian government.

Currently, Emirates Airline's expansion efforts into the Canadian market seem to rely on a change in Canada's airline protection policies. As a result, Emirates has launched multiple campaigns that portray the benefits that Canada could obtain from such an endeavor and focused its energy on further expansion within other North and South American countries. To that end, starting in January 2012, Emirates will be flying to six U.S. cities, some of which will be at the rate of two and three flights per day. Thus, it remains to be seen if Asian customers would start using Emirates routes to the United States as connection to Canadian cities.

1. An **ad valorem tariff** is assessed as a percentage of the market value of the imported good. For example, in Table 9.1 (which is drawn from the existing U.S. tariff code) a 2.1 percent ad valorem tariff is levied against imported pineapples preserved by sugar.

TABLE 9.1 A Section of the Harmonized Tariff Schedule of the United States

Heading/ Subheading	Stat. Suffix	Article Description	Units of Quantity	Rates of Duty
2006.00		Fruit, nuts, fruit peel, and other parts of plants, preserved by sugar (drained, glacé, or crystallized):		
2006.00.20	00	Cherries	kg	9.9¢/kg + 6.4%
2006.00.30	00	Ginger root	kg	2.4%
2006.00.40	00	Pineapples	kg	2.1%
		Other, including mixtures:		
2006.00.50	00	Mixtures	kg	16%
2006.00.60	00	Citrus fruit; peel of citrus or other fruit	kg	6¢/kg
2006.00.70	00	Other fruit and nuts	kg	8%
2006.00.90	00	Other	kg	16%

Source: U.S. International Trade Commission, *Harmonized Tariff Schedule of the United States* (Washington, DC: ITC Trade Data Base as of June 6, 2011).

2. A **specific tariff** is assessed as a specific dollar amount per unit of weight or other standard measure. As Table 9.1 shows, imported citrus fruit preserved by sugar bears a specific tariff of 6 cents per kilogram.

3. A **compound tariff** has both an ad valorem component and a specific component. Imported cherries preserved in sugar are levied a 6.4 percent ad valorem tariff and a 9.9 cents per kilogram specific tariff.

In practice, most tariffs imposed by developed countries are ad valorem. The tariff applies to the product's value, which is typically the sales price at which the product enters the country. Suppose Target buys a large shipment of canned pineapples preserved by sugar from a Philippine food processor at $400 a ton. When the pineapples are delivered to the Port of Los Angeles, Target will have to pay the U.S. Customs Service a duty of 2.1 percent of $400, or $8.40, for each ton it imports, a cost Target will pass on to its customers.

Most countries have adopted a detailed classification scheme for imported goods called the **harmonized tariff schedule (HTS)**. Because of its complexity, the HTS can sometimes be difficult to use. The first problem facing an importer is anticipating what customs officials will decide is the appropriate tariff classification for an imported good. For example, leather ski gloves imported into the United States are assessed a 5.5 percent ad valorem tariff, but if the gloves are specifically designed for cross-country skiing, then the ad valorem tariff is only 3.5 percent.

The tariff code is very complex, and an importer's expected profit margin on a transaction can shrink or disappear if a customs official subjects the imported good to a higher tariff rate than the importer expected. To reduce this risk, U.S. importers can request an advance tariff classification on prospective importations by writing the U.S. Customs Service. Importers who ignore this advice often find themselves embroiled in costly litigation.

Tariffs historically have been imposed for two reasons:

1. Tariffs raise revenue for the national government. Tariff revenues account for a significant portion of government revenues of developing countries such as Uganda and Tanzania. Such countries depend heavily on subsistence agriculture and so find it difficult to collect significant tax revenues from domestic sources. Customs duties, however, are reasonably easy to collect. Further, imported goods tend to be purchased by the wealthier members of society, so heavy reliance on import tariffs adds progressivity to the domestic tax system. Conversely, taxes on international trade form a relatively small percentage of government revenues in more developed countries that have broader tax bases such as Thailand, Egypt, and Mexico.

2. A tariff acts as a trade barrier. Because tariffs raise the prices paid by domestic consumers for foreign goods, they increase the demand for domestically produced substitute goods.

FIGURE 9.3

Impact of an Import Tariff on Demand for U.S.-Made SUVs

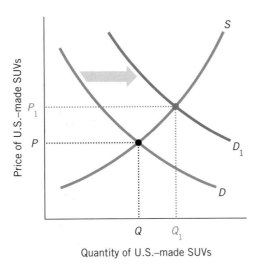

Quantity of U.S.–made SUVs

Tariffs affect both domestic and foreign special-interest groups. For example, suppose the U.S. government imposes a $2,000 specific tariff on imported SUVs. Foreign producers of SUVs will be forced to raise their U.S. prices, thereby reducing their U.S. sales. However, foreign-made SUVs and U.S.-made SUVs are substitute goods. Thus, the higher prices of foreign SUVs will increase the demand for U.S.-made SUVs. This is shown in Figure 9.3 by the shift in the demand for U.S.-made SUVs from D to D_1, resulting in more domestic vehicles being sold at higher prices. The $2,000 specific tariff creates both gainers and losers. Gainers include GM, Ford, and Chrysler dealerships selling domestic SUVs; suppliers to domestic producers; workers at domestic GM, Ford, and Chrysler SUV assembly plants; and the communities in which domestic SUV factories are located. Domestic consumers are losers because they pay higher prices for both domestic and foreign SUVs. Foreign producers also lose, as do people and firms that depend on them, including Toyota and Mazda dealerships in the United States, workers and suppliers in Japan, and communities in Japan in which the SUVs are manufactured.

Nontariff Barriers

Nontariff barriers are the second category of governmental controls on international trade. Any government regulation, policy, or procedure other than a tariff that has the effect of impeding international trade may be labeled a **nontariff barrier (NTB)**. In this section we discuss three kinds of NTBs: quotas, numerical export controls, and other nontariff barriers.

QUOTAS Countries may restrain international trade by imposing quotas. A **quota** is a numerical limit on the quantity of a good that may be imported into a country during some time period, such as a year. Quotas have traditionally been used to protect politically powerful industries, such as agriculture, automobiles, and textiles, from the threat of competition, as in the use of quotas to limit imports of rice by Japan, Korea, Taiwan, and the Philippines. However, as a result of trade agreements such as the Uruguay Round (see Chapter 10), many countries have replaced quotas with tariff rate quotas. A **tariff rate quota (TRQ)** imposes a low tariff rate on a limited amount of imports of a specific good; above that threshold, a TRQ imposes a prohibitively high tariff rate on the good. This situation is depicted in Figure 9.4, where the first 100,000 widgets imported into a country are subjected to a low tariff rate, T_L; all widgets after the first 100,000 are subjected to the high tariff rate, T_H. Canada, for example, has substituted a tariff rate quota for its previous quotas on imports of eggs, dairy products, and poultry. Imports of these goods above the threshold may carry tariffs as high as 350 percent. Japan imposes a 341-yen tariff on imported rice in excess of the quota, the equivalent of a 400 percent tariff.[9] Korea imposes tariffs of 243 percent on over-quota honey and 304 percent on over-quota potatoes.[10] In the short run, such high tariffs have the same effect as a quota: They normally limit imports of a good to the threshold level. However, at least in concept, exporters are allowed to increase their sales to the country as long as they are willing to pay the high tariff. And because tariffs are more visible than quotas, most experts believe that converting quotas to tariff rate quotas makes it easier to eliminate this type of trade barrier over time through trade negotiations.

FIGURE 9.4

Tariff Rate Quota on Widgets

A tariff rate quota imposes high tariff rates on imports above the threshold level.

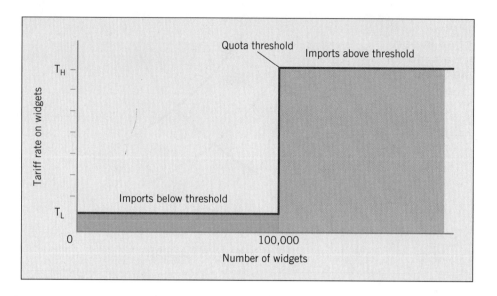

A quota or tariff rate quota helps domestic producers of the good in question but invariably hurts domestic consumers. Consider the impact on the U.S. market of the tariff rate quota on sugar. The U.S. government normally restricts the amount of foreign sugar that can be imported to less than 2 million tons annually by slapping a 17-cent specific tariff on each pound of sugar imported into the United States above that amount. (Domestic producers normally produce about 8 to 9 million tons per year.)[11] The price of sugar is higher in the United States than elsewhere in the world because the tariff rate quota prevents more imports from flowing into the U.S. market to equalize the prices. In August 2011, for instance, the U.S. price for sugar was 39¢ per pound, while the world price was only 28¢ per pound.

Who gains from the tariff rate quota? Domestic sugar producers, such as sugarcane growers in Louisiana and sugar beet growers in North Dakota, benefit because domestic production is increased and the price that domestic suppliers receive rises. Producers of sugar substitutes, such as Archer Daniels Midland, the largest domestic producer of corn-based fructose sweeteners, and Corn Belt farmers who supply the corn for the fructose sweeteners also gain as manufacturers of sweetened products substitute lower-cost fructose sweeteners for sugar. Losers from the policy include domestic candy manufacturers and soft drink makers, which must pay higher prices for sugar, as well as U.S. consumers, who pay a higher price—an estimated $1.5 billion a year—for all goods containing sugar. U.S. firms, such as San Francisco's Ghirardelli Chocolate Company (premium chocolates) or Corsicana, Texas's Collin Street Bakery (fruitcakes), which export goods with high sugar content, become less competitive in world markets because the sugar quota increases the cost of their ingredients.[12] A 2006 Department of Commerce study suggests that more than 10,000 Americans working for confectionary companies lost their jobs between 1997 and 2002 because of the sugar quota.[13]

Anyone with the right to import sugar into the United States within the 2-million-ton threshold also gains because the holder of such a right can buy sugar at the lower world price and resell it in the United States at the higher U.S. price. For this reason, the U.S. government uses such rights as instruments of foreign policy and foreign aid. Countries that are politically sympathetic to the United States or that the United States is trying to woo often receive generous rights, while countries hostile to the United States find their rights reduced or eliminated.

NUMERICAL EXPORT CONTROLS A country also may impose quantitative barriers to trade in the form of numerical limits on the amount of a good it will export. A **voluntary export restraint (VER)** is a promise by a country to limit its exports of a good to another country to a prespecified amount or percentage of the affected market. Often this is done to resolve or avoid trade conflicts with an otherwise friendly trade partner. For example, since 1982 the United States and Canada have been squabbling over whether Canada has been subsidizing its lumber industry by charging low stumpage fees (rights to harvest timber) in government-owned forests. To bring a truce to the conflict, Canada agreed in 1996 to adopt a VER for five years, limiting its annual exports to the United States of softwood lumber from Alberta, British Columbia, Ontario, and Quebec to 14.7 billion board feet. Canada also pledged to levy a substantial tax on any exports above that level bound for the United States. After the five-year window expired, however, the United States imposed a 27 percent duty on Canadian softwood lumber imports, which it later reduced to 10 percent. Canada filed a variety of complaints against the United States before tribunals sponsored by the North America Free Trade Agreement and the World Trade Organization; while its positions were generally upheld, Canada was disappointed by the American response. In 2006 the United States and Canada negotiated yet another settlement. The United States eliminated the tariff on Canadian softwood lumber exports and returned most of the monies it had collected to Canada. In return, Canada once again agreed to a VER, limiting its producers to a 34 percent share of the U.S. softwood lumber market. Given the contentious and long-term nature of the softwood lumber dispute, it is not surprising that the two countries have continued to squabble over the implementation of the 2006 agreement, which is scheduled to expire in 2013.[14]

Export controls may also be adopted to punish a country's political enemies. An **embargo**— an absolute ban on the exporting (and/or importing) of goods to a particular destination—is adopted by a country or international governmental authority to discipline another country. After Iraq invaded Kuwait in 1990, for example, the United Nations imposed an embargo on trade with Iraq, while the United States has had an embargo on trade with Cuba since the 1960s.

Numerical export controls may also be used to promote a country's industrial policy or to promote the competitiveness of other of its industries. Russia limits the export of logs and round wood to stimulate its wood-processing industry: The export controls lower the price paid by Russian wood processors but raise the input costs of their foreign competitors.[15] For similar reasons, China restricts exports of many minerals, such as antimony, bauxite, and fluorspar. For many of these minerals, China is one of the world's largest suppliers.[16] "Bringing the World into Focus" discusses the impact of China's export controls on the market for rare earths.

OTHER NONTARIFF BARRIERS Countries also use various other NTBs to protect themselves from foreign competition. Some NTBs are adopted for legitimate domestic public policy reasons but have the effect of restricting trade. Most NTBs, however, are blatantly protectionist. As we discuss in Chapter 10, international negotiations in the post–World War II era have reduced the use of tariffs and quotas. For this reason, nonquantitative NTBs have now become major impediments to the growth of international trade. These NTBs are more difficult to eliminate than tariffs and quotas because they often are embedded in bureaucratic procedures and are not quickly changeable. Among the most common forms of nonquantitative NTBs are the following:

- Product and testing standards
- Restricted access to distribution networks
- Public-sector procurement policies
- Local-purchase requirements
- Regulatory controls
- Currency controls
- Investment controls

We discuss these in the following sections.

PRODUCT AND TESTING STANDARDS A common form of NTB is a requirement that foreign goods meet a country's product standards or testing standards before the goods can be offered for sale in that country. Foreign firms often claim that these standards discriminate against their products. Brazil, for instance, requires that new pharmaceutical products undergo clinical testing in Brazil, even though they may have already undergone similar trials elsewhere and received approval from foreign regulators, such as the U.S. Food and Drug Administration.[17] Russia mandates that prior to its importation the country's Federal Security Service must test and approve any product utilizing encryption technology. The approval process may take as much as six months, thereby discouraging imports of such goods.[18] Korea requires that safety testing and certification for electrical equipment may only be performed by Korean nonprofit organizations, a restriction that disadvantages foreign producers of such goods and foreign testing labs.[19]

RESTRICTED ACCESS TO DISTRIBUTION NETWORKS Restricting foreign suppliers' access to the normal channels of distribution may also function as an NTB. China requires that imported sugar and petroleum be distributed only by state-owned trading enterprises.[20] In Thailand, foreign banks

BRINGING THE WORLD INTO FOCUS THE FIGHT OVER RARE EARTHS

Most trade conflicts arise from a country's erecting barriers against the importation of goods. In 2010, China decided to tighten its export controls on rare earths, announcing a 35 percent reduction in exports in 2011 from their 2010 levels. The intensity of the ensuing battle triggered over these obscure minerals reflects the globalization of supply chains and China's desire to transition its economy from manufacturing low value added goods to producing higher value added ones.

Rare earths is a term used to denote 17 different minerals that are critical for the production of many high-tech products, such as smartphones, computer chips, and batteries for hybrid cars. For example, cerium oxide is used to polish hard drives, while less than a penny's worth of neodymium allows cellphones to vibrate. Despite their name, rare earths are not that rare. However, they are expensive to produce, and environmental damage can ensue if the toxic chemicals used in their refining are not carefully handled. Moreover, bringing a new mine into production can take years.

China currently accounts for over 90 percent of the world's rare earth production, although it possesses only one-third of global reserves. It exported almost $1 billion of these minerals in 2010. China's dominance in the market is attributed to the low prices its mines charged starting in the 1990s. As prices fell, foreign producers closed their mines, unable to compete with the "China price."

China has claimed its export controls are motivated by its desire to protect the environment, save energy, and protect national resources. Critics in Europe, North America, and Japan see less benign reasons. They fear that the export controls are designed to boost Chinese production of high-tech goods by driving up the costs of key inputs to foreign users and encouraging foreign high-tech firms to relocate production facilities to China. They note that a 2009 policy paper issued by the country's Resource Ministry stressed that the quotas would enable the Ministry to promote the government's industrial policy and influence the demand-supply relationships in the market, allowing China to boost the prices it receives for its exports of rare earths. Moreover, it has announced plans to stockpile these minerals and has assured foreigners that any factories located in China will continue to have access to the rare earths they need.

China's policies have caused firms to seek to diversify their sourcing of rare earths. Japan is the largest importer of them, accounting for about 20 percent of annual usage. Its government is promoting recycling and funding R&D efforts in such areas as robotic deep-sea mining to lessen its dependence on Beijing. In late 2010, Japan's Toyota Tsusho Corporation signed an agreement with Indian Rare Earths Ltd. to construct a new rare-earths processing plant in India. Several companies, such as U.S.-based Molycorp, Australia's Lynas Corp., and Brazil's Vale, have announced plans to open or reopen rare-earth mines that had been closed due to low prices charged by Chinese competitors in the 1990s.

Free trade advocates fear that this overt manipulation of the rare-earths market by the Chinese government will cause other countries to retaliate, imposing their own quotas on critical resources or subsidizing new rare-earth mines and then raising trade barriers to rare-earth imports to reduce their dependence on Chinese mines. In their worst case scenario, they fear protectionists around the world will seize on China's rare-earths quotas as a justification for raising barriers to trade in goods they view as vital for their nations' economic security.

Sources: "Brazil's Vale gears up for rare earths," *Financial Times*, May 31, 2011, p. 13; "China rare earth metals soar as Beijing cuts sales," *Financial Times*, May 27, 2011, p. 21; "Rare-earth metals add heat," *Wall Street Journal*, March 23, 2011, p. B4; Office of the U.S. Trade Representative, *National Trade Estimate Report on Foreign Trade Barriers 2011*, p. 70; "Trade judges see flaw in China policies," *Wall Street Journal*, February 18, 2011; "India and Japan look to expand rare-earth alliance," *Wall Street Journal*, February 16, 2011; "China moves to strengthen grip over supply of rare-earth metals," *Wall Street Journal*, February 7, 2011, p. B1; "Rare action," *The Economist*, January 22, 2011; "Rare earth quotas: Big bark, less bite," *Wall Street Journal*, January 19, 2011; "Rare earths and China," *The Economist*, October 2, 2010.

are limited to a single branch and are forbidden from utilizing off-site ATM machines.[21] Foreign films may occupy only one-third of the screen time in Chinese movie theaters, a restriction that reduces the revenues of foreign movie studios and stimulates the widespread counterfeiting of DVDs (see Chapter 6's closing case, "Twenty-First Century Pirates"). Indonesia similarly limits the screen time of foreign films to 60 percent in its movie theaters.[22]

India has historically limited foreign participation in its retailing sector, fearing that competition from Western chains like Carrefour, Marks & Spencer, and Walmart would devastate the country's army of small mom-and-pop retailers. India has been pressured to eliminate these restrictions by its trading partners. The government has responded cautiously: In 2006, it relaxed the restrictions against single-brand stores, allowing foreign investors to own 51 percent of such establishments, subject to government approval. Foreigners are currently not permitted to own multibrand stores, however.[23]

PUBLIC-SECTOR PROCUREMENT POLICIES Public-sector procurement policies that give preferential treatment to domestic firms are another form of NTB. In the United States, "Buy American" restrictions are common at the federal, state, and local levels. The American Recovery and Reinvestment Act of 2009, for instance, requires that any iron, steel, and manufactured goods purchased using funds provided by the Act to build or repair a public building or public work must be produced in the United States. The federal government generally requires that international air travel purchased with U.S. government funds occur on U.S. airlines; China imposes similar restrictions on many employees of state-owned enterprises.

Public-sector procurement policies are particularly important in countries that have extensive state ownership of industry and in industries in which state ownership is common. If a national government adopts procurement policies that favor local firms, then foreigners are locked out of much of the market. Egypt gives state-owned enterprises a 15 percent bidding preference on public contracts, while Argentina grants domestically owned firms a 5 to 7 percent preference, Turkey a 15 percent preference, and Peru a 20 percent preference.[24] Kenya's Public Procurement and Disposal Act requires that certain government contracts be given only to Kenyan citizens.[25]

LOCAL-PURCHASE REQUIREMENTS Host governments may hinder foreign firms from exporting to or operating in the host countries by requiring the firms to purchase goods or services from local suppliers. Indonesia encourages pharmaceutical companies to manufacture locally if they wish their drugs to be approved for sale.[26] China requires that all travel agents use China's state-owned reservation service when booking flights for Chinese tourists.[27] Kazakhstan mandates that oil companies purchase any necessary services from Kazakh-owned companies.[28] The Philippines charges lower excise taxes on distilled spirits made from local raw materials.[29] Egypt requires that 60 percent of the managers of new computer-related companies be Egyptian nationals within three years of the firms' entry into the Egyptian market.[30]

The Canadian government requires that at least 60 percent of the programs broadcast by over-the-air TV stations be Canadian in origin; for cable stations, a majority of the programs must qualify as Canadian, as must 35 percent of the music played by radio stations.[31] The French government requires local TV services, such as TF1 or Canal Plus, to show French-made films at least 40 percent of the time and European-made films at least 60 percent of the time, thus restricting the market available to non-European films. Such quotas exist in radio broadcasting as well. During prime time, at least 40 percent of the songs played on France's 1,700 AM and FM stations must be written or sung by French or Francophone artists.[32] The European Union, Malaysia, South Korea, and Australia have similar requirements for broadcasters.[33] The U.S. government has strongly protested such requirements, arguing that they are designed to restrict competition from U.S. music, movie, and television producers.

REGULATORY CONTROLS Governments can create NTBs by adopting regulatory controls, such as conducting health and safety inspections, enforcing environmental regulations, requiring firms to obtain licenses before beginning operations or constructing new plants, and charging taxes and fees for public services that affect the ability of international businesses to compete in host markets. For example, Taiwan's National Health Insurance Bureau's reimbursement schedule for pharmaceuticals and medical devices favors domestically made products over foreign-produced ones.[34] Brazil requires that producers of health and fitness equipment, processed food, and cosmetics register their products with the Ministry of Health; approvals routinely take three to six months.[35] China's requirement that goods in 159 product categories—accounting for about one-fifth of U.S. exports to China—receive the China Compulsory Certification mark prior to their sale discourages importers. Typically such certifications may only be done in Chinese facilities, which are often backlogged. The additional expense and time delays reduce the competitiveness of imported goods in the Chinese market.[36]

CURRENCY CONTROLS Many countries, particularly developing countries and those with centrally planned economies, raise barriers to international trade through currency controls. Exporters of goods are allowed to exchange foreign currency at favorable rates so as to make foreign markets attractive sales outlets for domestic producers. Importers are forced to purchase foreign exchange from the central bank at unfavorable exchange rates, thus raising the domestic prices of foreign goods. Tourists may be offered a separate exchange rate that is designed to extract as much foreign exchange as possible from free-spending foreigners.

For example, Venezuela imposed currency controls to protect its currency reserves in 2003. It currently utilizes a dual exchange rate system, whereby certain favored transactions can obtain foreign exchange at the official exchange rate; the remaining transactions receive a less favorable rate. The controls made it more difficult for importers of nonessential goods to acquire foreign exchange.[37] Similarly, the National Bank of Ethiopia often makes it difficult for importers to obtain scarce foreign exchange, although state-owned enterprises or firms controlled by the ruling party normally have no such problems.[38]

FIGURE 9.5

Types of Barriers to International Trade: A Summary

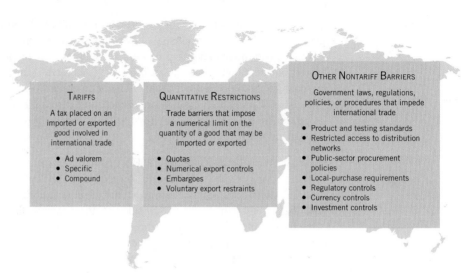

INVESTMENT CONTROLS Controls on foreign investment and ownership are common, particularly in key industries such as broadcasting, utilities, air transportation, defense contracting, and financial services. Such controls often make it difficult for foreign firms to develop an effective presence in such markets. The Philippines restricts foreign ownership in advertising to 30 percent and in telecommunications to 40 percent.[39] Malaysia caps foreign ownership of investment banks at 70 percent,[40] while foreigners may own no more than 49 percent of Peruvian broadcasters.[41] Indonesia limits foreign ownership in its telecommunications, film and video distribution, and construction industries. The United States similarly constrains foreign ownership of airlines and broadcast stations.

These NTBs are now more important impediments to international trade than tariffs are. And because they are sometimes imposed for sound domestic policy reasons but affect the competitiveness of foreign firms, NTBs can quickly cause intense international conflicts. International businesses whose operations are affected by NTBs often need the support of their home governments to help resolve these problems. Figure 9.5 summarizes the various forms that trade barriers can take.

Promotion of International Trade

We have just explored some techniques that governments use to restrict foreign business activity. In this section, we discuss government policies that promote international business, including subsidies, establishment of foreign trade zones, and export financing programs. Typically, these programs are designed to create jobs in the export sector or to attract investment to economically depressed areas.

Subsidies

Countries often seek to stimulate exports by offering subsidies designed to reduce firms' costs of doing business. Brazil and Kenya, for example, exempt imported inputs that are used to produce goods for export from taxes and tariffs.[42] Venezuela grants a 10 percent tax credit to firms exporting specific foodstuffs, including certain types of seafood and fruits.[43] Our opening case detailed the subsidies that the United States and the European Union utilize to promote their national champions in the commercial aircraft industry.

National, state, and local governments often provide economic development incentives—another type of subsidy—to entice firms to locate or expand facilities in their communities to provide jobs and increase local tax bases. These incentives may be in the form of property tax abatements, free land, training of workforces, reduced utility rates, new highway construction, and so on. Competition among different localities can be fierce. For instance, Georgia agreed to provide Kia Motors with $400 million in incentives to capture that firm's first U.S. plant and the

2,500 jobs it was estimated to produce.[44] Similarly, the U.S. Virgin Islands pledged to spend $100 million to help expand Fortune Brand's rum distillery on St. Croix and to build a new wastewater treatment facility for it.[45]

Because subsidies reduce the cost of doing business, they may affect international trade by artificially improving a firm's competitiveness in export markets or by helping domestic firms fight off foreign imports. Subsidies, however, can grow so large as to disrupt the normal pattern of international trade. The shipbuilding, wheat, and butter industries are notorious examples of markets in which trade is distorted because of the high level of subsidies. The big losers in the subsidy wars are efficient producers in countries that lack large-scale subsidies, such as Australia's wheat industry or New Zealand's dairy industry. "Emerging Opportunities" discusses the impact of subsidies on the market for cotton.

Foreign Trade Zones

A **foreign trade zone (FTZ)** is a geographic area where imported or exported goods receive preferential tariff treatment. An FTZ may be as small as a warehouse or a factory site (such as Caterpillar's diesel engine facility in Mossville, Illinois) or as large as the entire city of Shenzhen, China (which neighbors Hong Kong).[46] FTZs are used by governments worldwide to spur regional economic development. For example, an FTZ has played a key role in the economic development of the small African island nation of Mauritius (see Map 9.2). Through utilization of an FTZ, a firm typically can reduce, delay, or sometimes totally eliminate customs duties. Generally, a firm can import a component into an FTZ, process it further, and then export the processed good abroad and avoid paying customs duties on the value of the imported component.

The *maquiladora* system represents another example of the use of FTZs. A **maquiladora** is a factory located in an FTZ in Mexico; most are situated near the U.S. border. These factories import unfinished goods or component parts, further process the goods or parts, and reexport them. The goods produced by maquiladoras enjoy preferential customs and tax treatment. Mexico levies no customs duties on unfinished goods imported by a maquiladora, provided the goods are reexported after having been further processed in Mexico. Machinery imported into Mexico and used by a maquiladora is also exempt from customs duties. U.S. customs duties on maquiladoras' exports are applied only to the value of the processing performed in Mexico. Today the maquiladora industry is the second-largest sector of the Mexican economy (after oil production) and the second-largest source of Mexico's foreign-exchange earnings. However, as a result of the North American Free Trade Agreement, many tariff advantages once enjoyed only by the maquiladoras are now available

MAP 9.2
Foreign Trade Zone on Mauritius

Mauritius, which was once a French naval base, is a tropical island, roughly $10\frac{1}{2}$ times the area of Washington, D.C. For much of its history Mauritius's 1.2 million residents depended on sugarcane, and even today 90 percent of its cultivated land is devoted to this crop.

Mauritius has created a foreign trade zone (FTZ) to diversify its economy and encourage manufacturing. Today the country exports over $1.6 billion worth of textiles, apparel, and other goods to Europe and the United States. Because of the FTZ's success, the country's economy has enjoyed 5 percent annual growth during the last decade.

EMERGING OPPORTUNITIES   COTTON SUBSIDIES AND WORLD POVERTY

For years the United States and the European Union have poured money into subsidizing their agricultural sectors. These subsidies have been criticized by the Cairns Group, an organization of efficient agricultural producers who believe the U.S. and EU subsidies are distorting trade in agricultural goods. These critics have recently been joined by advocates concerned about alleviating poverty in developing countries; these advocates include NGOs like Oxfam and U-2's lead singer, Bono, who believe these subsidies contribute to the impoverishment of farmers in less-developed countries. Oxfam estimates that EU subsidies depress world butter prices by 20 percent, while its sugar subsidies cost Thailand $150 million and Brazil $500 million a year.

Cotton provides another example of this phenomenon. In a complaint filed with the World Trade Organization, Brazil argued that the $3 billion a year subsidies paid to American farmers increase U.S. cotton production by 29 percent, thereby depressing world cotton prices by 12.6 percent. Brazilian officials estimate these U.S. subsidies cost Brazilian farmers $600 million in lost sales. After the WTO found in Brazil's favor, the two countries negotiated a settlement requiring the U.S. government to provide $147 million in annual subsidies to Brazilian cotton farmers.

This settlement did not alleviate the impact of the U.S. cotton subsidies on parts of Central and Western Africa that are heavily dependent on cotton production. Ten million farmers in Benin, Burkina Faso, Chad, and Mali, many living below the poverty line, make their living farming cotton. Oxfam estimates that the subsidies paid to U.S. cotton farmers cost these countries $300 million a year and reduce their exports by a tenth. And the subsidies often neutralize whatever aid Western countries provide them. In 2001, for example, Oxfam estimates that U.S. cotton subsidies cost Mali $43 million, offsetting the $38 million in foreign aid the United States provided that country.

The United States is not the only country that subsidizes its cotton farmers. China provides an estimated $1.2 billion in subsidies to its farmers, while the EU subsidizes its cotton growers, primarily in Spain and Greece, to the tune of $700 million a year. China and the United States produce about 45 percent of the world's supply.

Sources: "Why the U.S. is also giving Brazilians farm subsidies," *Time*, April 9, 2010; "U.S. and Brazil reach agreement on cotton dispute," *New York Times*, April 6, 2010; "WTO allows Brazil to fine U.S.," *Wall Street Journal*, August 1, 2009; "In fight against farm subsidies, even farmers are joining foes," *Wall Street Journal*, March 14, 2006, p. A7; "Unpicking cotton subsidies," *The Economist*, April 30, 2004 (online); "Cultivating poverty," Oxfam Briefing Paper 30, Oxfam International; "A great yarn," *The Economist*, December 20, 2003, pp. 43ff.; "WTO chief leads cotton review," BBC News Online, September 12, 2003.

ISSOUF SANOGO/AFP/Getty Images/Newscom

Brazil filed a complaint with the World Trade Organization, urging it to end the large subsidies that the European Union and the United States offer their cotton farmers. Oxfam, one of the leading NGOs fighting world poverty, believes that such subsidies cost African cotton farmers over $300 million in lost sales and lowered prices, monies they can ill-afford to lose.

to factories throughout Mexico. Thus, interior cities such as Monterrey and Saltillo have been put on a more even footing with border communities such as Nuevo Laredo and Matamoros in terms of attracting new plants to serve the North American market.

Export Financing Programs

For many big-ticket items such as aircraft, offshore drilling rigs, and large construction projects, success or failure in exporting depends on a firm's producing a high-quality product, providing reliable repair service after the sale, and—often the deciding factor—offering an attractive financing package. For example, Boeing competes with Airbus to sell Air Canada 200-seat short-range aircraft. When Air Canada is deciding which firm's aircraft to buy, it carefully weighs price, after-sale technical support, aircraft operating costs, and financing expenses. All other things being equal, the financing terms offered to Air Canada may be critical in its decision of which firm wins the contract.

Because of the importance of the financing package, most major trading countries have created government-owned agencies to assist their domestic firms in arranging financing of export sales, both large and small. The **Export-Import Bank of the United States (Eximbank)** provides financing for U.S. exports through direct loans and loan guarantees; in 2010 it supplied financing for more than 3,500 export transactions worth $24.5 billion. Large firms such as Boeing are important clients, but the Eximbank also services small U.S. exporters. For example, it guaranteed $9.4 million in bank loans that helped three Midwestern companies, including two small businesses, to export equipment needed to construct a hydroelectric dam in Turkey.[47] Another U.S. government–sponsored organization, the **Overseas Private Investment Corporation (OPIC)**, provides a very different type of insurance—political-risk insurance, a subject covered in Chapter 3. If a foreign country confiscates an insured firm's goods or assets, OPIC will compensate the firm for its losses. Most major trading countries have similar organizations that provide export financing, commercial insurance, and political-risk insurance. In China, state-owned banks play a key role in supporting the growth of China's exports by offering such services.[48] Other countries, such as Malaysia, rely on their central bank to provide low-cost export financing.

Controlling Unfair Trade Practices

With governments around the world adopting programs designed to protect domestic industries from imports and other programs to promote their exports, it should not be surprising that competitors often cry foul. In response to these complaints, many countries have implemented laws protecting their domestic firms from unfair trade practices.

In the United States, complaints from firms affected by alleged unfair trade practices are first investigated by the International Trade Administration (ITA), a division of the U.S. Department of Commerce, which determines whether an unfair trade practice has occurred. The Department of Commerce transfers confirmed cases of unfair trading to the U.S. International Trade Commission (ITC), an independent government agency. If a majority of the six ITC commissioners decide that U.S. producers have suffered "material injury," the ITC will impose duties on the offending imports to counteract the unfair trade practice. The ITC, like the Canadian International Trade Tribunal and other similar government agencies worldwide, focuses on two types of unfair trade practices: government subsidies that distort trade and unfair pricing practices.

Countervailing Duties

Most countries protect local firms from foreign competitors that benefit from subsidies granted by their home governments. A **countervailing duty (CVD)** is an ad valorem tariff on an imported good that is imposed by the importing country to counter the impact of foreign subsidies. The CVD is calculated to just offset the advantage the exporter obtains from the subsidy. In this way, trade can still be driven by the competitive strengths of individual firms and the laws of comparative advantage, rather than by the level of subsidies that governments offer their firms. For instance, the EU and the United States each imposed countervailing duties on high-end glossy paper imported from China, in the belief that Chinese producers had benefited from cheap governmental financing and land sales.[49]

Not all government subsidies give a foreign firm an unfair advantage in the domestic market. Most countries impose CVDs only when foreign subsidization of a product leads to a distortion of international trade. For example, the U.S. government, in administering its CVD rules, tries to determine whether a particular subsidy is generally available to all industries in a country, in which case CVDs will not be applied; or whether the subsidy is restricted to a specific industry, in which case CVDs may be imposed. If a foreign government grants a tax credit to all employers for training handicapped workers, a CVD will not be applied because the tax credit is available to all the country's firms. If the tax credit is restricted to the footwear industry, however, a CVD may be imposed on imported footwear equal to the value of the tax credit.

CVD complaints are often triggered by some governmental action designed to overcome some other governmental action. For example, the EU's common agricultural policy has had the effect of raising the prices paid to European grain farmers. Unfortunately, the high cost of feed grains raised the costs of European swine producers and made their meat products uncompetitive in world markets. To undo the damage caused to swine producers by high grain prices, the EU agreed to provide an export subsidy for canned hams and other processed meat products. With the aid of this subsidy Danish and Dutch pork processors were able to capture 25 percent of the Canadian canned ham and canned luncheon meat market. As a result, Canadian pork-packing houses successfully petitioned the Canadian International Trade Tribunal to impose a countervailing duty on Danish and Dutch canned pork products.

Antidumping Regulations

Many countries are also concerned about their domestic firms being victimized by discriminatory or predatory pricing practices of foreign firms, such as dumping. There are two types of dumping. **Dumping** can occur when a firm sells its goods in a foreign market at a price below what it charges in its home market. This type of dumping is a form of international price discrimination. The second type of dumping involves the firm's selling its goods below cost in the foreign market, in which case the dumping is a form of predatory pricing. The concern with predatory pricing is that a foreign company may lower its prices in the host country, drive host country firms out of the market, and then charge monopoly prices to host country consumers once competitors have been eliminated. Antidumping laws protect local industries from dumping by foreign firms.

Determining whether the first type of dumping—price discrimination—has actually occurred is not always easy. For example, many Western politicians incorrectly accuse Japanese companies of dumping, noting that Japanese goods often retail for higher prices in Tokyo than in New York City. Retail prices, however, are irrelevant in determining whether dumping has occurred. The comparison should be made between the prices charged foreign customers and domestic customers at the factory gate; these prices are often difficult to obtain. The high retail prices in Tokyo might reflect the inefficient Japanese distribution system or high costs of retailing there rather than dumping by the manufacturer.

In the second type of dumping—predatory pricing—defining costs is complicated, particularly when dealing with a large, multidivisional MNC such as Toyota or Nissan. For example, when the ITA is determining the "cost" of a Toyota Sienna minivan, should it measure cost as the marginal cost of producing one more Sienna? Should it include some of Toyota's minivan-related R&D expenses, or should it simply recognize that these R&D costs would have been incurred whether or not the U.S. market existed? Should it include charges for Toyota's corporate overhead? Foreigners' guilt or innocence in dumping cases often turns on the answers to such accounting questions.

Should Countries Enforce Their Unfair Trade Practice Laws?

It may be surprising to learn that many economists argue for abolishing unfair trade practice laws. Who, after all, would support promoting unfair trade? Advocates of abolishing unfair trade practice laws generally agree with the objectives of these laws:

- Promote global efficiency by encouraging production in those countries that can produce a good most efficiently.
- Ensure that trade occurs on the basis of comparative advantage, not the size of government subsidies.
- Protect consumers from predatory behavior.

However, abolition advocates assert that in practice these laws do more harm than good. Much of their concern rests on how the laws are enforced. Foreign firms alleged to have dumped goods in the United States must provide comprehensive documentation of their pricing and cost-accounting procedures, in English, using U.S. generally accepted accounting principles (GAAP). Firms failing to comply with the short deadlines for supplying these documents find themselves at a disadvantage in defending themselves before the International Trade Commission. Moreover, critics of unfair trade practice laws argue that the ITC's costing methodology is flawed and biased toward finding dumping when none exists. New Zealand kiwi fruit was subjected to high dumping duties in the U.S. market for nearly a decade, for example, on what many experts consider to be flimsy evidence. Indeed, most major trading countries believe that U.S. enforcement of its unfair trade practice laws is based on politics, not the law, and thus the laws serve as a protectionist trade barrier.

Some economists go even further in their disdain for unfair trade practice laws. They believe the laws make no sense, either in theory or in practice, because of the harm they cause consumers. These economists are skeptical of the predatory pricing argument, contending that decades of economic research have failed to find many real-world examples of such behavior. With regard to international price discrimination or government subsidization, the economists argue that if foreigners are kind enough (or dumb enough) to sell their goods to our country below cost, why should we complain?

Safeguards

The previous sections refer to *unfair trade practices*. International trade law also allows countries to protect themselves from sudden surges in imported goods, even if the goods were traded fairly, in order to allow them time to adjust to the changed economic environment. Such actions utilize "safeguard clauses" or "escape clauses." In U.S. trade law, Section 201 of the Trade Act of 1974 permits the imposition of temporary tariffs, quotas, or other trade barriers by the federal government if the International Trade Commission finds that American firms have been seriously harmed by increased imports and if the president approves the ITC's findings.

For instance, in 2009, President Obama imposed temporary tariffs for three years on tires imported from China after the ITC ruled that American tire producers were harmed by rapid increases in imports, causing them to trim their workforces by 5,000 employees. Between 2004 and 2008, the ITC found that the U.S. market share of Chinese tires rose from 4.7 percent to 16.7 percent, and that four U.S. tire factories had shuttered their gates as a result. Obama chose to levy a 35 percent tariff on Chinese tires for one year. The president determined that the tariff should decline to 30 percent in the second year and to 25 percent in the final year. While the United Steelworkers, who filed the original complaint, were delighted by the president's decision, many American tire wholesalers, who rely on imports to keep their costs down, were not.[50]

MyManagementLab   Now that you have finished this chapter, go back to **www.pearsonglobaleditions.com/mymanagementlab** to continue practicing and applying the concepts you've learned.

CHAPTER REVIEW

Summary

Formulating trade policies that advance the economic interests of their citizens is an important task facing most national governments. Although some policymakers suggest that free trade is the most appropriate policy, numerous firms, government bureaucrats, and other interested parties argue for active governmental intervention in international trade.

Some rationales for governmental intervention focus on the specific needs of an industry (national defense, infant industry, maintenance of existing jobs, and strategic trade arguments), while others focus on the country's overall needs (economic development and industrial policy).

Over the centuries, governments have developed a variety of trade barriers. Import tariffs raise revenues for the government as well as help domestically produced goods compete with imported goods. Quotas and VERs place a numerical limitation on the amount of a good that can be imported or exported. Other NTBs may also disadvantage foreign products in the market. These barriers include product and testing standards, restricted access to distribution systems, public procurement policies that favor local firms, local-purchase requirements, regulatory powers, and currency and investment controls.

National governments also seek to promote the interests of domestic firms in international trade through other programs. The governments may subsidize local production of goods and services to make them more competitive in international markets. They also may authorize the establishment of FTZs to help domestic firms export goods. Export financing programs have been developed to assist exporters in marketing their goods.

National governments protect local producers from unfair foreign competition by enacting unfair trade laws. CVDs are imposed on foreign products that benefit from government subsidies that distort international trade. Antidumping laws protect domestic producers from being victimized by predatory pricing or price discrimination policies of foreign firms.

Review Questions

1. What is fair trade? Who benefits from it?
2. What is the infant industry argument?
3. What are the different types of tariffs?
4. Why is it useful for an importer to seek out an advance tariff classification from the U.S. Customs Service?
5. Why might a country adopt a VER?
6. What are the major forms of NTBs?
7. What is an FTZ?
8. What is the role of the Eximbank?
9. What is the purpose of a CVD?
10. What are the two definitions of *dumping*?

Questions for Discussion

1. What are the advantages and disadvantages of an industrial policy?
2. Because of Japan's success in competing in international markets, it has been the target of numerous complaints that it restricts foreign access to its local markets. As Japan reduces its barriers to imported goods, who is likely to gain from lowered barriers? Who is likely to lose from them?
3. Strategic trade theory applies to industries that are composed of only a few firms worldwide. List as many industries as possible that fit this description.
4. Refer back to Figure 9.2 on page 259. What would happen if Japan offered Toshiba a subsidy of $1.5 billion after it learns that France granted Areva a subsidy of $2 billion?
5. Indonesia has imposed high export taxes on the export of raw wood and sawn timber. Why would it do this? (Hint: What is the impact of these export tariffs on the domestic market for wood and timber? Which domestic industries would benefit from this impact?) Who is hurt by these high export taxes?
6. Should we worry if foreigners sell us goods cheaply?

Building Global Skills

Assessing Trade Barriers

The ability of firms to market their products in foreign countries is often affected by trade barriers imposed by individual countries. Your assignment is to pick an industry or product and report on the barriers to trade or investment that five countries impose on it. Because the members of the EU have common trade policies, only one of the five countries can be an EU member.

Fortunately, there are numerous sources of useful information available in published form and on the Internet. The Office of the U.S. Trade Representative publishes annually an analysis of trade barriers imposed by other nations titled the *National Trade Estimate Report on Foreign Trade Barriers*. This study also provides a detailed description of the evolution of current trade conflicts between the United States and the rest of the world. The European Commission provides similar information for the EU in the Trade section of its website (see http://ec.europa.eu/trade/). The U.S. Customs Service's website provides information on tariffs imposed by the United States. Other groups, such as the World Trade Organization and industry trade associations, also publish useful information.

CLOSING CASE   GREEN ENERGY AND FREE TRADE

The trauma of the global recession of 2008–2009 motivated politicians around the world to seek new ways of rejuvenating their struggling economies. Many of them focused on the promotion of green energy as a critical element of their economic recovery programs. (Green energy encompasses power generated by sustainable, renewable sources, such as solar, wind, waves and tide, geothermal deposits, biomass, and low-impact hydroelectric power.) In 2008, then presidential candidate Barack Obama proposed a "New Energy for America" initiative, which sought to invest $150 billion over 10 years to promote clean energy, reduce dependence on foreign oil, lower greenhouse gas emissions, and create 5 million new jobs. By stimulating new green energy technologies, candidate Obama believed that America would become a dominant exporter in the green energy markets of the future. During his 2010 election campaign, British Prime Minister David Cameron pledged to create a £20 billion green homes program. German Chancellor Angela Merkel announced her Nine-Point Program designed to increase over a 40-year period the role of renewable sources in generating Germany's electricity. For 2020, Merkel established a goal of having renewable sources provide 35 percent of Germany's electricity needs. The Canadian province of Ontario's Green Energy and Green Economy Act of 2009 promised to stimulate green energy production and to increase energy efficiency. Similar green energy programs were announced by the governments of China (with a price tag of $220 billion), South Korea ($60 billion), and Japan ($35 billion).

These green energy initiatives typically have dual goals: rejuvenate stagnating economies and address the global climate change problem. The Kyoto Protocols, the result of a 1997 enclave, and the Copenhagen Accord, the product of the 2009 U.N. Climate Change Conference, highlighted the need to reduce greenhouse gas emissions. Although these two international meetings were less successful than many climate experts wished—the United States did not ratify the Kyoto Protocol and the Copenhagen Accord was not framed as a legally binding treaty—national leaders recognized the magnitude of the global climate change threat.

The dual goals of these well-intentioned and politically-appealing green energy initiatives have created numerous problems for the world's trade officials, however. As we will discuss in detail in the next chapter, most countries are members of the World Trade Organization (WTO), and have pledged to reduce barriers to international trade. Yet many of these green energy initiatives contain provisions that are contrary to countries' obligations to the WTO. For example, to reduce its reliance on coal-fired electricity generation, Ontario's Green Energy and Green Economy Act mandates increased power generated by solar and wind. Unfortunately, the cost of producing electricity using solar panels or wind turbines is more expensive than by burning coal. To overcome this obstacle, Ontario requires electrical utilities to buy power produced by renewable providers at an above-market price.

Such "feed-in tariffs" are a common feature in laws promoting green energy use. Essentially they guarantee green energy producers a market for their expensive energy. The level of the feed-in tariff can be manipulated to promote other policy objectives. Spain's system, for example, offers higher tariffs for electricity generated by small suppliers than by large ones. Of course, by raising the average cost of producing electricity, they raise the price paid by users, both industrial and home, of electricity. Supporters of feed-in tariffs argue that in the short-run higher prices are necessary to induce investors to build green energy production facilities; in the long-run, they hope that by expanding the size of the green energy market, producers of green energy goods will capture economies of scale, thereby making green energy more cost competitive with coal-fired generators.

Feed-in tariffs do create political problems, however. They raise the cost of electricity to voters. They also raise the cost of electricity to local manufacturers, who may have to shut down if they no longer can compete with goods produced by distant rivals unaffected by the feed-in tariff. To address these concerns, Ontario mandated that 25 to 50 percent of the cost of the green energy facilities benefiting from the feed-in tariffs be locally sourced. In that way, while electricity costs might rise, local jobs would also be created. Indeed, Samsung, Siemens, SunEdison, and Celestica announced that they would build plants in Ontario to take advantage of the 2009 law.

Other countries have adopted local content rules in their green energy programs as well. China's wind energy program utilized a 70 percent local content rule. (It withdrew this requirement in 2009 under diplomatic pressure from U.S. trade officials.) India's Jawaharlal Nehru National Solar Mission envisions the country will add 20,000 megawatts of solar power by 2022. The government's $20 billion in subsidies include a 30 percent local content requirement. Unfortunately, such local content provisions may be contrary to the rules of the World Trade Organization. Japan, for example, has already filed a complaint with the WTO against Canada.

Many of the national programs promoting green energy provide subsidies for suppliers or consumers. The Indian government subsidizes homeowners 30 percent of the cost of installing rooftop solar panels. The American Recovery and Reinvestment Act of 2009 provided tax breaks for Americans who made their homes more energy efficient or purchased electric vehicles. The Chinese government subsidized local companies who entered the solar panel supply business by providing cheap credit from state-owned banks, as well as subsidizing solar-equipment purchases and generation of solar power. Total subsidies by China to its solar panel manufacturers are an estimated $30 billion. One Massachusetts solar panel factory, which had received $43 million in state subsidies, moved its production to China because China's subsidies were too attractive to ignore, costing 800 U.S. jobs.

Such subsidies raise concerns for the WTO and advocates of free trade. Direct subsidies to the manufacturers of goods embodying green technologies give recipients a competitive advantage in export markets and make it more difficult for manufacturers in countries who offer no subsidies to compete both domestically and internationally. For example, China has become the world's largest producer of solar panels, due in part to the subsidies offered producers by the Chinese government.

Another concern of free trade advocates involves proposed border tax adjustments (BTAs), or tariffs, on imported goods that have benefited from the regulatory "race to the bottom." Suppose country A requires its domestic manufacturers to adopt expensive technologies to reduce their greenhouse gas emissions while country B does not. Country A's manufacturers might argue that production and firms will move to country B where production is cheaper. Country B then benefits from the "race to the bottom." To deter countries from lowering their environmental regulations to attract new investment and industries, some countries, including the United States and the European Union, are proposing to impose BTAs on goods imported from countries whose environmental standards are lower than theirs. One study commissioned by the World Bank suggested that a $50 a ton tax on carbon dioxide would be equivalent to a 10 percent tariff on a typical Chinese import. Development specialists fear that BTAs of this magnitude could cripple the ability of small manufacturers, which form the backbone of China's manufacturing sector, to compete in developed markets. Environmental specialists conversely fear that attempts to control greenhouse gas emissions will come to naught unless such small manufacturers also comply with higher environmental standards.

Case Questions

1. Why have so many governments chosen to subsidize green energy initiatives? Can all of these programs be successful?
2. China has passed the United States as the largest emitter of greenhouse gases, which displeases environmentalists concerned about global climate change. China has subsidized its green energy manufacturers, allowing them to dominate key industries, such as solar panels, which displeases advocates of free trade. What would you recommend China do? Should it accommodate its critics? Should it ignore them?
3. What is the rationale for BTAs? Under what conditions, if any, should countries be allowed to impose BTAs?
4. What is the appropriate trade-off between promoting free trade and promoting green energy? Should the WTO rules be suspended when dealing with green energy?

Source: Office of the U.S. Trade Representative, *National Trade Estimate Report on Foreign Trade Barriers 2011*, pp. 54, 181; "Wind power hits a trough," *Wall Street Journal*, April 4, 2011; "Indian solar rules burn U.S.," *Wall Street Journal*, February 8, 2011; "U.S. seals energy deals as Hu arrives for visit," *Wall Street Journal*, January 19, 2011; "U.S. pushes India to lift solar import restrictions," *Wall Street Journal*, December 15, 2010; "Japan questions local-content requirements in Canadian province's energy programme," May 21, 2010, www.wto.org; "Asia's green tech rivals," *The Economist*, November 13, 2009; "Obama lays out clean-energy plans," *Washington Post*, March 24, 2009; "Barrack Obama and Joe Biden: New energy for America," www.barackobama.com; G. Atkinson, Hamilton G. Ruta, and D. van der Mensbrugghe, 2009, "Trade in 'Virtual Carbon': Empirical Results and Implications for Policy," Background paper for the World Development Report 2010; German government press release at http://www.germany.info/Vertretung/usa/en/_pr/P_Wash/2010/09/07_EnergyPlan_PR,archiveCtx=1992696.html

Endnotes

1. "WTO gives Airbus a mixed win," *Wall Street Journal*, May 19, 2011, p. B3; "Twin WTO ruling on Airbus dispute," *Financial Times*, May 19, 2011, p. 4; "W.T.O. ruling on Airbus subsidies upheld on appeal," *New York Times*, May 18, 2011; "WTO rules that Boeing received $5.3bn in aid," *Financial Times*, April 1, 2011, p. 19; "EU appeals Boeing ruling," *Wall Street Journal*, April 1, 2011; "WTO lowers boom on Boeing," *Wall Street Journal*, January 31, 2011, p. B1; "WTO finds EU aid to Airbus is illegal," *Wall Street Journal*, March 24, 2010, p. A10; "W.T.O. affirms ruling of improper Airbus aid," *New York Times*, March 23, 2010; Office of the U.S. Trade Representative, *National Trade Estimate Report on Foreign Trade Barriers 2006*, p. 253; "Balance of power starts to shift as Boeing fights back," *Financial Times*, June 13, 2005, p. 6; "Airbus's free ride," *Wall Street Journal*, March 10, 2005, p. A18; "Airbus beats Boeing in war over big order," *Financial Times,* October 15, 2002, p. 17; "Airbus wins first order for super jumbo from emirates," *Financial Times*, May 2, 2000, p. 1; "US critical of UK aid to Airbus super jumbo project," *Financial Times*, March 14, 2000, p. 1; "UK backing for Airbus 'superjumbo,'" *Financial Times*, March 14, 2000, p. 9; "Loan sparks US charge of illegal subsidy," *Financial Times*, March 14, 2000, p. 9; "U.S. questions need for loans by Britain to British Aerospace," *Wall Street Journal*, March 14, 2000, p. A27; "U.S. delay on Airbus challenge concerns Boeing," *Wall Street Journal*, January 24, 2000, p. A3.

2. U.S. International Trade Commission, *Shipbuilding Trade Reform Act of 1992: Likely Economic Effects of Enactment*, USITC Publication 2495 (June 1992), Washington, DC. The U.S. shipbuilding industry is so uncompetitive in world markets that from 1960 to 1994 the industry exported no commercial oceangoing vessels (p. 6).

3. "The trough," *The Economist*, June 27, 1992, p. 22.

4. Edward J. Lincoln, *Japan's Unequal Trade* (Washington, DC: The Brookings Institution, 1990), p. 112.

5. "Climbing through the clouds," *The Economist*, July 9, 2011 (online).

6. Paul Krugman and Maurice Obstfeld, *International Economics* (Reading, MA: Pearson Addison Wesley, 2005), Chapter 11.

7. "U.S. picks areas of technology it wants to back," *Wall Street Journal*, April 26, 1994, p. A4.

8. "Torpedo shipping protectionism," *Wall Street Journal*, November 26, 1991, p. A14.

9. Office of the U.S. Trade Representative, *National Trade Estimate Report on Foreign Trade Barriers 2011*, p. 195; Office of the U.S. Trade Representative, *National Trade Estimate Report on Foreign Trade Barriers 2006*, p. 352. Current tariff found at http://www.customs.go.jp/english/tariff/2011_4/data/i201104e_10.htm

10. Office of the U.S. Trade Representative, *National Trade Estimate Report on Foreign Trade Barriers 2011*, p. 226.

11. "U.S. faces sugar squeeze," *Wall Street Journal*, May 2, 2011, p. C8.

12. "Bitter about sugar prices," *Houston Chronicle*, April 27, 2006, p. D3.

13. "Shielding sugar industry 'costs thousands of jobs'," *Financial Times*, February 15, 2006, p. 6.

14. Office of the U.S. Trade Representative, *National Trade Estimate Report on Foreign Trade Barriers 2011*, pp. 52, 53; "U.S., Canada have tentative deal in dispute over softwood lumber," *Wall Street Journal*, April 28, 2006, p. A4; "U.S. will lift a lumber duty in a trade deal with Canada," *New York Times* (online), April 28, 2006.

15. Office of the U.S. Trade Representative, *National Trade Estimate Report on Foreign Trade Barriers 2011*, p. 309.

16. Office of the U.S. Trade Representative, *National Trade Estimate Report on Foreign Trade Barriers 2011*, pp. 69, 70.

17. Office of the U.S. Trade Representative, *National Trade Estimate Report on Foreign Trade Barriers 2011*, p. 40.

18. Office of the U.S. Trade Representative, *National Trade Estimate Report on Foreign Trade Barriers 2011*, p. 306.

19. Office of the U.S. Trade Representative, *2011 Report on Technical Barriers to Trade*, p. 81.

20. Office of the U.S. Trade Representative, *National Trade Estimate Report on Foreign Trade Barriers 2011*, p. 61.

21. Office of the U.S. Trade Representative, *National Trade Estimate Report on Foreign Trade Barriers 2011*, p. 349.

22. Office of the U.S. Trade Representative, *National Trade Estimate Report on Foreign Trade Barriers 2011*, pp. 80, 188.

23. Office of the U.S. Trade Representative, *National Trade Estimate Report on Foreign Trade Barriers 2011*, p. 179.

24. Office of the U.S. Trade Representative, *National Trade Estimate Report on Foreign Trade Barriers 2011*, pp. 24, 122, 291, 354.

25. Office of the U.S. Trade Representative, *National Trade Estimate Report on Foreign Trade Barriers 2011*, p. 222.

26. Office of the U.S. Trade Representative, *National Trade Estimate Report on Foreign Trade Barriers 2011*, p. 184.

27. Office of the U.S. Trade Representative, *National Trade Estimate Report on Foreign Trade Barriers 2011*, p. 81; Office of the U.S. Trade Representative, *National Trade Estimate Report on Foreign Trade Barriers 2008*, pp. 126ff.

28. Office of the U.S. Trade Representative, *National Trade Estimate Report on Foreign Trade Barriers 2011*, p. 219.

29. Office of the U.S. Trade Representative, *National Trade Estimate Report on Foreign Trade Barriers 2011*, p. 296.

30. Office of the U.S. Trade Representative, *National Trade Estimate Report on Foreign Trade Barriers 2011*, p. 123.

31. Office of the U.S. Trade Representative, *National Trade Estimate Report on Foreign Trade Barriers 2011*, p. 55.

32. Office of the U.S. Trade Representative, *National Trade Estimate Report on Foreign Trade Barriers 2011*, p. 141.

33. Office of the U.S. Trade Representative, *National Trade Estimate Report on Foreign Trade Barriers 2011*, pp. 30, 141, 229, and 246.

34. Office of the U.S. Trade Representative, *National Trade Estimate Report on Foreign Trade Barriers 2011*, p. 340.

35. Office of the U.S. Trade Representative, *National Trade Estimate Report on Foreign Trade Barriers 2011*, p. 40.

36. Office of the U.S. Trade Representative, *2011 Report on Technical Barriers to Trade*, p. 64.

37. Office of the U.S. Trade Representative, *National Trade Estimate Report on Foreign Trade Barriers 2011*, p. 370.

38. Office of the U.S. Trade Representative, *National Trade Estimate Report on Foreign Trade Barriers 2011*, p. 129.

39. Office of the U.S. Trade Representative, *National Trade Estimate Report on Foreign Trade Barriers 2011*, pp. 298, 299.

40. Office of the U.S. Trade Representative, *National Trade Estimate Report on Foreign Trade Barriers 2011*, p. 245.

41. Office of the U.S. Trade Representative, *National Trade Estimate Report on Foreign Trade Barriers 2011*, p. 293.

42. Office of the U.S. Trade Representative, *National Trade Estimate Report on Foreign Trade Barriers 2011*, pp. 41 and 222.

43. Office of the U.S. Trade Representative, *National Trade Estimate Report on Foreign Trade Barriers 2011*, p 373.

44. "US States Become Addicted to Use of Economic Sweeteners," *Financial Times*, March 23, 2006, p. 19.

45. "Rum Maker Wins Incentives," *Wall Street Journal*, October 7, 2009, p. B6.

46. Committee on Ways and Means, *Operation of the Foreign Trade Zones Program of the United States and Its Implications for the U.S. Economy and U.S. International Trade*, October 1989, Serial 101–56, pp. 281 and 326.

47. Export-Import Bank of the United States, *2010 Annual Report* (Washington, DC: Eximbank, 2011).

48. "U.S. export terms pose test for Beijing," *Wall Street Journal*, January 12, 2011, p. A11.

49. "Stakes raised in EU bid to curb China exports," *Financial Times*, May 16, 2011, p. 2; "Glossy paper from China, Indonesia to face U.S. anti-subsidy import duties," *Bloomberg News*, October 22, 2010.

50. "WTO backs U.S. in tire dispute with China," *Wall Street Journal*, December 13, 2010; "U.S. to impose tariff on tires from China," *Washington Post*, September 12, 2009; "U.S. adds tariffs on Chinese tires," *New York Times*, September 11, 2009.

CHAPTER 10

International Cooperation Among Nations

AFTER STUDYING THIS CHAPTER, YOU SHOULD BE ABLE TO:

1. Explain the importance of the GATT and the WTO to international businesses.

2. Contrast the different forms of economic integration among cooperating countries.

3. Analyze the opportunities for international businesses created by completion of the EU's internal market.

4. Describe the other major trading blocs in today's world economy.

Access a host of interactive learning aids at **www.pearsonglobaleditions.com/ mymanagementlab** to help strengthen your understanding of the chapter concepts.

MyManagementLab

Danita Delimont/Alamy

TRADE AND PROSPERITY: THE CASE OF MEXICO

Is trade or aid the best means of promoting economic development? For Mexico, the answer is clear: trade. From 1917 to 1982, Mexico relied on inward-looking economic policies: high tariffs to discourage imports; restrictions on foreign direct investment (FDI) to reduce foreign presence in its economy; government ownership of key industries; and powerful, conservative bureaucracies that strangled entrepreneurship and innovation. Although the Mexican economy grew during this time span, its performance did not match that of export-driven economies such as those of Hong Kong or South Korea. The last six presidents of Mexico have reversed these policies, in the process lowering tariffs, encouraging FDI, privatizing state-owned enterprises, and joining the General Agreement on Tariffs and Trade (GATT) and the World Trade Organization (WTO). Under their leadership, Mexico signed a series of free trade agreements with the United States and Canada, the European Union (EU), Israel, Japan, Chile, and five of its Central American neighbors.

While Mexico's treaty with Japan is its newest, the North American Free Trade Agreement (NAFTA) is the big story. Its implementation in 1994 opened up the U.S. and Canadian markets to Mexican firms, allowing the firms to take advantage of Mexico's lower labor costs. Although most newspaper headlines focused on NAFTA's likely impact on big industries such as autos or textiles, Mexican entrepreneurs have been quick to spot new opportunities. For example, a $100-million-a-year dental supply business has sprung up in Mexico as a result of NAFTA, producing labor-intensive products like buccal tubes (the straps that bind braces to teeth), endodontic files (stainless steel corkscrews used in root canals), and dental wax (a gummy paste used as a mold for crowns).

Another booming market is contract manufacturing (particularly in Guadalajara, Mexico's second largest city), which is being driven by the changing economics of the electronic goods market. Many electronics firms are outsourcing their manufacturing because they recognize they cannot methodically erect a facility to build each new product conjured up by their engineering wizards. By the time the factory is ready, the product may be obsolete. Thus, high-tech firms turn to contract manufacturers, who know the ins and outs of starting up a production line for the latest electronic gizmo and can ramp production up or down should demand for it soar—or collapse. Contract manufacturers like Flextronics International and Sanmina-SCI have invested more than $2 billion in Guadalajara plants to produce goods for companies like Cisco, Ericsson, and Hewlett-Packard. Even though labor costs are higher in Guadalajara than in China and other Asian countries, closeness to customers, not labor costs, is the key. UPS and Federal Express air freighters can deliver goods made in Guadalajara to Canadian and U.S. customers the next morning. Delivering Asian-made high-tech products is either too slow (a ship takes two weeks) or too expensive (long-distance air freight can be costly).

Mexican service industries are also booming. For example, Servicios Textiles de Baja California sorts, launders, folds, and delivers some 20 tons of linens a week to firms located on both sides of the Mexican–U.S. border. Other companies have located call centers, data-processing facilities, and other customer support services in Mexico. For example, Seagate Technology's Reynosa facility provides after-sales support for its North American customers. In 2010, Mexico's exports of such business services to the United States exceeded $2.7 billion.

Mexico still faces many challenges, of course. The escalation of violence among rival drug gangs has scared off some foreign investors. For instance, Electrolux AB, the giant Swedish appliance manufacturer, chose to locate its newest factory in Memphis, Tennessee, rather than Mexico, in part due to security concerns. China's joining the World Trade Organization has also threatened the trade-driven boom in the Mexican economy. China's entry, coupled with a slowdown in the U.S. economy in 2001, put a damper on Mexico's export surge. However, after a two-year slowdown, Mexico's economy regained its footing and exhibited healthy growth. While some manufacturers of low-margin, low-valued-added products like toys, apparel, and low-end electronics migrated to China to take advantage of low labor costs, Mexico still benefits from its proximity to the U.S. market and its integration into the supply chains of North American firms. For example, manufacturers of flat panel high-definition TVs, such as Samsung, Sony, and Vizio, find Mexico a convenient location to assemble their products for delivery to North American consumers. Querétaro, a colonial era city in the country's central highlands, is becoming a hub for aerospace firms. General Electric employs 1,300 engineers at its Querétaro R&D center designing engines for Airbus and Boeing widebody jets, while Bombardier's 1,600 workers are constructing the fuselage, electrical systems, and horizontal and vertical stabilizers for the company's newest line of corporate jets. Nonetheless, Mexican officials recognize that they have to raise the productivity of their workforce and improve the country's infrastructure if Mexico is to continue to compete successfully in the global economy.[1] ■

In Chapter 9 we explored the ways in which national governments intervene in international trade and investment. When a country adopts restrictions on international commerce, it can benefit at least some of its producers and workers. But other countries may retaliate with similar restrictions, thinking that they too will gain. As restrictions proliferate, international trading opportunities decline, and all countries end up losing. They often then realize that each is better off if they cooperate and agree to forswear trade restrictions. Such policy changes underlie the transformation of the Mexican economy, as we just noted.

International cooperative agreements form a major part of the economic environment in which international businesses operate. To be successful, international businesspeople must be knowledgeable about these agreements and use them to create business opportunities for their firms and counteract competitors' actions. Of particular importance is the growth of regional trading blocs, such as the Mercosur Accord and NAFTA, which are designed to reduce trade barriers among their members. By far the boldest of these regional economic integration efforts is that of the European Union (EU), most of whose members have replaced or are planning to replace their national currencies with a single currency, the euro.

The General Agreements on Tariffs and Trade and the World Trade Organization

The collapse of the international economy during the Great Depression between World Wars I and II has been blamed partly on countries' imposing prohibitive tariffs, quotas, and other protectionist measures on imported goods. Trading and investment opportunities for international businesses dried up as country after country adopted such "beggar-thy-neighbor" policies. By raising tariff and quota barriers, each nation believed that it could help its own industries and citizens, even though in doing so it might harm the citizens and industries of other countries. For example, in 1930 the United States sought to protect domestic industries from import competition by raising tariffs under the Smoot-Hawley Tariff Act to an average of 53 percent. However, as other countries, such as the United Kingdom, Italy, and France, constructed similarly high tariff walls, none gained a competitive advantage over another, and as international trade declined, all suffered from the contraction of export markets.

To ensure that the post–World War II international peace would not be threatened by such trade wars, representatives of the leading trading nations met in Havana, Cuba, in 1947 to create the International Trade Organization (ITO). The ITO's mission was to promote international trade; however, the organization never came into being because of a controversy over how extensive its powers should be. Instead the ITO's planned mission was taken over by the **General Agreement on Tariffs and Trade (GATT)**, which had been developed as part of the preparations for the Havana conference. From 1947 to 1994, the signatories to the GATT (the GATT was technically an agreement, not an organization) fought to reduce barriers to international trade. The GATT provided a forum for trade ministers to discuss policies and problems of common concern. In January 1995, it was replaced by the World Trade Organization, which adopted the GATT's mission.

The Role of the General Agreement on Tariffs and Trade

The GATT's goal was to promote a free and competitive international trading environment benefiting efficient producers, an objective supported by many multinational corporations (MNCs). The GATT accomplished this by sponsoring multilateral negotiations to reduce tariffs, quotas, and other nontariff barriers. Because high tariffs were initially the most serious impediment to world trade, the GATT first focused on reducing the general level

TABLE 10.1 GATT Negotiating Rounds

Round	Dates	Number of Participants	Average Tariff Cut (%)
Geneva	1947	23	35
Annecy	1949	13	NA
Torquay	1950–1951	38	25
Geneva	1956	26	NA
Dillon	1960–1962	45	NA
Kennedy	1964–1967	62	35
Tokyo	1973–1979	99	33
Uruguay	1986–1994	117	36

of tariff protection. It sponsored a series of eight negotiating "rounds," generally named after the location where each round of negotiations began (see Table 10.1), during its lifetime. The cumulative effect of the GATT's eight rounds was a substantial reduction in tariffs. Tariffs imposed by the developed countries fell from an average of more than 40 percent in 1948 to approximately 3 percent in 2005. As Figure 6.1 demonstrated (see page 172), the GATT negotiations have led to dramatic growth in world trade since the end of World War II.

To help international businesses compete in world markets regardless of their nationality, the GATT sought to ensure that international trade was conducted on a nondiscriminatory basis. This was accomplished through use of the **most favored nation (MFN) principle,** which requires that any preferential treatment granted to one country must be extended to all countries. (See "Bringing the World into Focus" for further discussion of MFN.) Under GATT rules, all members were required to utilize the MFN principle in dealing with other members. For example, if the United States cut the tariff on imports of British trucks to 20 percent, it also had to reduce its tariffs on imported trucks from all other members to 20 percent. Because of the MFN principle, multilateral, rather than bilateral, trade negotiations were encouraged, thereby strengthening the GATT's role.

There are two important exceptions to the MFN principle:

1. To assist poorer countries in their economic development efforts, the GATT permitted members to lower tariffs to developing countries without lowering them for more developed countries. Such reduced rates offered to developing countries are known as the **generalized system of preferences (GSP).** Each country is free to choose those developing countries to which it will apply GSP treatment. For instance, during the Cold War the United States

---

BRINGING THE WORLD INTO FOCUS   **MOST NATIONS ARE FAVORED**

As part of the rules of membership in the GATT and the WTO, each member must grant every other member most favored nation (MFN) status. However, members are also free to grant nonmembers MFN status as well. The United States, for example, grants MFN status to nearly all countries. The few countries excluded are those considered diplomatically hostile to it, such as Cuba and North Korea.

The Clinton administration decided to adopt the term "normal trade relations" (NTR) to replace MFN. It had two reasons for doing so. The public reason was that NTR was a more accurate description; if almost all countries receive such treatment, then the practice is "normal" rather than "most favored." There was also a political reason. The administration was in a battle to secure permanent MFN status for China as part of the administration's agreement to allow China to join the WTO. President Clinton judged that it would be easier to sway public opinion and win the vote in Congress if the United States were perceived to be treating China normally, rather than providing it favorable treatment. Hence, MFN became NTR in U.S. trade documents.

granted access to the lower GSP tariff rates to countries that were diplomatically allied with it against the Soviet Union. Obviously, by reducing these tariffs, the generalized system of preferences increases the pressures on domestic firms that are vulnerable to import competition from the developing countries. In contrast, MNCs can reduce their input and production costs by locating factories and assembly facilities in countries benefiting from the generalized system of preferences.

2. The second exemption is for comprehensive trade agreements that promote economic integration, such as the EU and NAFTA.

Although the GATT's underlying principles were noble, its framers recognized that domestic political pressures often forced countries to retreat from pure free trade policies. The GATT permitted countries to protect their domestic industries on a nondiscriminatory basis, although under GATT rules countries were supposedly restricted to the use of tariffs only. Quotas and other nontariff barriers can often be applied discriminatorily, and they are less "transparent"—that is, it is often harder to judge their impact on competition. However, there were loopholes in these rules, so many countries adopted quotas and other nontariff barriers yet remained in compliance with the GATT. For example, U.S. quotas restricting imports of peanuts, sugar, and other agricultural products that were granted a "temporary" waiver from GATT rules in 1955 remained in effect for decades. Countries were allowed exemptions to preserve national security or to remedy balance of payments problems. The GATT also permitted countries in certain circumstances to protect themselves against "too much" foreign competition.

The eighth, and final, round of GATT negotiations began in Uruguay in September 1986. Ratified by GATT members in Morocco in March 1994, the **Uruguay Round** agreement took effect in 1995. Like its seven predecessors, the Uruguay Round cut tariffs on imported goods—in this case, from an average of 4.7 percent to 3 percent. As average tariff rates declined, however, most countries recognized that nontariff barriers had become a more important impediment to the growth of world trade, so the Uruguay Round addressed them as well. For example, the participants made substantial progress in abolishing quotas by encouraging countries to convert existing quotas to tariff rate quotas (see Chapter 9). More importantly, Uruguay Round participants agreed to create the WTO. They established its initial agenda and granted it more power to attack trade barriers than the GATT had possessed.

The World Trade Organization

The **World Trade Organization** came into being on January 1, 1995. Headquartered in Geneva, Switzerland, the WTO includes 153 member and 30 observer countries. Members are required to open their markets to international trade and to follow the WTO's rules. The WTO has three primary goals:

1. Promote trade flows by encouraging nations to adopt nondiscriminatory, predictable trade policies. (Figure 10.1 details the WTO's principles for the world trading system.)
2. Reduce remaining trade barriers through multilateral negotiations. During the first several years of its existence the WTO emphasized negotiations focused on specific sectors of the world economy. For example, the WTO sponsored the 1996 Information Technology Agreement to eliminate tariffs on such products as computers, software, fax machines, and pagers. Similar agreements covering financial services and telecommunications were signed in 1997. In 2001, the WTO initiated the **Doha Round** of trade negotiations. The Doha negotiations were supposed to be completed by January 2005. The talks deadlocked over several troublesome issues. While reducing tariffs on manufactured goods exported to developing countries and freeing trade in services proved to be stumbling blocks, the most contentious issue facing the Doha negotiators was freeing trade in agricultural goods, a problem that also stymied the GATT. Trade in many agricultural products has been distorted by export subsidies, import restrictions, and other trade barriers. The **Cairns Group**, a group of major agricultural exporters led by Argentina, Australia, Brazil, Canada, and Thailand, has pressured other WTO members to ensure that the Doha

FIGURE 10.1

**The WTO's Principles
of the Trading System**

Source: "About the WTO,"
www.wto.org.

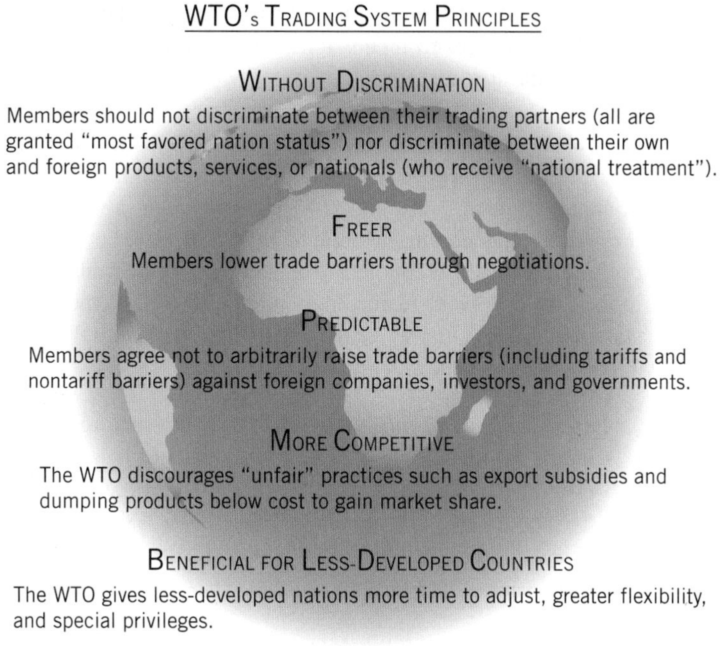

WTO's Trading System Principles

Without Discrimination

Members should not discriminate between their trading partners (all are
granted "most favored nation status") nor discriminate between their own
and foreign products, services, or nationals (who receive "national treatment").

Freer

Members lower trade barriers through negotiations.

Predictable

Members agree not to arbitrarily raise trade barriers (including tariffs and
nontariff barriers) against foreign companies, investors, and governments.

More Competitive

The WTO discourages "unfair" practices such as export subsidies and
dumping products below cost to gain market share.

Beneficial for Less-Developed Countries

The WTO gives less-developed nations more time to adjust, greater flexibility,
and special privileges.

Round significantly reduces barriers to agricultural trade, but has been unable as yet to
structure terms that satisfy China, India, Japan, and many other countries. Although the
Doha negotiations have not yet been terminated, few trade experts expect any significant
breakthroughs in the near term.[2]

3. Establish impartial procedures for resolving trade disputes among members.

The WTO was clearly designed to build on and expand the successes of the GATT; indeed, the GATT agreement was incorporated into the WTO agreement. The WTO differs
from the GATT in two important dimensions. First, the GATT focused on promoting trade in
goods, whereas the WTO's mandate is much broader: It is responsible for trade in goods,
trade in services, international intellectual property protection, and trade-related investment.
Second, the WTO's enforcement powers are much stronger than those possessed by
the GATT.

THE GENERAL AGREEMENT ON TRADE IN SERVICES (GATS) Another challenge facing the WTO is
reducing barriers to trade in services. The Uruguay Round developed a set of principles under
which such trade should be conducted. For instance, government controls on service trade
should be administered in a nondiscriminatory fashion. One nondiscriminatory approach is
the use of **national treatment**, whereby a country treats foreign firms the same way it treats
domestic firms. If, for example, national insurance regulators require domestic firms to maintain
reserves equal to 10 percent of their outstanding policies, then the identical requirement should
be imposed on foreign firms operating in that country. Service industries are very diverse,
however, and few concrete agreements regarding specific service industries were included in the
Uruguay Round. The WTO members began negotiating a new GATS agreement in 2000, but
progress has been slow.

AGREEMENT ON TRADE-RELATED ASPECTS OF INTELLECTUAL PROPERTY RIGHTS (TRIPS)
Entrepreneurs, artists, and inventors have been hurt by inadequate enforcement by many
countries of laws prohibiting illegal usage, copying, or counterfeiting of intellectual property.
These problems are particularly widespread in the music, filmed entertainment, and computer
software industries. On paper, the Uruguay Round agreement substantially strengthened the
protection granted to owners of intellectual property rights and developed enforcement and
dispute settlement procedures to punish violators. Unfortunately, many owners of intellectual
property believe that intellectual property theft has become more blatant and widespread

subsequent to the Uruguay Round, in large part because of lax enforcement of their property rights by many governments and those governments' unwillingness to live up to their Uruguay Round commitments.

TRADE-RELATED INVESTMENT MEASURES AGREEMENT (TRIMS) WTO members are well aware of the relationship between trade and investment: Approximately one-third of the $15.9 trillion of annual trade in goods and services is between subsidiaries of a parent organization. However, the developing countries believe that FDI can be an important mechanism for promoting economic growth, technology transfer, and industrialization and thus were unwilling to yield much control over it. Accordingly, the TRIMS agreement in the Uruguay Round is but a modest start toward eliminating national regulations on FDI that may distort or restrict trade. The TRIMS agreement affects:

- *Trade-balancing rules:* Countries may not require foreign investors to limit their imports of inputs to an amount equal to their exports of local production.
- *Foreign-exchange access:* Countries may not restrict foreign investors' access to foreign exchange.
- *Domestic sales requirements:* Countries may not require the investor to sell a percentage of a factory's output in the local market.[3]

Under certain circumstances, however, developing countries are able to waive these requirements.

ENFORCEMENT OF WTO DECISIONS The enforcement power of the GATT was notoriously weak. A country found to have violated its GATT obligations by an arbitration panel was in effect asked, "Is it okay if we punish you?" Most countries, as you might expect, answered "no," and there the matter ended. Under WTO rules, a country failing to live up to the agreement— for example, by imposing a nontariff barrier contrary to the WTO agreement—may have a complaint filed against it. If a WTO panel finds the country in violation of the rules, the panel will likely ask the country to eliminate the trade barrier. If the country refuses, the WTO will allow the complaining country to impose trade barriers on the offending country equal to the damage caused by the trade barrier. Furthermore, the offending country is not allowed to counterretaliate by imposing new trade barriers against the complainant. For instance, the WTO allowed Brazil to impose $248 million in trade sanctions on Canada after finding that Canada provided low-interest loans in violation of WTO rules that allowed Bombardier, a Canadian manufacturer of regional jets, to beat out Brazilian rival Embraer for a $1.7 billion order.[4] Similarly, the WTO will likely authorize sanctions to be imposed by the United States on the EU and by the EU on the United States once the Boeing-Airbus complaints discussed in Chapter 9's opening case exhaust the WTO's appeal process.

Although barriers to international trade and investment remain, no one believed they would come tumbling down like the walls of Jericho as soon as the WTO arrived on the scene. Most trade experts give the WTO good marks for its accomplishments during its first decade of existence, such as the sectoral agreements in telecommunications, information technology, and financial services. However, the failure of the WTO to break the deadlock over the Doha Round negotiations has raised some concerns about future reductions in trade barriers and the future effectiveness of the WTO.[5] Moreover, the growing importance of the WTO has attracted opposition to its actions. Environmentalists and human rights activists, for instance, believe that the WTO needs to incorporate more sensitivity to environmental and human needs in its decision making. Labor unions and workers' groups fear that the WTO's decisions weaken their bargaining power and threaten their members' job security.

Regional Economic Integration

Regional alliances to promote liberalization of international trade are an important feature of the post–World War II international landscape. More than 200 such agreements are in existence, although not all have had much practical impact. They present international businesses with myriad opportunities and challenges. The past decade in particular has seen a rise in the number of trading blocs, as countries seek to integrate their economies more closely in order to open new markets for their firms and lower prices for their consumers.

Forms of Economic Integration

Regional trading blocs differ significantly in form and function. The characteristic of most importance to international businesses is the extent of economic integration among a bloc's members, for it affects exporting and investment opportunities available to firms from member and nonmember countries. There are five different forms of regional economic integration: free trade area, customs union, common market, economic union, and political union. We discuss these next in order of ascending degree of economic integration.

FREE TRADE AREA A **free trade area** encourages trade among its members by eliminating trade barriers (tariffs, quotas, and other nontariff barriers [NTBs]) among them. An example of such an arrangement is NAFTA, which reduces tariffs and NTBs to trade among Canada, Mexico, and the United States.

Although a free trade area reduces trade barriers among its members, each member is free to establish its own trade policies against nonmembers. As a result, members of free trade areas are often vulnerable to the problem of **trade deflection**, in which nonmembers reroute (or deflect) their exports to the member nation with the lowest external trade barriers. Canada, for example, may use high tariffs or quotas to discourage imports of a given product from nonmembers, while the United States may impose few restrictions on imports of the same good from nonmembers. Taking advantage of the latter's low barriers, nonmembers may deflect their Canada-destined exports by first shipping the good to the United States and then reexporting it from the United States to Canada. To prevent trade deflection from destroying their members' trade policies toward nonmembers, most free trade agreements specify **rules of origin**, which detail the conditions under which a good is classified as a member good or a nonmember good. For example, under NAFTA rules of origin, most goods qualify for preferential treatment as a North American product only if they undergo substantial processing or assembly in Mexico, Canada, or the United States.

CUSTOMS UNION A **customs union** combines the elimination of internal trade barriers among its members with the adoption of common external trade policies toward nonmembers. Because of the uniform treatment of products from nonmember countries, a customs union avoids the trade deflection problem. A firm from a nonmember country pays the same tariff rate on exports to any member of the customs union.

Historically, the most important customs union was the *Zollverein,* created in 1834 by several independent principalities in what is now Germany. The eventual unification of Germany in 1871 was hastened by this customs union, which tightened the economic bonds among the Germanic principalities and facilitated their political union. A more contemporary example of a customs union is the Mercosur Accord, an agreement initially signed by Argentina, Brazil, Paraguay, and Uruguay to promote trade among themselves. In 2010, Russia, Belarus, and Kazakhstan similarly agreed to create a customs union.

COMMON MARKET A **common market** is a third step along the path to total economic integration. As in a customs union, members of a common market eliminate internal trade barriers among themselves and adopt a common external trade policy toward nonmembers. A common market goes a step further, however, by eliminating barriers that inhibit the movement of factors of production—labor, capital, and technology—among its members. Workers may move from their homeland and practice their profession or trade in any of the other member nations. Firms may locate production facilities, invest in other businesses, and utilize their technologies anywhere within the common market. Productivity within the common market is expected to rise because factors of production are free to locate where the returns to them are highest. An example of a common market is the European Economic Area, which is an agreement by EU members and several other European countries to promote the free movement of labor, capital, and technology among them.

ECONOMIC UNION An **economic union** represents full integration of the economies of two or more countries. In addition to eliminating internal trade barriers, adopting common external trade policies, and abolishing restrictions on the mobility of factors of production among members, an economic union requires its members to coordinate their economic policies (monetary policy, fiscal policy, taxation, and social welfare programs) in order to blend their economies into a single entity. The members of the European Union who have adopted the euro as their domestic currency are in the process of creating an economic union among themselves.

POLITICAL UNION A **political union** is the complete political as well as economic integration of two or more countries, thereby effectively making them one country. An example of a political union is the integration of the 13 separate colonies operating under the Articles of Confederation into a new country, the United States of America. Figure 10.2 summarizes the five forms of economic integration.

The Impact of Economic Integration on Firms

From the viewpoint of an individual firm, regional integration is a two-edged sword. Consider elimination of internal trade barriers, a feature common to all five forms of economic integration. Lowering tariffs within the regional trading bloc opens the markets of member countries to all member country firms. Firms can lower their average production and distribution costs by capturing economies of scale as they expand their customer base within the trading bloc. The lower cost structure will also help the firms compete internationally outside the trading bloc. For instance, many Canadian manufacturers supported their country's free trade agreements with the United States. They believed that improved access to the large U.S. market would allow longer production runs in Canadian factories, thereby lowering their average costs and making Canadian goods more competitive in international markets inside and outside the free trade area. However, elimination of trade barriers also exposes a firm's home market to competition from firms located in other member countries, thus threatening less efficient firms.

A regional trading bloc may also attract FDI from nonmember countries, as firms outside the bloc seek the benefits of insider status by establishing manufacturing facilities within the bloc. Most non-European MNCs, including General Mills, Toyota, and Samsung, have invested heavily in the EU to take advantage of Europe's increased economic integration. These investments bolster the productivity of European workers and increase the choices available to European consumers, but threaten established European firms such as Unilever, Renault, and Siemens.

Typically, each form of economic integration confers benefits on the national economy as a whole but often hurts specific sectors and communities within that economy. As a result,

FIGURE 10.2
Forms of Economic Integration

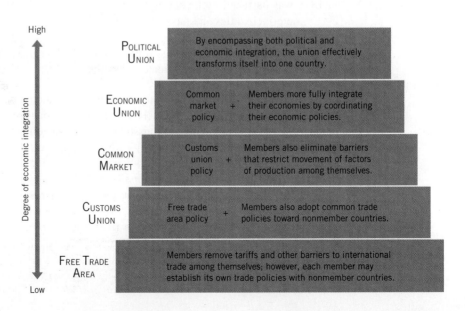

negotiating any form of economic integration is not easy. Special-interest groups that feel they will be harmed by an agreement will lobby against it. For example, U.S. and Canadian autoworkers lobbied against NAFTA, fearing that Ford, GM, and Chrysler would shift production to Mexico to take advantage of its lower-cost labor. As a result of such internal political pressures, few economic integration treaties are "pure"; most contain some exemptions to quiet politically powerful domestic special-interest groups.

The European Union

The most important regional trading bloc in the world today is the European Union (EU). The EU's 27 member countries, with a combined population of 499 million, compose one of the world's richest markets, with a total gross domestic product (GDP) of $16.4 trillion, or about 28 percent of the world economy. (See Table 10.2 and Map 10.1.)

Like the IMF, the World Bank, and the GATT, the creation of the EU was motivated by the desires of war-weary Europeans to promote peace and prosperity through economic and political cooperation. To further this objective, six European nations—France, West Germany, Italy, and

TABLE 10.2 The European Union, 2009 Data

Country	Total Population (millions)	Total GDP (billions)	Per Capita Income*	Date of Entry	Votes in Council	Votes in Parliament
Austria	8.4	381	46,850	1995	10	17
Belgium	10.8	471	45,310	1957	12	22
Bulgaria	7.6	49	5,770	2007	10	17
Cyprus	0.9	21	26,940	2004	4	6
Czech Republic	10.5	190	17,310	2004	12	22
Denmark	5.5	310	58,930	1973	7	13
Estonia	1.3	19	14,060	2004	4	6
Finland	5.3	238	45,680	1995	7	13
France	62.6	2,649	42,680	1957	29	72
Germany	81.9	3,330	42,560	1957	29	99
Greece	11.3	330	28,630	1981	12	22
Hungary	10.0	129	12,980	2004	12	22
Ireland	4.4	227	44,310	1973	7	12
Italy	60.2	2,113	35,080	1957	29	72
Latvia	2.3	26	12,390	2004	4	8
Lithuania	3.3	37	11,410	2004	7	12
Luxembourg	0.5	52	74,430	1957	4	6
Malta	0.4	7	16,690	2004	3	5
Netherlands	16.5	792	49,350	1957	13	25
Poland	38.1	430	12,260	2004	27	50
Portugal	10.6	232	20,940	1986	12	22
Romania	21.5	161	8,330	2007	14	33
Slovakia	5.4	88	16,130	2004	7	13
Slovenia	2.0	48	23,520	2004	4	7
Spain	46.0	1,460	31,870	1986	27	50
Sweden	9.3	406	48,930	1995	10	18
United Kingdom	61.8	2,174	41,520	1973	29	72
Total	498.6	16,373			345	736

Sources: World Bank, *World Development Report*, 2011; World Bank website; European Union website.
*In U.S. dollars.

MAP 10.1

The European Union

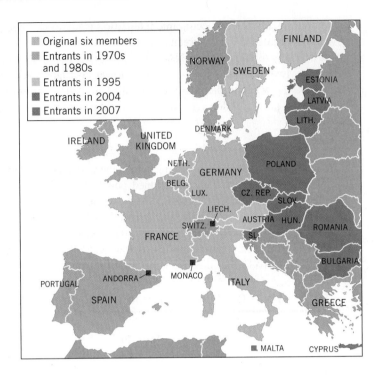

the **Benelux nations** (Belgium, the Netherlands, and Luxembourg)—signed the Treaty of Rome in 1957. The **Treaty of Rome** established the European Economic Community (EEC) and called for the development of a common market among the six member states.

Over the ensuing five decades, the EEC changed its name twice and expanded its membership dramatically. During the 1970s, the United Kingdom, Denmark, and Ireland joined the EEC, which became commonly referred to as the European Community (EC). During the 1980s, Greece, Portugal, and Spain entered the EC, bringing its membership to 12 countries. In 1993, the 12 EC members signed the Treaty of Maastricht; as a result of this agreement, the EC became known as the EU. In 1995, Austria, Finland, and Sweden joined the EU. Cyprus, the Czech Republic, Estonia, Hungary, Latvia, Lithuania, Malta, Poland, Slovakia, and Slovenia became EU members in 2004. Bulgaria and Romania joined the EU in 2007, bringing its total membership to 27.

Governing the European Union

The EU is a unique institution. Its members are sovereign nations that have agreed, sometimes begrudgingly, to cede certain of their powers to the EU. The EU can be characterized both as an "intergovernmental government" (because it is a government of national governments) and as a "supranational government" (because it exercises power above the national level). The EU is governed by five organizations that perform its executive, administrative, legislative, and judicial functions:

- The European Council (meets in Brussels, Belgium)
- The Council of the European Union (headquartered in Brussels, Belgium)
- The European Commission (also based in Brussels)
- The European Parliament (normally meets in Strasbourg, France)
- The European Court of Justice (sitting in Luxembourg)

Because most of the EU's employees are located in Brussels, many Europeans refer to the EU's government as "Brussels," the same way many Canadians refer to their national government as "Ottawa" or many Americans refer to theirs as "Washington."

THE EUROPEAN COUNCIL The **European Council** consists of the heads of government or of state of each of the member states, the President of the European Council, and the President of the European Commission. The EU's High Representative of the Union for Foreign Affairs and

Security Policy also participates in its meetings. Normally convening twice every six months, the European Council shapes the EU's political priorities and policy agendas. The European Council's decisions are usually based on consensus, unless the EU treaties require a different voting rule. In reaching these decisions, only the heads of government may vote. Although it has met informally beginning in 1974, the European Council became an official EU institution only in 2009, when the Treaty of Lisbon entered into force.

THE COUNCIL OF THE EUROPEAN UNION The **Council of the European Union** (previously named the Council of Ministers) is composed of 27 representatives, each selected directly by and responsible to his or her home government. Which representative a country sends to a Council meeting depends on the Council's agenda. For example, if the Council is dealing with farm policies, each country typically sends its minister of agriculture. The Council presidency rotates among the members every six months. In most Council decisions, a weighted voting system is used. France, Germany, Italy, and the United Kingdom have the most votes, 29 each, and tiny Malta has the fewest, 3. The allocation of votes is in rough proportion to the population and economic importance of the members.

The Council is the EU's most powerful decision-making body. Each representative pursues the interests of his or her home government. The Council's strong powers reflect the reluctance of the member states to surrender power to Brussels on issues they view as vital to their national interests. As a result, some Council decisions require unanimous approval—entry of new members, taxation, foreign and security policy initiatives, and amending EU treaties. On matters perceived to be less threatening to national interests, Council decisions require only a qualified majority (255 yes votes of a possible 345 votes, or 73.9 percent) for passage, subject to two other conditions, as "Bringing the World into Focus" reports. Effectively, a coalition of three large countries and one smaller country can block a decision. However, the EU strives to create consensus on all issues and often slows its deliberations to develop compromises amenable to all the members, even when unanimity is not required. As a result, an overwhelming percentage of Council decisions are made unanimously, regardless of the voting rules.

THE EUROPEAN COMMISSION The **European Commission** is composed of 27 people, one from each member state, selected for five-year terms. Once these individuals are in office, however, their loyalty is to the EU itself, not to their home countries. The Commission's primary mandate is to be the "guardian of the Treaties." The Commission also acts as the EU's administrative branch and manages the EU's €134 billion annual budget. Its functions include the following:

- It proposes legislation to be considered by the Council.
- It implements the provisions of the Treaty of Rome and other EU treaties.
- It protects the EU's interests in political debates, particularly in Council deliberations.
- It has extensive powers in implementing the EU's customs union, the Common Agricultural Policy (CAP), and the completion of the internal market.
- It administers the EU's permanent bureaucracy, which employs about 33,000 people—popularly known as "Eurocrats"—two-thirds of whom work at Commission headquarters in Brussels. Because the EU has 23 official languages, its translation budget is over $1 billion a year. It employs 1,750 linguists, who cumulatively are capable of translating any official language into any other official language—a possible 253 combinations.

THE EUROPEAN PARLIAMENT The **European Parliament** currently comprises 736 representatives elected in national elections to serve five-year terms. Seats are allocated in rough proportion to a country's population, although the smaller states (Malta, Cyprus, Luxembourg) are overrepresented on that basis. For example, Germany has 99 seats; France, Italy, and the United Kingdom are allocated 72 seats each; Cyprus and Luxembourg have 6 seats, and Malta 5 (refer back to Table 10.2). Of the EU's governing bodies the Parliament was originally the weakest. Initially it had only a consultative role in EU policymaking. However, it has used its budgetary powers to enlarge its influence within the EU's governing institutions, and it also gained additional powers under the Maastricht, Amsterdam, Nice, and Lisbon Treaties, as discussed later in this chapter.

The European Parliament was originally the weakest of the EU's governing bodies, but has gained increased powers as new agreements have amended the Treaty of Rome. It shares responsibility for adopting the EU's budget with the European Commission, and can dismiss the Commission with a vote of censure that obtains a two-thirds majority.

Gerard Cerles/AFP/Getty Images

THREE MAJORITIES ARE BETTER THAN ONE

The Treaty of Nice, like the Treaties of Maastricht and Amsterdam, broadened the number of areas where Council approval requires a qualified majority, rather than unanimity. However, because the number of votes allocated to member states for purposes of establishing a qualified majority is not strictly based on population, the larger members became concerned that they might lose power to the smaller members as the EU's membership expanded. As a result, the Treaty of Nice requires that a qualified majority can be obtained only if three conditions—the so-called triple majority—are met:

1. The decision receives 255 of a possible 345 votes in council, or 73.9 percent.

2. A majority of the member states approve the decision. (In some cases, two-thirds of the member states must approve.)
3. The decision is approved by members who represent at least 62 percent of the EU's population.

These rules are effective until November 2014, when new rules governing qualified majorities in the Council mandated by the Treaty of Lisbon are implemented.

Source: General Secretariat of the Council of the EU. *Information Note: Treaty of Lisbon,* December 2009. Office for Official Publications of the European Communities, "Who's Who in the European Union? What difference will the Treaty of Nice make?" Luxembourg, 2001.

The most telling example of the growing importance of the European Parliament was the mass resignation of all of the EU commissioners in 1999, after a Parliamentary inquiry uncovered fraud, inept management, favoritism, and a lack of accountability in several Commission-administered programs. Because many Europeans are concerned about the lack of accountability in the EU's programs and the lack of democracy in its decision-making processes, the role of the European Parliament is likely to continue to expand and its powers grow over time.

THE EUROPEAN COURT OF JUSTICE The **European Court of Justice** consists of 27 judges who serve six-year terms. The judges are selected jointly by the governments of the member states. The Court interprets EU law and ensures that members follow EU regulations and policies. Because national governments carry out the EU's policies, many cases reaching the European Court are referred from national courts asking it to interpret EU law. For example, the Court declared Germany's 450-year-old beer purity law regulating beer additives illegal, ruling that the law unreasonably restricted imports into Germany. Also, as discussed later in this chapter, its ruling in the *Cassis de Dijon* case smoothed the way for the creation of the common market called for in the Treaty of Rome.

THE LEGISLATIVE PROCESS The legislative process in the EU has never been simple, although it was once understandable, as captured in the catch phrase "the Commission proposes, the Parliament advises, and the Council disposes." As the Parliament has gained increased powers, the complexity of passing legislation has increased exponentially, as Figure 10.3, which depicts decision making under the **co-decision procedure**, shows. The co-decision procedure is used for settling most issues, including education, environmental protection, health, consumer policy, and free movement of workers. On issues where the co-decision process is not used, the process is simpler and the Parliament's power is weaker.

Because the EU prefers to develop a strong consensus on issues among its members before it adopts new legislation, transforming a Commission proposal into an EU law and then implementing that law into national legislation often takes years. The complicated governance arrangements of the EU reflect the ongoing struggle between the members' desire to retain their national sovereignty and their wish to create a supranational government with an international political and economic stature equal to those of the United States and Japan. As "Venturing Abroad" suggests, many MNCs exploit this power struggle to their benefit. The debate over national sovereignty versus supranational government is manifested in another way: Although the EU may formulate policies, in most circumstances they are implemented by members at a national level, giving the member states additional flexibility to tailor the policies to their unique circumstances.

The Struggle to Create a Common Market

The Treaty of Rome's goal of creating a common market was indeed visionary. Unfortunately, for the first 35 years of the EU's existence, it was nothing more than a cruel mirage. To establish a common market that would permit the free flow of goods, services, labor, capital, and technology, each EU member had to agree to change thousands of its national laws, product standards, and regulations to ensure that they were compatible with those of other EU members. In practice, the member nations moved cautiously because of political pressures from domestic special-interest groups.

As a result, conflicting national regulations, which affected nearly every good and service purchased by Europeans, hindered trade and the completion of the common market. For example, Spain required that keyboards sold within its borders contain a "tilde" key, an accent mark commonly used in the Spanish language. No other EU country prescribed such a regulation. Italy required pasta to be made of durum wheat, a requirement not decreed by other EU members.

The EU initially relied on a process of **harmonization** to eliminate such conflicts. The EU encouraged member countries to voluntarily adopt common, EU-wide ("harmonized") regulations affecting intra-EU trade in goods and services and movement of resources. The harmonization process moved slowly, however, as domestic political forces within the member states resisted change. For example, to protect the purity of its language, Spain refused to yield on the tilde issue. EU producers spent an estimated $260 billion (in 1988 dollars) annually to comply with different national regulations.[6] These increased costs raised the prices paid by European consumers and reduced the global competitiveness of European manufacturers.

FIGURE 10.3

The Co-Decision Procedure (Article 189b of the Treaty on European Union)

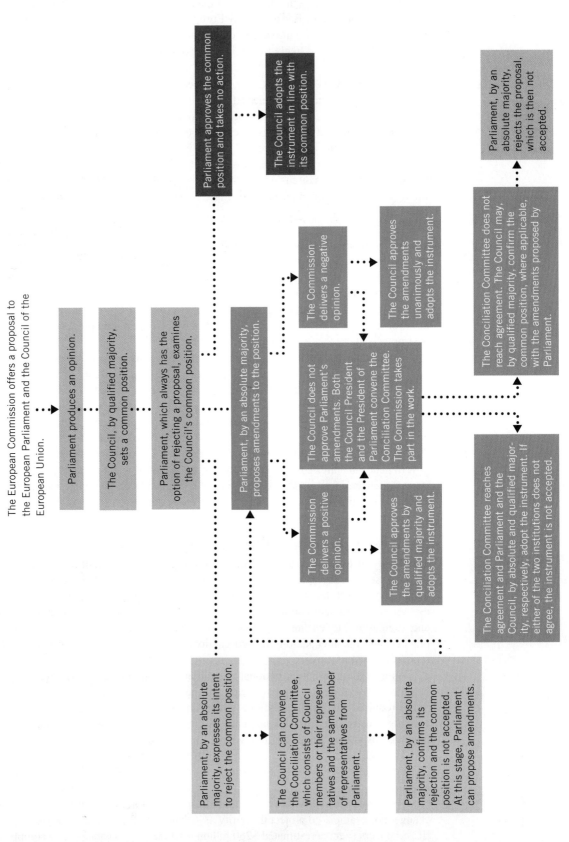

The European Commission offers a proposal to the European Parliament and the Council of the European Union.

Parliament produces an opinion.

The Council, by qualified majority, sets a common position.

Parliament, which always has the option of rejecting a proposal, examines the Council's common position.

Parliament approves the common position and takes no action.

The Council adopts the instrument in line with its common position.

Parliament, by an absolute majority, proposes amendments to the position.

The Commission delivers a negative opinion.

The Commission delivers a positive opinion.

The Council does not approve Parliament's amendments. Both the Council President and the President of Parliament convene the Conciliation Committee. The Commission takes part in the work.

The Council approves the amendments by qualified majority and adopts the instrument.

The Council approves the amendments unanimously and adopts the instrument.

Parliament, by an absolute majority, expresses its intent to reject the common position.

The Council can convene the Conciliation Committee, which consists of Council members or their representatives and the same number of representatives from Parliament.

Parliament, by an absolute majority, confirms its rejection and the common position is not accepted. At this stage, Parliament can propose amendments.

The Conciliation Committee reaches agreement and Parliament and the Council, by absolute and qualified majority, respectively, adopt the instrument. If either of the two institutions does not agree, the instrument is not accepted.

The Conciliation Committee does not reach agreement. The Council may, by qualified majority, confirm the common position, where applicable, with the amendments proposed by Parliament.

Parliament, by an absolute majority, rejects the proposal, which is then not accepted.

Source: The European Union, Luxembourg: Office for Official Publications of the European Communities, 1997, pp. 24–25.

VENTURING ABROAD   LOBBYING THE EUROPEAN UNION

The government of the European Union (EU) is engaged in many activities that affect international businesses, such as regulating payments to bumped passengers on overbooked airline flights or defining accounting standards. Because of the impact of the EU's decisions on the opening or closing of the enormous European market to international businesses, most countries maintain diplomatic relationships with the EU to ensure that it does not disregard their economic interests. The United States, for example, maintains a United States Mission to the European Union, led by a senior State Department official with ambassadorial status.

Savvy international businesspeople, however, do not rely solely on their home governments to protect them from adverse EU regulations. Indeed, an estimated 15,000 lobbyists work in Brussels, seeking to influence EU policy and decisions. A key to their success is understanding the power relationships within the EU—particularly between the Council of the European Union, which defends national interests, and the European Commission, which promotes the interests of an integrated Europe. Firms threatened by pending EU regulations can adopt two strategies:

1. They may lobby the Commission and its elaborate bureaucracy to adopt regulations more beneficial to their interests. Because the Commission must continually balance the often diverse interests

of EU members, firms can often influence the Commission to add their interests to the long list of other factors that it will consider in proposing legislation to the Council. Also, because of the Commission's commitment to completing the EU's internal market, firms have found that arguments promoting increased European integration are particularly well received by Eurocrats. For example, the Commission dropped proposed franchising regulations after U.S. firms convinced its staff that the pending regulations would hinder European integration.

2. Firms may lobby an ally on the Council. For example, remembering that "all politics is local," Japanese automakers that built assembly plants in the United Kingdom were able to enlist the help of the British representative on the Council—who was interested in preserving jobs in his country—when French and Italian automakers were urging the EU to adopt regulations prejudicial to those U.K. assembly plants.

Sources: "Europe proposes U.S.-style measures aimed at lobbyists," *Wall Street Journal*, May 4, 2006, p. A10; James N. Gardner, "Lobbying, European-style," *Europe*, November 1991 (Number 311), pp. 29–30; "European bureaucrats are writing the rules Americans will live by," *Wall Street Journal*, May 17, 1989, p. A1; "Lobbying Brussels in anticipation of 1992," *Wall Street Journal*, March 6, 1989, p. A12.

Progress toward eliminating conflicting product standards was so slow that some pessimists believed the EU would disintegrate. In 1979, however, the European Court of Justice heard the now famous *Cassis de Dijon* case. Rewe Zentral AG, a German wholesaler, wished to import Cassis de Dijon, a French liqueur made from black currants, into Germany. Cassis de Dijon failed to meet German regulatory standards, though—its alcohol content was too low. Rewe Zentral sued, arguing that Germany violated its obligations under the Treaty of Rome to promote the free movement of goods. The European Court of Justice found for the German wholesaler. In so doing, the Court created the concept of **mutual recognition**: if one member state determines that a product is appropriate for sale, then all other EU members are also obliged to do so under the provisions of the Treaty of Rome. Because France had determined Cassis de Dijon to be a legitimate liqueur, Germany was obligated to allow its sale as well.

Although the Court's findings contained some loopholes, the implications of the *Cassis de Dijon* case were profound. Adopting the concept of mutual recognition meant that the slow harmonization process could be bypassed, and conflicting product standards would no longer serve as barriers to trade among EU members. The timing of the case was also fortunate: Many European economic and political leaders were becoming increasingly concerned about the competitiveness of European firms in world markets. Their concerns reinvigorated the EU's commitment to completing the common market called for in the Treaty of Rome.

In 1985 the European Commission issued its *White Paper on Completing the Internal Market.* The *White Paper* called for accelerated progress on ending all trade barriers and restrictions on the free movement of goods, services, capital, and labor among members. Accepting the vision of the *White Paper*, the members in February 1986 signed the Single European Act, which took effect on July 1, 1987. The act was intended to help complete the formation of the *internal market* (the term developed by the Eurocrats to mean "common market") by December 31, 1992. Under the Single European Act, 279 broad regulatory changes had to be made to complete the internal market. Although not all these changes were fully implemented by the 1992 deadline, sufficient progress was made that many experts believed the Treaty of Rome's goal of creating a common market was close to being realized—but it took 35 years to do so! Still, if you think of the magnitude of the challenge—getting so many governments to cooperate peacefully on such a broad range of activities—perhaps 35 years is a remarkably short period of time.

The benefits of creating the common market are substantial to European firms, economies, and workers. The common market offers firms the opportunity to sell their goods in a large, rich market free from barriers to trade. However, although firms in EU member countries have gained improved access to a larger market, they also face increased competition in their home markets from other members' firms. This increased competition benefits consumers throughout the EU. Marketing, production, and research and development (R&D) costs have been reduced because firms generally have to comply with only one, EU-wide set of regulations instead of 27 separate sets of national regulations. Many firms have been able to restructure their European manufacturing operations to capture economies of scale and lower their production costs And the EU has been a magnet for new investment from other foreign firms eager to enter the lucrative European market and benefit from its common market. U.S. FDI in the EU has risen from $84 billion in 1985, when the *White Paper* was first issued, to $1.9 trillion in 2010. Similarly, more than 500 Japanese companies have established operations in the EU since 1985. More recently, Chinese firms have targeted the EU. From 2008 to 2010, Chinese companies invested $44 billion in EU companies, seeking to access the area's rich consumer market and sophisticated technologies.[7]

From Common Market to European Union

The EU members were justifiably proud of the progress made under the Single European Act. As the necessary changes were being finalized, the Cold War ended. The Soviet Union dissolved, the countries of Eastern Europe and Central Europe abandoned communism, and the threat of nuclear war diminished. The United States stood alone as the world's remaining superpower. Some European politicians believed that Europe should reassert itself on the world's stage and free itself from geopolitical domination by the United States. Meanwhile, many EU economists were arguing that European firms remained at a competitive disadvantage with regard to their North American and Asian rivals because of the risks and costs associated with doing business in so many different currencies. Addressing these concerns, the EU's Council of Ministers met in the Dutch city of Maastricht in December 1991 to discuss the EU's economic and political future. The result was a new treaty that amended the Treaty of Rome; this new treaty was known formally as the **Treaty on European Union** and informally as the **Maastricht Treaty.** After ratification by the then 12 EU members, the Maastricht Treaty came into force on November 1, 1993.

The Maastricht Treaty rests on three "pillars" designed to further Europe's economic and political integration:

1. A new agreement to create common foreign and defense policies among members
2. A new agreement to cooperate on police, judicial, and public safety matters
3. The old familiar European Community, with new provisions to create an economic and monetary union among member states

After the treaty was implemented, the European Community became commonly known as the European Union in recognition of the increasing integration of Europe. The Maastricht Treaty granted citizens the right to live, work, vote, and run for election anywhere within the EU and strengthened the powers of the EU's legislative body, the European Parliament, in budgetary, trade, cultural, and health matters. The treaty also created a new **cohesion fund**, a means of funneling economic development aid to countries whose per capita GDP is less than 90 percent of the EU average. The initial recipients of cohesion funds included Spain, Portugal, Greece, and Ireland, although Ireland's access to this aid terminated in 2004 because its then booming economy elevated Ireland's per capita income above the average for the EU; the 12 newest members of the EU also qualify for aid from the cohesion fund.

Without a doubt, the most important aspect of the Maastricht Treaty is the establishment of the **economic and monetary union (EMU)**. Its major task is to create a single currency, called the euro, to replace the existing national currencies. As of 2011, seventeen EU countries utilize the euro. Of the first 15 EU members, only Denmark, Sweden, and the United Kingdom chose not to become members of the single-currency bloc. Of the most

12 recent members, Cyprus, Estonia, Malta, Slovakia, and Slovenia have adopted the euro as their national currency, while the others have not yet met the convergence criteria necessary to do so.

The convergence criteria were developed because the architects of the economic and monetary union believed that convergence of the economic policies of its members was needed if the union was to be successful. Accordingly, any EU member wishing to adopt the euro has to meet five **convergence criteria**:

1. A country's inflation rate must be no more than 1.5 percentage points higher than the average of the three EU countries with the lowest inflation rates.
2. A country's long-term interest rates must be no more than 2 percentage points higher than that of the average of the three EU countries with the lowest long-term interest rates.
3. A country must have been a member of the EU's revised exchange-rate mechanism (ERM II) for two years, which commits the country to maintaining the value of its currency against the euro within a ±15 percent band, and it must not have devalued its currency during that time span.
4. A country's government budget deficit must be no more than 3 percent of its GDP.
5. A country's outstanding government debt must be trending toward no more than 60 percent of its GDP.

The euro came into being on January 1, 1999. On that date, the participants irrevocably fixed the value of their national currencies to the euro. However, euro coins and bank notes did not become immediately available. During a three-year transition period (1999 to 2001), the euro existed only as a bookkeeping currency to settle transactions among participating EU governments and banking systems. On New Year's Day 2002, euro coins and bills were placed into circulation, allowing ordinary citizens to use euros to transact their daily business. After a two-month transition period, the national currencies were withdrawn from circulation and no longer accepted as legal tender.

The creation of the euro reduced the exchange rate risks and currency conversion costs of firms doing business in the eurozone. Prior to the advent of the euro, firms conducting cross-border business within Europe were forced to pay fees to bankers typically ranging from 0.4 percent to 2 percent of the transaction amount anytime the firms wished to convert French francs into Belgian francs, Dutch guilders into Austrian schillings, and so on. Moreover, firms bore exchange rate risks in such transactions, as Chapter 8 discussed. Although the foreign-exchange market developed a variety of techniques to reduce (or hedge) this risk, these techniques nonetheless entailed paying fees to bankers or brokers. EU officials estimated that the creation of the euro saved Europeans $25 to $30 billion annually in currency conversion and hedging costs.

Creation of a single currency was not without controversy, however. Participating members lost control over their own domestic money supplies and economic destinies. The newly created **European Central Bank** is now responsible for controlling the eurozone's money supply, interest rates, and inflation. Moreover, under the terms of the **Stability and Growth Pact**, eurozone participants have agreed to limit their annual government deficits to no more than 3 percent of their GDPs, thus severely curtailing their ability to use fiscal policy to promote economic growth. In 2003, for instance, the German government raised taxes to comply with the 3 percent rule, despite the anemic growth of Germany's economy at the time—only 0.25 percent. As a result, national governments have become vulnerable to losing elections because of short-term pocketbook issues. Other critics fear that a "one size fits all" monetary policy for the entire eurozone will generate economic problems whenever the national economies of the eurozone countries are at different stages of the business cycle. In the mid-2000s, for example, the Irish economy was overheating, while the Italian, French, and German economies were stagnating. Irish government officials would have preferred that the European Central Bank aggressively raise interest rates in the hope of cooling down Ireland's economy, while officials from the other countries argued for more expansionary monetary policies.[8] The ensuing Irish housing bubble—and bursting of the housing bubble—contributed to the EU's bailout crisis of 2010–2011.

Eurozone consumers have benefited from the creation of the euro. A single currency makes pricing comparisons easier and eliminates currency conversion costs and hedging expenses among the eurozone countries.

The **Treaty for Europe** (more popularly known as the **Treaty of Amsterdam**) furthered the process of European integration. The most important components of the Treaty of Amsterdam, which was signed in 1997, include:

- A strong commitment to attack the EU's chronic high levels of unemployment, particularly among younger citizens
- A plan to strengthen the role of the European Parliament by expanding the number of areas that require use of the co-decision procedure
- Establishment of a two-track system, allowing groups of members to proceed with economic and political integration faster than the EU as a whole

The **Treaty of Nice**, which became effective in February 2003, continued the integration process by making modest adjustments in the EU's governance arrangements. For instance, to reduce the risk of political gridlock as the number of members increased, the treaty reduced the number of areas where unanimity is required for Council approval. The number of votes assigned to each Council member in determining a qualified majority was also adjusted.

European leaders acknowledged that more significant steps needed to be taken to reform the EU's decision-making processes: a governance structure designed for six members no longer met the needs of an enlarged EU. Some members believed the powers of the Council, which protects national interests, should be weakened, and the powers of the Commission, which represents Europe as a whole, strengthened. Other members resisted this proposal, fearing the loss of national sovereignty. The EU members agreed to establish a European Convention to resolve these conflicts.

The Convention, which began its deliberations in 2002, drafted a proposed Constitution, which was endorsed by the leaders of the EU's member states in 2004. The proposed Constitution then had to be approved unanimously by the member states, with each government determining its own approval process. Some governments chose to have their parliaments ratify the Constitution; others opted for voter referendums. France and the Netherlands decided to hold referendums on the issue. In May 2005, French voters rejected the Constitution, as did Dutch voters a week later, effectively killing the Constitution.

After a two-year "period of reflection" following the demise of the proposed Constitution, the EU member states agreed to support the **Treaty of Lisbon**—the so-called **Reform Treaty**—which adopted many of the governance changes proposed by the Constitutional Convention.

The Treaty of Lisbon entered into force in December 2009. The most important of these changes include creating a full-time President of the European Council with a 30-month term in office (with a possibility of a second term); designating a High Representative of the Union for Foreign Affairs and Security Policy, charged with representing the EU on the world stage in these areas; changing the voting rules governing Council decisions starting in 2014; permitting a reduction in the size of the European Commission to make it more manageable; and strengthening the powers of the European Parliament by extending the co-decision process to more areas, including justice and home affairs issues. The Treaty of Lisbon also grants national legislatures the formal right to voice concerns about proposed EU legislation. If some minimum number object to draft legislation (in most cases, one-third; one-quarter of the legislatures in the case of justice and home affairs legislation), then the Commission must reexamine the proposed legislation in light of the national legislatures' concerns.

FUTURE EU CHALLENGES The members of the EU have made remarkable progress in implementing the goals of the Treaty of Rome. Political conflicts still remain, of course. One divisive issue is state aid to industry. Under EU rules, national governments may not provide subsidies to firms that "distort" competition. Yet many governments are loath to let domestic firms go bankrupt, especially if local jobs are threatened. This became a particular problem during the recent global recession when national governments implemented programs to lessen domestic bank failures. Subsidies or programs designed to support local banks inevitably help them compete against banks from other EU countries, contrary to the spirit of the Treaty of Rome and the single market. Some national governments, including those of France, Italy, Poland, and Spain, have tried to protect their domestic corporations from unwanted takeovers by firms headquartered in other EU countries, contrary to the goal of the Treaty of Rome of creating an EU-wide capital market.[9] France and the United Kingdom continue to squabble over the EU's Common Agricultural Policy, which disproportionately benefits French farmers to the detriment of British interests and hurts European MNCs by poisoning the EU's relationships with the United States, the WTO, and the Cairns Group. Other countries are concerned about the paucity of democracy and lack of accountability within the EU. They believe more power should be given to the EU's only directly elected governing body, the European Parliament.

Other Regional Trading Blocs

The EU's success in enriching its members through trade promotion has stimulated the development of other regional trading blocs. Every inhabited continent now contains at least one regional trading group. Europe, for example, has many other smaller trading blocs, such as the **European Free Trade Association**. Its members are Iceland, Liechtenstein, Norway, and Switzerland. The first three of these countries have joined with the EU to create a common market known as the **European Economic Area**, which promotes the free movement of goods, services, labor, and capital among its members. Russia, Belarus, and Kazakhstan formed a customs union in 2010, with a goal of creating a common market in 2012.

The North American Free Trade Agreement

Another important example of regional economic integration is NAFTA. Implemented in 1994 to reduce barriers to trade and investment among Canada, Mexico, and the United States, NAFTA builds on the 1988 Canadian–U.S. Free Trade Agreement. Canada and the United States enjoy the world's largest bilateral trading relationship, with two-way trade totaling $609 billion in 2010. The United States is Mexico's largest trading partner, while Mexico is the third largest trading partner of the United States (after Canada and China). However, trade between Canada and Mexico, while growing, is rather small.

NAFTA increased the integration of the North American economies. Over a 15-year time span, tariff walls were lowered, NTBs reduced, and investment opportunities increased for firms located in the three countries. However, some industries received special treatment in the agreement. Negotiators from all three countries recognized the political sensitivity of certain issues and industries and chose to compromise on their treatment within NAFTA to ensure the

The North America Free Trade Agreement has lowered barriers to trade and increased commerce among Canada, Mexico, and the United States. To qualify for preferential treatment, NAFTA's rules of origin require that at least 62.5 percent of the value of this automobile be originated in the member countries.

agreement's ratification. For example, because Canada fears being dominated by U.S. media, NAFTA allows Canada to limit foreign investments in its culture industries (publishing, music, television, radio, cable, and film). Similarly, Mexico may restrain foreign investments in its energy sector, while the United States may bar foreign ownership in its airline and broadcasting industries.

U.S. and Canadian negotiators also were concerned that firms from nonmember countries might locate so-called screwdriver plants in Mexico as a means of evading U.S. and Canadian tariffs. A **screwdriver plant** is a factory in which very little transformation of a product is undertaken. Speaking metaphorically, in such factories the only tool workers need is the screwdriver they use to assemble a product. Therefore, the negotiators developed detailed rules of origin that defined whether a good was North American in origin and thus qualified for preferential tariff status. In the automobile industry, for example, U.S. and Canadian labor unions worried that European and Asian automakers would exploit the treaty by producing major components elsewhere and then establishing a North American factory merely to assemble motor vehicles, thereby causing the loss of jobs at Canadian and U.S. parts-producing factories. To diminish this problem, NAFTA specifies that for an automobile to qualify as a North American product, 62.5 percent of its value must be produced in Canada, Mexico, or the United States. Similarly, to protect textile industry jobs, clothing and other textile products must use North American–produced fibers to benefit from NAFTA's preferential tariff treatment.

Most experts believe that NAFTA has benefited all three countries, although the gains have been more modest in Canada and the United States than most NAFTA advocates expected. NAFTA's overall impact on the Mexican economy has been dramatic, as the chapter's opening case indicated.

Other Free Trade Agreements in the Americas

Many other countries are negotiating or implementing free trade agreements on a bilateral or multilateral basis. For example, Mexico has negotiated free trade pacts with five of its Central American neighbors—Costa Rica, El Salvador, Guatemala, Honduras, and Nicaragua.

THE CARIBBEAN BASIN INITIATIVE In 1983 the United States established the Caribbean Basin Initiative to facilitate the economic development of the countries of Central America and the Caribbean Sea. The **Caribbean Basin Initiative (CBI)** overlaps two regional free trade areas: the

TABLE 10.3 Major Regional Trade Associations

Acronym	Full Name/Members
AFTA	ASEAN Free Trade Area Brunei, Cambodia, Indonesia, Laos, Malaysia, Myanmar, Philippines, Singapore, Thailand, Vietnam
ANCOM	Andean Community Bolivia, Colombia, Ecuador, Peru; Associate Members: Argentina, Brazil, Chile, Paraguay, Uruguay
APEC	Asia-Pacific Economic Cooperation Australia, Brunei, Canada, Chile, China, Hong Kong, Indonesia, Japan, Malaysia, Mexico, New Zealand, Papua New Guinea, Peru, Philippines, Russia, Singapore, South Korea, Taiwan, Thailand, United States, Vietnam
CACM	Central American Common Market Costa Rica, El Salvador, Guatemala, Honduras, Nicaragua
CARICOM	Caribbean Community and Common Market Antigua and Barbuda, The Bahamas, Barbados, Belize, Dominica, Grenada, Guyana, Haiti, Jamaica, Montserrat, St. Kitts and Nevis, St. Lucia, St. Vincent and the Grenadines, Suriname, Trinidad and Tobago
CEMAC	Economic and Monetary Community of Central Africa Cameroon, Central African Republic, Chad, Republic of the Congo, Equatorial Guinea, Gabon
CER	Australia–New Zealand Closer Economic Trade Relations Agreement Australia, New Zealand
EAEC	Eurasian Economic Community Belarus, Kazakhstan, Kyrgyzstan, Russia, Tajikistan
ECOWAS	Economic Community of West African States Benin, Burkina Faso, Cape Verde, Cote d'Ivoire, The Gambia, Ghana, Guinea, Guinea-Bissau, Liberia, Mali, Niger, Nigeria, Senegal, Sierra Leone, Togo
EU	European Union Austria, Belgium, Bulgaria, Cyprus, Czech Republic, Denmark, Estonia, Finland, France, Germany, Greece, Hungary, Ireland, Italy, Latvia, Lithuania, Luxembourg, Malta, Netherlands, Poland, Portugal, Romania, Spain, Sweden, Slovenia, Slovakia, United Kingdom
EFTA	European Free Trade Association Iceland, Liechtenstein, Norway, Switzerland
GCC	Gulf Cooperation Council Bahrain, Kuwait, Oman, Qatar, Saudi Arabia, United Arab Emirates
MERCOSUR	Southern Cone Customs Union Argentina, Brazil, Paraguay, Uruguay; Associate Members: Bolivia, Chile, Colombia, Ecuador, Peru, Venezuela
NAFTA	North American Free Trade Agreement Canada, Mexico, United States
SADC	Southern African Development Community Angola, Botswana, Democratic Republic of the Congo, Lesotho, Madagascar, Malawi, Mauritius, Mozambique, Namibia, Seychelles, South Africa, Swaziland, Tanzania, Zambia, Zimbabwe

Central American Common Market and the Caribbean Community and Common Market (their members are listed in Table 10.3 and shown in Map 10.2). The CBI, which acts as a unidirectional free trade agreement, permits duty-free import into the United States of a wide range of goods that originate in Caribbean Basin countries, or that have been assembled there from U.S.–produced parts. However, numerous politically sensitive goods, many of which are traditional exports of the area, have been excluded from the CBI, including textiles, canned tuna, luggage, apparel, footwear, petroleum, and petroleum products. Through this pattern of duty-free access to the U.S. market, the

MAP 10.2

Free Trade Agreements in Central and South America and the Caribbean

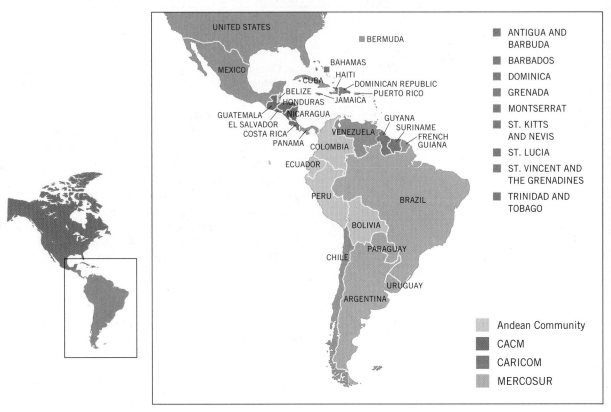

United States hopes to stimulate investment by domestic, U.S., and other foreign firms in new industries in the Caribbean Basin countries.

THE CENTRAL AMERICA–DOMINICAN REPUBLIC FREE TRADE AGREEMENT (CAFTA-DR) This agreement among the United States, five Central American countries (Costa Rica, El Salvador, Guatemala, Honduras, and Nicaragua), and the Dominican Republic was signed in 2004. The CAFTA-DR calls for the reduction of tariffs, nontariff barriers, and investment barriers in commerce among its members. Approximately 80 percent of U.S. exports to and imports from these countries will immediately be duty-free as a result of CAFTA-DR or other existing trade treaties. The remaining tariffs are to be phased out over a 10-year period.

THE MERCOSUR ACCORD In 1991, the governments of Argentina, Brazil, Paraguay, and Uruguay signed the Mercosur Accord, an agreement to create a customs union among themselves. They agreed to establish common external tariffs and to cut, over four years, their internal tariffs on goods that account for 85 percent of intra-Mercosur trade. Full implementation of the customs union began in 1995. Bolivia, Chile, Colombia, Ecuador, Peru, and Venezuela later joined Mercosur as associate members, allowing them to participate in the accord's free trade area component. Firms from the 10 countries have preferential access to a combined market of 388 million people and a total GDP of $2.9 trillion.

The Mercosur Accord is a direct response to the growth of other regional trading blocs. It is also a key element of the free-market-oriented economic reforms adopted by the Argentine and Brazilian governments elected in 1989 to revitalize their stagnating economies. Since its founding, Mercosur has been successful in stimulating trade among its members. In 2009, about 15 percent of the members' $217 billion in merchandise trade was to other Mercosur members. Mercosur—particularly Brazil—has proven to be a magnet for

FDI, driven in part by the booming demand for raw materials reported in Chapter 2's closing case, "China's Quest for Natural Resources," and by the expansion of the country's automobile manufacturing sector. The stock of FDI in Brazil rose from $122 billion in 2000 to $401 billion in 2009.[10]

ANDEAN COMMUNITY The Andean Community resulted from a 1969 agreement to promote free trade among five small South American countries—Bolivia, Chile, Colombia, Ecuador, and Peru—to make them more competitive with the continent's larger countries. Venezuela joined the pact in 1973, but Chile dropped out in 1976. During its first 20 years, the agreement was not very successful; trade among members totaled only 5 percent of their total trade. Geography played a role in this failure: The Andes mountain range, from which the agreement got its name, makes land transportation of goods between some members costly. More importantly, most members adopted protectionist, import substitution policies that hindered trade.

In response to the threat posed by the Mercosur Accord, in 1991 the Andean Community members agreed to reinvigorate their agreement. A year later the members established a customs union that provided for phased elimination of tariffs among themselves on most goods, a common external tariff, and harmonized regulations on capital movements, immigration, and agriculture. The new approach has had modest success: In 2009, about 8 percent of members' $78 billion in merchandise exports were purchased by other Andean Community members. Yet the liberalization has not gone smoothly. Creation of a common external tariff was stalled by political squabbling over the appropriate tariff level and structure. Peru suspended its membership in the group after judging that the customs union agreement permitted too many loopholes that allowed members to subsidize local firms and erect barriers to imported goods. Despite these setbacks, trade in the region is likely to become freer over time. In 2005, the Andean Community negotiated a cooperative agreement with Mercosur. As part of this agreement, Argentina, Brazil, Paraguay, and Uruguay joined the Andean Community as associate members, while the nations of the Andean Community became associate members of Mercosur. However, in 2006, Venezuela withdrew from the Andean Community in protest of Colombia's and Peru's signing trade promotion agreements with the United States.

Trade Arrangements in the Asia-Pacific Region

Trade groups are also growing in importance in the Asia-Pacific region. One of the longest standing is governed by the Closer Economic Relations Trade Agreement between Australia and New Zealand. More recently, the Association of Southeast Asian Nations has initiated a free trade agreement. Members of APEC (Asia-Pacific Economic Cooperation) have begun to reduce trade barriers among themselves as well.

THE AUSTRALIA–NEW ZEALAND AGREEMENT For most of their histories, Australia and New Zealand have been trade rivals because they are both commodities producers. As members of the British Commonwealth, both enjoyed preferential access to the U.K. market. After the United Kingdom joined the EU, however, both countries lost their privileged status in the British market. This change was particularly damaging to their agricultural sectors.

The ensuing poor performance by both the New Zealand and Australian economies during the 1970s, and the flow of human capital from the more depressed New Zealand to Australia, led to calls for closer economic ties between the two countries. The **Australia–New Zealand Closer Economic Relations Trade Agreement**, known as **ANZCERTA** or more simply as the **CER**, took effect on January 1, 1983. Over time, it eliminated tariffs and NTBs between the two countries. The CER also strengthened and fostered links and cooperation in fields as diverse as investment, marketing, movement of people, tourism, and transport. Although some areas have been excluded from the CER, such as broadcasting, postal services, and air traffic control, most analysts believe the CER has been one of the world's most successful free trade agreements.

MAP 10.3

The ASEAN Members

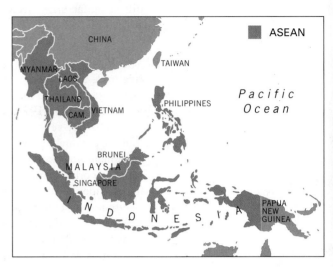

The ASEAN economy has been developing rapidly because its poorer members provide large pools of low-cost labor, receive preferential tariff rates under the U.S. generalized system of preferences and those of other WTO members, and have attracted significant Japanese, European, and North American direct investment.

ASSOCIATION OF SOUTHEAST ASIAN NATIONS The **Association of Southeast Asian Nations (ASEAN)** was established in August 1967 to promote regional political and economic cooperation (see Map 10.3). Its founding members were Brunei, Indonesia, Malaysia, the Philippines, Singapore, and Thailand. Cambodia, Laos, Myanmar, and Vietnam joined during the 1990s. These countries are by no means homogeneous: Oil-rich Brunei had a 2009 per capita income of $27,050 while Vietnam's was only $1,010.

To promote intra-ASEAN trade, members established the **ASEAN Free Trade Area (AFTA)**, effective January 1, 1993. AFTA members promised to slash their tariffs to 5 percent or less on most manufactured goods by 2003 and on all goods by 2010. To qualify for the preferential tariff, at least 40 percent of the value-added for the good must be performed within AFTA.[11] As with the Mercosur Accord and the Andean Community, creation of the ASEAN trading bloc stems from two factors: a decrease in government control of national economies that has stimulated local entrepreneurs and attracted FDI, and a defensive response to the growth of other regional trading blocs such as the EU and NAFTA.

Intra-ASEAN trade currently represents about 25 percent of the group's $814 billion in merchandise trade and has grown substantially as a result of AFTA. Recent meetings of ASEAN country ministers have addressed trade in services, removal of NTBs, and the creation of an ASEAN Free Investment Area. ASEAN increased its importance in the world market in 2003 by signing a free trade pact with China, with the first set of tariff cuts commencing in 2004.[12] As with other new trading blocs, firms have reacted quickly to take advantage of opportunities created by AFTA. Shortly after the agreement was negotiated, for instance, Philippine brewer San Miguel, which controls 90 percent of its home market, purchased Jakarta-based Delta brewery, which controls 40 percent of the Indonesian beer market. By moving rapidly, San Miguel hoped to dominate the entire ASEAN market prior to the fall of tariff rates triggered by AFTA.

THE ASIA-PACIFIC ECONOMIC COOPERATION INITIATIVE **Asia-Pacific Economic Cooperation (APEC)** includes 21 countries from both sides of the Pacific Ocean (see Map 10.4). It was founded in 1989 in response to the growing interdependence of the Asia-Pacific economies. A 1994 APEC meeting in Indonesia led to a declaration committing members to achieve free trade in goods, services, and investment among members by 2010 for developed economies and by 2020 for developing economies. This objective was furthered at APEC's 1996 meeting in Manila, where many countries made explicit pledges to reduce barriers to Asia-Pacific trade. In 2009, merchandise exports from APEC members

MAP 10.4
Asia-Pacific Economic Cooperation Initiative (APEC)

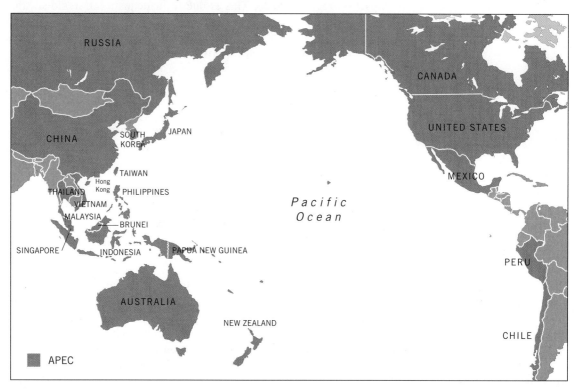

were valued at more than $6.8 trillion and represented about 55 percent of total world merchandise exports.[13]

African Initiatives

Many African countries have also established regional trading blocs. As shown in Table 10.3 and Map 10.5, the most important of these groups are the **Southern African Development Community (SADC)**, the **Economic and Monetary Community of Central Africa**

MAP 10.5

**Free Trade
Agreements in Africa**

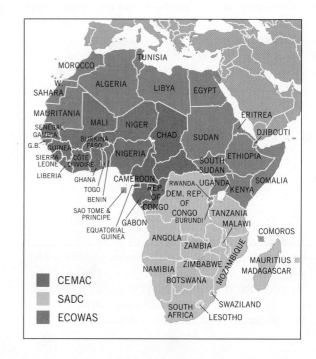

(CEMAC), and the **Economic Community of West African States (ECOWAS)**. Although these groups were established during the 1970s and early 1980s, they have not had a major impact on regional trade. This is due to inadequate intraregional transportation facilities[14] and the failure of most domestic governments to create economic and political systems that encourage significant regional trade. Intra-Africa trade to date accounts for less than 12 percent of the continent's total exports.

MyManagementLab Now that you have finished this chapter, go back to **www.pearsonglobaleditions.com/mymanagementlab** to continue practicing and applying the concepts you've learned.

CHAPTER REVIEW

Summary

Countries have come together to create numerous international agreements and organizations to promote their joint interests in international commerce. One of the most important was the GATT. The goal of this 1947 agreement was to promote global prosperity by reducing international trade barriers. Through a series of negotiating rounds over 47 years, the GATT significantly reduced the average level of tariffs facing exporters. The most recent series of GATT negotiations, the Uruguay Round, continued the trend of reducing tariffs and NTBs. In 1995, the GATT's mission was taken over by the WTO.

Countries may also band together in various ways to integrate their economies regionally. Free trade areas promote economic integration by abolishing trade barriers among their members. Members of a customs union carry regional economic integration a step farther by adopting common external trade barriers as well as abolishing internal barriers to trade. A common market combines the characteristics of a customs union with the elimination of controls on the free movement of labor, capital, and technology among its members. An economic union adds the coordination of economic policies to the features of a common market. A political union involves complete political as well as economic integration of two or more countries.

The most important example of a regional trading bloc is the EU, a market of 499 million consumers and a combined GDP of $16.4 trillion. Spurred by the passage of the Single European Act of 1987, EU members dismantled most of the physical, technical, and fiscal trade barriers among themselves. Under the Maastricht Treaty, many EU members have adopted a common currency and are attempting to create a true economic union, an effort that goes beyond the common market originally envisioned by the 1957 Treaty of Rome.

A second but much newer regional integration effort is occurring in North America. The United States, Mexico, and Canada have instituted NAFTA, which came into effect in January 1994. NAFTA's implementation signals a commitment to tightening the economic bonds among the North American countries.

The development of regional trading blocs in Europe and North America has stimulated efforts to promote regional economic integration on other continents. South America is home to the Mercosur Accord and the Andean Community. The chances of their future success have been increased by the economic reforms many South American countries have adopted, reforms that have increased the competitiveness of the countries' products in international markets. Australia and New Zealand and the ASEAN countries have similarly created free trade areas to promote regional economic integration. Several regional economic integration agreements negotiated by various African countries have yet to show much promise.

Review Questions

1. What does *most favored nation (MFN)* mean?
2. Under what conditions can WTO members not use MFN when dealing with one another?
3. How does the WTO differ from the GATT?
4. How do the various forms of economic integration differ?
5. Why do free trade areas develop rules of origin?
6. What was the goal of the Treaty of Rome?
7. Describe the five major organizations governing the EU.
8. What are NAFTA's major provisions?
9. What is the Caribbean Basin Initiative? What is its goal?
10. What efforts have South American countries made to regionally integrate their economies?

Questions for Discussion

1. Consider the opening case in this chapter. How has Mexico's success affected the Canadian and U.S. economies?
2. Suppose you are deciding whether to locate a factory in China or in Mexico in order to serve the U.S. market. What factors would influence your location decision? Suppose the price of oil suddenly rises. What impact would this have on your decision?
3. How does the WTO affect the operations of large MNCs? Did MNCs benefit from the successful completion of the Uruguay Round?
4. Should international businesses promote or fight the creation of regional trading blocs?
5. What strategies can North American and Asian firms adopt to ensure access to the enormous EU market?
6. Is the abandonment of import substitution policies by South American governments a necessary condition for the success of the Andean Community and the Mercosur Accord?
7. Of what importance are rules of origin to international businesses?
8. Why does the MFN principle promote multilateral, rather than bilateral, negotiations among WTO members?

Building Global Skills

NAFTA has been lauded by some as creating a major new market opportunity for U.S. businesses; it has been criticized by others because of the potential loss of domestic jobs as firms relocate production to Mexico to take advantage of lower-cost labor. This exercise will help you learn more about the effects of NAFTA on various firms.

Your instructor will divide the class into groups of four to five students each. Working with your group members, identify four products made by firms in each of the three countries that are part of NAFTA. The four products should include two that would seem to benefit from NAFTA and two that would seem to face increased threats from competitors in the two other member countries as a result of NAFTA. For example, identify two Canadian-made products that have considerable market potential in the United States and/or Mexico and two Canadian-made products that would seem to face new competition from U.S.

and/or Mexican firms. Each group should identify a total of 12 different products.

Next, work with your group members to determine and assess the appeal of each product in the NAFTA market. Investigate for each the current market share, domestic competitors, foreign competitors, and so forth. Research how well each was doing before and after NAFTA's passage. Discuss how NAFTA has affected and/or may potentially affect each product.

1. Has NAFTA provided new market opportunities for some of the products you identified? Why or why not?
2. Has NAFTA increased competition from other producers?
3. Have the effects of NAFTA on each product been consistent with what advocates or critics of NAFTA might have predicted?

CLOSING CASE — THE NEW CONQUISTADOR

The South American continent has emerged as one of the hottest markets as a result of economic policy changes initiated in the 1990s. Privatization, deregulation, and regional economic integration have unshackled the imaginations and energies of the continent's entrepreneurs and attracted the attention of foreign investors, while surging commodities exports have boosted the economies of such countries as Brazil (iron ore), Chile (copper), Bolivia (tin), and Venezuela (oil) (see Chapter 2's closing case, "China's Quest for Natural Resources").

One industry directly impacted by these policy changes is telecommunications. Once the sleepy preserve of inefficient and overstaffed state-owned enterprises, the industry has become a magnet for new firms and new technologies. The most aggressive entrant is Telefónica SA. Telefónica's managers knew all too well

the problems of state-owned telecommunications monopolists, for Telefónica was just such a firm in its former guise as government-run Telefónica de España. Telefónica de España first obtained its monopoly concession on telephone services in Spain in 1924. Originally privately owned, the company was nationalized in 1945, with the government owning outright 41 percent of the company's shares.

For four decades the company enjoyed the easy life of a monopolist. The seeds of change were planted in 1986, however, when Spain joined the European Union. Telefónica de España was ill-equipped to handle the explosive growth in telephone service or the chorus of complaints about poor service that followed. Moreover, as part of its single market initiative, the EU announced that state-sponsored telephone monopolies would be abolished by 1998. Any European telecommunications firm would then be able to provide service anywhere within the European Union.

Faced with the threat of new entry from European rivals that promised increased competition, lower prices, and smaller profit margins, Telefónica's managers realized they had to transform the company. A leaner and more competitive company emerged as managers trimmed fat, shed unprofitable operations, and pumped up investments in new technologies and facilities. With the EU-directed ending of state telephone monopolies, Telefónica's managers confronted a new strategic problem: Should they change the scope of their operations? Should they erect a fortress in Spain and keep out EU rivals, expand into other EU markets, or do something else?

In analyzing their strategic choices, Telefónica's managers recognized they had a strong position in Spain, and that domestic demand for telephone services would continue to grow in the relatively underserved Spanish market. Thus, they continued to invest in new equipment and technologies there. This approach has worked: Telefónica has over 13 million local fixed-line subscribers and 24 million cellular customers in its home market. Despite the EU's competition directive, at the end of 2010 Telefónica retained 69 percent of Spain's fixed-line business and about 41 percent of its mobile phone market.

In assessing their international prospects, Telefónica's managers decided that the company lacked a competitive advantage against European rivals like British Telecom and Deutsche Telekom, who had equal if not better access to the latest technology and managerial talent. That ruled out attacking other EU markets, at least initially. However, they noted that many South American countries were about to privatize their own state-owned telephone monopolies, and that investing in these companies made strategic sense. Telefónica did have a competitive advantage vis-à-vis local entrepreneurs in accessing technology, capital, and managerial talent. Moreover, because of linguistic and cultural ties between Spain and South America, Telefónica believed it had a competitive advantage over any of its European rivals who might wish to enter the South American market.

Telefónica de España launched its invasion of the South American market in 1990, when it acquired a minority interest in Compania de Telefonos de Chile and a contract to manage the southern half of Argentina's telephone system. In 1995, it purchased a majority interest in Telefónica del Peru, that country's state-owned monopoly provider of telephone services. A year later it acquired 35 percent of a regional Brazilian telephone company at a state-sponsored auction. Telefónica also acquired interests in Argentina's largest cable company and a digital satellite TV provider. The Spanish government then sold off the last of its ownership position, making Telefónica de España wholly privately owned. In 1998, the company changed its name—to Telefónica SA—and paid $4.9 billion at auction to acquire control of the fixed-line and cellular operations of Telebras, Brazil's former state-owned telephone giant. In 2000, Motorola sold its Mexican cellular service operations to Telefónica for $2.6 billion, while in 2006

Telefónica purchased 50 percent (plus one share) of state-owned Colombia Telecommunicaciones, making it the largest landline operator in that country as well.

All told, Telefónica has invested over $46 billion in South America. It is the largest telecommunications company on that continent and now has more landline customers there—24 million—than in Spain. Its wireless subsidiary, Telefónica Moviles, has 152 million customers in Latin America. It has followed the same pattern in each country it has entered: Trim excess payrolls ruthlessly and expand capacity aggressively. For example, it laid off half of the 22,000 workers in its Argentine subsidiary while doubling its network there to 4 million lines.

Telefónica's actions in South America have not lacked criticism, however. Telefónica's tactics have been denounced by local skeptics as "conquistador capitalism." After winning the Telebras auction, it moved quickly to expand service in Brazil's commercial center, São Paulo, while laying off thousands of workers. This strategy of doing more with less backfired, as chaotic disruptions in service led to numerous complaints. Minority shareholders also complained that Telefónica charges its South American subsidiaries exorbitant management fees that reduce the value of their interests. For example, its Argentine subsidiary pays 4.6 percent of its revenues to Telefónica for management services provided by the parent corporation.

Minority shareholders have also protested Telefónica's practice of transferring product lines with high growth potential from the subsidiaries to the parent. For example, Telefónica created Terra Networks SA to consolidate all of its South American Internet operations. It then sold to the public 30 percent of Terra Networks, retained the other 70 percent, and listed it on stock exchanges in Madrid and the United States. As part of this deal, Telefónica transferred the Internet operations of its Chilean subsidiary to Terra Networks for $40 million; minority owners believed that the price should have been double that figure. Minority shareholders in other subsidiaries have made similar complaints. Similarly, Telefónica has been transferring the telemarketing operations of its South American subsidiaries to an umbrella company in Madrid, arguing that they would benefit from the economies of scale that a consolidated operation would offer.

Telefónica also faces some operational challenges. Some are of its own doing: It was forced to pay $8 million in refunds in 1999 to São Paulo customers because of poor service. Others are not: It was forced to take a $300 million write-off for currency losses after Brazil devalued its currency in 1998 and a €1.8 billion markdown of its Venezuelan assets in 2010 after the bolivar was devalued. Moreover, changes in government policies have increased competitive pressures. For example, Argentina and Peru began to deregulate their telecommunications industries in 2000, ending their reliance on monopoly provision of telephone service. And Telefónica's success has attracted new competitors. In 1999, for instance, BellSouth signed up 1 million cellular phone subscribers in São Paulo, capturing nearly 50 percent of that market in only 10 months of operations. But BellSouth executives were unhappy with the venture's profitability, and in 2004

Telefónica purchased BellSouth's Latin American subsidiary for $5.9 billion, thereby eliminating a well-funded, technologically sophisticated competitor.

Having built strong bases in Spain and Latin America, in 2005 Telefónica turned its attentions back to Europe. It purchased Çesky Telecom, the leading provider of landline and mobile telecommunications services in the Czech Republic. In 2006, it acquired O2, the largest provider of mobile phone service in the United Kingdom. In 2007 it purchased a minority position in Telecom Italia. In 2009, it paid €913 million for HanseNet, a German provider of telecommunications services. Telefónica now serves some 51 million European customers outside its Spanish home market. It also purchased 5 percent of China Netcom in 2005, the second largest provider of landline service in China. In 2008, it agreed to buy an additional 2.2 percent of that company for €309 million. After China Unicom acquired China Netcom, Telefónica entered into a strategic alliance with China Unicom and increased its ownership of that company to 9.7 percent.

Overall, this strategy seems to be working. In 2010, Telefónica earned €10.2 billion on revenues of €60.7 billion. Under the direction of César Alierta, the firm's CEO since 2000, the company has become the world's second largest telecommunications company measured by market capitalization. Telefónica now operates in 25 countries, with 41 million landline customers and 223 million mobile phone customers.

Case Questions

1. How important was the EU's directive eliminating national telecommunications monopolies by 1998 in shaping Telefónica's strategy? What would the company look like today if Spain were not a member of the European Union?

2. How important were cultural ties in determining Telefónica's success in Latin America?

3. Why did Telefónica initially choose to enter the Czech market, rather than the larger French or German markets?

4. Considering Telefónica's large and persistent share of the Spanish telecommunications market, how successful has the EU's directive been in promoting competition within the European telecommunication industry?

5. Minority investors in Telefónica's South American subsidiaries are unhappy with the parent corporation. Suppose you are a senior manager at the parent corporation. How would you handle the problem of the minority investors? What would you recommend to the CEO should be done about the minority investors?

Sources: www.telefonica.com, accessed on June 8, 2011; "Telefónica to list stake in unit," *Wall Street Journal*, May 26, 2011; "Telefónica battles rising costs," *Wall Street Journal*, May 13, 2011; Telefónica Annual Report for the year ending December 31, 2010; "Brazil calling," *The Economist*, July 28, 2010; "Get off the line," *The Economist*, May 22, 2010; "Telecom Italia's shares plunge as debt-reduction plan disappoints," *Wall Street Journal*, March 7, 2008 (online); "Telefónica adds to stake in China Netcom Group," *Wall Street Journal*, January 21, 2008 (online); "Telefónica insists major deals are out," *Wall Street Journal*, July 16, 2007, p. A8; *Hoover's Handbook of World Business 2006*, p. 338; "Telefónica revamps its structure," *Financial Times*, July 27, 2006, p 18; "Telefónica's growing pains," *Wall Street Journal*, May 23, 2006, p. C4; "Enlarged EU expected to open opportunities for Telefónica," *Financial Times*, June 14, 2005, p. 4; "The information technology 100," *BusinessWeek* online (undated); "Telefónica aims to become world's fifth largest telecommunications group," *Financial Times*, December 21, 2002, p. 4; "Telefónica digs in to Mexican mobiles market," *Financial Times*, November 27, 2002, p. 19; "Wrong numbers dog Telecom Argentina," *Financial Times*, March 19, 2002, p. 17; "Telefónica makes its move into Mexico," *Wall Street Journal*, October 5, 2000, p. A19; "Telefónica posts 43% jump in earnings," *Wall Street Journal*, November 19, 1999, p. A18; "Spain's Telefónica jolts Latin America with tough tactics," *Wall Street Journal*, November 18, 1999, p. A1.

PART 2 CLOSING CASES | **THE SECOND CULTURAL REVOLUTION**

The explosive growth of the Internet has unleashed opportunities and challenges everywhere. New industries are being established before our very eyes. The traditional ways of buying and selling, purchasing and distributing, and disseminating and acquiring information are being subjected to the Darwinian imperative: adapt or die. The Internet revolution has created even more challenges for public policymakers, who must reconcile existing laws designed for the "old economy" with changes needed to accommodate the demands of e-commerce and the "new economy." And the boundaryless nature of the Internet presents other quandaries for those governments that would like to maintain walls between their citizens and the rest of the world.

The Internet challenges no government more than that of the People's Republic of China. For the past 40 years, the ruling Communist Party has navigated a tricky path in promoting China's economic growth. It has struggled to maintain its political hold over the country, while continually increasing the economic freedom allowed its people. China's leaders recognize that the country must embrace the Internet and master its underlying technologies if it is to continue on its upward economic trajectory.

The Internet is popular among the populace. China's Web surfers totaled some 450 million by early 2011, up thirteenfold from 34 million users in mid-2002, making China the world's largest Internet market. Surveys suggest that their primary use of the Internet is to acquire information and news. Therein lies the rub. To stimulate domestic development of Internet technology, China's leaders need to encourage Web surfing. But they also wish to maintain political control over the populace by reducing the influence of outsiders and limiting political debate among the citizenry.

The Chinese government fully recognizes the power of the Internet as a political weapon and as an independent source of information. For example, the Falun Gong, a million-person spiritual movement that has been banned by the Beijing government, often used the Internet to organize and coordinate its nationwide protests against the government's policy toward it. The Internet presents a threat to the state's commercial interests as well, particularly state-owned telecommunications and publishing monopolies. Millions of Chinese citizens have switched to Internet-based telephone service, thereby avoiding the high long-distance prices charged by the dominant state-owned telephone company, China Telecom.

The government has adopted a variety of measures to protect state-owned enterprises, suppress foreign influences, and maintain its political power. In 1999 it verbally banned foreign investment in Chinese Internet service providers (ISPs), Internet content providers, and other dot-com ventures, after hundreds of millions of dollars of foreign venture capital had already flowed into private dot-com start-ups. It tried to protect state-owned news media by restricting the development of private online news media.

The government proclaimed that its harsh laws against disseminating state secrets apply to the Internet as well. The State Bureau of Secrecy issued rules prohibiting the use of chat rooms, Internet bulletin boards, or e-mail to disseminate state secrets. To enforce these rules, it required that any ISP or Internet content provider must undergo a "security certification" before it can operate. It also established the Internet Information Management Bureau to eliminate "harmful" information from the Internet. While this may sound reasonable, recognize that a state secret is often defined as any information that has not yet been officially released to the public. Indeed, prior to the passage of these regulations, chat rooms played a major role in uncovering corruption in Fujian province and in the port city of Xiamen.

Another approach Chinese officials have adopted to reduce Western influence on China's Internet sector is to promote Linux (an open-source operating system) instead of Microsoft-based programs. Government agencies have been encouraged to use Red Flag, a Linux-based operating system developed by the state, and discouraged from using Windows Vista or Windows 7. Other domestic dot-com entrepreneurs are receiving funding from state agencies, such as the post office and the army, to develop Chinese-language software using Linux. While locally made Linux-based software is gaining market share, particularly in sales to provincial governments, many government offices have run into compatibility problems with peripheral equipment like external drives or printers. Moreover, the easy availability of pirated copies of Microsoft software reduces the incentives of nongovernmental users to switch to domestic software.

In 2005, the Ministry of Information Industry issued new regulations requiring online news services to post only "healthy and civilized news that is beneficial to the improvement of the quality of the nation... and conducive to social progress." Sites were enjoined from "spreading news and information that goes against state security and public interest." To enforce these regulations, the government employs an estimated 30,000 to 50,000 agents to cruise the Internet, trying to spot anti-Communist or antisocial news, blogs, and postings. The effectiveness of these efforts is spotty, however. Authorities claim to have shut down more than 2,000 porn and gambling sites, but new sites spring up quickly. Chinese officials have convinced the major search engine providers to ignore requests dealing with politically sensitive topics, like Falun Gong, human rights, or media censorship. For example, while protests in Tibet in 2008 were headline news around the world, popular Chinese portals like Baidu.com and Sohu.com carried only stories produced by China's official news agency, Xinhua. Yet such efforts have inspired so-called hacktivists to develop software and techniques to counteract the censors.

The government's often hostile and sometimes contradictory policies toward the Internet have created problems for foreign firms. Yahoo received much criticism after human rights activists learned that its Chinese subsidiary disclosed information to the Chinese government leading to the arrest and imprisonment of critics of government policies. Microsoft and Google have been condemned by other activists for cooperating with the government's attempts to filter out politically unacceptable postings, while Cisco has been criticized for selling routers and equipment that allow Chinese censors to monitor blogs and chat rooms. In 2006, Yahoo's executives, as well as those of Cisco and Microsoft, were asked at a congressional hearing to defend their willingness to cooperate with Chinese authorities. The companies responded that, like any business, they must operate within the laws and regulations of the host country. This defense did not sway all of the congresspersons in attendance. After listening to their testimony, Congressman Christopher Smith (R-NJ) castigated their "sickening collaboration," which "decapitat[ed] the voice of dissidents there." Representative Tom Lantos (D-CA) concluded, "I do not understand how your corporate leadership sleeps at night."

Questions

1. Assume you are the CEO of a North American search engine company. Perform a political risk assessment for your company's entrance into the Chinese market. What information would you need to conduct the study? What factors would you consider? On a scale of 1 to 10, with 10 being highest, how vulnerable is your company to political risk in China?
2. What strategies would you adopt to reduce your vulnerability to political risk in China?
3. Do you think the Chinese government will be successful in controlling the use of the Internet and minimizing Western influences in China?
4. What will be the impact of the government's efforts on the global competitiveness of China's high-tech industries?
5. Do you agree with the position of Yahoo and the other companies that they are constrained to act within the laws of the host country, or do you agree with their congressional critics? Defend your answer.

Sources: "Chinese Internet use surges past 450 million people in 2010," January 19, 2011, www.npr.org; "Numbers show China beats U.S. in net use, but which numbers?" *Wall Street Journal*, March 28, 2008; page B1; "News of protests is hard to find in China—in media or online," *Wall Street Journal*, March 18, 2008 p. A8; "China eases control over existing web sites," *Wall Street Journal*, February 6, 2008, page B4; "Yahoo officials questioned by Congress," *Wall Street Journal*, November 6, 2007 (online); "As Chinese students go online, little sister is watching," *New York Times*, May 9, 2006 (online); "Google chief rejects putting pressure on China," *New York Times*, April 13, 2006 (online); "The wild Web of China: Sex and drugs, not reform," *New York Times*, March 8, 2006 (online); "Inside the great firewall of China," *Fortune*, March 6, 2006, pp. 149ff.; "Outrunning China's Web cops," *BusinessWeek*, February 20, 2006, p. 38; "House member criticizes Internet companies for practices in China," *New York Times*, February 15, 2006 (online); "Chinese censors of Internet face 'hacktivists' in U.S.," *Wall Street Journal*, February 13, 2006, p. A1; "The fear of the Internet," *Houston Chronicle*, October 4, 2005, p. D6; "China tightens grip on Internet with new content, media rules," *Wall Street Journal*, September 27, 2005, p. B4; "China tightens Web-content rules," *Wall Street Journal*, September 26, 2005, p. B3; "Beijing takes on Microsoft to win control of desktop," *Financial Times*, April 25, 2005, p. 4; "China looks to Linux as a way not to get locked into Windows," *Wall Street Journal*, April 25, 2000, p. A11; "China creates office to regulate news on Internet sites," *Wall Street Journal*, April 24, 2000, p. A21; "State control gains upper hand among China websites," *Financial Times*, April 18, 2000, p. 7; "Beijing set to step up curbs on Internet," *Financial Times*, March 22, 2000, p. 6; "China reverses harsh Internet rules, easing threat to trade," *Wall Street Journal*, March 13, 2000, p. A21; "China restricts news further over Internet," *Wall Street Journal*, February 22, 2000, p. A26; "Microsoft is test case for Chinese rules," *Wall Street Journal*, February 17, 2000, p. A13; "Internet firms seek to sway lawmakers to see benefits in wider China trade," *Wall Street Journal*, February 15, 2000, p. A6; "China cracks down on Internet chat," *Houston Chronicle*, January 27, 2000, p. 15A; "Government shadow over China's 'Web' grows," *Wall Street Journal*, January 26, 2000, p. A17; "Internet phone service catches on with millions in China," *Wall Street Journal*, December 21, 1999, p. A14; "E-business is tapping China's online wonderlust," *Wall Street Journal*, October 27, 1999, p. A13.

WILL WHIRLPOOL CLEAN UP IN EUROPE?

For years, international businesses looked forward to the EU's emergence as a single, integrated market. Among these firms are ones that produce so-called white goods, or appliances such as refrigerators, dishwashers, ovens, washers, and dryers. (In the past kitchen and laundry room appliances mostly came in white, hence, the industry's name. Consumer electronics such as radios, televisions, and stereos came in brown, so these consumer durables are called "brown goods." Today's widespread use of color in appliances makes these labels somewhat anachronistic.)

The emergence of a single market in Europe has changed the way white-goods manufacturers do business. Previously, they had to customize their products to meet the often conflicting requirements of the EU's 27 national governments. Fortunately, the Single European Act promoted harmonized product standards, thus allowing the manufacturers to cut product development and production costs. Reduced barriers to intra-EU trade allow them to concentrate production in one factory that can serve markets throughout the EU. Reduced impediments to cross-border advertising make it easier to develop pan-European brands, which in turn reduce marketing and distribution costs. Elimination of physical barriers at border crossing points and of restrictions on trucking competition by national governments leads to productivity gains in logistics and physical distribution management.

One of the most aggressive firms seeking to conquer the European market is Whirlpool, the world's largest white-goods manufacturer. The firm's managers have a clearly defined view of this market:

> Among the truths about the European home-appliance market, there are two whose net effect Whirlpool has a particular interest in: first, consumers in Europe spend up to twice as many days of household income for appliances as do their U.S. counterparts, creating a consumer "value gap"; second, industry profit margins in the region are traditionally much lower than those of North American manufacturers. The reason for this truth is cultural: historically, the industry was organized to do business in individual, national markets, an approach with inherent cost inefficiencies. Now, however, with barriers to pan-European business disappearing, Whirlpool believes that it can use its unique regional position to deliver greater home-appliance value to customers and, in turn, establish a competitive advantage for itself. A strategy to do so suggests that the opportunity to eliminate costs which do not add to consumers' perceptions of value—and invest some of the savings into product and service characteristics that do add perceived value—will be substantial.[15]

For the past decade Whirlpool's managers have been attacking the European white-goods market by translating these words into concrete actions. One key element of the firm's strategy was the purchase of the appliance business of Philips Industries, the large Netherlands-based MNC; this gave Whirlpool control over Philips's European white-goods production facilities and distribution systems. Whirlpool has also sought many other operating and marketing economies:

1. It produces and markets three well-established pan-European brands: Bauknecht, a premium upscale product; Whirlpool, for the broad middle segment of the white-goods market; and Ignis, its low-price "value" brand aimed at price-sensitive consumers. This comprehensive product strategy allows Whirlpool to fully utilize its European production facilities and distribution systems and market its goods to Europeans at all income levels.

2. It consolidated 13 separate national sales offices for these three product lines into five regional operations in order to cut costs, coordinate pan-European promotional campaigns, and enhance the productivity of its sales force.

3. It centralized Whirlpool Europe's logistics, information technology, and consumer services operations to ease the task of warehousing products and distributing them throughout the EU.

4. It has redeployed its manufacturing capacity to take advantage of the elimination of national trade barriers. For example, it concentrates its production of refrigerators for its European customers in Trento, Italy, and that of automatic washers in Schondorf, Germany, thus allowing it to achieve significant manufacturing economies of scale. Similarly, its Wroclaw, Poland, factory—completed in 2005—produces cooktop and oven appliances for the entire European market.

5. It has encouraged technology transfer between its European and North American operations, a task made easier by the centralization of its European operations. For example, Whirlpool Europe now produces a line of clothes dryers that features easier loading and unloading and gentler treatment of clothes, features first developed by Whirlpool's Marion, Ohio, division. Conversely, European engineers are helping Whirlpool's U.S. engineers adapt energy-efficient, horizontal-axis washing machines (which are common in Europe) for the North American market in order to meet federal energy-efficiency standards.

Whirlpool is targeting two important segments of the European market: the emerging markets of Central and Eastern Europe, dominated by price-sensitive customers, and the richer countries of Western Europe, whose residents are willing to pay premium prices for premium products. To implement its European strategy, Whirlpool spent $3 billion to expand its manufacturing and distribution capabilities. In addition to upgrading and modernizing its European factories, Whirlpool also made strategic acquisitions. For example, Whirlpool acquired Polar SA, a Polish appliance manufacturer, which offers a low-cost production platform that can serve the entire EU market. In 2007, it introduced its upscale Kitchen Aid line of appliances to the European market to increase its share of this high-margin, fast-growing market segment.

Of course, Whirlpool's EU competitors have not stood still while Whirlpool has invaded their home markets. Germany's Bosch Siemens Hausgeräte, for example, has poured money into R&D to maintain the innovativeness of its appliances. It has dramatically increased the efficiency of its dishwashers, reducing their energy usage by 62 percent and their water usage by 34 percent compared to the machines it made two decades ago. It has also spent $350 million automating its production facilities in Germany and built new factories in Poland, Spain, and the Czech Republic to reduce its dependence on high-cost German labor. Sweden's Electrolux, which vies with Whirlpool for the title of the world's largest white-goods manufacturer, purchased the appliance business of AEG Hausgeräte from Daimler AG. Already controlling a 20 to 25 percent market share in Europe, Electrolux increased its market share by about 6 percentage points through this acquisition. Electrolux is also aggressively moving to control its costs by closing 25 factories and reducing its payrolls by 12,000.

Despite this intensified competition, Whirlpool remains optimistic that its European strategy will be successful. It has already established itself as the number-three white-goods manufacturer in Europe. In 2010, Europe generated $3.1 billion in revenue for Whirlpool, or 17 percent of its global sales revenue of $18.4 billion. And new product innovations, coupled with the increased penetration of the Whirlpool brand, have increased the company's market share and raised its profit margins in Europe.

Case Questions

1. What are the advantages of consolidating production of product lines at single factories in the EU? What are the disadvantages?
2. Should Whirlpool continue to produce and market in Europe its three product lines (Bauknecht, Whirlpool, and Ignis), which span the entire white-goods market, or should it focus on one market niche?
3. What benefits will Whirlpool gain by broadening the Whirlpool brand name from a North American brand to a global one?
4. In light of the aggressive responses of Electrolux and Bosch Siemens Hausgeräte, should Whirlpool revise or abandon its European strategy?
5. Do you think it is possible to design and sell the same basic appliance around the world?

Sources: Whirlpool Corporation, *2010 Annual Report;* "U.S. antitrust review backs Whirlpool-Maytag merger," *New York Times,* March 30, 2006 (online); "Suds law," *The Economist,* July 23, 2005, p. 60; "Whirlpool expected easy going in Europe, and it got a big shock," *Wall Street Journal,* April 10, 1998, p. A1; "Whirlpool net doubled in 4th quarter; gains in Europe, revamping are cited," *Wall Street Journal,* February 4, 1998, p. A6; "Despite setbacks, Whirlpool pursues overseas markets," *Wall Street Journal,* December 9, 1997, p. B4; "Rough and tumble industry," *Financial Times,* July 2, 1997, p. 13; "Whirlpool to build washing machines with European, fuel-efficient design," *Wall Street Journal,* August 19, 1994; Rahul Jacob, "The big rise," *Fortune,* May 30, 1994, pp. 74–90; "If you can't stand the heat, upgrade the kitchen," *Business Week,* April 25, 1994; "A chance to clean up in European white goods," *Financial Times,* December 13, 1993, p. 23; Maytag, *1993 Annual Report.*

Endnotes

1. "The newest Learjet ... now Mexican made," *Wall Street Journal,* July 29, 2011, p. B1; *Survey of Current Business,* July 2011, p. 103; "Mexico's GDP expands 4.6%, below expectations," *Wall Street Journal,* May 19, 2011; "Mexico plants back in business," *The Bryan College Station Eagle,* January 24, 2011, p. A13; "Companies shun violent Mexico," *Wall Street Journal,* December 17, 2010, p. B1; "Strains on auto parts industry in Mexico reflect U.S. woes," *Houston Chronicle,* January 2, 2008, p. D1; "Mexico seeks a lasting share of aerospace boom," *Wall Street Journal,* November 26, 2007, p. A2; "Flat-panel TVs display effects of globalization," *USA Today,* May 8, 2007, p. 1B; "Mexico industry: Maquiladoras get fitter," *The Economist Intelligence Unit,* March 13, 2006 (online); Organization for Economic Co-operation and Development, *Economic Survey of Mexico 2005: Economic Performance and Key Challenges* (Paris, 2005); "Mexico targets skilled U.S.

jobs,"*Wall Street Journal*, March 5, 2004, p. A8; "Mexico's maquiladoras may be putting a comeback together," *Wall Street Journal*, July 25, 2003, p. A12; "Wasting away," *BusinessWeek*, June 2, 2003, p. 42; "Toyota plans to build truck plant near Tijuana," *Houston Chronicle*, January 6, 2002, p. 2D; "Mexican truckers not rushing north," *Houston Chronicle*, December 29, 2001, p. 1C; "The world's new tiger on the export scene isn't Asian; it's Mexico," *Wall Street Journal*, May 9, 2000, p. A1; "A new market for Mexico's work force," *Wall Street Journal*, April 14, 2000, p. A15; "Mexico, EU sign free-trade agreement," *Wall Street Journal*, March 24, 2000, p. A15; "How a need for speed turned Guadalajara into a high-tech hub," *Wall Street Journal,* March 2, 2000, p. A1; "Mexico's Next Big Export: Your Teeth," *Wall Street Journal*, March 14, 2000, p. B6; "First came assembly; now, services soar," *Wall Street Journal*, February 28, 2000, p. A1; "European carmakers converge on Mexican gateway to the US," *Financial Times*, January 5, 2000, p. 5.

2. "A deadline for Doha," *The Economist*, January 29, 2011; "Mandelson says US largely alone on WTO farm demands," *New York Times*, May 4, 2006 (online); "Doha talks in crisis as farm reform deadline set to be missed," *Financial Times*, March 31, 2003, p. 1; "Sides line up to contest farm reform," *Financial Times*, February 14, 2003, p. 7; "WTO tries to break deadlock on medicines access," *Financial Times*, January 28, 2003, p. 6.

3. United Nations Conference on Trade and Development, *The Outcome of the Uruguay Round: An Initial Assessment* (Supporting Papers to the trade and Development Report, 1994) (New York: United Nations, 1994), p. 143.

4. "WTO rules in favor of Brazil," *Financial Times*, February 18, 2003, p. 4; "WTO allows Brazilian sanctions on Canada," *Wall Street Journal*, December 24, 2002, p. A8.

5. "Mandelson says US largely alone on WTO farm demands." *New York Times*, May 4, 2006 (online).

6. *Consumer Policy in the Single Market* (Luxembourg: Office for Official Publications of the European Communities, 1991), pp. 7–8.

7. "Chinese companies embark on shopping spree in Europe," *Wall Street Journal*, June 7, 2011, p. A1.

8. "Doubts swirl about EU future," *Wall Street Journal*, June 3, 2005, p. A2.

9. "GDF-Suez deal sets up EU-Paris fight," *Wall Street Journal*, September 4, 2007, p. A8.; "Europe's unreformed economies," *The Economist*, March 24, 2006; "Closing the borders to business," *The Economist*, February 27, 2006 (online); "Fighting for their slice of Europe," *Financial Times*, October 5, 2005, p. 13.

10. United Nations Conference on World Trade and Investment, *World Investment Report 2010*, Annex table 3.

11. "Doubts cloud South-East Asia's free trade dreams," *Financial Times*, December 30, 2002, p. 3.

12. "With aggressive trade pacts, China quietly builds clout in region," *Wall Street Journal*, March 19, 2003, p. A12.

13. APEC website at http://statistics.apec.org/index.php/ key_indicator/kid_result_list/1, accessed on June 8, 2011.

14. "Africa's trade flows clogged up at dockside," *Financial Times*, January 8, 2002, p. 6.

15. Whirlpool Corporation, *1993 Annual Report*, p. 15.

CHAPTER 11

International Strategic Management

AFTER STUDYING THIS CHAPTER, YOU SHOULD BE ABLE TO:

1. Characterize the challenges of international strategic management.
2. Assess the basic strategic alternatives available to firms.
3. Distinguish and analyze the components of international strategy.
4. Describe the international strategic management process.
5. Identify and characterize the levels of international strategies.

Access a host of interactive learning aids at **www.pearsonglobaleditions.com/ mymanagementlab** to help strengthen your understanding of the chapter concepts.

MyManagementLab

Pindiyath100/Dreamstime.com

GLOBAL MICKEY

Mickey Mouse is every bit as popular around the globe as Coca-Cola's soft drinks and McDonald's burgers. But the Walt Disney Company has done a surprisingly poor job of capitalizing on the global potential for its various products. In 2010, for instance, 74 percent of Disney's $38.1 billion in revenues came from the United States and Canada, which account for only 5 percent of the world's population. This contrasts markedly with Coca-Cola and McDonald's, which each derive about two-thirds of their revenue from outside the United States.

Perhaps Disney's most public effort at internationalization has been its theme park operations. Its first theme park, Disneyland, opened in Anaheim, California, in 1955 and was soon generating huge profits. The firm's next major theme park development, Walt Disney World, opened near Orlando, Florida, in 1971 and also was a major success. Because the two parks generate enormous profits, Disney has continued to invest in them by building new attractions and on-site hotels and by opening new parks adjacent to the existing ones. For example, the fourth Walt Disney World theme park, the Animal Kingdom, opened in 1998 and a new park adjacent to Disneyland, Disney's California Adventure, opened in 2001.

Given the enormous popularity of Disney characters abroad, the firm saw opportunities to expand theme park operations to foreign markets. Its first international venture, Tokyo Disneyland, opened in 1984. The Japanese have long been Disney fans, and many Japanese tourists visit Disneyland and Disney World each year. To limit its risk, though, the firm did not invest directly in the park—a decision Disney managers would eventually come to regret. Instead, a Japanese investment group called the Oriental Land Company financed and entirely owns Tokyo Disneyland. Disney oversaw the park's construction and manages it but receives only royalty income from it. Tokyo Disneyland has been an enormous success from the day it opened its gates: It greeted its 100 millionth visitor after only eight years, a milestone that Disneyland took twice as long to reach. And Tokyo Disneyland remains Japan's number one tourist attraction.

The success of Tokyo Disneyland inspired the firm to seek other foreign market opportunities. After evaluating potential sites throughout Europe, the firm narrowed its choice to one in France just outside Paris. This time, though, Disney decided to participate more fully in both the park's ownership and its profits. While the French government decreed that Disney's ownership in the new venture could be no more than 49 percent (with the remaining 51 percent made available for trade on European stock exchanges), Disney eagerly accepted this ownership structure. The French government's offer of numerous economic incentives also played a role in Disney's decision. The government sold the land for the park to Disney at bargain-basement prices and agreed to extend the Parisian rail system to the proposed park's front door. But as Euro Disney took shape, storm clouds loomed. The cultural elite in Paris lambasted the project as an affront to French cultural traditions. Farmers protested the manner in which the French government condemned their land so that it could be sold to Disney. And the firm found itself defending its conservative employee dress codes, regimented training practices, and plans to ban alcohol from park facilities. Amid the controversy, Euro Disney opened its doors to the public on April 12, 1992.

As it turned out, Disney's timing could not have been worse. First, a recession swept through Europe just as the park was opening. To aggravate matters, the British, Italian, and Spanish central banks devalued their respective currencies, raising the cost for their citizens of vacationing in France. Disney was forced to drop its plan to reduce its debt by selling land it owned near the park to local developers. And the carrying cost of its debt rose further as French interest rates climbed. Disney also severely misjudged the spending and lodging habits of its visitors. Visitors spent 12 percent less on food and souvenirs than expected. Disney planners had also presumed hotel guests would stay an average of three days, as they do in Orlando. But Euro Disney visitors typically stayed two days or less. Further, the firm had planned to sell the hotels shortly after the park's opening and use the proceeds to finance expansion in other areas. Unfortunately, the low occupancy rates made the properties less attractive, and Disney found no buyers. At this point, Euro Disney seemed to be burning money, and it actually came close to being shut down. Eventually, a complex and costly financial restructuring plan implemented in 1994 barely saved the park, and it has only been within the last few years that the park—renamed Disneyland Paris—has begun earning profits.

Disney did learn some things from its start-up problems in Europe. When it opened the Disney Studios theme park adjacent to Disneyland Paris in 2002, Disney made some small but significant changes in its operations. The voices of European actors such as Jeremy Irons, Nastassja Kinski, and Isabella Rossellini are featured on Disney Studios' tram rides, rather than those of American actors like Bruce Willis. Disneyland Paris originally offered only French sausages, upsetting German, Italian, and British visitors who preferred those of their own country. Disney Studios Paris's food outlets, however, offer a broader array of sausages. The setting of the park's featured stunt show is modeled after St. Tropez, rather than a Hollywood back lot. Small matters, perhaps, but such details are designed to make visitors to the theme park feel more at home.

In 2005, Disney's next major international foray came to fruition when Disneyland Hong Kong made its debut. Opening-day festivities included a traditional parade comprising mainly Disney characters coupled with a few local touches—fireworks, Chinese lion dancers, and clanging cymbals. The company received a 43 percent equity stake in the $3.6 billion project in exchange for an investment of only $314 million. The local government, in turn, invested over $2.9 billion in low-interest loans, land, and infrastructure improvements for the remaining 57 percent share. Disney was careful to incorporate feng shui concepts into the design of the Hong Kong park.

But as in Europe, Disney has had to go back to the drawing boards and revise its approach to running Disneyland Hong Kong. While attendance—and spending—fell slightly below initial projections when the park first opened, both dropped dramatically in 2006. Disney had again failed to understand its market. The Chinese were less familiar with many Disney characters and classic attractions than the company expected, and many visitors felt the park was too "foreign" for their tastes. To compensate, Disney has systematically reduced the presence of some of its traditional characters and replaced them with more Chinese figures such as Cai Shen Ye, the bearded Chinese god of wealth. It also changed the costuming of mainline favorites like Mickey and Minnie Mouse, putting the venerable characters into red Chinese New Year garb. And the iconic daily Disney parade has been changed to include such traditional Chinese favorites as dragons and puppets of birds, fish, and flowers. These efforts have worked; in 2011, Disney will begin a multiyear expansion of the Hong Kong park. The first addition will be Toy Story Land, featuring Buzz Lightyear, Woody, and friends.

Disney is nothing if not persistent. In addition to tinkering with Disneyland Hong Kong, the company established a branch office in Shanghai to coordinate its efforts in the 1.3 billion customer market. The Disney channel and Disney cartoons are now broadcast throughout China, while "Disney Corners" featuring Disney-branded merchandise are available in over 1,800 department stores in China. Disney operates 15 learning centers in Beijing and Shanghai, using a curriculum featuring Disney characters like the Little Mermaid and Mickey Mouse to teach English to 7,000 Chinese youngsters ranging in age from 2 to 12. It plans to expand this program to 150 facilities serving 150,000 students by 2015. Of course, this approach to language education familiarizes the new generation of Chinese with Disney characters as well as improving their English skills. Disney's methodical approach to the Chinese market has paid off: After a decade of negotiations, Disney broke ground on a new $4.4 billion theme park in Shanghai in 2011. Disney will own 43 percent of the new venture, with three city-owned businesses controlling the remainder.

The company also is targeting India as a lucrative market for its products. In 2004 it launched Disney Channel and Toon Disney programming customized for the Indian families. Disney developed an Indian takeoff on "High School Musical," although cricket replaced basketball in the movie's storyline. Chinese and Russian versions of "High School Musical" are also under way, as are live and animated films targeted to the Indian, Chinese, Arab, and Russian markets. Similarly, Disney has teamed up with local animation companies in Japan to produce Japan-specific television content. For instance, the Disney animated movie *Lilo and Stitch* was a huge hit in Japan, and so the company is planning a Japanese spin-off. But this version will be set in Okinawa, not Hawaii, and Lilo will be replaced with a Japanese girl named Hanako.

Nor is the company ignoring its opportunities elsewhere. Disney's Consumer Product Division has established dedicated sales teams to cater to the worldwide procurement needs of major international retailers like Carrefour, ASDA (the British subsidiary of Walmart), and Metro. Disney Channels Worldwide offers 95 channels in 35 languages in 168 countries, reaching an estimated 300 million homes. ESPN International has equity interests in 29 international TV networks and has developed customized programming, such as ESPN Classic Sport Europe, ESPN

Latin America, and ESPN Asia, to serve sports fans in those regions. ESPN UK, for example, obtained rights to broadcast Premier League and FA Cup games for the next four years. ESPN Latin America acquired the South American broadcast rights for the 2010 and 2012 Olympic games. Still, the company's international operations have much room for improvement. Company executives have calculated that if they can increase per capita consumer spending on Disney-related products in just five countries—the United Kingdom, Italy, Germany, France, and Japan—to 80 percent of the level in the United States, the firm would generate an additional $2 billion in annual revenues.[1] ∎

To survive in today's global marketplace, firms must be able to quickly exploit opportunities presented to them anywhere in the world and respond to changes in domestic and foreign markets as they arise. This requires a cogent definition of the firm's corporate mission, a vision for achieving that mission, and an unambiguous understanding of how the company intends to compete with other firms. To obtain this understanding, firms must carefully compare their strengths and weaknesses to those of their worldwide competitors; assess likely political, economic, and social changes among their current and prospective customers; and analyze the impact of new technologies on their ways of doing business.

Disney's decisions to build Tokyo Disneyland, Disneyland Paris, Disney Studios Paris, and Hong Kong Disneyland are consistent with its strategy to be a global entertainment firm. So, too, are its efforts to increase worldwide licensing of its characters and expand its audience for the Disney Channel to other countries. But the firm stumbled badly in its initial efforts with Disneyland Paris and knows its competitors will continue to fight for market share. European vacationers can enjoy other amusement parks, such as Denmark's Legoland or France's Parc Asterix. Mickey Mouse lunchboxes compete for the attention of the world's schoolchildren with those featuring England's Paddington Bear, France's Babar the Elephant, Japan's Hello Kitty, and Belgium's Smurfs. And Time Warner's Cartoon Network has been outperforming the mouse for years. Thus, Disney's top managers know that they are in a continuous battle for the entertainment dollars (and euros and yen and pounds) of the world's consumers and that it is up to them to deploy the firm's resources to achieve desired levels of profitability, growth, and market share.

The Challenges of International Strategic Management

Disney's managers, like those of other international businesses, utilize strategic management to address these challenges. More specifically, **international strategic management** is a comprehensive and ongoing management planning process aimed at formulating and implementing strategies that enable a firm to compete effectively internationally. The process of developing a particular international strategy is often referred to as **strategic planning.** Strategic planning is usually the responsibility of top-level executives at corporate headquarters and senior managers in domestic and foreign operating subsidiaries. Most large firms also have a permanent planning staff to provide technical assistance for top managers as they develop strategies. Disney's planning staff, for example, gathered demographic and economic data that the firm's decision makers used to select the French site for Euro Disney and the Shanghai site for its latest Asian park.

International strategic management results in the development of various **international strategies,** which are comprehensive frameworks for achieving a firm's fundamental goals. Conceptually, there are many similarities between developing a strategy for competing in a single country and developing one for competing in multiple countries. In both cases, the firm's strategic planners must answer the same fundamental questions:

- What products and/or services does the firm intend to sell?
- Where and how will it make those products or services?
- Where and how will it sell them?
- Where and how will it acquire the necessary resources?
- How does it expect to outperform its competitors?[2]

But developing an international strategy is far more complex than developing a domestic one.[3] Managers developing a strategy for a domestic firm must deal with one national government, one currency, one accounting system, one political and legal system, and, usually, a single language and a comparatively homogeneous culture. But managers responsible for developing a strategy for an international firm must understand and deal with multiple governments, multiple currencies, multiple accounting systems, multiple political systems, multiple legal systems, and a variety of languages and cultures.

Moreover, managers in an international business must also coordinate the implementation of their firm's strategy among business units located in different parts of the world with different time zones, different cultural contexts, and different economic conditions, as well as monitoring and controlling their performance. But managers usually consider these complexities acceptable trade-offs for the additional opportunities that come with global expansion. Indeed, international businesses have the ability to exploit three sources of competitive advantage unavailable to domestic firms.

- *Global efficiencies.* International firms can improve their efficiency through several means not available to domestic firms. They can capture *location efficiencies* by locating their facilities anywhere in the world that yields them the lowest production or distribution costs or that best improves the quality of service they offer their customers. Production of athletic shoes, for example, is very labor intensive, and Nike, like many of its competitors, centers its manufacturing in countries where labor costs are especially low.[4] Similarly, by building factories to serve more than one country, international firms may also lower their production costs by capturing *economies of scale*. For example, rather than splitting production of its first sports utility vehicle among several factories, Mercedes-Benz decided to initially produce this vehicle only at its Alabama assembly plant to benefit from economies of scale in production.[5] Finally, by broadening their product lines in each of the countries they enter, international firms may enjoy *economies of scope*, lowering their production and marketing costs and enhancing their bottom lines. Apple's transition from a seller of

Apple's extensive line of sophisticated consumer electronics generates economies of scope for the company. Its sleek Apple stores allow customers to test drive the company's latest iPads, iPhones, laptops, and desktops, which often share common design and operating features.

© Joseph Silva Photography/Alamy

only personal computers to a company with an extensive line of electronic communications equipment—desktops, laptops, iPhones, iPads, etc.—allows it to economize on research and development expenses, branding costs, and distribution expenses. As a result, its R&D, distribution, and branding costs per product are much lower than when it was simply a seller of computers.

- *Multinational flexibility.* As we discussed in Chapters 3 and 4, there are wide variations in the political, economic, legal, and cultural environments of countries. Moreover, these environments are constantly changing: New laws are passed, new governments are elected, economic policies are changed, new competitors may enter (or leave) the national market, and so on. International businesses thus face the challenge of responding to these multiple diverse and changing environments. But unlike domestic firms, which operate in and respond to changes in the context of a single domestic environment, international businesses may also respond to a change in one country by implementing a change in another country. Chicken processor Tyson Foods, for example, has benefited from the increased demand by health-conscious U.S. consumers for chicken breasts. In producing more chicken breasts, Tyson also produced more chicken legs and thighs, which are considered less desirable by U.S. consumers. Tyson capitalized on its surplus by targeting the Russian market, where dark meat is preferred over light, and the Chinese market, where chicken feet are considered a tasty delicacy. Tyson exports nearly $600 million worth of chicken thighs and legs to Russia and China.[6] In a variety of ways similar to this, international businesses are better able than purely domestic firms to exploit and respond to changes and differences in their operating environments.

- *Worldwide learning.* The diverse operating environments of MNCs may also contribute to organizational learning.[7] Differences in these operating environments may cause the firm to operate differently in one country than another. An astute firm may learn from these differences and transfer this learning to its operations in other countries.[8] For example, McDonald's U.S. managers believed that its restaurants should be freestanding entities located in suburbs and small towns. A Japanese franchisee convinced McDonald's to allow it to open a restaurant in an inner-city office building. That restaurant's success caused McDonald's executives to rethink their store location criteria. Nontraditional locations—office buildings, Walmart superstores, food courts, and airports—are now an important source of new growth for the firm. "Emerging Opportunities" provides another example of the benefits of worldwide learning.

Unfortunately, it is difficult to exploit these three factors simultaneously. Global efficiencies can be more easily obtained when a single unit of a firm is given worldwide responsibility for the task at hand. BMW's engineering staff at headquarters in Munich, for example, is responsible for the research and design of the company's new automobiles. By focusing its R&D efforts at one location, BMW engineers designing new transmissions are better able to coordinate their activities with their counterparts designing new engines. However, centralizing control of its R&D operations also hinders the firm's ability to customize its product to meet the differing needs of customers in different countries. Consider the simple question of whether to include cup holders in its cars. In designing cars to be driven safely at the prevailing high speeds of Germany's autobahn, the company's engineers initially decided that cup holders were both irrelevant and dangerous. Driving speeds in the United States, however, are much lower, and cup holders are an important comfort feature in autos sold to U.S. consumers. Lengthy battles were fought between BMW's German engineers and its U.S. marketing managers over this seemingly trivial issue. Only after a decade of argument did cup holders finally become a standard feature in the firm's automobiles sold in North America. And even then, in some BMW models the cup holders were placed in front of the air conditioner vents, making it harder to keep beverages at their desired temperature.

As this example illustrates, if too much power is centralized in one unit of the firm, it may ignore the needs of consumers in other markets. Conversely, multinational flexibility is enhanced when firms delegate responsibility to the managers of local subsidiaries. Vesting power in local managers allows each subsidiary to tailor its products, personnel policies, marketing techniques, and other business practices to meet the specific needs and wants of potential customers in each market the firm serves. However, this increased flexibility will reduce the firm's ability to obtain global efficiencies in such areas as production, marketing, and R&D.

While Toyota achieved its goal of being the world's largest car manufacturer in 2008, it initially struggled in the Chinese market, the fastest growing auto market in the world. In 2005, it sold a mere 183,000 cars there, ranking ninth in the market, far behind Volkswagen, General Motors, Hyundai, and Honda. And its performance fell well short of its ambitions: Toyota's goal was to sell one million cars a year in China by 2010. Part of Toyota's problem is that it was a late entrant. It delayed producing cars in China until 2002, when it entered into a joint venture with a local company, the First Auto Works Group (FAW). The first car manufactured by Toyota-FAW, the Vios, failed to attract much of a market, for, despite its unremarkable design, it was three times as expensive as most cars sold in China.

Toyota's real difficulty was not its slow start or poor product positioning, however. Rather, Toyota assumed the Chinese market would be similar to the Japanese market. It soon learned, the hard way, that the Chinese market more closely resembled the American market.

Sales personnel in Japan are paid a salary and succeed by slowly building a base of loyal clientele by providing first-class service to them. Similarly, most Japanese auto dealers sell but a single brand, thereby ensuring their loyalty to it. Japan is a relatively small country with an ethnically homogeneous population. Accordingly, Toyota utilized nationwide advertising to market its products in its home country.

Such is not the case in China. Salespersons live off their commissions, and most dealers sell numerous brands. Thus, loyalty plays little role in motivating either the sales staff or the dealers, who will ignore a slow-selling product should a more profitable one turn up. And China is a large, diverse country. For instance, an advertising campaign depicting the ruggedness of a Toyota SUV in conquering the harrowing terrain of inland China did little to spur sales in the populous, prosperous cities of the south.

To remedy its failures in the Chinese market, Toyota transferred Yoshi Inaba, a 38-year company veteran who had overseen the company's recent success in the United States. Inaba then recruited two senior American marketing executives who had worked for him in California to do the same in China. Their first task was to establish 32 FAW-Toyota regional dealership associations. In the American market, such associations develop cooperative advertising campaigns customized for their local markets. The new team also revamped its annual dealer meetings, shifting from the staid approach used in Japan to the more rah-rah, inspirational approach used in America to build enthusiasm for the Toyota brand. It also revamped Toyota's approach to allocating cars among its Chinese dealers, adopting the "turn and earn" system utilized in America: Dealers who sell (or turn) more cars earn favorable access to additional cars, particularly the hot-selling models. In this way, Toyota both rewards and motivates its dealers to focus their efforts on selling Toyotas rather than other vehicle brands.

Competition in the Chinese market is fierce, but transferring lessons learned in the American market to its operations in China appears to have been successful. Toyota sold nearly 800,000 vehicles there in 2010—a bit short of its ambitious million car goal, but a significant improvement from its 2005 sales—and is planning a $500 million plant expansion with joint venture partner FAW.

Sources: "After the quake," *The Economist*, May 19, 2011; "Toyota expands again in China," www.edmunds.com, March 11, 2008; "VW holds lead in China, Toyota comes in second," *Wall Street Journal*, January 11, 2008 (online); "In Chinese market, Toyota's strategy is made in U.S.A.," *Wall Street Journal*, May 26, 2006, p. A1; "The birth of the Prius," *Fortune*, March 6, 2006, p. 111; "China and Japan: So hard to be friends," *The Economist*, March 26, 2005, p. 23; "The Americanization of Toyota," *Fortune*, December 23, 2003, p. 165.

Furthermore, the unbridled pursuit of global efficiencies and/or multinational flexibility may stifle the firm's attempts to promote worldwide learning. Centralizing power in a single unit of the firm in order to capture global efficiencies may cause it to ignore lessons and information acquired by other units of the firm. Moreover, these other units may have little incentive or ability to acquire such information if they know that the "experts" at headquarters will ignore them. Decentralizing power in the hands of local subsidiary managers may create similar problems. A decentralized structure may make it difficult to transfer learning from one subsidiary to another. Local subsidiaries may be disposed to reject any outside information out of hand as not being germane to the local situation. Firms wishing to promote worldwide learning must utilize an organizational structure that promotes knowledge transfer among its subsidiaries and corporate headquarters. They must also create incentive structures that motivate managers at headquarters and in subsidiaries to acquire, disseminate, and act upon worldwide learning opportunities.

For example, in the late 1990s Procter and Gamble executives grew increasingly concerned that their organizational structure, which was organized along geographic lines, was hindering the ability of the firm to transfer hard-won knowledge in one region to other areas of the world. P&G underwent a drastic organizational restructuring, creating a complex matrix structure that shifted more power to product line managers while retaining the local expertise of regional managers. The process was neither easy nor quick. In fact, the CEO who initiated the restructuring was fired after 18 months on the job. His successor was more successful in implementing the change, which has allowed P&G to transfer products, such as the Swiffer Sweeper or the upscale SK-II skin care cleansing system developed by its Japanese subsidiaries, throughout the globe more quickly and profitably.[9]

SK-II was developed by P&G's Japanese subsidiary after a local scientist noticed the soft and youthful skin of women working in a sake brewery. Its expansion into other markets, including Asia, the United States, and the United Kingdom, was accelerated by an organizational restructuring designed to facilitate the transfer of new products and new technologies from one region to another.

General Electric adopted a different approach to facilitate learning transfer among its units. It established 12 management councils, composed of senior executives from different subsidiaries. At the quarterly meetings of these councils, each member must present a new idea that other subsidiaries can use in their businesses as well. In this way, hard-earned knowledge of new techniques or market opportunities can be quickly spread throughout GE's operations.[10]

Strategic Alternatives

Multinational corporations typically adopt one of four strategic alternatives in their attempt to balance the three goals of global efficiencies, multinational flexibility, and worldwide learning.

The first of these strategic alternatives is the *home replication strategy*. In this approach, a firm utilizes the core competency or firm-specific advantage it developed at home as its main competitive weapon in the foreign markets that it enters. That is, it takes what it does exceptionally well in its home market and attempts to duplicate it in foreign markets. Mercedes-Benz's home replication strategy, for example, relies on its well-known brand name and its reputation for building well-engineered, luxurious cars capable of traveling safely at very high speeds. It is this market segment that Mercedes-Benz has chosen to exploit internationally, despite the fact that only a very few countries have both the high income levels and the high speed limits appropriate for its products. Yet consumers in Asia, the rest of Europe, and the Americas, attracted by the car's mystique, eagerly buy it, knowing that they too could drive their new car 150 miles per hour, if only the local police would let them.

The *multidomestic strategy* is a second alternative available to international firms.[11] A multidomestic corporation views itself as a collection of relatively independent operating subsidiaries, each of which focuses on a specific domestic market. In addition, each of these subsidiaries is free to customize its products, its marketing campaigns, and its operations techniques to best meet the needs of its local customers. The multidomestic approach is particularly effective when there are clear differences among national markets; when economies of scale for production, distribution, and marketing are low; and when the cost of coordination between the parent corporation and its various foreign subsidiaries is high. Because each subsidiary in a multidomestic corporation must be responsive to the local market, the parent company usually delegates considerable power and authority to managers of its subsidiaries in various host countries. MNCs operating in the years prior to World War II often adopted this approach because of difficulties of controlling distant foreign subsidiaries given the communication and transportation technologies of those times.

The *global strategy* is the third alternative philosophy available for international firms. A global corporation views the world as a single marketplace and has as its primary goal the creation of standardized goods and services that will address the needs of customers worldwide. The global strategy is almost the exact opposite of the multidomestic strategy. Whereas the multidomestic firm believes that its customers in every country are fundamentally different and must be approached from that perspective, a global corporation assumes that customers are fundamentally the same regardless of their nationalities. Thus, the global corporation views the world market as a single entity as it develops, produces, and sells its products. It tries to capture economies of scale in production and marketing by concentrating its production activities in a handful of highly efficient factories and then creating global advertising and marketing campaigns to sell those goods. Since the global corporation must coordinate its worldwide production and marketing strategies, it usually concentrates power and decision-making responsibility at a central headquarters location.

The home replication strategy and the global strategy share an important similarity: Under either approach, a firm conducts business the same way anywhere in the world. There is also an important difference between the two approaches, however. A firm utilizing the home replication strategy takes its domestic way of doing business and uses that approach in foreign markets as well. In essence, a firm using this strategy believes that if its business practices work in its domestic market, then they should also work in foreign markets. Conversely, the starting point for a firm adopting a global strategy has no such home-country bias. In fact, the concept of a home market is irrelevant, for the global firm thinks of its market as a global one, not one divided into domestic and foreign segments. The global firm tries to figure out the best way to serve all of its customers in the global market, and then does so.

A fourth approach available to international firms is the *transnational strategy*. The transnational corporation attempts to combine the benefits of global scale efficiencies, such as those pursued by a global corporation, with the benefits and advantages of local responsiveness, which is the goal of a multidomestic corporation. To do so, the transnational corporation does not automatically centralize or decentralize authority. Rather, it carefully assigns responsibility for various organizational tasks to that unit of the organization best able to achieve the dual goals of efficiency and flexibility.

A transnational corporation may choose to centralize certain management functions and decision making, such as research and development and financial operations, at corporate headquarters. Other management functions, such as human resource management and marketing, however, may be decentralized, allowing managers of local subsidiaries to customize their business activities to better respond to the local culture and business environment. Often transnational corporations locate responsibility for one product line in one country and responsibility for a second product line in another. To achieve an interdependent network of operations, transnational corporations focus considerable attention on integration and coordination among their various subsidiaries. "Bringing the world into Focus" discusses how IKEA has tried to capture the benefits of global scale efficiencies while remaining responsive to local conditions.

Figure 11.1 assesses these four strategic approaches against two criteria, the need for local responsiveness and the need to achieve global integration. Firms must pay particular attention to local conditions when consumer tastes or preferences vary widely across countries, when large differences exist in local laws, economic conditions, and infrastructure, or when host-country governments play a major role in the particular industry. Pressures for global integration arise when the firm is selling a standardized commodity with little ability to differentiate its products through features or quality, such as agricultural goods, bulk chemicals, ores, and low-end semiconductor chips. If trade barriers and transportation costs are low, such firms must strive to produce their goods at the lowest possible cost. Conversely, if the product features desired by consumers vary by country or if firms are able to differentiate their products through brand names, after-sales support services, and quality differences, the pressures for global integration are lessened.

The home replication strategy is often adopted by firms when both the pressures for global integration and the need for local responsiveness are low, as the lower left-hand cell in

MASTER OF THE FURNITURE UNIVERSE

In 1943, when he was 17, Ingvar Kamprad established IKEA, a mail-order company selling assorted merchandise. A few years later, he added furniture to his product line but soon chose to design his own furniture products. IKEA developed the idea of shipping disassembled furniture to allow the use of less-expensive flat packaging. The firm opened Europe's first warehouse store in the small Swedish village of Älmhult in 1958. From these innovations, the pioneering retail firm has grown to encompass 316 stores in 37 countries.

The firm's products are known for their combination of Swedish-modern high style, practicality, and affordability. Sofas, for example, cost as little as $200 and are covered with washable, durable canvas. IKEA deliberately engages in social engineering, believing that better and lower-cost design can transform the lives of the average person. Peter Fiell, author of *Industrial Design A–Z*, claims that the retailer's philosophy is about "how to get the most quality to the greatest number of people for the least money." He adds, "That's the nucleus of modernism. It's inherently optimistic."

IKEA has developed a peculiarly Scandinavian culture, with emphasis on restraint and fairness, which it calls "democratic design." This slogan applies to products and also to organizational and task design. Bill Agee, an American employee who transferred to IKEA's Swedish headquarters, says, "It's a little religious or missionary in a sense, but it's who we are." Within the firm, private offices are rare and everyone is on a first-name basis. The no-frills facilities keep the emphasis on the downscale customers, who are referred to as "people with thin wallets." Josephine Rydberg-Dumont, the firm's managing director, speaks with evangelical fervor. "We're ready for modernism now," she says. "When it first came, it was for the few. Now it's for the many."

To cope with the needs of diverse customers around the world, IKEA relies on standardization, with global production and distribution. Customers in Russia, Malaysia, and the United States buy the same linens and cupboards. Customers walk through the identical warehouses along the same predetermined pathway. IKEA encourages ongoing consumption of "throw-away" furniture, long considered a durable good. Christian Mathieu, the firm's North American marketing manager, says of the traditional attitude, "Americans change their *spouse* as often as their dining-room table, about 1.5 times in a lifetime." To change that mind-set, IKEA launched a new ad campaign called Unböring, featuring a discarded lamp sitting out in the rain. The spokesman says, "Many of you feel bad for this lamp. That is because you are crazy." Rydberg-Dumont concurs, saying, "You value things that don't bog you down, that are easy to take

care of." The message is, you can and should update your home as often as you update your wardrobe.

IKEA made some mistakes in its early globalization efforts, not surprising for a firm whose 198 million catalogs are printed in more than 25 languages. In the United States, for example, beds didn't match standard sheet sizes. Another flop was the six-ounce drinking glass that was far too small for American preferences. Kent Nordin, a former IKEA manager, says, "People told us they were drinking out of our vases." Bedroom dressers contained numerous small drawers, a popular European feature, but they couldn't hold Americans' bulky sweaters. Storage units were not sized to hold standard coat hangers. Ultimately, top executives realized that telling American buyers to use smaller coat hangers wouldn't work. Today, IKEA has adapted its products to local tastes. The firm is one of the top furnishings retailers in the United States, and 1 in 10 American homes have at least one IKEA item.

In its newest venture, IKEA has expanded into designing and building entire communities of apartments that are furnished with IKEA products, down to the kitchen gadgets and the bath towels. They are able to provide housing that is 25 percent less expensive than comparable units. The firm's tendency toward social engineering informs every aspect of the design, from the community gardens to the cooperative governance. Many praise the developments, but some feel the concept will not work outside of Sweden. "The idea of building an ideal little street is quite laudable," says Ruth Eaton, author of *Ideal Cities: Utopianism and the (Un)Built Environment*. "But you can't put the same thing everywhere. That's where utopias go wrong. ... You can't take over the world, because conditions are too different, calling for different solutions. Yes for Stockholm, no for Timbuktu."

The retailer may master the furniture industry, but it's not clear whether those skills will translate into a flair for suburban development. IKEA still has a long way to go before realizing its vision of complete world domination in design for the home, but, with €23.8 billion in 2010 sales, it's obviously well on its way.

Sources: "The secret of IKEA's success," *The Economist*, February 24, 2011; www.ikea.com; "Ikea supersizes Beijing store," *Washington Times*, April 11, 2006 (online); "IKEA expects Vietnam business, with its cheap supplies, to surge," *Wall Street Journal*, September 24, 2003, p. B13A; "To Russia, with love: The multinationals' song," *BusinessWeek*, September 16, 2002, pp. 44–46; Eryn Brown, "Putting Eames within reach," *Fortune*, October 30, 2002, pp. 98–100; "A prefab utopia," *New York Times Magazine*, December 1, 2002, pp. 92–96.

Figure 11.1 shows. Toys "R" Us, for example, has adopted this approach to internationalizing its operations. It continues to use the marketing, procurement, and distribution techniques developed in its U.S. retail outlets in its foreign stores as well. The company's managers believe that the firm's path to success internationally is the same as it was domestically: build large, warehouse-like stores; buy in volume; cut prices; and take market share from smaller, high-cost toy retailers. Accordingly, they see little reason to adjust the firm's basic domestic strategy as they enter new international markets.

The multidomestic approach is often used when the need to respond to local conditions is high, but the pressures for global integration are low. Many companies selling brand-name food

FIGURE 11.1

Strategic Alternatives for Balancing Pressures for Global Integration and Local Responsiveness

Source: Adapted from Sumantra Ghoshal and Nitin Nohria, "Horses for courses: Organizational forms for multinational corporations," *Sloan Management Review* (Winter 1993), pp. 27 and 31.

PRESSURES FOR GLOBAL EFFICIENCIES — High

GLOBAL STRATEGY
The firm views the world as a single marketplace and its primary goal is to create standardized goods and services that will address the needs of customers worldwide.

TRANSNATIONAL STRATEGY
The firm attempts to combine the benefits of global scale efficiencies with the benefits of local responsiveness.

PRESSURES FOR GLOBAL EFFICIENCIES — Low

HOME REPLICATION
The firm uses the core competency or firm-specific advantage it developed at home as its main competitive weapon in the foreign markets it enters.

MULTIDOMESTIC STRATEGY
The firm views itself as a collection of relatively independent operating subsidiaries, each of which focuses on a specific domestic market.

Low — High
PRESSURES FOR LOCAL RESPONSIVENESS AND FLEXIBILITY

products have adopted this approach. While not unmindful of the benefits of reducing manufacturing costs, such marketing-driven companies as Kraft, Unilever, and Nestlé are more concerned with meeting the specific needs of local customers, thereby ensuring that these customers will continue to pay a premium price for the brand-name goods these companies sell. Moreover, they often rely on local production facilities to ensure that local consumers will readily find fresh, high-quality products on their supermarket shelves.

The global strategy is most appropriate when the pressures for global integration are high but the need for local responsiveness is low. In such cases, the firm can focus on creating standardized goods, marketing campaigns, distribution systems, and so forth. This strategy has been adopted by many Japanese consumer electronics firms such as Sony and Matsushita, which design their products with global markets in mind. Aside from minor adaptations for differences in local electrical systems and recording formats, these firms' digital cameras, TVs, smartphones, and Blu-ray players are sold to consumers throughout the world with little need for customization. Thus, these firms are free to seek global efficiencies by capturing economies of scale in manufacturing and concentrating their production in countries offering low-cost manufacturing facilities.

The transnational strategy is most appropriate when pressures for global integration and local responsiveness are both high. The Ford Motor Company has been attempting to employ this strategy. For example, Ford now has a single manager responsible for global engine and transmission development. Other managers have similar responsibilities for product design and development, production, and marketing. But each manager is also responsible for ensuring that Ford products are tailored to meet local consumer tastes and preferences. For instance, Ford products sold in the United Kingdom must have their steering wheels mounted on the right side of the passenger compartment. Body styles may also need to be slightly altered in different markets to be more appealing to local customer tastes.

Not addressed to this point has been the issue of worldwide learning. Worldwide learning requires the transfer of information and experiences from the parent to each subsidiary, from each subsidiary to the parent, and among subsidiaries. Neither the home replication, multidomestic, nor global strategy is explicitly designed, however, to accomplish such learning transfer. The home replication strategy is predicated on the parent company's transferring the firm's core competencies to its foreign subsidiaries. The multidomestic strategy decentralizes power to the local subsidiaries so that they can respond easily to local conditions. The global strategy centralizes decision making so that the firm can achieve global integration of its activities.

The transnational strategy would appear to be better able to promote global learning with its mix of centralization of certain functions and decentralization of others—a primary reason for adopting the transnational strategy in the first place. Transnational corporations utilize such techniques as matrix organizational designs, project teams, informal management networks, and corporate cultures to help promote transfer of knowledge among their subsidiaries. Such approaches to promoting worldwide learning are also available to firms adopting the home replication, multidomestic, and global approaches as well. However, such firms need to exert a systematic effort to successfully make use of these techniques.

Components of an International Strategy

After determining the overall international strategic philosophy of their firm, managers who engage in international strategic planning then need to address the four basic components of strategy development. These components are distinctive competence, scope of operations, resource deployment, and synergy.[12]

Distinctive Competence

Distinctive competence, the first component of international strategy, answers the question: "What do we do exceptionally well, especially as compared to our competitors?" A firm's distinctive competence may be cutting-edge technology, efficient distribution networks, superior organizational practices, or well-respected brand names. As our discussion of Dunning's eclectic theory in Chapter 6 suggested, a firm's possession of a distinctive competence (what Dunning called an ownership advantage) is thought by many experts to be a necessary condition for a firm to compete successfully outside its home market. Without a distinctive competence, a foreign firm will have difficulty competing with local firms that are presumed to know the local market better. The Disney name, image, and portfolio of characters, for example, is a distinctive competence that allows the firm to succeed in foreign markets. Similarly, the ready availability of software programs compatible with Windows operating systems gives Microsoft an advantage in competing with local firms outside the United States.

Whatever its form, this distinctive competence represents an important resource to the firm.[13] A firm often wishes to exploit this advantage by expanding its operations into as many markets as its resources allow. To a large degree, the internationalization strategy adopted by a company reflects the interplay between its distinctive competence and the business opportunities available in different countries.[14]

For example, Stuttgart-based Robert Bosch GmbH, the world's largest automotive electronic equipment supplier, was the first company to develop and sell electronic fuel injection and antilock brake systems. This head start resulted in a distinctive competence that other firms have found difficult to match. Bosch still enjoys a 50 percent share of these lucrative markets, selling to automobile manufacturers in all six inhabited continents.[15] Similarly, Frankfurt's Glasbau Hahn constructs glass showcases with self-contained climate controls and fiber-optic lighting. Because the showcases are perceived to be the world's best, museums pay Glasbau Hahn as much as $100,000 for a case in which to display priceless art, sculpture, or artifacts. Exploiting its distinctive competence in this specialized market, Glasbau Hahn has built a multimillion-dollar international business.[16]

Scope of Operations

The second component, the **scope of operations,** answers the question: "Where are we going to conduct business?" Scope may be defined in terms of geographical regions, such as countries, regions within a country, and/or clusters of countries. Or it may focus on market or product niches within one or more regions, such as the premium-quality market niche, the low-cost market niche, or other specialized market niches. Because all firms have finite resources and because markets differ in their relative attractiveness for various products, managers must decide which markets are most attractive to their firm. Scope is, of course, tied to the firm's distinctive competence: If the firm possesses a distinctive competence only in certain regions or in specific product lines, then its scope of operations will focus on those areas where the firm enjoys the distinctive competence.

For instance, the geographical scope of Disney's current theme park operations consists of the United States, Japan, France, and Hong Kong, while the geographical scope of its movie distribution and merchandise sales operations reaches almost two hundred countries. Other companies have chosen to participate in many lines of business but narrow their geographic focus, such as Grupo Luksics, a family-owned conglomerate with interests in beer, copper, banking, hotels, railroads, telecommunications, and ranching in Chile and neighboring countries. Conversely, Ballantyne Strong, a small ($136 million in annual revenues) Nebraska-based company, is sharply focused, just like its primary product: feature-film projectors, a market it has mastered in the United States and abroad.[17] Similarly, in the semiconductor industry, many firms have chosen to limit their operations to specific product niches. Asian semiconductor manufacturers like Samsung and Hynix dominate the global memory chip market. California-based Intel focuses on producing the microprocessors that power most personal computers. Texas Instruments specializes in digital signal processors, which convert analog signals into digital signals. Such chips have many uses, from computer modems to stereo systems to cellular phones. Infineon Technologies AG (which was spun off from Siemens in 1999) concentrates on chips that have automotive, industrial, and communications applications.[18] Thus, strategic planning results in some international businesses choosing to compete in only a few markets, some to compete in many, and others (such as Disney) to vary their operations across the different types of business operations in which they are involved.

Resource Deployment

Resource deployment answers the question: "Given that we are going to compete in these markets, how should we allocate our resources to them?" For example, even though Disney has theme park operations in four countries, the firm does not have an equal resource commitment to each market. Disney invested nothing in Tokyo Disneyland and limited its original investment in Disneyland Paris to 49 percent of its equity and in Hong Kong to 43 percent. But it continues to invest heavily in its U.S. theme park operations and in filmed entertainment.

Resource deployment might be specified along product lines, geographical lines, or both.[19] This part of strategic planning determines relative priorities for a firm's limited resources. Disney could have easily solved Disneyland Paris's financial difficulties without outside assistance. However, additional investment would have taken the firm's commitment far beyond the level it thought viable for its resource deployment goals and perhaps jeopardized its ability to build the California Adventure theme park in California or to purchase the ABC television network and its lucrative ESPN subsidiary.

Some large MNCs choose to deploy their resources worldwide. For example, Osaka-based Sharp Corporation manufactures its electronic goods in factories spread around the world. Other firms have opted to focus their production in one. Boeing, the leading U.S. exporter, concentrates final assembly of most of its commercial aircraft in the Seattle, Washington, region. And Daimler AG concentrates production of Mercedes-Benz automobiles in Germany; although it has production facilities in Alabama, South Africa, and Brazil, most Mercedes vehicles are still German-built.[20] Although these firms buy materials and sell products globally, they have limited most of their production resource deployment to their home countries.

Synergy

The fourth component of international strategy, **synergy,** answers the question: "How can different elements of our business benefit each other?" The goal of synergy is to create a situation in which the whole is greater than the sum of the parts. Disney has excelled at generating synergy in the United States. People know the Disney characters from television, so they plan vacations to Disney theme parks. At the parks they are bombarded with information about the newest Disney movies, and they buy merchandise featuring Disney characters, which encourage them to watch Disney characters on TV, starting the cycle all over again. However, as noted earlier, the firm has been more effective in capturing these synergies domestically than internationally.

Developing International Strategies

Developing international strategies is not a one-dimensional process. Firms generally carry out international strategic management in two broad stages, strategy formulation and strategy implementation. Simply put, strategy formulation is deciding what to do and strategy implementation is actually doing it.

In *strategy formulation*, the firm establishes its goals and the strategic plan that will lead to the achievement of those goals. In international strategy formulation, managers develop, refine, and agree on which markets to enter (or exit) and how best to compete in each. Much of what we discuss in the rest of this chapter and in the next two chapters primarily concerns international strategy formulation.

In *strategy implementation*, the firm develops the tactics for achieving the formulated international strategies. Disney's decision to build Hong Kong Disneyland was part of strategy formulation. But deciding which attractions to include, when to open, what to charge for admission, and how to leverage its investment in the park to penetrate the TV, movie, and character licensing markets in China is part of strategy implementation. Strategy implementation is usually achieved via the organization's design, the work of its employees, and its control systems and processes. Chapters 14 and 15 deal primarily with implementation issues.

While every strategic planning process is in many ways unique, there is nevertheless a set of general steps that managers usually follow as they set about developing their strategies. These steps, shown in Figure 11.2, are discussed next.

Mission Statement

Most organizations begin the international strategic planning process by creating a **mission statement,** which clarifies the organization's purpose, values, and directions. The mission statement is often used as a way of communicating with internal and external constituents and stakeholders about the firm's strategic direction. It may specify such factors as the firm's target customers and

FIGURE 11.2

Steps in International Strategy Formulation

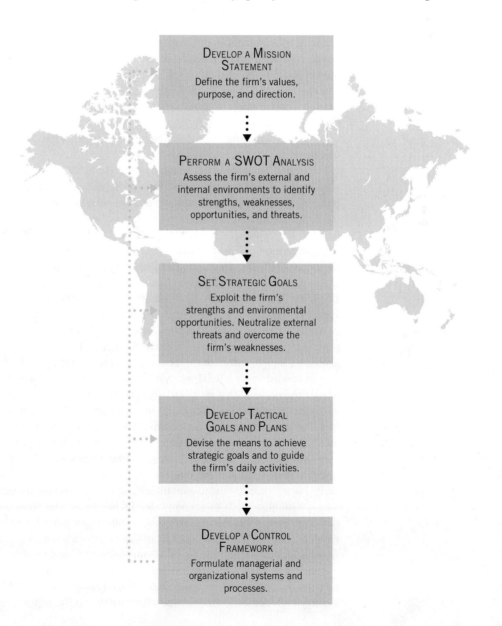

DEVELOP A MISSION STATEMENT
Define the firm's values, purpose, and direction.

PERFORM A SWOT ANALYSIS
Assess the firm's external and internal environments to identify strengths, weaknesses, opportunities, and threats.

SET STRATEGIC GOALS
Exploit the firm's strengths and environmental opportunities. Neutralize external threats and overcome the firm's weaknesses.

DEVELOP TACTICAL GOALS AND PLANS
Devise the means to achieve strategic goals and to guide the firm's daily activities.

DEVELOP A CONTROL FRAMEWORK
Formulate managerial and organizational systems and processes.

markets, principal products or services, geographical domain, core technologies, concerns for survival, plans for growth and profitability, basic philosophy, and desired public image.[21] For example, Wells Fargo's mission is to "satisfy all our customers' financial needs, help them succeed financially, be known as one of America's great companies and the number-one financial services provider in each of our markets," and Carpenter Technology specifies that its mission is to "satisfy customers while consistently earning in excess of our cost of capital and to be the best supplier worldwide for the specialty material needs of our customers." MNCs may have multiple mission statements—one for the overall firm and one for each of its various foreign subsidiaries. Of course, a firm that has multiple mission statements must ensure that they are compatible.

Environmental Scanning and the SWOT Analysis

The second step in developing a strategy is conducting a **SWOT analysis.** SWOT is an acronym for "Strengths, Weaknesses, Opportunities, and Threats." A firm typically initiates its SWOT analysis by performing an **environmental scan,** a systematic collection of data about all elements of the firm's external and internal environments, including markets, regulatory issues, competitors' actions, production costs, and labor productivity.[22]

When members of a planning staff scan the external environment, they try to identify both *opportunities* (the O in SWOT) and *threats* (the T in SWOT) confronting the firm. They obtain data about economic, financial, political, legal, social, and competitive changes in the various markets the firm serves or might want to serve. (Such data are also used for political risk analysis, discussed in Chapter 3, as well as the country market analysis discussed in Chapter 12.) For example, Boeing continuously monitors changes in political and economic forces that affect air travel. In China, political shifts in the early 1990s to allow more competition in the air travel market led the government to split the giant state-owned carrier CAAC into competing regional carriers and to allow Hong Kong's Cathay Pacific airline to offer air travel within China. Boeing's environmental scanning suggested that booming demand for air travel would make the Chinese market a particularly appealing opportunity. Accordingly, the firm chose to locate a new sales office in Beijing. The move paid off, and China has become one of Boeing's most important markets.

External environmental scanning also yields data about environmental threats to the firm, such as shrinking markets, increasing competition, the potential for new government regulation, political instability in key markets, and the development of new technologies that could make the firm's manufacturing facilities or product lines obsolete. Threats to Disney include increased competition in the U.S. market from Universal Studios, Six Flags, and other theme parks; potential competition in Europe from theme parks there; foreign resentment of American military and diplomatic policies; fluctuating exchange rates; and more stringent requirements for obtaining U.S. visas as a result of the 9/11 attacks on the Pentagon and World Trade Center. Threats to BMW include changing U.S. automobile fuel-efficiency standards, increased competition from Japanese producers in the luxury car market, the high value of the euro, and high German labor costs. The threats Federal Express faces include not only competition in the international express package delivery market from firms such as DHL Worldwide and TNT, but also the rapidly growing usage of information technology to send messages electronically.

In conducting a SWOT analysis, a firm's strategic managers must also assess the firm's internal environment, that is, its *strengths* and *weaknesses* (the S and W in SWOT). Organizational strengths are skills, resources, and other advantages the firm possesses relative to its competitors. Potential strengths, which form the basis of a firm's distinctive competence, might include an abundance of managerial talent, cutting-edge technology, well-known brand names, surplus cash, a good public image, and strong market shares in key countries. Disney's strengths include low corporate debt and the international appeal of its characters. BMW's strengths include its skilled workforce, innovative engineers, and reputation for producing high-quality automobiles.

A firm also needs to acknowledge its organizational weaknesses. These weaknesses reflect deficiencies or shortcomings in skills, resources, or other factors that hinder the firm's competitiveness. They may include poor distribution networks outside the home market, poor labor relations, a lack of skilled international managers, or product development efforts that lag behind competitors'. Disney's organizational weaknesses regarding Disneyland Paris include high capital costs, negative publicity, and underutilized hotel capacity. BMW's weaknesses include its extremely high domestic labor costs, which make it difficult for it to compete on the basis of price.

FIGURE 11.3

The Value Chain

Source: Based on *Competitive Advantage: Creating and Sustaining Superior Performance,* by Michael E. Porter, The Free Press, a Division of Simon & Schuster Copyright © 1985 by Michael E. Porter and *Strategic Management and Competitive Advantage: Concepts and Cases,* 4th edition, by Jay B. Barney and William S. Hesterly, © 2012 by Pearson Education, Inc., publishing as Prentice Hall.

One technique for assessing a firm's strengths and weaknesses is the value chain. Developed by Harvard Business School Professor Michael Porter, the **value chain** is a breakdown of the firm into its important activities—production, marketing, human resource management, and so forth—to enable its strategists to identify its competitive advantages and disadvantages. Each primary and support activity depicted in Figure 11.3 can be the source of an organizational strength (distinctive competence) or weakness. For example, the quality of Caterpillar's products (Research, Development, and Product Design in the figure) and the strength of its worldwide dealership network (Distribution and After-sales service in the figure) are among its organizational strengths, but a history of contentious labor relations (Human Resource Management in the figure) represents one of its organizational weaknesses.

Managers use information derived from the SWOT analysis to develop specific effective strategies. Effective strategies are those that exploit environmental opportunities and organizational strengths, neutralize environmental threats, and protect or overcome organizational weaknesses. For example, BMW's decision to build automobiles in South Carolina took advantage of its strong brand image in the United States. This decision also neutralized the firm's internal weakness of high German labor costs and its vulnerability to loss of U.S. customers if the euro were to rise in value relative to the U.S. dollar.

Nike has focused its corporate energies on one component of the value chain—marketing—and deemphasized another—manufacturing. Nike has outsourced production of its footwear and apparel to contract manufacturers throughout the world. An estimated 50,000 Vietnamese workers are employed in factories under contract with Nike.

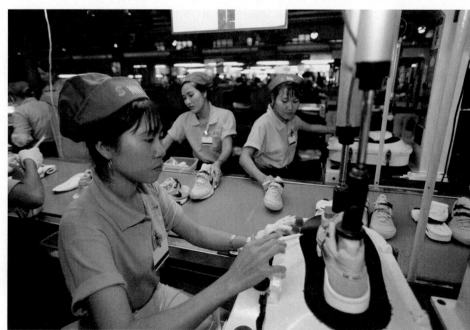

Strategic Goals

With the mission statement and SWOT analysis as context, international strategic planning is largely framed by the setting of strategic goals. **Strategic goals** are the major objectives the firm wants to accomplish through pursuing a particular course of action. By definition, they should be measurable, feasible, and time-limited (answering the questions: "how much, how, and by when?"). For example, Disney set strategic goals for Disneyland Paris for projected attendance, revenues, and so on. But, as the Scottish poet Robert Burns noted, "the best laid plans of mice and men" often go awry. Part of the park's resultant financial problems arose from the firm's goals not being met. Disney's strategic managers had to revise the firm's strategic plan and goals, taking into account the new information painfully learned from the first years of the park's unprofitable operation. And as e-World discusses, Nokia's strategy, which served them well for a decade, quickly became obsolete when new competitors like the iPhone entered their market.

Tactics

As shown in Figure 11.2, after a SWOT analysis has been performed and strategic goals set, the next step in strategic planning is to develop specific tactical goals and plans, or **tactics.** Tactics usually involve middle managers and focus on the details of implementing the firm's strategic goals. For example, Grand Metropolitan, a huge British food company, and Guinness, a major

---

E-WORLD | **NOKIA: NO LONGER KING OF THE HILL**

Nokia Corporation provides a useful case study of the opportunities and challenges facing firms competing in the global economy. It also offers an object lesson for firms who fail to react quickly and appropriately to changes in the global marketplace.

Nokia was formed by Fredrik Idestam, a Finnish engineer. Its early success is consistent with the theory of comparative advantage. Idestam's young company set up shop on the Nokia River in Finland (hence the firm's name) to manufacture pulp and paper using the area's lush forests as raw material. Nokia flourished in international anonymity for 100 years, focusing almost exclusively on its domestic market.

During the 1960s the firm's management decided to start expanding regionally. In 1967, with the government's encouragement, Nokia took over two state-owned firms, Finnish Rubber Works and Finnish Cable Works. In 1981, Nokia's destiny was altered dramatically by one seminal event: Because it had done so well with the rubber and cable operations, the Finnish government offered to sell Nokia 51 percent of the state-owned Finnish Telecommunications Company.

Because Nokia had already been developing competencies in digital technologies, it quickly seized this opportunity and pushed aggressively into a variety of telecommunications businesses. For example, Nokia created Europe's first digital telephone network in 1982. A series of other acquisitions and partnerships propelled the company to the number-one position in the global market for mobile telephones.

At face value it might seem that larger industrial countries like the United States, Germany, and Japan should be leading the way in this market. Conditions in Finland, however, provide a unique catalyst for Nokia's success. Many parts of the Finnish landscape are heavily forested, and vast regions of the country are very sparsely populated. Creating, maintaining, and updating land-based wired communication networks can be very slow and extremely expensive, making wireless digital systems a relative bargain. Thus, conditions were near perfect for an astute, forward-looking company like Nokia to strike gold.

During much of the past decade, Nokia hit a rich vein of pay dirt. It sold over 40 million of its premium-priced N-series handsets, which allow dedicated gamers to download and play video games that were more graphics-rich than those available on its competitors' products. Nokia aggressively targeted emerging markets as well, developing attractively priced mobile phones to meet the needs of those customers. By the end of 2007, Nokia was the world's largest seller of mobile phones, with a global market share of 40 percent. Moreover, it enjoyed the highest operating profit margins in the industry.

Unfortunately, Nokia's market dominance disappeared quickly, seemingly in the blink of an eye. In June 2007, Apple began selling the iPhone in the United States; five months later, the iPhone was available for sale in Europe. The iPhone redefined the rules of competition in the mobile phone industry. Software, not hardware, became the critical selling feature. Unfortunately, Nokia's strength lay in hardware, not software. Nokia's clumsy Symbian operating system was no match for the iPhone's easy to use iOS operating system. Apple's clever "There's an App for that" commercials reinforced the superiority of the iPhone over competing brands. To make matters worse, Nokia's share of emerging markets eroded in the face of increased competition from low-cost Android-based phones produced by Chinese rivals. By the first quarter of 2011, Nokia's global market share had fallen to 25 percent, and the company informed stock analysts that its profits in 2011 and 2012 would be well below previous expectations.

Sources: "Investors hang up on Nokia," *Wall Street Journal,* June 1, 2011, p. B1; "Nokia shares slump," *Wall Street Journal,* June 1, 2011; "Nokia to cut 7,000 globally," *Wall Street Journal,* April 28, 2011, p. B3; "The hands-on manager trying to revive a struggling giant," *Financial Times,* April 12, 2011, p. 10; "Downwardly mobile," *Financial Times,* February 25, 2011, p. 9; "Nokia rivals prepare to pounce on market share," *Financial Times,* February 17, 2011, pl 14; "Doomsday memo from Nokia," *Financial Times,* February 10, 2011, p. 15; "Nokia plays own game on phones," *Wall Street Journal,* April 4, 2008, p. B6; "Nokia moves subtly to regain U.S. share," *Wall Street Journal,* March 27, 2008, p. B1; *Hoover's Handbook of World Business 2006* (Austin, TX: Hoover's Business Press, 2006), pp. 236–237.

British spirits maker, merged to create Diageo PLC, one of the world's largest consumer products companies. The merger agreement reflected strategic decisions by the two companies. But after plans for the merger were announced, middle managers in both companies were faced with the challenges of integrating various components of the two original companies into a single new one. Tactical issues such as the integration of the firms' accounting and information systems; human resource procedures involving hiring, compensation, and career paths; and distribution and logistics questions ranging from shipping and transportation to warehousing all had to be addressed and synthesized into one new way of doing business.[23]

Control Framework

The final aspect of strategy formulation is the development of a **control framework,** the set of managerial and organizational processes that keep the firm moving toward its strategic goals. For example, Disneyland Paris had a first-year attendance goal of 12 million visitors. When it became apparent that this goal would not be met, the firm increased its advertising to help boost attendance and temporarily closed one of its hotels to cut costs. Had attendance been running ahead of the goal, the firm might have decreased advertising and extended its operating hours. Each set of responses stems from the control framework established to keep the firm on course. As shown by Figure 11.2's feedback loops, the control framework can prompt revisions in any of the preceding steps in the strategy formulation process.[24] We discuss control frameworks more fully in Chapter 14.

Levels of International Strategy

Given the complexities of international strategic management, many international businesses—especially MNCs—find it useful to develop strategies for three distinct levels within the organization. These levels of international strategy, illustrated in Figure 11.4, are corporate, business, and functional.[25]

Corporate Strategy

Corporate strategy attempts to define the domain of businesses in which the firm intends to operate. Consider three Japanese electronics firms: Sony competes in the global market for consumer electronics and entertainment but has not broadened its scope into home and kitchen appliances. Archrival Matsushita competes in all these industries, while Pioneer Electronic Corporation focuses only on electronic audio and video products. Each firm has answered quite differently the question of what constitutes its business domain. Their divergent answers reflect their differing corporate strengths and weaknesses, as well as their differing assessments of the opportunities

FIGURE 11.4

Three Levels of Strategy for MNCs

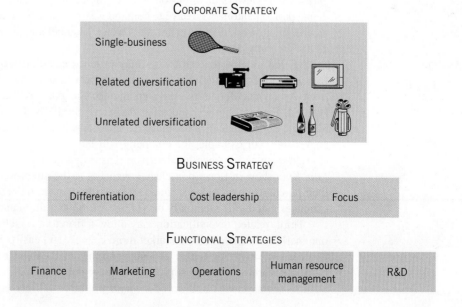

CORPORATE STRATEGY

Single-business

Related diversification

Unrelated diversification

BUSINESS STRATEGY

Differentiation | Cost leadership | Focus

FUNCTIONAL STRATEGIES

Finance | Marketing | Operations | Human resource management | R&D

and threats produced by the global economic and political environments. A firm might adopt any of three forms of corporate strategy. These are called a single-business strategy, a related diversification strategy, and an unrelated diversification strategy.

THE SINGLE-BUSINESS STRATEGY The **single-business strategy** calls for a firm to rely on a single business, product, or service for all its revenue. The most significant advantage of this strategy is that the firm can concentrate all its resources and expertise on that one product or service. However, this strategy also increases the firm's vulnerability to its competition and to changes in the external environment. For example, for a firm producing only floppy disk drives, a new innovation such as the thumb drive may make the firm's single product obsolete, and the firm may be unable to develop new products quickly enough to survive. Nonetheless, some MNCs, such as Singapore Airlines, McDonald's, and Dell, have found the single-business strategy a rewarding one.

RELATED DIVERSIFICATION **Related diversification,** the most common corporate strategy, calls for the firm to operate in several different but fundamentally related businesses, industries, or markets at the same time. This strategy allows the firm to leverage a distinctive competence in one market in order to strengthen its competitiveness in others. The goal of related diversification and the basic relationship linking various operations are often defined in the firm's mission statement.

Disney uses the related diversification strategy. Each of its operations is linked to the others via Disney characters, the Disney logo, a theme of wholesomeness, and a reputation for providing high-quality family entertainment. Disney movies and TV shows, many of which are broadcast over Disney-owned networks, help sell Disney theme parks, which in turn help sell Disney merchandise. Accor SA, one of the world's largest hotel operators, also uses a related diversification strategy. Originally the operator of a chain restaurant, this Paris-based firm began acquiring luxury hotel chains such as Sofitel and budget chains such as Motel 6. To keep its dining rooms and hotel beds full, Accor then branched out into the package tour business and the rental car business. To promote tourism, the firm even opened its own theme park north of Paris, based on the French cartoon character Asterix the Gaul.[26]

Related diversification has several advantages. First, the firm depends less on a single product or service, so it is less vulnerable to competitive or economic threats.[27] For example, if Disney faces increased competition in the theme park business, its movie, television, and licensing divisions can offset potential declines in theme park revenues. Moreover, these related businesses may make it more difficult for an outsider to compete with Disney in the first place. For example, non-Disney animated movies have trouble competing against new animated releases from the Disney Studios. Makers of these movies must buy advertising at commercial rates, while Disney can inexpensively promote its new releases to families waiting in line at its theme parks and to viewers of shows on ABC or the Disney Channel. Similar problems confront rival theme park operators, who have to contend with the constant exposure that Disney's theme parks receive on network television and the Disney Channel and on T-shirts and caps worn by kids of all ages worldwide.

Second, related diversification may produce economies of scale for a firm. For example, Limited Brands takes advantage of its vast size to buy new clothing lines at favorable prices from Asian manufacturers and then divides the purchases among its Victoria's Secret, The Limited, Express, Lerner, and other divisions. Similarly, Disney has created a division it calls Strategic Sourcing. This unit's purpose is to consolidate as much of the firm's global purchasing as possible. For example, the company will buy all its packaging materials from one supplier. Consumers who buy merchandise from Disneyland Paris, the Disney Store in Los Angeles, the *Lion King* show in London, a Disney website, or the direct-mail Disney catalog will all receive their purchases in the same size and style box bought from the same manufacturer. The company estimates that it will eventually be saving over $300 million annually from this approach.[28]

Third, related diversification may allow a firm to use technology or expertise developed in one market to enter a second market more cheaply and easily. For example, Pirelli SpA used its expertise in producing rubber products and insulated cables, refined over 100 years ago, to become the world's fifth largest producer of automobile tires. Pirelli has also transferred its knowledge of rubber cables to become a major producer of fiber-optic cables. More recently, Casio

Computer Company transferred the knowledge it gained in making hand-held electric calculators in the 1970s to the production of inexpensive electronic digital watches, musical synthesizers, and pocket televisions. Such potential synergies are a major advantage of the related diversification strategy.

One potential disadvantage of related diversification is the cost of coordinating the operations of the related divisions. A second is the possibility that all the firm's business units may be affected simultaneously by changes in economic conditions. For example, Accor can create synergies by steering travel customers to its hotels and restaurants. Yet all of Accor's divisions are vulnerable to a downturn in tourism. If another oil crisis erupts or an increase in terrorist actions keeps travelers at home, all Accor businesses will suffer.

UNRELATED DIVERSIFICATION A third corporate strategy international businesses may use is **unrelated diversification,** whereby a firm operates in several unrelated industries and markets. For example, General Electric (GE) owns such diverse business units as a lighting manufacturer, a medical technology firm, an aircraft engine producer, a home appliance manufacturer, and an investment bank. These operations are unrelated to each other, and there is little reason to anticipate synergy among such diverse operations and businesses.

During the 1960s, unrelated diversification was a popular investment strategy. Many large firms, such as ITT, Gulf and Western, LTV, and Textron became **conglomerates,** the term used for firms comprising unrelated businesses. The unrelated diversification strategy yields several benefits. First, the corporate parent may be able to raise capital more easily than any of its independent units can separately. The parent can then allocate this capital to the most profitable opportunities available among its subsidiaries. Second, overall riskiness may be reduced because a firm is less subject to business cycle fluctuations. For example, temporary difficulties facing one business might be offset by success in another. Third, a firm is less vulnerable to competitive threats, since any given threat is likely to affect only a portion of the firm's total operations. Fourth, a firm can more easily shed unprofitable operations because they are independent. It also can buy new operations without worrying about how to integrate them into existing businesses.

Nonetheless, the creation of conglomerates through the unrelated diversification strategy is out of favor on Wall Street today primarily because of the lack of potential synergy across unrelated businesses. Since the businesses are unrelated, no one operation can regularly sustain or enhance the others. For example, GE managers cannot use any of the competitive advantages they may have developed in the lighting business to help offset poor aircraft engine sales. Further, it is difficult for staff at corporate headquarters to effectively manage diverse businesses, because staff members must understand a much wider array of businesses and markets than if operations are related. This complicates the performance monitoring of individual operations. As a result, while some conglomerates, such as GE and Textron, have thrived, many others have changed their strategy or disappeared altogether. Daimler AG, for example, is reorienting its business away from unrelated diversification and more toward related diversification. The firm had operations in passenger cars and trucks, commercial vehicles, financial services and information technology, aerospace, rail, diesel engines, and auto electronics. But Daimler is consolidating some of its nonautomotive activities, selling others, and putting more and more emphasis on its automobile operations.[29]

Business Strategy

Whereas corporate strategy deals with the overall organization, business strategy focuses on specific businesses, subsidiaries, or operating units within the firm. Business strategy seeks to answer the question: "How should we compete in each market we have chosen to enter?"

Firms that pursue corporate strategies of related diversification or unrelated diversification tend to bundle sets of businesses together into **strategic business units (SBUs).** In firms that follow the related diversification strategy, the products and services of each SBU are somewhat similar to each other. For example, Disney defines its SBUs as Parks and Resorts, Studio Entertainment (Touchstone, Buena Vista, and Pixar studios), Consumer Products (Disney publishing, character licensing, Disney Stores), and Media Networks (ABC, the Disney Channel, ESPN). In firms that follow unrelated diversification strategies, products and services of each

SBU are dissimilar. Textron, for example, has created four SBUs: aircraft, automotive products, financial services, and industrial products.

By focusing on the competitive environment of each business or SBU, business strategy helps the firm improve its distinctive competence for that business or unit. Once a firm selects a business strategy for an SBU, it typically uses that strategy in all geographical markets the SBU serves. The firm may develop a unique business strategy for each of its SBUs, or it may pursue the same business strategy for all of them. The three basic forms of business strategy are differentiation, overall cost leadership, and focus.[30]

DIFFERENTIATION **Differentiation strategy** is a very commonly used business strategy. It attempts to establish and maintain the image (either real or perceived) that the SBU's products or services are fundamentally unique from other products or services in the same market segment. Many international businesses today are attempting to use quality as a differentiating factor. If successful at establishing a high-quality image, they can charge higher prices for their products or services. For example, Rolex sells its timepieces worldwide for premium prices. The firm limits its sales agreements to only a few dealers in any given area, stresses quality and status in its advertising, and seldom discounts its products. Other international firms that use the differentiation strategy effectively include Coca-Cola (nonalcoholic bottled beverages), Nikon (cameras), Calvin Klein (fashion apparel), and Waterford Wedgewood (fine china and glassware).

Other firms adopt value as their differentiating factor. They compete by charging reasonable prices for quality goods and services. Marks and Spencer has used the value factor to thrive in the department store market in the United Kingdom and on the European Continent. Lands' End, a Wisconsin mail-order clothing seller that was later purchased by Sears, has also used this differentiation strategy to grow into a billion-dollar company. It has established operations in the United Kingdom, Germany, and Japan. By translating its catalogs into the local language, providing local mailing addresses and telephone numbers, and accepting local currencies, its international operations have come to account for almost 10 percent of its sales. Ironically, this effort puts Lands' End and Marks and Spencer in direct competition with each other, with each stressing the value factor. They may have to switch to differentiation based on distribution mode—catalog versus retail outlet sales.

OVERALL COST LEADERSHIP The **overall cost leadership strategy** calls for a firm to focus on achieving highly efficient operating procedures so that its costs are lower than its competitors'. This allows it to sell its goods or services for lower prices. A successful overall cost leadership strategy may result in lower levels of unit profitability due to lower prices but higher total profitability due to increased sales volume. For example, France's Bic Pen Company has dominated the global ballpoint pen market since its founding in 1945. By concentrating on making those pens as cheaply as possible, the firm is able to sell them for a very low price. Taken together, volume production and a worldwide distribution network have allowed Bic to flourish. Other firms that use this strategy are Timex (watches), Vizio (high-definition TVs), Hyundai (automobiles), the LG Group (consumer electronics), and Hynix (DRAM memory chips).

FOCUS A **focus strategy** calls for a firm to target specific types of products for certain customer groups or regions, such as a retailer specializing in maternity clothes or "big and tall" clients. Doing this allows the firm to match the features of specific products to the needs of specific consumer groups. These groups might be characterized by geographical region, ethnicity, purchasing power, tastes in fashion, or any other factor that influences their purchasing patterns. For example, Hollister Co., a division of Abercrombie & Fitch, has targeted a narrow but lucrative slice of the apparel market. As its website proclaims, the company concentrates its energies on selling the "hottest southern Cali lifestyle clothing geared for outgoing guys and girls."[31] Denmark's Bang and Olufsen focuses on producing elegantly-designed high end audio products, thereby meeting the needs of customers with demanding standards in both form and function.

Functional Strategies

Functional strategies attempt to answer the question: "How will we manage the functions of finance, marketing, operations, human resources, and research and development (R&D) in ways consistent with our international corporate and business strategies?" We briefly introduce each common functional strategy here but leave more detailed discussion to later chapters.

International *financial* strategy deals with such issues as the firm's desired capital structure, investment policies, foreign-exchange holdings, risk-reduction techniques, debt policies, and working-capital management. Typically, an international business develops a financial strategy for the overall firm as well as for each SBU. We cover international financial strategy more fully in Chapter 18. International *marketing* strategy concerns the distribution and selling of the firm's products or services. It addresses questions of product mix, advertising, promotion, pricing, and distribution. International marketing strategy is the subject of Chapter 16.

International *operations* strategy deals with the creation of the firm's products or services. It guides decisions on such issues as sourcing, plant location, plant layout and design, technology, and inventory management. We return to international operations management in Chapter 17. International *human resource* strategy focuses on the people who work for an organization. It guides decisions regarding how the firm will recruit, train, and evaluate employees and what it will pay them, as well as how it will deal with labor relations. International human resource strategy is the subject of Chapter 19. Finally, a firm's international *R&D* strategy is concerned with the magnitude and direction of the firm's investment in creating new products and developing new technologies.

The next steps in formulating international strategy determine which foreign markets to enter and which to avoid. The firm's managers must then decide how to enter the chosen markets. These two issues are the subject of Chapters 12 and 13.

MyManagementLab   Now that you have finished this chapter, go back to **www.pearsonglobaleditions.com/mymanagementlab** to continue practicing and applying the concepts you've learned.

CHAPTER REVIEW

Summary

International strategic management is a comprehensive and on-going management planning process aimed at formulating and implementing strategies that enable a firm to compete effectively in different markets. Although there are many similarities in developing domestic and international strategies, international firms have three additional sources of competitive advantages unavailable to domestic firms. These are global efficiencies, multinational flexibility, and worldwide learning.

Firms participating in international business usually adopt one of four strategic alternatives: the home replication strategy, the multidomestic strategy, the global strategy, or the transnational strategy. Each of these strategies has advantages and disadvantages in terms of its ability to help firms be responsive to local circumstances and to achieve the benefits of global efficiencies.

A well-conceived strategy has four essential components. Distinctive competence is what the firm does exceptionally well. Scope of operations is the array of markets in which the firm plans to operate. Resource deployment specifies how the firm will distribute its resources across different areas. And synergy is the degree to which different operations within the firm can benefit one another.

International strategy formulation is the process of creating a firm's international strategies. The process of carrying out these strategies via specific tactics is called international strategy implementation. In international strategy formulation, a firm follows three general steps. First, a firm develops a mission statement that specifies its values, purpose, and directions. Next it thoroughly analyzes its strengths and weaknesses, as well as the opportunities and threats that exist in its environment. Finally, it sets strategic goals, outlines tactical goals and plans, and develops a control framework.

Most firms develop strategy at three levels. Corporate strategy answers the question: "What businesses will we operate?" Basic corporate strategies are single-business, related diversification, and unrelated diversification. Business strategy answers the question: "How should we compete in each market we have chosen to enter?" Fundamental business strategies are differentiation, overall cost leadership, and focus. Functional strategy deals with how the firm intends to manage the functions of finance, marketing, operations, human resources, and R&D.

Review Questions

1. What is international strategic management?
2. What are the three sources of competitive advantage available to international businesses that are not available to purely domestic firms?
3. Why is it difficult for firms to exploit these three competitive advantages simultaneously?

4. What are the four basic philosophies that guide strategic management in most MNCs?
5. How do international strategy formulation and international strategy implementation differ?
6. What are the steps in international strategy formulation? Are these likely to vary among firms?
7. Identify the four components of an international strategy.
8. Describe the role and importance of distinctive competence in international strategy formulation.

9. What are the three levels of international strategy? Why is it important to distinguish among the levels?
10. Identify and distinguish among three common approaches to corporate strategy.
11. Identify and distinguish among three common approaches to business strategy.
12. What are the basic types of functional strategies most firms use? Is it likely that some firms have different functional strategies?

Questions for Discussion

1. What are the basic differences between a domestic strategy and an international strategy?
2. Should the same managers be involved in both formulating and implementing international strategy, or should each part of the process be handled by different managers? Why?
3. Successful implementation of the global and the transnational approaches requires high levels of coordination and rapid information flows between corporate headquarters and subsidiaries. Accordingly, would you expect to find many companies adopting either of these approaches in the nineteenth century? Prior to World War II? Prior to the advent of personal computers?
4. Study mission statements from several international businesses. How do they differ, and how are they similar?
5. How can a poor SWOT analysis affect strategic planning?
6. Why do relatively few international firms pursue a single-product strategy?
7. How are the components of international strategy (scope of operations, resource deployment, distinctive competence, and synergy) likely to vary across different types of corporate strategy (single-business, related diversification, and unrelated diversification)?

8. The new Disney theme park in Shanghai will open later this decade. Develop a list of at least five ways other units of Disney can help promote and publicize the park's grand opening.
9. Is a firm with a corporate strategy of related diversification more or less likely than a firm with a corporate strategy of unrelated diversification to use the same business strategy for all its SBUs? Why or why not?
10. Identify products you use regularly that are made by international firms that use the three different business strategies.
11. Related and unrelated diversification represent extremes of a continuum. Discuss why a firm might want to take a mid-range approach to diversification, as opposed to being purely one or the other.
12. What are some of the issues that a firm might need to address if it decides to change its corporate or business strategy? For example, how would an MNC go about changing from a strategy of related diversification to a strategy of unrelated diversification?

Building Global Skills

Form a group with three or four of your classmates. Your group represents the planning department of a large, domestically oriented manufacturer that has been pursuing a corporate strategy of unrelated diversification. Currently, the firm makes four basic products, as follows:

1. All-terrain recreational vehicles. This product line consists of small two- and three-wheeled recreational vehicles, the most popular of which is a gasoline-powered mountain bike.
2. Color televisions. The firm concentrates on high-quality, wide-screen, LED televisions.
3. Luggage. This line is aimed at the low end of the market and comprises pieces made from inexpensive aluminum frames covered with ballistics material (high-strength, tear-resistant fabric). Backpacks are especially popular.

4. Writing instruments. The firm makes a full line of mechanical pens and pencils pitched to the middle-market segment, between low-end products such as Bic and high-end ones such as Montblanc.

Your firm's CEO is contemplating international expansion. However, the CEO also thinks that in order to raise its profitability the corporation should begin pursuing a strategy of related diversification. This may mean selling off some businesses and perhaps buying or starting new ones. The CEO has instructed you to develop alternatives, evaluate those alternatives, and then make recommendations as to how the company should proceed. With this in mind, follow these steps:

1. Characterize the current business strategies the company appears to be following with each of its four existing businesses.

2. Evaluate the extent to which there are any bases of relatedness among any of the four existing businesses.

3. Using any criterion your group prefers, select any single existing business and assume that you will recommend that it be kept and the other three sold.

4. Identify existing competitors for the business you chose to keep, including both domestic and international firms.

5. Identify three other countries where there might be potential for business expansion. Explain why.

6. Think of at least two other businesses that are related to the business you will keep and that might be targets for acquisition.

CLOSING CASE — GLOBAL SUCCESS OF SM ENTERTAINMENT

Since the late 2000s, Korean Pop (K-pop) has been gaining global popularity. K-pop initially gained its popularity in Asian countries but lately K-pop fans are not only from Asian countries but also from many European and American countries. K-pop stars' concerts were sold out in Tokyo, Japan; Shanghai, China; Paris, France; and New York, United States in 2011. Also, a prestigious U.S. music chart publisher Billboard launched a K-pop chart in the same year.

One of the key companies that lead to an interest in K-pop is SM Entertainment. SM Entertainment was built by Lee Soo Man, once a singer in 1995, and started idol groups such as H.O.T. and S.E.S. Both groups were a huge success in Korea during the late 1990s and since then SM Entertainment has successfully debuted many boy and girl groups: a solo singer BoA in 2000, a five-member boy group TVXQ in 2003, a thirteen-member boy group Super Junior in 2005, a nine-member girl group Girls' Generation in 2007, and five-member girl group f(x) in 2009. It entered the U.S. market by hosting SM Town Live, a sold-out showcase at Madison Square Gardens in November in 2011.

SM Entertainment aggressively attempted to enter the Asian market in early 2000. The first target country was Japan. Since the Japanese music market was the second largest in the world, entry into Japan provided a bigger opportunity for SM. In addition, Japanese pop culture was dominating the Asian music market. Successful entry into Japan would indicate the musical sophistication of SM Entertainment. In 2001, SM established a joint venture with VAP in Japan, and also signed a contract with Avex Entertainment to release albums of SM's pop singers. This contract was renewed in 2010. SM's singers become very successful in Japan. BoA's album ranked number 1 on the Oricon Charts in Japan multiple times. TVXQ sold out its Asia tour concerts in six countries including Korea, Thailand, Taiwan, Hong Kong, China, and Malaysia in 2007. SM entered the U.S. market in 2008 by forming a subsidiary, and in 2011 SM signed with Interscope Records for the release of the English-language version of the upcoming Girl's Generation album in the United States. In addition, to reinforce their stance in the Asian market, SM established a joint venture, SM True, with Thailand's True Visions Group in 2001.

A key success factor of SM Entertainment's global strategy is the auditions, which take place not only in Korea, but also in China, Japan, the United States, and Canada. In the entertainment industry, personal talent is a critical element that leads to success, and singers with talents are valuable resources for entertainment companies. Thus, finding talented young people is a determinant of the business success of entertainment companies. Global auditions from multiple countries expand the pool of talented young people, and help SM Entertainment increase the opportunities for finding future stars. Moreover, global auditions increase the diversity of music groups and allows them to easily enter other countries. For example, Amber in f(x) is of Taiwan origin and was discovered in the U.S. audition. Amber's background enables f(x) to get recognition in Taiwan relatively easy by making f(x) more familiar to the Taiwanese.

The apprenticeship is another element of SM Entertainments' global success. To promote and expand, SM fully subsidizes and oversees the professional lives and careers of trainees. The apprenticeship program includes training in languages (English, Chinese, and Japanese), global etiquette, and communication skills as well as vocal and dance training. This apprenticeship requires a minimum of two years before debut, and the cost of launching a new artist exceeds $400,000. Through this long and tough apprenticeship, trainees polish their voices, learn professional choreography, sculpt and shape their bodies, and acquire multiple language skills. Thus, their vocal and dance skills become better than other singers from many different countries, and the performance of these well trained singers is more glamorous.

Additionally, pop stars in SM Entertainment are less concerned with musical boundaries. SM Entertainment includes many young pop stars in various genres of music such as hip-hop, dance music, R&B, and ballad, etc. In addition, SM Entertainment attributes different images and identities to each pop star (such as cute and innocent for Girls Generation, and boyish and friendly for f(x)). Diverse music and identities can create synergy. By producing multiple genres of music with different images, SM Entertainment can attract diverse audiences with different preferences and tastes from different countries. Additionally, SM Entertainment has hosted SM Town concerts every year and all singers and groups in SM Entertainment appear in this joint concert. Since the singers' styles and music are different, the concert can be more dynamic and attractive.

Case Question

1. How is local responsiveness critical for the globalization in the music industry? What strategy does SM Entertainment adopt in responding to local responsiveness?
2. How does SM Entertainment develop the distinctive competencies of its singers, and why does it do this?
3. Internet social media such as YouTube and Facebook have become a major channel for music distribution.

What might be a potential strategy for SM Entertainment to exploit opportunities from such trends?

Sources: "Korean pop machine, running on innocence and hair gel," *The New York Times,* October 24, 2011; "New Korean wave led by idol group," *SERI Management Note,* October 14, 2010; "New Korean wave led by K-pop," *KOCCA Focus,* March 15, 2011; "Girls' Generation lead K-pop invasion of Japan," *The Guardian,* September 30, 2011; "Hallyu, yeah," *The Economist,* January 25, 2010; "Flying too high?" *The Time Magazine,* July 29, 2002.

Endnotes

1. *The Walt Disney Company 2010 Annual Report; The Walt Disney Company 10-K filing,* 2010; "Disney to expand language schools in China," *Financial Times,* July 7, 2010, p. 1; "Disney Indian adventure rewarded," *Financial Times,* November 12, 2008, p. 18; "Main Street, H.K.," *Wall Street Journal,* January 23, 2008, pp. B1, B2; "Disney tailors 'stitch' tale for the Japanese market," *Wall Street Journal,* March 7, 2008, p. B3; "Walt Disney to tap into Japanese animators," *Tokyo Financial Times,* March 6, 2008; "Disney rewrites script to win fans in India," *Wall Street Journal,* June 11, 2007, p. A1; "Chinese lessons for Disney," *Wall Street Journal,* June 12, 2006, p. B1; "Hong Kong Disneyland opens," *Wall Street Journal,* September 13, 2005, p. D6; "Transformer of a Mickey Mouse outfit," *Financial Times,* May 28, 2003, p. 10; "Euro Disney alters royalty payments plan," *Financial Times,* March 31, 2003, p. 23; "Euro Disney shares jump 8.5%," *Financial Times,* January 23, 2003, p. 1; "Disney hopes new theme park in Hong Kong opens up China," *Wall Street Journal,* January 15, 2003, p. B4B; "Empire of the mouse expands in Europe," *Financial Times,* March 17, 2002, p. 9; "A certain 'je ne sais quoi' at Disney's new park," *Wall Street Journal,* March 12, 2002, p. B1; *The Walt Disney Company 2002 Annual Report;* "Mickey stumbles at the border," *Forbes,* June 12, 2000, p. 58; "Euro Disney's sales climb 17%," *Wall Street Journal,* January 22, 1998, p. A15; "Fans like Euro Disney but its parent's goofs weigh the park down," *Wall Street Journal,* March 10, 1994, p. A1; "Euro Disney rescue package wins approval," *Wall Street Journal,* March 15, 1994, p. A3; "How Disney snared a princely sum," *BusinessWeek,* June 20, 1994, pp. 61–62; "Euro Disney—oui or non?" *Travel & Leisure,* August 1992, pp. 80–115.
2. See Charles W. L. Hill and Gareth R. Jones, *Strategic Management: An Analytical Approach,* 6th ed. (Boston: Houghton Mifflin, 2004), for an overview of strategy and strategic management. See also Bjorn Lovas and Sumantra Ghoshal, "Strategy as guided evolution," *Strategic Management Journal,* vol. 21, no. 9 (2000), pp. 875–896.
3. Howard Thomas, Timothy Pollock, and Philip Gorman, "Global strategic analyses: Frameworks and approaches," *Academy of Management Executive,* vol. 13, no. 1 (1999), pp. 70ff.
4. Kasra Ferdows, "Making the most of foreign factories," *Harvard Business Review* (March–April 1997), pp. 73–88.
5. "Mercedes bends rules," *USA Today,* July 16, 1997, pp. B1, B2.
6. *Tyson Foods, Inc. Fiscal 2010 Fact Book;* "Tyson foods' exports helped by weaker dollar," *The Morning News,* November 30, 2007 (online); "Russia bans U.S. chicken shipments, inspiring fears of tough trade battle," *Wall Street Journal,* February 23, 1996, p. A2.
7. Anil K. Gupta and Vijay Govindarajan, "Knowledge flows within multinational corporations," *Strategic Management Journal,* vol. 21, no. 4 (2000), pp. 473–496.
8. Christopher A. Bartlett and Sumantra Ghoshal, *Transnational Management,* 2nd ed. (Chicago: Richard D. Irwin, 1995), pp. 237–242. See also Tatiana Kostova, "Transnational transfer of strategic organizational practices: A contextual perspective," *Academy of Management Review,* vol. 24, no. 2 (1999), pp. 308–324.
9. Harvard Business School. "P&G Japan: The SK-II Globalization Project," Case 9-303-003 (March 2004).
10. "Conglomerate plays to its strength," *Financial Times,* November 23, 1999, p. 11.
11. Bartlett and Ghoshal label this strategy the *multinational strategy.* We have altered their terminology to avoid confusion with other uses of the term *multinational.*
12. See Hill and Jones, *Strategic Management.*
13. See T. S. Frost, J. M. Birkinshaw, and P. C. Ensign, "Centers of excellence in multinational corporations," *Strategic Management Journal,* vol. 23, no. 11 (November 2002), pp. 997–1018.
14. Bruce Kogut, "Designing global strategies: Comparative and competitive value-added chains," *Sloan Management Review* (Summer 1985), pp. 15–28.
15. *Hoover's Handbook of World Business 2006* (Austin, TX: Hoover's Business Press, 2006), pp. 283–284.
16. "Think small," *BusinessWeek,* November 4, 1991, p. 58.
17. BallantyneStrong, Annual Report for the Year 2010; Ballantyne of Omaha, Inc. 10-K Statement for Year Ending December 31, 2005; "Producer of feature-film projectors reels in fat profit as cinemas expand," *Wall Street Journal,* October 22, 1996, p. B5; "Chile's Luksics: Battle-tested and on the prowl," *Wall Street Journal,* December 1, 1995, p. A10.

18. "Infineon to split out memory unit in bid to gain agility in chip field," *Wall Street Journal*, May 11, 2006, p. B4; "Intel, backing its bets with big chips, wins," *Wall Street Journal*, September 24, 1992, p. B1; Michiyo Nakamoto, "Looking for smaller worlds to conquer," *Financial Times*, September 2, 1992.

19. Olav Sorenson, "Letting the market work for you: An evolutionary perspective on product strategy," *Strategic Management Journal*, vol. 21 (2000), pp. 577–592.

20. "European auto makers show signs of bouncing back," *Wall Street Journal*, September 15, 1994, p. B4.

21. John A. Pearce II and Fred David, "Corporate mission statements: The bottom line," *The Academy of Management Executive* (May 1987), pp. 109–115.

22. See Anil Gupta and Vijay Govindarajan, "Knowledge flows within multinational corporations," *Strategic Management Journal*, vol. 21 (2000), pp. 473–496.

23. "Grand Met, Guinness to form liquor colossus," The *Wall Street Journal*, May 13, 1997, pp. B1, B8.

24. D. E. W. Marginson, "Management control systems and their effects on strategy formation at middle-management levels: Evidence from a U.K. organization," *Strategic Management Journal* (November 2002), pp. 1019–1032.

25. Hill and Jones, op. cit.

26. "Accor SA, Europe's biggest hotel firm, takes on a new look under a new CEO," *Wall Street Journal*, January 30, 1998, p. B6A.

27. For example, see J. Michael Geringer, Stephen Tallman, and David M. Olsen, "Product and international diversification among Japanese multinational firms," *Strategic Management Journal*, vol. 21, no. 1 (2000), pp. 51–80.

28. *The Walt Disney Company Annual Report 1999*.

29. "DaimlerChrysler's focus may be narrowing," *Wall Street Journal*, October 18, 1999, pp. A37, A39.

30. C. Campbell-Hunt, "What have we learned about generic competitive strategy? A meta-analysis," *Strategic Management Journal*, vol. 21, no. 2 (2000), pp. 127–154.

31. "About Hollister Co.," www.hollisterco.com, October 19, 2006.

Strategies for Analyzing and Entering Foreign Markets

AFTER STUDYING THIS CHAPTER, YOU SHOULD BE ABLE TO:

1. Discuss how firms analyze foreign markets.

2. Outline the process by which firms choose their mode of entry into a foreign market.

3. Describe forms of exporting and the types of intermediaries available to assist firms in exporting their goods.

4. Identify the basic issues in international licensing and discuss the advantages and disadvantages of licensing.

5. Identify the basic issues in international franchising and discuss the advantages and disadvantages of franchising.

6. Analyze contract manufacturing, management contracts, and turnkey projects as specialized entry modes for international business.

7. Characterize the greenfield and acquisition forms of FDI.

Access a host of interactive learning aids at **www.pearsonglobaleditions.com/ mymanagementlab** to help strengthen your understanding of the chapter concepts.

MyManagementLab

Piero Cruciatti/Dreamstime.com

THE BUSINESS OF LUXURY

Christian Dior … Givenchy … Dom Pérignon … Louis Vuitton. To most of us, these names convey luxury, indulgence, the finer things in life. To Bernard Arnault, the chairman and CEO of the €20.3 billion fashion conglomerate LVMH Louis Vuitton Moët Hennessy SA—or more, simply, LVMH—it is his life's work. Like many French companies, LVMH is controlled by a family-owned group: In LVMH's case, the Arnault family owns 47.6 percent of its shares but 63.7 percent of the voting rights. Another 45 percent are owned by institutional investors in France, the United States, and other European countries. The remainder are owned by individuals.

LVMH is in the business of selling prestige. Consider the company's annual report: Displaying the company's portfolio of brands in glowing color, it looks more like a high-end fashion magazine than a boring compilation of the company's financial reports. LVMH plays upon the ancient heritage of its brands. In 2010, for example, bottles of Veuve Clicquot were discovered amid the remains of a nineteenth-century shipwreck in the Baltic Sea. LVMH publicists let it be known that the submerged champagne retained its "admirable organoleptic qualities"—a word choice sure to appeal to Veuve Clicquot's target market. Its sister brand, Dom Pérignon, dates back to 1688, while Louis Vuitton's luggage business began in 1854. Tag Heuer, celebrating its 150th anniversary, reissued a watch line in 2010 based upon its 1887 collection, while Chaumet launched its new Joséphine collection, named after its most important patron, the Emperor Napoleon's wife, to remind its customers of its imperial lineage.

LVMH is following a related-diversification strategy. It has stitched together a remarkable stable of luxury brands, organized into its Fashion and Leather Goods, Wines and Spirits, Perfumes and Cosmetics, Watches and Jewelry, and Selective Retailing strategic business units. LVMH has grown its portfolio of brands primarily by acquiring family-owned companies specializing in manufacturing and marketing luxury goods. While it typically operates the acquired firms as stand-alone subsidiaries, the corporate parent tries to reduce their behind-the-scenes costs by centralizing sourcing, advertising, financing, and acquisition of real estate. In March 2011, for example, LVMH offered $6 billion for high-end Italian jeweler Bulgari. The Bulgari family swapped its 51 percent stake in Bulgari for 16.5 million LMVH shares. The Bulgari acquisition will double LVMH's watch and jewelry revenues. While Bulgari will be run independently, Arnault believes that the jeweler's profit margins will benefit from LVMH's expertise and economies of scale in finance, store location, sourcing, and other behind-the-scenes operations. LVMH will also help Bulgari expand its presence in Asia. Of course, LVMH is not always successful, as its attempt to purchase Hermès International demonstrated. LVMH had quietly purchased 20 percent of the company's shares, but the descendants of founder Thierry Hermès created a family holding company to counter the proposed buyout.

Despite the luxury nature of its product line, LVMH weathered the global recession well. Although the company suffered flat revenues and reduced earnings at the nadir of the global recession in 2009, its revenues and profits boomed in 2010. Leading the way was its Fashion and Leather Goods group, which earned profits of €2.6 billion on revenues of €7.6 billion. The company believes its success rests on the "enduring values of our star brands, creativity as an absolute imperative, the quest for perfection in our products, and our efforts to ensure an environment of excellence."

For a company with a long and storied history in Europe, LMVH fully appreciates the need to broaden its appeal to customers outside the developed countries. Thirteen percent of its revenues come from its home, France, and another 21 percent from the rest of Europe. The United States accounts for 23 percent of its revenues, and Japan another 9 percent. What may be surprising is that the rest of Asia contributes 25 percent of its revenues, a reflection of the growing importance of that region to the world economy and LVMH's commitment to meeting the aspirations of the region's consumers. LVMH expects China to be the largest market for luxury goods by 2020. For instance, China has provided Hennessy, the company's prestigious cognac, with double-digit growth the past three years. In recognition of the country's growing clout, Louis Vuitton featured Godfrey Gao, a Taiwanese-Canadian model and TV star, in its recent commercials for the company's man bag.[1] ■

Chapter 11 focused on the process by which a firm formulates its international strategy. This chapter discusses the next steps in the implementation of strategy: choosing the markets the firm will enter and the modes of entry it will use to compete in these markets. As the opening case indicates, LVMH's primary mode of entry is to acquire purveyors of upscale goods that integrate easily into the company's portfolio of prestigious products. For some brands, LVMH operates its own retail outlets; for others, it relies on high-end retailers for distribution. In other cases, LVMH utilizes licensing agreements with local firms to promote its business interests or teams with local partners in joint ventures. As we discuss in this chapter, in deciding whether and how to enter a market, a well-managed firm will match its internal strengths and weaknesses to the unique opportunities and needs of that market. LVMH has successfully done this in the many national markets in which it participates.

Foreign Market Analysis

Regardless of their strategies, most international businesses have the fundamental goals of expanding market share, revenues, and profits. They often achieve these goals by entering new markets or by introducing new products into markets in which they already have a presence. A firm's ability to do this effectively hinges on its developing a thorough understanding of a given geographical or product market.[2] To successfully increase market share, revenue, and profits, firms must normally follow three steps: (1) assess alternative markets, (2) evaluate the respective costs, benefits, and risks of entering each, and (3) select those that hold the most potential for entry or expansion.

Assessing Alternative Foreign Markets

In assessing alternative foreign markets, a firm must consider a variety of factors, including the current and potential sizes of these markets, the levels of competition the firm will face, the markets' legal and political environments, and sociocultural factors that may affect the firm's operations and performance.[3] Table 12.1 summarizes some of the most critical of these factors.

Information about some of these factors is relatively objective and easy to obtain. For example, a country's currency stability is important to a firm contemplating exporting to or importing from that country or analyzing investment opportunities there. Objective information about this topic can be easily obtained from various published sources in the firm's home country or on the Internet. Other information about foreign markets is much more subjective and may be quite difficult to obtain. For instance, information about the honesty of local government officials or on the process of obtaining utility permits may be very hard to acquire in the firm's home country. Obtaining such information often entails visiting the foreign location early in the decision-making process to talk to local experts, such as embassy staff and chamber of commerce officials, or contracting with a consulting firm to obtain the needed data.[4]

MARKET POTENTIAL The first step in foreign market selection is assessing market potential. Many publications, such as those listed in "Building Global Skills" in Chapter 2, provide data about population, GDP, per capita GDP, public infrastructure, and ownership of such goods as automobiles and televisions. Such data permit firms to conduct a preliminary "quick and dirty" screening of various foreign markets.

The decisions a firm draws from this information often depend upon the positioning of its products relative to those of its competitors. A firm producing high-quality products at premium prices will find richer markets attractive but may have more difficulty penetrating a poorer market. Conversely, a firm specializing in low-priced, lower-quality goods may find the poorer market even more lucrative than the richer market. (See "Emerging Opportunities" for another aspect of this assessment.)

A firm must then collect data relevant to the specific product line under consideration. For instance, if Pirelli SpA is contemplating exporting tires to Thailand, its strategic managers must collect data about that country's transportation infrastructure, transportation alternatives, gasoline prices, and growth of vehicle ownership. Pirelli would also need data on the average age of motor vehicles and the production of automobiles in Thailand in order to assess whether to focus its marketing efforts on the replacement market or the OEM (original equipment manufacturer) market. In some situations, a firm may have to resort to using proxy data. For example, Whirlpool, in deciding whether to enter the dishwasher market in Indonesia, could examine sales of other household appliances, per capita electricity consumption, or the number of two-income families. Firms may also be concerned about the income distribution of the country.

But such data reflect the past, not the future. Firms must also consider the potential for growth in a country's economy by using both objective and subjective measures. Objective measures include changes in per capita income, energy consumption, GDP, and ownership of consumer durables such as private automobiles. More subjective considerations must also be

TABLE 12.1 Critical Factors in Assessing New Market Opportunities

Topic of Appraisal	Items to Be Considered
Product-market dimensions	How big is the product market in terms of unit size and sales volume?
Major product-market "differences"	What are the major differences relative to the firm's experience elsewhere in terms of customer profiles, price levels, national purchase patterns, and product technology?
	How will these differences affect the transferability of the firm's capabilities to the new business environment, and their effectiveness?
Structural characteristics of the national product market	What links and associations exist between potential customers and established national competitors currently supplying these customers?
	What are the major channels of distribution (discount structure, ties to present producers, levels of distribution separating producers from final customers, links between wholesalers, links between wholesalers and retailers, finance, role of government)?
	What links exist between established producers and their suppliers?
	Do industry concentration and collusive agreements exist?
Competitor analysis	What are major competitor characteristics (size, capacity utilization, strengths and weaknesses, technology, supply sources, preferential market arrangements, and relations with the government)?
	What is competitor performance in terms of market share, sales growth, and profit margins?
Potential target markets	What are the characteristics of major product-market segments?
	Which segments are potential targets upon entry?
Relevant trends (historic and projected)	What changes have occurred in total size of product market (short-, medium-, and long-term)?
	What changes have occurred in competitor performance (market share, sales, and profits)?
	What is the nature of competition (e.g., national or international)?
	What changes have occurred in market structure?
Explanation of change	Why are some firms gaining and others losing?
	Are foreign firms already operating here gaining or losing?
	Is there some general explanation of observed change, for example, product life cycle, change in overall business activity, and shift in nature of demand?
	What is the future outlook?
Success factors	What are the key factors behind success in this business environment, the pressure points that can shift market share from one firm to another?
	How are these different from those we have experienced in other countries?
	How do these success factors relate to our firm?
Strategic options	What elements emerge from the above analysis that point to possible strategies for this country?
	What additional information is required to identify our options more precisely?

Source: Reprinted with the permission of Lexington Books, an imprint of The Free Press, a Division of Simon & Schuster, from *Multinational Corporate Strategy: Planning for World Markets*, by James C. Leontiades. Copyright © 1985 by Lexington Books.

taken into account when assessing potential growth. For example, following the collapse of communist economies in Central and Eastern Europe, many Western firms ignored the data indicating negative economic growth in these countries. Instead they focused on the prospects for future growth as these countries adopted new economic policies and programs. As a result, firms such as Procter & Gamble and Unilever established production facilities, distribution channels, and brand recognition in order to seize first-mover advantages as these economies recovered from the process of adjusting to capitalism.

| EMERGING OPPORTUNITIES | THE BOTTOM OF THE PYRAMID |

As Figure 2.1 indicated, the majority of the world's economic activity is generated by the developed countries: the European Union, the United States, Canada, and the rich countries of Asia and Oceana—Japan, South Korea, Australia, New Zealand, Taiwan, Hong Kong, and Singapore. And there is little doubt that these lucrative markets have captured the attention of the world's entrepreneurs and international businesses.

C. K. Prahalad, in his influential 2004 book *The Fortune at the Bottom of the Pyramid*, argues that these businesspersons should turn their attention to the poorest of the 4 billion people in China, India, and other emerging markets who are now just becoming part of the market economy—what he calls the aspiring poor with incomes below $2 a day. After adjusting for purchasing power parity (PPP), Prahalad believes the potential size of this market is huge but recognizes that firms focused on developed markets may need to rethink how they make and market their products to meet the needs of the aspiring poor. For example, one simple approach is to sell products like toothpaste or shampoo in single-use sizes. Nonetheless, he argues that firms can boost their profitability and help alleviate poverty by targeting the bottom of the pyramid.

Other scholars are not so sure. Aneel Karnani notes that adjusting the incomes of the very poor for purchasing power may overstate the importance of the market to international businesses. After all, the revenue and profit potential of a market for MNCs denominated in their home currency is calculated using actual exchange rates, not PPP adjusted rates. Thus, Karnani believes the size of the bottom of the pyramid market in emerging markets is much smaller than Prahalad estimates. Then there is the problem of actually making a profit. Multinational corporations may find it very difficult to reduce their costs of production to a level necessary to be able to sell to people at the bottom of the pyramid. Moreover, much of the incomes of people at the bottom of the pyramid is spent on food and other necessities. And operating costs are often unexpectedly high because of infrastructure deficiencies in emerging markets.

Sources: Aneel Karnani, "Fortune at the bottom of the pyramid: A mirage," *California Management Review*, Vol. 49, No. 4 (Summer 2007); C. K. Prahalad, *The Fortune at the Bottom of the Pyramid: Eradicating Poverty through Profits* (Wharton School Publishing, 2004).

Similarly, although it accounts for only 2 percent of the world's GDP, sub-Saharan Africa is attracting much attention as a result of its huge potential. The area has enjoyed an annual growth rate of 5.7 percent in the past decade, driven by the run-up in commodities prices discussed in Chapter 2's closing case, "China's Quest for Natural Resources."[5] Google, for instance, is targeting the continent, believing that Africa's current low Internet penetration rates create enormous growth potential as its infrastructure improves. Moreover, mobile phone use is exploding—Nigeria alone added 75 million cell phone subscribers during the 2000s—creating demand for company services like Google maps and Gmail. Major global advertising groups like Publicis Groupe SA, WPP, and Omnicom are expanding their operations in numerous African countries or buying up local advertising agencies in response to their multinational customers' interest in marketing to African customers. Ghana, Kenya, Angola, and Nigeria have attracted particular attention, in addition to the continent's economic powerhouse, South Africa.[6]

LEVELS OF COMPETITION Another factor a firm must consider in selecting a foreign market is the level of competition in the market—both the current level and the likely future level. To assess the competitive environment, it should identify the number and sizes of firms already competing in the target market, their relative market shares, their pricing and distribution strategies, and their relative strengths and weaknesses, both individually and collectively. It must then weigh these factors against actual market conditions and its own competitive position. For example, Kia entered the crowded North American automobile market a few years ago believing low labor costs at its Korean factories would allow it to charge lower prices than entrenched competitors like GM, Ford, Toyota, and Volkswagen.

Most successful firms continually monitor major markets in order to exploit opportunities as they become available. This is particularly critical for industries undergoing technological or regulatory changes. The telecommunications industry provides an important example of this phenomenon. Once the home of inefficient, plodding state-owned monopolies, this industry is now the epicenter of the convergence of a variety of new technologies and products—fiber optics, smartphones, tablets, 4G cellular service, satellite networks, and so on. Many of these firms—particularly in Europe and Latin America—have been privatized. Privatization has been coupled with the tumbling of regulatory barriers to entry and innovation, allowing firms to enter new geographic and product markets, as Telefónica has done in Latin America as detailed in Chapter 10's closing case, "The New Conquistador.")

LEGAL AND POLITICAL ENVIRONMENT A firm contemplating entry into a particular market also needs to understand the host country's trade policies and its general legal and political environments. A firm may choose to forgo exporting its goods to a country that has high tariffs and other trade restrictions in favor of exporting to one that has fewer or less significant barriers. Conversely, trade policies and/or trade barriers may induce a firm to enter a market via FDI. For example, Ford, GM, Audi, and Mercedes-Benz built auto factories in Brazil to avoid that country's high tariffs and to use Brazil as a production platform to access other Mercosur members.[7] And some countries require foreign firms wanting to establish local operations to work with a local joint-venture partner.

Government stability is an important factor in foreign market assessment. Some less-developed countries have been prone to military coups and similar disruptions. Government regulation of pricing and promotional activities may need to be considered. For example, many governments restrict advertising for tobacco and alcohol products, so foreign manufacturers of those products must understand how those restrictions will affect their ability to market their goods in those countries. Care also often needs to be taken to avoid offending the political sensibilities of the host nation. Consider the political implications of the language used to describe the island of Taiwan. The leadership of the People's Republic of China (PRC) refuses to recognize the Republic of China (ROC) as an independent nation, viewing Taiwan as a breakaway province. Labeling Taiwan as the Republic of China might discourage sales of this textbook in the PRC; failure to do so might hurt sales in the ROC/Taiwan.

SOCIOCULTURAL INFLUENCES Managers assessing foreign markets must also consider sociocultural influences, which, because of their subjective nature, are often difficult to quantify. To reduce the uncertainty associated with these factors, firms often focus their initial internationalization efforts in countries culturally similar to their home markets.[8] For example, Canada was the location of Starbucks's and Hollister's first international outlets.

If the proposed strategy is to produce goods in another country and export them to the market under consideration, the most relevant sociocultural factors are those associated with consumers. Firms that fail to recognize the needs and preferences of host country consumers often run into trouble. For example, Denmark's Bang & Olufsen, a well-known stereo system manufacturer, floundered in some markets because its designers stress style rather than function. Japanese competitors, meanwhile, stress function and innovation over style and design. Bang & Olufsen's Danish managers failed to realize that consumers in markets such as the United States are generally more interested in function than in design and that they are more willing to pay for new technology than for an interesting appearance.[9]

A firm considering FDI in a factory or distribution center must also evaluate sociocultural factors associated with potential employees.[10] It must understand the motivational basis for work in that country, the norms for working hours and pay, and the role of labor unions. By hiring—and listening to—local managers, foreign firms can often avoid or reduce cultural conflicts.

Evaluating Costs, Benefits, and Risks

The next step in foreign market assessment is a careful evaluation of the costs, benefits, and risks associated with doing business in a particular foreign market.

COSTS Two types of costs are relevant at this point: direct and opportunity. Direct costs are those the firm incurs in entering a new foreign market and include costs associated with setting up a business operation (leasing or buying a facility, for example), transferring managers to run it, and shipping equipment and merchandise. The firm also incurs opportunity costs. Because a firm has limited resources, entering one market may preclude or delay its entry into another. The profits it would have earned in that second market are its opportunity costs—the organization has forfeited or delayed its opportunity to earn those profits by choosing to enter another market first. Thus, the firm's planners must carefully assess all the alternatives available to it.

BENEFITS Entering a new market presumably offers a firm many potential benefits; otherwise, why do it? Among the most obvious potential benefits are the expected sales and profits from the market. Others include lower acquisition and manufacturing costs (if materials and/or labor are cheap), foreclosing of markets to competitors (which limits competitors' ability to earn profits), competitive advantage (which allows the firm to keep ahead of or abreast with its competition), access to new technology, and the opportunity to achieve synergy with other operations.

RISKS Of course, few benefits are achieved without some degree of risk. Many of the earlier chapters provided overviews of the specific types of risks facing international businesses. Generally, a firm entering a new market incurs the risks of exchange rate fluctuations, additional operating complexity, and direct financial losses due to inaccurate assessment of market potential. In extreme cases, it also faces the risk of loss through government seizure of property or due to war or terrorism.

This list of factors a firm must consider when assessing foreign markets may seem burdensome. Nonetheless, successful international businesses carefully analyze these factors in order to uncover and exploit any and all opportunities available to them. At best, poor market assessments may rob a firm of profitable opportunities. At worst, a continued inability to reach the right decisions may threaten the firm's existence.

Choosing a Mode of Entry

Having decided which markets to enter, the firm is now faced with another decision: Which mode of entry should it use? Dunning's eclectic theory, discussed in Chapter 6, provides useful insights into the factors that affect the choice among either home country production (exporting), host country production in firm-owned factories (FDI and joint venture), or host country production performed by others (licensing, franchising, and contract manufacturing). Recall that the eclectic theory considers three factors: ownership advantages, location advantages, and internalization advantages.[11] Other factors a firm may consider include the firm's need for control, the availability of resources, and the firm's global strategy. The role of these factors in the entry mode decision is illustrated in Figure 12.1.

Ownership advantages are tangible or intangible resources owned by a firm that grant it a competitive advantage over its industry rivals. The ownership by Toronto-based Vale Canada, Ltd. (a subsidiary of Brazilian mining conglomerate Vale), of rich, nickel-bearing ores has

FIGURE 12.1

Choosing a Mode of Entry

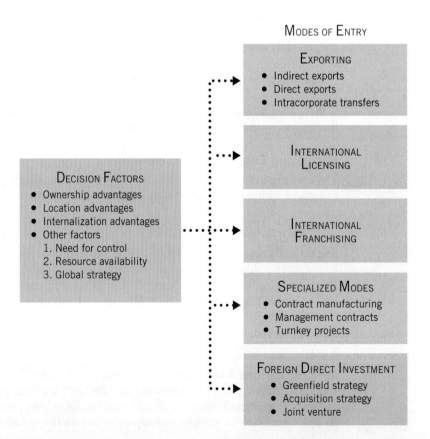

allowed the firm to dominate the production of both primary nickel and nickel-based metal alloys. The luxury appeal of Dom Pérignon champagne and Christian Dior perfumes—both products of France's LVMH Louis Vuitton Moët Hennessy—although a more intangible resource than a nickel ore mine, similarly grants the Parisian firm a competitive advantage over its rivals in international markets. Assuming that local firms know more about their home turf than foreigners do, a foreign firm contemplating entry into a new market should possess some ownership advantage that allows it to overcome the liability of foreignness. **Liability of foreignness** reflects the informational, political, and cultural disadvantages that foreign firms face when trying to compete against local firms in the host country market. As discussed later in this chapter, the nature of the firm's ownership advantage affects its selection of entry mode. Embedded technology, for example, is often best transferred through an equity mode, while firms whose competitive advantage is based on a well-known brand name sometimes enter foreign markets through a licensing or franchising mode. Further, firm advantages are primary determinants of bargaining strength; thus, they can influence the outcome of entry mode negotiations.

Location advantages are those factors that affect the desirability of host country production relative to home country production. Firms routinely compare economic and noneconomic characteristics of the home market with those of the foreign market in determining where to locate their production facilities. If home country production is found to be more desirable than host country production, the firm will choose to enter the host country market via exporting. For example, Siam Cement, one of the world's lowest cost producers, initially relied on exports from its modern domestic factories to serve the ASEAN market rather than setting up production facilities outside Thailand. Conversely, if host country production is more desirable, the firm may invest in foreign facilities or license the use of its technology and brand names to existing host country producers, as Starbucks has done in implementing its internationalization strategy.

The choice between home country and host country production is affected by many factors. Relative wage rates and land acquisition costs in the countries are important, but firms may also consider surplus or unused capacity in existing factories, access to R&D facilities, logistical requirements, the needs of customers, and the additional administrative costs of managing a foreign facility. Political risk must also be considered. The presence of civil war, official corruption, or unstable governments will discourage many firms from devoting significant resources to a host country.

Government policies can also have a major influence.[12] High tariff walls discourage exporting and encourage local production, while high corporate taxes or government prohibitions against repatriation of profits inhibit FDI. Even government inaction may affect location decisions. McDonald's built a bakery in Cairo in the late 1990s to supply its regional restaurants, in part because of its frustration in dealing with Egyptian customs bureaucrats, who required the company to obtain more than a dozen signatures each time it wished to import hamburger buns into Egypt.[13]

Location advantages may also be culture-bound. Turkey has benefited from its geographic, religious, linguistic, and cultural ties to the Central Asian and Caucasus republics of the former Soviet Union (see Map 12.1). MNCs like Siemens, JPMorgan Chase, and Goodyear have based their regional headquarters and export operations in Istanbul, viewing it as the ideal jumping-off point for doing business in the entire Eurasian region.[14]

Internalization advantages are those that make it desirable for a firm to produce a good or service itself rather than contracting with another firm to produce it. The level of transaction costs (costs of negotiating, monitoring, and enforcing an agreement) is critical to this decision. If such costs are high, the firm may rely on FDI and joint ventures as entry modes. If they are low, the firm may use franchising, licensing, or contract manufacturing. In deciding, the firm must consider both the nature of the ownership advantage it possesses and its ability to ensure productive and harmonious working relations with any local firm with which it does business. Toyota, for example, possesses two important ownership advantages: efficient manufacturing techniques and a reputation for producing high-quality automobiles. Neither asset is readily saleable or transferable to other firms; thus, Toyota has used FDI and joint ventures rather than franchising and licensing for its foreign production of automobiles.

Pharmaceutical firms routinely use licensing as their entry mode. In this industry, two common ownership advantages are the ownership of a patented drug that has unique medical properties and the ownership of local distribution networks. Obtaining either is expensive; researching, developing, and testing a new wonder drug can cost several hundred million dollars, while distribution networks

MAP 12.1

Turkey: The Gateway to the Central Asian Republics and the Caucasus

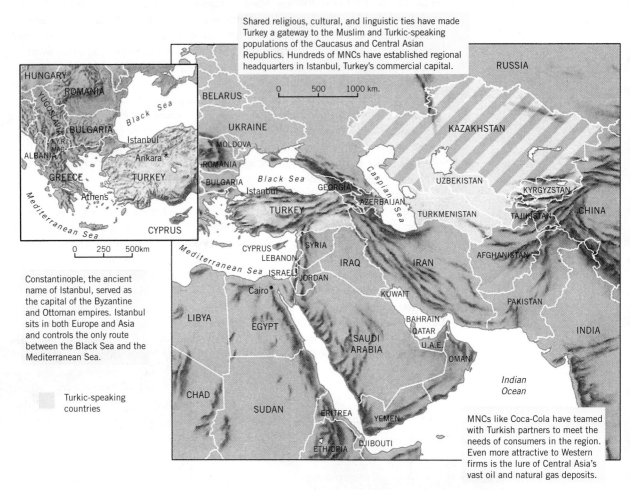

Shared religious, cultural, and linguistic ties have made Turkey a gateway to the Muslim and Turkic-speaking populations of the Caucasus and Central Asian Republics. Hundreds of MNCs have established regional headquarters in Istanbul, Turkey's commercial capital.

Constantinople, the ancient name of Istanbul, served as the capital of the Byzantine and Ottoman empires. Istanbul sits in both Europe and Asia and controls the only route between the Black Sea and the Mediterranean Sea.

Turkic-speaking countries

MNCs like Coca-Cola have teamed with Turkish partners to meet the needs of consumers in the region. Even more attractive to Western firms is the lure of Central Asia's vast oil and natural gas deposits.

must be large to be effective. In Japan, for example, a sales force of at least 1,000 employees is necessary to efficiently market prescription drugs.[15] Once a pharmaceutical firm has developed and patented a new drug, it is eager to amortize its R&D costs in both domestic and foreign markets. Many such firms prefer to forgo the expensive and time-consuming process of setting up overseas production facilities and foreign distribution networks. Instead they grant existing local firms the right to manufacture and distribute the patented drug in return for royalty payments. For example, Merck licensed Israel's Teva Pharmaceutical Industries to manufacture and market its pharmaceutical products in Israel, saving it the expense of establishing its own Israeli sales force. Licensing is also attractive because it is relatively inexpensive to monitor the sales and product quality of patented drugs sold in the host country by the licensee.

Other factors may also affect the choice of entry mode. For example, a firm is likely to consider its need for control and the availability of resources.[16] A firm's lack of experience in a foreign market may cause a certain degree of uncertainty. To reduce this uncertainty, some firms may prefer an initial entry mode that offers them a high degree of control.[17] However, firms short on capital or thin in executive talent may be unable or unwilling to commit themselves to the large capital investments this control entails; they may prefer an entry mode that economizes on their financial and managerial commitments, such as licensing. Cash-rich firms may view FDI more favorably, believing that it offers high profit potential and the opportunity to more fully internationalize the training of their young, fast-track managers.

A firm's overall global strategy also may affect the choice of entry mode. Firms such as Ford that seek to exploit economies of scale and synergies between their domestic and international operations may prefer ownership-oriented entry modes. Conversely, firms such as Microsoft and Nike, whose competitive strengths lie in flexibility and quick response to changing market conditions, are more likely to use any and all entry modes warranted by local conditions in a given host country.[18] A firm's choice may also be driven by its need to coordinate its activities across all markets as part of its global strategy. For example, IBM has for this reason traditionally favored ownership-oriented entry modes as part of its globalization strategy.[19]

In short, like most business activities, the choice of entry mode is often a trade-off between the level of risk borne by the firm, the potential rewards to be obtained from a market, the magnitude of the resource commitment necessary to compete effectively, and the level of control the firm seeks.

Exporting to Foreign Markets

Perhaps the simplest mode of internationalizing a domestic business is exporting, the most common form of international business activity. Its advantages and disadvantages, and those of the other modes of entry, are summarized in Table 12.2. Recall from Chapter 1 that exporting is the process of sending goods or services from one country to other countries for use or sale there. Merchandise exports in the world economy totaled $12.5 trillion in 2009, or 21 percent of the world's total economic activity, while service exports amounted to $3.4 trillion.

Exporting offers a firm several advantages. First, the firm can control its financial exposure to the host country market as it deems appropriate. Little or no capital investment may be needed if the firm chooses to hire a host country firm to distribute its products. In this case, the firm's

TABLE 12.2 Advantages and Disadvantages of Different Modes of Entry

Mode	Primary Advantages	Primary Disadvantages
Exporting	Relatively low financial exposure	Vulnerability to tariffs and NTBs
	Permit gradual market entry	Logistical complexities
	Acquire knowledge about local market	Potential conflicts with distributors
	Avoid restrictions on foreign investment	
Licensing	Low financial risks	Limited market opportunities/profits
	Low-cost way to assess market potential	Dependence on licensee
	Avoid tariffs, NTBs, restrictions on foreign investment	Potential conflicts with licensee
		Possibility of creating future competitor
	Licensee provides knowledge of local markets	
Franchising	Low financial risks	Limits market opportunities/profits
	Low-cost way to assess market potential	Dependence on franchisee
	Avoid tariffs, NTBs, restrictions on foreign investment	Potential conflicts with franchisee
		May be creating future competitor
	Maintain more control than with licensing	
	Franchisee provides knowledge of local market	
Contract manufacturing	Low financial risks	Reduced control (may affect quality, delivery schedules, etc.)
	Minimize resources devoted to manufacturing	Reduced learning potential
	Focus firm's resources on other elements of the value chain	Potential public relations problems—may need to monitor working conditions, etc.
Management contracts	Focus firm's resources on its area of expertise	Potential returns limited by contract
	Minimal financial exposure	May unintentionally transfer proprietary knowledge and techniques to contractee
Turnkey projects	Focus firm's resources on its area of expertise	Financial risks (cost overruns, etc.)
	Avoid all long-term operational risks	Construction risks (delays, problems with suppliers, etc.)
Foreign direct investment	High profit potential	High financial and managerial investments
	Maintain control over operations	Higher exposure to political risk
	Acquire knowledge of local market	Vulnerability to restrictions on foreign investment
	Avoid tariffs and NTBs	Greater managerial complexity

financial exposure is often limited to start-up costs associated with market research, locating and choosing its local distributor, and/or local advertising plus the value of the goods and services involved in any given overseas shipment. Alternatively, the firm may choose to distribute its products itself to better control their marketing. If the firm opts for this approach, it is then able to raise its selling prices because a middleman has been eliminated. However, its investment costs and its financial exposure may rise substantially, for the firm will have to equip and operate its own distribution centers, hire its own employees, and market its products.

Second, exporting permits a firm to enter a foreign market gradually, thereby allowing it to assess local conditions and fine-tune its products to meet the idiosyncratic needs of host country consumers. If its exports are well received by foreign consumers, the firm may use this experience as a basis for a more extensive entry into that market. For example, the firm may choose to take over distribution of its product from the host country distributor or to build a factory in the host country to supply its customers there, particularly if it finds it can reduce its production and distribution costs or improve the quality of its customer service. For instance, in 2011 Constellation Brands, the world's largest wine distributor, chose to develop its own marketing and distribution network in China to take advantage of the 20 percent annual growth in the Chinese consumption of wine.[20]

Firms may have proactive or reactive motivations for exporting. *Proactive motivations* are those that *pull* a firm into foreign markets as a result of opportunities available there. For example, San Antonio's Pace, Inc., a maker of Tex-Mex food products, began exporting proactively to Mexico after discovering that Mexican consumers enjoy its picante sauce as much as its U.S. customers do.[21] A firm also may export proactively in order to exploit a technological advantage or to spread fixed R&D expenses over a wider customer base, thereby allowing it to price its products more competitively in both domestic and foreign markets. For example, the breakeven price of commercial airliners produced by Airbus and Boeing would skyrocket if these firms limited their sales to their respective domestic markets.

Reactive motivations for exporting are those that *push* a firm into foreign markets, often because opportunities are decreasing in the domestic market. Some firms turn to exporting because their production lines are running below capacity or because they seek higher profit margins in foreign markets in the face of downturns in domestic demand. For instance, consider two suppliers of specialty services to the U.S. construction industry, which has been battered by the subprime meltdown (see Chapter 8's closing case). Hycrete Inc., a New Jersey firm that manufactures an additive to make concrete waterproof and corrosion proof, has shifted its emphasis from its domestic market to the booming Middle Eastern, Asian, and Eastern European markets. Illinois-based ProMark Associates, which manufactures and installs commercial air purifiers, has adopted a similar strategy in response to the slowdown in the U.S. construction market.[22]

Forms of Exporting

Export activities may take several forms (see Figure 12.2), including indirect exporting, direct exporting, and intracorporate transfers.

INDIRECT EXPORTING **Indirect exporting** occurs when a firm sells its product to a domestic customer, which in turn exports the product, in either its original form or a modified form. For example, if Kenworth, a leading American truck manufacturer, buys diesel engines from Cummins (also a U.S. firm) and then exports the completed trucks to Colombia, Cummins's engines have been indirectly exported. Or a firm may sell goods to a domestic wholesaler who then sells them to an overseas firm. A firm also may sell to a foreign firm's local subsidiary, which then transports the first firm's products to the foreign country.

Some indirect exporting activities reflect conscious actions by domestic producers. For example, the Association of Guatemala Coffee Producers sells bags of coffee to passengers boarding international flights in Guatemala City in order to gain export sales and to build consumer awareness of its product. In most cases, however, indirect exporting activities are not part of a conscious internationalization strategy by a firm. Thus, they yield the firm little experience in conducting international business. Further, for firms that passively rely on the actions of others, the potential short-term and long-term profits available from indirect exporting are often limited.

FIGURE 12.2
Forms of Exporting

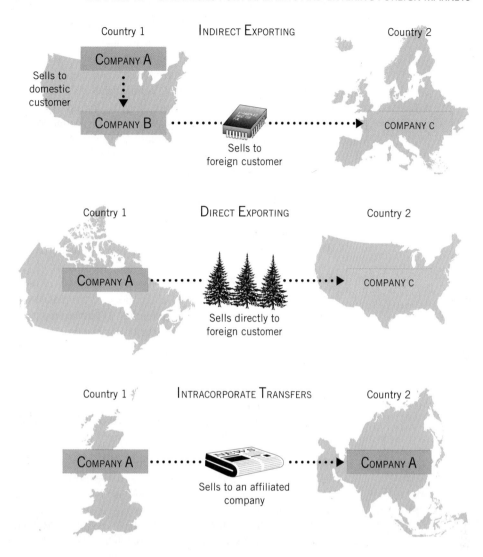

DIRECT EXPORTING **Direct exporting** occurs through sales to customers—either distributors or end-users—located outside the firm's home country. Research suggests that in one-third of cases, a firm's initial direct exporting to a foreign market is the result of an unsolicited order. However, its subsequent direct exporting typically results from deliberate efforts to expand its business internationally. In such cases, the firm actively selects the products it will sell, the foreign markets it will service, and the means by which its products will be distributed in those markets. Through direct exporting activities, the firm gains valuable expertise about operating internationally and specific knowledge concerning the individual countries in which it operates. And export success often breeds additional export success. Increasing experience with exporting often prompts a firm to become more aggressive in exploiting new international exporting opportunities.[23] Such experience also often proves useful if the firm later engages in FDI. Baskin-Robbins, for example, followed this deliberate approach in entering the Russian market. It began by shipping ice cream to that country in 1990 from company-owned plants in Canada and Texas. Over a five-year period, the company opened up 74 retail outlets with Russian partners, carefully observing the likes and dislikes of local consumers. Only after gaining a thorough understanding of the Russian market did Baskin-Robbins invest $30 million in a new ice cream plant in Moscow, ensuring a constant flow of Jamoca Almond Fudge and (at least) 30 other flavors to please Russian appetites.[24]

INTRACORPORATE TRANSFERS A third form of export activity is the intracorporate transfer, which has become more important as the sizes of MNCs have increased. An **intracorporate transfer** is the sale of goods by a firm in one country to an affiliated firm in another. For example, when BP ships crude oil from its storage facilities in Kuwait to its Australian subsidiary, the transaction is counted as a Kuwaiti export and an Australian import, but the revenues for the transaction remain within the same firm.

Intracorporate transfers are an important part of international trade. They account for about 40 percent of all U.S. merchandise exports and imports. Many MNCs constantly engage in such transfers, importing and exporting semifinished products and component parts in order to lower their production costs. By so doing, they use the productive capacity of both their domestic and foreign factories more efficiently, concentrating production of individual inputs at specific factories and shipping these inputs to other factories as needed. We will discuss these factors more thoroughly in Chapter 17 when we analyze the global sourcing strategies of MNCs.

Such transfers are also common in the service sector. For example, Dow Jones & Company publishes both Asian and European versions of the *Wall Street Journal* in addition to its U.S. edition. Although some of the stories in each edition are written locally and are intended for local audiences, others are written in one location and printed in all editions of the newspaper. The usage of stories first published by a Dow Jones subsidiary in one country by Dow Jones affiliates in other countries is an intracorporate transfer of services.

Additional Considerations

In considering exporting as its entry mode, a firm must consider many other factors besides which form of exporting to use, including (1) government policies, (2) marketing concerns, (3) logistical considerations, and (4) distribution issues.

GOVERNMENT POLICIES Export promotion policies, export financing programs, and other forms of home country subsidization encourage exporting as an entry mode. Conversely, host countries may impose tariffs and NTBs on imported goods, thereby discouraging the firm from relying on exports as an entry mode. Similarly, Japan's imposition of voluntary export restraints (VERs) on Japanese automobiles reduced Japanese exports, but it also encouraged Japanese automakers to construct assembly plants in the United States.

MARKETING CONCERNS Marketing concerns, such as image, distribution, and responsiveness to the customer, may also affect the decision to export. Often foreign goods have a certain product image or cachet that domestically produced goods cannot duplicate. For example, buyers of Dom Pérignon champagne are purchasing, at least in part, the allure of one of France's finest champagnes. This allure would be lost should LVMH choose to produce the product in Lubbock, Texas, even though Lubbock vineyards yield a regionally acclaimed wine, Llano Estacado. Swiss watches, German automobiles, Italian shoes, Cuban cigars, and Scottish wool are among the other product groups whose allure is closely associated with specific countries.

The allure of some goods—particularly luxury ones—is reinforced by their country of origin. The demand for Swiss watches rests in large part on the reputation for the craftsmanship of the skilled workers who carefully oversee their assembly.

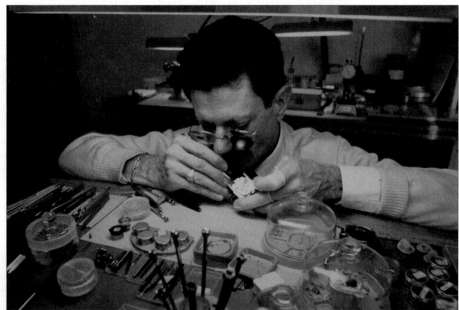

Raymond Reuter/Corbis Images

VENTURING ABROAD   DNATA: GLOBAL GROWTH STRATEGY

Founded in 1959, Dnata is an international travel management services company based in Dubai. It provides services in aircraft and cargo handling and engineering, information technology, as well as travel-related services and in-flight and institutional catering. Dnata has mainly three divisions: Dnata Airport Operations, Dnata Cargo, and Dnata Agencies. It is the fourth largest combined air services provider in the world with approximately 20,000 employees across five continents. As a key member of the Emirates Group, Dnata provides the Emirates Airline and other world major airlines with ground-handling services at 73 airports internationally. Today its business has expanded to 38 countries.

Despite the recent global economic recession, Dnata's revenues have increased dramatically, and nearly quadrupled over the past few years. The success is attributed largely to Dnata's management's forward thinking strategy and a global mindset. Dnata has been pursuing a global growth strategy and structured its business units in line with the strategy. It has one dedicated administration and management division called Dnata International, which oversees a number of Dnata's business operations including wholly owned and joint ventures in eight countries and a global network of sales offices outside the United Arab Emirates (UAE). Dnata has constantly scrutinized the world markets enabling it to capture opportunities to enter the markets based upon the strategic fit between the business opportunities, such as the growth pace of airline operations in a certain region and its existing resources. The president of Dnata described the approach as a result of extremely cautious planning with a focus on profitability. In 2004, Dnata entered the Singapore market which boasts one of the world's busiest and largest airports, and acquired Changi International Airport Services, called Dnata Singapore after the acquisition. Dnata Singapore offers a comprehensive range of ground-handling services to more than 30 scheduled airlines in Singapore. Over the past few years, Dnata has acquired stakes and/or established a number of joint ventures in Australia, China, Pakistan, Philippines, Switzerland, United Kingdom, and Iraq. Among them, the most important joint ventures are Toll Dnata Airport Services (TDAS), a joint venture between Toll Holdings (Australia) and Dnata, and Xi'an Dnata Aviation Services Co. Ltd., a joint venture between Dnata and China West Airport Group that provides airport ground-handling services at Xi'an Xianyang International Airport. In addition to expanding its business internationally through a number of strategic acquisitions outside the UAE, Dnata has entered strategic alliances with many travel agencies globally and established an extensive global network of sales offices. These strategic alliances expand Dnata's global reach and create win-win business opportunities without involving significant financial investment.

Following its global success, Dnata has most recently developed a new company logo and a mission statement in line with its brand strategy and brand architecture that are seen as an indication for further global growth. The new mission statement emphasizes its global value and unifies its 20,000 employees around the world. When asked about how Dnata protects itself from an increasingly competitive and volatile aviation industry, the president of Dnata considers that making the business less Dubai-centric and more global has helped the company to grow and sustain.

Sources: Dnata company website at http://www.dnata.com/english/; "Dnata reveals new brand identity following global success," at http://www.ameinfo.com/263500.html; "Dnata president on coping with Middle East and North Africa unrest," at http://www.bbc.co.uk/news/business-13314208.

The choice of exporting is also influenced by a firm's need to obtain quick and constant feedback from its customers. Such feedback is less important for standardized products whose designs change slowly, if at all, such as toothbrushes and coffeemakers. On the other hand, producers of goods such as personal computers and smartphones must continually monitor the marketplace to ensure that they are meeting the rapidly changing needs of their customers. For example, Hyundai shifted its production of personal computers from factories in its Korean homeland to the United States because it needed to be closer to its U.S. customer base.

LOGISTICAL CONSIDERATIONS Logistical considerations also enter into the decision to export. The firm must consider the physical distribution costs of warehousing, packaging, transporting, and distributing its goods, as well as its inventory carrying costs and those of its foreign customers. Typically, such logistical costs will be higher for exported goods than for locally produced goods. But logistical considerations go beyond mere costs. Because exporting means longer supply lines and increased difficulties in communicating with foreign customers, firms choosing to export from domestic factories must ensure that they maintain competitive levels of customer service for their foreign customers.

DISTRIBUTION ISSUES A final issue that may influence a firm's decision to export is distribution. A firm experienced in exporting may choose to establish its own distribution networks in its key markets. For example, Japanese consumer electronics manufacturers like Sony, Minolta, and Hitachi typically rely on wholly owned host country subsidiaries to distribute their products to wholesalers and retailers in the developed countries. The costs of establishing and operating these distribution networks are offset by two important benefits. First, a firm captures additional revenues by performing the distribution function. Second, it maintains control over the distribution process, thereby avoiding the problems that we discuss in the following paragraphs.

However, a firm—particularly a smaller business or one just beginning to export—often lacks the expertise to market its products abroad, so it will seek a local distributor to handle its products in the target market. Critical to the firm's success is the selection of this distributor, which must have sufficient expertise and resources (capital, labor, facilities, and local reputation) to successfully market the firm's products. However, often the best local distributors already handle the products of existing firms. Consequently, sometimes a firm must choose between an experienced local distributor and a less experienced one that will handle the firm's products exclusively.

The profitability and growth potential of exporting to a foreign market will be affected by the firm's agreement with the local distributor. The local distributor must be compensated for its services, of course. This compensation will reduce the exporter's profit margin. Further, the exporter and its local distributor depend on each other to ensure that a satisfactory business relationship is established and maintained. If the host country distributor inadequately markets, distributes, and/or services the exporter's products, it is the exporter that will suffer lost sales and damaged reputation. For example, Apple's initial share of the Japanese personal computer market was hurt by the performance of a Canon subsidiary hired to market and distribute the firm's products in Japan. Apple took over these tasks and quickly quintupled its market share.[25]

Problems may also arise if the business judgments of the local distributor and the exporter differ. The exporter and the importer may disagree on pricing strategies, with the exporter preferring lower retail prices to stimulate sales and the distributor favoring higher prices, which fatten its profit margins. The exporter may want its distributor to market its products more aggressively in hopes of building sales volume; the distributor may believe that the additional sales generated by this strategy will not cover the increased expenses incurred. Thus, the importance of selecting a distributor whose goals and business philosophy are compatible with those of the exporter cannot be overstressed.

Export Intermediaries

An exporter may also market and distribute its goods in international markets by using one or more **intermediaries,** third parties that specialize in facilitating imports and exports. These specialists may offer limited services such as handling only transportation and documentation. Or they may perform more extensive roles, including taking ownership of foreign-bound goods and/or assuming total responsibility for marketing and financing exports. Types of intermediaries that offer a broad range of services include export management companies, Webb-Pomerene associations, and international trading companies.

EXPORT MANAGEMENT COMPANY An **export management company (EMC)** is a firm that acts as its client's export department. Most are small operations that rely on the services of a handful of professionals. An EMC's staff typically is knowledgeable about the legal, financial, and logistical details of exporting and so frees the exporter from having to develop this expertise in-house. The EMC may also provide advice about consumer needs and available distribution channels in the foreign markets the exporter wants to penetrate.

EMCs usually operate in one of two ways. Some act as commission agents for exporters. They handle the details of shipping, clearing customs, and document preparation in return for an agreed-upon fee. In this case, the exporter normally invoices the client and provides any necessary financing it may need. Others take title to the goods. They make money by buying the goods from the exporter and reselling them at a higher price to foreign customers. Such EMCs may offer customer financing and design and implement advertising and promotional campaigns for the product.

WEBB-POMERENE ASSOCIATION A **Webb-Pomerene association** is a group of U.S. firms that operate within the same industry and that are allowed by law to coordinate their export activities without fear of violating U.S. antitrust laws. First authorized by the Export Trade Act of 1918, a Webb-Pomerene association engages in market research, overseas promotional activities, freight consolidation, contract negotiations, and other services for its members. It may also directly engage in exporting by buying goods domestically from members and selling the goods in foreign markets on the association's behalf. Although such associations were originally designed to allow smaller, related firms to cooperate in promoting exports, most are now dominated by larger firms. In general, Webb-Pomerene associations have not played a major role in international business. Fewer than 25 such associations exist today, and they tend to be concentrated in raw materials such as wood pulp, sulfur, and phosphate rock.

INTERNATIONAL TRADING COMPANY An **international trading company** is a firm directly engaged in importing and exporting a wide variety of goods for its own account. It differs from an EMC in that it participates in both importing and exporting activities. An international trading company provides a full gamut of services, including market research, customs documentation, international transportation and host country distribution, marketing, and financing. Typically, international trading companies have agents and offices worldwide. The economic intelligence information they glean from these far-flung operations is one of their most potent competitive weapons.

The most important international trading companies in the global marketplace are Japan's *sogo shosha*, which are an integral part of Japan's keiretsu system. The sogo shosha have prospered for several reasons. Because of their far-flung operations, they continuously obtain information about economic conditions and business opportunities in virtually every corner of the world. As part of a keiretsu, a sogo shosha enjoys ready access to financing (from the keiretsu's lead bank) and a built-in source of customers (its fellow keiretsu members). This customer base reduces the sogo shosha's costs of soliciting clients and builds up its business volume, thereby allowing it to reap economies of scale in its transportation and information-gathering roles. Nonmembers of the keiretsu are then attracted to doing business with the sogo shosha because of its low-cost structure and international expertise. Moreover, many of the sogo shosha have made investments in the natural resource sector, which, as Chapter 2's closing case "China's Quest for Natural Resources" indicates, have been extremely profitable in the past decade. Japan's international trading companies are among the world's largest service companies, measured by sales volume.[26] The five largest sogo shosha are featured in Table 12.3.

OTHER INTERMEDIARIES In addition to the intermediaries that provide a broad range of services to international exporters and importers, numerous other types offer more specialized services. **Manufacturers' agents** solicit domestic orders for foreign manufacturers, usually on a commission basis. **Manufacturers' export agents** act as a foreign sales department for domestic manufacturers, selling those firms' goods in foreign markets. **Export and import brokers** bring together international buyers and sellers of such standardized commodities as coffee, cocoa, and grains. **Freight forwarders** specialize in the physical transportation of goods, arranging customs documentation and obtaining transportation services for their clients. This list, however, is by no means complete. Indeed, specialists are available to provide virtually every service needed by exporters and importers in international trade.

International Licensing

Another means of entering a foreign market is **licensing,** in which a firm, called the **licensor,** leases the right to use its intellectual property—technology, work methods, patents, copyrights, brand names, or trademarks—to another firm, called the **licensee,** in return for a fee. This process is illustrated in Figure 12.3. The use of licensing as an entry mode may be affected by host country policies. Firms are not advised to use licensing in countries that offer weak protection for intellectual property, since they may have difficulty enforcing licensing agreements in the host country's courts. On the other hand, the use of licensing may be encouraged by high tariffs and NTBs, which discourage imports, or by host country restrictions on FDI or repatriation of profits.

Licensing is a popular mode for entering foreign markets because it involves little out-of-pocket cost. A firm has already incurred the costs of developing the intellectual property to be licensed; thus, revenues received through a licensing agreement often go straight to the firm's bottom line. Licensing also allows a firm to take advantage of any locational advantages of foreign production without incurring any ownership, managerial, or investment obligations.

TABLE 12.3 The Five Largest Sogo Shosha

Rank	Firm	2010 Sales ($ Millions)	Key Subsidiaries and Affiliates
1	Mitsubishi Corporation	60,793	Kirin Brewery (alcoholic beverages)
			The Mitsubishi Bank, Ltd.
			Mitsubishi Heavy Industries, Ltd. (construction)
			Mitsubishi Motor Corporation (automobiles)
			Nikon Corporation (cameras and video equipment)
			The Tokyo Marine and Fire Insurance Company
2	Mitsui & Company	54,635	Japan Steel Works, Ltd. (steel manufacturing)
			Mitsui Construction Company, Ltd. (construction)
			Mitsukoshi, Ltd. (department stores)
			Mitsui Mutual Life Insurance Company, Ltd.
			Onoda Cement Company, Ltd. (construction materials)
			Sakura Bank
3	Marubeni	43,011	Archer Pipe and Tube Company (steel pipe sales)
			Bactec Corporation (insecticides)
			Columbia Grain International (grain trading)
			Fremont Beef Company (meat processing)
			Kubota Tractor Company (farm equipment)
			Precision Tools Service, Inc. (machine tools)
4	Itochu Corporation	42,612	American Isuzu Motors (wholesaling)
			ATR Wires & Cable Company (steel tire cords)
			Century 21 Real Estate of Japan, Ltd. (real estate brokerage)
			Dunhill Group Japan, Inc. (men's clothing and accessories)
			Mazda Motor of America (wholesaling)
			Time Warner Entertainment of Japan (25 percent limited partnership)
			VIDEOSAT, Inc. (satellite transmission of video signals)
5	Sumitomo Group	36,218	Asahi Breweries, Ltd. (alcoholic beverages)
			NEC Corp. (electronics)
			Nippon Sheet Glass Company
			The Sumitomo Bank, Ltd.
			Sumitomo Cement Company, Ltd.
			Sumitomo Chemical Company, Ltd.
			Sumitomo Coal Mining Company, Ltd.
			Sumitomo Forestry Company, Ltd.
			Sumitomo Metal Industries, Ltd.
			Sumitomo Realty & Development Company, Ltd.

Source: Based on *Fortune*, July 25, 2011, pp. F1f.; various corporate websites.

FIGURE 12.3
The Licensing Process

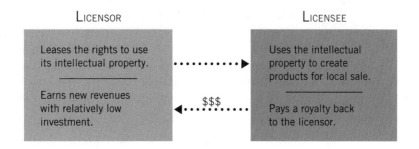

LICENSOR

Leases the rights to use its intellectual property.
_____
Earns new revenues with relatively low investment.

$$$

LICENSEE

Uses the intellectual property to create products for local sale.
_____
Pays a royalty back to the licensor.

BASIC ISSUES
1. Set the boundaries of the agreement.
2. Establish compensation rates.
3. Agree on the rights, privileges, and constraints conveyed in the agreement.
4. Specify the duration of the agreement.

Licensing is an important element of the strategies of many international firms. Consider the Nintendo Company. The firm manufactures electronic video game consoles and games. It also licenses dozens of firms worldwide to design and, in some cases, to manufacture games to be used in its game consoles. As part of its licensing arrangements, Nintendo provides game designers with technical specifications for how its game consoles work. The design firms create the games and then pay Nintendo a fee to manufacture them. Other firms manufacture the games themselves, but they must still pay a licensing fee to Nintendo. Through licensing, Nintendo not only generates new revenues; it also inspires the development of new video games, which in turn stimulate demand for Nintendo game consoles. Similar arrangements are used by many video game and software firms.[27]

Saks Inc. has similarly relied on licensing as part of its internationalization strategy. It licensed local companies to construct and operate stores in Saudi Arabia, Dubai, Bahrain, and Mexico City. Saks's executives believe they need to focus their attention on the highly competitive American market. Through the licensing arrangement, the company can establish a presence in the growing international market, generate royalty income with little risk and no investment, and not have to deal with the trials and tribulations of mastering the complexities of foreign retailing markets.[28]

Saks has relied on licensing as its primary mode of entering international markets. This Saks store in Dubai's prestigious BurJuman Mall features 80,000 square feet of retail space.

© Pictures Colour Library/SuperStock

Basic Issues in International Licensing

Nearly every international licensing arrangement is unique because of variations in corporate strategy, the levels of competition, the nature of the product, and the interests of the licensor and licensee. Normally the terms of a licensing agreement are specified in a detailed legal contract, which addresses such issues as (1) specifying the boundaries of the agreement, (2) determining compensation, (3) establishing rights, privileges, and constraints, and (4) specifying the duration of the contract.

SPECIFYING THE AGREEMENT'S BOUNDARIES The licensor and licensee must determine which rights and privileges are and are not being conveyed in the agreement. For example, Heineken is exclusively licensed to manufacture and sell Pepsi-Cola in the Netherlands. PepsiCo must either provide Heineken with the formula for its soft drink or supply concentrated cola syrup. Heineken is then allowed to add carbonated water to create the beverage, package it in appropriate containers, and distribute and sell it in the Netherlands. PepsiCo cannot enter into a competing licensing agreement with another firm to sell Pepsi-Cola in the Netherlands, nor can Heineken begin duplicating other products owned by PepsiCo (such as Lay's Potato Chips) without a separate agreement. Nor can it alter PepsiCo's formula, market the firm's products as its own, or ship them outside the Netherlands.

DETERMINING COMPENSATION Compensation is another basic issue that is specified in a licensing agreement. Obviously, the licensor wants to receive as much compensation as possible, while the licensee wants to pay as little as possible. Yet each also wants the agreement to be profitable for the other so that both parties will willingly perform their contractual obligations. Licensees must be careful to ensure that they can reach their target levels of profitability after paying licensing fees; the licensor will attempt to establish a rate that allows it to recoup its variable costs of negotiating and enforcing the licensing agreement plus recover at least part of its fixed investment in the intellectual property being licensed. Of course, from the licensor's perspective, the license fee, after deducting these variable costs, should also exceed its opportunity costs—that is, the profits it would have earned had it entered the market via a different entry mode.

Compensation under a licensing agreement is called a **royalty.** The royalty is usually paid to the licensor in the form of a flat fee, a fixed amount per unit sold, or, most commonly, a percentage of the sales of the licensed product or service. Although the royalty amount is often determined by prevailing market forces, royalties between 3 and 5 percent of sales are typical and have long been viewed as reasonable and appropriate. Some licensing agreements also guarantee a minimum royalty payment to ensure that the foreign licensee will take full advantage of the market value of whatever has been licensed, rather than merely acquiring and then shelving it to keep domestic rivals from obtaining it.

ESTABLISHING RIGHTS, PRIVILEGES, AND CONSTRAINTS Other basic issues to be addressed in licensing agreements are the rights and privileges given to the licensee and the constraints imposed by the licensor. For example, if a licensee began using inferior materials as a way to boost its profit margin, the image of the licensor's product could be severely damaged. Similarly, if the agreement included the transfer of technology, production processes, or work methods, the licensee might be tempted to sell this information to another firm, thereby harming the licensor. Or the licensee could simply underreport licensed sales as a means of reducing its licensing fees.

To prevent these practices, licensing agreements usually limit the licensee's freedom to divulge information it has obtained from the licensor to third parties, specify the type and form of records the licensee must keep regarding sales of the licensed products or services, and define standards that will be adhered to regarding product and service quality. To avoid costly litigation, the licensing agreement should also detail how the parties will resolve any disagreements. Many licensing agreements require, for example, that disputes be resolved through the use of a third-party mediator.

SPECIFYING THE AGREEMENT'S DURATION The licensor may view the licensing agreement as a short-term strategy designed to obtain knowledge about the foreign market at low cost and with little risk. If sales of its products and services are strong, it may want to enter the market itself after the agreement has ended. Thus, the licensor may seek a short-term agreement. However, if the contract's duration is too short, the licensee may be unwilling to invest in necessary consumer research, distribution networks, and/or production facilities, believing that it will be unable to amortize its investment over the life of the licensing contract. Normally the licensor wants the licensee to undertake these market development efforts. Accordingly, the greater the investment costs incurred by the licensee, the longer is the likely duration of the licensing agreement. For example, the licensees that built Tokyo Disneyland insisted on a 100-year licensing agreement with the Walt Disney Company before agreeing to invest the millions of dollars necessary to build the park. However, in most cases the term of the licensing agreement is far shorter than this.

Advantages and Disadvantages of International Licensing

Licensing carries relatively low financial risk, provided the licensor fully investigates its market opportunities and the abilities of its licensees. It also allows the licensor to learn more about the sales potential of its products and services in a new market without significant commitment of financial and managerial resources. Licensees benefit through the opportunity to make and sell, with relatively little R&D cost, products and services that have been successful in other international markets. Nintendo game designers, for example, have the relative safety of knowing there are millions of game system units available that will play their games.

However, licensing does have opportunity costs. It limits the market opportunities for both parties. For example, as long as the licensing agreement between PepsiCo and Heineken is in effect, PepsiCo cannot enter the soft-drink market in the Netherlands and Heineken cannot sell competing soft drinks such as Coca-Cola. Further, licensor and licensee depend on each other to maintain product quality and to promote the product's brand image. Improper actions by one party can damage the other party. Further, if the licensee or licensor does not adhere to the agreement, costly and tedious litigation may hurt both parties.

No matter how carefully worded a licensing agreement may be, there is always the risk of problems and misunderstandings. For example, several years ago Oleg Cassini licensed Jovan, a U.S. subsidiary of London's GlaxoSmithKline, to market the Cassini beauty products line in the United States. After signing the agreement, Jovan was approached by Diane Von Furstenberg Cosmetics with a similar proposal but better terms. Jovan subsequently signed a licensing agreement with Von Furstenberg to make and market its products instead of Cassini's. Cassini was left without a licensee in the United States. To complicate things even further, a clause in the contract between Jovan and Cassini prevented Cassini from licensing its name to any other U.S. firm. Cassini sued Jovan for $789 million. The dispute was eventually settled out of court, but it was more than three years beyond Cassini's original target date when the firm finally got its products into the United States.[29] Laura Ashley ran into similar problems after it granted L'Oréal exclusive rights for twenty years to develop Laura Ashley–branded cosmetics, toiletries, and perfumes. The British company later sued the French cosmetics company, claiming that L'Oréal had failed to develop the true potential of the Laura Ashley brand after it had only marketed one perfume under the agreement in six years.[30]

A final concern is the long-term strategic implications of licensing a firm's technology. Many firms are concerned that sharing their technology will inadvertently create a future competitor. The licensee, by producing under the licensing agreement, may be able to learn the manufacturing secrets of the licensor or to develop new production tricks of its own. The licensee can also build an independent reputation for manufacturing quality and service excellence while operating under the contract. Although the licensing agreement may restrict the geographical area in which the licensee can manufacture and sell the product, once it expires, the former licensee may choose to expand its operations into the licensor's existing territory. This is a risk the licensor must take if it chooses to license its product.

International Franchising

Still another popular strategy for internationalizing a business is franchising, actually a special form of licensing. **Franchising** allows the franchisor more control over the franchisee and provides for more support from the franchisor to the franchisee than is the case in the licensor-licensee relationship. International franchising is among the fastest-growing forms of international business activity today. A franchising agreement allows an independent entrepreneur or organization, called the **franchisee,** to operate a business under the name of another, called the

franchisor, in return for a fee. The franchisor provides its franchisees with trademarks, operating systems, and well-known product reputations, as well as continuous support services such as advertising, training, reservation services (for hotel operations), and quality assurance programs.

Basic Issues in International Franchising

International franchising is likely to succeed when certain market conditions exist. First, it may work when the franchisor has been successful domestically because of unique products and advantageous operating procedures and systems. McDonald's was successful initially because it provided a popular menu that was consistently prepared and service that was quick and efficient. Franchising may also be effective when the factors that contributed to domestic success are transferable to foreign locations. McDonald's prospered because "American" food is popular in other countries, efficiency and lower prices are valued by consumers worldwide, and foreign visitors to the United States usually seem to want to visit a McDonald's restaurant. Third, this may be a viable option if the franchisor has already achieved considerable success in franchising in its domestic market. For example, there were hundreds of franchised McDonald's restaurants in the United States before the first was built abroad. Finally, foreign investors must be interested in entering into franchise agreements. For well-established franchisors like McDonald's, this is typically not a problem.

Like licensing agreements, franchising agreements are spelled out in formal contracts, with a typical set of terms. The franchisor generally receives a fixed payment plus a royalty based on the franchisee's sales for the rights to use the franchisor's name, trademarks, formulas, and operating procedures. The franchisee usually agrees to adhere to the franchisor's requirements for appearance, financial reporting, and operating procedures. However, franchisors are likely to allow some degree of flexibility in order to meet local customs and tastes. In fact, as with other licensing arrangements, one of the services the franchisee offers the franchisor is knowledge about the local market's culture and customs. For example, McDonald's restaurants sell beer in Germany and Switzerland and wine in France. Finally, the franchisor almost always helps the franchisee establish the new business; provides expertise, advertising, and a corporate image; and is usually able to negotiate favorable arrangements with suppliers.

Numerous MNCs rely on franchising to internationalize their operations. Fast-food firms such as McDonald's, Dunkin' Donuts, Baskin-Robbins, Pizza Hut, and KFC have franchised restaurants worldwide. Benetton relies on franchised retail stores to distribute its clothing in over 120 countries. And Japan's Bridgestone Corporation franchises both Bridgestone and Firestone tire retail outlets in the United States as well as several other countries.

Advantages and Disadvantages of International Franchising

On the plus side, franchisees can enter a business that has an established and proven product and operating system, and franchisors can expand internationally with relatively low risk and cost. A franchisor also can obtain critical information about local market customs and cultures from host country entrepreneurs that it otherwise might have difficulty obtaining. It further can learn valuable lessons from franchisees that apply to more than the host country. McDonald's, for example, benefited from this worldwide learning phenomenon (see Chapter 11). Its U.S. managers once believed that the firm's restaurants would be successful only if they were freestanding entities located in suburbs and smaller towns. A Japanese franchisee convinced the firm to allow him to open a restaurant in an inner-city office building. It quickly became one of the firm's most popular restaurants. Because of the insight of its Japanese franchisee, McDonald's now has restaurants in downtown locations in many cities throughout the world.

On the negative side, as with licensing, both parties to a franchising agreement must share the revenues earned at the franchised location. International franchising may also be more complicated than domestic franchising. For example, when McDonald's expanded to Moscow, it had to teach local farmers how to grow potatoes that met its standards. Moreover, control is also an issue in international franchising. McDonald's was once forced to revoke the franchise it had awarded a French investor because his stores were not maintained according to McDonald's standards.

Specialized Entry Modes for International Business

A firm may also use any of several specialized strategies to participate in international business without making long-term investments. Such specialized modes include contract manufacturing, management contracts, and turnkey projects.

Contract Manufacturing

Contract manufacturing is used by firms, both large and small, that outsource most or all of their manufacturing needs to other companies. This strategy reduces the financial and human resources firms need to devote to the physical production of their products. Nike, for example, has chosen to focus its corporate energies on marketing its products and has contracted with numerous factories throughout Southeast Asia to produce its athletic footwear and apparel. Similarly, contract manufacturers in China assemble 70 percent of Kodak's cameras, allowing Kodak's engineers to devote their energies to fine-tuning the proprietary software that eliminates red-eye, balances colors and light, and facilitates cropping and printing of perfect photos.[31] By using this approach, international businesses can focus on that part of the value chain where their distinctive competence lies and yet benefit from any locational advantages generated by host country production. However, they also surrender control over the production process, which can lead to quality problems or other unexpected surprises. Nike, for example, suffered a string of blows to its public image—including a series of unflattering *Doonesbury* cartoons—because of reports of unsafe and harsh working conditions in Vietnamese factories churning out Nike footwear.[32] "Emerging Opportunities" discusses the growing importance of business process outsourcing, a service industry equivalent of contract manufacturing.

Management Contract

A **management contract** is an agreement whereby one firm provides managerial assistance, technical expertise, or specialized services to a second firm for some agreed-upon time in return for monetary compensation. For its services the first firm may receive either a flat fee or a percentage of sales. The management contract may also specify performance bonuses based on profitability, sales growth, or quality measures. Management contracts allow firms to earn additional revenues without incurring any investment risks or obligations. A subsidiary of Hilton Hotels, for example, offers hotel management and reservation services to hotels that bear the Hilton logo but that are not company-owned. Similarly, major airlines such as Air France, British Airways, and KLM often sell their management expertise to small state-owned airlines headquartered in developing countries.

Foxconn, an operating subsidiary of Taiwan's Hon Hai Precision Industries, employs over one million workers in China. One of the world's largest contract manufacturers and China's largest exporter, Foxconn is the primary manufacturer of such popular products as iPads and iPhones.

@ EPA/Photoshot

Turnkey Project

Another specialized strategy for participating in international business is the turnkey project. A **turnkey project** is a contract under which a firm agrees to fully design, construct, and equip a facility and then turn the project over to the purchaser when it is ready for operation. The turnkey contract may be for a fixed price, in which case the firm makes its profit by keeping its costs below the fixed price. Or the contract may provide for payment on a cost-plus basis, which shifts the risk of cost overruns from the contractor to the purchaser.

International turnkey contracts often involve large, complex, multiyear projects such as construction of a nuclear power plant, an airport, or an oil refinery. Managing such complex construction projects requires special expertise. As a result, most are administered by large construction firms such as Bechtel, KBR, Hyundai Group, New Zealand's Fletcher Challenge Ltd., and Germany's Friedrich Krupp GmbH. KBR, for example, was selected as the project manager for a $22 billion petrochemical complex being built by a joint venture between Saudi Aramco and Dow Chemical.[33] The awarding of lucrative turnkey projects is often based on the availability of home government financing, such as through the Eximbank of the United States, or on political ties between the host and home countries. U.S. construction engineering firms have secured many contracts in Saudi Arabia because of the friendly relations between the two countries, while French construction companies have done well in Francophone Africa.

An increasingly popular variant of the turnkey project is the so-called **B-O-T project,** in which the firm *builds* a facility, *operates* it, and later *transfers* ownership of the project to some other party. Through this approach, the contractor profits from operation and ownership of the project for some period of time but bears any financial risks associated with it during this period. For example, the government of Gabon wished to upgrade the quality of electrical service and fresh water delivered to its citizens. Aided by the International Finance Corporation, a branch of

---

EMERGING OPPORTUNITIES | **BUSINESS PROCESS OUTSOURCING**

Business process outsourcing (BPO) covers a variety of business functions, ranging from routine call centers focusing on telemarketing, customer service, and technical support to more sophisticated and expensive services like financial analysis, tax return preparation, and legal document review. India is the market leader in providing international BPO. Its initial success was based upon the large supply of well-trained English-speaking graduates that its universities produce each year. However, the BPO market has expanded so much that Indian BPO providers are finding it increasingly difficult to fill newly created positions, particularly in Bangalore and New Delhi. As a result, wages in the sector have increased, as has labor turnover. In response Indian BPO providers have targeted higher-value-added markets to maintain their profitability. For example, some large MNCs, such as Citigroup and General Electric, have begun outsourcing routine legal work like contract preparation and patent filings to Indian BPO firms, who charge a quarter to a third what a U.S. law firm would bill for the work. Other Indian firms have entered the remote infrastructure management business, offering to monitor from afar who enters and exits a client's buildings or to protect a client's computer network when hackers attempt to penetrate it.

Other countries have also benefited from the boom in BPO, often because they possess market-specific advantages unavailable to Indian firms. CendrisBSC, a Dutch call-center operator, has established a call center in Cape Town, South Africa, to service its customers in the Netherlands. Labor in the Netherlands is expensive, while South Africa suffers from high rates of unemployment—an estimated 30 to 40 percent. But low labor costs are not the country's only attraction. Europe and South Africa share a common time zone, and a

new submarine fiber-optic cable laid in 2003 connecting Europe to South Africa reduced communications costs. More importantly, 6 million South African citizens speak Afrikaans, a language that evolved from seventeenth-century Dutch. CendrisBSC has found that most Afrikaans speakers need only three months of intense training to become fluent in Dutch, although some cultural readjustments must be made, because South Africans usually exchange pleasantries before commencing a business conversation, while the Dutch often prefer to get down to business immediately.

Stockholm-headquartered Transcom Worldwide SA has adopted a different strategy. Taking advantage of the lower labor costs and language abilities of citizens of the EU's new entrants, Transcom has established call centers in the three Baltic republics, Hungary, and Poland. Many Estonians, for example, speak English, Estonian, Finnish, and Russian, allowing Transcom to serve the regional needs of clients like FedEx, IBM, and Shell. French customers are served by its operations in francophone Morocco. And, ironically, its Spanish call centers serve the Swedish market, for Transcom finds there is no shortage of Swedes living there who are trying to escape the cold.

Sources: " 'Sunnyvale, you have a problem'," *Wall Street Journal,* May 18, 2006, p. B2; "US law firms outsource to India," *Financial Times,* September 29, 2005, p. 30; "More U.S. legal work moves to India's low-cost lawyers," *Wall Street Journal,* September 28, 2005, p. B1; "Cape call center boom offers good hope for S. Africa jobs," *Financial Times,* June 1, 2005, p. 16; "Recruiting trails increasingly take call-center firms off beaten track," *Wall Street Journal,* March 15, 2005, p. A18; "Eastern Europe cuts in on India," *Wall Street Journal,* March 15, 2005, p. A18; "Africa eager for piece of call-center business," *Houston Chronicle,* February 3, 2005, p. D8.

the World Bank Group discussed in Chapter 7, Gabon contracted with Ireland's Electricity Supply Board International and France's Compagnie Générale des Eaux to operate the country's electrical and water systems for 20 years. The two companies invested $600 million to improve these basic services. After the 20-year contract expires, ownership of these assets will be transferred to the government of Gabon.

Foreign Direct Investment

Exporting, licensing, franchising, and the specialized strategies just discussed all allow a firm to internationalize its business without investing in foreign factories or facilities. However, many firms prefer to enter international markets through ownership and control of assets in host countries. Other firms may first establish themselves in a foreign market through exporting, licensing, franchising, or contract manufacturing. After gaining knowledge of and expertise in operating in the host country, they may then want to expand in the market through ownership of production or distribution facilities, as was Baskin-Robbins's strategy in Russia.

Such FDI affords the firm increased control over its international business operations, as well as increased profit potential. Control is particularly important to the firm if it needs to closely coordinate the activities of its foreign subsidiaries to achieve strategic synergies, as IBM has long done, or if it determines that the control is necessary in order to fully exploit the economic potential of proprietary technology, manufacturing expertise, or some other intellectual property right.

In one study, for example, British subsidiaries of U.S.-headquartered MNCs were found to be more effective and successful competitors in the United Kingdom than a matched set of British-owned firms, primarily because the U.S. parents were able to transfer their technological and managerial expertise to their British affiliates.[34]

FDI is also beneficial if host country customers prefer dealing with local factories. Many firms and governments participate in programs that favor locally made products—for example, "Buy American" or "Buy Korean"—in order to promote their local economies. Equally important, many purchasing managers perceive that local production implies more reliable supply, faster service, and better communication with suppliers.

On the other hand, FDI exposes the firm to greater economic and political risks and operating complexity, as well as the potential erosion of the value of its foreign investments if exchange rates change adversely. A firm's decision to engage in FDI may also be influenced by government policies. As noted in Chapter 3, host countries may discourage FDI through direct controls on foreign capital, bans on the acquisition of local companies by foreigners, or restrictions on repatriation of dividends and capital; home countries can promote FDI through such devices as political risk insurance. Firms using FDI must also meet the standard challenges of managing, operating, and financing their foreign subsidiaries while facing the additional hurdle of doing so in political, legal, and cultural milieus different from their own.

There are three methods for FDI: (1) building new facilities (called the greenfield strategy), (2) buying existing assets in a foreign country (called the **acquisition strategy** or the **brownfield strategy**), and (3) participating in a joint venture.

The Greenfield Strategy

The **greenfield strategy** involves starting a new operation from scratch (the word *greenfield* arises from the image of starting with a virgin green site and then building on it). The firm buys or leases land, constructs new facilities, hires and/or transfers in managers and employees, and then launches the new operation. Samsung's semiconductor chip fabrication facility in Texas represents a greenfield investment, as does the Mercedes-Benz automobile assembly plant in Alabama and Nissan's factory in Sunderland, England.

The greenfield strategy has several advantages. For one thing, the firm can select the site that best meets its needs and construct modern, up-to-date facilities. Local communities often offer economic development incentives to attract such facilities because they will create new jobs; these incentives lower the firm's costs. The firm also starts with a clean slate. Managers do not have to deal with existing debts, nurse outmoded equipment, or struggle to modify ancient work rules protected by intransigent labor unions. For example, GM's managers considered a major advantage of its building a new factory in Eisenach in the former East Germany to be its ability to implement Japanese-style production techniques and labor policies without having to battle workers wedded to the old way of doing things. In addition, the firm can acclimate itself to the new national business culture at its own pace, rather than having the instant responsibility of managing a newly acquired, ongoing business. Research indicates that the greater the cultural differences between the home and host countries, the more likely a firm is to choose to build a new factory rather than purchase an existing firm.[35]

However, the greenfield strategy also has some disadvantages. For one thing, successful implementation takes time and patience. For another, land in the desired location may be unavailable or very expensive. In building the new factory, the firm must also comply with various local and national regulations and oversee the factory's construction. It must also recruit a local workforce and train it to meet the firm's performance standards. And finally, by constructing a new facility, the firm may be more strongly perceived as a foreign enterprise.

Disney managers faced several of these difficulties in building Disneyland Paris. Although the French government sold the necessary land to Disney at bargain prices, Disney was not fully prepared to deal with French construction contractors. For example, Disney executives had numerous communications difficulties with a painter that applied 20 different shades of pink to a hotel before the firm approved the color. The park's grand opening was threatened when local contractors demanded an additional $150 million for extra work allegedly requested by Disney. And Disney clashed with its French employees, who resisted the firm's attempt to impose its U.S. work values and grooming standards on them.[36]

The Acquisition Strategy

A second FDI strategy is acquisition of an existing firm conducting business in the host country. Although the actual transaction may no doubt be very complex—requiring bankers, lawyers, regulators, and mergers and acquisitions specialists from several countries—the basic motivation for it is quite simple. By acquiring a going concern, the purchaser quickly obtains control over the acquired firm's factories, employees, technology, brand names, and distribution networks. The acquired firm can continue to generate revenues as the purchaser integrates it into its overall international strategy. And, unlike the greenfield strategy, the acquisition strategy adds no new capacity to the industry. In times of overcapacity, this is an obvious benefit. As the chapter's opening case indicated, the acquisition strategy is the approach Bernard Arnault favored in building LVMH.

Sometimes international businesses acquire local firms simply as a means of entering a new market. For instance, Cemex SA's purchase of Britain's RMC Group for $5.8 billion, which made the Mexican company the world's largest manufacturer of ready-mix concrete, allowed it to swiftly benefit from RMC's dominance of the European cement and concrete market.[37] Similarly, Best Buy chose to enter the Chinese market by buying a controlling interest in Jiangsu Five Star Appliance Co. The purchase of the 136-store appliance and retailing chain allowed Best Buy to quickly establish a presence in that country and to capture economies of scale in sourcing, marketing, and distribution.[38] While we noted earlier in the chapter that Best Buy is shuttering its Chinese outlets bearing the Best Buy brand, the American company is busily adding Five Star-branded stores, a format more attuned to the needs of Chinese consumers.[39]

At other times, acquisitions may be undertaken by a firm as a means of implementing a major strategic change. For example, the state-owned Saudi Arabian Oil Co. has tried to reduce its dependence on crude oil production by purchasing "downstream" firms, such as Petron Corporation, the largest petroleum refiner in the Philippines, and South Korea's Ssangyong Oil Refining Company. Similarly, to increase its presence in emerging markets and in non-carbonated beverages, PepsiCo agreed to pay $1.4 billion for 74 percent of Russia's largest juice producer, OAO Lebedyansky.[40]

The acquisition strategy does have some disadvantages, however. The acquiring firm assumes all the liabilities—financial, managerial, and otherwise—of the acquired firm. If the acquired firm has poor labor relations, unfunded pension obligations, or hidden environmental cleanup liabilities, the acquiring firm becomes financially responsible for solving the problem. The acquiring firm usually must also spend substantial sums up front. For example, when Kraft purchased Britain's Cadbury PLC for $19 billion in 2010, it had to pay out this vast sum shortly after the deal was closed. The greenfield strategy, in contrast, may allow a firm to grow slowly and spread its investment over an extended period.

Joint Ventures

Another form of FDI is the joint venture. **Joint ventures (JV)** are created when two or more firms agree to work together and create a jointly owned separate firm to promote their mutual interests. The number of such arrangements is burgeoning as rapid changes in technology, telecommunications, and government policies outstrip the ability of international firms to exploit opportunities on their own. Because of the growing importance of international intercorporate cooperation, as well as the unique set of challenges it offers international firms, we devote Chapter 13 to this subject.

MyManagementLab   Now that you have finished this chapter, go back to **www.pearsonglobaleditions.com/mymanagementlab** to continue practicing and applying the concepts you've learned.

CHAPTER REVIEW

Summary

An important aspect of international strategy formulation is determining which markets to enter. To make this decision, a firm must consider many factors, including market potential, competition, legal and political environments, and sociocultural influences. It must also carefully assess the costs, benefits, and risks associated with each prospective market. Once a firm has decided to expand its international operations and has assessed potential foreign markets, it must decide how to enter and compete most effectively in the selected foreign markets. An array of strategic options is available for doing this. Choosing an entry mode involves careful assessment of firm-specific ownership advantages, location advantages, and internalization advantages.

Exporting, the most common initial entry mode, is the process of sending goods or services from one country to other countries for use or sale there. Exporting continues to grow rapidly. There are several forms of exporting, including indirect exporting, direct exporting, and intracorporate transfer. In deciding whether to export, a firm must consider such factors as government policies, marketing concerns, consumer information needs, logistical considerations, and distribution issues. Export intermediaries are often used to facilitate exporting. These include export management companies, Webb-Pomerene associations, international trading companies, and export trading companies.

International licensing, another popular entry mode, occurs when one firm leases the right to use its intellectual property to another firm. Basic issues in international licensing include negotiating mutually acceptable terms, determining compensation, defining the rights and privileges of and the constraints imposed on the licensee, and specifying the duration of the agreement.

International franchising is also growing rapidly as an entry mode. International franchising is an arrangement whereby an independent organization or entrepreneur operates a business under the name of another. Several market conditions must exist in order for a firm to successfully franchise. As with licensing agreements, the terms of a franchising agreement are usually quite detailed and specific.

Three specialized entry modes are contract manufacturing, the management contract, and the turnkey project. Contract manufacturing permits a firm to outsource physical production of its product and focus its energies on some other element of the value chain. A management contract calls for one firm to provide managerial assistance, technical assistance, or specialized services to another firm for a fee. A turnkey project involves one firm agreeing to fully design, construct, and equip a facility for another.

The most complex entry mode is FDI. FDI involves the ownership and control of assets in a foreign market. The greenfield strategy for FDI calls for the investing firm to start a totally new enterprise from scratch. The acquisition strategy, in contrast, involves buying an existing firm or operation in the foreign market. In joint ventures, a third form of FDI, ownership and control are shared by two or more firms.

Review Questions

1. What are the steps in conducting a foreign market analysis?
2. What are some of the basic issues a firm must confront when choosing an entry mode for a new foreign market?
3. What is exporting? Why has it increased so dramatically in recent years?
4. What are the primary advantages and disadvantages of exporting?
5. What are three forms of exporting?
6. What is an export intermediary? What is its role? What are the various types of export intermediaries?

7. What is international licensing? What are its advantages and disadvantages?
8. What is international franchising? What are its advantages and disadvantages?
9. What are three specialized entry modes for international business, and how do they work?
10. What is FDI? What are its three basic forms? What are the relative advantages and disadvantages of each?

Questions for Discussion

1. Do you think it is possible for someone to make a decision about entering a particular foreign market without having visited that market? Why or why not?
2. How difficult or easy do you think it is for managers to gauge the costs, benefits, and risks of a particular foreign market?
3. How does each advantage in Dunning's eclectic theory specifically affect a firm's decision regarding entry mode?
4. Why is exporting the most popular initial entry mode?
5. What specific factors could cause a firm to reject exporting as an entry mode?
6. What conditions must exist for an intracorporate transfer to be cost-effective?
7. Your firm is about to begin exporting. In selecting an export intermediary, what characteristics would you look for?
8. Do you think trading companies like Japan's sogo shosha will ever become common in the United States? Why or why not?
9. What factors could cause you to reject an offer from a potential licensee to make and market your firm's products in a foreign market?
10. Under what conditions should a firm consider a greenfield strategy for FDI? An acquisition strategy?

Building Global Skills

Note: It might be helpful to review this chapter's closing before doing this exercise.

When property developers enter a new market, they need to ensure that they can maximize their potential profits in that market. The Gulf States, in particular, have expertise in developing infrastructure projects and recognize the opportunities in a developing nation such as Kazakhstan which is also rich in natural resources. To be attractive to investors, the country does not only have to be flexible and cooperative, it also needs to be politically and socially stable.

Kazakhstan has attracted investment from many different countries. The country is also seen as a vital link in the gateway between the east and the west. Early investors take the highest risk as involvement in the country is untested. However, these early investors stand to make the greatest profits and they are well placed to take advantage of new opportunities in Kazakhstan as they arise.

After reading and thinking about the types of investment in Kazakhstan, break up into groups of four or five people and proceed as follows:

1. Identify at least five products, brands or businesses you are familiar with that could consider being an early investor in a country such as Kazakhstan. Develop a clear rationale to support each example.
2. Identify at least five products, brands or businesses that probably would not consider early investment. Develop a clear rationale to support each example.
3. Randomly list the 10 examples you identified, keeping the rationale for each hidden. Exchange lists with another group. Each group should discuss the list given to it by the other group and classify the various products, brands or businesses into one of the two categories. Be sure to have some rationale for your decision.
4. Each pair of groups that exchanged lists should form one new group. Compare lists and note areas in which the smaller groups agreed and disagreed on their classifications. Discuss the reasons for any disagreements in classification.

Follow-Up Questions

1. What are the specific factors that enable Gulf States to use the approach described and simultaneously make it difficult for some other firms to copy it? What types of firms are most and least likely to be able to use this approach?
2. What does this exercise teach you about international business?

CLOSING CASE   MIDDLE AND FAR EAST INVESTORS TARGET KAZAKHSTAN

It is 2012 and alongside the Baiterek Tower and the Presidential Palace in Kazakhstan's capital Astana, there will be a new landmark. Designed by British architect Norman Foster and funded by the United Arab Emirates will be a structure that personifies Kazakhstan's economic growth, the Abu Dhabi Palace.

Aldar Properties, the developer of the new plaza, is just one of the many investors from the Middle East that is moving into the construction sector in Kazakhstan. Many of them are focusing on high profile projects, such as the Aktau City and providing the bulk of the $38 billion that is needed to complete the project. Abu Dhabi's International Petroleum Investment Company is also becoming involved in Kazakhstan's oil and gas industry.

Mortgages were introduced to Kazakhstan for the first time in the early years of the new millennium. The increase in real estate prices has kept many potential home buyers out of the market, and there has been unregulated speculation. The market reached its peak in the summer of 2007, and then the bubble burst and prices began to fall. Many potential home buyers, due to global liquidity problems, were cut off from potential sources of funds. Mortgage payments tripled, and many banks began to refuse to issue loans.

Consequently, the construction centre was also badly hit; many of the businesses lacked the funds to finish off projects and start new ones. Many home buyers and investors had bought properties off plan and now found themselves without a home or an asset.

There has been a switch in overseas investment in Kazakhstan in recent years. In 2007, the U.S. invested $2.4 billion, the Netherlands $3.1 billion, France $1 billion, Russia $751 million, Britain $720 million, Italy $512 million, and Turkey $327 million. With the liquidity problems around the world, it has been the Gulf States and South Korea that have moved in to take advantage of investment opportunities. Far Eastern companies, including those from Japan and China, are also moving in to make considerable investment. China's Jiuquan Iron and Steel Group has made a $4.4 billion investment in a joint venture; Japan has become involved in uranium production and nuclear energy (possibly to $2 billion); and South Korea's Kookmin Bank has bought shares in Bank CenterCredit. State-owned Samruk has entered into a joint venture with Datang from China and Kepco from South Korea to develop the $4.5 billion Balkhash Power Plant.

One of the most important infrastructure projects in Kazakhstan is the creation of a network of roads and railways, so that Kazakhstan can become a vital link in the overland transfer of products and resources between Europe and China. Deep in the Tian-Shan Mountains, trains line up at one of the busiest border crossings in Asia. Natural resources from Kazakhstan and beyond pour into China and manufactured goods head out of China, bound for Central Asia, Russia, and Europe.

Since 1956, the Alataw Pass has been the only rail crossing between China and Kazakhstan. It is expected that trade between the two countries will triple by 2020. A new railway is being built from China to the Caspian Sea and another rail link through the Khorgos Pass.

At the same time, Kazakhstan's Ministry of Transport and Communications is actively seeking potential investors for a major airport that can cope with large cargo planes. The project is seeking an investment of $500 million and will be located at Dostyk.

In November 2007, seven countries in the region agreed to spend more money on railways and roads to cross central Asia in order to connect China, Russia, the Middle East, and Europe. Most of the eight roads and rail corridors connect east to west, but some connect north to south and these are planned to be completed by 2018. Already Kazakhstan, Kyrgyzstan, and Tajikistan have signed an agreement, along with China, Mongolia, Afghanistan, and Azerbaijan. Kazakhstan is set to spend $7.5 billion on improving its railway infrastructure by 2012. There are 12 large-scale projects and of that total the government is spending $3.5 billion on just over 1,700 km of new railway and $1.07 billion to electrify 2,185 km of track.

In June 2008 the Kazakhstan Senate began looking at a draft law in order to encourage public –private partnerships in Kazakhstan. It was then passed onto the lower House of Parliament, the Majilis. The law will allow concessions to be granted for construction and reconstruction of state property. Further changes will be needed to tax and budgetary legislation. The idea is that it will be based on the British-style Private Finance Initiative Model.

In Dubai in 2007, at the world's largest real estate exhibition, Cityscape, Jordanian-based Saraya Holdings announced its intention to develop Aktau City on the Caspian Sea in Kazakhstan. They will build a 5-star resort hotel, serviced villas, a spa, branded villas, and an exclusive beach front, and they expect the project to be largely completed by 2011. Although Aktau is at the center of the emerging oil and gas industry in Kazakhstan, it is hoped Aktau could become a key tourist destination and a year-round destination for visitors.

As Kazakhstan is rich in natural resources and the Gulf States already have the knowledge and expertise in learning to exploit these commodities and drivers of the economy, a close association between Kazakhstan and the Gulf States was a natural development. In fact Kazakhstan's Prime Minister, Karim Massimov, can speak Arabic and has forged close relationships with many of the leading families and companies in the Gulf States.

Case Questions

1. What lessons should Kazakhstan learn from the collapse of the real estate market?
2. On average, how long does it take for goods to be shipped from China to Europe and how will the new route cut this time?

3. How is Kazakhstan intending to raise the funds for the massive expansion and modernisation programme of its railway infrastructure?

4. How does Kazakhstan intend to continue to forge relations with countries such as the United Arab Emirates and Gulf States in general for their mutual benefit?

Sources: Silk Road Intelligencer (www.silkroadintelligencer.com); Eurasia Net (www.eurasianet.org); Embassy of Kazakhstan to the United States and Canada (www.kazakhembus.com); World Nuclear Association (www.world-nuclear.org); US Department of State (www.state.gov); Asian Development Bank (www.adb.org); World Bank (www.worldbank.org.kz); The United Nations (www.un.org); European Commission (www.ec.europa.eu); Saudi Business Focus (www.sbfmedia.net); Saraya Holdings (www.sarayaholdings.com); Mubadala (www.mubadala.com) and Permanent Mission of Kazakhstan to the United Nations (www.kazakhstanun.org).

Endnotes

1. "Bulgari gives LVMH a bump," *Wall Street Journal*," March 8, 2011; "LVMH's highly priced Bulgari jewel," *Wall Street Journal*, March 8, 2011; "LVMH to take control of Italy's Bulgari," *New York Times Deal Book*, March 6, 2011 (online); LVMH Annual Report 2010; "China to be top luxury buyer by 2020," *Wall Street Journal*, February 5, 2011; "Luxury shoppers return to LVMH," *Wall Street Journal*, February 5, 2011; "At LV, this year's man is Chinese," *Wall Street Journal*, January 14, 2011; "Hermès clan wins approval for defensive move," *Wall Street Journal*, January 7, 2011.

2. Anoop Madhok, "Cost, value, and foreign market entry mode: The transaction and the firm," *Strategic Management Journal*, vol. 18 (1997), p. 37.

3. See George S. Yip and George A. Coundouriotis, "Diagnosing global strategy potential: The world chocolate confectionery industry," *Planning Review*, January–February 1991, pp. 4–14, for an example of how this can be done.

4. William H. Davidson, "The role of global scanning in business planning," *Organizational Dynamics*, Winter 1991, pp. 4–16.

5. "The Lion Kings?," *The Economist*, January 6, 2011 (online).

6. "Nigeria's mad men," *The Economist*, April 30, 2011, p. 72; "Global ad agencies flocking to Africa," *Wall Street Journal*, October 22, 2010; "In Africa, Google sows seeds for future growth," *Wall Street Journal*, May 18, 2010, p. B1.

7. "Ford plans $800m Brazil plant," *Financial Times*, October 3, 1997, p. 6; "GM plans to develop car in Brazil," *Financial Times*, June 3, 1997, p. 5.

8. M. Krishna Erramilli, "The experience factor in foreign market entry behavior of service firms," *Journal of International Business Studies*, vol. 22, no. 3 (Third Quarter 1991), pp. 479–501.

9. "A beautiful face is not enough," *Forbes*, May 13, 1991, pp. 105–106.

10. Susan C. Schneider and Arnoud De Mayer, "Interpreting and responding to strategic issues: The impact of national culture," *Strategic Management Journal*, vol. 12 (1991), pp. 307–320.

11. John H. Dunning, "Trade, location of economic activity and the MNE: A search for an eclectic approach," in Bertil Ohlin et al., eds., *The International Allocation of Economic Activity* (London: Macmillan, 1977); Alan M. Rugman, "A new theory of the multinational enterprise: Internationalization versus internalization," *Columbia Journal of World Business* (1980), pp. 23–29.

12. Jean J. Boddewyn, "Political aspects of MNE theory," *Journal of International Business Studies*, vol. 19, no. 1 (1988), pp. 341–363; Thomas L. Brewer, "Effects of government policies on foreign direct investment as a strategic choice of firms: An expansion of internalization theory," *The International Trade Journal*, vol. 7, no. 1 (Fall 1992), pp. 111–129.

13. "Egypt suddenly is a magnet for investors," *Wall Street Journal*, April 10, 1997, p. A6.

14. "Istanbul's location again makes it crucial to the entire region," *Wall Street Journal*, March 27, 1997, p. A1.

15. "Westerners profit as Japan opens its drug market," *Wall Street Journal*, December 2, 2002, pp. A1, A20; Kenichi Ohmae, "The global logic of strategic alliances," *Harvard Business Review* (March–April 1989), p. 151.

16. John M. Stopford and Louis T. Wells, *Managing the Multinational Enterprise: Organization of the Firm and Ownership of the Subsidiaries* (New York: Basic Books, 1972).

17. M. Krishna Erramilli, "The experience factor in foreign market entry behavior of service firms," *The Journal of International Business Studies*, vol. 22, no. 3 (Third Quarter 1991), pp. 479–502.

18. Bruce Kogut, "Designing global strategies: Profiting from operational flexibility," *Sloan Management Review* (Fall 1985), pp. 27–38; Edward W. Desmond, "Byting Japan," *Time*, October 5, 1992, pp. 68–69.

19. W. Chan Kim and Peter Hwang, "Global strategy and multinationals' entry mode choice," *Journal of International Business Studies*, vol. 23, no. 1 (First Quarter 1992), pp. 29–54; see also Sumantra Ghoshal, "Global strategy: An organizing framework," *Strategic Management Journal*, vol. 8 (1987), pp. 425–440.

20. "Wine firm ramps up its Chinese operations," *Wall Street Journal*, May 19, 2011, p. B8.

21. "Latin links," *Wall Street Journal*, September 24, 1992, p. R6.

22. "Looking abroad for a bigger boost in business," *Wall Street Journal*, September 9, 2008, p. B4.

23. Geir Gripsud, "The determinants of export decisions and attitudes to a distant market: Norwegian fishery

exports to Japan," *The Journal of International Business Studies*, vol. 21, no. 3 (Third Quarter 1990), pp. 469–494.

24. "Baskin-Robbins to open plant in Moscow," *Bryan College Station Eagle*, August 14, 1995, p. A1.

25. Desmond, op. cit.

26. "New tricks for Japan's old dogs," *Wall Street Journal*, April 7, 2005, p. A12.

27. "Nintendo to ease restrictions on U.S. game designers," *Wall Street Journal*, October 22, 1991, pp. B1, B4.

28. "Saks to follow luxury brands into China," *Wall Street Journal*, April 18, 2006, p. B1.

29. "Oleg Cassini, Inc., sues firm over licensing," *Wall Street Journal*, March 28, 1984, p. 5.

30. "L. Ashley sues L'Oréal for £18m," *Financial Times*, October 15, 2002, p. 23.

31. "In electronics, U.S. companies seize momentum from Japan," *Wall Street Journal*, March 10, 2005, p. A1.

32. "Unsafe conditions at Nike factory in Vietnam revealed in '96 audit," *Houston Chronicle*, November 10, 1997, p. 18A.

33. "Saudi Aramco and Dow Chemical select KBR," *news.dow.com*, July 12, 2007; "Dow Chemical, Aramco finalize venture," *Wall Street Journal*, May 14, 2007, p. A3.

34. J. H. Dunning, *American Investment in British Manufacturing Industry* (London: George Allen and Unwin, 1958).

35. Bruce Kogut and Harbir Singh, "The effect of national culture on the choice of entry mode," *Journal of International Business Studies*, vol. 19 (Fall 1988), pp. 411–432.

36. "Disney's rough ride in France," *Fortune*, March 23, 1992, p. 14.

37. "Cemex prowls for deals in both China and India," *Wall Street Journal*, January 27, 2006, p. C4.

38. "Best Buy will pay $180 million for majority of China's Jiangsu," *Wall Street Journal*, May 13–14, 2006, p. A6.

39. "Best Buy to close China stores," *Wall Street Journal*, February 21, 2010.

40. "Pepsi uncaps Russian juice deal," *Wall Street Journal*, March 21, 2008, p. B4.

CHAPTER 13

International Strategic Alliances

AFTER STUDYING THIS CHAPTER, YOU SHOULD BE ABLE TO:

1. Compare joint ventures and other forms of strategic alliances.

2. Characterize the benefits of strategic alliances.

3. Describe the scope of strategic alliances.

4. Discuss the forms of management used for strategic alliances.

5. Identify the limitations of strategic alliances.

Access a host of interactive learning aids at **www.pearsonglobaleditions.com/ mymanagementlab** to help strengthen your understanding of the chapter concepts.

MyManagementLab

Francis Dean/Dean Pictures/Newscom

THE EUROPEAN CEREAL WARS

Kellogg virtually created the market for breakfast cereals in Europe. The maker of such popular brands as Kellogg's Corn Flakes, Rice Krispies, and Frosted Flakes, Kellogg began introducing its products in the United Kingdom in the 1920s and on the continent in the 1950s. However, Europeans traditionally favored bread, fruit, eggs, and meats for breakfast, so the firm had a tough sell on its hands. Indeed, it took decades for Europeans to accept cereals as a viable breakfast choice.

Fortunately for cereal makers, during the 1980s and 1990s, demand for breakfast cereals in Europe began to accelerate as European consumers became more health-conscious and started looking for breakfast alternatives to eggs and meat. The busy schedules of the increasing number of dual-career families spurred demand for prepackaged foods. Another contributing factor has been the emergence of supermarkets in Europe. Traditionally most food products in Europe were sold at small specialty stores, which were often reluctant to stock cereals because they take up so much shelf space. In recent years, however, more full-line supermarkets have opened in Europe, and shelf space is now available for a wider array of products. Finally, the growth of commercial TV outlets in Europe has helped firms increase brand awareness and demand through advertising. Needless to say, the enormous potential of the European cereal market also attracted the interests of Kellogg's competitors.

One of Kellogg's biggest competitors in the United States is General Mills, which makes such popular brands as Cheerios and Golden Grahams. General Mills has traditionally concentrated on the North American market. But in 1989 General Mills's managers decided it was time for the company to enter the European market. However, they also recognized that taking on Kellogg, which controlled 50 percent of the worldwide cereal market and dominated the European market, would be a monumental battle.

After careful consideration, General Mills's CEO Bruce Atwater decided that the firm could compete most effectively in Europe if it worked with a strategic ally located there. It didn't take him long to choose one: Nestlé, the world's largest food-processing firm. Nestlé is a household name in Europe, has a well-established distribution system, and owns manufacturing plants worldwide. One major area in which Nestlé had never succeeded, however, was the cereal market. Thus, Atwater reasoned that Nestlé would be a logical and willing partner.

When he approached his counterpart at Nestlé, he was amazed to discover that that firm had already been considering approaching General Mills about just such an arrangement. From Nestlé's perspective, General Mills could contribute its knowledge of cereal technology, its array of proven cereal products, and its expertise in marketing cereals to consumers, especially children.

Top managers of the two firms met and quickly outlined a plan of attack. Each firm contributed around $80 million to create a new firm called Cereal Partners Worldwide (CPW). CPW's corporate offices were established in Lausanne, Switzerland. General Mills agreed to install its proprietary manufacturing systems in existing Nestlé factories, oversee the production of cereals, and help develop advertising campaigns. Nestlé, in turn, agreed to use its own globally recognized corporate name on the products and to handle sales and distribution throughout Europe. The two partners set two major goals for CPW: They wanted CPW to be generating annual sales of $1 billion and to be a strong number 2 in market share outside North America by the year 2000.

By almost any measure, CPW has been a roaring success. Among its first triumphs was a deal struck with Disneyland Paris to supply breakfast cereals to the restaurants and hotels at the French theme park and to use Disney characters to promote the firm's cereals. The firm quickly established itself as a major player in the European cereal market, with an impressive 25 percent of the United Kingdom market. Having solidified its beachhead in Europe, CPW then expanded its operations to Latin America and Asia. With revenues of $3 billion in 2010, it is now one of the world's largest cereal manufacturers. CPW operates in 130 countries and markets 50 brands, delivering a steady and growing stream of earnings for its parents, Nestlé and General Mills.[1] ■

Globalization can be a very expensive process, particularly when a firm must perfectly coordinate R&D, production, distribution, marketing, and financial decisions throughout the world in order to succeed. A firm may discover that it lacks all the necessary internal resources to effectively compete against its rivals internationally. The high costs of researching and developing new products alone may stretch its corporate budget. Thus, a firm may seek partners to share these costs. Or a firm may develop a new technology but lack a distribution network or production facilities in all the national markets it wants to serve. Accordingly, the firm may seek out other firms with skills or advantages that complement its own and negotiate agreements to work together. Such factors motivated Nestlé and General Mills to team together, as the opening case indicated.

International Corporate Cooperation

Cooperation between international firms can take many forms, such as cross-licensing of proprietary technology, sharing of production facilities, cofunding of research projects, and marketing of each other's products using existing distribution networks. Such forms of cooperation are known collectively as **strategic alliances,** business arrangements whereby two or more firms choose to cooperate for their mutual benefit. The partners in a strategic alliance may agree to pool R&D activities, marketing expertise, and/or managerial talent. For example, in the early 1990s, Kodak and Fuji—two fierce competitors in the film market—formed a strategic alliance with camera manufacturers Canon, Minolta, and Nikon to develop a new standard for cameras and film, the Advanced Photo System, to make picture taking easier and more goof-proof.[2]

A **joint venture (JV)** is a special type of strategic alliance in which two or more firms join together to create a new business entity that is legally separate and distinct from its parents. Joint ventures are normally established as corporations and are owned by the founding parents in whatever proportions they negotiate. Although unequal ownership is common, many are owned equally by the founding firms. Cereal Partners Worldwide represents this type of alliance.

A strategic alliance is only one method by which a firm can enter or expand its international operations. As Chapter 12 discussed, other alternatives exist: exporting, licensing, franchising, and FDI. In each of these alternatives, however, a firm acts alone or hires a second individual or firm—often one further down the distribution chain—to act on its behalf. In contrast, a strategic alliance results from cooperation among two or more firms. Each participant in a strategic alliance is motivated to promote its own self-interest but has determined that cooperation is the best way to achieve its goals.

Some means is required for managing any cooperative agreement. A joint venture, as a separate legal entity, must have its own set of managers and board of directors. It may be managed in any of three ways. First, the founding firms may jointly share management, with each appointing key personnel who report back to officers of the parent. Second, one parent may assume primary responsibility. And third, an independent team of managers may be hired to run it. The third approach is often preferred, because independent managers focus on what is best for the joint venture rather than attempting to placate bosses from the founding firms.[3] Other types of strategic alliances may be managed more informally—for example, by a coordinating committee, composed of employees of each of the partners, which oversees the alliance's progress.

A formal management organization allows a joint venture to be broader in purpose, scope (or range of operations), and duration than other types of strategic alliances. A non–joint-venture strategic alliance may be formed merely to allow the partners to overcome a particular hurdle that each faces in the short run. A joint venture will be more helpful if the two firms plan a more extensive and long-term relationship. A typical non–joint-venture strategic alliance has a narrow purpose and scope, such as marketing a new smartphone in Canada. A joint venture might be formed if firms wanted to cooperate in the design, production, and sale of a broad line of telecommunications equipment in North America. Non–joint-venture strategic alliances are often formed for a specific purpose that may have a natural ending. For example, the agreement among the camera manufacturers Canon, Minolta, and Nikon and the film manufacturers Fuji and Kodak to jointly create the Advanced Photo System for cameras and film terminated in 1996, after the new standards were developed. Each participant then marketed the resulting products on its own: Kodak called its new film Advantix; Minolta labeled its new cameras Vectis; and Nikon chose the name Nuvis.[4] But because joint ventures are separate legal entities, they generally have a longer duration. A venture such as Cereal Partners Worldwide has an indefinite time horizon in that it will continue to function so long as its two owners are satisfied with its performance.

Because of their narrow mission and lack of a formal organizational structure, non–joint-venture strategic alliances are relatively less stable than joint ventures. For example, in 1988 United Airlines and British Airways entered into an agreement to form a strategic marketing alliance involving their

North American and European routes. At the time, United was offering limited service to Europe and was losing market share to archrivals Delta and American Airlines, both of which offered more extensive service there. To solve its problem, United agreed to coordinate its flight schedules with British Airways, thereby making it more convenient for a Europe-bound U.S. traveler to board a domestic United flight and then transfer to a transatlantic British Airways flight. United and British Airways both prominently described the arrangement in their marketing campaigns and in the visits of their marketing reps to U.S. and European travel agencies. Within a year, however, Pan Am's routes to London were placed on the auction block. United quickly purchased those routes from Pan Am and severed relations with its strategic ally. British Airways was of little use to United once United could operate in London on its own. Needing a transatlantic partner, British Airways then entered into a similar strategic alliance with US Air in 1993. Three years later American Airlines and British Airways agreed to form a separate strategic alliance. US Air, believing that it would be the weakest partner in a three-way alliance, promptly sued British Airways and terminated their alliance.

Benefits of Strategic Alliances

Firms that enter into strategic alliances usually expect to benefit in one or more ways.[5] As summarized in Figure 13.1, international business may realize four benefits from strategic alliances: ease of market entry, shared risk, shared knowledge and expertise, and synergy and competitive advantage.[6]

Ease of Market Entry

A firm wishing to enter a new market often faces major obstacles, such as entrenched competition or hostile government regulations. Partnering with a local firm can often help it navigate around such barriers. In other cases, economies of scale and scope in marketing and distribution confer benefits on firms that aggressively and quickly enter numerous markets.[7] Yet the costs of speed and boldness are often high and beyond the capabilities of a single firm. A strategic alliance may allow the firm to achieve the benefits of rapid entry while keeping costs down.

For example, Imax recently targeted China as an important growth market for filmed entertainment. To speed its entry, it entered into a $40 million joint venture with Wanda Cinema Line, the operator of China's largest theater chain, to build 75 Imax theaters in China. Imax will supply its specialized projection equipment, while Wanda will build the theaters.[8] A similar meshing of strengths motivated a joint venture between Cigna, the U.S. insurance giant, and Banco Excel Economico, one of Brazil's largest privately owned banks, to sell personal insurance in Brazil. Cigna provides expertise in selling life, accident, and credit insurance to consumers, while Banco Excel supplies its knowledge of the Brazilian financial services industry, as well as access to its existing retail customer base. Each partner contributed half the $19 million invested in the new company, Excel Cigna Seguradora.[9]

Regulations imposed by national governments also influence the formation of joint ventures. Many countries are so concerned about the influence of foreign firms on their economies that they require MNCs to work with a local partner if they want to operate in these countries.[10]

FIGURE 13.1
Benefits of Strategic Alliances

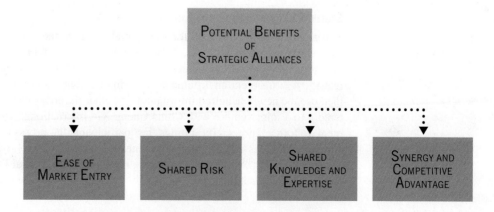

For example, the government of Namibia, an African nation, requires foreign investors operating fishing fleets off its coast to work with local partners. At other times governments strongly encourage foreign companies to participate in joint ventures in order to promote other policy goals. A case in point is China, which required foreign automobile companies to partner with local firms as a means of transferring technology to its automobile industry. A local partner may also make it easier to navigate through complex laws and customs. For instance, Rio Tinto, an Anglo-Australian mining company, formed a joint venture with Chinalco, China's leading aluminum company, to explore for ore deposits in China. The joint venture will benefit from Rio Tinto's expertise and Chinalco's knowledge of local law and ways of doing business.[11]

Shared Risk

Today's major industries are so competitive that no firm has a guarantee of success when it enters a new market or develops a new product. Strategic alliances can be used to either reduce or control individual firms' risks. For example, Boeing established a strategic alliance with several Japanese firms to reduce its financial risk in the development and production of the Boeing 777 jet. Researching, designing, and safety-testing a new aircraft model costs billions of dollars, much of which must be spent before the manufacturer can establish how well the airplane will be received in the marketplace. Even though Boeing has enjoyed much success as a manufacturer of commercial aircraft, it wanted to reduce its financial exposure on the 777 project. Thus, it collaborated with three Japanese partners—Fuji, Mitsubishi, and Kawasaki—agreeing to let them build 20 percent of the 777 airframe. Boeing, the controlling partner in the alliance, also hoped its allies would help sell the new aircraft to large Japanese customers such as Japan Air Lines and All Nippon Airways. The arrangement proved so successful that Boeing utilized it as well in designing and producing its latest jet, the 787 Dreamliner.

Or consider the strategic alliance involving Kodak and Fuji and three Japanese camera firms discussed previously. At face value, it might seem odd for Kodak to agree to collaborate with Fuji, its biggest competitor, to develop a new film that both would make and sell. Closer scrutiny, however, suggests that the arrangement reduced Kodak's risks considerably. Kodak managers realized that if they developed the film alone, Fuji would aggressively fight the innovation in the marketplace and Kodak would have to work hard to gain consumer acceptance of its new standard for film. Still worse, Fuji might have decided to develop its own new film standard, thereby jeopardizing Kodak's R&D investment should the Japanese-dominated camera-manufacturing industry adopt Fuji's approach rather than Kodak's. Mindful of the financial losses incurred by Sony when VHS rather than Betamax became the standard format for VCRs, Kodak chose to include Fuji in the deal. Through this strategic alliance, Kodak perhaps reduced its potential profits but also substantially reduced its risks. It was then free to compete on a playing field of its own choosing, able to harness its marketing clout, distribution networks, and formidable brand name against the efforts of its rivals.

Shared risk is an especially important consideration when a firm is entering a market that has just opened up or that is characterized by much uncertainty and instability. "Emerging Opportunities" discusses how one international business, Otis Elevator, uses joint ventures to slash its risks in such situations.

Shared Knowledge and Expertise

Still another common reason for strategic alliances is the potential for the firm to gain knowledge and expertise that it lacks. A firm may want to learn more about how to produce something, how to acquire certain resources, how to deal with local governments' regulations, or how to manage in a different environment—information that a partner often can offer.[12] The firm can then use the newly acquired information for other purposes. For instance, in 2006, Moody's entered into a joint venture with China Cheng Xin International Credit Rating Company to allow them to offer joint credit ratings for participants in cross-border financings; the Chinese company provides credit ratings for domestic firms, while Moody's provides ratings on international companies.[13] And, as our opening case discussed, Cereal Partners Worldwide has proved to be very successful, in part because it blended the knowledge and expertise of Nestle and General Mills.

EMERGING OPPORTUNITIES   **THE UPS AND DOWNS OF MARKET ENTRY**

Entering a new market is always a risky proposition, but when a firm is the first foreigner to enter, its risks are even greater. That's why many foreign firms who try to be first often look for a local partner for help. A good case in point is Otis Elevator.

A division of United Technologies, Otis has a strategy of trying to be the first foreign elevator manufacturer to enter emerging markets. For example, the firm entered China in 1984. The morning after the Berlin Wall fell, Otis executives began negotiating with prospective local partners in Central and Eastern Europe. And it was among the very first U.S. companies to announce plans to enter Vietnam when President Clinton lifted the trade embargo with that country.

Otis always looks for one or more local partners to ease its entry and reduce its risks. For example, the firm has eight joint ventures in China (see Map 13.1), employing over 8,000 people. These partners know the local landscape and can help the company avoid problems. They also aid the marketing of Otis's products. For example, Otis won the lucrative contract to provide 158 escalators for the Shanghai metro system thanks in part to its Chinese partners, as well as the elevators for the 101-story Shanghai World Financial Center, the tallest building in China. It was chosen to install 110 elevators and escalators for Tianjin's new subway system, as well as those for the Beijing Transit Center, which served thousands of visitors arriving for the 2008 Summer Olympics. On the other hand, Otis also often has to work hard to get its partners "up to speed." For example, it took Otis three years to get its first Chinese partner to phase out its own antiquated product line and replace it with newer Otis equipment. And convincing the partner about the benefits of customer service took even longer. To instill the service-oriented spirit vital to its success, Otis now spends over $2 million a year training its Chinese managers and employees.

Otis's strategy seems to be a sound one. Providing its local partner with cutting-edge technology, equipment, and training often yields high returns. Yet often low-tech solutions are equally as valuable. For example, the simple act of providing its new Russian workforce with vans boosted productivity; previously, these workers often transported spare parts by carrying them on the Moscow subway. Otis now services over 118,000 elevators throughout Russia and Ukraine. All told, 80 percent of Otis's $11.6 billion in revenues in 2010 were earned outside the United States. Perhaps more important, the company is perfectly positioned to benefit from the elevated growth prospects of many large emerging markets.

Sources: United Technologies Annual Report 2010; www.otis.com, various press releases; "The pioneers," *Wall Street Journal*, September 26, 1996, pp. R1, R14; "Overseas, Otis and its parent get in on the ground floor," *Wall Street Journal*, April 21, 1995, p. A6.

MAP 13.1

Otis Elevators' Eight Joint Ventures in China (shown in red)

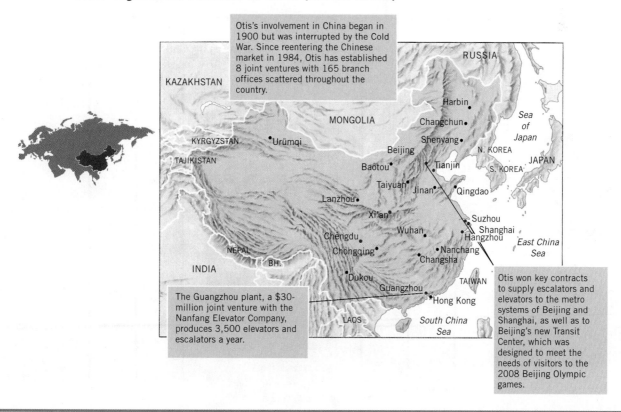

Otis's involvement in China began in 1900 but was interrupted by the Cold War. Since reentering the Chinese market in 1984, Otis has established 8 joint ventures with 165 branch offices scattered throughout the country.

The Guangzhou plant, a $30-million joint venture with the Nanfang Elevator Company, produces 3,500 elevators and escalators a year.

Otis won key contracts to supply escalators and elevators to the metro systems of Beijing and Shanghai, as well as to Beijing's new Transit Center, which was designed to meet the needs of visitors to the 2008 Beijing Olympic games.

Synergy and Competitive Advantage

Firms may also enter into strategic alliances in order to attain synergy and competitive advantage. These related advantages reflect combinations of the other advantages discussed in this section: The idea is that through some combination of market entry, risk sharing, and learning potential, each collaborating firm will be able to achieve more and to compete more effectively than if it had attempted to enter a new market or industry alone.[14]

For example, creating a favorable brand image in consumers' minds is an expensive, time-consuming process, as is creating efficient distribution networks and obtaining the necessary clout with retailers to capture shelf space for one's products. These factors led PepsiCo, the world's second-largest soft drink firm, to establish a joint venture with Thomas J. Lipton Co., a division of Unilever, to produce and market ready-to-drink teas in the United States. Lipton, which is the global market leader in ready-to-drink teas, provided the joint venture with manufacturing expertise and brand recognition in teas. PepsiCo supplied its extensive and experienced U.S. distribution network.[15] Similarly, Siemens and Motorola established a joint venture to produce DRAM computer chips. Motorola teamed with Siemens in part to help finance the new $1.5 billion factory the partners agreed to build, while Siemens sought to benefit from Motorola's manufacturing expertise and to improve its access to the huge U.S. market for DRAM memory chips.[16]

Scope of Strategic Alliances

The scope of cooperation among firms may vary significantly, as Figure 13.2 illustrates. For example, it may consist of a comprehensive alliance, in which the partners participate in all facets of conducting business, ranging from product design to manufacturing to marketing. Or it may

FIGURE 13.2

The Scope of Strategic Alliances

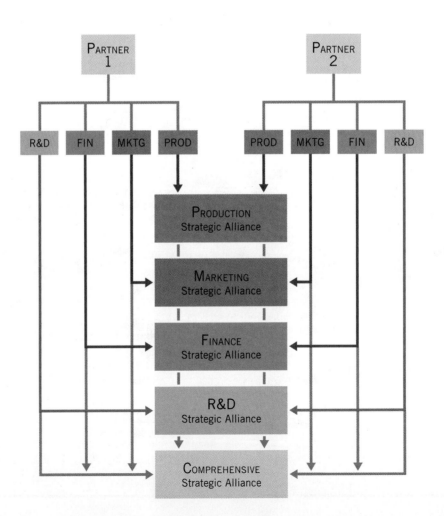

consist of a more narrowly defined alliance that focuses on only one element of the business, such as R&D. The degree of collaboration will depend on the basic goals of each partner.

Comprehensive Alliances

Comprehensive alliances arise when the participating firms agree to perform together multiple stages of the process by which goods or services are brought to the market: R&D, design, production, marketing, and distribution. Because of the broad scope of such alliances, the firms must establish procedures for meshing such functional areas as finance, production, and marketing for the alliance to succeed. Yet integrating the different operating procedures of the parents over a broad range of functional activities is difficult in the absence of a formal organizational structure. As a result, most comprehensive alliances are organized as joint ventures. As an independent entity, the joint venture can adopt operating procedures that suit its specific needs, rather than attempting to accommodate the often incompatible procedures of the parents, as might be the case with another type of strategic alliance.

Moreover, by fully integrating their efforts, participating firms in a comprehensive alliance are able to achieve greater synergy through sheer size and total resources. For instance, as the chapter's opening case discussed, General Mills and Nestlé created a comprehensive joint venture, Cereal Partners Worldwide, to market cereal in Europe in the face of fierce, entrenched competition from Kellogg. General Mills contributed its cereal-making technology to the joint venture, while Nestlé added its European distribution network and name recognition. Cereal Partners Worldwide would have had a major uphill battle in the European cereal market if the joint venture had covered only a single function, such as marketing. But a complete meshing of each firm's relative strengths resulted in a business unit that has emerged as a formidable competitor for Kellogg. Similarly, Dow Chemical and the Saudi Arabian Oil Co. (Aramco) agreed to build and operate a $22 billion petrochemical complex near Jubail that is scheduled to begin operation in 2015. Aramco will provide the feedstock for the plant, while Dow Chemical will contribute its technology and expertise in manufacturing petrochemicals.[17]

Functional Alliances

Strategic alliances may also be narrow in scope, involving only a single functional area of the business. In such cases, integrating the needs of the parent firms is less complex. Thus, functionally based alliances often do not take the form of a joint venture, although joint ventures are still the more common form of organization. Types of functional alliances include production alliances, marketing alliances, financial alliances, and R&D alliances.

PRODUCTION ALLIANCES A **production alliance** is a functional alliance in which two or more firms each manufacture products or provide services in a shared or common facility. A production alliance may utilize a facility one partner already owns. For example, as we discuss later in this chapter, the NUMMI joint venture between Toyota and GM was housed in a former GM assembly plant in California, which the American company had previously closed down. Alternatively, the partners may choose to build a new plant, as is the case for a new $3.5 billion joint venture between Sony and Sharp to manufacture liquid crystal display panels for high-definition televisions in western Japan.[18]

MARKETING ALLIANCES A **marketing alliance** is a functional alliance in which two or more firms share marketing services or expertise. In most cases, one partner introduces its products or services into a market in which the other partner already has a presence. The established firm helps the newcomer by promoting, advertising, and/or distributing its products or services. The established firm may negotiate a fixed price for its assistance or may share in a percentage of the newcomer's sales or profits. Alternatively, the firms may agree to market each others' products on a reciprocal basis. For example, U.S. toymaker Mattel and its Japanese rival Bandai established a strategic marketing alliance in 1999. Bandai agreed to distribute Mattel products like Barbie dolls, Hot Wheels, and Fisher Price toys in Japan, while Mattel agreed to market Bandai's Power Rangers and Digimon in Latin America, where Mattel's distribution network is strong but Bandai's nonexistent.[19] Marketing alliances are also very common in the international airline industry, as "Venturing Abroad" indicates. However, when forming a marketing alliance, partners must take care to ensure that their expectations and needs are mutually understood.

Marketing alliances are usually ad hoc in nature, established to remedy some problem a firm has in a specific market. In the international airline industry, however, mega-marketing alliances now dominate competition within the industry. Three mega-alliances together account for a majority of the world's air revenue passenger-miles. The Star Alliance, established in 1997, was the first of the mega-alliances to form and is the industry's largest. Its 27 members include United, USAir, Lufthansa, SAS, Air Canada, Air China, South African Airways, and Singapore Airlines. The Star Alliance provides 21,000 daily departures to 1,160 airports in 181 countries. The thirteen-member SkyTeam alliance includes Air France, KLM, Delta, Aeromexico, Korean Air Lines, and Aeroflot. This alliance offers 13,000 daily flights serving 900 cities in 169 countries. The OneWorld alliance, whose 12 members include American Airlines, British Airways, Qantas, Cathay Pacific, and Japan Airlines, is the third largest alliance. OneWorld carriers offer 9,300 daily departures to over 750 cities in 145 countries.

Alliances have become a critical component of competition in the international airline industry because of decisions made at the International Civil Aviation Conference held in Chicago in 1944. The Chicago Conference, like the Bretton Woods Conference of 1944, was convened to structure a portion of the post–World War II economic environment—in this case, that of the civil aviation industry. The Chicago conferees decided to grant each government control over international airline service to and from its country. Most countries chose to grant commercial airline rights on a reciprocal basis: Country A would grant country B the right to designate a carrier from country B to fly between a city in B and a city in A if country B granted country A the right to designate a carrier from country A to fly between a city in A and a city in B. Moreover, very few nations allowed cabotage—the carrying of passengers by a foreign carrier from one city in the host country to another city in the host country (e.g., Delta Airlines carrying a passenger from Vancouver to Montreal).

Thus, an airline like Delta could develop an elaborate hub-and-spoke system in Atlanta that would allow it to pick up a passenger in a U.S. city like Buffalo, transport her to Atlanta, and transfer her to a Delta flight going to Albuquerque. Using a hub-and-spoke system, Delta could provide convenient service to Buffalo-Albuquerque travelers, even though only a few passengers might wish to fly from Buffalo to Albuquerque on any given day. This advantage, however, stopped at the water's edge. Because of the Chicago Conference, Delta could not create a similar hub in Europe or Asia. However, by joining the SkyTeam Alliance, Delta can take advantage of Air France's hub in Paris, KLM's hub in Amsterdam, Aeroflot's hub in Moscow, and Korean Airlines' hub in Seoul. Thus, Delta and any other member of the SkyTeam alliance can advertise and offer service on over 13,000 flights a day to 900 cities in 169 countries even though it physically flies only a small percentage of these flights itself.

Besides offering customers more flights and more destinations, these marketing alliances make it easier for customers to transfer between alliance members' flights and allow customers to use frequent flyer miles earned on one carrier to fly free on the flights of other members of the alliance. The alliances also strive to maintain uniformly high standards of service and to promote consistent customer service policies. The SkyTeam alliance, for instance, coordinates its in-flight video offerings so that passengers flying different SkyTeam carriers on a given day see different movies on each leg of their journey.

Sources: www.staralliance.com; www.skyteam.com; www.oneworldalliance.com.

The Star Alliance is the largest of the three major consortia formed by international airlines to improve the service offered to travelers around the world. Among its newest members are Air China and Shanghai Airlines, whose entry into the Star Alliance led to this ceremony in Beijing.

FINANCIAL ALLIANCES A **financial alliance** is a functional alliance of firms that want to reduce the financial risks associated with a project. Partners may share equally in contributing financial resources to the project, or one partner may contribute the bulk of the financing while the other partner (or partners) provides special expertise or makes other kinds of contributions to partially offset its lack of financial investment. The strategic alliance between Boeing and its three Japanese partners was created primarily for financial purposes—Boeing wanted the other firms to help cover R&D and manufacturing costs. Those firms, in turn, saw a chance to gain valuable experience in commercial aircraft manufacturing as well as profits. Similarly, Marriott International and SAMHI Hotels Pvt Ltd., a hotel investment fund, created a financial alliance to introduce Marriott's midtier Fairfield hotel chain into the Indian market.[20] And 20th Century Fox and Paramount Pictures were financial allies in producing *Titanic,* one of the most successful movies in history.

RESEARCH AND DEVELOPMENT ALLIANCES Rapid technological change in high-technology industries and the skyrocketing cost of staying abreast of that change have prompted an increase in functional alliances that focus on R&D. In an **R&D alliance,** the partners agree to undertake joint research to develop new products or services. An example of a typical R&D alliance is one formed in 2000 among Intel, Micron Technology, Samsung, Hyundai, NEC, and Siemens to develop the next generation of DRAM chips.[21] Similarly, Bayer AG formed R&D alliances with smaller biotechnology companies like Millennium Pharmaceuticals and MorphoSys to strengthen their joint search for new miracle drugs.[22]

Such alliances are usually not formed as joint ventures, since scientific knowledge can be transmitted among partners through private research conferences, the exchange of scientific papers, and laboratory visits. Moreover, forming a separate legal organization and staffing it with teams of researchers drawn from the partners' staffs might disrupt ongoing scientific work in each partner's laboratory. Instead each partner may simply agree to cross-license whatever new technology is developed in its labs, thereby allowing its partner (or partners) to use its patents at will. Each partner then has equal access to all technology developed by the alliance, an arrangement that guarantees the partners will not fall behind each other in the technological race. Partners also are freed from legal disputes among themselves over ownership and validity of patents. For example, the alliance among Kodak, Fuji, and the three Japanese camera makers focused solely on R&D. Both Kodak and Fuji were licensed to make the new film they developed; the three camera makers were free to market the cameras to use it.

Because of the importance of high-tech industries to the world economy, many countries are supporting the efforts of R&D consortia as part of their industrial policies. An **R&D consortium** is a confederation of organizations that band together to research and develop new products and processes for world markets. It represents a special case of strategic alliance in that governmental support plays a major role in its formation and continued operation.[23] Japanese firms have successfully practiced this type of arrangement for many years. For example, more than two decades ago the Japanese government, Nippon Telephone and Telegraph, Mitsubishi, Matsushita, and three other Japanese firms agreed to work together to create new types of high-capacity memory chips. They were so successful that they dominated this market for many years. Similarly, the EU has developed a wide array of joint research efforts with clever acronyms—such as ESPRIT, RACE, BRITE, EURAM, JOULE, and SCIENCE—to ensure that its firms can compete against U.S. and Japanese firms in high-tech markets.

Implementation of Strategic Alliances

The decision to form a strategic alliance should develop from the firm's strategic planning process, discussed in Chapter 11. Having made this decision, its managers must then address several significant issues, which set the stage for how the arrangement will be managed.[24] Some of the most critical of these issues are the selection of partners, the form of ownership, and joint management considerations.

Selection of Partners

The success of any cooperative undertaking depends on choosing the appropriate partner(s). Research suggests that strategic alliances are more likely to be successful if the skills and resources of the partners are complementary—each must bring to the alliance some organizational strength the other lacks.[25] A firm contemplating a strategic alliance should consider at least four factors in selecting a partner (or partners): (1) compatibility, (2) the nature of the potential partner's products or services, (3) the relative safeness of the alliance, and (4) the learning potential of the alliance.

COMPATIBILITY The firm should select a compatible partner that it can trust and with whom it can work effectively. Without mutual trust, a strategic alliance is unlikely to succeed. But incompatibilities in corporate operating philosophies may also doom an alliance. For example, an alliance between General Electric Corporation (a U.K. firm unrelated to the U.S. firm of the same name) and the German firm Siemens failed because of incompatible management styles. The former firm is run by financial experts and the latter by engineers. General Electric Corporation's financial managers continually worried about bottom-line issues, short-term profitability, and related financial considerations. Siemens' managers, in contrast, paid more attention to innovation, design, and product development and less attention to financial issues.[26] In contrast, a key ingredient in Cereal Partners Worldwide's success is the high level of compatibility between General Mills and Nestlé.

NATURE OF A POTENTIAL PARTNER'S PRODUCTS OR SERVICES Another factor to consider is the nature of a potential partner's products or services. It is often hard to cooperate with a firm in one market while doing battle with that same firm in a second market. Under such circumstances, each partner may be unwilling to reveal all its expertise to the other partner for fear that the partner will use that knowledge against the firm in another market.

Most experts believe a firm should ally itself with a partner whose products or services are complementary to but not directly competitive with its own. The joint venture between General Mills and Nestlé is an example of this principle in action: Both are food-processing firms, but Nestlé does not make cereal, the product on which it is collaborating with General Mills. Similarly, PepsiCo and Lipton complement but do not compete with one another, thus raising the likelihood of success for their joint venture to market ready-to-drink tea in the United States.

THE RELATIVE SAFENESS OF THE ALLIANCE Given the complexities and potential costs of failed agreements, managers should gather as much information as possible about a potential partner before entering into a strategic alliance. For example, managers should assess the success or failure of previous strategic alliances formed by the potential partner. Also, it often makes sense to analyze the prospective deal from the other firm's side. What does the potential partner hope to gain from the arrangement? What are the partner's strengths and weaknesses? How will it contribute to the venture? Does the proposed arrangement meet its strategic goals? The probability of success rises if the deal makes good business sense for both parties.[27]

For example, Corning, Inc., created a joint venture—Asahi Video Products Company—by integrating its television glass production with the operations of Asahi Glass, a producer of large television bulbs. Corning believed this joint venture would be a sound one for several reasons:

- Asahi Glass's expertise in large television bulb technology complemented Corning's strength in other bulb sizes.
- The joint venture would benefit from Asahi Glass's ongoing business connections with the increasing number of Japanese television manufacturers that were establishing North American facilities.
- The combined strengths of the two firms would help both keep abreast of technological innovations in the video display industry.
- Asahi Glass would benefit from Corning's technology and marketing clout in the U.S. market.
- Corning had successfully operated another joint venture with Asahi Glass since 1965.

In fact, Corning is so good at developing joint ventures that almost half its profits are generated by joint ventures with leading MNCs like PPG, Dow Chemical, and Samsung.

THE LEARNING POTENTIAL OF THE ALLIANCE Before establishing a strategic alliance, partners should also assess the potential to learn from each other. Areas of learning can range from the very specific—for example, how to manage inventory more efficiently or how to train employees more effectively—to the very general—for example, how to modify corporate culture or

The New United Motor Manufacturing, Inc. (NUMMI) joint venture between Toyota and General Motors celebrated its 25th birthday in 2009. Located in a former GM assembly plant in Fremont, California, but managed by Toyota executives, NUMMI was created to allow each partner to acquire knowledge necessary to implement its future strategy. The joint venture was terminated after GM entered bankruptcy; its last vehicle was produced in 2010.

Jose Reyes/San Jose Mercury News/Newscom

how to manage more strategically. At the same time, however, each partner should carefully assess the value of its own information and not provide the other partner with any that will result in competitive disadvantage for itself should the alliance dissolve—a point we revisit in the next section.[28] "Venturing Abroad" discusses a successful alliance formed for learning purposes.

Form of Ownership

Another issue in establishing a strategic alliance is the exact form of ownership that is to be used. A joint venture almost always takes the form of a corporation, usually incorporated in the country in which it will be doing business. In some instances, it may be incorporated in a different country, such as one that offers tax or legal advantages. The Bahamas, for example, are sometimes seen as a favorable tax haven for the incorporation of joint ventures.

The corporate form enables the partners to arrange a beneficial tax structure, implement novel ownership arrangements, and better protect their other assets. This form also allows the

---

VENTURING ABROAD   LEARNING BY DOING

Toyota and GM enjoyed one of the more successful and long-lived joint ventures in the United States. In 1982 GM closed an old automobile manufacturing plant in Fremont, California, because it had become too costly and inefficient to run. In 1984 Toyota agreed to reopen the plant and manage it through a joint venture called NUMMI (New United Motor Manufacturing, Inc.). Although NUMMI was owned equally by the two partners, Toyota managed the facility and assembled automobiles for both. Each firm entered into the deal primarily to acquire knowledge. Toyota wanted to learn more about how to deal with labor and parts suppliers in the U.S. market; GM wanted to observe Japanese management practices firsthand. Toyota used its newly acquired information when it opened its own manufacturing plant in Georgetown, Kentucky, in 1988. GM used lessons learned from NUMMI in developing and operating its experimental automotive division, Saturn, and in organizing its newest European assembly plant in Eisenach, Germany. As a result,

productivity in this plant was double that of GM's plants in the United States. When GM entered into its $1.6 billion joint venture with Shanghai Automotive Industry Corporation to make Buicks in 1997, lessons learned at NUMMI played a critical role in the overwhelming success of that joint venture. However, by the late 2000s, the strategic and learning benefits of NUMMI to the partners had lessened. In the midst of its financial crisis and ensuing bankruptcy, in 2009 GM announced it would withdraw from the joint venture. Nonetheless, NUMMI must be rated a success: Both companies acquired the knowledge they sought through the creation of the joint venture.

Sources: "A giant falls," *The Economist*, June 4, 2009; "The car company in front," *The Economist*, January 27, 2005; "Testing GM's shock absorbers," *The Economist*, April 29, 1999; "Making a global alliance work," *Fortune*, December 17, 1990, pp. 121–126.

joint venture to create its own identity apart from those of the partners. Of course, if either or both of the partners have favorable reputations, the new corporation may choose to rely on those, perhaps by including the partners' names as part of its name.

A new corporation also provides a neutral setting in which the partners can do business. The potential for conflict may be reduced if the interaction between the partners occurs outside their own facilities or organizations. It may also be reduced if the corporation does not rely on employees identified with either partner and instead hires its own executives and workforce whose first loyalty is to the joint venture. For example, a joint venture formed by Corning and Genentech was not performing as well as expected. Corning soon discovered one source of the difficulties: Managers contributed by Genentech to the joint venture were actually on leave from Genentech. To ensure that these managers' loyalties were not divided between Genentech and the joint venture, Corning requested that they resign from Genentech. Once they did, the performance of the joint venture improved rapidly.[29]

In isolated cases, incorporating a joint venture may not be possible or desirable. For example, local restrictions on corporations may be so stringent or burdensome that incorporating is not optimal. The partners in these cases usually choose to operate under a limited partnership arrangement. In a limited partnership, one firm, the managing partner, assumes full financial responsibility for the venture, regardless of the amount of its own investment. The other partner (or partners) has liability limited to its own investment. Obviously, such arrangements are riskier for the managing partner.

PUBLIC-PRIVATE VENTURE   A special form of joint venture, a **public-private venture,** is one that involves a partnership between a privately owned firm and a government. Such an arrangement may be created under any of several circumstances.

When the government of a country controls a resource it wants developed, it may enlist the assistance of a firm that has expertise related to that resource. For example, South American countries have used several foreign lumber firms, such as Weyerhaeuser, to assist in the development of their rain forests and surrounding lands. A similar pattern exists in the discovery, exploration, and development of oil fields. National governments that control access to and ownership of oil fields may lack the technical expertise to drill for and manage the extraction of crude oil. International oil firms, on the other hand, possess the requisite knowledge and expertise but may lack the necessary drilling rights. A common result is a joint venture for which the government grants drilling rights and private oil firms provide capital and expertise. For example, in 2006 Exxon Mobil entered into a joint venture with the Abu Dhabi government, receiving a 28 percent interest in Abu Dhabi's Upper Zakum field; as part of the deal, the company agreed to establish a technology institute in Abu Dhabi and boost the field's production by 50 percent using advanced drilling and reservoir management techniques.[30]

Similarly, a firm may pursue a public-private venture if a particular country does not allow wholly owned foreign operations. If the firm cannot locate a suitable local partner, it may invite the government itself to participate in a joint venture, or the government may request an ownership share. Public-private ventures are typical in the oil industry. In assessing the opportunities and drawbacks of such a venture, a firm should consider the various aspects of the political and legal environment it will be facing. Foremost among these is the stability of the government. In a politically unstable country, the current government may be replaced with another, and the firm may face serious challenges. At best, the venture will be considered less important by the new government because of its association with the old government. At worst, the firm's investment may be completely wiped out, its assets seized, and its operation shut down. However, if negotiations are handled properly and if the local government is relatively stable, public-private ventures can be quite beneficial. The government may act benignly and allow the firm to run the joint venture. It may also use its position to protect its own investment—and therefore that of its partner—by restricting competing business activity.

A firm entering public-private partnerships should ensure that it thoroughly understands the expectations and commitments of both the host country's government and its prospective business partner. These concerns are most obvious in China. Because of the vast size and growth prospects of the Chinese market, many firms are interested in investment opportunities there, and joint ventures with state-owned firms are a common mode of entry for MNCs. Many Western firms have prospered through such arrangements. For example, Alcatel's joint venture with the Ministry of Post and Telecommunications, Shanghai Bell, captured more than half the market for switching equipment in the booming Chinese telecommunications market, much to the chagrin of its traditional rivals, Siemens and Nortel.

However, other Western firms have had their share of troubles with these arrangements, prompting a bitter joke among expatriates in China: "What qualities should you look for in a joint-venture partner?" "One who never comes to the office." For instance, Daimler-Benz signed an agreement in 1995 to establish a joint venture with state-owned Nanfang South China Motor Corporation to build minivans. Two years later, nothing had been done as the two partners bickered over a variety of issues. Nanfang, for example, wanted to assemble the minivans at two plant sites, while Daimler-Benz officials fought for a single plant so as to capture economies of scale.[31] Unilever had a different problem. Its joint venture partner in Shanghai not only continued to sell its own brand of detergent, White Cat, in competition with the Unilever product (Omo) produced by the joint venture, but it also began to copy Omo's formula and packaged its detergent in a box that looked almost identical to that of Omo. New Balance executives could sympathize with Unilever's plight. They discovered that their Chinese manufacturing partner was making counterfeit sneakers and selling them directly to discounters in England and Australia in addition to those it was legally making for New Balance itself.[32]

Joint Management Considerations

Further issues and questions are associated with how a strategic alliance will be managed.[33] Three standard approaches are often used to jointly manage a strategic alliance (see Figure 13.3): shared management agreements, assigned arrangements, and delegated arrangements.

Under a **shared management agreement,** each partner fully and actively participates in managing the alliance. The partners run the alliance, and their managers regularly pass on instructions and details to the alliance's managers. The alliance managers have limited authority of their own and must defer most decisions to managers from the parent firms. This type of agreement requires a high level of coordination and near-perfect agreement between the participating

FIGURE 13.3
Managing Strategic Alliances

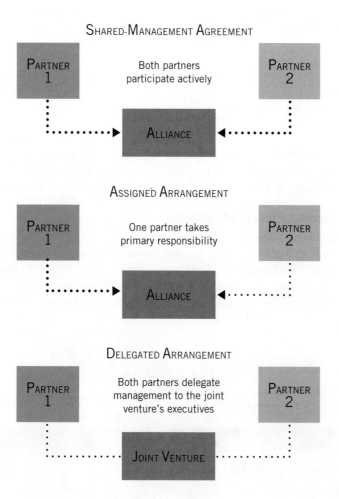

partners. Thus it is the most difficult to maintain and the one most prone to conflict among the partners. An example of this type of joint venture management is that used by Coca-Cola and France's Groupe Danone to distribute Coke's Minute Maid orange juice in Europe and Latin America. This joint venture combines Danone's distribution network and production facilities—Danone supplies between 15 and 30 percent of the dairy products sold by supermarkets in these countries—with the Minute Maid brand name. The joint venture operates under a shared management arrangement: Each company supplies three members of the JV's board of directors. Danone is responsible for the JV's operations, while Coke controls its marketing and finance.[34]

Under an **assigned arrangement,** one partner assumes primary responsibility for the operations of the strategic alliance. For example, GM, with a 67 percent stake in a joint venture with Raba, a Hungarian truck, engine, and tractor manufacturer, has assumed management control over the venture's operations.[35] Boeing controls the overall operations of its strategic alliance with Fuji, Mitsubishi, and Kawasaki for the design and production of its 777 and 787 commercial aircraft. Under an assigned arrangement, management of the alliance is greatly simplified because the dominant partner has the power to set its own agenda for the new unit, break ties among decision makers, and even overrule its partner(s). Of course, these actions may create conflict, but they keep the alliance from becoming paralyzed, which may happen if equal partners cannot agree on a decision.

Under a **delegated arrangement,** which is reserved for joint ventures, the partners agree not to get involved in ongoing operations and so delegate management control to the executives of the joint venture itself. These executives may be specifically hired to run the new operation or may be transferred from the participating firms. They are responsible for the day-to-day decision making and management of the venture and for implementing its strategy. Thus, they have real power and the autonomy to make significant decisions themselves and are much less accountable to managers in the partner firms. For example, both American Motors and the Beijing Automotive Works contributed experienced managers to the operation of Beijing Jeep so that its management team could learn both modern automobile assembly operations and operating conditions in China. Moreover, these managers were given responsibility for the joint venture's operations.

While it is important that both parties to the joint venture agree to the formal rules by which the venture will be managed, savvy international businesspersons recognize that in some instances the informal rules are equally important. Failure to appreciate the unwritten rules can sandbag foreign joint venture partners, as "Emerging Opportunities" explains.

Pitfalls of Strategic Alliances

Regardless of the care and deliberation a firm puts into constructing a strategic alliance, it still must consider limitations and pitfalls. Figure 13.4 summarizes five fundamental sources of problems that often threaten the viability of strategic alliances: incompatibility of partners, access to information, conflicts over distributing earnings, loss of autonomy, and changing circumstances.

Incompatibility of Partners

Incompatibility among the partners of a strategic alliance is a primary cause of the failure of such arrangements. At times, incompatibility can lead to outright conflict, although typically it merely leads to poor performance of the alliance. We noted earlier in the chapter the example of the conflict between Siemens's engineering-oriented management and General Electric Corporation's financially oriented management. Incompatibility can stem from differences in

FIGURE 13.4
Pitfalls of Strategic Alliances

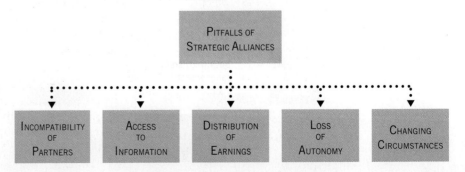

EMERGING OPPORTUNITIES | HU'S IN CHARGE

Webster's dictionary defines communism as a "social scheme which promotes the abolition of inequalities in the possession of wealth by distributing wealth equally or by holding all wealth in common for the benefit and use of all citizens." By that definition, contemporary China is not very communist. That does not mean that the Communist Party is unimportant, however, when doing business in or with China.

The most important person in the governance of any Chinese business organization of significant size is often the organization's party secretary. The party secretary is a member of the Chinese Communist Party (CCP), and is appointed by the CCP to be its representative within the organization. While a Chinese corporation or a joint venture with a Chinese partner may be formally governed by a board of directors, ultimate power resides with the party secretary. Appointments of executives and senior managers or major strategic decisions must be approved by the party secretary. Often, the party secretary informs the board as to decisions that have been made by the party, which the board must then implement. One telling example was the government's November 2004 decision to have the CEOs of the country's three largest telecommunications companies (China Telecom, China Mobile, and China Unicom) swap jobs among themselves. Although all three companies were state-owned enterprises, two of them were publicly listed with significant minority shareholders. Regardless of the formal role or wishes of their boards of directors, CCP leaders made the decision, which the three boards of directors then dutifully ratified.

Foreign companies must understand these informal, unwritten rules of governance or face the consequences, as New Zealand's Fonterra Corporation, the world's largest exporter of dairy products, learned to its chagrin. In 2005, Fonterra signed a joint venture agreement with Sanlu, China's premier dairy products firm. To implement the joint venture, Fonterra received a 43 percent ownership stake in Sanlu and was given three seats on Sanlu's board. Sanlu's rapid growth was attributable to its practice of buying milk in bulk from middlemen who in turn purchased it from local farmers. Sanlu began receiving scattered reports early in 2008 that some of the purchased milk, which it used to make its market-leading infant formula, was laced with melamine. Melamine boosted the apparent protein content of the milk, which raised the price that the seller received, but is highly toxic, causing kidney stones, bladder cancer, and damage to the reproductive system. By the end of July 2008 Sanlu's testing confirmed the problem.

Sanlu and its chairwoman Tian Wenhua—who also served as Sanlu's party secretary—faced a political as well as public health disaster. The Beijing Olympics were scheduled to begin on August 8, 2008, and the CCP made it clear it wanted no bad publicity to damage its desired triumphal staging of the summer games. When Sanlu's board met on August 2, it voted for a full product recall, according to Fonterra's minutes of the meeting. Sanlu's minutes indicate agreement on a limited product recall, the apparent result of intervention by the local vice-mayor in charge of product safety, who was mindful of the CCP's directive to suppress any food safety scandals while the eyes of the world's media and sports fans were focused on Beijing. A full product recall belatedly commenced in September, the result of New Zealand's ambassador notifying the Chinese government of the problem. While Fonterra executives claim that they first heard of the melamine contamination at the August 2nd board meeting, the damage to the firm's reputation will not be easy to repair. Fonterra learned too late that the party secretary, not the board of directors or the company's managers, is the one in charge.

Sources: Richard McGregor, *The Party* (New York: HarperCollins, 2010); "Convicted Sanlu boss blames Fonterra," *nzherald.co.nz*, January 28, 2009 (online); Xinting, Jia, "Corporate Governance in State Controlled Enterprises, *Journal of Business Systems, Governance, and Ethics*, Vol 1. No. 3; "China bank chiefs hit at Communist party role," *Financial Times*, April 28, 2005 (online); www.webster-dictionary.org.

Regardless of his or her formal role in the organization, the party secretary, who is appointed by the Communist Party, is the most powerful decision maker in many Chinese corporations and joint ventures. The General Secretary of the Chinese Communist Party—a position held by Hu Jintao since 2002—is the party's highest ranking official and the de facto leader of the country.

© vario images GmbH & Co.KG/Alamy

corporate culture, national culture, goals and objectives, or virtually any other fundamental dimension linking the two partners. For instance, General Motors' $340-million joint venture with Russian auto manufacturer OAO AvtoVAZ, which was established to build Chevrolet-branded compact sports utility vehicles designed by AvtoVAZ, has struggled as a result of disagreements between the partners over parts pricing, product design, market development, and adjustments in the joint venture's strategic direction.[36] Similarly, VW's management has been disappointed with the slow start of its joint venture with Suzuki, which it attributes to the methodical but time-consuming decision making of its Japanese partner.[37]

In many cases, compatibility problems can be anticipated if the partners carefully discuss and analyze the reasons why each is entering into the alliance in the first place. A useful starting point may be a meeting between top managers of the two partners to discuss their mutual interests, goals, and beliefs about strategy. The manner in which the managers are able to work together during such a meeting may be a critical clue to their ability to cooperate in a strategic alliance. Obviously, if the partners cannot agree on such basic issues as how much decision-making power to delegate to the alliance's business unit, what the alliance's strategy should be, how it is to be organized, or how it should be staffed, compromise will probably be difficult to achieve and the alliance is unlikely to succeed. For example, a marketing alliance between AT&T and Italy's Olivetti announced with great fanfare quickly failed after the firms could not reach agreement on a marketing strategy, what they wanted the alliance to accomplish, and how they planned to work together.

Access to Information

Limited access to information is another drawback of many strategic alliances. For a collaboration to work effectively, one partner (or both) may have to provide the other with information it would prefer to keep secret. It is often difficult to identify such needs ahead of time; thus, a firm may enter into an agreement not anticipating having to share certain information. When the reality of the situation becomes apparent, the firm may have to be forthcoming with the information or else compromise the effectiveness of the collaboration.[38]

For example, Unisys, a U.S. computer firm, negotiated a joint venture with Hitachi, a Japanese electronics firm. Only after the venture was well underway did Unisys realize that it would have to provide Hitachi with most of the technical specifications it used to build computers. Although Unisys managers reluctantly gave Hitachi the information, they feared they were compromising their own firm's competitiveness. And an alliance between Ford and Mazda to work on the design of a new Ford sedan almost stalled when Mazda officials would not allow their Ford counterparts to visit their research laboratory. After several weeks of arguing, a compromise was eventually reached whereby Ford engineers could enter the facility but only for a limited time.

Conflicts over Distributing Earnings

An obvious limitation of strategic alliances relates to the distribution of earnings. Because the partners share risks and costs, they also share profits. For example, General Mills and Nestlé split the profits from their European joint venture on a 50/50 basis. Of course, this aspect of collaborative arrangements is known ahead of time and is virtually always negotiated as part of the original agreement.

However, there are other financial considerations beyond the basic distribution of earnings that can cause disagreement. The partners must also agree on the proportion of the joint earnings that will be distributed to themselves as opposed to being reinvested in the business, the accounting procedures that will be used to calculate earnings or profits, and the way transfer pricing will be handled. For example, in the 1990s Rubbermaid ended its joint venture to manufacture and distribute rubber and plastic houseware products throughout Europe, North Africa, and the Middle East because its local partner, the Dutch chemical company DSM Group NV, resisted reinvesting profits to develop new products to expand the joint venture's sales as Rubbermaid preferred.[39]

Loss of Autonomy

Another pitfall of a strategic alliance is the potential loss of autonomy. Just as firms share risks and profits, they also share control, thereby limiting what each can do. Most attempts to introduce new products or services, change the way the alliance does business, or introduce any other significant organizational change first must be discussed and negotiated. To overcome such problems, FedEx chose to buy out its Chinese joint venture partner, Tianjin Datian W Group, for $400 million. The 2006 purchase freed FedEx to better integrate the joint venture's 90 parcel-processing facilities and its 3,000 workers into FedEx's global distribution network.[40] Conversely, as part of its contract with General Mills, Nestlé had to agree that if the joint venture is ever terminated, Nestlé cannot enter the North American cereal market for at least 10 years.

At the extreme, a strategic alliance may even be the first step toward a takeover. In the early 1980s, the Japanese firm Fujitsu negotiated a strategic alliance with International Computers, Ltd. (ICL), a British computer firm. After nine years of working together, Fujitsu bought 80 percent of ICL. One survey of 150 terminated strategic alliances found that more than three-fourths ended because a Japanese firm had taken over its non-Japanese partner.[41] In other cases, partners may accuse each other of opportunistic behavior, that is, trying to take unfair advantage of each other. For example, a joint venture between the Walt Disney Company and Sky Television, a British pay-TV channel operator, broke down after Sky accused Disney of deliberately delaying the supply of promised programming. Disney, in turn, accused Sky of proceeding too hastily and without consulting it.[42]

Changing Circumstances

Changing circumstances may also affect the viability of a strategic alliance. The economic conditions that motivated the cooperative arrangement may no longer exist, or technological advances may have rendered the agreement obsolete. For example, in 2008, Siemens announced it wished to terminate its joint venture with Fujitsu, Fujitsu Siemens Computers (FSC). Although FSC has been one of Europe's leading personal computer manufacturers since its creation in 1999, Siemens believed that the future profitability of the joint venture was unpromising due to increased competition from Hewlett-Packard, Dell, and Apple.[43] Similarly, in 2011, Johnson Controls sued to dissolve its joint venture with French battery manufacturer Saft Groupe SA to fabricate lithium-ion batteries for the automobile industry. The American company claimed that rapid technological change and the investments needed to maintain market leadership rendered the joint venture ineffective. Its French partner disagreed.[44]

MyManagementLab   Now that you have finished this chapter, go back to **www.pearsonglobaleditions.com/mymanagementlab** to continue practicing and applying the concepts you've learned.

CHAPTER REVIEW

Summary

Strategic alliances, in which two or more firms agree to cooperate for their mutual benefit, are becoming increasingly popular in international business. A joint venture, a common type of strategic alliance, involves two or more firms joining together to create a new entity that is legally separate and distinct from its parents.

Strategic alliances offer several benefits to firms that use them. First, they facilitate market entry. Second, they allow the partners to share risks. Third, they make it easier for each partner to gain new knowledge and expertise from the other partner(s). Finally, they foster synergy and competitive advantage among the partners.

The scope of strategic alliances can vary significantly. Comprehensive alliances involve a full array of business activities and operations. Functional alliances involving only one aspect of the business, such as production, marketing, finance, or R&D, are also common.

The decision to form a strategic alliance needs to be based on a number of different considerations. Selecting a partner is, of course, critically important and must take into account compatibility, the nature of the potential partner's products or services, the relative safety of the alliance, and the learning potential of the alliance. Selecting a form of organization is also very important to the success of the alliance. A special form of strategic alliance involves public and private partners. The management structure of the strategic alliance must also be given careful consideration.

Partners in a strategic alliance must be aware of several pitfalls that can undermine the success of their cooperative arrangement. These include incompatibility of the partners, access to information, conflicts over distributing earnings, loss of autonomy, and changing circumstances.

Review Questions

1. What are the basic differences between a joint venture and other types of strategic alliances?
2. Why have strategic alliances grown in popularity in recent years?
3. What are the basic benefits partners are likely to gain from their strategic alliance? Briefly explain each.
4. What are the basic characteristics of a comprehensive alliance? What form is it likely to take?
5. What are the four common types of functional alliances? Briefly explain each.
6. What is an R&D consortium?
7. What factors should be considered in selecting a strategic alliance partner?
8. What are the three basic ways of managing a strategic alliance?
9. Under what circumstances might a strategic alliance be undertaken by public and private partners?
10. What are the potential pitfalls of strategic alliances?

Questions for Discussion

1. What are the relative advantages and disadvantages of joint ventures compared to other types of strategic alliances?
2. Assume you are a manager for a large international firm, which has decided to enlist a foreign partner in a strategic alliance and has asked you to be involved in the collaboration. What effects, if any, might the decision to structure the collaboration as a joint venture have on you personally and on your career?
3. What factors could conceivably cause a sharp decline in the number of new strategic alliances formed?
4. Could a firm conceivably undertake too many strategic alliances at one time? Why or why not?
5. Can you think of any foreign products you use that may have been marketed in your country as a result of a strategic alliance? What are they?
6. What are some of the issues involved in a firm's trying to learn from a strategic alliance partner without giving out too much valuable information of its own?
7. Why would a firm decide to enter a new market on its own rather than using a strategic alliance?
8. What are some of the similarities and differences between forming a strategic alliance with a firm from your home country and forming one with a firm from a foreign country?
9. Otis Elevator has sought to obtain first-mover advantages by quickly entering emerging markets with the help of local partners. This strategy has proven very successful for Otis. Should all firms adopt this strategy? Under what conditions is this strategy most likely to be successful?

Building Global Skills

Break into small groups of four to five people. Assume your group is the executive committee (that is, the top managers) of Resteaze, Inc. Resteaze is a large manufacturer of mattresses, box springs, and waterbeds. The publicly traded firm is among the largest in the U.S. bedding market. It operates 15 factories, employs over 5,000 people, and last year generated $20 million in profits on sales of $380 million. Resteaze products are sold through department stores, furniture stores, and specialty shops and have the reputation of being of good quality and medium-priced.

Your committee is thinking about entering the European bedding market. You know little about the European market, so you are thinking about forming a joint venture. Your committee has identified three possible candidates for such an arrangement.

One candidate is Bedrest. Bedrest is a French firm that also makes bedding. Unfortunately, Bedrest products have a poor reputation in Europe and most of its sales stem from the fact that its products are exceptionally cheap. However, there are possibilities for growth in Eastern Europe. The consultant who recommended Bedrest suggests that your higher-quality products would mesh well with Bedrest's cheaper ones. Bedrest is known to be having financial difficulties because of declining sales. However, the consultant thinks the firm will soon turn things around.

A second candidate is Home Furnishings, Inc., a German firm that manufactures high-quality furniture. Its line of bedroom furniture (headboards, dressers, chests, and so on) is among the most popular in Europe. The firm is also known to be interested in entering the U.S. furniture market. Home Furnishings is a privately owned concern that is assumed to have a strong financial position. Because of its prices, however, the firm is not expected to be able to compete effectively in Eastern Europe.

Finally, Pacific Enterprises, Inc., is a huge Japanese conglomerate that is just now entering the European market. The firm does not have any current operations in Europe but has enormous financial reserves to put behind any new undertaking it might decide to pursue. Its major product lines are machine tools, auto replacement parts, communications equipment, and consumer electronics.

Your task is to assess the relative advantages and disadvantages of each of these prospective partners for Resteaze. The European market is important to you, this is your first venture abroad, and you want the highest probability for success. After assessing each candidate, rank the three in order of their relative attractiveness to your firm.

1. How straightforward or ambiguous was the task of evaluating and ranking the three alternatives?
2. Determine and discuss the degree of agreement or disagreement among the various groups in the class.

LOOK BEFORE YOU LEAP

Group Danone SA, the Paris-based marketer of yogurt, nonalcoholic beverages, and baby foods, has long been a savvy international competitor. Employing 101,000 persons, its sales in 2010 totaled €17 billion, 45 percent of which are outside its home base of Western Europe. It is the world's largest seller of fresh dairy products, and the second largest vendor of bottled water and infant nutrition products. Like many other MNCs, Danone believes emerging markets—which currently produce one-third of its sales—offer it significant opportunities for growth. Group Danone has adopted a strategy of allying with local companies to penetrate promising emerging markets. Danone contributes its financial clout, manufacturing expertise, and sophisticated marketing skills to these joint ventures, while the local partner contributes its knowledge of the host country's legal system, political process, distribution channels, and the consumption habits of local consumers.

In Bangladesh, for example, Danone created a joint venture with the Grameen Group (see page 167 for a fuller discussion of Grameen). Danone viewed Bangladesh's 159 million people as an untapped market. Grameen had two different, but complementary goals. It wished to improve nutrition in that country through the provision of healthier foods. It also wanted to reduce poverty by creating new markets for Bangladeshi farmers. To accommodate Grameen's goals, Danone had to make some changes in its normal business practices. For example, its local factory uses as little automation as possible, in order to maximize job creation, and Danone scientists tinkered with product formulas to eliminate the need for sugar, which would have had to have been imported. Grameen Danone's first product is low-priced Shoktidoi yogurt (Bengali for "yogurt that makes you strong"), which is fortified with vitamins to overcome nutritional deficiencies in the diet of rural children. Shoktidoi yogurt is made using milk provided by local farmers and is sweetened with molasses made from locally produced dates.

Danone adopted a similar strategy in entering the Chinese and Indian markets. In the former market, Danone established a partnership with Zong Qinghou, the entrepreneur who in the 1980s founded the Hangzhou Wahaha group, a drink manufacturer and owner of one of China's most famous brand names, Wahaha. Starting in 1996, Danone and the Wahaha group formed a series of joint ventures—a total of 38 in all—to produce soft drinks, sport drinks, tea, and bottled water. In most of these joint ventures, Danone had a 51 percent ownership share and Wahaha a 49 percent share.

On paper, these joint ventures were quite successful; most enjoyed large market shares with significant growth prospects. For example, Wahaha is the largest bottled-water marketer in China, with a 39 percent market share. Danone's joint venture with Hangzhou Wahaha and another small partner made Danone the country's largest soft drink seller, with an 18 percent market share. Its soft drink sales enjoyed annual growth rates between 10 and 15 percent in the past several years.

Despite the market successes of these companies, the relationship between Danone and Hangzhou fell apart. Danone argued that Zong Qinghou, the founder of Hangzhou Wahaha, set up without its permission 20 parallel soft-drink businesses, with cumulative sales of $1.46 billion, which operated outside of the Danone-Hangzhou agreement. Mr. Zong did not deny his creation of these parallel companies that compete with products made by the Danone-Hangzhou joint venture companies. Rather, he responded he was forced to do so to protect his rights to the Wahaha brand name and because Danone was not aggressive enough in building and investing in their joint venture operations. Zong also argued that Danone has been unfaithful as well, investing in other Chinese companies—such as the Mengui dairies and the Hui Yuan company, a manufacturer of fruit juices—that competed with their joint ventures.

Besides depriving it of its share of the profits, the parallel operations, in Danone's view, made it impossible to determine if the products sold to consumers were legitimate. Accordingly, Danone sued Mr. Zong and Hangzhou Wahaha in Chinese, Swedish, and American courts, alleging they had violated the joint-venture agreement. Danone did not fare well in Chinese courts. Danone claimed its joint ventures had the right to the Wahaha name. However, when Hangzhou Wahaha first submitted its request to transfer the Wahaha brand name to the joint ventures as was required by their contract, Chinese regulatory authorities failed to approve it. No reapplication of the request was ever made. Thus, in December 2007, the Hangzhou Arbitration Commission ruled that Danone had waited too long to demand that Wahaha transfer ownership of the Wahaha brand name to their joint ventures. Subsequent to this ruling, Danone suspended its lawsuits, hoping that the Chinese government would recognize the importance of protecting foreign companies' legal rights and that the Chinese and French governments would intervene to help settle the disputes. Its hopes for a political solution came to naught. Accordingly, in 2009, Danone chose to surrender: It sold its 51 percent share of the joint venture to Wahaha for €300 million, ending their dispute.

Danone had the opposite problem in India. Danone and the Wadia family each owned about one-quarter of their joint venture in India, Britannia Industries Ltd., with the remainder publicly held. Danone preferred to be more aggressive in introducing new products in India. Unfortunately, as part of its agreement with the Wadia family to market foodstuffs there, its 1995 contract stated it could only introduce new foodstuffs in the Indian market with the consent of the Wadia family, which is unwilling to do so. As was the case with its Wahaha joint ventures in China, in 2009 sold its stake in Britannia Industries to the Wadia family for $170 million.

Case Questions

1. Grameen Danone is a joint venture among two companies—the nonprofit Grameen Group and the for-profit Group Danone SA. What are the benefits of this joint venture to each of these companies? Why did each choose to participate in the joint venture?

2. From the perspective of each of the partners, are there any potential pitfalls to joining this joint venture?

3. Now consider Danone's joint venture in China. What were the benefits of this joint venture to each of these companies? Why did each choose to participate in the joint venture?

4. What could Danone have done to avoid the problems it is encountering in China and India?

Sources: "Danone's cheap trick," *Time*, August 23, 2010; "Danone exits China venture after years of legal dispute," *New York Times*, October 1, 2009; "Danone to quit joint venture with Wahaha," *Financial Times*, September 30, 2009; "Danone ends partnership with Wadia," *Financial Times*, April 14, 2009; "Danone's Wahaha appeal is dismissed," *Wall Street Journal*, August 6, 2008, p. B2; "Partners fight over Wahaha in China," *Wall Street Journal*, July 28, 2008, p. B1; "Arbiter rejects Danone's claims on China venture," *Wall Street Journal*, July 14, 2008, p. B3; "Danone willing to drop Wahaha suits," *Wall Street Journal*, December 14, 2007 (online); "Trademark ruling favors Wahaha," *Wall Street Journal*, December 11, 2007, p. B5; "Danone venture woes now crop up in India: Breakup may loom," *Wall Street Journal*, June 22, 2007, p. B3; "Danone's China strategy is set back," *Wall Street Journal*, June 15, 2007, p. A10; "China venture partner blames feud on Danone," *Wall Street Journal*, June 14, 2007 (online); "Danone seeks ways to fix China joint venture," *Wall Street Journal*, June 13, 2007, p. A8; "Danone China joint-venture chief quits amid feud," *Wall Street Journal*, June 8, 2007, p. A11; *Danone Social and Economic Report 2006*.

Endnotes

1. www.cerealpartners.co.uk/about-us/ accessed June 13, 2011; "Cereals—the next food frontier," *Wall Street Journal*, February 3, 2011; General Mills 2005 Annual Report; Ian Friendly, *Cereal Partners Worldwide: A World of Opportunity*, Vevey, Switzerland, June 8, 2005 (mimeo); "Breakfast cereals: The international market," *Euromonitor International*, June 9, 2000; "General Mills reports record earnings of 78 cents per share for fiscal 1997 third quarter," *PR Newswire*, March 12, 1997; "Cereal partners venture shakes up Kellogg's," *Eurofood*, July 1995, p. 24; Christopher Knowlton, "Europe cooks up a cereal brawl," *Fortune*, June 3, 1992, pp. 175-179; "Cafe au lait, a croissant-and Trix," *Business Week*, August 24, 1992, pp. 50–52.

2. "For Kodak's Advantix, double exposure as company re-launches camera system," *Wall Street Journal*, April 23, 1997, p. B1; "Camera system is developed but not delivered," *Wall Street Journal*, August 7, 1996, p. B1; "Kodak joins Fuji, others for project," *USA Today*, March 26, 1992, p. B1.

3. Peter J. Killing, "How to make a global joint venture work," *Harvard Business Review* (May–June 1982), pp. 120–127.

4. "Camera system is developed but not delivered," op. cit.

5. See Balaji Koka and John Prescott, "Strategic alliances as social capital: A multidimensional view," *Strategic Management Journal*, vol. 22 (2002), pp. 795–816.

6. David Lei and John W. Slocum, Jr., "Global strategic alliances: Payoffs and pitfalls," *Organizational Dynamics* (Winter 1991), pp. 44–62.

7. Michael E. Porter, *Competitive Strategy* (New York: Free Press, 1980), p. 275.

8. "Imax to open 75 China cinemas," *Financial Times*, March 25, 2011, p. 19.

9. "Cigna enters retail alliance in Brazil," *Financial Times*, March 21, 1997, p. 18.

10. Farok J. Contractor, "Ownership pattern of U.S. joint ventures abroad and the liberalization of foreign government regulations in the 1980s: Evidence from the benchmark surveys," *Journal of International Business Studies*, vol. 21, no. 1 (First Quarter 1990), pp. 55–73.

11. "Digging with the dragon," *The Economist*, December 18, 2010, p. 130.

12. Bruce Kogut, "Joint ventures: Theoretical and empirical perspectives," *Strategic Management Journal*, vol. 9 (1988), pp. 319–332; Andrew C. Inkpen and Paul W. Beamish, "Knowledge, bargaining power, and the instability of international joint ventures," *Academy of Management Review*, vol. 22, no. 1 (1997), pp. 177–202.

13. "Moody's grabs foothold in China," *Wall Street Journal*, April 14, 2006, p. C3.

14. See Duane Ireland, Michael Hitt, and Deepa Vaidyanath, "Alliance management as a source of competitive advantage," *Journal of Management*, vol. 28, no. 3 (2002), pp. 413–446.

15. "PepsiCo planning tea-drink venture with Unilever unit," *Wall Street Journal*, December 4, 1991, p. B8.

16. "Siemens, Motorola plan U.S. chip plant," *Wall Street Journal*, October 26, 1995, p. A18.

17. "Dow Chemical, Aramco finalize venture," *Wall Street Journal*, May 14, 2007, p. A3.

18. "Sony, Sharp form venture to make LCD-TV panels," *Wall Street Journal*, February 27, 2008, p. B2.

19. "Mattel forms an alliance with Bandai of Japan," *Wall Street Journal*, July 22, 1999, p. A20.

20. "Marriott plans India hotel expansion," *Wall Street Journal*, April 6, 2011, p. B8.

21. "Big chip makers join to develop new DRAM technology," *Wall Street Journal*, January 18, 2000, p. A21.

22. "Bayer forms research partnership for antibodies with MorphoSys," *Wall Street Journal*, December 23, 1999, p. A14.

23. Mariko Sakakibara, "Formation of R&D consortia: Industry and company effects," *Strategic Management Journal*, vol. 23 (2002), pp. 1033–1050.

24. See Yadong Luo, "Contract, cooperation, and performance in international joint ventures," *Strategic Management Journal*, vol. 23 (2002), pp. 903–919; see also Jeffrey Dyer, Prashant Kale, and Harbir Singh, "How to make strategic alliances work," *MIT Sloan Management Review* (Summer 2001), pp. 37–46.

25. J. Michael Geringer, "Strategic determinants of partner selection criteria in international joint ventures," *Journal of International Business Studies*, vol. 22, no. 1 (First Quarter 1991), pp. 41–62; Kathryn R. Harrigan, *Strategies for Joint Venture Success* (Lexington, MA: Lexington, 1985); Keith D. Brouthers, Lance Eliot Brouthers, and Timothy J. Wilkinson, "Strategic alliances: Choose your partners," *Long Range Planning*, vol. 28, no. 3 (1995), pp. 18–25.

26. Main, op. cit.

27. Stephen J. Kohn, "The benefits and pitfalls of joint ventures," *The Bankers Magazine* (May/June 1990), pp. 12–18.

28. See Eric Tsang, "Acquiring knowledge by foreign partners from international joint ventures in a transition economy," *Strategic Management Journal*, vol. 23 (2002), pp. 835–854.

29. Joseph E. Pattison, "Global joint ventures," *Overseas Business* (Winter 1990), pp. 24–29.

30. "The well," *Houston Chronicle*, April 2, 2006, p. D2; "Exxon Mobil gains piece of oil field in Abu Dhabi," *Houston Chronicle*, March 28, 2006, p. D10.

31. "Daimler-Benz may pull out of venture to build cars with Chinese company," *Wall Street Journal*, May 23, 1997, p. A8; "Going it alone," *The Economist*, April 19, 1997, pp. 54–55; "Ford hopes small investment in China will pay off big," *Wall Street Journal*, November 9, 1995, p. B3.

32. "A sneaker maker says China partner became its rival," *Wall Street Journal*, December 19, 2002, pp. A1, A8.

33. See R. Duane Ireland, Michael A. Hitt, and Deepa Vaidyanath, "Alliance management as a source of competitive advantage," *Journal of Management*, vol. 28, no. 3 (2002), pp. 413–446.

34. "Coke in venture with France's Danone to distribute orange juice overseas," *Wall Street Journal*, September 25, 1996, p. B8.

35. Nicholas Denton, "GM puts further DM100m into its Hungary venture," *Financial Times*, November 6, 1991, p. 7.

36. "Russian car maker comes under sway of old pal of Putin," *Wall Street Journal*, May 19, 2006, p. A1; "GM sees Russia as fertile ground," *Wall Street Journal*, April 7, 2006, p. A4.

37. "VW off to a slow start with Suzuki," *Financial Times*, March 11, 2011, p. 16.

38. Karen J. Hladik and Lawrence H. Linden, "Is an international joint venture in R&D for you?" *Research Technology Management* (July–August 1989), pp. 11–13.

39. "Rubbermaid ends venture in Europe, signaling desire to call its own shots," *Wall Street Journal*, June 1, 1994, p. A4.

40. "Flying start to FedEx's growth in China," *Financial Times*, February 15, 2006, p. 18.

41. Main, op. cit.

42. "Murdoch firm sues Disney, alleges violation of pact for pay TV in Britain," *Wall Street Journal*, May 17, 1989, p. B6.

43. "Siemens set to pull plug on venture with Fujitsu," *Wall Street Journal*, August 6, 2008, p. B1.

44. "Johnson controls seeks to dissolve battery venture," *Wall Street Journal*, May 18, 2011.

International Organization Design and Control

AFTER STUDYING THIS CHAPTER, YOU SHOULD BE ABLE TO:

1. Define and discuss the nature of international organization design and identify and describe the initial impacts of international business activity on organization design.

2. Identify and describe five advanced forms of international organization design and discuss hybrid global designs.

3. Identify and describe related issues in global organization design.

4. Explain the general purpose of control and the levels of control in international business.

5. Describe how international firms manage the control function.

Access a host of interactive learning aids at **www.pearsonglobaleditions.com/ mymanagementlab** to help strengthen your understanding of the chapter concepts.

MyManagementLab

QILAI SHEN/EPA/Newscom

LENOVO SPREADS ITS GLOBAL WINGS

Lenovo was started in Beijing by Chinese entrepreneur Liu Chuanzhi in 1984. The firm dabbled in a variety of high-tech industries before it began to focus on the personal computer market. Initially Lenovo made computers for other firms, most notably AST Research. In 1990, though, the firm launched its own brand of PC and by 1997 Lenovo was the top-selling PC company in its home country. As Lenovo grew, Liu structured his firm around the traditional functional areas such as operations, marketing, and finance, but also created a separate R&D group charged with exploring new technologies and commercializing existing technologies. The heads of each of these divisions worked directly with Liu as a team to make decisions and determine the firm's strategies.

Unfortunately, however, the company was not very successful in getting its computers accepted outside of China and the firm fell further and further behind leading computer firms such as IBM, Dell, Sony, and Toshiba. One reason for this was the lack of brand recognition. Another was that Lenovo simply did not have very many top managers with global experience. Hence, they did not have a deep understanding of foreign markets and how to penetrate those markets nor did they really know how to compete in a global marketplace.

But that began to change in 2005. During the early 2000s IBM, one of the world's most recognized computer companies, was developing a new strategy emphasizing informational technology and business services and concentrating on business clients. At the time IBM was also a major competitor in the personal computer market in both desktops and laptops (especially with its line of ThinkPad laptops). But IBM managers also felt that PCs were dropping in price so quickly that reasonable profit margins would be difficult to maintain. When the company finally decided to sell its PC operation in 2005, Lenovo was quick to jump on the opportunity and bought IBM's entire PC business for $1.75 billion. Lenovo was allowed to continue using the IBM name through 2007 but then began to brand all of its PCs with the Lenovo name.

Along with the PC business itself, Lenovo also got another extremely important asset—a team of skilled top managers well-versed in global PC markets. Senior IBM executives were quickly integrated throughout the top management structure and one of them, Stephen Ward, was appointed CEO of Lenovo. Liu, meanwhile, moved into the background but remained a director—he felt that Lenovo's best opportunity for the firm to gain international market share would be under the leadership of a seasoned global manager like Ward.

But almost from the start problems began to surface. Ward, for example, was extremely autocratic in how he made decisions and thought Lenovo should function in a highly centralized, command-and-control fashion. One of his first actions was to decrease the frequency of top management team meetings; he felt the functional vice presidents needed to spend more time running their own functional areas and less time meeting with him. Unfortunately, this alienated his new Chinese colleagues who believed that their roles were being diminished. Liu, for instance, had relied on a senior leadership team that worked together to make decisions, whereas Ward made most of the major decisions by himself. And at a more general level, the U.S. managers tried to impose a rigid, centralized, and bureaucratic structure throughout the new Lenovo. The Chinese, meanwhile, were highly resistant to these efforts, strongly preferring the more consensus-style structure that they had used previously.

Within a matter of months things came to a head. Among other changes, Ward was pushed out and replaced with William Amelio, a senior executive recruited from Dell Computer's highly successful Asia/Pacific operations. Amelio immediately indicated his intent to try to move Lenovo back toward the traditional Chinese structure. He also thought that the firm could benefit from an infusion of additional perspectives so he began to aggressively recruit new executives from other international high-tech firms such as Dell, Motorola, Samsung, and Toshiba. He also softened the rigid functional structure, and tried building more coordination across areas by creating cross-functional teams.

Unfortunately, though, Amelio's efforts at Lenovo yielded mixed results. On the one hand he led the development of a sophisticated and long-term international strategy that is still being followed today. He also successfully integrated numerous divisions and functions between the old IBM unit and Lenovo. But there were also major problems. For one thing, he never really made any major changes in how decisions were made, retaining much of the decision-making authority himself and continuing the command-and-control approach that had been Ward's downfall. For another, Lenovo began to lose market share. Its new products were not as well received in the marketplace as company directors had hoped, and profits began to drop. Internal conflict also became more significant, with the old-guard IBM executives in one camp, the Chinese executives who grew up in Lenovo from the beginning in a different camp, and the newly recruited executives from other firms in still a third camp.

Finally, in 2010 Liu Chuanzhi decided that he had to take action. He pushed Amelio to resign and took control of the firm himself. He then quickly restructured the upper ranks of Lenovo to fall more in line with the traditional Chinese approach. Under Amelio's U.S.-style approach, the

CEO had made most of the major decisions and then worked with business unit heads to execute them. Liu, though, re-formed the eight top managers at Lenovo into a close-knit team and then they all worked together to make decisions and formulate plans. After decisions and plans were made by consensus, the team continued to work together to ensure that they were implemented effectively and with buy-in from others throughout the organization. However, he also decided to continue Amelio's push away from functional divisions toward more cross-functional activity; he also increased the prominence of regional activities in different parts of the world.

Today Lenovo is headquartered in Hong Kong but has major operations in Beijing, Singapore, and Morrisville, North Carolina. The firm's products include PCs, workstations, servers, storage devices, and IT services. In 2010 Lenovo generated profits of $129 million on revenues of $16.6 billion and employed over 22,000 workers. Right now it's still too soon to know if the changes at Lenovo will improve its fortunes or not. But Liu believes that his new approach, which he calls a "blend of old Chinese thinking and modern global thinking," will soon carry the day.[1] ∎

The Lenovo case illustrates one of the most fundamental issues facing any international business—how much authority to retain at the top and how much to delegate to lower levels of the organization. In its earlier days the firm followed a consensus-oriented approach to authority. But as the firm sought to globalize, U.S. managers brought in to lead the firm installed a more centralized, command-and-control approach. Finally, though, as the firm's top management team again came to be dominated by Chinese executives Lenovo reverted back to its earlier consensus-based approach. As we will see in this chapter, this issue is an important component in managing international organization design and control.

In this chapter we describe the various organization designs that international businesses use to help achieve their strategic goals. Because these designs typically evolve along a well-defined path as firms become more international, we first discuss the initial forms of organization design firms use as they begin to internationalize their operations.[2] We then analyze the more advanced forms of organization design that firms adopt as they broaden their participation in international business to become true multinational corporations (MNCs). Next we discuss several related issues in global organization design. We conclude by describing another important management function related to organization design: control.

The Nature of International Organization Design

Organization design (sometimes called organization structure) is the overall pattern of structural components and configurations used to manage the total organization.[3] The appropriate design for any given organization may depend on the firm's size, strategy, technology, and environment, as well as the cultures of the countries in which the firm operates. Organization design is also the basic vehicle through which strategy is ultimately implemented and through which the work of the organization is actually accomplished.

A firm cannot function unless its various structural components are appropriately assembled.[4] Through its design the firm does four things. First, it allocates organizational resources. Second, it assigns tasks to its employees. Third, it informs those employees about the firm's rules, procedures, and expectations about the employees' job performances. Fourth, it collects and transmits information necessary for problem solving, decision making, and effective organizational control.[5] This last task is particularly important for large MNCs, which must manage sharing vast amounts of information between corporate headquarters and subsidiaries and staff spread worldwide.

An organization's structure is not created and then left alone; organization design is an ongoing process. Indeed, managers change the design of their firms almost continually. One study found that most firms and divisions of large firms make moderate design changes about once a year and one or more major design changes every four to five years.[6] These changes often result from changes in a firm's strategy because an important characteristic of a successful firm is its ability to match its strategy with a compatible organization design, as Lenovo has sought to do.[7] For example, even though Lenovo is less than 30 years old the firm has undergone dozens of major organization design changes as well as hundreds of smaller ones. And clearly, a strategy calling for increased internationalization will have an impact on the firm's organization design.

To see how this begins to happen, we will start by considering a domestic firm that has no international sales. Many entrepreneurs, particularly in larger economies such as those of the United States, Japan, and Germany, start new firms in response to some perceived need in the local market; they give little immediate thought to the international marketplace. Also, many small, domestically oriented firms enter international markets passively through indirect exporting, as discussed in Chapter 12. Because such indirect exporting occurs as a routine part of the firm's domestic business, the firm's organization design need not change at all.

Now assume that the hypothetical firm just described begins to engage in direct exporting on a modest level. Its initial response to international sales and orders is the **corollary approach,** whereby the firm delegates responsibility for processing such orders to individuals within an existing department, such as finance or marketing. Under this approach the firm continues to use its existing domestic organization design. This approach is typical of a firm that has only a very small level of international activity.

As a firm's export sales become more significant, however, its next step usually is to create a separate export department. The **export department** takes responsibility for overseeing international operations, marketing products, processing orders, working with foreign distributors, and arranging financing when necessary. Initially, the head of the export department may report to a senior marketing or finance executive. As exports grow in importance, however, the export department of a small- to medium-size firm may achieve equality on the organization chart with finance, marketing, human resources, and other functional areas.

When selling to foreign customers is not fundamentally different from selling to domestic ones, the export department may get by with knowing only a little about foreign markets. However, as international activities increase, firms often find that an export department no longer serves their needs. Once a firm begins to station employees abroad or establish foreign subsidiaries to produce, distribute, and/or market its products, managerial responsibilities, coordination complexities, and information requirements all swell beyond the export department's capabilities and expertise. Familiarity with foreign markets becomes more important and new methods for organizing may be required.

Firms respond to the challenges of controlling their burgeoning international business by changing their organization design through the creation of an international division that specializes in managing foreign operations. The **international division** allows a firm to concentrate resources and create specialized programs targeted on international business activity while simultaneously keeping that activity segregated from the firm's ongoing domestic activities.

Global Organization Designs

As a firm evolves from being domestically oriented with international operations to becoming a true multinational corporation with global aspirations, it typically abandons the international division approach. In place of that division it usually creates a global organization design to achieve synergies among its far-flung operations and to implement its organizational strategy.[8] For example, for several years Aetna maintained a separate division for its small but growing international operations. When its international revenues more than doubled during a three-year period, however, the firm announced plans to eliminate the international division and integrate Aetna's global initiatives into its existing structure. Executives at the firm indicated that their new structure would make it easier to transfer knowledge and technology between international markets.[9] Indeed, the global design adopted by any firm must deal with the need to integrate three types of knowledge to compete effectively internationally:[10]

- Area knowledge: Managers must understand the cultural, commercial, social, and economic conditions in each host country market in which the firm does business.
- Product knowledge: Managers must comprehend such factors as technological trends, customer needs, and competitive forces affecting the goods the firm produces and sells.
- Functional knowledge: Managers must have access to coworkers with expertise in basic business functions such as production, marketing, finance, accounting, human resource management, and information technology.

The five most common forms of global organization design are product, area, functional, customer, and matrix. As we will discuss, each form allows the firm to emphasize one type of knowledge, yet perhaps each also makes it more difficult to incorporate the other types of knowledge into the firm's decision-making processes. Accordingly, the global design the MNC chooses will reflect the relative importance of each of the three types of knowledge in the firm's operations, as well as its need for coordination among its units, the source of its firm-specific advantages, and its managerial philosophy about its position in the world economy.[11]

MNCs typically adopt one of three managerial philosophies that guide their approach to such functions as organization design and marketing. The ethnocentric approach is used by firms that operate internationally the same way they do domestically. The polycentric approach is used by firms that customize their operations for each foreign market they serve. The geocentric approach is used by firms that analyze the needs of their customers worldwide and then adopt standardized operations for all markets they serve. (We discuss these concepts more fully in Chapter 16.)

Global Product Design

The most common form of organization design adopted by MNCs is the global product design. The **global product design** assigns worldwide responsibility for specific products or product groups to separate operating divisions within a firm. This design works best when the firm has diverse product lines or when its product lines are sold in diverse markets, thereby rendering the need for coordination between product lines relatively unimportant. If the products are related, the organization of the firm takes on what is often called an M-form design; if the products are unrelated, the design is called an H-form design. The M in M-form stands for "multidivisional"—the various divisions of the firm are usually self-contained operations with interrelated activities. The H in H-form stands for "holding," as in "holding company"—the various unrelated businesses function with autonomy and little interdependence. After selling its specialty chemicals group (as discussed in this chapter's closing case), Unilever became an M-form business because the businesses it chose to retain were all somewhat related to one another.

Samsung Group is the largest business in Korea, with 2010 revenues of $134 billion and 277,000 employees. Samsung uses the H-form global product design, shown in Figure 14.1. The firm is organized into four major divisions: the electronics group, the chemical products group, the financial services group, and another group of smaller businesses. Each of these groups has little in common with the others and functions separately from them. Similarly, the other affiliated companies group includes businesses that are also unrelated, including a catering business, a small hotel chain, an amusement park, a professional baseball team, and a small group of hospitals and medical centers.

The global product design provides several potential competitive advantages. First, because a division focuses on a single product or product group, the division managers gain expertise in all aspects of the product or products, better enabling them to compete globally. Second, the global product design facilitates efficiencies in production because managers are free to manufacture the product wherever manufacturing costs are the lowest. It also allows managers to coordinate production at their various facilities, shifting output from factory to factory as global

FIGURE 14.1

Samsung Corporation's Global Product Design

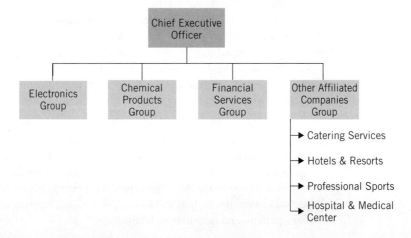

Samsung Group is a large and complex multinational business. This display board at the Samsung Electronics factory in Suwon, south of Seoul, illustrates the vast array of facilities the firm's managers oversee. And the electronics business is just one of four major divisions that constitute Samsung's overall operations.

Jung Yeon-Je/Getty Images, Inc.

demand or cost conditions fluctuate. Further, because managers have extensive product knowledge, they are better able to incorporate new technologies into their product(s) and respond quickly and flexibly to technological changes that affect their market. The global product design also facilitates global marketing of the product. The firm gains flexibility in introducing, promoting, and distributing each product or product group. Rather than being tied to one marketing plan that encompasses the whole firm, individual product line managers may pursue their own plans. Finally, because the global product design forces managers to think globally, it facilitates geocentric corporate philosophies. This is a useful mind-set as firms work to develop greater international skills internally.[12]

The global product design also has disadvantages, however. For one, it may encourage expensive duplication because each product group needs its own functional-area skills such as marketing, finance, and information management, and sometimes even its own physical facilities for production, distribution, and research and development (R&D). Similarly, each product group must develop its own knowledge about the cultural, legal, and political environments of the various regional and national markets in which it operates. Coordination and corporate learning across product groups also becomes more difficult. If such coordination is an important part of the firm's international strategy, a different global design, such as the global area design, may be preferable. Thus, businesses must carefully consider the relative advantages and disadvantages of using the global product design when deciding the best form of organization design for their particular circumstances.

Global Area Design

The **global area design** organizes the firm's activities around specific areas or regions of the world. This approach is particularly useful for firms with a polycentric or multidomestic corporate philosophy.[13] A global area design is most likely to be used by a firm whose products are not readily transferable across regions. "Emerging Opportunities" discusses how many firms doing business in China are using the global area design.

As shown in Figure 14.2, Adecco S.A. uses the global area design.[14] Adecco, a Swiss firm, is the world's largest temporary employment agency, serving over 100,000 clients from more than 5,500 offices worldwide. The firm has eight basic divisions, each representing a

FIGURE 14.2

Adecco S.A.'s Global Area Design

different area of the world where Adecco does business. Managers in each area division handle recruiting, distribution, promotion, advertising, client services, and other functions for their particular region.

The global area design is particularly useful for a firm whose strategy is marketing-driven rather than predicated on manufacturing efficiencies or technological innovation or for a firm whose competitive strength lies in the reputation of its brand name products. Both conditions apply to Adecco. Further, the geographical focus of this design allows a firm to develop expertise about the local market. Area managers can freely adapt the firm's products to meet local needs and can quickly respond to changes in the local marketplace. They also can tailor the product mix they offer within a given area. For example, Adecco managers must adapt their practices to local demand for temporary employment as well as different labor laws and cultural differences regarding employment relationships.

The global area design does have disadvantages, however. By focusing on the needs of the area market, the firm may sacrifice cost efficiencies that might be gained through global production. Diffusion of technology is also slowed because innovations generated in one area division may not be adopted by all the others. Thus, this design may not be suitable for product lines undergoing rapid technological change. Further, the global area design results in duplication of resources because each area division must have its own functional specialists, product experts, and, in many cases, production facilities. And finally, it makes coordination across areas expensive and discourages global product planning.

Global Functional Design

The **global functional design** calls for a firm to create departments or divisions that have worldwide responsibility for the common organizational functions—finance, operations, marketing, R&D, and human resources management. This design is used by MNCs that have relatively narrow or similar product lines. It results in what is often called a U-form organization, where the U stands for "unity." Lenovo used this design in the early years of its existence. Another example of the global functional design is that used by British Airways, shown in Figure 14.3. This firm is essentially a single-business firm—it provides air transport services—and has company-wide functional operations dedicated to marketing and operations, public affairs, engineering, corporate finance, human resources, and other basic functions.

The global functional design offers several advantages. First of all, the firm can easily transfer expertise within each functional area. For example, Exxon Mobil uses the global functional design, so production skills learned by Exxon Mobil's crews operating in the Gulf of Mexico can be used by its offshore operations in Malaysia's Jerneh field, and new catalytic cracking technology tested at its Baton Rouge, Louisiana, refinery can be adopted by its refineries in Singapore and Trecate, Italy. Second, managers can maintain highly centralized control over functional operations. For example, the head of Exxon Mobil's refinery division can rapidly adjust the production runs or product mix of refineries to meet changes in worldwide demand, thereby achieving efficient usage of these very expensive corporate resources. Finally, the global functional design focuses attention on the key functions of the firm. For example, managers can easily isolate a problem in marketing and distinguish it from activities in other functional areas.

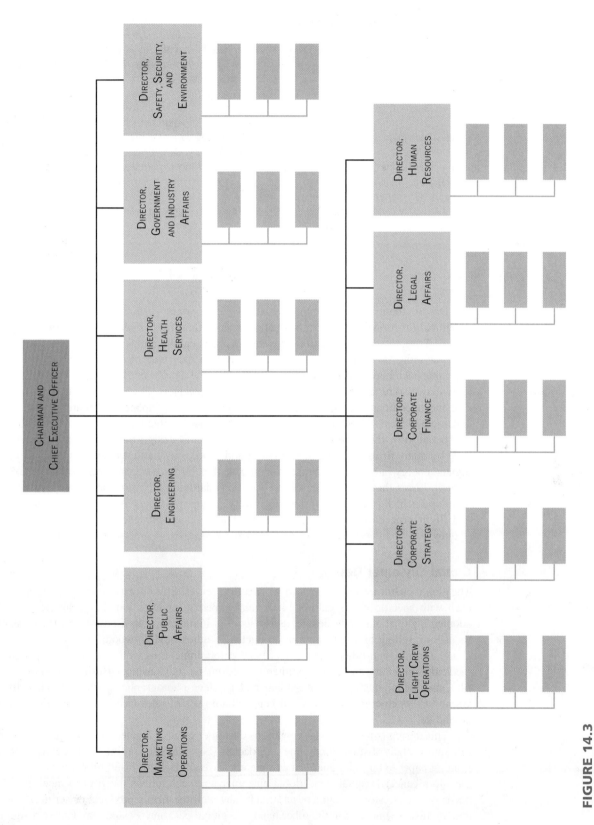

FIGURE 14.3
British Airways' Global Functional Design

EMERGING OPPORTUNITIES **FLYING SOLO IN CHINA**

When most foreign firms doing business in China first set up shop in that country, they used a local partner. Such partners were generally required by Chinese law, and they theoretically served an important role in helping foreign managers better navigate the Chinese bureaucratic maze. For instance, U.S. companies have signed well over 100,000 contracts to do business in China, and virtually all those contracts included one or more local partners.

But in recent years, however, observers have begun to notice some changes. As part of its efforts to be admitted into the World Trade Organization and wanting to put forward as business-friendly a face as possible, the country has started easing its requirements for local business partners in selected industries. (Telecommunications firms, automakers, and energy companies still require local partners.) Foreign firms have quickly started to take advantage of the new rules.

Many had found, for instance, that their local partners were serving little purpose and were instead a drain on assets. Others may have benefited from the local partner but had subsequently learned what they needed to know about doing business in China and were prepared to work alone.

As a result, two things have been happening. First, many foreign firms partnering with local firms have been buying out their joint venture partners. Second, foreign firms have been steering their new investments into wholly owned subsidiaries and businesses. Procter & Gamble, Kimberly-Clark, Dow Chemical, and Delphi Automotive are among the businesses moving aggressively in these new directions. In general firms that are taking this approach are setting up their Chinese operations as separate business units. This allows the firms to focus on the needs of local consumers and maintain a concentrated focus on the evolving Chinese marketplace.[15]

Despite these advantages, this design is inappropriate for many businesses. For one thing, the global functional design is practical only when the firm has relatively few products or customers. For another, coordination between divisions can be a major problem. For example, the manufacturing division and the marketing division may become so differentiated from each other that each may start pursuing its own goals to the detriment of the firm as a whole. Finally, there may also be duplication of resources among managers. For example, the finance, marketing, and operations managers may each hire an expert on Japanese regulation, when a single expert could have served all three functional areas just as effectively.

Because of these problems, the global functional design has limited applicability. It is used by many firms engaged in extracting and processing natural resources, such as the mining and energy industries, because in their case the ability to transfer technical expertise is important. Firms that need to impose uniform standards on all their operations also may adopt this approach. For example, to ensure safety, British Airways standardizes its maintenance and flight procedures regardless of whether a flight originates in London, Hong Kong, or Sydney.

Global Customer Design

The **global customer design** is used when a firm serves different customers or customer groups, each with specific needs calling for special expertise or attention. For example, Kodak has adopted a global customer design, as is shown in Figure 14.4. Its Commercial Business Group focuses on selling high-quality film products to studios in Hollywood, London, Munich, Hong Kong, Toronto, and other centers for filmed entertainment, as well as film and supplies to the medical community and other commercial customers. Its Consumer Business Group sells both film and digital media to professional and amateur photographers, while its New Business Group targets emerging markets and new technologies of relevance to leading-edge customers around the world.[16]

This design is useful when the various customer groups targeted by a firm are so diverse as to require totally distinct marketing approaches. For example, selling four packages of image printing paper to an individual is a completely different task from selling medical imaging supplies to a cancer hospital. The global customer approach allows the firm to meet the specific needs of each customer segment and track how well the firm's products or services are doing among those segments. On the other hand, the global customer design may lead to a significant duplication of resources if each customer group needs its own area and functional specialists. Coordination between the different divisions is also difficult because each is concerned with a fundamentally different market.

FIGURE 14.4

Eastman Kodak's Global Customer Design

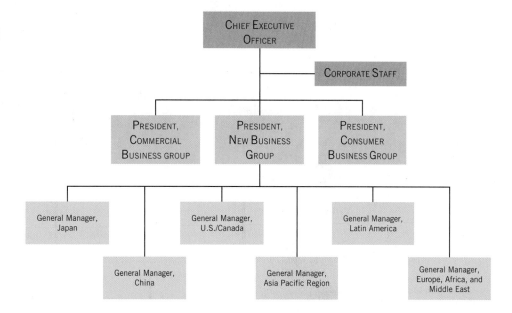

Global Matrix Design

The most complex form of international organization design is the global matrix design.[17] A **global matrix design** is the result of superimposing one form of organization design on top of an existing, different form. The resulting design is usually quite fluid, with new matrix dimensions being created, downscaled, and eliminated as needed. For example, the global matrix design shown in Figure 14.5 was created by superimposing a global product design (shown down the side) on an existing global functional design (shown across the top). This was the design that Lenovo's America managers attempted to use. Using a global matrix design, a firm can form specific product groups comprising members from existing functional departments. These product groups can then plan, design, develop, produce, and market new products with appropriate input from each functional area. In this way the firm can draw on both the functional and the product expertise of its employees. After a given product development task is completed, the product group may be dissolved; its members will then move on to new assignments. Of course, other matrix arrangements are possible. For example, an area design could be overlaid on a functional design, thereby allowing area specialists to coordinate activities with functional experts.

An advantage of the global matrix design is that it helps bring together the functional, area, and product expertise of the firm into teams to develop new products or respond to new challenges in the global marketplace. For example, Texas Instruments (TI) often uses a global matrix design for new product development, although its underlying organization design is based on function. At any one time TI has several product development groups in operation, which draw members from relevant functional groups and work toward creating new products or new uses for existing ones. If and when such breakthroughs are achieved, matrix-based product groups are used to transfer the new technology throughout the rest of the firm. After the task assigned to the product group is completed (for example, after the new product has been launched), the group may be dissolved.

The global matrix design thus promotes organizational flexibility. It allows firms to take advantage of functional, area, customer, and product organization designs as needed while simultaneously minimizing the disadvantages of each. Members of a product development team can be added or dropped from the team as the firm's needs change. The global matrix design also promotes coordination and communication among managers from different divisions.

The global matrix design has limitations, however. First of all, it is not appropriate for a firm that has few products and that operates in relatively stable markets. Second, it often puts employees in the position of being accountable to more than one manager. For example, at any given time an employee may be a member of his or her functional, area, or product group as

FIGURE 14.5

A Global Matrix Design

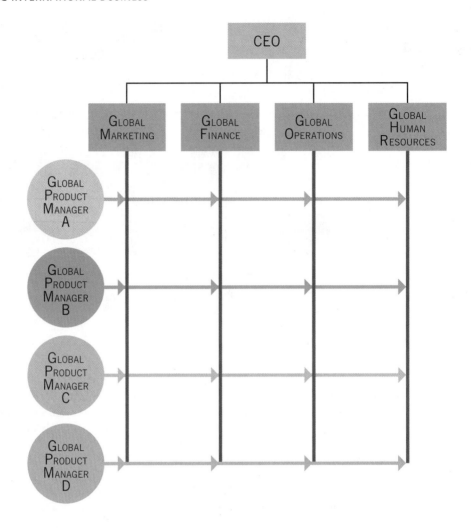

well as of two or three product development groups. As a result, the individual may have split loyalties—caught between competing sets of demands and pressures as the area manager to whom the employee reports wants one thing and the product line manager wants another. Similarly, the global matrix design creates a paradox regarding authority. On the one hand, part of the design's purpose is to put decision-making authority in the hands of those managers most able to use it quickly. On the other hand, because reporting relationships are so complex and vague, getting approval for major decisions may actually take longer. And finally, the global matrix design tends to promote compromises, or decisions based on the relative political clout of the managers involved.[18]

Hybrid Global Designs

Each global form of international organization design described in this section represents an ideal or pure type. Most firms, however, create a hybrid design that best suits their purposes, as dictated in part by the firms' size, strategy, technology, environment, and culture. Most MNCs are likely to blend elements of all the designs discussed. A firm may use a global product design as its overall approach, but it may have more of a functional orientation or area focus in some of its product groups than in others. In fact, if it were possible to compare the designs used by the world's 500 largest MNCs, no two would look exactly the same. A firm's managers start with the basic prototypes, merge them, throw out bits and pieces, and create new elements unique to their firm as they respond to changes in the organization's strategy and competitive environment. In many ways, Lenovo is using a hybrid design today. Specifically, its current design reflects functional, area, and matrix components.

Figure 14.6 illustrates how Nissan Motor Corporation uses a hybrid design to structure its U.S. operations. At the top level of the firm Nissan has some managers dedicated to products (such as the vice president and general manager for the Infiniti division) and others dedicated to

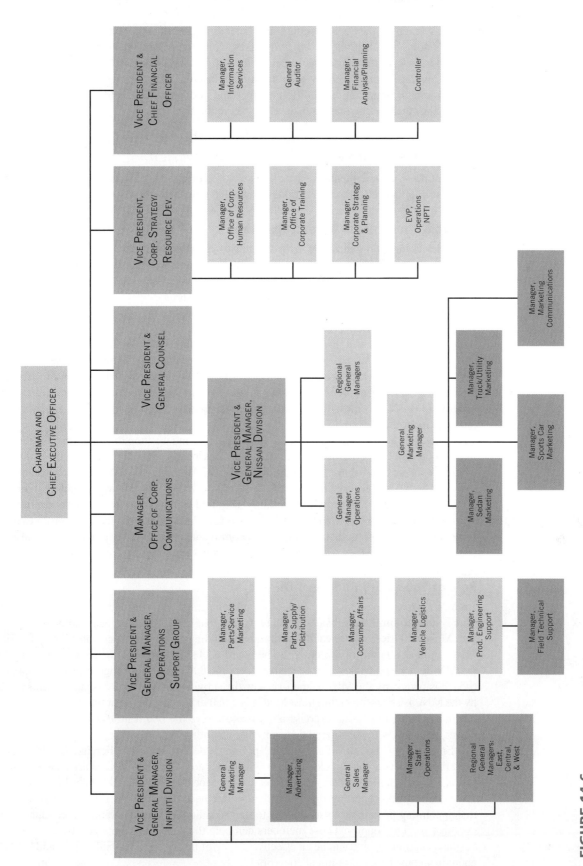

FIGURE 14.6
Nissan USA's Hybrid Design

functions (such as the vice president and chief financial officer). The marketing function for Nissan automobiles is broken down by product, with specific units responsible for sedans, sports cars, and trucks and utility vehicles. Both the Infiniti and Nissan divisions also have regional general managers organized by area. In similar fashion all large international firms mix and match forms of organization in different areas and at different levels to create hybrid organization designs that their managers believe best serve the firm's needs.

Related Issues in Global Organization Design

In addition to the fundamental issues of organization design we have addressed, MNCs also face a number of other related organizational issues that must be carefully managed.

Centralization versus Decentralization

When designing its organization, an MNC must make a particularly critical decision that determines the level of autonomy, power, and control it wants to grant its subsidiaries. Suppose it chooses to decentralize decision making by allowing individual subsidiaries great discretion over strategy, finance, production, and marketing decisions, thereby letting those decisions be made by managers closest to the market. These managers may then focus only on the subsidiary's needs rather than on the firm's overall needs. An MNC can remedy this deficiency by tightly centralizing decision-making authority at corporate headquarters. Decisions made by the corporate staff can then take into account the firm's overall needs. However, these decisions often hinder the ability of subsidiary managers to quickly and effectively respond to changes in their local market conditions. Because both centralization and decentralization offer attractive benefits to the MNC, most firms constantly tinker with a blend of the two to achieve the best outcome in terms of overall strategy.[19]

Numerous U.S. businesses have stumbled after setting up shop in China because they try to maintain centralized control from abroad. This has been especially problematic in industries where responsiveness to market conditions is critical. Both Google and eBay, for instance, have struggled in China because small local rivals have been more nimble in responding to customer preferences. Amazon, meanwhile, recently acquired a major online Chinese retailer called Joyo.com. Amazon founder and CEO Jeff Bezos has vowed to not replicate the mistakes of other firms, but instead insists that the local Joyo.com managers will have a great deal of discretion and control over how they responds to peculiarities in the Chinese market.[20]

Role of Subsidiary Boards of Directors

An MNC typically incorporates each of its subsidiaries in the subsidiary's country of operation. This is done to limit the subsidiary's liability and to allow it to attain legal status as a local citizen. Most countries require each corporation, including a wholly owned subsidiary of a foreign MNC, to have a board of directors.[21] The board is elected by corporate shareholders (which is the MNC), is responsible to those shareholders for the effective management of the subsidiary (which is owned by the MNC), and oversees the activities of top-level managers (who are hired by the MNC). The issue facing most MNCs is whether to view the creation of a subsidiary board of directors as a pro forma exercise and therefore give the board little real authority or to empower the board with substantial decision-making authority.[22]

Empowering the subsidiary's board promotes decentralization. Foreign subsidiaries may need the authority to act quickly and decisively without having to always seek the parent's approval. Also, if the MNC decentralizes authority to local levels, an active board provides a clear accountability and reporting link back to corporate headquarters. Some MNCs also have found that appointing prominent local citizens to the subsidiary's board is helpful in conducting business in a foreign country. These members can help the subsidiary integrate itself into the local business community and can be an effective source of information for both parent and subsidiary about local business and political conditions.

For example, prominent local business officials on the board of Apple's Japanese subsidiary were key to the firm's early success in the Japanese market. They enhanced the credibility of Apple's products in a country where corporate connections and status are an important marketing tool, while their appointment demonstrated Apple's long-term commitment to the

Japanese market. A subsidiary board also can help monitor the subsidiary's ethical and social responsibility practices. A potential disadvantage of empowering a subsidiary's board is that the subsidiary may become too independent as its board assumes substantial authority and thereby fails to maintain the desired level of accountability to the parent.[23]

In general a subsidiary board is most useful when the subsidiary has a great deal of autonomy, its own self-contained management structure, and a business identity separate from the parent's. Active subsidiary boards are particularly useful in H-form organizations because a holding company's subsidiaries are typically run independently of one another. For example, Nestlé's U.S. subsidiary, Carnation, meets each of the three criteria noted above. Not surprisingly, therefore, Carnation also has a very active board of directors. Honda, Matsushita, Hewlett-Packard, and Dow also empower their local boards of directors to make decisions and respond to local conditions.

Coordination in the Global Organization

Finally, as part of creating an effective design for itself, an international firm must address its coordination needs. **Coordination** is the process of linking and integrating functions and activities of different groups, units, or divisions. Coordination needs vary as a function of interdependence among the firm's divisions and functions. In other words, the higher the level of interdependence among divisions and functions, the more coordination is necessary among them.

MNCs can use any of several strategies to achieve and manage their desired level of coordination. The organizational hierarchy itself is one way to manage interdependence and promote coordination. An organization design that clearly specifies all reporting relationships and directions of influence facilitates coordination because each manager knows how to channel communications, decision making, and so on. Rules and procedures also facilitate coordination. For example, a standard operating procedure that requires the reporting of monthly and quarterly revenue, cost, and profit data to headquarters allows corporate staff to coordinate the firm's cash flows and to quickly identify troublesome markets.

MNCs also may adopt somewhat more temporary or ad hoc coordination techniques.[24] Using employees in liaison roles is one such technique. Suppose two divisions of an MNC are collaborating on an activity or function. Each may designate a specific manager as its liaison with the other. If any manager in one unit has information or questions that involve the other unit, they are channeled through the liaison to the appropriate person or unit. Toyota, for example, frequently uses this technique for managing relatively small-scale joint efforts.

When the magnitude of the collaboration is significant, task forces may be used for coordination. In such cases each participating unit or division assigns one or more representatives to serve on the task force. The assignment may be either full-time or part-time. Ford and Mazda, for example, used a task force when they collaborated on the design of the Ford Focus. Each firm designated members of its design, engineering, operations, and finance departments to serve on the task force. Employees of the two firms rotated on and off the task force depending on its needs and on the automobile's stage of development. When the final design was complete and the automobile was put into production, the task force was dissolved.

Many international firms also rely heavily on informal coordination mechanisms. Informal management networks can be especially effective. An **informal management network** is simply a group of managers from different parts of the world who are connected to one another in some way. These connections often form as a result of personal contact, mutual acquaintances, and interaction achieved via travel, training programs, joint meetings, task force experiences, and so on. Informal management networks can be very powerful for short-circuiting bureaucracy that may delay communication and decision making. They also can be effective for getting things done more quickly and more effectively than if normal and routine procedures were always followed.[25]

The Control Function in International Business

Another important role of organization design is to enable the firm to more effectively manage its control function. **Control** is the process of monitoring ongoing performance and making necessary changes to keep the organization moving toward its performance goals. Control is conceptually similar to a thermostat. A thermostat monitors room temperature and then turns on the cooling or heating system when the actual temperature moves too far from the ideal temperature. When the desired room temperature is reached, the system is turned off until it is needed again.

As illustrated in Figure 14.7, there are three main levels at which control can be implemented and managed in an international business. These three key levels of control are the strategic, organizational, and operations levels. Although each is important on its own merits, the three levels also are important collectively as an organizing framework for managers to use in approaching international control from a comprehensive and integrated perspective.

Strategic Control

Strategic control is intended to monitor both how well an international business formulates strategy and how well it goes about implementing that strategy.[26] Strategic control thus focuses on how well the firm defines and maintains its desired strategic alignment with the firm's environment and how effectively the firm is setting and achieving its strategic goals. For example, a few years ago Germany's largest automobile manufacturer, Daimler-Benz, bought Chrysler, the third largest automaker in the United States. At the time this decision seemed very logical. For instance, managers believed that the firms could learn from each other, that their existing product lines and organizational strengths complemented one another, and that the combined firm would be able to compete more effectively in global markets with other behemoths such as General Motors, Ford, and Toyota. As it turned out, though, this ended up being a poor strategic decision. The anticipated synergies and efficiencies could never be achieved and so Chrysler was subsequently sold to a group of private investors. (Those investors recently sold the firm to Fiat.)

FIGURE 14.7

Levels of International Control

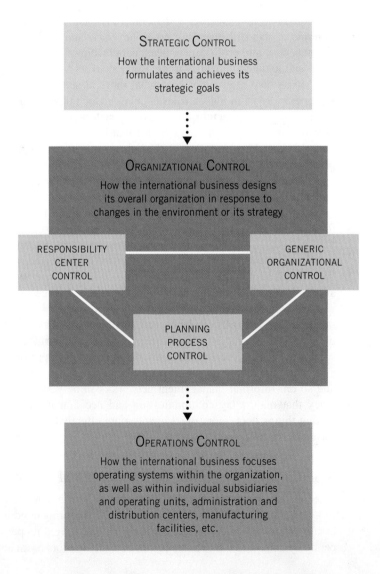

Strategic control also plays a major role in the decisions firms make about foreign-market entry and expansion. This is especially true when the market holds both considerable potential and considerable uncertainty and risk. For example, in the wake of India's overtures for foreign direct investment, many firms are expanding their operations in that country. Hindustan Lever, Unilever's Indian subsidiary, has increased its capacity for soap and detergent manufacturing and launched new food-processing operations as well. These steps represent a strategic commitment by the firm to the Indian market. As this strategy is implemented, strategic control systems will be used in making decisions about future operations there. If opportunities in the Indian market continue to unfold, Unilever no doubt will continue to expand. However, if uncertainty and risk become too great, the firm may become cautious, perhaps even reversing its expansion in India.

Often the most critical aspect of strategic control is control of an international firm's financial resources. Money is the driving force of any organization, whether that money is in the form of profits or of cash flow to ensure that ongoing expenses can be covered. Moreover, if a firm has surplus revenues, managers must ensure that those funds are invested wisely to maximize their payoff for the firm and its shareholders. Thus, it is extremely important that an international firm develop and maintain effective accounting systems. Such systems should allow managers to fully monitor and understand where the firm's revenues are coming from in every market in which the firm operates, to track and evaluate all its costs and expenses, and to see how its parts contribute to its overall profitability.[27]

Poor financial control can cripple a firm's ability to compete globally. For example, Mantrust, an Indonesian firm, bought Van Camp Seafood, packager of Chicken of the Sea tuna, for $300 million. Most of that money was borrowed from Indonesian banks. Mantrust's owner was unskilled at managing debt, and the firm had difficulties making its loan payments. Both Mantrust and Van Camp struggled for years until Mantrust sold Van Camp to Tri-Union Seafood, a limited partnership owned by investors in the United States and Thailand.

Financial control is generally a separate area of strategic control in an international firm. Most firms create one or more special managerial positions to handle financial control. Such a position is usually called controller. Large international firms often have a corporate controller responsible for the financial resources of the entire organization. Each division within the firm is likely to have a divisional controller who is based in a country where the division operates and who oversees local financial control. Divisional controllers usually are responsible both to the heads of their respective divisions and to the corporate controller. These control relationships are managed primarily through budgets and financial forecasts.

A special concern of an international controller is managing the inventory of various currencies needed to run the firm's subsidiaries and to pay its vendors.[28] For example, Coca-Cola has to manage its holdings of over 150 currencies as part of its daily operations. Each foreign subsidiary of an international firm needs to maintain a certain amount of local currency for the subsidiary's domestic operations. Each also needs access to the currency of the parent corporation's home country to remit dividend payments, reimburse the parent for the use of intellectual property, and pay for other intracorporate transactions. The subsidiary further must be able to obtain other currencies to pay suppliers of imported raw materials and component parts as their invoices are received.

Given the possibility of exchange rate fluctuations, the controller needs to oversee the firm's holdings of diverse currencies to avoid losses if exchange rates change. Many multinational corporations (MNCs) centralize the management of exchange rate risk at the corporate level. However, others, such as the Royal Dutch/Shell Group, allow their foreign affiliates to use both domestic and international financial and commodity markets to protect the affiliates against exchange rate fluctuations. Firms that decentralize this task need to maintain adequate financial controls on their subsidiaries or face financial problems. For example, a few years ago Shell's Japanese affiliate, Showa Shell Seikyu KK, engaged in widespread speculative trading in foreign-currency markets, a practice forbidden by Shell. Knowledge of this speculative trading was brought to light only when the Japanese affiliate reported a loss of over $1 billion. Clearly, Shell's internal controls had broken down and failed to detect the speculative activities. As a result, corporate officials implemented new procedures and tighter controls to better manage the firm's financial resources.

Another type of strategic control that is increasingly important to international firms is control of joint ventures and other strategic alliances.[29] As we discussed in Chapter 13, strategic alliances, particularly joint ventures, are being used more often by and becoming more important to international firms. It follows that strategic control systems also must account for the performances of such alliances. By definition a joint venture or other strategic alliance is operated as a relatively autonomous enterprise; therefore, most partners agree to develop an independent control system for each alliance in which they participate. The financial control of these alliances then becomes an ingredient in the overall strategic control system for each partner's firm. That is, the alliance maintains its own independent control systems, but the results are communicated not only to the managers of the alliance but also to each partner.

Organizational Control

Organizational control focuses on the design of the organization itself. As discussed earlier, there are many different forms of organization design that an international firm can use. However, selecting and implementing a particular design does not necessarily end the organization design process. For example, as a firm's environment or strategy changes, managers may need to alter the firm's design to better enable the firm to function in the new circumstances. Adding new product lines, entering a new market, or opening a new factory—all can dictate the need for a change in design.

The most common type of organizational control system is a decentralized one called **responsibility center control.** Using this system, the firm first identifies fundamental responsibility centers within the organization. Strategic business units are frequently defined as responsibility centers, as are geographical regions or product groups. Once the centers are identified, the firm then evaluates each on the basis of how effectively it meets its strategic goals. Thus, a unique control system is developed for each responsibility center. These systems are tailored to meet local accounting and reporting requirements, the local competitive environment, and other circumstances.

Nestlé uses responsibility center control for each of its units, such as Poland Springs, Alcon Labs, and Nestlé-Rowntree (see Map 14.1). These subsidiaries regularly provide financial performance data to corporate headquarters. Managers at Poland Springs, for example, file quarterly reports to Nestlé headquarters in Switzerland so that headquarters can keep abreast of how well its U.S. subsidiary is doing. By keeping each subsidiary defined as a separate and distinct unit and allowing each to use the control system that best fits its own competitive environment, corporate managers in Switzerland can see how each unit is performing within the context of its own market. Each report must contain certain basic information, such as sales and profits, but each also has unique entries that reflect the individual subsidiary and its market.

A firm may prefer to use **generic organizational control** across its entire organization; that is, the control systems used are the same for each unit or operation, and the locus of authority generally resides at the firm's headquarters. Generic organizational control most commonly is used by international firms that pursue similar strategies in each market in which they compete. Because there is no strategic variation between markets, responsibility center control would be inappropriate. The firm is able to apply the same centralized decision making and control standards to the strategic performance of each unit or operation. Moreover, international firms that use the same strategy in every market often have relatively stable and predictable operations; therefore, the organizational control system the firms use also can be relatively stable and straightforward. For example, United Distillers PLC markets its line of bourbon products in the United States, Japan, and throughout Europe. Because the product line is essentially the same in every market and the characteristics of its consumers vary little across markets, the firm uses the same control methods for each market.

A third type of organizational control, which could be used in combination with either responsibility center control or generic organizational control, focuses on the strategic planning process itself rather than on outcomes. **Planning process control** calls for a firm to concentrate its organizational control system on the actual mechanics and processes the firm uses to develop strategic plans. This approach is based on the assumption that if the firm controls its strategies, desired outcomes are more likely to result. Each business unit may then concentrate more on implementing its strategy, rather than worrying as much about the outcomes of that strategy.

In implementing planning process control, whenever a unit fails to meet its goals, the head of that unit meets with the firm's executive committee. The meeting focuses on how the original

MAP 14.1

A Sampling of Nestlé's Global Holdings, Subsidiaries, and Affiliates

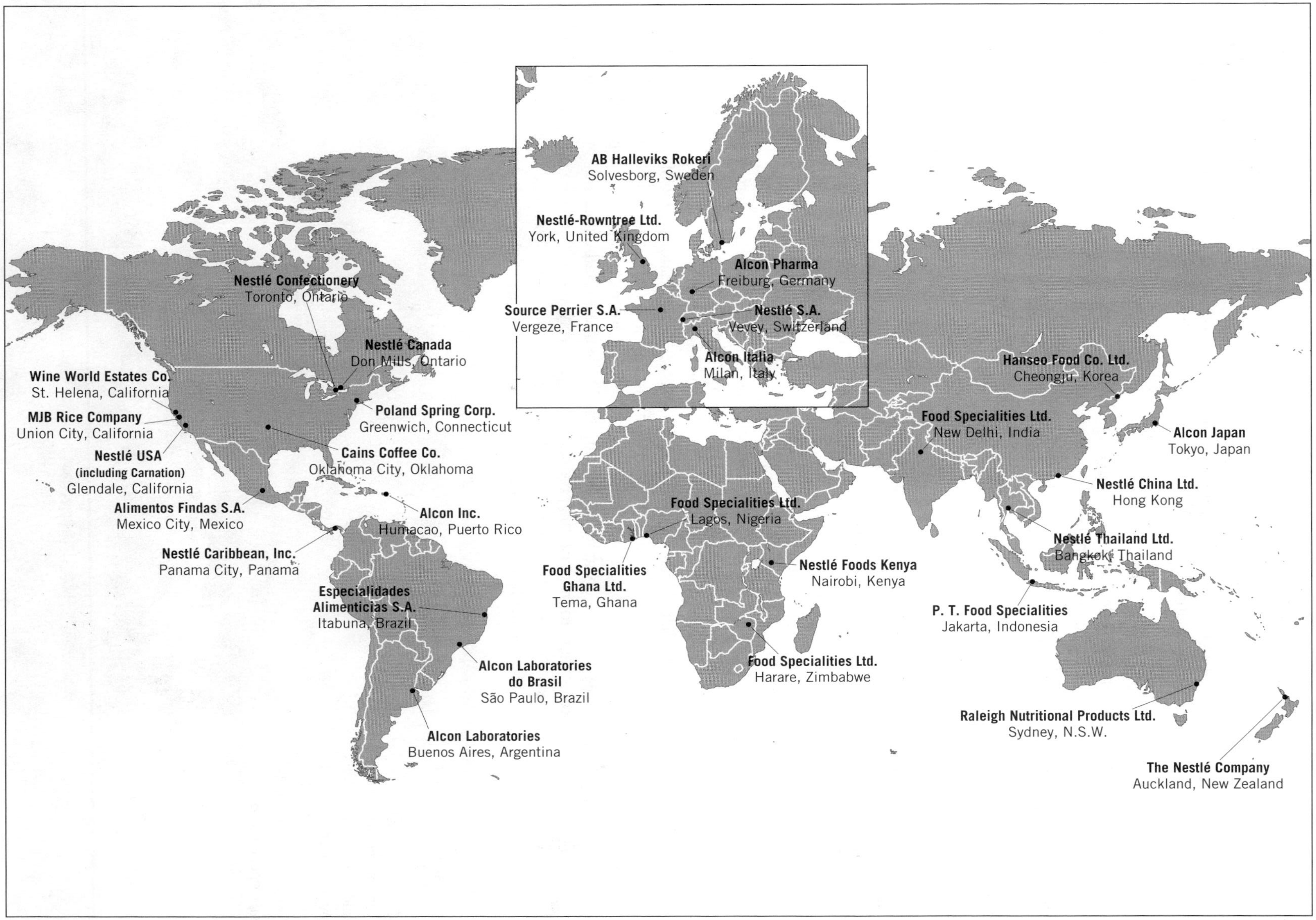

Alcon Japan
Tokyo, Japan

Nestlé China Ltd.
Hong Kong

Hanseo Food Co. Ltd.
Cheongju, Korea

Nestlé Thailand Ltd.
Bangkok, Thailand

Food Specialities Ltd.
New Delhi, India

P. T. Food Specialities
Jakarta, Indonesia

The Nestlé Company
Auckland, New Zealand

Raleigh Nutritional Products Ltd.
Sydney, N.S.W.

Nestlé Foods Kenya
Nairobi, Kenya

Food Specialities Ltd.
Harare, Zimbabwe

Alcon Pharma
Freiburg, Germany

Nestlé S.A.
Vevey, Switzerland

Alcon Italia
Milan, Italy

AB Halleviks Rokeri
Solvesborg, Sweden

Nestlé-Rowntree Ltd.
York, United Kingdom

Source Perrier S.A.
Vergeze, France

Food Specialities Ltd.
Lagos, Nigeria

Food Specialities Ghana Ltd.
Tema, Ghana

Alcon Laboratories do Brasil
São Paulo, Brazil

Alcon Laboratories
Buenos Aires, Argentina

Nestlé Canada
Don Mills, Ontario

Poland Spring Corp.
Greenwich, Connecticut

Cains Coffee Co.
Oklahoma City, Oklahoma

Alcon Inc.
Humacao, Puerto Rico

Especialidades Alimenticias S.A.
Itabuna, Brazil

Nestlé Confectionery
Toronto, Ontario

Wine World Estates Co.
St. Helena, California

MJB Rice Company
Union City, California

Nestlé USA
(including Carnation)
Glendale, California

Alimentos Findas S.A.
Mexico City, Mexico

Nestlé Caribbean, Inc.
Panama City, Panama

goals were set and why they were not met. Throughout the meeting the emphasis is on the process that was followed that led to the unsuccessful outcome. The goal is to correct shortcomings in the actual process each unit uses. For example, a unit might have based its unmet sales goals on outdated market research data because there were insufficient funds for new market research. Planning process control would focus not on correcting the sales shortfall but on enabling more accurate forecasting in the future.

There are clear and important linkages between strategic control and organizational control in an international firm. When a firm adopts a centralized form of organization design, strategic control is facilitated as a logical and complementary extension of that design. When a firm uses a decentralized design, strategic control is not as logically connected with that design.[30] A decentralized design gives foreign affiliates more autonomy and freedom while making it more difficult for the parent to maintain adequate control. The challenge facing managers of the parent is to foster the autonomy and freedom that accompany a decentralized design while simultaneously maintaining effective parent control of operating subsidiaries.

For a large international firm organizational control must be addressed at multiple levels. At the highest level the appropriate form of organization design must be maintained for the entire firm. At a lower level the appropriate form of organization design must be maintained for each subsidiary or operating unit. The firm also must ensure that these designs mesh with each other.

Operations Control

The third level of control in an international firm is operations control. **Operations control** focuses specifically on operating processes and systems within both the firm and its subsidiaries and operating units. The firm also may need an operations control system for each of its manufacturing facilities, distribution centers, and administrative centers.

Strategic control often involves time periods of several years, while organizational control may deal with periods of a few years or months. Operations control, however, involves relatively short periods of time, dealing with components of performance that need to be assessed on a regular—perhaps daily or even hourly—basis. An operations control system is also likely to be much more specific and focused than strategic and organizational control systems.

For example, a manufacturing firm may monitor daily output, scrappage, and worker productivity within a given manufacturing facility, while a retail outlet may measure daily sales. A firm that wants to increase the productivity of its workforce or enhance the quality of its products or services primarily will use operations control to pursue these goals. Operations control usually focuses on the lower levels of a firm, such as first-line managers and operating employees.

Aldi, the German grocery chain, has successfully exported its business model to the United States. Indeed, given the recent increases in energy and food prices, Aldi's focus on low prices and no-frills shopping has made the firm more successful than ever. This Aldi store recently opened in Batavia, Illinois.

PR NEWSWIRE/Newscom

Consider Aldi, a German grocery chain. Although people in the United States are used to sprawling, full-line supermarkets that carry everything from apples to zippers, typical European grocery stores tend to be smaller and less service oriented, to carry fewer product lines, and to charge higher prices. Aldi has prospered in Europe through an elaborate operations control system that relies heavily on cost control and efficiency. Aldi stores do not advertise or even list their numbers in telephone directories. Products are not unpacked and put on shelves but instead are sold directly from crates and boxes. The no-frills stores are also usually located in areas where rents are low. Customers bring their own sacks (or pay Aldi 5¢ each for sacks), bag their own purchases, and rent shopping carts for 25¢ (refunded if the customer returns the cart to the storage rack). Aldi does not accept checks or coupons and provides little customer service, but this austere approach allows the firm to charge rock-bottom prices. Aldi has effectively transferred its control methods to its U.S. operation. The result? Aldi's net profit margins and sales per square foot in the United States are about double the industry norm. With over 800 stores operating in 27 states (primarily from Kansas to the east coast), Aldi has become one of the country's most profitable grocery chains.

Managing the Control Function in International Business

Given the obvious complexities in control, it should come as no surprise that international firms must address a variety of issues in managing the control function. To effectively manage control, managers need to understand how to establish control systems, what the essential techniques for control are, why some people resist control, and what managers can do to overcome this resistance.

Establishing International Control Systems

As illustrated in Figure 14.8, control systems in international business are established through four basic steps: (1) set control standards for performance, (2) measure actual performance, (3) compare performance against standards, and (4) respond to deviations. There obviously will be differences in specificity, time frame, and sophistication, but these steps are applicable to any area and any level of control. "Bringing the World into Focus" describes how Ford has set goals and implemented a new control system targeting international growth.

SET CONTROL STANDARDS FOR PERFORMANCE The first step in establishing an international control system is to define relevant control standards. A control standard in this context is a target, or a desired level of the performance component the firm is attempting to control. Control standards need to be objective and consistent with the firm's goals. Suppose a firm is about to open its first manufacturing facility in Thailand. It might set the following four control standards

---

BRINGING THE WORLD INTO FOCUS   FORD AIMS HIGH

During the global recession of 2008–2009 the already-shaky Big Three U.S. automakers were especially hard hit. But while General Motors and Chrysler relied on government support to survive, Ford managed to stay afloat on its own. One reason for Ford's success was that under the leadership of Alan Mulally the firm was already well along its way to regaining its profitability. Among other things, Mulally has helped Ford reduce its overhead, boost productivity, and overhaul its product line to appeal more to younger auto buyers. For instance, while Ford SUVs still are the firm's largest selling products, new entrants like the Focus, Flex, Fusion, and Escape Hybrid have all been big hits.

But one area where Ford still lags is its international sales. In 2010, for example, Ford derived 54 percent of its revenue from North America but only 15 percent from China, currently the world's largest auto market. But in mid-2011 Mulally made it clear he intended to change things. Specifically, he announced a new corporate goal of increasing Ford's global sales by 50 percent by the end of 2015. He further specified that the Asia-Pacific region, India, and Africa were expected to account for most of the revenue growth.

Much of the growth is expected to come from sales of small cars. For instance, one of India's hottest-selling cars is the subcompact Ford Figo, recently named the 2011 India Car of the Year.

To make sure the firm stays on track, Mulally also put into place a series of annual growth goals for each region. These annual goals, in turn, will play a major control function. Each year area managers will be largely judged based on their contributions to the overall 50 percent growth goal. Their contributions, in turn, will impact their salary and other rewards for the year. Will this all work? Well, Mulally has so far done a masterful job of rebuilding the iconic Ford brand so few people want to bet against him.[31]

FIGURE 14.8

Steps in International Control

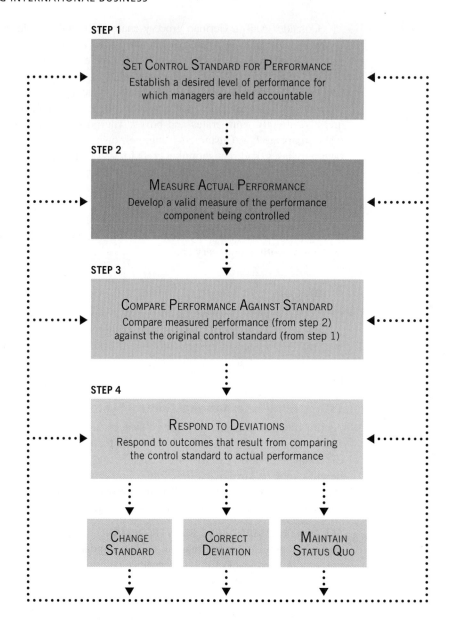

STEP 1

SET CONTROL STANDARD FOR PERFORMANCE
Establish a desired level of performance for which managers are held accountable

STEP 2

MEASURE ACTUAL PERFORMANCE
Develop a valid measure of the performance component being controlled

STEP 3

COMPARE PERFORMANCE AGAINST STANDARD
Compare measured performance (from step 2) against the original control standard (from step 1)

STEP 4

RESPOND TO DEVIATIONS
Respond to outcomes that result from comparing the control standard to actual performance

CHANGE STANDARD

CORRECT DEVIATION

MAINTAIN STATUS QUO

for the plant: (1) Productivity and quality in the new plant will exceed the levels in the firm's existing plants. (2) After an initial break-in period 90 percent of all management positions in the plant will be filled by local managers. (3) The plant will obtain at least 80 percent of its resources from local suppliers. (4) The plant will produce and sell 100,000 units per month.

These control standards help provide a road map for managers involved in opening and running the new plant. Managers can readily see that sales, productivity, and quality are critical and that the firm expects them to hire and buy locally. Where did these standards come from? The firm set them on the basis of its objectives for the new plant, its experience with similar operations, and its overall goals.[32] The second and third goals may have resulted from a conscious strategy of reducing political risk or the parent firm's desire to be a good corporate citizen in each country in which it operates.

MEASURE ACTUAL PERFORMANCE The second step in creating an international control system is to develop a valid measure of the performance component being controlled. Some elements of performance are relatively easy and straightforward to measure; examples are actual output, worker productivity, product quality, unit sales, materials waste, travel expenses, hiring practices, and employee turnover. Considerably more difficult are measuring the effectiveness of an advertising campaign to improve a firm's public image, measuring ethical managerial conduct, and measuring employee attitudes and motivation. For the firm introducing a new product in a

This tobacco processing facility in Nayarit, Mexico, must pay close attention to managing its control function. For instance, its managers must first create and then oversee appropriate systems to ensure acceptable product quality. They must also use meaningful accounting systems and procedures. Behavioral aspects of control must also be considered.

Gabriel M. Covian/The Image Bank

foreign market, performance may be based on the actual number of units sold. For the new plant in Thailand used as an example earlier, performance would be assessed in terms of sales, productivity, quality, and hiring and purchasing practices.

COMPARE PERFORMANCE AGAINST STANDARDS The third step in establishing an international control system is to compare measured performance (obtained in step 2) against the original control standards (defined in step 1). Again, when control standards are straightforward and objective and performance is relatively easy to assess, this comparison is easy. For example, comparing actual sales of 80,437 units against a target sales level of 100,000 is simple. Likewise, comparing the actual hiring of 20 Thai managers against a target of hiring 19 Thai managers is also straightforward. When control standards and performance measures are less concrete, however, comparing one against the other is considerably more complicated. Suppose a manager established a control standard of "significantly increasing market share" and now finds that market share has increased by 4 percent. Is this significant? Obviously, this comparison is ambiguous and difficult to interpret. Managers are advised to use specific and objective standards and performance measures whenever possible.

RESPOND TO DEVIATIONS The fourth and final step in establishing an international control system is responding to deviations observed in step 3. One of three different outcomes can result when comparing a control standard and actual performance: the control standard has been met, it has not been met, or it has been exceeded. For example, if the standard is sales of 100,000 units, actual sales of 99,980 units probably means the standard has been met, whereas sales of only 62,300 units means it has not been met. Actual sales of 140,329 units clearly surpasses the standard.

Depending on the circumstances, managers have many alternative responses to these outcomes. If a standard has not been met and a manager believes it is because of performance deficiencies by employees accountable for the performance, the manager may mandate higher performance, increase incentives to perform at a higher level, or discipline or even terminate those employees. Of course, the actual course taken depends on the nature of the standard versus performance expectations, the context within which the failure has occurred, and myriad other factors. Sometimes standards are not met for unforeseen reasons, such as unexpected competition, an unexpected labor strike, unpredictable raw material shortages, or local political upheavals. On the other hand, the original control standard may have been set too high to begin with, in which case it may be possible to adjust the standard downward or to make additional allowances.

Finally, actual performance occasionally exceeds the control standard. Again, there may be multiple explanations: Managers and employees may have expended extra effort, the original standard may have been too low, or competitors may have bungled their own opportunities. In this case managers may need to provide additional rewards or bonuses, adjust their control standards upward, or aggressively seize new opportunities.

Kenya Power & Lighting (KP&L) often finds it must react to deviations between control standards and actual performance in its distribution of electric power throughout Kenya. Businesses and municipalities in Kenya are more heavily dependent on hydroelectric power than are those in most other countries. Whenever Kenya experiences inadequate rain or prolonged dry spells (see Map 14.2), KP&L's water-powered electric plants have to ration electricity. Twice in the last 20 years, the government-run utility has been forced to enact nationwide rationing to ensure adequate power. It also has used smaller-scale rationing on numerous other occasions. During each rationing period continued supplies of electricity were guaranteed to hospitals and security installations, whereas big businesses were required to cut energy consumption by 30 percent, and homeowners were subjected to two-hour blackout periods each day. As soon as energy supplies reached an acceptable limit, rationing was phased out.

Essential Control Techniques

Because of the complexities of both the international environment and international firms themselves, those firms rely on a wide variety of different control techniques, as "Bringing the World into Focus" suggests. We do not describe them all but introduce a few of the most important ones.

MAP 14.2
Kenyan Rainfall

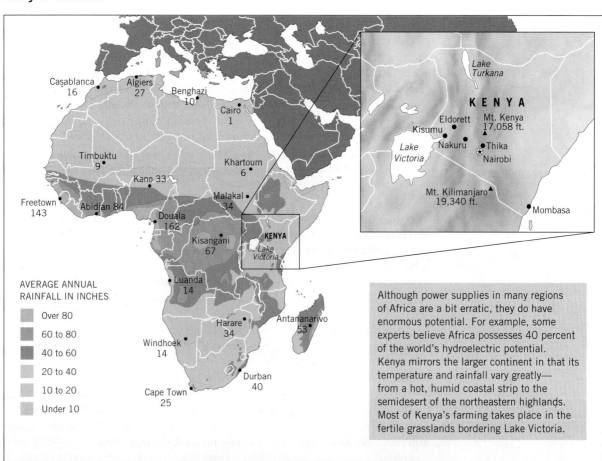

AVERAGE ANNUAL RAINFALL IN INCHES

- Over 80
- 60 to 80
- 40 to 60
- 20 to 40
- 10 to 20
- Under 10

Although power supplies in many regions of Africa are a bit erratic, they do have enormous potential. For example, some experts believe Africa possesses 40 percent of the world's hydroelectric potential. Kenya mirrors the larger continent in that its temperature and rainfall vary greatly— from a hot, humid coastal strip to the semidesert of the northeastern highlands. Most of Kenya's farming takes place in the fertile grasslands bordering Lake Victoria.

ACCOUNTING SYSTEMS Accounting is a comprehensive system for collecting, analyzing, and communicating data about a firm's financial resources. Accounting procedures are heavily regulated and must follow prescribed methods dictated by national governments. Because of these regulations, investors, government agencies, and other organizational stakeholders within a given country can better compare the financial performance of different organizations, have a common understanding of what various kinds of information mean, and place reasonable trust in the accuracy and meaning of that information. International firms face more difficulties in establishing their accounting procedures than do purely domestic firms. International businesses must develop accounting systems to control and monitor the performance of the overall firm and each division, operating unit, or subsidiary. These systems enable managers to keep abreast of the financial performance of every part of the firm.

Problems can arise when the accounting standards or procedures of the countries in which a firm operates are incompatible with each other, as is frequently the case. Each subsidiary must maintain its accounting records in accordance with local procedures and denominate its accounts in the local currency to satisfy local government regulations and meet the needs of local managers. Yet to meet the needs of investors, regulators, and tax collectors in the parent's home country, the parent needs the local accounting records of each subsidiary translated into the parent's currency using accounting procedures dictated by the parent's home country. The parent further must decide whether it will evaluate the performance of its subsidiaries and the subsidiaries' managers using the local currency, the parent's home country currency, or some combination of the two.

PROCEDURES Policies, standard operating procedures, rules, and regulations all help managers carry out the control function. For example, a firm may establish a policy that at least 75 percent of the raw materials it buys must be obtained from local suppliers. This policy guides plant managers in making purchasing decisions and allocations. A firm also could have a rule that each employee transferred to a foreign unit must attain basic proficiency in the local language within six months. This rule would serve as an ongoing and easily referenced measure of what is expected.

Firms often alter their procedures in the face of adversity. For example, during the crisis involving the Firestone/Ford recall of defective tires both firms had to deviate from their established procedures in order to satisfy both their customers and government regulators. Firestone replaced tires at no cost instead of prorating costs based on tread wear. Ford replaced many Firestone tires with more expensive Michelin tires at no extra cost. At times both firms even refused to sell new tires to unaffected customers to maintain a sufficient inventory for the recall program.

PERFORMANCE RATIOS International firms also use various performance ratios to maintain control. A performance ratio is a numerical index of performance that the firm wants to maintain. A common performance ratio used by many firms is inventory turnover. Holding excessive inventory is dysfunctional because the inventory ties up resources that could otherwise be used for different purposes and because the longer materials sit in inventory, the more prone they are to damage and loss. Based on a firm's unique circumstances, it may decide it does not want anything to sit in inventory for more than 30 days. Turnover rates are likely to differ among different types of retailers and among different countries depending on the amount of floor space, the sophistication of inventory management systems, and the reliability of suppliers. For example, because rents are so high in Tokyo, convenience stores like 7–Eleven have little room for storage. They must maintain high inventory turnover ratios to remain profitable. Often vendors resupply the 7–Elevens four or five times a day to ensure that goods are available for customers. Sophisticated electronic linkages allow the stores to communicate their inventory needs to suppliers on a real-time basis.

British Airways also uses performance ratios to maintain control of its airline operations. One key ratio for an airline is the percentage of seats filled on its flights. If this ratio falls below a set minimum, the firm looks into alternative ways to generate passenger demand, such as discounts or additional promotional activity. Another ratio of interest to British Airways is the

BRINGING THE WORLD INTO FOCUS **GETTING BACK TO BASICS**

While Japan's economy has been in the doldrums for the past few years, some experts believe that the problems facing many Japanese corporations are not related to economic woes, but rather to poor management. "Ninety percent of the Japanese economy is made up of domestic companies that are low-tech and low-productivity," claims consultant Masao Hirano. However, a few pioneering firms are starting to demonstrate that "by becoming better focused, [Japanese companies] can survive and even prosper," says analyst Satoru Oyama.

Cosmetics maker Shiseido held too much inventory and had overly high expenses, leading to a $550 million loss over two years. But rather than call for a government bailout, Shiseido executives focused on fundamental improvements. Better technology allowed them to control and forecast inventory more effectively. They cut costs throughout the corporation and curtailed their product line. After Shiseido returned to profitability, chief logistics officer Seiji Nishimori boasted, "We're showing other Japanese companies that it's possible to reverse a slide."

Canon, the world's leading maker of copiers and laser printers, has also taken a disciplined approach to performance improvement. CEO Fujio Mitarai replaced every manufacturing line at the firm's 29 Japanese factories with small, self-directed teams of half a dozen workers that do the work previously done by 30 laborers. The teams discovered more efficient inventory management techniques, and Canon was able to close 20 of its 34 parts warehouses. "Manufacturing is where most of the costs lie," Mitarai claims. Canon earnings improved by 53 percent, enabling Mitarai to conclude, "We're much more profitable today because of these changes."

The success of notable high performers such as multinational Toyota has caused Japanese firms to realize the benefit of global cost competitiveness. High-tech companies are abandoning manufacturing and switching attention to R&D to counteract an influx of inexpensive electronics from China, Taiwan, and Korea. For example, NEC has reduced its commitment to the unprofitable semiconductor chip-making business, and focused on more lucrative cell phones and software. Sharp, too, has given up on low-margin PC monitors and refocused its operations on innovative products such as liquid crystal displays for PDAs. Sony is working on revolutionary new computer chips while reducing its investment in consumer electronics.

All three companies say they now listen to their consumers more closely. "We were proud of our great technology, and [we] just pumped out products without thinking of our customers' needs," says NEC director Kaoru Tosaka. "Now, we're emphasizing efficiency, profits, and clients."

These companies are an exception in Japan, where so-called zombie firms are bailed out over and over again by a government that fears unemployment and chaos if businesses fail. But the zombies need to hear the lessons these stellar firms have learned: Watch inventory. Cut costs where possible. Use information technology more effectively. Simplify product lines. Experiment with new ways of organizing. Shut down money-losing businesses. Choose areas where the firm can add value. Listen to customer feedback. If the zombies could adopt these suggestions, the Japanese—and the rest of the world—would surely benefit.[33]

percentage of its flights that arrive and depart on time. If this ratio slips too much, managers try to identify and eliminate the reasons for delays.

Behavioral Aspects of International Control

Regardless of how well formulated and implemented a control system may be, managers must understand that human behavior plays a fundamental role in how well control works. Essential to this understanding is being aware that some people resist control. Also essential is recognizing that resistance can be minimized. Although resistance to control is likely to exist within most cultures, its magnitude will vary across cultures.

RESISTANCE TO CONTROL People in international firms may resist control for various reasons. One potential reason is overcontrol, whereby the firm tries to exert more control over individuals than they think is appropriate.[34] By definition control regulates and constrains behavior; most people accept this within what they perceive to be reasonable limits (with the limits being partially determined by the cultural context). However, if attempts to control behavior begin to exceed those perceived limits, people may balk and begin to resist. For example, when Disney first opened Disneyland Paris, it attempted to apply the same grooming standards for its employees there that it uses in the United States, banning beards and mandating trimmed hair. French employees saw this as overcontrol. They complained about the standards, vented their grievances in the media, and occasionally ignored the standards altogether. The resistance grew to the point where Disney eventually backed off and developed standards that were more acceptable to its European employees.

People also may resist control because it may be inappropriately focused; that is, the firm may inadvertently be trying to control the wrong things. For example, if a firm places so much emphasis on lowering costs that quality is compromised and employee morale suffers, employees may become indignant and attempt to circumvent the control system. Whistler Radar, a U.S. firm, encountered this problem in its assembly of radar detectors. Its control system focused on quality control only at the end of the assembly process. When managers discovered that 100 of the firm's 250 employees were doing nothing more than reworking defective units assembled by the other 150, the managers realized that control should have been focused on quality throughout the assembly process.

Finally, people may resist control because control increases their accountability. In the absence of an effective control system employees may be able to get by with substandard performance because managers do not understand what the employees are doing relative to what they should be doing. For example, if a foreign-branch manager has to submit financial performance data only annually, the manager may not do as good a job on a day-to-day basis as the firm would like. If the firm were to request performance reports more frequently, it could increase the manager's accountability. At the same time, if the firm demands too much reporting, it becomes prone to overcontrol. Thus, it is important to strike a balance between appropriate and acceptable levels of accountability without edging over into overcontrol.

OVERCOMING RESISTANCE TO CONTROL Although there are no guaranteed methods for eliminating resistance to control, there are a few that can help minimize it. The appropriate method, as well as its likely effectiveness, will vary by culture. In many cultures, for instance, one effective way to overcome resistance to control is to promote participation. Involving employees who are going to be affected by control in its planning and implementation will enable them to better understand the goal of the control system, how and why the system works, and how their jobs fit into the system. As a result, the employees may be less prone to resist it.

Another method to reduce resistance that works well in most cultures is to create a control system that has a clear appropriate focus and that creates reasonable accountability without overcontrolling. GlaxoSmithKline, the U.K.'s largest pharmaceutical firm, uses this method. The firm is very receptive to allowing scientists to explore ideas and possibilities for new prescription drugs, thereby motivating those scientists to pursue ideas and creating an atmosphere of creativity and innovation. At the same time Glaxo managers carefully monitor the progress of new product development. If costs start becoming excessive or if development begins to lag too far behind the competition, managers may choose to curtail a given project. Employees see this as a viable strategy because it gives them the opportunity to pursue their scientific interests while simultaneously keeping costs in check.[35]

A firm also may overcome resistance to control by providing a diagnostic mechanism for addressing unacceptable deviations. Suppose a plant manager reports productivity levels far below those expected by headquarters. Top managers should avoid jumping to a potentially wrong conclusion, such as simply assuming the manager has done a poor job and reprimanding the manager, or worse. Instead they first should learn why the poor performance occurred. For example, it may have resulted from the corporate purchasing manager's having bought inferior materials for the plant.

Again, it is important to account for cultural factors when planning how to deal with resistance to control. People from hierarchical cultures, for example, may be reluctant to actively participate in planning and implementing control because they view such activities as the domain of management.

Finally, behavioral aspects of control can be approached and managed from a cultural perspective. A firm may attempt to replace behaviors resulting from national culture with those more consistent with the firm's corporate culture. Being careful to hire people with values, experiences, work habits, and goals that are consistent with the firm's can go a long way toward this goal. Managers of Japanese-owned automobile factories in the United States, for example, spend thousands of dollars per worker selecting U.S. employees who will be receptive to the Japanese way of working as Chapter 19's closing case, "Training for the World," reports. Further refinements in behavior can be expedited through training and management development programs designed to impart the firm's cultural values and business methods.

MyManagementLab Now that you have finished this chapter, go back to **www.pearsonglobaleditions.com/mymanagementlab** to continue practicing and applying the concepts you've learned.

CHAPTER REVIEW

Summary

Organization design is the overall pattern of structural components and configurations used to manage the total organization. The most appropriate design of an organization depends on several factors. Managers also realize that organization design is an evolutionary process. When a firm first begins to operate internationally, it usually must change its design in one or more ways. Such change may involve following the corollary approach, then establishing an export department, and then creating an international division.

After a firm has established a significant international presence, it will usually develop a global organization design. The most common approaches to global organization design are the global product design, the global area design, the global functional design, the global customer design, and the global matrix design. Each of these approaches has unique advantages and disadvantages, and one approach may be more suitable for some firms than for others. Indeed, many firms actually use a hybrid global design best suited to their needs.

MNCs also must make other decisions related to organization design. Particularly important are those regarding centralization versus decentralization, the role of subsidiary boards of directors, and which coordination mechanisms to use. Informal management networks are especially powerful mechanisms for coordination.

Control is the process of monitoring and regulating activities of a firm so that a targeted component of performance is achieved or maintained. For an MNC control must be managed both at the corporate level and within each subsidiary. Most MNCs usually address control at three levels. Strategic control monitors how well an international firm formulates strategy and then goes about trying to implement it. Financial control is an especially important area of strategic control in international business, because poor financial control can cripple a firm's ability to compete globally. Organizational control

involves the design of the firm. Three basic forms of organizational control are responsibility center control, generic strategic control, and planning process control. Operations control focuses specifically on operating procedures and systems within the firm.

When international firms establish control systems, they first set control standards, then measure actual performance. Next they compare performance against the standards and respond to deviations. Essential control techniques include accounting systems, procedures, and performance ratios. International managers also need to understand behavioral aspects of control, such as why people resist control and how to overcome that resistance. Cultural factors are an important ingredient in addressing behavioral aspects of control.

Review Questions

1. What are some of the initial impacts of international activity on organization design?
2. What is the global product design? What are its strengths and weaknesses?
3. What is the global area design? What are its strengths and weaknesses?
4. What is the global functional design? What are its strengths and weaknesses?
5. What is the global customer design? What are its strengths and weaknesses?
6. What is the global matrix design? What are its strengths and weaknesses?
7. What are the three levels of control in international business?
8. Why is financial control so important?
9. What are the four basic steps in establishing an international control system?

Questions for Discussion

1. If a new organization starts out with a global perspective, will it necessarily experience any of the initial impacts of international activity on organization design? Why or why not?
2. Do managers of international firms need to approach organization design differently from their counterparts in domestic firms? Why or why not?
3. How do the global product, area, functional, and customer approaches to organization design differ? How are they similar?
4. Why is a global matrix design almost always transitional in nature?
5. Why is control an important management function in international business?

6. Do you think the three common types of international organizational control are mutually exclusive? Why or why not?
7. Which form of control system would you most and least prefer for your own work? Why?

8. Which control techniques are most likely to be tailored to international settings? Which can be merely extensions of domestic operations?

Building Global Skills

Form small groups of three or four students each. Assume that your group is the board of directors of a large firm, Unipro Incorporated, which for many years followed a single-product strategy. It manufactured small jet aircraft and sold them worldwide. Its products are market leaders in North America, Asia, and Europe and also sell well in South America and Africa. Because of the single-product strategy, Unipro set up a global functional organization design, which it still uses.

The board has been concerned about the firm's dependence on a single product, so several years ago it decided to diversify the firm. Over four years the firm has bought several other businesses:

- General Chemical (based in England; almost 90 percent of its revenues come from Europe)
- Total Software (based in Canada; most of its revenues come from North America and Europe)
- Pleasure Park (an amusement park in Japan)

- Fundamental Foods (a large food-processing firm with strong operations in the United States, Europe, and Japan)

Now that Unipro's diversification strategy has been fully implemented, the board (your group) sees that it needs to change the firm's organization design to better fit the new business mix. Based solely on the information you have, sketch a new organization design for the firm. When you are finished, draw your organization design on the blackboard. Be prepared to defend your design.

1. How is your group's organization design similar to and different from those of other groups?
2. What do you see as the biggest advantages and disadvantages of your group's organization design?
3. What additional information would have made it easier for you to develop a new organization design for Unipro?

CLOSING CASE   UNILEVER MATCHES STRATEGY AND STRUCTURE

Unilever is the world's second largest packaged consumer goods company; with $57 billion in annual sales, it trails only U.S. giant Procter & Gamble in the industry. Among its best-known brand names are Lipton, Dove, Knorr, Vaseline, and Q-tips. As the firm has grown, Unilever occasionally has set up other businesses to support its consumer products operations. For example, the firm once established a chemical unit to process the oils it uses to make margarine. At the time managers believed this route provided them with a predictable and controllable source of materials. Fragrances and food flavorings operations were created for the same reason. In similar fashion Unilever often has grown by acquiring other consumer products businesses, many of which had supporting operations as well.

About twenty years ago Unilever grew to the point where it was structured around five basic business groups: food products, personal-care products, soap/laundry products, cosmetics/perfume/hair products, and specialty chemicals. As the company continued to expand, however, this arrangement grew increasingly unwieldy. The methods and operations used to package, distribute, and promote the products and brands in the four consumer products groups were all very similar. Managers could be transferred across businesses easily, and knowledge about local market conditions in different countries was freely exchanged.

The specialty chemicals group, however, was an altogether different story. Because it had no consumer products, only indirect linkages existed between its operations and those in the consumer products groups. For example, in some markets the chemical companies made chemicals that were then "sold" to Unilever's consumer products businesses. These businesses in turn used the chemicals to create their consumer products for resale around the world. In the mid-1990s Unilever's board of directors grew concerned about the firm's seeming inability to gain market share from Procter & Gamble. A new CEO was hired to remedy this situation and to improve Unilever's financial performance.

After studying Unilever's operations, the new CEO concluded that the firm's specialty chemical businesses were part of the problem. For one thing, they did not meet the firm's profitability targets. For another, some of the chemicals they were making could be bought on the open market for the same—and sometimes lower—prices. Finally, the firm had higher administrative costs due to the lack of synergy between its dissimilar units (chemical and consumer products).

As a result of these conclusions, in 1997 Unilever executives decided to sell the specialty chemical units. The sale would eliminate inefficiencies created by the firm's structure and generate cash that could be used to reduce debt and to finance new acquisitions in Unilever's core business areas. The CEO argued that the new international organization design would allow Unilever to focus all its attention on competing with Procter & Gamble and other firms in the consumer products markets. Accordingly, Unilever negotiated the sale of its specialty chemical group to Britain's Imperial Chemical Industries PLC for approximately $8 billion.

Part of the proceeds from this sale were then used to acquire Ben & Jerry's Homemade Inc., the quirky ice cream maker, and SlimFast Foods Company, a leading diet products firm. However, managers soon realized that selling the chemicals business and buying new food products businesses were not really addressing Unilever's other problems, which were its slow decision making and weak control of worldwide marketing strategies. As a result, in 2000 the CEO announced another major restructuring of Unilever, reorganizing it into two units rather than four. One unit would be responsible for all food products and the other for all home and personal-care products. Each unit was then assigned its own chief executive responsible for all its global operations.

This new arrangement proved to be reasonably successful, but Unilever executives still felt there was room for improvement. In 2005 the CEO retired and was replaced by Patrick Cescau. Cescau agreed that the firms' structure was satisfactory but might benefit from some fine-tuning. So, he introduced a hybrid design for the home and personal-care products division. Basically, the division operates as a single entity with regard to procurement, operations, and manufacturing. But once products are manufactured, the division has two different units responsible for distribution, marketing, and sales. One handles all home-care products and the other concentrates on personal-care products. In 2008, this design was further refined by the creation of regional support centers. Clusters of neighboring countries now function as one entity, leveraging regional scale through shared services for functions such as human resource management, information technology, and finance. Unilever managers now believe they have

achieved the right structure and have turned their full attention to competing with their archrival, Procter & Gamble.

But, there is an old saying that "what goes around comes around." In 2010 newly installed CEO Michael Treschow (the first outsider to ever run Unilever) once again took Unilever back to the four-divisional model it had discarded ten years before. The newly formed product groups are (1) savory, dressings, and spreads, (2) personal care, (3) ice cream and beverages, and (4) home care and miscellaneous. Treschow's logic was based on literally dozens of acquisitions and divestitures Unilever had made during the first decade of this century. Essentially, the firm had exited the fragrance business altogether and bought numerous new businesses in the ice cream and dressings and spreads markets. So, will the new structure stick? Well, if history is any indication, it'll be around for awhile but Unilever will still look different in a few years.

Case Questions

1. Identify the basic organization design issues at Unilever.
2. What seems to account for the frequent changes in organization design at Unilever?
3. Do the frequent changes in organization design at Unilever seem to be, overall, relatively positive or relatively negative?
4. Identify the basic control issues at Unilever from all three levels.
5. How do you think the control function should be organized and managed at Unilever?

Sources: "Unilever Annual Report 2010," unilever.com; "Unilever refashions itself into two units," *Wall Street Journal*, August 7, 2000, p. A11; "Unilever to sell specialty-chemical unit to ICI of the U.K. for about $8 billion," *Wall Street Journal*, May 7, 1997, pp. A3, A12; "Unilever sells off four chemical units," *USA Today*, May 8, 1997, p. 3B; *Hoover's Handbook of World Business 2011* (Austin, TX: Hoover's Business Press, 2011), pp. 372–373.

Endnotes

1. "Lenovo's legend returns," *Time,* May 10, 2010, pp. 65–68; "Lenovo: A company without a country," *Business Week*, January 23, 2010, pp. 49–50; "Lenovo's turnaround man," *Forbes*, May 4, 2010, p. 88; *Hoover's Handbook of World Business 2011* (Austin: Hoover's Business Press, 2011), pp. 208–209; "IBM shows secret to corporate longevity," *USA Today*, June 16, 2011, pp. 1B, 3B.
2. J. M. Stopford and L. T. Wells, *Managing the Multinational Enterprise* (New York: Basic Books, 1972).
3. See Royston Greenwood and Danny Miller, "Tackling design anew: Getting back to the heart of organizational theory," *Academy of Management Perspectives*, November 2010, pp. 78–88. See also George P. Huber, "Organizations: Theory, design, future," in Sheldon Zedeck (Ed.), *Handbook of Industrial and Organizational*

Psychology (Washington, DC: American Psychological Association, 2010).
4. Alfred Chandler, Jr., *Strategy and Structure* (Cambridge, MA: MIT Press, 1962).
5. Monique Forte, James J. Hoffman, Bruce T. Lamont, and Erich N. Brockmann, "Organizational form and environment: An analysis of between-form and within-form responses to environmental change," *Strategic Management Journal*, vol. 21, no. 7 (2000), pp. 753–773.
6. John P. Kotter and Leonard A. Schlesinger, "Choosing strategies for change," *Harvard Business Review* (March–April 1979), pp. 106–119.
7. Chandler, op. cit.
8. Anant K. Sundaram and J. Stewart Black, "The environment and internal organization of multinational enterprises,"

Academy of Management Review, vol. 17, no. 4 (1992), pp. 729–757.

9. "Aetna to merge global, U.S. divisions," *Wall Street Journal*, January 10, 1999, pp. A3, A20.

10. Anil K. Gupta and Vijay Govindarajan, "Knowledge flows within multinational corporations," *Strategic Management Journal*, vol. 21, no. 4 (2000), pp. 473–496.

11. Kendall Roth, David M. Schweiger, and Allen J. Morrison, "Global strategy implementation at the business unit level: Operational capabilities and administrative mechanisms," *The Journal of International Business Studies*, vol. 22, no. 3 (1991), pp. 369–402.

12. See Tarun Khana and Krishna Palepu, "The right way to restructure conglomerates in emerging markets," *Harvard Business Review* (July–August 1999), pp. 125–134.

13. Christopher A. Bartlett, "Organizing for worldwide effectiveness: The transnational solution," *California Management Review* (Fall 1988), pp. 54–74.

14. *Hoover's Handbook of World Business 2011* (Austin: Hoover's Business Press, 2011), pp. 25–26.

15. "More U.S. firms expected to fly solo in China," *USA Today*, April 10, 2000, p. 1B; Jim Rohwer, "China's coming Telecom battle," *Fortune*, November 27, 2000, pp. 209–214.

16. Eastman Kodak Company website.

17. Christopher A. Bartlett and Sumantra Ghospal, "Matrix management: Not a structure, a frame of mind," *Harvard Business Review* (July–August 1990), pp. 138–145.

18. Lawton R. Burns and Douglas R. Wholey, "Adoption and abandonment of matrix management programs: Effects of organizational characteristics and interorganizational networks," *Academy of Management Journal*, vol. 36, no. 1 (1993), pp. 105–138.

19. C. K. Prahalad and Jan P. Oosterveld, "Transforming internal governance: The challenge for multinationals," *Sloan Management Review* (Spring 1999), pp. 31–41.

20. "Bezos says Amazon will boost investment in China," *Wall Street Journal*, June 6, 2007, p. A12.

21. See Steen Thomsen and Torben Pedersen, "Ownership structure and economic performance in the largest European companies," *Strategic Management Journal*, vol. 21, no. 6 (2000), pp. 689–705, for a recent discussion of these issues.

22. S. Watson O'Donnell, "Managing foreign subsidiaries: Agents of headquarters, or an interdependent network?" *Strategic Management Journal*, vol. 21, no. 5 (2000), pp. 525–548.

23. Ruth V. Aguilera and Gregory Jackson, "Comparative and international corporate governance," in *The Academy of Management Annals 2010*, James P. Walsh and Arthur P. Brief, Eds. (Philadelphia, PA: Taylor and Francis, 2010), pp. 485–556.

24. Jon I. Martinez and J. Carlos Jarillo, "The evolution of research on coordination mechanisms in multinational corporations," *The Journal of International Business Studies*, vol. 20 (1989), pp. 489–514.

25. Sumantra Ghoshal and Christopher A. Bartlett, "The multinational corporation as an interorganizational network," *Academy of Management Review*, vol. 15, no. 4 (1990), pp. 603–625.

26. David Asch, "Strategic control: A problem looking for a solution," *Long Range Planning* (February 1992), pp. 120–132.

27. John K. Shank and Joseph Fisher, "Target costing as a strategic tool," *Sloan Management Review* (Fall 1999), pp. 73–82.

28. Lane Daley, James Jiambalvo, Gary Sundem, and Yasumasa Kondon, "Attitudes toward financial control systems in the United States and Japan," *Journal of International Business Studies* (Fall 1985), pp. 91–110.

29. Hans Mjoen and Stephen Tallman, "Control and performance in international joint ventures," *Organization Science* (May–June 1997), pp. 257–268.

30. Michael Goold, "Strategic control in the decentralized firm," *Sloan Management Review* (Winter 1991), pp. 69–81.

31. "Ford hopes to raise sales by 50% in four years," *USA Today*, June 8, 2011, p. 2B; *Hoover's Handbook of American Business 2011* (Austin: Hoover's Business Press), pp. 374–376.

32. Robert S. Kaplan and David P. Norton, "The balanced scoreboard—measures that drive performance," *Harvard Business Review* (January–February 1992), pp. 71–79.

33. Clay Chandler, "Japan's horror show," *Fortune*, November 10, 2002, pp. 114–118; "Quick studies," *Business Week*, November 18, 2002, pp. 48–49.

34. See Mark Gimein, "CEOs who manage too much," *Fortune*, September 4, 2000, pp. 234–242.

35. "Why to kill new product Ideas," *Fortune*, December 14, 1992, pp. 91–94; Mark Keil and Ramiro Montealegre, "Cutting your losses: Extricating your organization when a big project goes awry," *Sloan Management Review* (Spring 2000), pp. 55–68.

Leadership and Employee Behavior in International Business

AFTER STUDYING THIS CHAPTER, YOU SHOULD BE ABLE TO:

1. Identify and discuss the basic perspectives on individual differences in different cultures.

2. Evaluate basic views of employee motivation in international business.

3. Identify basic views of managerial leadership in international business.

4. Discuss the nature of managerial decision making in international business.

5. Describe group dynamics and discuss how teams are managed across cultures.

Access a host of interactive learning aids at **www.pearsonglobaleditions.com/mymanagementlab** to help strengthen your understanding of the chapter concepts.

MyManagementLab

HADJ/SIPA/Newscom

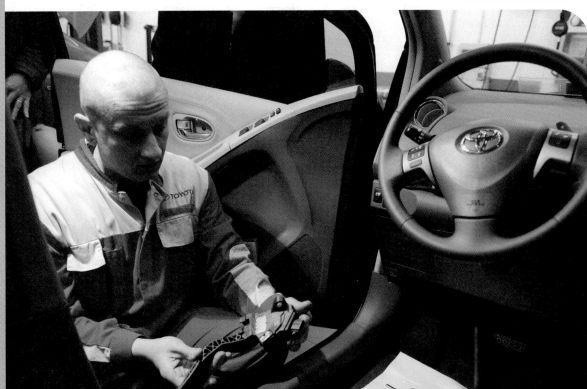

LEADERSHIP ISSUES AT TOYOTA

Until recently Toyota was among the most admired businesses in the world. Its products consistently earned top scores for quality and value, its financial base was among the strongest in its industry, and its leaders were respected for their integrity and strategic vision. But things have taken a different turn in recent times. After overtaking General Motors to become the world's largest automobile company in 2008, quality and safety problems with Toyota vehicles began to surface in 2010.

Specifically, word began to spread that certain Toyota vehicles were prone to uncontrolled acceleration that could lead to accidents—sometimes fatal. To make matters worse, it also became public knowledge that Toyota had known about the problems for some time and had chosen to do nothing about them. Over the next year, the company recalled over 8 million vehicles (5 million in the United States alone) to correct this and other safety problems. These recalls, in turn, cost the firm hundreds of millions of dollars and severely damaged its reputation for quality.

As it turns out, Toyota's leadership also came under intense scrutiny—and criticism—in the wake of these problems. Moreover, this scrutiny revealed not one but two different sets of leadership shortcomings at the company. One set of shortcomings may have played a pivotal role leading up to the quality crisis and the other served to further tarnish Toyota's reputation after the problems became public knowledge.

One of a leader's most important tasks is to thoroughly understand the organization culture at the company. It would follow logically, then, that if the culture is changed, the leader must understand the dynamics and potential outcomes of this change as well. And it is in this area that Toyota's leaders may have first stumbled. For decades Toyota's culture was centered on the principle of using "only reliable, thoroughly tested technology that services your people and processes." This translated into high-quality products and lean production processes and was known internally as "The Toyota Way."

But under the leadership of Fujio Cho and Katsuaki Watanabe, Toyota's chairman and vice chairman, respectively, the firm began to adjust its core operating principles. Cho was a strong advocate of environmentally friendly automotive technology, such as the hybrid-electric Prius, and led the company's effort to position Toyota as a market leader in this field. Watanabe, for his part, spearheaded Toyota's efforts to increase capability for building large gas-guzzling cars and small trucks in pursuit of increased U.S. market share. Indeed, the firm's strategic goal to become the world's number one automaker was based on using new know-how, new technology, and new materials to improve, perfect, and create new innovations in auto design and manufacturing. However, the strategy also required that Toyota shift its focus from manufacturing engineering and continuous improvement more toward research and development and product design.

But when a company shifts its focus from lean production to technology and innovation, the culture will also change. For instance, the essence of lean production dictates the elimination of waste. But the uncertainties in new product development require that the manufacturer build in redundancy to manage the risks of the unknown and ensure a high level of safety. Trying to balance lean production with the need for redundancy is a difficult act that requires the leadership to be instrumental in making key decisions as well as leading and managing the change. And by all accounts Cho and Watanabe failed to meet this obligation. That is, the new strategy called for a change in culture but this needed change was ignored.

Even worse, though, was that Toyota's leadership also allowed fundamental changes in human resource practices that may have also contributed to the problems. When the overarching goal is quality, performance is evaluated and rewards are distributed for producing high-quality products. But when growth becomes the goal, performance evaluations and rewards will also shift. So, under the previous system people were encouraged to correct quality problems. But under the new system correcting quality problems may detract from growth and hence actually (and presumably inadvertently) be discouraged. And compounding the problem was the fact that some experts think that the firm's longtime creed "The Toyota Way" became so biased toward positive information that employees "learned" to not make waves by raising concerns about product quality and safety.

A second leadership failure occurred after news of the safety problems became widely known. In times of crisis people often look to leaders to step forward, offer explanations, take responsibility, and outline corrective steps. But Toyota's leader, Akio Toyoda (promoted to president in 2009) was nowhere to be seen. Worse still, he allowed other senior managers to offer poorly worded apologies and make contradictory promises about how the company was addressing its problems. And some of Toyota's few consistent messages were that the problems were minor, could be easily corrected, and might have even been the fault of the drivers.

After several weeks of fumbling the company's response to the crisis, however, Toyoda eventually agreed to travel to the United States and appear before a congressional panel of inquiry. He also offered a contrite apology and initiated what would become one of the most massive product recalls in history. In 2009 the firm's net revenues fell by over 20 percent and it posted its first net loss since 1950. No doubt part of Toyota's decline was attributable to the global recession. And some of it would have happened no matter how well Toyoda had managed the crisis. But some of it also came as a result of the firm's leaders failing to carry out their jobs as effectively as they should have. Hopefully, though, these managers have also learned from their experiences and will be better equipped to handle the next crisis that comes along.[1] ▪

The story of Toyota's leadership shortcomings illustrates several important messages for all managers, but especially those who work in international businesses. For one thing, leaders must maintain a thorough knowledge of their firm, its culture, and its strategy. Second, leaders need to understand that changes in strategy may dictate changes in culture and rewards. Beyond these two points, it is also important for international managers to understand the symbolic role they play as the "face" of their organization. Clearly then, it is important that they represent their organization in the most effective manner possible.

To complicate their work further, while managers who operate in a domestic firm must understand and contend with a complex set of behavioral and interpersonal processes, managers in a multicultural firm have the additional challenge of managing people with diverse frames of reference and perspectives on work and organizations. International managers who develop insights into dealing with people from different cultural backgrounds will be far ahead of those who do not.

In Chapter 4, we discussed national culture and its implications for firms with international operations. We now look more closely at the actual behaviors of managers and employees in different cultures and how those behavioral differences affect the conduct of international business. We start by discussing the nature of individual differences in different cultures. Then we introduce and discuss four aspects of behavior that are especially important for international businesses: motivation, leadership, decision making, and groups and cross-cultural teams.[2]

Individual Behavior in International Business

Individual behavior in organizations is strongly influenced by a variety of individual differences—specific dimensions or characteristics of a person that influence that person.[3] Most patterns of individual differences are, in turn, based on personality. Other important dimensions that relate to individual behavior are attitudes, perception, creativity, and stress.

Personality Differences Across Cultures

Personality is the relatively stable set of psychological attributes that distinguishes one person from another.[4] A long-standing debate among psychologists—often referred to as the question of "nature versus nurture"—is the extent to which personality attributes are biologically inherited (the "nature" argument) or shaped by the social and cultural environment in which people are raised (the "nurture" argument). In reality, both biological factors and environmental factors play important roles in determining personalities.[5] Although the details of this debate are beyond the scope of our discussion here, international managers should recognize the limitations of sweeping generalizations about people's behavior based on their cultural backgrounds, and acknowledge that individual differences also exist within any given cultural group. That is, while culture may lead to certain behavioral tendencies, as outlined in Chapter 4, individual behavior within any given culture can also vary significantly.

THE "BIG FIVE" PERSONALITY TRAITS Psychologists have identified literally thousands of personality traits and dimensions that differentiate one person from another. But in recent years, researchers have identified five fundamental personality traits that are especially relevant to organizations. Because these five traits, illustrated in Figure 15.1, are so important and because they are currently the subject of so much attention, they are commonly referred to as the **"Big Five" personality traits.**[6]

Agreeableness refers to a person's ability to get along with others. Agreeableness causes some people to be gentle, cooperative, understanding, and good-natured in their dealings with

Within any given culture, even when two individuals are of the same age or professional standing, they are also different from each other in numerous fundamental ways. But when they are from different cultures, such as this European man and Asian man, their personality differences are magnified to a much greater degree.

others, but its absence results in those who are irritable, short-tempered, and uncooperative toward other people. **Conscientiousness** refers to the order and precision a person imposes on activities. This trait measures whether one is organized, systematic, responsible, and self-disciplined, or, conversely, disorganized, careless, and irresponsible. The third of the "Big Five" personality dimensions is **emotional stability,** which causes some individuals to be poised, calm, resilient, and secure; those who have less emotional stability will be excitable, insecure, reactive, and subject to extreme mood swings. **Extroversion,** a person's comfort level with relationships, indicates that some people are sociable, talkative, and assertive, whereas others are less sociable and more introverted. Finally, **openness** measures a person's rigidity of beliefs and

FIGURE 15.1

The "Big Five" Personality Traits

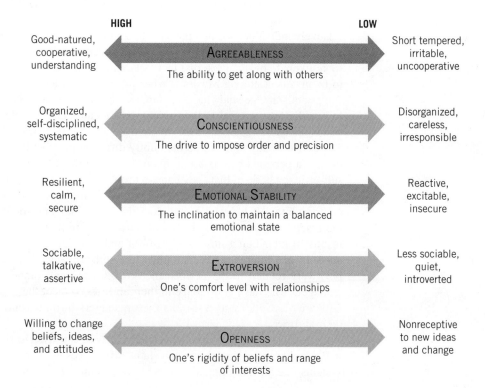

range of interests. This trait results in some people being willing to listen to new ideas and to change their own ideas, beliefs, and attitudes as a result of new information. Those who are less open are less receptive to new ideas and less willing to change their minds.

A growing body of research has emerged on the Big Five framework in the United States. In general, this work focuses on using one or more of the five traits to predict performance in various kinds of jobs. Recently this research has been extended to other countries. For instance, researchers have found that in the European Union, as in the United States, conscientiousness and emotional stability appear to be reasonable predictors of performance across a variety of job criteria and occupational groups. That is, Europeans with high conscientiousness and emotional stability are likely to perform at a higher level than those with low conscientiousness and less emotional stability. Similarly, extroversion is a useful predictor of managerial performance in China and among certain occupational groups in the European Union, most notably managers in sales and marketing. Openness and agreeableness predict performance across more occupational types, but only for certain performance criteria, most notably training proficiency.[7] There is also some evidence to suggest that the Big Five are reasonably good predictors of performance in Hong Kong, but predict even better when combined with traditional Chinese factors as harmony, face, and *ren qing* (personal connections).[8] Thus, when selecting individuals for job assignments in different countries, managers should take advantage of any valid and reliable personality measures that might help with their choices, but should also be sure to not overgeneralize the validity and reliability of such measures across cultures.

OTHER PERSONALITY TRAITS AT WORK Besides the Big Five, there are also several other personality traits that influence behavior in organizations. Among the most important are locus of control, self-efficacy, authoritarianism, and self-esteem.[9]

Locus of control is the extent to which people believe that their behavior has a real effect on what happens to them.[10] Some people, for example, trust that if they work hard, they will succeed. They also may believe that people who fail do so because they lack ability or motivation. People who maintain that individuals are in control of their lives are said to have an *internal locus of control*. Other people think that fate, chance, luck, or other people's behavior determines what happens to them. For example, an employee who fails to get a promotion may attribute that failure to a politically motivated boss or just bad luck, rather than to his own lack of skills or poor performance record. People who think that forces beyond their control dictate what happens to them are said to have an *external locus of control*.

While not yet demonstrated by research, it seems reasonable to suggest that people from relatively individualistic and power-tolerant cultures are more likely to have an internal locus of control, whereas people from relatively collectivistic and power-respecting cultures may be more likely to have an external locus of control. Similarly, an external locus of control is likely to be prevalent among Muslims, whereas an internal locus of control is more consistent with Protestantism. One study has found that samples of people in New Zealand and Singapore seem to be relatively internal in their orientation, as are many people in the United States.[11] It also seems likely, however, that locus of control will vary significantly across cultures.

Self-efficacy is a related but subtly different personality characteristic. Self-efficacy indicates a person's beliefs about his or her capabilities to perform a task.[12] People with high self-efficacy believe that they can perform well on a specific task, whereas people with low self-efficacy tend to doubt their ability to perform that task. While self-assessments of ability contribute to self-efficacy, so too does the individual's personality. Some people simply have more self-confidence than do others. This belief in their ability to perform a task effectively results in their being more self-assured and more able to focus their attention on performance. In one interesting recent study, the self-efficacy of senior managers was found to be positively related to the performance of international joint ventures. That is, joint-venture managers who have confidence in their abilities to meet the goals and objectives of the business are more likely to do so than are managers in joint ventures with lower confidence in their abilities.[13]

Another important personality characteristic is **authoritarianism,** the extent to which an individual believes that power and status differences are appropriate within hierarchical social systems like business organizations.[14] For example, a person who is highly authoritarian may accept directives or orders from someone with more authority purely because the other person is "the boss." On the other hand, even though a person who is not highly authoritarian may still carry out appropriate and reasonable directives from the boss, he or she is also more likely to question things, express disagreement with the boss, and even to refuse to carry out orders if they are for some reason objectionable. A highly authoritarian manager may be relatively autocratic and demanding, and highly authoritarian subordinates will be more likely to accept this behavior from their leader. A less authoritarian manager may allow subordinates a bigger role in making decisions, and less authoritarian subordinates will respond positively to this behavior. This trait is obviously quite similar to the concept of power orientation discussed in Chapter 4.

Self-esteem is the extent to which a person believes that he or she is a worthwhile and deserving individual. A person with high self-esteem is more likely to seek higher status jobs, be more confident in her ability to achieve higher levels of performance, and derive greater intrinsic satisfaction from her accomplishments. In contrast, a person with less self-esteem may be more content to remain in a lower-level job, be less confident of his ability, and focus more on extrinsic rewards.

Among the major personality dimensions, self-esteem is the one that has been most widely studied in other countries. More research is clearly needed, but the published evidence does suggest that self-esteem is an important personality trait in most Western European countries, throughout North America and South America, and in Australia. However, it has not been widely studied in Africa, the Middle East, and most Asian countries. In those societies where self-esteem does emerge as a meaningful personality trait, those individuals with high levels of self-esteem seem to be more motivated and to perform at a higher level than those with lower levels of self-esteem.[15]

Attitudes Across Cultures

Another dimension of individuals within organizations is their attitudes. **Attitudes** are complexes of beliefs and feelings that people have about specific ideas, situations, or other people. While some attitudes are deeply rooted and long-lasting, others can be formed or changed quickly. For example, attitudes toward political parties or major social issues, such as pollution control or abortion, evolve over an extended period of time. But attitudes about a new restaurant may be formed immediately after eating there for the first time.

Attitudes are important because they provide a way for most people to express their feelings. An employee's statement that he is underpaid by the organization reflects his feelings about his pay. Similarly, when a manager endorses the new advertising campaign, she is expressing her feelings about the organization's marketing efforts. In recent times, attitudes toward workplace privacy have become especially important in light of the increased use of e-mail, the Internet, and other forms of electronic communication.

JOB SATISFACTION   One especially important attitude in most organizations is job satisfaction. **Job satisfaction** or **dissatisfaction** is an attitude that reflects the extent to which an individual is gratified by or fulfilled in his or her work. Extensive research conducted on job satisfaction has indicated that personal factors such as an individual's needs and aspirations determine this attitude along with group and organizational factors such as relationships with coworkers and supervisors and working conditions, work policies, and compensation.[16] A satisfied employee also tends to be absent less often, to make positive contributions, and to stay with the organization. In contrast, a dissatisfied employee may be absent more often, may experience stress that disrupts coworkers, and may be continually looking for another job. However, high levels of job satisfaction do not necessarily lead to higher levels of performance.

Research has shown, at least in some settings, that expatriates who are dissatisfied with their jobs and foreign assignments are more likely to leave their employers than are more satisfied managers.[17] One survey measured job satisfaction among 8,300 workers in 106 factories in Japan and the United States. Contrary to what many people believe, this survey found that Japanese workers in general are less satisfied with their jobs than are their counterparts in the United States.[18] For instance, on a four-point scale the average U.S. worker scored 2.95 when asked "All in all, how satisfied would you say you are with your job?" The average

Japanese worker, in contrast, scored only 2.12. Another survey found that managers in the former USSR are relatively dissatisfied with their jobs, especially in terms of their autonomy to make important decisions.[19] Yet another study suggests that Vietnamese workers are relatively satisfied with their jobs, with younger workers (those born since 1975) especially satisfied.[20]

ORGANIZATIONAL COMMITMENT Another important job-related attitude is **organizational commitment,** which reflects an individual's identification with and loyalty to the organization. One comparative study of Western, Asian, and local employees working in Saudi Arabia found that the expatriate Asians reported higher levels of organizational commitment than did the Westerners and local Saudis.[21] Another found that U.S. production workers reported higher levels of organizational commitment than did Japanese workers.[22] More recently, a large study of organizational commitment among U.S. expatriates in four Asian and four European countries found that if those expatriates had a long service history with the firm, received extensive pretransfer training, and adjusted easily to the foreign culture after transfer, they retained high levels of commitment to their parent company. But expatriates with shorter service histories, who had less pretransfer training, and who had a more difficult adjustment period, actually developed stronger levels of commitment toward the *foreign* affiliate.[23] These findings seem reasonable: The first group of employees had made major personal investments in the parent organization and, because of the ease of their transfer, had less need to invest themselves emotionally in their new assignments. The second group had less attachment to their domestic employers, but needed to make larger personal investments in their new assignments to overcome the difficulties they were encountering. Similar "bonding" is observed among people who undergo stressful situations together, such as basic training in the military, initiation week in a fraternity or sorority, or the "ropes" course commonly used by many corporate trainers.

Perception Across Cultures

One important determinant of an attitude is the individual's perception of the object about which the attitude is formed. **Perception** is the set of processes by which an individual becomes aware of and interprets information about the environment. Perception obviously starts when we see, hear, touch, smell, or taste something. Each individual, however, then interprets that awareness through filtering processes that are unique to that person. For example, two people supporting different teams can watch the same play on a soccer or rugby field and "see" very different realities. An individual's cultural background obviously plays a role in shaping how the person's filtering mechanisms work.

Stereotyping is one common perceptual process that affects international business. *Stereotyping* occurs when we make inferences about someone because of one or more characteristics they possess. For example, some people in the United States hold stereotypes that Japanese managers work all the time, that Swiss managers are well organized, and that French managers are elitist. And some people in those countries stereotype U.S. managers as greedy. While such stereotypes may sometimes be useful as cultural generalizations, all managers should be aware that each individual is unique and may or may not fit preconceived impressions.

Aside from stereotyping, perception can affect international business in many other ways. For example, as described in Chapter 3, international managers must assess political and other forms of risk in foreign markets. However, there may be differences across cultures as to how risk is perceived. As illustrated in one recent study, managers from six Latin American countries perceived common business risks (such as political, commercial, and exchange-rate risks) very differently from one another.[24] Managers in Costa Rica saw risk as a definable and manageable part of the environment, whereas managers from Guatemala saw risk as an abstract force that was determined almost by chance.

Similarly, another study of Japanese expatriates and British locals working together in Japanese-owned banks in London found that the two groups perceived each other in very different ways.[25] The Japanese expatriates saw their British coworkers as being most interested in protecting their jobs and maintaining their income, whereas the British locals saw the Japanese as being most interested in profit and group harmony. And, finally, another study found that senior executives in the United States, the United Kingdom, Germany, and Austria perceived

Stress can be a powerful force in any organizational setting regardless of where it is located. Take this harried executive, for example. Her body language and facial expression clearly convey that she is experiencing stress. This stress is likely associated with the work she is performing and can result in a number of different consequences.

Bobby Deal/Dreamstime.com

ethical situations very differently from one another.[26] Clearly, then, international managers must consider the role of perception as they conduct business in different countries.

Stress Across Cultures

Another important element of behavior in organizations is stress. **Stress** is an individual's response to a strong stimulus.[27] This stimulus is called a *stressor*. We should note that stress is not all bad. In the absence of stress, we may experience lethargy and stagnation. An optimal level of stress can result in motivation and excitement; too much stress, however, can have negative consequences.

It is also important to understand that stress can be caused by "good" as well as "bad" things. Excessive pressure, unreasonable demands on our time, and bad news can all cause stress. But receiving a bonus and then having to decide what to do with the money can also be stressful. So, too, can receiving a promotion, gaining recognition, and similar positive events.

There are two different perspectives on stress that are especially relevant for international managers. One, managing stress resulting from international assignments, is covered in Chapter 19. The other is recognizing that people in different cultures may experience different forms of stress and then handle that stress in different ways. In one study that looked at stress patterns across 10 countries, Swedish executives experienced the least stress. Executives from the United States, the United Kingdom, and the former West Germany reported relatively moderate stress, and that they were managing this stress effectively. But managers from Japan, Brazil, Egypt, Singapore, South Africa, and Nigeria reported that they were experiencing very high levels of stress and/or that they were having difficulties managing stress.[28] Another study reported that managers in Germany do a better job of maintaining a healthy balance between work and nonwork activities and managing stress than do managers in the United Kingdom.[29]

Motivation in International Business

All international businesses face the challenge of motivating their workforces to reduce costs, develop new products, enhance product quality, and improve customer service. **Motivation** is the overall set of forces that causes people to choose certain behaviors from a set of available behaviors.[30] Yet the factors that influence an individual's behavior at work differ across cultures. An appreciation of these individual differences is an important first step in understanding how managers can better motivate their employees to promote the organization's goals, as "Bringing the World into Focus" indicates.

BRINGING THE WORLD INTO FOCUS | MIXING AND MATCHING IN A JOINT VENTURE

Because work teams have become so ubiquitous in management today, it follows that many new joint ventures and other alliances will have work teams as a critical component. But managers need to pay careful attention to the culturally based differences that can exist among people in such settings and how those differences can facilitate or hinder the new venture.

Consider, for example, the experiences that three multinational firms had several years ago when they decided to "venture abroad" together. It all started when IBM, Siemens, and Toshiba entered into a new joint venture to work together in developing an advanced type of computer chip. Each firm identified a set of research scientists for the project and the total group of around 100 people assembled for work at an IBM facility in East Fishkill, a small Hudson River Valley town in New York. The idea was that the best and brightest minds from three diverse companies would bring such an array of knowledge, insight, and creativity to the project that it was bound to succeed.

Unfortunately, things didn't start out well, and it took much longer than expected for the firms to really figure out how to work together. The biggest reasons cited for the early difficulties related to the cultural differences and barriers that existed among the group members. For example, the Japanese scientists were accustomed to working in one big room where everyone could interact with everyone else and it was easy to overhear what others were saying. The IBM facility, in contrast, had small, cramped offices that could only hold a few people at a time. The Germans were unhappy because most of their offices lacked windows—they claimed that back home no one would be asked to work in a windowless office.

Interpersonal styles also caused conflict at times. Both the U.S. and Japanese scientists criticized their German colleagues for planning and organizing too much, while the Japanese were criticized for their unwillingness to make clear decisions. The German and Japanese scientists felt that their U.S. hosts did not spend enough time socializing with them after work. There were also problems with employee privacy and workplace rights. The office doors at the IBM facility all had small windows that visitors could use to peek in to see if the occupant was busy before knocking. Both the Germans and Japanese, however, saw this as an invasion of their privacy and often hung their coats over the windows. And they also objected to IBM's strict no-smoking policy that mandated that people go outside to smoke, regardless of weather conditions.

Because of these problems, the group's initial lack of progress was discouraging. Managers felt that a big part of the problem was that they did not do an adequate job of training the group members before transferring them to the project, and that better cultural training in particular would have been useful. Fortunately for the joint venture, the group members eventually started to train and socialize themselves about how to overcome the cultural differences. Indeed, after the early rough spots, the new venture finally took off and the new chip was developed only a few months behind schedule.[31]

Needs and Values Across Cultures

The starting point in understanding motivation is to consider needs and values. **Needs** are what an individual must have or wants to have. **Values,** meanwhile, are what people believe to be important. Not surprisingly, most people have a large number of needs and values. Primary needs are things that people require in order to survive, such as food, water, and shelter. Thus, they are instinctive and physiologically based. Secondary needs, on the other hand, are more psychological in character and are learned from the environment and culture in which the individual lives. Examples of secondary needs include the needs for achievement, autonomy, power, order, affiliation, and understanding. Secondary needs often manifest themselves in organizational settings. For example, if an individual is to be satisfied with her job the rewards provided by the organization must be consistent with her needs. Offering a nice office and job security may not be sufficient if the individual is primarily seeking income and promotion opportunities. Values, meanwhile, are learned and developed as a person grows and matures. These values are influenced by one's family, peers, experiences, and culture.

Motivational Processes Across Cultures

Most modern theoretical approaches to motivation fall into one of three categories. *Need-based models of motivation* are those that attempt to identify the specific need or set of needs that results in motivated behavior. *Process-based models of motivation* focus more on the conscious thought processes people use to select one behavior from among several. Finally, the *reinforcement model* deals with how people assess the consequences of their behavioral choices and how that assessment goes into their future choice of behaviors. This model incorporates the roles of rewards and punishment in maintaining or altering existing behavioral patterns.

Need-Based Models Across Cultures

Hofstede's work, discussed in Chapter 4, provides some useful insights into how need-based models of motivation are likely to vary across cultures.[32] Common needs incorporated in most models of motivation include the needs for security, for being part of a social network, and for having opportunities to grow and develop. By relating these need categories to four of Hofstede's dimensions—social orientation, power orientation, uncertainty orientation, and goal orientation—we can draw several inferences about differences in motivation across cultures.

For example, managers and employees in countries that are individualistic may be most strongly motivated by individually based needs and rewards. Opportunities to demonstrate personal competencies and to receive recognition and rewards as a result may be particularly attractive to such people. In contrast, people from collectivistic cultures may be more strongly motivated by group-based needs and rewards. Indeed, they may be uncomfortable in situations in which they are singled out for rewards apart from the group with which they work.

Conflicts can easily arise when an international firm's mechanisms for motivating workers clash with cultural attitudes. Many U.S. managers working for Japanese MNCs have difficulty with the seniority-based, group-performance-oriented compensation systems of their employers. Similarly, Michigan autoworkers resisted the attempts by Mazda officials to get them to "voluntarily" wear Mazda baseball caps as part of their work uniforms.[33] And U.S. professional baseball players playing for Japanese teams, accustomed to the "star system" at home that accords them status, prestige, and special privileges, are often shocked by the team-based approach in Japan, which discourages attention to individuals.

Power-respecting individuals are those who accept their boss's right to direct their efforts purely on the basis of organizational legitimacy. As a consequence of this power respect, they may be motivated by the possibility of gaining their boss's approval and acceptance. Thus, they may willingly and unquestioningly accept and attempt to carry out directives and mandates. In contrast, power-tolerant people attach less legitimacy to hierarchical rank. Thus, they may be less motivated by gaining their boss's approval than by opportunities for pay raises and promotions.

Managers and employees in uncertainty-avoiding cultures may be highly motivated by opportunities to maintain or increase their perceived levels of job security and job stability. Any effort to reduce or eliminate that security or stability may be met with resistance. In contrast, people in uncertainty-accepting cultures may be less motivated by security needs and less inclined to seek job security or stability as a condition of employment. They also may be more motivated by change and by new challenges and opportunities for personal growth and development. For example, recent studies comparing U.S. and German workers reveal substantial differences in their preferences regarding job values. Job security and shorter work hours were valued more highly by the German workers than the U.S. workers. Income, opportunities for promotion, and the importance of one's work were much more highly valued by the U.S. workers than by their German counterparts.[34]

Finally, people from more aggressive goal behavior cultures are more likely to be motivated by money and other material rewards. They may pursue behavioral choices that they perceive as having the highest probability of financial payoff. They also may be disinclined to work toward rewards whose primary attraction is mere comfort or personal satisfaction. In contrast, workers in passive goal behavior cultures may be more motivated by needs and rewards that can potentially enhance the quality of their lives. They may be less interested in behavioral choices whose primary appeal is a higher financial payoff. For example, Swedish firms provide generous vacations and fringe benefits.

Various studies have tested specific motivation theories in different cultural settings. The theory receiving the most attention has been Abraham Maslow's hierarchy of five basic needs: physiological, security, social, self-esteem, and self-actualization.[35] International research on

Maslow's hierarchy provides two different insights. First, managers in many different countries, including the United States, Mexico, Japan, and Canada, usually agree that the needs included in Maslow's hierarchy are all important to them. Second, the relative importance and preference ordering of the needs vary considerably by country.[36] For example, managers in less-developed countries such as Liberia and India place a higher priority on satisfying self-esteem and security needs than do managers from more developed countries.[37]

Results from research based on another motivation theory, David McClelland's learned needs framework, have been slightly more consistent. In particular, the need for achievement (to grow, learn, and accomplish important things) has been shown to exist in many different countries. McClelland has also demonstrated that the need for achievement can be taught to people in different cultures.[38] However, given the role of Hofstede's cultural differences, it follows that McClelland's needs are not likely to be constant across cultures. In particular, individualistic, uncertainty-accepting, power-tolerant, and aggressive goal behavior cultures seem more likely to foster and promote the needs for achievement and power (to control resources) than the need for affiliation (to be part of a social network). In contrast, collectivistic, uncertainty-avoiding, power-respecting, and passive goal behavior cultures may promote the need for affiliation more than the needs for achievement and power.[39]

Frederick Herzberg's two-factor theory is another popular need-based theory of motivation.[40] This theory suggests that one set of factors affects dissatisfaction and another set affects satisfaction. It, too, has been tested cross-culturally with varied results. For example, research has found different patterns of factors when comparing U.S. managers with managers from New Zealand and Panama.[41] Results from U.S. employees suggested that supervision contributed to dissatisfaction but not to satisfaction. But supervision did contribute to employees' satisfaction in New Zealand. Unfortunately, Herzberg's theory often fails to yield consistent results even within a single culture. Thus, even though the theory is well known and popular among managers, managers should be particularly cautious in attempting to apply it in different cultural contexts.

Process-Based Models Across Cultures

In contrast to need-based theories, expectancy theory takes a process view of motivation.[42] The theory suggests that people are motivated to behave in certain ways to the extent that they perceive that such behaviors will lead to outcomes they find personally attractive. The theory acknowledges that different people have different needs—one person may need money, another recognition, another social satisfaction, and still another prestige. But each will be willing to improve his or her performance if he or she believes the result will be fulfillment of the needs he or she finds most important.

Relatively little research has explicitly tested expectancy theory in countries other than the United States. It does seem logical, however, that the basic framework of the theory should have wide applicability. Regardless of where people work, they are likely to work toward goals they think are important. However, cultural factors will partially determine both the nature of those work goals and people's perceptions of how they should most fruitfully pursue them.

One particularly complex factor that is likely to affect the expectancy process is the cultural dimension of social orientation. The expectancy theory is essentially a model of individual decisions regarding individual behavioral choices targeted at individual outcomes. Thus, it may be less able to explain behavior in collectivistic cultures, but otherwise may be one of the most likely candidates for a culturally unbiased explanation of motivated behavior. For example, expectancy theory helps explain the success Sony has enjoyed. People who go to work for Sony know they will be able to pursue diverse opportunities and will be kept informed about what is happening in the firm. People who see these conditions as especially important will be most strongly motivated to work for Sony.

The Reinforcement Model Across Cultures

Like expectancy theory, the reinforcement model has undergone relatively few tests in different cultures. This model says that behavior that results in a positive outcome (reinforcement) will likely be repeated under the same circumstances in the future. Behavioral choice that results in negative consequences (punishment) will result in a different choice under the same circumstances in the future. Since this model makes no attempt to specify what people will find reinforcing or punishing, it may also be generalizable to different cultures.

Like expectancy theory, the reinforcement model may have exceptions. In Muslim cultures, for example, people tend to believe that the consequences they experience are the will of God rather than a function of their own behavior. Thus, reinforcement and punishment are likely to have less effect on their future behavioral decisions. Aside from relatively narrow exceptions such as this, however, the reinforcement model, like expectancy theory, warrants careful attention from international managers, provided they understand that what constitutes rewards and punishment will vary across cultures.

Leadership in International Business

Another important behavioral and interpersonal consideration in international business is leadership. **Leadership** is the use of noncoercive influence to shape the goals of a group or organization, to motivate behavior toward reaching those goals, and to help determine the group or organizational culture.[43] Leadership in international business takes on additional complexities due in part to the more diverse workforces that are likely to be found in international organizations.[44] [See Chapter 5 for discussions of both effective (Patagonia) and less-effective (BP) leadership in multinational firms.]

Some people mistakenly equate management and leadership. However, there are clear and substantive differences between these two important processes. Management tends to rely on formal power and authority and to focus on administration and decision making. Leadership, in contrast, relies more on personal power and focuses more on motivation and communication. Leadership has been widely studied by organizational scientists for decades. Early studies attempted to identify physical traits or universal behaviors that most clearly distinguished leaders from nonleaders. More recently, attention has focused on matching leadership with situations. Although some studies still focus on traits, most leadership models suggest that appropriate leader behavior depends on situational factors.[45]

Contemporary leadership theories recognize that leaders cannot succeed by always using the same set of behaviors in all circumstances. Instead, leaders must carefully assess the situation in which they find themselves and then tailor one or more behaviors to fit that situation. Common

The leadership of diverse groups can pose a variety of challenges to those in positions of authority. For instance, when South Africa was governed by apartheid, white leaders and white citizens had superior standing while the rights of non-whites were severely limited. But following the abolishment of apartheid, Nelson Mandela, the former leader of the black opposition, was elected president. His first big challenge was to reconcile the former ruling white population with the formerly oppressed blacks and other nonwhite groups.

AP Images/Kim Ludbrook

situational factors that affect appropriate leader behavior include individual differences among subordinates; characteristics of the group, the organization, and the leader; and subordinates' desire to participate.[46]

Clearly, cultural factors will affect appropriate leader behavior, and the way in which managers spend their workday will vary among cultures.[47] Figure 15.2 summarizes some interesting findings from an early international study of leadership. Managers were asked to indicate the extent to which they agreed with the statement, "It is important for a manager to have at hand precise answers to most of the questions that subordinates may raise about their work." As shown in the figure, more than half of the managers in Japan and Italy agreed with this statement, whereas a much smaller percentage of managers in Sweden, Germany, Great Britain, and the United States did so. In general, agreement with the statement would suggest that managers and leaders are perceived as experts who should know all the answers. Those who disagree with the statement believe that managers and leaders are supposed to be problem solvers who may not know the answer to a question but can figure it out or know how to find the answer. In the United States, therefore, a manager who failed to refer a subordinate to a more knowledgeable authority would be seen as arrogant. But in Indonesia, a manager who refers a subordinate to someone else for answers is likely to be seen as incompetent.[48]

Several implications for leaders in international settings can be drawn from the cultural factors identified in Hofstede's work. In individualistic cultures, leaders may need to focus their behavior on individual employees rather than the group. In contrast, in a collectivistic culture, leader behaviors will clearly need to focus on the group rather than on individual group members. In a group-oriented culture such as that of Japan, an effective leader must guide subordinates while preserving group harmony. At Sony, for example, managers are expected to allow their employees to transfer at will to more interesting job settings because such transfers are believed to be in the firm's overall best interests. The Japanese management system focuses on consensus-building efforts to ensure that both leader and subordinates reach a common decision. A leader would destroy group harmony if he dictatorially commanded his subordinates to implement his decisions. One problem that may develop, however, is that junior managers attempt to anticipate what their boss's preferred strategy is and then offer it as their own. A leader confronted with such a strong tendency toward conformity must seek ways to encourage creative solutions from subordinates to new problems as they arise. A Japanese manager may thus distance himself from pending decisions,

FIGURE 15.2

The Role of Managers Varies Across Cultures

Source: Based on *International Studies of Management and Organization,* vol. XIII, Nos. 1–2 (Spring–Summer 1983), by permission of M. E. Sharpe, Inc., Armonk, NY 10504.

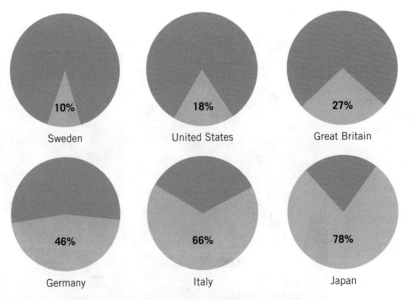

Sweden 10%   United States 18%   Great Britain 27%

Germany 46%   Italy 66%   Japan 78%

"It is important for a manager to have at hand precise answers to most of the questions that subordinates may raise about their work."

(Percentages refer to those in agreement.)

thereby encouraging subordinates to discuss a variety of options among themselves. Only then will the manager lead by dropping subtle hints regarding what he sees as the correct solution to an issue.[49]

Power orientation carries even more direct implications for situational leadership. In power-respecting cultures employees may expect leaders to take charge, to make decisions, and to direct their efforts. Leaders may therefore need to concentrate on performance-oriented behaviors (direct, structured, and goal-oriented behaviors), avoid employee-oriented behaviors (caring, concern, and interpersonally oriented behaviors), and make little attempt to foster participation. But if power tolerance is the more pervasive cultural value, a leader should spend less time on performance-oriented behaviors. Instead, employee-oriented behaviors and more employee participation may result in higher levels of effectiveness.

Attempts at blurring the distinctions between managers and workers may not be well received in more authoritarian, hierarchical societies. For example, one U.S. firm exported the "company picnic" concept to its Spanish subsidiary, complete with company executives serving food to the Spanish employees. However, this informality was not well received by the employees, who were embarrassed at being served by their "superiors."[50]

Uncertainty orientation is also an important situational factor to consider. Where uncertainty avoidance is the rule, employees will have a strong desire for structure and direction. Thus, performance-oriented behaviors are likely to be more successful, whereas employee-oriented behaviors and attempts to use participation may be less so. For example, German managers tend to be autocratic and task-oriented, making decisions with reference to existing corporate rules and procedures. Having determined departmental objectives, they then confidently delegate tasks to subordinates, whom they expect to competently carry out the tasks necessary to achieve the objective.[51]

In contrast, employees more prone toward uncertainty acceptance may respond more favorably to opportunities for participation. They may even prefer participative behaviors on the part of their leaders. But performance-oriented leadership may be undesirable or unnecessary, while employee-oriented leadership may have little impact. That is, employees may have such a strong desire to participate and be involved in their work that they see performance-oriented or employee-oriented behaviors from their supervisor as being redundant with or even negating their own opportunities for participation.

Finally, differences in goal orientation will affect leader behavior. Recall that people in aggressive goal behavior cultures tend to value money and other material rewards. If performance-oriented leadership or higher levels of participation are perceived by followers to result in higher rewards, those behaviors will be more acceptable. In contrast, outcomes enhancing quality of life are more desirable in passive goal behavior cultures. To the extent that employee-oriented leader behaviors may cause followers to feel more satisfied with their work and the organization, such behaviors may be more effective in these settings.

Cultural factors are among the most difficult and complex to assess and understand. They may also be among the most critical in determining leader effectiveness. It is important that leaders attempt to match their behaviors with the context—the people they are leading and the organization in which they are functioning.[52] For example, one study analyzed the productivity of U.S. and Mexican factories owned by the same MNC. Cultural differences clearly exist between the two countries. Mexico ranks high on power respect relative to the United States. U.S. residents are far more individualistic than those of Mexico, while the family is more highly valued in Mexico than in the United States. Mexican cultural values translate into the paternalistic, authoritarian management style adopted by managers of the MNC's Mexican facilities. Managers of its U.S. facilities, however, adopted less paternalistic and more participative styles in managing their employees. By allowing management styles to adapt to national culture, the MNC enjoyed equally high levels of productivity from both facilities.[53]

Decision Making in International Business

Another area of international business in which large cultural differences exist is decision making. **Decision making** is the process of choosing one alternative from among a set of alternatives in order to promote the decision maker's objectives.

Models of Decision Making

There are two very different views of how managers go about making decisions, as illustrated in Figure 15.3. The *normative model of decision making* suggests that managers apply logic and rationality in making the best decisions. In contrast, the *descriptive model of decision making* argues that behavioral processes limit a manager's ability to always be logical and rational.[54]

The normative model suggests that decision making starts when managers recognize that a problem exists and a decision has to be made. For example, a Shell refinery manager recently noticed that turnover among a certain group of workers had increased substantially. The second step is for the manager to identify potential alternatives for addressing the problem. The Shell manager determined that since turnover can be caused by low wages, poor working conditions, or poor supervision, her alternatives included raising wages, improving working conditions, or changing the group's supervisor.

The third step in the normative model is to evaluate each alternative in light of the original problem. The Shell manager knew that the group's wages were comparable to what others in the refinery were making. She also realized that the group's work area had recently been refurbished, so she assumed working conditions were not a problem. In addition, she also discovered that a new supervisor had recently been appointed for the group. Using this information, the manager proceeded to step four in the normative process, selecting the best alternative. She felt that the problem was one of poor supervision, so she looked more closely at that particular part of the situation.

After scrutinizing the new supervisor's records, the plant manager saw that the supervisor had been promoted during a very hectic period and had not gone through the refinery's normal supervisory training program. Since step five of the normative model suggests that the chosen alternative be implemented, the plant manager arranged for the new supervisor to complete his training. After six months, turnover in the group had dropped significantly and the plant manager was certain from this follow-up and evaluation that her chosen course of action was the correct one.

The descriptive model acknowledges that this is perhaps how managers should make their decisions. But the model also notes that, in reality, managers are affected by two important behavioral processes. The first is called bounded rationality. *Bounded rationality* suggests that decision makers are constrained in their ability to be objective and rational by limitations of the human mind. Thus, they often use incomplete and imperfect information. Notice that the Shell

FIGURE 15.3

Models of the Decision-Making Process

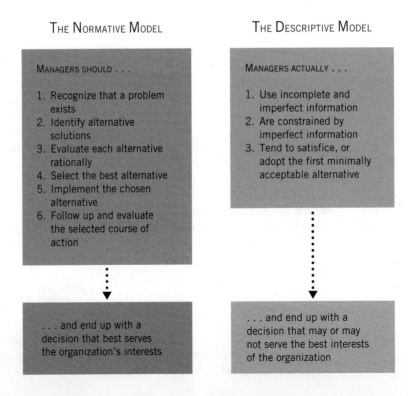

THE NORMATIVE MODEL

MANAGERS SHOULD . . .

1. Recognize that a problem exists
2. Identify alternative solutions
3. Evaluate each alternative rationally
4. Select the best alternative
5. Implement the chosen alternative
6. Follow up and evaluate the selected course of action

. . . and end up with a decision that best serves the organization's interests

THE DESCRIPTIVE MODEL

MANAGERS ACTUALLY . . .

1. Use incomplete and imperfect information
2. Are constrained by imperfect information
3. Tend to satisfice, or adopt the first minimally acceptable alternative

. . . and end up with a decision that may or may not serve the best interests of the organization

manager in the example above did not consult with the members of the group to find out why turnover had increased. Had she done so, she might have gained additional information. The other behavioral process is called satisficing. *Satisficing* suggests that managers sometimes adopt the first minimally acceptable alternative they identify, when a further search might suggest an even better alternative. For example, since the supervisor had an opportunity to gain some experience, he might have been able to improve his skills with an abbreviated or accelerated training program. "Bringing the World into Focus" highlights the role of decision making at Porsche.

The Normative Model Across Cultures

We can draw several possible implications from applying our basic understanding of the normative and descriptive models to decision making in other cultures.[56] To explore those implications, we first walk through the steps in the normative model.

STEP 1: PROBLEM RECOGNITION People from different cultures are likely to recognize and define problem situations in very different ways. For example, in individualistic cultures, problems are likely to be defined in terms of individual scenarios and consequences. In collectivistic cultures, the focus will be more on group-related issues and situations. In an uncertainty-accepting culture, managers are more likely to take risks in solving problems and making decisions. In uncertainty-avoiding cultures, they may be much more cautious and strive to reduce uncertainty as much as

---

BRINGING THE WORLD INTO FOCUS   **RISKY DECISIONS LEAD THE WAY FOR PORSCHE**

The word *Porsche* conjures up images of speed and glamour and can cause an adrenaline rush among just about any car enthusiast. Hence, it might come as a bit of a surprise to learn that one of the firm's greatest leaders was not some jaunty and dashing jet setter but instead an unassuming and quiet man who wore white shirts and old-fashioned glasses. That leader was Wendelin Wiedeking, CEO until mid-2010. "All" he did during his tenure as CEO was to increase Porsche's profits for 10 years running and achieve profit margins that often exceeded 50 percent! How did he accomplish these feats? One key to his success was his willingness to make tough—and risky—decisions.

For instance, the German government once offered the firm $97.5 million as an incentive for it to build a new factory. Wiedeking turned the money down, however, because he didn't want Porsche customers to be criticized for having the government support their expensive habits. He also mandated that no Porsche executive could receive stock options—indeed, during his tenure they cannot even buy company stock. Why? Because he feared that in a small company like Porsche virtually any major decision could affect share price, thus opening up possible claims of insider trading.

Wiedeking was also about to list Porsche on the New York Stock Exchange when a new law was enacted requiring senior executives to swear that their financial reporting is accurate. He argued that since hundreds of people prepare Porsche's financial documents, he could not always be sure that each and every one was precisely correct. A recent Wiedeking comment reflects his view of the firm: "Those who make concessions will lose. If we were just a small copy of a major player, our continued existence would certainly be unjustified."

A great example of Wiedeking's willingness to take risks involved one of the most significant decisions in the firm's long and storied history. As auto companies across the globe consolidated into fewer but larger firms, Porsche—by comparison—became smaller and smaller. Eventually, the differential became so great that Wiedeking and his senior executives knew that they either had to agree to become taken over by a larger firm or else substantially increase Porsche's sales base. Wiedeking initially chose to go the latter route. Among his first steps was the introduction of the Boxster, a lower-priced sports car that today accounts for nearly half of the firm's annual revenues.

But then he made a much riskier decision—to design and build a sports utility vehicle. There was considerable internal debate, and Porsche enthusiasts howled in protest. But Wiedeking quickly decided to proceed to put the prototype into full-scale production. The new vehicle, called the Cayenne, went on sale in 2003; Porsche sold all 25,000 units it made that year. Since that time, the firm has modestly increased production each year. In defense of the controversial new vehicle, Wiedeking commented that "It was not easy to make the decision, but now everybody at Porsche is happy with the Cayenne. It rides like a Porsche and drives like a Porsche. It is 100% Porsche." Perhaps emboldened by Cayenne's success, Porsche next developed and launched a four-door sedan called the Panamera.

Eventually, though, Wiedeking came to realize that the best hope for Porsche's future was for the firm to merge with or be taken over by another, larger company. Carefully working behind the scenes, he managed to orchestrate a takeover by Volkswagen. For its part, Volkswagen agreed to retain the Porsche brand as a separate product line. As plans for the takeover were finalized in 2010, Wiedeking stepped down from his leadership position. But his legacy as both an astute leader and a manager willing to make risky decisions will be a long-lasting part of the storied Porsche history.[55] (Note: Several financial and legal complications arose as the merger was being finalized. As a result, the timetable for completing the deal has been pushed back until at least 2012.)

possible before making a decision. As a result, they may fall back on firm policies and rules to provide a course of action ("We can't do that because it's against company policy").

STEP 2: IDENTIFYING ALTERNATIVES The processes through which alternatives are identified will also vary across cultures. For example, in power-respecting cultures, managers may be much less willing to consider an alternative that potentially threatens the hierarchy—for example, that a suggestion from a subordinate might be valid or that a problem might exist at a higher level in the organization. But in power-tolerant cultures, such hierarchical issues are more likely to be considered possible remedies to organizational problems.

In collectivistic societies, the desire for group harmony and conflict avoidance may be so strong that decision making is approached in unique ways. For example, the Japanese concern for maintaining group harmony has given rise to the ringi system for identifying alternatives and making decisions. The **ringi system** provides that decisions cannot be made unilaterally; doing that would be too individualistic and therefore destructive of group harmony. To encourage creative solutions, a manager may draw up a document, called the *ringisho*, which defines the problem and sets out a proposed solution. The Japanese corporate belief is that those who implement a solution should be those most affected by the problem, since they understand the problem and are motivated to solve it. Thus, most ringisho originate from middle managers.

Although the ringisho originates from an individual, it is soon subsumed by the group. The document is circulated to all members of the originator's work group, as well as to other groups affected by it. As the ringisho passes through the workplace, it may be accepted, rejected, or modified. Only a document that is approved by all its reviewers is passed to a more senior manager for approval or disapproval. But before the ringisho reaches this stage, any senior manager worth his salt will have already dropped hints if he had any objections to any parts of it. Appropriate changes then would have been incorporated into the document by some subordinate before the ringisho arrived at the senior manager's desk. Through the ringi system, creativity, innovation, and group harmony are all promoted.[57]

In contrast, the German business structure is both strongly hierarchical and compartmentalized. Decision making tends to be slow and drawn out, designed to build consensus within a department of a firm. Data are painstakingly gathered, then communicated to the appropriate employees within the hierarchy. However, information often does not flow easily between departments, and a decision, once reached, may be difficult to change. Also, established operating procedures are followed carefully. These factors substantially reduce the firm's flexibility and responsiveness to rapidly changing conditions. The resulting inflexibility often hinders the performance of foreign subsidiaries of German MNCs, which have difficulty getting the home office to acknowledge that their operating conditions may differ from those in Germany.[58]

STEP 3: EVALUATING ALTERNATIVES Evaluating alternatives can also be affected by cultural phenomena. For example, an alternative that results in financial gain may be more attractive in an aggressive goal behavior culture than in a passive goal behavior culture, which may prefer an alternative that results in improved quality of work life. Uncertainty avoidance will also be a consideration; alternatives with varying levels of associated uncertainty may be perceived to be more or less attractive.

Evaluating alternatives is further complicated in countries where people tend to avoid taking responsibility for making decisions. China's economic policies, for example, have changed so quickly and drastically over the past five decades that those supporting today's economic policies may find themselves in political difficulties tomorrow. A Chinese proverb, "The tall tree gets broken off in the wind," suggests the tendency of many Chinese officials to avoid association with any decision that could haunt them later. Group decision making reduces the potential blame an individual bureaucrat may suffer.[59]

STEP 4: SELECTING THE BEST ALTERNATIVE Cultural factors can affect the actual selection of an alternative. In an individualistic culture, for example, a manager may be prone to select an alternative that has the most positive impact on him or her personally; in a collectivistic culture, the impact of the alternative on the total group will carry more weight. Not surprisingly, a manager trained in one culture will often use the same techniques when operating in a different culture, even though they may be ineffective there. In one recent study comparing U.S. managers operating in the United States with U.S. managers operating in Hong Kong, the managerial behaviors of the two groups were found to be the same. These behaviors included managerial supportiveness of subordinates, problem solving, openness of communication, disciplining of subordinates, and so on. However, although these behaviors positively affected firm performance in the United States, they had no effect on firm performance in Hong Kong.[60]

Cultural differences in problem solving and decision making may be particularly troublesome for partners in a joint venture or other strategic alliance because they must develop mutually acceptable decisions. U.S. managers often deliberately use conflict (in the form of devil's advocate or dialectical inquiry techniques) as a means of improving the decision-making process. Managers from more consensus-oriented societies, such as Japan, find this disharmonious approach very distasteful and unproductive.[61]

STEP 5: IMPLEMENTATION In a power-respecting culture, implementation may be mandated by a manager at the top of the organization and accepted without question by others. But in a power-tolerant culture, participation may be more crucial in order to ensure acceptance. In an uncertainty-avoiding culture, managers may need to carefully plan every step of the implementation before proceeding so that everyone knows what to expect. In an uncertainty-accepting culture, however, managers may be more willing to start implementation before all the final details have been arranged.

STEP 6: FOLLOW-UP AND EVALUATION Follow-up and evaluation also have cultural implications, most notably regarding power orientation. In a power-respecting culture, a manager may be unwilling to find fault with an alternative suggested by a higher-level manager. Also, too much credit may be given to a higher-level manager purely on the basis of his or her position in the hierarchy. But in a power-tolerant culture, responsibility, blame, and credit are more likely to be accurately attributed.

The Descriptive Model Across Cultures

The behavioral processes of bounded rationality and satisficing are more difficult to relate to cultural differences. Few research efforts have specifically explored these phenomena in different cultures, and their very nature makes it hard to draw reasonable generalizations. Thus, while it is likely that they do have some impact on business decisions made in different cultures and therefore need to be understood by managers, more research needs to be conducted on their precise influence. In particular, all managers need to understand the potential limitations of applying different modes of decision making in different cultural settings. For example, several years ago the Japanese owners of the Dunes Hotel and Casino in Las Vegas tried to implement a variety of Japanese management practices in the casino operation. One was decision making by consensus. They quickly recognized, however, that it was far too slow for the intensely competitive, fast-changing casino industry.

Groups and Teams in International Business

Other important behavioral processes that international managers should understand are those associated with groups and teams. Regardless of whether a firm is a small domestic company or a large MNC, much of its work is accomplished by people working together as a part of a team, task force, committee, or operating group.

The Nature of Group Dynamics

Firms use groups frequently because, in theory, people working together as a group can accomplish more than they can working individually. While organizations use a wide array of different kinds of groups, teams are especially popular today. Indeed, many managers now refer to all their groups as teams. Technically, a *group* is any collection of people working together to accomplish a common purpose, while a *team* is a specific type of group that assumes responsibility for its own work. Because teams are so ubiquitous today and the term is so common among managers, we will use this term in our discussion.

A mature team in a firm generally has certain characteristics:

1. It develops a well-defined role structure; each member has a part to play on the team, accepts that part, and makes a worthwhile contribution.
2. It establishes norms for its members. Norms are standards of behavior, such as how people should dress, when team meetings or activities will begin, the consequences of being absent, how much each member should produce, and so on.

3. It is cohesive. That is, team members identify more and more strongly with the team, and each member respects, values, and works well with the others.

4. Some teams identify informal leaders among their members—individuals whom the team accords special status and who can lead and direct the team without benefit of formal authority.

If a team's role structure promotes efficiency, its norms reinforce high performance, it truly is cohesive, and its informal leaders support the firm's goals, then it can potentially reach maximum effectiveness. Sony's computer development group took on all of these characteristics, which no doubt helped contribute to the group's ability to reach its goal ahead of schedule. However, if the team's role structure is inefficient, its performance norms are low, it is not cohesive, and/or its informal leaders do not support the firm's goals, then it may become very ineffective from the firm's standpoint.

Managing Cross-Cultural Teams

The composition of a team plays a major role in the dynamics that emerge from it. A relatively homogeneous team generally has less conflict, better communication, less creativity, more uniform norms, higher cohesiveness, and clear informal leadership. A more heterogeneous team often has more conflict, poorer communication, more creativity, less uniform norms, a lower level of cohesiveness, and more ambiguous informal leadership.

Managers charged with building teams in different cultures need to assess the nature of the task to be performed and, as much as possible, match the composition of the team to the type of task. For example, if the task is relatively routine and straightforward, a homogeneous team may be more effective. Similarities in knowledge, background, values, and beliefs can make the work go more smoothly and efficiently. But if the task is nonroutine, complex, and/or ambiguous, a heterogeneous team may be more effective because of members' diverse backgrounds, experiences, knowledge, and values.

Other cultural factors may also play a role in team dynamics. For example, in an individualistic culture, establishing shared norms and cohesiveness may be somewhat difficult, while in a collectivistic culture, team cohesiveness may emerge naturally. In a power-respecting culture, team members should probably be from the same level of the organization, since members from lower levels may be intimidated and subservient to those from higher levels. In a power-tolerant culture, variation in organizational level may be less of a problem. Uncertainty avoidance and team dynamics may also interact as a function of task. If a task is vague, ambiguous, or unstructured, an uncertainty-avoiding group may be unable to function effectively; in contrast, an uncertainty-accepting group may actually thrive. Finally, teams in an aggressive goal behavior culture may work together more effectively if their goal has financial implications, whereas teams in a passive goal behavior culture may be more motivated to work toward attitudinal or quality-of-work outcomes.[62]

Matching business behavior with the cultural values of the workforce is a key ingredient in promoting organizational performance. Much of the competitive strength of Japanese firms, for example, is due to their incorporation of Japanese cultural norms into the workplace. Japanese culture emphasizes the importance of group harmony and respect for superiors. "Silent leaders," ones who guide rather than command subordinates and who preserve group harmony, are more admired than are authoritarian managers. The ringi system ensures that new approaches are granted group approval before being implemented. The traditional lifetime employment practices that some major Japanese firms use promote employee loyalty to the organization. All these features are reinforced by careful selection of new employees. Only those persons who are willing to subordinate their individual goals to the needs of the group are hired. This corporate philosophy carries over to foreign operations of Japanese MNCs. For example, many U.S. newspapers have reported on the extraordinary amounts of testing and interviewing that such firms operating in North America do before hiring an employee. (See Chapter 19's closing case, "Training for the World.")

CHAPTER REVIEW

Summary

Behavioral and interpersonal processes are vitally important in any organization. Both their importance and their complexity are magnified in international firms. Individual differences provide the cornerstone for understanding behavioral patterns in different cultures. Personality traits, attitudes, perceptions, and stress are all important individual differences that international managers should understand.

Motivation is the overall set of forces that causes people to choose certain behaviors from a set of available behaviors. Need-based, process-based, and reinforcement models of motivation each explain different aspects of motivation. Although none of these models is generalizable to all cultures, each can provide insights into motivation in similar cultures.

Leadership is the use of noncoercive influence to shape the goals of a group or organization, to motivate behavior toward reaching those goals, and to help determine the group or organizational culture. People from different cultures react in different ways to each type of leadership behavior. These different reactions are determined partially by cultural dimensions and partially by the individuals themselves.

Decision making is the process of choosing an alternative from among a set of alternatives designed to promote the decision maker's objectives. People from different cultures approach each step in the decision-making process differently. Again, variation along cultural dimensions is a significant determinant of variations in decision-making processes.

Groups and teams are part of all organizations. A team's role structure, cohesiveness, norms, and informal leadership all contribute to its success or failure. Culture plays a major role in determining the team's degree of heterogeneity or homogeneity, which in turn helps determine its overall level of effectiveness.

Review Questions

1. Define *personality* and explain how personality differences affect individual behavior.
2. Explain how attitudes vary across cultures.
3. Discuss the basic perceptual process and note how it differs across cultures.
4. Explain how attitudes and perception can affect each other.
5. Discuss stress and how it varies across cultures.
6. Identify some of the basic issues managers must confront when attempting to motivate employees in different cultures.
7. How do needs and values differ in different cultures?
8. Summarize the steps in the normative model of decision making and relate each to international business.
9. Why are teams so important? What are the basic implications of teams for an international business?

Questions for Discussion

1. Which do you think is a more powerful determinant of human behavior—cultural factors or individual differences?
2. Think of two or three personality traits that you believe are especially strong in your culture, and two or three that are especially weak. Relate these to Hofstede's cultural dimensions.
3. Assume that you have just been transferred by your company to a new facility in a foreign location. Which of your own personal dimensions do you think will be most effective in helping you deal with this new situation? Does your answer depend on which country you're sent to?
4. How might perception affect motivation in different cultures?
5. How might organizations in different cultures go about trying to enhance leadership capabilities?
6. Do you think it will ever be possible to develop a motivation framework that is applicable in all cultures? Why or why not?
7. How do motivation and leadership affect corporate culture?
8. What advice would you give a Japanese, an Australian, and an Italian manager just transferred to the United States?
9. Assume that you are leading a team composed of representatives from British, Mexican, Brazilian, and Egyptian subsidiaries of your firm. The team must make a number of major decisions.

   a. What guidelines might you develop for yourself for leading the team through its decision-making process?

   b. What steps might you take to enhance the team's cohesiveness? How successful do you think such an effort would be?

Building Global Skills

Select a country in which you have some interest and about which you can readily find information (for example, Japan as opposed to Bhutan). Go to your library or use the Internet and learn as much as you can about the behavior of people from the country you selected. Concentrate on such culturally based social phenomena as the following:

- The meaning people from the country attach to a few common English words
- The meaning they attach to common gestures
- How they interpret basic colors
- The basic rules of business etiquette they follow
- Their preferences regarding personal space
- How the country is characterized along Hofstede's dimensions

Team up with a classmate who chose a different country. Each of you should pick a product or commodity that is produced in the country you studied (such as stereos, bananas, oil, or machine parts). Attempt to negotiate a contract for selling your product or commodity to the other. As you negotiate, play the role of someone from the country you studied as authentically as possible. For example, if people from that culture are offended by a certain gesture and your counterpart happens to make that gesture while negotiating, act offended!

Spend approximately 15 minutes negotiating. Then spend another 15 minutes discussing with your classmate how the cultural background each of you adopted affected (or could have affected) the negotiation process.

1. How easy or difficult is it to model the behavior of someone from another country?
2. What other forms of advance preparation might a manager need to undertake before negotiating with someone from another country?

CLOSING CASE **IKEA'S TRANSFORMATIONAL LEADER**

Pernille Spiers-Lopez grew up in a small town in Denmark. After finishing college she worked as a journalist for a short time, but she found that profession to be unsatisfying. Her next move was to relocate to the United States and open a business importing Danish furniture. Unfortunately, that venture failed. She then took a minimum wage job selling furniture in Florida. Through hard work and determination within two years Spiers-Lopez was supervising 24 stores. The regional furniture company where she was working was then purchased by IKEA in 1993.

She quickly advanced through the management ranks at IKEA, where she was the only woman on the company's North American board. A 1997 businesswomen's leadership conference led her to reassess her priorities and her role at IKEA. In response, she chose to alter her career path and moved into human resource management. She subsequently became the U.S. director of human resources; one of her first actions was to implement programs to recruit more minority and female managers. Today, half of the firm's 75 top earners are female. Five women now serve on the management board. She also increased pay and benefits throughout the firm, especially for the lowest-paid employees. Today, thanks in large part to Spiers-Lopez, IKEA offers one of the most generous benefits packages for full-time and part-time workers in the retailing sector. And along the way she was promoted to the position of President of IKEA North America.

Yet it was a very personal, frightening experience that led to the most dramatic change. Spiers-Lopez is a working mother whose husband is a public school principal. As her IKEA career developed, the couple chose not to uproot the family. Instead, Spiers-Lopez commuted home several times each week from distant worksites. In 1999, Spiers-Lopez was working long hours and commuting frequently. Her competitive, Type A personality caused her to push herself harder and harder without regard to the consequences. One night as she left work she experienced tremendous pain in the chest and arms. Rushing to the emergency room, convinced she was having a heart attack, Spiers-Lopez found the problem instead was exhaustion and stress.

She decided she wanted to continue working but with more limits. "I'd been in denial for some time about my own strength. I'd been emotionally numb, ignored things and moved ahead, and put my family on automatic pilot," Spiers-Lopez says. "Now I've acted on that wake-up signal and am working on balancing life and work."

One of her coping mechanisms was a reduction in working hours so that she could relax with family. She says, "For years I've struggled with questions of whether I'm a good mother, a good friend, and a good wife. … [Now] I avoid business travel on weekends, try to keep regular hours at work and leave the job at the office." Her coworkers help, too. "We have meetings, and they know if they don't say, 'Let's take a break,' they won't get a break. So they say, 'Pernille, in order to help you, we're going to all take a break.'" A perfectionist, she struggles to keep from being overwhelmed but adds, "I am continuing to learn how to 'wing' things." Her career and personal life have both flourished as a result of better balance.

Her personal experiences with balancing career and family have affected her choices as a manager. She is a strong advocate for telecommuting, alternative work arrangements, and job sharing. IKEA'S policy of generous leave for new or adoptive mothers and fathers was designed by Spiers-Lopez. The organization has also flourished under Spiers-Lopez's leadership. The number of American stores has doubled and sales are the fastest growing of all the IKEA regions.

The combination of hard-driving competition and a culture that values people has resulted in an organization that is both supportive of its workers and profitable. Author Andy Meisler calls it "high-yield humanism." Spiers-Lopez admits that it is not easy for her to walk the line between challenge and nurture. "I want things done quickly," she says. "But in big organizations you have to be careful not to move too many things too quickly. Elevators have to stop at every floor."

Case Questions

1. Can you speculate about the personality traits that personify Pernille Spiers-Lopez?

2. Describe the role that motivation has played in the choices made by Pernille Spiers-Lopez in her career.

3. Discuss how her experiences with stress may have been impacted by international issues.

4. Describe Pernille Spiers-Lopez's approach to leadership at IKEA.

Sources: "The Ikea concept," IKEA website, www.ikea.com on May 16, 2008; Joseph Roth, "Unique training program key to timing for recruitment," IKEA press release, April 24, 2007, www.ikea.com on May 16, 2008; Andy Meisler, "Success, Scandinavian style," *Workforce Management*, August 2004, pp. 26–32; "Pernille Spiers-Lopez has designs for IKEA," *WomensBiz.US*, June 2005, www. womensbiz.us on May 16, 2008.

PART 3 CLOSING CASES REINVENTING NISSAN

During the 1980s it was hard to pick up a copy of *Business Week*, *Fortune*, or *Forbes* that did not feature some article extolling the virtues of Japanese management techniques and the Japanese way of doing business. Many Western commentators urged U.S. and European firms to adopt such Japanese corporate policies as lifetime employment, group-oriented compensation, and reliance on tight customer-supplier networks like those found in the keiretsu system. Among the most admired of these firms were Japan's premier automakers—Toyota, Nissan, and Honda.

The 1990s, however, were disastrous for many Japanese firms. The collapse of Japan's so-called bubble economy at the end of the 1980s condemned Japan to a decade of slow growth, stagnant stock markets, and loss of confidence. Among Japan's corporate elite, Nissan perhaps suffered the greatest fall of all. Although Nissan had prospered during the 1980s, the 1990s were far less kind. Expansion of its domestic automaking capacity during the 1980s left Nissan with far too many factories and workers, and it was forced to battle for market share in the crowded Japanese domestic market by keeping its prices low. (Japan has more major domestic automobile manufacturers than any other country.) The company suffered from excess capacity in its European operations as well. And the high value of the yen during the first half of the 1990s made it difficult for the company to export its way out of its difficulties. The Asian currency crisis of 1997–1998 dried up that region's demand for the company's products in the waning years of the twentieth century. Confronted with these diverse challenges, the company eked out a small profit in 1991 but lost money in 1992 and 1993.

To restore the company to profitability, Nissan's executives announced a major cost-cutting program in 1994. As one part of this program, Nissan pledged to slash the number of suppliers the firm would buy from in the future. It hoped this would result in better prices for auto parts by increasing the size of its orders to individual suppliers. Nissan also decided to trim its workforce and to reduce the number of parts used in the company's cars, thereby simplifying its procurement operations and reducing its inventory costs. Unfortunately, these efforts did not work, in part because the program's targets were not met. As a result, Nissan continued to lose money in 1994 and 1995. Although the company earned a modest profit in 1996, its profits turned negative once again in 1997. Profit performance for 1998 and 1999 was no better.

Unable to overcome its mounting problems, Nissan suffered the ultimate humiliation for a Japanese company: It was taken over by a foreigner. In May 1999 France's Renault SA purchased 37 percent of Nissan's common stock for $5.4 billion, effectively transferring control of Japan's second largest auto manufacturer to the French firm. Renault empowered one of its most highly respected executives, Carlos Ghosn, to clean up the mess at Nissan. Ghosn first spent five months carefully reviewing Nissan's operations. In October 1999 the Brazilian-born Ghosn announced a "revival plan" for the company designed to reduce Nissan's annual costs by nearly $10 billion. To reach this goal, five Nissan factories in Japan would have to be shuttered and 21,000 jobs eliminated. About 16,000 of the job cuts would occur in Nissan's domestic operations. Mindful of Japan's distaste for layoffs and Japanese labor laws that make firing employees expensive, the employment reductions were to be implemented via attrition, which averages about 2,000 domestic employees per year.

Other options, such as voluntary retirement programs, were initially shelved due to opposition from Nissan's union leaders, although the options have not been permanently ruled out. Further cost reductions were to be implemented by eliminating regional offices in such cities as New York and Washington and cutting the number of different vehicle models produced and marketed by Nissan. To ensure that no one misunderstood the importance of cost cutting to revive the company, Ghosn announced that "No one in purchasing, engineering, or administration will receive a pay raise until they [show] what their contribution is to this [cost cutting]."[63]

Ghosn recognized the need to hack away at Nissan's mountain of debt—some 2.4 trillion yen (in early 2001, 117 yen were worth 1 U.S. dollar)—and set a target of halving it by 2002. Ghosn also sought to streamline Nissan's dealership networks in Japan and North America. In Japan, for example, Nissan owns about half of its distributorships. Unfortunately, many of its distributors act like employees, rather than entrepreneurs, an attitude that Ghosn hopes to change by trimming company-owned outlets.

Review of the firm's marketing operations unearthed another set of problems. Ghosn quickly recognized that Nissan's product image differed from country to country, making it hard to launch cost-effective cross-border advertising campaigns. Far worse, he discovered that Nissan suffered from a "brand deficiency," causing consumers to value rivals' vehicles over those produced by Nissan. In the United States, for example, comparable cars sold by Honda, Toyota, Chrysler, and Ford might sell for $1,000 more than Nissan's product. To sharpen its brand identity and develop a uniform global image for its products, Nissan contracted with TBWA Worldwide to handle all of its advertising throughout the world—an account worth an estimated $1.1 billion in annual billings.

Perhaps the most controversial of Ghosn's initiatives dealt with parts procurement. He estimated that Nissan's parts procurement costs were 10 percent higher than those of Renault. Ghosn believed that by combining, centralizing, and globalizing Renault's and Nissan's parts procurement, these costs could be cut by 20 percent. To accomplish this, however, Ghosn needed to overcome a key element of the Japanese environment—the keiretsu system. The keiretsu system, in which members of a keiretsu group own shares in each other, has been a mainstay of the Japanese economy since World War II. The system is designed to build trust and promote stable, long-term cooperative relationships among suppliers and customers. Under this system Nissan funneled orders for parts and components to keiretsu affiliates, many of which were partially owned by Nissan. Ghosn's criticism of the keiretsu system was blunt. He believed that Nissan's purchase of parts and components from keiretsu affiliates promoted inefficiency and mediocrity. Because they were guaranteed business from Nissan, Ghosn felt that many of Nissan's keiretsu members failed to continue to innovate and cut costs:

> About 60 percent of our costs are in the suppliers. You have to have suppliers that are innovative. You want suppliers offering products to many customers so there is a flow of information about best standards. That won't happen with keiretsu companies.[64]

Accordingly, Ghosn announced he would liquidate Nissan's holdings in all but four of its 1,394 keiretsu partners. In a separate but related announcement he also said Nissan would halve the number of its suppliers to about 600. Instead of purchasing the same part from several suppliers, Nissan would now concentrate its purchases among a smaller number of suppliers, allowing them to achieve economies of scale and reduce their costs. Offering a carrot and a stick, he announced that suppliers cutting their prices to Nissan by 20 percent would get more of Nissan's business. Those failing to do so, however, risked losing Nissan as a customer. Not surprisingly, these tough measures were not embraced by everyone. For example, the then prime minister of Japan, Keizo Obuchi, promptly denounced Ghosn's plan, fearing job losses in the tens of thousands as Nissan cut back parts purchases from inefficient affiliates and suppliers.

Perhaps an even bigger challenge to Ghosn was to change Nissan's corporate culture. He learned that too many Nissan executives were focused on protecting their turf rather than on promoting the company's objectives. Moreover, he discovered to his horror that communication among divisions was nonexistent:

> Country [organizations] were not talking to each other, people were not talking to each other. … This company is very territorial, very divisional; this goes deep into the history and tradition of Nissan. There is nothing that upsets me more than turfism.[65]

Ghosn knew he needed to redirect the company's managers, refocusing their efforts on improving profits and enhancing customer satisfaction. To implement this objective, he created a network of multinational, cross-functional teams to reexamine and reinvigorate each of the firm's activities, from research and development to purchasing to manufacturing to distribution. These teams were also charged with spreading the restructuring gospel and tearing down the walls that have divided Nissan's operating divisions. Further down the line Ghosn plans to implement American-style compensation schemes, such as stock options and bonuses based on profitability and performance, for managerial and nonmanagerial employees alike. If implemented, compensation will no longer be based merely on seniority, as it traditionally has been in Japan. And to drive home the point that Nissan could no longer operate as it did in the past, he made English Nissan's official language.

Not all of Nissan's critics were convinced that Ghosn's strategy would work. One skeptic noted that many of the senior managers surrounding Ghosn were the same ones who were in charge of Nissan's operations while it hemorrhaged red ink during the 1990s. Others believed that any outsider—even a Brazilian from a French company—lacked the understanding of the Japanese business culture and the credibility necessary to motivate domestic managers and workers. Eventually, though, things seemed to be headed back in the right direction. In 2008, for example, Nissan posted record profits. And in 2010 the firm announced a joint venture with Daimler in which Nissan would provide transmissions for some of Daimler's models and Daimler would provide engines for some of Nissan's Infiniti automobiles.

Questions

1. What benefits will Nissan gain if its procurement of parts is combined with Renault's parts procurement on a global basis? Are there any costs to this change? What problems does Nissan create if it abandons the keiretsu system for purchasing parts? In what ways might the Internet facilitate this change?

2. Suppose natural attrition fails to allow Nissan to reach its goal of reducing its workforce by 21,000 people. If this occurs, what would you advise Carlos Ghosn to do? Should he abandon the planned job cuts? Or should he begin to fire workers and risk violating one of Japan's strongest cultural norms?

3. Given Japan's culture, will the introduction of performance-based compensation schemes create any problems for Nissan in Japan? If so, what is the nature of these problems? Do you have any suggestions for overcoming these problems?

4. Prime Minister Obuchi's comments send a clear signal that Japanese politicians will resist any restructuring of Nissan's operations that lead to significant losses of domestic jobs. How important is this political threat to Ghosn's plans? What advice would you give to Ghosn to overcome or address Obuchi's concerns?

5. As it turned out, Ghosn's strategies paid off. Nissan has become one of the most dramatic turnaround success stories

in years. The firm returned to profitability in 2001 and since that time has been systematically cutting costs, boosting profits, and growing market share. Some observers are now arguing that only a foreigner (a non-Japanese) could have turned Nissan around so quickly. Do you agree?

Sources: Hoover's Handbook of World Business 2011 (Austin, TX: Hoover's Business Press, 2011), pp. 247–248; "Nissan set to announce record $6.1 billion profit," *Financial Times*, April 23, 2003, p. 18; "Look! Up in the sky! It's Nissan's chief executive," *Wall Street Journal*, December 27, 2001, p. B1; "Feared 'cost killer' who became a corporate hero," *Financial Times*, December 17, 2001, p. II.; "Renault's Nissan deal begins to come up trumps," *Financial Times*, July 18, 2001, p. 20; "Nissan sizes up TBWA for $1 bil global ad prize," *Advertising Age*, December 6, 1999, pp. 1ff; "Remaking Nissan," *Business Week*, November 15, 1999, pp. 70ff; "The circle is broken," *Financial Times*, November 9, 1999, p. 18; "'Le cost-killer' makes his move," *Financial Times*, November 9, 1999, p. 15; "Nissan's ambitious restructuring plan delivers a blow to Japan's longstanding system of corporate families," *Wall Street Journal*, October 20, 1999, p. A20; "Nissan's cost cutter shows how he got his nickname," *Financial Times*, October 19, 1999, p. 20; "Nissan outlines restructuring to get into the black," *Wall Street Journal*, October 19, 1999, p. A18; "Nissan's Ghosn faces obstacles in carrying out 'revival plan'," *Wall Street Journal*, October 18, 1999, p. A37; "'Killer' to make unkindest cut," *Financial Times*, October 18, 1999, p. 14; "Can Japan keep 11 carmakers?" *Financial Times*, July 22, 1998, p. 13; "Nissan finds the road is rough despite cost cutting," *Wall Street Journal*, April 4, 1994, p. B4; "The world's top automakers change lanes," *Fortune*, October 4, 1993, p. 73ff.

SLIMLINE: MARCHING TO A DIFFERENT DRUMMER

Globalization means different things to different people. To the CEO of a multinational enterprise, globalization reflects the changing business world: access to new consumers, opportunities to reduce production costs by siting factories in low-cost areas, and the threat of competition from foreign firms. To workers in developed countries, globalization often implies job insecurity and no raises. To human rights activists, globalization implies exploitation of workers and denial of human rights.

Many multinational enterprises have been confronted with allegations of mistreatment of workers in developing countries. Nike, for example, has been the target of accusations that its subcontractors in China, Indonesia, and other Asian countries abuse their workers. One enterprise that has never been subjected to such criticism is Slimline, Ltd., an apparel manufacturer in Pannala, Sri Lanka. Indeed, Slimline's way of doing business stands in marked contrast to that of many apparel manufacturers in developed and developing countries alike. The company employs 5,000 workers, who produced $50 million worth of apparel annually. Many of them have undergraduate or graduate degrees. Its payrolls have included a mathematician (a Ph.D. from Yale), a physicist, and an investment banker. Slimline goes out of its way to provide its workers with working conditions that exceed industry standards. Entry-level wages are deliberately set higher than those in the local market.

Like most apparel manufacturers, most of its employees are female sewing machine operators. Even here Slimline defies the sweatshop stereotypes that plague the industry. Its production workers utilize advanced pneumatic sewing machines instead of the manual models prevalent in most Asian apparel factories. Work stations are ergonomically designed, and the factory is air-conditioned. As a result, Slimline has attracted a premier workforce, and the HR office maintains a waiting list for prospective employees.

The job is intense and demanding, to be sure. Base pay is $80 to $100 per month (breakfast included). Computers monitor the output of each worker, who must match factory-wide production standards to earn her monthly bonus. But, contrary to industry norms, the standards are racheted down for pregnant workers. All employees have access to a new gymnasium, staffed by a full-time trainer and equipped with modern exercise machines.

Why has Slimline adopted this approach? Slimline's managers have concluded that Sri Lanka can't compete with Bangladesh or China on the basis of low wages. Instead, they believe that they must focus on producing high-quality goods for their customers, brand-name retailers like Victoria's Secret, Express, and Marks and Spencer. But these retailers are vulnerable to anti-sweatshop campaigns by human rights activists in Europe and North America. Notes one Slimline official:

> … in today's global economy Sri Lankan manufacturers must tie themselves to big Western retailers to survive, and the more they do that the more their factory standards have to meet the workplace norms demanded by Western consumers.[66]

Slimline was founded in 1993 as a joint venture among Mast Industries, Courtaulds, and MAS Holdings Ltd. Slimline has benefited from the unique knowledge and expertise of the joint venture partners. Mast Industries, a subsidiary of Limited Brands, is a U.S.-based contract manufacturer of apparel, with annual sales of $1.5 billion. Among its major customers are The Limited, Intimate Brands, Victoria's Secret, Marks and Spencer, Liz Claiborne, The Gap, Ralph Lauren, C&A, and Tommy Hilfiger. Mast operates 36 factories in Sri Lanka through joint ventures, employing over 16,300 people. Courtaulds Textiles PLC was the U.K.'s largest apparel manufacturer until its purchase by Sara Lee in 2000. (Sara Lee sold its Courtaulds subsidiary in 2006 but retained its stake in Slimline.) The third partner, MAS Holdings Ltd., is a privately owned Sri Lankan company that has rapidly become Sri Lanka's largest apparel manufacturer and one of the island's largest employers. MAS is Victoria's Secret's largest source of goods, supplying an estimated 30–32 percent of the U.S.-based retailer's merchandise. MAS later developed the world's first carbon-neutral textile facility.

The driving force behind Slimline is Dian Gomes. In 1993, Gomes was 36 years old and employed as the finance director of another apparel factory when he was approached by Mahesh Amalean, the chairman of MAS Holdings Ltd., to launch a new business, Slimline. Gomes rose to the challenge, but the goals he set for himself and the venture were neither modest or easy:

> I had a dream, and … I set out to make it a reality at Slimline. To make an ambitious garment project a state-of-the-art plant. A super efficient monolith. My aim was to be number one, and stay number one![67]

The first task confronting Gomes and his new management team was to build a state-of-the-art garment factory. Courtaulds sent an experienced team of production managers from its British operations to oversee the construction and start-up of the factory. Gomes added Japanese inventory control and production methods that cut costs and raised productivity and team-building techniques that he learned at executive education programs at Wharton and Harvard to build employee morale and commitment. He later incorporated a $4-million computer system into the factory's operations to monitor quality and production. The system is integrated with the computer systems of its major customers, facilitating distribution and improving service to its customers. It also facilitates communication between the factory, customers, and the marketplace, allowing the factory to quickly shift production to the styles most in demand.

While its state-of-the art facilities and technology have played a critical role in Slimline's success, Gomes and his staff have worked to instill pride in the company. One way Slimline has bolstered its company image and enhanced employee morale is by sponsoring company sports teams. Its teams won the National Women's Cricket Championship four years in a row, while the company boxing team captured the National Boxing Championship. Slimline also sponsored Ruwini Abeymanne, who placed a respectable thirty-first among pistol shooters in the 2000 Sydney Olympics and won a bronze medal at the Commonwealth pistol championship in 2001. Nor has the company forgotten about the community. Slimline built a new auditorium for the local high school and equipped its computer and science labs. It also provided scholarships allowing local high school graduates to attend the local university.

Although less than two decades old, Slimline has been recognized by numerous groups for its innovative approaches and commitment to its workers and the community. The company has received, for example, the Sri Lankan National Safety Award, the National Productivity Award, the Best Corporate Citizen Award, the Akimoto Award (for incorporating Japanese productivity and quality techniques into its manufacturing processes), Courtauld's Risk Management Award (placing first among Courtauld's 123 manufacturing facilities), and Mast Industries' Quality Award. In 2007 it was certified by the Sri Lankan government as a "Garments without Guilt" participant, meaning its human resources practices were in compliance with the standards established by the International Labor Organization. And with such successes has come growth: The company now operates four factories that produce over 50 million units of women's sleepwear and intimate apparel.[68]

Questions

1. Slimline is a joint venture among three companies— a local Sri Lankan firm, a British firm, and a U.S. firm. What are the benefits of this joint venture to each of these companies?

2. Why did each choose to participate in the joint venture rather than operate its own wholly owned subsidiary?

3. From the perspective of each of the partners, are there any potential pitfalls to joining this joint venture?

DAIMLER AND CHRYSLER: DREAM OR NIGHTMARE?

In 1998 Daimler-Benz and Chrysler, two of the world's largest automakers, announced that they had agreed to merge. Executives at the two firms called the deal a "marriage of equals." To reinforce this idea, Daimler CEO Jurgen Schrempp indicated that he and Chrysler's CEO, Robert Eaton, would serve as co-chairs for at least three years. In reality, however, rather than a merger the deal was more accurately an acquisition, with Daimler Benz owning 58 percent ownership of the new company and retaining most of the senior management positions. The new enterprise was dubbed DaimlerChrsyler and would become the third largest automaker in the world.

Investors and other analysts hailed the deal as a dream partnership and a perfect match. For example, Daimler engineers could teach Chrysler about quality and technology, and Chrysler could give the Germans lessons in efficiency and speed to market. Daimler's well-developed distribution network could boost Chrysler's expansion in Europe, and while Chrysler could help Mercedes-Benz with logistics and other support in the United States. And their products were almost perfectly complimentary, with Mercedes-Benz having the cachet of expensive, finely-engineered, and high-performance passenger cars and Chrysler providing a nice mix of lower-priced cars and minivans plus the valuable Jeep brand name for its sports utility vehicles. Finally, DaimlerChrysler would also have more combined muscle to attack emerging markets in Asia and South America. All in all, then, the reunion seemed to be a corporate marriage made in heaven.

By 2000, however, investors and observers alike were calling it more like a marriage made in hell rather than one made in heaven. None of the anticipated advantages had been achieved, and innumerable problems had the firm so mired down that at one point its market value was lower than it had been for either Daimler or Chrysler before the merger. In 2001 DaimlerChrysler announced it would reduce Chrysler's payrolls by 26,000, about 20 percent of its workforce. How did such a dream partnership end up as a nightmare? Several different factors can be identified.

One notable factor was the major differences between operating procedures that existed at Daimler and Chrysler. Chrysler had been one of the world's most profitable automobile makers by being nimble and responsive—decisions were made quickly, there were few long meetings to slow things down, and management reports were kept to a minimum. Just the opposite circumstances existed at Daimler-Benz. Most major decisions were made in marathon meetings that sometimes went on for days, and most operations were driven by lengthy and detailed management reports. Reconciling the two systems proved to be harder than expected, and most meetings seemed to end in shouting matches.

Another problem was that Chrysler was not in as good a condition as observers thought at the time of the merger. Although it was selling lots of automobiles and sports utility vehicles and racking up big profits, its product lines were also growing stale. Some of its most popular products, such as the Jeep Grand Cherokee, needed major redesign and others, such as its best-selling line of minivans, were gradually losing market share to aggressive competitors such as Toyota and Honda. Although some new models were introduced, most notably the funky PT Cruiser, Chrysler had few other new products in the pipeline. Finally, Chrysler was so intent on improving product quality that it was adding about $2,000 in costs to many of its top sellers for improvements that many consumers did not want and that could not be seen, such as more sound-proofing material and stronger braking systems.

The new firm also seemed to have trouble curbing its spending. For example, shortly after the merger was announced, Daimler wanted to start using Chrysler's U.S. distributors to transport parts and equipment to Mercedes dealers. However, the dealers did not want Chrysler or Dodge vans on their premises, so at considerable expense all of Chrysler's vans were repainted and a new discreet DaimlerChrysler logo affixed.

Similarly, during the implementation of the merger there were repeated clashes over travel expenses. Chrysler executives were accustomed to flying coach and staying in Holiday Inns; Daimler executives flew first class and stayed in expensive suites. One Chrysler executive estimated that during the first year of the merger, senior executives of the combined firm spent over $5 million on rooms and meals just for meetings in New York City, meetings that served little or no purpose. At some meetings every executive in attendance got a $500-per-night suite at the Waldorf-Astoria or St. Regis, even though many of the executives were not even spending the night in the city.

Morale was also became a problem. Although originally billed as a merger of equals, everyone quickly saw that Daimler was actually overwhelming Chrysler. Most senior Chrysler executives were systematically replaced by German executives from the parent company, and Chrysler procedures and policies were routinely replaced with those already in place at Daimler. As a result, turnover among key people was high, shareholders sued the firm because they feel they were misled about the original merger, and UAW labor leaders in the United States and Canada threatened to strike if the company attempted to lower their wages or reduce their benefits, something the firm had been hinting about.

DaimlerChrysler executives were criticized for not giving the merger time to be properly implemented before undertaking new ventures. For example, shortly after the two firms started being combined, the firm announced it was considering buying Nissan, Japan's second largest automaker. After extended negotiations, however, the firm backed off and instead invested heavily in two other auto companies, Mitsubishi and Hyundai. So far these deals also have been a bust as both firms have failed to meet profit goals.

Finally, in 2007 DaimlerChrysler executives decided it was time to throw in the towel. They announced that they were interested in selling controlling interest in the Chrysler unit, and subsequently spun off 80% of Chrysler to an investment firm named Cerberus. Daimler retained 20% ownership and agreed to continue to partner with Chrysler in a few specific areas, such as sales, financial services, and global sourcing. In early 2008 DaimlerChrysler also officially changed its name to Daimler AG. Daimler is now looking at joint venture opportunities in China. The firm also posted profits in both 2007 and 2008 before the global recession hit the firm with a loss in 2009. But by 2010 Daimler was again in the black.

As for Chrysler, its travails continue. The firm was spun off from Cerberus in 2008 just as the global recession was hitting businesses everywhere. As a result, Chrysler, like General Motors, had to seek protection under Chapter 11 bankruptcy laws and relied on government bail-out funds to stay afloat. It was eventually sold to Italian automaker Fiat. Fiat, meanwhile, plans to systematically introduce its full line of products to existing Chrysler dealerships as a way to increase market share for both brands. Chrysler is also investing heavily in electric engines.

Questions

1. Identify the basic strategic management issues faced by top managers at Daimler and at Chrysler before the merger, during the merger, and after the merger.
2. In what ways, if any, might elements of organization design have affected the failure of the Daimler and Chrysler merger?
3. Identify the basic control issues at Daimler from all three levels.
4. How do you think the control function should be organized and managed at Daimler? At Chrysler?
5. Describe how behavioral issues may have played a role in DaimlerChrysler's problems.

Sources: "Germans bring cool back to Chrysler," *Houston Chronicle*, January 6, 2002, p. 2D; "Chrysler's New Bosses Give Refresher Course On Thrift and Style," *Wall Street Journal*, January 4, 2002, p. A1; "Chrysler's Rescue Team," *Business Week*, January 15, 2001, pp. 48–50; "Purging Chrysler," *Time*, December 4, 2000, pp. 58–60; "DaimlerChrysler Hit by More Lawsuits, Labor Unrest," *USA Today*, November 30, 2000, p. 3B; "For Two Car Giants, a Megamerger Isn't the Road to Riches," *Wall Street Journal*, October 27, 2000, pp. A1, A8; "The Merger That Can't Get in Gear," *Business Week*, July 31, 2000, pp. 46–47; Bill Vlasic and Bradley A. Stertz, "Taken for a Ride," *Business Week*, June 5, 2000, pp. 84–92; *Hoover's Handbook of World Business 2011* (Austin: Hoover's Business Press, 2011), pp. 113–114.

Endnotes

1. "Why CEOs fail: The Toyota edition," *Washington Post*, February 11, 2010, p. B1; William George, "Tragedy at Toyota: How not to lead in crisis," *Harvard Business School Weekly*, February 22, 2010; Alan Pang, "Toyota off the cliff? Lessons in leadership," *Aon Consulting Global Research Center Newsletter*, February 2010; *Hoover's Handbook of World Business 2011* (Austin: Hoover's Business Press, 2011), pp. 365–367.

2. For a review of behavioral processes and concepts in organizations, see Ricky W. Griffin and Gregory Moorhead, *Organizational Behavior*, 11th ed. (Cincinnati, OH: Cengage, 2011).

3. Ibid.; see also Miriam Erez, "Cross-cultural and global issues in organizational psychology," in Sheldon Zedeck ed., *Handbook of Industrial and Organizational Psychology* (Washington, DC: American Psychological Association, 2010).

4. Lawrence Pervin, "Personality," in Mark Rosenzweig and Lyman Porter, eds., *Annual Review of Psychology*, vol. 36 (Palo Alto, CA: Annual Reviews, 1985), pp. 83–114.

5. Jennifer George, "The role of personality in organizational life: Issues and evidence," *Journal of Management*, vol. 18 (1992), pp. 185–213.

6. L. R. Goldberg, "An alternative 'description of personality': The Big Five factor structure," *Journal of Personality and Social Psychology*, vol. 59 (1990), pp. 1216–1229; M. R. Barrick and M. K. Mount, "The Big Five personality dimensions and job performance," *Personnel Psychology*, vol. 44 (1991), pp. 1–26.

7. Jesus F. Salgado, "The Five Factor model of personality and job performance in the European Community," *Journal of Applied Psychology*, vol. 82, no. 1 (1997), pp. 30–43.

8. "'Big 5' test may not fit HK," *The Standard*, March 15, 2004, p. B-6.

9. Ya-Ru Chen, Kwok Leung, and Chao C. Chen, "Bringing national culture to the table: Making a difference with cross-cultural differences and perspectives," in James P. Walsh and Arthur P. Brief, eds., *The Academy of Management Annals 2009* (Philadelphia PA: Taylor and Francis, 2009), pp. 217–250.

10. J. B. Rotter, "Generalized expectancies for internal vs. external control of reinforcement," *Psychological Monographs*, vol. 80 (1966), pp. 1–28; Bert De Brabander and Christopher Boone, "Sex differences in perceived locus of control," *The Journal of Social Psychology*, vol. 130 (1990), pp. 271–276.

11. Colleen Ward and Antony Kennedy, "Locus of control, mood disturbance, and social difficulties during cross-cultural transitions," *International Journal of Intercultural Relations*, vol. 16 (1992), pp. 175–194.

12. Marilyn E. Gist and Terence R. Mitchell, "Self-efficacy: A theoretical analysis of its determinants and malleability," *Academy of Management Review* (April 1992), pp. 183–211.

13. J. Michael Geringer and Colette A. Frayne, "Self-efficacy, outcome expectancy and performance of international joint venture general managers," *Canadian Journal of Administrative Sciences*, vol. 10, no. 4 (1993), pp. 322–333.

14. T. W. Adorno, E. Frenkel-Brunswick, D. J. Levinson, and R. N. Sanford, *The Authoritarian Personality* (New York: Harper & Row, 1950).

15. Michael Harris Bond and Peter B. Smith, "Cross-cultural social and organizational psychology," in Janet Spence, ed., *Annual Review of Psychology*, vol. 47 (Palo Alto, CA: Annual Reviews, 1996), pp. 205–235.

16. Patricia C. Smith, L. M. Kendall, and Charles Hulin, *The Measurement of Satisfaction in Work and Behavior* (Chicago: Rand-McNally, 1969).

17. Meg G. Birdseye and John S. Hill, "Individual, organizational/work and environmental influences on expatriate turnover tendencies: An empirical study," *Journal of International Business Studies* (Fourth Quarter 1995), pp. 787–813.

18. James R. Lincoln, "Employee work attitudes and management practice in the U.S. and Japan: Evidence from a large comparative study," *California Management Review* (Fall 1989), pp. 89–106.

19. Daniel J. McCarthy and Sheila M. Puffer, "Perestroika at the plant level—Manager's job attitudes and views of decision-making in the former USSR," *The Columbia Journal of World Business* (Spring 1992), pp. 86–99.

20. Thang Van Nguyen and Nancy Napier, "Work attitudes in Vietnam," *Academy of Management Executive*, vol. 14, no. 4 (2000), pp. 142–143.

21. Abdul Rahim A. Al-Meer, "Organizational commitment: A comparison of Westerners, Asians, and Saudis," *International Studies of Management and Organization*, vol. 19, no. 2 (1989), pp. 74–84.

22. Janet Near, "Organizational commitment among Japanese and U.S. workers," *Organization Studies*, vol. 10, no. 3 (1989), pp. 281–300.

23. Hal B. Gregersen and J. Stewart Black, "Antecedents to commitment to a parent company and a foreign operation," *Academy of Management Journal*, vol. 35, no. 1 (1992), pp. 65–90.

24. Kent D. Miller, "Industry and country effects on managers' perceptions of environmental uncertainties," *Journal of International Business Studies* (Fourth Quarter 1993), pp. 693–714.

25. Satoko Watanabe and Ryozo Yamaguchi, "Intercultural perceptions at the workplace: The case of the British subsidiaries of Japanese firms," *Human Relations*, vol. 48, no. 5 (1995), pp. 581–607.

26. Bodo B. Schlegelmilch and Diana C. Robertson, "The influence of country and industry on ethical perceptions of senior executives in the U.S. and Europe," *Journal of International Business Studies* (Fourth Quarter 1995), pp. 859–881.

27. For a recent overview of the stress literature, see Frank Landy, James Campbell Quick, and Stanislav Kasl, "Work, stress, and well-being," *International Journal of Stress Management*, vol. 1, no. 1 (1994), pp. 33–73.

28. "Executive stress: A ten-country comparison," *The Chicago Tribune*, March 31, 1988.

29. Bruce D. Kirkcaldy and Cary L. Cooper, "Stress differences among German and U.K. managers," *Human Relations*, vol. 46, no. 5 (1993), pp. 669–680.

30. James M. Diefendorff and Megan M. Chandler, "Motivating employees," in Sheldon Zedeck, ed., *Handbook of Industrial and Organizational Psychology* (Washington, DC: American Psychological Association, 2010).

31. "Siemens climbs back," *Business Week*, June 5, 2000, pp. 79–82; "Computer chip project brings rivals together, but the cultures clash," *Wall Street Journal*, May 3, 1994, pp. A1, A8; *Hoover's Handbook of American Business 2011* (Austin, TX: Hoover's Business Press, 2011), pp. 745–746; *Hoover's Handbook of World Business 2011* (Austin, TX: Hoover's Business Press, 2011), pp. 529–530, 622–623.

32. Geert Hofstede, "Motivation, leadership, and organization: Do American theories apply abroad?" *Organizational Dynamics* (Summer 1980), pp. 42–63.

33. Joseph J. Fucini and Suzy Fucini, *Working for the Japanese: Inside Mazda's American Auto Plant* (New York: Free Press, 1990).

34. Charles Weaver and Michael Landeck, "Cross-national differences in job values: A segmented comparative analysis of United States and West German workers" (Laredo State University, 1991), mimeo.

35. Abraham Maslow, "A theory of human motivation," *Psychological Review* (July 1943), pp. 370–396.

36. Nancy Adler, *International Dimensions of Organizational Behavior*, 3rd ed. (Cincinnati: South-Western, 1997), pp. 130–138.

37. P. Howell, J. Strauss, and P. F. Sorenson, "Research note: Cultural and situational determinants of job satisfaction among management in Liberia," *Journal of Management Studies* (May 1975), pp. 225–227.

38. David McClelland, *The Achieving Society* (Princeton, NJ: Van Nostrand, 1961).

39. Adler, op. cit.

40. Frederick Herzberg, Bernard Mausner, and Barbara Snyderman, *The Motivation to Work* (New York: Wiley, 1959).

41. G. H. Hines, "Achievement, motivation, occupations and labor turnover in New Zealand," *Journal of Applied Psychology*, vol. 58, no. 3 (1973), pp. 313–317.

42. Victor Vroom, *Work and Motivation* (New York: Wiley, 1964).

43. Gary Yukl, *Leadership in Organizations*, 6th ed. (Upper Saddle River, NJ: PrenticeHall, 2005).

44. Luciara Nardon and Richard Steers, "The new global manager: Learning cultures on the fly," *Organizational Dynamics*, January–March 2008, pp. 47–57; see also Julian Barling, Amy Christie, and Colette Hoption, "Leadership," in Sheldon Zedeck, ed., *Handbook of Industrial and Organizational Psychology* (Washington, DC: American Psychological Association, 2010).

45. David A. Ralston, David J. Gustafson, Fanny M. Cheung, and Robert H. Terpstra, "Differences in managerial values: A study of U.S., Hong Kong, and PRC managers," *Journal of International Business Studies* (Second Quarter 1993), pp. 249–275.

46. See Joseph A. Petrick, Robert F. Scherer, James D. Brodzinski, John F. Quinn, and M. Fall Ainina, "Global leadership skills and reputational capital: Intangible resources for sustainable competitive advantage," *Academy of Management Executive*, vol. 13, no. 1 (1999), pp. 58–69.

47. Robert H. Doktor, "Asian and American CEOs: A comparative study," *Organizational Dynamics*, vol. 18, no. 3 (1990), pp. 46–56.

48. See Mansour Javidan, Peter Dorfman, Mary Sully de Luque, and Robert House, "In the eye of the beholder: Cross cultural lessons in leadership from Project GLOBE," *Academy of Management Perspectives* (February 2006), pp. 67–90.

49. Jon P. Alston, *The American Samurai* (New York: Walter de Gruyter, 1986), pp. 103–113.

50. "The Spanish-American business wars," *Worldwide P & I Planning* (May–June 1971), pp. 30–40.

51. Arvin Parkhe, "Interfirm diversity, organizational learning, and longevity in global strategic alliances," *Journal of International Business Studies*, vol. 22, no. 4 (Fourth Quarter 1991), pp. 592–593; Edward T. Hall and Mildred Reed Hall, *Understanding Cultural Differences* (Yarmouth, ME: Intercultural Press, 1990), pp. 55–62.

52. For example, see Manfred F.R. Kets de Vries, "Leadership style and organizational practices in Russia," *Organizational Dynamics*, vol. 28, no. 4 (2000), pp. 67–81.

53. Tom Morris and Cynthia M. Pavett, "Management style and productivity in two cultures," *Journal of International Business Studies*, vol. 23, no. 1 (First Quarter 1992), pp. 169–179.

54. Herbert A. Simon, *Administrative Behavior*, 3rd ed. (New York: Free Press, 1976). See also Gerd Gigerenzer and Wolfgang Gaissmaier, "Heuristic decision making," in Susan T. Fiske, Daniel L. Schacter, and Shelley Taylor, eds, *Annual Review of Psychology 2011* (Palo Alto CA: Annual Reviews, 2011), pp. 451–482

55. Alex Taylor III, "Porsche's risky recipe," *Fortune*, February 17, 2003, pp. 90–94; *Hoover's Handbook of World Business 2011* (Austin, TX: Hoover's Business Press, 2011), pp. 253–254.

56. Adler, op. cit.

57. Alston, op. cit., pp. 181–186.

58. Hall and Hall, op. cit., pp. 33–84.

59. Lawrence C. Wolken, "Doing business in China," *Texas A&M Business Forum* (Fall 1987), pp. 39–42.

60. J. Stewart Black and Lyman W. Porter, "Managerial behaviors and job performance: A successful manager in Los Angeles may not succeed in Hong Kong," *Journal of International Business Studies*, vol. 22, no. 1 (First Quarter 1991), pp. 99–113.

61. Parkhe, op. cit., pp. 579–601.

62. See Chantell E. Nicholls, Henry W. Lane, and Mauricio Brehm Brechu, "Taking self-managed teams to Mexico," *Academy of Management Executive*, vol. 13, no. 3 (2000), pp. 15–25.

63. "Remaking Nissan," *Business Week*, November 15, 1999, p. 71.

64. "The circle is broken," *Financial Times*, November 9, 1999, p. 18.

65. "'Le cost-killer' makes his move," *Financial Times*, November 9, 1999, p. 15.

66. Thomas L. Friedman, *The Lexus and the Olive Tree* (New York: Anchor Books, 2000), p. 178.

67. Dian Gomes, "Introduction," *A Place in the Sun* (Pannala, Sri Lanka [privately printed]) 2001), p. xiii.

68. Web sites of Slimline (www.slimline.lk), Mast Industries (www.mast.com), Sara Lee Courtaulds (www.saralee.com), and www.diangomes.com; "Not many pluses," *The Economist*, August 16, 2008, p. 42; "Get your green pants here," *The Economist*, May 31, 2008, p. 71; "Sri Lanka Gears Up for Asian Garment Competition," www.tdctrade.com, January 8, 2004; Dian Gomes, "Introduction," *A Place in the Sun* (Pannala, Sri Lanka [privately printed], 2001), p. xiii; Thomas L. Friedman, *The Lexus and the Olive Tree* (New York: Anchor Books, 2000), pp. 177–178; "Sri Lanka Keeps Victoria's Secret: Toiling in Comfort," *Wall Street Journal*, July 14, 1999.

CHAPTER 16

International Marketing

AFTER STUDYING THIS CHAPTER, YOU SHOULD BE ABLE TO:

1. Characterize the nature of marketing management in international business.

2. Discuss the basic kinds of product policies and decisions made in international business.

3. Identify pricing issues and evaluate pricing decisions in international business.

4. Identify promotion issues and evaluate promotion decisions in international business.

5. Discuss the basic kinds of distribution issues and decisions in international business.

Access a host of interactive learning aids at **www.pearsonglobaleditions.com/ mymanagementlab** to help strengthen your understanding of the chapter concepts.

MyManagementLab

© Robert Morris/Alamy

"TUNE IN TO BUDGET INN": BUDGET HOTEL BRANDS GO GLOBAL

Historically, budget hotel brands have existed primarily in Europe and North America. Today they are expanding into other parts of the world as hotel construction booms in emerging markets. Budget hotels charge lower prices than their upscale and luxury counterparts, while still providing basic amenities important to business travellers like clean, comfortable rooms with workspace and Internet access. Although limited breakfast offerings may also be available on-site, full-service restaurants and room service typically are not in the deal. Yet, depending on the specific brand, some scaled-down business, entertainment, and fitness services may be available.

India in particular is a target for budget hotel expansion. For example, Intercontinental Hotel Group is extending its brand presence in the country more than tenfold over the next 10 years, and has said about 75 percent of that growth will come from its mid-market Holiday Inn brand. Other chains are also introducing their budget brands in India, including Marriott's Fairfield by Marriott, Hilton's Hampton Inn, and Starwood's Aloft.

In Latin America, budget hotels are part of the overall construction pipeline as well, with Brazil in particular preparing to host the World Cup in 2014 and the Olympics in 2016. More broadly, La Quinta Inns & Suites is expanding aggressively throughout Central and South America, including in Panama and Mexico. Finally, though very little new hotel construction is currently planned in Europe or North America, Etap, an Accor budget hotel brand, recently expanded its presence in Madrid and has indicated potential for further investment in Spain.

Tune Hotels, after launching in Malaysia and Indonesia, recently opened in London. Fifteen hotels are planned in London by 2017. Tony Fernandes, the Malaysian businessman behind the low-cost airline AirAsia, is the founder of Tune Hotels.

As we compare a luxury hotel and budget hotel's price strategy, most companies are unwilling to be this focused in their choice of target market, value proposition, and business model. Unlike the luxury hotels, Tune Hotels offer customers a simple value proposition in what some call a "bloated hotel price" market. The hotel promotes "5 star beds at 1 star prices." This no-frills hotel operates on a business model that charges for everything except the bed and the lavatory. For the price of £50 (approx. USD 80) for a double room, Tunes offers its customers a great bed but little else. All other amenities, or what some travellers might call "essentials," cost extra. Even towels and soap are noticeably absent, but are available for around £1.50 (approx. USD 2.4). Air-conditioning units, televisions, telephones, and minibars are available on rent for a prebooked time period. Housekeeping is provided only on checkout, but can be purchased as a daily service for an additional fee. The buildings are brand new, but facilities like pools, gyms, and conference rooms are nowhere to be found. Tune Hotels is an excellent example of a firm that knows how to compete as a fierce price value leader. It targets a customer who wants only the barest quality level in a hotel room. Its rock-bottom low price in London, where even simple rooms routinely sell for £100–200 (approx. USD 160–320) per night, is like a breath of fresh air to travellers who don't care about anything but a good night's sleep. By splurging on a 5-star bed and cutting all the rest from the hotel experience, Tunes is likely to hit a sweet spot in the London market (and around the world for that matter). This strategy delivers what its target market wants and nothing more. Like Ginger Hotel in India and other low-cost service providers across the travel industry, Tune built its strategy first by knowing exactly what its customers want and then by ruthlessly eliminating everything else.

Tune Hotels Sdn. Bhd. operates hotels in Asia. The company has a strategic partnership with Apodis Hospitality Group to develop its hotels in India. Tune Hotels was founded in 2007 and is based in Petaling Jaya, Malaysia, with locations in Kuala Lumpur, Sabah, Sarawak, Penang, Selangor Darul Ehsan, and Kelantan in Malaysia; and in Bali, Indonesia, as well as in the United Kingdom.

Tune Hotels Sdn. Bhd. announced it aims to open 30 new hotels in 2012 for between USD 180 million and USD 240 million and all will be eco-friendly certified. Tune Hotels is aiming for 100 hotels in its global portfolio by 2015. It now has 13 hotels in Malaysia, Indonesia, and the United Kingdom. Tune Hotels Group will also open four more hotels in Thailand by 2012.[1] ■

The opening example underscores the importance and the value of marketing in international business. Identifying the right products, matching those products with the right customers, promoting the products to those customers, and then developing an effective distribution mechanism for getting products to customers can lead to a successful enterprise regardless of where it might be located.

Marketing is "the process of planning and executing the conception, pricing, promotion, and distribution of ideas, goods, and services to create exchanges that satisfy individual and organizational objectives."[2] **International marketing** is the extension of these activities across national boundaries. Firms expanding into new markets in foreign countries must deal with different political, cultural, and legal systems, as well as unfamiliar economic conditions, advertising media, and distribution channels. An international firm accustomed to promoting its products on television will have to alter its approach when entering a less developed market in which relatively few people have televisions. Advertising regulations also vary by country. French law, for instance, discourages advertisements that disparage competing products; comparative advertisements must contain at least two significant, objective, and verifiable differences between products.[3] New Zealand regulators may ban ads for a variety of reasons. A Nike ad was banned for being too violent, and a Coca-Cola ad featuring aboriginal dancers was banned for being "culturally insensitive."[4]

In addition to dealing with national differences, international marketing managers confront two tasks their domestic counterparts do not face: capturing synergies among various national markets and coordinating marketing activities among those markets. Synergies are important because they provide opportunities for additional revenues and for growth and cross-fertilization. Coordination is important because it can help lower marketing costs and create a unified marketing effort.

International Marketing Management

An international firm's marketing activities often are organized as a separate and self-contained function within the firm. Yet that function both affects and is affected by virtually every other organizational activity, as shown in Figure 16.1. These interrelationships make international marketing management a critical component of international business success. International marketing management encompasses a firm's efforts to ensure that its international marketing activities mesh with the firm's corporate strategy, business strategy, and other functional strategies.

International Marketing and Business Strategies

A key challenge for a firm's marketing managers is to adopt an international marketing strategy that supports the firm's overall business strategy.[5] As we discussed in Chapter 11, business strategy can take one of three forms: differentiation, cost leadership, or focus.

A differentiation strategy requires marketing managers to develop products as well as pricing, promotional, and distribution tactics that differentiate the firm's products or services from those of its competitors in the eyes of customers. Differentiation can be based on perceived

FIGURE 16.1

International Marketing as an Integrated Functional Area

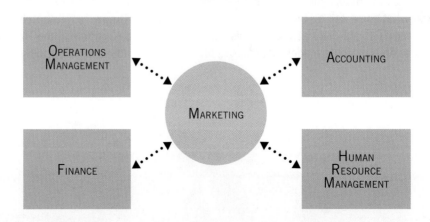

A differentiation strategy based on perceived quality or fashion allows companies to charge higher prices for their products. Rolex, for instance, has carefully cultivated an image that allows it to charge prices several times higher than those of most watchmakers. The Swiss-based firm has enjoyed great success in extending its differentiation strategy throughout most Asian markets.

TEH ENG KOON/AFP/Getty Images

quality, fashion, reliability, or other salient characteristics, as the marketing managers of such products as Rolex watches, BMW automobiles, and Montblanc pens successfully have shown. Assuming the differentiation can be communicated effectively to customers, the firm will be able to charge higher prices for its product or insulate itself from price competition from lesser brands. For example, Rolex, which has successfully implemented a differentiation strategy, does not need to cut the price for its diamond-faced $15,000 watches whenever Target advertises Timex quartz watches for $39.95.

Alternatively, a firm may adopt an international business strategy that stresses its overall cost leadership. Cost leadership can be pursued and achieved through systematic reductions in production and manufacturing costs, reductions in sales costs, the acceptance of lower profit margins, the use of less expensive materials and component parts, or other means. Marketing managers for a firm adopting this strategy will concentrate their promotional efforts on advertising the low price of the product and will utilize channels of distribution that allow the firm to keep the retail price low—for example, by selling through discounters rather than through fashionable boutiques. Casio calculators, Kia automobiles, and Bic pens all are marketed using a cost leadership strategy. And Timex's cost leadership approach has allowed it to thrive in the large market for low-price watches.

A firm also may adopt a focus strategy. In this case marketing managers will concentrate their efforts on particular segments of the consumer market or on particular areas or regions within a market. International marketing managers will need to concentrate on getting the appropriate message regarding the firm's products or services to the various selected target markets. For example, the Swiss watchmaker Ste. Suisse Microelectronique et d'Horlogerie SA (SMH), which manufactures Swatch watches, focuses its marketing efforts on selling this inexpensive line of watches to young, fashion-oriented consumers in Europe, North America, and Asia. "Emerging Opportunities" demonstrates how one Chinese entrepreneur used the Internet as a key ingredient in implementing his focus strategy.

A critical element for a firm's success is the congruency of its international marketing efforts with its overall business strategy. Timex, Rolex, and SMH—all watchmakers—have chosen different strategies, yet all are successful internationally because they match their international marketing efforts to their business strategies. Timex's cost leadership strategy implies that the firm must seek out low-cost suppliers globally and sell its watches in discount stores such as Walmart and Target, rather than in fashionable department stores such as Saks Fifth Avenue and Harrod's. Rolex's differentiation strategy, based on the firm's carefully nurtured worldwide image, might collapse if Rolex distributed its watches through armies of street vendors stationed in front of subway stations throughout the world, rather than through a handful of chic and expensive horologists located on the most fashionable avenues of the world's most glamorous cities. Similarly, SMH does not advertise Swatch watches to the upper-class, middle-aged audiences of *Town and Country* and *Architectural Digest* or to the predominantly male readership of *Field and Stream* and *Popular Electronics*. It does advertise its wares in the U.S., Chinese, and French editions of *Elle*, which are read by demographically similar young, trendy female audiences—the target of its focus strategy.

Having adopted an overall international business strategy, a firm must assess where it wants to do business. Decisions about whether to enter a particular foreign market are derived from and must be consistent with the firm's overall business strategy. For example, the steady economic growth of such low-to-middle-income countries as Costa Rica, Namibia, Poland, and Turkey offers exciting new business opportunities for Timex but not necessarily for Rolex.

Because of budget and resource limitations, international firms must carefully assess countries and rank them according to their potential for the firms' products. Influencing this ranking

---

EMERGING OPPORTUNITIES | **PRETTY GARLIC**

When Yafod International was founded, a little more than a decade ago, it sold but one product: garlic. John Huang, at the time the managing director of the small exporting company based in China's Shandong province, faced an interesting challenge: how to convince the world's food-processing companies and vegetable wholesalers to order his garlic, despite his lack of a marketing budget.

Huang's solution was to use the Internet to build worldwide recognition of his company and its simple product line. He developed a clever brand name—Pretty Garlic—and designed an attractive website—www.prettygarlic.com—that provides much of the information a prospective buyer of garlic needs—varieties, prices, ordering information, payment terms, shipping arrangements, and packaging details. The website also provides information of use to garlic retailers, such as the plant's health benefits. It is probably the first site on the Internet that features color photos showcasing the different sizes and types of Chinese garlic. Although most Web surfers have no need to see a photo of a 5.5-centimeter pure-white Jinxiang garlic bulb, buyers for the world's food processors and grocery chains do. Over half of Huang's orders are generated by the Internet, and the company now ships over 15,000 tons of garlic a year.

Needless to say, the Internet provided a perfect means for Huang to reach his small but focused target market. Boosted by its imaginative Internet-driven marketing strategy, Yafod has broadened its product line to include other fruits, vegetables, beans, and spices. It now has offices in Canada, Colombia, Iran, India, Poland, and the United Kingdom. While not as big or as well-known as Amazon or eBay, Pretty Garlic's success similarly demonstrates the power of Internet to reach customers world-wide. In reflecting on his company's growth, Huang notes the "Internet has played a major role in our development. We continuously develop our online e-business platform and promote our products on leading search engines ... Daily we receive new inquiries from various countries in the world." Creative use of the Internet, coupled with a commitment to quality and customer service, are the foundations of the young company's achievements. Indeed, *Fortune* magazine recently described Pretty Garlic as the "industry's equivalent of Nike or Coca-Cola."

Sources: Correspondence with John Huang, August 23, 2011 and March 25, 2010; "Inside China's garlic bubble," *Fortune*, March 23, 2010 (online); "The Web @ Work," *Wall Street Journal*, August 7, 2000, p. B4; www.prettygarlic. com website.

may be factors such as culture, levels of competition, channels of distribution, and availability of infrastructure. Depending on the nature of the product and other circumstances, a firm may choose to enter simultaneously all markets that meet certain acceptability criteria. For example, consumer goods marketers like Nike and Coca-Cola often introduce new products broadly throughout North America or Europe to maximize the impact of their mass media advertising campaigns. Alternatively, a firm may choose to enter markets one by one, in an order based on their potential to the firm. Caterpillar, for example, uses this approach because its marketing strategy is based on the painstaking development of strong local dealerships, not glitzy TV campaigns highlighting the endorsements of the latest music and sports stars.

The Marketing Mix

After an international firm has decided to enter a particular foreign market, further marketing decisions must be made.[6] In particular, international marketing managers must address four issues:

1. How to develop the firm's product(s)
2. How to price those products
3. How to sell those products
4. How to distribute those products to the firm's customers.

These elements are collectively known as the **marketing mix** and colloquially referred to as the *four Ps of marketing*: product, pricing, promotion, and place (or distribution). The role of the four Ps in international marketing is illustrated in Figure 16.2.

International marketing-mix issues and decisions parallel those of domestic marketing in many ways, although are more complex. The array of variables international marketing managers must consider is far broader, and the interrelationships among those variables far more intricate, than is the case for domestic marketing managers. Before we discuss these complexities, however, we need to focus on another important issue in international marketing—the extent to which an international firm should standardize its marketing mix in all the countries it enters.

Standardization versus Customization

A firm's marketers usually choose from three basic approaches in deciding whether to standardize or customize their firm's marketing mix:

1. Should the firm adopt an *ethnocentric approach*, that is, simply market its goods internationally the same way it does domestically?

FIGURE 16.2

The Elements of the Marketing Mix for International Firms

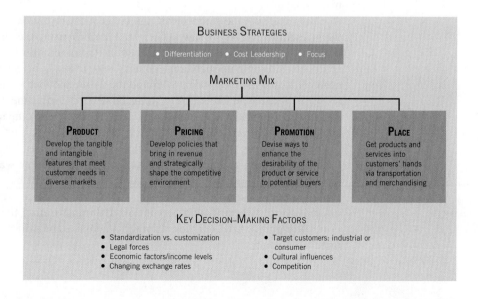

BUSINESS STRATEGIES

• Differentiation   • Cost Leadership   • Focus

MARKETING MIX

PRODUCT	**PRICING**	**PROMOTION**	**PLACE**
Develop the tangible and intangible features that meet customer needs in diverse markets	Develop policies that bring in revenue and strategically shape the competitive environment	Devise ways to enhance the desirability of the product or service to potential buyers	Get products and services into customers' hands via transportation and merchandising

KEY DECISION-MAKING FACTORS

- Standardization vs. customization
- Legal forces
- Economic factors/income levels
- Changing exchange rates

- Target customers: industrial or consumer
- Cultural influences
- Competition

2. Should it adopt a *polycentric approach*, that is, customize the marketing mix to meet the specific needs of each foreign market it serves?
3. Should it adopt a *geocentric approach*, that is, analyze the needs of customers worldwide and then adopt a standardized marketing mix for all the markets it serves?[7]

The **ethnocentric approach** is relatively easy to adopt. The firm simply markets its goods in international markets using the same marketing mix it uses domestically, thereby avoiding the expense of developing new marketing techniques to serve foreign customers. When some firms first internationalize, they adopt this approach, believing that a marketing mix that worked at home should be as successful abroad. For example, when Lands' End targeted the German mail-order market—which on a per capita basis is the largest in the world—it deliberately replicated its U.S. marketing strategy. Stressing its "down home" roots, the company trumpets to its U.S. consumers its location next to a rural Wisconsin cornfield, the friendliness of its operators and production staff, and its generous return policy—consumers can return all Lands' End products, even if they are used or worn out, with no questions asked. When it entered the German market, Lands' End established its local headquarters in an old schoolhouse in the tiny, picturesque village of Mettlach on the Saar River. The company spent months training its telephone operators to ensure they would meet its standards for friendly, helpful service. It also transplanted its "no questions asked" return service, much to the consternation of its German competitors, whose policy was to accept returns only if the goods were flawed or inaccurately described in their catalogs and then only if the goods were unused and in good condition.[8] The ethnocentric approach may not be desirable, however, if the firm loses sales because it fails to take into account the idiosyncratic needs of its foreign customers. Should this be the case, successful firms will modify their marketing mixes to meet local conditions and needs after the firms learn more about the local market.

The **polycentric approach** is far more costly because international marketers attempt to customize the firm's marketing mix in each market the firm enters in order to meet the idiosyncratic needs of customers in that market. Customization may increase the firm's revenues if its marketers are successful in this task. Firms that adopt this approach believe customers will be more willing to buy and more willing to pay a higher price for a product that exactly meets their needs than a product that does not. Often international firms that view themselves as multidomestic adopt this approach.

The **geocentric approach** calls for standardization of the marketing mix, allowing the firm to provide essentially the same product or service in different markets and to use essentially the same marketing approach to sell that product or service globally. Coca-Cola was one of the first international businesses to adopt this approach. It sells its popular soft drink worldwide and uses essentially the same packaging, product, and advertising themes everywhere. Indeed, the contoured shape of a Coca-Cola bottle is one of the world's most widely recognized images.

Note that both the ethnocentric and the geocentric approaches argue for standardization of the marketing mix. As we saw in Chapter 11, a firm using the ethnocentric approach standardizes on the basis of what the firm does in its home country. A firm using the geocentric approach starts with no such home country bias. Instead, the geocentric approach considers the needs of all the firm's customers around the world and then standardizes on that basis.

Standardization became a popular buzzword during the 1980s, as proponents such as Kenichi Ohmae (then managing director of McKinsey & Company's Tokyo office) argued that customers in the rich countries of North America, Europe, and Asia were becoming increasingly alike, with similar incomes, educational achievements, lifestyles, and aspirations, so that expensive customization of the marketing mix by country was less necessary.[9] Similarly, Harvard Business School marketing guru Theodore Levitt believes that standardization of a firm's products and other elements of its marketing mix creates huge economies of scale in production, distribution, and promotion. By transforming these cost savings into reduced prices worldwide, Levitt argues, a firm that adopts standardization can outperform its international competitors.[10]

The trade-offs between standardization and customization are clear. Standardization allows a firm to achieve manufacturing, distribution, and promotional efficiencies and to maintain simpler and more streamlined operations.[11] However, the firm may suffer lost sales if its products fail to meet the unique needs of customers in a given market. Customization allows a firm to tailor its products to meet the needs of customers in each market, although the firm may sacrifice cost efficiencies by so doing. In essence, standardization focuses on the cost side of the profit equation; by driving down costs, the firm's profits are enhanced. Customization focuses on the revenue side of the profit equation; by attending to the unique customer needs in each market, the firm is able to charge higher prices and sell more goods in each market. In practice, most firms avoid the extremes of either approach.[12] Many successful firms have adopted a strategy of "think globally, act locally" to gain the economies of scale of a global marketing mix while retaining the ability to meet the needs of customers in different national markets. Even Coca-Cola, a pioneer in the use of global marketing, has begun to encourage more localized thinking within its global marketing framework. For instance, it allows its South African distributor to package Coca-Cola in three different size cans and also markets a sweeter-tasting cola in that country called Iron Brew.

The home appliance market provides a useful example of this strategy. U.S. kitchens tend to be large and spacious, and consumers prefer large stoves, refrigerators, and dishwashers. The smaller kitchens of Europe and Japan dictate the use of much smaller appliances. Further, within Europe there are marked differences in power supply characteristics and in consumer preferences for various design features and alternatives. Thus, appliance manufacturers must develop specific and unique product lines for each country in which the firms do business. Whirlpool has tried to reduce some of the costs of customization by designing its products to meet the needs of market niches that cross national boundaries. For example, Whirlpool designers have developed a World Washer, a small, stripped-down automatic washing machine targeted to meet the needs of the emerging middle classes in such countries as Brazil, Mexico, and India. Whirlpool, however, stands ready to customize even the World Washer when needed. It modified the agitators of World Washers sold in India to ensure the machines would not shred or tangle the delicate saris traditionally worn by Indian women.[13]

The degree of standardization or customization a firm adopts depends on many factors, including product type, the cultural differences between the home country and the host countries, and the host countries' legal systems. The firm may adopt one approach for one element of the marketing mix and another for a second element. Often firms standardize product designs to capture manufacturing economies of scale but customize advertisements and the channels of distribution to meet specific local market needs. The degree of standardization also may be influenced by the firm's perception of the global marketplace, which is similar to the conundrum "Is the glass half full or half empty?" A firm tilting toward standardization assumes consumers around the world are basically similar but then adjusts for differences among them. A firm tilting toward customization assumes consumers are different but then adjusts for similarities among them.

An international firm also must consider its own organizational structure. Standardization implies that power and control should be centralized, often at the firm's headquarters, whereas customization suggests that headquarters must delegate considerable decision-making power to local managers. Thus, a strongly centralized firm (see Chapter 14) can more easily standardize its international marketing mix than can a decentralized firm. Often international firms address these organizational issues by adopting a two-step process:

1. The decision to standardize some elements of the marketing mix, such as product design, brand name, packaging, and product positioning, is made centrally.
2. Then local managers are called on to critique the global marketing program and to develop plans to implement customized elements of the marketing mix, such as promotion and distribution.[14]

Table 16.1 summarizes some factors that may lead a firm to adopt standardization or customization for all or part of its international marketing efforts.

TABLE 16.1 Advantages and Disadvantages of Standardized and Customized International Marketing

Standardized International Marketing	
Advantages	Disadvantages
1. Reduces marketing costs	1. Ignores different conditions of product use
2. Facilitates centralized control of marketing	2. Ignores local legal differences
3. Promotes efficiency in R&D	3. Ignores differences in buyer behavior patterns
4. Results in economies of scale in production	4. Inhibits local marketing initiatives
5. Reflects the trend toward a single global marketplace	5. Ignores other differences in individual markets

Customized International Marketing	
Advantages	Disadvantages
1. Reflects different conditions of product use	1. Increases marketing costs
2. Acknowledges local legal differences	2. Inhibits centralized control of marketing
3. Accounts for differences in buyer behavior patterns	3. Creates inefficiency in R&D
4. Promotes local marketing initiatives	4. Reduces economies of scale in production
5. Accounts for other differences in individual markets	5. Ignores the trend toward a single global marketplace

Product Policy

The first P of the international marketing mix is the product itself. Here, **product** comprises both the set of tangible factors that the consumer can see or touch (the physical product and its packaging) and numerous intangible factors such as image, installation, warranties, and credit terms. Critical to a firm's ability to compete internationally is its success in developing products with tangible and intangible features that meet the wants and needs of customers in diverse national markets.[15] For instance, Toyota's success in selling its automobiles in Europe, Asia, and the Americas reflects its product-related achievements in designing and producing mechanically reliable vehicles, offering competitive warranties, building a solid brand name for its products, providing spare parts and repair manuals, and furnishing financing to its dealers and retail customers.

Standardized Products or Customized Products?

A key product policy decision facing international marketers is the extent to which their firms' products should be standardized across markets or customized within individual markets. For example, Toyota, like many international firms, has adopted a blend of customization and standardization. It has standardized its corporate commitment to building high-quality, mechanically reliable automobiles and to maintaining the prestige of the Toyota brand name. Yet it customizes its products and product mix to meet the needs of local markets. It sells right-hand-drive motor vehicles in Japan, Australia, South Africa, and the United Kingdom and left-hand-drive vehicles in the Americas and continental Europe. It also adjusts its warranties from country to country based on the warranties offered by its competitors. The name under which it sells a product also may vary by country. For years Toyota sold the Lexus Sports Coupe (a U.S. brand) in its own country as a Toyota Soarer because the Lexus brand was not introduced in Japan until recently.

Sometimes firms learn they have customized their products not by design but by accident. For example, a few years ago managers at Unilever realized that for no apparent reason the firm was using 85 different recipes for its chicken soups and 15 different cone shapes for its Cornetto ice creams in Europe. Once this problem was identified, Unilever quickly standardized its ice cream cone design and slashed the number of chicken soup flavors it offered European customers, thereby reducing its production and inventory costs and simplifying its distribution requirements.[16]

Many firms use a combination of product standardization and customization. Automakers, for example, can use the same basic seat designs, control buttons, and compact disc players in many parts of the world. But they also have to adapt to right-hand versus left-hand driving customs and metric versus non-metric mileage and gasoline measurements.

© Richard Naude/Alamy

The extent to which products should be customized to meet local needs varies according to several factors. One is the nature of the product's target customers—are they industrial users or are they individual consumers? Although some industrial products are customized and some consumer products are standardized, generally speaking, industrial products are more likely to be standardized than consumer products. For example, Caterpillar's bulldozers and front-end loaders are sold throughout the world with only minor modifications to meet local operating and regulatory requirements. Products sold as commodities also are typically standardized across different markets; examples include agricultural products, petroleum, 512MB computer memory chips, and chemicals. A general rule of thumb is that the closer to the body a product is consumed, the more likely it will need to be customized. For example, to boost its sales in Japan, Eddie Bauer altered the styles of clothing it sells there, adding to its store shelves stretchy shirts and straight-legged pants that the Japanese prefer.[17] The Big Boy burger chain added pork omelettes and fried rice to its menus in Thailand to attract local consumers.[18]

Legal Forces

The laws and regulations of host countries also may affect the product policies adopted by international firms. Some countries, for instance, have imposed detailed labeling requirements and health standards on consumer products that firms, both foreign and domestic, must follow strictly. International firms must adjust the packaging and even the products themselves to meet these consumer protection regulations. For example, Grupo Modelo SA, the brewer of Corona beer, had to reduce the nitrosamine levels of the beer it sells in Germany, Austria, and Switzerland to meet those countries' health standards.[19] Countries also may regulate the design of consumer products to simplify purchase and replacement decisions. Saudi Arabia, for instance, requires electrical connecting cords on consumer appliances to be 2 meters long. GE suffered the embarrassment (and a loss of profits) of having its goods turned back at a Saudi port when an inspector determined GE's connecting cords were only 2 yards long.[20] Widely varying technical standards adopted by countries for such products as electrical appliances and broadcasting and telecommunications equipment also force firms to customize their products. For example, the electrical plugs of home appliances sold in Europe must be modified on a country-by-country basis to fit the array of electrical outlets found there.

Cultural Influences

International firms often must adapt their products to meet the cultural needs of local markets. One typical adaptation is to change the labeling on the product's package into the primary language of the host country. ("E-World" examines the unique language problems facing e-commerce.)

However, in some cases a foreign language may be used to connote quality or fashion. For instance, after the fall of communism, Procter & Gamble added German words to the labels of detergents sold in the Czech Republic. Market researchers had determined that products in packages labeled in English or German were viewed by Czechs as being of higher quality than products labeled in Czech.[21] Often the ingredients of food products are modified to better please local palates. Gerber, for example, customizes its baby food to meet the requirements of the local culture. The company found that Polish mothers refused to purchase its mashed bananas for their infants because the fruit was viewed as an expensive luxury. Instead, Polish mothers favor such Gerber flavors as Vegetable and Rabbit Meat to help nurture their infants; Japanese mothers choose Gerber's Freeze Dried Sardines and Rice for their children.[22] Pepsi's Frito-Lay division also has modified its snack foods to better meet the needs of foreign consumers, offering, for example, paprika-flavored chips to Poles and Hungarians and shrimp-flavored chips to Koreans.[23] Its food scientists also are busily working on a squid-peanut snack food Frito-Lay believes will be very successful among Southeast Asians. Presumably for cultural reasons, neither Gerber nor Frito-Lay has yet made plans to market these items in North America.

Culture may affect product policy in other ways. For example, foreign automobile makers have learned that Japanese consumers are extremely quality conscious. For many Japanese consumers an automobile is more a status symbol than a mode of transportation—the average car in Japan is driven only 5,000 miles per year, about one-third the U.S. average. Thus, the way the car looks is often more important than the way it drives. A Japanese customer may reject a car if the paint underneath the hood is uneven or the gas tank cover fits loosely.[24] Many German consumers are very environmentally conscious. As a result, firms often must redesign products they sell in Germany to allow for easier disposal and recycling.

In a similar vein, firms may also find it necessary to adjust or modify their packaging in different countries. For instance, when German grocery retailer Metro entered the market in Southeast Asia it initially used the same methods for packaging fresh fruits and vegetables as it used elsewhere—corrugated containers of shrink-wrapped food. But consumers in Vietnam insisted on ripping such packages open, wanting to insure there were no rotten items on the bottom. They also indicated a strong need to touch, feel, and smell their food. So Metro altered its methods and simply stacked its fruits and vegetables just as they are in street market stalls.[25]

At other times culture may force changes in a foreign product. For example, although U.S. films are very popular in Asia, HBO often has to edit its movies before they can be broadcast in Asia's culturally conservative countries. HBO could not show *Schindler's List* or *Amistad* in Malaysia because both films contained brief nudity, and their director, Steven Spielberg, refuses to allow others to cut scenes from his movies. Similarly, musicians embarking on international tours may have to adjust to local sensibilities. Artists Gwen Stefani and Beyoncé Knowles changed their costuming and other artistic elements of their shows when performing in Malaysia.[26]

Both Nike and Adidas have been experimenting with ways to make their normal "Americanized" products blend more readily into foreign cultures. For instance, each has been launching new products in China with standard designs embellished with local cultural touches. Adidas has introduced a line of sportswear that follows normal western design (polo-type shirts, for instance) decorated with ancient Chinese swirling "lucky cloud" patterns. Nike, meanwhile, has been marketing its products using various Chinese slogans and traditional sayings.[27]

Economic Factors

A country's level of economic development may affect the desired attributes of a product. Consumers in richer countries often favor products loaded with extra performance features; more price-sensitive consumers in poorer countries typically opt for stripped-down versions of the same products. Sometimes a firm may have to adjust package size or design to meet local conditions. For example, firms selling toothpaste or shampoo in poorer countries often package their goods in single-use sizes to make the products more affordable to local citizens. The quality of a country's infrastructure also may affect the customization decision; thus, manufacturers may reinforce the suspension systems of motor vehicles sold in countries where road maintenance is poor. The availability and cost of repair services also can affect product design. Automobiles sold in poorer countries often use simpler technology, which allows more repairs to be done by backyard mechanics.

E-WORLD **E-TRANSLATION**

Americans were the first enthusiastic adopters of the Internet. So it's not surprising that most websites are created in English. Most users, wherever they were located and whatever language they spoke, could read at least some of what they saw. But in the last few years, the strongest online growth has occurred outside the United States. That has led to an explosion in websites that are explicitly designed for users in other cultures. And marketers around the world are trying to determine how to best meld language and content to achieve the best results.

One key factor is that 50 percent of current Internet users are not fluent in English. Website designers rely on language translation tools, provided by companies such as TRADOS. One TRADOS customer is Kelly Services, which provides staffing support to 200,000 customers worldwide. The company needed to translate its Web content, including training materials, software documentation, and performance appraisals, from English into Spanish, French, German, Dutch, and Italian. Kelly used to perform translations with a permanent staff of 10 at a cost of $255,000 annually. With TRADOS, the work is performed by two employees and expenses have dropped by half. Translation time was cut 70 percent.

But a mere word-for-word translation often is unsatisfactory because users in different regions follow different conventions. For instance, firms developing websites for overseas use must take into account variations in currencies and measurements. When a language is read from right to left or in vertical rows, so too are the local websites. Net icons may not be familiar to non-English speakers. In countries where high-speed connections are less common, sites that are rich in graphics may be unacceptably slow in loading.

American firms are finding that they must reach out to a multi-cultural customer base of overseas clients and immigrants, or risk losing out to foreign competitors. The online auction giant eBay, for example, has 20 national sites, from Argentina to the United Kingdom. Amazon, Yahoo!, and AOL have all developed international content. However, 55 percent of U.S. business websites are still offered only in English. Brigitte E. Biver, a German working in the United States, prefers sites in her native language. "It gives you an incentive to use a service—if it's multilingual," she claims. On the Internet, diverse customers are speaking up and U.S. firms had better listen.

Sources: "Babel.net," *BusinessWeek*, December 17, 2000, pp. 78–80; "The next Web," *BusinessWeek*, March 4, 2002, pp. 99–101; "Surfing in tongues," *BusinessWeek*, December 11, 2000, pp. 84–86.

Brand Names

One element international firms often like to standardize is the brand name of a product. A firm that does this can reduce its packaging, design, and advertising production costs. It also can capture spillovers of its advertising messages from one market to the next. For example, Avon's entry into the China market was made easier by the fact that millions of consumers had seen its products advertised on Hong Kong television.[28] Mars, Inc., sought to capture the benefits of standardization by dropping its successful local brand names for the Marathon bar in the British market and the Raider chocolate biscuit on the Continent in favor of the more universally known Snickers and Twix brands.[29] However, sometimes legal or cultural factors force a firm to alter the brand names under which it sells its products. For example, Grupo Modelo SA markets Corona beer in Spain as Coronita because a Spanish vineyard owns the Corona brand name.[30] Coca-Cola calls its low-calorie soft drink Diet Coke in weight-conscious North America but Coca-Cola Light in other markets.

Marvel Comics has recently undertaken an interesting approach to customizing a brand name to local markets. Its popular character Spider-Man was already well-known in India, and Spider-Man comics had reasonable sales levels. But Marvel decided to introduce a new version of Spider-Man in that country. The "new" Spider-Man's alter ego is Pavitr Prabhakar (not Peter Parker), he got his powers from a yogi (instead of a radioactive spider), and he wears a loincloth into battle (instead of the famous spider suit). As a result, sales of Spider-Man comics and Spider-Man licensed merchandise in India has skyrocketed. Certain characters from Disney, Sesame Street, and the Powerpuff Girls have also been modified to better fit the Indian market.[31]

Pricing Issues and Decisions

The second P of the international marketing mix is pricing. Developing effective pricing policies is a critical determinant of any firm's success.[32] Pricing policies directly affect the size of the revenues earned by a firm. The policies also serve as an important strategic weapon by allowing the firm to shape the competitive environment in which it does business. For example, Toys 'R' Us has achieved success in Germany, Japan, the United States, and other countries by selling low-priced toys in low-cost warehouse-like settings. Its low prices have placed enormous pressure on its competitors to slash their costs, alter their distribution systems, and shrink their profit margins. The firm's aggressive pricing strategy has effectively forced its competitors to fight the battle for Asian, European, and North American consumers on terms dictated by Toys 'R' Us. Walmart is doing much the same in foreign markets where it competes.

Both domestic and international firms must strive to develop pricing strategies that will produce profitable operations, but the task facing an international firm is more complex than that facing a purely domestic firm. To begin with, a firm's costs of doing business vary widely by country. Differences in transportation charges and tariffs cause the landed price of goods to vary by country. Differences in distribution practices also affect the final price the end customer pays. For example, intense competition among distributors in the United States minimizes the margin between retail prices and manufacturers' prices. In contrast, Japan's inefficient multilayered distribution system, which relies on a chain of distributors to get goods into the hands of consumers, often inflates the prices Japanese consumers pay for goods.

Exchange rate fluctuations also can create pricing problems. If an exporter's home currency rises in value, the exporter must choose between maintaining its prices in the home currency (which makes its goods more expensive in the importing country) and maintaining its prices in the host currency (which cuts its profit margins by lowering the amount of home country currency it receives for each unit sold).

International firms must consider these factors in developing their pricing policies for each national market the firms serve. They must decide whether they want to apply consistent prices across all those markets or customize prices to meet the needs of each. In reaching this decision, the firms must remember that competition, culture, distribution channels, income levels, legal requirements, and exchange rate stability may vary widely by country.

Pricing Policies

International firms generally adopt one of three pricing policies:[33]

1. Standard price policy
2. Two-tiered pricing
3. Market pricing

An international firm following a geocentric approach to international marketing will adopt a **standard price policy,** whereby the firm charges the same price for its products and services regardless of where they are sold or the nationality of the customer. Firms selling goods that are easily tradable and transportable often adopt this pricing approach out of necessity. For example, if a firm manufacturing DRAM memory chips charged different customers vastly different prices, some of its favored customers might begin to resell the chips to less-favored customers—an easy task, given the small size and high value of the chips. Similarly, firms that sell commodity goods in competitive markets often use this pricing policy. Producers of crude oil, such as Aramco, Kuwait Oil, and Pemex, sell their products to any and all customers at prices determined by supply and demand in the world crude oil market. Other commodities produced and traded worldwide, such as coal and agricultural goods, also are sold at competitive prices with suitable adjustments for quality differentials and transportation costs and little regard to the purchaser's nationality.

An international firm that follows an ethnocentric marketing approach will use a **two-tiered pricing policy,** whereby the firm sets one price for all its domestic sales and a second price for all its international sales. A firm that adopts a two-tiered pricing policy commonly allocates to domestic sales all accounting charges associated with research and development, administrative overhead, capital depreciation, and so on. The firm then can establish a uniform foreign sales price without having to worry about covering these costs. Indeed, the only costs that need to be covered by the foreign sales price are the marginal costs associated with foreign sales, such as the product's unit manufacturing costs, shipping costs, tariffs, and foreign distribution costs.

Two-tiered pricing often is used by domestic firms just beginning to internationalize. In the short run charging foreign customers a price that covers only marginal costs may be an appropriate approach for such firms. However, the strong ethnocentric bias of two-tiered pricing suggests it is not a suitable long-run pricing strategy. A firm that views foreign customers as marginal—rather than integral—to its business is unlikely to develop the international skills, expertise, and outlook necessary to compete successfully in the international marketplace.

Firms that adopt a two-tiered pricing policy also are vulnerable to charges of dumping. Recall from Chapter 9 that dumping is the selling of a firm's products in a foreign market for a price lower than that charged in the firm's domestic market—an outcome that easily can result from a two-tiered pricing system. Most major trading countries have issued regulations intended to protect domestic firms from dumping by foreign competitors. For example, Toyota and Mazda were charged with dumping minivans in the U.S. market. Although the Japanese automakers were not penalized in this case, both subsequently raised their minivan prices to avoid future dumping complaints.

Market Pricing

An international firm that follows a polycentric approach to international marketing will use a **market pricing policy.** Market pricing is the most complex of the three pricing policies and the one most commonly adopted. A firm utilizing market pricing customizes its prices on a market-by-market basis to maximize its profits in each market.

As you may remember from your microeconomics class, the profit-maximizing output (the quantity the firm must produce to maximize its profit) occurs at the intersection of the firm's marginal revenue curve and its marginal cost curve. The profit-maximizing price is found by reading across from the point on the firm's demand curve where the profit-maximizing output occurs. In Figure 16.3(a) the intersection of the marginal revenue curve (MR) and the marginal cost curve (MC) occurs at Q, which is the profit-maximizing output. If you read straight up from Q until you reach the demand curve (D), then move left to the y-axis, you find the profit-maximizing price, P, the maximum price at which quantity Q of the good can be sold. With market pricing the firm calculates and charges the profit-maximizing price in each market it serves. Figure 16.3(b) shows two markets in which a firm has identical demand and marginal revenue curves but faces different marginal cost curves. The firm faces higher marginal costs in country 1 (MC_1) than in country 2 (MC_2). Accordingly, its profit-maximizing price in country 1 (P_1) is higher than that in country 2 (P_2).

Two conditions must be met if a firm is to successfully practice market pricing:

1. The firm must face different demand and/or cost conditions in the countries in which it sells its products. This condition usually is met because taxes, tariffs, standards of living, levels of competition, infrastructure costs and availability, and numerous other factors vary by country.
2. The firm must be able to prevent arbitrage, a concept discussed in Chapter 8. The firm's market pricing policy will unravel if customers are able to buy the firm's products in a low-price country and resell them profitably in a high-price country. Because of tariffs, transportation costs, and other transaction costs, arbitrage is usually not a problem if country-to-country price variations are small. If prices vary widely by country, however, arbitrage can upset the firm's market pricing strategy.

FIGURE 16.3

Determining the Profit-Maximizing Price

a. Finding the profit-maximizing price

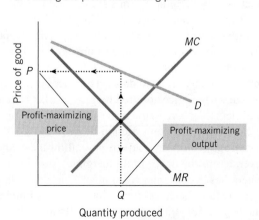

b. Finding the profit-maximizing price for two markets

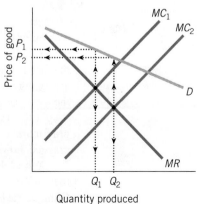

Assuming these conditions are met, the advantages of this polycentric approach are obvious. The firm can set higher prices where markets will tolerate them and lower prices where necessary to remain competitive. It also can directly allocate relevant local costs against local sales within each foreign market, thereby allowing corporate strategists and planners to better allocate the firm's resources across markets. Such flexibility comes with a cost, however. To capture the benefits of market pricing, local managers must closely monitor sales and competitive conditions within their markets so that appropriate and timely adjustments can be made. Also, corporate headquarters must be willing to delegate authority to local managers to allow them to adjust prices within their markets.

A market pricing policy, however, can expose a firm to complaints about dumping (as discussed earlier) as well as to three other risks: (1) damage to its brand name, (2) development of a gray market for its products, and (3) consumer resentment against discriminatory prices.

The firm needs to ensure that the prices it charges in one market do not damage the brand image it has carefully nurtured in other markets. For example, suppose Kirin encouraged its North American and European brand managers to market Chivas Regal as a premium scotch whiskey sold at a premium price but allowed its Japanese brand managers to sell Chivas Regal as a nonprestigious brand sold at rock-bottom prices. Because of its marketing approach in Japan, Kirin would risk deterioration of Chivas Regal's premium brand image in North America and Europe. Thus any international firm that sells brand name products and adopts market pricing should review the prices charged by local managers to ensure that the integrity of its brand names and its market images is maintained across all of its markets.

A firm that follows a market pricing policy also risks the development of gray markets for its products as a result of arbitrage. A **gray market** is a market that results when products are imported into a country legally but outside the normal channels of distribution authorized by the manufacturer. (This phenomenon also is known as **parallel importing.**) A gray market may develop when the price in one market is sufficiently lower than the price the firm charges in another market that entrepreneurs can buy the good in the lower-price market and resell it profitably in the higher-price market. Thus, the firm that has large price differences among markets is vulnerable to having these differentials undercut by gray markets. Gray markets frequently arise when firms fail to adjust local prices after major fluctuations in exchange rates. Coca-Cola, for example, faced such a problem in the mid-1990s after the yen strengthened relative to the U.S. dollar. Japanese discounters were able to purchase and import Coke made in the United States for 27 percent less than the price of Coke made in Japan, thereby disrupting the firm's pricing strategy in both countries.[34] Merck had a similar problem when the British pound rose relative to other European Union (EU) currencies. The company was forced to cut the prices in the United Kingdom of many of its drugs, such as the recently developed AIDS drug Crixivan, because of parallel importing from other EU countries.[35]

Products commonly influenced by gray markets include big-ticket items such as automobiles, cameras, computers, ski equipment, and watches. Gray markets also are more prevalent in free-market economies, where fewer government regulations make it easier for gray markets to emerge. One estimate suggests gray-market sales in the United States approach $130 billion each year.[36] Many multinational corporations (MNCs) have attempted to eliminate or control gray markets through legal action, but few have had much success.

Gray-market sales undermine a firm's market pricing policy and often lower the firm's profits. Gray-market sales also cause friction between the firm and its distributors, who lose sales but often are stuck with the costs of either providing customer support and honoring product guarantees on gray-market goods or explaining to unhappy customers why they will not do so. For example, Charles of the Ritz reports that over 10,000 retailers sell its Opium perfume, although the firm has authorized only 1,300 to do so. The prices its authorized dealers charge are continually being undercut by the prices offered by gray-market sellers, thereby making it difficult for the authorized dealers to adhere to the firm's suggested pricing schedule. Charles of the Ritz has sought to smooth over the resulting friction by helping its authorized dealers compete with the gray marketers through additional advertising allowances and special price reductions. This practice, however, harms the firm's profit margins.

A third danger lies in consumer resentment. Consumers in the high-priced country may feel they are being gouged by such pricing policies. Estee Lauder, for example, charges $40 for Clinique facial soap in Tokyo; the same soap sells for only $10 in the United States. J. Crew charges Japanese customers $130 for wool sweaters that sell for $48 in the United States. Japanese newspapers and television stations have highlighted this issue, claiming that foreign companies take advantage of Japanese consumers. Although spokespersons from various companies have argued that the price differences are due to the high cost of doing business in Japan, the ill will engendered by the controversy has not helped the companies' sales.[37]

Promotion Issues and Decisions

Promotion, the third P of the international marketing mix, encompasses all efforts by an international firm to enhance the desirability of its products among potential buyers. Although many promotional activities are specifically targeted at buyers, successful firms recognize they also must communicate with their distributors and the general public to ensure favorable sentiment toward the firms themselves and their products. Because promotion relies on communication with audiences in the host country, it is the most culture bound of the four Ps. Thus, a firm must take special care to ensure that the message host country audiences receive is in fact the message the firm intended to send. International marketing managers must therefore effectively blend and utilize the four elements of the **promotion mix**—advertising, personal selling, sales promotion, and public relations—to motivate potential customers to buy their firms' products.

Advertising

For most international firms, especially those selling consumer products and services, advertising is the most important element in the promotion mix. As a firm develops its advertising strategy, it must consider three factors:

1. The message it wants to convey
2. The media available for conveying the message
3. The extent to which the firm wants to globalize its advertising effort

At the same time the firm must take into account relevant cultural, linguistic, and legal constraints found in various national markets.

MESSAGE The **message** of an advertisement is the facts or impressions the advertiser wants to convey to potential customers. An automaker may want to convey a message of value (low price), reliability (quality), and/or style (image and prestige). The choice of message is an important reflection of the way the firm sees its products and services and the way it wants them to be seen by customers. Coca-Cola, for example, believes its products help consumers enjoy life, and its advertising messages consistently stress this theme worldwide. Products that are used for different purposes in different areas will need to be marketed differently. For instance, in the United States motorcycles are seen primarily as recreational products, but in many other countries they are seen mainly as a means of transportation. Thus, Honda's and Kawasaki's ads in the United States stress the fun and excitement of riding. In poorer countries they stress the reliability and functionalism of motorcycles as a mode of inexpensive transportation.[38]

A product's country of origin often serves as an important part of the advertising message.[39] Among fashion-conscious teenagers and young adults in Europe and Japan, U.S. goods often are viewed as being very trendy. Thus, Harley-Davidson, Gibson guitars, Stetson hats, and the National Basketball Association, among others, highlight the U.S. origins of their products. Japanese products often are perceived to be of high quality, so international marketers stress the Japanese origin of such products as Toyota automobiles and Sony electronics goods.

MEDIUM The **medium** is the communication channel used by the advertiser to convey a message. A firm's international marketing manager must alter the media used to convey its message from market to market based on availability, legal restrictions, standards of living, literacy rates, the cultural homogeneity of the national market, and other factors. In bilingual or multilingual countries such as Belgium, Switzerland, and Canada, international firms must adjust their mix of media outlets to reach each of the country's cultural groups. For example, Nestlé communicates to its French-speaking Swiss audience by advertising in French-language newspapers and to its German-speaking Swiss audience via ads in German-language newspapers.

A country's level of economic development also may affect the media firms use. In many less-developed countries television ownership may be limited and literacy rates low. This eliminates television, newspapers, and magazines as useful advertising media but raises the importance of radio. Some firms have developed innovative solutions to communicate with potential consumers. For example, Colgate-Palmolive wished to increase its sales in rural India. Unfortunately, only one-third of rural Indians own television sets, and more than half are illiterate. To reach these customers, the company's marketers outfitted "video vans" to tour the rural countryside. After showing rural villagers a half-hour infomercial extolling the virtues of the company's oral hygiene products, sales representatives handed out samples of Colgate toothpaste and toothbrushes. This technique has proved successful, doubling tooth-paste consumption in rural areas during the past decade.[40] "Bringing the World into Focus" illustrates another unusual but innovative approach to developing advertising media customized for the local market.

Legal restrictions also may prompt the use of certain media. Most national governments limit the number of TV stations as well as the amount of broadcast time sold to advertisers. Countries often outlaw the use of certain media for advertising products that may be harmful to their societies. For example, South Korea, Malaysia, Hong Kong, China, and Singapore ban cigarette advertising on television. South Korea has broadened the ban to magazines read primarily by women and by persons under the age of 20; Hong Kong has extended it to radio; China to radio, newspapers, and magazines; and Singapore to all other media.[41] As in the United States, however, this ban has prompted tobacco firms to sponsor athletic events and to purchase display ads at stadiums that will be picked up by TV cameras.[42] Legal restrictions on the advertising of alcoholic products also are common throughout the world.

GLOBAL VERSUS LOCAL ADVERTISING A firm also must decide whether advertising for its product or service can be the same everywhere or must be tailored to each local market the firm serves.[43] Some products, such as Coca-Cola soft drinks, Bic pens, Levi jeans, and McDonald's hamburgers, have almost universal appeal. Such companies frequently advertise globally, utilizing the same advertising campaign in all of the markets they serve. For example, in the late 1990s Coca-Cola introduced a series of ads shown globally that featured its "Always Coca-Cola" slogan.[44]

BRINGING THE WORLD INTO FOCUS | **SAILING FOR SALES**

When advertisers start promoting their products in new countries, one of their first actions should be to develop a complete understanding of both advertising channels and local customs and mores. For instance, many Egyptian advertisers pitch their products through cheap billboards that line the country's highways or television ads featuring dancing women. A few years ago, though, Coca-Cola decided to look for alternative methods for reaching local consumers. As it turned out, all its executives had to do was look out of their Cairo offices to the Nile River.

For centuries, Egyptians have relied on feluccas—sailboats that glide up and down the mighty Nile—for transportation and recreation. Ancient versions of the felucca helped transport workers and supplies to the construction sites of the pyramids and allowed the pharaohs to rule their realm. Today's feluccas are propelled by large, triangular white sails. Tourists and Egyptian families on holiday can catch a ride on a felucca at many places along the Nile, including Cairo, Aswan, and Luxor. Coca-Cola executives realized that felucca sails would be the ideal place to promote their signature soft drink.

After some negotiation, the firm signed a two-year deal with a large felucca operator for 27,000 Egyptian pounds (around $8,000) plus new sails. Coke did have to make one significant concession to local values: while its executives would have preferred that the feluccas hoist red sails showcasing Coke's logo, local custom required the sails be white. Recognizing that it's difficult to fight a three millennia-old tradition, Coke agreed to white sails displaying Coke's red logo.

There's an old saying that imitation is the sincerest form of flattery. Other consumer goods companies quickly realized the brilliance of Coke's advertising innovation. Perrier and Al Ahram Beverages (now a part of Heineken) quickly followed suit, inking their own advertising agreements with other large felucca operators.

Sources: "Felucca ride in Cairo," localyte.com, accessed on July 6, 2011; Barbara Mueller, *Dynamics of International Advertising* (New York: Peter Lang, 2006), p. 250; "Advertising breezes along the Nile River with signs for sails," *Wall Street Journal*, July 18, 1997, pp. A1, A11.

Sometimes international businesses may choose to make subtle adaptations to meet the needs of the local market. Unilever applied this approach to an advertising campaign for Dove soap. The company's TV commercials were identical in each market, but the actors were not. On the same stage and set, U.S., Italian, German, French, and Australian models were filmed in succession, each stating in her own language, "Dove has one-quarter cleansing cream."[45] Nestlé used a single theme in promoting Kit Kat candy to its European customers—"Have a break, have a Kit Kat"—but changed the backgrounds to better appeal to customers across national markets.

Other firms have opted for a regionalization strategy. IBM, for instance, began advertising its products in European markets by creating a pan-European advertising campaign. Instead of customizing its ads by country, IBM featured the same text and visual images in all its European ads, altering only the language used for its broadcast and print ads. IBM determined that this approach saved $22 to $30 million in creative and production expenses (of a total advertising budget of $150 million). However, maintaining uniformity of the product's image was of paramount concern. The campaign was designed specifically to ensure that IBM's European clients, regardless of the country in which they were located, received the same message about its product.[46] Similarly, Levi Strauss used the same TV ad to sell its 501 jeans in six European markets. Because each of its commercials costs about $500,000 to shoot, Levi Strauss would have spent about $3 million on six ads and thus saved $2.5 million in production costs alone by choosing this regional strategy.[47]

Whether to choose a standardized or a specialized advertising campaign also is a function of the message the firm wants to convey. Standardized advertisements tend to contain less concrete information than do more specialized advertisements. Ads for products such as candy and soft drinks often can be standardized because the ads stress the warm, emotional aspects of consuming the good, whereas ads for products such as credit cards, automobiles, and airline services tend to be customized to meet the needs of local consumers.[48]

Personal Selling

The second element of the promotion mix is **personal selling**—making sales on the basis of personal contacts. The use of sales representatives, who call on potential customers and attempt to sell them a firm's products or services, is the most common approach to personal selling.[49] Because of the close contact between the salesperson and the potential customer, sellers are likely to rely on host country nationals to serve as their representatives. A firm just starting international operations often will subcontract personal selling to local sales organizations that handle product lines from several firms. As the firm grows and develops a sales base in new markets, it may establish its own sales force. Colgate-Palmolive, for example, made very effective use of personal selling to gain market share in Central Europe. The firm opened a sales office in Warsaw after the Iron Curtain fell and used it to develop a well-trained professional sales staff. That staff has made Colgate-Palmolive the consumer products market leader in Poland.[50]

The importance of personal selling as an element of the promotion mix differs for industrial products and for consumer products. For industrial products (such as complex machinery, electronic equipment, and customized computer software) customers often need technical information about product characteristics, usage, maintenance requirements, and availability of after-sales support. Well-trained sales representatives often are better able to convey information about the intricacies of such products to customers than are print or broadcast media. For consumer products personal selling normally is confined to selling to wholesalers and to retail chains. Most consumer products firms find that advertising, particularly in print and broadcast media, is a more efficient means of communicating with consumers than is personal selling. However, personal selling can be used to market some goods. Avon and Amway, for example, have successfully exported to the Asian and European markets the personal selling techniques they developed in the United States. Similarly, American International Group (AIG) carefully built its 5,000-person sales force in Shanghai over a four-year period; today AIG is the leading foreign-owned insurance company in the country.[51]

In Amway's case personal selling and the ethnic ties of its existing distributors have played a critical role in the firm's internationalization strategy. When Amway decided to enter the Philippines in 1997, it encouraged distributors of Philippine heritage from the United States,

New Zealand, and Australia to act as ambassadors, recruiting new distributors there. Because the ambassadors receive a percentage of the sales generated by the persons they recruit, over 100 existing distributors eagerly traveled to the Philippines at their own expense to develop Amway's sales force. The company has used a similar approach to break into the Korean and Chinese markets.[52]

Personal selling has several advantages for an international firm:

- Firms that hire local sales representatives can be reasonably confident that those individuals understand the local culture, norms, and customs. For example, a native of India selling products in that country will be better informed about local conditions than will someone sent from Spain to sell products in India.
- Personal selling promotes close, personal contact with customers. Customers see real people and come to associate that personal contact with the firm.
- Personal selling makes it easier for the firm to obtain valuable market information. Knowledgeable local sales representatives are an excellent source of information that can be used to develop new products and/or improve existing products for the local market.

On the other hand, personal selling is a relatively high-cost strategy. Each sales representative must be adequately compensated even though each may reach relatively few customers. An industrial products sales representative, for example, may need a full day or more to see just one potential customer. After a sale is closed, the sales representative may still find it necessary to spend large blocks of time with the customer explaining how things work and trying to generate new business. Most larger international firms also find it necessary to establish regional sales offices staffed by sales managers and other support personnel, which add more sales-related costs.

Sales Promotion

Sales promotion comprises specialized marketing efforts such as coupons, in-store promotions, sampling, direct mail campaigns, cooperative advertising, and trade fair attendance. Sales promotion activities focused on wholesalers and retailers are designed to increase the number and commitment of these intermediaries working with the firm. Many international firms participate in international trade shows such as the Paris Air Show or the Tokyo Auto Mart to generate interest among existing and potential distributors for the firms' products. Participation in international trade shows often is recommended as a first step for firms wanting to internationalize their sales. The U.S. Department of Commerce often will help small U.S. firms participate in overseas trade shows as part of its export promotion efforts. Agencies with a similar mission exist in the governments of most major trading nations. Firms also may develop cooperative advertising campaigns or provide advertising allowances to encourage retailers to promote the firms' products.

Sales promotion activities may be narrowly targeted to consumers and/or offered for only a short time before being dropped or replaced with more permanent efforts. This flexible nature of sales promotions makes them ideal for a marketing campaign tailored to fit local customs and circumstances. For example, British American Tobacco, Philip Morris, and R.J. Reynolds competed in the Taiwanese market by handing out free cigarettes, a practice not utilized in the U.S. market. Philip Morris and R.J. Reynolds built market share by offering Korean consumers free cigarette lighters and desk diaries emblazoned with the firms' logos in return for cigarette purchases.[53] U.S. airlines have effectively used direct mail and email to lure international travelers away from foreign airlines.

Public Relations

Public relations consists of efforts aimed at enhancing a firm's reputation and image with the general public, as opposed to touting the specific advantages of an individual product or service. The consequence of effective public relations is a general belief that the firm is a good "corporate citizen," that it is reputable, and that it can be trusted.

Savvy international firms recognize that money spent on public relations is money well spent because it earns them political allies and makes it easier to communicate the firms' needs to the general public. They also recognize that, as "foreigners," they often are appealing political targets; thus, the firms attempt to reduce their exposure to political attacks. Toyota provides a case in point. The company received large financial incentives from the state of Kentucky to build its first wholly owned U.S. auto assembly plant in Georgetown. During the first few years it operated that plant, Toyota received a fair amount of criticism for its lack of community concern—Japanese firms, unlike their U.S. counterparts, do not have a tradition of corporate philanthropy. The firm eventually realized it had to adapt its corporate attitudes to local customs if it wanted to maintain the goodwill of local politicians. Toyota subsequently became a model corporate citizen, providing grants to local charities, funding college scholarships to graduating high school students, and sponsoring local youth sports teams.

The impact of good public relations is hard to quantify, but over time an international firm's positive image and reputation are likely to benefit the firm in a host country. Consumers are more likely to resist "buy local" pitches when the foreign firm also is perceived to be a good guy. Good public relations also can help the firm when it has to negotiate with a host country government for a zoning permit or an operating license or when it encounters a crisis or unfavorable publicity. For example, Toshiba once found itself in deep trouble when one of its subsidiaries was discovered to have been illegally selling to the Soviet Union advanced technology designed to make the detection of nuclear submarines harder. Normally, few citizens would be aware of the importance of such a breach of security. Unfortunately for Toshiba, one of the best-selling novels that year was Tom Clancy's *The Hunt for Red October*, which had educated U.S. readers about the technological nature of submarine warfare. Fortunately for Toshiba, the firm had been a good corporate citizen in the United States. Relying on the goodwill it had previously fostered with local government officials, community leaders, and its workforce, Toshiba was able to avoid trade sanctions that would have jeopardized its standing in the United States.

Distribution Issues and Decisions

The fourth P of the international marketing mix is place—more commonly referred to as distribution. **Distribution** is the process of getting products and services from the firm into the hands of customers. (As we discuss in Chapter 17, distribution is also one component of international logistics management.) An international firm faces two important sets of distribution issues:

1. Physically transporting its goods and services from where they are created to the various markets in which they are to be sold
2. Selecting the means by which to merchandise its goods in the markets it wants to serve

International Distribution

The most obvious issue an international firm's distribution managers must address is the selection of a mode (or modes) of transportation for shipping the firm's goods from their point of origin to their destination. This choice entails a clear trade-off between time and money, as Table 16.2 indicates. Faster modes of transportation, such as air freight and motor carrier, are

TABLE 16.2 Advantages and Disadvantages of Different Modes of Transportation for Exports

Transportation Mode	Advantages	Disadvantages	Sample Products
Train	Safe	Limited to rail routes	Automobiles
	Reliable	Slow	Grains
	Inexpensive		
Airplane	Safe	Expensive	Jewelry
	Reliable	Limited access	Medicine
Truck	Versatile	Small size	Consumer goods
	Inexpensive		
Ship	Inexpensive	Slow	Automobile
	Good for large products	Indirect	Furniture
Electronic media	Fast	Unusable for many products	Information

more expensive than slower modes, such as ocean shipping, railroad, pipeline, and barge. However, the transportation mode selected affects the firm's inventory costs and customer service levels, as well as the product's useful shelf life, exposure to damage, and packaging requirements. International air freight, for example, scores high on each of these dimensions, whereas ocean shipping ranks very low.

Consider the impact of transportation mode on the firm's inventory expenses and the level of customer service. If the firm relies on slower modes of transportation, it can maintain a given level of inventory at the point of sale only by maintaining higher levels of inventory in transit. If the firm selects unreliable modes that make it difficult to predict when shipments will actually arrive, the firm will have to increase buffer stocks in its inventory to avoid stock-outs that will lead to disappointed customers. Slower modes of transportation also increase the firm's **international order cycle time**—the time between the placement of an order and its receipt by the customer—for any given level of inventories. Longer order cycle times lower the firm's customer service levels and may induce its customers to seek alternative supply sources.

The product's shelf life affects the selection of transportation mode. Goods that are highly perishable because of physical or cultural forces—such as cut flowers or fashionable dresses—are typically shipped by air freight because of their short shelf life. Less perishable products, such as coal, crude oil, or men's socks, are shipped using less expensive modes. In some cases the transportation mode may affect the product's packaging requirements. For example, goods sent on long ocean voyages may need special packaging to protect them from humidity and damage due to rough seas; the firm could avoid the extra costs of packaging if it chose a faster mode such as air freight. Of course, a simple solution is sometimes available: When Calpis, a Colorado-based agricultural goods processor, entered the Japanese orange juice market, the firm switched its packaging from glass bottles to cans to reduce breakage.[54]

Channels of Distribution

An international firm's marketing managers also must determine which distribution channels to use to merchandise the firm's products in each national market it serves. Figure 16.4 shows the basic channel options used by most international manufacturing firms. Note that a distribution channel can consist of as many as four basic parts:

1. The manufacturer that creates the product or service
2. A wholesaler that buys products and services from the manufacturer and then resells them to retailers
3. The retailer that buys from wholesalers and then sells to customers
4. The actual customer, who buys the product or service for final consumption

FIGURE 16.4
Distribution Channel Options

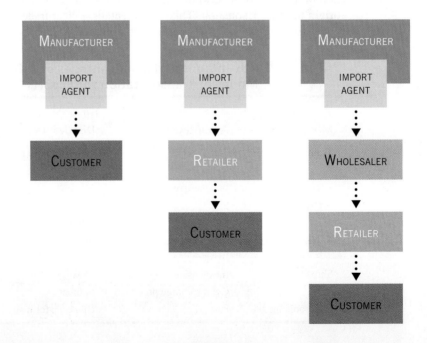

Product shelf life affects the modes of transportation international firms can use to distribute their products. Unilever, for example, can use slower labor-intensive modes of transportation, such as this delivery cart in the West African country of Burkina Faso, to distribute Omo, one of its laundry detergents. But the firm's ice cream products cannot be distributed in the same manner. Refrigerated containers must be used for perishable products like ice cream, milk, and cheese.

Ron Giling/Photolibrary/Peter Arnold, Inc.

Import agents (discussed in Chapter 11) also may be used as intermediaries, especially by smaller firms.

One important factor illustrated by Figure 16.4 is **channel length,** the number of stages in the distribution channel. A firm that sells directly to its customers, which then pay the business directly, bypasses wholesalers and retailers and therefore has a very short distribution channel. This approach is called **direct sales** because the firm is dealing directly with its final consumer. Dell Computer started out as a direct-sales business, taking customer orders over toll-free, 24-hour telephone lines. The advantage of this approach is that the firm maintains control over retail distribution of its products and retains any retailing profits it earns. Unfortunately, the firm also bears the costs and risks of retailing its products.

A slightly longer channel of distribution involves selling to retailers, which then market and sell the products to customers. This is easiest to do when retailers in a given market are heavily concentrated. When there are relatively few large retailers, selling directly to each is easier for manufacturers; when a larger number of smaller retailers are present, selling to each is more complex. For example, huge supermarkets with vast selections of foods and toiletries exist throughout the United States. In Europe, however, many consumers still buy food from small neighborhood stores, and few of these carry toiletries. A consumer products firm therefore will have to use very different approaches to distributing its products in the two markets. For example, in the United States Procter & Gamble (P&G) may sell directly to Kroger or Safeway, which will routinely stock several hundred tubes of toothpaste of various sizes on its shelves and store cartons of inventory in its warehouses. A European retailer, however, may have retail space for only a few tubes and little storage space for backup inventory, thereby making it more difficult for P&G to sell directly to such outlets.

The longest distribution channel involves the use of wholesalers. Wholesalers are separate businesses that buy from manufacturers and then resell to retailers or, in some cases, to other wholesalers. For example, small farmers cannot easily sell their produce to large grocery chains because those chains find it inefficient to deal with large numbers of small suppliers. Instead, farmers sell their produce to wholesalers, which then sell it to grocery stores; thus the grocery stores must deal with only a few large suppliers. Similarly, in markets with little retail concentration, a consumer products firm like P&G generally finds it easier to sell to a few wholesalers rather than attempt to deal with a huge number of small retailers. The use of wholesalers makes it easier to market in countries with little retail concentration and also allows the firm to maintain a smaller sales staff. On the other hand, profit margins tend to be smaller because there are more businesses involved, each of which expects to make a profit. Rather than keeping all the profits for itself, as in the case of direct sales, a firm must share them with wholesalers and retailers.

The challenge for international marketing managers is to find the optimal distribution channel to match the firm's unique competitive strengths and weaknesses with the requirements of each national market it serves. In practice, as with other elements of international marketing, most international firms develop a flexible distribution strategy—they may use a short channel in some markets and a longer channel in others.

The firm's distribution strategy also may be an important component of its promotion strategy. For example, SMH manufactures not only relatively inexpensive Swatch watches but also high-priced watches such as Omega and Tissot. It distributes its expensive watches through exclusive jewelry stores and its Swatch watches through department stores like Macy's and Dillard's.[55] Toyota initially adopted different distribution strategies for its luxury cars in the United States and Japan. In the United States it named the model Lexus and set up an independent dealership network to strengthen the prestige of that brand name. In Japan, where the firm had less need to bolster its image, the same model was sold under the Toyota name through existing Toyota dealerships. And Unilever has developed a unique approach for distributing and promoting its products in rural Tanzania. Its brigade of pedaling peddlers journeys into the countryside each morning on bicycles to hawk small packets of the company's soaps, toothpaste, and laundry powders.[56]

As noted in Chapter 12, some international firms, particularly producers of more specialized products, may hire a sales or import agent to distribute their goods. For example, the National Football League contracted with Japan Marketing Services to promote NFL-licensed goods in Japan. Annual Japanese sales of T-shirts, sweatshirts, and other clothing bearing the names of U.S. football teams exceed $50 million.[57] Many governments, as part of their efforts to stimulate exports, have developed programs to help firms locate suitable international import agents. For instance, the U.S. and Foreign Commercial Service, a branch of the U.S. Department of Commerce, provides lists of foreign firms that have expressed a willingness to distribute given products in their market areas. These data can be obtained by contacting local offices of the U.S. and Foreign Commercial Service or through the National Trade Data Bank.

Firms should exercise caution when selecting a foreign distributor. The distributor is the firm as far as local customers are concerned, so a poor distributor jeopardizes the firm's reputation and performance in that market, often for a very long time. Further, local laws may make it difficult for a firm to terminate the distributor. In Saudi Arabia, for example, a foreign firm must hire a local national to represent it, and firing that agent is virtually impossible without the agent's consent.

Some international firms attempt to transfer to international markets the distribution systems developed in their home countries. McDonald's, for example, gained its status as the leading food service company in the United States by taking great care in selecting its franchisees and by nurturing their enterprises to the mutual benefit of both the franchisees and McDonald's. The firm has followed a similar distribution strategy to capture fast-food dollars in Europe, Asia, Australia, Africa, and Central and South America. Similarly, Coca-Cola utilizes a network of subsidiaries and independent bottlers to market its soft drinks in virtually every country—a distribution strategy identical to that used by the firm in its home market.

At other times a firm may adapt its distribution practices to match local customs. In Russia, for example, many goods are sold at street-side kiosks; Pepsi-Cola and Coca-Cola are sold at hundreds of these stands in Moscow alone.[58] And Kodak, recognizing the desire of many Chinese to run their own businesses, developed a turnkey program that provided local entrepreneurs a fully furnished and equipped photo-processing lab for 99,000 yuan (less than $12,000). For budding owners without cash, Kodak offered financing through an agreement with the Bank of China. Thanks to this initiative, Kodak had 8,000 stores spread throughout China and enjoyed a 63 percent share of the Chinese market. China quickly became the company's second largest market, trailing only the United States.[59] But little in international business is permanent: the benefits of this effort diminished once digital photography displaced film-based photography.

Local laws may affect distribution strategies. For many years the ability of foreigners to establish distribution systems was limited in India, Mexico, and China. As a result, most MNCs established joint ventures with local firms in order to distribute their products in those countries. Similarly, the complexities of Japan's culture and the complicated nature of its distribution networks have prompted many Western firms to seek joint-venture partners to help the firms penetrate the Japanese market. KFC, for example, teamed up with Mitsubishi to create a joint venture to market KFC's products in Japan. Mitsubishi contributed chicken (one of its subsidiaries is a major chicken producer), distribution networks, and an understanding of the cultural nuances of dealing with Japanese consumers. KFC contributed its brand name, an American image that appealed to fashion-conscious Japanese, and its technology and trade secrets—including, of course, the secret spices that make its chicken so finger-lickin' good.

MyManagementLab	Now that you have finished this chapter, go back to **www.pearsonglobaleditions.com/mymanagementlab** to continue practicing and applying the concepts you've learned.

CHAPTER REVIEW

Summary

International marketing is the process of planning and executing the conception, pricing, promotion, and distribution of ideas, goods, and services across national boundaries to create exchanges that satisfy individual and organizational objectives.

International marketing management is a critical organizational operation that should be integrated with other basic functions such as operations and human resource management. International marketing is generally based on one of three business strategies: differentiation, cost leadership, or focus. Determining the firm's marketing mix involves making decisions about product, pricing, promotion, and place (distribution). A related basic issue that marketing managers must address is the extent to which the marketing mix will be standardized or customized for different markets. A variety of factors must be considered in making this decision.

Product policy focuses on the tangible and intangible factors that characterize the product itself. Standardization versus customization is again a consideration. Industrial products and consumer products usually require different types of product policies. Legal, cultural, and economic forces also affect product policy and must be carefully evaluated.

Pricing issues and decisions constitute the second element of the marketing mix. The three basic pricing philosophies are standard pricing, two-tiered pricing, and market pricing. Market pricing, the most widely used and complex policy, involves setting different prices for each market. Basic economic analyses are used to arrive at the prices. Concerns related to gray markets, dumping, and potential consumer resentment must be addressed by firms that use this approach. Otherwise, serious problems may result.

Promotion issues and decisions generally concern the use of advertising and other forms of promotion. The promotion mix is a blend of advertising, personal selling, sales promotion, and public relations. Each of these elements is usually carefully tailored for the market in which it will be used and implemented accordingly.

Finally, international marketing managers also must plan for distribution—getting products and services from the firm to customers. International distribution may involve a variety of transportation modes, each with its own unique set of advantages and disadvantages. A firm must also develop appropriate distribution channels, which may involve wholesalers and retailers in addition to the firm and its customers. Effective distribution can have a significant impact on a firm's profitability.

Review Questions

1. What are the basic factors involved in deciding whether to use standardization or customization?
2. How do legal, cultural, and economic factors influence product policy?
3. Why are brand names an important marketing tool for international business?
4. What are the three basic pricing policies?
5. What are the problems that a firm using market pricing might encounter?
6. What are some of the fundamental issues that must be addressed in international advertising?
7. What is a distribution channel? What options does an international firm have in developing its channels?

Questions for Discussion

1. What are the similarities and differences between domestic and international marketing?
2. Identify several products you think could be marketed in a variety of foreign markets with little customization. Identify other products that clearly would require customization.
3. How do legal, cultural, and economic factors in your home country affect product policy for foreign firms?
4. What are the pros and cons of trying to use a single brand name in different markets, as opposed to creating unique brand names for various markets?

5. What are the advantages and disadvantages of each pricing policy? Why do most international firms use market pricing?
6. The ethnocentric approach and the geocentric approach both suggest standardization of the marketing mix. What is the difference between these two approaches, if both lead to standardization?

7. What are some basic differences you might expect to see in TV ads broadcast in France, Japan, Saudi Arabia, and the United States?

Building Global Skills

Ajax Alarms is a medium-sized U.S. firm that sells alarm clocks. It subcontracts the production of its clocks to a Korean firm, which manufactures them based on Ajax designs and specifications and then ships the clocks directly to the Ajax warehouse in Kansas. Ajax markets and distributes the clocks throughout the United States and Canada. The clocks themselves are brightly colored novelty items. For example, one of the firm's biggest sellers is a plastic rooster that crows in the morning. Last year Ajax reported profits of $5 million on total revenues of slightly more than $50 million.

Ajax managers have determined that the firm has few growth opportunities in the United States and Canada and so must enter new markets if it is to continue to expand. The managers have decided to start by selling in Mexico. They have hired you, an internationally famous marketing consultant, to advise them.

Your assignment is to outline a marketing plan for Ajax. Ajax wants you to consider product policy, pricing, promotion, and distribution issues. In developing your marketing plan, be sure to consider the factors discussed in this chapter, including standardization versus customization, legal forces, cultural influences, economic factors, and brand name questions. Note specific areas where you can make recommendations to your client. For example, if you believe a certain advertising medium will be beneficial to Ajax, make that recommendation (be sure to provide some rationale or justification). If you feel you lack sufficient information to make a recommendation in some area, identify the factors that must be addressed by Ajax in that particular area. For example, if you cannot recommend a pricing policy, describe the information Ajax needs to acquire and evaluate when making that decision.

CLOSING CASE | **A CALL FOR PROGRESS**

As Chapter 1 noted, one of the drivers of globalization is technological change in communications, which has made it easier for entrepreneurs and organizations to identify promising opportunities in foreign markets. Conversely, inadequate communication facilities can be an important factor limiting economic progress in developing countries. In many of these countries, provision of telephone service was often left in the hands of undercapitalized, inefficient state-run monopolies, staffed by inadequately trained and poorly motivated bureaucrats. The advent of the cell phone, however, has allowed many countries plagued by poor land-line service to bypass these problems. Some studies indicate that increasing the cell phone penetration rate (the percentage of the population with cell phone service) by 10 percentage points boosts per capita GDP by 0.59 percent.

Increased access to communication services promotes economic growth in many ways, some obvious, some subtle. Improved communications make it easier for entrepreneurs to learn about new market opportunities; but they also make markets more efficient, lowering prices and reducing the waste of resources. For example, one small Indian farmer decided to rent his tractor to other local farmers when he didn't need it for his own crops. Before he owned a cell phone, he often had to leave his own farm for an entire day to handle a routine tractor rental,

a matter that now takes but a few minutes on the cell phone. Cell phones have also aided small fishermen in Kerala, a state in the south of India. After catching a good haul of sardines, they typically headed for their home port without knowing what price their catch would bring at the dock. If other local fisherman had good luck as well, they might find the price for their catch depressed, even though the price might be higher at the next port up the coast. Sometimes they were forced to dump their catch if the local market were oversupplied and there were simply no buyers. Now, though, they can call all the buyers within the region and head for the port that offers the best price. The simple introduction of cell phones made the market more efficient and eliminated the wasteful dumping of fish: Fishermen's profits rose by 8 percent while average prices paid by consumers fell 4 percent.

Cell phone manufacturers and equipment suppliers are eagerly pursuing opportunities in emerging markets. The industry's goal is to sell more than a billion units annually. But in most developed countries, cell phone penetration is high. Some Western European countries have more cell phone accounts than people, suggesting very limited growth prospects there. In the United States, 80 percent of Americans have a cell phone account, and only 1.2 million new accounts are created each month. China, meanwhile, has the most cell users of any country in the world at 900 million (as of mid-2011). India, though, claims the title of the fastest-growing market with 791 million users, but 35 percent of the country's population still does not have a cell phone (as of mid-2011).

Of course, emerging markets offer the cell phone industry new challenges. Because of their lower per capita incomes, consumers in these markets are more price sensitive than their European or Japanese counterparts. Millicom International Cellular found it needed to adapt its marketing and pricing strategies accordingly. Its typical customer in Africa and Latin American spends less than $10 a month on his or her phone service, and often lacks a credit history. Millicom's initial approach was to rely on prepaid calling cards rather than monthly subscriptions, which eliminated the need to check its customers' credit histories, as no credit was being extended. But Millicom found that prepaid calling cards were relatively expensive to service. The company then developed e-PIN, which eliminates the need to rely on the prepaid calling cards. Customers of the Millicom can go to a company-authorized outlet—such as a local bodega or other shop—and buy extra minutes—often as little as 30 cents worth—from the vendor. The shopkeeper collects the funds and sends a text-message to Millicom, along with the phone number of the customer, requesting that more minutes be added to the customer's account. Alternatively, a friend or relative can text Millicom, asking that some of their prepaid minutes be transferred to the friend's phone. To make its service even more affordable, Millicom's calling rates are calculated per second, rather than per minute.

The need to cut costs and the unique operating environments in emerging markets has stimulated much innovation in the industry. A significant part of the costs of providing cell service are the costs of the cell towers themselves. In India, towers need air-conditioning and backup power generators because of the country's frequent power outages. One leading Indian cell company, Bharti, encouraged its suppliers to make their equipment smaller, in order to reduce its cost and power consumption. Bharti was able to slash the cost of each of its towers by 40 percent to $75,000 per tower. Another Indian cell company contracted with Chinese factories to manufacture easily assembled towers, thereby reducing installation costs. Nokia Siemens Networks has developed a small, cheap antenna that can be placed on the highest building in a village, obviating the need for a costly cell tower. Ericsson has teamed up with an Indian cell provider to develop a generator powered by used cooking oil, having previously abandoned an experiment using methane produced by cow dung.

There are other surprises facing cell service providers in emerging markets. Phone manufacturers had originally assumed that plain vanilla, inexpensive phones would be the most popular, given the level of per capita income in these countries. Among young urban consumers in China, however, a cell phone is a status symbol: Many eagerly upgrade their phones to make sure they contain the latest features. Nokia estimates that 60 percent of its sales in emerging markets in 2007 were replacement sales; two years earlier, replacement sales constituted only 43 percent of emerging market sales. As the iPhone and other so-called "smart phones" have cut into Nokia's market share, though, the same facts seemed to hold true—users want a phone with multiple functions. India's Bharti Airtel Ltd. believes a typical urban cell phone user replaces his or her phone every 8 to 12 months. GrameenPhone of Bangladesh reports a similar phenomenon. Even in that poor country, young consumers in Dacca and other cities want stylish, well-designed phones with the latest bells and whistles.

Case Questions

1. Identify and describe the roles of product policy, pricing, promotion, and distribution in the cell phone market in developed countries.
2. Identify and describe the roles of product policy, pricing, promotion, and distribution in emerging markets.
3. What are the relative opportunities for standardization and customization in the cell phone industry?
4. What are the roles of legal forces and cultural influences in the cell phone industry?

Sources: "Nokia rivals prepare to pounce on market share," *Financial Times*, February 17, 2011, p. 14; engadget.com, June 9, 2011; "In India, rural poor are key to cellular firm's expansion," *Wall Street Journal*, September 24, 2007, p. A1; "Upgrading a call on emerging markets," *Wall Street Journal*, September 6, 2007, p. B3; "Connecting with developing world," *Wall Street Journal*, August 28, 2007, p. A8; "To do with the price of fish," *The Economist*, May 10, 2007 (online).

Endnotes

1. http://www.dailymail.co.uk/travel/article-1288557/ AirAsias-low-cost-Tune-Hotels-mark-London-opening-1p-rooms.html#ixzz1dJpw4hNd; http://www.scribd.com/ doc/4089502/Tune-Hotel by Mohd Rizal Kismath Bacha (2007); http://www.strategyfromtheoutsidein.com/blog/ page/3/; http://www.cwtindustrywatch.com/industry_ watch/en/global/article/2011-04/article3.html.

2. From "AMA board approves new marketing definition," *Marketing News*, March 31, 1985, p. 1.
3. "France retreats from 'knocking' adverts," *Financial Times*, August 14, 1995, p. 3.
4. "New Zealand bans Reebok, other ads it deems politically incorrect for TV," *Wall Street Journal*, July 25, 1995, p. A12.

5. David Lei, "Strategies for global competition," *Long Range Planning*, vol. 22, no. 1 (1989), pp. 102–109. See also Yoram Wind and Susan Douglas, "International portfolio analysis and strategy: The challenge of the 1980s," *Journal of International Business Studies* (Fall 1981), pp. 69–82.

6. Nicholas Papadopoulos and Louise A. Heslop (Eds.), *Product-Country Images—Impact and Role in International Marketing* (New York: International Business Press, 1993).

7. For an overview see David McCutcheon, Amitabh Raturi, and Jack Meredith, "The customization-responsiveness squeeze," *Sloan Management Review* (Winter 1994), pp. 89–100.

8. "U.S. catalog firms go after Europeans," *Wall Street Journal*, January 6, 1998, p. A15.

9. Kenichi Ohmae, "The triad world view," *Journal of Business Strategy*, vol. 7, no. 4 (Spring 1987), pp. 8–19.

10. Theodore Levitt, "The globalization of markets," *Harvard Business Review* (May–June 1983), pp. 92–102.

11. Aysegul Ozsomer, Muzzafer Bodur, and S. Tamer Cavusgil, "Marketing standardisation by multinationals in an emerging market," *European Journal of Marketing*, vol. 25, no. 12 (1991), pp. 50–63.

12. John A. Quelch and Edward J. Hoff, "Customizing global marketing," *Harvard Business Review* (May–June 1986), pp. 59–68.

13. "The right way to go global: An interview with Whirlpool CEO David Whitwam," *Harvard Business Review* (March–April 1994), pp. 134–145; "A little washing machine that won't shred a sari," *Business Week*, June 3, 1991, p. 100; "Creativity overflowing," *Business Week*, May 8, 2006, pp. 50–53.

14. Quelch and Hoff, op. cit.

15. Judie Lannon, "Developing brand strategies across borders," *Marketing and Research Today* (August 1991), pp. 160–167.

16. Guy de Jonquires, "Just one Cornetto," *Financial Times*, October 28, 1991.

17. "U.S. superstores find Japanese are a hard sell," *Wall Street Journal*, February 14, 2000, p. B1.

18. "Big Boy's adventures in Thailand," *Wall Street Journal*, April 12, 2000, p. B1.

19. "Mexico's Corona brew wins back cachet lost during the late '80s," *Wall Street Journal*, January 19, 1993, p. B6.

20. "U.S. firms are letting Saudi market slip," *Wall Street Journal*, January 20, 1994, p. A10.

21. "Eastern Europe poses obstacles for ads," *Wall Street Journal*, July 30, 1992, p. B6.

22. "It's goo, goo, goo, goo vibrations at the Gerber lab," *Wall Street Journal*, December 4, 1996, p. A1.

23. "Pepsi mounts effort to make potato chips international snack," *Wall Street Journal*, November 30, 1995, p. B10.

24. "Adapting a U.S. car to Japanese tastes," *Wall Street Journal*, June 26, 1995, p. B1.

25. "Don't Wrap the Veggies," *Forbes*, April 28, 2005, pp. 94–97.

26. "Asia proves unexpectedly tough terrain for HBO, Cinemax channels," *Wall Street Journal*, August 23, 2000, p. B1.

27. "Stylish sportswear with designs on China," *Wall Street Journal*, March 29, 2008, p. B1.

28. "U.S. companies in China find patience, persistence and salesmanship pay off," *Wall Street Journal*, April 3, 1992, p. B1.

29. "In pursuit of the elusive Euroconsumer," *Wall Street Journal*, April 23, 1992, p. B1.

30. "Mexico's Corona brew wins back cachet," op. cit.

31. "Cartoon characters get a big makeover for overseas fans," *Wall Street Journal*, October 16, 2007, p. A1.

32. Clive Sims, Adam Phillips, and Trevor Richards, "Developing a global pricing strategy," *Marketing and Research Today* (March 1992), pp. 3–14.

33. William Pride and O. C. Ferrell, *Marketing* (Boston: Houghton Mifflin, 2006).

34. "Coca-Cola faces a price war," *Wall Street Journal*, July 7, 1994, p. A1; "Cola price war breaks out in Japan," *Financial Times*, July 14, 1994, p. 1.

35. "Merck cuts price of AIDS drug," *Financial Times*, March 20, 1997, p. 8.

36. "Copyrights can't stop gray markets," *Houston Chronicle*, March 10, 1998, p. 1C.

37. "Luxury prices for U.S. goods no longer pass muster in Japan," *Wall Street Journal*, February 8, 1996, p. B1.

38. "World marketing: Going global or acting local? Five expert viewpoints," *Journal of Consumer Marketing* (Spring 1986), pp. 5–26.

39. Martin S. Roth and Jean B. Romeo, "Matching product category and country image perceptions: A framework for managing country-of-origin effects," *Journal of International Business Studies*, vol. 23, no. 3 (Third Quarter 1992), pp. 477–498; John R. Darling and Van R. Wood, "A longitudinal study comparing perceptions of U.S. and Japanese consumer products in a third/neutral country: Finland 1975 to 1985," *Journal of International Business Studies*, vol. 21, no. 3 (Third Quarter 1990), pp. 427–450.

40. "In rural India, video vans sell toothpaste and shampoo," *Wall Street Journal*, January 10, 1996, p. B1.

41. "U.S. cigarette firms are battling Taiwan's bid to stiffen ad curbs like other Asian nations," *Wall Street Journal*, May 5, 1992, p. C25.

42. General Accounting Office, *Advertising and Promoting U.S. Cigarettes in Selected Asian Countries,* Report GAO/GGD-93-38 (December 1992), p. 38ff.

43. Barbara Mueller, "Multinational advertising: Factors influencing the standardised vs. specialised approach," *International Marketing Review*, vol. 8, no. 1 (1991), pp. 7–18.

44. "Coke global image ads," *Wall Street Journal*, April 29, 1997, p. B15.

45. "Global ad campaigns, after many missteps, finally pay dividends," *Wall Street Journal*, August 27, 1992, p. A1.

46. "IBM strives for a single image in its European ad campaign," *Wall Street Journal*, April 16, 1991, p. B12.

47. "A universal message," *Financial Times*, May 27, 1993.

48. Barbara Mueller, "An analysis of information content in standardized vs. specialized multinational advertisements," *Journal of International Business Studies*, vol. 22, no. 1 (First Quarter 1991), pp. 23–40.

49. For a review of the issues involved, see Sudhir H. Kale and John W. Barnes, "Understanding the domain of cross-national buyer-seller interactions," *Journal of International Business Studies*, vol. 23, no. 1 (First Quarter 1992), pp. 101–132.

50. "Colgate-Palmolive is really cleaning up in Poland," *Business Week*, March 15, 1993, pp. 54–56.
51. "AIG reshapes China's insurance industry," *Wall Street Journal*, February 9, 1996, p. A8.
52. "Amway grows abroad, sending 'ambassadors' to spread the word," *Wall Street Journal*, May 14, 1997, p. A1.
53. General Accounting Office, *Advertising and Promoting U.S. Cigarettes in Selected Asian Countries,* op. cit., pp. 37ff.
54. Ashley Blaker, "For global assistance, Dyal a marketer," *San Antonio Business Journal*, August 7, 1989, p. 8.
55. "SMH leads a revival of Swiss watchmaking industry," *Wall Street Journal*, January 20, 1992, p. B4.
56. "Bicycle brigade takes Unilever to the people," *Financial Times*, August 17, 2000, p. 8.
57. Jean Downey, "Touchdown!" *Business Tokyo*, March 1992, p. 34.
58. "Coca-Cola to open plant in Moscow," *Wall Street Journal*, January 17, 1992, p. A3.
59. "Cracking the Chinese market," *Wall Street Journal*, January 9, 2003, p. B1.

International Operations Management

AFTER STUDYING THIS CHAPTER, YOU SHOULD BE ABLE TO:

1. Describe the nature of international operations management.

2. Analyze the supply chain management and vertical integration decisions facing international production managers.

3. Analyze the meaning of productivity and discuss how international firms work to improve it.

4. Explain how firms control quality and discuss total quality management in international business.

5. Analyze how international firms control the information their managers need to make effective decisions.

Access a host of interactive learning aids at **www.pearsonglobaleditions.com/ mymanagementlab** to help strengthen your understanding of the chapter concepts.

MyManagementLab

© Peter Erik Forsberg/Prague/Alamy

RACING TO MARKET

Like two heavyweight fighters, Benetton Group SpA, the trendy Italian clothing chain, and Inditex, the Spanish parent of hot retailer Zara, have been constantly maneuvering for the last several years to see who can gain the upper hand in the mass-market trendy clothing industry. Benetton had a head-start, growing from a two-person operation in 1955 to a multinational clothing empire. The first Benetton retail store opened in a fashionable ski resort in the Italian Alps in 1968. Other stores quickly followed in the leading fashion capitals of Europe. It now has hundreds of stores throughout the former communist bloc, as well as stores in such far-flung locations as Turkey, Japan, and Egypt. Benetton has been opening stores in China at a steady pace, and also has plans for expansion in the Middle East (especially Dubai). In total, Benetton distributes its goods through 5,000 outlets in some 120 countries. Almost all Benetton outlets are independently owned; Benetton licenses its name to these shop owners, who in turn must carry only Benetton goods. Italian styling and reasonable prices are two of the critical ingredients in Benetton's success.

The first Zara store, meanwhile, was opened in 1975 in La Coruna, a port town near Artexio in northern Spain. Its first international store was opened in Portugal in 1989, followed soon thereafter by one in New York. There are now over 3,700 Zara stores in 68 countries; the firm plans to continue an aggressive expansion campaign to open several hundred new stores per year. In addition to Zara, Inditex also owns and operates Massimo Dutti (more upscale stores located in high-fashion centers) and Bershka (more youth-oriented stores, often located in shopping malls). Unlike Benetton, though, Inditex does not franchise—it owns all of its stores.

The real battlefield between the two firms, though, has been behind-the-scenes. Both Benetton and Inditex have world-class operations management systems that have allowed them to stay a step ahead of the rest of the pack. Benetton centralizes design and production in Italy so the firm can maintain tight control over manufacturing costs, quality, and related considerations. Each retail transaction in a Benetton store is electronically coded and transmitted to a central information-processing center in Italy. Managers there can track sales levels, sales trends and patterns, and inventory distributions, and they can do so for individual stores, for clusters of stores in an area, by country, or on a global basis. Managers use this sales information to plan and adjust production activity. Whenever a new garment is designed, its creators try to plan for possible variations and alterations. For example, a new shirt will be designed so it can be produced with short, midlength, or full-length sleeves and with or without a collar. Early production runs and shipments will include all six possible styles. A portion of those runs also will be devoted to making shirt bodies without sleeves or collars. As sales figures begin to arrive, managers very quickly can tailor production adjustments to these inventoried shirt bodies to finish them out according to customer demand. If shirts with midlength sleeves and a collar sell much faster than other variations, more of this type of shirt can be finished quickly and shipped to stores. The same approach also is used for colors.

Bar codes and scanners are used throughout Benetton factories and warehouses. Using fully networked computer workstations, managers can plan and initiate production runs based on style and color demand. Partially completed products are pulled from shelves by robots and placed on final production lines. As those products are finished out, bar codes are attached, and the products are automatically wrapped, packaged, and shipped to those stores that need inventory replenishment. Through the use of this sophisticated system Benetton can fill an order from any of its 5,000 stores spread throughout the globe in 13 to 27 days.

Zara, meanwhile, has taken some of these same techniques to a whole new level. Inditex makes its garments in Spain and surrounding countries such as Portugal, Turkey, and Morocco. But it actually stocks its stores with new designs twice a week. New collections are often small, and the more successful ones sell out quickly. But this allows the firm to both maintain an air of exclusivity and avoid marking unsold merchandise down to lower prices. Like Benetton, though, Zara can quickly restock virtually any of its items quickly and efficiently. Zara is also constantly looking for new ways to get products into the hands of consumers at an ever faster pace. For instance, most retailers have store employees attach inventory control tags to new products after the items arrive in the stockroom. They also routinely replace the inexpensive hangers used to ship products with more substantial ones before taking the garments out to the sales floor. But Zara ships its products with the tags already affixed—saving several hours at the store level. Moreover, employees hang the garments on their original shipping hangers and only later replace them with standard display hangers. This practice has even had some unexpected bonus effects—savvy young shoppers know that garments still on their shipping hangers have just arrived and are thus the very latest styles!

By mid-2011 industry experts were declaring Zara the winner. The real issues turned out to require even more finesse than managers at Benetton imagined. For instance, even though Benetton was a pioneer in mass customization, it still only changes its basic product lines once per season. But Zara can actually alter its entire line within a few weeks. This has allowed Zara to slowly but surely creep ahead of its rival in terms of fashion cachet. The other end of the supply chain has also had an impact as well. For instance, because most of its stores are franchised, Benetton has less control over how retailers display and promote products. Meanwhile, though, Zara's company-owned store layouts can be tweaked and merchandise rearranged on the basis of a quick e-mail from company headquarters.

But Zara cannot afford to rest on its newfound laurels. American retailers like Abercrombie & Fitch and Gap have made inroads in many European cities currently controlled by Benetton and Zara. H&M, a Swedish fashion retailer, is also coming on strong. And Urban Outfitters is also moving cautiously into this arena as well. Indeed, Urban Outfitters might eventually pose the greatest challenge to Zara. While Zara and its competitors offer essentially the same product lines at each of their stores (just varying the mix), Urban Outfitters has invested in creating a separate design center in Europe; the firm has also indicated that as it finalizes plans for a big push into Asia it will establish yet another design center there as well. And the firm has also invested heavily in its own supply chain and has reached the point where it has the lowest manufacturing, warehousing and shipping costs of all of the major chains, and has reduced the time it takes to get new stock to a store to an astonishing 24 hours![1] ▪

First Benetton and more recently Zara and Urban Outfitters have flourished for various reasons. Among them are their ability to track demand for various products and then to take the appropriate steps to satisfy that demand promptly and efficiently. By centralizing design and manufacturing systems in their home countries of Italy and Spain, Benetton and Zara are able to maintain tight control over those and related functions. By building flexibility into design, production, and distribution, the firms are able to get new inventory to their stores around the world much faster than most of their competitors. But upstarts like H&M and Urban Outfitters are closing the gap, not necessarily on the basis of style but instead by getting new products to market quickly and efficiently. The basis for planning and implementing these activities is operations management.

Some firms, such as Shell, Exxon Mobil, and BP, are concerned with physically transforming natural resources into various products through complex refining processes. Others, such as Dell, Sony, and Philips, purchase completed component parts from suppliers and then assemble the parts into electronics products. Still others, such as Emirates, United, British Airways, and JAL, use a global travel network to provide transportation services to people. Regardless of a firm's product, however, the goal of its international operations managers is to design, create, and distribute goods or services that meet the needs and wants of customers worldwide—and to do so profitably.

The Nature of International Operations Management

Operations management is the set of activities an organization uses to transform different kinds of inputs (materials, labor, and so on) into final goods and services.[2] **International operations management** refers to the transformation-related activities of an international firm. Figure 17.1 illustrates the international operations management process. As shown, a firm's strategic context provides a necessary backdrop against which it develops and then manages its operations functions. Flowing directly from the strategic context is the question of standardized versus customized production. The positioning of a firm along this continuum in turn helps dictate the appropriate strategies and tactics for other parts of the operations management process. The next part of international operations management is the activities and processes connected with the acquisition of the resources the firm needs to produce the goods or services it intends to sell. Location decisions—where to build factories and other facilities—are also important. In addition, international operations managers are concerned with logistics and materials management—the efficient movement of materials into, within, and out of the firm. We use this framework to organize this chapter's discussion of international operations management.

Operations management is also closely linked with quality, productivity, and information technology. A firm's operations management system largely determines how inputs are transformed into goods or services. Properly designed and managed operating systems and procedures

FIGURE 17.1

The International Operations Management Process

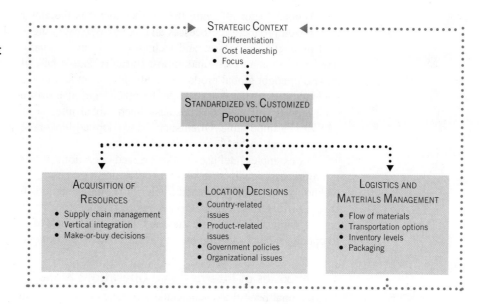

play a major role in determining product quality and productivity. For example, Zara is able to squeeze extra measures of productivity from its distribution centers because of its highly efficient and flexible design. Conversely, poorly designed operating systems are a major cause of poor quality and lower productivity. They promote inefficiency and can contribute in various ways to higher costs and suboptimal profit performance. Hence, we also describe productivity, quality, and information in this chapter as well.

The Strategic Context of International Operations Management

The central role of operations management is to create the potential for achieving superior value for the firm. That is, operations management is a value-adding activity intended to create or add new value to the organization's inputs in ways that directly impact outputs. If operations can take $2 worth of inputs to create $10 worth of goods or services, it has created considerable value. However, if it requires $9 worth of inputs to create the same $10 worth of goods or services, it has created much less value.

Figure 17.1 indicates that international operations management must be aligned closely with a firm's business strategy. Indeed, the business strategy set by top managers at the firm's corporate and regional levels will affect all facets of the planning and implementing of operations management activities, such as supply chain management strategies, location decisions, facilities design, and logistics management.[3] For a company pursuing a differentiation strategy, the operations management function must be able to create goods or services that are clearly different from those of the company's competitors. For a firm like Porsche or Rolex that wants to compete on the basis of product performance and status, costs will be less important than product quality and design. As a result, production facilities may need to be located where there is a skilled labor force, even if the cost of employing that labor is relatively high.[4] For example, Porsche has never considered shifting its production from Stuttgart to a lower-labor-cost locale because its highly skilled and committed workforce is vital to producing its high-quality cars.

Conversely, for a firm following a cost leadership strategy, the operations management function must be able to reduce the costs of creating goods or services to the absolute minimum so the firm can lower its prices while still earning an acceptable level of profits. In this case cost and price issues are central, whereas quality may be less critical. As a result, locating production facilities where labor costs are especially low may be highly appropriate. Hong Kong's Roly International Holdings, for example, annually sells over $300 million worth of low-priced home decorations, such as Christmas tree lights and plaster birdbaths, made in its factories in China. Its goods are shipped via slow but low-cost cargo ships to be distributed by retailers such as Walmart and Walgreens.

Another factor affecting the firm's choices is the extent to which it uses standardized or customized production processes and technologies. On the one hand, if the firm uses standardized production processes and technologies in every market where it does business, then its operations systems can—and almost certainly should be—globally integrated. Such firms may choose to adopt global product designs, for example, to capture more easily global efficiencies generated by their operations. On the other hand, if a firm uses a unique operations system in each market where it does business, such global integration is not only unnecessary but also likely to be impossible. Often such firms adopt a global area design to promote responsiveness of their operations managers to local conditions.

For example, Intel uses a standardized operations management strategy in that it makes its microprocessors using the same manufacturing processes around the world. Thus, it can share technology between plants and freely ship component parts between factories in different countries. Conversely, Nestlé tailors its mix of products, as well as their ingredients and packaging, across markets. So although there may be some sharing of production technology, Nestlé tends to operate each production facility as more of a self-contained unit.

Complexities of International Operations Management

International operations management presents one of the most complex and challenging set of tasks managers face today. The basic complexities inherent in operations management stem from the production problem itself—where and how to produce various goods and services. Operations managers typically must decide important and complex issues in three areas:

1. *Resources:* Managers must decide where and how to obtain the resources the firm needs to produce its products. Key decisions relate to supply chain management and vertical integration.
2. *Location:* Managers must decide where to build administrative facilities, sales offices, and plants; how to design them; and so on.
3. *Logistics:* Managers must decide on modes of transportation and methods of inventory control.

All firms, whether domestic or international, must address these issues. However, resolving them is far more complicated for international firms. A domestic manufacturer may deal with only local suppliers, be subject to one set of government regulations, compete in a relatively homogeneous market, have access to an integrated transportation network, and ship its goods relatively short distances. An international manufacturer, in contrast, is likely to deal with suppliers from different countries and confront different government regulations wherever it does business, as well as very heterogeneous markets, disparate transportation facilities and networks, and relatively long shipping distances. International operations managers must choose the countries in which to locate production facilities, taking into account factors such as costs, tax laws, resource availability, and marketing considerations. They also must consider potential exchange rate movements and noneconomic factors such as government regulations, political risk, and predictability of a country's legal system. Further, they must consider the impact of facilities' locations on the firm's ability to respond to changes in customer tastes and preferences. Finally, they must factor in logistical problems. Just as long supply lines doomed Napoleon's invasion of Russia, locating factories far from one's suppliers may impede timely access to resources and materials.

Production Management

Although some similarities exist between creating goods and creating services for international markets, there also are major fundamental differences. Operations management decisions, processes, and issues that involve the creation of tangible goods are called **production management,** and those involving the creation of intangible services are called **service operations management.** This section focuses on production management; service operations management is addressed later in the chapter.

Manufacturing is the creation of goods by transforming raw materials and component parts in combination with capital, labor, and technology. Some examples of manufacturing activities are Sony's production of digital cameras, BMW's production of automobiles, and Michelin's production of tires. BMW, for example, takes thousands of component parts, ranging from sheet metal to engine parts to upholstery to rubber molding, and combines them to make different types of automobiles.

Most successful manufacturers use many sophisticated techniques to produce high-quality goods efficiently. These techniques are best covered in more advanced and specialized production management courses, so we focus here on three important dimensions of international production management: international supply chain management, international facilities location, and international logistics.

Supply Chain Management and Vertical Integration

Because the production of most manufactured goods requires a variety of raw materials, parts, and other resources, the first issue an international production manager faces is deciding how to acquire those inputs.[5] **Supply chain management** is the set of processes and steps a firm uses to acquire the various resources it needs to create its products (other common terms for this activity include *sourcing* and *procuring*). Supply chain management clearly affects product cost, product quality, and internal demands for capital. Because of these impacts, most international firms approach supply chain management as a strategic issue to be carefully planned and implemented by top management.[6]

The first step in developing a supply chain management strategy is to determine the appropriate degree of vertical integration. **Vertical integration** is the extent to which a firm either provides its own resources or obtains them from other sources. At one extreme, firms that practice relatively high levels of vertical integration are engaged in every step of the operations management process as goods are developed, transformed, packaged, and sold to customers. Various units within the firm can be seen as suppliers to other units within the firm, which can be viewed as the customers of the supplying units. At the other extreme, firms that have little vertical integration are involved in only one step or just a few steps in the production chain. They may buy their inputs and component parts from other suppliers, perform one operation or transformation, and then sell their outputs to other firms or consumers.[7]

BP is a vertically integrated international business. One unit of the firm is engaged in the worldwide exploration for natural gas and crude oil. After oil is discovered, another unit is

As a vertically integrated refiner of natural gas and crude oil, BP owns and manages exploration units, refineries, pipelines, trucks, and retail outlets. This level of integration across what are really disparate businesses adds substantial complexity to the company's operations and considerable challenges to the jobs of its operations managers. At the same time, though, it reduces BP's dependence on other companies and increases the possibilities for highly efficient operations.

© Roger Bamber/Alamy

responsible for its extraction. The oil then is transported through company-owned pipelines and on company-owned tanker ships to company-owned refineries. Those refineries transform the crude oil into gasoline, processed petroleum, and other petroleum-based fuels. Next, the fuel is transported by company-owned trucks to company-owned service stations and convenience stores, where it is sold to individual consumers. Thus, BP's exploration and extraction business supplies its pipeline business, which supplies its refinery business, which supplies its retailing business. Although the firm occasionally uses third-party suppliers and may sometimes sell its products to other firms or franchise retailers to distribute its products, it primarily seeks to maintain an unbroken and efficient chain of vertically integrated operations from the beginning of the production process to the final sale of the product to individual consumers.[8]

In contrast, Heineken NV, the world's third largest brewer, practices relatively little vertical integration. The firm buys the grains and other ingredients it needs to brew beer from local farmers and agricultural cooperatives. From various container suppliers it buys the bottles, labels, and cartons it uses to package its beers. After brewing and bottling its beers, Heineken sells them to distributors, which subsequently resell them to retailers, which in turn resell them to consumers.

The extent of a firm's vertical integration is the result of a series of supply chain management decisions made by production managers. In deciding how to acquire the components necessary to manufacture a firm's products, its production managers have two choices: The firm can make the inputs itself, or it can buy them from outside suppliers. This choice is called the **make-or-buy decision.** It is also important to note, though, that the make-or-buy decision carries with it other decisions as well. For example, a decision to buy rather than make dictates the need to choose between long-term and short-term supplier relationships. Similarly, a decision to make rather than buy leaves open the option of making by self or making in partnership with others. If partnership is the choice, yet another decision relates to the degree of control the firm wants to have.

The make-or-buy decision can be influenced by a firm's size, scope of operations, and technological expertise and by the nature of its product. For example, because larger firms are better able to benefit from economies of scale in the production of inputs, larger automakers such as GM and Fiat are more likely to make their parts themselves, whereas smaller automakers such as Saab or BMW are more likely to buy parts from outside suppliers. Components embodying relatively new technologies, such as satellite navigation systems and hands-free cellular telephones, are more likely to be purchased from outside suppliers, whereas more standardized components, such as conventional braking systems and AM/FM automotive radios, are more likely to be produced in-house. At other times the make-or-buy decision will depend on existing investments in technology and manufacturing facilities. For example, personal computer manufacturers such as Dell and Sony must decide whether they want to make or buy microprocessors, memory chips, disk drives, motherboards, and power supplies. Because of its extensive manufacturing expertise, Sony is more likely to make a component in-house, whereas Dell is more likely to rely heavily on outside suppliers.

All else being equal, a firm will choose to make or buy simply on the basis of whether it can obtain the resource cheaper by making it internally or by buying it from an external supplier. "All else being equal" seldom occurs, however, so strategic issues also must be considered. For example, the firm must balance competitive advantage against strategic vulnerability when resolving the make-or-buy decision. If a high potential for competitive advantage exists along with a high degree of strategic vulnerability, the firm is likely to maintain strategic control by producing internally. However, if the potential for competitive advantage and the degree of strategic vulnerability are both low, the firm will need less control and therefore will be more likely to buy "off the shelf." Finally, when intermediate potential for competitive advantage and moderate degree of strategic vulnerability call for moderate control, special ventures or contract arrangements may be most appropriate.

In addition to these strategic considerations, other factors may play a role with respect to the make-or-buy decision. In particular, international firms typically must make trade-offs between costs and control, risk, investment, and flexibility.[9]

CONTROL Making a component has the advantage of increasing the firm's control over product quality, delivery schedules, design changes, and costs. A firm that buys from external suppliers may become overly dependent on those suppliers. If a given supplier goes out of business, raises its prices, or produces poor-quality materials, the firm will lose its source of inputs, see its costs increase, or experience its own quality-related problems.

Another issue of control relates to the ability to enforce contracts with outside suppliers. Enforcing contracts with foreign suppliers may be difficult or costly because of differences in national legal systems. For example, if laws protecting intellectual property of foreigners are weak in a certain country, entertainment firms such as Sony Records and BMG may be unwilling to license firms in that country to duplicate their CDs and DVDs. When such considerations are important, a firm may prefer to make rather than buy necessary inputs. One strength of the Japanese keiretsu system, for instance, is its ability to reduce the problem of enforcing contracts between a firm and its suppliers. Cross-ownership of shares among keiretsu members, which strengthens trust among members, increases their willingness to enter into long-term contracts and to share intellectual property with each other.[10]

RISK Buying a component from an external supplier has the advantage of reducing the firm's financial and operating risks. BP, for example, has risk associated with its drilling platforms, pipelines, and every other stage in its production chain. If the firm simply bought crude oil from other firms, it would not have to worry about equipment failure or injuries on drilling platforms because those risks would be assumed by the supplier. The firm also would not have to worry about earning an adequate rate of return on those assets. Equally important, the firm that buys rather than makes can reduce its political risk in a host country. For example, BP runs the risk that politicians elected on anti-British or antiforeigner platforms in the United States, Nigeria, Colombia, or elsewhere may someday expropriate its refineries. Indeed, this did happen in 1951, when Iran's rulers seized a major BP operation in that country. "Bringing the World Into Focus" illustrates another form of supply chain risk—natural disasters.

INVESTMENTS IN FACILITIES, TECHNOLOGY, AND PEOPLE Buying from others lowers the firm's level of investment. By not having to build a new factory or learn a new technology, a firm can free up capital for other productive uses. Benetton, for example, primarily uses licensees to retail its goods, allowing the firm to concentrate on what it does best—manufacturing. Honda provides another example of this approach. As production at Honda's U.S. manufacturing plant in Ohio grew, the firm needed an increased supply of mirrors for its cars. It convinced a local supplier, Donnelly Corp., to build a new factory to assemble mirrors for its automobiles. Thus, Honda obtained a convenient and dependable supplier without having to invest its own money in building a mirror factory.[11] Of course, by buying rather than making the mirrors, Honda surrendered the profits of mirror manufacturing to Donnelly.

Buying from others also reduces a firm's training costs and expertise requirements. By contracting with Donnelly, Honda avoided having to develop expertise in designing, manufacturing, and marketing automobile mirrors. BP, in contrast, needs a wide range of expertise and talent among the ranks of its managers to take full advantage of its highly vertically integrated global operations. At the same time, though, "Bringing the World Into Focus" illustrates how unexpected events like the earthquake and tsunami that devastated parts of Japan in 2011 can severely disrupt supply chains.

FLEXIBILITY A firm that buys rather than makes retains the flexibility to change suppliers as circumstances dictate. This is particularly helpful in cases in which technology is evolving rapidly or delivered costs can change as a result of inflation or exchange rate fluctuations. Most personal computer manufacturers, for example, have chosen to buy disk drives, USB ports, and microprocessors from outside suppliers. By so doing, they avoid the risk of product obsolescence and the large research and development expenditures needed to stay on the cutting edge of each of the technologies embedded in the component parts of personal computers. Similarly, Dallas's Peerless Manufacturing buys components from numerous European subcontractors that produce filters and separators. Peerless can shift its sourcing around the continent depending on currency fluctuations and flows of orders from its customers.

Of course, sometimes a firm must make trade-offs that reduce flexibility. In the case of Honda and Donnelly, Donnelly was concerned it would be at Honda's mercy once it invested in the new mirror factory. To induce Donnelly to agree to build the new factory, the automaker had

BRINGING THE WORLD INTO FOCUS   DEALING WITH THE UNEXPECTED

Relations between manufacturers and their suppliers can be vitally important to each. Manufacturers depend on their suppliers to provide them with high-quality parts and supplies on a timely basis, whereas suppliers depend on their manufacturing customers for revenue. In general, both parties work to create and maintain a sound relationship. But sometimes Mother Nature can get in the way—and create big problems.

In March 2011 a massive earthquake in Japan triggered an equally devastating tsunami. Between the two natural disasters, manufacturing facilities and shipping routes throughout the country were shut down. These events created obvious problems for just about every manufacturer in Japan. But the ripple effects were also felt in North America as well. For instance, Toyota's North American manufacturing plants get about 15 percent of their parts from suppliers back in Japan. As inventory was depleted, the North American plants began to cut back on production. Two months later they were operating at only 30 percent of normal capacity when they experienced critical shortages of 150 important component parts. And experts predicted that they might not be able to resume normal production until the end of 2011. Nissan and Honda faced similar problems.

Nor were problems limited to Toyota and other Japanese firms. General Motors, for instance, spends about 2 percent of its parts budget in Japan and so it too was affected. But GM managers responded very effectively to the crisis. Four days after the earthquake, GM assembled hundreds of employees into teams that began working around the clock to identify critical parts likely to be affected and developing plans for dealing with anticipated shortages. The teams identified 118 parts most likely to be affected and quickly located alternative suppliers. Had GM run out of any of those products, production would have been halted for days.

One lesson that all of the major automakers say they learned was the need for more comprehensive crisis plans in the event of future disasters or other supply chain disruptions. One GM executive, for example, noted that while GM had a standing contingency plan for supply chain disruptions, it was not ready for anything "on this kind of scale or scope." Meanwhile, other sectors ranging from electronics to clothing manufacturing to food production also had to assess the impact of the earthquake and tsunami and make their own decisions about being better prepared in the future.

Sources: "Toyota rations Japanese parts; Honda to cut hours," *USA Today,* March 30, 2011, p. 1B; "Supply shortages likely following Japanese tsunami," *Supply Chain Review*, March 11, 2011, p. 1; "Asian supply chain rattled by Japan quake, tsunami," *International Business Times*, March 14, 2011, p. 1; "G.M. pieces together Japanese supply chain," *New York Times*, May 13, 2011, p. 5.

to assure Donnelly managers that the firm would get all of Honda's mirror business for at least 10 years. By so doing, Honda reduced its capital investment but sacrificed the flexibility of changing suppliers during the 10-year period. This example also illustrates a major trend in buyer-supplier relationships. Not long ago, managers assumed it was useful to use a variety of suppliers to avoid becoming too dependent on a single one. A drawback of this approach, however, is the complexity associated with dealing with a large network of suppliers, especially if that network is global. More recently, some firms have come to realize that by engaging in exclusive or semi-exclusive long-term relationships with fewer suppliers, the firms can better benefit from these suppliers' experience and product knowledge. In the automobile industry many manufacturers are relying on so-called first-tier suppliers such as Johnson Controls or Magna International to work with the automakers' engineers to design component systems, such as seating systems or dashboard assemblies, for new vehicles. Companies also are saving additional money by relying on first-tier suppliers to manage and monitor the acquisition of parts and subassemblies from second-tier suppliers.

Location Decisions

An international firm that chooses to make rather than buy inputs faces another decision: Where should it locate its production facilities? In reaching a location decision, the firm must consider country-related issues, product-related issues, government policies, and organizational issues.

COUNTRY-RELATED ISSUES Several features of countries can influence the decision about where to locate an international facility. Chief among these are resource availability and cost, infrastructure, and country-of-origin marketing effects.

Resource availability and cost constitute a primary determinant of whether an individual country is a suitable location for a facility. As suggested by the classical trade theories and the Heckscher-Ohlin theory (see Chapter 6), countries that enjoy large, low-cost endowments of a

Abundant and low-cost labor represents a significant advantage for businesses that can locate production facilities in China. Take these factory workers, for instance. They work hard, do high-quality work, and are willing to accept wages much lower than their counterparts in most other parts of the world. Little wonder, then, that China has become one of the world's most important and attractive locations for manufacturing across a wide variety of industries.

© Lou Linwei/Alamy

factor of production will attract firms needing that factor of production. For example, BP has little choice but to situate drilling platforms where crude oil reserves are located. China has attracted toy, footwear, and textile manufacturers due to the availability of low-cost labor. At the same time, though, the migration of factories to countries with low labor costs has generated much controversy.

Infrastructure also affects the location of production facilities. Most facilities require at least some minimal level of infrastructural support. To build a facility requires construction materials and equipment as well as materials suppliers and construction contractors. More important, electrical, water, transportation, telephone, and other services are necessary to utilize the facility productively. In addition, access to medical care, education, adequate housing, entertainment, and other related services are almost certain to be important for the employees and managers who will work at the facility as well as for their families.

Country-of-origin effects also may play a role in locating a facility. Certain countries have "brand images" that affect product marketing. For example, Japan has a reputation for manufacturing high-quality products, whereas Italy often is credited with stylishly designed products. In one interesting experiment a researcher found that consumer preference for Timex watches fell by only 6 percent when interviewees were told the watches were made in Pakistan rather than Germany. However, when consumers were confronted with an unfamiliar brand called Tempomax, their willingness to buy the watches fell by 74 percent when they were told the watches were made in Pakistan instead of Germany. All else being equal, it obviously is easier to sell watches made in Germany than ones made in Pakistan to consumers in industrialized countries, particularly if the product is not backed by a strong brand name. Firms must take into account these country-of-origin effects in deciding where to site a production facility. A firm interested in marketing its product as high quality might choose to locate in Japan or Germany rather than in Pakistan or Indonesia, whereas a firm competing on the basis of low costs and prices might make the opposite choice.

PRODUCT-RELATED ISSUES Product-related characteristics also may influence the location decision. Among the more important of these are the product's value-to-weight ratio and the required production technology.[12]

The product's value-to-weight ratio affects the importance of transportation costs in the product's delivered price. Goods with low value-to-weight ratios, such as iron ore, cement, coal, bulk chemicals, and raw sugar and other agricultural goods, tend to be produced in multiple locations to minimize transportation costs. Conversely, goods with high value-to-weight ratios, such as microprocessors or diamonds, can be produced in a single location or handful of locations without loss of competitiveness.

The production technology used to manufacture the good also may affect facility location. A firm must compare its expected product sales with the efficient size of a facility in the industry. If a firm's sales are large relative to an efficient-sized facility, the firm is likely to operate many facilities in various locations. If its sales are small relative to an efficient-sized facility, the firm probably will utilize only one plant. For example, the minimum efficient size of a petroleum refinery is about 200,000 barrels per day. Thus, BP, which can produce up to 5 million barrels per day, has chosen to operate 17 refineries located in such countries as the United Kingdom, Spain, and Colombia.

The relative importance of customer feedback also may influence the location decision. Products for which firms desire quick customer feedback often are produced close to the point of final sale. For example, a general rule of thumb in the U.S. apparel industry is that, all else being equal, the more fashionable the item, the more likely it will be produced near or in the United States so the manufacturer can respond quickly to market trends. At the beginning of each selling season women's sportswear buyers for Macy's, Nordstrom's, and Sak's Fifth Avenue carefully monitor which new items are hot sellers. The buyers quickly reorder the hot items and mercilessly dump goods that fashion-conscious shoppers ignore. Because the selling season for such goods may last only two or three months—and no one can predict with certainty what the fashion fanatics will buy—apparel manufacturers in the United States are better able to respond to the sportswear buyers' demands than are producers in Taiwan or Indonesia. Conversely, low-fashion items are more likely to be produced outside the United States to take advantage of lower production costs. For example, J.C. Penney can predict with reasonable certainty how many athletic socks and white cotton briefs it will sell each summer. If for some reason it overestimates summer sales of these items, it can continue to sell them in the fall. Accordingly, Penney's menswear buyers often enter into long-term contracts with Asian knitting mills. In this case cost is a more important variable than speed or flexibility of delivery.

GOVERNMENT POLICIES Government policies also may play a role in the location decision. Especially important are the stability of the political process, national trade policies, economic development incentives, and the existence of foreign trade zones.

The stability of the political process within a country can clearly affect the desirability of locating a factory there. Firms like to know what the rules of the game are so they can make knowledgeable investment, production, and staffing decisions. A government that alters fiscal, monetary, and regulatory policies seemingly on whim and without consulting the business community raises the risk and uncertainty of operating in that country. Unforeseen changes in taxation policy, exchange rates, inflation, and labor laws are particularly troublesome to international firms.

National trade policies also may affect the location decision. To serve its customers, a firm may be forced to locate a facility within a country that has high tariff walls and other trade barriers. For example, Toyota, Nissan, and Mazda built factories in the United States to evade a voluntary export restraint imposed by the Japanese government to limit the exports of Japanese-built automobiles to the United States. Similarly, Hewlett-Packard located a personal computer manufacturing facility in São Paulo to avoid Brazilian import taxes.

Economic development incentives may influence the location decision. Communities eager to create jobs and add to the local tax base often seek to attract new factories by offering international firms inexpensive land, highway improvements, job-training programs, and discounted water and electric rates. For example, the government of France sold the Walt Disney Company suburban land on which to build Disneyland Paris at a greatly discounted rate. Similarly, Mississippi outbid dozens of North American cities, provinces, and states for an $800-million Nissan assembly plant, offering the firm a $295-million package of incentives.[13]

An international firm also may choose a site based on the existence of a foreign trade zone (FTZ). As discussed in Chapter 9, an FTZ is a specially designated and controlled geographical area in which imported or exported goods receive preferential tariff treatment. A country may establish FTZs near its major ports of entry and/or major production centers. It then allows international firms to import products into those zones duty free for specified purposes, sometimes with express limitations; for example, there may be limitations on the types and value of products allowed and on the kind of work that may be performed.

A firm may decide to locate in a particular area because the existence of an FTZ gives the firm greater flexibility regarding importing or exporting and creates avenues for lowering costs.[14] For example, the Port of Houston operates a large FTZ used primarily for storage by non-U.S. automakers. Toyota and Nissan can ship all their automobiles bound for sale in the southern part of North America to Houston, where they are stored without any payment of import tariffs being required. Only when specific automobiles are removed from the zone and shipped to dealerships must the manufacturers pay the duty. However, some automobiles eventually are shipped to Mexico or various Caribbean countries. The firms then pay only whatever duty those countries levy and avoid paying U.S. duties altogether.

Costs can be lowered through the creative use of FTZs. A firm may be able to import component parts, supplement them with other component parts obtained locally, and assemble them all into finished goods. The duty paid on the imported components incorporated into the products assembled in the FTZ may be lower than the duty imposed on imported components in general. For this reason most automobiles produced in the United States are assembled in FTZs. Further, some duties are calculated on the basis of the good's total weight, including packaging. So a firm may lower its duties by bringing goods into the FTZ in lightweight, inexpensive packaging, and then, after duties have been paid, repackaging them with heavier, more substantial materials obtained locally.

ORGANIZATIONAL ISSUES An international firm's business strategy and its organizational structure also may affect the location decision. Inventory management policies are important considerations as well.

A firm's business strategy may affect its location decisions in various ways. A firm that adopts a cost leadership strategy must seek out low-cost locations, whereas a firm that focuses on product quality must locate facilities in areas that have adequate skilled labor and managerial talent. A firm may choose to concentrate production geographically to better meet organizational goals. Benetton does this with its Italian production facilities so as to better control product design and quality. Other firms find that strategic goals can be better met by dispersing facilities in various foreign locations. Most electronics firms take this approach. For example, Intel has manufacturing and assembly plants in Ireland, Israel, Malaysia, China, Costa Rica, and Vietnam to take advantage of the relatively low-cost resources available in each of these markets. Further, shipping the firm's computer chips to distant markets from those manufacturing facilities is relatively easy and inexpensive. Multiple production facilities also protect a firm against exchange rate fluctuations. FMC, for example, often shifts orders for its food-packaging machinery from plants in Chicago to plants in Italy or vice versa, depending on the relative values of the dollar and the euro.

A firm's organizational structure also influences the location of its factories. For example, as noted in Chapter 14, adoption of a global area structure decentralizes authority to area managers. These managers, seeking to maintain control over their area, are likely to favor locating factories within their area to produce goods sold within the area. For example, Ford once was structured as three area groups: North America, Europe, and Asia Pacific. The firm exported few automobiles from these regions: Rather, each area focused on producing automobiles to meet the needs of consumers in its area. Ford later abandoned this organizational structure, believing it hindered the company's ability to truly globalize its automobile production. Conversely, a firm having a global product structure will locate factories anywhere in the world to meet the firm's cost and quality performance goals.

A firm's inventory management policies are also affected by plant location decisions. Inventory management is a complex task all operations managers must confront. They must balance the costs of maintaining inventory against the costs of running out of materials and/or finished goods. The costs of maintaining inventory include those associated with storage (operating a warehouse, for example), spoilage and loss (some stored inventory gets ruined, damaged, or stolen), and opportunity costs (an investment in inventory cannot be put

A just-in-time inventory management system requires suppliers to deliver their products directly to the buyer's manufacturing center, usually in small batches, just as they are needed for production. This allows the buyer to lower its inventory storage costs and reduce shrinkage and damage while goods are being warehoused. But it also requires extra coordination and may raise the costs for suppliers. This supplier is loading a shipment on a truck to be delivered to a local manufacturer "just in time."

Baloncici/Dreamstime.com

to other business uses). Factory location affects the level of inventory that firms must hold because of the distances and transit times involved in shipping goods. For example, if Walmart purchases private-label televisions for its U.S. stores from a Taiwanese factory, Walmart's inventory levels will be higher than if it purchases the televisions from a Mexican factory. Factory location becomes particularly critical when the **just-in-time (JIT)** inventory management system is adopted. With this approach a firm's suppliers deliver their products directly to the firm's manufacturing center, usually in frequent small shipments, just as they are needed for production. The JIT system requires careful coordination between a firm and its internal and external suppliers. Often parts suppliers locate their facilities near the factories of their major customers to meet the JIT requirements of their customers. For example, many car-part makers, such as TRW Steering Systems, Denso, Bosch, and Johnson Controls, have located in Wales or the West Midlands region of England to better serve major customers like Jaguar and Range Rover. Parts manufacturers also have gravitated to the midwestern United States, Ontario, Brazil, Thailand, and other areas where auto assembly plants are clustered.

International Logistics and Materials Management

Regardless of the location of an international firm's factories, its operations management must address issues of international logistics. **International logistics** is the management of the flow of materials, parts, supplies, and other resources from suppliers to the firm; the flow of materials, parts, supplies, and other resources within and between units of the firm itself; and the flow of finished products, services, and goods from the firm to customers.

The first two sets of activities usually are called **materials management,** and the third set often is called physical distribution, or, more simply, distribution.[15] Recall that we discussed distribution issues in Chapter 16 because they often are managed as part of the firm's marketing function. Thus, our focus here is on the materials management area of logistics. The role of logistics is particularly important for firms that have developed integrated, but geographically dispersed, manufacturing and distribution networks where parts may be made in one country for assembly in a second country for sale in a third country.[16] Three basic factors differentiate domestic and international materials management functions. The first is simply the distance involved in shipping. Shipments within even the largest countries seldom travel more than a couple of thousand miles, and many shipments travel much less. For example, the road distance between New York City and Los Angeles is around 2,800 miles, but

CUTTING COSTS TO THE BONE

Ratan Tata is a quiet, unassuming leader. In spite of his wealth, he lives a quiet life in Mumbai. He avoids publicity and is often alone. He worked hard to get where he is today, spending years in various remote units of the Tata Group. Yet his humble early career and simple lifestyle show that Ratan Tata is a man who deeply identifies with average Indians. His "people's car," the new Tata Nano, is made for them.

In 1998, Ratan Tata vowed to develop an affordable four-person car, designed and built in India and retailing for 100,000 rupees (US $2,400). The constraints: low cost, assembly-line manufacturing, aesthetically pleasing, and efficient to build. Instead of viewing these as crippling limitations, Tata's engineers considered them opportunities to innovate.

"A promise is a promise," says Ratan Tata, demonstrating his low-cost commitment. Thousands of innovations were made in the 10-year quest to reach the goal. In addition, development costs were $70 million in India, compared to $350 million in the West. Factory workers' wages were $1.20 hourly. Nanos will ship as kits for local assembly, for more savings. The result is the first affordable car for India's growing middle class.

Of course, the Nano is not perfect. It's so stripped down that it wouldn't meet safety standards in many countries, although it does meet India's. "It's safer than putting four people on a scooter, but that's it," says Sandy Munro, an industry expert, citing a common practice among the Indian middle class. Luxuries such as air-conditioning, reclining seats, and radio are not available. In addition, as materials prices have increased substantially in recent years Tata has had no choice but to increase the price of the Nano. For instance, in early 2011 the cheapest Nano was around $3000—still a very low-cost automobile.

Some competitors are rushing to imitate. Nissan chairman Carlos Ghosn says, "If Tata can do it, we can do it." So far, even the best designs cost thousands more. Other automakers are uninterested in the slim profit margins Tata will obtain. Yet Ratan Tata's company is aiming to make vehicle ownership possible for the first time for millions of Indians.

Sources: C. K. Prahalad, "A nano leap into the future," *The Times of India* (Delhi), January 13, 2008, on June 1, 2008; "My other car is a Tata," *Business Week*, January 3, 2008, pp. 56–57; John Elliott, "'Nano' achieves Ratan Tata's dream," *Fortune*, January 10, 2008, pp. 105–109.

the distances between New York and Warsaw, Tokyo, and Sydney are 4,300 miles, 6,700 miles, and 9,900 miles, respectively.[17] Thus, assembling component parts in Kansas City, Chicago, and St. Louis and then shipping them to Cincinnati for final assembly is much easier than assembling component parts in San Diego, Montreal, and Cairo and then shipping them to Singapore for final assembly.

The second basic difference between domestic and international materials management functions is the sheer number of transport modes that are likely to be involved. Shipments within the same country often use only a single mode of transportation, such as truck or rail. However, shipments that cross national boundaries, and especially shipments traveling great distances, almost certainly involve multiple modes of transportation.[18] For example, a shipment bound from Kansas City to Berlin may use truck, rail, ship, and then rail and truck again.

Third, the regulatory context for international materials management is much more complex than for domestic materials management. Most countries regulate many aspects of their internal transportation systems—price, safety, packaging, and so on. Shipments that cross through several countries are subject to the regulations of each of those countries. Although various economic trade agreements, such as the North American Free Trade Agreement, have sought to streamline international shipping guidelines and procedures, transporting goods across national boundaries is still complex and often involves much red tape.

Seemingly simple logistics and materials management issues often become much more complex in an international context. Packaging issues, which might at first glance seem minor, are in reality a significant consideration in managing international logistics. Packaging protects the goods in transit, helps make the goods easier to handle, and facilitates delivery and/or sale of finished goods at their final destination. International shipping complicates packaging decisions, however, because of the use of multiple modes of transportation as well as the variation in conditions that will be encountered.[19]

Consider the problems confronted by a firm that wants to ship a large quantity of delicate electronics equipment from a plant in California, where the equipment was produced, to a facility in Saudi Arabia, where the equipment will be used. During the course of shipment the equipment likely will be on trucks, railcars, and a ship. These transport settings will have variations in humidity, temperature, and amount of dust. Moreover, each time the equipment is loaded and unloaded, it will be handled with varying degrees of roughness or delicacy. Thus, the equipment must be packaged to handle everything it will encounter during its travels.

The weight of the packaging itself also is a consideration, especially for finished goods en route to customers. As noted earlier in the chapter, weight sometimes determines the amount of import duty, so firms frequently repackage goods after shipment. Sometimes customers even go so far as to specify precise total weights, including packaging, they will accept, and may require that packaging meet certain preset specifications.

Logistical considerations may play a critical role in the decision of where to locate a factory. Production costs may be lower in a domestic factory than in a foreign factory. However, the firm also must consider the materials management costs of warehousing, packaging, transporting, and distributing its goods, as well as its inventory carrying costs and those of its foreign customers. Typically, such logistical costs will be higher for exported goods than for locally produced goods. There also are logistical considerations besides costs. Because of longer supply lines and increased difficulties in communicating with foreign customers, a firm that chooses to export from domestic factories must ensure that it maintains competitive levels of service for its foreign customers.

Needless to say, the ongoing globalization of the world's economy has magnified the importance of international logistics. Globalization would be much less extensive and much slower to develop had it not been for rapid changes in information technology (IT). Although the development of personal computers, fax machines, electronic mail, smartphones, the Internet, and the like are widely known, less visible IT breakthroughs such as satellite communications, electronic data interchange, and bar coding have been equally significant. By integrating such technological changes into their logistical operations, firms are able to increase their productivity and enhance customer satisfaction. Firms such as Zara and Urban Outfitters that have aggressively and innovatively harnessed these new information technologies have improved the efficiency of their overall operations as well as their logistical operations. Cost savings can be huge. Volkswagen, for example, believes it can trim its overall operating costs by 1 percent using electronic data interchange for all of its internal and external transactions.

IT also has promoted a reconceptualization of the logistics process and a rethinking of the supplier-customer relationship. By harnessing IT, firms are able to analyze how to promote the efficiency and productivity of the entire supply chain, rather than just their particular component of it. Indeed, by using IT creatively, companies not only enhance their own productivity but also raise the satisfaction of their customers. IT has other advantages as well. Investments in IT can act as substitutes for investments in inventory and warehousing capacity, reducing capital costs and improving rates of return on assets. Moreover, IT helps firms monitor their progress toward attainment of their strategic goals.

International Service Operations

The service sector has emerged in recent years as an increasingly important part of many national economies, especially those of developed countries. For example, the service sector accounts for almost three-fourths of the U.S. gross domestic product and is the source of most new U.S. jobs.[20] It therefore should come as no surprise that services are becoming a more integral part of international trade and of the global economy. An **international service business** is a firm that transforms resources into an intangible output that creates utility for its customers. Examples of international services are British Airways' transporting of passengers from London to New Delhi; PricewaterhouseCooper's assistance with the accounting and auditing functions of firms such as BP, Baxter, and IBM; and Dai-Ichi Kangyo Bank's handling of international corporate business accounts.

Characteristics of International Services

Services have several unique characteristics that create special challenges for firms that want to sell services in the international marketplace. In particular, services often are intangible, are not storable, require customer participation, and may be linked with tangible goods.

SERVICES ARE INTANGIBLE A consumer who goes to a store and buys an Apple iPad has a tangible product, one that can be held, manipulated, used, stored, damaged, and/or returned. A consumer who goes to an accountant to obtain financial advice leaves with intangible knowledge that cannot be held or seen. (The pieces of paper or electronic documents sometimes associated with services—tax statements, insurance policies, and so on—although tangible themselves, are actually just symbols or representations of the service product itself.) Because of this intangibility, assessing a service's value or quality often is more difficult than assessing the value or quality of a good.

SERVICES GENERALLY ARE NOT STORABLE Often they cannot be created ahead of time and inventoried or saved for future usage. A service call to repair a broken washing machine can occur only when the technician is physically transported to the site of the broken appliance—and is wasted if no one is home to unlock the door. An empty airline seat, an unused table in a restaurant, and an unsold newspaper all lose their economic value as soon as their associated window of opportunity closes, that is, after the plane takes off, the restaurant kitchen closes, and the next day's newspaper is printed. The high degree of perishability of services makes capacity planning a critical problem for all service providers. **Capacity planning** is deciding how many customers a firm will be able to serve at a given time. Failure to provide sufficient capacity often means permanently lost sales, whereas provision of too much capacity raises the firm's costs and lowers its profits.

SERVICES OFTEN REQUIRE CUSTOMER PARTICIPATION International services such as tourism cannot occur without the physical presence of the customer. Because of customer involvement in the delivery of the service, many service providers need to customize the product to meet the purchaser's needs. Thomas Cook, for example, can sell more bus tours in London if it provides Spanish-speaking guides for its Mexican, Venezuelan, and Argentinean clients and Japanese-speaking guides for its Japanese customers. Further, an identical service can be perceived quite differently by each of its customers, thereby creating strategic and marketing problems. The London bus tour, for instance, may be viewed with great excitement by Japanese honeymooners on their first trip outside of Osaka but with boredom by a harried Toshiba executive who has visited the city many times.

MANY SERVICES ARE TIED TO THE PURCHASE OF OTHER PRODUCTS Many firms offer **product-support services**—assistance with operating, maintaining, and/or repairing products for customers. Such services may be critical to the sale of the related product. For example, Swedish appliance maker AB Electrolux manufactures vacuum cleaners, refrigerators, washing machines, and other appliances under such names as Eureka, Frigidaire, Tappan, and Weed Eater. The firm also has service operations set up to repair those products for consumers who buy them, to provide replacement parts, and so on. The firm's ability to sell its appliances would be harmed substantially if it did not offer these related services. Moreover, not only must it offer the services at its corporate headquarters in Stockholm, Sweden; if Electrolux wants to compete in the U.S., Canadian, and British markets, it must provide repair and parts distribution services there as well.

The Role of Government in International Services Trade

An important dimension of the international services market is the role of government. Many governments seek to protect local professionals and to ensure that domestic standards and credentials are upheld by restricting the ability of foreigners to practice such professions as law, accounting, and medicine. Government regulations often stipulate which firms are allowed to enter service markets and the prices they may charge. For instance, in the United States foreign banks and insurance firms are heavily regulated and must follow the directives of numerous state and federal regulatory agencies. In many countries telecommunications, transportation, and utility firms typically need governmental permission to serve individual markets. For example, airline routes between the United States and Australia are defined by a bilateral agreement between those two countries. Qantas, Australia's leading airline, can fly passengers between Sydney and San Francisco and between Sydney and Dallas, but it cannot board passengers in San Francisco and fly them to Dallas.

The past decade has seen a reduction in domestic and international regulation of many service industries. Continued reductions in barriers to service trade is a high priority of the World Trade Organization. Deregulation and reduced trade barriers have created opportunities for firms in industries such as banking and telecommunications and spurred them to aggressively seek new domestic markets and expand their operations to foreign markets. These changes have also triggered numerous strategic alliances, cross-border investments, and new start-up companies in every corner of the globe.

Managing Service Operations

The actual management of international service operations involves a number of basic issues, including capacity planning, location planning, facilities design and layout, and operations scheduling.

Recall that capacity planning is deciding how many customers the firm will be able to serve at one time. Because of the close customer involvement in the purchase of services, capacity planning affects the quality of the services provided to customers. For example, McDonald's first restaurant in Russia was considerably larger than many of its other restaurants in order to accommodate an anticipated higher level of sales volume. Despite this larger size, customer waiting times at the Moscow restaurant were much longer than those in the United States. The lack of restaurant alternatives made Muscovites more willing to stand in long lines for their "Big Mek." In contrast, if customers had to wait a half-hour to be served in Boulder, Columbus, or even Paris, McDonald's would lose much of its business.

As with production management, location planning is important for international service operations. By definition most service providers must be close to the customers they plan to serve (exceptions might be information providers that rely on electronic communication). Indeed, most international service operations involve setting up branch offices in each foreign market and then staffing each office with locals.

International service facilities also must be carefully designed so the proper look and layout are established. At times firms operating internationally may highlight their foreign identity or blend their home country heritage with the local culture. At Disneyland Paris, for example, signs are in both English and French. At other times firms may chose to downplay their foreign identity. Most American donut dunkers, for instance, were unaware that Dunkin' Donuts was owned by a British conglomerate for many years.

Finally, international service firms must schedule their operations to best meet the customers' needs. For example, airlines transporting passengers from the United States to Europe generally depart late in the evening. Doing this gives passengers the opportunity to spend some of the day working before they depart, and they arrive in the early morning the next day. In contrast, westbound flights usually leave Europe in midmorning and arrive in the United States late that same afternoon. This scheduling provides an optimal arrangement because it factors in customer preferences, time zones, jet lag, and aircraft utilization and maintenance requirements.

Managing Productivity in International Business

A key consideration in operations management for many international firms is productivity. At its simplest level **productivity** is an economic measure of efficiency that summarizes the value of outputs relative to the value of the inputs used to create the outputs.[21] Productivity is important for various reasons. For one thing, it helps determine a firm's overall success and contributes to its long-term survival. For another, productivity contributes directly to the overall standard of living within a particular country. If the firms within a country are especially productive, the country's citizens will have more products and services to consume. Moreover, the firm's goods and services can be exported to other countries, thereby bringing additional revenues back into the country of origin. Each of these factors positively impacts gross domestic product and thus benefits the whole country.

Regardless of where a firm operates, one of its fundamental goals must be to continue to enhance its productivity. There are several general strategies a firm can pursue in its efforts to maintain and/or boost productivity. Three approaches in particular often help firms become more productive: (1) spend more on research and development (R&D), (2) improve operations, and (3) increase employee involvement.

The starting point in improving productivity is often to invest more heavily in R&D. Through R&D firms identify new products, new uses for existing products, and new methods for making products. Each of these outcomes in turn contributes directly to higher productivity. U.S. firms often spend more on R&D than do their foreign competitors, but the gap is narrowing as more foreign firms increasingly invest in R&D. Moreover, U.S. firms have a long and painful history of achieving significant scientific breakthroughs but then being ineffective in getting them to market.[22]

Another important way to increase productivity is to improve operations. This is where control comes in; a firm seeking to increase productivity needs to examine how it does things and then look for ways to do them more efficiently. Replacing outmoded equipment, automating selected tasks, training workers to be more efficient, and simplifying manufacturing processes are all ways to improve operations and boost productivity. Japanese manufacturers have been especially successful at increasing productivity through improved operations. Just-in-time manufacturing and inventory control techniques, consistent investments in technology, and a concentration on efficiency have paid big dividends for many Japanese firms. U.S. firms also are paying more attention to operations. For example, General Electric once required three weeks to fill an order for a custom-made industrial circuit breaker box. Further, the firm had six plants making the boxes. Through improved operations—more efficient manufacturing methods and product simplification, among other improvements—the firm now fills such an order in only three days and makes all its circuit breaker boxes in a single facility.

Finally, productivity can be improved by increasing employee involvement. The idea is that if managers give employees more say in how they do their jobs, those employees will become more motivated to work and more committed to the firm's goals. Further, because they are the ones actually doing the jobs, the employees probably have more insights than anyone else into how to do the jobs better.[23] Increased involvement is generally operationalized through the use of self-managed teams. Groups of workers are formed into teams, each of which has considerable autonomy over how it does its job. Self-managed teams were pioneered in Sweden and the United Kingdom, refined in Japan, and are now used extensively worldwide.[24]

For example, Lufthansa currently uses employee participation in its efforts to cut costs. The firm's overhead had grown out of control, and it needed to be reduced for the firm to remain competitive. Lufthansa wanted to cut its payroll in Germany but was stymied because of two strong national unions. So the firm enlisted the assistance of the unions to meet its cost-cutting goals. Representatives from the firm and both unions now meet regularly to devise ways to trim payroll costs without resorting to massive layoffs. So far the cuts have focused on reducing work rules and eliminating jobs through attrition and early retirement.

Managing Quality in International Business

Operations management also helps firms maintain and enhance the quality of their products and/or services. Indeed, quality has become such a significant competitive issue in most industries that control strategies invariably have quality as a central focus. The American Society for Quality has defined **quality** as the totality of features and characteristics of a product or service that bear on its ability to satisfy stated or implied needs.[25] The International Organization for Standardization (ISO) has been working to develop and refine an international set of quality guidelines. These guidelines, called collectively ISO 9000, provide the basis for a quality certification that is becoming increasingly important in international business. The guidelines were updated and revised in 2000.

The ISO 9000 standards cover such areas as product testing, employee training, record keeping, supplier relations, and repair policies and procedures. Firms that want to meet these standards apply for certification and are audited by a firm chosen by the ISO's domestic affiliate. These auditors review every aspect of the firm's business operations in relation to the standards. Many firms report that merely preparing for an ISO 9000 audit has been helpful. Many firms today, including General Electric, DuPont, Eastman Kodak, British Telecom, and Philips Electronics are urging—or in some cases requiring—that their suppliers achieve ISO 9000 certification. All told, more than 157 countries have adopted ISO 9000 as a national standard, and more than 400,000 certificates of compliance have been issued. ISO 14000 is an extension of the same concept to environmental performance. Specifically, ISO 14000 requires that firms document how they are using raw materials more efficiently, managing pollution, and reducing their impact on the environment.

Quality is of vital importance for several reasons. First, many firms today compete on the basis of quality.[26] Firms whose products or services have a poor reputation for quality are unlikely to succeed. For example, some Korean companies initially had difficulty competing in Europe because their products were not perceived by Europeans as being of the same quality as those made by European firms. Such country-of-origin factors play a major role in the marketing and location decisions of international firms. The South Korean chaebols overcame this perceived shortcoming by opening plants in Europe, establishing strategic alliances with European firms, and working to meet ISO 9000 guidelines and standards.

Second, quality is important because it is directly linked with productivity. Higher quality means increased productivity because of fewer defects, fewer resources devoted to reworking defective products, and fewer resources devoted to quality control itself. Finally, higher quality helps firms develop and maintain customer loyalty. Customers who buy products and services that fulfill quality expectations are more likely to buy again from the same firm.

Because of the increasing importance of quality, firms worldwide are putting more and more emphasis on improving the quality of their products and services. Many of these firms call their efforts total quality management. **Total quality management (TQM)** is an integrated effort to systematically and continuously improve the quality of an organization's products and/or services.

TQM programs vary by firm and must be adapted to fit each firm's unique circumstances. As shown in Figure 17.2, TQM must start with a strategic commitment to quality. This means the quality initiative must start at the top of the firm, and top managers must be willing to commit the resources necessary to achieve continuous improvement. Firms that only pay lip service to quality and try to fool employees and customers into believing they care about it are almost certain to fail.[27]

FIGURE 17.2

The Essential Components of Total Quality Management

With a strong strategic commitment as a foundation TQM programs rely on four operational components to implement quality improvement. Employee involvement almost always is cited as a critical requirement in quality improvement. All employees must participate in helping to accomplish the firm's quality-related objectives. Materials also must be scrutinized. Firms often can improve the quality of their products by requiring higher-quality parts and materials from their suppliers and procuring inputs only from suppliers whose commitment to quality matches their own. The firm also must be willing to invest in new technology to become more efficient and to achieve higher-quality manufacturing processes. Finally, the firm must be willing to adopt new and improved methods of getting work done.

Firms using TQM have a variety of tools and techniques from which they can draw, including statistical process control and benchmarking. **Statistical process control** is a family of mathematically based tools for monitoring and controlling quality. Its basic purposes are to define the target level of quality, specify an acceptable range of deviation, and then ensure that product quality is hitting the target. For example, Source Perrier SA uses statistical process control to monitor its bottling operations. Managers there have determined that a large bottle of Perrier water should contain 23 fluid ounces. Of course, regardless of how careful managers are, few bottles will have exactly 23 ounces—some will have a bit more, some a bit less. However, if too many bottles are filled with either too much or too little, adjustments must be made. An acceptable range for this situation might be an actual content of between 22.8 and 23.2 ounces, with a target of 99.9 percent of all bottles having content within this range. Samples of finished products are taken and their actual content measured. As long as 99.9 percent of all samples have between 22.8 and 23.2 ounces, production continues. However, if only 97 percent of one sample falls within the acceptable range, managers may stop production and adjust their bottling equipment.

Another important TQM technique is benchmarking. **Benchmarking** is the process of legally and ethically studying how other firms do something in a high-quality way and then either imitating or improving on their methods. Xerox started the benchmarking movement in the United States as a result of competitive pressures from foreign rivals. Canon, a Japanese firm, once introduced a midsized copier that sold for less than $10,000. Xerox was sure Canon was selling it below cost to gain market share. To learn more about what was going on, Xerox sent a team of managers to Japan to work with Fuji-Xerox, a joint venture a Xerox affiliate had established with Fuji to make copiers in Asia. While there, the managers bought a Canon copier and took it apart. To their surprise they found the Canon copier to be of higher quality and lower cost than the copiers Xerox was making. By imitating various materials and methods used by Canon, Xerox was able to begin making its own higher-quality and lower-cost equipment.

Managing Information in International Business

A final and increasingly important aspect of operations in international business involves information. **Information** is data in a form that is of value to a manager in making decisions and performing related tasks.

Information is vitally important to any firm. Managers use it in every phase of their work because it is necessary to the decision-making process. Obtaining accurate and timely information is of particular importance to international firms. Managers use information to better understand their firm's environment—its customers, competitors, and suppliers; the government policies that affect its hiring, producing, and financing decisions; and virtually every other element of its environment.

Managers also use information to help them decide how to respond to the environment. Meetings, reports, data summaries, telephone calls, and electronic mail messages are all used as managers set strategic goals and map out strategic plans. Information is also critical to implementing those strategic plans. For example, top managers must communicate their goals and expectations to managers of their foreign operations. Information is needed continually as managers make decisions daily and provide feedback to others in the firm about the consequences of those decisions. Finally, information is an important part of the control process itself as managers monitor and assess how well they are meeting goals and executing plans. No manager likes to be taken by surprise. Having ready access to information that can be used to gauge ongoing performance and actual accomplishments is an important part of a manager's ability to function effectively.[28]

The importance of information management depends on the type of strategy and organization design the firm uses. If a firm is using related diversification, it is very important that various parts of the firm be able to communicate with other parts so the firm can most effectively capitalize on the potential synergies of this strategy. If the firm is highly centralized, information systems are vital for top managers so they can maintain the control they seek from using this particular design. On the other hand, if a firm is using unrelated diversification, its information systems needs will be quite different. Communication among the various businesses within the firm will be far less important. Finally, if the firm is using a decentralized form of organization design, its top managers will need and expect somewhat less information reporting by managers of various divisions and units.

The nature of international business adds considerable complexity to information and its role in a firm. In a domestic firm information is almost certain to be in a common language, within the same legal context (the same accounting standards, financial reporting requirements, and so on will apply), and stored, manipulated, and accessed through common computer software and hardware configurations. In an international firm information is likely to be in different languages and subject to different legal contexts. For example, foreign partners and foreign governments may constrain the flow of information into and/or out of their countries. Moreover, computer software and hardware configurations are not always compatible. Thus, managing information is not only very important for an international firm; it also is more complex than for a domestic firm.

Firms increasingly are working to develop integrated information systems to more effectively manage their information. An **information system** is a methodology created by a firm to gather, assemble, and provide data in a form or forms useful to managers. Most information systems are computerized, although they do not necessarily have to be—routing slips, files, and file storage systems can effectively manage information in small firms. Larger firms today almost always use computerized systems to manage their information. For example, managers at Laura Ashley, a British fashion and home furnishings chain, use a computerized information system to help the firm manage its information more effectively. Each sale is electronically recorded and used by managers to make decisions about reordering hot-selling merchandise. And, as the chapter opening case indicated, a primary source of Benetton's competitive advantage lies in mastery of information.

To the extent possible international firms would like to use information systems to link their operations, so their managers in any part of the world can access information and communicate with counterparts from any of the firm's operations. The sheer size of this undertaking, however, along with computer software and hardware limitations, makes it difficult for firms to achieve true global integration of their information systems. Thus, most firms develop information subsystems for specific functional operations or divisions.

Texas Instruments is further along the path toward a truly global system than are most firms. One of its subsidiaries, TIRIS (Texas Instruments Registration and Identification Systems), is headquartered in the United Kingdom; its product development units are in Germany and the Netherlands, and its manufacturing facilities are in Japan and Malaysia. Managers and engineers at each facility communicate with each other over an integrated computer-based information system that enables them to function as if they were across the hall from each other rather than thousands of miles apart. A manager in England might respond to a new customer order by sending a request electronically to a designer in Germany to make a small modification in a part to meet the customer's specifications. After the modification is made, the design specifications and order information can be sent electronically to Japan where the products will be manufactured. The original manager in England receives verification that the parts have been made and shipped and can call the customer with the news. At any time during the entire process any manager or designer can electronically monitor what is being done with the order and where it will be sent next. This approach helps Texas Instruments compete internationally by enabling it to reduce its costs and meet differing needs of customers in different countries.

CHAPTER REVIEW

Summary

International operations management is the set of activities used by an international firm to transform resources into goods or services. Effective operations management is a key ingredient in any firm's success. A firm's business strategy provides the major direction it will take regarding its operations management activities.

Production management refers to the creation of tangible goods. One of the first decisions production managers must make concerns supply chain management and vertical integration. Supply chain management, also called sourcing or procuring, encompasses the set of processes and steps used in acquiring resources and materials. Vertical integration refers to the extent to which a firm either provides its own resources or obtains them externally.

A key decision is whether to make or buy inputs. Several options exist. Production managers attempting to select from among them must consider strategic issues as well as risks, flexibility, investments in facilities, and questions of control.

Location decisions are also of paramount importance to effective international operations management. Country-related considerations include resource availability and costs, infrastructure, and country-of-origin marketing effects. Product-related issues are the value-to-weight ratio, production technology, and the importance of customer feedback. Governmental factors that must be considered include stability of the political process, tariffs and other trade barriers, economic development incentives, and the existence of FTZs. Finally, organizational issues include the firm's strategy, its structure, and its inventory management policies.

International logistics and materials management are also a basic part of production management. Several factors differentiate international from domestic materials management, including shipping distance, transportation modes, and the regulatory context. Packaging, weight, and factory location also must be considered. Technological changes in information technology are revolutionizing logistics and redefining relationships between suppliers and end users.

Service operations management is concerned with the creation of intangible products. The service sector is an increasingly important part of the global economy. International services are generally characterized as being intangible, not storable, requiring customer participation, and linked with tangible goods. The basic issues involved in managing service operations include capacity planning, location planning, design and layout, and operations scheduling.

Productivity is an economic measure of efficiency that summarizes the value of outputs relative to the value of inputs used to create the outputs. Productivity can be assessed at a variety of levels and in many different forms. Experts agree that a firm can improve productivity by spending more on R&D, improving operations, and increasing employee involvement.

Quality is the total set of features and characteristics of a product or service that bears on its ability to satisfy stated or implied needs. Quality has become a critical factor in both domestic and global competition. To improve quality, many firms are relying on TQM. TQM starts with a strategic commitment and is based on employee involvement, high-quality materials, up-to-date technology, and effective methods. Quality improvement tools include statistical process control and benchmarking.

Information is data in a form that is of value to a manager. It plays a major role in international business. Managers use information to understand their environment and to make decisions. Information is also an important element in effective control. Managing information in an international firm is complex, and many firms use sophisticated electronic information systems to do so more effectively.

Review Questions

1. How does a firm's corporate strategy affect its operations management?
2. How do production management and service operations management differ?
3. What is supply chain management? What is vertical integration?
4. What basic set of factors must a firm consider when selecting a location for a production facility?
5. What basic factors must be addressed when managing international service operations?
6. Why is it important for organizations to control productivity?

Questions for Discussion

1. How does international operations management relate to international marketing (discussed in Chapter 16)?
2. How are a firm's strategy and operations management interrelated?
3. How do each of the basic business strategies (differentiation, cost leadership, and focus) relate to operations management?
4. What are the basic similarities and differences between production management and service operations management?

5. Why are services most closely associated with developed, industrialized economies?
6. List 10 products you use for which quality is important in your purchasing decision. Which countries, if any, have reputations (good or bad) for each of these particular products?
7. What types of information are particularly important to an international firm?

Building Global Skills

Bluebonnet Creameries is a large U.S. ice cream company. The family-owned enterprise makes premium ice cream using only fresh, natural ingredients. Its butter-fat content is lower than that of Ben & Jerry's and Haagen-Dazs but higher than that of such national brands as Dreyer's. This allows the firm to hit the true "middle" of the market—Bluebonnet has a premium taste and image but is sold for a lower price than the high-end brands but is also only slightly more expensive than national mass-produced brands.

One ingredient in Bluebonnet's success has been its production and distribution model. Transporting ice cream over long distances requires that it be "deep frozen." This process, unfortunately, also requires the addition of preservatives and produces a slightly altered taste. As a result, Bluebonnet has built a number of mid-sized creameries near its major market centers throughout the United States. The firm also has its own fleet of delivery trucks and drivers to transport the ice cream and stock grocery shelves. Using this model, Bluebonnet doesn't have to "deep freeze" its products because its ice cream is made within a one-day drive of each market where it's delivered. Thus, a truck can leave a creamery with a full-load early in the morning, spend the day making deliveries, and have an empty truck by the end of that same day.

Consumers can also order Bluebonnet products online. The order is packed in Styrofoam containers, refrigerated with dry ice, and shipped via FedEx or UPS with next day delivery. Because distances are so short and export requirements clear, Bluebonnet can also fulfill orders to Canada, Mexico, Central America, and the Caribbean. A potential international customer from Europe, Asia, or elsewhere is informed early in the order process that Bluebonnet cannot ship to that individual's address. The primary reasons that Bluebonnet cannot fulfill orders from these locations are that normal shipping times are simply too long and customs regulations too complicated.

The manager in charge of online service has been monitoring foreign orders for several years and has noticed a steady but dramatic increase in online order attempts from Asia, especially China. Indeed, the attempted order volume has grown to the point where the online service manager has brought it up to a couple of senior managers (both members of the family that owns Bluebonnet). He recently informed them that the requested order volume from China would, if orders could be fulfilled, increase the firm's total revenues by 25 percent.

The family council (family members) recently met and identified the following options.

- Continue to follow their current business model and ignore the Asian market.
- Build a dedicated creamery designed for international distribution. The creamery would be built near a major FedEx or UPS shipping hub, and the ice cream produced there would include preservatives. Overseas orders from Asia, as well as Europe, Australia, Africa, and South America would be fulfilled from this creamery. The ice cream would be "deep frozen," packed with strong refrigerating chemicals, and shipped to individuals placing orders. Current technology would allow a window of 10 days for shipping-to-delivery. This process would be expensive, but the shipping and distribution costs would all be passed along to consumers.
- Contract with a Chinese distribution partner. Build a dedicated creamery near a west coast shipping port. Mass produce ice cream with preservatives at that creamery, "deep freeze" the ice cream, and pack it in large refrigerated shipping containers. Ship the containers via freighters across the Pacific to China, and allow the local partner there to handle distribution to interested retailers.
- Contract with a Chinese partner. Build a creamery near a major city such as Beijing, Shanghai, or Hong Kong. Manufacture ice cream there using the same model as used in the United States (no preservatives, controlled distribution, etc.).

Form groups with three or four of your classmates and do the following:

1. Identify the major advantages, disadvantages, and risks of each of the options identified above.
2. Rank order the options in terms of what you would recommend to the family that owns Bluebonnet.

3. Discuss and potentially identify other options that might be considered.
4. Each group should share the results of its deliberations with the rest of the class, and areas of agreement and disagreement discussed.

OUT SUPPLY-CHAINING THE KING OF SUPPLY CHAINERS

It's no secret that Walmart is the largest retailer (indeed, the largest corporation) on the planet, with total revenues in 2010 of $419 billion. It's over six times bigger than the number-two retailer in the United States, Home Depot (2010 revenue: $66 billion), and it's bigger than Europe's three largest retailers—France's Carrefour, Britain's Tesco, and Germany's Metro AG—combined. It is, according to the business-information service Hoover's, "an irresistible (or at least unavoidable) retail force that has yet to meet any immovable objects." One key to Walmart's success has been astute supply chain management. For example, Walmart was among the first to use point-of-sale scanners to track product sales and re-order quickly to meet shifting consumer buying patterns. And Walmart has also been ruthless at forcing its suppliers to continuously lower their own costs.

But some experts have recently noted that Walmart is actually getting beaten at its own game by one of its European rivals, Tesco. Food-retail analyst Kevin Coupe points out that "there isn't a place in the world where Tesco has gone one-on-one with Walmart and Tesco hasn't won." In Britain, for example, U.K.-owned Tesco, the world's third-largest retailer, commands a 34-percent market share—double that of Walmart-owned Asda. In 2007, moreover, Tesco launched a bold counteroffensive against Walmart on the retail super-power's home turf. In November, Tesco rolled out a chain of food stores called Fresh & Easy in California, Arizona, and Nevada, and by mid-2008, 145 Fresh & Easy outlets were up and running. Tesco has temporarily slowed its push into the U.S. market due to the global recession but many analysts agree that, by 2020, Tesco could have 5,000 stores in the United States with sales of $60 billion.

Fast & Easy outlets are about the size of a Trader Joe's, offer the kind of products that you'd find at Whole Foods, and feature prices calculated to make you think of Costco. The format is one of five that Tesco operates among nearly 4,000 stores in 13 countries, and its ability to manage stores in multiple formats as well as multiple markets is one of the company's greatest strengths. The key to this core competence is technology—or more precisely, data management, which is critical in any effort to optimize inventory selection, size, and distribution. Tesco, reports retail-industry analyst Scott Langdoc, "is ruthless in supply-chain management." In the United Kingdom,

for instance, a wireless network connecting all Tesco stores facilitates real-time management of distribution and transportation. Workers use handheld PDAs for data entry and reporting, and radio frequency identification (RFID) tags allow them to conduct crates and pallets to stores carrying anywhere from 3,500 to 60,000 different products in markets located anywhere from Sussex to Seoul.

The same expertise in data management, of course, is being brought to bear in Tesco's efforts to establish a beachhead in the $500 billion U.S. grocery business. And Tesco is good not only at applying data management to supply chain management, it has also developed considerable skill in applying data management to the analysis of consumer preferences in different markets. Tesco relies on a data-mining firm called Dunnhumby (of which it has majority control) to manage everything from targeting sales promotions to designing store formats and, perhaps most importantly, developing private-label products. Along with its ability to manage multiple store formats, many analysts regard Tesco's ability to provide a better and broader range of private brands—products manufactured for retailers who sell them under their own names—as one of the most important factors in the company's marketing success. U.S. retailers, on the other hand, have never been quite able to convince consumers that private-label products are as good as their brand-name counterparts. Walmart, for example, struggles to get 35 percent of its sales from private-label goods. In many countries, however, Tesco gets as much as 60 percent of its revenue from private-label sales, and 70 percent of Fast & Easy sales come from private-label products.

The difference? Tesco, explains New York retail consultant Burt P. Flickinger III, knows which products to develop, how to price them, and how to integrate them into the product lines of its various stores. "[our] range of high-quality own-label products," says CEO Terry Leahy, " … is an integral part of our offer in every market in which we operate." Tesco offers about 12,000 private-label and specialty brands at every price point. Some high-range products, such as Tesco Finest Chocolates, even sell at 50-percent premiums to established brands like Cadbury, and all of them sell at significantly higher margins than national brands.

According to Flickinger, "Tesco is arguably the finest food retailer in the world," and he suggests that, armed with a unique set of competencies with which to invade the U.S. market, the

British grocer may well be "Walmart's worst nightmare." On a less dramatic note, he predicts that, at the very least, Tesco will "take a little piece out of everybody from Walmart to Whole Foods."

Case Questions

1. What might Walmart do to counter Tesco's actions?
2. Tesco, of course, is a food retailer. How vulnerable might Walmart be to similar competition from a non-food retailer?

3. The global recession slowed down Tesco's plans for expansion. Why might Tesco have been more harmed by the recession that Walmart?

Sources: "Walmart, Inc.," Hoover's website, www.hoovers.com on June 2, 2011; "British grocery chain hits America with fresh ideas," *USA Today*, April 11, 2010, pp. B1, B2; "Tesco: 'Walmart's worst nightmare,' " *Business Week*, December 29, 2009, "Walmart, Kroger, Safeway better watch out: The British are coming!" CNNMoney.com, June 5, 2011; "Sir Terry Leahy: Pilot of world-class enterprise," *Private Label Magazine*, March/April 2010.

Endnotes

1. *Hoover's Handbook of World Business 2011* (Austin, TX: Hoover's Business Press, 2011), pp. 65–66; "The families that own Europe," *Time*, March 24, 2003, p. 46; "Pace-setting Zara seeks more speed to fight its rising cheap-chic rivals," *Wall Street Journal*, February 20, 2008, p. B1; "Benetton: A must-have becomes a has-been," *Business Week*, March 14, 2011, pp. 28–29; "Urban Outfitters improves supply chain management," computing.co.uk, June 5, 2011.
2. See Anil Lhurana, "Managing complex production processes," *Sloan Management Review* (Winter 1999), pp. 85–98.
3. Robert H. Hayes and Gary P. Pisano, "Beyond world-class: The new manufacturing strategy," *Harvard Business Review* (January–February 1994), pp. 77–87.
4. Michael McGrath and Richard Hoole, "Manufacturing's new economies of scale," *Harvard Business Review* (May–June 1992), pp. 94–103.
5. Masaaki Kotabe and Janet Y. Murray, "Linking product and process innovations and modes of international sourcing in global competition: A case of foreign manufacturing firms," *Journal of International Business Studies* (Third Quarter, 1990), pp. 383–408.
6. James Brian Quinn and Frederick G. Hilmer, "Strategic outsourcing," *Sloan Management Review* (Summer 1994), pp. 43–55; James Brian Quinn, "Outsourcing innovation: The new engine of growth," *Sloan Management Review* (Summer 2000), pp. 13–28.
7. Stephen J. Kobrin, "An empirical analysis of the determinants of global integration," *Strategic Management Journal*, vol. 12 (1991), pp. 17–31.
8. Peter Siddall, Keith Willey, and Jorge Tavares, "Building a transnational organization for British Petroleum," *Long Range Planning*, vol. 25, no. 1 (1992), pp. 18–26.
9. See Paul S. Adler, Barbara Goldoftas, and David I. Levine, "Flexibility versus efficiency," *Organization Science*, vol. 10, no. 1 (1999), pp. 43–52.
10. Jeffrey K. Liker and Yen-Chun Wu, "Japanese automakers, U.S. suppliers and supply chain superiority," *Sloan Management Review* (Fall 2000), pp. 81–93.
11. "An efficiency guru refits Honda to fight auto giants," *Wall Street Journal*, September 15, 1999, pp. B1, B4.
12. Andrew D. Bartmess, "The plant location puzzle," *Harvard Business Review* (March–April 1994), pp. 20–22.
13. "Nissan to say 'We're back' with new Mississippi plant," *Houston Chronicle*, November 9, 2000, p. 3C.
14. "The supplier moves next door," *Financial Times*, July 24, 1997, p. IV.
15. David Arnold, "Seven rules of international distribution," *Harvard Business Review* (November–December 2000), pp. 131–137.
16. Stanley E. Fawcett, Linda L. Stanley, and Sheldon R. Smith, "Developing a logistics capability to improve the performance of international operations," *Journal of Business Logistics*, vol. 18, no. 2 (1997), p. 102.
17. Walter Zinn and Robert E. Grosse, "Barriers to globalization: Is global distribution possible?" *The International Journal of Logistics Management*, vol. 1 (1990), pp. 13–18.
18. Adam J. Fein and Sandy D. Jap, "Manage consolidation in the distribution channel," *Sloan Management Review* (March 29, 1999), pp. A1, A8.
19. Clyde E. Witt, "Packaging: From the plant floor to the global customer," *Material Handling Engineer* (October 1992), pp. 3–31.
20. Richard B. Chase and Warren J. Erikson, "The service factory," *Academy of Management Executive* (August 1988), pp. 191–196.
21. John W. Kendrick, Understanding Productivity: An Introduction to the Dynamics of Productivity (Baltimore: Johns Hopkins, 1977).
22. Gene Bylinsky, "Look Who's Doing R&D," *Fortune*, November 27, 2000, pp. 232[B]–232[F].
23. See Rob Cross and Lloyd Baird, "Technology is not enough: Improving performance by building organizational memory," *Sloan Management Review* (Spring 2000), pp. 69–78.
24. Brian Dumaine, "Who needs a boss?" *Fortune*, May 7, 1990, pp. 52–60; Brian Dumaine, "The trouble with teams," *Fortune*, September 5, 1994, pp. 86–92.

25. Ross Johnson and William O. Winchell, *Management and Quality* (Milwaukee: American Society for Quality Control, 1989).

26. See Sandra Vandermerwe, "How increasing value to customers improves business results," *Sloan Management Review* (Fall 2000), pp. 27–38.

27. Marshall Sashkin and Kenneth J. Kiser, *Putting Total Quality Management to Work* (San Francisco: Berrett-Koehler, 1993).

28. Donald A. Marchand, William J. Kettinger, and John D. Rollins, "Information orientation: People, technology, and the bottom line," *Sloan Management Review* (Summer 2000), pp. 69–80.

CHAPTER 18

International Financial Management

AFTER STUDYING THIS CHAPTER, YOU SHOULD BE ABLE TO:

1. Analyze the advantages and disadvantages of the major forms of payment in international trade.

2. Identify the primary types of foreign-exchange risk faced by international businesses.

3. Describe the techniques used by firms to manage their working capital.

4. Evaluate the various capital budgeting techniques used for international investments.

5. Discuss the primary sources of investment capital available to international businesses.

Access a host of interactive learning aids at **www.pearsonglobaleditions.com/ mymanagementlab** to help strengthen your understanding of the chapter concepts.

MyManagementLab

© Gordon Tipene/Dreamstime.com

SINGAPORE AIRLINES' WORLDWIDE FINANCIAL MANAGEMENT

Singapore Airlines lives or dies in the international market. It has no domestic market because the land mass of its home, the city-state of Singapore, is only 693 square kilometers. Singapore Airlines competes head-to-head against other major international carriers, including Air France, American, British Airways, Cathay Pacific, KLM, Japan Air Lines, United, and Qantas.

The foundation of Singapore Airlines' global success is its reputation for providing high-quality service. It has lured passengers of all nationalities to its flights, particularly highly valued business travelers, who are willing to pay a premium for safe and reliable service. Only 27 percent of its business is done within the friendly turf of East Asia. European operations account for 24 percent of its revenue, while flights to the Americas provide 18 percent. The carrier also provides West Asian, Pacific, and African services.

A truly international carrier, Singapore Airlines flies to more than 60 cities in 30 countries on all six inhabited continents. But its international success brings a major financial challenge—managing its holdings of dozens of currencies it uses in the normal conduct of business. Singapore Airlines receives from its customers a rainbow of currencies, including baht, ringgit, rupees, rand, krone, dollars (Australian, Canadian, Hong Kong, New Zealand, and United States), as well as yen, yuan, pounds, Swiss francs, euros, and of course its home currency, the Singapore dollar. It also must pay in local currency for local services—landing fees, ground-handling services, travel agent commissions, and so on—in each country in which it does business.

Managing the firm's revenues, expenses, assets, and liabilities, all denominated in various foreign currencies, is a major task for Singapore Airlines' financial officers. To pay local expenses, they must maintain local-currency cash balances in each country. They also must search worldwide for sources of low-cost capital to modernize the firm's aircraft fleet and thereby maintain its reputation for high-quality service. In addition, they must protect the carrier from exchange rate fluctuations, which will change the value in its home currency that it receives for its services and the costs it incurs for aircraft, fuel, flight services, and ground handling. These executives must thoroughly understand how the contemporary international monetary system operates. They must monitor changes in the foreign-exchange market, be knowledgeable about potential shifts in government economic policies in their major markets, and constantly shop for the best credit terms in such capital markets as Amsterdam, London, Frankfurt, New York, Singapore, and Tokyo.[1] ▪

In many business transactions, the receipt of goods by the buyer and the receipt of payment by the seller in a form the seller can use immediately do not coincide. Even when a customer pays for goods with a check, the seller will not have access to the funds until the check clears. Until then, the seller risks having the check returned because of insufficient funds. Thus, some type of financing and some degree of trust between buyer and seller are necessary to allow business transactions to occur.

Although these problems affect both domestic and international businesses, the problems of financing and credit checking are far greater for international transactions. Differences in laws, customs, financial practices, and currency convertibility among countries mean that an international firm must know the practices both of its home country and of each country in which it does business—or else hire experts who do. A firm also must acquire specific credit information about the foreign firms with which it wants to deal. On top of these problems is that of transacting in a foreign currency—a problem that either the buyer or the seller must face. Financial officers of international businesses such as Singapore Airlines are well aware of the challenges created by using different currencies. How international businesses address these myriad problems is the subject of this chapter.

Financial Issues in International Trade

We begin by considering the problems associated with financing international trade. In any business transaction, the buyer and the seller must negotiate and reach agreement on such basic issues as price, quantity, and delivery date. However, when the transaction involves a buyer and a seller from two countries, several other issues arise:

- Which currency to use for the transaction
- When and how to check credit
- Which form of payment to use
- How to arrange financing

Choice of Currency

One problem unique to international business is choosing the currency to use to settle a transaction. Exporters and importers usually have clear—and conflicting—preferences as to which currency to use. The exporter typically prefers payment in its home currency so it can know the exact amount it will receive from the importer. The importer generally prefers to pay in its home currency so it can know the exact amount it must pay the exporter. Sometimes an exporter and an importer may elect to use a third currency. For example, if both parties are based in countries with relatively weak or volatile local currencies, they may prefer to deal in a more stable currency such as the Japanese yen or the U.S. dollar. By some estimates, more than 70 percent of the exports of less-developed countries and 85 percent of the exports of Latin American countries are invoiced using the U.S. dollar, while the exports of many of the new entrants into the European Union favor the euro.[2] In some industries one currency is customarily used to settle commercial transactions. In the oil and commercial aircraft industries, for instance, the U.S. dollar serves this function.[3] Among the major exporting countries, the most common practice is for the exporter to invoice foreign customers using its home currency. However, smaller exporting countries may choose to use the currency of a major trading partner; most of Thailand's exports are invoiced in U.S. dollars, for example.

Credit Checking

Another critical financial issue in international trade concerns the reliability and trustworthiness of the buyer. If an importer is a financially healthy and reliable company and one with whom an exporter has had previous satisfactory business relations, the exporter may choose to simplify the payment process by extending credit to the importer. However, if the importer is financially troubled or known to be a poor credit risk, the exporter may demand a form of payment that reduces its risk.

In commercial transactions it is wise to check customers' credit ratings. For most domestic business transactions firms have simple and inexpensive mechanisms for doing this. In North America, for instance, firms may ask for credit references or contact established sources of credit information such as Dun & Bradstreet or Moody's. Similar sources are available in other countries; however, many first-time exporters are unaware of them. Fortunately, an exporter's domestic banker often can obtain credit information on foreign customers through the bank's foreign banking operations or through its correspondent bank in a customer's country. Most national government agencies in charge of export promotion also offer credit-checking services. For example, the International Trade Administration, a branch of the U.S. Department of Commerce, provides financial information about foreign firms for a fee. Numerous commercial credit-reporting services also are available. Country desk officers of the U.S. and Foreign Commercial Service are available to steer new exporters to these services.

The firm that ignores the credit-checking process may run into serious payment problems. For example, one small U.S. manufacturer exported $127,000 worth of fan blades to a new customer in Africa. However, it failed to first contact any of the customer's credit references. Frustrated by the subsequent lack of payment, the manufacturer turned the account over to a collection agency, which discovered that the supposed customer had vanished and its credit references were nonexistent.[4]

Implicit in this discussion is an important lesson that many successful international businesspeople have learned the hard way. Because the physical and cultural gaps between the exporter and the importer are often large, finding partners, customers, and distributors with whom to build long-term, trusting relationships is invaluable to any international business.

Method of Payment

Parties to the international transaction normally negotiate a method of payment based on the exporter's assessment of the importer's creditworthiness and the norms of their industry. Many forms of payment have evolved over the centuries, including payment in advance, open account, documentary collection, letters of credit, credit cards, and countertrade. As with most aspects of finance, each form involves different degrees of risk and cost.

PAYMENT IN ADVANCE **Payment in advance** is the safest method of payment from the exporter's perspective: The exporter receives the importer's money prior to shipping the goods. Using this method, the exporter reduces its risk and receives payment quickly, which may be important if its working capital balance is low. Exporters prefer payments in advance to be made by wire transfer, which allows immediate use of the funds. Payment by ordinary check may take four to six weeks to clear the banking systems of the two countries involved, depending on the size and sophistication of their financial services sectors.

From the importer's perspective, payment in advance is very undesirable. The importer must give up the use of its cash prior to its receipt of the goods and bears the risk that the exporter will fail to deliver the goods in accordance with the sales contract. For these reasons exporters that insist on payment in advance are vulnerable to losing sales to competitors willing to offer more attractive payment terms. Nonetheless, payment in advance may be the preferred form if the importer is a poor credit risk.

OPEN ACCOUNT From the importer's perspective the safest form of payment is the **open account,** whereby goods are shipped by the exporter and received by the importer prior to payment. The exporter then bills the importer for the goods, stipulating the amount, form, and time at which payment is expected. Open accounts also can be used as a marketing tool because they offer potential buyers short-term financing. Use of an open account enables the importer to avoid the fees charged by banks for alternative means of payment such as letters of credit or documentary collection, which will be discussed shortly. An open account has the further advantage of requiring less paperwork than these other forms of payment.

From the exporter's perspective, an open account may be undesirable for several reasons. First, the exporter must rely primarily on the importer's reputation for paying promptly. Second, because the transaction does not involve a financial intermediary such as a bank, the exporter cannot fall back on such an intermediary's expertise if a dispute arises with the importer. Third, the exporter may pay a price for the advantage of doing less paperwork: If the importer refuses to pay, the lack of documentation can hamper the exporter's pursuit of a claim in the courts of the importer's home country. Finally, the exporter must tie up working capital to finance foreign accounts receivable. Borrowing working capital collateralized by foreign receivables is often expensive because it may be difficult for domestically oriented lenders to evaluate the riskiness of a firm's portfolio of foreign receivables. Such borrowing is not impossible, however. Numerous firms engage in a specialized international lending activity called **factoring,** in which they buy foreign accounts receivable at a discount from face value. The size of the fees these firms charge (in the form of the discount from face value of the receivables) reflects both the time value of money and the factor's assessment of the portfolio's riskiness.

As a result, an open account is best suited for dealing with well-established, long-term customers or larger firms with impeccable credit ratings and reputations for timely payment of their bills. For example, U.S. restaurant suppliers that deal with McDonald's in the United States on an open account basis might offer the same arrangement to McDonald's subsidiary in the United Kingdom, particularly if McDonald's pledged to honor its subsidiary's trade obligations. Similarly, foreign subsidiaries owned by a common parent corporation often deal with each other on an open account basis because the risk of default in such circumstances is minimal. About 40 percent of U.S. international trade involves transactions between subsidiaries of a parent firm.[5]

Payment in advance and an open account share a basic similarity. Both shift the cash flow burden and risk of default to one party in the transaction: to the buyer in the case of payment in advance and to the seller in the case of an open account.

DOCUMENTARY COLLECTION To get around the cash flow and risk problems caused by the use of payment in advance and open accounts, international businesses and banks have developed

FIGURE 18.1

Using a Sight Draft

Note: In the case of a time draft, the importer makes a promise to pay, not the actual payment, in step 5.

Source: Based on *Dynamics of Trade Finance*, Chase Manhattan Bank, 1989, p. 42.

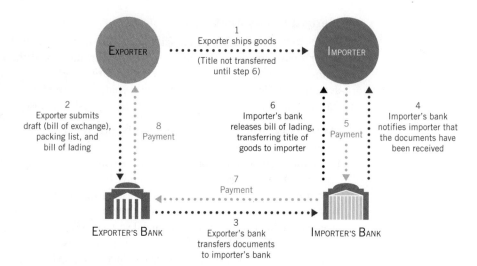

several other methods to finance transactions. One is **documentary collection,** whereby commercial banks serve as agents to facilitate the payment process. To initiate this method of payment, the exporter draws up a document called a **draft** (often called a *bill of exchange* outside the United States), in which payment is demanded from the buyer at a specified time. After the exporter ships its goods, it submits to its local banker the draft and appropriate shipping documents, such as the packing list and the bill of lading.[6] The **bill of lading** plays two important roles in documentary collection: It serves both as a contract for transportation between the exporter and the carrier and as a title to the goods in question. Acting on the exporter's instructions, the exporter's bank then contacts its correspondent bank in the importer's country (or one of its own branches there, if it has any). The latter bank is authorized to release the bill of lading, thereby transferring title of the goods, when the importer honors the terms of the exporter's draft.[7] This process is shown in Figure 18.1.

There are two major forms of drafts:

1. A **sight draft** requires payment upon the transfer of title to the goods from the exporter to the importer. When the bank in the importer's country receives the bill of lading and the sight draft from the exporter's bank, it notifies the importer, which then pays the draft. On payment the bank gives the bill of lading to the importer, which then can take title to the goods.
2. A **time draft** extends credit to the importer by requiring payment at some specified time, such as 30 or 60 days, after the importer receives the goods. (A variant of the time draft, the **date draft,** specifies a particular date on which payment will be made.)

To obtain title to the goods when a time draft is used, the importer must write "accepted" on the draft, thereby incurring a legal obligation to pay the draft when it comes due. An accepted time draft is called a **trade acceptance,** which under the laws of most countries is a legally enforceable and negotiable debt instrument. For a fee the importer's bank also may accept a time draft, thereby adding its own obligation to pay the draft to the importer's obligation. In this case the time draft becomes a **banker's acceptance.**

The exporter may hold either a trade acceptance or a banker's acceptance until it comes due. However, banks and other commercial lenders often are willing to buy acceptances at a discount, thereby allowing the exporter to receive immediate cash. Some acceptances are sold **without recourse,** meaning the buyer of the acceptance is stuck with the loss if the importer does not pay. Others are sold **with recourse,** meaning the exporter will have to reimburse the buyer of the acceptance in the case of nonpayment by the importer. Exporters planning to sell their accepted time drafts must balance the prices they will receive for the drafts against the additional banking fees they must pay (in the case of banker's acceptances) and the degree of risk they are willing to bear (in the case of acceptances sold with recourse). Because of their greater riskiness, acceptances sold without recourse are sold at bigger discounts from face value than acceptances sold with recourse. Similarly, because banker's acceptances are guaranteed by the bank as well as by the importer, they are less risky and usually are discounted less than trade acceptances are.

For an exporter, payment through documentary collection has several advantages over the use of open accounts. First, the bank fees for documentary collection are quite reasonable because the banks act as agents rather than risk takers (except in the case of a banker's acceptance). The typical fees charged the exporter and the importer by a large international bank might range from $75 to $150 each.[8] Second, a trade acceptance or a banker's acceptance is an enforceable debt instrument under the laws of most countries, thereby solidifying the exporter's legal position if the importer defaults on its promise to pay. Third, using banks simplifies the collection process for the exporter and substitutes the banks' superior expertise in effecting international payments for the exporter's presumably inferior knowledge. Further, because the collection agent is a local bank, and the importer does not want to jeopardize its business reputation with a local lender, the importer is more likely to pay a time draft promptly than an invoice sent under an open account. Finally, because of the enforceability of acceptances in courts of law, arranging financing for foreign accounts receivable is easier and less expensive when documentary collection is used than when open accounts are used.

With documentary collection the exporter still bears some risks, however. Suppose local business conditions change or the importer finds a cheaper supply source. In such a case, an importer may simply refuse the shipment and decline to accept the draft, perhaps under a false pretext that the shipment was late or the goods improperly packed. The importer's default on the sales contract places the exporter in the unenviable position of having its goods piled up on a foreign loading dock (and running up storage fees known as *demurrage*) while receiving no payment for them. Alternatively, the importer may default on the time draft when it comes due. The exporter may have legal remedies in either case, but pursuing them is often costly in terms of time, energy, and money.

LETTERS OF CREDIT To avoid such difficulties, exporters often request payment using a **letter of credit,** a document that is issued by a bank and contains its promise to pay the exporter on receiving proof that the exporter has fulfilled all requirements specified in the document. Because of the bank's pledge, the exporter bears less risk by using a letter of credit than by relying on documentary collection. However, cautious bankers are unlikely to issue a letter of credit unless they fully expect the importer to reimburse them. Thus, using a letter of credit has the additional advantage that the exporter benefits from the bank's knowledge of the importer's creditworthiness, the requirements of the importer's home country customs service, and any restrictions the importer's home country government imposes on currency movements.

Usually, an importer applies to its local bank—in most cases, one with which it has an ongoing relationship—for a letter of credit. The bank then assesses the importer's creditworthiness, examines the proposed transaction, determines whether it wants collateral, and, assuming everything is in order, issues the letter of credit. The letter of credit details the conditions under which the importer's bank will pay the exporter for the goods. The conditions imposed by the issuing bank reflect normal sound business practices. Most letters of credit require the exporter to supply an invoice, appropriate customs documents, a bill of lading, a packing list, and proof of insurance. Depending on the product involved, the importer's bank may demand additional documentation before funding the letter, such as the following:

- *Export licenses* are issued by an agency of the exporter's home country. They may be required for politically sensitive goods, such as nuclear fuels, or for high-technology goods that may have military uses.
- *Certificates of product origin* confirm that the goods being shipped were produced in the exporting country. They may be required by the importing country so it can assess tariffs and enforce quotas.
- *Inspection certificates* may be needed to provide assurance that the products have been inspected and conform to relevant standards. For example, imported foodstuffs often must meet rigorous standards regarding pesticide residues, cleanliness, sanitation, and storage.

After issuing the letter of credit, the importer's bank sends it and the accompanying documents to the exporter's bank, which advises the exporter of the terms of the instrument, thereby creating an **advised letter of credit.** The exporter can also request its bank to add its own guarantee of payment to the letter of credit, thereby creating a **confirmed letter of credit.** This type of instrument is particularly appropriate when the exporter is concerned about political risk. If the importer's home country government later imposes currency controls or otherwise blocks payment by the importer's bank, the exporter can look to the confirming bank for payment.

Another type of letter of credit is the **irrevocable letter of credit,** which cannot be altered without the written consent of both the importer and the exporter. A bank may also issue a **revocable letter of credit,** which the bank may alter at any time and for any reason. An irrevocable letter of credit offers the exporter more protection than a revocable letter of credit. However, amending such an instrument can be cumbersome, expensive, and time consuming.

Banks that issue, advise on, and/or confirm letters of credit charge for their services. Typically the issuing bank charges from 0.5 percent to 1.5 percent of the transaction amount for the letter of credit, depending on the importer's creditworthiness. Often the importer and the exporter agree to split this cost between them.[9] When goods are sold under a letter of credit, payment does not depend on meeting the terms of the sales contract between the buyer and seller. Rather, the bank issuing the letter of credit will make payment only when the terms of that letter have been fulfilled. Thus, the exporter must carefully analyze the letter's terms before agreeing to them, to be sure they are compatible with the sales contract.

Surprisingly, it is this feature of letters of credit—that they are paid when their terms are met, not when the sales contract is fulfilled—that makes them so useful in international trade. Once the exporter meets the letter's terms, the importer's bank is obligated to pay the exporter even if the importer refuses the shipment or fails to pay for the goods. Such difficulties become the problem of the importer's bank, not the exporter. However, the likelihood of such difficulties arising are reduced because the importer is unlikely to jeopardize its business reputation or credit lines with its bank. Figure 18.2 shows how a letter of credit is used in a typical international transaction.

Although the issuing bank will not pay the exporter until all the terms of the letter of credit have been met, the exporter can often sell the letter prior to the expected payment date to its bank or another commercial lender at a discount from the face value. The discount will reflect the time value of money, the risk the buyer of the instrument bears if the issuing bank defaults on the transaction, and the buyer's administrative costs. Because confirmed and irrevocable letters of credit reduce the risk of secondary buyers, such letters sell for higher prices (or lower discounts from face value) than do letters of credit without these features. Thus, an exporter planning to sell a letter of credit prior to delivery must trade off the inconvenience or higher fees paid for these less risky types against the higher prices it will receive from secondary buyers of them.

CREDIT CARDS For small international transactions, particularly those between international merchants and foreign retail customers, credit cards such as American Express, VISA, and MasterCard may be used. A firm may tap into the well-established credit card network to facilitate international transactions, subject to the normal limitations of these cards. The credit card

FIGURE 18.2
Using a Letter of Credit

Source: Based on *Dynamics of Trade Finance,* Chase Manhattan Bank, 1989, pp. 62–63.

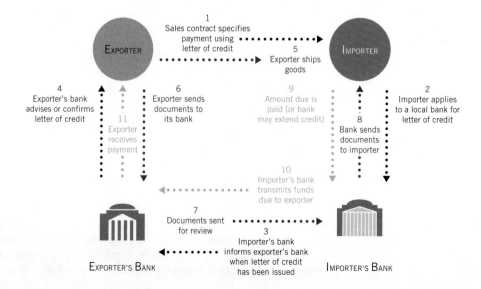

companies collect transaction fees (usually 2 to 4 percent) from the merchant and in return assume the costs of collecting the funds from the customer and any risks of nonpayment. The companies typically charge an additional 1 to 3 percent for converting currencies. However, they offer exporters and importers none of the help banks do in dealing with the paperwork and documentation requirements of international trade.

COUNTERTRADE An additional method used for payment in international transactions is countertrade. **Countertrade** occurs when a firm accepts something other than money as payment for its goods or services. Forms of countertrade include barter, counterpurchase, buy-back, and offset purchase.

The simplest form of countertrade is **barter,** in which each party simultaneously swaps its products for the products of the other. In the late 1990s, for instance, the State Trading Corporation of India agreed to exchange wheat and other grains to Turkmenistan in return for cotton. Similarly, Azerbaijan agreed to import 100,000 tons of wheat from Romania, following a poor harvest in Azerbaijan and a bumper crop in Romania. Payment by Azerbaijan was in the form of crude oil.

A more sophisticated form of countertrade is **counterpurchase,** whereby one firm sells its products to another at one point in time and is compensated in the form of the other's products at some future time. Counterpurchase is the most common form of countertrade. It is sometimes called **parallel barter,** because it disconnects the timing of contract performance by the participating parties. In this way, one part of the transaction can go ahead even if the second requires more time. Boeing, for example, has used counterpurchase to sell aircraft to Saudi Arabia in return for oil and to India in return for coffee, rice, castor oil, and other goods.

Another variant of countertrade involves **buy-back,** or compensation arrangements whereby one firm sells capital goods to a second firm and is compensated in the form of output generated as a result of their use. For example, Japan's Fukusuke Corporation sold 10 knitting machines and raw materials to Chinatex, a Shanghai-based clothing manufacturer, in exchange for 1 million pairs of underwear to be produced on the knitting machines.[10] Similarly, Internationale Vine of Latvia agreed to buy equipment for producing apple juice concentrate from PKL of Switzerland and to pay for the equipment with output from the machinery. Because it links payment with output from the purchased goods, a buy-back is particularly useful when the buyer of the goods

Countertrade occurs when a firm accepts something other than money as payment for its products. For example, Turkmenistan sent cotton from this and other factories in Ashgabat to the State Trading Corporation in India in exchange for Indian wheat.

A3116 Tim Brakemeier Deutsche Presse-Agentur/Newscom

needs to ensure the exporter will provide necessary after-sale services such as equipment repairs or instructions on how to use the equipment.[11]

Another important type of countertrade involves **offset purchases,** whereby part of the cost of an exported good is offset by production in the importing country. Offset arrangements are particularly important in sales to foreign governments of expensive military equipment such as fighter jets or tanks. For instance, for a defense contract greater than $10 million, the United Arab Emirates requires the seller to establish joint ventures with local companies that will cumulatively generate profits to offset 60 percent of the contract's cost within seven years.[12] Similarly, export sales of the new American F-35 Joint Strike Fighter have been boosted by offset arrangements. A Fiat subsidiary is responsible for production of the aircraft's turbine motor, while BAE, the British aerospace giant, is manufacturing its tail section.[13] Balancing export sales and counterpurchase obligations on a deal-by-deal basis is often cumbersome. To facilitate countertrade, firms may agree to establish **clearinghouse accounts,** in which the exporting firm incurs a counterpurchase obligation of an equivalent value, which is recorded in its clearinghouse account. When the exporting firm eventually buys goods from its partner, its clearinghouse obligation is reduced. Thus, a firm does not need to balance any single countertrade transaction, although it must honor its cumulative set of obligations by the time its clearinghouse account expires.

Sometimes firms enter into countertrade agreements to expand their international sales, without having experience in or desire to engage in countertrade. In this case countertrade agreements often permit the use of **switching arrangements,** whereby countertrade obligations are transferred from one firm to another. A variety of consulting firms, many headquartered in either London (because of access to capital markets) or Vienna (because of access to the former communist countries), is available to provide financing, marketing, and legal services needed by international businesses engaging in switching arrangements.[14] Japan's soga shosha (large trading companies discussed in Chapter 12) are particularly skillful in the use of switching arrangements and clearinghouse accounts because of the soga shosha's extensive worldwide operations. A soga shosha might assist in the sale of Mitsubishi trucks in Ghana, taking payment in cocoa, which then can be sold to keiretsu-linked food processors back in Japan or to independent candy makers anywhere in the world.[15]

Some firms specialize in exploiting countertrade opportunities by constructing complicated multiple-market trades as part of the firms' normal business. Consider, for example, Marc Rich & Co., which did over $3 billion in business annually in the former Soviet Union. (Marc Rich & Co. later morphed into Swiss-headquartered Glencore International plc, a leading multinational commodities trading and mining conglomerate.) Soon after the Soviet Union broke up in the early 1990s, the firm engineered a complicated deal among several cash-poor countries that began with its buying 70,000 tons of Brazilian raw sugar on the open market (see Map 18.1). It then hired a

MAP 18.1

Countertrade by Marc Rich

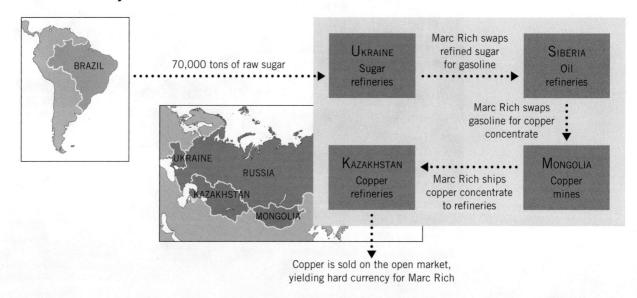

Copper is sold on the open market,
yielding hard currency for Marc Rich

Ukrainian firm to refine the sugar and paid the refinery with part of the sugar. Next, it swapped the rest of the refined sugar to oil refineries in Siberia, which needed the sugar for their workers, in return for gasoline. It then swapped 130,000 tons of gasoline to Mongolia in return for 35,000 tons of copper concentrate. The copper concentrate was shipped to copper refineries in Kazakhstan, which received payment in kind. The refined copper then was sold on the world market. At that point, Marc Rich—after several months of efforts—was able to extract its profits on these countertrades in the form of hard currency.[16]

Informed estimates suggest countertrade accounts for 15 to 20 percent of world trade, although some published reports claim the proportion approaches 40 percent.[17] Countertrade is of particular importance to countries that lack a convertible currency and is often used as a means of reducing the drain on scarce holdings of convertible foreign currencies. The former Soviet Union, for example, was a major countertrade user. Often goods were traded between the Soviet Union and its former allies using clearinghouse accounts. The former communist countries also engaged in countertrade with capitalist countries. Moreover, when countries are gripped by financial crisis, countertrade may be used as a last resort. In 2002, for example, Argentina's economy was devastated by a series of financial problems. To keep its local auto business afloat, DaimlerChrysler announced it would accept harvested grain in payment from its Argentine customers.[18]

Table 18.1 summarizes the benefits and costs of the various methods of payment. Techniques that reduce risk for the exporter generally are more expensive. Thus, the exporter

TABLE 18.1   Payment Methods for International Trade

Method	Timing of Payment	Timing of Delivery of Goods	Risk(s) for Exporter	Risk(s) for Importer	Availability of Financing for Exporter	Condition(s) Favoring Use
Payment in advance	Prior to delivery of goods	After payment, when goods arrive in importer's country	None	Exporter may fail to deliver goods	N/A	Exporter has strong bargaining power; importer unknown to exporter
Open account	According to credit terms offered by exporter	When goods arrive in importer's country	Importer may fail to pay account balance	None	Yes, by factoring of accounts receivable	Exporter has complete trust in importer; exporter and importer are part of the same corporate family
Documentary collection	At delivery if sight draft is used; at specified later time if time draft is used	Upon payment if sight draft is used; upon acceptance if time draft is used	Importer may default or fail to accept draft	None	Yes, by discounting draft from its face value	Exporter trusts importer to pay as specified; when risk of default is low
Letter of credit	After terms of letter are fulfilled	According to terms of sales contract and letter of credit	Issuing bank may default; documents may not be prepared correctly	Exporter may honor terms of letter of credit but not terms of sales contract	Yes, by discounting letter from its face value	Exporter lacks knowledge of importer; importer has good credit with local bank
Credit card	According to normal credit card company procedures	When goods arrive in importer's country	None	Exporter fails to deliver goods	N/A	Transaction size is small
Countertrade	When exporter sells countertraded goods	When goods arrive in importer's country	Exporter may not be able to sell countertraded goods	None	No	Importer lacks convertible currency; importer or exporter wants access to foreign distribution network

must decide how much risk it is willing to bear. In dealing with a new and unknown customer, an exporter may choose a safer but more expensive means of securing payment. In dealing with well-established clients, less expensive but riskier payment methods may be acceptable.

Financing Trade

Financing terms are often important in closing an international sale. In most industries standard financing arrangements exist, and an international firm must be ready to offer those terms to its foreign customers. Depending on the product, industry practice may be to offer the buyer 30 to 180 days to pay after receipt of an invoice. For the sale of complex products such as commercial aircraft, which will be delivered several years in the future, the payment terms may be much more complicated. They may include down payments, penalty payments for cancellation or late delivery, inflation clauses, and concessionary interest rates for long-term financing. In many emerging markets, capital markets are often not well developed, and local lenders may charge extremely high interest rates, especially to smaller borrowers. Thus, exporters with access to low-cost capital can gain a competitive advantage by offering financing to foreign customers who lack access to cheaper financing. Of course, by acting as a lender, the exporter increases the risk of not being paid for its goods. Before deciding to extend credit, the exporter must examine the trade-off between the benefits of increased sales and the higher risks of default.

As noted earlier in this chapter, banks and other commercial lenders often are willing to finance accounts receivable of exporters by purchasing letters of credit or time drafts or factoring open accounts at a discount from face value. Many developed countries supplement the services of these commercial lenders with government-supported financing programs to promote exports. For example, the Export-Import Bank of the United States (Eximbank) offers a working capital guarantee loan program to encourage U.S. exports. Under this program, commercial loans made to finance exportable inventory and foreign accounts receivable will be reimbursed 90 percent if the importer defaults on its obligations. Eximbank activities aided $24.5 billion of exports in 2010. Eximbank has made a special effort to serve the needs of small businesses; in 2010, it provided $5 billion of support for U.S. small businesses exports.[19] Eximbank also offers medium-term loan guarantees (up to 7 years' duration) and long-term guarantees (more than 10 years' duration) for telecommunications, electrical generation, and transportation infrastructure projects.

Managing Foreign Exchange Risk

By using contracts denominated in a foreign currency, Singapore Airlines and other firms that conduct international business are exposed to the risk that exchange rate fluctuations may affect the firms adversely. Experts have identified three types of foreign-exchange exposure confronting international firms: transaction, translation, and economic.

Transaction Exposure

A firm faces **transaction exposure** when the financial benefits and costs of an international transaction can be affected by exchange rate movements that occur after the firm is legally obligated to complete the transaction. Many typical international business transactions denominated in a foreign currency can lead to transaction exposure, including the following:

- Purchase of goods, services, or assets
- Sales of goods, services, or assets
- Extension of credit
- Borrowing of money

Suppose that Saks Fifth Avenue, in order to meet its Christmas needs, agrees on April 10 to buy 5 million Swiss francs' worth of Rolex watches from Rolex's Swiss manufacturer, payable upon delivery on October 10. Saks now faces the risk that exchange rate fluctuations will raise the cost of the watches denominated in its home currency—in this case, U.S. dollars—by the time the transaction is completed on October 10. (Of course, exchange rate movements could lower its costs.) Saks could avoid this risk by contracting in dollars, but then Rolex would face transaction exposure. In most international transactions, one of the parties has to bear transaction exposure.

Saks has several options for responding to this transaction exposure, which we will discuss next. In particular it can

- Go naked
- Buy Swiss francs forward
- Buy Swiss franc currency options
- Acquire an offsetting asset

GO NAKED Saks can ignore the transaction exposure and deliberately assume the foreign-exchange risk by choosing to buy the necessary Swiss francs on October 10 when it needs to pay for the watches. By doing so, Saks is betting that the U.S. dollar will rise in value relative to the franc between April and October. This approach has several advantages. First, Saks does not have to tie up any capital in April for the transaction because its only obligation is to pay 5 million Swiss francs on October 10. Second, Saks can benefit from any appreciation of the U.S. dollar versus the Swiss franc. If this happens, Saks can pay its bill on October 10 using fewer dollars than it otherwise would have used. This advantage, of course, can turn sour if the dollar falls relative to the franc. In this unfortunate circumstance, Saks would be forced to pay more U.S. dollars for the watches than it had anticipated. By going naked, however, Saks avoids paying fees to any intermediaries, an expense it would incur if it adopted any of the three other strategies, discussed next.

BUY SWISS FRANCS FORWARD Saks has several ways of avoiding the transaction exposure if it wants. For example, it could buy Swiss francs forward in the foreign-exchange market for delivery on October 10, thereby locking in the price in April that it will pay for the 5 million francs in October. This strategy has two advantages. First, Saks guarantees the dollar price it will pay for the imported watches and protects itself from declines in the value of the dollar. Second, it ties up none of its capital until it receives the goods because its only agreement is to buy the currency on October 10 and pay Rolex the 5 million francs on delivery of the watches. On the other hand, with this strategy Saks will miss the opportunity to benefit from any appreciation of the U.S. dollar relative to the Swiss franc. It also will bear some transaction costs in the form of fees and markups charged by the bank through which Saks buys the forward Swiss francs.

A variant of this approach is for Saks to purchase Swiss franc currency futures, as discussed in Chapter 8. Whether the firm chooses to buy currency futures or use the forward market depends on the price of francs in these two markets as well as the relative transaction costs of using the two markets.

BUY SWISS FRANC CURRENCY OPTIONS Alternatively, Saks could acquire a currency options contract allowing it to buy 5 million Swiss francs in October. As discussed in Chapter 8, the purchase of an options contract gives the buyer the opportunity, but not the obligation, to buy a certain currency at a given price in the future. By buying an option, Saks can guarantee it will pay no more for its francs than the price stated in its options contract. When payment for the watches is due in October, Saks can exercise the option if the U.S. dollar has declined in value relative to the franc or let the option expire if the U.S. dollar has increased in value—hence, the advantage of an options contract over a forward contract or a futures contract.

Saks is equally protected against depreciation of the dollar by all three types of foreign-exchange transactions; however, it can benefit from an appreciation of the U.S. dollar with an options contract (by letting it expire unused) but not with a forward or a futures contract. The options contract's disadvantage is that it is more expensive than other hedging techniques. Options typically cost from 3.0 to 5.5 percent of the transaction's total value. Accordingly, some multinational corporations (MNCs), such as Merck, prefer currency options to currency futures or forward contracts when hedging their transaction risk because of the "heads I win, tails I don't lose" feature of options. Other MNCs find options too expensive relative to their expected benefit.[20]

ACQUIRE AN OFFSETTING ASSET Another option for Saks is to neutralize its liability of 5 million Swiss francs pending on October 10 by acquiring an offsetting asset of equivalent size denominated in Swiss francs. For example, suppose the interest rate in April on a six-month certificate of deposit (CD) in Switzerland is 8 percent annually (4 percent for six months). By purchasing a six-month CD in April from a Swiss bank such as Credit Suisse for 4,807,692 francs, Saks will receive 5 million francs (4,807,692 × 1.04) in October when its payment obligation to Rolex comes due. By matching its assets denominated in francs with its liabilities denominated in francs, Saks will suffer no net transaction exposure. The disadvantage of this approach is that Saks has to tie up some of its capital in a Swiss bank until October. Saks will earn interest on the Swiss CD, but it may have been able to earn a higher rate of return if it utilized its capital elsewhere.

Of course, if Saks (or a member of its corporate family) already had an existing franc-denominated CD or receivable due in October, Saks could have used that asset to offset its pending franc-denominated liability to Rolex. Suppose, for example, Saks had licensed a Swiss T-shirt manufacturer to use the Saks logo on its shirts. If Saks expected to receive 5 million Swiss francs in royalties in October from the licensing deal, it could have offset those funds against its October liability to Rolex in order to neutralize its transaction exposure, rather than buying the Swiss CD. If the licensing deal were to yield only 2 million Swiss francs instead of 5 million, Saks could still pair up the two transactions. To eliminate its exposure totally, Saks would then need to cover its *net* transaction exposure of 3 million francs using one of the means just discussed.

Table 18.2 summarizes the benefits and costs of these different techniques available to manage transaction exposure. Unfortunately, in many developing markets these techniques are unavailable or very expensive to utilize. As a result, many companies operating in such economies choose to go naked. A survey conducted by Goldman Sachs of large Indonesian companies with large foreign debts suggested that half of them went naked (i.e., did not hedge these debts), and most of the rest hedged only a small portion of their foreign debts. No doubt the cost of hedging played an important role in their behavior. Consider the case of one Indonesian company that did hedge, Indo-Rama Synthetics. In 1997, just before the Asian currency crisis struck, it borrowed $175 million from a consortium of foreign lenders, payable over a five-year period, to finance an expansion of its operations. Indo-Rama paid a premium of about 10 percent of the face value of the loan to lock in an exchange rate of 2,650 rupiah per dollar for its loan repayments. In hindsight this turned out to be a very fortunate move because within a year the rupiah had fallen in value by over 70 percent against the dollar. Many of Indo-Rama's compatriots, such as Astra International (discussed in Chapter 7), were not so farsighted—or perhaps were unwilling at the time to pay the 10 percent premium to lock in a forward rate for repayment of their debts. There is little doubt that the 1997–1998 Asian currency crisis was worsened by the failure of many Asian firms to manage their transaction exposure effectively.[21]

TABLE 18.2 Strategies for Managing Transaction Exposure

Strategy	Benefit(s)	Cost(s)
Go naked	No capital outlay; potential for capital gain if home currency rises in value	Potential for capital loss if home currency falls in value
Buy forward currency	Elimination of transaction exposure; flexibility in size and timing of contract	Fees to banks; lost opportunity for capital gain if home currency rises in value
Buy currency future	Elimination of transaction exposure; ease and relative inexpensiveness of futures contract	Small brokerage fee; inflexibility in size and timing of contract; lost opportunity for capital gain if home currency rises in value
Buy currency option	Elimination of transaction exposure; potential for capital gain if home currency rises in value	Premium paid up front for option because of its "heads I win, tails I don't lose" nature; inflexibility in size and timing of option
Acquire offsetting asset	Elimination of transaction exposure	Effort or expense of arranging offsetting transaction; lost opportunity for capital gain if home currency rises in value

Translation Exposure

As part of reporting its operating results to its shareholders, a firm must integrate the financial statements of its subsidiaries into a set of consolidated financial statements. Problems can arise, however, when the financial statements of a foreign subsidiary are denominated in a foreign currency rather than the firm's home currency. **Translation exposure** is the impact on the firm's consolidated financial statements of fluctuations in exchange rates that change the value of foreign subsidiaries as measured in the parent's currency. If exchange rates were fixed, translation exposure would not exist. (Because translation exposure develops from the need to consolidate financial statements into a common currency, it is often called *accounting exposure*.)

Consider this simple example of translation exposure. Suppose GM transfers $20 million to Barclays Bank to open an account for a new British distribution subsidiary, General Motors Import & Distribution Company Ltd., so the subsidiary can begin operations. Further assume that the exchange rate on the day of the transfer is £1 = $2.00. Thus, the subsidiary's sole asset is a bank account containing £10 million. If the value of the dollar were to rise to £1 = $1.95, the subsidiary still would have £10 million. However, when GM's accountants prepare the firm's consolidated financial statements, its investment in the British subsidiary would be worth only $19,500,000 (10 million pounds × $1.95). GM thus would suffer a translation loss of $500,000 ($20,000,000 − $19,500,000).

Financial officers can reduce their firm's translation exposure through the use of a balance sheet hedge. A **balance sheet hedge** is created when an international firm matches its assets denominated in a given currency with its liabilities denominated in that same currency. This balancing occurs on a currency-by-currency basis, not on a subsidiary-by-subsidiary basis. For example, Georgia-based AFLAC Inc. is the largest foreign provider of supplemental insurance in Japan. To protect its $8.8-billion net investment in Japan from translation exposure, the company utilizes a two-pronged balance sheet hedge. Its Japanese insurance subsidiary owns $5.6 billion of U.S. dollar-denominated securities. To finance its other operations, the parent corporation borrowed $1.0 billion worth of yen from Japanese banks. Through these transactions, only a net $2.2 billion of AFLAC's assets are vulnerable to translation exposure should the yen fall in value.[22] The Walt Disney Company, Pfizer, Procter & Gamble, and McDonald's follow similar strategies to reduce their translation exposure.[23]

A controversy exists among financial experts over whether or not firms should protect themselves from translation exposure. Some experts believe managers should ignore translation exposure and instead focus on reducing transaction exposure, arguing that transaction exposure can produce true cash losses to the firm, whereas translation exposure produces only paper, or

As if it didn't have enough problems educating consumers about its company's insurance products, the AFLAC duck also has to worry about translation exposure. Because the majority of AFLAC's revenues, assets, and profits are generated by its Japanese subsidiary, AFLAC's corporate treasurer manages the company's exposure to changes in the yen–dollar exchange rate by using a balance sheet hedge.

PRNewsFoto/Aflac Incorporated

accounting, losses. Other experts disagree, stating that translation exposure should not be ignored. For instance, firms forced to take write-downs of the value of their foreign subsidiaries may trigger default clauses in their loan contracts if their debt-to-equity ratios rise too high. Further, in AFLAC's case its Japanese operations are so large relative to the rest of the company—75 percent of its premium income is generated there—that the company feels compelled to manage its translation exposure.

Economic Exposure

The third type of foreign-exchange exposure is **economic exposure,** the impact on the value of a firm's operations of unanticipated exchange rate changes. From a strategic perspective, the threat of economic exposure deserves close attention from the firm's highest policy makers because it affects virtually every area of operations, including global production, marketing, and financial planning. Unanticipated exchange rate fluctuations may affect a firm's overall sales and profitability in numerous markets. In the first half of 2011, for example, the value of the yen and the euro rose relative to the U.S. dollar in world currency markets. Japanese and European exporters to the United States faced the unhappy choice of either raising the prices in dollars that they charged their American customers and seeing their market shares erode or holding the line on the dollar prices they charged their American customers and seeing their profit margins cut.

Long-term investments in property, plant, and equipment are particularly vulnerable to economic exposure, even if they are located in a firm's home country. If the yen continues to rise in value, for instance, Japanese automakers like Toyota and Nissan will discover that their Japanese factories will become less competitive relative to automobile factories located in countries whose currencies are declining in value.

One approach firms can use to address the problem of economic exposure is to utilize an **operational hedge** (or natural hedge) by trying to match their revenues in a given currency with an equivalent flow of costs. Some firms, such as Sony, have tried to cut their economic exposure to exchange rate fluctuations by localizing their manufacturing, research and development, and parts procurement to better match their revenue flows and cost flows by country.[24] Similarly, Japanese auto companies like Toyota and Honda or European manufacturers like BMW and Mercedes-Benz generate enormous revenues denominated in U.S. dollars because of their success in the American market. By assembling vehicles in the United States, they can limit their economic exposure by offsetting their dollar-denominated revenue flows with significant costs denominated in dollars.[25]

As these examples suggest, an important element of managing economic exposure is analyzing likely changes in exchange rates. (Map 18.2 shows exchange rate changes versus the dollar over a four-year period ending in August 2011.) A wide variety of exchange rate experts and expertise is available to assist international businesses in this task. These range from private consultants to the staffs of international banks to the published forecasts of international organizations such as the World Bank and the International Monetary Fund. Exchange rate experts scrutinize many of the factors discussed in Chapter 8. The theory of purchasing power parity, for example, provides guidance regarding long-term trends in exchange rates between countries. In the short term, forward exchange rates have been found to be unbiased predictors of future spot rates. Because of the importance of interest arbitrage in establishing equilibrium exchange rates, experts also may forecast countries' monetary policies to predict future currency values. Balance of payments performance also is useful because it provides insights into whether a country's industries are remaining competitive in world markets and whether foreigners' short-term claims on a country are increasing. Prospects for inflation also are carefully assessed because inflation can affect a country's export prospects, demand for imports, and future interest rates.

Management of Working Capital

Managing foreign-exchange exposure is related to another task that financial officers of international businesses perform—managing working capital, or cash, balances. This task is more complicated for MNCs than for purely domestic firms. An MNC's financial officers must consider the firm's working capital position for each of its foreign subsidiaries and in each currency in which the subsidiaries do business, as well as for the firm as a whole. Singapore Airlines, for

MAP 18.2

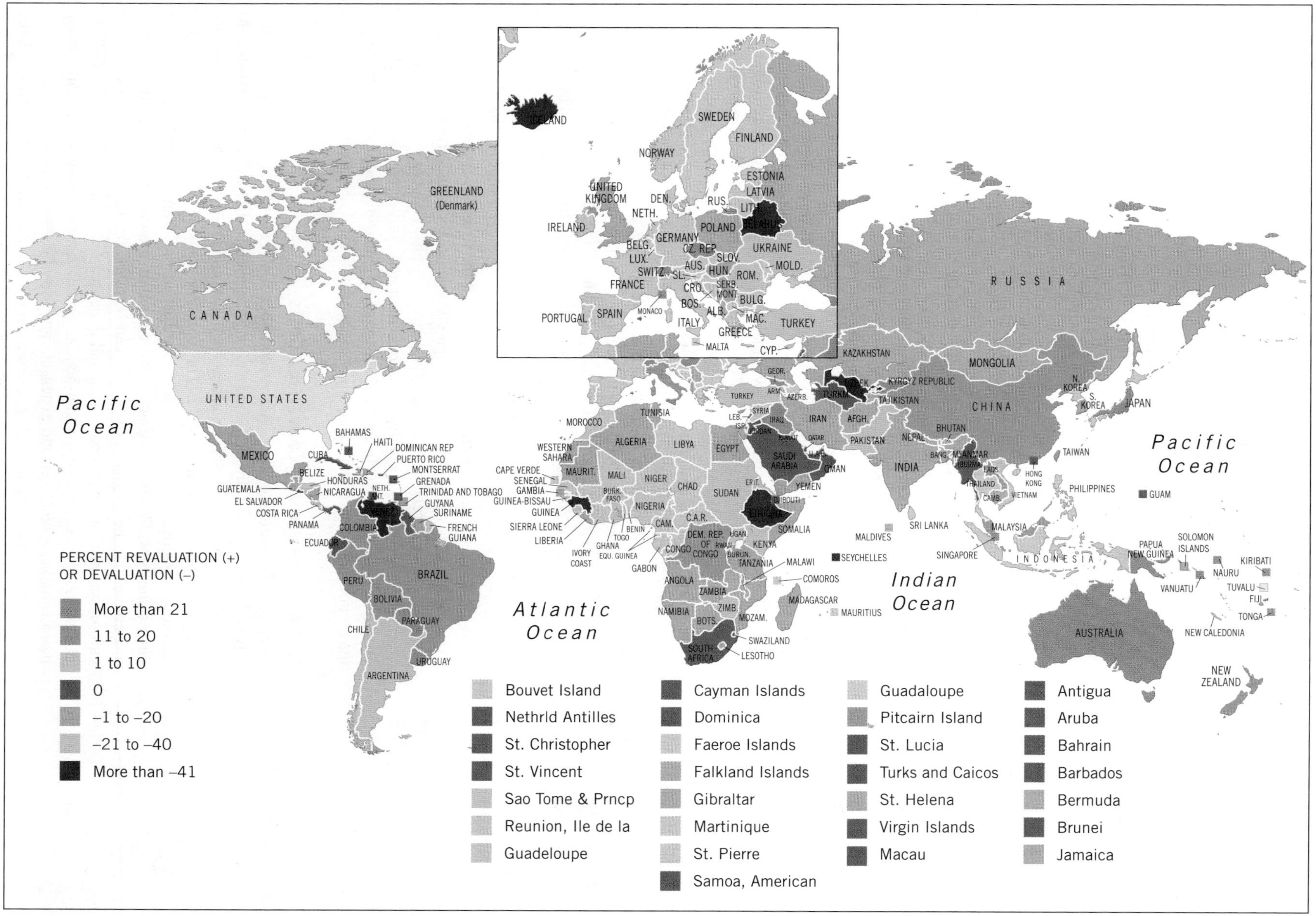

Changes in Currency Values Relative to the U.S. Dollar, August 2011 versus August 2007

instance, routinely uses more than 20 currencies in its operations, and its financial officers must monitor its holdings of each of these currencies. In the process, they must balance three corporate financial goals:

1. Minimizing working capital balances
2. Minimizing currency conversion costs
3. Minimizing foreign-exchange risk

Minimizing Working Capital Balances

Financial officers seek to minimize the firm's working capital balances. Both domestic and international firms must hold working capital for two reasons: to facilitate day-to-day transactions and to cover the firm against unexpected demands for cash. (Note that the term *cash* refers here to actual cash, checking account balances, and highly liquid marketable securities that normally carry low yields.) Obviously, a firm does not want to run out of cash on hand. Failure to have sufficient cash to pay workers or suppliers can lead, at a minimum, to expensive emergency borrowings or, in the worst case, to an embarrassing loss of reputation that may cause suppliers and lenders to cut off future lines of credit. However, the rate of return on working capital is extremely low, and financial officers prefer to capture higher rates of return, if possible, by investing surplus funds in some other form than cash. Thus, they need to balance the firm's needs for cash against the opportunity cost of holding the firm's financial assets in such low-yielding forms.

One technique MNCs can use to minimize their company-wide cash holdings is **centralized cash management.** A centralized cash manager, typically a member of the MNC's corporate treasury staff, coordinates the MNC's worldwide cash flows. Each of the MNC's subsidiaries sends to the centralized cash manager a daily cash report and an analysis of the subsidiary's expected cash balances and needs over the short run, which may range from a week to a month depending on the parent corporation's operating requirements. These reports then are assembled by the centralized cash manager's staff, who uses them to reduce the precautionary balances held by the corporation as a whole and to plan short-term investment and borrowing strategies for the MNC. Instead of each subsidiary holding precautionary, "just in case" cash balances, the staff may direct each subsidiary to send cash in excess of its operational needs to a central corporate bank account. The centralized cash manager will pool these funds, funneling them to subsidiaries when and if emergencies arise. The unexpected need for additional cash by one subsidiary often will be offset by an unexpected excess of cash generated by a second. Thus, the centralized cash manager is able to reduce the precautionary cash balances held by the firm as a whole and thereby reduce the amount of the firm's assets tied up in such a low-yielding form.

Further, the expertise of the centralized cash manager's staff can be used to seek out the best short-term investment opportunities available for the firm's excess cash holdings and to monitor expected changes in the values of foreign currencies. By transferring these tasks from the subsidiaries to the parent corporation, this approach also reduces the number of highly trained, high-salaried financial specialists that the corporate family needs. It is more efficient and cost effective to concentrate such financial information gathering and decision making in one unit of the corporation, rather than compelling each subsidiary to develop such expertise in-house.

Minimizing Currency Conversion Costs

International businesses face another complication. Their foreign subsidiaries may continually buy and sell parts and finished goods among themselves. For example, Samsung, Korea's largest chaebol, has major assembly plants as well as company-owned parts suppliers and distribution companies throughout the world. The constant transfer of parts and finished goods among Samsung subsidiaries generates a blizzard of invoices and a constant need to transfer funds among the subsidiaries' bank accounts. Cumulative bank charges for transferring these funds and converting the currencies involved can be high. For large transactions involving two major currencies, currency conversion fees and expenses may average 0.3 percent of the value of the transaction. For smaller-sized transactions or for transactions involving minor currencies with narrow markets, such fees and expenses can easily be three or four times higher.

Let us consider Samsung's operations in just three countries: Mexico, the United Kingdom, and South Korea. As depicted in Figure 18.3, the gross trade among the firm's subsidiaries in the three countries is $21 million (= 1 + 3 + 6 + 4 + 5 + 2). (We have denominated their trade in

FIGURE 18.3

Payment Flows without Netting

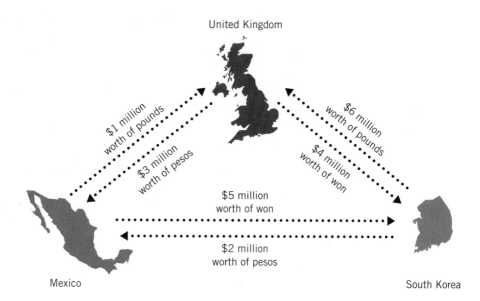

a common currency—U.S. dollars—for simplicity.) If the costs of converting currencies total 0.5 percent of the transactions' value, Samsung would pay 0.5 percent times $21 million, or $105,000, to convert the currencies necessary to settle these transactions among its subsidiaries.

This cost can be cut considerably, however, if the subsidiaries engage in **bilateral netting,** in which two subsidiaries net out their mutual invoices. Consider Samsung's Mexican and British subsidiaries. Rather than have the Mexican subsidiary convert $1 million worth of pesos into pounds and the British subsidiary convert $3 million worth of pounds into pesos, it makes more sense for them to net out the difference. In this case, the British subsidiary simply should pay the Mexican subsidiary $2 million in pesos, making them even. In similar fashion, the South Korean subsidiary can pay the British subsidiary $2 million worth of pounds ($6 million − $4 million = $2 million), and the Mexican subsidiary can pay the Korean subsidiary $3 million worth of Korean won ($5 million − $2 million = $3 million). By engaging in bilateral netting, Samsung reduces its currency conversion costs to $35,000 (0.5 percent × $7 million).

Currency conversion costs can be reduced further if Samsung engages in **multilateral netting,** which is done among three or more business units. As shown in Table 18.3, the British subsidiary owes the equivalent of $7 million to the other two subsidiaries but also is owed $7 million by them. The South Korean subsidiary is owed $9 million but owes $8 million, for a net receipt of $1 million. The Mexican subsidiary is owed $5 million but owes $6 million, for a net debt of $1 million. When accompanied by the appropriate bookkeeping entries, all transactions among the three subsidiaries can be settled by the Mexican subsidiary transferring $1 million worth of won to the South Korean subsidiary. Because only $1 million is being converted physically in the foreign-exchange market and transferred through the banking system, Samsung's conversion costs shrink to $5,000 (0.5 percent * $1 million) as a result of the multilateral netting operation.

TABLE 18.3   Multilateral Netting in Action (all quantities in millions of U.S. dollar equivalents)

		Payments Owed by				
		South Korean Subsidiary	Mexican Subsidiary	British Subsidiary	Total Receipts	Net Transfer
Receipts Due to	South Korean subsidiary	—	5	4	9	+ 1
	Mexican subsidiary	2	—	3	5	− 1
	British subsidiary	6	1	—	7	0
	Total payments	8	6	7	21	

In concept, multilateral netting differs little from what children do on the playground all the time: "David owes Karen a quarter, but Karen owes LaTisha 20 cents, so David owes LaTisha 20 cents and Karen 5 cents, and Karen doesn't owe anyone anything." To complicate matters, however, some countries impose restrictions on netting operations to support their local banking industries, which benefit from the fees charged for currency exchange. MNCs wanting to engage in netting operations often have to work around such government-imposed barriers.

Minimizing Foreign-Exchange Risk

Financial officers also typically adjust the mix of currencies that make up the firm's working capital to minimize foreign-exchange risk. Often firms use a **leads and lags strategy** to try to increase their net holdings of currencies that are expected to rise in value and to decrease their net holdings of currencies that are expected to fall in value. For example, if the Thai baht were expected to decline in value, the financial officers would try to minimize the MNC's baht-denominated liquid assets, perhaps by demanding quicker (or *leading*) payment on baht-denominated accounts receivable or by reducing baht-denominated bank balances. The officers also would try to increase the firm's baht-denominated short-term liabilities, perhaps by slowing (or *lagging*) payment on baht-denominated accounts payable or by increasing short-term borrowing from Thai banks. Conversely, if the Mexican peso were expected to rise in value, the financial officers would try to maximize the firm's net holdings of pesos through reverse techniques.

Avon adopted these tactics as the Asian currency crisis worsened in late 1997. It bought most of the raw materials needed by its Asian factories locally; the working capital needs of these factories were supplied by local banks with the loans repayable in the local currency. Avon thus increased its liabilities denominated in weakened currencies like the Indonesian rupiah, the Malaysian ringgit, and the Philippine peso. Its Asian subsidiaries were required to repatriate their earnings to headquarters on a weekly basis rather than on the monthly basis they had used previously. In this way Avon minimized its holdings of these vulnerable currencies.[26]

In summary, an MNC's financial officers face a complex task. They must ensure each subsidiary maintains sufficient cash balances to meet expected ordinary day-to-day cash outflows, as well as an appropriate level of precautionary balances to respond quickly to sudden, unexpected increases in cash outflow. They also must balance each subsidiary's expected and unexpected demands for cash against the opportunity cost of holding the firm's financial assets in such low-yielding forms, while simultaneously controlling working capital-related currency conversion costs and foreign-exchange risk. Typically, such tasks are performed by a single unit of the firm, such as the treasury department of the parent corporation. For example, Tate & Lyle, a large British food processor, has followed this approach. Its centralized treasury provides cash management, in-house banking, currency conversion, and foreign-exchange risk management services for all of the company's far-flung subsidiaries. Its centralized treasury handles over $6 billion of intracorporate cash flows a year.[27]

International Capital Budgeting

Another task that financial officers of any business face is capital budgeting. Firms have limited funds for investment and often a seemingly endless set of projects from which to choose. Financial officers must establish mechanisms for developing, screening, and selecting projects in which the firm will make significant new investments. Numerous approaches for evaluating investment projects are available, but the most commonly used methods include net present value, internal rate of return, and payback period.

Net Present Value

The net present value approach is based on a basic precept of finance theory that a dollar today is worth more than a dollar in the future. To calculate the net present value of a project, a firm's financial officers estimate the cash flows the project will generate in each time period and then discount them back to the present. For many projects, the cash flow in the early years will be negative because the firm must outlay cash for the initial investment and be prepared to suffer start-up operating losses in the first year or two. In later years, of course, the firm expects cash flows to be positive. Financial officers must decide which interest rate, called the *rate of discount,* to use in the calculation, based on the firm's cost of capital. For example, if the firm's cost of capital is 10 percent, then financial officers will use an annual interest rate of 10 percent to discount the cash flows generated by the project through time in order to calculate the present value. The firm will undertake only projects that generate a positive net present value.

The net present value approach can be used for both domestic and international projects. However, several additional factors must be considered when determining whether to undertake an international project. These factors are risk adjustment, currency selection, and choice of perspective for the calculations.

RISK ADJUSTMENT Because a foreign project may be riskier than a domestic project, international businesses may adjust either the discount rate upward or the expected cash flows downward to account for a higher level of risk. The amount of risk adjustment should reflect the degree of riskiness of operating in the country in question. For example, little if any risk adjustment is needed for Germany because of its political stability, well-respected court system, and superb infrastructure. In contrast, political conflict in Syria and civil war in Libya warrant the use of much larger risk adjustments for potential investments in those countries.

CHOICE OF CURRENCY The determination of the currency in which the project should be evaluated depends on the nature of the investment. If the project is an integral part of the business of an overseas subsidiary, use of the foreign currency is appropriate. For example, GM's German subsidiary Adam Opel AG invested millions of German marks to build a new factory in Eisenach, Germany, in the 1990s. Constructing the plant was central to Opel's overall business plan, and the subsidiary's financial officers thus made the net present value calculation in German marks. For foreign projects that are more properly viewed as integrated parts of a firm's global procurement strategy, translation into the home country currency may make sense. For instance, Hewlett-Packard allocates production between its U.S. and foreign factories as part of an overall strategy of global reduction of production costs. If Hewlett-Packard invests £10 million to expand the output of its Scottish production facilities, it should calculate the project's net present value in U.S. dollars instead of pounds. To do this, it must estimate revenues and costs for the project and then convert them into dollars. It also must account for any expected changes in the exchange rate between the dollar and the pound over the life of the project.

WHOSE PERSPECTIVE: PARENT'S OR PROJECT'S? Another factor is determining whether the cash flows that contribute to the net present value of the capital investment should be evaluated from the perspective of the parent or that of the individual project. In practice, some international businesses analyze the cash flows of the individual project, others focus on the project's impact on the parent, and others do both.[28]

The cash flows to the parent can differ from those to the project for several reasons. MNCs often impose arbitrary accounting charges on the revenues of their operating units for the units' use of corporate trademarks or to cover general corporate overhead. These arbitrary charges may reduce the *perceived* cash flows generated by the project but not the *real* cash flows returned to the parent. For example, suppose that when the corporate parent's accountants are calculating a subsidiary's profitability, they routinely assess a 5 percent fee against revenues for general corporate and administrative expenses. This technique may be a reasonable mechanism for allocating general corporate expenses across all the firm's operations. The 5 percent charge, however, does not represent a true drain on the cash flow generated by the subsidiary. Thus, the charge should be ignored in the calculation of the net present value to the parent of a project the subsidiary proposes. Similarly, fees assessed against the subsidiary for the use of corporate trademarks, brand names, or patents should not be considered in the net present value calculation because the parent firm incurs no additional costs regardless of whether the subsidiary undertakes the project.

Financial officers also must consider any governmental restrictions on currency movements that would affect the firm's ability to repatriate profits when it wants. A project proposed by a foreign subsidiary may be enormously profitable, but if the profits can never be repatriated to the parent, the project may not be desirable from the perspective of the parent and its shareholders. The importance of currency controls in determining the attractiveness of a project also may be a function of the parent's overall strategy. For example, PepsiCo has made a long-term commitment to the Ukrainian soft-drink market. Any current Ukrainian restrictions on profit repatriation are of little concern to PepsiCo and its shareholders because the firm expects to increase its investments in the country in the short and medium term. However, PepsiCo's shareholders would be concerned if the firm were never allowed to repatriate profits from its Ukrainian operations.

Internal Rate of Return

A second approach commonly used for evaluating investment projects is to calculate the internal rate of return. With this approach, financial officers first estimate the cash flows generated by each project under consideration in each time period, as in the net present value analysis. They then calculate the interest rate—called the *internal rate of return*—that makes the net present value of the project just equal to zero. As with the net present value approach, the financial officers must adjust their calculations for any accounting charges that have no cash flow implications (intracorporate licensing fees, overhead charges for general corporate and administrative expenses, and so on). They then compare the project's internal rate of return with the **hurdle rate**—the minimum rate of return the firm finds acceptable for its capital investments. The hurdle rate may vary by country to account for differences in risk. The firm will undertake only projects for which the internal rate of return is higher than the hurdle rate.

Payback Period

A third approach for assessing and selecting projects is to calculate a project's **payback period**—the number of years it will take the firm to recover, or pay back, the original cash investment from the project's earnings. The payback period technique has the virtue of simplicity: All one needs is simple arithmetic to calculate the payback period. This approach ignores, however, the profits generated by the investment in the longer run. A project that earns large early profits but whose later profits diminish steadily over time may be selected over a project that suffers initial start-up losses but makes large continuous profits after that.

Because of its simplicity, many firms use the payback period technique for a quick-and-dirty screening of projects and then follow with a more sophisticated method for further analysis of those projects that pass the preliminary screening.[29] A firm may choose different payback criteria for international projects than for domestic ones. Here too adjustments must be made to eliminate intracorporate charges that have no real effect on corporate cash flows.

Sources of International Investment Capital

Firms use capital budgeting techniques to allocate their financial resources toward those domestic and international projects that promise the highest rates of return. Having identified such profitable opportunities, firms must secure sufficient capital to fund them, from either external or internal sources. In doing so, an international business wants to minimize the worldwide cost of its capital, while also minimizing its foreign-exchange risk, political risk, and global tax burden.

External Sources of Investment Capital

When raising external financing for their investment projects, international businesses may choose from a rich source of debt and equity alternatives. Investment bankers, such as Goldman Sachs, and securities firms, such as Merrill Lynch and Nomura, can help firms acquire capital from external sources. For example, if a firm wants to increase its equity base, such an intermediary can place the firm's stock with investors in the home country, in the host country, or in other countries. To facilitate the raising of equity internationally, many MNCs list their common stock on stock markets in several different countries. For example, Sony's stock is listed on the New York, London, Tokyo, and Osaka stock exchanges. Through multiple foreign listings, international businesses assure foreign investors they can easily dispose of their shares should the need arise.

International firms also have many opportunities to borrow funds internationally on either a short-term or a long-term basis. They may shop for the best credit terms in their home country market, in the host country market, or in other markets. For example, consider New Jersey's Baltek Corporation, which annually produces $30 million worth of balsa wood products at its factory in Ecuador. Baltek relied on local Ecuadorian banks to finance its expansion into shrimp farming in the Gulf of Guayaquil. The firm found those banks more eager for its business than

U.S. banks were—an example of the advantages of being a big fish in a small pond.[30] Larger MNCs may rely on syndicated short- and medium-term loans in which a consortium of international banks and pension fund managers join together to provide the capital. Often these syndicated loans use Eurocurrencies because the absence of expensive central bank regulations reduces the cost of Eurocurrency-based loans. MNCs also may secure longer-term loans in the form of home country bonds, foreign bonds, and Eurobonds, as discussed in Chapter 8.

Securities firms and investment banks are continually developing innovative financing techniques to reduce the costs of borrowing for their MNC clients or to exploit gaps in national financial regulations.[31] For example, an MNC may issue dual-currency bonds, whereby it borrows money and pays interest in one currency but repays the principal in a second currency. Alternatively, bonds may be denominated as a basket of several currencies or be redeemable in gold. Some firms get very creative. For instance, in the early 1990s the Walt Disney Company issued $400 million in Eurobonds that had a different twist: Their interest rate depended on the success of 13 Disney movies. Investors were guaranteed at least a 3 percent rate, with a possible return of 13.5 percent. Comparable quality bonds were yielding only 7 to 8 percent. Eager investors snapped up the bonds, betting that *The Muppet Christmas Carol* and other Disney movies would be box office hits.[32] Pleased with its ability to shift some movie-making risks to the bondholders through low minimum interest rates, several years later Disney offered a similar note linked to a new set of motion pictures.[33]

A particularly important facet of the international capital market is the **swap market,** in which two firms can exchange their financial obligations. Swaps are undertaken to change the cost and nature of a firm's interest obligations or to change the currency in which its debt is denominated. For example, suppose firm A has a fixed-rate obligation but prefers a floating-rate one, whereas firm B has a floating-rate obligation and wants a fixed-rate one. The two firms can swap their obligations. As noted by one financial officer, "The advantage of the swap market is that it allows you to adjust exposure profiles without having to undo the underlying transactions."[34] Often an international bank will facilitate such swaps by acting as a broker or by undertaking half of a swap for its own account.

MNCs also often engage in currency swaps to shift their interest and payment obligations from a less preferred currency to a more preferred one. An MNC may consider its net obligations in one currency to be too large or may expect exchange rate fluctuations to adversely affect its loan repayment costs. A swap may be arranged between two firms that have differing currency preferences. International banks play a key role in the currency swap market. Because they continually monitor foreign-exchange markets as well as their own net currency exposures, they usually can accommodate any MNC's currency swap needs. Most international banks engage in currency swaps with corporate clients on an ongoing basis.

Internal Sources of Investment Capital

Another source of investment capital for international businesses is the cash flows generated internally—for example, profits from operations and noncash expenses such as depreciation and amortization earned by the parent firm and its various subsidiaries. The amount from such sources is significant: In 2008, foreign subsidiaries of U.S.-owned firms earned $956 billion. However, U.S. subsidiaries of foreign-owned parents lost $4 billion in 2008, due in large part to $63 billion in losses suffered by subsidiaries in the financial services industry resulting from the subprime meltdown discussed in Chapter 8's closing case. (In 2007, a more normal year, U.S. subsidiaries of foreign-owned parents earned $115 billion.)[35]

Subject to legal constraints, the parent firm may use the cash flow generated by any subsidiary to fund the investment projects of any member of the corporate family. The corporate parent may access the cash flow directly via the subsidiary's dividend payments to the parent. The parent then can channel those funds to another subsidiary through either a loan or additional equity investments in that subsidiary. Alternatively, one subsidiary can invest in or lend funds directly to a second subsidiary. Figure 18.4 summarizes the various internal sources of capital available to the parent and its subsidiaries.

Two legal constraints may affect the parent's ability to shift funds among its subsidiaries. First, if the subsidiary is not wholly owned by the parent, the parent must respect the rights of the subsidiary's other shareholders. Any intracorporate transfers of funds must be done on a

FIGURE 18.4

Internal Sources of Capital for International Businesses

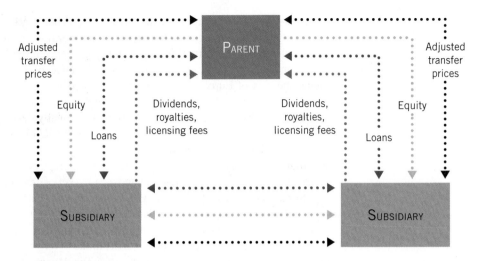

fair-market basis. This ensures that the parent does not siphon off the subsidiary's profits through self-dealing, thereby harming the other shareholders' interests. If the subsidiary is wholly owned, transfers of funds do not raise this issue. Second, some countries impose restrictions on the repatriation of profits, thus blocking their intracorporate transfer.

Strategic Use of Transfer Pricing

A significant percentage of world trade involves transactions between subsidiaries of the same corporation, such as a production subsidiary of Toyota Motor Company selling Lexus sedans made in Japan to Toyota's sales subsidiary in the United States. Intracorporate shipments account for an estimated 40 percent of U.S. international trade in goods, for instance.

A **transfer price** is the price paid for goods and services involved in intracorporate transactions between a subsidiary and other branches of the corporate family. In practice, transfer prices are calculated in one of two ways:

1. Market-based method
2. Nonmarket-based methods

MARKET-BASED TRANSFER PRICES The market-based method utilizes prices determined in the open market to transfer goods between units of the same corporate parent. Suppose Samsung wants to export memory chips from South Korea for use in assembling personal computers at one of its U.S. subsidiaries. It can establish the transfer price for the memory chips between its U.S. and Korean subsidiaries by using the open market price for such chips.

This market-based approach has two main benefits. First, it reduces conflict between the two units over the appropriate price. The higher the price charged in the intracorporate transfer, the better the selling subsidiary's performance appears and the poorer the buying subsidiary's performance appears. To the extent that the parent allocates managerial bonuses or investment capital to its subsidiaries on the basis of profitability, the unit managers have incentives to squabble over the transfer price because they care about how the MNC's accounting system reports their unit's performance. From the parent's perspective, however, such arguments waste firm resources. Once the firm's accounting records are consolidated, its overall before-tax profits will remain the same regardless of whether the transfer price overstates unit A's profitability and understates unit B's, or vice versa. Assuming both subsidiaries recognize the basic fairness of the market-based price, such intracorporate conflict will be reduced.

Second, the market-based approach promotes the MNC's overall profitability by encouraging the efficiency of the selling unit. If the price the unit can charge for intracorporate sales is limited to the market price, its managers know the unit's profitability depends on their ability to control its costs. Moreover, they recognize that if they successfully produce the product in question more cheaply than their international competitors can, the parent's market-based transfer pricing will acknowledge their efforts in full. Motivated by the prospects of bonuses and lucrative promotions, unit managers have every incentive to improve the efficiency and profitability of their operations.

NONMARKET-BASED TRANSFER PRICES Transfer prices also may be established using nonmarket-based methods. Prices may be set by negotiations between the buying and selling units or on the basis of cost-based rules of thumb, such as production costs plus a fixed markup. Some services of the corporate parent may be assessed as a percentage of the subsidiary's sales, such as charges for general corporate overhead and administrative services or for the right to use technology or intellectual property owned by the parent. In 2009, for instance, foreign subsidiaries paid their U.S.-owned parents $55.4 billion in royalties and licensing fees, and U.S. subsidiaries paid their foreign-owned parents $13.8 billion for the same purpose.[36]

MNCs commonly use nonmarket-based prices partly because, for some goods and services, no real market exists outside the firm. For example, the sole market for an engine produced in a Ford factory in Spain may consist of Ford automobile assembly plants in Belgium, Germany, and the United Kingdom. Because no external market exists for this engine, Ford may establish a transfer price for the engine based on production costs plus an allowance for overhead and profit. Similarly, Toyota's ability to design and develop new automobile models is not a service that is bought and sold in the open market. Yet Toyota may want to charge its North American, European, and Australian subsidiaries an appropriate fee for the use of its research, design, and development services.

The use of nonmarket-based prices has both disadvantages and advantages. One disadvantage is that managers of the buying and selling units may waste time and energy arguing over the appropriate transfer price because it will affect their reported profits even though it will have no overall impact on the parent's consolidated before-tax income. Nonmarket-based transfer prices also may reduce the selling unit's efficiency. A transfer price based on the seller's costs plus some markup may reduce the seller's incentive to keep its costs low because it can pass along any cost increases to other members of the corporate family through the nonmarket-based transfer price.

However, strategic use of nonmarket-based transfer prices may benefit an international business, as Table 18.4 shows. Creative rearranging of intracorporate prices may allow the parent to lower its overall tax bill. For example, an MNC can lessen the burden of an ad valorem import tariff by reducing the price the selling unit charges the buying unit, thereby lowering the basis on which the tariff is calculated. Clever structuring of transfer prices can also allow a firm to evade host country restrictions on repatriation of profits. Suppose, for example, that a host country blocks repatriation by forbidding dividend payments from the subsidiary to the parent. The parent can evade this restriction by raising the transfer prices it charges the subsidiary for goods and services produced by other units of the corporate family or by charging fees for general corporate services. By means of this technique cash will flow from the subsidiary to other parts of the

TABLE 18.4   Strategic Use of Nonmarket-Based Transfer Prices

Goal	Technique	Effect
Decrease tariff paid on components imported from a subsidiary	Lower transfer price charged by the subsidiary	Lowering the price on which an ad valorem tariff is based decreases total amount of import tariff
Decrease overall corporate income tax	Raise transfer prices paid by subsidiaries in high-tax countries and/or lower transfer prices charged by those subsidiaries; lower transfer prices paid by subsidiaries in low-tax countries and/or raise transfer prices charged by those subsidiaries	Reported profits of subsidiaries in high-tax countries decrease, and reported profits of subsidiaries in low-tax countries increase; total corporate tax burden decreases
Repatriate profits from a subsidiary located in a host country that blocks repatriation	Raise transfer prices paid by the subsidiary; lower transfer prices charged by the subsidiary	Cash flows from the subsidiary to other units, circumventing restriction on repatriation

firm in the form of payments for goods or services, rather than through the forbidden dividend payments. The net effect is the same, however: Funds (in some form) are repatriated from the host country.

The most significant strategic use of transfer pricing, however, is to reduce a firm's total income tax payments. A firm's transfer prices often reflect a trade-off between tax consequences and legal constraints imposed by countries in which the firm operates. Numerous studies conducted by researchers indicate that MNCs routinely engage in tax-shifting behavior through transfer pricing and other devices.[37] Suppose an MNC operates in two countries, one with high corporate income tax rates and the second with low rates. The firm can raise the transfer prices charged to the subsidiary in the high-tax country and lower those charged to the subsidiary in the low-tax country. Doing this will reduce the profitability of the first subsidiary, as measured by its accounting records, while increasing the profitability of the second. The net effect is to shift the location of the MNC's profits from the high-tax country to the low-tax country, thereby reducing the firm's overall tax burden. Ireland, for example, offers low income tax rates on corporate profits to encourage MNCs to locate factories and service facilities in that country. Yet this tax break also encourages MNCs to manipulate the transfer prices charged by their Irish subsidiaries so as to increase the profits reported by those subsidiaries and lower the profits reported by their non-Irish subsidiaries (see the chapter's closing case, "Double Irish and a Dutch Sandwich").[38] "Venturing Abroad" explores how the U.S. government addresses such tax-shifting behavior.

Although such intracorporate transfers of funds may theoretically benefit the entire firm, they can create serious problems at the subsidiary and managerial levels. From the parent's perspective shifting cash flows to minimize taxes may be beneficial. However, it may cause operational problems and increased expenses for the subsidiary. The parent may consider it wise policy to siphon off the subsidiary's working capital and reduce its reported profitability by inflating royalty fees, administrative charges, or other transfer prices. Yet such approaches may result in a misleading picture of the subsidiary's performance in the marketplace. If the parent rewards managerial performance without making adjustments for these financial manipulations, morale among the subsidiary's managers may plummet, to the detriment of the parent.

VENTURING ABROAD | **TAXATION OF FOREIGN SUBSIDIARY INCOME BY THE U.S. GOVERNMENT**

Subsidiaries incorporated in a foreign country are legally distinct from the home country parent corporation. In general, for U.S. tax purposes, a U.S. parent corporation does not need to include the earnings of its foreign subsidiaries in calculating its taxable income, as long as those earnings are reinvested in the foreign subsidiaries. The **deferral rule** in the U.S. tax code states such earnings will be taxed only when they are remitted to the parent in the form of dividends, thus allowing the parent to defer paying U.S. taxes on foreign subsidiaries' reinvested earnings.

The deferral rule is intended to stimulate international business activity by U.S. firms. Consider Caterpillar. More than half its sales are outside the United States, and the deferral rule, by annually saving it millions of dollars in taxes, has helped it penetrate key markets in Europe and Asia. However, one important exception to the deferral rule ensures that U.S. firms do not establish shell corporations in tax havens that do little but provide the parent with the ability to defer U.S. taxes. U.S. tax law requires a parent corporation to determine whether each of its foreign subsidiaries is a controlled foreign corporation. A **controlled foreign corporation (CFC)** is a foreign corporation in which U.S. shareholders—each of which holds at least 10 percent of the firm's shares—together own a majority of its stock. This definition may seem strange, but it is designed to focus on foreign firms that are controlled by a single U.S. firm or a group of U.S.

firms acting in concert, rather than foreign firms owned by many small U.S. investors.

According to the U.S. tax code, the income of CFCs is divided into two types: active income and passive income (also called Subpart F income). **Active income** is income generated by traditional business operations such as production, marketing, and distribution. **Subpart F income,** or **passive income,** is generated by passive activities such as the collection of dividends, interest, royalties, and licensing fees—the type of activities typically performed by subsidiaries incorporated in tax havens. U.S. firms may defer active income earned by CFCs they control. In calculating their U.S. taxes, however, they generally may not defer Subpart F income. In the absence of this restriction U.S. firms could escape federal corporate income taxes on earnings generated by their intellectual property and investment portfolios. The firms could do this by establishing subsidiaries in tax havens and transferring to those subsidiaries legal title to the firms' trademarks, patents, brand names, and investment portfolios. The U.S. government, by treating active and passive earnings of foreign subsidiaries differently, is walking a fine line between stimulating U.S. firms' international business activities and limiting the firms' ability to avoid U.S. taxes through the creation of subsidiaries in tax havens. Not surprisingly, U.S. companies are continually probing the limits of the law in their attempts to cut their tax bills, as the chapter's closing case, "Double Irish and a Dutch Sandwich," indicates.

SUN, SAND, AND SHELLS

Being a tax haven can create a thriving economy, as the 51,000 residents of the Cayman Islands are well aware. The per capita income of this British Overseas Territory is an estimated $47,000. While the islands' white coral sand beaches and luxurious hotels draw upwards of two million visitors a year, the Caymans are equally attractive to the world's financiers, for its government imposes no income taxes on personal or corporate earnings. Almost 100,000 foreign firms are registered there, outnumbering local citizens by nearly two to one. Many of these registered companies are mere corporate shells, allowing their owners to shift their reported profits to these shells through the artful use of transfer pricing. The Cayman Islands' success as a tax haven reflects the high-quality services it provides to international businesses; an MNC can create and incorporate a Cayman Islands subsidiary within 24 hours if needed.

The firms create demand for highly paid professionals such as accountants, bankers, and lawyers. As a result, the Cayman Islands is a major world banking and finance center. The Cayman Islands are now home to 246 active banks with assets totaling $1.7 trillion, over 700 insurance companies, and 9,000 mutual funds. From the Cayman Islands' perspective the tax-haven sector of the local economy represents the ultimate "clean" industry so beloved by economic development officials. However, the existence of tax havens creates numerous headaches for the taxing authorities of other countries.

Sources: World Factbook found at www.cia.gov; Cayman Islands Monetary Authority website, www.cimoney.com.ky, June 21, 2011; "Generation of huge changes," *Financial Times*, February 2, 2000, p. III.

Tax Havens

The ability of multinational corporations to lower their tax burdens by the strategic use of transfer prices is facilitated by the existence of **tax havens,** countries that impose little or no corporate income taxes. For a relatively small fee an MNC may set up a wholly owned subsidiary in a tax haven. By manipulating payments such as transfer prices, dividends, interest, royalties, and capital gains between its various subsidiaries, an MNC may divert income from subsidiaries in high-tax countries to the subsidiary operating in the tax haven. By booking its profits in the tax haven subsidiary, the MNC escapes the clutches of revenue agents in other countries. For example, an MNC may give ownership of its trademarks to a subsidiary located in Bermuda. That subsidiary then can charge each of the corporation's operating subsidiaries a fee for the use of the trademarks. The fees paid by the operating subsidiaries reduce their profitability and thus the corporate income taxes they must pay to their host governments. The government of Bermuda, however, imposes no income tax on the trademark licensing fees earned by the subsidiary located there—or on income, profits, capital gains, or dividends. Thus, the MNC reduces its overall income tax burden.

Several other smaller countries, including the Cayman Islands (see "Emerging Opportunities" and Map 18.3), the Bahamas, the Channel Islands, Liechtenstein, and the Netherlands Antilles,

While thousands of tourists annually visit the Cayman Islands to sunbathe and collect seashells along its white sandy beaches, the islands also attract companies seeking a different kind of shell. The islands are home to thousands of shell corporations, established to take advantage of the islands' lack of income taxes.

© Danita Delimont/Alamy

MAP 18.3

The Cayman Islands

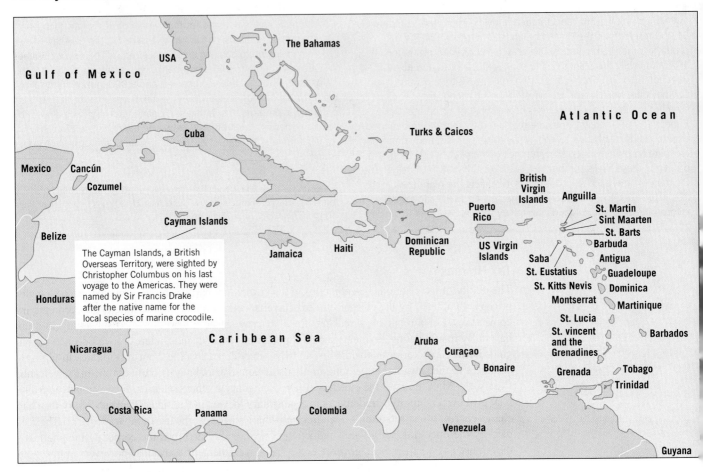

The Cayman Islands, a British Overseas Territory, were sighted by Christopher Columbus on his last voyage to the Americas. They were named by Sir Francis Drake after the native name for the local species of marine crocodile.

also have gone into the business of being tax havens. To attract MNCs, a tax haven must not only refrain from imposing income taxes but also provide a stable political and business climate, an efficient court system, and sophisticated banking and communications industries. In return, the tax haven is able to capture franchising and incorporation fees and generate numerous lucrative professional jobs far beyond what an economy of its size normally could.

Government agencies, such as the U.S. Internal Revenue Service, are well aware of these opportunities to play accounting games. As a result, both home and host countries scrutinize the transfer-pricing policies of MNCs operating within their borders to ensure the firms do not evade their tax obligations and the governments receive their "fair share" of taxes from the firms. A common approach is to use an **arm's length test** whereby government officials attempt to determine the price that two unrelated firms operating at arm's length would have agreed on. In many cases, however, an appropriate arm's length price is difficult to establish, leading to conflict between international businesses and tax authorities. For example, in 1999 the U.K.'s Inland Revenue agency launched a study of whether IBM inappropriately raised the 8 percent royalty rate paid by its British subsidiary to the U.S. parent to 12 percent for a five-year period beginning in 1991. The effect of the increased royalty rate was to shift $260 million of profits from its U.K. operations to its U.S. operations, thus reducing the taxes IBM owed the British government.[39] Of course, determining the appropriate arm's length price for a unique asset like IBM's trademarks and technology is not simple. Similarly, in 2004, the U.S. Internal Revenue Service claimed that British drug company GlaxoSmithKline owed it $2.7 billion, plus interest, alleging that the company overcharged its American subsidiaries for the cost of

R&D done in the United Kingdom.[40] Such conflicts are rarely resolved easily or quickly. To remedy the cost and uncertainty of the resolution of complex transfer pricing conflicts, firms may negotiate an **advance pricing agreement** (APA) with the U.S. Internal Revenue Service. The APA, which represents a binding contract between the firm and the IRS, details the methodology that will be used to establish the firm's transfer prices. The IRS agrees it will not retroactively review or challenge the firm's transfer prices as long as the firm abides by the methodology established in the APA.

MyManagementLab   Now that you have finished this chapter, go back to **www.pearsonglobaleditions.com/mymanagementlab** to continue practicing and applying the concepts you've learned.

CHAPTER REVIEW

Summary

International firms face financial management challenges that are far more complex than those confronting purely domestic firms. Conflicts may arise between exporters and importers over the currency to use in invoicing international transactions. Exporting firms often find it difficult to check the creditworthiness of their foreign customers. Also, obtaining payment for goods from foreign customers may be more difficult because of greater geographic distances, differing legal systems, and unfamiliar business customs. Fortunately, many methods of payment have been developed over the centuries, including payment in advance, open accounts, letters of credit, documentary collection, credit cards, and countertrade.

International firms must strive to minimize the impact of exchange rate fluctuations on the firms' operations. Three main types of exchange rate exposure exist. Transaction exposure refers to the impact of exchange rate fluctuations on the profitability of a business transaction denominated in a foreign currency. Translation exposure reflects the impact of exchange rate fluctuations on the book value of foreign operations in a firm's accounting records. Economic exposure is the impact unanticipated exchange rate movements have on the value of the firm's operations.

Management of working capital balances presents international businesses with unique challenges. A firm and each of its operating subsidiaries must have sufficient cash to facilitate day-to-day operations and to meet unexpected demands for cash. Also, the firm must monitor its holdings of each currency in which it and its subsidiaries do business. MNCs often use centralized cash management and currency netting operations to control their working capital balances, reduce currency conversion costs, and minimize their exposure to adverse changes in exchange rates.

Financial officers of international firms must adjust capital budgeting techniques to meet the unique requirements of international business. Standard investment evaluation techniques, such as net present value, internal rate of return, and payback period analysis, must be changed to account for differences in risk, government restrictions on currency movements, and various payments between the parent firm and its foreign subsidiaries that do not affect net cash flows generated by an investment project.

Finally, financial officers must look worldwide for low-cost sources of capital. Ongoing operations of the parent firm and its foreign subsidiaries are often an important internal source of investment capital. Well-developed international debt and equity markets can provide external sources of such capital. Also, international businesses often use the swap market to reduce their exposure to adverse changes in currency values or interest rates.

Review Questions

1. What special problems arise in financing and arranging payment for international transactions?
2. What are the major methods of payment used for international transactions?
3. What are the different types of letters of credit?
4. How do a time draft and a sight draft differ? How do a trade acceptance and a banker's acceptance differ?
5. How do the various types of countertrade arrangements differ from one another?
6. What techniques are available to reduce transaction exposure? Discuss each.
7. What is translation exposure? What effect does a balance sheet hedge have on translation exposure?
8. Why do MNCs engage in currency netting operations?
9. What capital budgeting techniques are available to international businesses?
10. What is a transfer price? How do firms determine them?

Questions for Discussion

1. What are the advantages and disadvantages of each method of payment for international transactions from the exporter's perspective?
2. Which type of letter of credit is most preferable from the exporter's point of view?
3. Why do firms use countertrade? What problems do they face when they do?
4. How does capital budgeting for international projects differ from that for domestic projects?

5. How can firms use transfer prices and tax havens to reduce their corporate income tax bills? What do governments do in response?
6. Are firms that create shell corporations in tax havens being socially responsible?
7. Why would a firm want to negotiate an Advance Pricing Agreement with the Internal Revenue Service? Why would the Internal Revenue Service want to negotiate an Advance Pricing Agreement?

Building Global Skills

Consider Belgian Lace Products (BLP), a hypothetical table linens manufacturer. BLP consists of a parent corporation, a wholly owned manufacturing subsidiary in Belgium, and four wholly owned distribution subsidiaries in Belgium, the United Kingdom, Japan, and the United States. Its manufacturing subsidiary buys inputs from various suppliers, manufactures high-quality lace napkins and tablecloths, and sells the output to the four BLP-owned distribution subsidiaries. The four distribution subsidiaries in turn sell the products to retail customers in the subsidiaries' marketing areas. The distribution subsidiaries buy certain inputs, such as labor, warehouse space, electricity, and computers, from outside suppliers as well.

The following summarizes typical monthly transactions for each of the BLP operating units (note that the symbol for the euro is €):

Manufacturing Subsidiary

Sales to Belgian distribution subsidiary: €15,000
Sales to British distribution subsidiary: €12,500
Sales to Japanese distribution subsidiary: €17,500
Sales to U.S. distribution subsidiary: €11,250
Costs of inputs purchased from Belgian suppliers: €7,500
Costs of inputs purchased from British suppliers: £25,000
Costs of inputs purchased from Japanese suppliers:
   ¥3,000,000
Costs of inputs purchased from U.S. suppliers: $5,000

Belgian Distribution Subsidiary

Sales to retail customers: €50,000
Payments to BLP manufacturing subsidiary: €15,000
Payments to external suppliers: €750 and £10,000

British Distribution Subsidiary

Sales to retail customers: £75,000
Payments to BLP manufacturing subsidiary: €12,500
Payments to external suppliers: £5,000, €1,000, and $9,000

Japanese Distribution Subsidiary

Sales to retail customers: ¥5,000,000
Payments to BLP manufacturing subsidiary: €17,500
Payments to external suppliers: ¥3,000,000 and $8,000

U.S. Distribution Subsidiary

Sales to retail customers: $40,000
Payments to BLP manufacturing subsidiary: €11,250
Payments to external suppliers: $10,000 and ¥300,000

Exchange Rates

€1.33 = £1
€1 = $1.00
€1 = ¥120

Use the above information to answer the following questions:

1. Calculate the profitability of each of BLP's five subsidiaries. (Because BLP is Belgian, perform the calculations in terms of euros, which Belgium began using as its national currency in 2002.) Are any of the subsidiaries unprofitable? On the basis of the information provided, would you recommend shutting down an unprofitable subsidiary? Why or why not?
2. Suppose it costs each subsidiary 1 percent of the transaction amount each time it converts its home currency into another currency to pay its suppliers. Develop a strategy by which BLP as a corporation can reduce its total currency conversion costs. Suppose your strategy costs BLP 400 euros per month to implement. Should the firm still adopt your approach?
3. If the United Kingdom decided to join the EU's single-currency bloc and use the euro, what effect would this have on BLP? What effect would it have on the benefits and costs of the strategy you developed to reduce BLP's currency conversion costs?

DOUBLE IRISH AND A DUTCH SANDWICH

Note: You may find it helpful to re-read "Venturing Abroad: Taxation of Foreign Subsidiary Income by the U.S. Government" on page 528 and "Emerging Opportunities: Sun, Sand, and Shells" on page 529.

Taxation of business income is always a contentious public policy issue. Firms, tax lawyers, and accountants continually engage in cat-and-mouse clashes with their national tax authorities. The former group strives to minimize the tax burden imposed on their businesses, asserting that they have a fiduciary duty to their shareholders to do so. The latter group responds that they are charged with the task of ensuring that all the taxes owed to the government are appropriately and legally collected. While the battle of wits, lawsuits, and lobbying is intense between domestic firms and domestic tax authorities, it pales in comparison to the company-government wars fought over international taxation.

Most politicians care little about the nuances of the benefits of comparative advantage, the productivity gains generated by specialization of labor, or the deleterious impact of trade barriers. Their concerns are focused on job creation and tax revenue, and they are willing to adjust their national tax codes if doing so stimulates the local economy. The result is wide variations in corporate income taxes among countries. For instance, in the United States the federal corporate income tax rate is 35 percent, while in Canada it is 16.5 percent, but only 12.5 percent in Ireland. In many tax havens, no taxes are imposed on corporate earnings. Another complicating factor is differences in how various types of income are taxed. When taxing dividends, some countries, such as Australia and Mexico, provide dividend tax credits to the shareholder for income taxes paid by the corporation; others, such as the United States and Sweden, do not. Estonia and the Slovak Republic choose not to tax dividend income at all. Ireland offers generous tax credits for research and development expenditures and exemptions for income generated by intellectual property. The effective rate on royalty income imposed by Ireland can be as low as zero, for example.

These variations in tax codes generate opportunities for firms to locate or relocate their economic activities to lower their overall taxation costs. Firms can also creatively fashion the transfer prices they charge for intracorporate transactions. Much of the attention of the world's tax collectors has been focused on so-called tax havens (see "Emerging Opportunities" on page 529). But Ireland has become the new focal point for imaginative structuring of corporate transactions to reduce tax bills. Of the OECD nations, Ireland has been the most aggressive user of its corporate tax code to promote economic development. The Industrial Development Agency Ireland, a governmental agency responsible for promoting inward FDI, believes nearly 1,000 MNCs have located their European headquarters in Ireland, drawn in large part by the country's low taxes and pro-business policies.

Google is one company that has benefitted from Ireland's pro-business tax code. It has taken advantage of two strategies created by international tax lawyers, dubbed the "Double Irish" and the "Dutch Sandwich," which allowed it to reduce its taxes by $3.1 billion over the past three years. In 2006, Google entered into an advance pricing agreement with the U.S. Internal Revenue Service, establishing the terms under which it could transfer its intellectual property to its foreign subsidiaries. After signing the agreement with the U.S. tax authorities, Google licensed its intellectual property to Google Ireland Holdings, a wholly owned subsidiary. While established in Ireland, Google Ireland Holdings is managed in Bermuda, making it a nonresident corporation that is not subject to Irish taxation under Irish law. Google Ireland Holdings, however, is the owner of an Irish resident corporation, Dublin-based Google Ireland Limited— hence, the term "Double Irish." Google Ireland Limited's 2,000 employees sell advertising and provide support services to customers in Europe, the Middle East, and Africa, and account for about 88 percent of Google's non-U.S. revenues. Even though its California engineers and scientists developed most of Google's technology, this arrangement allows Google to avoid immediate U.S. taxation of its non-U.S. profits. That takes care of the U.S. Internal Revenue Service. To avoid Ireland's Revenue Commissioners, Google Ireland Limited then transmits what would appear to be its profits from selling this advertising to another Google subsidiary, Google Netherlands Holdings (the "Dutch sandwich"), in the form of royalty payments, thereby slashing Google Ireland Limited's Irish tax bill. (Payments are made to Google Netherlands Holdings because of favorable provisions in the Irish tax code dealing with royalty payments to companies based in other EU countries.) Google Netherlands Holdings, which has no employees, then remits 99.8 percent of the royalty payments it receives to Google Ireland Holdings, eliminating most of its tax liability to the Netherlands. And, of course, Bermuda has no corporate income tax, so the "profits" earned by Google Ireland Holdings remain untaxed so long as these profits are not repatriated to the parent corporation back in the United States.

Other technology-intensive companies, such as Microsoft and Oracle, have established Irish subsidiaries for similar purposes. A Microsoft subsidiary in Ireland, Round Island One Ltd., "localizes" Microsoft products developed by American employees for the European, African, and Middle Eastern markets. The customized products are then licensed by a Round Island One subsidiary in Ireland, Flat Island Company, to customers in those markets. Earnings from these sales are taxed at Ireland's relatively low 12.5 percent corporate income tax rate. From the U.S. perspective, because the U.S.-developed products undergo transformation in Ireland, Round Island One's earnings are characterized as active income, allowing Microsoft to take advantage of the IRS's deferral rule and avoid U.S. taxation of that income.

Case Questions

1. Why do tax rates and tax treatment of corporate income vary so dramatically among countries?
2. Explain the use of the Double Irish and the Dutch Sandwich by Google.
3. How important is the advance pricing agreement that Google negotiated with the Internal Revenue Service to the success of its tax-minimization strategy?
4. Google's corporate motto is "Don't be evil." Is Google's use of the Double Irish and the Dutch Sandwich honoring that motto?
5. Explain how Microsoft uses its Irish subsidiary to cut its U.S. taxes. How does it get around U.S. regulations regarding passive income?
6. What is the impact of Microsoft's Irish subsidiary on the Irish economy?
7. Are Google and Microsoft acting ethically? Are they being socially responsible?

Sources: Microsoft Annual Report 2010; Google Annual Report 2010; "Zambia demands more taxes from Glencore," *Wall Street Journal*, June 7, 2011; "Microsoft Ireland profits rise by 76% to €1.43bn," *The Irish Times*, April 20, 2011; "G.E.'s strategies let it avoid taxes altogether," *New York Times*, March 24, 2011; IDA Ireland, 2010 Guide to Tax in Ireland; "Google uses 'transfer pricing' to pay less taxes," www.Bloomberg.com, October 21, 2010; "Tax enforcers intensify focus on multinationals," *New York Times*, January 5, 2010; "GlaxoSmithKline, IRS tangle in tax court," *Wall Street Journal*, May 22, 2009, p. B1; "Irish subsidiary lets Microsoft slash taxes in U.S. and Europe," *Wall Street Journal*, November 7, 2005, p. A1.

Endnotes

1. Singapore Airlines Annual Report 2009/2010.
2. Linda S. Goldberg, "Trade invoicing in the accession countries: Are they suited to the Euro?" *Federal Reserve Bank of New York Staff Reports*, No. 222, October 2005.
3. "EADS urges Boeing to adopt Euro as the industry's currency," *Financial Times*, March 25, 2003, p. 17.
4. "Small firms hit foreign obstacles in billing overseas," *Wall Street Journal*, December 8, 1992, p. B2.
5. *Survey of Current Business*, July 2005, p. 13 and August 2005, p. 209.
6. Richard Schaffer, Beverly Earle, and Filiberto Agusti, *International Business Law and Its Environment* (St. Paul, MN: West Publishing, 1990), pp. 154–155.
7. Chase Manhattan Bank, *Dynamics of Trade Finance* (New York: Chase Manhattan, 1984), pp. 41–58; Steve Murphy, *Complete Export Guide Manual* (Manhattan Beach, CA: Tran Publishing House, 1980).
8. "Age-old question of international trade," *Wall Street Journal*, May 29, 2007, p. B4.
9. Ibid., p. B4.
10. Pompiliu Verzariu, *Countertrade Practices in East Europe, the Soviet Union and China: An Introductory Guide to Business* (Washington, DC: Department of Commerce, International Trade Administration, November 1984), pp. 98, 101.
11. Rolf Mirus and Bernard Yeung, "Economic incentives for countertrade," *Journal of International Business Studies* (Fall 1986), pp. 27–39.
12. Office of the U.S. Trade Representative, National Trade Estimate Report on Foreign Trade Barriers 2011, p. 360.
13. "U.S., 8 countries meet to discuss fighter-jet project," *Wall Street Journal*, June 5, 2006, p. A5; "Dutch govt sticking to F-35 JSF as successor to F-16," www. DefenseTalk.com, May 16, 2006 (online); "U.S. woos allies with unique deal on new fighter jet," *Wall Street Journal*, July 22, 2002, p. A1; "BAE opens office for fighter crews," *Fort Worth Star-Telegram*, July 10, 2002 (online); "Fiat unit is in deal on fighter jets," *Wall Street Journal*, June 11, 2002, p. B2.
14. Grant T. Hammond, *Countertrade, Offsets and Barter in International Political Economy* (New York: St. Martin's, 1990), p. 75.
15. Max Eli, *Japan Inc.* (Chicago: Probus Publishing, 1999), pp. 101–104.
16. "Marc Rich & Co. does big deals at big risk in former U.S.S.R.," *Wall Street Journal*, May 15, 1993, p. A1.
17. Hammond, op. cit., p. 11.
18. "Daimler allows Argentines to pay with grain," *Wall Street Journal*, November 22, 2002, p. A11.
19. Export-Import Bank of the United States, *2010 Annual Report*.
20. *Merck 10-K for the Fiscal Year Ended December 31, 2007*, p. 74; "Foreign currency trades slow at Merck as firms back away," *Wall Street Journal*, October 20, 1992, p. C1.
21. "What made the Indonesian currency plummet," *Wall Street Journal*, December 30, 1997, p. A4.
22. AFLAC Incorporated, *2010 10-K filing*, p. 89.
23. The Walt Disney Company 2007 Annual Report, p. 95; Pfizer 2007 Financial Report, p. 55; Procter & Gamble Annual Report 2007, p. 60; McDonald's Corporation 2007 Annual Report, p. 51.
24. Sony Annual Report Year Ended March 31, 1996, p. 31.
25. "BMW's outlook bullish despite stronger Euro," *Wall Street Journal*, March 19, 2008, p. C5; "Tested by the mighty Euro," *The Economist*, March 20, 2004, p. 61; "European auto makers rev up output where dollar is king," *Wall Street Journal*, January 7, 2004, p. A2.
26. "How U.S. firm copes with Asia crisis," *Wall Street Journal*, December 26, 1997, p. A2.
27. "Centralization lessens the risk," *Financial Times*, April 18, 1997, p. III.
28. Marjorie Stanley and Stanley Block, "An empirical study of management and financial variables influencing capital budgeting decisions for multinational corporations in the 1980s," *Management International Review*, vol. 23, no. 3 (1983), pp. 61–71.

29. U. Rao Cherukuri, "Capital budgeting in India," in S. Kerry Cooper, ed., *Southwest Review of International Business Research* (1992), pp. 194–204.

30. "When it's smart to use foreign banks," *International Business* (January 1992), pp. 17–18.

31. Gunter Dufey and Ian H. Giddy, "Innovation in the international financial market," *The Journal of International Business Studies* (Fall 1981), pp. 33–51.

32. "A Eurobond issue tied to film results," *Wall Street Journal*, October 12, 1992, p. C17.

33. "Walt Disney to sell notes tied to films' results, with initial yield linked to U.S. 7-year issue," *Wall Street Journal*, February 17, 1994, p. C20.

34. "Vital tool in minimizing costs," *Financial Times*, November 11, 1992, p. iii.

35. *Survey of Current Business*, November 2010, pp. 55f and August 2010, p. 224.

36. *Survey of Current Business*, October 2010, pp. 44f.

37. "Tax authorities step up pressure on multinationals," *Financial Times*, November 16, 2005, p. 4; David Harris, Randall Morck, Joel Slemrod, and Bernard Yeung, "Income shifting in U.S. multinational corporations," University of Michigan, mimeo, 1991; James R. Hines and Eric Rice, "Fiscal paradise: Foreign tax havens and American business," N.B.E.R. Working Paper #3477 (Cambridge, MA, 1990); James Wheeler, "An academic look at transfer pricing in a global economy," *Tax Notes*, July 4, 1988.

38. J. C. Stewart, "Transfer pricing: Some empirical evidence from Ireland," *Journal of Economic Studies*, vol. 16, no. 3 (1989), pp. 40–56.

39. "IBM probed over payments of U.K. taxes," *Wall Street Journal*, August 6, 1999, p. A3.

40. "GlaxoSmithKline gets big tax bill," *Wall Street Journal*, January 8, 2004, p. A8.

International Human Resource Management and Labor Relations

AFTER STUDYING THIS CHAPTER, YOU SHOULD BE ABLE TO:

1. Describe the nature of human resource management in international business.

2. Detail how firms recruit and select managers for international assignments.

3. Explain how international businesses train and develop expatriate managers.

4. Discuss how international firms conduct performance appraisals and determine compensation for their expatriate managers.

5. Analyze retention and turnover issues in international business.

6. Explain basic human resource issues involving nonmanagerial employees.

7. Describe labor relations in international business.

Access a host of interactive learning aids at **www.pearsonglobaleditions.com/ mymanagementlab** to help strengthen your understanding of the chapter concepts.

MyManagementLab

© Aurora Photos/Alamy

AN EMERGING VOICE FOR WORKERS

It's no secret, of course, that China has become the largest manufacturing center in the world. Products marked "Made in China" are just about impossible to avoid in any retail outlet, factory, warehouse, supply chain, or other marketplace. It's also no secret about why this is true—China provides a vast army of relatively compliant workers with a wide array of skills who are willing to work long hours for low pay. This combination has made China an emerging global powerhouse and fueled its explosive economy to ever greater heights.

But cracks may be appearing in its manufacturing machine that could slow China's economic ascension. In some ways it's almost reminiscent of the kinds of labor problems that plagued the U.S. railroad and steel industries more than 100 years ago. In a nutshell, as the overall economic climate in China has improved, so too has the awareness of its workers of their own economic value and their willingness to stand up to their employers. Consider, for example, the words of Lan Yimin, a 22-year-old factory worker in China's Pearl River Delta: "The young generation has a wider social circle; we talk more about factory conditions and we know more about our legal rights."

The Chinese government, for its part, has allowed wages to increase and improved working conditions in many manufacturing facilities. Part of the impetus for these changes has been the recognition that higher wages translate into more spending, which can serve as an economic stimulus. But the government also walks a fine line. If it invests too heavily in its workers and their working conditions, it risks losing its standing as a low-cost manufacturing center. On the other hand, though, repressing wages and maintaining substandard working conditions may lead to growing worker discontent and unwanted international media attention.

The unspoken words in all this, of course, are "labor unions." But that too is tricky. In the United States, for instance, unions are formed by collectives of workers within a defined bargaining group (defined by profession, business, and/or location). While the formation and operation of unions are regulated, the workers are responsible for forming a union, managing it, and engaging in collective bargaining with their employers. There are approximately 25,000 different unions in the United States. But in China, there is only one legal union—the state-controlled All-China Federation of Trade Unions (ACFTU). And the government is actually encouraging companies to unionize under the ACFTU umbrella. The thinking is that this form of union membership will give workers an avenue to air their grievances, forestalling harsher and more extreme actions.

But strikes are also becoming increasingly common. So far, at least, the Chinese government has taken a low-key approach to these strikes, though, because for the most part they have been directed at foreign-owned operations. Honda, for one, was hit by several strikes in 2010 and 2011. And Foxconn, a Taiwanese-owned electronics firm that makes electronic goods for Apple and Dell, has had a spate of suicides largely attributed to low wages and poor working conditions. Official information about the frequency and magnitude of strikes is unavailable. But according to Chinese government data, labor complaints heard by arbitration committees more than doubled from 2000 through 2007 to 350,182. And in 2008, arbitrated cases surged to almost 700,000 after a new law took effect, making it cheaper for workers to pursue arbitration and requiring employers to provide written contracts.

No one knows what the future holds, of course. But many experts agree that China still has a long way to go before it achieves a reasonable framework for dealing with organized labor. And the surge in strikes and lawsuits may indicate that workers are no longer willing to work for minimal wages while their country's economy booms. Interestingly, China's growing labor movement has also attracted attention in other parts of the region—workers in Vietnam and Cambodia have gone on strike in recent times as well, crediting their Chinese colleagues for inspiring them to take action. As the movement spreads, we can only be reminded of the words of the Greek poet Homer, who noted that "There is a strength in the union ... of ... men."[1]

At its most basic level any organization—from a small neighborhood convenience store to the largest multinational corporation (MNC)—is nothing more than a collection of jobs, clusters of jobs, and interconnections among those jobs. The people who fill the jobs are a vital ingredient in determining how effectively the organization will be able to meet its goals, remain competitive, and satisfy its constituents. Businesses in China, like those in many other countries, are having to grapple with achieving the right balance between worker prosperity and business profitability. Finding this balance, in turn, requires both strategic oversight and effective human resource management.

The Nature of International Human Resource Management

Human resource management (HRM) is the set of activities directed at attracting, developing, and maintaining the effective workforce necessary to achieve a firm's objectives. HRM includes recruiting and selecting nonmanagers and managers, providing training and development, appraising performance, and providing compensation and benefits. HR managers, regardless of whether they work for a purely domestic firm or an international one, must develop procedures and policies for accomplishing these tasks.

International HR managers, however, face challenges beyond those confronting their counterparts in purely domestic companies.[2] Specifically, differences in cultures, levels of economic development, and legal systems among the countries in which a firm operates may force it to customize its hiring, firing, training, and compensation programs on a country-by-country basis. Particularly troublesome problems develop when conflicts arise between the culture and laws of the home country and those of the host country. For example, prohibitions against gender discrimination in U.S. equal employment opportunity laws conflict with Saudi Arabian custom and law regarding the role, rights, and privileges of women. Such conflicts cause problems for U.S. MNCs that want to ensure their female executives receive overseas assignments equivalent to those given to their male colleagues.[3]

The international firm also must determine where various employees should come from—the home country, the host country, or third countries. The optimal mix of employees may differ according to the location of the firm's operations. A firm is likely to hire more employees from its home country to work in production facilities there than to work in foreign facilities. Local laws also must be considered because they may limit or constrain hiring practices. For example, immigration laws may limit the number of work visas granted to foreigners, or employment regulations may mandate the hiring of local citizens as a requirement for doing business in a country.

International businesses also face more complex training and development challenges. HR managers must provide cross-cultural training for corporate executives chosen for overseas assignments. Similarly, training systems for production workers in host countries must be adjusted to reflect the education offered by local school systems. For example, because of the tradition of employment as a lifetime commitment, Toyota, like other large Japanese corporations, goes to great lengths to hire just the right people to work in its factories and offices. To help accomplish this, the firm has nurtured partnerships with local public school systems in Japan to help train and select future employees. However, Toyota cannot rely on this approach in each country in which it does business because local school systems often are not prepared to operate such training partnerships with individual firms. The German secondary school system provides extensive vocational training for its students, but that training is less firm-specific. The United States, on the other hand, emphasizes general education and provides only modest vocational training opportunities through its public schools. Moreover, many countries have labor pools that, when measured along any dimension, are uneducated and unskilled. Toyota thus has adjusted its selection, recruitment, and training practices to meet the requirements of the countries in which it does business.

Finally, because working conditions and the cost of living may vary dramatically by country, international HR managers often must tailor compensation systems to meet the needs of the host country's labor market. They must take into account variations in local laws, which may require the payment of a minimum wage or may mandate certain benefits, such as annual bonuses or health care coverage. These managers also must determine how to compensate executives on overseas assignments, who potentially face higher costs of living, reductions in the quality of their lifestyle, and unhappiness or stress due to separation from friends and relatives.[4]

Strategic Significance of HRM

As with marketing, operations, and finance, the firm's managers must design an HRM strategy that promotes the company's overall corporate and business strategies. The cultural nuances inherent in international business heighten the complexities of developing an effective human resource strategy.[5] The basic elements of the international HRM process are shown in Figure 19.1, which provides the framework around which this chapter is organized.

FIGURE 19.1

The International Human Resource Management Process

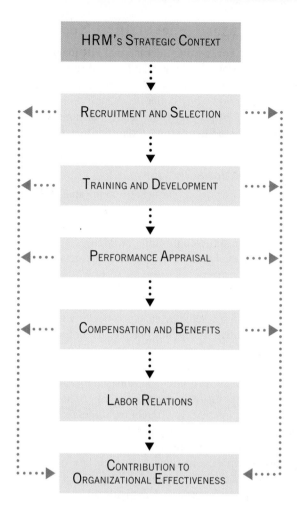

The starting point is recognizing and appreciating HRM's strategic position within the firm and the interconnection between overall firm strategy and HRM strategy. For example, suppose a firm decides to adopt a cost leadership strategy and subsequently identifies the opportunity to undercut competing firms by aggressively pricing its products in new international markets. In implementing this strategy, the firm could decide to purchase more inputs from outside suppliers, or it could shift production to a country with low-cost labor, such as China or Indonesia. This production location decision could result in less need for home country workers and more need for workers at the foreign facility. The firm's HR managers thus would have to develop severance packages and provide outplacement services for released workers in the home country as well as select, recruit, and train the new workers in the foreign country. Over time the firm's HR managers would have to adjust their HR practices to meet the conditions in the host country, which are likely to differ from those in the home country.

The decision to shift production overseas has other HR consequences. HR managers have to select key managerial personnel to oversee the transfer of the firm's technology, operating policies, and proprietary skills to its new overseas factories. Regardless of the skills or abilities of the selected international managers, few of them will be able to walk into a foreign operation and know exactly how to do things from the first day they arrive. Thus, HR managers must provide them with training to help them function more effectively in a new culture.

HR managers also must be prepared to define performance effectiveness and assess how well each international manager is doing relative to that definition. Moreover, international managers must be compensated for their work. Further, companies invest a lot in their international managers, so HR managers must carefully assess how effectively their firm manages retention and turnover.

International Managerial Staffing Needs

The staffing issues confronting international HR managers can be divided into two broad categories. One of these is recruiting, training, and retaining managerial and executive employees. The other is recruiting, training, and retaining nonmanagerial employees, such as blue-collar production workers and white-collar office staff. For managerial employees strategic and developmental issues are of primary importance. For nonmanagerial workers differences in cultural, political, and legal conditions among countries may be of greater significance.[6]

Scope of Internationalization

We begin by focusing on recruiting, training, and retaining managers. The size of this task depends on the scope of the firm's international involvement. Obviously, a firm's needs in the beginning stages of internationalization, such as in indirect exporting, are far less complex and comprehensive than those confronting an MNC with extensive investments in numerous countries. Consider the evolution of organizational structure discussed in Chapter 14:

1. *Export department*: A firm's initial foray into international business usually involves small-scale exporting using output from existing domestic production facilities. Its international activities are administered by an export department, whose manager reports to an existing company executive such as the vice president of marketing. The manager is likely to be a citizen of the home country and may or may not have special training in overseas marketing and financing. As export sales increase, however, the firm quickly recognizes it must increase its staff's expertise, so it hires specialists in export documentation, international trade financing, and overseas distribution and marketing. These specialists often are recruited from international banks, international freight forwarders, or export management companies.

2. *International division*: As its international operations grow in importance, a firm often creates a separate international division to administer all of its international activities. Typically, a firm's international division is housed at corporate headquarters in its home country and is headed by a home country citizen to facilitate communication and coordination between the domestic and international operations. The heads of the firm's foreign subsidiaries in turn report to the vice president of the international division. These foreign subsidiaries' managers (including their presidents as well as heads of functional departments such as finance, marketing, and production) may be either home country or host country citizens. Use of a home country manager facilitates communication and coordination with corporate headquarters because of shared cultural and educational backgrounds.[7] Use of a host country manager often improves the subsidiary's ability to adjust to changes in local economic and political conditions. As we discuss later in this chapter, cost considerations also play a major role in the choice between home country and host country managers.

3. *Global organization*: A firm further along in the internationalization process often adopts a global organization form. (Chapter 14 discussed the global product, global functional, global area, and global customer forms.) Because of the complexity of its operations, a global organization must assemble a team of managers that have the expertise to produce, finance, and market its products worldwide while simultaneously coordinating its activities to achieve global production, financing, and marketing economies and synergies. To operate successfully, a global firm needs a team of managers that collectively possess expertise in and knowledge of the following:

   - The firm's *product line*: Product managers must be aware of such factors as the latest manufacturing techniques, research and development opportunities, and competitors' strategies.
   - The *functional skills* (accounting, logistics, marketing, manufacturing management, and so on) necessary to ensure global competitiveness: Functional specialists strive to capture global economies of scale and synergies in a firm's financial, marketing, and production activities.
   - The *individual country markets* in which the firm does business: Country managers must understand such factors as local laws, culture, competitors, distribution systems, and advertising media. These managers play a key role in meeting the needs of local

customers, ensuring compliance with host country rules and regulations, and enlarging the firm's market share and profitability in the host country.

● The firm's *global strategy*: High-level executives at corporate headquarters must formulate a global strategy for the firm and then control and coordinate the activities of the firm's product, functional, and country managers to ensure that its strategy is successfully implemented.

Centralization versus Decentralization of Control

An international business's HRM needs also are affected by whether the firm wants decision making to be centralized at corporate headquarters or delegated (decentralized) to operating subsidiaries. Firms that use a centralized approach often favor employing home country managers; firms that follow a decentralized decision-making philosophy are more likely to employ host country managers.

Certain organizational approaches and forms affect the choice of centralization or decentralization. Firms that view themselves as multi*domestic* rather than multi*national* are likely to favor decentralization of decision making. The global area form facilitates delegating responsibility to managers of the firm's foreign subsidiaries. Conversely, the international division form favors centralizing decision making at corporate headquarters.

Recall from Chapter 14 that most international businesses operate somewhere along the continuum from pure centralization to pure decentralization. In managing human resources, most adopt an overall HRM strategy at the corporate headquarters level but delegate many day-to-day HR issues to local and regional offices. Doing this allows each foreign operation to meet its own needs and to more effectively deal with local conditions, cultures, and HR practices.

Staffing Philosophy

The extent of the firm's internationalization and its degree of centralization or decentralization affects (and is affected by) its philosophy regarding the nationality of its international managers. Firms can hire from three groups: parent country nationals, host country nationals, and third-country nationals.

Parent country nationals (PCNs) are residents of the international business's home country. Use of PCNs in an MNC's foreign operations provides many advantages to the firm. Because PCNs typically share a common culture and educational background with corporate headquarters staff, they facilitate communication and coordination with corporate headquarters. If the firm's global strategy involves exploiting new technologies or business techniques that were developed in the home market, PCNs often are best able to graft those innovations to a host country setting. For example, Mercedes sent a team of executives from Germany to oversee the start-up of its U.S. operations. It wanted to ensure that its manufacturing techniques and corporate commitment to quality were successfully transplanted to Alabama.

However, using PCNs has several disadvantages. PCNs typically lack knowledge of the host country's laws, culture, economic conditions, social structure, and political processes. Although PCNs can be trained to overcome these knowledge gaps, such training is expensive (particularly when the opportunity cost of the manager's time is considered) and is not a perfect substitute for having been born and raised in the host country. Further, PCNs are often expensive to relocate and maintain in the host country. Finally, many host countries restrict the number of foreign employees who can be transferred in and/or mandate that a certain percentage of an international firm's payroll must be paid to employees from the host country. Thus, an international business may not have total freedom to hire whomever it wants for international assignments. Because of these factors, PCNs are most likely to be used in upper-level and/or technical positions in host countries.

Host country nationals (HCNs) are residents of the host country. HCNs are commonly used by international businesses to fill middle-level and lower-level jobs, but they also often appear in managerial and professional positions. Experienced MNCs such as Intel, Canadian Imperial Bank of Commerce, IBM, and Halliburton often hire HCNs instead of transferring home country employees to work in professional positions in the firms' foreign operations. Many smaller firms setting up operations abroad hire HCNs because the firms do not have enough managerial talent at home to send someone on a foreign assignment.[8] "Emerging Opportunities" provides more examples of how many firms are using this strategy in both China and India.

Using HCNs offers two primary advantages. First, HCNs already understand the local laws, culture, and economic conditions. Second, the firm avoids the expenses associated with expatriate managers, such as relocation costs, supplemental wages paid for foreign service, and private schooling for children. However, using HCNs can have disadvantages. HCNs may be unfamiliar with the firm's business culture and practices, thus limiting the effectiveness of the HCNs. As noted earlier in this chapter, Mercedes used German executives to shepherd the development of its U.S. operations to ensure that its new employees understood the firm's emphasis on producing quality automobiles.

Finally, an international firm may hire **third-country nationals (TCNs),** who are not citizens of the firm's home country or of the host country. Like PCNs, TCNs are most likely to be used in upper-level and/or technical positions. TCNs and PCNs collectively are known as **expatriates,** or people working and residing in countries other than their native country. In the past TCNs were likely to be used when they had special expertise that was not available to the firm through any other channel. Today they are consciously being employed by some firms to promote a global outlook throughout their operations. Firms such as Nestlé and Philips NV rely heavily on TCNs because they believe those managers bring broader perspectives and experiences to the firms' host country operations. Further, some firms are recruiting more TCNs to serve on their boards of directors to help bring a more global orientation to the boards.

Most international firms develop a systematic strategy for choosing among HCNs, PCNs, and TCNs for various positions. Some firms rely on the **ethnocentric staffing model,** whereby they primarily use PCNs to staff higher-level foreign positions. This approach is based on the assumption that home office perspectives should take precedence over local perspectives and that expatriate PCNs will be most effective in representing the views of the home office in the foreign operation. Other international firms follow a **polycentric staffing model;** that is, they emphasize the use of HCNs in the belief that HCNs know the local market best. Finally, the **geocentric staffing model** puts PCNs, HCNs, and TCNs on an equal footing. Firms that adopt this approach want to hire the best person available, regardless of where that individual comes from.[9]

National culture often affects the staffing model chosen by a firm. European MNCs are more likely than U.S. or Japanese MNCs to adopt the geocentric approach. This approach is encouraged by the European Union to improve the mobility of workers and managers throughout

EMERGING OPPORTUNITIES   THINKING GLOBALLY BUT HIRING LOCALLY

When international businesses first began to aggressively move into China and India, they generally transferred expatriate managers from their home company to run these new operations. Among other reasons, the firms felt a need to try to export their corporate cultures and work procedures to the emerging markets they were entering; they also felt there was a lack of local managerial talent.

As recently as the mid-1990s, for example, virtually every U.S. company doing business in China filled most of its middle and upper management positions in that country with Americans. And the few positions not held by Americans were often filled with managers groomed in Singapore and Hong Kong, markets where these firms had operated for many years.

But in the 1990s things began to change. In China, for instance, many locals sharpened their English language skills, developed more leadership and decision-making skills, and became increasingly familiar and comfortable with the international business world. As a result, more and more locals are entering the ranks of middle and upper level managers today. It's estimated, for instance, that around 70 percent of foreign firms' top management positions in China are today filled by Chinese managers. This trend is not restricted to China; the same pattern is also occurring in India as well.

Nor is this pattern found only among U.S. firms in China. The German company Siemens, for instance, has Chinese nationals holding seven of its nine regional management positions there. And Ericsson, a Swedish telecommunications giant, currently fills 90 percent of its middle management positions and half of its top management positions in China with local managers.

Why are firms moving in this direction? There are several reasons. For one thing, hiring local managers is much cheaper. The company avoids costly relocation expenses and does not risk expatriate failure. Further, the compensation package for a local Chinese manager is only around 20 percent to 25 percent of that of a comparable manager transferred from a Western country. Local managers have a strong understanding of local market conditions, competitive behaviors, and government regulations. In addition, hiring locally can boost employee morale and motivation. The local manager has a rich understanding of cultural issues in the workplace and also serves as a symbol of advancement and success for other rising local managers.

Sources: "Firms in China think globally, hire locally," *Wall Street Journal,* February 27, 2006, pp. B1, B3; *Hoover's Handbook of World Business 2011* (Austin: Hoover's Business Press, 2011), pp. 132–133; 315–316.

BRINGING THE WORLD INTO FOCUS   ## SCHLUMBERGER PROFITS FROM GEOCENTRIC STAFFING

Schlumberger is one of the world's largest oil field services companies. The firm offers a complete range of oil and gas services, including engineering, construction, and project management. Schlumberger has over 70,000 employees, does business around the world, and, in 2010, earned more than $4.3 billion in profits. But while the firm has little trouble finding oil these days, attracting and keeping the right people—a fundamental human resource management issue—is proving to be an ongoing challenge.

Schlumberger and other large companies in energy-related industries depend heavily on a steady inflow of new employees. But an aging workforce and an unevenly distributed supply of talent continues to create challenges. For instance, there is a significant shortage of geosciences and petroleum engineering students in both North America and the Middle East—the very regions where more people are needed.

More than 40 years ago Schlumberger adopted an aggressive and innovative human resource strategy that is based on diversity and partnerships with colleges and universities. As a result, the firm has long hired in every country where it operates. In addition, it took a geocentric approach to all of its global assignments, hiring the best people regardless of where they are from and moving them to work assignments that are mutually beneficial regardless of the location of those assignments. Schlumberger also established a long-term emphasis on hiring and developing women engineers.

As a result of these efforts, Schlumberger has maintained a human resource advantage over many of its key competitors. But these same competitors have shown their own brands of creativity as they, too, have taken a more global and integrated approach to human resource management. Among other things, other firms in the industry often look to current Schlumberger employees when they need to recruit experienced people.

To maintain the competitive advantages Schlumberger gets from its workforce, the firm continues to develop and implement new systems, policies, and practices to retain the strong workforce it has attracted. For example, a rigorous and comprehensive training and development program helps keep its engineers at the forefront of their fields. Competitive salaries and performance-based incentives helps retain the best and brightest of its employees, and well-defined career paths helps Schlumberger continue to grow and nourish the talent it needs to remain competitive in an increasingly competitive world.

Sources: Schlumberger Annual Report 2007; *Hoover's Handbook of American Business 2011* (Austin, Texas: Hoover's Business Press, 2011), pp. 737–738.

---

its member countries. Japanese firms favor the ethnocentric staffing model, partly because their consensus-oriented approach to decision making is facilitated by employing Japanese managers in key roles in the firms' foreign subsidiaries. Japanese firms sometimes rely too heavily on this model, to their own disadvantage. Although they usually hire HCNs for lower-level positions, the firms are reluctant to use non-Japanese managers in higher-level positions. When the firms do hire an HCN as a local manager, they have been accused of being too quick to send in a troubleshooter from the home office at the first sign of a problem. Further, the non-Japanese managers often face a glass ceiling because the top positions in the firms are reserved for Japanese managers. Thus, the ethnocentric policy often results in the loss of the best HCN managers, who seek more challenge and responsibility by shifting to non-Japanese employers.

Recruitment and Selection

A firm's scope of internationalization, level of centralization, and staffing philosophy help determine the skills and abilities its international managers need. As shown in Figure 19.2, these skills and abilities fall into two general categories: those needed to do the job and those needed to work in a foreign location.

The firm first must define the actual business skills necessary to do the job. For example, a firm that has an assembly plant in a foreign market needs a plant manager who understands the technical aspects of what is to be manufactured, what manufacturing processes will be utilized, and so on. The firm's marketing managers must be knowledgeable about advertising media availability, distribution channels, market competition, and local consumers' demographic characteristics.

The firm next must determine the skills and abilities a manager must have to work and function effectively in the foreign location. These include the manager's ability to adapt to cultural change, ability to speak the local language, overall physical and emotional health, levels of independence and self-reliance, and appropriate levels of experience and education. Obviously, an HCN can meet these requirements far easier than a PCN or TCN can. Firms relying on the ethnocentric or geocentric staffing models thus must devote more resources to selecting and training PCNs and TCNs for foreign assignments than do firms that rely on the polycentric model.

FIGURE 19.2

Necessary Skills and Abilities for International Managers

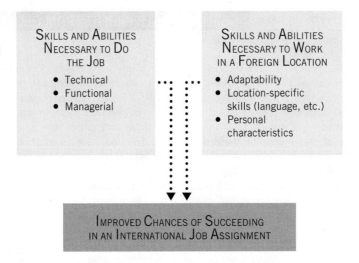

Recruitment of Managers

Once the international business determines the skills and abilities an international manager must have, it next must develop a pool of qualified applicants for the job and then recruit and select the best candidate.

RECRUITMENT OF EXPERIENCED MANAGERS International businesses recruit experienced managers through a variety of channels. A common source of recruits is within the firm itself—among employees already working for the firm in the host country or those who, although currently employed in the home country, might be prepared for an international assignment in the host country. The latter group may include both managers who have never held an international assignment and managers who have already completed previous international assignments. For example, when Kal Kan's Canadian subsidiary entered the animal-food market in Poland, the firm relied on a team of Polish-born Canadian executives to start up the new operation. Other companies dip into their pool of retired executives to fill short-term international assignments. Whirlpool rehired one of its retired senior engineers to help expand its Shanghai washing machine factory, and Quaker Oats sent a team of five retired employees to oversee the start-up of a cereal plant in that same city. Retired employees often are eager to take on such tasks. For example, Verizon has a pool of 725 former employees willing to tackle short-term foreign assignments.[10]

An international business also may attempt to identify prospective managers who work for other firms. These may be home country managers who are deemed to be qualified for an international assignment or managers already working in an international assignment for another firm. For higher-level positions firms often rely on so-called **headhunters** to help them locate prospective candidates. Headhunters are recruiting firms that actively seek qualified managers and other professionals for possible placement in positions in other organizations. In many parts of the world, including Japan, switching employers has long been frowned on; until recently, headhunting in Europe was considered unethical. Both of these views are changing, however. More firms are finding they can even entice highly qualified Japanese employees away from Japanese firms.

A firm may sometimes find it useful to relocate its facilities to be closer to a pool of qualified employees. For example, when Upjohn and Pharmacia (U.S. and Swedish pharmaceutical firms, respectively) merged in the mid-1990s, they initially selected London for their new corporate headquarters. However, it quickly became apparent there was not an adequate pool of managerial and technical talent available locally to staff the enterprise. Because London is among the world's most expensive cities, transferring in managers from other locations was not cost effective. Thus, the firm subsequently moved its headquarters to New Jersey, where many other drug companies are located. Managers reasoned this would place them closer to a large

International businesses rely on a number of approaches to recruit new managers. While the Internet has become the most widely used approach, many firms still also rely heavily on traditional print media, especially publications geared to international audiences. *The Economist,* a magazine, and the *International Herald Tribune,* a newspaper, often feature advertisements seeking managers and other professionals. This ad, for example, is seeking a Marketing Executive for an international company.

pistolseven/Shutterstock

talent pool of managers with pharmaceutical industry experience and therefore make recruiting a bit easier.[11]

One trend seems clear: As a result of the globalization of business, the market for executive talent also is becoming globalized. Firms increasingly value performance more than nationality. Nomura Securities, Japan's largest stock brokerage firm, typifies this trend. Concerned about losses in its global market share, the firm turned to a seasoned U.S. securities executive, Max Chapman, to reinvigorate its global operations, which are headquartered in London.

RECRUITMENT OF YOUNGER MANAGERS It is uncommon for large MNCs to hire new college graduates for immediate foreign assignments. Some firms, however, will hire new graduates they ultimately intend to send abroad and, in the short term, give the graduates domestic assignments. Particularly attractive are graduates with foreign-language skills, international travel experience, and a major in international business or a related field. A few firms have started taking a longer-term view of developing international managerial talent. Coca-Cola, for example, has developed an innovative strategy for recruiting managers for future international assignments. It actively seeks foreign students who are studying at U.S. colleges and universities and who intend to return to their home countries after receiving their degrees. The firm recruits and hires the best of these graduates and puts them through a one-year training program. The new managers then return home as Coca-Cola employees and take assignments in the firm's operations in their home countries.

Selection of Managers

After the pool of prospective managers has been identified, HR managers must decide which persons from that pool are the best qualified for the assignment. The most promising candidates share the following characteristics:

- Managerial competence (technical and leadership skills, knowledge of the corporate culture)
- Appropriate training (formal education, knowledge of the host market and its culture and language)
- Adaptability to new situations (ability to deal simultaneously with adjusting to a new work and job environment, adjusting to working with HCNs, and adjusting to a new national culture)

The importance of the selection process cannot be overstated when dealing with expatriate managers. The costs to a firm of expatriate failure are extremely high. **Expatriate failure** is the early return of an expatriate manager to the home country because of an inability to perform in the overseas assignment. Experts suggest these costs range from $200,000 to as much as $1.2 million (these figures include the expatriate's original training, moving expenses, and lost managerial productivity but do not include the decreased performance of the foreign subsidiary itself). Expatriate failure occurs far too often. Failure rates of 20 to 50 percent are common for many U.S. firms, and rates appear to be much higher for them than for European and Japanese firms.[12]

The primary cause of expatriate failure is the inability of the managers and/or their spouse and family to adjust to the new locale. As a result, international HR managers increasingly are evaluating the nontechnical aspects of a candidate's suitability for a foreign assignment. Assessing certain skills and abilities is relatively easy. For example, measuring a prospect's language proficiency is a straightforward undertaking. Assessing a person's cultural adaptability is more difficult and must be accomplished through a variety of means. Most firms use a combination of tests (such as personality and aptitude tests) and interviews in their selection process. Assessment centers, which offer programs of exercises, tests, and interviews that last several days, are also useful because they provide an in-depth look at a set of prospective candidates under the same circumstances.

Another important consideration is the prospect's motivation for and interest in the foreign assignment.[13] Some managers are attracted to foreign assignments, perhaps because they relish the thought of living abroad or because they see the experience as being useful in their future career plans. Others balk at the thought of uprooting their family and moving to a foreign environment, particularly one that is culturally distant from their own. As previously noted, failure of the family to adjust to the new culture is a prominent cause of expatriate failure. Thus, most firms also consider the family's motivation for and interest in the foreign assignment. The manager's job performance often will deteriorate if the manager has an unhappy spouse cut off from friends and family and frustrated by dealing with a new culture. Clearly a foreign relocation is far more disruptive to the family than a domestic relocation. Dependent children may face problems integrating into a new school culture—particularly if they do not speak the local language—and may find that material covered in the courses at their new school is well ahead (or well behind) that at their home school.[14] In addition, there is the dual-career problem. Trailing spouses may find it difficult to take leave from their current position, thereby forcing a disruption in their career advancement. Still worse, labor laws in the new country may make it difficult or impossible for the spouse to obtain employment there legally.

Because of the risk of expatriate failure, firms often devote considerable resources to selection and training.[15] AT&T, for example, prides itself on doing an especially thorough job of selecting managers for foreign assignments. The firm has long used personality tests and interviews as part of its selection process. It now also uses psychologists to help assess prospects and is investing more into learning about family considerations. In addition, the prospects complete a self-assessment checklist designed to help them probe their motivations for seeking a foreign transfer. AT&T reports that this exercise increases managers' self-awareness. As a result, more managers now remove themselves from consideration for foreign assignments.

Some international businesses are concerned with not only how well a prospective manager will adapt to the foreign culture but also how well the person will fit into that culture.[16] For example, for years some U.S. firms hesitated to send women managers on foreign assignments to some countries, such as Japan, because the firms assumed the women would not be accepted in a culture that frowned on women working outside the home. However, research indicates that this fear is overstated. Host country citizens react primarily to these executives' foreignness, rather than to their gender.

Expatriation and Repatriation Issues

PCNs on long-term foreign assignments face great acculturation challenges. Working in and coping with a foreign culture can lead to **culture shock,** a psychological phenomenon that may lead to feelings of fear, helplessness, irritability, and disorientation. New expatriates may experience a sense of loss regarding their old cultural environment as well as confusion, rejection, self-doubt, and decreased self-esteem from working in a new and unfamiliar cultural setting.[17] Acculturation, as shown in Figure 19.3, typically proceeds through four phases.[18]

Culture shock reduces an expatriate's effectiveness and productivity, so international businesses have developed various strategies to mitigate its effects. One simple solution is to provide expatriates (and their families) with predeparture language and cultural training, so they can better understand and anticipate the cultural adjustments they must undergo. In addition to straightforward training, firms also might make initial foreign assignments relatively brief and make sure the expatriates understand the role each assignment plays in their overall career prospects.

FIGURE 19.3
Phases in Acculturation

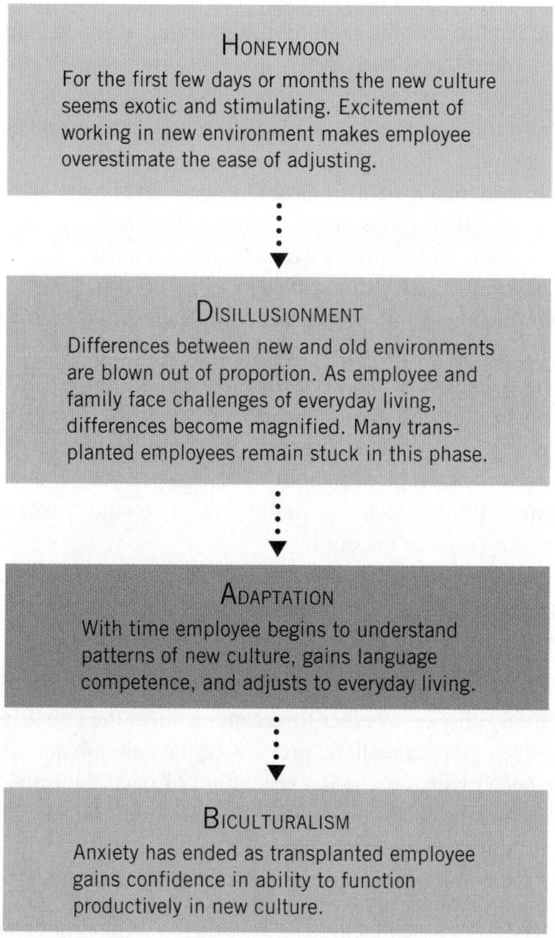

HONEYMOON
For the first few days or months the new culture seems exotic and stimulating. Excitement of working in new environment makes employee overestimate the ease of adjusting.

DISILLUSIONMENT
Differences between new and old environments are blown out of proportion. As employee and family face challenges of everyday living, differences become magnified. Many transplanted employees remain stuck in this phase.

ADAPTATION
With time employee begins to understand patterns of new culture, gains language competence, and adjusts to everyday living.

BICULTURALISM
Anxiety has ended as transplanted employee gains confidence in ability to function productively in new culture.

Managers in global organizations need to recognize the importance of expatriation and repatriation issues in determining the success of an international assignment. The U.S. military pays close attention to these issues when it deploys soldiers to foreign locations. For instance, the military makes sure that its members have access to e-mail as well as other "reminders" of home.

A3528 Armin Weigel Deutsche Presse-Agentur/Newscom

Interestingly, international businesses should pay almost as much attention to **repatriation**—bringing a manager back home after a foreign assignment has been completed—as they do to expatriation. If managers and their families have been successfully expatriated, they become comfortable with living and working in the foreign culture. Returning home can be almost as traumatic to them as was the original move abroad. One reason for the difficulty of repatriation is that people tend to assume nothing has changed at home. They look forward to getting back to their friends, familiar surroundings, and daily routines. Yet their friends may have moved or developed new social circles, and their coworkers may have been transferred to other jobs. Some expatriates who have returned to the United States have even been denied credit because they have not had a domestic financial history for several years![19]

Repatriated managers also have to cope with change and uncertainty at work. The firm may not be sure what their job is going to entail. Further, they may have been running the show at the foreign operation and enjoying considerable authority. Back home, however, the managers are likely to have much less authority and to be on a par with many other managers reporting to more senior managers. Also, repatriated managers and their families may have enjoyed a higher social status in the host country than they will enjoy after returning home. Thus, readjustment problems may be severe and need the attention of both the managers and the firm.

The repatriation problem can be expensive for a firm. By some estimates one-quarter of all repatriated employees leave their employer within a year after returning home. The average U.S. expatriate costs the employer about $300,000 per year and stays three to four years on an overseas assignment; thus, each repatriated executive who leaves the firm represents a million-dollar investment walking out the door.

The bottom line is that expatriation and repatriation problems can be reduced if international businesses systematically provide organizational career development programs for their expatriate managers.[20] Recent research indicates that the likelihood of managers being successful at an overseas assignment increases if the managers:

- Can freely choose whether to accept or reject the expatriate assignment
- Have been given a realistic preview of the new job and assignment
- Have been given a realistic expectation of what their repatriation assignment will be
- Have a mentor back home who will guard their interests and provide corporate and social support during the assignment
- See a clear link between the expatriate assignment and their long-term career path

Of these five elements, the last is the most critical in determining expatriate success.

Training and Development

The international firm's HR managers also must provide training and development for its home and host country managers to help them perform more effectively. **Training** is instruction directed at enhancing specific job-related skills and abilities. For example, training programs might be designed to help employees learn to speak a foreign language, to use new equipment, or to implement new manufacturing procedures. Special acculturation training is important for employees who are given international assignments. **Development** is general education concerned with preparing managers for new assignments and/or higher-level positions. For instance, a development program could be aimed at helping managers improve their ability to make decisions or to motivate subordinates to work harder.

Assessing Training Needs

Before a firm can undertake a meaningful training or development program, it must assess its exact training and development needs. This assessment involves determining the difference between what managers and employees can do and what the firm feels they need to be able to do. For example, suppose a firm that does business in Latin America wants its employees to be able to speak Spanish fluently. If most of its employees are fluent in Spanish, its language-training needs may be minimal, but if relatively few employees are fluent, extensive training may be called for. The assessment of training needs is an extremely important element of international HRM. Firms that underestimate training needs can encounter serious difficulties. Indeed, lack of knowledge about foreign customers and markets is a major barrier to successful entry into such markets, as Figure 19.4 shows.

A firm just moving into international markets has different training and development needs from those of an established global firm. The newly internationalizing firm is likely to have few, if any, experienced international managers. Thus, its training and development needs will be substantial. In contrast, a global firm has a cadre of trained and experienced managers with international backgrounds, skills, and abilities. Yet even then, organization change may necessitate training. For instance, when Jaguar took over a plant in England that had formerly been making Ford Escorts, managers found a workforce that was dispirited and unwilling to accept responsibility for making decisions. All employees were thus sent to several training workshops intended to both enhance their technical skills and to empower them to make key decisions for themselves.[21]

Basic Training Methods and Procedures

The first issue an international business must consider as it plans its training and development efforts is whether to rely on standardized programs or to develop its own customized programs. Certain kinds of training can be readily obtained in common retail outlets—for example, self-paced language

FIGURE 19.4

Barriers to Entering Foreign Markets

Source: From "Cross-cultural training helps in leap abroad," *Houston Chronicle*, September 25, 1994, p. 1E. Reprinted with permission. Data: Ernst & Young survey.

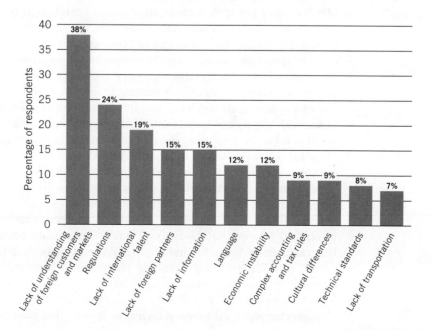

training on CDs or DVDs. Prudential Insurance even offers packaged training programs for families of expatriates, a good idea in light of the importance of family problems in causing expatriate failure. One advantage of standardized programs is that they tend to be less expensive than customized ones. On the other hand, a standardized program may not precisely fit the firm's needs.

As a result, most training and development programs often are customized to a firm's particular needs. Larger MNCs often have training and development departments that develop customized programs for the unique needs of individual managers and/or business units. Training and development activities may take place in regular classroom settings within the firm, on actual job sites, or off premises in a conference center or hotel. Customized programs are more costly than standardized programs; however, they ensure that employees get the precise information deemed necessary. Regardless of whether training and development programs are standardized or customized, most use a variety of methods as instructional vehicles. Lectures and assigned readings are common, as are videotaped and Web-based instruction. Multimedia technologies are increasingly being incorporated into cross-cultural training. According to Sanjyot Dunung, president of Atma Global, one of the innovators in this area, MNCs increasingly desire globally consistent but flexible delivery of cross-cultural training for their employees. Multimedia approaches allow employees spread throughout the globe to access training materials at their convenience at any time of day or night.

Role-playing and other forms of experiential exercises are useful for helping people better understand other cultures. Motorola uses a workplace simulation to help prepare its managers for foreign assignments.[22] Case studies also are used, although not as frequently as other methods. Training materials often must be altered to fit different cultural contexts. For example, a consultant hired to make training videos for Bally of Switzerland initially assumed he could use the same basic video for each of Bally's regional offices, with only minor script modifications. As the project progressed, however, he found that so many language and cultural differences affected the video that he essentially had to reshoot it for each office.

The trainers themselves also may need to adapt how they do things. One professional trainer reported difficulties in using her normal style when running a training program in Thailand. She preferred to be informal and to involve the participants through role-playing and other forms of interaction. She found, however, that Thai managers were uncomfortable with her informality and resisted the role-playing approach. She eventually had to adopt a more formal style and use a straightforward lecture approach to get her points across.[23]

Developing Younger International Managers

The increasing globalization of business has prompted most MNCs to recognize the importance of internationalizing their managers earlier in their careers. Until the late 1980s most U.S. MNCs delayed giving their managers significant overseas assignments until they had spent 7 to 10 years with the firm. Today many of these MNCs are beginning to recognize that they need to develop the international awareness and competence of their managers earlier and to systematically integrate international assignments into individual career plans. For example, GE provides language and cross-cultural training to its professional staff even though they may not be scheduled for overseas postings. Such training is important because these employees, even if they never leave their home countries, are likely to work with GE employees from other countries and to deal with visiting executives from GE's foreign partners, suppliers, and customers. Such training also helps the employees gain a better understanding of the firm's international markets. Other firms, such as American Express and Johnson & Johnson, occasionally post managers to overseas assignments after only 18 to 20 months on the job. PepsiCo and Raychem are bringing young managers from the firms' foreign operations to the United States to enrich the managers' understanding of their firms' cultures and technologies.

U.S. firms are not the only ones integrating international assignments into career development plans for younger managers. Honda's U.S. manufacturing subsidiary has been sending U.S. managers to Tokyo for multiyear assignments so they can learn more about the firm's successful manufacturing and operating philosophies. Samsung regularly sends its executives abroad for various assignments. One of its more interesting strategies is to send younger managers to certain foreign locations for as long as a year with no specific job responsibilities. The managers are supposed to spend their time learning the local language and becoming familiar with the culture. The idea is that if they are transferred back to that same location in the future—when they are in a higher-level position—they will be able to function more effectively. Even though the program costs Samsung about $80,000 per person per year, executives believe the firm will quickly recoup its investment.

Performance Appraisal and Compensation

Another important part of international HRM consists of conducting performance appraisals and determining compensation and benefits. Whereas recruitment, selection, and training and development tend to focus on preassignment issues, performance appraisal and compensation involve ongoing issues that continue to have an effect well past the initial international assignment.

Assessing Performance in International Business

Performance appraisal is the process of assessing how effectively people are performing their jobs. The purposes of performance appraisal are to provide feedback to individuals on how well they are doing; to provide a basis for rewarding top performers; to identify areas in which additional training and development may be needed; and to identify problem areas that may call for a change in assignment.

Performance appraisals of an international business's top managers must be based on the firm's clear understanding of its goals for its foreign operations. A successful subsidiary in a mature and stable foreign market will have different goals than will a start-up operation in a growing but unstable market. Thus, a firm assigning two new managers to head these different subsidiaries must understand that it cannot expect the same outcome from each of them. Similarly, managers of foreign subsidiaries that serve as cost centers must be judged by different standards from those used for managers of profit centers.

In assessing a manager's actual performance, the firm may consider sales, profit margin, market share growth, or any other measures or indicators it deems important. If a subsidiary has been having problems, performance may be more appropriately assessed in terms of how well the manager has helped to solve those problems. For example, reducing net losses or halting a decline in market share might be considered good performance, at least in the short term.

Expected and actual performance must be compared, and differences must be addressed. This step needs to have a strong diagnostic component: Why and how has the manager's performance been acceptable or unacceptable? Are any problems attributable to the manager's lack of skills? Are some problems attributable to unforeseen circumstances? Is the home office accountable for some of the problems that may have arisen, perhaps because the manager was inadequately trained? Of course, cultural values may shape expectations—an individualistic culture will attribute more of the organization's performance to the individual manager than a collectivist one—thus complicating performance appraisal when the appraiser and the appraisee come from different cultures.

Circumstances will dictate how frequently performance appraisals occur. In a domestic firm they may occur as often as every quarter. Geographical factors, however, can limit the frequency with which international performance appraisals can occur. Generally, international managers are expected to submit reports on performance-based results to headquarters regularly. As long as these reports fall within acceptable parameters, the firm is likely to conduct a formal performance appraisal perhaps on an annual basis. However, if standard reports reveal a problem, performance appraisals may be done more often in an effort to get things back on track.

Determining Compensation in International Business

Another important issue in international HRM is determining managerial compensation. To remain competitive, firms must provide prevailing compensation packages for their managers in a given market. These packages include salary and nonsalary items and are determined by labor market forces such as the supply and demand of managerial talent, occupational status, professional licensing requirements, standards of living, government regulations, tax codes, and similar factors. For example, in Germany employers customarily reimburse their executives for car expenses. In Japan the executive may actually get a car plus expenses. Japanese executives also receive generous entertainment allowances and an allowance for business gifts. Similarly, British companies typically provide company cars to managers. In the United States firms offer managers health care benefits because such benefits are free from income taxes.

COMPENSATING EXPATRIATE MANAGERS A more complex set of compensation issues apply to expatriate managers. Most international businesses find it necessary to provide these managers with differential compensation to make up for dramatic differences in currency valuation, standards of living, lifestyle norms, and so on.[24] When managers are on short-term assignments abroad, their home country salaries normally continue unchanged. (Of course, the managers are reimbursed for short-term living expenses such as for hotel rooms, meals, and transportation.) If foreign assignments are indefinite or longer term, compensation is routinely adjusted to allow the managers to maintain their home country standard of living. This adjustment is particularly important if a manager is transferred from a low-cost location to a high-cost location or from a country with a high standard of living to one with a lower standard of living. Map 19.1 identifies the 50 most expensive cities in the world. For example, in 2011, Angola's capital of Luanda was the most expensive city in the world for expatriates. Oslo, Norway, was number 11, New York was number 27, and Frankfurt, Germany, and Abu Dhabi in the UAE were tied for number 50.

The starting point in differential compensation is a **cost-of-living allowance.** This allowance is intended to offset differences in the cost of living in the home and host countries. The premise is that a manager who accepts a foreign assignment is entitled to the same standard of living the manager enjoyed at home. If the cost of living in the foreign country is higher than that at home, the manager's existing base pay will result in a lower standard of living, and the firm will supplement the base pay to offset this difference. Of course, if the cost of living in the foreign location is lower than at home, no such allowance is needed.

Sometimes firms find they must supplement base pay to get a manager to accept an assignment in a relatively unattractive location. Although it may not be difficult to find people willing to move to England or Japan, it may be much more difficult to entice people to move to Sudan or Afghanistan. Called either a **hardship premium** or a **foreign-service premium,** this supplement is essentially an inducement to the individual to accept the international assignment. For instance, the French oil company Total wanted to transfer managers back to its operations in Angola when that country's bloody civil war ended; it found that it had to offer a substantial foreign-service premium to entice anyone to go. Even then, those executives also insisted that their assignment in Angola would last for one year or less.

Finally, many international businesses also find they must set up a tax equalization system. A **tax equalization system** is a means of ensuring that the expatriate's after-tax income in the host country is similar to what the person's after-tax income would be in the home country. Each country has unique tax laws that apply to the earnings of its own citizens, to earnings within its borders by foreign citizens, and/or to earnings in another country by its own citizens. The most common tax equalization system has the firm's own accounting department handling the taxes of its expatriates. An accountant from the firm determines what a manager's taxes will be where the manager is living and what they would be at home on the same income and then makes the appropriate adjustment to equalize the two.

Figure 19.5 shows how one major oil company creates compensation packages for its expatriate managers. The blocks in the center reflect an individual's U.S. base compensation prior to being posted to an international assignment. After an assignment has been made, the blocks above and below are used to calculate appropriate adjustments to the employee's compensation. For example, suppose a U.S. executive being transferred abroad currently earns $100,000, of which $25,000 is paid in taxes, $10,000 is saved, and the remaining $65,000 consumed. Further suppose that the executive currently spends $2,000 a month on housing (mortgage plus utilities). The firm will adjust the executive's total compensation to make it as equal as possible to that currently earned in the United States. Assume that housing and utilities in the host country cost about 20 percent more than in the United States, and other consumables cost about 10 percent more. Thus, the firm will pay the executive a supplemental housing allowance that is equal to what the executive currently pays times 20 percent, or a total of $400 a month. The remaining part of the executive's consumption spending will be increased by 10 percent. Similar adjustments will be made to the other components of Figure 19.5.

BENEFITS PACKAGES FOR EXPATRIATE MANAGERS International businesses must provide not only salary adjustments but also special forms of benefits for their expatriate managers in addition to standard benefits such as health insurance and vacation allowances. Special benefits include housing, education, medical treatment, travel to the home country, and club memberships.

MAP 19.1

Global Cost of Living Survey

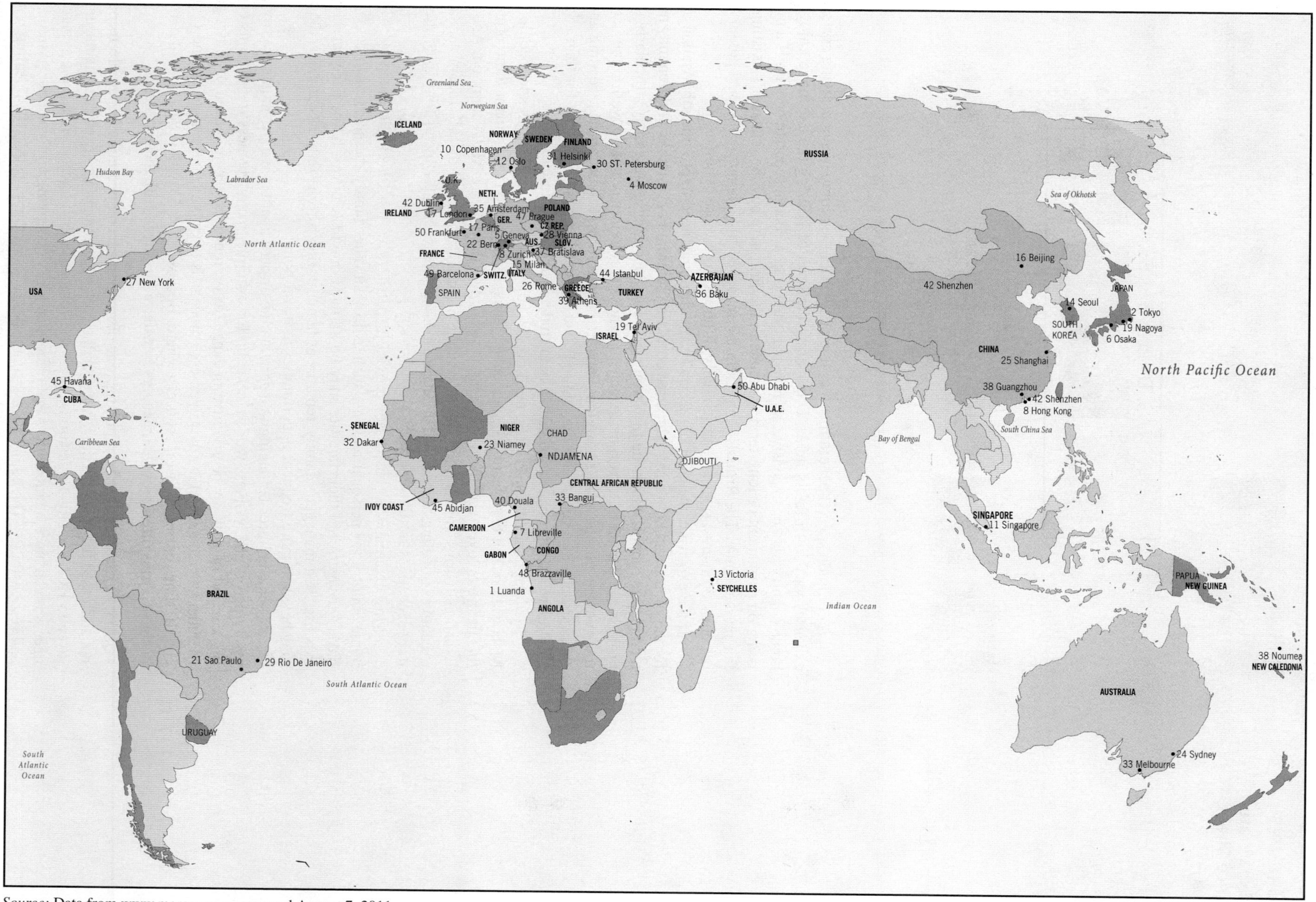

North Pacific Ocean

Sea of Okhotsk

2 Tokyo
19 Nagoya
6 Osaka
JAPAN
14 Seoul
SOUTH KOREA
16 Beijing
25 Shanghai
42 Shenzhen
38 Shenzhen
8 Hong Kong
South China Sea
CHINA
42 Shenzhen

38 Nouméa
NEW CALEDONIA

24 Sydney
33 Melbourne
AUSTRALIA

PAPUA NEW GUINEA

SINGAPORE
11 Singapore

RUSSIA

Bay of Bengal

Indian Ocean

50 Abu Dhabi
U.A.E.

13 Victoria
SEYCHELLES

DJIBOUTI

AZERBAIJAN
36 Baku
30 St. Petersburg
4 Moscow
44 Istanbul
TURKEY
19 Tel Aviv
ISRAEL

CENTRAL AFRICAN REPUBLIC
33 Bangui

FINLAND
31 Helsinki
SWEDEN
NORWAY
12 Oslo
10 Copenhagen
POLAND
CZECH REP.
AUS.
SLOV.
28 Vienna
37 Bratislava
26 Rome
15 Milan
ITALY
39 Athens
GREECE
35 Amsterdam
NETH.
GER.
17 Frankfurt
47 Prague
5 Geneva
3 Bern
22 Zurich
SWITZ.
17 London
50 Paris
FRANCE
49 Barcelona
SPAIN
42 Dublin
IRELAND
ICELAND

Greenland Sea
Norwegian Sea

CHAD
NDJAMENA
NIGER
23 Niamey
40 Douala
CAMEROON
GABON
7 Libreville
CONGO
48 Brazzaville
1 Luanda
ANGOLA

45 Abidjan
IVORY COAST

SENEGAL
32 Dakar

North Atlantic Ocean
Labrador Sea
Hudson Bay

USA
27 New York

45 Havana
CUBA
Caribbean Sea

South Atlantic Ocean

BRAZIL
29 Rio De Janeiro
21 Sao Paulo
URUGUAY

South Atlantic Ocean

South Atlantic Ocean

Source: Data from www.mercer.com, accessed August 7, 2011.

553

FIGURE 19.5

An Expatriate Balance Sheet

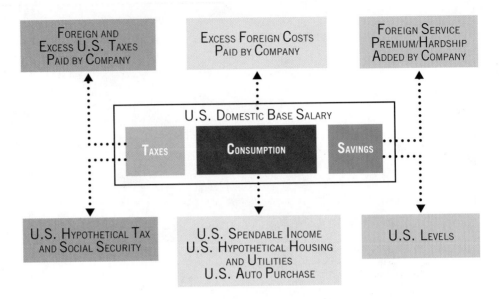

A common special benefit involves housing. Like other components of living costs, housing expenses vary in different areas. Duplicating the level of housing the executive enjoyed in the home country may be expensive, so housing often is treated as a separate benefit. If a manager is going on permanent or long-term assignment, the firm may buy the manager's existing home at fair-market value. The firm also may help the manager buy a house in the host country if housing costs or interest rates are substantially different from those at home.

If the expatriate manager has a family, the firm may need to provide job location assistance for the spouse and help cover education costs for children. For example, children may need to attend private school, which the firm would pay for. Schooling represents a particularly important problem for Japanese expatriate managers, whose children may not do well in the national entrance exams for the most prestigious Japanese universities if their Japanese reading and writing skills atrophy as a result of living abroad. Thus, many Japanese firms pay for their expatriates' children to attend private schools that help students cram for those exams.

Medical benefits also may need to be adjusted. For example, some people consider Malaysian health care facilities inadequate. Thus, managers on assignment there often request that their employer send them to Singapore whenever they need medical attention. And many international firms are routinely incorporating immunizations and dietary recommendations for executives traveling abroad, and arranging medical exams and treatments for expatriates and visiting executives from overseas.[25]

Most international businesses provide expatriates with a travel allowance for trips to the home country for personal reasons, such as to visit other family members or to celebrate holidays. Managers and their families may be allowed one or two trips home per year at company expense. If a manager's family remains at home during a short-term assignment, the manager may be given more frequent opportunities to travel home.

In some cultures belonging to a certain club or participating in a particular activity is a necessary part of the business world. In Japan, for example, many business transactions occur during a round of golf. To be effective in Japan, a foreign manager may need to join a golf club. Memberships in such clubs, however, cost thousands of dollars, and a single round of golf may cost 10 times or more what it costs elsewhere. Because such activities are a normal part of doing business, firms often provide managers transferred to Japan with these benefits.

EQUITY IN COMPENSATION Thus far, our discussion of compensating expatriate managers has not addressed the issue of equity between the compensation granted expatriate managers and that given to HCNs in similar positions. Often the compensation package offered the expatriate manager is much more lucrative than that offered an HCN occupying an equivalent position of power and responsibility. The equity issue becomes even more complicated when dealing with TCNs. For example, if a U.S. international oil firm transfers a Venezuelan executive to its Peruvian operations, should the Venezuelan be paid according to Peruvian, Venezuelan, or U.S. standards?

Unfortunately there is no simple solution to this problem, and MNCs use a variety of approaches in grappling with it. Hewlett-Packard pays expatriates on short-term assignments according to home country standards and those on long-term assignments according to host country standards. Minnesota Mining & Manufacturing (3M) compares the compensation package it offers in the expatriate's home country with what it normally pays HCNs and then gives the expatriate the higher pay package. Phillips Petroleum pegs a TCN's salary to that of the person's home country but offers housing allowances, educational benefits, and home leaves based on costs in the host country.

The failing value of the dollar and recent changes in the U.S. tax codes have caused some firms to begin an intensive study and review of their expatriate compensation and benefits programs. For instance, the taxes expatriates pay on their foreign housing allowance has recently been increased; some firms pay this cost for their employees and so the higher rates are passed on to the employer. Higher costs have also led some firms to rethink the best people to consider for a new international assignment. If a multinational has a large operation in both Eastern Europe and the United States, for instance, it might find that an executive from the Czech Republic will accept more modest living arrangements for an assignment in Singapore than will his or her colleague from New York.[26]

BRINGING THE WORLD INTO FOCUS | **JAPANESE MANAGEMENT TECHNIQUES IN CHINA**

Japanese multinational corporations operating in China have invariably brought Japanese management techniques and practices to their factories and operations in China. On the one hand, Japanese management seems to be a fairly good fit, but many Chinese employees suggest that there are fundamental problems, ranging from seating arrangements to incentive structures. Certainly an enormous number of Chinese employees resign from Japanese companies. Most university graduates stay no longer than three years and Japanese companies rank very low for Chinese workers as businesses they would like to work for. Sony was only ranked twenty-fourth and Matsushita forty-sixth.

One of the key cultural differences that caused problems for Chinese employees is the layout of the offices. Japanese companies use open-office layouts, with no partitions and desks arranged in clusters.

The second key criticism was the fact that Japanese businesses are too process orientated. They demand that all tasks are carried out using a particular work procedure, even down to teaching employees how to file. Working time is also a key issue. Overtime is part of the culture of Japanese companies and Chinese employees are expected to work 40 or more hours overtime per month. The feeling is that overtime equals hard work. In compensation, Japanese companies do pay for overtime in China, which is not always the case in Japan. Paid leave is also an issue—the Chinese seeing paid leave as an entitlement and the Japanese seeing it as a concession.

Remuneration is also a concern for the Chinese workers. European and American multinational companies tend to pay more than the Japanese. Career development is problematic too. Senior management is almost exclusively reserved for Japanese nationals. If Japanese employees leave (which is rare), the parent company sends a replacement Japanese manager to fill the post, rather than offering it to similarly qualified Chinese employees.

There are still anti-Japanese sentiments in China, so it is reasonable to consider the points with a degree of caution. The Japanese may have believed that in wholesale export of their management style they would have been able to replicate Japanese management systems and decision-making processes. However, in instances this may have been undermined by an over reliance on ex-patriot Japanese management.

Sources: International Journal of Human Resource Management (www.palgrave-journals.com); Japanese Institute for Labor Policy and Training (www.jil.go.jp).

Retention and Turnover

Another important element of international HRM focuses on retention and turnover. **Retention** is the extent to which a firm is able to retain valued employees. **Turnover,** essentially the opposite, is the rate at which people leave a firm.

People choose to leave a firm for any number of reasons—for example, dissatisfaction with their current pay or promotion opportunities or receipt of a better offer to work elsewhere. Turnover is often a result of job transitions such as those associated with expatriation and repatriation: A worker contemplating changing work locations also may consider changing employers. Turnover is a particular problem in international business because of the high cost of developing managers' international business skills. Managers with strong reputations for having those skills are in high demand. As noted earlier, some firms even rely on headhunters to help them locate prospective managers currently working for other firms. For exactly the same reason—a scarcity of skilled, experienced managers—keeping successful managers should be a high priority for any international business. One way to control managerial turnover is to develop strategies designed to reduce expatriate failure and repatriate failure. These may include providing career development counseling or cross-cultural training to ease the stress of relocation.

A firm also may have to provide special inducements or incentives to its most valuable international managers. They may receive higher salaries or be given a greater say in choosing their assignments. The firm also may make stronger guarantees to them regarding the time frame of their assignments. For example, a firm may want to hire a particularly skillful TCN to run its operation in Italy. Because of the costs and other problems associated with relocation, the individual may consider the assignment only if the firm guarantees the assignment will last for a minimum of, say, five years.

Another important element of turnover management is the **exit interview.** An exit interview is an interview with an employee who is leaving a firm. Its purpose is to find out as much as possible about why the person decided to leave. Given the distances involved in international business, however, firms may be reluctant to do exit interviews. Yet the potential value of the information gleaned is high: Managers can use it to reduce future employee losses. Thus, firms should give careful consideration to using such interviews as part of their strategy for reducing turnover.

Dubai-based Emirates airlines has been growing rapidly in recent years. In order to maintain the necessary cadre of skilled pilots, Emirates has routinely been hiring pilots from other countries. For example, there are over 100 former U.S. pilots currently working for Emirates. By providing strong salaries and benefits packages, the airline has become a very attractive place to work. Some airlines in China and India have also adopted this model.

© bronstein/Alamy

The U.S. airline industry has been facing mounting challenges in retaining its best pilots. For years, as the airlines went through one financial difficult after another, pilots saw their salaries cut, their benefits reduced, and/or their job security eliminated. As new foreign airlines have sprung up, they have come to see the U.S. labor pool a ready source of pilots. For example, Dubai-based Emirates air offers its pilots a freshly pressed uniform and a chauffer-driven ride to the airport each day they fly. Emirates pilots also get twice the vacation time as their U.S. counterparts, as well as guaranteed annual raises and strong benefits. All told, there are over 100 former U.S. pilots now working for Emirates. New start-up airlines in China and India are also aggressively recruiting U.S. pilots.[27]

Human Resource Issues for Nonmanagerial Employees

Next, we shift the focus of our discussion of HR issues to nonmanagerial employees in host countries. The standard HRM tasks associated with nonmanagerial employees—recruitment, selection, training, compensation, and so on—are strongly influenced by local laws, culture, and economic conditions. To prosper in the host country environment, HR managers must not fall prey to their own self-referencing criteria. They must be willing to do things the way the locals want, not the way things are done at home. In short, "When in Rome, do as the Romans do." Thus, many MNCs hire HCNs to staff their HR operations, so the local knowledge of the HCNs can be incorporated into the policies and procedures of the HR department.

Recruitment and Selection

In international firms' foreign operations nonmanagerial employees, such as blue-collar production workers and white-collar office workers, are typically HCNs. In most cases there are economic reasons for this decision: HCNs are usually cheaper to employ than are PCNs or TCNs. HCNs also are used because local laws often promote the hiring of locals. Immigration and visa laws, for example, typically restrict jobs to citizens and legal residents of the country. A few exceptions to this rule exist. Construction firms in rich countries like Saudi Arabia and Kuwait often use Bangladeshi or Pakistani labor because local citizens dislike the working conditions. Oil firms and airlines often employ PCNs and TCNs for high-skilled jobs such as drilling supervisor and pilot.

Nonetheless, an international business must develop and implement a plan for recruiting and selecting its employees in a host country market.[28] This plan should include assessments of the firm's human resources needs, sources of labor, labor force skills and talents, and training requirements, and also should account for special circumstances that exist in the local labor market.

When firms are hiring PCNs for foreign assignments, the firms must adhere to their home country's hiring regulations, laws, and norms. When hiring HCNs, the firms must be aware of those regulations, laws, and norms within the host country. For example, in the United States laws and regulations prohibit a firm from discriminating against someone on the basis of gender, race, age, religion, and other characteristics. Because of these restrictions, the selection process in the United States emphasizes job relatedness. Job-related criteria such as skills, abilities, and education can be used to hire employees; non-job-related criteria such as gender or age cannot. In some countries characteristics such as gender, religion, and skin color are commonly used in hiring decisions. For example, firms in Israel and Northern Ireland often discriminate on the basis of religion, and those in Saudi Arabia discriminate on the basis of gender.

Training and Development

HR managers also must assess the training and development needs of the host country's workforces to help them perform their jobs more effectively. The training and development needs of local workforces depend on several factors. An important one is the location of the foreign operation. In highly industrialized markets firms usually find a nucleus of capable workers who may need only a bit of firm-specific training. In an area that is relatively underdeveloped, training needs will be much greater. For example, when Hilton began operating hotels in Eastern Europe after the Soviet Union disintegrated, it found that waiters, hotel clerks, and other customer service employees lacked the basic skills necessary to provide high-quality service to guests. These employees were so accustomed to working in a planned economy, where there was little or no need to worry about customer satisfaction, that they had difficulty recognizing why they needed to change their workplace behavior. Hilton had to invest much more in training new employees there than it had anticipated.

Training also is a critical element if an international business wants to take full advantage of locating production abroad. In recent years MNCs have shown a marked tendency to move facilities to certain areas, such as Honduras, Malaysia, and Indonesia, to capitalize on inexpensive labor. But often the productivity of this labor is low, unless the firm is willing to invest in workforce training. In Malaysia, for example, only one-third of adults have more than a sixth-grade education; thus, training costs there can be quite high. The owner of Quality Coils, Inc., a U.S. maker of electromagnetic coils, closed the firm's plant in Connecticut and opened a plant in Ciudad Juarez, Mexico, because hourly wage rates there were one-third the wage rates in Connecticut. The owner soon discovered, however, that productivity was also only one-third of what it had been in Connecticut. This, combined with higher absenteeism and the personal costs of running a facility in Mexico, prompted the owner to move the operation back to Connecticut.[29]

Training costs sometimes arise for reasons the firm might not have anticipated. For example, when Merrill Lynch bought Japan's fourth-largest brokerage company, Yamaichi Securities, it thought it was also gaining a cadre of 2,000 talented and experienced brokers familiar with their domestic market. But Merrill Lynch soon discovered that while Yamaichi brokers knew how to handle stock transactions, they were unfamiliar with concepts associated with customer service and working to understand customer investment goals before making stock recommendations. Hence, Merrill had to invest heavily in training its new brokers in how it wanted them to work with clients.[30]

Compensation and Performance Appraisal

Compensation and performance appraisal practices for nonmanagerial employees also differ dramatically among countries, depending on local laws, customs, and cultures. Individualistic cultures such as that of the United States focus on assessing the individual's performance and then compensating the person accordingly. More group-oriented cultures such as Japan's emphasize training and motivating the group and place less emphasis on individual performance appraisal and compensation. The HR manager at each foreign operation must develop and implement a performance appraisal and reporting system most appropriate for that setting, given the nature of the work being performed and the cultural context. For example, although U.S. workers often appreciate feedback from the appraisal system—thereby allowing them to do better in the future—German workers are often resentful of feedback, believing it requires them to admit failures and shortcomings.[31]

Compensation practices also reflect local laws, culture, and economic conditions. Prevailing wage rates vary among countries, which has caused many labor-intensive industries to migrate to countries such as Malaysia, Indonesia, and Guatemala. To attract workers, HR managers must ensure their firms' wage scales are consistent with local norms.

Compensation packages entail incentive payments and benefit programs in addition to wages. International business researchers have found that the mix among wages, benefits, and incentive payments varies as a function of national culture. For example, wages on average accounted for 85 percent of the total compensation package for workers in 41 manufacturing industries in four Asian countries. However, wages amounted to only 56 percent of the total compensation package for workers in those same industries in five "Latin European" countries. By adjusting the composition of the compensation package to meet local norms, HR managers ensure their workers (and the firm) get the maximum value from each compensation dollar spent.[32] Local laws also affect an international firm's compensation policies. For example, Mexican law requires employers to provide paid maternity leave, a Christmas bonus of 15 days' pay, and at least three months' severance pay for dismissed workers. Local norms may also have an impact on compensation costs. In Sweden, workers use more sick leave than is the case in other countries—an average of 24.4 days per year, four times as much as U.S. workers and twice as much as the average Danish, German, or Spanish employee.[33]

Labor Relations

A final component of international HRM is labor relations. Because of their complexity and importance, labor relations often are handled as a separate organizational function, apart from human resource management.

Comparative Labor Relations

Labor relations in a host country often reflect its laws, culture, social structure, and economic conditions. For example, membership in U.S. labor unions has been steadily declining in recent years and today constitutes less than 15 percent of the country's total workforce. Labor relations in the United States are heavily regulated by various laws, and both the actions of management toward labor and the actions of labor toward management are heavily restricted. Further, the formal labor agreement negotiated between a firm and a union is a binding contract enforceable in a court of law. Because of the heavy regulation, most negotiations are relatively formal and mechanical, with both parties relying on the letter of law.

A different situation exists in many other countries. In some countries union membership is very high and continues to grow. In Europe labor unions are much more important than in the United States. Labor unions in many European countries are aligned with political parties, and their fortunes ebb and flow as a function of which party currently controls the government. Throughout most of Europe temporary work stoppages are frequently used by unions in a bid for public backing for their demands. For example, the transport workers' union in Paris often calls for day-long work stoppages that result in the city's buses, subways, and railroads being totally shut down. The union hopes the inconvenienced public will call on elected officials to do whatever it takes to avoid such disruptions in the future. Foreign firms that try to alter prevailing host country labor relations may be buying trouble. For example, the unwillingness of Toys 'R' Us to adopt the standard collective bargaining agreement used by most Swedish retailers led to a three-month strike against the firm and denunciations by labor leaders who branded the firm "an anti-union interloper bent on breaking established traditions in Sweden," which was not the public image the firm was trying to create.[34] Likewise, German retail unions used short but frequent work stoppages to try to get Walmart to meet more of their demands.

In contrast, labor relations in Japan tend to be cordial. Labor unions usually are created and run by businesses themselves. Unions and management tend to work cooperatively toward their mutual best interests. The Japanese culture discourages confrontation and hostility, and these norms carry over into labor relations. Disputes are normally resolved cordially and through mutual agreement. In the rare event that a third-party mediator is necessary, there is seldom any hard feelings or hostility after a decision has been rendered. Thus, strikes are relatively rare in Japan.

Collective Bargaining

Collective bargaining is the process used to make agreements between management and labor unions. As already noted, collective bargaining in the United States is highly regulated. Aside from passing the laws that regulate the process, however, government plays a relatively passive role in establishing labor agreements. Union and management representatives meet and negotiate a contract. That contract governs their collective working relationship until the contract expires, when a new one is negotiated. Bargaining normally takes place on a firm-by-firm and union-by-union basis. For example, United Air Lines must bargain with a pilots union, a flight attendants union, a mechanics union, and so on, one at a time. Further, each of these unions negotiates individually with each airline whose employees it represents.

In many other countries the government is much more active in collective bargaining. In some European countries collective bargaining is undertaken by representatives of several firms and unions, along with government officials. The outcome is an umbrella agreement that applies to entire industries and collections of related labor unions. In Japan collective bargaining also usually involves government officials but is done on a firm-by-firm basis. A government official serves more as an observer, recording what transpires and answering any questions that arise during the negotiation.

Union Influence and Codetermination

Union influence can be manifested in various ways, including membership, strikes, and public relations. In Europe much of the influence of labor unions arises from the premise of industrial democracy—the belief that workers should have a voice in how businesses are run. In some countries, most notably Germany, union influence extends far beyond traditional boundaries of labor-management relations. The approach taken in Germany is called codetermination and provides for cooperation between management and labor in running the business.

Codetermination is the result of a 1947 German law that required firms in the coal and steel industries to allow unions to have input into how the firms were run. The law has been amended several times, and today it applies to all German firms with 2,000 or more employees. The law requires all covered firms to establish a supervisory board. Half the seats on this board are elected by the firm's owners (much like the board of directors of a U.S. corporation); the other half are appointed or elected by labor. Of the labor seats one-third are union officials and two-thirds are elected by the workforce. One seat elected by labor must be occupied by a managerial employee, so management essentially controls a potential tie-breaking vote. The supervisory board oversees another board called the board of managers. This board, composed of the firm's top managers, actually runs the business on a day-to-day basis.

The German model promotes a high level of industrial democracy. Some other European countries, including Sweden, the Netherlands, Norway, Luxembourg, Denmark, and Austria, take similar approaches in requiring some form of labor representation in running businesses. In contrast, Italy, Ireland, the United Kingdom, and Latvia have little or no mandated labor participation. However, the EU has been attempting to standardize labor practices, employment regulations, and benefits packages throughout its member states. The ongoing implementation of its **social charter** (sometimes called the **social policy**) focuses on such concerns as maternity leave, job training, and superannuation (pension) benefits. One motivation for the social charter is to reduce the potential loss of jobs from richer countries, such as Germany or Belgium, to countries with lower wages and poorer benefit programs, such as Portugal, Greece, and Spain. Worker participation reform also is spreading into Pacific Asia. For example, workers in Singapore have been given a considerably stronger voice in how businesses are operated. Even though Japanese workers do not have a particularly strong voice in the management of their firms, they traditionally have enjoyed an abundance of personal power and control over how they perform their own jobs.

MyManagementLab   Now that you have finished this chapter, go back to **www.pearsonglobaleditions.com/mymanagementlab** to continue practicing and applying the concepts you've learned.

CHAPTER REVIEW

Summary

Human resource management is the set of activities directed at attracting, developing, and maintaining the effective workforce necessary to achieve a firm's objectives. Because the HR function is central to a firm's success, top managers should adopt a strategic perspective on it.

International human resource needs are partially dictated by a firm's degree of internationalization. The relative degree of centralization versus decentralization of control also plays an important role. A basic staffing philosophy should be developed and followed.

Recruitment and selection are important elements of international HRM. Some firms choose to recruit experienced managers for foreign assignments, whereas others hire younger, and more likely inexperienced, managers. Various avenues may be

used for either approach to recruiting. The selection of managers for foreign assignments usually involves consideration of both business and international skills. Managers and firms must address a variety of expatriation and repatriation issues.

Training and development also are important aspects of international HRM. The two principal components of this activity are the assessment of training needs and the selection of basic training methods and procedures.

A firm also must assess the performance of its international managers and determine their compensation. Compensation for expatriate managers usually includes a cost-of-living adjustment as well as special benefits.

Given the high cost of training and development of expatriates, firms need to focus special attention on managing retention and turnover. Each part of international HRM also must be addressed for the firm's nonmanagerial employees.

Labor relations pose an especially complex task for HR managers and often are handled by a special department. One key aspect of labor relations is collective bargaining, or negotiating agreements with unions.

Review Questions

1. Along what dimensions does domestic HRM differ from international HRM?
2. How does the degree of centralization or decentralization affect international staffing?
3. What are the basic issues involved in recruiting and selecting managers for foreign assignments?
4. What issues are at the core of expatriation and repatriation problems?
5. Why is performance appraisal important for international firms?
6. What special compensation and benefits issues arise in international HRM?
7. How does international HRM for nonmanagerial employees differ from that for managerial employees?

Questions for Discussion

1. How does HRM relate to other functional areas such as marketing, finance, and operations management?
2. Why and how does the scope of a firm's internationalization affect its HRM practices?
3. How are the different approaches to recruiting and selecting managers for foreign assignments similar and dissimilar?
4. Which are easier to assess, business skills or international skills? Why?
5. If you were being assigned to a foreign position, what specific training requests would you make of your employer?
6. Do you agree or disagree with the idea that some international assignments require special compensation?
7. How easy or difficult do you think it is to handle the equity issue in international compensation?
8. What does the high cost of replacing an international manager suggest regarding staffing philosophy?
9. Which do you think is easier, HRM for managerial employees or HRM for nonmanagerial employees? Why?

Building Global Skills

Assume you are the top HR manager for a large international firm. The head of your company's operation in Japan has just resigned unexpectedly to take a job with another firm. You must decide on a replacement as quickly as possible. You have developed the following list of potential candidates for the job:

- Jack Henderson: Henderson is a senior vice president based in your Chicago headquarters. Jack has a long and distinguished career with your firm, is well regarded by everyone, and plans to retire in three years. He has never worked outside the United States but is strongly and visibly lobbying for the job in Japan. Because you and your spouse socialize with Jack and his wife outside of work, you know she does not want to move from Chicago.
- Takeo Takahashi: Takahashi is the number two manager in your Japanese operation, although he has served in that role for only three months. He was born and raised in Japan. After attending college in the United States, he returned to Japan and went to work for your firm. Takeo is considered an emerging star in the company but is also relatively young and inexperienced. Your CEO prefers to appoint someone for the Japanese job with at least 15 years of company experience, and Takeo has only eight years of experience. He was being groomed to eventually take over the operation,

but the just-departed top executive had been expected to serve until he reached retirement age in another seven years.
- Jane Yamaguchi: Yamaguchi is a Hawaiian-born manager currently heading up a major division for your company in the United States. She was a dual economics and Asian studies major at the University of Hawaii. For the last several years she has been studying the Japanese market and has become a true expert on that country. She enjoys traveling and spends as much time in Asia as possible. You know she would be very interested in this job if it were offered, although you are concerned that her husband and two high-school-age children may not share her enthusiasm about living in Japan. In addition, you worry that if she is not offered a new challenge soon, she might start looking for another position.
- Jacques Moine: Moine is your most experienced international manager. Originally from France, Jacques has held senior management positions in your firm's operations in Germany, Spain, Canada, Argentina, and Mexico. Moine appears to be quite satisfied with his current posting in Mexico. Because that operation is both stable and very efficient, it likely could be run by someone with less experience.

Working alone, carefully consider the strengths and weaknesses of each of the four leading candidates for the job. Select the individual you think is the best candidate.

Then form small groups of four or five students. Share with each other your individual choices for the job in Japan, along with the reasons for making those choices.

THE CHICAGO FOOD AND BEVERAGE COMPANY

The Chicago Food and Beverage Company (CFBC) is an American multinational with subsidiaries in North America, Europe, and Asia. Paul Fierman, a 34-year-old American manager, was appointed general director of CFBC Vietnam with a mission to lead the subsidary and implement the new organizational strategy.

Obtaining this expatriate position had not been difficult for Paul. In 1995 he earned his bachelor's degree in marketing from Cornell University. After graduation, Paul took a position as product vice manager in the marketing department at the New York subsidiary of CFBC. Three years later, he became carbonated nonalcoholic beverages' manager for the Eastern American region. After two years in this position, Paul was put in charge of both carbonated and noncarbonated nonalcoholic drinks in the U.S. market. As a country manager, he was paid an annual base salary of $300,000 and 10 to 15 percent commission on sales. Although Paul was satisfied with his job, he wanted to reorientate his career toward general management positions in the company. Therefore, in 2002 he decided to undertake a full-time Master in Business Administration studies in international management at Harvard Business School. After completing his MBA, Paul wanted to return to CFBC, but in order be able to reach the pinnacle of his career, he thought he needed to acquire some international professional experience. The only international experience he had so far was a year spent in Oxford, Great Britain, as an exchange program student.

Paul kept in touch with his former supervisor at his first position within CFBC, Allan Roger, marketing director of the New York subsidiary. Just before graduating from his MBA, Paul called Allan to discuss his potential return to the company. Allan was very enthusiastic about this prospect :

"The expatriate Managing Director of CFBC Haiphong, Vietnam, has just returned to the U.S. unexpectedly due to health problems, the headquarters are desperate to replace him as soon as possible. If you are interested, you can send me your application for the position of Managing Director in Vietnam, and I will forward it to the General Manager in Chicago. You have high potential in this company! Your lack of international experience is a problem...but it does not mean that you would not be able to prepare and

implement, in collaboration with the regional director of Pacific Rim, the new strategy to integrate the three Asian subsidiaries. This expatriation would be an exceptional training experience for you, preparing you for a higher level managing position within the Chicago headquarters on your return to the U.S. three years later."

With his experience within CFBC and his high recommendations, Paul Fierman was a good candidate for this three-year expatriate position. He was perceived as a promising young manager due to his excellent academic background and the outstanding professional results he achieved during his employment within the company.

At that point, things moved very quickly. In March 2004, thanks to Allan's intervention and contacts, Paul met directly with the general manager in Chicago. Two weeks later, a notice of approval had been sent to Paul from the Chicago HR department, officially confirming his managing position in Vietnam. Robert Greenberg, managing director in charge of the Asia Pacific region, had been informed about Paul's nomination by Chicago's general manager himself. One month later, in April 2004, Paul began his new position in Haiphong. Before his departure he spent a couple of weeks preparing his move and organizing the rental of his house in New York. His wife Carrie and their seven-year-old daughter Rachel joined him two months later in Haiphong. These two extra months gave Carrie enough time to have her resignation accepted by her employer. In the meantime, Paul settled into their new Vietnamese house and enrolled their daughter at Haiphong international school. Before his departure, Paul bought three books on Vietnam in order to get some preliminary knowledge about the general business context of the country. However, his readings on culture and the economic and political history of Vietnam seemed to be too disconnected from today's business reality.

One week before his arrival in Vietnam, Paul had a three-hour meeting with Robert Greenberg in New York. Robert showed him the outlines of the corporate strategy aiming at creating synergies among the three Asian subsidiaries. Since then, they never spoke to each other directly. Six months after his arrival in Vietnam, Paul was feeling extremely frustrated.

"I feel very frustrated by the results of my work in the subsidiary and the relationships I have with my Vietnamese colleagues. The financial situation of the subsidiary six months after my arrival is very bad: declining revenues, decreasing motivation of Vietnamese plant workers and staff, lack of cooperation on behalf of local management, etc. The implementation of the new organizational strategy is far from even getting off the ground! I have to handle all these problems alone. I have the impression that my work does not produce any of the expected results."

Case Questions

1. Which staffing philosophy do you recognize at CFBC?
2. How would you have organized the recruitment and selection of the right candidate?
3. How well was Paul prepared for his expatriation?

Source: V. Bodolica and M. F. Waxin, International HRM Case Study, "Chicago Food and Beverage Company: The Challenges of Managing International Assignments," *Journal of International Academy For Case Studies, 13*, 3(2007): 31–43.

PART 4 CLOSING CASES   THE ARAMCO ADVANTAGE

Between the years 1979 and 1981 Saudi Arabia had a major disagreement with the other members of the Organization of Petroleum Exporting Countries (OPEC) about the appropriate price to charge for a barrel of crude oil. So-called OPEC hawks wanted to keep the price of oil high. Saudi Arabia, fearful that high prices would encourage other countries to explore for new, low-cost oil fields and stimulate consumers to conserve on energy usage, believed the most profitable long-run strategy was to keep prices low. The Saudis' actions resulted in the creation of the "Aramco advantage" and the world's largest tax refund involving transfer pricing.

Aramco was a consortium of four U.S. oil companies—Chevron, Exxon, Mobil, and Texaco—that originally controlled the Saudi oil fields. (Exxon and Mobil have subsequently merged, as have Chevron and Texaco.) After its oil reserves were expropriated by the Saudi government in the 1970s, Aramco continued to play a major role in marketing Saudi oil. The Aramco advantage began in January 1979 when Ahmed Zaki Yamani, the Saudi oil minister, wrote a letter to Aramco forbidding it to sell Saudi oil for more than the price set by Yamani's ministry. This price was well below the world market price for crude oil. The Aramco partners, not wishing to displease the Saudi government, dutifully complied with Yamani's request. They sold the crude oil to their foreign refineries at Yamani's price and then refined the oil into gasoline, diesel fuel, and other petroleum products. Yamani's directive, however, covered only the price of crude oil. Each company was free to sell the refined products at their market prices, which the four companies did. Because they were buying the crude oil at less than the market price, the refining operations of the Aramco partners were soon making money hand over fist. (In case you are wondering, Yamani was not ignorant of the impact of his letter. He had numerous political reasons for his actions.)

The impact of the Aramco advantage was enormous. Exxon's refineries earned an additional $4.5 billion from 1979 to 1981, and Texaco's refineries netted an estimated $1.8 billion. Because these profits were earned by the companies' foreign refinery subsidiaries, the profits could be sheltered from U.S. taxation thanks to the deferral rule—or so the companies thought. The U.S. Internal Revenue Service (IRS) had a different view, arguing that it was the marketing activities of the two companies that were responsible for the profits, not the refining operations. Accordingly, the IRS claimed that $4.5 billion in income should be transferred to Exxon (the parent corporation) from its foreign refineries and that Texaco should make a similar shift of $1.8 billion. Having done so, the companies then should be required to pay U.S. corporate income taxes on these earnings.

Not surprisingly, the companies resisted the IRS's interpretation. They said they were following the explicit instructions of the minister of a sovereign, friendly nation. Because of Yamani's directive, Texaco and Exxon asserted that the parent companies were unable to directly benefit from lower crude oil prices because the companies were forbidden to resell the oil at the market price. Rather, they noted that the Aramco advantage could be captured only by someone operating further down in the production-distribution chain. As things turned out, it was the next link in the chain—the foreign refineries owned by the individual Aramco partners—that garnered the Aramco advantage. Exxon and Texaco also pointed out that the United States had been putting great diplomatic pressure on the Saudis to lower the price of crude oil and that U.S. officials were well aware that the result of this policy would be increased refining profits.

Texaco's case was the first to complete its long journey through the U.S. judicial system. The U.S. Tax Court agreed with Texaco's interpretation. The court found that the $1.8

billion in additional profits generated by the Aramco advantage were earned by Texaco's foreign refining subsidiaries and not subject to U.S. corporate income taxes unless and until the profits were repatriated back to the parent corporation in the form of dividends. A federal appeals court upheld the verdict of the Tax Court, and in April 1997 the U.S. Supreme Court refused to hear the IRS's appeal of the appeals court decision. Texaco's tax refund was estimated to be $700 million.

Questions

1. Which unit of Texaco really "earned" the Aramco advantage? Aramco itself? Texaco's foreign refineries? Texaco's marketing operations? Or the parent corporation?
2. Had Aramco sold the crude oil to Texaco's U.S. refineries, would Texaco have been able to avoid U.S. taxation on the Aramco advantage?
3. Because Minister Yamani created the Aramco advantage partly in response to U.S. diplomatic pressure, should Exxon and Texaco have been required to sell their allotment of Saudi crude oil to their domestic refineries?
4. The IRS lawyers argued that the appeals court ruling amounted to a "blueprint for the evasion of U.S. taxes. [It] … creates substantial tax incentives for United States corporations to encourage or to endure the adoption of profitable foreign 'legal restrictions' that 'require' such corporations to avoid United States taxation." Do you agree with the IRS position? Or is it just being a crybaby because it lost?

Sources: "Court blocks challenge of big tax refund for Texaco," *New York Times,* April 22, 1997, p. C1; "Texaco wins billion-dollar tax battle," *Houston Chronicle,* April 22, 1997, p. 1C.

TOXIC MILK

Back in 2004, China experienced a scandal that saw dozens of Chinese babies die from malnutrition after being fed fake or inferior quality baby milk powders. Some children died whilst others were hospitalized. An analysis of the formula revealed that it contained only traces of proteins and nutrients that would be found in normal milk powder.

A full-scale inquiry discovered that no less than 45 types of sub-standard powder were being produced by 141 factories across China. It was an example of counterfeit goods that often flood rural areas of China. The rural areas are targeted because supervision is relatively slack and the customers are badly informed.

Four years later, there was another toxic milk scandal in China. Approximately 400 babies had been taken ill in China by mid-September 2008. It was discovered that the milk had been contaminated with an industrial chemical, melamine. Melamine is banned from food products and is generally used to make plastics. Melamine is rich in nitrogen and therefore registers higher protein levels.

By the middle of September, 19 arrests had been made and it had become clear that melamine had been used by some Chinese suppliers of animal feed to make them appear to have more protein content. As the days passed in September, more and more Chinese babies were suffering from kidney stones; a rare complaint in young children. It also transpired that some 700 tons of the contaminated milk powder were in circulation.

By September 17, around 6,000 children had been taken ill after drinking the powdered milk and around 160 had experienced acute kidney failure. Still at the center of the scandal was the Sanlu Group, based in Shijiazhuang in Hebei province.

The police had launched an investigation and were arresting suspects. Some of those had sold the melamine, whilst others had knowingly sold the contaminated milk. The chairperson and general manager of the Sanlu Group, Tian Wenhua, was also arrested. By September 19, child deaths had risen to four and it was becoming clear that the melamine contamination was even wider than anyone had ever possibly feared.

In the seven days leading up to September 19, hospitals had been inundated with terrified families bringing in their children to look for signs of sickness caused by the toxic milk powder. In the Renmin Hospital in Shijiazhuang staff were seeing 500 children a day.

Despite China's assurances that the milk products had not been exported, there were health scares in Brunei, Indonesia, Singapore, Malaysia, Hong Kong, Taiwan, Japan, Bangladesh, Gabon, Burundi and the Philippines. All were testing Chinese dairy products or immediately recalling them from sale. Starbucks in China immediately stopped serving drinks with milk; Malaysia instituted a blanket ban to include chocolate and other confectionery; in Japan, bread products containing Chinese milk were pulled from the stores.

Beijing hospitals were besieged by anxious parents. There were long waiting lists for children to be scanned and tested and 69 batches of milk products made by 22 dairy companies had been revealed to contain melamine by September 19.

Singapore banned all Chinese dairy products on September 20, and the Chinese government was desperately searching for solutions to deal with the crisis. Medical authorities were instructed to provide free examination and treatment for children and more resources were thrown into rural areas to improve screening.

China's State Administration for Industry and Commerce (SAIC) launched a nationwide investigation into dairy producers and sellers. SAIC had so far received 106,143 complaints and had refunded 304.38 tons of dairy products.

In the six days before September 21, sales of baby milk powder brands involved in the contamination scandal had dropped by 33 percent. The Chinese dairy industry was concerned that foreign brands would now dominate the market. Most of the foreign branded baby milk powder sold for up to three times more than the price charged by Sanlu. As far as investigations were concerned, melamine had been added to milk since at least 2005. There were obviously loopholes in the management and supervision of manufacturers by the government watchdogs.

By September 22, it was clear that the bulk of the children that had been affected by the contaminated milk had actually drunk the Sanlu formula milk. By this stage, the toll of ill children had reached 53,000 and at least four were dead. Over a 100 children were seriously ill. The Chinese government had also worked out precisely why melamine had been added to the raw milk. Milk sellers would dilute the milk with water to increase the supply. They would then add melamine to boost the apparent protein content.

Consumer confidence in China had reached an all time low as far as the dairy industry was concerned, but anger was even greater. By October 15, 6,000 children were still in hospitals across China being treated for kidney diseases and 6 were in a serious condition. By late October, of the 300,000 Beijing families with children under 3 years of age, 74,000 families had a child that had been fed with the tainted milk.

Case Questions

1. What was the reaction of Fonterra to the discovery that Sanlu was selling contaminated milk?
2. There were criticisms that the Chinese authorities took too long to respond. How fair is this criticism?
3. Why would a business like Starbucks choose to curtail the sale of their products with milk ingredients?
4. How did the crisis affect the share price of Mengniu, Yili Group and Bright Dairy?

Sources: China Daily (www.chinadaily.com); Chinese government (www .english.gov.cn); Dairy Reporter (www.dairyreporter.com); Danwei (www.danwei .org); Shanghaiist (www.shanghaiist.com); Just Food (www.just-food.com); Fonterra (www.fonterra.com).

Endnotes

1. "The end of cheap labor in China," *Time*, June 27, 2011, pp. B1–B4; "Workers are finding their voice in China," *USA Today*, November 19, 2010, pp. B1, B2; "China's labor unrest leading to wage raises in several industries," *International Business Times*, December 17, 2011, pp. 5–7; "China labor unrest spreads as workers seek more," *Reuters*, June 10, 2011; Homer, *The Iliad*, Book XIII, Line 237.

2. Angelo S. DeNisi and Ricky W. Griffin, *Human Resource Management* (Cincinnati: Cengage, 2012); see also Kwok Leung and Mark F. Peterson, "Managing a globally distributed workforce: Social and interpersonal issues," in Sheldon Zedeck (Ed.), *Handbook of Industrial and Organizational Psychology* (Washington, DC: American Psychological Association, 2010).

3. "To get shipped abroad, women must overcome prejudice at home," *Wall Street Journal*, June 29, 1999, p. B1.

4. See Miriam Erez, "Cross-cultural and global issues in organizational psychology," in Sheldon Zedeck (Ed.), *Handbook of Industrial and Organizational Psychology* (Washington, DC: American Psychological Association, 2010).

5. Peter Cappelli, "Talent management for the twenty-first century," *Harvard Business Review*, March 2008, pp. 74–81.

6. Ya-Ru Chen, Kwok Leung, and Chao C. Chen, "Bringing national culture to the table: Making a difference with cross-cultural differences and perspectives," in James P. Walsh and Arthur P. Brief (Eds.), *The Academy of Management Annals 2009* (Philadelphia, PA: Taylor and Francis, 2009), pp. 217–250.

7. Nakiye Boyacigiller, "The role of expatriates in the management of interdependence, complexity, and risk in multinational corporations," *Journal of International Business Studies*, vol. 21, no. 3 (Third Quarter 1990), pp. 357–382.

8. Gretchen M. Spreitzer, Morgan W. McCall, Jr., and Joan D. Mahoney, "Early identification of international executive potential," *Journal of Applied Psychology*, vol. 82, no. 1 (1997), pp. 6–29.

9. See DeNisi and Griffin, *Human Resource Management*.

10. "Companies send Intrepid retirees to work abroad," *Wall Street Journal*, March 2, 1998, p. B1.

11. "Pharmacia to move headquarters to U.S. East Coast," *Wall Street Journal*, October 14, 1997, p. B14.

12. See J. Stewart Black and Hal B. Gregersen, "The right way to manage expats," *Harvard Business Review* (March–April 1999), pp. 52–62.

13. See Paula M. Caligiuri, "The big five personality characteristics as predictors of expatriate's desire to terminate the assignment," *Personnel Psychology*, vol. 53, no. 1 (2000), pp. 67–78.

14. "To smooth a transfer abroad, a new focus on kids," *Wall Street Journal*, January 26, 1999, pp. B1, B14.

15. Andrea C. Poe, "Destination everywhere," *HRMagazine*, October 2000, pp. 67–77.

16. Ann Marie Ryan, Lynn McFarland, Helen Baron, and Ron Page, "An international look at selection practices: Nation and culture as explanations for variability in practice," *Personnel Psychology*, vol. 52, no. 2 (1999), pp. 58–70.

17. Joel D. Nicholson, Lee P. Stepina, and Wayne Hochwarter, "Psychological aspects of expatriate effectiveness," in Ben B. Shaw and John E. Beck (guest eds.), Gerald R. Ferris and Kendrith M. Rowland (eds.), *Research in Personnel and Human Resources Management* (Supplement 2: International Human Resources Management) (Greenwich, CT: JAI Press, 1990), pp. 127–145.

18. Gary P. Ferraro, *The Cultural Dimension of International Business* (Upper Saddle River, NJ: Prentice Hall, 1990), pp. 143–144.

19. "Before going overseas, smart managers plan their homecoming," *Wall Street Journal*, September 28, 1999, p. B1; "Expatriates find long stints abroad can close doors to credit at home," *Wall Street Journal*, May 17, 1993, pp. B1, B6.

20. Juan I. Sanchez, Paul E. Spector, and Cary L. Cooper, "Adapting to a boundaryless world: A developmental expatriate model," *Academy of Management Executive* (May 2000), pp. 96–105.

21. "New plant gets Jaguar in gear," *USA Today*, November 27, 2000, p. 4B.

22. "Distractions make global manager a difficult role," *Wall Street Journal*, November 21, 1999, pp. B1, B18.

23. Michael J. Marquardt and Dean W. Engel, "HRD competencies for a shrinking world," *Training & Development* (May 1993), pp. 59–60.

24. Shirley Fung, "How should we pay them?" *Across the Board* (June 1999), pp. 37–41.

25. See Joann Greco, "Executive checkup," *Continental* (in-flight magazine), April 2008, pp. 74–78.

26. Lin Grensing-Pophal, "Expat lifestyles take a hit," *HR Magazine*, March 2008, pp. 51–54.

27. "International departures," *Time*, April 14, 2008, p. Global 4.

28. Lawrence A. West, Jr., and Walter A. Bogumil, Jr., "Foreign knowledge workers as a strategic staffing option," *Academy of Management Executive* (November 2000), pp. 71–84.

29. "Some U.S. companies find Mexican workers not so cheap after all," *Wall Street Journal*, September 15, 1993, pp. A1, A16.

30. "How Merrill lost its way in Japan," *BusinessWeek*, November 12, 2001, p. 104.

31. Christopher Lorenz, "Learning to live with a cultural mix," *Financial Times*, April 26, 1993, p. 18.

32. Anthony M. Townsend, K. Dow Scott, and Steven E. Markham, "An examination of country and culture-based differences in compensation practices," *Journal of International Business Studies*, vol. 21, no. 4 (Fourth Quarter 1990), pp. 667–678.

33. "Sick Swedes a high-cost headache to employers," *Houston Chronicle*, September 8, 2002, p. 3D.

34. "Bitter Swedish dispute set to end," *Financial Times*, May 30, 1995, p. 3.

Glossary

Absolute advantage, theory of. Theory stating that trade between nations occurs when one nation is absolutely more productive than other nations in the production of a good and thus should export that good.

Accounting reserves. Reserves created by firms for foreseeable expenses.

Accommodative stance. A firm that meets its ethical and legal requirements but also will go further than those in selected cases.

Acculturation. Process of understanding and learning how to operate in a new culture.

Acquisition strategy. Form of foreign direct investment involving the purchase of existing assets in a foreign country.

Active income. Income generated by active business operations such as production, marketing, and distribution.

Ad valorem tariff. Tax assessed as a percentage of the market value of an imported good.

Adjustable peg. Feature of the Bretton Woods system by which a country had a limited right to adjust the value of its currency in terms of gold.

Advance pricing agreement (APA). A binding contract between a firm and the IRS, detailing the methodology that will be used to establish the firm's transfer prices; used to remedy the cost and uncertainty of the resolution of complex transfer pricing conflicts.

Advised letter of credit. Letter of credit in which the seller's bank advises the seller about the creditworthiness of the bank issuing the letter of credit.

Affiliated bank. Partly owned, separately incorporated overseas banking operation of a home country bank.

Agglomeration economies. Occur when a firm's costs of production decline as the number of firms in that industry increase within a given area.

Aggressive goal behavior. Behavior based on the cultural belief that material possessions, money, and assertiveness underlie motivation and reflect the goals that a person should pursue.

Agreeableness. A "big five" personality trait referring to a person's ability to get along with others.

Aktiengesellschaft (AG). A form of corporate organization in Germany; typically, a large, publicly held firm with limited liability; it must have a management board and a board of directors.

Alien Tort Claims Act. Holds a company responsible for human rights abuses by foreign governments if the company benefited from those abuses.

Andean Community. Customs union composed of Bolivia, Chile, Colombia, Ecuador, and Peru; Argentina, Brazil, Paraguay, and Uruguay are associate members.

Anti-Bribery Convention of the Organization for Economic Cooperation and Development. To eliminate bribery in international business transactions, mandates jail sentences for those convicted of paying bribes.

Arbitrage. Riskless purchase of a product in one market for immediate resale in a second market to profit from price differences between the markets.

Arbitration. An alternate dispute resolution technique in which parties to a dispute submit their cases to a private party or body whose decision they will honor.

Arm's length test. Imposed by the IRS to determine the appropriateness of transfer prices; reflects the price that one independent company would charge another for a good or service.

ASEAN Free Trade Area (AFTA). Established in January 1993 to promote intra-ASEAN trade.

Asia-Pacific Economic Cooperation (APEC). A group of countries on both sides of the Pacific working to promote trade among themselves by reducing or eliminating trade barriers.

Assigned arrangement. Management arrangement in which one partner in a strategic alliance assumes primary responsibility for the operations of the alliance.

Association of Southeast Asian Nations (ASEAN). Established in August 1967 to promote regional political and economic cooperation.

Attitudes. Complexes of beliefs and feelings about specific ideas, situations, or other people.

Australia–New Zealand Closer Economic Relations Trade Agreement (ANZCERTA or CER). An agreement between Australia and New Zealand to eliminate trade barriers between them.

Authoritarianism. Personality trait determining the extent to which a person believes that power and status differences are appropriate within hierarchical social systems like organizations.

Backtranslation. Technique used to check for translation errors; after one person translates a document from language A to language B, a second person translates the document from B back to A to check if the intended message is actually being sent.

Baker Plan. Plan developed in 1985 by U.S. Treasury Secretary James Baker to solve the international debt crisis; stressed debt rescheduling, tight controls over domestic monetary and fiscal policies, and continued loans to debtor nations.

Balance of payments (BOP) accounting system. Records commercial transactions between the residents of one country and residents of other countries.

Balance on merchandise trade. Difference between a country's merchandise exports and imports.

Balance on services trade. Difference between a country's service exports and imports.

Balance sheet hedge. Technique for eliminating translation exposure in which a firm matches its assets and liabilities denominated in a given currency on a consolidated basis.

Banker's acceptance. Time draft endorsed by a bank, signifying the bank's promise to guarantee payment at the designated time.

Barter. Form of countertrade involving simultaneous exchange of goods or services between two parties.

Beggar-thy-neighbor policies. Domestic economic policies that ignore the economic damage done to other countries.

Benchmarking. Legally and ethically studying how other firms do something in a high-quality way and then imitating or improving on their methods.

Benelux nations. Belgium, the Netherlands, and Luxembourg.

Besloten vennootschap (BV). Term used in the Netherlands to refer to a privately held, limited liability firm.

"Big five" personality traits. Popular personality model based on five dominant traits—agreeableness, conscientiousness, emotional stability, extroversion, and openness.

Big Ten countries. Argentina, Brazil, China, India, Indonesia, Mexico, Poland, South Africa, South Korea, and Turkey.

Bilateral netting. Netting of transactions between two business units.

Bill of lading. International trade document that serves (1) as a contract between the exporter and the transporter and (2) as a title to the exported goods.

B-O-T project. Variant of a turnkey project for market entry in which a firm builds a facility, operates it, and later transfers ownership to another party.

Brady Plan. Plan developed in 1989 by U.S. Treasury Secretary Nicholas Brady to solve the international debt crisis; involves writing off part of the debtor nations' debts or repurchase of their debts at less than face value.

Branch bank. Overseas banking operation of a home country bank that is not separately incorporated.

Bribery Act. A 2010 British law that outlaws corrupt actions done anywhere in the world by firms with a business presence in the United Kingdom.

BRIC countries. Brazil, Russia, India, and China.

Brownfield strategy. See acquisition strategy.

Bureaucratic law. Legal system based on interpretations, actions, and decisions of government employees.

Buy-back. Form of countertrade in which a firm is compensated in the form of goods produced by equipment or technology that it has sold to another firm.

Cairns Group. Group of major agricultural exporting nations, led by Argentina, Australia, and Canada, that lobbies for reductions in agricultural subsidies.

Call option. Publicly traded contract granting the owner the right, but not the obligation, to buy a specific amount of foreign currency at a specified price at a stated future date.

Capacity planning. Deciding how many customers a firm will be able to serve at a given time.

Capital account. BOP account that records capital transactions between residents of one country and those of other countries.

Caribbean Basin Initiative (CBI). Program developed by the United States to spur the economic development of countries in the Caribbean Basin; allows duty-free importation of selected goods from these countries into the United States.

Carry trade. Uncovered interest arbitrage technique which exploits differences in the interest rates between countries.

Centralized cash management. System controlled by a parent corporation that coordinates worldwide cash flows of its subsidiaries and pools their cash reserves.

Chaebol. Any of the large business conglomerates that dominate the Korean economy.

Channel length. Number of stages in a distribution channel.

Civil law. Law based on detailed codification of permissible and nonpermissible activities; world's most common form of legal system.

Clearinghouse accounts. Accounting system used to facilitate international countertrade; a firm must balance its overall countertrade transactions but need not balance any single countertrade transaction.

Clustering. Phenomenon in which firms within an industry locate in the same geographic area to benefit from agglomeration economies.

Co-decision procedure. Procedure that shares decision-making power between the European Parliament and the Council of the European Union.

Codes of ethics. Written statements of the values and ethical standards that guide firms' actions.

Codetermination. German system that provides for cooperation between management and labor in running a business.

Cohesion fund. Means of funneling economic development aid to countries whose per capita GDP is less than 90 percent of the EU average.

Collectivism. The belief that the group comes first.

Common law. Law that forms the foundation of the legal system in Anglo-American countries; based on cumulative findings of judges in individual cases.

Common market. Form of regional economic integration that combines features of a customs union with elimination of barriers inhibiting the movement of factors of production among members.

Commonwealth of Independent States (CIS). Organization formed by 12 former Soviet republics to promote free trade and discuss issues of common concern.

Comparative advantage, theory of. Theory stating that trade between countries occurs when one country is relatively more productive than others in the production of a good.

Compound tariff. Tax that combines elements of an ad valorem tariff and a specific tariff.

Comprehensive alliance. Strategic alliance in which the participants agree to perform together multiple stages of the process by which goods or services are brought to market.

Confirmed letter of credit. Letter of credit in which the seller's bank adds its promise to pay should the issuing bank fail to pay the seller.

Confiscation. Involuntary transfer of property, with little or no compensation, from a privately owned firm to the host government.

Conglomerate. Firm that uses a strategy of unrelated diversification.

Conscientiousness. A "big five" personality trait referring to the order and precision a person imposes on activities.

Contract manufacturing. Process of outsourcing manufacturing to other firms to reduce the amount of a firm's financial and human resources devoted to the physical production of its products.

Control. Process of monitoring and regulating activities in a firm so that targeted measures of performance are achieved or maintained.

Control framework. Managerial and organizational processes used to keep a firm on target toward its strategic goals.

Controlled foreign corporation (CFC). Foreign corporation in which certain U.S. shareholders (each of which must own at least 10 percent of the foreign corporation's stock) cumulatively own at least 50 percent of the foreign corporation's stock.

Convergence criteria. Criteria imposed on EU members wishing to adopt the euro as their national currency.

Convertible currencies. Currencies that are freely traded and accepted in international commerce; also called hard currencies.

Coordination. Process of linking and integrating functions and activities of different groups, units, or divisions.

Core competency. A distinctive strength or advantage of a firm which allows it to compete effectively with its rivals.

Corollary approach. Approach whereby a firm delegates responsibility for processing international sales orders to individuals within an existing department, such as finance or marketing.

Corporate social audit. A formal and thorough analysis of the effectiveness of a firm's social performance.

Correspondent relationship. Agency relationship whereby a bank in country A acts as an agent for a bank from country B, providing banking services in country A for both the B bank and its clients; typically done on a reciprocal basis.

Cost-of-living allowance. Compensation for managers on international assignment designed to offset differences in living costs.

Council of the European Union. Main decision-making body of the EU.

Counterpurchase. Form of countertrade in which one firm sells its products to another at one point in time and is compensated in the form of the other's products at some future time.

Countertrade. Form of payment in which a seller accepts something other than money in compensation.

Countervailing duty (CVD). Ad valorem tariff placed on imported goods to offset subsidies granted by foreign governments.

Country fund. Mutual fund that specializes in investing in stocks and bonds issued by firms in a specific country.

Country similarity theory. Theory stating that international trade in manufactured goods will occur between countries with similar income levels and at similar stages of economic development.

Covered-interest arbitrage. Arbitrage that exploits geographic differences in interest rates and differences in exchange rates over time.

Crawling peg. Allowing the currency peg to change gradually over time.

Cross-cultural literacy. Ability to understand and operate in more than one culture.

Cross rate. Exchange rate between two currencies, A and B, derived by using currency A to buy currency C and then using currency C to buy currency B.

Cultural cluster. Group of countries that share many cultural similarities.

Cultural convergence. Convergence of two or more cultures.

Culture. Collection of values, beliefs, behaviors, customs, and attitudes that distinguish and define a society.

Culture shock. Psychological phenomenon arising from being in a different culture; may lead to feelings of fear, helplessness, irritability, and disorientation.

Currency future. Publicly traded contract involving the sale or purchase of a specific amount of foreign currency at a specified price with delivery at a stated future date.

Currency option. Publicly traded contract giving the owner the right, but not the obligation, to sell or buy a specific amount of foreign currency at a specified price at a stated future date (see also call option; put option).

Current account balance. Net balance resulting from merchandise exports and imports, service exports and imports, investment income, and unilateral transfers.

Customs union. Form of regional economic integration that combines features of a free trade area with common trade policies toward nonmember countries.

Date draft. Draft that requires payment at some specified date.

Decision making. Process of choosing one alternative from among a set of alternatives to promote the decision maker's objectives.

Defensive stance. When an organization does everything legally required of it but nothing more.

Deferral rule. Rule permitting U.S. companies to defer paying U.S. income taxes on profits earned by their foreign subsidiaries.

Delegated arrangement. Management arrangement in which partners in a strategic alliance play little or no management role, delegating responsibility to the executives of the alliance itself.

Development. General education aimed at preparing managers for new assignments and/or higher-level positions.

Differentiated goods. Goods for which brand names and product reputations play an important role in consumer decision making (e.g., automobiles, expensive electronics equipment, and personal care products).

Differentiation strategy. Business-level strategy that emphasizes the distinctiveness of products or services.

Direct exchange rate. Price of a foreign currency in terms of the home currency; also called a direct quote.

Direct exporting. Product sales to customers, either distributors or end users, located outside the firm's home country.

Direct quote. See direct exchange rate.

Direct sales. Selling products to final consumers.

Dirty float. See managed float.

Distinctive competence. Component of strategy that answers the question "What do we do exceptionally well, especially as compared to our competitors?"

Distribution. Process of getting a firm's products and services to its customers.

Documentary collection. Form of payment in which goods are released to the buyer only after the buyer pays for them or signs a document binding the buyer to pay for them.

Doha Round. World Trade Organization negotiations that began in 2001.

Draft. Document demanding payment from the buyer.

Dual use. Products that may be used for both civilian and military purposes.

Dumping. Sale of imported goods either (1) at prices below what a company charges in its home market or (2) at prices below cost.

Eclectic theory. Theory that foreign direct investment occurs because of location advantages, ownership advantages, and internalization advantages.

Economic and monetary union (EMU). Goal established by the Maastricht Treaty to create a single currency for the EU, thereby eliminating exchange rate risks and the costs of converting currencies for intra-EU trade.

Economic and Monetary Community of Central Africa (CEMAC). Organization promoting regional economic cooperation in Central Africa.

Economic Community of West African States (ECOWAS). Organization promoting regional economic cooperation created by 16 West African countries.

Economic exposure. Impact on the value of a firm's operations of unanticipated exchange rate changes.

Economic union. Form of regional economic integration that combines features of a common market with coordination of economic policies among its members.

Embargo. Ban on the exporting and/or importing of goods to a particular country.

Emerging markets. Countries whose recent growth or prospects for future growth exceed that of traditional markets.

Emotional stability. A "big five" personality trait defining a person's poise, calmness, and resilience.

Environmental scanning. The systematic collection of data about all elements of a firm's external and internal environments.

Errors and omissions account. BOP account that results from measurement errors; equals the negative of the sum of the current account, the capital account, and the official reserves account.

Ethical behavior. Behavior that conforms to generally accepted social norms.

Ethical compliance. The extent to which the members of the organization follow basic ethical and legal standards of behavior.

Ethics. An individual's beliefs about whether a decision, behavior, or action is right or wrong.

Ethnocentric approach. Managerial approach in which a firm operates internationally the same way it does domestically.

Ethnocentric staffing model. Approach that primarily uses PCNs to staff upper-level positions.

Eurobonds. Bonds denominated in one country's currency but sold to residents of other countries.

Eurocurrency. Currency on deposit in banks outside its country of issue.

Eurodollars. U.S. dollars deposited in banks outside the borders of the United States.

European Central Bank. The central bank responsible for controlling monetary policy for all EU countries adopting the euro as their currency.

European Commission. 27-person group that acts as the EU's administrative branch of government and proposes all EU legislation.

European Council. Consists of the heads of government or state of each of the member states, the President of the European Council, and the President of the European Commission.

European Court of Justice. 27-member court charged with interpreting EU law; also interprets whether the national laws of the EU members are consistent with EU laws and regulations.

European Economic Area. Common market created by the EU and Iceland, Liechtenstein, and Norway.

European Free Trade Association. Trading bloc in Europe that works closely with the EU to promote intra-European trade; current members are Iceland, Liechtenstein, Norway, and Switzerland.

European Monetary System (EMS). System based on 1979 agreement among members of the European Union to manage currency relationships among themselves.

European Parliament. Legislature elected from member countries that has a consultative role in EU decision making.

Exchange rate. Price of one currency in terms of a second currency.

Exchange rate mechanism (ERM). Agreement among European Union members to maintain fixed exchange rates among themselves within a narrow band.

Exit interview. Interview with an employee who is leaving the organization.

Expatriate failure. Early return of an expatriate manager to his or her home country because of an inability to perform in the overseas assignment.

Expatriates. Collective name for parent country nationals (PCNs) and third-country nationals (TCNs).

Export and import brokers. Agents who bring together international buyers and sellers of standardized commodities such as coffee, cocoa, and grains.

Export department. The part of the firm that has responsibility for overseeing international operations, marketing products, processing orders, working with foreign distributors, and arranging financing when necessary.

Export-Import Bank of the United States (Eximbank). U.S. government agency that promotes U.S. exports by offering direct loans and loan guarantees

Export management company (EMC). Firm that acts as its clients' export department.

Export of the services of capital. Income that a country's residents earn from their foreign investments.

Export promotion. Economic development strategy based on building a vibrant manufacturing sector by stimulating exports, often by harnessing some advantage the country possesses, such as low labor costs.

Export promotion strategy. See export promotion.

Export tariff. Tax levied on goods as they leave the country.

Exporting. Selling products made in one's own country for use or resale in other countries.

Expropriation. Involuntary transfer of property, with compensation, from a privately owned firm to a host country government.

Extraterritoriality. Application of a country's laws to activities occurring outside its borders.

Extroversion. A "big five" personality trait defining a person's comfort level with relationships, resulting in some people being sociable, talkative, and assertive, and others being less sociable and more introverted.

Factoring. Specialized international lending activity in which firms buy foreign accounts receivable at a discount from face value.

Fair trade. Trade between nations that takes place under active government intervention to ensure that the companies of each nation receive their fair share of the economic benefits of trade; also called managed trade.

Financial alliance. Strategic alliance in which two or more firms work together to reduce the financial risks associated with a project.

Fixed exchange rate system. International monetary system in which each government promises to maintain the price of its currency in terms of other currencies.

Flexible (or floating) exchange rate system. System in which exchange rates are determined by supply and demand.

Flight capital. Money sent out of politically or economically unstable countries by investors seeking a safe haven for their assets.

Float. To allow a currency's value to be determined by forces of supply and demand.

Focus strategy. Business-level strategy targeting specific types of products for certain customer groups or regions.

Foreign bonds. Bonds issued by residents of one country to residents of a second country and denominated in the second country's currency.

Foreign Corrupt Practices Act (FCPA). U.S. law enacted in 1977 prohibiting U.S. firms, their employees, and agents acting on their behalf from paying or offering to pay foreign government officials to influence official actions or policies or to gain or retain business.

Foreign direct investment (FDI). Investments made for the purpose of actively controlling property, assets, or companies located in a host country.

Foreign exchange. Currencies issued by countries other than one's own.

Foreign portfolio investments (FPI). Investments made in a host country by foreign investors not for purposes of control.

Foreign service premium. See hardship premium.

Foreign Sovereign Immunities Act of 1976. U.S. law that limits the ability of U.S. citizens to sue foreign governments in U.S. courts.

Foreign trade zone (FTZ). Geographical area in which imported or exported goods receive preferential tariff treatment.

Forum shopping. Attempt to seek a court system or judge that will be most sympathetic to an attorney's client.

Forward discount. Difference between the forward and the spot price of a currency expressed as an annualized percentage (assumes the forward price is less than the spot price (see also forward premium).

Forward market. Market for foreign exchange involving delivery of currency at some point in the future.

Forward premium. Difference between the forward and the spot price of a currency expressed as an annualized percentage (assumes the forward price is more than the spot price (see also forward discount).

Franchisee. Independent entrepreneur or organization that operates a business under the name of another.

Franchising. Special form of licensing in which the licensor authorizes the licensee to utilize its operating systems, brand names, trademarks, and logos in return for a royalty payment.

Franchisor. Firm that allows an independent entrepreneur or organization to operate a business under its name.

Free trade. Trade between nations that is unrestricted by governmental actions.

Free trade area. Regional trading bloc that encourages trade by eliminating trade barriers among its members.

Freight forwarders. Agents who specialize in the physical transportation of goods, arranging customs documentation and obtaining transportation services for their clients.

General Agreement on Tariffs and Trade (GATT). International agreement that sponsors negotiations to promote world trade.

Generalized system of preferences (GSP). System of reduced tariff rates offered on goods exported from developing countries.

Generic organizational control. Form of organizational control based on centralized generic controls across the entire organization.

Geocentric approach. Management approach in which a firm analyzes the needs of its customers worldwide and then adopts standardized operating practices for all markets it serves.

Geocentric staffing model. Approach using a mix of PCNs, HCNs, and TCNs to staff upper-level foreign positions.

Geographic arbitrage. See two-point arbitrage.

Gesellschaft mit beschränkter Haftung (GmbH). A form of corporate organization in Germany; a typical GmbH is a small, privately held company.

Global area design. Form of organization design that centers a firm's activities around specific areas or regions of the world.

Global bonds. Large, liquid bond issues designed to be traded in numerous capital markets.

Global customer design. Form of organization design centered around different customers or customer groups, each requiring special expertise or attention.

Global functional design. Form of organization design based on departments or divisions having worldwide responsibility for a single organizational function such as finance, operations, or marketing; also called U-form organization.

Globalization. The increasing integration of the world economy and the world's countries.

Global matrix design. Complex form of international organization design created by superimposing one form of design on top of an existing different form.

Global product design. Form of organization design that assigns worldwide responsibility for specific products or product groups to separate operating divisions within a firm.

Goal orientation. Cultural beliefs about motivation and the different goals toward which people work.

Gold standard. International monetary system based on the willingness of countries to buy or sell their paper currencies for gold at a fixed rate.

Goodwill. Accounting term used to measure the difference between the price paid for a company and the fair value of its tangible net assets.

Gray market. Market created when products are imported into a country legally but outside the normal channels of distribution authorized by the manufacturer.

Greenfield investment. Form of investment in which the firm designs and builds a new factory from scratch, starting with nothing but a "green field."

Greenfield strategy. Form of foreign direct investment that involves building new facilities.

Gross domestic product (GDP). The total market value of all goods and services produced in a country during some time period, such as a year.

Gross national income (GNI). GDP plus net income, such as dividends and interest received from residents of other countries minus those paid to residents of other countries.

Hard currencies. Currencies that are freely tradable; also called convertible currencies.

Hard loan policy. World Bank lending policy requiring that loans be made only if they are likely to be repaid.

Hardship premium. Supplemental compensation to induce managers to accept relatively unattractive international assignments; also called foreign service premium.

Harmonization. Voluntary adoption of common regulations, policies, and procedures by members of a regional trading bloc to promote internal trade.

Harmonized tariff schedule (HTS). Classification scheme used by many nations to determine tariffs on imported goods.

Headhunters. Recruiting firms that actively seek qualified managers and other professionals for possible placement in positions in other organizations.

Heckscher-Ohlin theory. See relative factor endowments, theory of.

High-context culture. A culture context in which a discussion is held is equally as important as the actual words that are spoken in conveying the speaker's message to the listener.

Home country. Country in which a firm's headquarters is located.

Host country. Country other than a firm's home country in which it operates.

Host country nationals (HCNs). Employees who are citizens of the host country where an international business operates.

Human resource management (HRM). Set of activities directed at attracting, developing, and maintaining the effective workforce necessary to achieve a firm's objectives.

Hurdle rate. Minimum rate of return a firm finds acceptable for its capital investments.

IMF conditionality. Restrictions placed on economic policies of countries receiving IMF loans.

Import of the services of capital. Payments that a country's residents make on capital supplied by foreigners.

Import substitution policy. Economic development strategy that relies on the stimulation of domestic manufacturing firms by erecting barriers to imported goods.

Import substitution strategy. Economic development approach that relies on the promotion of domestic manufacturing by erecting barriers to imported goods

Import tariff. Tax levied on goods as they enter a country.

Importing. Buying products made in other countries for use or resale in one's own country.

Inconvertible currencies. Currencies that are not freely traded because of legal restrictions imposed by the issuing country or that are not generally accepted by foreigners in settlement of international transactions; also called soft currencies.

Indirect exchange rate. Price of the home currency in terms of the foreign currency; also called indirect quote.

Indirect exporting. Sales of a firm's products to a domestic customer, which in turn exports the product, in either its original form or a modified form.

Indirect quote. See indirect exchange rate.

Individualism. The cultural belief that the person comes first.

Industrial policy. Economic development strategy in which a national government identifies key domestic industries critical to the country's economic future and then formulates policies that promote the international competitiveness of these industries.

Infant industry argument. Argument in favor of governmental intervention in trade: a nation should protect fledgling industries for which the nation will ultimately possess a comparative advantage.

Informal management network. Group of managers from different parts of the world who are connected to one another in some way.

Information. Data in a form that is of value to a manager.

Information system. Methodology created by a firm to gather, assemble, and provide data in a form or forms useful to managers.

Interindustry trade. International trade involving the exchange of goods produced in one industry in one country for goods produced in another industry in a different country.

Intermediaries. Third parties that specialize in facilitating imports and exports.

Internalization advantages. Factors that affect the desirability of a firm's producing a good or service itself rather than relying on other firms to control production.

Internalization theory. Theory stating that foreign direct investment occurs because of the high costs of entering into production or procurement contracts with foreign firms.

International Accounting Standards Board (IASB). International organization, formed in 2001 from the restructuring of the IASC, to issue international accounting standards.

International Bank for Reconstruction and Development (IBRD). Official name of the World Bank, established by the Bretton Woods agreement to reconstruct the war-torn economies of Western Europe and whose mission changed in the 1950s to aid the development of less developed countries.

International banking facility (IBF). Entity of a U.S. bank that is exempted from domestic banking regulations as long as it provides only international banking services.

International business. Business that engages in cross-border commercial transactions with individuals, private firms, and/or public-sector organizations; also refers to cross-border transactions.

International Development Association (IDA). World Bank affiliate that specializes in loans to less developed countries.

International division. Organizational unit whose responsibility is to manage foreign operations, allowing the firm to concentrate resources and create specialized programs for international business activities.

International Finance Corporation (IFC). World Bank affiliate whose mission is the development of the private sector in developing countries.

International Financial Reporting Standards (IFRS). Accounting standards promulgated by the International Accounting Standards Board.

International Fisher effect. Observation that differences in nominal interest rates among countries are due to differences in their expected inflation rates.

International investments. Capital supplied by residents of one country to residents of another.

International Labor Organization (ILO). Watchdog that monitors working conditions in factories in developing countries.

International licensing. Transaction in which a firm in one country (the licensor) sells the right to use its intellectual property to a firm located in a second country (the licensee) for a fee.

International logistics. Management functions associated with the international flow of materials, parts, supplies, and finished products from suppliers to the firm, between units of the firm itself, and from the firm to customers.

International marketing. Extension of marketing activities across national boundaries; see also marketing.

International Monetary Fund (IMF). Agency created by the Bretton Woods Agreement to promote international monetary cooperation after World War II.

International monetary system. System by which countries value and exchange their currencies.

International operations management. Transformation-related activities of an international firm.

International order cycle time. Time between placement of an order and its receipt by the customer.

International service business. Firm that transforms resources into an intangible output that creates utility for its customers.

International strategic management. Comprehensive and ongoing management planning process aimed at formulating and implementing strategies that enable a firm to compete effectively internationally.

International strategies. Comprehensive frameworks for achieving a firm's fundamental goals.

International trade. Voluntary exchange of goods, services, or assets between a person or organization in one country and a person or organization in another country.

International trading company. Firm directly engaged in importing and exporting a wide variety of goods for its own account.

Intracorporate transfer. Selling of goods by a firm in one country to an affiliated firm in another country.

Intraindustry trade. Trade between two countries involving the exchange of goods produced by the same industry.

Invoicing currency. Currency in which an international transaction is invoiced.

Irrevocable letter of credit. Letter of credit that cannot be changed without the consent of the buyer, the seller, and the issuing bank.

Jamaica Agreement. Agreement among central bankers made in 1976, allowing each country to adopt whatever exchange rate system it wished.

Job satisfaction/dissatisfaction. An attitude that reflects the extent to which an individual is gratified by or fulfilled in his or her work.

Joint venture (JV). Special form of strategic alliance created when two or more firms agree to work together and jointly own a separate firm to promote their mutual interests.

Just-in-time (JIT) systems. Systems in which suppliers are expected to deliver necessary inputs just as they are needed.

Kabushiki kaisha (KK). In Japan, term used to represent all limited-liability companies.

Keiretsu. Family of Japanese companies, often centered on a large bank or trading company, having extensive cross-ownership of shares and interacting with one another as suppliers or customers.

Kommanditgesellschaft auf Aktien (KGaA). A form of corporate organization in Germany; a typical KGaA is primarily owned by partners with limited liability, although at least one shareholder must have unlimited liability.

Leadership. Use of noncoercive influence to shape the goals of a group or organization, to motivate behavior toward reaching those goals, and to help determine the group or organizational culture.

Leads and lags strategy. Money management technique in which an MNC attempts to increase its holdings of currencies and assets denominated in currencies that are expected to rise in value and to decrease its holdings of currencies

and assets denominated in currencies that are expected to fall in value.

Legal compliance. The extent to which an organization conforms to regional, national, and international laws.

Leontief paradox. Empirical finding that U.S. exports are more labor intensive than U.S. imports, which is contrary to the predictions of the theory of relative factor endowments.

Letter of credit. Document issued by a bank promising to pay the seller if all conditions specified in the letter of credit are met.

Liability of foreignness. The informational, political, and cultural disadvantages that foreign firms face when trying to compete against local firms in the host country.

Licensing. Transaction in which a firm (the licensor) sells the rights to use its intellectual property to another firm (the licensee) for a fee.

Licensee. Firm that buys the rights to use the intellectual property of another firm.

Licensor. Firm that sells the rights to use its intellectual property to another firm.

Lingua franca. Common language.

Location advantages. Factors that affect the desirability of host country production relative to home country production.

Locus of control. Personality trait determining the extent to which people believe that their behavior has a real effect on what happens to them.

London Interbank Offer Rate (LIBOR). Interest rate that London banks charge each other for short-term Eurocurrency loans.

Long-term foreign portfolio investments. Portfolio investments with maturities of more than one year.

Louvre Accord. Agreement made in 1987 among central bankers to stabilize the value of the U.S. dollar.

Low-context culture. Culture in which the words being spoken explicitly convey the speaker's message to the listener.

Ltd. Abbreviation used in the United Kingdom to indicate a privately held, limited-liability company.

Maastricht Treaty. Common name given to the Treaty on European Union.

Macropolitical risk. Political risk that affects all firms operating within a country.

Make-or-buy decision. Decision for an organization to either make its own inputs or buy them from outside suppliers.

Managed float. Flexible exchange system in which government intervention plays a major role in determining exchange rates; also called a dirty float.

Managed trade. See fair trade.

Management contract. Agreement whereby one firm provides managerial assistance, technical expertise, or specialized services to a second firm for an agreed-upon time for a fee.

Manufacturers' agents. Agents who solicit domestic orders for foreign manufacturers, usually on a commission basis.

Manufacturers' export agents. Agents who act as an export department for domestic manufacturers, selling those firms' goods in foreign markets.

Maquiladoras. Mexican factories, mostly located along the U.S.-Mexico border, that receive preferential tariff treatment.

Marketing. Process of planning and executing the conception, pricing, promotion, and distribution of ideas, goods, and services to create exchanges that satisfy individual and organizational objectives.

Marketing alliance. Strategic alliance in which two or more firms share marketing services or expertise.

Marketing mix. How a firm chooses to address product development, pricing, promotion, and distribution.

Market pricing policy. Pricing policy under which prices are set on a market-by-market basis.

Materials management. Part of logistics management concerned with the flow of materials into the firm from suppliers and between units of the firm itself.

Medium. Communication channel used by an advertiser to convey a message.

Message. Facts or impressions an advertiser wishes to convey to potential customers.

Mercantilism. Economic philosophy based on the belief that a nation's wealth is measured by its holdings of gold and silver.

Merchandise export. Sale of a good to a resident of a foreign country.

Merchandise exports and imports. Trade involving tangible products.

Merchandise import. Purchase of a good from a resident of a foreign country.

Micropolitical risk. Political risk that affects only specific firms or a specific industry operating within a country.

Mission statement. Definition of a firm's values, purpose, and directions.

Most favored nation (MFN) principle. Principle that any preferential treatment granted to one country must be extended to all countries.

Motivation. Overall set of forces that cause people to choose certain behaviors from a set of available behaviors.

Multilateral Investment Guarantee Agency (MIGA). World Bank affiliate that offers political risk insurance to investors in developing countries.

Multilateral netting. Netting of transactions between three or more business units.

Multinational enterprise (MNE). Business that may or may not be incorporated and has extensive involvement in international business.

Multinational organization (MNO). Any organization—business or not-for-profit—with extensive international involvement.

Mutual recognition. Legal concept created by the European Court of Justice; implies that if one EU member determines that a product is valid for sale within its borders, then other EU members must also recognize its validity and allow it to be sold within their borders.

Naamloze vennootschap (NV). Term used in the Netherlands to refer to a publicly held, limited-liability firm.

National competitive advantage, theory of.. States that success in international trade is based on the interaction of factor conditions, demand conditions, related and supporting industries, and firm strategy, structure, and rivalry.

National defense argument. Argument in favor of governmental intervention in trade, holding that a nation should be self-sufficient in critical raw materials, machinery, and technology.

National treatment. Imposing the same standards, regulations, and so forth on foreign firms that are imposed on domestic firms.

Nationalization. Transfer of property from a privately owned firm to the government.

Natural hedge. See operational hedge.

Needs. The things an individual must have or wants to have.

Neomercantilists. Modern supporters of mercantilism, who hold that a country should erect barriers to trade to protect its industries from foreign competition; also called protectionists.

New trade theory. Extends Linder's analysis by incorporating the impact of economies of scale on trade in differentiated goods.

Newly Independent States (NIS). Refers to the 15 independent countries created as a result of the breakup of the Soviet Union.

Nontariff barrier (NTB). Any governmental regulation, policy, or procedure other than a tariff that has the effect of impeding international trade.

Obstructionist stance. A firm doing as little as possible to address social or environmental problems.

Official reserves account. BOP account that records changes in official reserves owned by a central bank.

Official settlements balance. BOP balance that measures changes in a country's official reserves.

Offset purchases. Form of countertrade in which a portion of the exported good is produced in the importing country.

Open account. Type of payment in which the seller ships goods to the buyer prior to payment; the seller relies on the promise of the buyer that payment will be forthcoming.

Openness. A "big five" personality trait referring to a person's rigidity of beliefs and range of interests.

Operational hedge. When a firm tries to match its revenues in a given currency with an equivalent flow of costs; also called natural hedge.

Operations control. Level of control that focuses on operating processes and systems within both the organization and its subsidiaries and operating units.

Operations management. Set of activities used by an organization to transform different kinds of resource inputs into final goods and services.

Opportunity cost. Value of what is given up to get the good or service in question.

Organization for Economic Cooperation and Development (OECD). A group of 34 market-oriented democracies formed to promote economic growth.

Organizational commitment. An attitude reflecting an individual's identification with and loyalty to the organization.

Organizational control. Level of control that focuses on the design of the organization itself.

Organizational stakeholders. People and organizations that are directly affected by the practices of an organization and that have a stake in its performance.

Organization design. Overall pattern of structural components and configurations used to manage the total organization; also called organization structure.

Organization structure. See organization design.

Overall cost leadership strategy. Business-level strategy that emphasizes low costs.

Overseas Private Investment Corporation (OPIC). U.S. government agency that promotes U.S. international business activities by providing political risk insurance.

Ownership advantages. Resources owned by a firm that grant it a competitive advantage over its industry rivals.

Ownership advantage theory. Theory stating that foreign direct investment occurs because of ownership of valuable assets that confer monopolistic advantages in foreign markets.

Par value. Official price of a currency in terms of gold.

Parallel barter. See counterpurchase.

Parallel importing. Market that results from products being imported into a country legally but outside the normal channels of distribution authorized by a manufacturer (synonymous with gray market).

Parent country nationals (PCNs). Employees who are citizens of an international business's home country and are transferred to one of its foreign operations.

Passive goal behavior. Behavior based on the cultural belief that social relationships, quality of life, and concern for others are the basis of motivation and reflect the goals that a person should pursue.

Passive income. See Subpart F income.

Payback period. Number of years it takes a project to repay a firm's initial investment.

Payment in advance. When an exporter receives the importer's money prior to shipping the goods.

Pegged. Tied to, as in "The gold standard created a fixed exchange rate system because each country pegged the value of its currency to gold."

Per capita income. Average income per person in a country.

Perception. The set of processes by which an individual becomes aware of and interprets information about the environment.

Performance appraisal. Process of assessing how effectively a person is performing his or her job.

Personal selling. Making sales on the basis of personal contacts.

Personality. The relatively stable set of psychological attributes that distinguish one person from another.

Philanthropic giving. Awarding funds or gifts to charities or other social programs.

Planning process control. Form of organizational control that focuses on the actual mechanics and processes a firm uses to develop strategic plans.

Plaza Accord. Agreement made in 1985 among central bankers to allow the U.S. dollar to fall in value.

PLC. Abbreviation used in the United Kingdom to indicate a publicly held, limited-liability company.

Political risk. Change in the political environment that may adversely affect the value of a firm.

Political risk assessment. Systematic analysis of the political risks that a firm faces when operating in a foreign country.

Political union. Complete political and economic integration of two or more countries.

Polycentric approach. Management approach in which a firm customizes its operations for each foreign market it serves.

Polycentric staffing model. Approach primarily using HCNs to staff upper-level foreign positions.

Power orientation. Cultural beliefs about the appropriateness of power and authority in hierarchies such as business organizations.

Power respect. Cultural belief that the use of power and authority is acceptable simply on the basis of position in a hierarchy.

Power tolerance. Cultural belief that the use of power and authority is not acceptable simply on the basis of position in a hierarchy.

Principle of comity. Provides that a country will honor and enforce within its own territory the judgments and decisions of foreign courts, with certain limitations.

Privatization. Sale of publicly owned property to private investors.

Proactive stance. When a firm exhibits the highest degree of social responsibility, viewing itself as a citizen in society and actively seeking ways to contribute.

Product. A good produced either by man or nature.

Product life cycle theory. A theory that traces the evolution of international trade and investment as a product evolves through the stages of new product, maturing product, and standardized product.

Product-support services. Assistance a firm provides for customers regarding the operation, maintenance, and/or repair of its products.

Production alliance. Strategic alliance in which two or more firms each manufacture products or provide services in a shared or common facility.

Production management. International operations management decisions and processes involving the creation of tangible goods.

Productivity. Economic measure of efficiency that summarizes the value of outputs relative to the value of inputs used to create them.

Promotion. Set of all efforts by an international firm to enhance the desirability of its products among potential buyers.

Promotion mix. Mix of advertising, personal selling, sales promotion, and public relations used by a firm to market its products.

Protectionists. See neomercantilists.

Protestant ethic. Belief that hard work, frugality, and achievement are means of glorifying God.

Public choice analysis. Branch of economics that analyzes public decision making.

Public-private venture. Joint venture involving a partnership between a privately owned foreign firm and a government.

Public relations. Efforts aimed at enhancing a firm's reputation and image.

Purchasing power parity (PPP), theory of. Theory stating that the prices of tradable goods, when expressed in a common currency, will tend to equalize across countries as a result of exchange rate changes.

Put option. Publicly traded contract granting the owner the right, but not the obligation, to sell a specific amount of foreign currency at a specified price at a stated future date.

Quality. Totality of features and characteristics of a product or service that bear on its ability to satisfy stated or implied needs.

Quota. Deposit paid by a member nation when joining the International Monetary Fund.

R&D alliance. Strategic alliance in which two or more firms agree to undertake joint research to develop new products or services.

R&D consortium. Confederation of organizations that band together to research and develop new products and processes for world markets.

Reexporting. Process of importation of a good into a country for immediate exportation, with little or no transformation of the good.

Reform Treaty. Common name given to the Treaty of Lisbon.

Regional development banks. Banks whose mission is to promote economic development of poorer nations within the region they serve.

Related diversification. Corporate-level strategy in which the firm operates in several different but related businesses, industries, or markets at the same time.

Relative factor endowments, theory of. Theory stating that a country will have a comparative advantage in producing goods that intensively use factors of production it has in abundance; also called Hecksher-Ohlin theory.

Religious law. Law based on officially established rules governing the faith and practice of a particular religion.

Repatriate. To return to a home country.

Repatriation. Moving a manager back home after a foreign assignment has been completed.

Resource deployment. Component of strategy that answers the question "Given that we are going to compete in these markets, how will we allocate our resources to them?"

Responsibility center control. Form of organizational control based on decentralized responsibility centers.

Retention. Extent to which a firm is able to retain its employees.

Revocable letter of credit. Letter of credit that can be changed by the bank without the consent of the buyer and the seller.

Ringi system. Japanese approach to ensuring that decisions are made collectively rather than by an individual.

Royalty. Compensation paid by a licensee to a licensor.

Rules of origin. Rules to determine which goods will benefit from reduced trade barriers in regional trading blocs.

Sales promotion. Specialized marketing efforts using such techniques as coupons and sampling.

Sanctions. Government-imposed restraints against commerce with a foreign country.

Scope of operations. Component of strategy that answers the question "Where are we going to conduct business?"

Screwdriver plant. Domestic factory that assembles imported parts in which little value is added to the parts.

Self-efficacy. Personality trait determining a person's beliefs about his or her capabilities to perform a task.

Self-esteem. Personality trait determining the extent to which a person believes that he or she is a worthwhile and deserving individual.

Self-reference criterion. The unconscious use of one's own culture to help assess new surroundings.

Service export. Sale of a service to a resident of a foreign country.

Service exports and imports. Trade involving intangible products.

Service import. Purchase of a service from a resident of a foreign country.

Service operations management. International operations management decisions and processes involving the creation of intangible services.

Shared management agreement. Management arrangement in which each partner in a strategic alliance fully and actively participates in managing the alliance.

Short-term foreign portfolio investments. Portfolio investments with maturities of one year or less.

Sight draft. Draft that requires payment upon transfer of the goods to the buyer.

Single-business strategy. Corporate-level strategy that calls for a firm to rely on a single business, product, or service for all its revenue.

Smithsonian Conference. Meeting held in Washington, DC, in December 1971, during which central bank representatives from the Group of Ten agreed to restore the fixed exchange rate system but with restructured rates of exchange between the major trading currencies.

Social charter. EU policy promoting common job-related benefits and working conditions throughout the EU; also called social policy.

Social mobility. The ability of individuals to move from one stratum of society to another.

Social orientation. Cultural beliefs about the relative importance of the individual and the groups to which an individual belongs.

Social policy. See social charter.

Social responsibility. The set of obligations an organization undertakes to protect and enhance the society in which it functions.

Social stratification. Organization of society into hierarchies based on birth, occupation, wealth, educational achievements, and/or other characteristics.

Società per azioni (SpA). A form of corporate organization in Italy in which owners of the firm enjoy limited liability.

Société anonyme (SA). A form of corporate organization in France in which owners of the firm enjoy limited liability.

Soft currencies. See inconvertible currencies.

Soft loans. Loans made by the World Bank Group that bear significant risk of not being paid.

Sogo shosha. Large Japanese export trading company.

Southern African Development Community (SADC). Free trade area created by 12 Southern African countries.

Sovereign wealth funds. Investment companies owned and esablished by national governments.

Special drawing rights (SDRs). Credits granted by the IMF that can be used to settle transactions among central banks; also called paper gold.

Specific tariff. Tax assessed as a specific dollar amount per unit of weight or other standard measure.

Spot market. Market for foreign exchange involving immediate delivery of the currency in question.

Stability and Growth Pact. Limits annual government deficits of eurozone participants to no more than 3 percent of their GDPs.

Standard price policy. Pricing policy under which a firm charges the same price for its products and services regardless of where they are sold.

Statistical process control. Family of mathematically based tools for monitoring and controlling quality.

Statutory laws. Laws enacted by legislative action.

Sterling-based gold standard. Gold standard in which the British pound is commonly used as an alternative means of settlement of transactions.

Strategic alliance. Business arrangement in which two or more firms choose to cooperate for their mutual benefit.

Strategic business units (SBUs). "Bundles" of businesses created by a firm using a corporate strategy of either related or unrelated diversification.

Strategic control. Process of monitoring how well an international business formulates and implements its strategies.

Strategic goals. Major objectives a firm wants to accomplish through the pursuit of a particular course of action.

Strategic planning. Process of developing a particular international strategy.

Strategic trade theory. Theory addressing the optimal policies through which a government may benefit its country by aiding domestic firms in monopolistic or highly oligopolistic industries.

Stress. An individual's response to a strong stimulus.

Subpart F income. Income earned from financial transactions, such as dividends, interest, and royalties; also called passive income.

Subsidiary bank. Separately incorporated overseas banking operation.

Supply chain management. Set of processes and steps a firm uses to acquire raw materials, parts, and other resources it needs to create its own products.

Swap market. Facet of international capital market in which two firms can exchange financial obligations.

Swap transaction. Transaction involving the simultaneous purchase and sale of a foreign currency with delivery at two different points in time.

Switching arrangements. Agreement under which firms may transfer their countertrade obligations to a third party.

SWOT analysis. Analysis of a firm and its environment to determine its strengths, weaknesses, opportunities, and threats.

Synergy. Component of strategy that answers the question "How can different elements of our business benefit one another?"

Tactics. Methods used by middle managers to implement strategic plans.

Tariff. Tax placed on a good involved in international trade.

Tariff rate quota (TRQ). A type of quota that imposes a low tariff rate on a limited amount of imports of a specific good into the country but then subjects all imports above that threshold to a prohibitively high tariff.

Tax equalizational system. System for ensuring that an expatriate's after-tax income in the host country is comparable to what the person's after-tax income would be in the home country.

Tax havens. Countries that charge low, often zero, taxes on corporate incomes and that offer an attractive business climate.

Technology transfer. The transmittal of technology from one country to another.

Theocracy. Country whose legal system is based on religious law.

Theory of absolute advantage. See absolute advantage, theory of.

Theory of comparative advantage. See comparative advantage, theory of.

Theory of national competitive advantage. See national competitive advantage, theory of.

Theory of purchasing power parity (PPP). See purchasing power parity (PPP), theory of.

Theory of relative factor endowments. See relative factor endowments, theory of.

Third-country nationals (TCNs). Employees of an international business who are not citizens of the firm's home or host country.

Three-point arbitrage. Arbitrage based on exploiting differences between the direct rate of exchange between two currencies and their cross rate of exchange using a third currency.

Time draft. Draft that requires payment at some specified time after the transfer of goods to the buyer.

Time orientation. Cultural beliefs regarding long-term versus short-term outlooks on work, life, and other aspects of society.

Total quality management (TQM). Integrated effort to systematically and continuously improve the quality of an organization's products and/or services.

Trade. Voluntary exchange of goods, services, assets, or money between one person or organization and another.

Trade acceptance. Time draft that has been signed by the buyer signifying a promise to honor the payment terms.

Trade deflection. Rerouting of exported goods to the member of a free trade area with the lowest barriers to imports from nonmember countries.

Trade in invisibles. British term denoting trade in services.

Trade in visibles. British term referring to merchandise trade.

Training. Instruction directed at enhancing job-related skills and abilities.

Transaction costs. Costs of negotiating, monitoring, and enforcing a contract.

Transaction currency. Currency in which an international transaction is denominated.

Transaction exposure. Financial risks that occur because the financial benefits and costs of an international transaction may be affected by exchange rate movements occurring after the firm is legally obligated to the transaction.

Transfer price. Prices that one branch or subsidiary of a parent firm charges for goods, services, or property sold to a second branch or subsidiary of the same parent firm.

Transit tariff. Tax levied on goods as they pass through one country bound for another.

Translation exposure. Impact on a firm's consolidated financial statements of fluctuations in foreign exchange rates that change the value of foreign subsidiaries as measured in the parent's currency.

Treaty for Europe. See Treaty of Amsterdam.

Treaty of Amsterdam. 1997 treaty furthering integration among EU members.

Treaty of Lisbon. An agreement among EU members to adopt many of the reforms proposed by the EU's Constitutional Convention.

Treaty of Nice. Became effective in February 2003, furthering the integration of the EU.

Treaty of Rome. Treaty signed in 1957 that established the European Economic Community.

Treaty on European Union. Signed in 1992 and came into force on November 1, 1993, furthering economic and political integration of the EC's members; important provisions include the creation of an economic and monetary union, a cohesion fund, a pledge to cooperate on foreign and defense policies, and the renaming of the EC as the European Union; commonly known as the Maastricht Treaty.

Triffin paradox. Paradox that resulted from reliance on the U.S. dollar as the primary source of liquidity in the Bretton Woods system; for trade to grow, foreigners needed to hold more dollars; the more dollars they held, however, the less faith they had in the U.S. dollar, thereby undermining the Bretton Woods system.

Turnkey project. Contract under which a firm agrees to fully design, construct, and equip a facility and then turn the project over to the purchaser when it is ready for operation.

Turnover. Rate at which people leave an organization.

Two-point arbitrage. Riskless purchase of a product in one geographic market for immediate resale in a second geographic market to profit from price differences between the markets; also called geographic arbitrage.

Two-tiered pricing policy. Pricing policy under which a firm sets one price for all its domestic sales and a second price for all its international sales.

Uncertainty acceptance. Cultural belief that uncertainty and ambiguity are stimulating and present new opportunities.

Uncertainty avoidance. Cultural belief that uncertainty and ambiguity are unpleasant and should be avoided.

Uncertainty orientation. Cultural beliefs about uncertainty and ambiguity.

Undifferentiated goods. Goods for which brand names and product reputations play a minor role in consumer purchase decisions (e.g., coal, petroleum products, and sugar).

Unethical behavior. Behavior that does not conform to generally accepted social norms.

Unilateral transfers. Gifts made by residents of one country to residents of another country.

Unrelated diversification. Corporate-level strategy that calls for a firm to operate in several unrelated businesses, industries, or markets.

Uruguay Round. GATT negotiations (1986–1994) that created the World Trade Organization, slashed tariff rates, and strengthened enforcement of intellectual property rights.

Values. The things that people believe to be important.

Value chain. A breakdown of the firm into its important activities—production, marketing, human resource management, and so forth—to enable its strategists to identify its competitive advantages and disadvantages.

Vertical integration. Extent to which a firm either provides its own resources or obtains them from other sources.

Voluntary export restraint (VER). Promise by a country to limit its exports of a good to another country.

Webb-Pomerene association. Group of U.S. firms that operate within the same industry and that are allowed by law to coordinate their export activities without fear of violating U.S. antitrust laws.

Whistle-blowing. The disclosure by an employee of illegal or unethical conduct by others within the organization.

With recourse. Term signifying that should a trade acceptance or banker's acceptance sold by an exporter to an investor fail to be paid, the exporter will reimburse the investor; the exporter retains the risk of default by the signer of the acceptance.

Without recourse. Term signifying that should a trade acceptance or banker's acceptance sold by an exporter to an investor fail to be paid, the exporter is not obligated to reimburse the investor; the investor retains the risk of default by the signer of the acceptance.

World Bank. See International Bank for Reconstruction and Development.

World Bank Group. Organization consisting of the World Bank and its affiliated organizations, the International Development Agency, the International Finance Corporation, and the Multilateral Investment Guarantee Agency.

World Trade Organization (WTO). Successor organization to the GATT founded in 1995; created by the Uruguay Round negotiations.

Name Index

Company Index

Subject Index